D1609380

ANDERSON'S
Law School Publications

Administrative Law Anthology
Thomas O. Sargentich

Administrative Law: Cases and Materials
Daniel J. Gifford

An Admiralty Law Anthology
Robert M. Jarvis

Alternative Dispute Resolution: Strategies for Law and Business
E. Wendy Trachte-Huber and Stephen K. Huber

The American Constitutional Order: History, Cases, and Philosophy
Douglas W. Kmiec and Stephen B. Presser

American Legal Systems: A Resource and Reference Guide
Toni M. Fine

Analytic Jurisprudence Anthology
Anthony D'Amato

An Antitrust Anthology
Andrew I. Gavil

Appellate Advocacy: Principles and Practice, *Third Edition*
Ursula Bentele and Eve Cary

Arbitration: Cases and Materials
Stephen K. Huber and E. Wendy Trachte-Huber

Basic Accounting Principles for Lawyers: With Present Value and Expected Value
C. Steven Bradford and Gary A. Ames

Basic Themes in Law and Jurisprudence
Charles W. Collier

The Best-Kept Secrets of Evidence Law: 101 Principles, Practices, and Pitfalls
Paul R. Rice

A Capital Punishment Anthology (and Electronic Caselaw Appendix)
Victor L. Streib

Cases and Materials in Juvenile Law
J. Eric Smithburn

Cases and Materials on Corporations
Thomas R. Hurst and William A. Gregory

Cases and Materials on the Law Governing Lawyers
James E. Moliterno

Cases and Problems in California Criminal Law
Myron Moskovitz

Cases and Problems in Criminal Law, *Fourth Edition*
Myron Moskovitz

The Citation Workbook: How to Beat the Citation Blues, *Second Edition*
Maria L. Ciampi, Rivka Widerman, and Vicki Lutz

Civil Procedure Anthology
David I. Levine, Donald L. Doernberg, and Melissa L. Nelken

Civil Procedure: Cases, Materials, and Questions, *Third Edition*
Richard D. Freer and Wendy Collins Perdue

Civil Procedure for Federal and State Courts
Jeffrey A. Parness

Clinical Anthology: Readings for Live-Client Clinics
Alex J. Hurder, Frank S. Bloch, Susan L. Brooks, and Susan L. Kay

Commercial Transactions Series: Problems and Materials
Louis F. Del Duca, Egon Guttman, Alphonse M. Squillante, Fred H. Miller, Linda Rusch, and Peter Winship
Vol. 1: Secured Transactions Under the UCC
Vol. 2: Sales Under the UCC and the CISG
Vol. 3: Negotiable Instruments Under the UCC and the CIBN

Communications Law: Media, Entertainment, and Regulation
Donald E. Lively, Allen S. Hammond, Blake D. Morant, and Russell L. Weaver

A Conflict-of-Laws Anthology
Gene R. Shreve

Constitutional Conflicts
Derrick A. Bell, Jr.

A Constitutional Law Anthology, *Second Edition*
Michael J. Glennon, Donald E. Lively, Phoebe A. Haddon, Dorothy E. Roberts, and Russell L. Weaver

Constitutional Law: Cases, History, and Dialogues, *Second Edition*
Donald E. Lively, Phoebe A. Haddon, Dorothy E. Roberts, Russell L. Weaver, and William D. Araiza

The Constitutional Law of the European Union
James D. Dinnage and John F. Murphy

The Constitutional Law of the European Union: Documentary Supplement
James D. Dinnage and John F. Murphy

Constitutional Torts
Sheldon H. Nahmod, Michael L. Wells, and Thomas A. Eaton

A Contracts Anthology, *Second Edition*
Peter Linzer

Contract Law and Practice
Gerald E. Berendt, Michael L. Closen, Doris Estelle Long, Marie A. Monahan, Robert J. Nye, and John H. Scheid

Contracts: Contemporary Cases, Comments, and Problems
Michael L. Closen, Richard M. Perlmutter, and Jeffrey D. Wittenberg

A Copyright Anthology: The Technology Frontier
Richard H. Chused

Corporate Law Anthology
Franklin A. Gevurtz

Corporate and White Collar Crime: An Anthology
Leonard Orland

Criminal Law: Cases and Materials, *Second Edition*
Arnold H. Loewy

Criminal Procedure: Cases, Materials, and Questions
Arnold H. Loewy

Criminal Procedure: Arrest and Investigation
Arnold H. Loewy and Arthur B. LaFrance

Criminal Procedure: Trial and Sentencing
Arthur B. LaFrance and Arnold H. Loewy

Economic Regulation: Cases and Materials
Richard J. Pierce, Jr.

Elder Law: Readings, Cases, and Materials
Thomas P. Gallanis, A. Kimberley Dayton, and Molly M. Wood

Elder Law: Statutes and Regulations
Thomas P. Gallanis, A. Kimberley Dayton, and Molly M. Wood

Elements of Law
Eva H. Hanks, Michael E. Herz, and Steven S. Nemerson

Ending It: Dispute Resolution in America Descriptions, Examples, Cases and Questions
Susan M. Leeson and Bryan M. Johnston

An Environmental Law Anthology
Robert L. Fischman, Maxine I. Lipeles, and Mark S. Squillace

Environmental Law Series

Environmental Decisionmaking, *Third Edition*
Robert L. Fischman and Mark S. Squillace

Water Pollution, *Third Edition*
Jackson B. Battle and Maxine I. Lipeles

Air Pollution, *Third Edition*
Mark S. Squillace and David R. Wooley

Hazardous Waste, *Third Edition*
Maxine I. Lipeles

Environmental Protection and Justice Readings and Commentary on Environmental Law and Practice, *Second Edition*
Kenneth A. Manaster

European Union Law Anthology
Karen V. Kole and Anthony D'Amato

An Evidence Anthology
Edward J. Imwinkelried and Glen Weissenberger

Family Law in Action: A Reader
Margaret F. Brinig, Carl E. Schneider, and Lee E. Teitelbaum

Federal Antitrust Law: Cases and Materials, *Second Edition*
Daniel J. Gifford and Leo J. Raskind

Federal Income Tax Anthology
Paul L. Caron, Karen C. Burke, and Grayson M.P. McCouch

Federal Rules of Civil Procedure
Publisher's Staff

Federal Rules of Evidence Handbook
Publisher's Staff

Federal Rules of Evidence: Rules, Legislative History, Commentary and Authority
Glen Weissenberger and James J. Duane

Federal and State Civil Procedure Handbook, *Second Edition*
Jeffrey A. Parness

Federal Wealth Transfer Tax Anthology
Paul L. Caron, Grayson M.P. McCouch, Karen C. Burke

First Amendment Anthology
Donald E. Lively, Dorothy E. Roberts, and Russell L. Weaver

The History, Philosophy, and Structure of the American Constitution
Douglas W. Kmiec and Stephen B. Presser

Individual Rights and the American Constitution
Douglas W. Kmiec and Stephen B. Presser

International Environmental Law Anthology
Anthony D'Amato and Kirsten Engel

International Human Rights: Law, Policy, and Process, *Third Edition*
David Weissbrodt, Joan Fitzpatrick, and Frank Newman

Selected International Human Rights Instruments and Bibliography for Research on International Human Rights Law, *Third Edition*
David Weissbrodt, Joan Fitzpatrick, Frank Newman, Marci Hoffman, and Mary Rumsey

International Intellectual Property Anthology
Anthony D'Amato and Doris Estelle Long

International Law Anthology
Anthony D'Amato

International Taxation: Cases, Materials, and Problems
Philip F. Postlewaite

Introduction to the Study of Law: Cases and Materials, *Second Edition*
John Makdisi

Judicial Externships: The Clinic Inside the Courthouse, *Second Edition*
Rebecca A. Cochran

A Land Use Anthology
Jon W. Bruce

Law and Economics Anthology
Kenneth G. Dau-Schmidt and Thomas S. Ulen

The Law of Disability Discrimination, *Third Edition*
Ruth Colker and Bonnie Poitras Tucker

The Law of Disability Discrimination Handbook: Statutes and Regulatory Guidance, *Third Edition*
Ruth Colker and Bonnie Poitras Tucker

The Lawyer's Craft: An Introduction to Legal Analysis, Writing, Research, and Advocacy
Cathy Glaser, Jethro K. Lieberman, Robert A. Ruescher, and Lynn Boepple Su

Lawyers and Fundamental Moral Responsibility
Daniel R. Coquillette

Mediation and Negotiation: Reaching Agreement in Law and Business
E. Wendy Trachte-Huber and Stephen K. Huber

Microeconomic Predicates to Law and Economics
Mark Seidenfeld

Natural Resources: Cases and Materials
Barlow Burke

Patients, Psychiatrists and Lawyers: Law and the Mental Health System, *Second Edition*
Raymond L. Spring, Roy B. Lacoursiere, and Glen Weissenberger

Preventive Law: Materials on a Non Adversarial Legal Process
Robert M. Hardaway

Principles of Evidence, *Fourth Edition*
Irving Younger, Michael Goldsmith, and David A. Sonenshein

Problems and Simulations in Evidence, *Second Edition*
Thomas F. Guernsey

A Products Liability Anthology
Anita Bernstein

Professional Responsibility Anthology
Thomas B. Metzloff

A Property Anthology, *Second Edition*
Richard H. Chused

Property Law: Cases, Materials, and Questions
Edward E. Chase

Public Choice and Public Law: Readings and Commentary
Maxwell L. Stearns

The Question Presented: Model Appellate Briefs
Maria L. Ciampi and William H. Manz

Readings in Criminal Law
Russell L. Weaver, John M. Burkoff, Catherine Hancock, Alan Reed, and Peter J. Seago

Science in Evidence
D.H. Kaye

A Section 1983 Civil Rights Anthology
Sheldon H. Nahmod

Sports Law: Cases and Materials, ***Fourth Edition***
Ray L. Yasser, James R. McCurdy, C. Peter Goplerud, and Maureen A. Weston

State and Local Government Law: A Transactional Approach
John Martinez and Michael E. Libonati

A Torts Anthology, ***Second Edition***
Julie A. Davies, Lawrence C. Levine, and Edward J. Kionka

Trial Practice
Lawrence A. Dubin and Thomas F. Guernsey

Understanding Negotiation
Melissa L. Nelken

Unincorporated Business Entities, ***Second Edition***
Larry E. Ribstein

FORTHCOMING PUBLICATIONS

The Art and Science of Trial Advocacy
L. Timothy Perrin, H. Mitchell Caldwell, and Carol A. Chase

Bankruptcy Anthology
Charles J. Tabb

Cases and Materials on Comparative Military Justice
Eugene R. Fidel, Michael F. Noone, and Elizabeth Lutes Hillman

Clinical Legal Education–A Textbook for Law School Clinical Programs
David F. Chavkin

First Amendment Law: Cases, Comparative Perspectives, and Dialogues
Donald E. Lively, William D. Araiza, Phoebe A. Haddon, John C. Knechtle, and Dorothy E. Roberts

Taxation: A Skills Approach
Michael A. Livingston and Nancy C. Staudt

Federal Antitrust Law Cases and Materials

Second Edition

FEDERAL ANTITRUST LAW
CASES AND MATERIALS

SECOND EDITION

DANIEL J. GIFFORD
Robins, Kaplan, Miller & Ciresi Professor of Law
University of Minnesota Law School

LEO J. RASKIND
Professor of Law
Brooklyn Law School

ANDERSON PUBLISHING CO.
CINCINNATI, OHIO

NOTE TO USERS

To ensure that you are using the latest materials available in this area, please be sure to periodically check Anderson Publishing's web site for downloadable updates and supplements at www.andersonpublishing.com

FEDERAL ANTITRUST LAW: CASES AND MATERIALS, SECOND EDITION
DANIEL J. GIFFORD AND LEO J. RASKIND

Anderson Publishing Co.
2035 Reading Road / Cincinnati, Ohio 45202
800-582-7295 / e-mail lawschool@andersonpublishing.com / Fax 513-562-5430
www.andersonpublishing.com

ISBN: 1-58360-789-7

To Ann and Mollie

Table of Contents

Preface to the Second Edition

In this edition we have retained the basic framework of the earlier work. The book has been written and edited to provide an effective teaching tool. In adding the new decisions, we have followed the existing format and added Commentaries designed to probe the doctrinal and policy issues raised by the new cases. In keeping with our objective of providing the economic analysis that may amplify and clarify the legal and policy issues, we have also taken into account recent trends in the relevant economic literature.

We acknowledge our debt to our respective schools. Both Law Library staffs have facilitated our work. At Minnesota, we acknowledge the valuable assistance of Suzanne Thorpe, Vicente Garces, George Jackson, Mary Rumsey, and April Schwartz. John Allen and Ben Johnson assisted in providing direct network communication between us. At Brooklyn, valuable assistance was provided by Sara Robbins, Jean Davis, Linda Holmes, Deborah Paulus, and Victoria Szymczak.

We express our appreciation to Deans E. Thomas Sullivan and Joan G. Wexler.

We express also our special gratitude to Sean Caldwell and Keith Moore for their substantial editorial assistance in the publication process.

D.J.G.
L.J.R.
October 2001

Preface to the First Edition

> . . . [T]he ideas of economists and political philosophers, both when they are right and when they are wrong, are more powerful than is commonly understood. Indeed the world is ruled by little else. Practical men, who believe themselves to be quite exempt from any intellectual influences, are usually the slaves of some defunct economist. . . . I am sure that the power of vested interests is vastly exaggerated compared with the gradual encroachment of ideas.
>
> John Maynard Keynes, THE GENERAL THEORY OF EMPLOYMENT, INTEREST, AND MONEY 383 (1936).

In preparing this edition we have two objectives: First, to present the material in the most current form. Second, to sharpen the focus on the underlying ideas that have infused and directed the development of substantive antitrust principles. To this end, we have drawn more widely on economic writings in this edition. Although the selection of the appropriate economic models to guide antitrust law has been the subject of substantial debate in recent years, we have sought to avoid taking sides or espousing one viewpoint. Rather, we have sought to follow the competitive principle inherent in this discipline by setting out the competing positions in a balanced fashion. It is not that we are without our individual preferences in these matters, but rather that we believe that doctrinal disputes are less productive than illuminating the trade-offs involved in adopting various economic models. Our interest is with the development of rules that will permit the exercise of the full sweep of private initiative, consistent with the public interest. The overriding issue is that of determining if, when, and the extent to which government intervention in private markets is in the public interest. This issue has, in turn, proven to be a function of the mode of economic theorizing that is dominant at the time.

The first chapter begins this approach with an historical review of antitrust law in terms of the political and economic ideas which have shaped it throughout its development. In the successive chapters we have sought to continue this theme and to provide a sense of the manner in which changes in the underlying economic analysis have shaped the application of the statutes by the enforcement agencies and the courts. Much of the complexity and uncertainty that surrounds the antitrust laws are also attributable to the development of antitrust substantive principles in application to the technology of the time. For example, the technology undergirding the world wide web was developed by a new, electronics-based industry, the nature and function of which requires the adaptation of traditional antitrust principles. Thus, antitrust issues raised by the new electronics and information age were met initially by principles rooted in the technology of blast furnaces, the steam locomotive, and traditional methods of inventorying, marketing, and distributing goods. Economists have responded to these changes with doctrines of network externalities and a theory of innovation markets, which are set out in context in relevant chapters. The changes in these techniques and methods have led to further antitrust complexity. Not only has this new electronic technology dramatically changed the mode of gathering and transmitting the information central to the functioning of free markets, but another level of antitrust analysis is invoked. Since this technology itself is frequently in the form of intangible property, *i.e.* patented and copyrighted materials, the exclusionary rights inherent in intellectual property also press this level of traditional antitrust principles. Recent events require one further factor of adjustment to traditional principles. As global markets and regional trading areas expand, it may be necessary to adjust such principles as the definition of a relevant market and other doctrines to this wider arena. A broader approach to our competition policy may be required. For example, if the rules governing vertical restraints or horizontal mergers in the European Union are materially different than the rules in the United States, the difference may impede trading relations and generate an issue before the World Trade Organization.

Such macroeconomic considerations serve also to re-focus the concern with markets. As political authorities of various nation states seek to manage the rate of growth of their economies with a view to the level of employment and the general welfare of their populations, the rules of competition come into focus. The macroeconomic concern with employment also raises collateral issues with labor associations and with exporters as market actors. Are the traditional antitrust exemptions for these groups functional in the current environment? A further example of the macroeconomic emphasis is the concern with the delivery of health care. The dramatic, but expensive technological changes in medicine have created a demand for these services that outstrips the resources that the governments have traditionally devoted to these markets. While Canada, the U.K., and the Northern European countries have delivered health care by substantial governmental involvement in the markets for these services, the U.S. state and federal governments had historically intervened only in the markets for hospital construction, for research, and in subsidizing medical education and training. Recent governmental initiatives more directly affecting the markets for the delivery of medical services have spurred a chain reaction among private providers. As the several economic actors in the health care arena in the U.S. are adapting to change by merger of hospitals, by various associations of physicians, by new initiatives among insurers, and by changes in the trading practices of pharmaceutical firms, traditional antitrust principles have been invoked in a new and different context.

We have addressed the antitrust issues raised by these changes in technology, in the rise of global markets, in the structure of health care markets by devoting three separate chapters to Intellectual Property, International Trade, and Health Care.

We express appreciation to Richard H. Stern and to E. Thomas Sullivan for sharing their learning and experience.

We want to express appreciation for the several persons who materially facilitated the preparation of this manuscript. At Brooklyn Law School, Sara Robbins, Jean Davis, and Linda Holmes provided excellent library reference services. Golda Lawrence assisted in manuscript preparation. At the University of Minnesota, Suzanne Thorpe, Marci Hoffman, George Jackson, and April Schwartz provided excellent library reference services. Nancy McCormick, Ed Zale, and Ingrid Miza mobilized the library resources of the Twin Cities when needed. Computer assistance was provided routinely by Laurie Neubauer, Rosemary Rogers, Harriet Carlson, Barbara Damchik-Dykes, and Jon Flanders.

D.J.G
L.J.R.
November 1997

Table of Cases

Table of Authorities

Leo J. Raskind, *Licensing Under United States Antitrust Law*, 20 BROOK. J. INT'L L. 49 (1993) 764

Eric B. Rasmusen, J. Mark Ramseyer & John S. Wiley, *Naked Exclusions*, 81 AM. ECON. REV. 1137 (1991) 313

James R. Ratner, *Should There Be an Essential Facility Doctrine?*, 21 U.C. DAVIS L. REV. 327 (1988) 473

Robert B. Reich, *Bailout: A Comparative Study in Law and Industrial Structure*, 2 YALE J. ON REG. 163 (1984) 52

David Reiffen & Andrew N. Kleit, Terminal Railroad *Revisited: Foreclosure of an Essential Facility or Simple Horizontal Monopoly?*, 33 J.L. ECON. 419 (1990) 473

Patrick Rey & Joseph Stiglitz, *Vertical Restraints and Producers' Competition*, 32 EUR. ECON. REV. 561 (1988) 165

Patrick Rey & Jean Tirole, *The Logic of Vertical Restraints*, 76 AM. ECON. REV. 921 (1986) 165

Gary L. Roberts & Steven C. Salop, *Efficiencies in Dynamic Merger Analysis*, 19 WORLD COMPETITION 5 (1996) 571-73

E.A.G. Robinson, MONOPOLY (1941) 510

Mark D. Rollinger, *Interstate Banking and Branching Under the Riegle-Neal Act*, 33 HARV. J. LEGIS. 183 (1996) 564

Norman E. Rosen, *Intellectual Property and the Antitrust Pendulum: Recent Developments at the Interface Between the Antitrust and Intellectual Property Laws*, 62 ANTITRUST L.J. 669 (1994) 815-16

Peter D. Rosenberg, PATENT LAW FUNDAMENTALS (1994) 822

G. Rosenbluth, *Measures of Concentration*, in BUSINESS CONCENTRATION AND PRICE POLICY (1955) 416

Stephen F. Ross, PRINCIPLES OF ANTITRUST LAW (1993) 63, 172

Eugene V. Rostow, *The New Sherman Act: A Positive Instrument of Progress*, 14 U. CHI. L. REV. 567 (1947) 337-38

Mark E. Roszkowski, *Vertical Maximum Price Fixing: In Defense of* Albrecht, 23 LOYOLA U. CHI. L. REV. 209 (1992) 190

Steven C. Salop, *The Noisy Monopolist: Imperfect Information, Price Dispersion, and Price Discrimination*, 44 REV. ECON. STAT. 393 (1977) 65

Pamela Samuelson, Randall Davis, Mitchell D. Kapor & J.H. Reichman, *A Manifesto Concerning the Legal Protection of Computer Programs*, 94 COLUM. L. REV. 2308 (1994) 270

Tim R. Sass & David S. Saurman, *Mandated Exclusive Territories and Economic Efficiency: An Empirical Analysis of the Malt Beverage Industry*, 36 J.L. & ECON. 153 (1993) 313

Antonin Scalia, *The Rule of Law as a Law of Rules*, 56 U. CHI. L. REV. 1175 (1989) 525

Fredric M. Scherer, *Antitrust, Efficiency, and Progress*, 62 N.Y.U. L. REV. 998 (1987) 629

F.M. Scherer, INDUSTRIAL MARKET STRUCTURE AND ECONOMIC PERFORMANCE (1970) 479

F.M. Scherer, INDUSTRIAL MARKET STRUCTURE AND ECONOMIC PERFORMANCE (2d ed. 1980) 393, 551

Chapter 1
Antitrust Law in Historical Perspective

> Antitrust in the United States is not, in the conventional sense, a set of laws by which men may guide their conduct. It is rather a general, sometimes conflicting statement of articles of faith and economic philosophy, which takes specific form as the courts and governmental agencies apply its generalities to the facts of individual cases in the economic and ideological setting of the time.[1]

In the above quotation, the late Justice Fortas has broadly summarized the shifting objectives and analyses of antitrust law. Since Justice Fortas wrote those words, the antitrust enforcement agencies as well as economic theorists have increasingly concerned themselves with conduct. The *Microsoft* litigation was initiated by the Justice Department's Antitrust Division based on allegations by Microsoft's competitors that its market conduct was "unfair" and "anticompetitive." Concern with conduct is reinforced from another perspective. Recent empirical work on economic decision-making by psychologists and economists has produced a new literature of law and economics—Behavioral Law and Economics, which is noted in some detail below.[2] This introductory chapter identifies the several periods of rise and decline of the different economic analyses and ideologies that have shaped antitrust law. This chapter also describes the approach of this book, namely, to provide materials from which teachers and students can critically examine the objectives and the various legal doctrines employed by enforcement agencies, courts, and commentators concerned with implementing a federal policy of achieving competitive markets.

---

1 Abe Fortas, *Forward* to A.D. NEALE & D.G. GOYDER, THE ANTITRUST LAWS OF THE UNITED STATES OF AMERICA v (3rd ed. 1980).

2 At page 12, below. *See also* BEHAVIORAL LAW AND ECONOMICS 1-3 (Cass Sunstein ed., 2000).

A. Congressional Action

The distinctive body of federal statutes known as the antitrust laws include the Sherman Act, the Clayton Act, and the Federal Trade Commission Act.[3] The Sherman Act of 1890 reflects the economic and political views dominant in the United States of 1865 to 1890, a period of intense economic activity stimulated by the Civil War. The introduction of a resolution in the United States Senate on July 10, 1888 addressed the conflict between the agrarian interests in the South and West and the newly emerging industrial sectors of the East and Midwest. In resolving this conflict between the agrarian and the industrial interests, the statute bearing Senator Sherman's name emerged as the expression of a federal competition policy. The 1888 resolution directed the Senate Finance Committee to give its attention to specific commercial practices, as follows:

> . . . all arrangements, contracts, agreements, trusts, or combinations between persons or corporations, made with a view, or which tend to prevent free and full competition in the production, manufacture, or sale of articles of domestic growth or production, . . . or which, against public policy, are designed or tend to foster monopoly or to artificially advance the cost to the consumer of necessary articles of human life. . . .[4]

One source of the tension between the agrarian sector and the emerging industrial sector was rising railroad freight rates for agricultural products. As the industrial products of greater weight and density than agricultural products began to constitute a larger fraction of railroad freight, the new traffic exerted an upward pull on freight rates for agricultural commodities. The increase in rates, coupled with the decreased availability of railroad cars at harvest time caused farmers to view themselves as victims of discriminatory treatment by the railroads.

Seeking relief from this onerous situation at a time when agricultural prices were depressed, farmers mobilized into a powerful and vocal political force that came to be known as the Granger Movement. The primary objective of this organization was to seek relief from these railroad rate differentials through legislation, initially from state legislatures and subsequently from Congress. Originating as a social and educational organization of agrarian interests around 1867, known initially as the Patrons of Husbandry, the Movement became a vital organization consisting of some 19,000 local granges.[5] By 1873 it is estimated that the movement had a membership of 1.6 million.[6] The results of this organizational activity at the

---

[3] According to 15 U.S.C. § 12 (1994), the Federal Trade Commission Act is not defined as an antitrust law. Accordingly, private actions authorized by §§ 4 and 16 of the Clayton Act may not be based on the Federal Trade Commission Act.

[4] 19 CONG. REC. 7 (July 7, 1888).

[5] SOLON BUCK, THE GRANGER MOVEMENT 58 (1913).

[6] FREDRIC L. PAXON, HISTORY OF THE AMERICAN FRONTIER 1763-1893, 530 (1924); *see also* Drew, *The Present Farmers Movement*, 6 POL. SCI. Q. 282 (1891); BUCK, THE AGRARIAN CRUSADE Chs. 6 & 10 (1920).

state level were reflected in a spate of state statutes regulating both the rates charged by public carriers and by grain elevators that became known as the Granger Laws.[7] Indeed, even state constitutions were modified as a result of Granger agitation as shown by the Illinois Constitution of 1870 which directed the legislature to: ". . . pass laws to correct abuses and to prevent unjust discrimination and extortion in the rates of freight . . . ."[8] Shortly thereafter, Illinois, Minnesota, Wisconsin, Nebraska, Ohio, Missouri, Michigan, California, and Massachusetts enacted legislation regulating rail freight rates.[9] Congress responded to these complaints in 1887 by enacting the Interstate Commerce Commission Act, which established the first modern federal administrative agency, the Interstate Commerce Commission, to assure "just and reasonable [railroad] rates" and to prohibit discriminatory rates.[10]

During this same period from the end of the Civil War to 1890, a vast wave of innovation and applied technology facilitated both growth and concentration in the industrial sector. For example, new technology together with a national rail network transformed the prior system of local and regional markets into a national market for many commodities and services. A partial list of new devices of the period describes the contribution of technology to this process of expansion. On the agricultural side, mechanical mowers, reapers, and seeding machines dramatically increased output. On the communications side, the telegraph, telephone, and transoceanic cable linked the Western territories of the United States into a single network that could serve national and international markets. Electricity made its contribution by powering the rotary printing press, and lifting devices, including elevators. The commercial development of petroleum products, the refinement of the internal combustion engine, analine dyes, and wire rope were also among the new products and processes attributable to the technology of the period.[11]

As production facilities expanded, the corporate form emerged as the business unit of choice, a fact that is reflected in the numerous state incorporation laws enacted during this period.[12] As markets expanded and the size of corporate firms grew, the moderate tone of commercial rivalry receded. Trading relationships as previously conducted by local and regional individual proprietorships and part-

---

[7] ERNEST BOGART & CHARLES M. THOMPSON, THE INDUSTRIAL STATE 1870-1893, 84-86 (1920).

[8] *See* BUCK, THE GRANGER MOVEMENT, *supra* note 4, at 130.

[9] *Id.* at 159-64.

[10] The Interstate Commerce Act, 49 U.S.C. § 1(5) (1992); H.R. 876, 103rd Cong., 1st Sess., was introduced in 1993 to repeal the Interstate Commerce Act and the Interstate Commerce Commission, transferring all of the latter's authority to the Secretary of Transportation. Under § 2 of the bill, the purpose is:

> . . . to reduce unnecessary and burdensome Government regulations and to improve the productivity and competitiveness of United States industries in domestic and world markets.

See also I. LEO SHARFMAN, 1 THE INTERSTATE COMMERCE COMMISSION Ch. 1 (1931) (the definitive work on this agency); CHARLES BEARD, THE RISE OF AMERICAN CIVILIZATION Ch. 21 (1930).

[11] These technological changes were recorded by a leading economist, David A. Wells, in RECENT ECONOMIC CHANGES 64 (1899).

[12] ADOLF A. BERLE & GARDINER C. MEANS, THE MODERN CORPORATION AND PRIVATE PROPERTY 136 (1932).

nerships gave way to more intensive, if more impersonal, modes of competition. One description of this new mode of rivalry among corporate competitors is given as follows:

> The National Cash Register Co., organized in 1882, set out deliberately to destroy its competitors. It hired their employees away from them. It bribed their employees and the employees of common carriers and telephone and telegraph companies to spy on them and disclose their business secrets. It spread false rumors concerning their solvency. It instructed its agents to misrepresent the quality of their goods, interfere with their sales, and damage the mechanism of their machines. . . .[13]

This heightened commercial rivalry coupled with the newly-perceived benefits of economies of scale served as a spur for corporations to combine and to expand. The emergence of a rapidly growing corporate sector evoked requests for increased enforcement of the new state legislation directed at specific practices that were perceived as inimical to agrarian interests. Discriminatory pricing by railroads and by grain elevators were of particular concern to farmers.[14] Rockefeller's ability to obtain discriminatory rail rates in his expansion of Standard Oil, impacted also on the railroad freight rates for agrarian products.[15] In addition to action against the corporations, pressure was also exerted for rigorous enforcement action by the Interstate Commerce Commission against the practice of obtaining secret rebates from the railroads in contravention of the posted tariffs required by the new federal Interstate Commerce Act.[16]

A rising tide of public hostility to perceived corporate misconduct developed. One commentator notes, "Public feeling against the oil monopoly was an important factor in causing passage of the Sherman Antitrust Act in 1890."[17] This sentiment generated pressure in Congress directly to curb the abusive practices of the "trusts." The trust became central to this controversy because, as an instrumentality of splitting legal ownership from effective control, it provided a technical means of moving a corporation from the state whose charter gave it existence, to another state in which a trust was created, without moving the physical assets. This device

---

[13] Clair Wilcox, Competition and Monopoly In American Industry, U.S. Temporary National Economic Committee Monograph No. 21, 68 (1940).

[14] The state court cases seeking to regulate these practices became known as the "Granger cases." They are reviewed by Charles F. Adams, *The Granger Movement*, 120 N. Am. Rev. 394 (1875).

[15] Elizabeth Granitz & Benjamin Klein, *Monopolization by Raising Rivals' Costs: The Standard Oil Case,* 39 J.L. & Econ. 1 (1996) (arguing that Rockefeller's ability to cartelize petroleum transportation and raise rail costs to rivals enabled him to force rival refiners to sell out).

[16] Ida M. Tarbell's articles in McClure's Magazine that appeared as a series from 1902 to 1904, and later published as a book, The History of the Standard Oil Company (1925), drew widespread public attention to the harsh competitive practices and secret railroad rebates. *See* Simon N. Whitney, 1 Antitrust Policies 101-02 (1958). In 1903, Congress amended the Interstate Commerce Act by the Elkins Act, 32 Stat. 847 (1903), expressly to outlaw discriminatory rail rates.

[17] *See* Whitney, *supra* note 15, at 101.

effectively deprived the attorneys general of states of their ability to seek revocation of the charter of those corporations engaging in "monopolistic" and abusive commercial practices. To avoid the jurisdiction of state attorneys general, corporate advisers had turned to the instrumentality of the trust as early as 1879.

An example of the response by a state to complaints of price-fixing and other anticompetitive practices was the successful charter revocation suit against a combination of sugar refiners in New York.[18] In that case, 17 New York refiners had formed a combination and constituted a board to manage price and output limitations on the members. Since all parties were subject to the jurisdiction of the New York courts, the charter revocation proceedings effectively ended the combination.

As the trust became the approved means of removing a corporate enterprise from the jurisdiction of state courts, it became the prevailing organizational form for many major industries. By the end of the nineteenth century many basic products such as steel, petroleum, tobacco, sugar, and whiskey, were produced by firms controlled through trusts. Even where successful, state court litigation seeking to revoke corporate charters did not expressly address price-fixing, secret railroad rebates, and related anticompetitive practices that were the subject of complaints. Thus, the quest began for a federal solution to control these abusive business practices directly.[19]

The "trust problem" became a political issue in the presidential campaign of 1888. In accepting the nomination of the Republican Party for the presidency, Benjamin Harrison wrote approvingly of the platform plank stating opposition to the "trust." As he put it in his letter accepting the nomination,

> The declaration of the convention against all combinations of capital, organized in trusts or otherwise . . . is in harmony with the view entertained and publicly expressed by me long before the assembling of the convention.[20]

Against this background of conflict between major elements of the society at the turn of the last century, the Sherman Act was enacted as a response to the dominant political phrases of the day—"trusts," and "monopolies." As the legislative history of the Sherman Act attests, the congressional debates that led to its enactment did not provide a clear direction for interpreting the statute as enacted.[21] A dic-

---

[18] The State of New York prevailed in a suit against a combination of 17 sugar refineries in which the Court of Appeals held that the transfer of management powers to a board exceeded the corporation's power under its New York charter. *People v. North River Sugar Refining Co.*, 3 N.Y. Supp. 401 (1889), *aff'd*, 24 N.E. 834 (1890). *See also* HENRY R. SEAGER & CHARLES A. GULICK, JR., TRUST AND CORPORATION PROBLEMS 49-71 (1929).

[19] *See* HANS THORELLI, THE FEDERAL ANTITRUST POLICY 76-85 (1954); WILLIAM LETWIN, LAW AND ECONOMIC POLICY IN AMERICA 71-73 (1965).

[20] CHARLES HEDGES, SPEECHES OF BENJAMIN HARRISON 113 (1892).

[21] OSWALD W. KNAUTH, THE POLICY OF THE UNITED STATES TOWARD INDUSTRIAL MONOPOLY 1-10 (1914); Charles Bullock, *Trust Literature: A Survey and a Criticism*, 15 Q.J. ECON. 167 (1901). There is not unanimity among commentators as to the forces that produced the Sherman Act. One view is that this was major legislation expressing a desire to limit political power by decentralizing economic power. *See* David Millon, *The Sherman*

tum of Chief Justice Stone effectively conveys the judicial perception of the Sherman Act as legislation drawn in broad, almost constitutional terms:

> The prohibitions of the Sherman Act were not stated in terms of precision or of crystal clarity and the Act itself does not define them. In consequence of the vagueness of its language, perhaps not uncalculated, the courts have been left to give content to the statute, and in the performance of that function it is appropriate that courts should interpret its words in the light of its legislative history and the particular evils at which the legislation was aimed.[22]

A leading industrial organization economist attributes the generality of the language of the Sherman Act to congressional uncertainty in addressing the "trust" problem. He wrote,

> A close reading of the debates and committee hearings that preceded passage of the Sherman Act can convey a good idea of the fears that inspired it. The Congress of 1890 had quite a few growing out of the appearance of cartels, the plight of farmers, railroad rates, so-called destructive competition, the size of eastern banks, and above all, the activities of the Standard Oil Company. But the debates and committee hearings do not indicate that Congress in 1890 meant to lay out any detailed agenda for dealing with its worries. The most that we can assume is that Congress wanted some sort of action from the Attorney General and the courts.[23]

The broad Congressional grant of authority given the federal judiciary by the Sherman Act has left room for various economic and political objectives to be imputed to this legislation. The objective of this book is to illuminate the process of interpreting these statutes.

Act and the Balance of Power, 61 S. CAL. L. REV. 1219 (1988). George Stigler rejected the conclusion that agrarian interests, which were primarily consumers of land and credit, were directly affected by "monopolies." He found also unsupportable the conclusion that railroad rates were a material factor in the pressure for enactment of the Sherman Act. Rather he noted the prior enactment of antitrust legislation by some 16 states prior to 1890 and the near unanimity of the voting on the Sherman Act in Congress (141 - 0 in the House and 51 - 1 in the Senate). Accordingly, he concluded that the Sherman Act represented a modest statement of public policy to extend the common law rule against restraints of trade, a position which was adopted by politicians and thus became subject to party discipline. *See* George J. Stigler, *The Origin of the Sherman Act*, 14 J. LEGAL STUD. 1 (1985).

[22] *Apex Hosiery Co. v. Leader*, 310 U.S. 469, 489 (1940).

[23] Donald Dewey, *Economists And Antitrust: The Circular Road*, 35 ANTITRUST BULL. 349, 354 (1990).

B. Economic Analyses and Ideologies

The breadth of the Congressional mandate to provide for competitive markets reflected a societal ambivalence concerning the appropriate governmental role in economic affairs. In contrast to the current practice, during the period of gestation of the Sherman Act, 1875-1890, the economists of the day contributed little to the debate. *Laissez-faire* reigned as the dominant view; the "Trust Problem" was considered a political issue outside the scope of economics. By 1885, however, a group of young economists who had studied in Germany began to question the conventional wisdom concerning the minimal role of government in economic affairs.[24] In 1885, Richard T. Ely and others formed the American Economic Association to articulate an alternative viewpoint. The initial statement of principles for the Association rejected *laissez-faire* as a controlling principle of economic organization as follows:

> We regard the state as an agency whose positive assistance is one of the indispensable conditions of human progress . . . we believe in a progressive development of economic conditions which must be met by a corresponding development of legislative policy.[25]

The enactment of the Sherman Act served to attract the attention of economists to the "Trust Problem."[26] Prior to 1890, the prevailing view among economists of the "trust" and "monopoly" problem was that expressed by John Bates Clark. Like Alfred Marshall, the great English neo-classical economist, Clark saw the ultimate goal of economic analysis to be the betterment of society through technological progress. Thus, Clark wrote in 1901 that: ". . . progress is in itself the *summum bonum* in economics, and that society is essentially the best which improves the fastest."[27] Since Clark perceived of economics as an instrument of social betterment, his analysis reflected his concern with paths to economic improvement. Accordingly, he rejected the traditional static analysis in his pursuit of a process of betterment. As he applied this perspective to the economic analysis of competition, he wrote, ". . . a static state . . . is imaginary. All natural societies

---

[24] ALFRED MARSHALL, PRINCIPLES OF ECONOMICS, Preface (1st ed. 1890).

[25] RICHARD T. ELY, REPORT OF THE ORGANIZATION OF THE AMERICAN ECONOMIC ASSOCIATION 35 (1886). For a review of this period see also Herbert Hovenkamp, *The First Law & Economics Movement*, 42 STAN. L. REV. 993, 1021-24 (1990).

[26] Of the lack of interest in antitrust issues prior to the enactment of the Sherman Act, a leading economist of the 1950's wrote,

> One shudders to think of what the position of an editor of an economic . . . journal in search of manuscripts must have been before the passage of the Sherman law.

Edward S. Mason, *Market Power and Business Conduct: Some Comments*, 46 AM. ECON. REV. 471 (1956) (a commentary on the 1955 Report of the Attorney General To Study the Antitrust Laws).

[27] JOHN BATES CLARK, THE CONTROL OF TRUSTS 82 (1901). Marshall emphasized the core concern ". . . with human beings who are impelled . . . to change and progress. . . . The central idea of economics . . . must be that of living force and movement." PRINCIPLES OF ECONOMICS xv (8th ed. 1920).

are dynamic. . . . [T]he most important thing that is included . . . is a theory of progress."[28]

Clark viewed the monopoly problem as a potential impediment to economic betterment, but he also saw that research and innovation were related to size and consolidation. While acknowledging the growth of the trust, he also recognized the dynamic power of competition. He thus articulated a theme of antitrust analysis that has endured as a topic of contention. Namely, the selection of a normative model of competition against which to assess specific practices to determine whether enforcement action should be taken. Clark selected the purely competitive model as the reference point for enforcement activity. He believed that free markets serve best to protect the public interest even in the case of a complete monopoly by a single seller. He analyzed the pricing practices of such a firm as follows:

> . . . the price may conceivably be a normal one. It may stand not much above the cost of production to the monopoly itself. If it does . . . [sell at a substantially higher price], it . . . would invite competition. The great company prefers to sell all the goods that are required at a moderate price rather than to invite rivals into its territory. This is monopoly in form but not in fact, for it is shorn of its injurious power; and the thing that holds it firmly in check is *potential competition*. . . .[29]

Thus, Clark was not an advocate of vigorous antitrust enforcement. Rather, he considered the mere expression of governmental policy, such as the Sherman Act, as an important factor in reminding large firms to "keep the field open for competitors" and to discourage unfair and predatory methods of commercial rivalry.[30] Implicit, but not expressly stated in Clark's writings and those of the leading English economists was the understanding of competition as a process to be considered in terms of the workings of actual markets, rather than as a process represented by a pure, abstract model of perfect competition.[31] For example, A.C. Pigou, Alfred Marshall's successor at Cambridge University, named the theoretical model of pure competition, "simple competition," reserving the phrase, "adequate competition," for markets that failed to meet the conditions of the theoretical model, but which

---

[28] JOHN BATES CLARK, THE DISTRIBUTION OF WEALTH 442 (1899).

[29] *Id.* at 380. J.B. Clark placed substantial reliance on the efficacy of potential competition as a safeguard against monopolistic practices. *See* J.B. CLARK, THE PHILOSOPHY OF WEALTH 120 (1886).

[30] Clark, *supra* note 27, at 383-85.

[31] A.C. Pigou, Marshall's successor at Cambridge, distinguished the analytical model of perfect competition as "simple competition," but would, like Clark, rely on "adequate" competition as well as an acceptance of government intervention in limited circumstances. *See* THE ECONOMICS OF WELFARE Ch. 21 (4th ed. 1950).

In his earlier writing, Clark made the distinction between "conservative and easy competition" and the "fiercer variety" in which the extermination of rivals, called "cut-throat" competition is the mode of rivalry. He concluded that, "Easy and tolerant competition is the antithesis of monopoly; the cut-throat process is the father of it." JOHN BATES CLARK, THE PHILOSOPHY OF WEALTH 120 (1886).

should not require government intervention.[32] It remained for Clark's son, J.M. Clark, to bring the phrase, "workable competition," into the economic and antitrust law vocabulary.[33]

This characterization of competition by reference to a dynamic competitive norm that is noted in the writings of Clark and others, continues as a topic of contemporary antitrust law discourse. Thus, for example, Clark's emphasis on potential competition is mirrored in the current debate precipitated by the Supreme Court decision in *Eastman Kodak, Inc. v. Image Technical Services, Inc.*,[34] a case involving tie-in arrangements (discussed in Chapter 6, below). One recent commentator articulates the differences between applying a static or a dynamic model as follows:

> . . . [these] theories [that tying arrangements do not cause anticompetitive results absent the existence of monopoly power] might best describe a world of omniscient buyers and well-capitalized, informed competitors, facing no entry barriers, no economies of scale, and no cartel behavior.
>
> A further limitation of . . . [this] analysis is . . . the implicit premise that static efficiency is the critical economic measure of harm.[35]

In their writings, Clark and his contemporaries seemed to have anticipated the recent controversy surrounding the contribution of the Chicago School, which has relied primarily on static, micro-economic analysis.

In subsequent chapters, this book will explore the characterization of market conduct under the antitrust statutes in terms of the shifting conceptions of competitive norms that have marked their application. Identifying conduct inimical to effective competition is the substance of antitrust law. Like the debates among the nineteenth century courts and commentators, contemporary discourse, now enlightened by a rich literature of theoretical, empirical, and caselaw analysis, still revolves around the basic issue of identifying norms of acceptable competitive behavior. Like their nineteenth century precursors, courts and contemporary commentators continue the debate about the assumptions underlying the characterization of anti-competitive conduct.

The chapters that follow are devoted to the exposition of antitrust doctrines and their application to transactions and arrangements in domestic and global markets. Antitrust aspects of current issues of public debate, such as health care, trade issues, and information technology afford an opportunity for studying the process of adapting traditional antitrust principles to rapidly changing new circumstances. The historical survey of antitrust enforcement that follows provides an

---

32 A.C. Pigou, The Economics of Welfare Ch. 21 (4th ed. 1950).

33 J.M. Clark, *Toward A Concept of Workable Competition*, 30 Am. Econ. Rev. 241 (Proceedings (1940)).

34 *Eastman Kodak Co. v. Image Technical Services, Inc.*, 504 U.S. 451 (1992).

35 Warren S. Grimes, *Antitrust Tie-In Analysis After* Kodak*: Understanding the Role of Market Imperfections,* 62 Antitrust L.J. 263, 272 (1994).

awareness of a constant societal concern with such common issues as efficient management of resources and the curbing of abuses of economic power, a concern that has infused the debate over the decades. In flux are institutional, contractual, and technological arrangements in the economy, as well as the analytical tools that guide the application of antitrust principles. There are tensions among the various possible objectives of antitrust doctrines. The art of antitrust analysis lies in identifying and articulating the trade-offs between attaining efficiencies, and at various costs, of accepting increased market power or of diminished consumer choices. A recent historical study makes this point as follows:

> This . . . [historical] review . . . provides a framework for understanding the history of American competition policy as the outcomes of struggles and confrontations, both among political and idealogical factions and, at another level, between utopian aspirations and material conditions. [36]

The remainder of this chapter is devoted to an historical overview of the development of antitrust law. This historical material is designed to provide a context for assessing the contemporary antitrust debate in the courts and in the journals over the selection of the appropriate economic models for antitrust analysis and enforcement. This present discourse is illustrated by the difference in behavioral assumptions between Judge Posner and Professors Krattenmaker and Salop. The judge, an advocate of strict application of microeconomic models, assumes that the conduct of market actors is governed by narrowly rational economic motives focused on short-run cost minimization, which he expresses as follows:

> Economics is not a theory about consciousness. Behavior is rational when it conforms to a model of rational choice whatever the state of mind of the chooser. . . .
>
> The concept of man as a rational maximizer of self-interest implies that people respond to incentives—that if a person's surroundings change in such a way that he could increase his satisfaction by altering his behavior, he will do so. From this proposition derive the . . . fundamental principles of economics.[37]

Recent economic analysis undertakes to question this unqualified assumption of rational economic conduct. Kenneth Arrow has summed up this body of theory as follows: "I hope to make the case for the proposition that an important class of intertemporal markets shows systematic deviations from individual rational behavior . . . ."[38] While this analysis has not yet progressed to offer antitrust policy recommendations, it underscores the recognition of the complexity of economic behavior. As one recent theorist states:

---

[36] Rudolph J.R. Peritz, Competition Policy in America, 1888-1992, 5 (1996).

[37] Richard A. Posner, Economic Analysis of Law 4 (4th ed. 1992).

[38] Kenneth Arrow, *Risk Perception in Psychology and Economics,* 20 Economic Inquiry 1 (1982).

> . . . [W]e start to explore the implications of irrationality for economics. . . . We show that the knee-jerk reaction of some economists that competition will render irrationality irrelevant is apt only in very special cases, probably rarely observed in the real world. Our analysis highlights the important roles played by arbitrageurs and entrepreneurs. We find that, perhaps counter to intuition, more competition can actually make things worse by leaving no possibility of a profit to an entrepreneur who offers education or information.[39]

A parallel branch of economic analysis, game theory, applies assumptions of bounded rationality to economic behavior to posit alternative market outcomes derived from various assumptions of economic strategies by the market participants.[40] Yet another variant of the assumption of rational economic behavior is offered by Herbert A. Simon. He urges the adoption of a "substantive theory" of rationality in which:

> . . . we accept the proposition that both the knowledge and the computational power of the decision maker are severely limited. . . . [W]e must construct a theory (and test it empirically) of the processes of the decision.
>
> * * *
>
> . . . The rational person . . . [thus described] goes about making his or her decisions in a way that is procedurally reasonable in the light of the available knowledge and the means of computation.[41]

Professors Krattenmaker and Salop have undertaken to explore market conduct other than maximizing revenue by reducing short-run costs. Called strategic behavior, the practice is described as follows.

> Firms employing . . . strategies seek to increase their profits not by reducing their own costs, which is competitive; nor by excluding rivals from a market altogether, which is often anticompetitive; nor by convincing rivals to engage in price fixing, also anticompetitive; but rather by increasing the costs of rivals while imposing smaller or no . . . [costs] on the strategizing firm. Many . . . strategies of raising rivals' costs are anticompetitive. . . .
>
> The . . . strategies for raising rivals' costs vary from quite simple to extremely complex. . . . Some strategies require concerted behavior by firms collectively controlling a significant market share. Others require not market dominance but rather success in convincing a legislative or

---

39 Thomas Russell & Richard Thaler, *The Relevance of Quasi Rationality in Competitive Markets,* 75 AM. ECON. REV. 1071 (1985).

40 DAVID M. KREPS, GAME THEORY AND ECONOMIC MODELLING Ch. 3 (1990).

41 Herbert A. Simon, *Rationality in Psychology and Economics,* 59 J. BUS. §§ 209, 211 (1989).

administrative body to impose cost raising regulations. Still others can be effected by single, perhaps even nondominant, firms.[42]

Different assumptions about the goals of market conduct will support different conclusions and characterizations of anti-competitive behavior. Similarly, assumed specific behavior within a static model of competition will invite different conclusions from similar behavior in assumptions of a dynamic model, as J.B. Clark noted at the turn of the century. It is characteristic of antitrust law that differing perceptions of anti-competitive conduct in different cases come about from varying premises in the underlying economic model that is applied to the problem. As a commentator has noted as an example of such a shift in the antitrust analysis of predatory pricing:

> During the past 30 years, the Court's approach to predatory pricing has ranged from one broadly protective of competitors . . . with little or no attention to market structure . . . to one in which the now-generally accepted rarity of predatory pricing is fully embraced. . . .
>
> As currently conceived, antitrust law embodies national policies furthering productive and allocative efficiency. These policy goals are susceptible to economic analysis, and analysis that is generally not beyond the power of courts to apply but that is generally beyond the power of courts to formulate and to articulate in the first instance.
>
> Indeed, the courts have been most successful in antitrust law when they have adopted broad schemas worked out by others.[43]

An emerging literature of behavioral law and economics extends Herbert Simon's concept of bounded rationality by suggesting that some economic decisions can display a pattern of predictable responses which are guided as much by shortcuts, rules of thumb, and interactive responses as by the traditional calculus of utility. This new discipline lies at the intersection of economics and psychology. Psychologists and other behavioral scientists report studies and experiments in economic decision-making of individuals. Comparison of their experimental results with the traditional behavioral assumptions of micro-economic analysis has identified some departures from the traditional norm. This new literature claims to have identified patterns of economic decision-making that are not predicted by the utility-maximizing concept of economic behavior. This new approach rests on the premise that certain cognitive biases are consistent and predictable.[44]

---

[42] Herbert Hovenkamp, *Antitrust Policy, Restricted Distribution, and the Market for Exclusionary Rights,* 71 MINN. L. REV. 1293, 1294 (1987). *See also* Thomas G. Krattenmacher & Steven C. Salop, *Anticompetitive Exclusion: Raising Rivals' Costs to Achieve Power Over Price*, 96 YALE L.J. 209 (1986).

[43] Daniel J. Gifford, *Predatory Pricing Analysis in the Supreme Court*, 39 ANTITRUST BULL. 431, 432, 480 (1994).

[44] Matthew Rabin, *Incorporating Fairness Into Game theory and Economics,* 83 AMER. ECON. REV. 1281, 1292 (1993); Daniel Kahneman et al., *Fairness as a Constraint on Profit Seeking: Entitlements in the Market,* 76 AMER. ECON. REV. 728 (1986).

At this early state of its development, behavioral law and economics has yet to produce a workable framework suited to economic analysis. Yet, as Richard A. Posner (and others) have noted, the new work has promise. Thus Posner writes:

> [This work] is critical of the efforts of economists to enrich the model of rational choice . . . yet, its own approach is ad hoc; and though it prides itself on empirical rigor and predictive accuracy, it is deficient in both qualities. These are remediable deficiencies, however, and I expect that they will be remedied in future work by these and other scholars.[45]

Practitioners of behavioral economics do not perceive their objective to be the elimination of the traditional model of rational economic behavior. Rather, they perceive the challenge for the new discipline to be the development of a more refined model, one capable of incorporating the new learning. It is claimed that providing empirically verified patterns of behavior outside the present formulation can enhance the predictive power of such a refined model. One group of behavioral scholars has noted the prospect of discerning discrete behavioral patterns in various markets as follows:

> [W]hile human beings often display bounded rationality, willpower, and self-interest, markets can sometimes lead to behavior consistent with conventional economic assumptions. Then the question becomes when, exactly, do market forces make it reasonable to assume that people behave in accordance with those assumptions? What circumstances apply to most of the domains in which law and economics is used? [46]

At this writing the new discipline, as such, has not yet been applied to antitrust law. Perhaps the concept of strategic behavior noted earlier can qualify both as a precursor as well as a validation of this perspective. For example, some recent economic studies of tying arrangements also identify the dynamic, interactive behavior that is a feature of the new approach.[47] While it is possible that the discipline of behavioral law and economics may not redeem its promise of producing a full-blown theory of economic behavior, some legal writers have already found this perspective useful. In two articles, Hanson and Kysar have applied the behavioral perspective to products liability. By coupling consumers' risk assessment behavior

---

[45] Richard A. Posner, *Rational Choice, Behavioral Economics, and The Law,* 50 STAN. L. REV. 1551 (1998).

[46] Christine Jolls, Cass R. Sunstein & Richard Thaler, *A Behavioral Approach to Law and Economics, in* BEHAVIORAL LAW AND ECONOMICS 13, 19 (Cass R. Sunstein ed., 2000); *see also* Richard A. Posner, *Rational Choice, Behavioral Economics, and the Law,* 50 STAN. L. REV. 1551 (1998); Matthew Rabin, *Psychology and Economics,* 36 J. ECON. LIT. 11 (1998).

[47] *See also* Dennis W. Carlton & Michael Waldman, *Strategic Use of Tying to Preserve and Create Market Power in Evolving Industries,* WORKING PAPER NO. 145, GEORGE J. STIGLER CENTER FOR THE STUDY OF THE ECONOMY AND THE STATE (1998); Michael D. Whinston, *Tying, Foreclosure, and Exclusion,* 80 AMER. ECON. REV. 837 (1990) (showing the use of tying arrangements as a method of inducing the exit of competitors in the tied product market).

with methods by which manufacturers seek to modify that behavior, these authors develop their concept of "market manipulation" as a predicate for imposing tort liability on manufacturers.[48] Since, as the chapters which follow will demonstrate, much of antitrust law concerns itself with conduct and patterns of behavior, it is foreseeable that this perspective will also infuse antitrust law in the future.

In each of the chapters that follow, the different modes of economic analysis and their underlying assumptions will be set out for critical review. This treatment will include the examination of the "Harvard School," the "Chicago School," the "Post-Chicago School," the "Institutionalists," as well as the new behavioral law and economics scholarship. This latter body of work may refine the traditional assumptions of rational economic behavior in some fact-specific situations.[49] A commentator has characterized the current mode of antitrust analysis as being in an excessively empirical phase of this cyclical process—one characterized by "hyper-complexity" because of the increased attention courts are giving to all aspects of market conduct. This view is stated as follows:

> Seen in perspective, the hyper-complexity of current antitrust represents a predictable phase in a jurisprudential cycle. Modern antitrust jurisprudence has regularly adopted highly assumptive modes of analysis, only to reject them for more fact-intensive methodologies. [50]

C. Enforcement

Given this cyclical development of antitrust analysis, it is not surprising to observe a meandering history of enforcement. At least four stages of antitrust history can be identified.[51] In each phase, it becomes apparent that different policy objectives and different modes of economic analysis were responsible for the various approaches to interpreting and enforcing the antitrust laws.

1. 1890-1902

This first period after the enactment of the Sherman Act was one of limited acceptance of the new statute by the courts. In 1895, the Supreme Court held that the conduct of the largest sugar refiner was outside the purview of the Sherman Act

---

48 Jon D. Hanson & Douglas A. Kysar, *Taking Behavioralism Seriously: The Problem of Market Manipulation,* 74 N.Y.U. L. REV. 630 (1999); *Taking Behavioralism Seriously: Some Evidence of Market Manipulation,* 112 HARV. L. REV. 1420 (1999).

49 Michael S. Jacobs, *The New Sophistication in Antitrust*, 79 MINN. L.J. 1 (1994).

50 *Id.* at 52.

51 *See* SIMON N. WHITNEY, 1 ANTITRUST POLICIES 6-11 (1958).

because its pricing conduct lacked the requisite nexus to interstate commerce. In *United States v. E.C. Knight*,[52] the first Sherman Act case to reach the Supreme Court, the monopoly position of the American Sugar Refining Company under the Sherman Act was recognized by the Court. However, the lower court's dismissal of the complaint was affirmed on the ground that the refining of sugar bore no distinct relation to interstate commerce. Accordingly, the acquisition of four competitors by the defendant was not actionable under the Sherman Act.

However, three subsequent government victories in Sherman Act cases laid the basis for a fundamental caselaw doctrine holding price-fixing agreements illegal. In *United States v. Trans-Missouri Freight Association*,[53] the Court held that the Sherman Act applied and made illegal an agreement among fifteen competing railroads to form an association, a committee of which would determine and announce reasonable uniform freight rates to be quoted by each member to its shippers. Under the articles of association, the chairman was authorized to investigate all departures from the association prices. A finding of willful departures from stated association prices would subject a member to a fine not to exceed one hundred dollars for each violation, payable to the Association. Mr. Justice Peckham, representing a majority of five justices wrote:

> . . . [W]e are . . . asked to hold that . . . [the Sherman Act] excepts contracts which are not in unreasonable restraint of trade, and which only keep rates up to a reasonable price, notwithstanding the language of the act makes no such exception. In other words, we are asked to read into the act by way of judicial legislation an exception that is not placed there by the law-making branch of the Government, and this is to be done on the theory that the impolicy [sic] of such legislation is so clear that it cannot be supposed that Congress intended the natural import of the language it used. This we cannot and ought not to do. The impolicy [sic] is not so clear, nor are the reasons for the exception so potent as to permit us to interpolate an exception into the language of the act, and thus to alter its meaning and effect.
>
> * * *
>
> The conclusion which we have drawn . . . is that the Anti-Trust Act . . . applies to railroads, and that it renders illegal all agreements which are in restraint of trade or commerce.
>
> * * *
>
> . . . [T]he suit of the Government can be maintained without proof of the allegation that the agreement was entered into for the purpose of restrain-

---

52 *United States v. E.C. Knight,* 156 U.S. 1 (1895).

53 *United States v. Trans-Missouri Freight Ass'n,* 166 U.S. 290 (1897).

> ing trade or commerce or for maintaining rates above what was reasonable. The necessary effect of the agreement is to restrain trade or commerce no matter what the intent was on the part of those who signed it.[54]

The four dissenters urged that the interpretation of the statutory phrase, "restraint of trade" be made in the light of the common law doctrine that contracts in restraint of trade were void and unenforceable only if the restraint that is produced is unreasonable. Under this view, if there was agreement among competitors as to price, but the price collectively determined was a reasonable one, that contract was not in violation of Section 1 of the Sherman Act.

In *United States v. Joint Traffic Association,*[55] some thirty one competing railroad companies operating between Chicago and the eastern seaboard, formed an association with the stated purpose of cooperating with each other and with other such railroad associations to establish and maintain reasonable and just rates and fares. This association functioned jointly to set freight rates and established severe fines for failure of a member to observe rates set by the association. Again writing for a majority of five, Mr. Justice Peckham stated: "An agreement of the nature of this one, which directly and effectually stifles competition, must be regarded under the statute as one in restraint of trade . . . ."[56]

The third foundation case in the interpretation of Section 1 of the Sherman Act is *United States v. Addyston Pipe & Steel Co.*[57] Judge (later Chief Justice) Taft's opinion (discussed in Chapter 3, *infra*) is widely considered as providing most of the analytical basis for the contemporary interpretation of Section 1.[58] As an historical irony, it may be noted that these governmental enforcement successes had the perverse effect of encouraging mergers, enhancing consolidation between and among competitors, and often restricting competition. The record shows that within a year of the government's victory in the *Addyston Pipe* case, which held illegal price-fixing and territorial division, the defendant firms merged and presumably continued their price-fixing activity with impunity within one larger corporate shell, because the "contract, combination, . . . or conspiracy" language of Section 1 requires a plurality of actors, and divisions within a single corporate shell are not so recognized. Given the absence of any explicit statutory prohibition against mergers prior to 1914, such arrangements may not have violated the Sherman Act.[59]

---

54 *Id.* at 340-41.

55 *United States v. Joint Traffic Ass'n,* 171 U.S. 505 (1898).

56 *Id.* at 577.

57 *United States v. Addyston Pipe & Steel Co.,* 85 F. 271 (6th Cir. 1898), *aff'd,* 175 U.S. 211 (1899).

58 *See* Edward Bittlingmayer, *Decreasing Cost and Competition: A New Look at the* Addyston Pipe *Case,* 25 J.L. & ECON. 201 (1982).

59 SIMON N. WHITNEY, 2 ANTITRUST POLICIES 6-7 (1958). *Compare Northern Securities Co. v. United States,* 193 U.S. 197 (1904), *infra* page 17. All the defendants in the *Addyston Pipe* case, plus a few of their prior competitors were consolidated into one firm within a year after the final decree by Judge Taft.

2. 1903-1915

This period began with the first Supreme Court case ordering dissolution of merged corporations as a remedy under the Sherman Act—the split-up of the Great Northern-Northern Pacific railroad combination.[60] The leading economists of the day did not advocate vigorous enforcement of the Sherman Act.[61] Rather, they placed their reliance on actual and potential competition as a regulator of abusive economic conduct.[62]

During this period, the political process began to take note of antitrust enforcement. From 1904 to 1915, the "big stick" approach of President Theodore Roosevelt began, a policy that was carried over to the administrations of Presidents Taft and Wilson. This period began with the activation of the Antitrust Division, which was established in 1903, and culminated with substantial government successes in the Supreme Court with victories over the Standard Oil Company and the American Tobacco Company.[63] These cases, however, also produced the "rule of reason" as a judicial standard for evaluating restrictive market conduct. One result of the announcement of the "rule of reason" in the *Standard Oil* and the *American Tobacco* opinions was to give impetus to the advocates of more vigorous antitrust enforcement. During the presidential campaign of 1912, all three political parties promised stronger action against monopolies. These pressures resulted in the enactment of the Clayton Act, which brought mergers and certain specific practices, such as tying arrangements, under judicial scrutiny. The contemporaneous passage of the Federal Trade Commission Act established an administrative agency to screen practices not otherwise designated, under the heading of "unfair methods of competition." The theory of this legislation was to end anticompetitive practices before they led to full blown restraints of trade or to monopolies.[64] The Clayton Act also initiated the Congressional practice of exempting certain activities from antitrust scrutiny. The 1914 version of the Clayton Act exempted labor unions and farm organizations from application of the antitrust laws.

---

60 *Northern Securities Co. v. United States*, 193 U.S. 197 (1904).

61 John Bates Clark considered large-scale enterprise as the basis of achieving the benefits of economies of scale. Moreover, he considered potential competition the best safeguard of the competitive process. *See* John Bates Clark, *The Limits of Competition*, 2 POL. SCI. Q. 45 (1887); JOHN BATES CLARK, THE PHILOSOPHY OF WEALTH 120 (1886). *See also* RICHARD T. ELY, PROBLEMS OF TODAY—A DISCUSSION OF PROTECTIVE TARIFF, TAXATION, AND MONOPOLIES 126 (1888).

62 See the text at note 28, *supra*. Some economists favored a regulatory approach of industry rather than antitrust enforcement. Thus, Richard T. Ely wrote, "I oppose private monopolies. What I favor is the management of certain monopolies by public authorities, and in the interest of the public." PROBLEMS OF TODAY 253 (1890).

63 *Standard Oil Co. of New Jersey v. United States,* 221 U.S. 1 (1911); *United States v. American Tobacco Co.*, 221 U.S. 106 (1911).

64 *See* GERARD HENDERSON, THE FEDERAL TRADE COMMISSION 27-32 (1924).

3. 1916-1935

This period was dominated by the government's loss in 1920 of its case against the United States Steel Corporation, the largest of the existing trusts.[65] Seemingly in response to this defeat, and notwithstanding the rule of reason analysis of *Board of Trade of the City of Chicago v. United States,*[66] the enforcement activity of the Antitrust Division shifted to cases involving "agreements" used by trade associations as facades and to cases that permitted invoking the *per se* rule against price-fixing.[67] Meanwhile, the Federal Trade Commission began its efforts to enjoin such practices as misbranding of goods.[68] During this period the Federal Trade Commission began its extended battle against the basing point system, a practice primarily employed in three industries—cement, corn products, and steel.[69] The decision by the Supreme Court in *Appalachian Coals, Inc. v. United States,*[70] holding that the joint sales agency was subjected to rule of reason analysis, extended the reasoning of *United States v. Trenton Potteries*,[71] a position soon to be in conflict with *United States v. Socony-Vacuum Oil Co.*[72]

The closing years of this period were dominated by the Great Depression. The New Deal's initial response to the Depression was to abandon enforcement of the antitrust laws. In the pursuit of a national remedy to revive the economy, the antitrust laws were expressly abrogated by the National Industrial Recovery Act of 1933.[73] Contrary to the conventional economic wisdom of the day, which advocated balancing the budget and cutting wages and other costs, the NRA was an attempt

---

65 *United States v. United States Steel Corp.*, 252 U.S. 417 (1920).

66 *Board of Trade of the City of Chicago v. United States,* 246 U.S. 231 (1918)

67 *Maple Flooring Manufacturers' Ass'n. v. United States*, 268 U.S. 563 (1925); *United States v. American Linseed Oil Co.*, 262 U.S. 371 (1923); *United States v. Trenton Potteries*, 273 U.S. 392 (1927).

68 *FTC v. Winstead Hosiery Co.*, 258 U.S. 483 (1922).

69 Basing point pricing is discussed at pages 340-47, *infra.* One academic economist, Frank A. Fetter, was the principal opponent of the basing point system. He inveighed against this practice with great fervor as a breach of fair competition, as follows:

> It is . . . also a false idea of true competition in trade that it necessarily or usually leads to the business destruction of competitors. This notion, repeatedly suggested in the confused pleadings of lawyers, has appeared also in the confused opinions of the courts. . . . [U]nder *fair* competition, the more efficient have a chance to succeed and less successful competitors are led to confine themselves in the long run to other territory. . . ."

THE MASQUERADE OF MONOPOLY 32 (1931, 1971 reprint).

70 *Appalachian Coals Co. v. United States,* 288 U.S. 344 (1933).

71 *United States v. Trenton Potteries,* 273 U.S. 392 (1927).

72 *United States v. Socony-Vacuum Oil Co.,* 310 U.S. 150 (1940).

73 15 U.S.C. §§ 703-712 (repealed 1935). Enacted by a special session of the 73rd Congress, the Act effectively repealed the antitrust laws for entire industries, if that industry adopted codes of "fair" competition. Some 22 volumes of detailed terms regulated the hours of work, wages, and the terms and conditions of sale of products and services. *See* M. GALLAGHER, GOVERNMENT RULES INDUSTRY 1-5 (1934). For example, the Code of the Artificial Flower and Feather Industry was adopted by agreement of industry and labor groups and was promulgated by the National Industrial Recovery Administration. The Code, as adopted, specified prices, permissible discounts, the manner of crediting returned merchandise, advertising allowances, gifts to buyers, and required NRA approval for the assignment of accounts receivable.

to "reflate" the economy by forming cartels in the major sectors of the economy. The NRA administrator ordered former competitors to meet together, to include labor organizations and consumer groups, and jointly to prepare codes governing each industry that restricted or eliminated competition in that industry. The Codes specified every commercial aspect including prices, conditions of work, and the terms of trade for each product and service in the economy.[74] In the last year of this period, the National Industrial Recovery Act was declared unconstitutional by the Supreme Court, thus ending the only experiment in abrogating the antitrust laws across all sections of the economy.[75]

4. 1936-1973

When the National Industrial Recovery Act was declared unconstitutional by the Supreme Court in 1935, the policy of a managed, cartelized economy was discarded. After the demise of the National Industrial Recovery Act, there was a renewed interest in the extent of competition in the economy. In 1938, Congress authorized the Temporary National Economic Commission to study and to make empirical findings on the structure of the economy.[76] In the same year, the Antitrust Division came under the stewardship of a colorful advocate of vigorous enforcement. In his famous iconoclastic book, Thurman Arnold criticized the prior enforcement of the antitrust laws:

> The actual result of the antitrust laws was to promote the growth of great industrial organizations by deflecting the attack on them into purely moral and ceremonial channels. . . . [T]he courts soon discovered that it was only 'unreasonable' combinations which were bad. . . . In various . . . ways the actual enforcement of the antitrust laws was completely emasculated by the courts. . . .[77]

---

[74] *See* M. Gallagher, *supra* note 67.

[75] *Schechter Poultry Corp. v. United States*, 295 U.S. 495 (1935) (holding the Act invalid as an undue delegation of congressional power to the President and, as applied, exceeding congressional power under the Commerce Clause). A recent study of the effect of the NIRA on prices and output reaches the counter-intuitive conclusion that the legislation had a salutary macroeconomic effect, generating an increase in durable goods output and in stock prices. *See* George Bittlingmayer, *Output and Stock Prices When Antitrust Is Suspended: The Effects of the NIRA,* in THE CAUSES AND CONSEQUENCES OF ANTITRUST 287, 318 (Fred S. McChesney & William F. Shughart II eds. 1996).

[76] *See, e.g.,* TNEC Monograph No. 13, RELATIVE EFFICIENCY OF LARGE, MEDIUM-SIZED, AND SMALL BUSINESS (1938); *see also* ELLIS W. HAWLEY, THE NEW DEAL AND THE PROBLEM OF MONOPOLY: A STUDY IN ECONOMIC AMBIVALANCE 12 (1966).

[77] THURMAN ARNOLD, THE FOLKLORE OF CAPITALISM 212 (1937); see also THURMAN ARNOLD, THE BOTTLENECKS OF BUSINESS Ch. 1 (1940) (in which Arnold emphasized the need for antitrust scrutiny of the channels of distribution); Thurman Arnold, *Theories About Economic Theories*, 172 ANNALS AM. ACAD. POL. & SOC. SCI. 26 (1934); Douglas Ayer, *In Quest of Efficiency: The Idealogical Journey of Thurman Arnold in the Interwar Period*, 23 STAN. L. REV. 1049 (1971).

The year 1938 began a period of vigorous antitrust enforcement. Between 1890 and 1938, the Division had brought a total of 433 cases. Under Thurman Arnold, in the period from July of 1938 to June of 1943, a total of 347 cases were filed.[78] This active approach to enforcement policy initiated by Arnold was, in part, based upon the new theories of competition developed by Edward H. Chamberlin and Joan Robinson, the origins of which were rooted in inquiries about the role of markets in causing and extending the Great Depression. The renewed interest in vigorous antitrust enforcement was reinforced by the new market models of economists.[79] Beginning in the 1930s, economists began to develop models that more closely mirrored the observed workings of markets in the economy. Rejecting the presumption that there was a tendency for the classical competitive model to prevail in the economy, economists posited imperfect markets with tendencies toward monopoly, as being more representative of the real world.[80] The new theories of imperfect and monopolistic competition filled the continuum between polar models of perfect competition and monopoly, neither of which were considered representative of substantial portions of the economy of the 1930s.

Thus, the model of monopolistic competition incorporated the realism of trademark and brand name usage by adding the theoretical construct of product differentiation. Broadening the classical model that had dealt exclusively with homogeneous goods, Edward H. Chamberlin addressed the sale of heterogeneous goods—goods that are close, but not perfect substitutes. Each seller's efforts to differentiate its product to attract buyers, provided such seller with some market power over the particularly designated products—hence the title of his work—monopolistic competition. Joan Robinson took a different analytical route to refute the classical assumption of a tendency for markets always to be perfectly competitive. Although neither Chamberlin nor Robinson made direct policy recommendations, their work served to draw attention to the structure of markets, and in particular, to distinguish markets by the numbers of sellers participating in them.[81] An outgrowth of the renewed interest in market structure developed into a body of economic analysis concerned with the interaction of sellers in markets with few

---

78 Victor H. Kramer, *The Antitrust Division and the Supreme Court: 1890-1953*, 40 VA. L. REV. 433 (1954).

79 In Edward H. Chamberlin's THE THEORY OF MONOPOLISTIC COMPETITION (1933) and Joan Robinson's THE ECONOMICS OF IMPERFECT COMPETITION (1933), shortcomings of the classical model of competition were addressed from differing analytical perspectives.

80 ARTHUR R. BURNS, THE DECLINE OF COMPETITION 40 (1936).

81 The original foundation of oligopoly theory was laid by a French economist, Augustin Cournot in 1838, in a work that was commercially published in English in the U.S. in 1963 as RESEARCHES IN THE MATHEMATICAL PRINCIPLES OF THE THEORY OF WEALTH (1963). Cournot provided analysis for a stable price/quantity equilibrium as a function of the number of sellers. A market with a single seller produces a monopoly price, with two sellers he assumed that each would assume the quantity to be marketed by the rival to be fixed and would maximize its own output. As the number of sellers increases, the equilibrium price for the industry declines through competition, until in a market with many sellers price equals marginal cost. Chamberlin extended the Cournot analysis in an article, *Duopoly: Value Where Sellers Are Few*, 44 Q.J. ECON. 63 (1929), and incorporated the substance of his article as Chapter III in the THEORY OF MONOPOLISTIC COMPETITION (1933).

sellers—oligopoly theory.[82] The substance of this analysis has been described as follows:

> Oligopoly, like monopolistic competition, occupies an intermediate position between the extremes of perfect competition and monopoly.
>
> . . . [W]ith oligopoly . . . the number of firms is not so large that any one of them can expect its actions to go unnoticed by the other firms. . . . [T]he number of firms in an oligopolistic industry is small enough for each to recognize their *mutual interdependence*.
>
> The basic problem posed by oligopoly is to account for the mutual interdependences among firms . . . to model how a given firm reacts to the pricing and output decisions of its rivals.[83]

This analysis provided a basis for antitrust scrutiny of oligopoly markets for the existence of collusive behavior. Reinforced by the descriptions of widespread concentration contained in the Temporary National Economic Commission's industry studies, there developed a climate of support for vigorous antitrust enforcement activity directed to markets with relatively few sellers. Adding to this concern was a substantial body of empirical work showing substantial concentration in many sectors of the economy. Gardiner Means' study of highly concentrated industries concluded that rigid pricing practices were characteristic of such markets. An ancillary finding was that concentrated industries had deepened and prolonged the Depression.[84] There is, however, little current support for this belief.

These empirical studies of actual markets and industries contributed to an active interest in antitrust enforcement policy. Beginning in the 1940s, the substantial volume of industry studies became the basis of a separate branch of economics known as industrial organization.[85] These studies built upon the work that had begun in the Temporary National Economic Commission.[86] During this period, the Federal Trade Commission contributed a study of asset holdings by manufacturing corporations.[87] The statistical measurement of the structure of the economy framed the question of whether this data also showed a trend toward concentration.

---

[82] The literature of oligopoly theory is reviewed in WILLIAM FELLNER, COMPETITION AMONG THE FEW 55 (1949). *See also* R.H. Coase, *The Problem of Duopoly Reconsidered,* 17 REV. ECON. & STATISTICS 137 (1935); P.M. Sweezy, *Demand Under Conditions of Oligopoly,* 46 J. POL. ECON. 568 (1939); G. Stigler, *The Kinky Oligopoly Demand Curve and Rigid Prices,* 55 J. POL. ECON. 434 (1947).

[83] WILLIAM F. SHUGHART II, THE ORGANIZATION OF INDUSTRY 34 (1990).

[84] Gardiner Means, *Notes on Inflexible Prices*, 26 AM. ECON. REV. 23 (Supp. 1936).

[85] THE STRUCTURE OF AMERICAN INDUSTRY: SOME CASE STUDIES (Walter Adams ed. 1954); SIMON N. WHITNEY, ANTITRUST POLICIES (1958) (a two-volume study of 20 industries); J.W. McKie, *The Decline of Monopoly in the Metal Container Industry*, 45 AM. ECON. REV. 499 (1955); Joe S. Bain, *Market Classifications In Modern Price Theory*, 56 Q.J. ECON. 560 (1941); *A Note On Pricing In Monopoly and Oligopoly*, 39 AM. ECON. REV. 448 (1949).

[86] WILLARD THORP, ET AL., THE STRUCTURE OF INDUSTRY (TNEC Monograph No. 27, Part V (1941)).

[87] FEDERAL TRADE COMMISSION, REPORT ON THE CONCENTRATION OF PRODUCTIVE FACILITIES, 1947 (1949).

However, as the data was released, it depicted a picture of change without demonstrating clear trends.

A leading commentator summarized this literature in 1951 as follows:

> . . . [In] explor[ing] a segment of American economic history since 1900 by way of the available statistical record . . . [w]e have . . . found no continuing growth in concentration, but rather a surprising stability. It is clear that among nonmanufacturing industries, the railroads underwent both gigantic growth and great concentration before 1900; but they have not changed much . . . since then. . . . As for the field of distribution, the rise of chain stores and mail-order houses have not increased their share of the retail market.[88]

The data on the structure of industry initiated a debate over the relationship between the structure of a given market and the behavior of the managers and the performance of the firms within it. This literature generated a debate about the scope and direction of antitrust policy that continues to the present. A leading writer reviewed this debate as follows:

> If technological and institutional conditions are not compatible with pure competition . . . [but] are not deemed to be such as to justify a public utility regulation of the firms in question, there arises a problem of defining an acceptable kind of competition in terms of market structure such that it can normally be expected to be accompanied by the kind of performance that is considered acceptable in the use of resources.[89]

Antitrust enforcement policy, as well as the decisional law of this period was influenced by the growing theoretical and empirical literature that underscored the possibility that concentration in markets created an environment in which collusion and other anticompetitive conduct could develop. Congress, too, seemed responsive to the data on concentration, as well as to the implications in the new oligopoly literature that suggested the potential for collusive conduct, albeit while also advancing a definition of workable competition.[90] For example, the Federal Trade

---

[88] M.A. Adelman, *The Measurement of Industrial Concentration, in* Readings In Industrial Organization and Public Policy 40 (Richard Heflebower & George W. Stocking eds. 1958).

[89] Edward S. Mason, *The Current Status of the Monopoly Problem in the United States*, 62 Harv. L. Rev. 1265, 1266 (1949).

[90] John M. Clark, the son of John Bates Clark, emphasized the existence of a free option of the buyer to deal with a rival. *See* J.M. Clark, *Toward A Concept of Workable Competition*, 30 Am. Econ. Rev. 241 (Proceedings, 1940). George J. Stigler's definition was a market consisting of a considerable number of firms not in collusion, in which market the long-run average cost curve for a new firm would not be materially higher than that of an established firm. *See* George J. Stigler, *The Extent and Bases of Monopoly*, 32 Am. Econ. Rev. 1 (Proceedings, 1942). Corwin Edwards accepted the same basic conditions, but added the absence of a dominant firm. *See* Corwin D. Edwards, Maintaining Competition 9 (1949).

Cases in which violations of the Sherman Act were found that involved large market shares and findings of anticompetitive conduct were: *United States v. Aluminum Co. of America*, 148 F.2d 416 (2d Cir. 1945); *American Tobacco Co. v. United States*, 328 U.S. 781 (1946); and *United States v. National Lead Co.*, 332 U.S. 319 (1947).

Commission study of the wave of mergers that occurred after the Second World War, energized Congress to amend § 7 of the Clayton Act to reach asset acquisitions, previously exempt.[91] Antitrust enforcement and the decisional law were also influenced by the economic literature stressing the importance of market structure and the corollary that concentrated markets can induce collusive and anticompetitive conduct by firm managers.

On occasion, policy outran the analysis. For example, with regard to merger activity there was substantial divergence between the data and the policy recommendation.[92] The Federal Trade Commission's 1948 Report on the Postwar Merger Movement urged the amendment of Section 7 of the Clayton Act in the following terms,

> . . . if nothing is done to check the growth in concentration either the giant corporations will ultimately take over the country, or the government will be impelled to step in and impose some form of direct regulation. . . .[93]

Yet, a critical review of the statistical methods employed in this Report concluded that the data showed that the post-World War II merger movement had produced little or no effect on concentration.[94] Another commentator says of the FTC Merger Report,

---

[91] FEDERAL TRADE COMMISSION, THE MERGER MOVEMENT: A SUMMARY REPORT (1948); *see also* The Report of the Federal Trade Commission on THE PRESENT TREND OF CORPORATE MERGERS AND ACQUISITIONS (1947); *Brown Shoe Co. v. United States*, 370 U.S. 294, 311-22 (1962) (citing the Congressional as well as the Court's reliance on these reports).

The Federal Trade Commission Report was criticized both for its conclusions and for its methodology in a work by John Lintner, John K. Butters, and William Cary, EFFECTS OF TAXATION: CORPORATE MERGERS Ch. X (1951). A lively debate erupted in the Journals involving a defense of the Report and further statistical errors in the defense. *See* M.A. Adelman, *The Measurement of Industrial Concentration,* in READINGS IN INDUSTRIAL ORGANIZATION AND PUBLIC POLICY 71 n.3 (Richard Heflebower & George W. Stocking eds. 1958).

Empirical work of Joe Bain tended to dominate economic analysis of the period. His studies concluded that economies of scale were not significant in most markets. Moreover, he found that in such concentrated markets, the existing firms erected barriers to entry against new competitors. He also associated coordinated pricing policies with relatively low levels of concentration. Accordingly, concentration in markets of large firms was not justified on economic grounds. *See* Joe Bain, *Relation of Profit Rate to Industry Concentration: American Manufacturing, 1936-1940,* 65 Q.J. ECON. 293 (1951); BARRIERS TO NEW COMPETITION: THEIR CHARACTER AND CONSEQUENCES IN MANUFACTURING INDUSTRIES 53 (1956). *See also* Leonard W. Weiss, *The Structure-Conduct-Performance Paradigm and Antitrust*, 127 U. PA. L. REV. 1104 (1979) (showing further corroboration of the thesis that concentration induces higher prices and profits).

[92] William H. Nicholls, *The Tobacco Case of 1946*, 39 AM. ECON. REV. 284 (Proceedings, 1949); James W. McKie, *The Decline of Monopoly in the Metal Container Industry*, 45 AM. ECON. REV. 499 (Proceedings, 1955); Walter Adams, *The Aluminum Case,* 41 AM. ECON. REV. 923 (1951); M.A. Adelman, *The A & P Case: A Study in Applied Economic Theory*, 63 Q.J. ECON. 238 (1949); Joel B. Dirlam, *Leadership and Conflict in the Pricing of Gasoline*, 61 YALE L.J. 818 (1952); Albert Nicols, *The Cement Case*, 39 AM. ECON. REV. 297 (Proceedings, 1949).

[93] FEDERAL TRADE COMMISSION, THE MERGER MOVEMENT: A SUMMARY REPORT 28 (1948).

[94] John Lintner & James Butters, *Effect of Mergers on Industrial Concentration*, 32 REV. ECON. & STAT. 30 (1950).

> The statement of the Federal Trade Commission is in part a policy judgment. . . . It is also a statement of fact, and as such it is doubly wrong: there has been no increase in concentration, and mergers have not been important enough to be of any effect, one way or the other.[95]

Not only was there a lack of unanimity among economists as to the implications of these various studies for antitrust enforcement policy, there was also a body of literature rejecting the need for vigorous antitrust enforcement. For example, Joseph Schumpeter, a famous Harvard economist, conceived of a different mode of economic rivalry—one in which various markets were dominated by one or two large firms possessing technological superiority. He considered that competition among firms for technological superiority was a continuous process—one that was adequate to protect the public interest. Schumpeter, like John Bates Clark and Alfred Marshall, considered industrial progress as the ultimate economic objective. Unlike them, he deemed beneficial certain restraints of trade as well as some market power. Supra-competitive profits could be justified to fund research and development activity for new and improved products and processes.[96] But Schumpeter's was clearly the minority view of antitrust enforcement policy during this period. Schumpeter's view is discussed further in Chapter 12, which deals with mergers.

The enforcement activity of the New Deal carried over into the decade of the 1950s, and into the early years of the 1960s. Within this period, the Antitrust Division succeeded in divesting the motion picture studios of their theater chains,[97] in obtaining antitrust scrutiny of patent licensing practices,[98] as well as in modifying specific exclusionary practices in selected industries.[99] The concern with structure was also evidenced by the group of merger and vertical restraint cases brought in the 1960s.[100] By 1963, the government victories in these cases stimulated a vast literature of economic analysis devoted to the antitrust cases.[101] The thrust of this intense, critical scrutiny of the case law consequently brought into question the eco-

---

95 M.A. Adelman, *supra* note 82, at 46.

96 Joseph A. Schumpeter, Capitalism, Socialism, and Democrary Chs. 7 & 8 (2d ed. 1947). This view was supported by David E. Lilienthal, Big Business: A New Era (1953).

97 *United States v. Griffith,* 334 U.S. 100 (1948); *United States v. Paramount Pictures, Inc.,* 334 U.S. 131 (1948); *Schine Chain Theaters, Inc. v. United States,* 334 U.S. 110 (1948).

98 *International Business Machine, Inc. v. United States*, 298 U.S. 131 (1936); *Ethyl Gasoline Corp. v. United States,* 309 U.S. 436 (1940); *United States v. Univis Lens, Inc.*, 316 U.S. 241 (1942); *United States. v. Masonite Corp.*, 316 U.S. 265 (1942); *International Salt Co. v. United States*, 332 U.S. 392 (1947); *United States v. Line Material Co.*, 333 U.S. 287 (1948).

99 *American Medical Assoc. v. United States*, 317 U.S. 519 (1943); *Associated Press v. United States,* 326 U.S. 1 (1945).

100 *See, e.g., Brown Shoe Co. v. United States*, 370 U.S. 294 (1962); *United States v. Philadelphia National Bank,* 374 U.S. 321 (1963); *United States v. Von's Grocery Co.,* 384 U.S. 270 (1966).

101 Carl Kaysen & Donald F. Turner, Antitrust Policy: An Economic and Legal Analysis (1959); George W. Stocking, Workable Competition and Antitrust Policy (1961); M. Massel, Competition and Monopoly: Legal and Economic Issues (1962); Richard Caves, American Industry: Structure, Behavior, and Public Policy (1964).

nomic justification of antitrust enforcement itself. A leading economist has recently summarized the literature on this point as follows:

> Over the years, and especially after World War II . . . antitrust issues began to be studied by economists with much better training, tools, and data. The result . . . has been increasing skepticism about the economic case for antitrust. . . . Most . . . [economists] now accept the criticism of antitrust as forcefully set forth by such writers as . . . Armentano, . . . Stigler, . . . Demsetz, and . . . Posner. This criticism sees hardly any merit in . . . [antitrust policy] other than the rule that price-fixing agreements are illegal per se. The views of Oliver Williamson on antitrust deriving from his emphasis on . . . transactions costs are not quite so negative. Still he does make clear that the older economists were too quick to label as anticompetitive innovations in business structure and conduct that could have no place in the perfectly competitive market that was their reference point.[102]

Toward the end of this period, the government prevailed in cases involving vertical restraints and vertical mergers. *See* Chapters 5 and 12.

5. 1974 to Date

In the 1970s the gap between the industrial organization literature, which suggested that many concentrated markets were workably competitive, and antitrust enforcement policy, that took the perfectly competitive model as its objective, brought antitrust case law and analysis under critical scrutiny. A debate erupted about the goals and doctrines of antitrust law that originated in the writings of scholars associated with the University of Chicago and which, accordingly, came to be identified as the "Chicago School" approach.[103] Robert H. Bork's ANTITRUST PARADOX made the case for antitrust law to be interpreted solely in terms of the economics of efficiency. Consequently, he advocated a "minimalist" approach to enforcement, *i.e.*, enforcement should focus principally on price-fixing—while market concentration, vertical arrangements, and mergers should be presumptively, if not conclusively, recognized as inherently reflecting efficiency conditions.[104] There developed a lively debate in the journals over the appropriate goals of the antitrust

---

[102] Donald Dewey, *Economics and Antitrust: The Circular Road*, 35 ANTITRUST BULL. 349, 364 (1990).

[103] The phrase "Chicago School" describes a group of antitrust scholars associated with the University of Chicago Law School and Economics Department. The oral tradition of economic analysis that began with Frank H. Knight, Henry Simons, George Stigler, and Aaron Director, was brought to bear on the conventional wisdom of antitrust law. *See* Richard A. Posner, *The Chicago School of Antitrust Analysis*, 127 U. PA. L. REV. 925 (1979); Aaron Director & Edward H. Levi, *Law and the Future: Trade Regulation,* 51 NW. U. L. REV. 281 (1956).

[104] ROBERT H. BORK, THE ANTITRUST PARADOX: A POLICY AT WAR WITH ITSELF 91 (1978); Frank H. Easterbrook, *Workable Antitrust Policy*, 84 MICH L. REV. 1696, 1703 (1986).

laws and the optimum means of achieving them. Some commentators consider the antitrust laws to have served historically as an appropriate restraint on undue concentration and exercise of economic power and that they continue to do so.[105]

At present, it is widely accepted that the critical approach of the "Chicago School" has served to refine and advance the understanding of antitrust analysis. As one commentator sums up this debate: "The Chicago School of antitrust analysis has made an important and lasting contribution to antitrust policy."[106] However, as the twentieth century draws to a close, there remain substantial differences as to the goals and means of antitrust law. One view urges the complete repeal of the antitrust laws stating,

> . . . antitrust regulation appears to have lost all of its claim to political legitimacy. In a rapidly changing information and technological world, with an inevitable internationalization of markets, the burden of proof is clearly now on those who would retain the law to demonstrate why all antitrust regulation should not be abolished.[107]

An alternative viewpoint is offered by a former head of the Antitrust Division. He suggests that formulating and administering antitrust policy is in the nature of aiming at a moving target, one in which the direction cannot always be discerned. Thus, as the late Donald F. Turner wrote,

> I made some mistakes. I should not have appealed the *Von's Grocery* merger case to the Supreme Court; and my 1968 merger guidelines were too severe. . . . [A]nother mistake I made—not requesting the Solicitor General to file amicus briefs objecting to plaintiffs' claims in *Utah Pie* and *Albrecht.*
>
> * * *
>
> With populist goals set aside, the function of courts is to formulate antitrust rules promotive of economic competitive goals.
>
> * * *

---

105 Robert Pitofsky, *The Political Content of Antitrust*, 127 U. PA. L. REV. 1051 (1979); Harlan Blake & William Jones, *The Goals of Antitrust: A Dialogue on Policy,* 65 COLUM L. REV. 377 (1965).

This debate over the goals and analysis appropriate to antitrust law is reviewed in ANTITRUST POLICY IN TRANSITION (Eleanor M. Fox & James Halverson eds. 1984). *See also* INDUSTRIAL CONCENTRATION: THE NEW LEARNING (Harvey Goldschmid, Henry Mann & James Weston eds. 1974); Eleanor M. Fox, *The Battle For The Soul Of Antitrust*, 75 CAL. L. REV. 917 (1987).

106 Herbert Hovenkamp, *Antitrust Policy After Chicago*, 84 MICH. L. REV. 213, 283 (1985). *See also* William E. Kovacic, *The Antitrust Paradox Revisited: Robert Bork and the Transformation of Modern Antitrust Policy*, 36 WAYNE L. REV. 1413 (1990); James May, *Historical Analysis In Antitrust Law*, 35 N.Y.L. SCH. L. REV. 857 (1990).

107 D.T. Armentano, *Time To Repeal Antitrust Regulation?,* 35 ANTITRUST BULL. 311, 328 (1990).

> However, it is often difficult to formulate rules that are both clear and economically rational. . . . First, there may be gaps in economic theory, such as the absence of economic analysis of novel practices. Second, there may be conflicts among economists as to the competitive effects of particular practices. Third, economic analysis often indicates that assessment of the effects of particular conduct requires consideration of several market factors, and both short-run and long-run effects. This points in the direction of complex rather than simple rules. . . . [I]t may be difficult to get and assess adequate facts for deciding individual cases where the outcome depends on assessing various factors and balancing anticompetitive and procompetitive effects.
>
> * * *
>
> Economic analysis problems do not warrant a severe cutback on the scope of antitrust law.[108]

Yet another statement of the objective(s) of antitrust law is that it "preserves and protects markets as an alternative to a more intrusive government regulation or control of the economy."[109] The recent decision in *United States v. Microsoft Corp.,* 97 F. Supp. 2d 59 (D.D.C. 2000), again ignited the question of the appropriate goals of the antitrust laws. Some argued that the antitrust laws have become obsolete and thus unsuited to dealing with practices of firms in the new technology of digital information. Others have taken the position that abusive market practices are a perennial problem and not a function of technology. *See* Chapters 6, 9, and 15 for a full treatment of the *Microsoft* litigation.

---

[108] Donald F. Turner, *The Virtues and Problems of Antitrust Law*, 35 ANTITRUST BULL. 297, 298-301 (1990). For divergent opinions about the goals of the antitrust laws among economists of an earlier era, see Dexter M. Keezer, *The Effectiveness of the Antitrust Law: A Symposium*, 39 AMER. ECON. REV. 689. (1949). Among the contributors to this symposium is another former Attorney General (during the Nixon Administration) and antitrust law scholar, Edward H. Levi, who wrote,

> I think there are three principal reasons for the relative ineffectiveness of the antitrust laws:
>
> 1. The courts are not sufficiently aware of the monopoly problem. . . . [T]he courts have not sufficiently considered size rather than the abuse of monopoly position to be the violation of the law.
>
> * * *
>
> 2. The Department of Justice has never had a sufficiently sustained and energetic policy of enforcement.
>
> * * *
>
> 3. Economists, in general, I think must bear a great share of the blame. The general impression of the public is that monopoly is inevitable. . . .
>
> * * *
>
> I think economists have failed to distinguish between descriptions of our present economy and analysis of what can or ought to be done.

39 AM. ECON. REV. 703 (1949).

[109] LAWRENCE A. SULLIVAN & WARREN S. GRIMES, THE LAW OF ANTITRUST: AN INTEGRATED HANDBOOK 10 (2000).

Other commentators characterize the present state of antitrust doctrine as emphasizing an empirical approach, with a diminished emphasis on a theoretical framework.[110] The 1992 decision in *Kodak* [at page 256, below] provides the basis for this assertion.[111]

One conclusion that may be drawn from this cursory historical overview is that a certain skepticism toward labeling is warranted. From the origins of the Sherman Act and throughout its history, a list of terms of ambiguous content seem to have influenced both enforcement initiatives as well as the caselaw. In the beginning there were such terms as "trusts," "monopolies," and "cut-throat competition." During the Depression and beyond, "bigness," "concentration," "collusion," "conscious parallelism," "leverage," "coercion," "foreclosure," "market power," "monopoly power," and "merger movement" became the basis of enforcement action. More recently, "consumer welfare," "free-rider," "competitiveness," "global economy," "productivity," "strategic behavior," and "raising a rival's costs" have been in vogue.

Over the enforcement history of the antitrust laws each of these various phrases has been a stated, if not a dominant concept in interpreting the statutes. By the late 1970s, it had become clear that allocative efficiency had emerged as the dominant criterion in the judicial interpretation of the antitrust laws. The leading treatise thus states,

> . . . [D]espite occasional implications to the contrary the courts have given efficiency and progressiveness priority over "populist" . . . [*i.e.*, dispersing wealth, broadening entrepreneurial opportunities, and reliance on market forces] goals.[112]

However, economic efficiency is a multifaceted concept that is in continuous process of theoretical and empirical refinement. A leading industrial organization economist refers to the policy choices presented by reliance on efficiency criteria as a guide to antitrust policy as follows.

> How does antitrust affect the level of economic efficiency, construed from both narrow and broad perspectives? Is there a tradeoff among diverse efficiency achievements? Can we identify specific policies that have had clear, important efficiency-retarding impacts? . . . Although antitrust policy may have had some negative effect on "efficiency" (in the senses defined below), the efficiency losses are probably small. . . .[113]

---

[110] *See* Jacobs, *supra* note 43.

[111] *See* William H. Page, *Legal Realism and the Shaping of Modern Antitrust*, 44 EMORY L.J. 1, 66-69 (1995).

[112] PHILLIP AREEDA & DONALD F. TURNER, ANTITRUST LAW 9 (1977). *See also* HERBERT HOVENKAMP, FEDERAL ANTITRUST POLICY 71-72 (1994).

[113] F.M. Scherer, *Antitrust, Efficiency and Progress*, 62 N.Y.U. L. REV. 998 (1987).

There are at least three distinct aspects in which the phrase, economic efficiency, can be interpreted. First, there is allocative efficiency in the sense that societal resources are allocated to the production of goods and services and their distribution to consumers in a manner that no reallocation would make some consumers better off without making others worse off. Then there is X-efficiency (or productive efficiency), the production of goods and services under least cost/maximum profit conditions in the short-run. Finally, there is long-run innovation or technological efficiency that reflects the rate of technological progress in society over time.

Scherer concludes his analysis of efficiency as the foundation of antitrust policy by illustrating its complexity as follows:

> There are a few things we know about the links between antitrust and efficiency, and too much that we do not know. . . . X-efficiency is much more important quantitatively than allocative efficiency, and dynamic . . . [technological] efficiency is surely even more important. We know that the links between antitrust, competition, and both X-efficiency and dynamic efficiency are complex and difficult to pin down precisely. Maintaining relatively fragmented market structures probably imposes modest foregone scale-economy costs, but vigorous competition keeps enterprises at fighting weight. Our quantitative insights are too limited to let us know whether a lean, tough welterweight is not to be preferred over a flabby heavyweight. The dynamic efficiency nexus is even more complex. . . . By striving to maintain a diversity of competitors and keeping entry barriers from being raised unnecessarily, antitrust is at least pointing in the right direction.[114]

Against this evolving conceptual background, the question remains, how should enforcement policy of the antitrust laws in the coming years be determined? Emphasis on all aspects of efficiency concerns is surely the start in considering antitrust enforcement action to the participants in a specific market. Most would agree that our national experience with antitrust enforcement illustrates the complexity of conforming a domestic legal system to a dynamic and complex market economy that increasingly is influenced both by rapid technological change and international trade.[115] There would probably be a broad consensus among commentators that antitrust enforcement policy should be aimed at those market practices that: 1) materially impede progress (the production of better goods and

---

[114] *Id.* at 1018-19. *See also* Joseph F. Broadley, *Efficiency, Consumer Welfare, and Technological Progress*, 62 N.Y.U. L. REV. 1020, 1028 (1987) (urging the primary importance of innovation and production efficiencies).

[115] Forecasting the future of antitrust law enforcement is usual with a change of administrations in Washington. *See* Robert H. Lande, *Beyond Chicago: Will Activist Antitrust Arise Again?*, 39 ANTITRUST BULL. 1 (1994). *See also* Donald F. Turner, *Symposium: Anticipating Antitrust's Centennial: Comment, Antitrust in the Next 100 Years*, 75 CAL. L. REV. 797 (1987).

services) to the detriment of consumers, 2) breach accepted norms of commercial rivalry without promoting efficient use of resources, and 3) impact a significant sector of the economy. Also, many would agree that the antitrust laws should not be used by private litigants to cast up contract, due process, warranty, licensing disputes, denials of hospital privileges, and like claims in the guise of antitrust violations to avail themselves of the federal courts, of treble damages, and of other antitrust remedies. Such litigation has often resulted in distorted development of antitrust doctrines.

Judge Easterbrook sounded an appropriate theme when he wrote: "What characterizes . . . [the Chicago school of antitrust analysis] is skepticism, not adherence to a set model."[116] While a skeptical attitude is appropriate, a positive framework of analysis is also required to formulate an antitrust policy. In the last decade of the twentieth century, new analytical tools have become available. The doctrinal disputes that pervaded the discussions of the 1980s are being supplanted by the advancement of new models as well as by the empirical testing of older ones. In large measure these changes are the result of a different division of labor among the contributors. The source of the new analysis of the 1970s, identified as the "Chicago School" had its origins in the Department of Economics of the University of Chicago and in the work of Frank H. Knight, Henry Simons, Aaron Director, Ronald Coase, and George Stigler. Director, an economist, who adhered to the oral tradition of scholarship, did not himself publish much of his innovative analysis; this was done by others.[117] As a teacher in the Law School at the University of Chicago of such courses as Competition and Monopoly and Industrial Organization, Professor Director conveyed his analysis to lawyers. In the 1970s, it was the lawyers—Robert H. Bork, Richard A. Posner, and Frank Easterbrook—who applied Director's analysis to recast the antitrust doctrines of the 1960s and early 1970s. The ensuing intellectual ferment stimulated interest in antitrust law among economists.

By the 1980s the economists had regained the analytical initiative from the lawyers. New theories and refined empirical work are currently infusing antitrust analysis. An early innovative contribution to the then conventional view of industry structure was made by the theory of contestable markets.[118] This analysis drew

---

116 Frank H. Easterbrook, *Workable Antitrust Policy,* 84 MICH. L. REV. 1696, 1708 (1986).

117 There is one joint published work. *See* Aaron Director & Edward H. Levi, *Law and the Future: Trade Regulation*, 51 NW. U. L. REV. 281 (1956). Director's influence by discussion is acknowledged in the introductory paragraph to the first footnote, in Ward Bowman's, *Tying Arrangements And The Leverage Problem*, 67 Yale L.J. 19, n.1 (1957):

> I have reconstructed . . . [two explanations formulated by Professor Aaron Director] as I understood them from previous discussions with him over a period of years ending in 1956 at the University of Chicago Law School.

See also Richard A. Posner, *The Chicago School of Antitrust Analysis*, 127 U. PA. L. REV. 931 (1979) (also noting the oral tradition and the influence of Aaron Director on antitrust doctrines). There is an anecdote attributed to Edward H. Levi, who brought Aaron Director to his Antitrust course, that his approach was initially received as a form of lunacy only to end up reshaping the then conventional wisdom.

118 WILLIAM J. BAUMOL, JOHN C. PANZAR & ROBERT D. WILLIG, CONTESTABLE MARKETS AND THE THEORY OF INDUSTRIAL STRUCTURE (1982). This analysis may be seen as a technically updated version of J.B. Clark's doctrine of potential competition.

attention to industries characterized by costless reversible entry. The theory of contestable markets has been described by its authors as follows:

> A perfectly contestable market is . . . one in which entry and exit are easy and costless. . . . Potential entrants are assumed to face the same set of productive techniques and market demands as those available to incumbent firms. There are no legal restrictions on market entry or exit and no special costs that must be borne by an entrant that do not fall on incumbents as well.
>
> An entrepreneur will enter the market if he expects to obtain a positive profit by undercutting the incumbent's price and serving the entire market demand at the new lower price. If the incumbent readjusts his price, reducing it beneath that of the entrant, then the new competitor can readily exit from the market without loss of investment.[119]

Although the authors conceived of this analysis to ". . . transform the field . . . [of industrial organization] and render it far more applicable to the real world,"[120] the theory of contestable markets has not initiated a body of empirical work to test it. However, the theory of contestability was reflected in the Merger Guidelines. *See* Chapter 12. Beyond describing the activities of small airlines shortly after deregulation of that industry, it lapsed from consideration, although this analysis served to refine the concept of economies of scale.[121]

A more recent example of innovative theorizing is found in the literature of network externalities.[122] This body of work is narrowly directed to industries characterized by new technology. The theory that has emerged has shifted the focus in competition modeling from concern with individual products to a model in which competition among sellers is shaped by the consumers' adoption of clusters of complementary products. The concept of systems markets poses antitrust issues because

---

119 *Id.* at xx.

120 *Id.* at xiii.

121 HERBERT HOVENKAMP, FEDERAL ANTITRUST POLICY 36 (1994), states:

> The minimum conditions for contestability (costless exit and instantaneous entry) must obtain very strictly, and contestable market performance deteriorates very quickly in response to minor imperfections. . . .
>
> . . . [These limitations] may have made contestability a flash in the pan, so to speak, as economic theories of industrial organization go.

122 Avinash Dixit & Joseph Stiglitz, *Monopolistic Competition and Optimal Product Diversity*, 67 AMER. ECON. REV. 297 (1977); Michael Katz & Carl Shapiro, *Network Externalities, Competition, and Compatibility*, 75 AMER. ECON. REV. 424 (1985); Brian Arthur, *Competing Technologies, Increasing Returns, and Lock-in By Historical Events*, 99 ECON. J. 116 (1989); Nicholas Economides & Steven Salop, *Competition and Integration Among Complements, and Network Market Structures,* 40 J. OF INDUST. ECON. 105 (1992); Michael Katz & Carl Shapiro, *Systems Competition and Network Effects,* 8 J. OF ECON. PERSPECTIVES 93 (1994); Stanley M. Besen & Joseph Farrell, *Choosing How to Compete: Strategies and Tactics in Standardization,* 8 J. OF ECON. PERSPECTIVES 117 (1994); S.J. Liebowitz & Stephen E. Margolis, *Network Externality: An Uncommon Tragedy*, 8 J. OF ECON. PERSPECTIVES 133 (1994).

such markets involve new technology whose rapid evolution and acceptance requires a decision among the producers on the standardization of some basic element—in the fax machine, the common signal; in the personal computer, the size of the disk. Once the standard is fixed—as by the adoption of ASCI language for software, competition between the adopted standard commodity and its former alternatives is ended.

In such industries, the theory of network externalities posits increasing returns on the demand side.[123] A network externality arises when the value of a fax to the initial buyer(s) increases as more buyers of fax machines join the network. Network externalities generate increasing returns from consumption in the same way economies of scale reflect increasing returns from production. The similarity between network externalities and economies of scale is that both generate increasing returns. In the case of economies of scale, it is the size of the capital investment that generates the increased return. In the network case, it is the increased use of the fax by others that adds the incremental value for the initial buyer(s). The distinction between economies of scale and network externality is that scale economies are associated with production—the supply side—and contrariwise, network externalities arise on the consumption—the demand side. In this way, as the network of consumers widens, the added value to the consumer of the initial purchase also accrues to the benefit of the producer and accordingly gives the producer of the accepted product an increased advantage over its rivals.

The implications of this manner of theorizing for antitrust enforcement policy is the subject of a current debate. The case for a more lenient enforcement policy is stated as follows:

> In network industries, most sales . . . will likely be made by a few leading vendors. Network externalities, like economies of scale, tend to produce concentration and departures from the competitive model. They may even lead firms to engage in anticompetitive practices on occasion. But competition for leadership position in network markets is often intense. Leadership is often precarious and transitory.
>
> A well-informed antitrust policy for network industries therefore cannot focus on short-run market structure. Nor should it apply unusually strict standards to network industries. Instead, the focus should be on business practices that do not have competitive justifications within a network industry.
>
> . . . The inevitability of complex business strategies in technology-intensive network industries does not . . . justify cartel behavior. . . . Moreover, the frequency and speed with which . . . [an extensive, irreversible network] occurs in some network industries significantly

---

123 For a fuller exposition, see David S. Evans & Richard Schmalensee, *A Guide to the Antitrust Economics of Networks*, 10 ANTITRUST 36 (1996).

reduces the value of current market shares as predictors of future competitive significance.[124]

Antitrust enforcement concerns remain regarding technology-intensive industries characterized by network externalities. Given the importance of such industries to the economy and the speed at which an entrenched network may develop, there is no assurance for society that as between rival technologies in the cluster, the superior technology rather than the first-adopted technology will prevail. These factors, it is urged, require strict antitrust scrutiny to be applied early because once the network is formed, competition between alternative technologies is ended.[125]

Another response by economists and policy makers to newly emerging technologies has been the introduction of the concept of innovation market analysis in the Intellectual Property Guidelines of 1995 [Appendix D, page 1133]. Some technological innovations of a method (including a method of doing business), process, or apparatus meet the standard for patent protection [Appendix A]. Other innovations resulting in creative expression, including computer software, may be protected by copyright. When products are protected under the patent or copyright regimes, the right holders seek to recoup the value of their investment by licensing the manufacture or distribution of the protected product. Chapter 15 contains material explaining the manner and extent of antitrust scrutiny of intellectual property licensing and related practices of patent holders and copyright owners. Also, the enforcement agencies are increasingly employing arguments based upon an alleged reduction in innovative activities to support claims of illegal practices. They are employing these arguments beyond the area of intellectual property licensing to merger analysis, tying arrangements, and monopolization litigation (as illustrated in the case of *Microsoft*). As noted in Chapter 12, innovation-market analysis can be relevant in merger analysis both in the determination of potential competition as well as in the determination of the appropriate remedy.

New technology also refines the tools of the economist. Empirical work is fostered by advanced econometric computing capabilities. For example, the discourse on the impact of foreign competition on domestic markets has traditionally been conducted in terms of case studies of specific industries, often bolstered by anecdotal evidence.[126] A recent study developed a model to take existing data from the Department of Commerce, Bureau of Labor Statistics, Federal Trade Commission, and National Bureau of Economic Research on labor productivity, concentration ratios, selling and research expenses, among others, to establish that foreign competition resulted in labor productivity increases in concentrated industries after a lag

---

[124] *Id.* at 39.

[125] Memorandum of *Amici Curiae* in Opposition to Proposed Final Judgement, in *United States v. Microsoft Corp.*, Civ. Action No. 94-1564 (D.D.C. Jan. 10, 1994).

[126] Robert C. Clark, *The Interdisciplinary Study of Legal Evolution*, 90 YALE L.J. 1265 (1981); ALFRED D. CHANDLER, STRATEGY AND STRUCTURE (1966) (a study of business history).

period, but had little impact on less concentrated industries.[127] Using available government data such as the Census of Manufactures and the Standard Industrial Classification codes, as well as TRINET, the electronic data base, an econometric model showed recently that little overall change in concentration had occurred between 1981 and 1989.[128] Similarly, this kind of research can serve to refine the manner in which basic government data about concentration in the economy is gathered.[129]

One conclusion that emerges from this historical perspective is that the emerging economic analysis, when coupled with the rapid rate of change in technology and its licensing practices, in health care markets, and in global competition requires refinements in enforcement approaches. It is possible that economic analysis of industrial organization will advance to dynamic modelling of entire industries. Enforcement decisions of the not far distant future might be made with the assistance of such an industry model. Some economists have begun to prepare an algorithm to provide a formal model which sets out the likely changes that will take place in price and output after a merger.[130]

In the end, economists have stressed that policy decisions must rest on models related to institutional practices. As Ronald Coase, a pioneer of the Chicago School cautioned, model-building alone cannot support antitrust policy. The choice is always to compare alternative institutional arrangements in terms of "viable institutional alternatives." As he put it:

> Contemplation of an optimal system may suggest ways of improving the system. . . . But in general its influence has been pernicious. It has directed economists' attention away from the main question, which is how alternative arrangements will work in practice. . . .[131]

Similarly, the task of fashioning policy based on economic analysis has been characterized as: "The task of linking concepts with observations . . . [is one which] demands a great deal of detailed knowledge of the realities of economic life."[132]

To this end, we have sought to include in relevant chapters some of the substantial body of economic analysis, "institutional economics," which rests on the work of Ronald Coase and for which he was awarded the Nobel Prize.[133] Institu-

---

127 James M. McDonald, *Does Import Competition Force Efficient Production?*, 76 Rev. Econ. & Statistics 721 (1994).

128 Julia Porter Liebeskind, Tim C. Opler & Donald E. Hatfield, *Corporate Restructuring and the Consolidation of US Industry,* 44 J. Indust. Econ. 54 (1996).

129 Amos Golan, George Judge & Jeffrey M. Perloff, *Estimating the Size Distribution of Firms Using Government Summary Statistics*, 44 J. Indust. Econ. 69 (1996).

130 Ariel Pakes, *New Economic Tools for Merger Analysis,* (unpublished paper presented at Charles River Assoc. Conference (April 1997)); *see also* Ariel Pakes & Paul McGuire, *Computing Markov-Perfect Nash Equilibria: Numerical Implications of a Dynamic Differentiated Product Model, 29* Rand J. Econ. 555 (1994).

131 Ronald H. Coase, *The Regulated Industries: Discussion*, 54 Amer. Econ. Rev. 195 (1964).

132 Tjalling Koopmans, Three Essays On the State of Economic Science 145 (1957).

133 Ronald H. Coase, *The Nature of the Firm*, 4 Economica (n.s.) 1 (1937).

tional economics was further developed in the writings of Oliver Williamson and others.[134] Prior to the identification of transaction costs by Coase, the economists' conception of the firm was as a center of decision-making over productive activity adhering solely to the profit-maximizing principle. The identification by Coase of transactions costs as a material factor in economic decisions, became the basis of the studies by Williamson and others of the firm as a governance structure in relation to actual markets—hence the title institutional economics. This perspective shifted economic analysis away from markets in which actors were posited as having only profit-maximizing goals, to a theoretical and an empirical analysis of firm organization and managerial behavior in actual markets.

From this institutional perspective, the use of exclusive contracts or the implementation of a variety of vertical restraints represents bounded rationality in a context of a battery of long- and short-run market objectives. An added consequence of the literature of institutional economics had been to mute, albeit not to void entirely doctrinal differences between the various schools noted earlier in this chapter. As Judge Posner, often identified with the Chicago School of law and economics, put it recently,

> The subject matter of law and economics overlaps that of the new institutional economics at a number of points. Vertical integration, corporate governance, and long-term contracts are foci of law and economics, just as they are foci of the new institutional economics.
>
> * * *
>
> The overlap between the new approaches is not total, and this leads to a difference not in theory but in theoretical emphasis. The new institutional economists' preoccupation with transaction costs leads them away from price theory toward theoretical concepts tailormade as it were for transaction-cost problems.[135]

In the chapters that follow, we hope to convey this sense of adventure in adapting and extending legal doctrines to rapidly changing technology, business practices, and marketing arrangements in order to formulate appropriate antitrust policies.[136]

---

[134] OLIVER WILLIAMSON, MARKETS AND HIERARCHIES: ANALYSIS AND ANTITRUST IMPLICATIONS (1975); George A. Akerlof, *The Market for "Lemons,"* 48 Q.J. ECON. 488 (1970); Armin A. Alchian & Harold Demsetz, *Production, Information Costs, and Economic Organization*, 62 AM. ECON. J. 777 (1972); Paul L. Jaskow, *Vertical Integration and Long Term Contracts: The Case of Coal-Burning Electric Generating Plants*, 1 J.L. ECON. & ORG. 33 (1985).

[135] Richard A. Posner, *The New Institutional Economics Meets Law and Economics*, 149 J. OF INSTITUTIONAL & THEORETICAL ECON. 73, 83 (1993).

[136] Antitrust policy includes also the absence of enforcement activity. A former head of the Antitrust Division of the Department of Justice states that before 1980, antitrust policy had reflected:

> . . . a pattern of meddlesome, interventionist antitrust policy, sometimes petty and mechanical as in the tie-in area, sometimes discretionary and at times potentially disastrous as in the concept of no-fault monopoly that characterized the old *Alcoa* decision and underlay the attack on *IBM*.

William F. Baxter, *Antitrust Policy*, in AMERICAN ECONOMIC POLICY IN THE 1980S, 600 (Martin Feldstein ed. 1994).

Although this book consists of a series of chapters in which each of the subtopics—the substantive compartments—of antitrust law is developed and analyzed, it is appropriate to keep sight of the larger significance of antitrust law. Accordingly, Judge Bork relies on allocative efficiency as the touchstone of antitrust enforcement. He is not concerned with the distributive effects of the performance of markets. His criticisms were directed at the failure of courts to accept this model. As a result, Judge Bork charged, courts were invoking outworn doctrines, such as foreclosure and predation, to bar commercial practices which actually could enhance consumer welfare. Overall, the adherents of this position tended to consider antitrust scrutiny as an intrusive economic regulation of business decisions. They advocate limited enforcement activity guided by micro-economic analysis. In the years since Judge Bork began the discourse which shifted the objectives of the antitrust laws, a group of economists and lawyers, too varied in their outlook to be considered a "school," have offered various other relevant factors as appropriate objectives of antitrust enforcement policy. For example, Victor Fuchs urges that distributional issues be considered along with efficiency considerations.[137] Krattenmacher and Salop urge taking account of "strategic behavior," as a qualification of the theoretical premise of rational economic behavior.[138] F.M. Scherer emphasizes the importance of further empirical study of the relationship between market structure and the performance of the decision-makers of the firms in it.[139] He also considers the dispersion of economic power an appropriate topic for further debate.[140]

In the last decade, the public choice scholars have raised these two issues about the antitrust laws.[141] First, they question the existence of empirical evidence to support the contention that antitrust enforcement has enhanced consumer welfare.[142] Secondly, they accuse both schools in the debate of uncritical acceptance of antitrust enforcement as the work of public servants acting in the public interest. The public choice perspective of the persons engaged in antitrust enforcement is one which emphasizes the pursuit of personal interest over the public interest. As one such study of the Federal Trade Commission has concluded:

> Our results lend support to a private-interest theory of FTC behavior over the entire period that we investigated [1961-1979]. . . . We would claim

---

137 Victor R. Fuchs, *Economics, Values, and Health Care Reforms,* 86 AM. ECON. REV. 1, 15-16 (1996).

138 Thomas G. Krattenmacher & Steven C. Salop, *Anticompetitive Exclusion: Raising Rivals' Costs to Achieve Power Over Price,* 96 YALE L.J. 209 (1986).

139 F.M. SCHERER & DAVID ROSS, INDUSTRIAL MARKET STRUCTURE AND ECONOMIC PERFORMANCE 684 (1990).

140 *Id.* at 482-83.

141 THE CAUSES AND CONSEQUENCES OF ANTITRUST (Fred S. McChesney & William F. Shugart II eds. 1995) (containing a collection of essays from the public choice perspective).

142 Fred S. McChesney, *Be True to Your School: Chicago's Contradictory Views of Antitrust and Regulation,* in THE CAUSES AND CONSEQUENCES OF ANTITRUST, *supra* note 135, at 323.

> that those observers who see the FTC as acting more in congruence with the public interest (whatever this may mean) . . . have been misled in their analysis.[143]

Other public choice investigators cite the recent enforcement agency actions against *Microsoft* (discussed in Chapter 15) in support of their belief that it is politics, rather than economic analysis, that drives antitrust enforcement policy. McChesney and Shugart support their conclusion that political considerations control, by citing the conduct of the enforcement agencies in the initial *Microsoft* litigation. Noting that the decision of the Federal Trade Commission not to take action against Microsoft was quickly followed by the filing of a complaint against the company by the Department of Justice, they give their interpretation as follows:

> . . . [N]o one could discern the White House's position on the Microsoft matter. "Part of the commissioners' problem," one observer said at the time, "has been trying to divine what the administration wants to do."
>
> . . . The DOJ's intervention in the Microsoft investigation occurred only after calls from Capitol Hill to Anne Bingaman, President Clinton's Assistant Attorney General for antitrust.[144]

Aside from the public choice perspective, there is also the criticism that the economic analysis, which has molded antitrust enforcement, is itself lacking in an empirical foundation. A former Director of the Federal Trade Commission's Bureau of Economics notes the following limitation in contemporary economic analysis of markets as follows:

> . . . [There is] . . . a weakness at the core of economics—we do not have a good model of the firm that explains much of the reality that we observe. This has been a very long standing deficiency in economics. . . .
>
> I believe that this deficiency can be remedied by bringing into economics much more of the reality of actual firms and tapping what is useful in the disciplines of marketing, accounting, and business strategy. . . . It is well past time for economists at the antitrust agencies to produce papers on topics such as what has been learned about actual companies' pricing strategy and market-level effects from the many thorough company investigations. Such research could benefit both antitrust and economic theorists who need a much richer empirical basis on which to develop new theoretical models.[145]

---

[143] Roger L. Faith, Donald R. Leavens & Robert D. Tollison, *Antitrust Pork Barrel,* in THE CAUSES AND CONSEQUENCES OF ANTITRUST, *supra* note 135, at 201, 212.

[144] Fred S. McChesney & William F. Shugart II, *The Unjoined Debate,* in THE CAUSES AND CONSEQUENCES OF ANTITRUST, *supra* note 135, at 344.

[145] David T. Scheffman, *Antitrust, Economics, and "Reality,"* in THE ECONOMICS OF THE ANTITRUST PROCESS 238, 240 (Malcolm B. Coate & Andrew N. Kleit eds. 1996).

In the preparation of the chapters which follow, we have sought to provide material to illuminate the historical development of each topic, its economic and legal underpinnings, and sufficient current materials from which the reader may consider the merits of these various criticisms of contemporary antitrust law. From whatever perspective one approaches this subject, it seems clear that it is a subject in flux. Despite changes in analysis and in interpretation, the enforcement of the antitrust laws is a fixture of government macroeconomic policy. In a recent REPORT OF THE COUNCIL OF ECONOMIC ADVISERS, the function of the antitrust laws is described as follows:

> The antitrust laws are the public policy instrument for preventing . . . anticompetitive collusion and mergers.
>
> * * *
>
> . . . [M]arkets efficiently . . . [perform] and provide proper incentives only when sellers compete with enough intensity to drive prices down to cost. But in some circumstances, firms can impede the forces of competition by agreeing among themselves to maintain high prices, or by merging to the point where individual production decisions substantially affect prices.[146]

These materials address the issues posed by this public policy instrument. There is a range of differences among economists, antitrust lawyers, and the public regarding the objectives to which antitrust enforcement should be directed. The authors hope that these materials may serve to illuminate this discourse.

While the antitrust laws express the congressional preference for competitive markets, they are not applicable to all markets in the economy. Because the core of the antitrust laws rests on the economic premise that competitive markets offer allocation, production, and dynamic efficiencies as well as advancing consumer choice, Congress has determined that there are some markets that are unable to provide the benefits of competition without some regulatory assistance. For example, in the markets for securities, banking services, and prescription drugs the information required for informed consumer choice is not generated in the ordinary course of business. For such markets regulatory legislation has established federal agencies and assigned them the task of ameliorating the perceived market failures. Thus, the Securities and Exchange Commission requires a prospectus, the Food and Drug Administration requires adequate labels, and the Federal Reserve System requires member banks to provide pamphlets describing borrowers' rights.

With the markets of the economy thus divided into regulated and unregulated sectors, the application of the antitrust laws is confined largely, but not exclusively to the unregulated sector. In this latter sector, as the chapters which follow indicate, the antitrust laws attack price-fixing, monopolization, boycotts, uneconomic merg-

---

[146] ECONOMIC REPORT OF THE PRESIDENT 129 (1997).

ers, and like conduct that impedes competition. However, the application of the antitrust laws is not entirely barred from the regulated sector, but may reach conduct and transactions not covered by the regulatory legislation. Moreover, there is not uniformity among the regulatory statutes. There are a group of statutes which provide for express, albeit limited, exemption from the antitrust laws for various markets. Cooperation among competitors is permitted by statute for agricultural cooperatives,[147] fishery associations,[148] ocean carriers,[149] telecasting of professional football,[150] small businesses,[151] jointly owned export trading companies,[152] and joint publishing ventures between one or more failing newspapers,[153] among other statutes. Finally, it should be noted that the boundary between the regulated and the unregulated sector is not necessarily fixed.

Congress has provided for further limitations on the scope of the antitrust laws in order to achieve specific policy objectives, such as permitting collective wage determination. Although determining prices by agreement among sellers is illegal *per se* in the unregulated sector, antitrust scrutiny is expressly withdrawn from collaborative determination of wages in labor markets. Section 6 of the Clayton Act [App. B] states that labor is not an article of commerce and § 20 of that Act provides that federal courts have very limited power to issue injunctions in cases involving labor disputes.[154] Chapter 16, *infra,* is devoted to explaining the scope of this labor exemption. Similarly, § 2 of the McCarran-Ferguson Act exempts the "business of insurance" from the antitrust laws to the extent that the business is regulated by state law.[155] Like labor negotiations, the setting of insurance rates and the evaluation of risks involve collaborative activity.

Given the great variation in the statutory regimes regulating the different industries, it is sometimes not clear when regulation preempts antitrust scrutiny. Some of the regulatory statutes contain an express exemption from antitrust liability;[156] courts may also consider claims of an implied repeal of antitrust liability in the absence of an express repeal provision.[157] Moreover, the boundaries of the

---

[147] 7 U.S.C.A. § 7 (1998)

[148] 15 U.S.C.A. § 521 (1998).

[149] 46 U.S.C.A. § 1706 (1998)

[150] 15 U.S.C.A. § 1291 (1998).

[151] 15 U.S.C.A. § 640(b) (1997).

[152] 15 U.S.C.A. § 4016(a) (1998).

[153] 15 U.S.C.A. § 1802(5) (1997).

[154] 15 U.S.C.A. § 17 (1997); 29 U.S.C.A. § 52 (1998).

[155] 15. U.S.C.A. §§ 1011-1015, 1011 (1997).

[156] The Sports Broadcasting Act, codified at 15 U.S.C.A. § 1291 *et seq.*, provides in § 1294 that shelter from the antitrust laws is provided for the joint agreements authorized by § 1291.

[157] *Eleven Line, Inc. v. North Texas State Soccer Assoc., Inc.*, 213 F.3d 198 (5th Cir. 2000) (no implied immunity from antitrust liability under the Ted Stevens Olympic and Amateur Sports Act, 36 U.S.C.A. §§ 220501-29 (2000)).

regulated sector are not fixed. "Privatization" and "deregulation" are terms which describe the process of the congressional withdrawal from some areas of regulation.[158] A further source of exemption from antitrust liability is made by case law. Chapter 18, *infra*, presents those cases which preclude antitrust liability if the disruption to competition is caused either by an intervention of a state government (the State Action Doctrine) or by the petitioning of a legislative body by a competitor (the *Noerr-Pennington* Doctrine).

Finally, the enactment of statutes designed to modulate the competitive process which began in the United States with the Sherman Act has been emulated abroad, principally in Europe. The Treaty of Rome, 298 U.N.T.S. 11 (1957), as amended by the Treaty of Amsterdam, O.J. (C 340) (1997) (renumbered provisions effective May 1, 1999), provided legal authority akin to the Sherman and Clayton Acts governing commerce and mergers in the European Economic Community. In applying these Treaty Provisions, the judiciary of the European Economic Community frequently refers to United States Supreme Court antitrust opinions interpreting our antitrust statutes. *See* VALENTINE KORAH, AN INTRODUCTORY GUIDE TO EEC COMPETITION LAW AND PRACTICE (7th ed. 2000); MARK FURSE, COMPETITION LAW OF THE UK AND THE EC (1999).

---

158 *See, e.g.*, The Telecommunications Act of 1996, codified as 47 U.S.C.A. §251(a) *et seq.* (2000) (not permitting competition in local and long distance telephone markets, permitting video service by telephone companies and telephone service by cable companies and reducing cable rate regulation).

Chapter 2

The Development of the *Per Se* Rule and the Rule of Reason as Applied to Horizontal Price-Fixing Agreements

A. Introduction

1. The *Per Se* Rule

At one time it was unclear whether the Sherman Act condemned all agreements in restraint of trade or only those which were in unreasonable restraint of trade. At least since 1911, it is clear that the Sherman Act condemns only the latter, *i.e.*, agreements which restrain trade unreasonably. The Courts have been willing, however, to treat some types of agreements—which they believe to have clear anticompetitive tendencies—as unreasonable on their face. These categories of agreements are treated as *per se* illegal.

The advantage of identifying categories of agreements as *per se* illegal is that it dispenses with the need to expend enforcement resources in repeatedly proving the unreasonableness of these agreements in every case in which they occur and, similarly, of repeatedly using judicial resources in adjudicating their reasonableness in every case. If identifiable categories of agreements are deemed illegal *per se*, then enforcement and adjudication are made less burdensome and more efficient. Moreover, to the extent that *per se* rules make the law more predictable, business firms benefit from their greater ability to avoid the unintentional violation of legal prohibitions.

2. The Rule of Reason

In the law of contracts, the common law had developed a doctrine of reasonable restraints. Contracts which were unreasonably in restraint of trade were not enforced by the courts as against public policy. Contracts which restrained trade "reasonably," however, were enforced.

When the Sherman Act was enacted, many observers believed that legislation had incorporated the common-law doctrine of "reasonable" restraints. Section 1 of the Sherman Act, however, literally prohibited "[e]very contract, combination . . . or conspiracy, in restraint of trade . . . ." The pressing question of the day was whether that provision should be read literally or whether it should be construed to have incorporated the common-law doctrine of reasonable restraints. In the *Addys-*

ton Pipe & Steel Co. case, Judge (later Chief Justice) Taft, sitting on the Sixth Circuit, incorporated the common-law doctrine of reasonable restraints into his opinion upholding a government case under the Sherman Act.

In *United States v. Addyston Pipe & Steel Co.*, 85 F. 271 (6th Cir. 1898), *aff'd*, 175 U.S. 211 (1899), six defendant manufacturers of cast-iron pipe, comprising 30 percent of the nation's productive capacity, formed an association whose objective was to eliminate price competition among its members by substituting a collective response to a potential buyer's request for a price quotation from any member. Prior to the formation of the association, a municipal government office would have received a range of individually determined price quotations from the member firms. After the formation of the association, the range of announced prices was collectively determined by the members of the association.

The essence of the plan was to divide the market for cast-iron pipe into three zones. The first category was the "reserved cities," which consisted of those customer municipalities located nearest to the designated association member. As the association functioned, the member firm closest to a reserved city obtained the right to submit the lowest bid on that job by agreeing to pay the association a fee for the privilege. It was agreed that the other member firms, not designated as the "reserved city" firm, would submit simultaneously higher bids to the same customer. The second zone designated by the association's rules as "free territory," consisted of some dozen states in the Northeast. In this region, association members were permitted to make bids entirely on their own. This region was dominated by nine competitor mills which possessed a combined productive capacity slightly in excess of that of the membership of the association. The third zone, "pay territory," comprised the rest of the United States. In this zone the association rules required that any price quoted by a member must have been determined by the association. Once the governing board of the association had determined the actual price to be quoted, the right to use that price was auctioned among the association members. The bidding consisted of offers by members to pay a bonus to the association. The firms which did not prevail at this auction were bound to bid high. The funds collected from bonus payments were distributed periodically to those members who were not successful at the internal auction.

The government sued the members of the association, claiming violations of the Sherman Act. Judge Taft, sitting on the Sixth Circuit, wrote a classic Sherman Act opinion, upholding the government's claim. Although the case antedated the Supreme Court's rule of reason decisions of 1911, Taft did not dismiss arguments based on reasonableness out of hand. Rather, drawing from the common law, he ruled that an agreement could be said to be in reasonable restraint of trade only if it was incidental or ancillary to another agreement whose main purpose was consistent with a competitive market:

> . . . covenants in partial restraints of trade are generally upheld as valid when they are agreements (1) by the seller of property or business not to compete with the buyer in such a way as to derogate from the value of

> the property or business sold; (2) by a retiring partner not to compete with the firm; (3) by a partner pending the partnership not to do anything to interfere, by competition or otherwise, with the business of the firm; (4) by the buyer of property not to use the same in competition with the business retained by the seller; and (5) by an assistant, servant, or agent not to compete with his master or employer after the expiration of this time of service. . . .
>
> . . . The main purpose of the contract suggests the measure of protection needed and furnishes a sufficiently uniform standard by which the validity of such restraints may be judicially determined.

Taft ruled that where there was no legitimate main purpose—as in the association agreements—then the restraints could not be upheld:

> . . . where the sole object of both parties . . . is merely to restrain competition, and enhance or maintain prices, it would seem that there was nothing to justify or excuse the restraint, that it would necessarily have a tendency to monopoly, and therefore would be void.

Evaluating the agreements before him under this standard, Taft ruled that the court below had improperly dismissed the case and ordered it reinstated.

3. The Rule of Reason in the Supreme Court

In two early Sherman Act cases, the Supreme Court construed the Act literally to prohibit concerted "restraint[s] of trade," regardless of their reasonableness. *United States v. Trans-Missouri Freight Ass'n*, 166 U.S. 290 (1897); *United States v. Joint Traffic Ass'n*, 171 U.S. 505 (1898).

In 1911, the Supreme Court abandoned its literal approach to the Sherman Act and adopted a doctrine that has come to be known as the rule of reason. In the famous *Standard Oil* opinion, the Court held that despite the express reference in § 1 of the Sherman Act to "Every contract, combination, . . . or conspiracy in restraint of trade . . . ," the Act did not condemn all agreements in restraint of trade, but only those which accomplished an unreasonable restraint of trade.

This turnaround was occasioned by two cases: *Standard Oil Co. of New Jersey v. United States*, 221 U.S. 1 (1911), and *United States v. American Tobacco Co.*, 221 U.S. 106 (1911). After holding in these cases that the Sherman Act prohibits only agreements in unreasonable restraint of trade, the Court felt obliged to explain or reconcile its newly articulated approach with its first two decisions, *United States v. Trans-Missouri Freight Ass'n*, *supra,* and *United States v. Joint Traffic Ass'n*, *supra*, decisions which had seemingly rejected a rule of reason approach.

4. The Relation of the *Per Se* Rule to the Rule of Reason

In its attempt to reconcile the rule of reason with these earlier decisions which had applied the § 1 prohibition literally, the Court explained that some agreements, because of their "nature and character" were inherently unreasonable. Thus while the Sherman Act forbade only agreements in unreasonable restraint of trade, there were some types of agreements which were inherently unreasonable. The latter type of agreements—being inherently unreasonable—could be condemned out of hand, without a special inquiry into their reasonableness. This rationale was, of course, the origin of the *per se* rule.

At present, these two categories function both as substantive rules as well as rules of procedure. When the trier of fact, after reviewing the evidence, makes findings that the practice at issue is truly a price-fixing agreement, as a matter of substantive law the practice is illegal *per se*.

Much of the confusion that bedevils antitrust law students at the beginning of the course can be reduced by placing the two rules in the context of an actual trial and distinguishing between the conduct of the trial and the rendering of judgment. In each case, the court must decide which of the two rules should control that case for purposes of rendering judgment.

The formulation of the *per se* rule determines the matters which must be proved in a *per se* case. Under Justice Douglas's formulation of the rule in *Socony-Vacuum* below, the plaintiff need only prove an agreement among competitors about price. The earlier version articulated in *Trenton Potteries*, 273 U.S. 392 (1927) (discussed in the *Socony-Vacuum* decision below and at page 52, *infra*), required that the plaintiff also prove market power. In identifying the matters to be proved, the rule governs the presentation of the plaintiff's case and plays a procedural role.

In the absence of the *per se* rule, a plaintiff, suing under § 1 of the Sherman Act, must prove concerted action by the defendants which unreasonably restrains trade. As the cases indicate, an unreasonable restraint is one in which the supply of goods on the market is limited to levels below those which would be offered in a competitive market. In many situations it is difficult or impossible for a plaintiff to prove this market effect.

Because the *per se* rule is designed to be a short-cut method for reaching similar overall results which would be reached under the rule of reason, tension between the two rules arises in those cases in which a plaintiff would be able to prove its case under the *per se* rule but would not be able to prove a case under the rule of reason. Then the precise formulation of the *per se* rule takes on a new importance: not only is the *per se* rule a less costly way for the plaintiff to prove its case, but it may be the only way.

In some of the cases you will read, the government or a private plaintiff charges the defendants with price fixing, but the defendants respond by attempting to convince the court that the arrangement in question does not fall within the scope of the *per se* rule against price fixing. In these cases, the courts are called upon to determine the boundaries of behavior which fall within the *per se* rule against price fixing agreements.

While the cases have to speak for themselves, a widely held contemporary view is that the *per se* rule applies to "naked" price-fixing agreements, *i.e.*, price fixing agreements among competitors whose sole purpose is to fix market price. Other agreements involving price determinations which are "ancillary" or incidental to an arrangement which plausibly furthers overall competition in the market place do not fall within the *per se* rule but are governed by the rule of reason. Robert Bork has forcefully articulated this distinction and there is support for it in the cases.

When the court is uncertain whether the agreement under attack is one which plausibly furthers competition in the overall market, it may require that all of the facts about the operation of the agreement be brought out at trial. In such a case, the court is required initially and during the course of the trial to rule on the admissibility of evidence adduced to establish all the details of the practice under antitrust scrutiny; thus, a rule of reason approach is effectively taken for purposes of determining the admissibility of the evidence.

In its most recent decision addressing the determinants of the rule of reason, *California Dental Association v. F.T.C.*, 526 U.S. 756 (1999), the Court effectively showed that a complex, multi-part analysis is often required in order to distinguish *per se* from rule of reason analysis in a given case. Justice Souter, writing for a divided court, described the difficult task of determining the proper mode of analysis as follows:

> [T]here is generally no categorical line to be drawn between restraints that give rise to an intuitively obvious inference of anticompetitive effect and those that call for a more detailed treatment. What is required, rather, is an inquiry meet for the case, looking to the circumstances, details, and logic of a restraint. The object is to see whether the experience of the market has been so clear, or necessarily will be, that a confident conclusion about the principal tendency of a restriction will follow from a quick look (or at least a quicker) look, in place of a more sedulous one.

526 U.S. at 780-81. *See also* page 77, *infra*, for a full discussion of this case. Note that the Court in *California Dental* recognizes two variants of the rule of reason—the quick look and the full inquiry into the procompetitive and anticompetitive aspects of a given practice. This material is covered later in the Chapter.

B. Price-Fixing Agreements

1. *Per Se* Rules

United States v. Socony-Vacuum Oil Co.
310 U.S. 150 (1940)

[Respondents, twelve major oil companies and five individuals, were convicted by a jury under an indictment which charged the oil companies with having "combined and conspired together for the purpose of artificially raising and fixing the tank car price of gasoline" in the "spot markets" in the East Texas and Mid-Continent fields. Respondents were convicted by a jury in District Court. The Court of Appeals for the Seventh Circuit reversed and remanded for a new trial and the Supreme Court granted certiorari.

[The Events and Their Background

[Beginning about 1926 crude oil was being produced in excessive quantities. As Oklahoma and Kansas attempted to restrict production through proration laws, a vast new oil field was discovered in East Texas. Production of crude oil from the latter field forced the price of crude oil to ten to fifteen cents a barrel and gasoline was sold in the East Texas field for 2¢ a gallon.

[When the price of crude oil fell to such levels, it fell below the cost of production from so-called "pumping" and "stripper" wells, forcing their abandonment. Since these wells accounted for about 40 percent of the known national reserves and since abandoned pumping and stripper wells often could not be brought back into production, the low price of crude oil threatened to waste significant amounts of resources. Proration laws enacted by the oil-producing states were designed to limit production within those states in the interest of conservation, but those laws were widely evaded when oil produced in violation of those laws ("hot oil") was shipped for sale to other states. Independent refineries using legally-produced crude oil found much of their market lost to lower-priced gasoline produced from "hot" oil. As a result many refiners had no outlet for much of their production and yet were compelled to continue operations in order to avoid losing their supply sources and their regular customers. Unordered gasoline which they produced ("distress gasoline") was dispatched to market in railroad tank cars and sold for whatever price it would bring. This distress gasoline, of course, depressed the spot market for gasoline.

[In 1933 Congress passed the National Industrial Recovery Act as a response to the Great Depression. Section 9(c) of that Act authorized the President to forbid the interstate and foreign shipment of petroleum produced in violation of state laws. The Act also authorized the establishment of so-called codes of fair competition, and such a code was thereafter established for the petroleum industry. These codes of fair competition were means by which the Roosevelt Administration sought to utilize industry-wide cooperative price fixing to raise prices and thereby to raise incomes. The philosophy embodied in the National Industrial Recovery Act was, needless to say, antithetical to that of the antitrust laws. Accordingly, that Act immunized conduct performed under its mandate from those laws. After the Supreme Court held the National Industrial Recovery Act unconstitutional in *Schechter Poultry Corp. v. United States,* 295 U.S. 495 (1935) (see page 47, *infra*), the codes lost their legal footing. When the defendants then continued to cooperate as they had done previously under the shelter of the petroleum code, the Department of Justice instituted suit.

[The Administrator of the petroleum industry code was the Secretary of the Interior. Under the petroleum code, an industry Planning and Coordination Committee was appointed, one member of which was respondent Charles E. Arnott, a vice president of Socony-Vacuum. Soon thereafter several buying programs were instituted under which distress gasoline produced by unintegrated refiners would be purchased by the major oil companies, thus relieving the spot markets from the downward pressure of this distress gasoline on price. These buying programs were at first unsuccessful because of the continuing influx of hot gasoline. Enforcement of § 9(c) was enjoined in a number of lawsuits and on January 7, 1935 the Supreme Court held § 9(c) to be unconstitutional in *Panama Refining Co. v. Ryan,* 293 U.S. 388 (1934).

[Representatives of the major oil companies meeting as the General Stabilization Committee under the code set up a new buying program which was to go into effect when Congress enacted new legislation to replace § 9(c). A Tank Car Stabilization Committee and a Mechanical Sub-Committee were appointed to administer the buying program. On February 22, 1935 the Connally Act forbidding the interstate shipment of hot oil and gasoline became law and a buying program was soon instituted under which the major oil companies purchased distress gasoline from the Mid-Continent buying program as follows:]

The major companies regularly reported to Bourque, the trade association representative of the Mid-Continent independent refiners, the volume of their purchases under the program and the prices paid. Representatives of one of the corporate respondents repeatedly characterized its purchases as "quotas," "obligations," or "allocations." They spoke of one of its "dancing partners" under the buying program as "one of the babies placed in our lap last spring when this thing was inaugurated." And they stated that "we don't have much choice as to whose material we are to take, when we purchase outside third grade gasoline in connection with the Buying Program Committee's operations. On such purchases, we have refineries 'assigned' to us." This was doubtless laymen's, not lawyers', language. As we have said, there does not appear to have been any binding commitment to purchase; the plan was *wholly voluntary*; there is nothing in the record to indicate that a participant would be penalized for failure to cooperate. But though the arrangement was informal, it was nonetheless effective, as we shall see. And, as stated by the Circuit Court of Appeals, there did appear to be at least a moral obligation to purchase the amounts specified at the fair market prices "recommended." That alone would seem to explain why some of the major companies cancelled or declined to enter into profitable deals for the exchange of gasoline with other companies in order to participate in this buying program.

[On May 27, 1935 the National Industrial Recovery Act was held unconstitutional in *Schechter Poultry Corp.* The Tank Car Stabilization Committee nevertheless decided to continue with the buying program. Because the East Texas market price could adversely affect the Mid-Continent price if the differential became larger than the freight rate, the majors became involved in an East Texas buying program instituted in the spring of 1935 aimed at removing distress gasoline from the East Texas market.

[The Respondents' Marketing and Distribution Methods

[In 1935 the respondent companies sold about 20 percent of their mid-western gasoline through their own retail outlets, and they sold about 12 percent of their midwestern gasoline through those outlets during the first seven months of 1936. The retail price of gasoline was set by Standard Oil Company (Indiana) under a formula based upon the Mid-Continent spot market price, and most of the other retail outlets customarily followed Standard's posted price. About 24 percent of the respondents' sales in the midwestern area in 1935 were to jobbers under long-term supply contracts which generally provided that the sales price was to be Mid-Continent spot market price on the date of shipment. Thus the higher was the Mid-Continent spot market price, the higher were the respondents' proceeds from retail and jobber sales in the midwestern area. The Court thought the "conclusion . . . . irresistible that defendants' purpose was not merely to raise the spot market prices but, as the real and ultimate end, to raise the price of gasoline in their sales to jobbers and consumers in the Mid-Western Area."

[An extract from Justice Douglas' opinion for the Court follows:]

The court charged the jury that it was a violation of the Sherman Act for a group of individuals or corporations to act together to raise the prices to be charged for the commodity which they manufactured where they controlled a substantial part of the interstate trade and commerce in that commodity. The court stated that where the members of a combination had the power to raise prices and acted together for that purpose, the combination was illegal; and that it was immaterial how reasonable or unreasonable those prices were or to what extent they had been affected by the combination. . . .

The Circuit Court of Appeals held this charge to be reversible error, since it was based upon the theory that such a combination was illegal *per se*. In its view respondents' activities were not unlawful unless they constituted an unreasonable restraint of trade. . . . In answer to the government's petition respondents here contend that the judgment of the Circuit Court of Appeals was correct, since there was evidence that they had affected prices only in the sense that the removal of the competitive evil of distress gasoline by the buying programs had permitted prices to rise to a normal competitive level; that their activities promoted rather than impaired fair competitive opportunities; and therefore that their activities had not unduly or unreasonably restrained trade. . . .

In *United States v. Trenton Potteries Co.*, 273 U.S. 392 (1927), this Court sustained a conviction under the Sherman Act where the jury was charged that an agreement on the part of the members of a combination, controlling a substantial part of an industry, upon the prices which the members are to charge for their commodity is in itself an unreasonable restraint of trade without regard to the reasonableness of the prices or the good intentions of the combining units. . . .

Respondents seek to distinguish the *Trenton Potteries* case from the instant one. They assert that in that case the parties substituted an agreed-on price for one determined by competition; that the defendants there had the power and purpose to suppress the play of competition in the determination of the market price; and therefore that the controlling factor in that decision was the destruction of market competition, not whether prices were higher or lower, reasonable or unreasonable. Respondents contend that in the instant case there was no elimination in the spot tank car market of competition which prevented the prices in that market from being made by the play of competition in sales between independent refiners and their jobber and consumer customers; that during the buying programs those prices were in fact determined by such competition; that the purchases under those programs were closely related to or dependent on the spot market prices; that there was no evidence that the purchases of distress gasoline under those programs had any effect on the competitive market price beyond that flowing from the removal of a competitive evil; and that if respondents had tried to do more than free competition from the effect of distress gasoline and to set an arbitrary non-competitive price through their purchases, they would have been without power to do so.

But we do not deem those distinctions material.

In the first place, there was abundant evidence that the combination had the purpose to raise prices. And likewise, there was ample evidence that the buying programs at least contributed to the price rise and the stability of the spot markets, and to increases in the price of gasoline sold in the Mid-Western area during the indictment period. That other factors also may have contributed to that rise and stability of the markets is immaterial. . . . So far as cause and effect are concerned it is sufficient in this type of case if the buying programs of the combination resulted in a price rise and market stability which but for them would not have happened. . . . Proof that there was a conspiracy, that its purpose was to raise prices, and that it caused or contributed to a price rise is proof of the actual consummation or execution of a conspiracy under § 1 of the Sherman Act.

Secondly, the fact that sales on the spot markets were still governed by some competition is of no consequence. For it is indisputable that competition was restricted through the removal by respondents of a part of the supply which but for the buying programs would have been a factor in determining the going prices on those markets. But the vice of the conspiracy was not merely the restriction of supply of gasoline by removal of a surplus. As we have said, this was a well organized program. The timing and strategic placement of the buying orders for distress gasoline played an important and significant role. Buying orders were carefully placed so as to remove the distress gasoline from weak hands. Purchases were timed. Sellers were assigned to the buyers so that regular outlets for distress gasoline would be available. . . . And as a result of the payment of fair going market prices a floor was placed and kept under the spot markets. . . .

The elimination of so-called competitive evils is no legal justification for such buying programs. The elimination of such conditions was sought primarily for its effect on the price structures. Fairer competitive prices, it is claimed, resulted when distress gasoline was removed from the market. But such defense is typical of the protestations usually made in price-fixing cases. . . . Any combination which tampers with price structures is engaged in an unlawful activity. Even though the members of the price-fixing group were in no position to control the market, to the extent that they raised, lowered, or stabilized prices they would be directly interfering with the free play of market forces. The Act places all such schemes beyond the pale and protects that vital part of our economy against any degree of interference. Congress has not left with us the determination of whether or not particular price-fixing schemes are wise or unwise, healthy or destructive. It has not permitted the age-old cry of ruinous competition and competitive evils to be a defense to price-fixing conspiracies. It has no more allowed genuine or fancied competitive abuses as a legal justification for such schemes than it has the good intentions of the members of the combination. . . . Hence prices are fixed within the meaning of the *Trenton Potteries* case if the range within which purchases or sales will be made is agreed upon, if the prices paid or charged are to be at a certain level or on ascending or descending scales, if they are to be uniform, or if by various formulae they are related to the market prices. They are fixed because they are agreed upon. And the fact that, as here, they are fixed at the fair going market price is immaterial. . . . Respondents . . . argue that there was no correlation between the amount of gasoline which the major companies were buying and the trend of prices on the spot markets. They point to the fact that such purchasing was lightest during the period of the market rise in the spring of 1935, and heaviest in the summer and early fall of 1936 when the prices declined; and that it decreased later in 1936 when the prices rose. But those facts . . . are wholly consistent with the maintenance of a floor under the market . . . since the need for purchases . . . might well decrease as prices rose and increase as prices declined. . . .

Under the Sherman Act a combination formed for the purpose and with the effect of raising, depressing, fixing, pegging, or stabilizing the price of a commodity in interstate or foreign commerce is illegal *per se*. Where the machinery for price-fixing is an agreement on the prices to be charged or paid for the commodity in the interstate or foreign channels of trade, the power to fix prices exists if the combination has control of a substantial part of the commerce in that commodity. Where the means for price-fixing are purchases or sales of the commodity in a market operation or, as here, purchases of a part of the supply of the commodity for the purpose of keeping it from having a depressive effect on the markets, such power may be found to exist though the combination does not control a substantial part of the commodity. In such a case that power may be established if as a result of market conditions, the resources available to the combinations, the timing and the strategic placement of orders and the like, effective means are at hand to accomplish the desired objective. But there may be effective influence over the market though the group in question does not control it. Price-fixing agreements may have utility to members of the group though the power possessed or exerted falls far short of domination and control. . . . Proof that a combination was formed for the purpose of fixing prices and that it caused them to be fixed or contributed to that result is proof of the completion of a price-fixing conspiracy under § 1 of the Act.[59] . . .

COMMENTARY

1. Justice Douglas' condemnation of price-fixing is cast in strong and sweeping language. Note his emphasis in the text on both "purpose" and "effect." Is "purpose" alone sufficient to violate § 1? Consider whether this broad indictment of collective price determination should be interpreted as a rejection of the prior precedents, such as *Appalachian Coals, Inc. v. United States,* 288 U.S. 344 (1933), *Board of Trade of the City of Chicago v. United States,* 246 U.S. 231 (1918), or *Addyston Pipe*? These cases are more fully discussed at pages 42-43, *supra,* and pages 58-65, *infra.*

Can *Appalachian Coals* be distinguished from the decisions in *Joint Traffic*, *Addyston Pipe*, and *Trenton Potteries* as a judicial recognition of an industry in dis-

---

[59] Under this indictment proof that prices in the Mid-Western area were raised as a result of the activities of the combination was essential, since sales of gasoline by respondents at the increased prices in that area were necessary in order to establish jurisdiction in the Western District of Wisconsin. Hence we have necessarily treated the case as one where exertion of the power to fix prices (*i.e.*, the actual fixing of prices) was an ingredient of the offense. But that does not mean that both a purpose and a power to fix prices are necessary for the establishment of a conspiracy under § 1 of the Sherman Act. That would be true if power or ability to commit an offense was necessary in order to convict a person of conspiring to commit it. But it is well established that a person "may be guilty of conspiring, although incapable of committing the objective offense." . . . And it is likewise well settled that conspiracies under the Sherman Act are not dependent on any overt act other than the act of conspiring. . . . It is the "contract, combination . . . or conspiracy, in restraint of trade or commerce" which § 1 of the Act strikes down, whether the concerted activity be wholly nascent or abortive on the one hand, or successful on the other. . . . In view of these considerations a conspiracy to fix prices violates § 1 of the Act though no overt act is shown, though it is not established that the conspirators had the means available for accomplishment of their objective, and though the conspiracy embraced but a part of the interstate or foreign commerce in the commodity. . . . Price-fixing agreements may or may not be aimed at complete elimination of price competition. The group making those agreements may or may not have power to control the market. But the fact that the group cannot control the market prices does not necessarily mean that the agreement as to prices has no utility to the members of the combination. . . .

tress? How should distress be defined for this purpose? Were not the defendant major oil companies in *Socony-Vacuum* also in distress? Were the defendant firms in *Addyston Pipe* responding collectively to a sharp fall in the demand for their product? What factors might have led the Department of Justice to bring an antitrust action against the major oil companies when those companies decided to carry on the practices that began with the blessing of the government under the National Industrial Recovery Act? Might the Justice Department have brought the *Socony-Vacuum* case, in part, to clarify the scope of the *per se* rule after *Appalachian*? Consider this question after reading the material on pages 58-63.

2. Does the group of cases discussed above illuminate the choice that firms in economic distress face between private cartel-like self-help and asking for direct governmental assistance? Consider the course taken by the Chrysler and Lockheed Aircraft corporations. Each sought and received governmental loan assistance. *See* Chrysler Corporation Loan Guarantee Act of 1979, Pub. L. No. 96-185, 93 Stat. 1324 (1980); Emergency Loan Guarantee Act, Pub. L. 92-70, 85 Stat. 178 (1971). Although the latter statute did not specifically mention the Lockheed Corporation, this statute was stimulated by its financial problems. *See* H.R. Rep. No. 379, 97th Cong., 1st Sess. 1271 (1971).

Is it sound public policy to subject private action among firms in a distressed industry to antitrust sanctions? Does this not create an incentive to seek direct financial assistance from the government? In this posture, what is the government's policy toward competition as the rule of the marketplace? Is it the case that competition is fostered by the antitrust laws, but if competition puts a large firm in financial straits, the government stands prepared to assist a firm that may be inefficient?

About the time the Chrysler Corporation received government help from Washington, AEG-Telefunken, A.G., was assisted by the German government and a consortium of banks. A decade earlier, British Leyland was formed by a merger of two government-owned automobile manufacturing companies in order better to meet foreign competition. In 1975, when British Leyland was in financial difficulty, Prime Minister Wilson persuaded Parliament to advance the company $426 million. In 1979, Prime Minister Margaret Thatcher persuaded Parliament to advance $600 million and in 1981 an additional $1.2 billion was advanced. In Japan, the government and a private bank assisted Toyo Kogyo, the maker of Mazda automobiles, with substantial loans to avert a financial crisis in 1975.

In each instance the governmental assistance enabled the companies to return to profitability, albeit after also making substantial organizational changes. Do these episodes suggest that the scope of antitrust laws should be narrowed so that large firms that provide many jobs and income to a cluster of suppliers are outside the ambit of enforcement when they undertake self-help, *i.e.*, cartel-like measures, in the face of financial stringency? One commentator notes a pattern in governmental assistance as follows:

> When large companies that employ substantial portions of a region's workforce begin to falter, political pressures invariably mount to "save

> jobs." Even if politics did not intercede initially, rapid dissolution of such companies might so disrupt social and economic life that governments and other institutions would be compelled to respond.

(Former Secretary of Labor) Robert B. Reich, *Bailout: A Comparative Study in Law and Industrial Structure*, 2 YALE J. ON REG. 163, 222 (1984). For a detailed description of these foreign cases, see *id.* at 166-87.

3. Should the growing policy of bailouts (including the savings and loan institutions) require an adjustment of the scope of antitrust enforcement? If the policy of the antitrust laws is to establish competition as the rule of the marketplace in the private, unregulated sector, does that not imply that some firms should not survive? Would not the Chicago School urge that with efficiency and consumer welfare as the objectives, competition requires the demise of inefficient firms? Would Areeda and Turner deem it within the broad, populist, view of the goals of antitrust policy to rescue inefficient firms?

Consider the U.S. Department of Justice and Federal Trade Commission Merger Guidelines in Chapter 12 and Appendix C. Does the failing company exception not state a limitation in antitrust enforcement of § 7 of the Clayton Act on account of financial stringency? Should there be such for §§ 1 and 2 of the Sherman Act? For a review of bailouts, see Cheryl D. Block, *Overt and Covert Bailouts: Developing a Public Bailout Policy*, 67 IND. L. REV. 951, 962 (1992).

4. Although both Japan and the European Union have antitrust or competition laws, both jurisdictions sometimes allow the firms in distressed industries to adopt a plan for revitalization involving agreed-upon capital reductions. Observe that in an industry suffering from an excessive amount of obsolete capacity, the excess capacity deters each firm from replacing its existing obsolete plant with a state-of-the-art plant. An agreement which contemplates simultaneous reduction in capacity with reinvestment in an efficient plant at an overall lower level of industry capacity removes these disincentives. In Japan and the European Union, industries in this situation have been able to enter into such agreements with official approval. *See* MITSUO MATSUSHITA, INTERNATIONAL TRADE AND COMPETITION LAW IN JAPAN 283-85 (1993); Synthetic Fiber Agreement, Commission Decision of July 14, 1984, Com. Mkt. Rep. (CCH) ¶ 10,606.

5. Consider what conduct and evidence it takes to violate § 1 under the holding of *Socony-Vacuum*. Will the government prevail as a party plaintiff if it proves the existence of an agreement among competitors in interstate commerce to set price? Does the government also have to prove that the competitors adhering to the agreement possess the power to make that price prevail in the actual market? How do you interpret footnote 59 in *Socony*?

In *United States v. Trenton Potteries Co.*, 273 U.S. 392 (1927), one of the earlier *per se*, price-fixing precedents, Justice Stone began the opinion by noting that the defendant companies together, as horizontal competitors, controlled 82 percent of the supply of the product. Should agreement among such competitors be held to violate § 1 only if the competitors control a substantial share of the market? Does Justice Douglas reject the necessity of a finding of market power in his opinion in *Socony*? If courts are to ignore market power in horizontal price fixing cases, is it an efficient use of the scarce enforcement resources of the Antitrust Division to bring cases against firms without market power? Might such cases better be left to the force of competition for correction?

6. The apparent clarity of the *per se* rule condemning horizontal price-fixing agreements deters most business firms from joining price-fixing agreements. Yet periodically the government uncovers blatant price-fixing as it did in an international cartel involving citric acid. In that case, Archer Daniels Midland Company recently pled guilty to fixing prices on citric acid and even more recently the American subsidiary of Bayer A.G. of Germany entered a guilty plea in the same conspiracy. *See* N.Y. TIMES January 30, 1997, at C1. According to the government, the conspiracy was well developed:

> A group of senior executives at the companies involved were responsible for negotiating the broad terms of the scheme. The group of executives was dubbed "the masters." A second level of executives, known as "the sherpas," then worked out the details and technicalities of the broad agreement reached by the "masters." Those details, Government officials said, involved such items as the precise percentage of the total citric acid market that each participant was allowed to sell.
>
> The scheme even had its own policing and enforcement system. Under that, each company shared monthly sales figures with co-conspirators—something also done in the lysine scheme. At the end of the year, the performance of the conspirators was reviewed. Then, any company that sold more than its allotted share in one year was required to purchase the excess from another conspirator the following year.

Id. at C5.

During the 1980s, the president of American Airlines asked the president of Braniff to participate in joint price-fixing. The scheme never materialized because Braniff's president taped the solicitation and gave the tape to the Justice Department. The Justice Department then charged American Airlines and its president with attempted monopolization. *See United States v. American Airlines, Inc.*, 743 F.2d 1114 (5th Cir. 1984) (excerpted at page 485, *infra*).

7. Is the *per se* bar against collective price determination validated by economic theory? How should economic analysis provide content to the following Supreme Court statement of the objective of the Sherman Act?

> The Sherman Act was designed to be a comprehensive charter of economic liberty aimed at preserving free and unfettered competition as the

> rule of trade. It rests on the premise that the unrestrained interaction of competitive forces will yield the best allocation of our economic resources, the lowest prices, the highest quality and the greatest material progress . . . .

Northern Pacific Railway v. United States, 356 U.S. 1, 4 (1958). To what norm of competition should the law conform? The economic model of perfect competition rests on assumptions not characteristic of most actual markets. For example,

> The conditions . . . which obtain . . . in an economic model of "perfect competition," are: 1) all sellers make an absolutely homogeneous product . . . 2) each seller in the market is . . . small in proportion to the entire market . . . 3) all resources are completely mobile . . . 4) all participants in the market have perfect knowledge of price, output and other information about the market.

HERBERT HOVENKAMP, ECONOMICS AND FEDERAL ANTITRUST LAW 2 (1985). Should it be the focus of antitrust policy to restructure actual markets to approach these theoretical norms? What roles (if any) should these theoretical norms play in antitrust administration?

As economic theorists refine the analysis of competition, these basic assumptions have come under critical scrutiny. One line of critical inquiry undertakes to broaden the explanation of the economic behavior of firms by incorporating organizational theory and game theory. *See* OLIVER E. WILLIAMSON, MARKETS AND HIERARCHIES Ch. 1 (1975); JEAN TIROLE, THE THEORY OF INDUSTRIAL ORGANIZATION Ch. 11 (1992). Another approach questions the basic assumptions, *e.g.*, the condition of perfect information.

For example, once the assumption of perfect knowledge is withdrawn in favor of a premise that information is a good that can only be acquired at some cost, the character of competition is altered. As one leading theorist has put it:

> Costly information gives rise to monopoly power; firms are able to charge more than the competitive price. . . . Even with relatively small search costs, prices may be well in excess of the marginal cost of production. . . . Models are more aptly described by a model of monopolistic competition than by either a model of perfect competition or monopoly.

Joseph E. Stiglitz, *Imperfect Information in the Product Market, in* 1 HANDBOOK OF INDUSTRIAL ORGANIZATION 769, 818 (Richard Schmalensee & Robert D. Willig eds. 1989).

8. If economic theory suggests that actual markets are imperfectly competitive, how should the law be applied to achieve the norm of making them more competitive? By what economic analysis should the law be guided? Time is deemed of the essence in one branch of the law of contracts. How should considerations of time be an element of enforcement of the antitrust laws? The story is told of John Maynard Keynes that he remonstrated with a colleague who repeatedly defended an economic model in terms of its long-run effects, by stating in exasperation, "In the long-run, we are all dead."

Consider the facts of the *Socony-Vacuum* case and assume that the defendants were not prosecuted, but that they set the price for their product high enough to yield substantial monopoly profits. Consider a long-run perspective, *i.e.*, a time period in which competing producers were able to acquire and operate competing crude oil facilities. Would not the new entrants to this market be able to divert Socony customers to themselves by charging a slightly lower price, but one that was above the marginal cost of the new entrants? As other entrants are similarly attracted to this market by the prospect of supra-competitive profits, would not the monopoly profits of the Socony cartel be eroded away, so that at some point in time a competitive price would prevail in this market?

Given this long-run corrective potential, are the antitrust laws needed at all? Or is there a role for antitrust legislation as a means of nipping in the bud the emergence of monopoly profits?

The objectives of the antitrust laws are continuous issues of concern. One view, stated by Judge Bork, is that the sole and exclusive role of the antitrust laws is to maximize consumer welfare through efficient allocation of scarce resources. *See* ROBERT H. BORK, THE ANTITRUST PARADOX 62 (1978); *see also* Frank Easterbrook, *The Limits of Antitrust*, 63 TEX. L. REV. 1, 39 (1984) (who writes: "[I]f there is no market power, if the defendant cannot profit by reducing output . . . [there ought be no finding of an antitrust violation].").

The competing view concedes that efficiency concerns are within the ambit of the antitrust laws, but urges a wider concern as follows:

> In addition to maintaining public confidence in the market system, reasonably precise goals delimit American antitrust policy . . . . These goals generally fall into four categories: (1) consumer welfare goals, including the efficient allocation of existing resources and avoiding wealth transfers to participants with market power; (2) fostering innovation and technological progress; (3) protecting individual firms through fairness and equity goals; and (4) maintaining decentralized power.

LAWRENCE A. SULLIVAN & WARREN S. GRIMES, THE LAW OF ANTITRUST: AN INTEGRATED HANDBOOK § 1.5b (2000).

Some commentators reject allocative efficiency as an inappropriately limited goal and prefer in the alternative the multivalued goals of Sullivan & Grimes, above. *See* John J. Flynn & James F. Ponsoldt, *Legal Reasoning and the Jurisprudence of Vertical Restraints: The Limitations of Neoclassical Economic Analysis in the Resolution of Antitrust Disputes*, *in* REVITALIZING ANTITRUST IN ITS SECOND CENTURY 271 (Harry First, Eleanor M. Fox & Robert Pitofsky eds. 1991).

Did Justice Stone articulate multifaceted goals for the antitrust laws when he began his opinion in the *Trenton Potteries* case in 1927 as follows: ". . . [T]he Sherman law is not only a prohibition against . . . a particular type of public injury. It is a limitation of rights . . . which may be pushed to evil consequences"?

9. Suppose there were no state or federal antitrust laws and suppose further that in the above variant (in the preceding Note) of the *Socony* facts the cartel continues to enjoy the monopoly profit because there are no new entrants. In this textbook example of a monopoly, there exists a misallocation of resources. Would society be as well served, absent antitrust legislation, if there were legal requirements for reinvesting monopoly profits in research and development, improving skills of the workforce, making compensation a function of increased productivity, and denying an income tax deduction to a firm that pays compensation to managers in excess of productivity increases, among other measures designed to obtain the benefits of the competitive norm? Despite the possibility of obtaining the results of efficient allocation of resources by such alternative measures, one commentator has suggested that the antitrust laws can serve to achieve multiple social goals. In some circumstances monopoly profits might be permitted in exchange for greater efficiency. He would urge a calculation of the tradeoff (gain in other valued social goals, as those set out above) against some loss of allocative efficiency. Presumably he would be willing to trade some allocative efficiency loss in exchange for a high rate of technological innovation. Oliver Williamson writes:

> It should be understood . . . [from this perspective] that allocative efficiency is . . . [not] all that matters. Allocative efficiency is, however, a valued social goal. Moreover, as between alternative public policy instruments—which include taxes, government spending, transfer payments, . . . and the like—antitrust enforcement is unusually well suited to promote efficiency goals.

Oliver E. Williamson, *Economies as an Antitrust Defense Revisited*, 125 U. PA. L. REV. 699, 734 (1977).

Consider the organization of the executive branch of the federal government. Does the President's cabinet serve as an appropriate forum to coordinate antitrust policy with tax policy and considerations of subsidies for certain markets, such as Williamson suggests? Does the President's Counsel of Economic Advisers now perform this function? Does President Clinton's Economic Council provide a means of providing such coordination?

Does Williamson's analysis accomplish a synthesis between the views of Judge Bork and that of Areeda and Turner by use of a wider time frame for assessing the impact of given market conduct?

10. As the antitrust laws, enacted in 1890, enter the second century of their application, how, if at all, should their objectives be reviewed and adjusted to serve in the emerging global economy? In 1890, the United States was an emerging industrial economy with an expanding western frontier. In 1993, the United States is a mature economy, the world's largest debtor, required to meet rigorous competition from state-assisted German and Japanese firms with superior trained work forces. German antitrust laws permit cartels and interlocking directorates among competing firms. Japan supports and oversees the operation of private enterprises in competition with U.S. firms, as in automobiles and semiconductor products. Should antitrust enforcement continue to require individual firms to act independently in the face of such competition? One school of thought suggests that collective action should be met by collective action. *See* LESTER THUROW, HEAD TO HEAD 124-36 (1991); CLYDE V. PRESTOWITZ, TRADING PLACES 81-85, 218-25, 248-85 (1989).

---

2. The Philosophy of the *Per Se* Approach

Justice Douglas formulated the requirements for violating § 1 in a way that would minimize the enforcement burden on the government. The enforcement authorities in the Department of Justice would have to prove merely the (1) existence of an agreement (2) among competitors (3) about their prices. This proof would establish a violation. Not only would the burden on the enforcement authorities be minimized. The burden on the courts would also be minimized: As the elements of a violation were narrowed, trials would be shortened as well.

Prior to *Socony-Vacuum*, the *Trenton Potteries* case (*United States v. Trenton Potteries Co.*, 273 U.S. 392 (1927)) had applied an earlier version of the *per se* rule against price-fixing agreements. That case had involved an agreement among business firms controlling 82 percent of the business of manufacturing and distributing vitreous pottery for use in bathrooms and lavatories. Against the defense that the prices agreed upon were reasonable ones, the Court ruled that the reasonableness of the prices was irrelevant. Rather, the offense consisted in the agreement itself which created the power to establish prices. In so deciding, the Court was attempting to relieve the government from the burden of proving unnecessary matters:

> The aim and result of every price-fixing agreement, if effective, is the elimination of one form of competition. The power to fix prices, whether reasonably exercised or not, involves power to control the market and to fix arbitrary and unreasonable prices. The reasonable price fixed today may through economic and business changes become the unreasonable price of tomorrow. Once established, it may be maintained unchanged because of the absence of competition secured by the agreement for a price reasonable when fixed. Agreements which create such potential power may well be held to be in themselves unreasonable or unlawful restraints, without the necessity of minute inquiry whether a particular price is reasonable or unreasonable as fixed and without placing on the government in enforcing the Sherman Law the burden of ascertaining from day to day whether it has become unreasonable through the mere variation of economic conditions. Moreover, in the absence of express legislation requiring it, we should hesitate to adopt a construction making the difference between legal and illegal conduct in the field of business relations depend upon so uncertain a test as whether prices are reasonable—a determination which can be satisfactorily made

> only after a complete survey of our economic organization and a choice between rival philosophies.

Accordingly, in *Trenton Potteries*, the Court held that:

> . . . uniform price-fixing by those controlling in any substantial manner a trade or business in interstate commerce is prohibited by the Sherman Law, despite the reasonableness of the particular prices agreed upon.

Id. at 397-98. Under the *Trenton Potteries* formulation, the defendants' market power was an element which had to be proved.

The reformulation of the *per se* rule in Douglas' *Socony-Vacuum* opinion dispenses with the need to prove the defendants' market power. In Douglas' view, there is no need to expend enforcement and judicial resources in exploring such matters as the defendants' power to control market price. Their agreement itself should be sufficient to show that they possessed the power to carry it out.

The weakness in the *Socony-Vacuum* formulation—a weakness which has become increasingly apparent over time—is that agreements between competitors about price may not always be anticompetitive. As we will observe below, some agreements among competitors may be innocuous and others may produce efficiencies. When a group of competing business firms lack market power, it means that the competitive process is functioning in that market, so that agreements among them need not produce substantial anticompetitive effects. If they do enter into an agreement, therefore, that agreement can have some purpose other than an anticompetitive one. Too literal an application of the *per se* rule forecloses the opportunity for firms to come forward and to offer justification for an agreement that might even enhance competition and contribute to consumer welfare.

As the cases which follow will illustrate, courts have increasingly declined to decide antitrust cases in *per se* terms, without considering whether the disputed practice generally produces an anticompetitive impact. In *State Oil Company v. Khan* [at page 183, *infra*], the Supreme Court found no economic justification for finding maximum price-fixing illegal *per se*. Greater judicial concern with competitive impact and potential pro-competitive consequences is also apparent in the development of rule of reason analysis. In *California Dental Assoc. v. F.T.C.* [at page 77, *infra*], the Supreme Court rejected "quick look" rule of reason analysis in favor of a more extended consideration of possible pro-competitive consequences of a professional society's rules barring some advertising.

NOTE: THE CASELAW BACKGROUND TO *SOCONY-VACUUM*

Besides *Trenton Potteries*, which the Court had decided in 1927, the background to *Socony-Vacuum* included *Board of Trade of the City of Chicago v. United States*, 246 U.S. 231 (1918), and *Appalachian Coals, Inc. v. United States*, 288 U.S. 344 (1933).

The *Board of Trade* case involved the largest grain trading center in the world. Each day, special trading sessions, termed the "Call" and usually about one-half hour in length, were held immediately after the close of the regular daily session for grain "to arrive." This trading involved agreements to deliver on arrival grain which was already in transit to Chicago or which was to be shipped there within a time specified. In 1906 the Board adopted the so-called "Call rule." Under the Call rule, members of the Board of Trade who wished to trade after the close of the Call and prior to the resumption of public trading on the next morning were required to trade at the bid price ending the Call session on the evening before.

The trial court had upheld the government's attack on the Call rule without even publishing an opinion. In reversing the trial court, Justice Brandeis' opinion of the Court contained a classic statement of the rule of reason:

> . . . The Government proved the existence of the rule and described its application and the change in business practice involved. It made no attempt to show that the rule was designed to or that it had the effect of limiting the amount of grain shipped to Chicago; or of retarding or accelerating shipment; or of raising or depressing prices; or of discriminating against any part of the public; or that it resulted in hardship to any one. The case was rested upon the bald proposition, that a rule or agreement by which men occupying positions of strength in any branch of trade, fixed prices at which they would buy or sell during an important part of the business day, is an illegal restraint of trade under the Anti-Trust Law. But the legality of an agreement or regulation cannot be determined by so simple a test, as whether it restrains competition. Every agreement concerning trade, every regulation of trade, restrains. To bind, to restrain, is of their very essence. The true test of legality is whether the restraint imposed is such as merely regulates and perhaps thereby promotes competition or whether it is such as may suppress or even destroy competition. To determine that question the court must ordinarily consider the facts peculiar to the business to which the restraint is applied; its condition before and after the restraint was imposed; the nature of the restraint and its effect, actual or probable. The history of the restraint, the evil believed to exist, the reason for adopting the particular remedy, the purpose or end sought to be attained, are all relevant facts. This is not because a good intention will save an otherwise objectionable regulation or the reverse; but because knowledge of intent may help the court to interpret facts and to predict consequences.

246 U.S. at 238.

Justice Brandeis concluded that because the rule applied "to only a small part of the grain shipped to Chicago," "to that only during a part of the business day" and did not apply at all to grain shipped to other markets, "the rule had no appreciable effect on general market prices; nor did it materially affect the total volume of grain coming to Chicago."

"But within the narrow limits of its operation," Brandeis determined that "the rule helped to improve market conditions" because:

> (a) It created a public market for grain "to arrive." Before its adoption, bids were made privately. Men had to buy and sell without adequate knowledge of actual market conditions. This was disadvantageous to all concerned, but particularly so to country dealers and farmers.
>
> (b) It brought into the regular market hours of the Board sessions, more of the trading in grain "to arrive."
>
> (c) It brought buyers and sellers into more direct relations; because on the Call they gathered together for a free and open interchange of bids and offers.
>
> (d) It distributed the business in grain "to arrive" among a far larger number of Chicago receivers and commission merchants than had been the case before.
>
> (e) It increased the number of country dealers engaging in this branch of the business; supplied them more regularly with bids from Chicago; and also increased the number of bids received by them from competing markets.
>
> (f) It eliminated risks necessarily incident to a private market, and thus enabled country dealers to do business on a smaller margin. In that way the rule made it possible for them to pay more to farmers without raising the price to consumers.
>
> (g) It enabled country dealers to sell some grain "to arrive" which they would otherwise have been obliged either to ship to Chicago commission merchants or to sell for "future delivery."
>
> (h) It enabled those grain merchants of Chicago who sell to millers and exporters, to trade on a smaller margin and by paying more for grain or selling it for less, to make the Chicago market more attractive for both shippers and buyers of grain.
>
> (i) Incidentally it facilitated trading "to arrive" by enabling those engaged in these transactions to fulfill their contracts by tendering grain arriving at Chicago on any railroad, whereas formerly shipments had to be made over the particular railroad designated by the buyer.

In *Appalachian Coals, Inc. v. United States*, 288 U.S. 344 (1933), the Court extended the approach of the *Chicago Board of Trade* case to uphold the distressed coal industry's self-help program. Prompted by the wartime demands in 1917, the coal industry had dramatically expanded to a capacity of 700,000,000 tons; the postwar demand was for less than 500,000,000 tons. Expanding production of a coal mine means reaching deeper seams of coal, which in turn requires extending elevator shafts, rail facilities, and air and water pumping equipment. Given the high, fixed capital costs of expansion, the mine operators have an economic incentive to cover the variable costs of running the pumps and air handling equipment, if they cannot cover all costs. Shutting down a coal mine is not economical, since the water will rise in the deeper shafts and undercut the structural security as well as destroy the rail and other equipment.

After the war, demand fell off sharply. As the price for coal plummeted, most mines continued to operate in the hope of covering variable costs until demand improved. In the Appalachian region, producers organized Appalachian Coals, Inc. Appalachian Coals, Inc. was set up to function as the common selling agency for the producers who organized and jointly owned it. This agency was given the exclusive right to sell the coal produced by its owner-producers and the right to determine the price at which the coal was sold.

The Government successfully enjoined the selling agency before it began its work, the trial court relying on *Addyston Pipe*, *Trenton Potteries*, and other price-fixing precedents. In resisting the injunction, the producers contended unsuccessfully that the common selling agency was designed to remedy certain destructive trade practices which had developed in the industry. These consisted largely of "distress" production, "pyramiding" and "misrepresentation" of the size of coal. The defendants also argued that, given the market conditions, they lacked power to set prices yielding monopoly profits. The trial court rejected these arguments stating:

> If it be thought that the law should permit agreements eliminating competition as between the parties thereto and fixing as between them prices at which goods shall be sold, in cases where monopolistic control of the market is not intended and does not result, the remedy is with Congress.

1 F. Supp. 339, 349 (N.D. Tex. 1932).

Consider the economic circumstances underlying the defendant's argument. Distress production occurred when a customer ordered a particular size of coal as required by furnaces of varying designs, (*viz.*, nut and slack, stove coal, egg coal, lump coal). Under the prevailing coal-sizing technology, the conversion of the original lumps into a given boiler size left a residual amount of coal that did not necessarily conform to another market size. Because there was often no place to store this excess coal, it was loaded into railroad cars and shipped to a billing point. If the coal was not disposed of at its destination, the producer incurred demurrage charges (*i.e.*, rent) for use of the railroad car, which continued to accrue as long as the coal remained unsold in the railroad car. The producer was thus pressured to dispose of the coal at almost any price covering some or all of the variable costs in order to avoid further demurrage charges. This, in turn, served further to depress the market price for coal.

Given the pressure on the coal company to avoid demurrage charges, pyramiding occurred when a producer hired several selling agents in the hope of increasing the chance of disposing of its inventory. Thus that practice meant that several selling agents were offering the identical consigned lot of coal. As the Court understood the effect of pyramiding, the existence of several selling agents for the same coal made it appear that the supply of coal was greater than it was, exerting a depressing effect on the market price of coal: "the coal competes with itself, thereby resulting in abnormal and destructive competition which depresses the price for all coals in the market."

Another destructive practice was misrepresentation, which occurred when sellers, hoping to dispose of excess coal, misdescribed their coal to buyers as the type of coal (*e.g.*, nut and slack, stove coal, egg coal, lump coal) which the buyer desired, thereby both injuring the buyer and taking away a sale from a rival seller who actually had the desired type of coal. Misrepresentation was facilitated because standards for the various types of coal were lacking.

Although the selling agency accounted for 74.4 percent of the coal independently produced in the Appalachian Territory, the selling agency accounted for only part of the coal mined east of the Mississippi. Little coal was consumed in the producing territory, however, and the coal was in fact marketed in the "highly competitive" coal market existing in the industrial area east of the Mississippi and north of the Ohio Rivers, where it accounted for only 11.96 percent of the coal sold.

In reversing the trial court and upholding the selling agency against government attack, the Court used language which superficially appears inconsistent with some of the language of *Socony-Vacuum*:

> The contention is, and the court below found, that while defendants could not fix market prices, the concerted action would "affect" them, that is, that it would have a tendency to stabilize market prices and to raise them to a higher level than would otherwise obtain. But the facts found do not establish . . . that any effect will be produced which in the circumstances of this industry will be detrimental to fair competition. A cooperative enterprise, otherwise free from objection, which carries with it no monopolistic menace, is not to be condemned as an undue restraint merely because it may effect a change in market conditions, where the change would be in mitigation of recognized evils and would not impair, but rather foster, fair competitive opportunities. Voluntary action to rescue and preserve these opportunities, and thus to aid in relieving a depressed industry and in reviving commerce by placing competition upon a sounder basis, may be more efficacious than an attempt to provide remedies through legal processes. The fact that the correction of abuses may tend to stabilize a business, or to produce fairer price levels, does not mean that the abuses should go uncorrected or that co-operative endeavor to correct them necessarily constitutes an unreasonable restraint of trade. The intelligent conduct of commerce through the acquisition of full information of all relevant facts may properly be sought by the co-operation of those engaged in trade, although stabilization of trade and more reasonable prices may be the result. . . . Putting an end to injurious practices, and the consequent improvement of the competitive position of a group of producers is not a less worthy aim and may be entirely consonant with the public interest, where the group must still meet effective competition in a fair market and neither seeks nor is able to effect a domination of prices.

288 U.S. at 373-74.

The task for the antitrust lawyer is to reconcile the two apparently inconsistent lines of authority represented on the one hand by *Socony-Vacuum* and *Trenton Potteries* and on the other by *Board of Trade* and *Appalachian Coals.* How would Judge Taft's early decision in *Addyston Pipe* relate to these two lines? Does the early approach of Professors Jaffe and Tobriner set forth below present a workable reconciliation of the two lines of authority? To the extent that their analysis is valid, how would you restate the holding of *Socony-Vacuum* and its predecessors?

Writing before the decision in *Appalachian Coals* by the Supreme Court, these commentators stress the importance of properly characterizing the underlying economic circumstances, as follows:

> It is an economic fact that there may be effective (and salutary) power over the market without controlling it. . . .
>
> It would seem, therefore, that the primary assumption of the Court in the *Trenton Potteries* case is unsound. And the additional and secondary assumption on which the decision rests is equally fallacious.
>
> . . . Assuming that all price agreements are monopolies, the [*Trenton Potteries*] Court considers that the only question of "reasonableness" can be one of *reasonable price*, which is a confusion of two different concepts. Many price agreements are not monopolies or attempts to form monopolies, and may be "reasonable" precisely for that reason. . . . [I]t does not follow that the alternative before the Court is to hold all price agreements bad, or even to hold some good or bad as the prices named might be fair. Position in the industry, tactics toward competitors not in the group, method of arriving at the price policy, all these would be pertinent in testing the price agreement. . . .

Louis L. Jaffe & Mathew O. Tobriner, *The Legality of Price-Fixing Agreements*, 45 HARV. L. REV. 1164, 1180-81 (1932). How would the Jaffe and Tobriner approach compare with that of Robert Bork who distinguishes between "naked" and "ancillary" restraints? *See Rothery Storage & Van. Co. v. Atlas Van Lines, Inc.*, 792 F.2d 210 (D.C. Cir. 1986), at page 109, *infra*.

Another (and more recent) commentator considers the state of the business cycle in explaining *Socony* and *Appalachian Coals* as follows:

> What explains the sharply differing approaches, coming just seven years apart, taken by Chief Justice Hughes and Justice Douglas? Hughes wrote at the height of the Depression, when the Justices' personal views no doubt reflected society's shaken faith in free enterprise. Douglas wrote as the nation was gearing up for World War II and pulling its way out of the Depression, with a restored faith in competition.

STEPHEN F. ROSS, PRINCIPLES OF ANTITRUST LAW 133 (1993).

3. Information and a Public Market

Both *Chicago Board of Trade* and *Appalachian Coals* raise the matter of the availability of adequate trading information to market participants. In *Chicago Board of Trade* there were a small number of specialist members who engaged in trading in "to arrive" grain. Brandeis' opinion shows that he believed that the farmers and country dealers who communicated with the specialists after the close of public trading operated at an informational disadvantage. The specialists, located in Chicago at the center of trading and able easily to communicate with each other, had a better picture of the "to arrive" market than did the relatively isolated farmers and country dealers. When the markets were open, information possessed and acted upon by any one trader would be rapidly incorporated into the public trading price, effectively giving all traders the benefit of that information. Note Brandeis' references to traders prior to the promulgation of the Call rule having to buy and sell "without adequate knowledge of actual market conditions" as well as his references to the creation of a "public market" where the benefit of information was effectively shared replacing "private market" where it was not.

Similarly, in the *Appalachian Coals* situation, the distress production, pyramiding, and misrepresentation all reflect inadequate market information by traders. In a market in which all participants had access to relevant information, the problem of distress production, as it existed in the coal industry, would not exist. Because of lack of market information, buyers who wanted a particular type of coal, say egg coal, often ordered it from a seller who had to produce it, even though a second seller already had egg coal available and did not know what to do with it. With better market information, the buyers who wanted egg coal would purchase it from those sellers who already had produced the egg coal as a byproduct in responding to an earlier order. Sellers with the needed coal already produced as a byproduct would always make the sale because their marginal cost of supplying the needed coal would be effectively zero and thus could always underbid a seller who had not already produced the desired type of coal. Thus widely disseminated market information would have eliminated the distress production problem.

The Court's description of the pyramiding problem is one in which market participants are misled by inaccurate information. Similarly, the problem of misrepresentation is also one based in a lack of information.

In the standard economic models of marketplace behavior, market participants possess adequate information to make intelligent decisions. Indeed, the textbook model of a competitive market only works because the participants are fully informed. If the participants in the coal market were fully informed, the problems identified in the Court's opinion would not have existed. The common selling agency then can be seen as a device to overcome the participants' lack of information and one which helps the market to operate more like an ideal competitive market. Thus both *Chicago Board of Trade* and *Appalachian Coals* can be viewed as upholding agreements which operate to help their respective markets more closely resemble an ideal competitive market. Accordingly, those agreements should be viewed as "reasonable" in so far as they further the operation of the competitive process in this manner.

Is the effect of Justice Brandeis' opinion in *Board of Trade* to add an element of competitive market analysis to the "Call rule" session? Does this opinion hold that the case does not involve price-fixing and therefore, the *per se* rule is not invoked? Or does this opinion hold that there was an agreement about price, but that the resulting prices were reasonable? Characterize the opinion in *Appalachian Coals* in these same terms. Does the *Appalachian Coals* opinion hold that although there was an agreement about price, the participants lacked the market power to enforce that price? Formulate a rule making price-fixing illegal under § 1 of the Sherman Act.

For further discussion of the effect of information on the competitive process, see Steven Salop, *The Noisy Monopolist: Imperfect Information, Price Dispersion, and Price Discrimination*, 44 REV. ECON. STAT. 393 (1977); George Stigler, *The Economics of Information*, 69 J. POL. ECON. 213 (1961).

Broadcast Music, Inc. v. Columbia Broadcasting System, Inc.

441 U.S. 1 (1979)

Mr. Justice WHITE delivered the opinion of the Court.

This case involves an action under the antitrust and copyright laws brought by respondent Columbia Broadcasting System, Inc. (CBS), against petitioners, American Society of Composers, Authors and Publishers (ASCAP) and Broadcast Music, Inc. (BMI), and their members and affiliates. The basic question presented is whether the issuance by ASCAP and BMI to CBS of blanket licenses to copyrighted musical compositions at fees negotiated by them is price fixing *per se* unlawful under the antitrust laws.

. . . .

Since 1897, the copyright laws have vested in the owner of a copyrighted musical composition the exclusive right to perform the work publicly for profit, but the legal right is not self-enforcing. In 1914, Victor Herbert and a handful of other composers organized ASCAP because those who performed copyrighted music for profit were so numerous and widespread, and most performances so fleeting, that as a practical matter it was impossible for the many individual copyright owners to negotiate with and license the users and to detect unauthorized uses. . . . As ASCAP operates today, its 22,000 members grant it nonexclusive rights to license nondramatic performances of their works, and ASCAP issues licenses and distributes royalties to copyright owners in accordance with a schedule reflecting the nature and amount of the use of their music and other factors.

BMI, a nonprofit corporation owned by members of the broadcasting industry, was organized in 1939, is affiliated with or represents some 10,000 publishing companies and 20,000 authors and composers, and operates in much the same manner as ASCAP. Almost every domestic copyrighted composition is in the repertory either of ASCAP . . . or of BMI. . . .

Both organizations operate primarily through blanket licenses, which give the licensees the right to perform any and all of the compositions owned by the members or affiliates as often as the licensees desire for a stated term. Fees for blanket licenses are ordinarily a percentage of total revenues or a flat dollar amount, and do not directly depend on the amount or type of music used. . . .

. . . CBS argued that ASCAP and BMI are unlawful monopolies and that the blanket license is illegal price fixing, an unlawful tying arrangement, a concerted refusal to deal, and a misuse of copyrights. The District Court . . . dismissed the complaint, rejecting . . . the claim that the blanket license was price fixing and a *per se* violation of § 1 of the Sherman Act, and holding that since direct negotiation with individual copyright owners is available and feasible there is no undue restraint of trade, illegal tying, misuse of copyrights, or monopolization. . . .

Though agreeing with the District Court's factfinding and not disturbing its legal conclusions on the other antitrust theories of liability, the Court of Appeals held that the blanket license issued to television networks was a form of price fixing illegal *per se* under the Sherman Act. . . .

To the Court of Appeals and CBS, the blanket license involves "price fixing" in the literal sense: the composers and publishing houses have joined together into an organization that sets its price for the blanket license it sells.[13] But this is not a question simply of determining whether two or more potential competitors have literally "fixed" a "price." As generally used in the antitrust field, "price fixing" is a shorthand way of describing certain categories of business behavior to which the *per se* rule has been held applicable. The Court of Appeals' literal approach does not alone establish that this particular practice is one of those types or that it is "plainly anticompetitive" and very likely without "redeeming virtue." Literalness is overly simplistic and often overbroad. When two partners set the price of their goods or services they are literally "price fixing," but they are not *per se* in violation of the Sherman Act. . . . Thus, it is necessary to characterize the challenged conduct as falling within or without that category of behavior to which we apply the label "*per se* price fixing." That will often, but not always, be a simple matter.

[The government brought an antitrust action against ASCAP in 1941 which was settled by a consent decree that same year. The 1941 decree was reopened and extensively modified in 1950.]

Under the amended decree, which still substantially controls the activities of ASCAP, members may grant ASCAP only nonexclusive rights to license their works for public performance. Members, therefore, retain the rights individually to license public performances, along with the rights to license the use of their compositions for other purposes. ASCAP itself is forbidden to grant any license to perform one or more specified compositions in the ASCAP repertory unless both the user and the owner have requested it in writing to do so. ASCAP is required to grant to any user making written application a nonexclusive license to perform all ASCAP compositions either for a period of time or on a per-program basis. ASCAP may not insist on the blanket license, and the fee for the per-program license, which is to be based on the revenues for the program on which ASCAP

---

[13] CBS also complains that it pays a flat fee regardless of the amount of use it makes of ASCAP compositions and even though many of its programs contain little or no music. We are unable to see how that alone could make out an antitrust violation or misuse of copyrights: "Sound business judgment could indicate that such payment represents the most convenient method of fixing the business value of the privileges granted by the licensing agreement. . . . Petitioner cannot complain because it must pay royalties whether it uses Hazeltine patents or not. What it acquired by the agreement into which it entered was the privilege to use any or all of the patents and developments as it desired to use them." *Automatic Radio Mfg. Co. v. Hazeltine Research, Inc.*, 339 U.S. 827, 834 (1950). . . .

music is played, must offer the applicant a genuine economic choice between the per-program license and the more common blanket license. If ASCAP and a putative licensee are unable to agree on a fee within 60 days, the applicant may apply to the District Court for a determination of a reasonable fee, with ASCAP having the burden of proving reasonableness.[20]

. . . [T]he Court of Appeals' holding would appear to be quite difficult to contain. If, as the court held, there is a *per se* antitrust violation whenever ASCAP issues a blanket license to a television network for a single fee, why would it not also be automatically illegal for ASCAP to negotiate and issue blanket licenses to individual radio or television stations or to other users who perform copyrighted music for profit? Likewise, if the present network licenses issued through ASCAP on behalf of its members are *per se* violations, why would it not be equally illegal for the members to authorize ASCAP to issue licenses establishing various categories of uses that a network might have for copyrighted music and setting a standard fee for each described use?

Although the Court of Appeals apparently thought the blanket license could be saved in some or even many applications, it seems to us that the *per se* rule does not accommodate itself to such flexibility and that the observations of the Court of Appeals with respect to remedy tend to impeach the *per se* basis for the holding of liability.[27]

CBS would prefer that ASCAP be authorized, indeed directed, to make all its compositions available at standard per-use rates within negotiated categories of use. . . . But if this in itself or in conjunction with blanket licensing constitutes illegal price fixing by copyright owners, CBS urges that an injunction issue forbidding ASCAP to issue any blanket license or to negotiate any fee except on behalf of an individual member for the use of his own copyrighted work or works. Thus, we are called upon to determine that blanket licensing is unlawful across the board. We are quite sure, however, that the *per se* rule does not require any such holding.

. . . .

The blanket license, as we see it, is not a "naked restrain[t] of trade with no purpose except stifling of competition," . . . but rather accompanies the integration of sales, monitoring, and enforcement against unauthorized copyright use. . . .

---

[20] BMI is in a similar situation. The original decree against BMI [was entered in 1941]. . . . A new consent judgment was entered in 1966 following a monopolization complaint filed in 1964. . . . The ASCAP and BMI decrees do vary in some respects. The BMI decree does not specify that BMI may only obtain nonexclusive rights from its affiliates or that the District Court may set the fee if the parties are unable to agree. Nonetheless, the parties stipulated, and the courts below accepted, that "CBS could secure direct licenses from BMI affiliates with the same ease or difficulty, as the case may be, as from ASCAP members." . . .

[27] . . . The Court of Appeals would apparently not outlaw the blanket license across the board but would permit it in various circumstances where it is deemed necessary or sufficiently desirable. It did not even enjoin blanket licensing with the television networks, the relief it realized would normally follow a finding of *per se* illegality of the license in that context. Instead, as requested by CBS, it remanded to the District Court to require ASCAP to offer in addition to blanket licensing some competitive form of per-use licensing. But per-use licensing by ASCAP, as recognized in the consent decrees, might be even more susceptible to the *per se* rule than blanket licensing.

The rationale for this unusual relief in a *per se* case was that "[t]he blanket license is not simply a 'naked restraint' ineluctably doomed to extinction." . . . To the contrary, the Court of Appeals found that the blanket license might well "serve a market need" for some. . . . This, it seems to us, is not the *per se* approach, which does not yield so readily to circumstances, but in effect is a rather bobtailed application of the rule of reason, bobtailed in the sense that it is unaccompanied by the necessary analysis demonstrating why the particular licensing system is an undue competitive restraint.

With the advent of radio and television networks, market conditions changed, and the necessity for and advantages of a blanket license for those users may be far less obvious than is the case when the potential users are individual television or radio stations, or the thousands of other individuals and organizations performing copyrighted compositions in public. But even for television network licenses, ASCAP reduces costs absolutely by creating a blanket license that is sold only a few, instead of thousands, of times, and that obviates the need for closely monitoring the networks to see that they do not use more than they pay for. ASCAP also provides the necessary resources for blanket sales and enforcement, resources unavailable to the vast majority of composers and publishing houses. Moreover, a bulk license of some type is a necessary consequence of the integration necessary to achieve these efficiencies, and a necessary consequence of an aggregate license is that its price must be established.

This substantial lowering of costs, which is of course potentially beneficial to both sellers and buyers, differentiates the blanket license from individual use licenses. The blanket license is composed of the individual compositions plus the aggregating service. Here, the whole is truly greater than the sum of its parts; it is, to some extent, a different product. The blanket license has certain unique characteristics: It allows the licensee immediate use of covered compositions, without the delay of prior individual negotiations and great flexibility in the choice of musical material. . . . Thus, to the extent the blanket license is a different product, ASCAP is not really a joint sales agency offering the individual goods of many sellers, but is a separate seller offering its blanket license, of which the individual compositions are raw material.[40] . . .

Finally, we have some doubt—enough to counsel against application of the *per se* rule—about the extent to which this practice threatens the "central nervous system of the economy," . . . that is, competitive pricing as the free market's means of allocating resources. Not all arrangements among actual or potential competitors that have an impact on price are *per se* violations of the Sherman Act or even unreasonable restraints. Mergers among competitors eliminate competition, including price competition, but they are not *per se* illegal, and many of them withstand attack under any existing antitrust standard. Joint ventures and other cooperative arrangements are also not usually unlawful, at least not as price-fixing schemes, where the agreement on price is necessary to market the product at all.

Here, the blanket-license fee is not set by competition among individual copyright owners, and it is a fee for the use of any of the compositions covered by the license. But the blanket license cannot be wholly equated with a simple horizontal arrangement among competitors. ASCAP does set the price for its blanket license, but that license is quite different from anything any individual owner could issue. The individual composers and authors have neither agreed not to sell individually in any other market nor use the blanket license to mask price fixing in such other markets. Moreover, the substantial restraints placed on ASCAP and its members by the consent decree must not be ignored. The District Court found that there was no legal, practical, or conspiratorial impediment to CBS's obtaining individual licenses; CBS, in short, had a real choice.

---

40 Moreover, because of the nature of the product—a composition can be simultaneously "consumed" by many users—composers have numerous markets and numerous incentives to produce, so the blanket license is unlikely to cause decreased output, one of the normal undesirable effects of a cartel. And since popular songs get an increased share of ASCAP's revenue distributions, composers compete even within the blanket license in terms of productivity and consumer satisfaction.

With this background in mind, which plainly enough indicates that over the years, and in the face of available alternatives, the blanket license has provided an acceptable mechanism for at least a large part of the market for the performing rights to copyrighted musical compositions, we cannot agree that it should automatically be declared illegal in all of its many manifestations. Rather, when attacked, it should be subjected to a more discriminating examination under the rule of reason. It may not ultimately survive that attack, but that is not the issue before us today.

. . . .

The judgment of the Court of Appeals is reversed, and the cases are remanded to that court for further proceedings consistent with this opinion.

It is so ordered.

COMMENTARY

1. If it were impractical for CBS to negotiate individually with each copyright holder, would this fact lend support to the reasonableness of the ASCAP blanket license? Conversely, if it were practical for CBS to negotiate individually with each copyright holder, would this fact lend support to the reasonableness of the ASCAP blanket license (on the theory that the availability of this practical alternative exerted a constraining effect on ASCAP's market power)? Imagine yourself as counsel for ASCAP trying to justify the blanket license. Consider whether either or both of these arguments can be supported.

2. In his dissenting opinion in *Broadcast Music*, Justice Stevens differed with the majority in both procedure and substance. As to procedure, he saw no need to remand, given the fullness of the record. On substance, he would have affirmed the Court of Appeals because the record

> . . . describes a market that could be competitive and is not, and since that market is dominated by two firms engaged in a single, blanket method of dealing, it surely seems logical to conclude that trade has been restrained unreasonably.

441 U.S. at 1878. Is this too "literal" a perception of the practices involved? Does Justice Stevens dismiss entirely the need for an efficient institutional method for copyright holders to receive royalties? How does the majority deal with this issue?

3. One study of collective organizations like ASCAP and BMI states:

> The primary justification advanced for the formation of collecting societies is that they permit copyright owners to enforce their rights at lower costs than if each rights holder were required to enforce his rights separately.

STANLEY M. BESEN & SHEILA N. KIRBY, COMPENSATING CREATORS OF INTELLECTUAL PROPERTY 2 (1989). This study of institutional combinations of copyright holders to collect royalties states that cooperative pricing may be inevitable, but that such arrangements are more efficient. Should efficiency considerations withdraw the *per se* rule from the agreement about price?

4. Is the arrangement in *Broadcast Music* better analyzed as a joint venture among composers and the copyright collectives? If the proper characterization of these arrangements is that of a joint venture, does the ancillary analysis of *Rothery* control? For further consideration of joint ventures, see Chapter Eight.

5. *Catalano, Inc. v. Target Sales, Inc.*, 446 U.S. 643 (1980), is another Supreme Court opinion in a price-fixing case under § 1 of the Sherman Act. The plaintiffs, a group of beer retailers, brought a class action against their beer wholesalers alleging price-fixing in the combined refusal of the wholesalers to continue extending free, short-term credit on sales to the retailers. Prior to the agreement retailers received credit from 30 to 42 days; after the agreement all purchases were to be paid for in cash on delivery or in advance of delivery. Plaintiffs alleged that fixing the terms of sale to cash only constituted a fixing of credit terms and, indirectly, fixing price. The trial court granted summary judgment to the wholesalers on the ground that no *per se* illegality had been shown, but certified the issue to the Court of Appeals under 28 U.S.C. § 1292 (permitting certification where an order involves a controlling question of law ". . . as to which there is substantial ground for difference of opinion.").

On appeal, a majority of the Ninth Circuit dismissed the *per se* count, but remanded for a hearing on the damages issue. In rejecting the allegation that credit-fixing was indirect price-fixing, the Court of Appeals noted that such an agreement might enhance competition by removing a possible entry barrier for sellers and by making price more "visible," given the absence of the non-price component of the transaction, *i.e.*, credit.

Judge Sneed wrote: ". . . it has not been established that the agreement . . . [to refuse credit] was entered into with the purpose, or had the effect, of restraining price competition. . . ." *Catalano, Inc. v. Target Sales, Inc*, 605 F.2d 1097, 1100 (9th Cir. 1979). In dissent, Judge Blumenfeld, citing *Socony-Vacuum*, considered the practice to be indirect price-fixing and illegal *per se*. As he saw it:

> Allowing a retailer interest-free short-term credit on beer purchases effectively reduces the price of beer, when compared to a requirement that the retailer pay the same amount immediately in cash; . . . the elimination of free credit is the equivalent of a price increase.

605 F.2d at 1103. The Supreme Court reversed *per curiam*, stating:

> It is virtually self-evident that extending interest-free credit for a period of time is equivalent to giving a discount equal to the value of the use of the purchase price for that period of time. An agreement to terminate the

> practice of giving credit is thus tantamount to an agreement to eliminate discounts and thus falls squarely within the traditional *per se* rule against price fixing.

446 U.S. 643, 648 (1979). If the practice at issue is as "virtually self-evident" as the Court states, why did the various judges below differ as to its characterization? Is the difficulty in stating the scope of the *per se* rule as to price-fixing as much a problem of defining the practice as of applying the doctrine? How proximate must the restriction be to the calculus of a final price to come within the *Socony-Vacuum* formula? To what extent are the purpose and effect criteria of *Socony-Vacuum* still being applied? What does "purpose" and "effect" mean in this context?

National Collegiate Athletic Association v. Board of Regents of the University of Oklahoma

468 U.S. 85 (1984)

Justice Stevens delivered the opinion of the Court.

The University of Oklahoma and the University of Georgia contend that the National Collegiate Athletic Association has unreasonably restrained trade in the televising of college football games. After an extended trial, the District Court found that the NCAA had violated § 1 of the Sherman Act and granted injunctive relief. . . . The Court of Appeals agreed that the statute had been violated but modified the remedy in some respects. . . . We granted *certiorari* . . . and now affirm.

I

The NCAA

Since its inception in 1905, the NCAA has played an important role in the regulation of amateur collegiate sports. It has adopted and promulgated playing rules, standards of amateurism, standards for academic eligibility, regulations concerning recruitment of athletes, and rules governing the size of athletic squads and coaching staffs. . . . With the exception of football, the NCAA has not undertaken any regulation of the televising of athletic events.

The NCAA has approximately 850 voting members. The regular members are classified into separate divisions to reflect differences in size and scope of their athletic programs. Division I includes 276 colleges with major athletic programs; in this group only 187 play intercollegiate football. Divisions II and III include approximately 500 colleges with less extensive athletic programs. . . .

The Current Plan

The plan adopted [by the NCAA] . . . for the 1982-1985 seasons is at issue in this case. This plan, like each of its predecessors, recites that it is intended to reduce, insofar as possible, the adverse effects of live television upon football game attendance. It provides that "all forms of television of the football games of NCAA member institutions during the Plan control periods shall be in accordance with this Plan." . . .

In separate agreements with each of the carrying networks, ABC and the Columbia Broadcasting System (CBS), the NCAA granted each the right to telecast the 14 live "exposures" described in the plan, in accordance with the "ground rules" set forth therein.

Each of the networks agreed to pay a specified "minimum aggregate compensation to the participating NCAA member institutions" during the 4-year period in an amount that totaled $131,750,000. In essence the agreement authorized each network to negotiate directly with member schools for the right to televise their games. . . . [T]he practice . . . that the District Court found would be followed under the current agreement involved the setting of a recommended fee by a representative of the NCAA for different types of telecasts, with national telecasts being the most valuable, regional telecasts being less valuable, and Division II or Division III games commanding a still lower price. . . . Except for differences in payment between national and regional telecasts, and with respect to Division II and Division III games, the amount that any team receives does not change with the size of the viewing audience, the number of markets in which the game is telecast, or the particular characteristic of the game or the participating teams. Instead, the "ground rules" provide that the carrying networks make alternate selections of those games they wish to televise, and thereby obtain the exclusive right to submit a bid at an essentially fixed price to the institutions involved. . . .

The plan also contains "appearance requirements" and "appearance limitations" which pertain to each of the 2-year periods that the plan is in effect. The basic requirement imposed on each of the two networks is that it must schedule appearances for at least 82 different member institutions during each 2-year period. . . . [N]o member institution is eligible to appear on television more than a total of six times and more than four times nationally, with the appearances to be divided equally between the two carrying networks. . . . The number of exposures specified in the contracts also sets an absolute maximum on the number of games that can be broadcast.

Thus, . . . the current plan . . . limits the total amount of televised intercollegiate football and the number of games that any one team may televise. No member is permitted to make any sale of television rights except in accordance with the basic plan.

. . . .

The District Court found that competition in the relevant market had been restrained in three ways: (1) NCAA fixed the price for particular telecasts; (2) its exclusive network contracts were tantamount to a group boycott of all other potential broadcasters and its threat of sanctions against its own members constituted a threatened boycott of potential competitors; and (3) its plan placed an artificial limit on the production of televised college football.

. . . .

The Court of Appeals held that the NCAA television plan constituted illegal *per se* price-fixing. . . . It rejected each of the . . . arguments advanced by NCAA to establish the procompetitive character of its plan. . . . [T]he Court of Appeals refused to view the NCAA plan as competitively justified by the need to compete effectively with other types of television programming, since it entirely eliminated competition between producers of football and hence was illegal *per se*.

II

There can be no doubt that the challenged practices of the NCAA constitute a "restraint of trade" in the sense that they limit members' freedom to negotiate and enter into their own television contracts. . . .

It is also undeniable that these practices share characteristics of restraints we have previously held unreasonable. . . . Because it places a ceiling on the number of games member institutions may televise, the horizontal agreement places an artificial limit on the quantity of televised football that is available to broadcasters and consumers. By restraining the quantity of television rights available for sale, the challenged practices create a limitation on output; our cases have held that such limitations are unreasonable restraints of trade. Moreover, the District Court found that the minimum aggregate price in fact operates to preclude any price negotiation between broadcasters and institutions, thereby constituting horizontal price fixing, perhaps the paradigm of an unreasonable restraint of trade.

. . . Nevertheless, we have decided that it would be inappropriate to apply a *per se* rule to this case. This decision is not based on a lack of judicial experience with this type of arrangement, on the fact that the NCAA is organized as a nonprofit entity, or on our respect for the NCAA's historic role in the preservation and encouragement of intercollegiate amateur athletics. Rather, what is critical is that this case involves an industry in which horizontal restraints on competition are essential if the product is to be available at all.

. . . What the NCAA and its member institutions market in this case is competition itself—contests between competing institutions. Of course, this would be completely ineffective if there were no rules on which the competitors agreed to create and define the competition to be marketed. A myriad of rules affecting such matters as the size of the field, the number of players on a team, and the extent to which physical violence is to be encouraged or proscribed, all must be agreed upon, and all restrain the manner in which institutions compete. Moreover, the NCAA seeks to market a particular brand of football—college football. . . . In order to preserve the character and quality of the "product," athletes must not be paid, must be required to attend class, and the like. And the integrity of the "product" cannot be preserved except by mutual agreement; if an institution adopted such restrictions unilaterally, its effectiveness as a competitor on the playing field might soon be destroyed. Thus, the NCAA plays a vital role in enabling college football to preserve its character, and as a result enables a product to be marketed which might otherwise be unavailable. In performing this role, its actions widen consumer choice—not only the choices available to sports fans but also those available to athletes—and hence can be viewed as procompetitive.

. . . Respondents concede that the great majority of the NCAA's regulations enhance competition among member institutions. Thus, despite the fact that this case involves restraints on the ability of member institutions to compete in terms of price and output, a fair evaluation of their competitive character requires consideration of the NCAA's justifications for the restraints. . . .

Per se rules are invoked when surrounding circumstances make the likelihood of anticompetitive conduct so great as to render unjustified further examination of the challenged conduct. But whether the ultimate finding is the product of a presumption or actual market analysis, the essential inquiry remains the same—whether or not the challenged restraint enhances competition. Under the Sherman Act the criterion to be used in judging the validity of a restraint on trade is its impact on competition.

III

Because it restrains price and output, the NCAA's television plan has a significant potential for anticompetitive effects. The findings of the District Court indicate that this potential has been realized. The District Court found that if member institutions were free to sell television rights, many more games would be shown on television, and that the NCAA's output restriction has the effect of raising the price the networks pay for television rights. . . .

The anticompetitive consequences of this arrangement are apparent. Individual competitors lose their freedom to compete. Price is higher and output lower than they would otherwise be, and both are unresponsive to consumer preference. This latter point is perhaps the most significant, since "Congress designed the Sherman Act as a 'consumer welfare prescription.'" . . . A restraint that has the effect of reducing the importance of consumer preference in setting price and output is not consistent with this fundamental goal of antitrust law. Restrictions on price and output are the paradigmatic examples of restraints of trade that the Sherman Act was intended to prohibit. . . .

Petitioner argues, however, that its television plan can have no significant anticompetitive effect since the record indicates that it has no market power—no ability to alter the interaction of supply and demand in the market. We must reject this argument for two reasons, one legal, one factual.

As a matter of law, the absence of proof of market power does not justify a naked restriction on price or output. To the contrary, when there is an agreement not to compete in terms of price or output, "no elaborate industry analysis is required to demonstrate the anticompetitive character of such an agreement." [Citing *National Society of Professional Engineers v. United States*, 435 U.S. 679, 692 (1978).] . . . Petitioner does not quarrel with the District Court's finding that price and output are not responsive to demand. Thus the plan is inconsistent with the Sherman Act's command that price and supply be responsive to consumer preference. We have never required proof of market power in such a case. This naked restraint on price and output requires some competitive justification even in the absence of a detailed market analysis.

As a factual matter, it is evident that petitioner does possess market power. . . . Petitioner's argument that it cannot obtain supracompetitive prices from broadcasters since advertisers, and hence broadcasters, can switch from college football to other types of programming simply ignores the findings of the District Court. It found that intercollegiate football telecasts generate an audience uniquely attractive to advertisers and that competitors are unable to offer programming that can attract a similar audience. These findings amply support its conclusion that the NCAA possesses market power. Indeed, the District Court's subsidiary finding that advertisers will pay a premium price per viewer to reach audiences watching college football because of their demographic characteristics is vivid evidence of the uniqueness of this product. Moreover, the District Court's market analysis is firmly supported by our decision in *International Boxing Club v. United States*, 358 U.S. 242 (1958), that championship boxing events are uniquely attractive to fans and hence constitute a market separate from that for non-championship events. . . . Thus, respondents have demonstrated that there is a separate market for telecasts of college football which "rest[s] on generic qualities differentiating" viewers. . . . It inexorably follows that if college football broadcasts be defined as a separate market—and we are convinced they are—then the NCAA's complete control over those broadcasts provides a solid basis for the District Court's conclusion that the NCAA possesses market power with respect to those broadcasts. . . .

Thus, the NCAA television plan on its face constitutes a restraint upon the operation of a free market, and the findings of the District Court establish that it has operated to raise price and reduce output. Under the Rule of Reason, these hallmarks of anticompetitive behavior place upon petitioner a heavy burden of establishing an affirmative defense which competitively justifies this apparent deviation from the operations of a free market. . . . We turn now to the NCAA's proffered justifications.

IV

Relying on *Broadcast Music*, petitioner argues that its television plan constitutes a cooperative "joint venture" which assists in the marketing of broadcast rights and hence is procompetitive. . . .

The District Court did not find that the NCAA's television plan produced any procompetitive efficiencies which enhanced the competitiveness of college football television rights; to the contrary it concluded that NCAA football could be marketed just as effectively without the television plan. There is therefore no predicate in the findings for petitioner's efficiency justification. . . . If the NCAA's television plan produced procompetitive efficiencies, the plan would increase output and reduce the price of televised games. The District Court's contrary findings accordingly undermine petitioner's position. . . .

V

Throughout the history of its regulation of intercollegiate football telecasts, the NCAA has indicated its concern with protecting live attendance. This concern, it should be noted, is not with protecting live attendance at games which are shown on television; that type of interest is not at issue in this case. Rather, the concern is that fan interest in a televised game may adversely affect ticket sales for games that will not appear on television.

. . . The NCAA's argument that its television plan is necessary to protect live attendance is not based on a desire to maintain the integrity of college football as a distinct and attractive product, but rather on a fear that the product will not prove sufficiently attractive to draw live attendance when faced with competition from televised games. At bottom the NCAA's position is that ticket sales for most college games are unable to compete in a free market. The television plan protects ticket sales by limiting output—just as any monopolist increases revenues by reducing output. By seeking to insulate live ticket sales from the full spectrum of competition because of its assumption that the product itself is insufficiently attractive to consumers, petitioner forwards a justification that is inconsistent with the basic policy of the Sherman Act. . . .

VII

The NCAA plays a critical role in the maintenance of a revered tradition of amateurism in college sports. There can be no question but that it needs ample latitude to play that role, or that the preservation of the student-athlete in higher education adds richness and diversity to intercollegiate athletics and is entirely consistent with the goals of the Sherman Act. But consistent with the Sherman Act, the role of the NCAA must be to *preserve* a tradition that might otherwise die; rules that restrict output are hardly consistent with this role. Today we hold only that the record supports the District Court's conclusion that by curtailing output and blunting the ability of member institutions to respond to consumer preference, the NCAA has restricted rather than enhanced the place of intercollegiate athletics in the Nation's life. Accordingly, the judgment of the Court of Appeals is

Affirmed.

Justice WHITE, with whom Justice REHNQUIST joins, dissenting.

. . . The legitimate noneconomic goals of colleges and universities should not be ignored in analyzing restraints imposed by associations of such institutions on their members. . . . The primarily noneconomic values pursued by educational institutions differ fundamentally from the "overriding commercial purpose of [the] day-to-day activities" of engineers, lawyers, doctors, and businessmen . . . and neither *Professional Engineers* nor any other decision of this Court suggests that associations of nonprofit educational institutions must defend their self-regulatory restraints solely in terms of their competitive impact, without regard for the legitimate noneconomic values they promote.

When these values are factored into the balance, the NCAA's television plan seems eminently reasonable. Most fundamentally, the plan fosters the goal of amateurism by spreading revenues among various schools and reducing the financial incentives toward professionalism. . . .

COMMENTARY

1. Justice Stevens, who wrote the majority opinion in *NCAA*, also wrote the majority opinion in *Maricopa County* (excerpted in Section C, *infra*) where he applied the *per se* rule to condemn a maximum-price-fixing agreement, despite claims that the agreement helped to overcome a market failure. Can you explain his rationale for rejecting the rule of reason in the former and accepting it in the latter? Are the reasons for invoking the *per se* rule over the rule of reason rule any more compelling in *NCAA?*

2. When the rule of reason has been invoked in price-fixing cases, what rationale have the courts employed? Recall *Broadcast Music Inc. v. Columbia Broadcasting System* on page 65 above. Did the blanket license there constitute an agreement as to price by competing sellers of a license to perform music? Contrast the stated reasons for invoking rule of reason analysis in *Chicago Board of Trade*, *Broadcast Music*, and *NCAA*.

3. A commentator, reviewing the opinions in *Broadcast Music*, *Maricopa County*, and *NCAA* states that the problem of analysis in them is:

> . . . to define those classes of price-fixing agreements that qualify for exceptional treatment. In the case of conventional or "straight" price-fixing—agreements on price unaccompanied by any agreement to collaborate in other potentially procompetitive activity—there is a powerful argument for an absolute prohibition, regardless of purpose or effect. . . . It is where the agreement on price functions as part of a larger potentially procompetitive undertaking that serious questions about *per se* illegality arise.

Richard S. Wirtz, *Rethinking Price-Fixing*, 20 IND. L.J. 591 (1987).

4. In determining when to characterize an agreement involving pricing as illegal price-fixing, is a trial court obligated to allow the introduction of all evidence of possible procompetitive benefits? Who are the beneficiaries of such alleged beneficial effects: consumers, competitors, or the competitive process? To what extent are the procompetitive effects to be viewed in terms solely of the effect of the practice on price and output?

5. Isn't it odd that the Court could state that "the anticompetitive consequences of this arrangement are apparent" and yet still apply the rule of reason? What test did the Court employ to evaluate the restraint under the rule of reason? Ultimately, the NCAA television arrangement was evaluated under a standard of whether, within the relevant market, it reduced output and raised prices in relation to competitively-determined output and prices. Since the NCAA arrangement clearly failed this test, its "anticompetitive consequences" were "apparent."

6. Did *Chicago Board of Trade*, *Broadcast Music*, and *NCAA* permit the introduction of evidence of pro-competitive justification to overcome an otherwise applicable presumption that illegal price-fixing was the proper characterization of the practice at issue?

7. Consider the definition of the product in *NCAA*. Do the majority and dissenting opinions contain a definition of the market in which the various forces operate? Do these two opinions differ as to whether the market is televised college football or the entire television market? Although definition of the relevant market is associated with § 2 of the Sherman Act and § 7 of the Clayton Act (*see* Chapters 3 and 12, *infra*), are not the concepts of market and product definition also useful in applying § 1?

8. The Court's analysis vastly simplifies Justice Brandeis' description of a rule of reason inquiry. The Court makes explicit that the goal of the Sherman Act is the avoidance of restrictions on market supply. If it can be shown that an agreement not to deal—or any agreement, for that matter—results in a decrease in industry output and an increase in market price (vis-à-vis price and output in a competitive market), the agreement is unlawful.

California Dental Association v. Federal Trade Commission

526 U.S. 756 (1999)

SOUTER, J., delivered the opinion for a unanimous Court with respect to Parts I and II, and the opinion of the Court with respect to Part III, in which REHNQUIST, C.J., and O'CONNOR, SCALIA, and THOMAS, JJ., joined. BREYER, J., filed an opinion concurring in part and dissenting in part, in which STEVENS, KENNEDY, and GINSBURG, JJ., joined.

... We hold that the Commission's jurisdiction under the Federal Trade Commission Act (FTC Act) extends to an association that, like the CDA, provides substantial economic benefit to its for-profit members, but that where, as here, any anticompetitive effects of given restraints are far from intuitively obvious, the rule of reason demands a more thorough enquiry into the consequences of those restraints than the Court of Appeals performed.

I

The CDA is a voluntary nonprofit association of local dental societies to which some 19,000 dentists belong, including about three-quarters of those practicing in the State. . . . The CDA is exempt from federal income tax . . . although it has for-profit subsidiaries that give its members advantageous access to various sorts of insurance, including liability coverage, and to financing for their real estate, equipment, cars, and patients' bills. . . .

The dentists who belong to the CDA through these associations agree to abide by a Code of Ethics (Code) including the following § 10:

> Although any dentist may advertise, no dentist shall advertise or solicit patients in any form of communication in a manner that is false or misleading in any material respect. In order to properly serve the public, dentists should represent themselves in a manner that contributes to the esteem of the public. Dentists should not misrepresent their training and competence in any way that would be false or misleading in any material respect. . . .

The CDA has issued a number of advisory opinions interpreting this section,[1] and through separate advertising guidelines intended to help members comply with the Code and with state law the CDA has advised its dentists of disclosures they must make under state law when engaging in discount advertising.[2]

---

[1] The advisory opinions, which substantially mirror parts of the California Business and Professions Code, *see* CAL. BUS. & PROF. CODE ANN. §§ 651, . . . include the following propositions:

> A statement or claim is false or misleading in any material respect when it:
>
> a. contains a misrepresentation of fact;
>
> b. is likely to mislead or deceive because in context it makes only a partial disclosure of relevant facts;
>
> c. is intended or is likely to create false or unjustified expectations of favorable results and/or costs;
>
> d. relates to fees for specific types of services without fully and specifically disclosing all variables and other relevant factors;
>
> e. contains other representations or implications that in reasonable probability will cause an ordinarily prudent person to misunderstand or be deceived.
>
> Any communication or advertisement which refers to the cost of dental services shall be exact, without omissions, and shall make each service clearly identifiable, without the use of such phrases as "as low as," "and up," "lowest prices," or words or phrases of similar import.
>
> Any advertisement which refers to the cost of dental services and uses words of comparison or relativity—for example, "low fees"—must be based on verifiable data substantiating the comparison or statement of relativity. The burden shall be on the dentist who advertises in such terms to establish the accuracy of the comparison or statement of relativity.
>
> Advertising claims as to the quality of services are not susceptible to measurement or verification; accordingly, such claims are likely to be false or misleading in any material respect.

128 F.3d 720, 723-24 (9th Cir. 1997) (some internal quotation marks omitted).

[2] The disclosures include:

> 1. The dollar amount of the nondiscounted fee for the service[.]
>
> 2. Either the dollar amount of the discount fee or the percentage of the discount for the specific service[.]
>
> 3. The length of time that the discount will be offered[.]
>
> 4. Verifiable fees[.]
>
> 5. [The identity of] [s]pecific groups who qualify for the discount or any other terms and conditions or restrictions for qualifying for the discount.

Id. at 724.

Responsibility for enforcing the Code rests in the first instance with the local dental societies, to which applicants for CDA membership must submit copies of their own advertisements and those of their employers or referral services to assure compliance with the Code. The local societies also actively seek information about potential Code violations by applicants or CDA members. Applicants who refuse to withdraw or revise objectionable advertisements may be denied membership; and members who, after a hearing, remain similarly recalcitrant are subject to censure, suspension, or expulsion from the CDA. . . .

The Commission brought a complaint against the CDA, alleging that it applied its guidelines so as to restrict truthful, nondeceptive advertising, and so violated § 5 of the FTC Act . . . .[3] The complaint alleged that the CDA had unreasonably restricted two types of advertising: price advertising, particularly discounted fees, and advertising relating to the quality of dental services. . . . An Administrative Law Judge . . . found a violation of § 5 of the FTC Act. . . .

. . . The Commission treated the CDA's restrictions on discount advertising as illegal *per se*. . . . In the alternative, the Commission held the price advertising (as well as the non-price) restrictions to be violations of the Sherman and FTC Acts under an abbreviated rule-of-reason analysis. . . .

The Court of Appeals for the Ninth Circuit affirmed, sustaining the Commission's assertion of jurisdiction over the CDA and its ultimate conclusion on the merits.The court thought it error for the Commission to have applied *per se* analysis to the price advertising restrictions, finding analysis under the rule of reason required for all the restrictions. But the Court of Appeals went on to explain that the Commission had properly,

> applied an abbreviated, or "quick look," rule of reason analysis designed for restraints that are not *per se* unlawful but are sufficiently anticompetitive on their face that they do not require a full-blown rule of reason inquiry. . . . ("The essential point is that the rule of reason can sometimes be applied in the twinkling of an eye.") . . . It allows the condemnation of a "naked restraint" on price or output without an "elaborate industry analysis." . . .

The Court of Appeals thought truncated rule-of-reason analysis to be in order for several reasons. As for the restrictions on discount advertising, they "amounted in practice to a fairly 'naked' restraint on price competition itself." The CDA's procompetitive justification, that the restrictions encouraged disclosure and prevented false and misleading advertising, carried little weight because "it is simply infeasible to disclose all of the information that is required," . . . and "the record provides no evidence that the rule has in fact led to increased disclosure and transparency of dental pricing" . . . . As to non-price advertising restrictions, the court said that

> [t]hese restrictions are in effect a form of output limitation, as they restrict the supply of information about individual dentists' services. . . . The restrictions may also affect output more directly, as quality and comfort advertising may induce some customers to obtain nonemergency care when they might not oth-

[3] The FTC Act's prohibition of unfair competition and deceptive acts or practices, . . . [under § 5 of the Federal Trade Commission Act] overlaps the scope of § 1 of the Sherman Act, . . . aimed at prohibiting restraint of trade . . . . [T]he Commission relied upon Sherman Act law in adjudicating this case . . . .

> erwise do so. . . . Under these circumstances, we think that the restriction is a sufficiently naked restraint on output to justify quick look analysis. . . .

* * *

We granted certiorari to resolve conflicts among the Circuits on the Commission's jurisdiction over a nonprofit professional association and the occasions for abbreviated rule-of-reason analysis. . . . We now vacate the judgment of the Court of Appeals and remand.

II

The FTC Act gives the Commission authority over "persons, partnerships, or corporations," . . . [including "associations"] which is organized to carry on business for its own profit or that of its members" . . . .

* * *

. . . Through for-profit subsidiaries, the CDA provides advantageous insurance and preferential financing arrangements for its members, and it engages in lobbying, litigation, marketing, and public relations for the benefit of its members' interests. This congeries of activities confers far more than de minimis or merely presumed economic benefits on CDA members; the economic benefits conferred upon the CDA's profit-seeking professionals plainly fall within the object of enhancing its members' "profit," which the FTC Act makes the jurisdictional touchstone. There is no difficulty in concluding that the Commission has jurisdiction over the CDA.

* * *

III

. . . Because we decide that the Court of Appeals erred when it held as a matter of law that quick-look analysis was appropriate (with the consequence that the Commission's abbreviated analysis and conclusion were sustainable), we do not reach the question of the substantiality of the evidence supporting the Commission's conclusion.[8]

In *National Collegiate Athletic Assn. v. Board of Regents of Univ. of Okla.*, 468 U.S. 85 (1984), . . . we held that a "naked restraint on price and output requires some competitive justification even in the absence of a detailed market analysis." . . . Elsewhere, we held that "no elaborate industry analysis is required to demonstrate the anticompetitive character of" horizontal agreements among competitors to refuse to discuss prices, *National Soc. of Professional Engineers v. United States*, 435 U.S. 679, 692 (1978), . . . or to withhold a particular desired service, *FTC v. Indiana Federation of Dentists*, 476 U.S. 447, 459 (1986). . . . In each of these cases, which have formed the basis for what has come to be called abbreviated or "quick-look" analysis under the rule of reason, an observer with even a rudimentary understanding of economics could conclude that the arrangements in question would have an anticompetitive effect on customers and markets. In *National Collegiate Athletic Assn.*, the league's television plan expressly limited output (the number of games that could be televised) and fixed a minimum price. 468 U.S. at 99-100. . . . In *National Soc.*

---

[8] We leave to the Court of Appeals the question whether on remand it can effectively assess the Commission's decision for substantial evidence on the record, or whether it must remand to the Commission for a more extensive rule-of-reason analysis on the basis of an enhanced record.

of Professional Engineers, the restraint was "an absolute ban on competitive bidding." 435 U.S. at 692 . . . . In *Indiana Federation of Dentists*, the restraint was "a horizontal agreement among the participating dentists to withhold from their customers a particular service that they desire." 476 U.S. at 459. . . . As in such cases, quick-look analysis carries the day when the great likelihood of anticompetitive effects can easily be ascertained. *See Law v. National Collegiate Athletic Assn.*, 134 F.3d 1010, 1020 (10th Cir. 1998) (explaining that quick-look analysis applies "where a practice has obvious anticompetitive effects"); *Chicago Professional Sports Limited Partnership v. National Basketball Assn.*, 961 F.2d 667, 674-76 (7th Cir. 1992) (finding quick-look analysis adequate after assessing and rejecting logic of proffered procompetitive justifications); *cf. United States v. Brown University*, 5 F.3d 658, 677-78 (3d Cir. 1993) (finding full rule-of-reason analysis required where universities sought to provide financial aid to needy students and noting by way of contrast that the agreements in *National Soc. of Professional Engineers* and *Indiana Federation of Dentists* "embodied a strong economic self-interest of the parties to them").

The case before us, however, fails to present a situation in which the likelihood of anticompetitive effects is comparably obvious. Even on Justice BREYER's view that bars on truthful and verifiable price and quality advertising are *prima facie* anticompetitive, . . . and place the burden of procompetitive justification on those who agree to adopt them, the very issue at the threshold of this case is whether professional price and quality advertising is sufficiently verifiable in theory and in fact to fall within such a general rule. Ultimately our disagreement with Justice BREYER turns on our different responses to this issue. Whereas he accepts, as the Ninth Circuit seems to have done, that the restrictions here were like restrictions on advertisement of price and quality generally, . . . it seems to us that the CDA's advertising restrictions might plausibly be thought to have a net procompetitive effect, or possibly no effect at all on competition. The restrictions on both discount and nondiscount advertising are, at least on their face, designed to avoid false or deceptive advertising[6] in a market characterized by striking disparities between the information available to the professional and the patient.[7] *C.f.* Carr & Mathewson, *The Economics of Law Firms: A Study in the Legal Organization of the Firm*, 33 J. LAW & ECON. 307, 309 (1990) (explaining that in a market for complex professional services, "inherent asymmetry of knowledge about the product" arises because "professionals supplying the good are knowledgeable [whereas] consumers demanding the good are uninformed"); Akerlof, *The Market for "Lemons": Quality Uncertainty and the Market Mechanism*, 84 Q.J. ECON. 488 (1970) (pointing out quality problems in market characterized by asymmetrical information). In a market for professional services, in which advertising is relatively rare and the comparability of service packages not easily established, the difficulty for customers or potential competitors to get

---

6 That false or misleading advertising has an anticompetitive effect, as that term is customarily used, has been long established. *Cf. FTC v. Algoma Lumber Co.*, 291 U.S. 67, 79-80, 54 S. Ct. 315, 78 L. Ed. 655 (1934) (finding a false advertisement to be unfair competition).

7 The fact that a restraint operates upon a profession as distinguished from a business is, of course, relevant in determining whether that particular restraint violates the Sherman Act. It would be unrealistic to view the practice of professions as interchangeable with other business activities, and automatically to apply to the professions antitrust concepts which originated in other areas. The public service aspect, and other features of the professions, may require that a particular practice, which could properly be viewed as a violation of the Sherman Act in another context, be treated differently.

Goldfarb v. Virginia State Bar, 421 U.S. 773, 788-89, n.17, 95 S. Ct. 2004, 44 L. Ed. 2d 572 (1975).

and verify information about the price and availability of services magnifies the dangers to competition associated with misleading advertising. What is more, the quality of professional services tends to resist either calibration or monitoring by individual patients or clients, partly because of the specialized knowledge required to evaluate the services, and partly because of the difficulty in determining whether, and the degree to which, an outcome is attributable to the quality of services (like a poor job of tooth-filling) or to something else (like a very tough walnut). *See* Leland, *Quacks, Lemons, and Licensing: A Theory of Minimum Quality Standards*, 87 J. Pol. Econ. 1328, 1330 (1979); 1 B. Furrow, T. Greaney, S. Johnson, T. Jost, & R. Schwartz, Health Law § 3-1, p. 86 (1995) (describing the common view that "the lay public is incapable of adequately evaluating the quality of medical services"). Patients' attachments to particular professionals, the rationality of which is difficult to assess, complicate the picture even further. *C.f.* Evans, *Professionals and the Production Function: Can Competition Policy Improve Efficiency in the Licensed Professions?, in* Occupational Licensure and Regulation 235-236 (S. Rottenberg ed. 1980) (describing long-term relationship between professional and client not as "a series of spot contracts" but rather as "a long-term agreement, often implicit, to deal with each other in a set of future unspecified or incompletely specified circumstances according to certain rules," and adding that "[i]t is not clear how or if these [implicit contracts] can be reconciled with the promotion of effective price competition in individual spot markets for particular services"). The existence of such significant challenges to informed decisionmaking by the customer for professional services immediately suggests that advertising restrictions arguably protecting patients from misleading or irrelevant advertising call for more than cursory treatment as obviously comparable to classic horizontal agreements to limit output or price competition.

The explanation proffered by the Court of Appeals for the likely anticompetitive effect of the CDA's restrictions on discount advertising began with the unexceptionable statements that "price advertising is fundamental to price competition," . . . and that "[r]estrictions on the ability to advertise prices normally make it more difficult for consumers to find a lower price and for dentists to compete on the basis of price" . . . . The court then acknowledged that, according to the CDA, the restrictions nonetheless furthered the "legitimate, indeed procompetitive, goal of preventing false and misleading price advertising." The Court of Appeals might, at this juncture, have recognized that the restrictions at issue here are very far from a total ban on price or discount advertising, and might have considered the possibility that the particular restrictions on professional advertising could have different effects from those "normally" found in the commercial world, even to the point of promoting competition by reducing the occurrence of unverifiable and misleading across-the-board discount advertising. Instead, the Court of Appeals confined itself to the brief assertion that the "CDA's disclosure requirements appear to prohibit across-the-board discounts because it is simply infeasible to disclose all of the information that is required," . . . followed by the observation that "the record provides no evidence that the rule has in fact led to increased disclosure and transparency of dental pricing" . . . .

But these observations brush over the professional context and describe no anticompetitive effects. Assuming that the record in fact supports the conclusion that the CDA disclosure rules essentially bar advertisement of across-the-board discounts, it does not obviously follow that such a ban would have a net anticompetitive effect here. Whether advertisements that announced discounts for, say, first-time customers, would be less effective at conveying information relevant to competition if they listed the original and discounted prices for checkups, X-rays, and fillings, than they would be if they simply specified a percentage discount across the board, seems to us a question susceptible to empirical but not *a priori* analysis. In a suspicious world, the discipline of specific example may well be a necessary condition of plausibility for professional claims that for all practical purposes defy comparison shopping. It is also possible in principle that, even if across-the-board discount advertisements were more effective in drawing customers in the short run, the recurrence of some measure of intentional or accidental misstatement due to the breadth of their claims might leak out over time to make potential patients skeptical of any such across-the-board advertising, so undercutting the method's effectiveness. *Cf.* Akerlof, 84 Q.J. ECON. at 495 (explaining that "dishonest dealings tend to drive honest dealings out of the market"). It might be, too, that across-the-board discount advertisements would continue to attract business indefinitely, but might work precisely because they were misleading customers, and thus just because their effect would be anticompetitive, not procompetitive. Put another way, the CDA's rule appears to reflect the prediction that any costs to competition associated with the elimination of across-the-board advertising will be outweighed by gains to consumer information (and hence competition) created by discount advertising that is exact, accurate, and more easily verifiable (at least by regulators). As a matter of economics this view may or may not be correct, but it is not implausible, and neither a court nor the Commission may initially dismiss it as presumptively wrong.[12]

* * *

The Court of Appeals was . . . tolerant in accepting the sufficiency of abbreviated rule-of-reason analysis as to the nonprice advertising restrictions. The court began with the argument that "[t]hese restrictions are in effect a form of output limitation, as they restrict the supply of information about individual dentists' services." . . . Although this sentence does indeed appear as cited, it is puzzling, given that the relevant output for antitrust purposes here is presumably not information or advertising, but dental services themselves. The question is not whether the universe of possible advertisements has been limited (as assuredly it has), but whether the limitation on advertisements obviously tends to limit the total delivery of dental services. The court came closest to addressing this latter question when it went on to assert that limiting advertisements regarding quality and safety "prevents dentists from fully describing the package of services they offer," . . . adding that "[t]he restrictions may also affect output more directly, as quality and comfort advertising may induce some customers to obtain nonemergency care when they might not otherwise do so" . . . . This suggestion about output is also puzzling. If quality advertising actually induces some patients to obtain more care than they would in its absence, then restricting such advertising would reduce the demand for dental services, not the supply; and it is of course the producers' sup-

---

12 Justice BREYER suggests that our analysis is "of limited relevance," . . . because "the basic question is whether this . . . theoretically redeeming virtue in fact offsets the restrictions' anticompetitive effects in this case," *ibid.* He thinks that the Commission and the Court of Appeals "adequately answered that question," *ibid.*, but the absence of any empirical evidence on this point indicates that the question was not answered, merely avoided by implicit burden-shifting of the kind accepted by Justice BREYER. The point is that before a theoretical claim of anticompetitive effects can justify shifting to a defendant the burden to show empirical evidence of procompetitive effects, as quick-look analysis in effect requires, there must be some indication that the court making the decision has properly identified the theoretical basis for the anticompetitive effects and considered whether the effects actually are anticompetitive. Where, as here, the circumstances of the restriction are somewhat complex, assumption alone will not do.

ply of a good in relation to demand that is normally relevant in determining whether a producer-imposed output limitation has the anticompetitive effect of artificially raising prices,[13] *see General Leaseways, Inc. v. National Truck Leasing Assn.*, 744 F.2d 588, 594-595 (C.A. 7 1984) ("An agreement on output also equates to a price-fixing agreement. If firms raise price, the market's demand for their product will fall, so the amount supplied will fall too—in other words, output will be restricted. If instead the firms restrict output directly, price will as mentioned rise in order to limit demand to the reduced supply. Thus, with exceptions not relevant here, raising price, reducing output, and dividing markets have the same anticompetitive effects").

Although the Court of Appeals acknowledged the CDA's view that "claims about quality are inherently unverifiable and therefore misleading," . . . it responded that this concern "does not justify banning all quality claims without regard to whether they are, in fact, false or misleading" . . . . As a result, the court said, "the restriction is a sufficiently naked restraint on output to justify quick look analysis." . . . The court assumed, in these words, that some dental quality claims may escape justifiable censure, because they are both verifiable and true. But its implicit assumption fails to explain why it gave no weight to the countervailing, and at least equally plausible, suggestion that restricting difficult-to-verify claims about quality or patient comfort would have a procompetitive effect by preventing misleading or false claims that distort the market. It is, indeed, entirely possible to understand the CDA's restrictions on unverifiable quality and comfort advertising as nothing more than a procompetitive ban on puffery . . . .

The point is not that the CDA's restrictions necessarily have the procompetitive effect claimed by the CDA; it is possible that banning quality claims might have no effect at all on competitiveness if, for example, many dentists made very much the same sort of claims. And it is also of course possible that the restrictions might in the final analysis be anticompetitive. The point, rather, is that the plausibility of competing claims about the effects of the professional advertising restrictions rules out the indulgently abbreviated review to which the Commission's order was treated. The obvious anticompetitive effect that triggers abbreviated analysis has not been shown.

In light of our focus on the adequacy of the Court of Appeals's analysis, Justice BREYER's thorough-going, *de novo* antitrust analysis contains much to impress on its own merits but little to demonstrate the sufficiency of the Court of Appeals's review. The obligation to give a more deliberate look than a quick one does not arise at the door of this Court and should not be satisfied here in the first instance. Had the Court of Appeals engaged in a painstaking discussion in a league with Justice BREYER's (compare his 14 pages with the Ninth Circuit's 8), and had it confronted the comparability of these restrictions to bars on clearly verifiable advertising, its reasoning might have sufficed to justify its conclusion. Certainly Justice BREYER's treatment of the antitrust issues here is no "quick look." Lingering is more like it, and indeed Justice BREYER, not surprisingly, stops short of endorsing the Court of Appeals's discussion as adequate to the task at hand.

---

[13] Justice BREYER wonders if we "mea[n] this statement as an argument against the anticompetitive tendencies that flow from an agreement not to advertise service quality." . . . But as the preceding sentence shows, we intend simply to question the logic of the Court of Appeals's suggestion that the restrictions are anticompetitive because they somehow "affect output," . . . presumably with the intent to raise prices by limiting supply while demand remains constant. We do not mean to deny that an agreement not to advertise service quality might have anticompetitive effects. We merely mean that, absent further analysis of the kind Justice BREYER undertakes, it is not possible to conclude that the net effect of this particular restriction is anticompetitive.

Saying here that the Court of Appeals's conclusion at least required a more extended examination of the possible factual underpinnings than it received is not, of course, necessarily to call for the fullest market analysis. Although we have said that a challenge to a "naked restraint on price and output" need not be supported by "a detailed market analysis" in order to "requir[e] some competitive justification," . . . it does not follow that every case attacking a less obviously anticompetitive restraint (like this one) is a candidate for plenary market examination. The truth is that our categories of analysis of anticompetitive effect are less fixed than terms like "*per se*," "quick look," and "rule of reason" tend to make them appear. We have recognized, for example, that "there is often no bright line separating *per se* from Rule of Reason analysis," since "considerable inquiry into market conditions" may be required before the application of any so-called "*per se*" condemnation is justified. . . . "[W]hether the ultimate finding is the product of a presumption or actual market analysis, the essential inquiry remains the same—whether or not the challenged restraint enhances competition." . . .

. . . As the circumstances here demonstrate, there is generally no categorical line to be drawn between restraints that give rise to an intuitively obvious inference of anticompetitive effect and those that call for more detailed treatment. What is required, rather, is an enquiry meet for the case, looking to the circumstances, details, and logic of a restraint. The object is to see whether the experience of the market has been so clear, or necessarily will be, that a confident conclusion about the principal tendency of a restriction will follow from a quick (or at least quicker) look, in place of a more sedulous one. And of course what we see may vary over time, if rule-of-reason analyses in case after case reach identical conclusions. For now, at least, a less quick look was required for the initial assessment of the tendency of these professional advertising restrictions. Because the Court of Appeals did not scrutinize the assumption of relative anticompetitive tendencies, we vacate the judgment and remand the case for a fuller consideration of the issue.

It is so ordered.

Justice BREYER, with whom Justice STEVENS, Justice KENNEDY, and Justice GINSBURG join, . . . dissenting . . . .

. . . In my view, a traditional application of the rule of reason to the facts as found by the Commission requires affirming the Commission—just as the Court of Appeals did below.

I

. . . I would not simply ask whether the restraints at issue are anticompetitive overall. Rather, like the Court of Appeals (and the Commission), I would break that question down into four classical, subsidiary antitrust questions: (1) What is the specific restraint at issue? (2) What are its likely anticompetitive effects? (3) Are there offsetting procompetitive justifications? (4) Do the parties have sufficient market power to make a difference?

A

The most important question is the first: What are the specific restraints at issue? . . . Those restraints do not include merely the agreement to which the California Dental Association's (Dental Association or Association) ethical rule literally refers, namely, a promise to refrain from advertising that is "'false or misleading in any material respect.'" . . . Instead, the Commission found a set of restraints arising out of the way the Dental Association implemented this innocent-sounding ethical rule in practice, through advisory opinions, guidelines, enforcement policies, and review of membership applications. As implemented, the ethical rule reached beyond its nominal target, to prevent truthful and nondeceptive advertising. In particular, the Commission determined that the rule, in practice:

> (1) "precluded advertising that characterized a dentist's fees as being low, reasonable, or affordable," . . .
> (2) "precluded advertising . . . of across the board discounts," . . . ; and
> (3) "prohibit[ed] all quality claims" . . . .

Whether the Dental Association's basic rule as implemented actually restrained the truthful and nondeceptive advertising of low prices, across-the-board discounts, and quality service are questions of fact. . . . [B]oth the ALJ and the Commission ultimately found against the Dental Association in respect to these facts. . . .

The Court of Appeals referred explicitly to some of the evidence that it found adequate to support the Commission's conclusions. It pointed out, for example, that the Dental Association's "advisory opinions and guidelines indicate that . . . descriptions of prices as 'reasonable' or 'low' do not comply" with the Association's rule; that in "numerous cases" the Association "advised members of objections to special offers, senior citizen discounts, and new patient discounts, apparently without regard to their truth"; and that one advisory opinion "expressly states that claims as to the quality of services are inherently likely to be false or misleading," all "without any particular consideration of whether" such statements were "true or false." . . .

* * *

B

Do each of the three restrictions mentioned have "the potential for genuine adverse effects on competition"? . . . I should have thought that the anticompetitive tendencies of the three restrictions were obvious. An agreement not to advertise that a fee is reasonable, that service is inexpensive, or that a customer will receive a discount makes it more difficult for a dentist to inform customers that he charges a lower price. If the customer does not know about a lower price, he will find it more difficult to buy lower price service. That fact, in turn, makes it less likely that a dentist will obtain more customers by offering lower prices. And that likelihood means that dentists will prove less likely to offer lower prices. But why should I have to spell out the obvious? To restrain truthful advertising about lower prices is likely to restrict competition in respect to price—"the central nervous system of the economy." . . . [C.]f., *e.g.*, *Bates v. State Bar of Ariz.*, 433 U.S. 350, 364 (1977) . . . (price advertising plays an "indispensable role in the allocation of resources in a free enterprise system"); *Virginia Bd. of Pharmacy v. Virginia Citizens Consumer Council, Inc.*, 425 U.S. 748, 765 (1976). The Commission thought this fact sufficient to hold (in the alternative) that the price advertising restrictions were unlawful *per se*. . . . For present purposes, I need not decide whether the Commission was right in applying a *per se* rule. I need only assume a rule of reason applies, and note the serious anticompetitive tendencies of the price advertising restraints.

The restrictions on the advertising of service quality also have serious anticompetitive tendencies. This is not a case of "mere puffing," as the FTC recognized. . . . The days of my youth, when the billboards near Emeryville, California, home of AAA baseball's Oakland Oaks, displayed the name of "Painless" Parker, Dentist, are long gone—along with the Oakland Oaks. But some parents may still want to know that a particular dentist makes a point of "gentle care." Others may want to know about 1-year dental work guarantees. To restrict that kind of service quality advertisement is to restrict competition over the quality of service itself, for, unless consumers know, they may not purchase, and dentists may not compete to supply that which will make little difference to the demand for their services. That, at any rate, is the theory of the Sherman Act. . . .

* * *

The upshot, in my view, is that the Court of Appeals, applying ordinary antitrust principles, reached an unexceptional conclusion. It is the same legal conclusion that this Court itself reached in *Indiana Federation*—a much closer case than this one. There the Court found that an agreement by dentists not to submit dental X rays to insurers violated the rule of reason. The anticompetitive tendency of that agreement was to reduce competition among dentists in respect to their willingness to submit X rays to insurers—a matter in respect to which consumers are relatively indifferent, as compared to advertising of price discounts and service quality, the matters at issue here. The redeeming virtue in *Indiana Federation* was the alleged undesirability of having insurers consider a range of matters when deciding whether treatment was justified—a virtue no less plausible, and no less proved, than the virtue offered here. *See id.* at 462-64, 106 S. Ct. 2009. The "power" of the dentists to enforce their agreement was no greater than that at issue here (control of 75% to 90% of the relevant markets). *See id.* at 460, 106 S. Ct. 2009. It is difficult to see how the two cases can be reconciled.

* * *

I would note that the form of analysis I have followed is not rigid; it admits of some variation according to the circumstances. The important point, however, is that its allocation of the burdens of persuasion reflects a gradual evolution within the courts over a period of many years. That evolution represents an effort carefully to blend the procompetitive objectives of the law of antitrust with administrative necessity. It represents a considerable advance, both from the days when the Commission had to present and/or refute every possible fact and theory, and from antitrust theories so abbreviated as to prevent proper analysis. The former prevented cases from ever reaching a conclusion . . . and the latter called forth the criticism that the "Government always wins" . . . . I hope that this case does not represent an abandonment of that basic, and important, form of analysis.

For these reasons, I respectfully dissent from Part III of the Court's opinion.

COMMENTARY

1. What does Justice Souter identify as the Ninth Circuit's reversible error? Did the Supreme Court opinion state that the Dental Association's restraints were probably lawful? Did this opinion state that a full blown rule of reason analysis was required on the remand? Does the absence of any criticism of the Federal Trade Commission for failing to define a relevant market and for failing to find an exercise of market power suggest that a court may consider a plaintiff's assertion of anticompetitive effects without a full scale rule of reason analysis?

2. On the remand the Ninth Circuit vacated the judgment of the Federal Trade Commission and instructed it to dismiss its complaint, *California Dental Association v. Federal Trade Commission,* 224 F.3d 942 (9th Cir. 2000). In her opinion, Judge Hall noted that the Supreme Court found reversible error in the earlier Ninth Circuit opinion's use of a "quick look"/abbreviated rule of reason analysis. However, Justice Souter had also stated that this case did not necessarily call for the fullest market analysis. Judge Hall characterized the Ninth Circuit's analysis on the remand as:

> [S]omewhere on the rule-of-reason continuum between abbreviated and full-blown, we employ a level of inquiry closer to the latter, bearing in mind that our ultimate task is to determine whether the challenged restraint enhances competition.

Id. at 947. In explaining her disposition of the remand, Judge Hall noted that counsel for the Commission has "focused on winning the case under *per se* or abbreviated rule of reason," *id.* at 959, by not calling an expert witness to testify in opposition the Association's expert.

Is it likely that the Commission will in a future case introduce limited evidence and rely on *per se* analysis by a reviewing court?

3. An earlier judicial effort to distinguish *per se* disposition from full-scale rule of reason analysis was made by Judge Cowen in *United States v. Brown University,* 5 F.3d 658 (3d Cir. 1993). In that litigation, the Antitrust Division sued the Ivy Overlap Group, a consortium of eight Ivy League colleges and universities which collectively reviewed financial need applications of applicants and collectively determined the actual amount of financial assistance to be offered commonly admitted applicants. The Third Circuit reversed the trial court's determination of *per se* illegality, citing the lower court's failure to consider the procompetitive and social welfare justifications of the educator's collaboration. Under a full rule of reason analysis how do the anticompetitive consequences on price or output of the defendant's conduct enter into the analysis? Does the plaintiff bear the burden of establishing this anticompetitive impact? In which of the cases in this Chapter would the plaintiff have been able to establish such impact? Is the discussion of market power in these cases a surrogate for proof of the anticompetitive impact? Judge Easterbrook has urged that requiring a plaintiff to establish defendant's market power is a useful way to distinguish a meritorious case from a frivolous one. *See* Frank H. Easterbrook, *The Limits of Antitrust,* 63 TEX. L. REV. 1 (1984). Do Justice Breyer's four criteria stated in his dissenting opinion give priority to market power? How does a plaintiff's burden of showing anticompetitive effects or market power change in order to succeed in obtaining a "quick look," "abbreviated," or "structured" rule of reason analysis instead of a full-blown rule of reason disposition? When a court requires a plaintiff to sustain the burden of showing the anticompetitive effect of a practice, does the burden then shift to the defendant to come forward with an efficiency-based justification? At this point, what is the defendant's burden? Is the defendant required to prove the actual procompetitive impact? Does the *California Dental* decision direct a lower court to apply full rule of reason analysis if the defendant can show "facially plausible" efficiencies resulting from the challenged restraint? After *California Dental,* when is "quick look" rule of reason analysis invoked—by a "naked restraint"? by a restraint on price or output that is "facially" or "inherently"restrictive, or when? How is the Court's direction for a "less quick look" to be implemented on the remand—from the existing voluminous trial record or from further hearings? *See* Stephen Calkins, California Dental Association*: Not a Quick Look But Not the Full Monty,* 67 ANTITRUST L.J. 495 (2000).

Were the schools participating in price fixing agreements? How did the subject of their agreements differ from typical price-fixing agreements held illegal *per se*?

Did the agreements among the Ivy League schools enable them to earn monopoly profits? Did the schools earn profits at all? Does the rationale of the *per se* rule condemning price fixing agreements fit in a situation in which nonprofit (I.R.C. § 501(c)(3)) institutions are intentionally and continuously operating at a loss? Should tax-exempt, educational institutions be the object of Department of Justice Antitrust Division scrutiny?

4. After the Third Circuit's decision in *United States v. Brown University*, the parties settled. Subsequently, Congress intervened by enacting a two-year antitrust exemption for the parties and permitting the Overlap Group to function essentially as before, except barring agreement on awards to specific students, Pub. L. No. 102-325, 106 Stat. 448, 837 (1992). Further extension of the antitrust exemption for educators' collaboration in awarding financial aid until September 30, 2001 was provided by the The Need-Based Educational Aid Antitrust Protection Act of 1997, Pub. L. No. 105-43, 112 Stat. 58 (1997).

Does the congressional action following the *Brown University* case suggest congressional concern that the Antitrust Division unwisely brought this case against the universities that were collaborating as not-for-profit competitors in order to increase minority enrollment?

5. Congress has also demonstrated concern with the application of the antitrust law by private litigants when broader societal concerns are raised. A grand-niece and a guardian brought an antitrust price-fixing claim to upset a donative transfer through the use of a charitable remainder trust of a 96-year-old donor afflicted with dementia and Alzheimer's disease. The principal named defendant, The American Council on Gift Annuities, is a nonprofit entity formed to suppress unwanted competition in the valuation of charitable remainder trusts among institutional donee-benficiaries to the detriment of federal income tax revenue. Charitable gift annuities and charitable remainder trusts are controlled by I.R.C. §§ 501(m)(5) and 664(d). A donor may obtain a charitable contribution deduction by entering into a charitable remainder trust agreement with an I.R.C. § 501(c)(3) charitable, religious, or educational entity to transfer property in exchange for an annuity providing a fixed income for the life of the donor. The coordinated price-determining conduct of the defendant Council consisted of providing a uniform annuity rate, based on the Council's determination of the fair market value of the gift. Prior to the formation of the Council, donors would shop among several prospective charitable donee-entities for the most favorable valuation, a practice that resulted in excessive federal income tax deductions by donors. To end this practice, the Council, in agreement with the prospective donee-charities, sets valuations, warns charities not to exceed them, and monitors compliance. After this first antitrust challenge to the Council was brought in *Richie v. American Council on Gift Annuities*, 943 F. Supp. 685 (N.D. Tex. 1996), Congress enacted the Charitable Gift Annuity Antitrust Relief Act of 1995, Pub. L. No. 104-63, 109 Stat. 687, 688 (1995) (codified at 15 U.S.C. §§ 37, 37a (1995)). This Act provides:

> . . . [I]t shall not be unlawful under any of the antitrust laws . . . for 2 or more persons . . . that are *exempt from taxation* under . . . title 26 to use, or to agree to use, the same annuity rate for the purpose of issuing . . . charitable gift annuities. [emphasis added]

In *Ozee v. The American Council on Gift Annuities*, 110 F.3d 1082 (5th Cir. 1997), the court dismissed the defense of antitrust immunity under the Act because among the several donees there were taxable entities. Congress undertook to reverse the result in *Ozee* by introducing H.R. 1902, The Charitable Donation Antitrust Immunity Act of 1997. H. Rep. No. 105-146 at 3 (1997), states the purpose of the bill as follows:

> A recent decision by the . . . Court of Appeals for the Fifth Circuit . . . [*Ozee*] . . . indicates that the Charitable Gift Annuity Antitrust Relief Act of 1995 is not being interpreted as broadly as it was intended by Congress.
>
> H.R. 1902 replaces current law with language drafted in broader terms. . . . Enactment is . . . intended to obviate the need for further litigation over the antitrust . . . [issues], in that it extends complete immunity to all defendants being sued for participation in the issuance of a charitable gift annuity or charitable remainder trust.
>
> The Committee believes that given the valuable role our charities serve in our communities, the importance of gift annuities and charitable remainder trusts as a source of funding for them, and the tremendous legal and financial uncertainty caused by pending and possibly future antitrust challenges, H.R. 1902 is well justified . . . and the Antitrust Division of the Department of Justice has voiced no opposition to it.

If the Antitrust Division in the exercise of its discretion did not oppose H.R. 1902, how might it justify bringing the *Brown University* litigation against tax-exempt educational institutions?

6. In *National Society of Professional Engineers v. United States*, 435 U.S. 679 (1978), the Court held that the rule of reason could not be used to explore the factual basis proffered as a justification for an ethical canon of a professional association forbidding competitive bidding. Apparently concerned that competitive bidding might adversely impact the quality of the work performed by structural engineers, the association contended that the canon was designed to forestall the public harm which might be produced by unrestrained competitive bidding. On review, the Court held that this concern could not justify collective price-fixing. According to the Court, the association could defend its canon only if it could show that the canon enhanced competition:

> Contrary to its name, the Rule [of Reason] does not open the field of antitrust inquiry to any argument in favor of a challenged restraint that may fall within the realm of reason. Instead, it focuses directly on the challenged restraint's impact on competitive conditions.
>
> . . . Petitioner's ban on competitive bidding prevents all customers from making price comparisons in the initial selection of an engineer, and imposes the Society's views of the costs and benefits of competition on the entire marketplace. It is this restraint that must be justified under the Rule of Reason, and petitioner's attempt to do so on the basis of the potential threat that competition poses to the public safety and the ethics of its profession is nothing less than a frontal assault on the basic policy of the Sherman Act.

435 U.S. at 688, 695. In thus ruling that the association was foreclosed from defending its canon under the rule of reason, the Court clarified the scope of the rule of reason as permitting only those justifications which could be based upon enhancing competition in the marketplace.

7. Are the decisions in *BMI*, *NCAA* and *California Dental Association* consistent with the rationale of *Professional Engineers*?

4. Maximum Price-Fixing Agreements as *Per Se* Illegal

Arizona v. Maricopa County Medical Society
457 U.S. 332 (1982)

Justice Stevens delivered the opinion of the Court.

The question presented is whether § 1 of the Sherman Act . . . has been violated by agreements among competing physicians setting, by majority vote, the maximum fees that they may claim in full payment for health services provided to policyholders of specified insurance plans. The United States Court of Appeals for the Ninth Circuit held that the question could not be answered without evaluating the actual purpose and effect of the agreements at a full trial. . . . Because the undisputed facts disclose a violation of the statute, we granted *certiorari* . . . and now reverse.

I

In October 1978 the State of Arizona filed a civil complaint against two county medical societies and two "foundations for medical care" that the medical societies had organized. The complaint alleged that the defendants were engaged in illegal price-fixing conspiracies. After the defendants filed answers . . . the State moved for partial summary judgment on the issue of liability. The District Court denied the motion, but entered an order . . . certifying for interlocutory appeal the question [of whether the maximum-fee agreements are illegal *per se*. The Court of Appeals affirmed the District Court's order refusing to grant summary judgment]. . . .

II

The Maricopa Foundation for Medical Care is a nonprofit Arizona corporation composed of licensed doctors of medicine, osteopathy, and podiatry engaged in private practice. Approximately 1,750 doctors, representing about 70% of the practitioners in Maricopa County, are members.

The Maricopa Foundation was organized in 1969 for the purpose of promoting fee-for-service medicine and to provide the community with a competitive alternative to existing health insurance plans.[7] The foundation performs three primary activities. It establishes the schedule of maximum fees that participating doctors agree to accept as payment in full for services performed for patients insured under plans approved by the foundation. It reviews the medical necessity and appropriateness of treatment provided by its members to such insured persons. It is authorized to draw checks on insurance company accounts to pay doctors for services performed for covered patients. In performing these functions, the foundation is considered an "insurance administrator" by the Director of the Arizona Department of Insurance. Its participating doctors, however, have no financial interest in the operation of the foundation.

The Pima Foundation for Medical Care, which includes about 400 member doctors,[8] performs similar functions. For the purposes of this litigation, the parties seem to regard the activities of the two foundations as essentially the same. . . .

. . . .

The fee schedules limit the amount that the member doctors may recover for services performed for patients insured under plans approved by the foundations. To obtain this

---

7 Most health insurance plans are of the fee-for-service type. Under the typical insurance plan, the insurer agrees with the insured to reimburse the insured for "usual, customary, and reasonable" medical charges. The third-party insurer, and the insured to the extent of any excess charges, bears the economic risk that the insured will require medical treatment. An alternative to the fee-for-service type of insurance plan is illustrated by the health maintenance organizations authorized under the Health Maintenance Organization Act of 1973. . . . Under this form of prepaid health plan, the consumer pays a fixed periodic fee to a functionally integrated group of doctors in exchange for the group's agreement to provide any medical treatment that the subscriber might need. The economic risk is thus borne by the doctors.

8 The record contains divergent figures on the percentage of Pima County doctors that belong to the foundation. A 1975 publication of the foundation reported 80%; a 1978 affidavit by the executive director of the foundation reported 30%.

approval the insurers—including self-insured employers as well as insurance companies[11]—agree to pay the doctors' charges up to the scheduled amounts, and in exchange the doctors agree to accept those amounts as payment in full for their services. The doctors are free to charge higher fees to uninsured patients, and they also may charge any patient less than the scheduled maxima. A patient who is insured by a foundation-endorsed plan is guaranteed complete coverage for the full amount of his medical bills only if he is treated by a foundation member. He is free to go to a nonmember physician and is still covered for charges that do not exceed the maximum-fee schedule, but he must pay any excess that the nonmember physician may charge.

The impact of the foundation fee schedules on medical fees and on insurance premiums is a matter of dispute. The State of Arizona contends that the periodic upward revisions of the maximum-fee schedules have the effect of stabilizing and enhancing the level of actual charges by physicians, and that the increasing level of their fees in turn increases insurance premiums. The foundations, on the other hand, argue that the schedules impose a meaningful limit on physicians' charges, and that the advance agreement by the doctors to accept the maxima enables the insurance carriers to limit and to calculate more efficiently the risks they underwrite and therefore serves as an effective cost-containment mechanism that has saved patients and insurers millions of dollars. . . . [W]e must assume that the respondents' view of the genuine issues of fact is correct.

This assumption presents, but does not answer, the question whether the Sherman Act prohibits the competing doctors from adopting, revising, and agreeing to use a maximum-fee schedule in implementation of the insurance plans.

III

The respondents recognize that our decisions establish that price-fixing agreements are unlawful on their face. But they argue that the *per se* rule does not govern this case because the agreements at issue are horizontal and fix maximum prices, are among members of a profession, are in an industry with which the judiciary has little antitrust experience, and are alleged to have procompetitive justifications. . . .

The respondents' principal argument is that the *per se* rule is inapplicable because their agreements are alleged to have procompetitive justifications. The argument indicates a misunderstanding of the *per se* concept. The anticompetitive potential inherent in all price-fixing agreements justifies their facial invalidation even if procompetitive justifications are offered for some. Those claims of enhanced competition are so unlikely to prove significant in any particular case that we adhere to the rule of law that is justified in its general application. Even when the respondents are given every benefit of the doubt, the limited record in this case is not inconsistent with the presumption that the respondents' agreements will not significantly enhance competition.

The respondents contend that their fee schedules are procompetitive because they make it possible to provide consumers of health care with a uniquely desirable form of insurance coverage that could not otherwise exist. The features of the foundation-endorsed insurance plans that they stress are a choice of doctors, complete insurance coverage, and

---

[11] Seven different insurance companies underwrite health insurance plans that have been approved by the Maricopa Foundation, and three companies underwrite the plans approved by the Pima Foundation. The record contains no firm data on the portion of the health care market that is covered by these plans. The State relies upon a 1974 analysis indicating that insurance plans endorsed by the Maricopa Foundation had about 63% of the prepaid health care market, but the respondents contest the accuracy of this analysis.

lower premiums. The first two characteristics, however, are hardly unique to these plans. Since only about 70% of the doctors in the relevant market are members of either foundation, the guarantee of complete coverage only applies when an insured chooses a physician in that 70%. If he elects to go to a nonfoundation doctor, he may be required to pay a portion of the doctor's fee. It is fair to presume, however, that at least 70% of the doctors in other markets charge no more than the "usual, customary, and reasonable" fee that typical insurers are willing to reimburse in full. Thus, in Maricopa and Pima Counties as well as in most parts of the country, if an insured asks his doctor if the insurance coverage is complete, presumably in about 70% of the cases the doctor will say "Yes" and in about 30% of the cases he will say "No."

It is true that a binding assurance of complete insurance coverage—as well as most of the respondents' potential for lower insurance premiums[25]—will be obtained only if the insurer and the doctor agree in advance on the maximum fee that the doctor will accept as full payment for a particular service. Even if a fee schedule is therefore desirable, it is not necessary that the doctors do the price fixing.[26] The record indicates that the Arizona Comprehensive Medical/Dental Program for Foster Children is administered by the Maricopa Foundation pursuant to a contract under which the maximum-fee schedule is prescribed by a state agency rather than by the doctors. This program and the Blue Shield plan challenged in *Group Life & Health Insurance Co. v. Royal Drug Co.*, 440 U.S. 205 (1979), indicate that insurers are capable not only of fixing maximum reimbursable prices but also of obtaining binding agreements with providers guaranteeing the insured full reimbursement of a participating provider's fee. In light of these examples, it is not surprising that nothing in the record even arguably supports the conclusion that this type of insurance program could not function if the fee schedules were set in a different way.

---

[25] We do not perceive the respondents' claim of procompetitive justification for their fee schedules to rest on the premise that the fee schedules actually reduce medical fees and accordingly reduce insurance premiums, thereby enhancing competition in the health insurance industry. Such an argument would merely restate the long-rejected position that fixed prices are reasonable if they are lower than free competition would yield. It is arguable, however, that the existence of a fee schedule, whether fixed by the doctors or by the insurers, makes it easier—and to that extent less expensive—for insurers to calculate the risks that they underwrite and to arrive at the appropriate reimbursement on insured claims.

[26] According to a Federal Trade Commission staff report: "Until the mid-1960's, most Blue Shield plans determined in advance how much to pay for particular procedures and prepared fee schedules reflecting their determinations. Fee schedules are still used in approximately 25 percent of Blue Shield contracts." Bureau of Competition, Federal Trade Commission, Medical Participation in Control of Blue Shield and Certain Other Open-Panel Medical Prepayment Plans 128 (1979). We do not suggest that Blue Shield plans are not actually controlled by doctors. Indeed, as the same report discusses at length, the belief that they are has given rise to considerable antitrust litigation. *See also* D. Kass & P. Pautler, Bureau of Economics, Federal Trade Commission, Staff Report on Physician Control of Blue Shield Plans (1979). Nor does this case present the question whether an insurer may, consistent with the Sherman Act, fix the fee schedule and enter into bilateral contracts with individual doctors. That question was not reached in *Group Life & Health Insurance Co. v. Royal Drug Co.*, 440 U.S. 205 (1979). . . . In an amicus curiae brief, the United States expressed its opinion that such an arrangement would be legal unless the plaintiffs could establish that a conspiracy among providers was at work. . . . Our point is simply that the record provides no factual basis for the respondents' claim that the doctors must fix the fee schedule.

The most that can be said for having doctors fix the maximum prices is that doctors may be able to do it more efficiently than insurers. The validity of that assumption is far from obvious,[28] but in any event there is no reason to believe that any savings that might accrue from this arrangement would be sufficiently great to affect the competitiveness of these kinds of insurance plans. It is entirely possible that the potential or actual power of the foundations to dictate the terms of such insurance plans may more than offset the theoretical efficiencies upon which the respondents' defense ultimately rests.[29]

. . . .

C

Our adherence to the *per se* rule is grounded not only on economic prediction, judicial convenience, and business certainty, but also on a recognition of the respective roles of the Judiciary and the Congress in regulating the economy. . . . Given its generality, our enforcement of the Sherman Act has required the Court to provide much of its substantive content. By articulating the rules of law with some clarity and by adhering to rules that are justified in their general application, however, we enhance the legislative prerogative to amend the law. The respondents' arguments against application of the *per se* rule in this case therefore are better directed to the Legislature. Congress may consider the exception that we are not free to read into the statute.

IV

Having declined the respondents' invitation to cut back on the *per se* rule against price fixing, we are left with the respondents' argument that their fee schedules involve price fixing in only a literal sense. For this argument, the respondents rely upon *Broadcast Music, Inc. v. Columbia Broadcasting System, Inc.*, 441 U.S. 1 (1979).

In *Broadcast Music* we were confronted with an antitrust challenge to the marketing of the right to use copyrighted compositions derived from the entire membership of the American Society of Composers, Authors and Publishers (ASCAP). The so-called "blanket license" was entirely different from the product that any one composer was able to sell by himself.[31] Although there was little competition among individual composers for their separate compositions, the blanket-license arrangement did not place any restraint on the right of any individual copyright owner to sell his own compositions separately to any buyer

---

28 In order to create an insurance plan under which the doctor would agree to accept as full payment a fee prescribed in a fixed schedule, someone must canvass the doctors to determine what maximum prices would be high enough to attract sufficient numbers of individual doctors to sign up but low enough to make the insurance plan competitive. In this case that canvassing function is performed by the foundation; the foundation then deals with the insurer. It would seem that an insurer could simply bypass the foundation by performing the canvassing function and dealing with the doctors itself. Under the foundation plan, each doctor must look at the maximum-fee schedule fixed by his competitors and vote for or against approval of the plan (and, if the plan is approved by majority vote, he must continue or revoke his foundation membership). A similar, if to some extent more protracted, process would occur if it were each insurer that offered the maximum-fee schedule to each doctor.

29 In this case it appears that the fees are set by a group with substantial power in the market for medical services, and that there is competition among insurance companies in the sale of medical insurance. Under these circumstances the insurance companies are not likely to have significantly greater bargaining power against a monopoly of doctors than would individual consumers of medical services.

31 "Thus, to the extent the blanket license is a different product, ASCAP is not really a joint sales agency offering the individual goods of many sellers, but is a separate seller offering its blanket license, of which the individual compositions are raw material." 441 U.S. at 22 (footnote omitted).

at any price.[32] But a "necessary consequence" of the creation of the blanket license was that its price had to be established. . . . We held that the delegation by the composers to ASCAP of the power to fix the price for the blanket license was not a species of the price-fixing agreements categorically forbidden by the Sherman Act. The record disclosed price fixing only in a "literal sense." . . .

This case is fundamentally different. Each of the foundations is composed of individual practitioners who compete with one another for patients. Neither the foundations nor the doctors sell insurance, and they derive no profits from the sale of health insurance policies. The members of the foundations sell medical services. Their combination in the form of the foundation does not permit them to sell any different product.[33] Their combination has merely permitted them to sell their services to certain customers at fixed prices and arguably to affect the prevailing market price of medical care.

. . . .

The judgment of the Court of Appeals is reversed.

It is so ordered.

Justice BLACKMUN and Justice O'CONNOR took no part in the consideration or decision of this case.

Justice POWELL, with whom THE CHIEF JUSTICE and Justice REHNQUIST join, dissenting.

The medical care plan condemned by the Court today is a comparatively new method of providing insured medical services at predetermined maximum costs. It involves no coercion. Medical insurance companies, physicians, and patients alike are free to participate or not as they choose. On its face, the plan seems to be in the public interest.

. . . .

. . . [T]he two agreements [in *Maricopa* and in *Broadcast Music*] are similar in important respects. Each involved competitors and resulted in cooperative pricing. Each arrangement also was prompted by the need for better service to the consumers. And each arrangement apparently makes possible a new product by reaping otherwise unattainable efficiencies. The Court's effort to distinguish *Broadcast Music* thus is unconvincing.[12]

---

[32] "Here, the blanket-license fee is not set by competition among individual copyright owners, and it is a fee for the use of any of the compositions covered by the license. But the blanket license cannot be wholly equated with a simple horizontal arrangement among competitors. ASCAP does set the price for its blanket license, but that license is quite different from anything any individual owner could issue. The individual composers and authors have neither agreed not to sell individually in any other market nor use the blanket license to mask price fixing in such other markets." . . .

[33] It may be true that by becoming a member of the foundation the individual practitioner obtains a competitive advantage in the market for medical services that he could not unilaterally obtain. That competitive advantage is the ability to attract as customers people who value both the guarantee of full health coverage and a choice of doctors. But, as we have indicated, the setting of the price *by doctors* is not a "necessary consequence" of an arrangement with an insurer in which the doctor agrees not to charge certain insured customers more than a fixed price.

[12] . . . .

In the same manner [as in *Broadcast Music*], the foundations set up an innovative means to deliver a basic service—insured medical care from a wide range of physicians of one's choice—in a more economical manner. The foundations' maximum-fee schedules replace the weak cost containment incentives in typical "usual, customary, and reasonable" insurance agreements with a stronger cost control mechanism: an absolute ceiling on maximum fees that can be charged. The conduct of the insurers in this case indicates that they believe that the foundation plan as it presently exists is the most efficient means of developing and administering such schedules. At this stage in the litigation, therefore, we must agree that the foundation plan permits the more economical delivery of the basic insurance service—"to some extent, a different product.". . .

. . . .

V

I believe the Court's action today loses sight of the basic purposes of the Sherman Act. As we have noted, the antitrust laws are a "consumer welfare prescription." *Reiter v. Sonotone Corp.*, 442 U.S. 330, 343 (1979). In its rush to condemn a novel plan about which it knows very little, the Court suggests that this end is achieved only by invalidating activities that *may* have some potential for harm. But the little that the record does show about the effect of the plan suggests that it is a means of providing medical services that in fact benefits rather than injures persons who need them.

In a complex economy, complex economic arrangements are commonplace. It is unwise for the Court, in a case as novel and important as this one, to make a final judgment in the absence of a complete record and where mandatory inferences create critical issues of fact.

COMMENTARY

1. Do you think the Court should have applied the *per se* rule to the arrangement in *Maricopa County*? Should the case have gone to trial to determine what the effects of the arrangement were? Would this be tantamount to a decision to apply the rule of reason? Would a trial court be required to apply a full-scale rule of reason analysis after *California Dental*?

2. The Court suggested that when the Ninth Circuit formulated the issue to be whether the arrangement facilitated or obstructed the matching of marginal cost to marginal revenue, it was adopting "a legal standard based on the reasonableness of the fixed prices, an inquiry we have so often condemned." Is there force in the Court's criticism?

3. The defendants claimed that their arrangement produced procompetitive effects. Do you think that they made a plausible case that their arrangement furthered competition or efficiency?

4. Consider the Court's footnote 25. It says that reduced prices are of no relevance; only reduced costs. Is this an endorsement of Bork's position that the antitrust laws are designed to further the combination of producer and consumer surplus? This approach makes it easier to reconcile *Broadcast Music* with the condemnation of the price agreement in *Maricopa*.

5. Judge Frank H. Easterbrook has argued that in many situations maximum-price agreements (both horizontal and vertical) are pro-competitive. Commenting upon the Maricopa County case, he has suggested that the maximum-fee arrangements served the purpose of lowering search costs for low-priced physicians and that they thus enhanced price competition:

> A maximum-price agreement can help to reduce search costs. . . . Those adhering to the agreement are identified as low-price sellers, and this identification should lead to an increase in the sales by those so identified. . . .
>
> Medical services are a textbook example of goods in which quality is uncertain, search costs are high (patients sometimes cannot search at all), purchases are infrequent, and third-party payments reduce the incentive for patients to search even when they can do so at low cost. A maximum-price agreement may identify low-price sellers to the insurance companies, which may instruct the insureds to use a member of the foundation for medical care. Insurers participating in the plan will have lower costs, and the insureds will pay lower premiums. Physicians willing to accept the established maximum may join the foundation; others will not do so. The process should lead to a reduction in the cost of service. . . .

Frank H. Easterbrook, *Maximum Price Fixing*, 48 U. CHI. L. REV. 886, 896 (1981).

6. Are you persuaded by Easterbrook or by the Court? In the Court's opinion it suggested that if maximum-fee schedules facilitated low-cost medical insurance, it was not necessary that doctors themselves set the maximum fees. Could the insurance companies or other agencies set maximum fees as well as doctors? If the insurance companies each establish their own maximum-fee schedules, how would the situation differ—legally and economically—from that involved in the *Maricopa County* case?

C. Agreements Among Buyers

Since there is no apparent difference in the way agreements among sellers affect the operation of the market from the way agreements among buyers affect the market, the same rules *prima facie* should apply to both groups. In *Socony-Vacuum*, Justice Douglas broadened the *per se* rule condemning price-fixing agreements from the rule articulated in *Trenton Potteries*. In *Socony-Vacuum*, the *per se* rule was said to apply even in cases in which the parties lacked power to control the market.

Consider the impact of *Socony-Vacuum* upon agreements among buyers. (Actually in *Socony-Vacuum*, the participants in the price-fixing agreement were buyers, weren't they? It was the major oil companies which contracted to purchase the excess production of the independent refineries in an effort to maintain the prices for gasoline on the spot market. Thus although the defendants in *Socony-Vacuum* were in fact buyers, they were not trying to affect the prices which they paid for gasoline. Rather, their buying activities were designed to affect the price at which gasoline was sold on the spot market.) Should (or does) the rule condemning horizontal price fixing agreements as *per se* illegal apply to horizontal agreements among buyers about the prices which they will pay?

If all or most buyers in a market agreed together about the prices they would pay for supplies, they would be acting like a monopsonist—the buyer counterpart of a monopolist. A group composed of all or most buyers in a market would be able to restrict their purchases, so as to force down market price. There is no question that, in the absence of offsetting efficiencies,[1] such an agreement would be illegal *per se*.

What about the legality of a joint purchasing agreement among a group of buyers too small in the aggregate to possess market power? It is a common practice for groups of buyers—frequently (but not always) commercial buyers—to combine in a joint purchasing agency, which enables them to reduce their purchasing costs. Often buyers engaged in joint purchasing also are engaged in joint warehousing, another practice which often reduces their costs. But joint purchasing also enables buyers to exert more "buying power" and thereby receive a more favorable price than the individual buyers might receive on their own. In order to make a large sale, sellers are often willing to offer a discount. Should it be unlawful for buyers to form a joint purchasing agency in order to bargain down the prices of sellers? Does your answer depend upon whether the joint purchasing agency pressures down prices by restricting its purchases or whether it obtains lower prices as a result of competitive bids from rival sellers? Note that in the former case output is restricted whereas in the latter case it is not. Indeed the tendency of the behavior described in the latter case is towards increased purchases (and greater output) rather than the opposite.

Does Justice Douglas' apparent extension of the *per se* rule condemning horizontal price-fixing agreements to embrace agreements in which the participants lack market power cast a cloud over the lawfulness of joint selling or marketing agreements? The joint selling agency in *Appalachian Coals* was upheld on the rationale that it lacked market power, a rationale no longer available under *Socony-Vacuum*. The joint selling agency in *BMI* could be defended on the ground that it produced efficiencies. So long as joint selling and buying agencies present a plausible case that their activities are efficiency enhancing, they may be able to avoid application of the *per se* rule. Yet these selling and marketing agencies may bear the effective burden of showing the existence of these efficiencies. And to the extent that they fail to persuade courts that they have carried that burden, they may be penalized for innocuous activity. And what if a buying agency lacks efficiencies and its sole effect is to bargain down the price to a level which the individual buyers could not obtain? Why should hard bargaining constitute an antitrust offense, if output is not restricted?

---

1 *Mandeville Island Farms v. American Crystal Sugar*, 334 U.S. 219 (1948) (illegal price-fixing for sugar refiners to adopt a pricing formula that resulted in a uniform price for raw sugar beets). *See also* ROGER D. BLAIR & JEFFREY L. HARRISON, MONOPSONY: ANTITRUST LAW AND ECONOMICS, Ch. 4 (1993).

Since the majority of litigated cases under § 1 of the Sherman Act involving collective action concern sellers affecting other sellers of goods or services, should the same analysis apply when the collective action is by buyers against other buyers?

In *Mandeville Island Farms v. American Crystal Sugar Co.*, 334 U.S. 219 (1948), a group of sugar refiners in Northern California combined to offer uniform low prices to the farmers in that region. The Court, noting that this was agreement among buyers rather than sellers, applied the traditional rule against price-fixing. Does agreement among buyers have the same anticompetitive impact as agreement among competing sellers?

Mandeville Island is supportable because when the refiners offered a uniform price, that price might have been set at a level depriving the farmers of a rate of return that would ensure their continued planting of sugar beets. In that event, output would be restricted by an artificially set price—the same injury as in agreement among sellers. But would buyers intentionally set those prices so low as to drive their suppliers out of business?

Cooperative buying arrangements carry a potential for achieving purchasing efficiencies. Yet they can be misused when their combined buying power results in a restriction of market supply. It has therefore been suggested that the appropriate application of § 1 is neither a *per se* nor a rule of reason approach. Instead, a flexible or "escapable" rule is urged. The advocates of this position explain it as follows:

> When sellers fix prices, the problem is that too few units are sold. In the case of colluding buyers, too few units are purchased. If a buying cooperative seeks to achieve procompetitive efficiencies, then the cooperative may have redeeming virtues. Society should not lose these benefits because of an inflexible rule. Thus, joint pricing agreements among buyers should be evaluated under a flexible or "escapable" standard.

Roger D. Blair & Jeffrey L. Harrison, *Cooperative Buying, Monopsony Power, and Antitrust Policy*, 86 Nw. U. L. Rev. 331, 342 (1992). This proposal would employ a presumption of illegality to a pricing agreement or a boycott among buyers, shifting the burden to the buyers to offer credible evidence of achieving some efficiencies. These commentators credit their proposal to the analysis of ancillary restraints in *Trenton Potteries*.

D. Other *Per Se* Practices Under Section One

The rationale for the *per se* rule is articulated in *Broadcast Music* as follows:

> . . . certain agreements or practices are so plainly anticompetitive . . . and so often . . . lack . . . any redeeming virtue, that they are conclusively presumed illegal without further examination under the rule of reason generally applied in Sherman Act cases. This *per se* rule is a valid and useful tool of antitrust policy and enforcement.

441 U.S. at 8. The *per se* rule is also applied to agreements for the division of sales territory and to certain boycotts when these practices are adopted by horizontal competitors.

Territorial division merits *per se* treatment because it forecloses the competition among the agreeing parties by coupling customers (as well as products) to the designated conspiring sellers based on the location of the customer. An agreement among a group of firms that controls a significant percentage of the product in an industry as to the territory in which each will sell effectively grants the designated seller a competition-free license to charge a price of its own choosing within that geographic area. Eliminating that competition would permit each of the sellers in the group to reduce output below efficient levels, to raise prices to monopoly levels, and to earn monopoly profits. The resulting misallocation of resources directly conflicts with antitrust goals, so that territorial division properly qualifies for *per se* illegality.

Similarly, certain boycotts have been thought to merit *per se* treatment because they, too, foreclose preexisting competition by coupling or identifying eligible suppliers or customers for a group of conspiring sellers. Boycotts are a tool which, when strategically employed, have enabled groups of firms to induce suppliers or customers to deny patronage to rivals, thereby raising the costs of those rivals or eliminating them altogether. Typically a boycott would be used against a more efficient rival or to or punish a rival who deviated from a price-fixing agreement. Again, the targets of boycotts are often identified either individually or by status, rather than by geographic location, although the two criteria are not mutually exclusive. For example, if all the residential housing mortgage lenders in a city were to agree among themselves not to finance houses for low-income buyers of a given ethnic, racial, or gender identity, the clustered location of low-priced houses may produce a geographic, territorial effect to the defined objects of the boycott. (Such an agreement would be *per se* illegal. The economic motivation for such an agreement, however, is unclear.)

Like price-fixing, there are definitional problems in applying each term. Because a market division among all or most of the firms competing in an industry eliminates preexisting competition and establishes regional or product monopolies, and because boycotts constitute a weapon used by inefficient or noncompetitive firms against their rivals, there is little doubt that the *per se* rule should apply to some identifiable core of these activities. The problem, of course, is identifying that core. Territorial divisions and boycotts are the subjects of the following two chapters.

As the *California Dental Association* case illustrates, the by-laws and standards of a professional organization may be subjected to antitrust scrutiny if the by-laws address prices (of services) even indirectly. In *United States v. American Bar Ass'n*, 1996 WL 426832 (D.D.C.), Judge Richey issued a consent decree barring a series of practices by the Accreditation Committee of the Section of Legal Education and Admissions to the Bar of the American Bar Association. In the Complaint the government had alleged that the legal educators, as members of the Accreditation Committee, had "captured" the law school accreditation process, *id.* at 8, to accomplish "anticompetitive guild objectives," *id.* at 9, by rules conditioning ABA accreditation of a law school on minimum salaries of full-time law school teachers, deans, library directors, and librarians; by limiting student-to-faculty ratios; by defining "faculty" solely as full-time, tenure track teachers; by setting limits on the number of hours taught per semester; by requiring periodic leave for teachers; by requiring a minimum volume count of books and other library resources; by requiring certain physical facilities; by denying course credit for bar review courses; and by barring the transfer of course credit by a student from a non-accredited school to an accredited school, *id.* at 7-8. As part of the initial accreditation application of a new law school, the salary structure of the applicant school is required to be reported. To provide a basis for comparison, the Accreditation Committee gathers annually comparable data by academic rank and term of service of the teachers in all accredited law schools.

In June of 1995, responding to the complaint of a law school dean whose school was denied accreditation for failing to have sufficient full-time faculty and conforming facilities, the Department of Justice filed a civil suit alleging violation of § 1 of the Sherman Act by restraining competition among professional personnel at ABA-approved law schools by fixing their compensation levels and working conditions, and thereby limiting competition from non-ABA-approved schools. The complaint further alleged that

> . . . rather than setting minimum standards for law school quality and thus providing valuable information to consumers, the legitimate purposes of accreditation, the ABA at times acted as a guild that protected the interests of professional school personnel.

Id. at 5.

In his Final Judgment, Judge Richey ordered the ABA to institute a Compliance Program, to designate a Compliance Officer, to eliminate the dominance of academic lawyers over the accreditation process, and to end the adoption or enforcement of any rule or standard that imposes requirements as to base salary, stipends, fringe benefits, or other compensation paid to law school faculty and other law school employees. In addition, the ABA is prohibited from accrediting only law schools organized as non-profit entities. *Id.* at 8. Judge Richey also retained jurisdiction for a ten year period.

For a review of the case, see 82 ABA J. 44 (1996). Does this litigation pose the public policy question of a choice between allowing free market forces to determine the value of a law degree or permitting a professional association to set minimum conditions? Do you find credible the allegation that the teacher who is in front of this class today is a participant in a price-fixing cartel? Should it be of interest to the ABA or to you when you filed your application for admission to law school, whether the faculty pay scale of a non-accredited school is the same of that of a comparable accredited school? What rules can you formulate besides those dealing with salary structure to inhibit the establishment of proprietary medical schools? Can salary structure be a useful surrogate for a cluster of quality criteria? Can an absolute rule of antitrust liability for any agreement involving price become a force of attraction to overwhelm any rule of reason analysis?

Chapter 3
Market Divisions

When all or most of the business firms competing with each other in a broad market divide that market among themselves, allocating regions (or products) to each firm, they transform that market from a competitive one into a number of smaller markets which are uncompetitive. Such arrangements make each of the participating firms monopolists in the areas respectively allocated to them. Arrangements of this type produce restraints analogous to price-fixing agreements, the principal difference being that in most of the market division cases, a single firm sets monopoly prices in the area assigned to it whereas in the price-fixing cases all of the firms cooperate in setting a monopoly price at which they all sell.

In one of the earliest Sherman Act cases, Judge Taft ruled in *United States v. Addyston Pipe & Steel Co.*, 85 F. 271 (6th Cir. 1898), *aff'd*, 175 U.S. 211 (1899), that market division was an illegal restraint. The Supreme Court indicated that market division agreements were unlawful in *Timken Co. v. United States*, 341 U.S. 593 (1951). Because a market division agreement among all or most of the firms competing in an industry eliminates preexisting competition and establishes regional or product monopolies, there can be little doubt that such agreements are illegal *per se*.

Interesting issues arise, however, when agreements allocating products or territories are made by a number of firms which—because they comprise only a small part of the total number of competing firms—lack market power. What considerations are relevant in considering whether such agreements should be subject to the *per se* rule? Two such agreements came before the Supreme Court in *United States v. Sealy, Inc.*, 388 U.S. 350 (1967), and *United States v. Topco Associates, Inc.*, 405 U.S. 596 (1972).

In *United States v. Sealy, Inc.*, 388 U.S. 350 (1967), approximately 30 mattress manufacturers owned all of the stock of Sealy, Inc., a corporation which owned the Sealy name and trademarks and issued licenses to its stockholder members to use the Sealy name and trademarks in designated areas. Each licensee agreed not to manufacture or sell "Sealy products" outside its assigned area but was free to make and sell its private label products anywhere. Partially influenced by retail price-fixing in which the stockholder-licensees had been engaging, the Court asserted that "Sealy, Inc., is an instrumentality of the licensees for the purposes of . . . horizontal territorial allocation," and the arrangement was accordingly condemned as a *per se* violation of the Sherman Act. The price fixing "underlines," the Court stated, "the horizontal nature of the enterprise" and "refutes appellee's claim that the territorial restraints were mere incidents of a lawful program of trademark licensing."

In *United States v. Topco Associates, Inc.*, 405 U.S. 596 (1972), Topco was a cooperative association of approximately 25 small- and medium-sized regional grocery supermarket chains whose basic function was to serve as a purchasing agent for its members. Topco's purchasing operations enabled its members "to obtain high quality merchandise under private labels in order to compete more effectively with larger national and regional chains." According to the Court, there was "much evidence in the record that Topco members are frequently in as strong a competitive position in their respective areas as any other chain. The strength of this competitive position is due, in some measure, to the success of Topco-brand products. Although only 10% of the total goods sold by Topco members bear the association's brand names, the profit on these goods is substantial and their very existence has improved the competitive potential of Topco members with respect to other large and powerful chains." The problematic part of the Topco arrangement was an agreement between each Topco member and the association designating the territory in which the member was permitted to sell Topco-brand products, forbidding sales of such products outside that area, and providing each member with a practical veto power over the admission of new members. Although Topco argued that it needed "territorial divisions to compete with larger chains; that the association could not exist if the territorial divisions were anything but exclusive; and that by restricting competition in the sale of Topco-brand goods, the association actually increases competition by enabling its members to compete successfully with larger regional and national chains," the Court held that the arrangement was a "horizontal" allocation of territories and therefore a *per se* violation of § 1.

COMMENTARY

1. Note that an agreement among all of the firms competing in a market which allocates each firm an exclusive territory eliminates all competition analogous to the way a price-fixing agreement among all of the firms competing in a market eliminates competition. When a small number of firms join together in a cooperative venture in order to sell more effectively, competition is likely intensified if the cooperation reduces the participants costs. When a *per se* rule was effectively applied to a market division agreement in *Addyston Pipe* and *Timken*, the courts were treating those ventures as they would have treated a price-fixing agreement among competitors.

2. There is some question, however, whether the current version of the *per se* rule against price-fixing agreements is too broadly phrased. To the extent that it literally appears to condemn cooperative ventures which either intensify competition or enhance efficiency, it unnecessarily deters procompetitive behavior. In *Broadcast Music*, the Court was forced to reject a "literal" view of price fixing. Much of the trouble with the present formulation can be traced to Justice Douglas' *Socony-*

Vacuum opinion which eliminated the need to establish the market power of the defendants before condemning an agreement on prices.

The same question arises in connection with applying a *per se* rule to all agreements among competitors to allocate or divide markets. Such a *per se* rule may be too broadly phrased. If the present formulation of the *per se* rule condemning market division agreements condemns agreements which—rather than lessening competition—intensify competition, then such a formulation conflicts with the basic purpose of the antitrust laws, which is the promotion of competition.

In the light of these considerations, consider whether you believe that *Topco* requires *per se* condemnation of cooperative agreements which, by bringing into the market new or more efficient competitors, carry the potential for enhancing competition. Try to distinguish the market division agreements which lessen or eliminate competition from those which enhance competition.

After the remand, in which the Supreme Court directed the entry of judgment not inconsistent with its opinion, the district court entered its Final Judgment in which it permitted Topco to allocate areas of prime responsibility among its members and to terminate membership of a firm that did not adequately promote Topco brands. In a subsequent proceeding, the Department of Justice moved to strike these two provisions of the Final Judgment, 1973-1 Trade Cas. ¶ 74,485. In denying the government's motion the district court stated:

> . . . [T]here is no basis in fact for the government's omniscient assertion that such assignment (or a territory of prime responsibility) "can only result in a limitation upon the territories" in which Topco members will sell.
>
> * * *
>
> . . . [T]ermination solely for failure to promote adequately the sale of Topco products would be perfectly proper.

Id. at 94, 155.

In light of the ultimate disposition of this litigation, was this a case in which a rule of reason analysis would have been more appropriate? Should Topco's small market share have been dispositive in the decision to bring this case?

Palmer v. BRG of Georgia, Inc.

498 U.S. 46 (1990)

PER CURIAM.

In preparation for the 1985 Georgia Bar Examination, petitioners contracted to take a bar review course offered by respondent BRG of Georgia, Inc. (BRG). In this litigation they contend that the price of BRG's course was enhanced by reason of an unlawful agreement between BRG and respondent Harcourt Brace Jovanovich Legal and Professional Publications (HBJ), the Nation's largest provider of bar review materials and lecture services. The central issue is whether the 1980 agreement between respondents violated § 1 of the Sherman Act.

HBJ began offering a Georgia bar review course on a limited basis in 1976, and was in direct, and often intense, competition with BRG during the period from 1977-1979. BRG and HBJ were the two main providers of bar review courses in Georgia during this time period. In early 1980, they entered into an agreement that gave BRG an exclusive license to market HBJ's material in Georgia and to use its trade name "Bar/Bri." The parties agreed that HBJ would not compete with BRG in Georgia and that BRG would not compete with HBJ outside of Georgia.[2] Under the agreement, HBJ received $100 per student enrolled by BRG and 40% of all revenues over $350. Immediately after the 1980 agreement, the price of BRG's course was increased from $150 to over $400.

On petitioners' motion for partial summary judgment as to the § 1 counts in the complaint and respondents' motion for summary judgment, the District Court held that the agreement was lawful [and the United States Court of Appeals for the Eleventh Circuit affirmed]. . . .

In *United States v. Topco Associates, Inc.*, 405 U.S. 596 (1972), we held that agreements between competitors to allocate territories to minimize competition are illegal:

> "One of the classic examples of a *per se* violation of § 1 is an agreement between competitors at the same level of the market structure to allocate territories in order to minimize competition. . . . This Court has reiterated time and time again that '[h]orizontal territorial limitations . . . are naked restraints of trade with no purpose except stifling of competition.' Such limitations are *per se* violations of the Sherman Act."

Id. at 608 (citations omitted). The defendants in *Topco* had never competed in the same market, but had simply agreed to allocate markets. Here, HBJ and BRG had previously competed in the Georgia market; under their allocation agreement, BRG received that market, while HBJ received the remainder of the United States. Each agreed not to compete in the other's territories. Such agreements are anticompetitive regardless of whether the parties split a market within which both do business or whether they merely reserve one market for one and another for the other. Thus, the 1980 agreement between HBJ and BRG was unlawful on its face.

The petition for a writ of *certiorari* is granted, the judgment of the Court of Appeals is reversed, and the case is remanded for further proceedings consistent with this opinion.[7]

It is so ordered.

---

[2] The 1980 agreement contained two provisions, one called a "Covenant Not to Compete" and the other called "Other Ventures." The former required HBJ not to "directly or indirectly own, manage, operate, join, invest, control, or participate in or be connected as an officer, employee, partner, director, independent contractor or otherwise with any business which is operating or participating in the preparation of candidates for the Georgia State Bar Examination." Plaintiffs' Motion for Partial Summary Judgment, Attachment E, at 10. The latter required BRG not to compete against HBJ in states in which HBJ currently operated outside the state of Georgia. *Id.* at 15.

[7] In 1982, in connection with the settlement of another lawsuit, respondents made certain changes in their arrangement. Because the District Court found that the 1980 agreement did not violate § 1 of the Sherman Act, it did not address whether the 1982 modified agreement constituted a withdrawal from or abandonment of the conspiracy. In *United States v. Kissel*, 218 U.S. 601 (1910), we held that antitrust conspiracies may continue in time beyond the original conspiratorial agreement until either the conspiracy's objectives are abandoned or succeed. *Id.* at 608-609. Thus, it is an unsettled factual issue whether the conspiratorial objectives manifest in the 1980 agreement between HBJ and BRG have continued in spite of the 1982 modifications.

COMMENTARY

Consider whether the circumstances in this case are comparable to *Topco*, the authority invoked by the Court for its decision. Consider whether the application of the *per se* rule in this case is more appropriate than in *Topco*. In addition to the fact—pointed out by the Court—that BRG and HBJ were actual (rather than potential) competitors in Georgia, there are additional reasons why application of the *per se* rule fits better here.

In *Topco*, the companies attempted to justify the market division on the basis that they were collectively creating a new and more valuable product, the low-cost, high-value Topco brand line and that the market division was essential to the pursuit of that objective. Consider whether or not the companies involved in the *BRG* case are jointly creating a new product or service for which the market division is essential.

Consider the extent to which the Court took account of the market power (or market shares) of BRG and HBJ. Does a fair reading of *BRG* suggest that market power is irrelevant to a market division case?

Rothery Storage & Van Co. v. Atlas Van Lines, Inc.

792 F.2d 210 (D.C. Cir. 1986)

BORK, Circuit Judge:

Appellants, plaintiffs below, seek review of the district court's decision dismissing their antitrust action against Atlas Van Lines, Inc. ("Atlas"). . . .

I.

Atlas operates as a nationwide common carrier of used household goods under authority granted by the Interstate Commerce Commission. It contracts to provide moving services to individuals and to businesses transferring employees. Like most national moving companies, Atlas exercises its interstate authority by employing independent moving companies throughout the country as its agents. These companies execute a standard agency contract with Atlas, agreeing to adhere, when making shipments on Atlas' authority, to such things as standard operating procedures, maintenance and painting specifications, and uniform rates. Typically, such an agreement will contain a provision barring an agent affiliated with a particular van line from dealing with any other line. The agency agreement is supplemented by Atlas' bylaws, rules, and regulations governing the agents' interstate operations.

Some of these independent moving companies, the "non-carrier agents," have no interstate authority of their own and can move goods interstate only on Atlas' authority. Until recently, other companies, the "carrier agents," possessed their own interstate authority and could move goods to the extent of that independent authority as principals for their own accounts. Both types of agent may engage in intrastate carriage without Atlas' permission or governance. A carrier agent, however, could act in interstate commerce both as an agent of the van line it serves and as a competitor of that van line. The carrier agents could, and some did, use Atlas equipment, training, and the like for interstate carriage under their own authorities and pay Atlas nothing.

A van line and its agents constitute an enterprise on a scale not easily obtainable by a single carrier. Atlas, which is the sixth largest van line in the nation, provides a network of 490 agents capable of carrying household goods between any two points in the nation. Atlas coordinates and supports the agents' operations. The use of agents spares a van line the necessity of obtaining enormous amounts of capital to perform the same services and, quite possibly, avoids diseconomies of scale, i.e., the inefficiencies of a single management large and complex enough to perform all the functions that are now divided between the van line and its agents. The agents find customers and do the packing, loading, hauling, and storage. Atlas sets the rates, dispatches shipments, chooses routes, arranges backhauls so the agent's truck need not return empty, arranges services at the origin and destination of shipments, collects all revenues and pays the agents, establishes uniform rules for the appearance and quality of equipment, trains salespeople and drivers, purchases and finances equipment for use by the agents, and maintains insurance on all shipments made under Atlas' authority. In addition, Atlas conducts national advertising and promotional forums. With the assistance of agents, it handles customer claims. In short, Atlas, and its agents make up an enterprise or firm integrated by contracts, one which is indistinguishable in economic analysis from a complex partnership.

. . . .

The deregulation of the moving industry, beginning in 1979, produced changes that had a profound impact on the relationship between van lines and their agents. Prior to the regulatory changes, independent moving companies had little ability to obtain their own interstate transportation authority. . . .

This increased potential for the diversion of interstate business to its carrier agents posed two potential problems for Atlas. Each of these problems is a version of what has been called the "free ride." A free ride occurs when one party to an arrangement reaps benefits for which another party pays, though that transfer of wealth is not part of the agreement between them. The free ride can become a serious problem for a partnership or joint venture because the party that provides capital and services without receiving compensation has a strong incentive to provide less, thus rendering the common enterprise less effective. The first problem occurs because, by statute, a van line incurs strict liability for acts of its agents exercising "actual or apparent authority." 49 U.S.C. § 10934(a) (1982). Thus, an increase of shipments made on the agents' independent authority, but using Atlas' equipment, uniforms, and services would create the risk of increased liability for Atlas although Atlas received no revenue from those shipments. Second, because carrier agents could utilize Atlas services and equipment on non-Atlas interstate shipments, the possible increase of such shipments meant that Atlas might make large outlays for which it received no return. . . .

To meet these problems . . . Atlas announced that it . . . would terminate the agency contract of any affiliated company that persisted in handling interstate carriage on its own account as well as for Atlas. Under the new policy, any carrier agent already affiliated with Atlas could continue to exercise independent interstate authority only by transferring its independent interstate authority to a separate corporation with a new name. These new entities could not use the facilities or services of Atlas or any of its affiliates.

. . . .

When the Atlas policy challenged in this case went into effect, every agent in the system was an actual or potential competitor of Atlas. The carrier agents were actual competitors and the non-carrier agents, because of the ICC's increased willingness to grant interstate moving authority, were potential competitors. Every carrier that stayed in the Atlas network adhered to a policy of ending or lessening its competition with Atlas (by abandoning its interstate authority or transferring that authority to a separate company with a new trade name) or of not entering into full competition with Atlas (by not obtaining interstate authority). Agents required to ship on Atlas' interstate authority must, of course, abide by Atlas' rates. Thus, all of these legally separate corporations agreed to a policy that restricted competition.

. . . .

IV.

Appellants contend, however, that Atlas' restraints include horizontal price maintenance since the agents must ship on rates established by Atlas. We take this to be a claim that the horizontal elimination of competition within the system is illegal *per se* or, failing that, is nevertheless unlawful under a rule-of-reason analysis.

. . . .

Atlas has required that any moving company doing business as its agent must not conduct independent interstate carrier operations. Thus, a carrier agent, in order to continue as an Atlas agent, must either abandon its independent interstate authority and operate only under Atlas' authority or create a new corporation (a "carrier affiliate") to conduct interstate carriage separate from its operation as an Atlas agent. Atlas' agents may deal only with Atlas or other Atlas agents.

The result of this is an interstate system for the carriage of household goods in which legally separate companies integrate their activities by contract. In this way the participants achieve many of the same benefits or efficiencies that would be available if they were integrated through ownership by Atlas. At the outset of this opinion . . . , we set out the functions performed by Atlas and by the agents and stated that the system is a contract integration, one identical, in economic terms, to a partnership formed by agreement. Analysis might begin and end with the observation that Atlas and its agents command between 5.1 and 6% of the relevant market, which is the interstate carriage of used household goods. It is impossible to believe that an agreement to eliminate competition within a group of that size can produce any of the evils of monopoly. *See, e.g.,* 3 J. VON KALINOWSKI, ANTITRUST LAWS AND TRADE REGULATION § 8.02[3], at 8-34 to 8-34.2 & n.71 (1986). A monopolist (or those acting together to achieve monopoly results) enhances its revenues by raising the market price. It can do that only if its share of the market is so large that by reducing its output of goods or services the amount offered by the industry is substantially reduced so that the price is bid up. If a group of Atlas' size reduced its output of services, there would be no effect upon market price because firms making up the other 94% of the market would simply take over the abandoned business. The only effect would be a loss of revenues to Atlas. Indeed, so impotent to raise prices is a firm with a market share of 5 or 6% that any attempt by it to engage in a monopolistic restriction of output would be little short of suicidal.

. . . .

We might well rest, therefore, upon the absence of market power as demonstrated both by Atlas' 6% national market share and by the structure of the market. If it is clear that Atlas and its agents by eliminating competition among themselves are not attempting to restrict industry output, then their agreement must be designed to make the conduct of their business more effective. No third possibility suggests itself. But we need not rely entirely upon that inference because the record made in the district court demonstrates that the challenged agreement enhances the efficiency of the van line. The chief efficiency, as already noted, is the elimination of the problem of the free ride.

A carrier agent can attract customers because of Atlas' "national image" and can use Atlas' equipment and order forms when undertaking carriage for its own account. . . . The carrier agents "benefit from use of the services of moving and storage firms affiliated with Atlas, for origin or destination work at remote locations, when operating independently of Atlas." . . . This benefit involves not only the availability of a reliable network of firms providing such services, but also includes the benefit of Atlas' "mediating collection matters" among its affiliates. . . . To the degree that a carrier agent uses Atlas' reputation, equipment, facilities, and services in conducting business for its own profit, the agent enjoys a free ride at Atlas' expense. The problem is that the van line's incentive to spend for reputation, equipment, facilities, and services declines as it receives less of the benefit from them. That produces a deterioration of the system's efficiency because the things consumers desire are not provided in the amounts they are willing to pay for. In the extreme case, the system as a whole could collapse.

By their own assertions, appellants establish that the carrier agents in the Atlas organization have benefitted from Atlas' business infrastructure in carrying shipments made for their own accounts. Rothery suggests free riding does not occur, and that the district court erred in concluding that it did. That argument, however, cannot withstand scrutiny, for Rothery has conceded that the carrier agents associated with Atlas do derive significant benefits from Atlas in dealing with customers for their own profit. We find the district court's conclusion that free riding existed to be amply supported and by no means clearly erroneous.

A few examples will suffice. Plaintiff-appellants conceded below that the carrier agents "benefitted" from their association with Atlas' "national image." . . . We cannot rationally infer that this consumer identification advantage did not benefit the carrier agents in operating on their own accounts while using Atlas equipment and personnel trained by Atlas. Rothery also allowed that, while the carrier agents bore the bulk of costs associated with their operations, Atlas did make "some small contributions" to the group advertising programs and "some contributions" to the painting of trucks on which the Atlas logo appeared. . . .

Rothery also credited Atlas with providing a dispatching service, a clearinghouse service for the settlement of accounts among its affiliates, assistance in settling claims among affiliates, certain written forms, sales meetings to provide exposure to national customers, driver and employee training programs, and the screening of the quality and reliability of affiliated firms that provided origin and destination services for the carrier agents. . . .

Rothery did not assert . . . nor may we infer, that the carrier agents could not avail themselves of the benefits derived from these services when operating for their own accounts. Many of these services confer intangible advantages that redound to the benefit of the carrier agent as a whole, and do not admit of easy segregation as between shipments on Atlas' interstate authority and shipments on the carrier agent's authority. For example, if Atlas provides superior training to the employees of its carrier agents, that training improves the quality of work not only on shipments undertaken for Atlas but also on shipments made on the carrier agent's own interstate authority. And because carrier agents may elect to use their own or Atlas' interstate authority for a given shipment . . . exposure to national clients at Atlas' sales meetings can provide them with interstate customers for their own, as well as for Atlas' accounts.

These examples are not exhaustive, but they illustrate the point. Even though entitled to every favorable inference . . . Rothery . . . could not seriously contend that the carrier agents' association with Atlas did not provide them with benefits that aided them in conducting business in competition with Atlas. Thus, because the plaintiff-appellants asserted that the carrier agents paid Atlas only for its clearinghouse service and for the provision of written forms, we agree with the district court's finding that many of the services supplied as part of Atlas' arrangement with the carrier agents' arrangement resulted in Atlas subsidizing its competitors. . . .

If the carrier agents could persist in competing with Atlas while deriving the advantages of their Atlas affiliation, Atlas might well have found it desirable, or even essential, to decrease or abandon many such services. . . . Of that tendency there can be no doubt. When a person or business providing goods or services begins to receive declining revenues, then, other things being equal, that person or firm will provide fewer goods or services. As marginal revenue drops, so does output. Thus, when Atlas' centralized services, equipment, and national image amount to a subsidy of competing carrier agents, this cuts down the marginal revenue derived from the provision of such things so that less will be offered than the market would reward.

On the other side, the firm receiving a subsidized good or service will take more of it. As cost declines, then, other things being equal, demand increases. Carrier agents, that is, will increase the use of Atlas' services, etc., on interstate carriage for their own accounts, over-consuming that which they can obtain at less than its true cost. In this way, free riding distorts the economic signals within the system so that the van line loses effectiveness in serving consumers. The restraint at issue in this case, therefore, is a classic attempt to counter the perceived menace that free riding poses. By compelling carrier agents to transfer their interstate authority to a separate entity, Atlas can continue providing services at optimal levels, confident that it will be paid for those services.

The Atlas agreements thus produce none of the evils of monopoly but enhance consumer welfare by creating efficiency. There seems no reason in the rationale of the Sherman Act, or in any comprehensible policy, to invalidate such agreements. . . .

V.

The law concerning contract integrations and the restraints of trade that augment their effectiveness has been a variable growth. At times, courts have thought integrations or partnerships with restraints like Atlas' obviously not only lawful but desirable. At other times, courts have treated the restraints as illegal *per se*, beyond any possibility of justification. The question is the state of the law today. We begin with the law's earliest analysis of such restraints, then discuss later cases that implicitly repudiated that analysis, and, finally, seek to discover the degree to which the law has now returned to its original formulation.

. . . .

In *United States v. Addyston Pipe & Steel Co.* . . . Judge (later Chief Justice) William Howard Taft framed a rule of *per se* illegality for "naked" price-fixing and market-dividing agreements, i.e., agreements between competitors who cooperated in no other integrated economic activity. But Taft recognized that such a rule would not do where fusions or integrations of economic activity occurred and, further, that agreements eliminating rivalry within such an enterprise were means of enhancing the firm's efficiency. He explained the reasons for the validity of an agreement "by a partner pending the partnership not to do anything to interfere, by competition or otherwise, with the business of the firm."

. . . .

If Taft's formulation is the law today, it is obvious that the Atlas agreements are legal, for *Addyston Pipe & Steel*'s analysis of ancillary restraints fits this case exactly.[3] The Atlas

3 A hypothetical was posed at oral argument which seems instructive. If there were a number of law firms in a given location of a size distribution like that of the van lines in this case, the extraction of a promise by each

network involves a union of the parties' enterprise to carry on a useful business, the challenged agreements are ancillary in that they enhance the efficiency of that union by eliminating the problem of the free ride, and, given Atlas' small market share, the agreements cannot be part of a plan to gain monopoly control of the market.

. . . .

B.

The argument that horizontal eliminations of competition among legally independent persons or companies are automatically illegal, even though the restraint is ancillary to a partnership or a joint venture, rests primarily upon *United States v. Topco Associates, Inc.*, 405 U.S. 596 (1972). The business arrangement in *Topco* very closely resembles Atlas' policy.

. . . .

C.

The Supreme Court reformed the law of horizontal restraints in *Broadcast Music, Inc. v. Columbia Broadcasting System*, 441 U.S. 1 (1979) ("*BMI*"), *National Collegiate Athletic Association v. Board of Regents*, 468 U.S. 85 (1984) ("*NCAA*"), and *Northern Wholesale Stationers, Inc. v. Pacific Stationery & Printing Co.*, ___ U.S. ___, 105 S. Ct. 2613, 86 L. Ed. 2d 202 (1985) ("*Pacific Stationery*").

. . . .

BMI, *NCAA*, and *Pacific Stationery* dictate the result in this case. All horizontal restraints are alike in that they eliminate some degree of rivalry between persons or firms who are actual or potential competitors. This similarity means that the rules applicable to all horizontal restraints should be the same. At one time, as we have seen, the Supreme Court stated in *Topco* and *Sealy* that the rule for all horizontal restraints was one of *per se* illegality. The difficulty was that such a rule could not be enforced consistently because it would have meant the outlawing of very normal agreements (such as that of law partners not to practice law outside the firm) that obviously contributed to economic efficiency. The alternative formulation was that of Judge Taft in *Addyston Pipe & Steel*: a naked horizontal restraint, one that does not accompany a contract integration, can have no purpose other than restricting output and raising prices, and so is illegal *per se*; an ancillary horizontal restraint, one that is part of an integration of the economic activities of the parties and appears capable of enhancing the group's efficiency, is to be judged according to its purpose and effect. In *BMI*, *NCAA*, and *Pacific Stationery*, the Supreme Court returned the law to the formulation of *Addyston Pipe & Steel* and thus effectively overruled *Topco* and *Sealy* as to the *per se* illegality of all horizontal restraints.

---

partnership that its members and associates not compete with the firm could, by no one's estimation, be construed as running afoul of § 1 of the Sherman Act. Indeed, it is with respect to the legal profession that the law has properly distinguished between lawful ancillary and unlawful naked restraints. Although literally price fixing among competitors, fee schedules imposed by a law partnership are accepted, even taken for granted. Yet in *Goldfarb v. Virginia State Bar*, 421 U.S. 773 (1975), the Supreme Court held that a minimum fee schedule applicable to the entire bar of a state violated § 1 of the Sherman Act. Thus, in its actual operation, the law has recognized the propriety of horizontal restraints ancillary to an efficiency-producing economic integration as distinct from the imposition of such restraints by competitors who have integrated none of their productive endeavors.

The application of these principles to Atlas' restraints is obvious because . . . these restraints are ancillary to the contract integration or joint venture that constitutes the Atlas van line. The restraints preserve the efficiencies of the nationwide van line by eliminating the problem of the free ride. There is, on the other hand, no possibility that the restraints can suppress market competition and so decrease output. Atlas has 6% or less of the relevant market, far too little to make even conceivable an adverse effect upon output. If Atlas should reduce its output, it would merely shrink in size without having any impact upon market price. . . . Under the rule of *Addyston Pipe & Steel*, *BMI*, *NCAA*, and *Pacific Stationery*, therefore, it follows that the Atlas agreements do not violate section 1 of the Sherman Act.

A joint venture made more efficient by ancillary restraints, is a fusion of the productive capacities of the members of the venture. That, in economic terms, is the same thing as a corporate merger. Merger policy has always proceeded by drawing lines about allowable market shares and these lines are based on rough estimates of effects because that is all the nature of the problem allows. If Atlas bought the stock of all its carrier agents, the merger would not even be challenged under the Department of Justice Merger Guidelines because of inferences drawn from Atlas' market share and the structure of the market. We can think of no good reason not to apply the same inferences to Atlas' ancillary restraints.

The judgment of the district court is

Affirmed.

COMMENTARY

Does the Supreme Court's reliance upon *Topco* in deciding *BRG* mean that Judge Bork's careful analysis of the caselaw in *Rothery* is no longer valid? Is the distinction between a "naked" and an "ancillary" restraint a valid one? Bork traces that distinction back to Judge Taft in *Addyston Pipe*. Do you agree with Judge Bork that the same distinction is incorporated into *Broadcast Music*?

Bork provides a persuasive case that the distinction between "naked" and "ancillary" restraints was ignored in *Topco*, although the law both before and after *Topco* observed that distinction. Consider how it would be possible both to accept Bork's historical analysis and reconcile it with the Supreme Court's *per curiam* opinion in *BRG*.

Chapter 4

Boycotts and Agreements Not to Deal

A. Introduction

Collaborative actions by sellers or by customers have been subjected to differential antitrust analysis by courts depending both on the form as well as on the effect of the arrangements. Boycott and refusal to deal are the terms which identify certain types of non-price restraints of trade subject to § 1 of the Sherman Act or to the provisions of § 2 dealing with conspiracies to monopolize. In these § 1 cases as elsewhere in antitrust law, there is the choice between *per se* or rule of reason analysis. The choice by a court between these two approaches is often a function of whether the practices involved as are characterized as horizontal—*i.e.,* agreement among individuals or firms at the same level of economic activity, such as manufacturing, wholesale, or retail distribution—or as vertical arrangements—between market actors at different levels in the process of production and distribution. An appellate judge has recently characterized his perspective on applying § 1 in a refusal to deal case as a difficult task in which:

> [C]ourts are asked to categorize various complex commercial arrangements into a rigid legal taxonomy, *e.g.* horizontal restraint, vertical restraint, . . . concerted refusal to deal, and so on. The initial categorization is often outcome-determinative. Under one category, the arrangement may be *per se* illegal, while under another, it may be found permissible under the rule of reason. Due to the complexity of modern business transactions, . . . courts often find that commercial arrangements can be classified theoretically under a number of different categories.

Discon, Inc. v. NYNEX Corp., 93 F.3d 1055, 1058-59 (2d Cir. 1996), *rev'd,* 525 U.S. 128 (1998).

The opinion in *Klor's Inc. v. Broadway-Hale Stores, Inc.,* 359 U.S. 207 (1959), has dominated the analysis of boycotts and restraint of trade despite the fact that it was a case in which there was no trial record before the Supreme Court and that its opinion does not articulate the form of the restraint, but only implies that there was a horizontal agreement among manufacturers with one vertical retailer-participant. The litigation in *Klor's* involved a suit by a single discount retailer of major household appliances against Broadway-Hale, a chain department store which also sold such appliances, alleging that the manufacturers and distributors of these trademarked items had conspired with Broadway-Hale either not to sell to Klor's or to sell only at highly unfavorable terms. The complaint further alleged that

Broadway-Hale had used its "monopolistic" buying power to bring about this concerted refusal to deal. In reversing the court of appeals which had dismissed the complaint, Justice Black emphasized the collaborative nature of the arrangement, which he characterized as a boycott, stating:

> Group boycotts, or concerted refusals by traders to deal with other traders, have long been held to be in the forbidden category. . . .
>
> Plainly the allegations of this complaint disclose such a boycott. . . . Alleged in this complaint is a wide combination consisting of manufacturers, distributors, and a retailer.

Id. at 212-13. In his opinion, Justice Black did not note the vertical nature of the agreement between the appliance manufacturers and Broadway-Hale, rather he based his ruling of illegality on the existence of a "wide combination." This combination, in turn, supported the characterization of the arrangement as a group boycott, which Justice Black considered to be in the "forbidden category"—*i.e.,* illegal *per se.*

Justice Black's determination that the defendants had engaged in a group boycott evoked critical comment as follows:

> Probably the most that the plaintiff could ever establish would be that Hale approached each supplier separately and persuaded him to agree to stop selling to Klor's. Thus, there would be about 18 agreements between Hale and a supplier that the latter refuse to deal with Klor's. Can these eighteen agreements be aggregated together to form one boycott (1) if each of the eighteen suppliers does not know that the others have been approached, or even (2) if the eighteen are aware of the other agreements?

Friedrich Kessler & Richard H. Stern, *Competition, Contract, and Vertical Integration,* 69 YALE L.J. 1 (1959). For the treatment of an agreement among a seller and buyers not to deal with rivals where there is knowledge that others have entered into a similar agreement, see the material on "hub and spoke" conspiracies, Chapter 8, page 354, *infra.*

The decision in *Klor's* left uncertain both the definition of a boycott as a subset of refusals to deal, as well as the prospect of identifying the possible pro-competitive effects of some vertical restrictions. Despite its limitations, however, the *Klor's* case became the basis on which courts subsequently applied the concept of group boycott as an expandable doctrine. By the late 1970s, after the Supreme Court had recognized the enhancement of inter-brand competition by vertical restrictions, *see Continental T.V., Inc. v. GTE Sylvania, Inc.*, 433 U.S. 36 (1977), at page 202, *infra*, lower courts began to distinguish vertical collaborative arrangements from horizontal restrictions in boycott cases as a means of limiting the scope of the group boycott category. For example, in *Oreck Corp. v. Whirlpool Corp.*, 579 F.2d 126, 131 (2d Cir. 1978), the plaintiff alleged, relying on *Klor's*, that its exclusive distributorship was not renewed by the manufacturer because of a group boycott arranged by the manufacturer and a larger customer. In reversing the trial court's verdict for the plaintiff, the Second Circuit stated,

> It is important to distinguish between "horizontal" restraints . . . and "vertical" restraints . . . .
>
> The present case, involving as it does an alleged agreement between a single manufacturer and a single dealer is, in essence, an exclusive distributorship controversy, and the "group boycott" is . . . not applicable.

The *NYNEX* case which follows represents the latest attempt by the Supreme Court to clarify the law governing refusals to deal. This case moved to the Supreme Court on appeal from the Second Circuit's ruling that a vertical non-price agreement to exclude a competing supplier may constitute a group boycott illegal *per se*, *Discon, Inc. v. NYNEX Corp.*, 93 F.3d 1055 (2d Cir. 1996).

NYNEX Corp. v. Discon, Inc.

525 U.S. 128 (1998)

Justice BREYER delivered the opinion of the Court.

In this case we ask whether the antitrust rule that group boycotts are illegal *per se* as set forth in *Klor's, Inc. v. Broadway-Hale Stores, Inc.*, 359 U.S. 207, 212 (1959), applies to a buyer's decision to buy from one seller rather than another, when that decision cannot be justified in terms of ordinary competitive objectives. We hold that the *per se* group boycott rule does not apply.

I

Before 1984, American Telephone and Telegraph Company (AT & T) supplied most of the Nation's telephone service and, through wholly owned subsidiaries such as Western Electric, it also supplied much of the Nation's telephone equipment. In 1984, an antitrust consent decree took AT & T out of the local telephone service business and left AT & T a long-distance telephone service provider, competing with such firms as MCI and Sprint. *See* M. KELLOGG, J. THORNE & P. HUBER, FEDERAL TELECOMMUNICATIONS LAW § 4.6, p. 221 (1992). The decree transformed AT & T's formerly owned local telephone companies into independent firms. At the same time, the decree insisted that those local firms help assure competitive long-distance service by guaranteeing long-distance companies physical access to their systems and to their local customers. *See United States v. American Telephone & Telegraph Co.*, 552 F. Supp. 131, 225, 227 (D.D.C. 1982), *aff'd. sub nom. Maryland v. United States*, 460 U.S. 1001 (1983). To guarantee that physical access, some local telephone firms had to install new call-switching equipment; and to install new call-switching equipment, they often had to remove old call-switching equipment. This case involves the business of removing that old switching equipment (and other obsolete telephone equipment)—a business called "removal services."

Discon, Inc., the respondent, sold removal services used by New York Telephone Company, a firm supplying local telephone service in much of New York State and parts of Connecticut. New York Telephone is a subsidiary of NYNEX Corporation. NYNEX also owns Materiel Enterprises Company, a purchasing entity that bought removal services for New York Telephone. Discon, in a lengthy detailed complaint, alleged that the NYNEX defendants (namely, NYNEX, New York Telephone, Materiel Enterprises, and several NYNEX related individuals) engaged in unfair, improper, and anticompetitive activities in order to hurt Discon and to benefit Discon's removal services competitor, AT & T Technologies, a lineal descendant of Western Electric. The Federal District Court dismissed Discon's complaint for failure to state a claim. The Court of Appeals for the Second Circuit affirmed that dismissal with an exception, and that exception is before us for consideration.

The Second Circuit focused on one of Discon's specific claims, a claim that Materiel Enterprises had switched its purchases from Discon to Discon's competitor, AT & T Technologies, as part of an attempt to defraud local telephone service customers by hoodwinking regulators. According to Discon, Materiel Enterprises would pay AT & T Technologies more than Discon would have charged for similar removal services. It did so because it could pass the higher prices on to New York Telephone, which in turn could pass those prices on to telephone consumers in the form of higher regulatory-agency-approved telephone service charges. At the end of the year, Materiel Enterprises would receive a special rebate from AT & T Technologies, which Materiel Enterprises would share with its parent, NYNEX. Discon added that it refused to participate in this fraudulent scheme, with the result that Materiel Enterprises would not buy from Discon, and Discon went out of business.

These allegations, the Second Circuit said, state a cause of action under § 1 of the Sherman Act, though under a "different legal theory" from the one articulated by Discon. 93 F.3d 1055, 1060 (1996). The Second Circuit conceded that ordinarily "the decision to discriminate in favor of one supplier over another will have a pro-competitive intent and effect." *Id.* at 1061. But, it added, in this case, "no such pro-competitive rationale appears on the face of the complaint." *Ibid.* Rather, the complaint alleges Materiel Enterprises' decision to buy from AT & T Technologies, rather than from Discon, was intended to be, and was, "anti-competitive." *Ibid.* Hence, "Discon has alleged a cause of action under, at least, the rule of reason, and possibly under the *per se* rule applied to group boycotts in *Klor's*, if the restraint of trade '"has no purpose except stifling competition."'" *Ibid.* (quoting *Oreck Corp. v. Whirlpool Corp.*, 579 F.2d 126, 131 (2d Cir.) (en banc) (in turn quoting *White Motor Co. v. United States*, 372 U.S. 253, 263 (1963)), *cert. denied*, 439 U.S. 946 (1978)). For somewhat similar reasons the Second Circuit believed the complaint stated a valid claim of conspiracy to monopolize under § 2 of the Sherman Act. *See* 93 F.3d, at 1061-1062.

The Second Circuit noted that the Courts of Appeals are uncertain as to whether, or when, the *per se* group boycott rule applies to a decision by a purchaser to favor one supplier over another (which the Second Circuit called a "two-firm group boycott"). . . . We granted *certiorari* in order to consider the applicability of the *per se* group boycott rule where a single buyer favors one seller over another, albeit for an improper reason.

II

. . . .

The case before us involves *Klor's*. The Second Circuit did not forbid the defendants to introduce evidence of "justification." To the contrary, it invited the defendants to do so, for it said that the "*per se* rule" would apply only if no "pro-competitive justification" were to be found. 93 F.3d at 1061; *cf.* 7 P. AREEDA & H. HOVENKAMP, ANTITRUST LAW ¶ 1510, p. 416 (1986) ("Boycotts are said to be unlawful *per se* but justifications are routinely considered in defining the forbidden category"). Thus, the specific legal question before us is whether an antitrust court considering an agreement by a buyer to purchase goods or services from one supplier rather than another should (after examining the buyer's reasons or justifications) apply the *per se* rule if it finds no legitimate business reason for that purchasing decision. We conclude no boycott-related *per se* rule applies and that the plaintiff here must allege and prove harm, not just to a single competitor, but to the competitive process, *i.e.*, to competition itself.

Our conclusion rests in large part upon precedent, for precedent limits the *per se* rule in the boycott context to cases involving horizontal agreements among direct competitors. . . . Although *Klor's* involved a threat made by a single powerful firm, it also involved a horizontal agreement among those threatened, namely, the appliance suppliers, to hurt a competitor of the retailer who made the threat. . . .

This Court subsequently pointed out specifically that *Klor's* was a case involving not simply a "vertical" agreement between supplier and customer, but a case that also involved a "horizontal" agreement among competitors. *See Business Electronics*, 485 U.S. at 734, 108 S. Ct. 1515. And in doing so, the Court held that a "vertical restraint is not illegal *per se* unless it includes some agreement on price or price levels." *Id.* at 735-736, 108 S. Ct. 1515. This precedent makes the *per se* rule inapplicable, for the case before us concerns only a vertical agreement and a vertical restraint, a restraint that takes the form of depriving a supplier of a potential customer. *See* 11 HOVENKAMP, *supra*, ¶ 1902d, at 198.

Nor have we found any special feature of this case that could distinguish it from the precedent we have just discussed. We concede Discon's claim that the petitioners' behavior hurt consumers by raising telephone service rates. But that consumer injury naturally flowed not so much from a less competitive market for removal services, as from the exercise of market power that is lawfully in the hands of a monopolist, namely, New York Telephone, combined with a deception worked upon the regulatory agency that prevented the agency from controlling New York Telephone's exercise of its monopoly power.

To apply the *per se* rule here—where the buyer's decision, though not made for competitive reasons, composes part of a regulatory fraud—would transform cases involving business behavior that is improper for various reasons, say, cases involving nepotism or personal pique, into treble-damages antitrust cases. And that *per se* rule would discourage firms from changing suppliers—even where the competitive process itself does not suffer harm. *Cf. Poller v. Columbia Broadcasting System, Inc.*, 368 U.S. 464, 484 (1962) (Harlan, J., dissenting) (citing *Packard Motor Car Co. v. Webster Motor Car Co.*, 243 F.2d 418, 421 (D.C. Cir. 1957)).

The freedom to switch suppliers lies close to the heart of the competitive process that the antitrust laws seek to encourage. . . . At the same time, other laws, for example, "unfair competition" laws, business tort laws, or regulatory laws, provide remedies for various "competitive practices thought to be offensive to proper standards of business morality." . . . Thus, this Court has refused to apply *per se* reasoning in cases involving that kind of activity. . . .

Discon points to another special feature of its complaint, namely, its claim that Materiel Enterprises hoped to drive Discon from the market lest Discon reveal its behavior to New York Telephone or to the relevant regulatory agency. That hope, says Discon, amounts to a special anticompetitive motive.

We do not see how the presence of this special motive, however, could make a significant difference. That motive does not turn Materiel Enterprises' actions into a "boycott" within the meaning of this Court's precedents. . . . Nor, for that matter, do we understand how Discon believes the motive affected Materiel Enterprises' behavior. Why would Discon's demise have made Discon's employees less likely, rather than more likely, to report the overcharge/rebate scheme to telephone regulators? Regardless, a *per se* rule that would turn upon a showing that a defendant not only knew about but also hoped for a firm's demise would create a legal distinction—between corporate knowledge and corporate motive—that does not necessarily correspond to behavioral differences and which would be difficult to prove, making the resolution of already complex antitrust cases yet more difficult. We cannot find a convincing reason why the presence of this special motive should lead to the application of the *per se* rule.

Finally, we shall consider an argument that is related tangentially to Discon's *per se* claims. The complaint alleges that New York Telephone (through Materiel Enterprises) was the largest buyer of removal services in New York State . . . and that only AT & T Technologies competed for New York Telephone's business . . . . One might ask whether these accompanying allegations are sufficient to warrant application of a *Klor's*-type presumption of consequent harm to the competitive process itself.

We believe that these allegations do not do so, for, as we have said . . . antitrust law does not permit the application of the *per se* rule in the boycott context in the absence of a horizontal agreement. . . . The complaint itself explains why any such presumption would be particularly inappropriate here, for it suggests the presence of other potential or actual competitors, which fact, in the circumstances, could argue against the likelihood of anticompetitive harm. The complaint says, for example, that New York Telephone itself was a potential competitor in that New York Telephone considered removing its equipment by itself, and in fact did perform a few jobs itself. . . . The complaint also suggests that other nearby small local telephone companies needing removal services must have worked out some way to supply them. . . . The complaint's description of the removal business suggests that entry was easy, perhaps to the point where other firms, employing workers who knew how to remove a switch and sell it for scrap, might have entered that business almost at will. . . . To that extent, the complaint suggests other actual or potential competitors might have provided roughly similar checks upon "equipment removal" prices and services with or without Discon. At the least, the complaint provides no sound basis for assuming the contrary. Its simple allegation of harm to Discon does not automatically show injury to competition.

III

The Court of Appeals also upheld the complaint's charge of a conspiracy to monopolize in violation of § 2 of the Sherman Act. It did so, however, on the understanding that the conspiracy in question consisted of the very same purchasing practices that we have previously discussed. Unless those agreements harmed the competitive process, they did not amount to a conspiracy to monopolize. We do not see, on the basis of the facts alleged, how Discon could succeed on this claim without prevailing on its § 1 claim. . . . Given our conclusion that Discon has not alleged a § 1 *per se* violation, we think it prudent to vacate this portion of the Court of Appeals' decision and allow the court to reconsider its finding of a § 2 claim.

. . . .

V

For these reasons, the judgment of the Court of Appeals is vacated, and the case is remanded for further proceedings consistent with this opinion.

It is so ordered.

COMMENTARY

1. In the Supreme Court, the enforcement agencies, the Antitrust Division and the Federal Trade Commission, jointly filed an *amicus* brief urging the Court to reject the lower court's characterization of the arrangement as a group boycott illegal *per se*.[1] The brief stated that vertical restriction may have procompetitive effect and thus did not warrant the absolute, *per se* condemnation. Rather, the brief urged that rule of reason analysis be applied.

2. Was the district court applying *Klor's* when it dismissed Discon's claim because its complaint stated a vertical agreement between one buyer, NYNEX, and one seller, AT&T Technologies, to exclude other bidders? Did the court of appeals also apply *Klor's* when it reversed the trial court on the reasoning that two vertically related firms may violate § 1 by a boycott because in *Klor's* the Supreme Court "found that the intent and effect . . . was a horizontal market impact." *Discon,* 93 F.3d at 1060-61. Assume the agreement in *Klor's* had been established by a trial record, how would it be decided under the reasoning in *NYNEX*? Does Justice Breyer's opinion mean that in an agreement between one buyer and one vertically related supplier to restrict other suppliers, the vertical relationship forecloses the finding of a boycott that is illegal *per se*? Under Justice Breyer's analysis, what are the determinants of illegality under a rule of reason analysis?

3. What is the Court saying about the relationship between § 1 and § 2? Under *NYNEX*, could a plaintiff successfully raise a § 2 claim given the same fact pattern? If so, what would the plaintiff need to plead and establish in order to prevail? Justice Breyer noted that NYNEX was subject to the jurisdiction of a regulatory agency. Does injury to the regulatory process give rise to an antitrust violation?

4. Who were the alleged conspirators? Were they corporate affiliates? To what extent can affiliated corporations conspire? *See Copperweld Corp. v. Independence Tube Co.*, 467 U.S. 752 (1984), *supra* page 347.

5. *Fashion Originators Guild of America, Inc. v. FTC*, 312 U.S. 457 (1941):

> The Fashion Originators Guild of America (FOGA) was composed of 176 garment manufacturers who developed original and distinctive designs of fashionable clothing for women. These garment manufacturers accounted for 38% of all women's garments wholesaling at $6.75 and up and for more than 60% of those wholesaling for $10.75 and up. Concerned about rivals copying their original designs, the garment manufacturers used the organization of the FOGA to boycott retail stores which handled garments made by so-called style pirates. A group of

[1] <http://www.usdoj.gov/atr/cases/f1800/1820.htm>

approximately 100 textile manufactures (belonging to the National Federation of Textiles, Inc.) which developed original fabric designs also was concerned about copyists. The Guild and the Federation cooperated in coordinating a boycott of noncooperating retailers. Both the Guild and the Federation maintained design registration bureaus and employed "shoppers" to check on retail stores. An elaborate system of trial and appellate tribunals was established for determining whether a given garment was in fact a copy of a Guild design. In a proceeding brought by the FTC, the FTC held that the Guild and the Federation had committed an "unfair method of competition" in violation of § 5 of the Federal Trade Commission Act.

When the case reached the Supreme Court, that Court ruled that if the activities challenged "ru[n] counter to the public policy declared in the Sherman and Clayton Acts, the Federal Trade Commission has the power to suppress it as an unfair method of competition." It then declared that the Guild's activities ran counter to the policy contained in § 3 of the Clayton Act as well as counter to the policies of the Sherman Act. Rejecting a defense that the actions of the Guild and Federation were reasonable restraints, because necessary to protect their members from the pirating of original designs, the Court asserted:

> The purpose and object of this combination, its potential power, its tendency to monopoly, the coercion it could and did practice upon a rival method of competition, all brought it within the policy of the prohibitions declared by the Sherman and Clayton Acts. . . . Under these circumstances it was not error to refuse to hear evidence offered, for the reasonableness of the methods pursued by the combination to accomplish its unlawful object is no more material than would be the reasonableness of the prices fixed by unlawful combination.

312 U.S. at 467-68.

Did the Court adopt a *per se* rule against boycotts? Consider how you would phrase that rule. Was there a market power component of that rule? Does the boycott have to target a competitor or a group of competitors to fall under the ban? Is there a "public interest" in discouraging style piracy? Does the holding in the *Northwest Wholesale Stationers* case that follows rest on a finding of a horizontal agreement among competitors to exclude one class of competitors?

6. Is there an adequate remedy against style piracy at state or other federal law? For a discussion of the inadequacy of federal design patent and copyright protection of the style of utilitarian articles, see Note, *Protection of the Artistic Aspects of Articles of Utility*, 72 HARV. L. REV. 1520 (1959). For a discussion of the use of trademark law to protect design, see Daniel J. Gifford, *The Interplay of Product Definition, Design and Trade Dress*, 75 MINN. L. REV. 769 (1991).

7. Note that the Court in *Fashion Originators* includes a market power component in the description of the activity which it condemns. The parallel here (in the boycott realm) with the early articulation of the *per se* rule against horizontal price-fixing agreements in *Trenton Potteries* is striking. Yet *Fashion Originators* was decided in 1941, subsequent to Justice Douglas' *Socony-Vacuum* opinion, jettisoning of the market power requirement in the *per se* rule condemning horizontal price-fixing agreements.

Northwest Wholesale Stationers, Inc. v. Pacific Stationery & Printing Co.
472 U.S. 284 (1985)

Justice BRENNAN delivered the opinion of the Court.

This case requires that we decide whether a *per se* violation of § 1 of the Sherman Act, 15 U.S.C. § 1, occurs when a cooperative buying agency comprising various retailers expels a member without providing any procedural means for challenging the expulsion. The case also raises broader questions as to when *per se* antitrust analysis is appropriately applied to joint activity that is susceptible of being characterized as a concerted refusal to deal.

I

. . . Certain background facts are undisputed. Petitioner Northwest Wholesale Stationers is a purchasing cooperative made up of approximately 100 office supply retailers in the Pacific Northwest States. The cooperative acts as the primary wholesaler for the retailers. Retailers that are not members of the cooperative can purchase wholesale supplies from Northwest at the same price as members. At the end of each year, however, Northwest distributes its profits to members in the form of a percentage rebate on purchases. Members therefore effectively purchase supplies at a price significantly lower than do nonmembers.[1] Northwest also provides certain warehousing facilities. The cooperative arrangement thus permits the participating retailers to achieve economies of scale in purchasing and warehousing that would otherwise be unavailable to them. In fiscal 1978 Northwest had $5.8 million in sales. . . .

Respondent Pacific Stationery & Printing Co. sells office supplies at both the retail and wholesale levels. Its total sales in fiscal 1978 were approximately $7.6 million; the record does not indicate what percentage of revenue is attributable to retail and what percentage is attributable to wholesale. Pacific became a member of Northwest in 1958. In 1974 Northwest amended its bylaws to prohibit members from engaging in both retail and wholesale operations. . . . A grandfather clause preserved Pacific's membership rights. . . .

---

[1] Although this patronage rebate policy is a form of price discrimination, § 4 of the Robinson-Patman Act specifically sanctions such activity by cooperatives: "Nothing in this Act shall prevent a cooperative association from returning to its members, producers, or consumers the whole, or any part of, the net earnings or surplus resulting from its trading operations, in proportion to their purchases or sales from, to, or through the association." 49 Stat. 1528, 15 U.S.C. § 13b. A relevant state-law provision provides analogous protection. Ore. Rev. Stat. § 646.030 (1983).

In 1977 ownership of a controlling share of the stock of Pacific changed hands . . . and the new owners did not officially bring this change to the attention of the directors of Northwest. This failure to notify apparently violated another of Northwest's bylaws. . . .

In 1978 the membership of Northwest voted to expel Pacific. Most factual matters relevant to the expulsion are in dispute. No explanation for the expulsion was advanced at the time, and Pacific was given neither notice, a hearing, nor any other opportunity to challenge the decision. . . . It is undisputed that Pacific received approximately $10,000 in rebates from Northwest in 1978, Pacific's last year of membership. Beyond a possible inference of loss from this fact, however, the record is devoid of allegations indicating the nature and extent of competitive injury the expulsion caused Pacific to suffer.

Pacific brought suit in 1980 in the United States District Court for the District of Oregon alleging a violation of § 1 of the Sherman Act. The gravamen of the action was that Northwest's expulsion of Pacific from the cooperative without procedural protections was a group boycott that limited Pacific's ability to compete and should be considered *per se* violative of § 1. . . . [T]he District Court rejected application of the *per se* rule and held instead that rule-of-reason analysis should govern the case. Finding no anticompetitive effect on the basis of the record as presented, the court granted summary judgment for Northwest. . . .

The Court of Appeals for the Ninth Circuit reversed, holding "that the uncontroverted facts of this case support a finding of *per se* liability." . . .

We granted *certiorari*. . . . We reverse.

II

A

[The Court considered and rejected the view of the Court of Appeals that the expulsion would be exempt from *per se* condemnation only if the affected member was afforded certain procedural safeguards.]

B

This case . . . turns . . . on whether the decision to expel Pacific is properly viewed as a group boycott or concerted refusal to deal mandating *per se* invalidation. "Group boycotts" are often listed among the classes of economic activity that merit *per se* invalidation under § 1. . . . Exactly what types of activity fall within the forbidden category is, however, far from certain. "[T]here is more confusion about the scope and operation of the *per se* rule against group boycotts than in reference to any other aspect of the *per se* doctrine." L. SULLIVAN, LAW OF ANTITRUST 229-230 (1977). Some care is therefore necessary in defining the category of concerted refusals to deal that mandate *per se* condemnation. . . .

Cases to which this Court has applied the *per se* approach have generally involved joint efforts by a firm or firms to disadvantage competitors by "either directly denying or persuading or coercing suppliers or customers to deny relationships the competitors need in the competitive struggle." *Sullivan*, *supra*, at 261-262. *See, e.g.*, *Silver*, *supra* (denial of necessary access to exchange members); *Radiant Burners, Inc. v. Peoples Gas Light & Coke Co.*, 364 U.S. 656 (1961) (denial of necessary certification of product); *Associated Press v. United States*, 326 U.S. 1 (1945) (denial of important sources of news); *Klor's, Inc.*, *supra* (denial of wholesale supplies). In these cases, the boycott often cut off access to a supply, facility, or market necessary to enable the boycotted firm to compete, *Silver*, *supra*; *Radiant Burners, Inc.*, *supra*, and frequently the boycotting firms possessed a dominant position in the relevant market. . . . In addition, the practices were generally not justified by plausible arguments that they were intended to enhance overall efficiency and make markets more competitive. Under such circumstances the likelihood of anticompetitive effects is clear and the possibility of countervailing procompetitive effects is remote.

Although a concerted refusal to deal need not necessarily possess all of these traits to merit *per se* treatment, not every cooperative activity involving a restraint or exclusion will share with the *per se* forbidden boycotts the likelihood of predominantly anticompetitive consequences. . . .

Wholesale purchasing cooperatives such as Northwest are not a form of concerted activity characteristically likely to result in predominantly anticompetitive effects. Rather, such cooperative arrangements would seem to be "designed to increase economic efficiency and render markets more, rather than less, competitive." *Broadcast Music, Inc. v. Columbia Broadcasting System, Inc., supra*, 441 U.S. at 20. The arrangement permits the participating retailers to achieve economies of scale in both the purchase and warehousing of wholesale supplies, and also ensures ready access to a stock of goods that might otherwise be unavailable on short notice. The cost savings and order-filling guarantees enable smaller retailers to reduce prices and maintain their retail stock so as to compete more effectively with larger retailers.

Pacific, of course, does not object to the existence of the cooperative arrangement, but rather raises an antitrust challenge to Northwest's decision to bar Pacific from continued membership.[2] It is therefore the action of expulsion that must be evaluated to determine whether *per se* treatment is appropriate. The act of expulsion from a wholesale cooperative does not necessarily imply anticompetitive animus and thereby raise a probability of anticompetitive effect. . . . Wholesale purchasing cooperatives must establish and enforce reasonable rules in order to function effectively. Disclosure rules, such as the one on which Northwest relies, may well provide the cooperative with a needed means for monitoring the creditworthiness of its members.[3] Nor would the expulsion characteristically be likely to result in predominantly anticompetitive effects, at least in the type of situation this case presents. Unless the cooperative possesses market power or exclusive access to an element essential to effective competition, the conclusion that expulsion is virtually always likely to have an anticompetitive effect is not warranted. . . . Absent such a showing with respect

---

[2] Because Pacific has not been wholly excluded from access to Northwest's wholesale operations, there is perhaps some question whether the challenged activity is properly characterized as a concerted refusal to deal. To be precise, Northwest's activity is a concerted refusal to deal with Pacific on substantially equal terms. Such activity might justify *per se* invalidation if it placed a competing firm at a severe competitive disadvantage. *See generally* Brodley, *Joint Ventures and Antitrust Policy*, 95 HARV. L. REV. 1521, 1532 (1982) ("Even if the joint venture does deal with outside firms, it may place them at a severe competitive disadvantage by treating them less favorably than it treats the [participants in the joint venture]").

[3] Pacific argues, however, that this justification for expulsion was a pretext because the members of Northwest were fully aware of the change in ownership despite lack of formal notice. According to Pacific, Northwest's motive in the expulsion was to place Pacific at a competitive disadvantage to retaliate for Pacific's decision to engage in an independent wholesale operation. Such a motive might be more troubling. If Northwest's action were not substantially related to the efficiency-enhancing or procompetitive purposes that otherwise justify the cooperative's practices, an inference of anticompetitive animus might be appropriate. But such an argument is appropriately evaluated under the rule-of-reason analysis.

to a cooperative buying arrangement, courts should apply a rule-of-reason analysis. At no time has Pacific made a threshold showing that these structural characteristics are present in this case. . . .

. . . A plaintiff seeking application of the *per se* rule must present a threshold case that the challenged activity falls into a category likely to have predominantly anticompetitive effects. The mere allegation of a concerted refusal to deal does not suffice because not all concerted refusals to deal are predominantly anticompetitive. When the plaintiff challenges expulsion from a joint buying cooperative, some showing must be made that the cooperative possesses market power or unique access to a business element necessary for effective competition. Focusing on the argument that the lack of procedural safeguards required *per se* liability, Pacific did not allege any such facts. Because the Court of Appeals applied an erroneous analysis in this case, the court never evaluated the District Court's rule-of-reason analysis rejecting Pacific's claim. A remand is therefore appropriate for the limited purpose of permitting appellate review of that determination.

III

"The rule is a valid and useful tool of antitrust policy and enforcement." . . . It does not denigrate the approach to suggest care in application. In this case, the Court of Appeals failed to exercise the requisite care and applied analysis inappropriately. The judgment of the Court of Appeals is therefore reversed, and the case is remanded for further proceedings consistent with this opinion.

It is so ordered.

COMMENTARY

1. Consider the *Northwest Wholesale Stationers* case in relation to earlier applications of § 1 to collective refusals to deal in which the objective was the denial of membership in an association or a joint venture was denied.

In *United States v. Terminal Railroad Ass'n of St. Louis*, 224 U.S. 383 (1912), the Supreme Court ordered an association of railroads serving St. Louis that had acquired control of all the railroad bridge facilities linking the east and west banks of the Mississippi River, to grant equal access to non-member railroads.

In *Associated Press v. United States*, 326 U.S. 1 (1945), the by-laws of Associated Press (AP), a cooperative association of 1200 newspapers, prohibited members from furnishing gathered news to non-members and enabled members to bar competing newspapers from being admitted to AP. Without access to AP as a source of national and international news, a local newspaper would be at a substantial competitive disadvantage against an AP member. The by-laws of AP effectively denied access to a newspaper when a member objected to its admission by imposing on the prospective entrant the money cost of aggregate retroactive association dues from October 1, 1900. As this formula would apply to a New York newspaper in 1944, the cost would be about $1.4 million. The trial court granted the government's motion for summary judgment and enjoined the members from observing the by-laws of the Association. The Supreme Court affirmed, without reference to the rule. In an implied rule of reason analysis, Justice Black rejected AP's contentions that 1) news was not a commodity, 2) local readers were not deprived of access to AP news, and 3) First Amendment considerations were paramount to Sherman Act policy. In a separate concurring opinion, Justice Douglas stressed the dominance of AP in news gathering market, while Justice Frankfurter concurred expressly on a rule of reason analysis.

Silver v. New York Stock Exchange, 373 U.S. 341 (1963), involved a refusal by the Exchange, a membership association, to permit a telecommunication connection between a member of the Exchange and a non-member securities broker. Justice Goldberg, writing for the majority, affirmed the grant of petitioner's motion for summary judgment, stating:

> It is plain, to begin with, that removal of the wires by collective action of the Exchange and its members would, had it occurred in a context free from other federal regulation, constitute a violation of Sec. 1 of the Sherman Act. The concerted action of the Exchange and its members here was, in simple terms, a group boycott depriving petitioners of a valuable business service which they needed in order to compete effectively as broker-dealers in the over-the-counter securities market.

Id. at 347.

2. In the above cases, the defendant association controlled access to the market or to the preferred means of access to the market. Would you describe the defendants in those cases as controlling an "essential facility" as possessing market power? For a further discussion of the essential facility doctrine, see pages 472-76, *infra*.

3. Consider whether, in a concerted refusal to deal, the participants' possession of market power is a critical issue. Consider the extent to which market power is essential (or helpful) to the application of a rule. Consider the extent to which market power is essential (or helpful) to the proof of illegality in a rule of reason case.

4. What kind of a prima facie showing did the Court require from the plaintiff in order to apply a *per se* rule to a concerted refusal to deal? In contrast to the proposal of Blair and Harrison, the Court is demanding an initial showing from the plaintiffs before it is willing to apply a *per se* rule. The presumption, in other words, is of the lawfulness of the behavior. It is the plaintiff who must overcome that presumption.

5. In this case, the Court tried to explain its prior decisions as applying the rule only to concerted refusals to deal which targeted competitors of the participants:

> Cases to which this Court has applied the approach have generally involved joint efforts by a firm or firms to disadvantage competitors by

> "either directly denying or persuading or coercing suppliers or customers to deny relationships the competitors need in the competitive struggle."

472 U.S. 284, 294 (1985). Thus, according to the Court, those concerted refusals to deal which have been subjected to the *per se* rule have been horizontal not only in that the participants have been in a competitive relationship with each other but the relation between the participants in the concerted refusal to deal and the ultimate target has been horizontal as well. This description may fit *Fashion Originators* in the sense that the style pirates who were the targets of the conspiracy were competitors of the Guild members, although when we take account of the textile manufacturers who participated in the boycott, the application of this description becomes a more complex task.

6. Consider the procedural aspect of *Northwest Stationers* and of *Silver*. In the former, Pacific was excluded from continued membership without notice or hearing. In the latter, for reasons connected with the Securities Act policy of self-regulation by exchanges, notice and hearing were necessary elements in an expulsion process. Without notice and hearing, the expulsion would not be shielded from the antitrust laws by the Securities Act.

In *Northwest Stationers*, the Court of Appeals had construed *Silver* to mandate notice and hearing prior to expulsion from an association. In reversing, the Supreme Court explained that notice and hearing were unnecessary because no federal system of regulation existed over buying cooperatives.

Federal Trade Commission v. Indiana Federation of Dentists
476 U.S. 447 (1986)

Justice WHITE delivered the opinion of the Court.

This case concerns commercial relations among certain Indiana dentists, their patients, and the patients' dental health care insurers. The question presented is whether the Federal Trade Commission correctly concluded that a conspiracy among dentists to refuse to submit x rays to dental insurers for use in benefits determinations constituted an "unfair method of competition" in violation of § 5 of the Federal Trade Commission Act . . . .

I

Since the 1970s, dental health insurers, responding to the demands of their policyholders, have attempted to contain the cost of dental treatment by, among other devices, limiting payment of benefits to the cost of the "least expensive yet adequate treatment" suitable to the needs of individual patients. Implementation of such cost-containment measures, known as "alternative benefits" plans, requires evaluation by the insurer of the diagnosis and recommendation of the treating dentist, either in advance of or following the provision of care. In order to carry out such evaluation, insurers frequently request dentists to submit, along with insurance claim forms requesting payment of benefits, any dental x rays that have been used by the dentist in examining the patient as well as other information concerning their diagnoses and treatment recommendations. Typically, claim forms and accompanying x rays are reviewed by lay claims examiners, who either approve payment of claims or, if the materials submitted raise a question whether the recommended course of treatment is in fact necessary, refer claims to dental consultants, who are licensed dentists, for further review. On the basis of the materials available, supplemented where appropriate by further diagnostic aids, the dental consultant may recommend that the insurer approve a claim, deny it, or pay only for a less expensive course of treatment.

Such review of diagnostic and treatment decisions has been viewed by some dentists as a threat to their professional independence and economic well-being. . . . In 1976, a group of . . . dentists formed the Indiana Federation of Dentists, respondent in this case, in order to [resist] . . . insurers' requests for x rays. The Federation, which styled itself a "union" . . . immediately promulgated a "work rule" forbidding its members to submit x rays to dental insurers in conjunction with claim forms. Although the Federation's membership was small, numbering less than 100, its members were highly concentrated in and around three Indiana communities: Anderson, Lafayette, and Fort Wayne. The Federation succeeded in enlisting nearly 100% of the dental specialists in the Anderson area, and approximately 67% of the dentists in and around Lafayette. In the areas of its strength, the Federation was successful in continuing to enforce the . . . policy of refusal to submit x rays to dental insurers.

[In 1978, the Federal Trade Commission issued a complaint against the Federation, alleging in substance that its efforts to prevent its members from complying with insurers' requests for x rays constituted an unfair method of competition in violation of § 5 of the Federal Trade Commission Act. Following lengthy proceedings the Commission ruled that the Federation's policy constituted a violation of § 5 and issued an order requiring the Federation to cease and desist from further efforts to organize dentists to refuse to submit x rays to insurers. The Commission's order, however, was overturned on review by the U.S. Court of Appeals for the Seventh Circuit.]

We granted *certiorari* . . . in order to consider the Commission's claim that in vacating the Commission's order the Court of Appeals misconstrued applicable principles of antitrust law and "'misapprehended or grossly misapplied' the substantial evidence test." . . . We now reverse.

. . . .

IV

The question remains whether these findings are legally sufficient to establish a violation of § 1 of the Sherman Act—that is, whether the Federation's collective refusal to cooperate with insurers' requests for x rays constitutes an "unreasonable" restraint of trade. Under our precedents, a restraint may be adjudged unreasonable either because it fits within a class of restraints that has been held to be "unreasonable," or because it violates what has come to be known as the "Rule of Reason," under which the "test of legality is whether the restraint imposed is such as merely regulates and perhaps thereby promotes competition or whether it is such as may suppress or even destroy competition." *Chicago Board of Trade v. United States*, 246 U.S. at 238.

The policy of the Federation with respect to its members' dealings with third-party insurers resembles practices that have been labeled "group boycotts": the policy constitutes a concerted refusal to deal on particular terms with patients covered by group dental insurance. . . . Although this Court has in the past stated that group boycotts are unlawful, *see United States v. General Motors Corp.*, 384 U.S. 127 (1966); *Klor's, Inc. v. Broadway-Hale*

Stores, Inc. 359 U.S. 207 (1959), we decline to resolve this case by forcing the Federation's policy into the "boycott" pigeonhole and invoking the rule. As we observed last Term in *Northwest Wholesale Stationers, Inc. v. Pacific Stationery & Printing Co.*, 472 U.S. 284 (1985), the category of restraints classed as group boycotts is not to be expanded indiscriminately, and the approach has generally been limited to cases in which firms with market power boycott suppliers or customers in order to discourage them from doing business with a competitor—a situation obviously not present here. Moreover, we have been slow to condemn rules adopted by professional associations as unreasonable, *see National Society of Professional Engineers v. United States*, 435 U.S. 679 (1978), and, in general, to extend analysis to restraints imposed in the context of business relationships where the economic impact of certain practices is not immediately obvious, see *Broadcast Music, Inc. v. Columbia Broadcasting System, Inc.*, 441 U.S. 1 (1979). Thus, as did the FTC, we evaluate the restraint at issue in this case under the Rule of Reason rather than a rule of illegality.

Application of the Rule of Reason to these facts is not a matter of any great difficulty. The Federation's policy takes the form of a horizontal agreement among the participating dentists to withhold from their customers a particular service that they desire—the forwarding of x rays to insurance companies along with claim forms. "While this is not price fixing as such, no elaborate industry analysis is required to demonstrate the anticompetitive character of such an agreement." . . . A refusal to compete with respect to the package of services offered to customers, no less than a refusal to compete with respect to the price term of an agreement, impairs the ability of the market to advance social welfare by ensuring the provision of desired goods and services to consumers at a price approximating the marginal cost of providing them. Absent some countervailing procompetitive virtue—such as, for example, the creation of efficiencies in the operation of a market or the provision of goods and services, *see Broadcast Music, Inc. v. Columbia Broadcasting System, Inc., supra*; *Chicago Board of Trade, supra*; *cf., National Collegiate Athletic Assn. v. Board of Regents of Univ. of Okla.*, 468 U.S. 85 (1984)—such an agreement limiting consumer choice by impeding the "ordinary give and take of the market place,". . . cannot be sustained under the Rule of Reason. No credible argument has been advanced for the proposition that making it more costly for the insurers and patients who are the dentists' customers to obtain information needed for evaluating the dentists' diagnoses has any such procompetitive effect.

The Federation advances three principal arguments for the proposition that, notwithstanding its lack of competitive virtue, the Federation's policy of withholding x rays should not be deemed an unreasonable restraint of trade. First, as did the Court of Appeals, the Federation suggests that in the absence of specific findings by the Commission concerning the definition of the market in which the Federation allegedly restrained trade and the power of the Federation's members in that market, the conclusion that the Federation unreasonably restrained trade is erroneous as a matter of law, regardless of whether the challenged practices might be impermissibly anticompetitive if engaged in by persons who together possessed power in a specifically defined market. This contention, however, runs counter to the Court's holding in *National Collegiate Athletic Assn. v. Board of Regents of Univ. of Okla., supra*, that "[a]s a matter of law, the absence of proof of market power does not justify a naked restriction on price or output," and that such a restriction "requires some competitive justification even in the absence of a detailed market analysis." . . . Moreover, even if the restriction imposed by the Federation is not sufficiently "naked" to call this principle into play, the Commission's failure to engage in detailed market analysis is not fatal to its finding of a violation of the Rule of Reason. The Commission found that in two localities in the State of Indiana (the Anderson and Lafayette areas), Federation dentists constituted heavy majorities of the practicing dentists and that as a result of the efforts of the Federation, insurers in those areas were, over a period of years, actually unable to obtain compliance with their requests for submission of x rays. Since the purpose of the inquiries into market definition and market power is to determine whether an arrangement has the potential for genuine adverse effects on competition, "proof of actual detrimental effects, such as a reduction of output," can obviate the need for an inquiry into market power, which is but a "surrogate for detrimental effects." 7 P. AREEDA, ANTITRUST LAW ¶ 1511, p. 429 (1986). In this case, we conclude that the finding of actual, sustained adverse effects on competition in those areas where IFD dentists predominated, viewed in light of the reality that markets for dental services tend to be relatively localized, is legally sufficient to support a finding that the challenged restraint was unreasonable even in the absence of elaborate market analysis.

Second, the Federation, again following the lead of the Court of Appeals, argues that a holding that its policy of withholding x rays constituted an unreasonable restraint of trade is precluded by the Commission's failure to make any finding that the policy resulted in the provision of dental services that were more costly than those that the patients and their insurers would have chosen were they able to evaluate x rays in conjunction with claim forms. This argument, too, is unpersuasive. Although it is true that the goal of the insurers in seeking submission of x rays for use in their review of benefits claims was to minimize costs by choosing the least expensive adequate course of dental treatment, a showing that this goal was actually achieved through the means chosen is not an essential step in establishing that the dentists' attempt to thwart its achievement by collectively refusing to supply the requested information was an unreasonable restraint of trade. A concerted and effective effort to withhold (or make more costly) information desired by consumers for the purpose of determining whether a particular purchase is cost justified is likely enough to disrupt the proper functioning of the price-setting mechanism of the market that it may be condemned even absent proof that it resulted in higher prices or, as here, the purchase of higher priced services, than would occur in its absence. . . . Moreover, even if the desired information were in fact completely useless to the insurers and their patients in making an informed choice regarding the least costly adequate course of treatment—or, to put it another way, if the costs of evaluating the information were far greater than the cost savings resulting from its use—the Federation would still not be justified in deciding on behalf of its members' customers that they did not need the information: presumably, if that were the case, the discipline of the market would itself soon result in the insurers' abandoning their requests for x rays. The Federation is not entitled to pre-empt the working of the market by deciding for itself that its customers do not need that which they demand.

. . . .

V

The factual findings of the Commission regarding the effect of the Federation's policy of withholding x rays are supported by substantial evidence, and those findings are sufficient as a matter of law to establish a violation of § 1 of the Sherman Act, and, hence, § 5 of the Federal Trade Commission Act. . . . The judgment of the Court of Appeals is accordingly

Reversed.

COMMENTARY

1. Does this case show that § 5 of the Federal Trade Commission Act is read in parity with § 1 of the Sherman Act? In several opinions, the Supreme Court has read § 5 as supplementary to the Sherman and Clayton Acts and can be invoked against conduct that violates the Sherman Act. *See, e.g., FTC v. Beech-Nut Packing Co.*, 257 U.S. 441 (1922). *See also Fashion Originators Guild of America, Inc. v. FTC*, 312 U.S. 457 (1941) (discussed at page 123, *supra*).

2. This case involves the antitrust laws as applied to a licensed profession and its policies and standards. The Federation was formed by dentists, licensed to practice in Indiana, in response to the cost containment program of a group of health care insurance companies. The insurance companies wanted the x-rays to evaluate the need for treatment and the reasonableness of that treatment. The Federation dentists took the position that the submission of x-rays for review to persons not licensed to practice was unsound and aided and abetted the practice of dentistry by unlicensed persons. As an alternative to submission of x-rays alone, the Federation offered the x-rays as part of the entire patient record for review on the dentists' premises by competent persons.

The Federal Trade Commission issued its complaint under § 5 of the Federal Trade Commission Act alleging that the Federation had engaged in ". . . unfair methods of competition . . . affecting commerce" by hindering and eliminating competition among dentists by failing to submit information that would aid the determination of the least expensive course of treatment.

The Administrative Law Judge found that the action of the Federation constituted a group boycott that was illegal under § 5. The Commission, noting that the conduct of the Federation was consistent with the Quality of Care standards of the American Dental Association which provided that "Proper dental treatment is predicated on a diagnosis from many types of examination and not radiographs alone," rejected the analysis, but held the conduct illegal under the rule of reason. 101 F.T.C. 138 (1983).

The Court of Appeals for the Seventh Circuit reversed, holding that the evidence did not support a finding of a group boycott. It stated:

> The evidence in this case establishes that the IFD member dentists collectively adhered to their policy of quality and proper dental care, refusing to comply with the group dental health care insurers' directive to submit . . . x-rays without the benefit of examining and reviewing all diagnostic aids . . . case history, and all clinical findings.

Indiana Federation of Dentists v. FTC, 745 F.2d 1124, 1135 (7th Cir. 1984). Moreover, this court found no evidence to support the finding of anticompetitive effect.

3. In its decision, the Supreme Court reiterated the caution it expressed in *Northwest Wholesale* about scope of the category of illegal restraints.

> . . . [T]he category of restraints classed as group boycotts is not to be expanded indiscriminately, and the approach has generally been limited to cases in which firms with market power boycott suppliers or customers in order to discourage them from doing business with a competitor—a situation obviously not present here.

4. How should the existence of market power be determined in this case? Is the adherence by 88% of the dentists in the region to the Quality of Care standards of the American Dental Association probative of their market power? How should the market power of the Federation be determined?

5. By reaffirming its approach in *Northwest Wholesale*, the Court was unable to apply a *per se* approach to the Indiana Federation's concerted agreement not to comply with the insurers' directive, in the absence of a finding of market power. Yet it was nonetheless clear that the agreement was restrictive.

6. Did the Court treat the dentists' concerted refusal to submit x-rays as a concerted refusal to deal? How did the Court treat the dentists' agreement differently from the way that the Court would treat a price-fixing agreement?

7. Consider the extent to which the agreement in this case was, as the Court put it, a "naked restriction on price or output." How did the Federation restrict output? Did the refusal to submit x-rays serve to reinforce higher prices for dental procedures? Explain.

8. Why could we not say that a "naked restriction on price or output" is illegal? Would such a formulation be helpful? The problem with such a statement is that the rule is a shortcut to an evaluation which ultimately determines whether industry output is reduced below the competitive level or whether market price is raised above the competitive level. A "naked" restriction is one which is not likely to generate efficiencies. If we have determined that the restriction is efficiency enhancing, we have determined that the restriction is not likely to restrict output. Does this make the proposed formulation conclusory? Explain.

9. In both the *Indiana Federation* and *NCAA* cases the defendants contended that they had not been shown to have possessed market power. If the defendants lacked market power they could not affect industry output or market prices. In each case, the Court ruled that—contrary to the defendants' assertions—the record showed that they possessed market power.

10. In each case, the Supreme Court also ruled that the agreements involved could be condemned without a showing of market power. They could be condemned because they were "naked restrictions on price or output." The Supreme Court held that the agreements were restrictions on price or output for which the defendants offered no plausible economic or business justification. That meant that these restrictions were "naked" ones, *i.e.,* restrictions without any plausible justification. Do you find the proposed justifications of their refusals to deal by the defendants in each case equally unpersuasive? Explain. Should the dentists' case come out the same way if there were no Federation, but each dentist refused submission individually, claiming reliance on the Quality Care Standards? In the latter instance, would competition among dentists be affected differently? Did Justice White apply a full scale or a "quick look" rule of reason analysis in *Indiana Federation of Dentists*? Would Justice White's rule of reason analysis pass muster under *California Dental Association*? Explain.

Federal Trade Commission v. Superior Court Trial Lawyers Association

493 U.S. 411 (1990)

Justice STEVENS delivered the opinion of the Court.

[In the District of Columbia, the Public Defender System provides counsel to indigent criminal defendants in the most serious felony cases. In the less serious felony cases and misdemeanor cases, representation is provided by court-appointed counsel. These counsel are compensated under the District of Columbia Criminal Justice Act (CJA). At the time of the events giving rise to the litigation, court-appointed counsel were paid $30 per hour for court time and $20 per hour for out-of-court time. The bulk of the work under the CJA was performed by about 100 lawyers who derived almost all of their income from CJA work.

[When the city refused to increase their hourly compensation, these lawyers—organized into the Superior Court Trial Lawyers Association (SCTLA)—refused to accept additional cases until they were granted a substantial increase in their hourly rate. After ten days the city capitulated. The Mayor offered to support an immediate increase of all CJA hourly rates to $35 hourly and pledged to support a permanent increase to $45 an hour for out-of-court time and $55 for in-court time. The SCTLA accepted the Mayor's proposal and its members returned to work representing indigent defendants as before.

[The Federal Trade Commission (FTC) instituted a proceeding against the SCTLA and four of its officers (respondents) which culminated in an order "to prohibit the respondents from initiating another boycott . . . whenever they become dissatisfied with the results or pace of the city's legislative process."]

The Court of Appeals vacated the FTC order and remanded for a determination whether respondents possessed "significant market power." The court began its analysis by recognizing that absent any special First Amendment protection, the boycott "constituted a classic restraint of trade within the meaning of Section 1 of the Sherman Act." . . . The Court of Appeals . . . noted that boycotts have historically been used as a dramatic means of expression and that respondents intended to convey a political message to the public at large. It therefore concluded that . . . a restriction on this form of expression could not be justified unless it is no greater than is essential to an important governmental interest. This test, the court reasoned, could not be satisfied by the application of an otherwise appropriate rule, but instead required the enforcement agency to "prove rather than presume that the evil against which the Sherman Act is directed looms in the conduct it condemns." . . .

III

Reasonable lawyers may differ about the wisdom of this enforcement proceeding. The dissent from the decision to file the complaint so demonstrates. So, too, do the creative conclusions of the ALJ and the Court of Appeals. Respondents' boycott may well have served a cause that was worthwhile and unpopular. We may assume that the preboycott rates were unreasonably low, and that the increase has produced better legal representation for indigent defendants. Moreover, given that neither indigent criminal defendants nor the lawyers who represent them command any special appeal with the electorate, we may also assume that without the boycott there would have been no increase in District CJA fees at least until the Congress amended the federal statute. These assumptions do not control the case, for it is not our task to pass upon the social utility or political wisdom of price-fixing agreements.

As the ALJ, the FTC, and the Court of Appeals all agreed, respondents' boycott "constituted a classic restraint of trade within the meaning of Section 1 of the Sherman Act." . . . As such, it also violated the prohibition against unfair methods of competition in § 5 of the FTC Act. . . . Prior to the boycott CJA lawyers were in competition with one another, each deciding independently whether and how often to offer to provide services to the District at CJA rates. The agreement among the CJA lawyers was designed to obtain higher prices for their services and was implemented by a concerted refusal to serve an important customer in the market for legal services and, indeed, the only customer in the market for the particular services that CJA regulars offered. "This constriction of supply is the essence of 'price-fixing,' whether it be accomplished by agreeing upon a price, which will decrease the quantity demanded, or by agreeing upon an output, which will increase the price offered.". . . The horizontal arrangement among these competitors was unquestionably a "naked restraint" on price and output. *See National Collegiate Athletic Assn. v. Board of Regents of Univ. of Okla.*, 468 U.S. 85, 110 (1984).

It is, of course, true that the city purchases respondents' services because it has a constitutional duty to provide representation to indigent defendants. It is likewise true that the quality of representation may improve when rates are increased. Yet neither of these facts is an acceptable justification for an otherwise unlawful restraint of trade. As we have remarked before, the "Sherman Act reflects a legislative judgment that ultimately competition will produce not only lower prices, but also better goods and services." *National Society of Professional Engineers v. United States*, 435 U.S. 679, 695 (1978). This judgment "recognizes that all elements of a bargain—quality, service, safety, and durability—and not just the immediate cost, are favorably affected by the free opportunity to select among alternative offers." *Ibid.* That is equally so when the quality of legal advocacy, rather than engineering design, is at issue.

The social justifications proffered for respondents' restraint of trade thus do not make it any less unlawful. The statutory policy underlying the Sherman Act "precludes inquiry into the question whether competition is good or bad." *Ibid.* Respondents' argument, like that made by the petitioners in *Professional Engineers*, ultimately asks us to find that their boycott is permissible because the price it seeks to set is reasonable. But it was settled shortly after the Sherman Act was passed that it "is no excuse that the prices fixed are themselves reasonable. See, *e.g., United States v. Trenton Potteries Co.*, 273 U.S. 392, 397-398 (1927); *United States v. Trans-Missouri Freight Assn.*, 166 U.S. 290, 340-341 (1897); *Catalano, Inc. v. Target Sales, Inc.*, 446 U.S. 643, 647 (1980). Respondents' agreement is not outside the coverage of the Sherman Act simply because its objective was the enactment of favorable legislation.

Our decision in *Noerr* in no way detracts from this conclusion. In *Noerr*, we "considered whether the Sherman Act prohibited a publicity campaign waged by railroads" and "designed to foster the adoption of laws destructive of the trucking business, to create an atmosphere of distaste for truckers among the general public, and to impair the relationships existing between truckers and their customers." *Claiborne Hardware*, 458 U.S. at 913. Interpreting the Sherman Act in the light of the First Amendment's Petition Clause, the Court noted that "at least insofar as the railroads' campaign was directed toward obtaining governmental action, its legality was not at all affected by any anticompetitive purpose it may have had." 365 U.S. at 139-140.

It of course remains true that "no violation of the Act can be predicated upon mere attempts to influence the passage or enforcement of laws," . . . even if the defendants' sole purpose is to impose a restraint upon the trade of their competitors. . . . But in the *Noerr* case the alleged restraint of trade was the intended *consequence* of public action; in this case the boycott was the *means* by which respondents sought to obtain favorable legislation. The restraint of trade that was implemented while the boycott lasted would have had precisely the same anticompetitive consequences during that period even if no legislation had been enacted. In *Noerr*, the desired legislation would have created the restraint on the truckers' competition; in this case the emergency legislative response to the boycott put an end to the restraint.

Indeed, respondents' theory of *Noerr* was largely disposed of by our opinion in *Allied Tube & Conduit Corp. v. Indian Head, Inc.*, 486 U.S. 492 (1988). We held that the *Noerr* doctrine does not extend to "every concerted effort that is genuinely intended to influence governmental action." 486 U.S. at 503. We explained:

> If all such conduct were immunized then, for example, competitors would be free to enter into horizontal price agreements as long as they wished to propose that price as an appropriate level for governmental ratemaking or price supports. . . . Horizontal conspiracies or boycotts designed to exact higher prices or other economic advantages from the government would be immunized on the ground that they are genuinely intended to influence the government to agree to the conspirators' terms. . . . Firms could claim immunity for boycotts or horizontal output restrictions on the ground that they are intended to dramatize the plight of their industry and spur legislative action. . . .

IV

SCTLA argues that if its conduct would otherwise be prohibited by the Sherman Act and the Federal Trade Commission Act, it is nonetheless protected by the First Amendment rights recognized in *NAACP v. Claiborne Hardware Co.*, 458 U.S. 886 (1982). That case arose after black citizens boycotted white merchants in Claiborne County, Mississippi. The white merchants sued under state law to recover losses from the boycott. We found that the "right of the States to regulate economic activity could not justify a complete prohibition against a nonviolent, politically motivated boycott designed to force governmental and economic change and to effectuate rights guaranteed by the Constitution itself." . . . We accordingly held that "the nonviolent elements of petitioners' activities are entitled to the protection of the First Amendment." . . .

SCTLA contends that because it, like the boycotters in *Claiborne Hardware*, sought to vindicate constitutional rights, it should enjoy a similar First Amendment protection. It is, of course, clear that the association's efforts to publicize the boycott, to explain the merits of its cause, and to lobby District officials to enact favorable legislation—like similar activities in *Claiborne Hardware*—were activities that were fully protected by the First Amendment. But nothing in the FTC's order would curtail such activities, and nothing in the FTC's reasoning condemned any of those activities.

The activity that the FTC order prohibits is a concerted refusal by CJA lawyers to accept any further assignments until they receive an increase in their compensation; the undenied objective of their boycott was an economic advantage for those who agreed to participate. It is true that the *Claiborne Hardware* case also involved a boycott. That boycott, however, differs in a decisive respect. Those who joined the *Claiborne Hardware* boycott sought no special advantage for themselves. They were black citizens in Port Gibson, Mississippi, who had been the victims of political, social, and economic discrimination for many years. They sought only the equal respect and equal treatment to which they were constitutionally entitled. They struggled "to change a social order that had consistently treated them as second class citizens." . . . As we observed, the campaign was not intended "to destroy legitimate competition." . . . Equality and freedom are preconditions of the free market, and not commodities to be haggled over within it.

The same cannot be said of attorney's fees. As we recently pointed out, our reasoning in *Claiborne Hardware* is not applicable to a boycott conducted by business competitors who "stand to profit financially from a lessening of competition in the boycotted market." *Allied Tube & Conduit Corp. v. Indian Head, Inc., supra*, at 508. No matter how altruistic the motives of respondents may have been, it is undisputed that their immediate objective was to increase the price that they would be paid for their services. Such an economic boycott is well within the category that was expressly distinguished in the *Claiborne Hardware* opinion itself. . . .

V

Respondents' concerted action in refusing to accept further CJA assignments until their fees were increased was thus a plain violation of the antitrust laws. The exceptions derived from *Noerr* and *Claiborne Hardware* have no application to respondents' boycott. For these reasons we reject the arguments made by respondents in the cross-petition.

The Court of Appeals, however, crafted a new exception to the rules, and it is this exception which provoked the FTC's petition to this Court. The Court of Appeals derived its exception from *United States v. O'Brien*, 391 U.S. 367 (1968). In that case O'Brien had burned his Selective Service registration certificate on the steps of the South Boston Courthouse. He did so before a sizable crowd and with the purpose of advocating his antiwar beliefs. We affirmed his conviction. We held that the governmental interest in regulating the "nonspeech element" of his conduct adequately justified the incidental restriction on First Amendment freedoms. Specifically, we concluded that the statute's incidental restriction on O'Brien's freedom of expression was no greater than necessary to further the Government's interest in requiring registrants to have valid certificates continually available.

However, the Court of Appeals held that, in light of *O'Brien*, the expressive component of respondents' boycott compelled courts to apply the antitrust laws "prudently and with sensitivity," . . . with a "special solicitude for the First Amendment rights" of respondents.

The Court of Appeals concluded that the governmental interest in prohibiting boycotts is not sufficient to justify a restriction on the communicative element of the boycott unless the FTC can prove, and not merely presume, that the boycotters have market power. Because the Court of Appeals imposed this special requirement upon the government, it ruled that *per se* antitrust analysis was inapplicable to boycotts having an expressive component.

There are at least two critical flaws in the Court of Appeals' antitrust analysis: it exaggerates the significance of the expressive component in respondents' boycott and it denigrates the importance of the rule of law that respondents violated. Implicit in the conclusion of the Court of Appeals are unstated assumptions that most economic boycotts do not have an expressive component, and that the categorical prohibitions against price fixing and boycotts are merely rules of "administrative convenience" that do not serve any substantial governmental interest unless the price-fixing competitors actually possess market power.

It would not much matter to the outcome of this case if these flawed assumptions were sound. *O'Brien* would offer respondents no protection even if their boycott were uniquely expressive and even if the purpose of the rules were purely that of administrative efficiency. We have recognized that the government's interest in adhering to a uniform rule may sometimes satisfy the *O'Brien* test even if making an exception to the rule in a particular case might cause no serious damage. . . . The administrative efficiency interests in antitrust regulation are unusually compelling. The rules avoid "the necessity for an incredibly complicated and prolonged economic investigation into the entire history of the industry involved, as well as related industries, in an effort to determine at large whether a particular restraint has been unreasonable." *Northern Pacific R. Co. v. United States*, 356 U.S. 1, 5 (1958). If small parties "were allowed to prove lack of market power, all parties would have that right, thus introducing the enormous complexities of market definition into every price-fixing case." R. BORK, THE ANTITRUST PARADOX 269 (1978). For these reasons, it is at least possible that the *Claiborne Hardware* doctrine, which itself rests in part upon *O'Brien*, exhausts *O'Brien*'s application to the antitrust statutes.

In any event, however, we cannot accept the Court of Appeals' characterization of this boycott or the antitrust laws. Every concerted refusal to do business with a potential customer or supplier has an expressive component. At one level, the competitors must exchange their views about their objectives and the means of obtaining them. The most blatant, naked price-fixing agreement is a product of communication, but that is surely not a reason for viewing it with special solicitude. At another level, after the terms of the boycotters' demands have been agreed upon, they must be communicated to its target: "[W]e will not do business until you do what we ask." That expressive component of the boycott conducted by these respondents is surely not unique. On the contrary, it is the hallmark of every effective boycott.

At a third level, the boycotters may communicate with third parties to enlist public support for their objectives; to the extent that the boycott is newsworthy, it will facilitate the expression of the boycotters' ideas. But this level of expression is not an element of the boycott. Publicity may be generated by any other activity that is sufficiently newsworthy. Some activities, including the boycott here, may be newsworthy precisely for the reasons that they are prohibited: the harms they produce are matters of public concern. Certainly that is no reason for removing the prohibition.

In sum, there is thus nothing unique about the "expressive component" of respondents' boycott. A rule that requires courts to apply the antitrust laws "prudently and with sensitivity" whenever an economic boycott has an "expressive component" would create a gaping hole in the fabric of those laws. Respondents' boycott thus has no special characteristics meriting an exemption from the rules of antitrust law.

Equally important is the second error implicit in respondents' claim to immunity from the rules. In its opinion, the Court of Appeals assumed that the antitrust laws permit, but do not require, the condemnation of price fixing and boycotts without proof of market power. The opinion further assumed that the rule prohibiting such activity "is only a rule of 'administrative convenience and efficiency,' not a statutory command." . . . This statement contains two errors. The rules are, of course, the product of judicial interpretations of the Sherman Act, but the rules nevertheless have the same force and effect as any other statutory commands. Moreover, while the rule against price fixing and boycotts is indeed justified in part by "administrative convenience," the Court of Appeals erred in describing the prohibition as justified only by such concerns. The rules also reflect a longstanding judgment that the prohibited practices by their nature have "a substantial potential for impact on competition." *Jefferson Parish Hospital District No. 2 v. Hyde*, 466 U.S. 2, 16 (1984).

As we explained in *Professional Engineers,* the rule of reason in antitrust law generates

> "two complementary categories of antitrust analysis. In the first category are agreements whose nature and necessary effect are so plainly anticompetitive that no elaborate study of the industry is needed to establish their illegality—they are 'illegal.' In the second category are agreements whose competitive effect can only be evaluated by analyzing the facts peculiar to the business, the history of the restraint, and the reasons why it was imposed." 435 U.S. at 692.

"Once experience with a particular kind of restraint enables the Court to predict with confidence that the rule of reason will condemn it, it has applied a conclusive presumption that the restraint is unreasonable." *Arizona v. Maricopa County Medical Society*, 457 U.S. 332, 344 (1982).

The rules in antitrust law serve purposes analogous to restrictions upon, for example, stunt flying in congested areas or speeding. Laws prohibiting stunt flying or setting speed limits are justified by the State's interest in protecting human life and property. Perhaps most violations of such rules actually cause no harm. No doubt many experienced drivers and pilots can operate much more safely, even at prohibited speeds, than the average citizen.

If the especially skilled drivers and pilots were to paint messages on their cars, or attach streamers to their planes, their conduct would have an expressive component. High speeds and unusual maneuvers would help to draw attention to their messages. Yet the laws may nonetheless be enforced against these skilled persons without proof that their conduct was actually harmful or dangerous.

In part, the justification for these rules is rooted in administrative convenience. They are also supported, however, by the observation that every speeder and every stunt pilot poses some threat to the community. An unpredictable event may overwhelm the skills of the best driver or pilot, even if the proposed course of action was entirely prudent when initiated. A bad driver going slowly may be more dangerous than a good driver going quickly, but a good driver who obeys the law is safer still.

So it is with boycotts and price fixing. Every such horizontal arrangement among competitors poses some threat to the free market. A small participant in the market is, obviously, less likely to cause persistent damage than a large participant. Other participants in the market may act quickly and effectively to take the small participant's place. For reasons including market inertia and information failures, however, a small conspirator may be able to impede competition over some period of time. Given an appropriate set of circumstances and some luck, the period can be long enough to inflict real injury upon particular consumers or competitors.

. . . .

Of course, some boycotts and some price-fixing agreements are more pernicious than others; some are only partly successful, and some may only succeed when they are buttressed by other causative factors, such as political influence. But an assumption that, absent proof of market power, the boycott disclosed by this record was totally harmless—when overwhelming testimony demonstrated that it almost produced a crisis in the administration of criminal justice in the District and when it achieved its economic goal—is flatly inconsistent with the clear course of our antitrust jurisprudence. Conspirators need not achieve the dimensions of a monopoly, or even a degree of market power any greater than that already disclosed by this record, to warrant condemnation under the antitrust laws.

VI

The judgment of the Court of Appeals is accordingly reversed insofar as that court held the rules inapplicable to the lawyers' boycott.[19] The case is remanded for further proceedings consistent with this opinion.

It is so ordered.

Justice BRENNAN, with whom Justice MARSHALL joins, concurring in part and dissenting in part.

. . . .

B

Underlying the majority opinion are apprehensions that the Trial Lawyers' boycott was really no different from any other, and that requiring the FTC to apply a rule-of-reason analysis in this case will lead to the demise of the rule in the boycott area. I do not share the majority's fears. The boycott before us today is readily distinguishable from those with which the antitrust laws are concerned, on the very ground suggested by the majority: the Trial Lawyers intended to and in fact did "communicate with third parties to enlist public support for their objectives." . . . As we have seen, in all likelihood the boycott succeeded not due to any market power wielded by the lawyers but rather because they were able to persuade the District government through political means. Other boycotts may involve no expressive features and instead operate solely on an economic level. Very few economically coercive boycotts seek notoriety both because they seek to escape detection and because they have no wider audience beyond the participants and the target.

Furthermore, as the Court of Appeals noted, there may be significant differences between boycotts aimed at the government and those aimed at private parties. . . . The government has options open to it that private parties do not; in this suit, for example, the boycott was aimed at a legislative body with the power to terminate it at any time by requiring

[19] In response to Justice BRENNAN'S opinion, and particularly to its observation that some concerted arrangements that might be characterized as "group boycotts" may not merit condemnation . . . , we emphasize that this case involves not only a boycott but also a horizontal price-fixing arrangement—a type of conspiracy that has been consistently analyzed as a violation for many decades. All of the "group boycott" cases cited in Justice BRENNAN'S footnote involved nonprice restraints. There was likewise no price-fixing component in any of the boycotts listed on pages 787-788 of Justice BRENNAN'S opinion. Indeed, the text of the opinion virtually ignores the price-fixing component of respondents' concerted action.

all members of the District Bar to represent defendants *pro bono*. If a boycott against the government achieves its goal, it likely owes its success to political rather than market power.

The Court's concern for the vitality of the rule, moreover, is misplaced, in light of the fact that we have been willing to apply rule-of-reason analysis in a growing number of group-boycott cases. *See, e.g., Indiana Federation of Dentists*, 476 U.S. at 458-459; *Northwest Wholesale Stationers, Inc. v. Pacific Stationery & Printing Co.*, 472 U.S. 284, 293-298 (1985); *National Collegiate Athletic Assn.*, 468 U.S. at 101; *Broadcast Music, Inc. v. Columbia Broadcasting System, Inc.*, 441 U.S. 1, 9-10 (1979) (criticizing application of rule because "[l]iteralness is overly simplistic and often overbroad").[9] We have recognized that "there is often no bright line separating *per se* from Rule of Reason analysis. *Per se* rules may require considerable inquiry into market conditions before the evidence justifies a presumption of anticompetitive conduct." *National Collegiate Athletic Assn., supra*, at 104, n.26.

In short, the conclusion that analysis is inappropriate in this boycott case would not preclude its application in many others, nor would it create insurmountable difficulties for antitrust enforcement. The plainly expressive nature of the Trial Lawyers' campaign distinguishes it from boycotts that are the intended subjects of the antitrust laws.

I respectfully dissent.

COMMENTARY

1. The court of appeals would have imposed a requirement that the FTC prove market power before entering its order against the trial lawyers. In reversing the court of appeals, the Supreme Court is indicating that market power is not a component of the trial lawyers' offense, is it not? The Court is thus both reaffirming the *per se* rule over boycotts and is defining it to exclude a market power component. Is the Court clear otherwise on the scope of the rule?

The court of appeals also would have required the Commission to "apply the antitrust laws to . . . this case with a special solicitude for . . . First Amendment rights . . . . " 856 F.2d 226, 233. Should First Amendment considerations be part of the balance in a rule of reason analysis or should such considerations be a factor in the decision of the enforcement agency to bring a case? An FTC Commissioner dis-

---

[9] Although "group boycotts" often are listed among the types of activity meriting condemnation, *see, e.g., Silver v. New York Stock Exchange*, 373 U.S. 341, 348 (1963); *White Motor Co. v. United States*, 372 U.S. 253, 259-260 (1963); *Klor's, Inc. v. Broadway-Hale Stores, Inc.*, 359 U.S. 207, 212 (1959); *Northern Pacific R. Co. v. United States*, 356 U.S. 1, 5 (1958); *Associated Press v. United States*, 326 U.S. 1, 12 (1945); *Fashion Originators' Guild of America, Inc. v. FTC*, 312 U.S. 457, 465-468 (1941), we have recognized that boycotts "are not a unitary phenomenon." *St. Paul Fire & Marine Ins. Co. v. Barry*, 438 U.S. 531, 543 (1978). In fact, "there is more confusion about the scope and operation of the rule against group boycotts than in reference to any other aspect of the doctrine." *Northwest Wholesale Stationers, Inc. v. Pacific Stationery & Printing Co.*, 472 U.S. at 294 (quoting L. SULLIVAN, LAW OF ANTITRUST 229-230 (1977)). We have observed that "the category of restraints classed as group boycotts is not to be expanded indiscriminately, and the *per se* approach has generally been limited to cases in which firms with market power boycott suppliers or customers in order to discourage them from doing business with a competitor." *FTC v. Indiana Federation of Dentists*, 476 U.S. at 458. These considerations provide additional reason to analyze the instant case with great care, because the Trial Lawyers' boycott is certainly *sui generis*.

sented in this case because he deemed it a poor use of prosecutorial discretion, since the dispute had been settled and there was no evidence of harm to consumers. 107 F.T.C. 510, 512.

2. Do the criteria identified in *Northwest Wholesale* indicate that *Trial Lawyers* is a case of a group boycott that is illegal *per se*? Should it matter that the activity in question is that of professionals? Is this decision consistent with *Indiana Dentists* and *California Dental Association*?

3. The "boycott" undertaken by the trial lawyers was really a strike, wasn't it? In the latter part of the nineteenth century and the early part of the twentieth century, federal courts often enjoined strikes as conspiracies in restraint of trade. In 1914 Congress, in §§ 6 and 20 of the Clayton Act, sought to exempt labor union activity from the antitrust laws. Section 6 provides that the labor of a human being is not an article of commerce and § 20 specifically bars federal courts from enjoining strikes. Later Congress enacted the Norris-LaGuardia Act divesting the federal courts of jurisdiction to issue injunctions in labor disputes, except in unusual cases. If the labor of a human being is not an article of commerce, how was it that the FTC could order the lawyers not to "boycott" the District's trial courts? The labor/antitrust interface is the subject of Chapter 16, *infra*.

4. The court of appeals would have bent the antitrust rules to take account of the "expressive" nature of the trial lawyers' behavior. Do you agree? disagree? What problems in the administration of the antitrust laws would be generated by the approach of the court of appeals? Is the rule of reason analysis of *California Dental Association* consistent with that of *Northwest Wholesale*?

5. Do you find Justice Brennan persuasive in his argument that the Court is applying the rule of reason in a growing number of boycott cases? How would Justice Brennan identify the scope of the rule? He would expand the applicable scope of the rule of reason beyond the criteria identified in *Northwest Wholesale*, would he not? Does Justice Brennan suggest a predictable approach for sorting out the rule of reason cases and the *per se* cases?

Alvord-Polk, Inc. v. F. Schumacher & Co.

37 F.3d 996 (3d Cir. 1994)

OPINION OF THE COURT

LEWIS, Circuit Judge.

For over a decade, retailers who market wallpaper by providing sample books and showroom displays have feuded with dealers who sell at a discount through toll-free "1-800" telephone numbers. In this case, ten 800-number dealers have accused the retailers' trade association and one of the leading wallpaper manufacturers of violating antitrust laws in an attempt to force them out of business. The district court granted summary judgment to the defendants on these and certain state-law claims. We will reverse the grant of summary judgment as to some federal and state antitrust claims but will affirm as to others and as to the 800-number dealers' tort claims.

. . . .

IV.

. . . .

At Count I, in which plaintiffs named only NDPA [National Decorating Products Association, a trade association of independent retailers—Eds.] as a defendant, they alleged that conventional retailers, acting through the NDPA, conspired to pressure manufacturers to eliminate them from the marketplace. The district court examined the record for evidence of "officially sanctioned NDPA activity," found none, and ruled that plaintiffs could not meet the "concerted action" requirement because "[t]he NDPA can only act pursuant to a resolution from its board and no such resolution has been identified." . . . We will reverse.

A.

It is both uncontested and uncontestable that NDPA is an association of competing wallpaper dealers. As such, when NDPA takes action it has engaged in concerted action so as to trigger potential section 1 liability. . . .

B.

Having focused our inquiry not just upon whether Petit or other NDPA agents might have acted with apparent authority but also upon whether their actions could constitute an antitrust violation in the absence of that authority, we believe that a rational jury could find for the plaintiffs if the evidence presented to us is proven at trial. As noted previously, Petit has acknowledged that since the entry of the FTC consent decree he has continued to urge manufacturers to take steps to hinder 800-number dealers in the conduct of their business. . . . He described himself as conveying "the concerns of NDPA" . . . , and he stated that he views it as part of his job to convey those concerns. . . . Additionally, once FSC [F. Schumacher & Co., a manufacturer—Eds.] announced its local trading policy, Petit circulated a copy of it to the NDPA board of directors along with a memorandum which could be read as triumphant. . . . From this, a rational juror could infer that Petit viewed himself as being authorized by the NDPA to make the statements he made.

Moreover, the record contains evidence from which a rational juror could also infer that Petit's actions represented concerted action. That is, a jury could find that, while representing NDPA, Petit went beyond merely voicing complaints to manufacturers to actually coercing (or attempting to coerce) them into cooperating in eliminating 800-number dealers. There is some evidence that Petit emphasized to manufacturers with whom he met "the anger felt by the retailers in [the] lack of support from the wallcovering industry." . . . Such evidence, when viewed against the existing backdrop of urgings from NDPA officers and editors that retailers should support only those manufacturers who supported them, could imply a threat of a retailers' boycott if manufacturers did not take steps to help eliminate 800-number dealers from the marketplace.

In sum, nothing in either the antitrust laws or the FTC consent decree prohibits NDPA from voicing complaints. Granting all reasonable inferences to the plaintiffs, however, a rational jury could find that NDPA did more than serve as a conduit for members' complaints in this case. It could, for example, find that NDPA, acting through its officers, threatened a retailers' boycott of manufacturers and thus could hold NDPA liable for a section 1 violation. For these reasons, we will reverse the district court's grant of summary judgment at Count I.

V.

At Count II, plaintiffs alleged that FSC responded to pressure from the NDPA by conspiring with it to eliminate 800-number wallpaper dealers from the marketplace. Their allegations flow directly from evidence of FSC's taking actions to eliminate free riders from the marketplace in response to conventional retailers' complaints (and, possibly, threats of boycott). There is no dispute that plaintiffs are free riders, and there is no question as to the legitimacy of a manufacturer's desire to rid the marketplace of free riders. *See Continental T.V., Inc. v. GTE Sylvania, Inc.*, 433 U.S. 36, 55 (1977); *cf. Big Apple BMW*, 974 F.2d at 1377-78. Therefore, the scenario which is the focus of Count II is as consistent with procompetitive activity as with allegedly illegal activity. *Monsanto*, 465 U.S. at 763.

. . . .

In marked contrast to *Big Apple BMW* and *Arnold Pontiac*, here the 800-number dealers concede that they are free riders. It is also undisputed that FSC has for years sold sample books and promotional materials and has encouraged its dealers to invest in these and other overhead costs in order to provide better service to their customers. A jury could find that, because FSC had for years recognized the importance of selling service, its actions aimed at 800-number dealers were entirely consistent with its previously held view of its own self-interest and do not tend to demonstrate that it acted in conjunction with anyone in implementing its policies.

On the other hand, however, the record also contains evidence that may indicate concerted action between FSC and NDPA. Specifically, plaintiffs highlight two examples of what they claim to be FSC's assertion of pretextual reasons for its actions. If FSC in fact advanced reasons for its actions which were pretextual, this would tend to support an inference that it acted as part of a conspiracy with conventional retailers. *See Big Apple BMW*, 974 F.2d at 1374-80.

First, plaintiffs point to evidence in FSC's management committee minutes which contrast the "objective" of its drop shipment surcharge ("To make statement to industry that we are trying to help them") with the "rationale" for this surcharge ("To protect legitimate customers, [t]o increase margins in this area"). . . . They also point to a parallel distinction between FSC's original and published press releases announcing the surcharge. The original press release stated:

> In direct response to retailer requests, we at F. Schumacher & Company are proud to announce that we will assertively support our dealers in their local trading areas and protect them from sales piracy by adding a seven percent surcharge onto all drop shipments. . . . While bar coding is a breakthrough for the industry in terms of product identification we feel that it alone is not an entirely effective deterrent against sales piracy. . . . Our approach attacks the problem at its root and makes the accounts who drop ship feel the effects, rather than leaving the responsibility of policing to the retailers.

. . . The final press release stated that the policy was not designed to combat "piracy" but rather to

> help insure that our consumers receive the best possible service and that our wallcovering brands are supported in the most effective and appropriate manner at retail. . . . This policy seeks to encourage all dealers to concentrate their selling efforts exclusively within their own trading areas where they can provide service directly to the consumers to whom they sell the product.
>
> . . . .

Plaintiffs argue that these inconsistencies in and contrasts between the internal and the public explanations of the drop shipment policy reveal that FSC was attempting to disguise the true reason for its actions. We agree; while the two statements and the two press releases could be seen as being in harmony with FSC's explanation that it took the action it did to protect the investments made by traditional retailers, a jury might view FSC's apparent desire to use more genteel language when explaining its actions to the public as implying a sinister motive.

Second, plaintiffs argue that although FSC acknowledges that dealer complaints were part of the reason for its surcharge, at one time it also stated that the surcharge was intended in part to recoup increased costs associated with drop shipments. FSC did not, however, use mathematical calculations to arrive at its surcharge figure; it neither consulted anyone regarding nor studied such costs, and the record contains statements by another manufacturer indicating that his costs for drop shipments were no higher than for shipments to stores. This, plaintiffs argue, underscores the arbitrariness of the surcharge and evinces FSC's true, sinister motive.

A lack of market research, while perhaps adding luster to plaintiffs' contention that the surcharge was arbitrarily determined, does not necessarily invite an inference that FSC's statement was an attempt to conceal a conspiracy. It is true that the seven percent figure did not reflect an analysis of FSC's costs; however, this does not indicate that FSC was not pursuing its self interests in imposing it. Nevertheless, viewing this evidence in conjunction with the press releases and the retailer pressure on FSC, it is not an implausible conclusion that FSC may have imposed the surcharge without first undertaking mathematical calculations because it had agreed with others to impose the surcharge whether it made economic sense or not.

Accordingly, because there is some evidence from which a rational jury could infer that FSC advanced pretextual reasons for its policies, and might in turn infer that FSC had acted in concert with NDPA in deciding to implement policies designed to injure 800-number dealers, we will reverse the district court's grant of summary judgment at Count II.

COMMENTARY

1. Did *Alvord-Polk* involve a horizontal boycott? Did their behavior threaten a competitor? Did the dealers' behavior constitute a offense? Did the dealers possess market power? Did the dealers' behavior meet the standards of *Northwest Wholesale* for application of the rule?

2. For purposes of antitrust analysis, would it matter whether the dealers were joined by one or more wallpaper manufacturers?

3. The trade association of the dealers is in a difficult position. It can legitimately act as a conduit for its members' complaints. But it cannot act as a vehicle for its members to threaten a boycott or to carry out a boycott.

4. A manufacturer (like Schumacher) is also in a difficult position. It possesses an economic interest in keeping its dealers satisfied, so that they will promote its product. To a large extent, therefore, its economic interest coincides with its dealers. Yet when it acts upon its dealers' complaints, it runs the danger of being found to have conspired with them.

5. In the next Chapter, we will examine more closely the (vertical) relations between manufacturers and suppliers on the one hand and their dealers on the other. The Supreme Court has decided a number of cases which attempt to make it less dangerous for a manufacturer to listen to its dealers and to follow their suggestions when it is in the manufacturer's interest to do so. Yet the *Alvord-Polk* situation—involving as it does a (horizontal) association among the dealers—remains a hazardous one for a manufacturer.

B. Insurance and the McCarran-Ferguson Act

In 1944 the Supreme Court decided *United States v. South-Eastern Underwriters Ass'n*, 322 U.S. 533 (1944). In that case the Court held (1) that insurance was "commerce" within the meaning of the commerce clause and therefore subject to regulation by Congress, and (2) that Congress had intended to include the insurance industry within the scope of the Sherman Act. In response to the Court's holding in *South-Eastern Underwriters*, Congress enacted the McCarran-Ferguson Act. 15 U.S.C. §§ 1011-1015 (1994). The McCarran-Ferguson Act recognizes the rights of the states to regulate insurance and further provides that the Sherman and Clayton Acts shall apply to the business of insurance to the extent that such business is not regulated by state law. Thus, under the McCarran-Ferguson Act, the applicability of the Sherman and Clayton Acts depends upon whether the states are regulating insurance. Congress further provided that limited federal antitrust regulation of the insurance industry would continue, regardless of the presence or extent of state regulation: Congress provided that nothing contained in the McCarran-Ferguson Act would "render inapplicable the said Sherman Act to any agreement to boycott, coerce, or intimidate, or act of boycott, coercion, or intimidation." 15 U.S.C. § 1013(b) (1994). The latter provision means that the meaning of the terms "boycott," "coercion" and "intimidation" is critical to the application of the McCarran-Ferguson Act. In the *Hartford Fire Insurance* case below, Justice Scalia addressed the meaning of the term "boycott" as it is used in the McCarran-Ferguson Act.

Hartford Fire Insurance Co. v. California
509 U.S. 764 (1993)

[Most commercial general liability (CGL) insurance in the United States is written upon standard forms provided by the Insurance Services Office, Inc. (ISO), an insurance trade association. The ISO is the almost exclusive source of support services for GCL insurance. ISO develops standard policy forms and files or lodges them with each State's insurance regulators. For each of its standard policy forms, ISO supplies actuarial and rating information: it collects, aggregates, interprets, and distributes data on the premiums charged, claims filed and paid, and defense costs expended with respect to each form, and on the basis of this data it predicts future loss trends and calculates advisory premium rates. Most ISO members cannot afford to continue to use a form if ISO withdraws these support services.

[In this case, nineteen States and several private parties charged that four insurance companies had conspired with the ISO and with domestic and foreign reinsurers to bring about certain changes in the standard ISO GCL form: they wanted the form changed from an occurrence to a claims made basis; they wanted the claims made policy to have a retroactive date provision restricting coverage to claims based on incidents occurring subsequent to a certain date; they wanted to eliminate coverage for "sudden and accidental" pollution; and they wanted legal defense costs to be counted against the stated policy limits.

[According to the complaints, the four insurance companies sought and obtained the assistance of reinsurance companies. The reinsurance companies agreed to deny reinsurance unless the CGL form were changed to contain the desired provisions.

[The Supreme Court dealt with two major issues. A majority of the Court upheld the application of the Sherman Act to foreign insurance companies agreeing abroad to demand the changes to American insurance policies. That part of the Court's action is the subject of our consideration in Chapter 14. Here we are concerned with whether the defendants were exempted from the Sherman Act by the McCarran-Ferguson Act. As noted above, the McCarran-Ferguson Act exempts the "business of insurance" from the Sherman Act, except for activities constituting, *inter alia,* a "boycott."

[Justice Scalia wrote for the majority in addressing the question of whether the defendants' conspiracies constituted one or more "boycotts."]

With respect to the petition in No. 91-1111, I join the Court's judgment and Part I and II-A of its opinion. I write separately because I do not agree with Justice SOUTER'S analysis, set forth in Part II-B of his opinion, of what constitutes a "boycott" for purposes of § 3(b) of the McCarran-Ferguson Act. . . .

I

Determining proper application of § 3(b) of the McCarran-Ferguson Act to the present case requires precise definition of the word "boycott."[1] It is a relatively new word, little more than a century old. It was first used in 1880, to describe the collective action taken against Captain Charles Boycott, an English agent managing various estates in Ireland. The Land League, an Irish organization formed the previous year, had demanded that landlords reduce their rents and had urged tenants to avoid dealing with those who failed to do so. Boycott did not bend to the demand and instead ordered evictions. In retaliation, the ten-

---

[1] Section 3(b) of the McCarran-Ferguson Act, 15 U.S.C. § 1013(b), provides: "Nothing contained in this Act shall render the said Sherman Act inapplicable to any agreement to boycott, coerce, or intimidate, or act of boycott, coercion, or intimidation."

ants "sen[t] Captain Boycott to Coventry in a very thorough manner." J. McCARTHY, ENGLAND UNDER GLADSTONE 108 (1886). "The population of the region for miles round resolved not to have anything to do with him, and, as far as they could prevent it, not to allow any one else to have anything to do with him. . . . [T]he awful sentence of excommunication could hardly have rendered him more helplessly alone for a time. No one would work for him; no one would supply him with food." *Id.* at 108-109; *see also* H. LAIDLER, BOYCOTTS AND THE LABOR STRUGGLE 23-27 (1968). Thus, the verb made from the unfortunate Captain's name has had from the outset the meaning it continues to carry today. To "boycott" means "[t]o combine in refusing to hold relations of any kind, social or commercial, public or private, with [a neighbour], on account of political or other differences, so as to punish him for the position he has taken up, or coerce him into abandoning it." 2 THE OXFORD ENGLISH DICTIONARY 468 (2d ed. 1989).

Petitioners have suggested that a boycott ordinarily requires "an absolute refusal to deal on any terms," which was concededly not the case here. . . . We think not. As the definition just recited provides, the refusal may be imposed "to punish [the target] for the position he has taken up, or *coerce him into abandoning it.*" The refusal to deal may, in other words, be *conditional*, offering its target the incentive of renewed dealing if and when he mends his ways. This is often the case—and indeed seems to have been the case with the original Boycott boycott. Cf. McCARTHY, *supra*, at 109 (noting that the Captain later lived "at peace" with his neighbors). Furthermore, other dictionary definitions extend the term to include a partial boycott—a refusal to engage in some, but not all, transactions with the target. *See* WEBSTER'S NEW INTERNATIONAL DICTIONARY 321 (2d ed. 1950) (defining "boycott" as "to withhold, wholly *or in part*, social or business intercourse from, as an expression of disapproval or means of coercion") (emphasis added).

It is, however, important—and crucial in the present case—to distinguish between a conditional boycott and a concerted agreement to seek particular terms in particular transactions. A concerted agreement to terms (a "cartelization") is "a way of obtaining and exercising market power by concertedly exacting terms like those which a monopolist might exact." L. SULLIVAN, LAW OF ANTITRUST 257 (1977). The parties to such an agreement (the members of a cartel) are not engaging in a boycott, because:

> "They are not coercing anyone, at least in the usual sense of that word; they are merely (though concertedly) saying '*we will deal with you only on the following trade terms.*'
>
> ". . . Indeed, if a concerted agreement, say, to include a security deposit in all contracts is a 'boycott' because it excludes all buyers who won't agree to it, then by parity of reasoning every price fixing agreement would be a boycott also. The use of the single concept, boycott, to cover agreements so varied in nature can only add to confusion."

Ibid. (emphasis added). Thus, if Captain Boycott's tenants had agreed among themselves that they would refuse to renew their leases unless he reduced his rents, that would have been a concerted agreement on the terms of the leases, but not a boycott.[2] The tenants, of

---

[2] Under the Oxford English Dictionary definition, of course, this example would not be a "boycott" because the tenants had not suspended all relations with the Captain. But if one recognizes partial boycotts (as we and Justice SOUTER do), and if one believes (as Justice SOUTER does but we do not) that the purpose of a boycott can be to secure different terms in the very transaction that is the supposed subject of the boycott, then it is impossible to explain why this is not a boycott. Under Justice SOUTER'S reasoning, it would be a boycott, at least if the

course, did more than that; they refused to engage in other, unrelated transactions with Boycott—e.g., selling him food—unless he agreed to their terms on rents. It is this expansion of the refusal to deal beyond the targeted transaction that gives great coercive force to a commercial boycott: unrelated transactions are used as leverage to achieve the terms desired.

The proper definition of "boycott" is evident from the Court's opinion in *Eastern States Retail Lumber Dealers' Assn. v. United States*, 234 U.S. 600 (1914). . . . The associations of retail lumber dealers in that case refused to buy lumber from wholesale lumber dealers who sold directly to consumers. The boycott attempted "to impose as a condition . . . on [the wholesale dealers'] trade that they shall not sell in such manner that a local retailer may regard such sale as an infringement of his exclusive right to trade." . . . We held that to be an "artificial conditio[n]," since "the trade of the wholesaler with strangers was directly affected, not because of any supposed wrong which he had done to them, but because of a grievance of a member of one of the associations." . . . In other words, the associations' activities were a boycott because they sought an objective—the wholesale dealers' forbearance from retail trade—that was collateral to their transactions with the wholesalers.

Of course as far as the Sherman Act (outside the exempted insurance field) is concerned, concerted agreements on contract terms are as unlawful as boycotts. For example, in *Paramount Famous Lasky Corp. v. United States*, 282 U.S. 30 (1930), and *United States v. First National Pictures, Inc.*, 282 U.S. 44 (1930), we held unreasonable an agreement among competing motion picture distributors under which they refused to license films to exhibitors except on standardized terms. We also found unreasonable the restraint of trade in *Anderson v. Shipowners Assn. of Pacific Coast*, 272 U.S. 359 (1926), which involved an attempt by an association of employers to establish industry-wide terms of employment. These sorts of concerted actions, similar to what is alleged to have occurred here, are not properly characterized as "boycotts," and the word does not appear in the opinions.[3] In fact, in the 65 years between the coining of the word and enactment of the McCarran-Ferguson Act in 1945, "boycott" appears in only seven opinions of this Court involving commercial (nonlabor) antitrust matters, and not once is it used . . . to describe a concerted refusal to engage in particular transactions until the terms of those transactions are agreeable.[4]

. . . .

---

tenants acted "at the behest of" (whatever that means) . . . the Irish Land League. This hypothetical shows that the problems presented by partial boycotts (which we agree fall within § 3(b)) make more urgent the need to distinguish boycotts from concerted agreements on terms.

[3] Justice SOUTER points out that the Court in *St. Paul Fire & Marine Ins. Co. v. Barry,* 438 U.S. 531 . . . (1978), found the term boycott "does not refer to 'a unitary phenomenon,'" . . . (quoting *Barry, supra,* at 543 (quoting P. AREEDA, ANTITRUST ANALYSIS 381 (2d ed. 1974)), and asserts that our position contradicts this. . . . But to be not a "unitary phenomenon" is different from being an all-encompassing one. "Boycott" is a multifaceted "phenomenon" that includes conditional boycotts, punitive boycotts, coercive boycotts, partial boycotts, labor boycotts, political boycotts, social boycotts, etc. It merely does not include refusals to deal because of objections to proposed terms. [Justice Souter considered the majority definition of "boycott" to be "overly narrow," 509 U.S. at 785—Eds.]

[4] *See United States v. Frankfort Distilleries, Inc.,* 324 U.S. 293, 295-296, 298 (1945) (refusal to engage in all transactions with targeted companies unless they agreed to defendants' price-fixing scheme); *United States v. South-Eastern Underwriters Assn.,* 322 U.S. 533, 535, 536, 562 (1944) (discussed *infra* . . .); *United States v. Bausch & Lomb Optical Co.,* 321 U.S. 707, 722 (1944) (word used in reference to a refusal to deal as means of enforcing resale price maintenance); *Fashion Originators' Guild of America, Inc. v. FTC,* 312 U.S. 457, 461, 465, 467 (1941) (boycott of retailers who sold competitors' products); *United States v. American Livestock Commission Co.,* 279 U.S. 435, 436-438 (1929) (absolute boycott of a competing livestock association, intended to drive it out of business); *Eastern States Lumber Assn., supra,* 234 U.S. at 610-611 (discussed *supra* . . .); *Nash v. United States,* 229 U.S. 373, 376 (1913) (word used in passing).

The one case in which we have found an activity to constitute a "boycott" within the meaning of the McCarran-Ferguson Act is *St. Paul Fire & Marine Ins. Co. v. Barry*, 438 U.S. 531 (1978). There the plaintiffs were licensed physicians and their patients, and the defendant (St. Paul) was a malpractice insurer that had refused to renew the physicians' policies on an "occurrence" basis, but insisted upon a "claims made" basis. The allegation was that, at the instance of St. Paul, the three other malpractice insurers in the State had collectively refused to write insurance for St. Paul customers, thus forcing them to accept St. Paul's renewal terms. Unsurprisingly, we held the allegation sufficient to state a cause of action. The insisted-upon condition of the boycott (not being a former St. Paul policyholder) was "artificial": it bore no relationship (or an "artificial" relationship) to the proposed contracts of insurance that the physicians wished to conclude with St. Paul's competitors.

Under the standard described, it is obviously not a "boycott" for the reinsurers to "refus[e] to reinsure coverages written on the ISO CGL forms until the desired changes were made," . . . because the terms of the primary coverages are central elements of the reinsurance contract—they are *what* is reinsured. . . . The "primary policies are . . . the basis of the losses that are shared in the reinsurance agreements." . . . Indeed, reinsurance is so closely tied to the terms of the primary insurance contract that one of the two categories of reinsurance (assumption reinsurance) substitutes the reinsurer for the primary or "ceding" insurer and places the reinsurer into contractual privity with the primary insurer's policyholders. . . . And in the other category of reinsurance (indemnity reinsurance), either the terms of the underlying insurance policy are incorporated by reference (if the reinsurance is written under a facultative agreement) . . . or (if the reinsurance is conducted on a treaty basis) the reinsurer will require full disclosure of the terms of the underlying insurance policies and usually require that the primary insurer not vary those terms without prior approval. . . .

Under the test set forth above, there are sufficient allegations of a "boycott" to sustain the relevant counts of complaint against a motion to dismiss. For example, the complaints allege that some of the defendant reinsurers threatened to "withdra[w] entirely from the business of reinsuring primary U.S. insurers who wrote on the occurrence form." . . . Construed most favorably to the respondents, that allegation claims that primary insurers who wrote insurance on disfavored forms would be refused all reinsurance, even as to risks written on other forms. If that were the case, the reinsurers might have been engaging in a boycott—they would, that is, unless the primary insurers' other business were relevant to the proposed reinsurance contract (for example, if the reinsurer bears greater risk where the primary insurer engages in riskier businesses). . . . Other allegations in the complaints could be similarly construed. For example, the complaints also allege that the reinsurers "threatened a boycott of North American CGL risks," not just CGL risks containing dissatisfactory terms . . . ; that "the foreign and domestic reinsurer representatives presented their agreed upon positions that there would be changes in the CGL forms or no reinsurance," . . . ; that some of the defendant insurers and reinsurers told "groups of insurance brokers and agents . . . that a reinsurance boycott, and thus loss of income to the agents and brokers who would be unable to find available markets for their customers, would ensue if the [revised] ISO forms were not approved." . . .

Many other allegations in the complaints describe conduct that may amount to a boycott if the plaintiffs can prove certain additional facts. For example, General Re, the largest American reinsurer, is alleged to have "agreed to either coerce ISO to adopt [the defendants'] demands or, failing that, 'derail' the entire CGL forms program." . . . If this means that General Re intended to withhold all reinsurance on all CGL forms—even forms having no objectionable terms—that might amount to a "boycott." Also, General Re and several other domestic reinsurers are alleged to have "agreed to boycott the 1984 ISO forms unless a retroactive date was added to the claims-made form, and a pollution exclusion and a defense cost cap were added to both [the occurrence and claims made] forms." . . . Liberally construed, this allegation may mean that the defendants had linked their demands so that they would continue to refuse to do business on either form until both were changed to their liking. Again, that might amount to a boycott. "[A] complaint should not be dismissed unless 'it appears beyond doubt that the plaintiff can prove no set of facts in support of his claim which would entitle him to relief.'" . . . Under that standard, these allegations are sufficient to sustain the First, Second, Third, and Fourth Claims for Relief in the California Complaint and the First and Second Claims for Relief in the Connecticut Complaint.

COMMENTARY

1. Congress enacted the McCarran-Ferguson Act in 1945 as a response to the decision of the Supreme Court in *United States v. South-Eastern Underwriters Ass'n*, 322 U.S. 533 (1944). In that case the Supreme Court held that insurance was interstate commerce and therefore subject to the Sherman Act. Congress' concern was to preserve the power of the states to regulate insurance, a power which it feared was called into question by the *South-Eastern Underwriters* decision. In enacting the McCarran-Ferguson Act, Congress provided, *inter alia,* that the "business of insurance" would be subject to state regulation and taxation; that the federal antitrust laws would be applicable to the business of insurance only to the extent that that business was not regulated by state law; but that the exemption from the federal antitrust laws would not extend to "any agreement to boycott, coerce, or intimidate, or any act of boycott, coercion, or intimidation." *See* 15 U.S.C. §§ 1011-15 (1988). *See, e.g., Group Life & Health Ins. Co v. Royal Drug Co.*, 440 U.S. 205, 217-24 (1979) (describing enactment of McCarran-Ferguson Act).

2. The meaning of the term "boycott" can be critical for determining when the antitrust exception of the McCarran-Ferguson Act applies. But the definition of that term for McCarran-Ferguson Act purposes does not necessarily affect the application of the Sherman Act to concerted refusals to deal which do not fall within the definition of "boycott" under that Act. Justice Scalia's opinion above makes this clear.

3. It was commonly stated that "boycotts" were illegal *per se*. As *Northwest Wholesale Stationers* and *Indiana Federation* have now indicated, the scope of the *per se* rule is narrow: normally it applies to agreements among competitors possessing market power to deny to a rival something essential to the rival's ability to compete. Thus the general applicability and scope of the rule is more appropriately articulated in economic terms than through the linguistic approach which the Court majority employed in *Hartford Fire Insurance Co.* to determine the applicability of the McCarran-Ferguson antitrust exception.

4. Note that the Court applied the Sherman Act to foreign insurance companies for their conduct in their home countries. For the extraterritorial application of the Sherman Act's criminal provisions to a foreign corporation for its acts abroad which were intended to and did have substantial effect on commerce in the United States, see *United States v. Nippon Paper Industries Co., Ltd.*, 109 F.3d 1 (1st Cir. 1997). *See also* Chapter 14, *infra.*

Chapter 5

Vertical Restraints: The Basic Focus

A. Introduction

Vertical restraint issues may arise from the commercial arrangements between business firms in supplier-customer relations with each other. A prerequisite for a problem under § 1 of the Sherman Act is, of course, the existence of a combination or agreement. In some cases, whether or not a given arrangement is properly characterized as a combination or agreement will itself be problematic.

The benefits of controlling various aspects of distribution and the benefits of cost savings are the two dominant factors in the manufacturer's decision of whether to own and operate retail outlets or whether to utilize contractual arrangements in distribution. Gasoline distribution in which major-brand firms sell refined petroleum products through substantial numbers of owned outlets lie at one end of the distribution spectrum, and the distribution of convenience items and branded food products, such as toothpaste, soap, and over-the-counter medications by independent retailers lie at the other end. Ownership and contractual arrangements are alternative means of achieving the control and cost saving associated with vertical integration. Each mode has its costs and benefits. Ownership permits direct control and the saving of interim marketing costs, but requires substantial outlay of capital and the supervision of a substantial number of employees. Contractual arrangements avoid the capital outlay, yet provide the manufacturer with indirect control by means of contract clauses. The cost of this means of control, however, is that contract remedies become the sole instrumentality by which the manufacturer can exercise leverage over the retailer. Traditional contract remedies—damages, rescission, and termination or (possibly) the threat of non-renewal ultimately become subject to scrutiny under § 1 of the Sherman Act. If a manufacturer acquires an existing vertical distribution facility by merger, § 7 of the Clayton Act may provide a basis for antitrust scrutiny. *See* Chapter 12.

When a manufacturer agrees with a distributor that it will not sell its product to another distributor in the same geographic area as the first distributor, that restraint on the manufacturer's freedom to establish distributorships is called a "vertical" restraint. This terminology serves to identify separate commercial functions such as manufacturing from that of mere selling. Because the parties to vertical restraints perform different functions, they are not generally in direct competition with each other for the same customers. Thus, there is not the same prospect of anticompetitive harm as is posed by horizontal restraints, where the sellers are in direct competition. Many of the products in these verticle distribution cases are trademark-protected branded items. Accordingly, the terminology—intrabrand and interbrand—distinguishes the competition between identical brands from the rivalry with other marks.

The law of vertical restraints has been made uncertain and unduly complex by shifting views as to the scope of *per se* illegality to be applied to vertical arrangements. In 1911, the Supreme Court held unlawful an agreement between a dealer and a manufacturer imposing minimum resale prices in *Dr. Miles Medical Co. v. John D. Park & Sons Co.*, 220 U.S. 373 (1911). Although the Court did not employ the words "*per se* illegal" in its opinion, the case has been understood to impose a rule of *per se* illegality upon vertical price-fixing agreements. In 1961, the Supreme Court underscored the economic differences between horizontal and vertical agreements for purposes of applying § 1 as follows:

> Horizontal . . . limitations, like group boycotts, or concerted refusals by traders to deal with other traders . . . are naked restraints of trade with no purpose except stifling of competition. A vertical . . . limitation may or may not have that purpose or effect. We do not know enough of the economic and business stuff out of which these arrangements emerge to be certain. . . . We need to know more than we do about the actual impact of these arrangements on competition to decide whether . . . they should be classified as *per se* violations of the Sherman Act.

White Motor Co. v. United States, 372 U.S. 253, 263 (1963). Justice Clark's dissenting opinion, however, in which Chief Justice Warren and Justice Black joined, characterized White Motor's arrangement as ". . . one of the most brazen violations of the Sherman Act that I have experienced. . . ." *Id.* at 276.

The majority reversed and remanded for a determination of the legality of White Motor's territorial and customer restraints by a full trial. The case was settled by the entry of a consent decree (*see* Chapter 12, *infra*) that barred White Motor from entering: "[I]nto any agreement to limit, allocate or restrict the territories in which, or the persons or classes of persons to whom, any distributor, dealer or other person may sell trucks." *United States v. White Motor Co.*, 1964 Trade Cas. ¶ 71,195, 79,763 (N.D. Ohio 1964). The *White Motor* opinion by the Supreme Court seemed to tell lower court judges to apply rule of reason analysis, but without identifying the factors to consider. *See Continental T.V., Inc. v. GTE Sylvania Inc.*, 433 U.S. 36 (1977) (discussed below) for a refinement of the rule of reason analysis.

In 1967 the Court also imposed *per se* illegality upon agreements between suppliers and their distributors or dealers who purchased the supplier's products for resale when their agreements restricted the territory in which the distributors or dealers were permitted to resell or restricted the customers to whom distributors or dealers were permitted to resell. *United States v. Arnold, Schwinn & Co.*, 388 U.S. 365 (1967). However, in *Schwinn*, the Court held that a rule of reason governed the evaluation of distribution agreements imposing identical restrictions when the distributors or dealers took the goods on consignment rather than purchasing them.

Ten years later, in response to widespread dissatisfaction with, and scathing academic criticism of the *Schwinn* rule, the Court overruled *Schwinn* in *Continental T.V., Inc. v. GTE Sylvania Inc.*, 433 U.S. 36 (1977) (discussed below). In *Sylvania*, the Court held that the rule of reason would govern all restrictions which were imposed upon distributors or dealers, so long as the restrictions did not govern the resale prices of the distributors or dealers.

The result of *Sylvania* was to divide vertical agreements into two classes for purpose of antitrust treatment: Agreements which set resale prices were *per se* illegal, while other (nonprice) vertical agreements were governed by the rule of reason. Since it is generally more costly to assemble the evidence of market conditions required for a rule of reason case against a vertical restriction than to present a *per se,* price-fixing case, plaintiffs perceived a powerful incentive to characterize their claims as price-fixing cases when at all possible. The diminished probability of prevailing in a rule of reason vertical restraint case reinforced this incentive to cast all restraints in the mold of price-fixing agreements.

The law of vertical restraints has remained complicated after the *Sylvania* decision, however, by the distinction between price restraints and nonprice restraints recognized in the *Sylvania* case. Under the analysis of that opinion, plaintiffs undertake to characterize as price-fixing the broadest range of commercial arrangements plausibly related to pricing, in order to obtain the advantages available under a *per se* rule. As a result of this practice, many of the cases reflect the efforts of courts to prevent expansive definitions of price-fixing in order to avoid unduly expanding the scope of the *per se* rule. In addition, economic analysis has subjected *per se* rules condemning vertical price-fixing agreements—even narrowly drawn ones—to severe challenge. As will become apparent from the material in this chapter, the antitrust law governing vertical restraints continues in a state of flux.

We begin our examination of the cases with the development of the *per se* rule governing vertical price-fixing agreements.

B. Vertical Price-Fixing

Dr. Miles Medical Co. v. John D. Park & Sons Co.

220 U.S. 373 (1911)

[Dr. Miles Medical Co. manufactured proprietary medicines which it distributed through wholesale and retail dealers who had executed distribution contracts with it. The distribution contracts sought to treat the wholesale and retail dealers as "agents" of the Dr. Miles Company to whom the medicines had been shipped on consignment and attempted to reserve title to the medicines in the Dr. Miles Company. Provisions in these distribution contracts attempted to control the identity of the dealers handling those medicines and the prices at which the medicines were sold.

[The John D. Park & Sons Company was a wholesale drug concern which had refused to execute a distribution contract with Dr. Miles and which was charged by Dr.

Miles with procuring medicines manufactured by the Dr. Miles Company for sale at "cut prices" by inducing Dr. Miles dealers to violate the restrictive provisions of their distribution contracts. The trial court dismissed Dr. Miles' complaint on demurrer; the Court of Appeals for the Sixth Circuit affirmed; and the Supreme Court granted *certiorari*.

[Because of the careless drafting of the distribution contracts, the Supreme Court concluded that at least some of the medicines in the hands of dealers had been purchased outright by them. In such cases, the dealers would not be "agents," selling supplies whose title had been reserved to Dr. Miles. Since the John D. Park & Sons Co. could have acquired its supplies of medicines from dealers who held title themselves, the Court addressed itself to the validity of the other relevant contractual restriction on the Dr. Miles dealers: a contractual restriction pursuant to which the manufacturer seeks to control the prices charged by its dealers in reselling products which they have purchased from the manufacturer.]

Mr. Justice HUGHES . . . delivered the opinion of the court:

. . . [I]t is insisted . . . (1) That the restrictions are valid because they relate to proprietary medicines manufactured under a secret process; and (2) that, apart from this, a manufacturer is entitled to control the prices on all sales of his own products. . . . If a manufacturer, in the absence of statutory privilege, has the control over the sales of the manufactured article for which the complainant here contends, it is not because the process of manufacture is kept secret. In this respect, the maker of so-called proprietary medicines, unpatented, stands on no different footing from that of other manufacturers. . . .

Second. We come, then, to the second question,—whether the complainant, irrespective of the secrecy of its process, is entitled to maintain the restrictions by virtue of the fact that they relate to products of its own manufacture.

The basis of the argument appears to be that, as the manufacturer may make and sell, or not, as he chooses, he may affix conditions as to the use of the article or as to the prices at which purchasers may dispose of it. The propriety of the restraint is sought to be derived from the liberty of the producer.

But because a manufacturer is not bound to make or sell, it does not follow in case of sales actually made he may impose upon purchasers every sort of restriction. Thus, a general restraint upon alienation is ordinarily invalid. . . .

The bill asserts the importance of a standard retail price, and alleges generally that confusion and damage have resulted from sales at less than the prices fixed. But the advantage of established retail prices primarily concerns the dealers. The enlarged profits which would result from adherence to the established rates would go to them, and not to the complainant. It is through the inability of the favored dealers to realize these profits, on account of the described competition, that the complainant works out its alleged injury. If there be an advantage to the manufacturer in the maintenance of fixed retail prices, the question remains whether it is one which he is entitled to secure by agreements restricting the freedom of trade on the part of dealers who own what they sell. As to this, the complainant can fare no better with its plan of identical contracts than could the dealers themselves if they formed a combination and endeavored to establish the same restrictions, and thus to achieve the same result, by agreement with each other. If the immediate advantage they would thus obtain would not be sufficient to sustain such a direct agreement, the asserted ulterior benefit to the complainant cannot be regarded as sufficient to support its system.

. . . .

Judgment affirmed.

COMMENTARY

1. Consider the relationship between the law of contracts and the federal antitrust laws. Is the determination of which body of law controls a function of federal jurisdiction? What is the antitrust significance of having the distributor as the legal agent of the manufacturer? Had the lawyers for the Dr. Miles Company drafted the distribution contracts more carefully, title would have been retained—as intended—in the Dr. Miles Company until the sale to the consumer. In such circumstances, the distribution would have taken the form of Dr. Miles consigning supplies to "agents" at the wholesale and retail levels. Because the distribution contracts forbade the distributors and dealers from selling outside of the Dr. Miles distribution system, the defendant would then have been able to obtain its supplies only by "inducing breach of trust by an agent" as charged in the complaint.

In such circumstances, all of the Dr. Miles distributors and dealers would have been Dr. Miles' agents, selling goods consigned to them, title to which was held by Dr. Miles. The question of whether a manufacturer could lawfully control by contract the resale prices of its dealers who had acquired title by purchase would not have arisen. Consider the significance of this formality for § 1. Does it take a plurality of actors to form a "contract, combination, or . . . conspiracy"? Is an agent sufficiently independent from its principal to count as a separate actor?

Justice Holmes dissented in *Dr. Miles*, stating among other grounds that under the reasoning of the majority opinion, the manufacturer:

> . . . [B]y a slight change in the form of the contract . . . can accomplish the result [of obtaining the dealer's adherence to the manufacturer's suggested resale price] in a way that would be beyond successful attack.

Dr. Miles Medical Co. v. Park & Sons, Co., 220 U.S. 373, 411 (1911) (Holmes, J., dissenting). Why can this formal change make a substantive difference? Consider whether the Court adopted this view in the next case.

2. Consider how the Court reached the result that agreements between a manufacturer and its dealers governing the resale prices of the dealers are unenforceable. Did the Court reach its conclusion as a result of the public policy declared in the Sherman Act? Did the Court consider the vertical agreements the equivalent of a dealers' cartel? Did the Court invoke the common law of contracts? Did the Court consider any of the business reasons for making the challenged agreements, as explored in Note 5, below? Did the Court find that the profits from the agreed on prices inured to the benefit of the dealers or to the manufacturers? Did the court acknowledge the difference between interbrand and intrabrand competition?

The Court failed adequately to analyze a critical issue in the case: The Court raised the question of why the manufacturer wanted to control the resale prices of its dealers but never attempted an answer. Perhaps if the Court had discovered why the manufacturer wanted to control dealer resale prices, it would have reached a different result.

3. Consider the Court's reference to a "restraint upon alienation" in the light of Chaffee's comments in Note 5, below. One policy underlying the doctrine is the furtherance of competition. This policy is reflected in copyright and patent law as the "first sale" or "exhaustion" doctrine, 17 U.S.C. § 109 (1992). As applied to copyrighted material, control over the price on resale by a buyer lapses after the first sale by the rightholder.

The first application of the Sherman Act to vertical price restraints was in 1907 in *J.D. Park and Sons v. Hartman*, 153 F. 24 (6th Cir. 1907), in which the practice was found illegal under a rule of reason analysis. In two cases involving book dealers, *Bobbs-Merrill v. Straus*, 210 U.S. 399 (1908), and *Scribner v. Straus*, 210 U.S. 352 (1908), the Supreme Court held that the copyright statute did not grant the rightholder-publisher the power to control the resale price of a retail bookseller.

4. Judge Bork writes that Justice Hughes laid down the "wrong premise" in *Dr. Miles*:

> In holding a resale price maintenance program illegal *per se*, Justice Hughes reasoned from the *per se* illegality of horizontal agreements among competitors. . . . The Court has been unwilling to reexamine that proposition, though it is obviously incorrect.

Robert H. Bork, *Vertical Restraints:* Schwinn *Overruled*, 1977 SUP. CT. REV. 171, 179-80.

5. As the cases below indicate, the antitrust treatment and the economic analysis of vertical price and non-price restraints has been intertwined and sometimes conflicting. In *Dr. Miles* the Supreme Court invoked *per se* treatment. In *Sylvania,* the Court rejected this rule in favor of rule of reason analysis based, in Justice White's phrase, "on the new economics of vertical relationships." *Continental T.V. Inc. v. GTE Sylvania Inc.*, 433 U.S. 36, 69 (1977). In making this doctrinal shift, the Court reflected the influence of an economic literature that rejected the holding in *Dr. Miles*, that such restraints were always to be condemned as abusive consequences of market power.

From the date of the decision in *Dr. Miles* until 1950, antitrust law and economic analysis were in agreement. The traditional economist's view of vertical restraints was that they reflected the existence of market power to the detriment of competition. When, for example, resale price maintenance was initiated by a group of manufacturers, under certain circumstances, this was considered a collusive effort aimed at fixing prices at the manufacturing level. When initiated at the distributor level, this could reflect a collusive effort among the distributors. Alternatively, the distributors could be proposing the establishment of a resale price maintenance regime at the behest of the manufacturers. *See* Basil S. Yamey, *Origins of Resale Price Maintenance*, 62 ECON. J. 147 (1952); Walter Adams, *Resale Price Maintenance: Fact and Fancy*, 64 YALE L.J. 967 (1955).

In 1950 the economic analysis of vertical restraints shifted away from conventional monopoly analysis and directed its inquiry into the reasons and benefits of these arrangements. *See* J.J. Spengler, *Vertical Integration and Antitrust Policy*, 58 J. POL. ECON. 347 (1950). Lester Telser extended Spengler's analysis of the pro-competitive or neutral effects of vertical integration to vertical price and non-price restraints. *See* Lester Tesler, *Why Should Manufacturers Want Fair Trade?*, 3 J.L. & ECON. 86 (1960). Telser addressed the question that was avoided by the majority in the *Dr. Miles* opinion: what are the business reasons for these arrangements? The same question was posed some years earlier as follows:

> Actually, the manufacturer by his advertising and other commercial devices has brought the consumers into a direct relation with himself. He is trying to make them buy *his* product, and they think of themselves as buying *his* product. Legally, it ceased to be owned by him some time before it reaches them, for he is separated from them by a succession of sales through wholesalers and retailers. . . . Consequently, what . . . [the manufacturer] wants is a new legal (or equitable) device to throw a bridge across to the consumers over the heads of these intervening dealers. . . . [The manufacturer] wants to make the intermediary transfers of title legally immaterial . . . and to be able to treat the entire process of marketing . . . goods from the factory to the consumer as a unified transaction. . . . Furthermore, he [the manufacturer] desires that his dealers, though not agents, shall be interrelated members of a unified selling organization, which will run much less smoothly and steadily if they are constantly differing with each other or with him as to the margin of profit. . . .

Zechariah Chafee, *Equitable Servitudes on Chattels,* 41 HARV. L. REV. 945, 947-48 (1928).

Telser replaced the traditional economic analysis of vertical restrictions as reflecting the pursuit or exercise of monopoly power with an efficiency explanation for vertical price and non-price arrangements. His analysis stressed the need for pre-sales services and information that is a fixture of contemporary marketing practice. As Chafee noted above, the manufacturer has an interest in having his product offered with full information about its attributes and quality. Given the diversity of consumer tastes and preferences, some consumers would be motivated entirely by price. Foreseeably, some dealers would address the preferences of those consumers by not incurring the costs of pre-sales services, *i.e.*, advertising, promotional activity, product demonstrations, as well as delivery, credit, and repair services. Telser points out that those dealers who did incur the costs of such services would then be at a competitive disadvantage. While the tastes, preferences, and income position of some customers would support those dealers providing the services and offering the product at a higher price to cover the costs of the services, there was a de-stabilizing element—some consumers would shop the product at the high price, information and service-providing dealer, but actually purchase the product from the cost-cutting, no-service dealer.

Telser concluded: "... [T]he retailers who do not provide special services get a free ride at the expense of those who have convinced customers to buy the product." Tesler, *supra,* at 91. *See also* George Stigler, *The Economics of Information*, 69 J. POL. ECON. 213 (1961).

To remain competitive with "free rider" dealers, service-providing dealers will tend to lower prices and preserve profit margins by saving the cost of services. Thus, there is created a tendency toward an equilibrium in which fewer promotional services will be offered and the total sales of the product will tend to fall.

Telser, accordingly, placed the conduct of manufacturers establishing minimum retail prices in the context of inducing retailers to continue to provide the services. Eliminating price competition was needed to eliminate the "free rider" problem and to induce the retailers to compete by providing better services. This analysis removed the taint of collusion that was the presumption under the traditional economist's analysis.

6. How did the new economic analysis affect the interpretation of the Sherman Act treatment of vertical restraints?

Telser's analysis became the bedrock for some antitrust commentators to propose a complete revision of the way the Sherman Act treats vertical price restraints. *See* Richard A. Posner, *The Next Step in the Antitrust Treatment of Restricted Distribution: Per Se Legality*, 48 U. CHI. L. REV. 6 (1981). Judge Bork, taking Telser's analysis as the general case, initially took the position that, absent evidence of manufacturer or retailer collusion, vertical restraints could never be anticompetitive.

Bork began his analysis by assuming that the manufacturer risked a fall in output and in sales by imposing a minimum retail price. Thus, the manufacturer would only impose the minimum price if, in return, the distributor provided the requisite services to induce increased sales. Accepting Telser's analysis, he wrote:

> ... the manufacturer's motive can never be restriction of output. ... [T]he only satisfactory alternative hypothesis is that the manufacturer believes the restraint will increase its net revenue by increasing distributive efficiency. ...

Robert H. Bork, *The Rule of Reason and the Per Se Concept: Price-Fixing and Market Division (pt.2)*, 75 YALE L.J. 373, 403 (1966).

Critics questioned Judge Bork's conclusion that only one characterization of this conduct was possible, citing four cases in which imposing minimum prices would result in smaller output and higher price to the consumer,

> The novelty of Bork's approach lies not in its recognition that in some circumstances the use of ... [resale price maintenance or r.p.m.] may increase manufacturer's sales and be of advantage to consumers, but in

> its attempted demonstration that, in the absence of cartels, the use of r.p.m. cannot fail to have this effect. . . .

J.R. Gould & B.S. Yamey, *Professor Bork on Vertical Price Fixing*, 76 YALE L.J. 722 (1967).

The critics pointed out that once the restraints were imposed, the economic analysis was more complex than Bork had assumed.

Before the restraint, there was the product and its cost and demand functions; after the imposition, the product had two elements to be taken into the economic calculus—the physical product and the added dealer services. Thus, the calculation of the social benefit from the vertical restraint centered on whether the increase in services was worth the increase in price. This calculation, in turn, involved aggregating the differences in consumer preference.

Bork acknowledged the validity of Gould & Yamey's point about the two elements of the product and added an assumption about consumer preferences:

> The composition of the product has changed. Using . . . [the vertical restraint] . . . the manufacturer has purchased and added to his manufactured article the information and promotion supplied by the reseller. . . . [I]f the new product becomes more profitable, it means that consumers prefer the new allocation of services.

Robert H. Bork, *A Reply to Professors Gould and Yamey*, 76 YALE L.J. 731, 733-34 (1967).

Now the validity of Bork's conclusion rests on the assumption that the manufacturer will not impose the minimum price unless the consumers find that the value of the services exceeds the increase in price.

7. What is the current state of the economic analysis of vertical restraints? What should the rule be? There is criticism of Bork's position, but not unanimity. One economist states:

> Telser's free-rider analysis and Bork's efficiency argument have become conventional economic wisdom on vertical restraints. Although Telser's analysis appears valid, Bork's efficiency argument is open to doubt.
>
> * * *
>
> Economic theory alone cannot predict whether the imposition of vertical restraints—and dealer's provision of additional services—will benefit consumers and enhance efficiency. Whether consumers benefit depends on whether gains to . . . [service seeking] consumers outweigh losses to . . . [price-seeking consumers]. . . .
>
> * * *
>
> When vertical restraints are used to promote the provision of distribution services, the critical issue for antitrust purposes remains whether con-

> sumers are better served by lower prices and fewer services or by higher prices and more services.

William S. Comanor, *Vertical Price-Fixing, Vertical Restrictions, and the New Antitrust Policy,* 98 HARV. L. REV. 983, 990, 999, 1001 (1985). If rule of reason analysis is required, what factors should be taken into account? This commentator continues:

> Because vertical restraints can either enhance or diminish consumer welfare . . . it is tempting to apply the rule of reason analysis on a case-by-case basis. . . . Yet it is no easy task to determine whether particular restraints increase or decrease efficiency: the answer in each case depends largely on the relative preferences of different groups of consumers.

Id.

Other economists have questioned the scope of Telser's premise as follows:

> It is necessary to recognize the limitations of Telser's scenario. First, only pre-sale service (including advertising, on-site demonstration, and generous inventory stocking) qualifies. On post-sale services, the free rider problem is less likely to arise. If . . . nonwarranty repairs are needed, the high-service outlet can charge for them without fearing the competition of low-service rivals. . . . Second, most of the presale service implied in Telser's argument is unnecessary when the customer already knows what she wants and why. . . . [M]ost of the goods sold in supermarkets, clothing stores, furniture outlets, and much else are ruled out. Third, the free-riding argument applies mainly for purchases of reasonably high value.
>
> * * *
>
> A dynamic model is needed. . . .

F.M. SCHERER & DAVID ROSS, INDUSTRIAL MARKET STRUCTURE AND ECONOMIC PERFORMANCE 551-52 (3d ed. 1990).

If the Telser analysis is grounded in a static economic model, one in which the assumptions apply to a fixed time period, how should the policy of antitrust treatment of vertical price fixing be adjusted to reflect the dynamic model—one that takes account of reactions of the participants to change over time?

Scherer and Ross characterize this policy issue as follows:

> Whether resale price maintenance agreements quite generally should be evaluated under a rule of reason rather than under the *per se* rules embedded in the main . . . legal precedents recalls many difficult issues. . . . On one hand, some resale price maintenance arrangements [RPM] facilitate new entry or the provision of desirable services, and except when RPM spreads to cover the bulk of an industry's output, depriving consumers of a meaningful choice between high-service and low-price outlets, most are probably innocuous. On the other hand, . . . claims that

> strictly vertical RPM cannot impair economic efficiency are plainly wrong and . . . [the] estimates of the benefits from RPM are correspondingly exaggerated. The overall balance between benefits and costs is probably close. The remaining question is whether the courts are able to sort out desirable from harmful conduct under a rule of reason approach without excessive litigation costs and error rates.

Id.

In the cases that follow, consider the extent to which the courts have been successful in distinguishing harmful conduct from appropriate competitive conduct.

The extent of competition at the producer's level is also identified as a factor in determining the effect on price and output of the producer's vertical restraint. Some investigators find that:

> . . . producers' competition is in fact a crucial element for the analysis of vertical arrangements. . . . [When] several producers are imperfectly competing at the upper level, then vertical restraints may serve to facilitate collusion. . . . [C]ontractual arrangements may be efficient, in . . . that joint profits are higher, but the gains to the producers and distributors are at the expense of consumers. Vertical restraints may not thus be socially desirable.

Patrick Rey & Joseph Stiglitz, *Vertical Restraints and Producers' Competition*, 32 EUR. ECON. REV. 561, 562 (1988).

Other economists have considered theoretical models taking into account the extent of the manufacturer's information about the retailer's costs in assessing the impact of vertical restraints. They posit a series of outcomes, but reject the view that vertical restraints should be deemed legal *per se* under § 1. *See* Patrick Rey & Jean Tirole, *The Logic of Vertical Restraints*, 76 AM. ECON. REV. 921 (1986).

Two investigators developed a model to suggest a variant of Telser's hypothesis—that providing [or not providing] services is a method for differentiating the product. They concluded that resale price maintenance enhances distributive efficiency only where consumers are not price shoppers. Their conclusion is:

> There is ample evidence that manufacturers of a wide variety of products, from beer to bicycles, are worried about retailers' incentives to use . . . services as an instrument of vertical differentiation. Coors . . . pointed out how refrigeration and product rotation services could affect the quality of its beer and specifically complained about distributors who would not offer these services and sell the beer at a discount. . . . Raleigh insisted . . . the quality of its bicycles depended both on pre-delivery services (pre-sales inspection, final assembly, and adjustments) and post-delivery services (repairs, technical advice, . . . [availability of spare parts]). . . . Raleigh's main concern was with discount stores that would not offer these services. . . .

Patrick Bolton & Giacomo Bonanno, *Vertical Restraints in a Model of Vertical Differentiation*, 103 Q.J. ECON. 355, 365-66 (1988).

Other investigators have applied econometric techniques to the facts set out in the record of *United States v. Sealy* (page 105, *supra*) and have concluded that the vertical restraints there reflected abuse of market power rather than a response to the free rider problem. *See* Willard F. Mueller & Frederick E. Geithman, *An Empirical Test of the Free Rider and Market Power Hypotheses*, 73 REV. OF ECON. & STATISTICS 301 (1991).

Another empirically-based criticism of Telser's analysis is provided by Benjamin Klein and Kevin M. Murphy in *Vertical Restraints as Contract Enforcement Mechanisms*, 31 J.L. & ECON. 265, 266-67 (1988). They state:

> . . . [S]tandard economic analysis of vertical restraints is fundamentally flawed. Vertical restraints, by themselves, do not create a direct incentive for retailers to supply desired services. . . . No matter how large a margin is created by resale price maintenance, there appears to be no incentive for competitive free-riding retailers to supply the desired demonstration services. . . . For example, free-riding retailers of personal computers could encourage consumers to obtain a product demonstration from a full-service retailer before purchasing the product from them with, say, lower priced tied accessories. [F]ree riding entails an extra short-run profit to the retailer . . . no matter how large a margin is created by the vertical restraint, retailers will have no incentive to incur the added costs of supplying the desired services.
>
> Our . . . alternative theory of how vertical restraints operate to induce desired dealer services . . . [posits that] manufacturers are assumed to induce desired dealer services through a private enforcement mechanism by which active manufacturer monitoring and the threat of manufacturer termination assures dealer performance.
>
> * * *
>
> Manufacturers employ vertical restraints, not to avoid consumer free riding, but to optimally compensate dealers on a per unit of sales basis for an increased supply of product promotion services and to prevent price competition that would eliminate the targeted marketing scheme. This analysis is . . . consistent with the use of exclusive dealing arrangements, with the use of resale price maintenance in the marketing of brand name clothing such as Levi Strauss jeans, and with the facts of *Monsanto*.

See also Peter C. Carstensen & Richard S. Dahlson, *Vertical Restraints in Beer Distribution: A Study of the Business Justifications for and Legal Analysis of Restricting Competition*, 1986 WIS. L. REV. 1 (concluding that vertical territorial restraints in this study reduced consumer welfare and stifled competition).

A recent reviewer of all reported resale price maintenance cases between 1976 and 1982 found that there was a settlement rather than trial in 70 percent of the filed cases, plaintiffs won judgments in only 28 percent of the cases that went to trial, and that the practices in the cases were highly varied. She concluded:

> The current dearth of empirical evidence on the use of vertical restraints and of RPM in particular seriously limits the development of economic understanding of these practices. . . . This empirical vacuum is especially pressing in the policy setting, where the relative importance of the efficiency and inefficiency theories is fundamental.

Pauline M. Ippolito, *Resale Price Maintenance: Empirical Evidence from Litigation*, 34 J.L. & ECON. 263, 292 (1991).

In the cases that follow, consider the analysis of the decisions in the light of the variables these various commentators have identified as significant for determining the antitrust consequences of the vertical restraint at issue.

United States v. Colgate & Co.

250 U.S. 300 (1919)

[Colgate, a large manufacturer of soap and related toilet articles, distributed its products through independent wholesalers and retailers. Colgate had allegedly specified the resale price of each item thus marketed and announced that it would not sell further to those distributors failing to adhere to the specified prices. Dealers and Colgate agents, according to the indictment, identified non-complying distributors from whom Colgate sought assurances and promises of further compliance before it would resume sales.

[The government indicted Colgate, charging a criminal conspiracy violating § 1.]

Mr. Justice MCREYNOLDS delivered the opinion of the Court.

We are confronted by an uncertain interpretation of an indictment itself couched in rather vague and general language. . . .

In the course of its opinion the trial court said:

> "No charge is made that any contract was entered into by and on the part of the defendant, and any of its retail customers, in restraint of trade and commerce—the averment being, in effect, that it knowingly and unlawfully created and engaged in a combination with certain of its wholesale and retail customers, to procure adherence on their part . . . to resale prices fixed by the defendant . . . .
>
> ". . . [The defendant] agrees with his wholesale and retail customers, upon prices claimed by them to be fair and reasonable, . . . and declines to sell his products to those who will not thus stipulate as to prices. This . . . presents for the determination of the court how far one may control and dispose of his own property. . . .
>
> "The pregnant fact should never be lost sight of that no averment is made of any contract or agreement having been entered into whereby the defendant, the manufacturer, and his customers bound themselves to enhance and maintain prices. . . ."

Our problem is to ascertain, as accurately as may be, what interpretation the trial court placed upon the indictment—not to interpret it ourselves; and then to determine whether, so construed, it fairly charges violation of the Sherman Act. Counsel for the government maintain, in effect, that, as so interpreted, the indictment adequately charges an unlawful combination . . . resulting from restrictive agreements between defendant and sundry dealers whereby the latter obligated themselves not to resell except at agreed prices. . . .

Considering all said in the opinion (notwithstanding some serious doubts) we are unable to accept the construction placed upon it by the government. We cannot, *e.g.*, wholly disregard the statement that—"The retailer, after buying, could, if he chose, give away his purchase or sell it at any price he saw fit, or not sell it at all, his course in these respects being affected only by the fact that he might by his action incur the displeasure of the manufacturer who could refuse to make further sales to him, as he had the undoubted right to do." And we must conclude that, as interpreted below, the indictment does not charge Colgate & Company with selling its products to dealers under agreements which obligated the latter not to resell except at prices fixed by the company.

. . . .

The purpose of the Sherman Act is to prohibit monopolies, contracts and combinations which probably would unduly interfere with the free exercise of their rights by those engaged, or who wish to engage, in trade and commerce—in a word to preserve the right of freedom to trade. In the absence of any purpose to create or maintain a monopoly, the act does not restrict the long recognized right of [*sic*] trader or manufacturer engaged in an entirely private business, freely to exercise his own independent discretion as to parties with whom he will deal. And, of course, he may announce in advance the circumstances under which he will refuse to sell. . . .

Affirmed.

COMMENTARY

1. Can you reconcile *Dr. Miles* with *Colgate*? Does the manufacturer in each case seek to control the resale price of the dealer? Did the Supreme Court accept the trial court's characterization of the indictment? Is this opinion constrained by the procedural posture of case? Explain.

2. What analysis does this opinion provide for the interpretation of the contract or combination language of § 1 of the Sherman Act? The *Colgate* case is often cited as holding that a "unilateral" refusal to deal does not violate § 1. Was there the traditional offer and acceptance between the parties in *Colgate*? Is there implied acceptance by the distributors? Coerced acceptance? In what sense was the conduct of Colgate unilateral?

3. Does *Colgate* announce a privilege for a manufacturer to select its distributor-customers? Is the privilege absolute and free of § 1 scrutiny?

Consider whether the understanding of the *Colgate* precedent expressed in the following cases remain valid today after reading *Monsanto,* page 218, *infra*, and other recent cases set forth later in the Chapter. Does Justice Breyer's opinion in *NYNEX v. Discon* rely on *Colgate* for the conclusion that consumers are entitled to choose their suppliers?

United States v. Parke, Davis & Co.

362 U.S. 29 (1960)

[The government sought to enjoin Parke, Davis & Co. from maintaining the resale prices of its products. The District Court dismissed the complaint after the government completed the presentation of its evidence; and the government appealed.]

Mr. Justice BRENNAN delivered the opinion of the Court.

. . . Parke Davis makes some 600 pharmaceutical products which it markets nationally through drug wholesalers and drug retailers. The retailers buy these products from the drug wholesalers or make large quantity purchases directly from Parke Davis. Sometime before 1956 Parke Davis announced a resale price maintenance policy in its wholesalers' and retailers' catalogues.

. . . [D]uring the spring and early summer of 1956 drug retailers in [Washington, D.C. and Richmond, Virginia] . . . advertised and sold several Parke Davis vitamin products at prices substantially below the suggested minimum retail prices. . . . The Baltimore office manager of Parke Davis . . . sought advice from his head office on how to handle this situation. The Parke Davis attorney advised that the company could legally "enforce an adopted policy arrived at unilaterally" to sell only to customers who observed the suggested minimum resale prices. He further advised that this meant that "we can lawfully say 'we will sell you only so long as you observe such minimum retail prices' but cannot say 'we will sell you only if you agree to observe such minimum retail prices,' since except as permitted by Fair Trade legislations [*sic*] agreements as to resale price maintenance are invalid." Thereafter in July the branch manager put into effect a program for promoting observance of the suggested minimum retail prices by the retailers involved. The program contemplated the participation of the five drug wholesalers. In order to insure that retailers who did not comply would be cut off from sources of supply, representatives of Parke Davis visited the wholesalers and told them, in effect, that not only would Parke Davis refuse to sell to wholesalers who did not adhere to the policy announced in its catalogue, but also that it would refuse to sell to wholesalers who sold Parke Davis products to retailers who did not observe the suggested minimum retail prices. Each wholesaler was interviewed individually but each was informed that his competitors were also being apprised of this. The wholesalers without exception indicated a willingness to go along.

Representatives called contemporaneously upon the retailers involved, individually, and told each that if he did not observe the suggested minimum retail prices, Parke Davis would refuse to deal with him, and that furthermore he would be unable to purchase any Parke Davis products from the wholesalers. Each of the retailers was also told that his competitors were being similarly informed.

. . . The branch manager [of Parke Davis] testified at the trial that thereafter he talked to a vice-president of Peoples [Drug chain] and that the following occurred:

> "Q: Well, now, you told Mr. Downey [the vice-president of Peoples] at this meeting, did you not, Mr. Powers, [the assistant branch manager of Parke Davis] that you noticed that Peoples were cutting prices?
>
> "A: Yes.
>
> "Q: And you told him, did you not, that it had been the Parke, Davis policy for many years to do business only with individuals that maintained the scheduled prices?

"A: I told Mr. Downey that we had a policy in our catalog, and that anyone that did not go along with our policy, we were not interested in doing business with them.

"Q: . . . Now, Mr. Downey told you on the occasion of this visit, did he not, that Peoples would stop cutting prices and would abide by the Parke, Davis policy, is that right?

"A: That is correct.

"Q: When you went to call on Mr. Downey, you solicited his support of Parke, Davis policies, is not that right?

"A: That is right.

"Q: And he said, I will abide by your policy?

"A: That is right."

. . . [The *Colgate* doctrine] meant no more than that a simple refusal to sell to customers who will not resell at prices suggested by the seller is permissible under the Sherman Act. In other words, an unlawful combination is not just such as arises from a price maintenance *agreement*, express or implied; such a combination is also organized if the producer secures adherence to his suggested prices by means which go beyond his mere declination to sell to a customer who will not observe his announced policy. . . .

The program upon which Parke Davis embarked to promote general compliance with its suggested resale prices plainly exceeded the limitations of the *Colgate* doctrine and . . . effected arrangements which violated the Sherman Act. Parke Davis did not content itself with announcing its policy regarding retail prices and following this with a simple refusal to have business relations with any retailers who disregarded that policy. Instead Parke Davis used the refusal to deal with the wholesalers in order to elicit their willingness to deny Parke Davis products to retailers and thereby help gain the retailers' adherence to its suggested minimum retail prices. . . . In thus involving the wholesalers to stop the flow of Parke Davis products to the retailers, thereby inducing retailers' adherence to its suggested retail prices, Parke Davis created a combination with the retailers and the wholesalers to maintain retail prices and violated the Sherman Act. . . .

Moreover, Parke Davis also exceeded the "limited dispensation which [*Colgate*] confers," . . . in another way. . . . With regard to the retailers' suspension of advertising, Parke Davis did not rest with the simple announcement to the trade of its policy in that regard followed by a refusal to sell to the retailers who would not observe it. First it discussed the subject with Dart Drug. When Dart indicated willingness to go along the other retailers were approached and Dart's apparent willingness to cooperate was used as the lever to gain their acquiescence in the program. Having secured those acquiescences Parke Davis returned to Dart Drug with the report of the accomplishment. Not until all this was done was the advertising suspended and sales to all the retailers resumed. In this manner Parke Davis sought assurances of compliance and got them, as well as the compliance itself. It was only by actively bringing about substantial unanimity among the competitors that Parke Davis was able to gain adherence to its policy. It must be admitted that a seller's announcement that he will not deal with customers who do not observe his policy may tend to engender confidence in each customer that if he complies his competitors will also. But if a manufacturer is unwilling to rely on individual self-interest to bring about general voluntary acquiescence which has the collateral effect of eliminating price competition, and takes affirmative action to achieve uniform adherence by inducing each customer to adhere to avoid such price competition, the customers' acquiescence is not then a matter of individual free choice prompted alone by the desirability of the product. The product then comes packaged in a competition-free wrapping—a valuable feature in itself—by virtue of concerted action induced by the manufacturer. The manufacturer is thus the organizer of a price-maintenance combination or conspiracy in violation of the Sherman Act. . . .

Judgment reversed. . . .

COMMENTARY

1. Did the Parke Davis attorney give that company legal advice which was accurate at the time he gave it? Do you find it credible that the Parke Davis branch manager understood the attorney's distinction? Lawyers are often unsuccessful when they attempt to communicate fine legal distinctions to business people who do not normally think in those terms.

2. Did Parke Davis "go beyond the simple refusal to sell to customers who [did] . . . not resell at stated prices"? If a manufacturer sees a dealer selling below its suggested resale prices, can the manufacturer remind the dealer of its sales policy, including its policy to cease doing business with nonconforming dealers? If a manufacturer reminded a dealer of its policy and the dealer then conformed, could their actions be construed as an offer for a unilateral contract, *i.e.,* an offer by the manufacturer to continue to sell if the dealer raises its price, followed by the acceptance of that offer by the dealer when it did in fact raise its price? Then there would be a contract between the manufacturer and its dealer to maintain price and a violation of the Sherman Act under *Dr. Miles*.

3. *Parke Davis* completely unsettled the *Colgate* doctrine. The dissenters said that the majority opinion "eviscerate[d] *Colgate*." 362 U.S. at 57 (Harlan, Frankfurter & Whittaker, J.J., dissenting). Lower court judges continued to invoke *Colgate*. In *House of Materials, Inc. v. Simplicity Pattern*, 298 F.2d 867, 870 (2d Cir. 1962), *Colgate* was characterized as having been "substantially limited, but not expressly overruled," citing with approval an earlier Second Circuit opinion that noted that after *Parke Davis*: "The Supreme Court has left a narrow channel through which a manufacturer may pass."

Determining the scope of *Colgate* after *Parke Davis* engaged courts and commentators. Justice Stewart in his concurrence characterized the majority opinion as

> . . . [A]mply demonstrat[ing] that the . . . record shows an illegal combination to maintain retail prices. I therefore find no occasion to question, even by innuendo, the continuing validity of the *Colgate* decision.

362 U.S. at 49 (Stewart, J., concurring).

Others were less certain of the remaining scope of *Colgate*. One commentator wrote: "Although *Parke Davis* is surely unsympathetic to *Colgate*, it does not purport . . . to treat willing or unwilling compliance as an agreement." 7 PHILLIP E.

AREEDA, ANTITRUST LAW 111 (1986). Is Areeda stressing the word "agreement"? Did the Court find a "combination" between Parke Davis and the wholesalers? Distinguish combination from agreement in this context.

Another commentator casts the issue in procedural terms as follows:

> . . . [T]he scope of *Colgate* has always been unclear. Narrowly construed, . . . [it] merely holds that under section 1 of the Sherman Act a plaintiff must allege an agreement between the manufacturer and the dealers.

George A. Hay, *Vertical Restraints After* Monsanto, 66 CORNELL L. REV. 418, 424 (1985). On a motion by a defendant manufacturer for summary judgment, what evidence would the plaintiff be required to present in order to prevail?

The *Colgate* case has also been criticized on policy grounds as follows:

> *Colgate*'s privilege is clearly unsound as a matter of economic policy. Whatever one thinks of resale price maintenance, its economic impact is the same whether enforced by explicit written contracts or by a *Colgate*-protected refusal to deal. *Colgate* thus has no place in an economically rational antitrust doctrine.

STEPHEN F. ROSS, PRINCIPLES OF ANTITRUST LAW 264 (1993).

Does *Parke Davis* hold that a manufacturer cannot implement a resale price maintenance plan through a two-tier distribution system (by cutting off supplies to wholesalers who sell to nonconforming retailers)? If the wholesalers acquiesce in the manufacturer's demand to terminate supplies to the nonconforming retailers, but acquiesce unwillingly and only to assure themselves continuing supplies, they would be forming a "combination" with the supplier within the meaning of the Sherman Act's section one. The *Albrecht* case, in its description of *Parke Davis,* offers a more precise analysis of the resulting combination(s) than is found in *Parke Davis* itself. *See* Note 7-10 in Commentary following *State Oil Co. v. Khan, infra.*

4. Is *Parke Davis* inconsistent with *Colgate*? If a combination can be formed when unwilling retailers are pressured into conforming to the suggested prices, then why is not all unwilling acquiescence adequate to form a combination? In *Russell Stover Candies, Inc. v. FTC*, 718 F.2d 256 (8th Cir. 1983), the FTC was reversed on the authority of *Colgate* for the erroneous conclusion that:

> the *Colgate* doctrine, as it stands today, does not preclude, as a matter of law, a finding of an agreement when a buyer unwillingly complies with a supplier's pricing policy to avoid termination.

Id. at 258.

5. *Parke Davis* raised the possibility that the Court might overrule *Colgate*. The pendulum has now swung in a different direction, and *Colgate* is currently regarded as a procompetitive safeguard. *See Monsanto Co. v. Spray-Rite Service Corp.,* 465 U.S. 752 (1984), and *Business Electronics Corp. v. Sharp Electronics Corp.,* 485 U.S. 717 (1988), both of which are excerpted in Section E, *infra.*

Is the following characterization of *Colgate* still valid in the light of the cases that follow?

> ... Since, in the absence of an attempt to achieve or maintain a monopoly, *Colgate* guarantees the right of customer selection, a manufacturer must be free, in so far as the antitrust laws are concerned, to replace an existing distributor with a new one regardless of the hardship for the former and even in the absence of any plausible justification.

Carl H. Fulda, *Individual Refusals to Deal: When Does Single-Firm Conduct Become Vertical Restraint?*, 30 LAW & CONTEMP. PROBS. 590, 597 (1965).

6. Note that no mention is made in these § 1 cases of the market share of the manufacturer imposing the vertical restraint. *See Otter Tail Power Co. v. United States*, 410 U.S. 366 (1973), *Lorain Journal Co. v. United States*, 342 U.S. 143 (1951) and *Aspen Skiing v. Aspen Highlands Skiing Corp.*, 472 U.S. 585 (1985), Chapters 9 and 10, below, for the significance of refusal to deal by a firm having a dominant market position.

7. Unilateral refusals to deal may be subjected to antitrust scrutiny under § 2. *See* Chapter 9, *infra*.

Toys "R" Us, Inc. v. Federal Trade Commission

221 F.3d 928 (7th Cir. 2000)

Diane P. WOOD, Circuit Judge.

The antitrust laws, which aim to preserve and protect competition in economically sensible markets, have long drawn a sharp distinction between contractual restrictions that occur up and down a distribution chain—so-called vertical restraints—and restrictions that come about as a result of agreements among competitors, or horizontal restraints. Sometimes, however, it can be hard as a matter of fact to be sure what kind of agreement is at issue. This was the problem facing the Federal Trade Commission . . . when it brought under . . . [antitrust scrutiny] the large toy retailer Toys "R" Us (. . . we will abbreviate the company's name as TRU . . .).

The Commission concluded, upon an extensive administrative record, that TRU had acted as the coordinator of a horizontal agreement among a number of toy manufacturers. The agreements took the form of a network of vertical agreements between TRU and the individual manufacturers, in each of which the manufacturer promised to restrict the distribution of its products to lowpriced warehouse club stores, on the condition that other manufacturers would do the same. This practice, the Commission found, violated § 5 of the Federal Trade Commission Act . . . . It also found that TRU had entered into a series of vertical agreements that flunked scrutiny under antitrust's rule of reason. TRU appealed that decision to us. It attacks both the sufficiency of the evidence supporting the Commission's conclusions and the scope of the Commission's remedial order. It is hard to prevail on either type of challenge: the former is fact-intensive and faces the hurdle of the substantial evidence standard of review, while the latter calls into question the Commission's exercise of its discretion to remedy an established violation of the law. We conclude that, while reasonable people could differ on the facts in this voluminous record, the Commission's decisions pass muster, and we therefore affirm.

I

TRU is a giant in the toy retailing industry. The Commission found that it sells approximately 20% of all the toys sold in the United States, and that in some metropolitan areas its share of toy sales ranges between 35% and 49%. The variety of toys it sells is staggering: over the course of a year, it offers about 11,000 individual toy items, far more than any of its competitors. As one might suspect from these figures alone, TRU is a critical outlet for toy manufacturers. It buys about 30% of the large, traditional toy companies' total output and it is usually their most important customer. According to evidence before the Commission's administrative law judge, or ALJ, even a company as large as Hasbro felt that it could not find other retailers to replace TRU—and Hasbro, along with Mattel, is one of the two largest toy manufacturers in the country, accounting for approximately 12% of the market for traditional toys and 10% of a market that includes video games. Similar opinions were offered by Mattel and smaller manufacturers.

Toys are sold in a number of different kinds of stores. At the high end are traditional toy stores and department stores, both of which typically sell toys for 40 to 50% above their cost. Next are the specialized discount stores—a category virtually monopolized by TRU today—that sell at an average 30% markup. General discounters like Wal-Mart, K-Mart, and Target are next, with a 22% mark-up, and last are the stores that are the focus of this case, the warehouse clubs like Costco and Pace. The clubs sell toys at a slender mark-up of 9% or so.

The toys customers seek in all these stores are highly differentiated products. The little girl who wants Malibu Barbie is not likely to be satisfied with My First Barbie, and she certainly does not want Ken or Skipper. The boy who has his heart set on a figure of Anakin Skywalker will be disappointed if he receives Jar-Jar Binks, or a truck, or a baseball bat instead. Toy retailers naturally want to have available for their customers the season's hottest items, because toys are also a very faddish product, as those old enough to recall the mania over Cabbage Patch kids or Tickle Me Elmo dolls will attest.

What happened in this case, according to the Commission, was fairly simple. For a long time, TRU had enjoyed a strong position at the low price end for toy sales, because its only competition came from traditional toy stores who could not or did not wish to meet its prices, or from general discounters like Wal-Mart or K-Mart, which could not offer anything like the variety of items TRU had and whose prices were not too far off TRU's mark.

The advent of the warehouse clubs changed all that. They were a retail innovation of the late 1970s: the first one opened in 1976, and by 1992 there were some 600 individual club stores around the country. Rather than earning all of their money from their mark-up on products, the clubs sell only to their members, and they charge a modest annual membership fee, often about $30. As the word "warehouse" in the name suggests, the clubs emphasize price competition over service amenities. Nevertheless, the Commission found that the clubs seek to offer name-brand merchandise, including toys. During the late 1980s and early 1990s, warehouse clubs selected and purchased from the toy manufacturers' full array of products, just like everyone else. In some instances they bought specialized packs assembled for the "club" trade, but they normally preferred stocking conventional products so that their customers could readily compare the price of an item at the club against the price of the same item at a competing store.

To the extent this strategy was successful, however, TRU did not welcome it. By 1989, its senior executives were concerned that the clubs were a threat to TRU's low-price image and, more importantly, to its profits. A little legwork revealed that as of that year the clubs carried approximately 120-240 items in direct competition with TRU, priced as much as 25 to 30% below TRU's own price levels.

TRU put its President of Merchandising, a Mr. Goddu, to work to see what could be done. The response Goddu and other TRU executives formulated to beat back the challenge from the clubs began with TRU's decision to contact some of its suppliers, including toy manufacturing heavyweights Mattel, Hasbro, and Fisher Price. At the Toy Fair in 1992 (a major event at which the next Christmas season's orders are placed), Goddu informed the manufacturers of a new TRU policy, which was reflected in a memo of January 29, 1992. The policy set forth the following conditions and privileges for TRU:

- The clubs could have no new or promoted product unless they carried the entire line.
- All specials and exclusives to be sold to the clubs had to be shown first to TRU to see if TRU wanted the item.
- Old and basic product had to be in special packs.
- Clearance and closeout items were permissible provided that TRU was given the first opportunity to buy the product.
- There would be no discussion about prices.

TRU was careful to meet individually with each of its suppliers to explain its new policy. Afterwards, it then asked each one what it intended to do. Negotiations between TRU and the manufacturers followed, as a result of which each manufacturer eventually agreed that it would sell to the clubs only highly differentiated products (either unique individual items or combo packs) that were not offered to anything but a club (and thus of course not to TRU). As the Commission put it, "[t]hrough its announced policy and the related agreements discussed below, TRU sought to eliminate the competitive threat the clubs posed by denying them merchandise, forcing the clubs' customers to buy products they did not want, and frustrating customers' ability to make direct price comparisons of club prices and TRU prices." . . .

The agreements between TRU and the various manufacturers were, of course, vertical agreements, because they ran individually from the supplier/manufacturer to the purchaser/retailer. The Commission found that TRU reached about 10 of these agreements. After the agreements were concluded, TRU then supervised and enforced each toy company's compliance with its commitment.

But TRU was not content to stop with vertical agreements. Instead, the Commission found, it decided to go further. It worked for over a year and a half to put the vertical agreements in place, but "the biggest hindrance TRU had to overcome was the major toy companies' reluctance to give up a new, fast-growing, and profitable channel of distribution." . . . The manufacturers were also concerned that any of their rivals who broke ranks and sold to the clubs might gain sales at their expense, given the widespread and increasing popularity of the club format. To address this problem, the Commission found, TRU orchestrated a horizontal agreement among its key suppliers to boycott the clubs. The evidence on which the Commission relied showed that, at a minimum, Mattel, Hasbro, Fisher Price, Tyco, Little Tikes, Today's Kids, and Tiger Electronics agreed to join in the boycott "*on the condition that their competitors would do the same.*" . . .

The Commission first noted that internal documents from the manufacturers revealed that they were trying to expand, not to restrict, the number of their major retail outlets and to reduce their dependence on TRU. They were specifically interested in cultivating a relationship with the warehouse clubs and increasing sales there. Thus, the sudden adoption of measures under which they decreased sales to the clubs ran against their independent economic self-interest. Second, the Commission cited evidence that the manufacturers were unwilling to limit sales to the clubs without assurances that their competitors would do likewise. . . . Goddu himself testified that TRU communicated the message "I'll stop if they stop" from manufacturer to competing manufacturer. . . . He specifically mentioned having such conversations with Mattel and Hasbro, and he said more generally "We communicated to our vendors that we were communicating with all our key suppliers, and we did that I believe at Toy Fair 1992. We made a point to tell each of the vendors that we spoke to that we would be talking to our other key suppliers." . . .

Evidence from the manufacturers corroborated Goddu's account. A Mattel executive said that it would not sell the clubs the same items it was selling to TRU, and that this decision was "based on the fact that competition would do the same." *Id.* at 32. A Hasbro executive said much the same thing: "because our competitors had agreed not to sell loaded [that is, promoted] product to the clubs, that we would . . . go along with this." *Id.* TRU went so far as to assure individual manufacturers that no one would be singled out.

Once the special warehouse club policy (or, in the Commission's more pejorative language, boycott) was underway, TRU served as the central clearinghouse for complaints about breaches in the agreement. The Commission gave numerous examples of this conduct in its opinion. . . .

Last, the Commission found that TRU's policies had bite. In the year before the boycott began, the clubs' share of all toy sales in the United States grew from 1.5% in 1991 to 1.9% in 1992. After the boycott took hold, that percentage slipped back by 1995 to 1.4%. Local numbers were more impressive. Costco, for example, experienced overall growth on sales of all products during the period 1991 to 1993 of 25%. Its toy sales increased during same period by 51%. But, after the boycott took hold in 1993, its toy sales decreased by 1.6% even while its overall sales were still growing by 19.5%. The evidence indicated that this was because TRU had succeeded in cutting off its access to the popular toys it needed. In 1989, over 90% of the Mattel toys Costco and other clubs purchased were regular (*i.e.* easily comparable) items, but by 1993 that percentage was zero. Once again, the Commission's opinion is chock full of similar statistics.

The Commission also considered the question whether TRU might have been trying to protect itself against free riding, at least with respect to its vertical agreements. It acknowledged that TRU provided several services that might be important to consumers, including "advertising, carrying an inventory of goods early in the year, and supporting a full line of products." . . . Nevertheless, it found that the manufacturers compensated TRU directly for advertising toys. . . . A 1993 TRU memorandum confirms that advertising is manufacturer-funded and is "essentially free." . . .

In short, the Commission found, there was no evidence that club competition without comparable services threatened to drive TRU services out of the market or to harm customers. Manufacturers paid each retailer directly for the services they wanted the retailer to furnish.

Based on this record, the Commission drew three central conclusions of law: (1) the TRU-led manufacturer boycott of the warehouse clubs was illegal *per se* under the rule enunciated in *Northwest Wholesale Stationers, Inc. v. Pacific Stationery & Printing Co.*, 472 U.S. 284, 105 (1985); . . . (2) the boycott was illegal under a full rule of reason analysis because its anticompetitive effects "clearly outweigh[ed] any possible business justification"; and (3) the vertical agreements between TRU and the individual toy manufacturers, "entered into seriatim with clear anticompetitive effect, violate section 1 of the Sherman Act."

. . . These antitrust violations in turn were enough to prove a violation of FTC Act § 5, which for present purposes tracks the prohibitions of the Sherman and Clayton Acts. After offering a detailed explanation of these conclusions . . ., it turned to the question of remedy and affirmed the order the ALJ had entered.

In the Commission's words, its order:

> prohibits TRU from continuing, entering into, or attempting to enter into, vertical agreements with its suppliers to limit the supply of, or refuse to sell, toys to a toy discounter. . . . The order also prohibits TRU from facilitating, or attempting to facilitate, an agreement between or among its suppliers relating to the sale of toys to any retailer. . . . Additionally, TRU is enjoined from requesting information from suppliers about their sales to any toy discounter, and from urging or coercing suppliers to restrict sales to any toy discounter. . . . These four elements of relief are narrowly tailored to stop, and prevent the repetition of, TRU's illegal conduct. . . .

TRU complained that the order trampled on its ability to exercise its rights under *United States v. Colgate & Co.*, 250 U.S. 300 (1919), to choose unilaterally the companies with which it wanted to deal. The Commission rejected the point, because it found that TRU had repeatedly crossed the line from unilateral to concerted behavior in illegal ways, and that it was entitled to include remedial provisions that were necessary to prevent recurrence of the illegal behavior . . . .

. . . .

II

On appeal, TRU makes four principal arguments: (1) the Commission's finding of a horizontal conspiracy is contrary to the facts and impermissibly confuses the law of vertical restraints with the law of horizontal restraints; (2) whether the restrictions were vertical or horizontal, they were not unlawful because TRU has no market power, and thus the conduct can have no significant anticompetitive effect; (3) the TRU policy was a legitimate response to free riding; and (4) the relief ordered by the Commission goes too far. We review the Commission's legal conclusions *de novo*, but we must accept its findings of fact if they are supported by such relevant evidence as a reasonable mind might accept as adequate to support a conclusion. *FTC v. Indiana Fed'n of Dentists*, 476 U.S. 447, 454 (1986).

A. Horizontal Conspiracy

As TRU correctly points out, the critical question here is whether substantial evidence supported the Commission's finding that there was a horizontal agreement among the toy manufacturers, with TRU in the center as the ringmaster, to boycott the warehouse clubs. It acknowledges that such an agreement may be proved by either direct or circumstantial evidence, under cases such as *Matsushita Electric Indus. Co. v. Zenith Radio Corp.*, 475 U.S. 574 (1986) (horizontal agreements), *Monsanto Co. v. Spray-Rite Service Corp.*, 465 U.S. 752 (1984) (vertical agreements), and *Interstate Circuit, Inc. v. United States,* 306 U.S. 208 (1939). When circumstantial evidence is used, there must be some evidence that "tends to exclude the possibility" that the alleged conspirators acted independently. *Monsanto*, 465 U.S. at 764, *quoted in Matsushita*, 475 U.S. at 588. This does not mean, however, that the Commission had to exclude all possibility that the manufacturers acted independently. As we pointed out in *In re Brand Name Prescription Drugs Antitrust Litigation,* 186 F.3d 781 (7th Cir.1999), that would amount to an absurd and legally unfounded burden to prove with 100% certainty that an antitrust violation occurred. *Id.* at 787. The test states only that there must be some evidence which, if believed, would support a finding of concerted behavior. In the context of an appeal from the Commission, the question is whether substantial evidence supports its conclusion that it is more likely than not that the manufacturers acted collusively.

In TRU's opinion, this record shows nothing more than a series of separate, similar vertical agreements between itself and various toy manufacturers. It believes that each manufacturer in its independent self-interest had an incentive to limit sales to the clubs, because TRU's policy provided strong unilateral incentives for the manufacturer to reduce its sales to the clubs. . . .

We do not disagree that there was some evidence in the record that would bear TRU's interpretation. But that is not the standard we apply when we review decisions of the Federal Trade Commission. Instead, we apply the substantial evidence test. . . . [T]he Commission painstakingly explained in a long opinion exactly what evidence in the record supported its conclusion. We need only decide whether the inference the Commission drew of horizontal agreement was a permissible one from that evidence, not if it was the only possible one.

The Commission's theory, stripped to its essentials, is that this case is a modern equivalent of the old *Interstate Circuit* decision. [*See* Chapter 8, page 327, *infra*—Eds.] . . .

The Commission is right. Indeed, as it argues in its brief, the TRU case if anything presents a more compelling case for inferring horizontal agreement than did *Interstate Circuit*, because not only was the manufacturers' decision to stop dealing with the warehouse clubs an abrupt shift from the past, and not only is it suspicious for a manufacturer to deprive itself of a profitable sales outlet, but the record here included the direct evidence of communications that was missing in *Interstate Circuit*. Just as in *Interstate Circuit*, TRU tries to avoid this result by hypothesizing independent motives. . . . If there were no evidence in the record tending to support concerted behavior, then we agree that *Matsushita* would require a ruling in TRU's favor. But there is. The evidence showed that the companies wanted to diversify from TRU, not to become more dependent upon it; it showed that each manufacturer was afraid to curb its sales to the warehouse clubs alone, because it was afraid its rivals would cheat and gain a special advantage in that popular new market niche. The Commission was not required to disbelieve the testimony of the different toy company executives and TRU itself to the effect that the only condition on which each toy manufacturer would agree to TRU's demands was if it could be sure its competitors were doing the same thing.

That is a horizontal agreement. . . . [I]t has nothing to do with enhancing efficiencies of distribution from the manufacturer's point of view. The typical story of a legitimate vertical transaction would have the manufacturer going to TRU and asking it to be the exclusive carrier of the manufacturer's goods; in exchange for that exclusivity, the manufacturer would hope to receive more effective promotion of its goods, and TRU would have a large enough profit margin to do the job well. But not all manufacturers think that exclusive dealing arrangements will maximize their profits. Some think, and are entitled to think, that using the greatest number of retailers possible is a better strategy. These manufacturers were in effect being asked by TRU to reduce their output (especially of the popular toys), and as is classically true in such cartels, they were willing to do so only if TRU could protect them against cheaters.

Northwest Stationers also demonstrates why the facts the Commission found support its conclusion that the essence of the agreement network TRU supervised was horizontal. There the Court described the cases that had condemned boycotts as "*per se*" illegal as those involving "joint efforts by a firm or firms to disadvantage competitors by either directly denying or persuading or coercing suppliers or customers to deny relationships the competitors need in the competitive struggle." 472 U.S. at 294.

... The boycotters had to have some market power, though the Court did not suggest that the level had to be as high as it would require in a case under Sherman Act § 2. Here, TRU was trying to disadvantage the warehouse clubs, its competitors, by coercing suppliers to deny the clubs the products they needed. It accomplished this goal by inducing the suppliers to collude, rather than to compete independently for shelf space in the different toy retail stores. *See also NYNEX Corp. v. Discon, Inc.*, 525 U.S. 128 (1998); *Klor's, Inc. v. Broadway-Hale Stores, Inc.*, 359 U.S. 207 (1959).

B. Degree of TRU's Market Power

TRU's efforts to deflate the Commission's finding of market power are pertinent only if we had agreed with its argument that the Commission's finding of a horizontal agreement was without support. Horizontal agreements among competitors, including group boycotts, remain illegal *per se* in the sense the Court used the term in *Northwest Stationers*. We have found that this case satisfies the criteria the Court used in *Northwest Stationers* for condemnation without an extensive inquiry into market power and economic pros and cons: (1) the boycotting firm has cut off access to a supply, facility or market necessary for the boycotted firm (*i.e.* the clubs) to compete; (2) the boycotting firm possesses a "dominant" position in the market (where "dominant" is an undefined term, but plainly chosen to stand for something different from antitrust's term of art "monopoly"); and (3) the boycott, as we explain further below, cannot be justified by plausible arguments that it was designed to enhance overall efficiency. 472 U.S. at 294. We address the market power point here, therefore, only in the alternative.

TRU seems to think that anticompetitive effects in a market cannot be shown unless the plaintiff, or here the Commission, first proves that it has a large market share. This, however, has things backwards. As we have explained elsewhere, the share a firm has in a properly defined relevant market is only a way of estimating market power, which is the ultimate consideration. *Ball Memorial Hospital, Inc. v. Mutual Hospital Insurance*, 784 F.2d 1325, 1336 (7th Cir.1986). The Supreme Court has made it clear that there are two ways of proving market power. One is through direct evidence of anticompetitive effects. *See FTC v. Indiana Fed'n of Dentists*, 476 U.S. 447, 460-61 ("the finding of actual, sustained adverse effects on competition in those areas where IFD dentists predominated, viewed in light of the reality that markets for dental services tend to be relatively localized, is legally sufficient to support a finding that the challenged restraint was unreasonable even in the absence of elaborate market analysis."). The other, more conventional way, is by proving relevant product and geographic markets and by showing that the defendant's share exceeds whatever threshold is important for the practice in the case. *See, e.g., United States v. E.I. duPont de Nemours & Co.*, 351 U.S. 377 (1956); *United States v. Grinnell Corp.*, 384 U.S. 563 (1966); *United States v. Aluminum Co. of America*, 148 F.2d 416 (2d Cir.1945) (suggesting that more than 90% is enough to constitute a monopoly for purposes of Sherman Act § 2 and 33% is not); *Jefferson Parish Hospital Dist. No. 2 v. Hyde*, 466 U.S. 2 (1984) (indicating that something more than 30% would be needed to show the kind of power over a tying product necessary for a violation of Sherman Act § 1).

The Commission found here that, however TRU's market power as a toy retailer was measured, it was clear that its boycott was having an effect in the market. It was remarkably successful in causing the 10 major toy manufacturers to reduce output of toys to the warehouse clubs, and that reduction in output protected TRU from having to lower its prices to meet the clubs' price levels. Price competition from conventional discounters like Wal-Mart and K-Mart, in contrast, imposed no such constraint on it, or so the Commission found. In addition, the Commission showed that the affected manufacturers accounted for some 40% of the traditional toy market, and that TRU had 20% of the national wholesale market and up to 49% of some local wholesale markets. Taking steps to prevent a price collapse through coordination of action among competitors has been illegal at least since *United States v. Socony-Vacuum Oil Co.*, 310 U.S. 150 (1940). Proof that this is what TRU was doing is sufficient proof of actual anticompetitive effects that no more elaborate market analysis was necessary.

C. Free Riding Explanation

TRU next urges that its policy was a legitimate business response to combat free riding by the warehouse clubs. We think, however, that it has fundamentally misunderstood the theory of free riding.

. . . .

Here, the evidence shows that the freeriding story is inverted. The manufacturers wanted a business strategy under which they distributed their toys to as many different kinds of outlets as would accept them: exclusive toy shops, TRU, discount department stores, and warehouse clubs. Rightly or wrongly, this was the distribution strategy that each one believed would maximize its individual output and profits. The manufacturers did not think that the alleged "extra services" TRU might have been providing were necessary. This is crucial, because the most important insight behind the free rider concept is the fact that, with respect to the cost of distribution services, the interests of the manufacturer and the consumer are aligned, and are basically adverse to the interests of the retailer (who would presumably like to charge as much as possible for its part in the process). *See Premier Electrical Construction Co. v. Nat'l Electrical Contractors Ass'n*, 814 F.2d 358, 369-70 (7th Cir. 1987) ("[The rationale for permitting restricted distribution policies] depends on the alignment of interests between consumers and manufacturers. Destroy that alignment and you destroy the power of the argument.").

What TRU wanted or did not want is neither here nor there for purposes of the free rider argument. Its economic interest was in maximizing its own profits, not in keeping down its suppliers' cost of doing business. Furthermore, we note that the Commission made a plausible argument for the proposition that there was little or no opportunity to "free" ride on anything here in any event. The consumer is not taking a free ride if the cost of the service can be captured in the price of the item. As our earlier review of the facts demonstrated, the manufacturers were paying for the services TRU furnished, such as advertising, full-line product stocking, and extensive inventories. These expenses, we may assume, were folded into the price of the goods the manufacturers charged to TRU, and thus these services were not susceptible to free riding. On this record, in short, TRU cannot prevail on the basis that its practices were designed to combat free riding.

D. Remedy

Last, we consider TRU's challenge to the remedial provisions the Commission ordered. TRU's basic point here is that the Commission has commanded it to do things that it would have been free to refuse, and conversely to refrain from actions it would have been free to take, in the absence of its violation of FTC Act § 5. So that its arguments can be fully understood, we set forth Section II of the decree in its entirety here:

> IT IS ORDERED that respondent, directly or indirectly, through any corporation, subsidiary, division or other device, in connection with the actual or potential purchase or distribution of toys and related products, in or affecting commerce, as "commerce" is defined in the Federal Trade Commission Act, forthwith cease and desist from:
>
> A. Continuing, maintaining, entering into, and attempting to enter into any agreement or understanding with any supplier to limit supply or to refuse to sell toys and related products to any toy discounter.
>
> B. Urging, inducing, coercing, or pressuring, or attempting to urge, induce, coerce, or pressure, any supplier to limit supply or to refuse to sell toys and related products to any toy discounter.
>
> C. Requiring, soliciting, requesting or encouraging any supplier to furnish information to respondent relating to any supplier's sales or actual or intended shipments to any toy discounter.
>
> D. Facilitating or attempting to facilitate agreements or understandings between or among suppliers relating to limiting the sale of toys and related products to any retailer(s) by, among other things, transmitting or conveying complaints, intentions, plans, actions, or other similar information from one supplier to another supplier relating to sales to such retailer(s).
>
> E. For a period of five years, (1) announcing or communicating that respondent will or may discontinue purchasing or refuse to purchase toys and related products from any supplier because that supplier intends to sell or sells toys and related products to any toy discounter, or (2) refusing to purchase toys and related products from a supplier because, in whole or in part, that supplier offered to sell or sold toys and related products to any toy discounter.
>
> PROVIDED, however, that nothing in this order shall prevent respondent from seeking or entering into exclusive arrangements with suppliers with respect to particular toys.

TRU makes a perfunctory, one-paragraph argument that paragraphs II(B), II(C), II(D), and II(E)(1) impose a "gag order" that contravenes the Supreme Court's recognition in *Monsanto Co. v. Spray-Rite Corp.*, . . . that manufacturers and distributors have a legitimate need for a free flow of information between them. This order, they claim, will create an irrational dislocation in the market to the detriment of toy suppliers, retailers, and consumers. With respect to paragraph II(E)(2), it argues that the five-year restriction on refusals to deal impermissibly cabins its *Colgate* rights to choose the suppliers with which it wants to deal. In effect, it claims, the decree will force it to purchase all toys that are offered to anyone, unless it can somehow prove that its refusal was because of a safety defect or other similar flaw.

We consider first TRU's challenges to parts II(B) through II(D) of the order. (It has not mentioned II(A) in its brief, and thus it has waived any challenge to that part of the order.) In general, if a retailer had some kind of restricted distribution arrangement with a manufacturer, *Monsanto* holds that it is permissible for the retailer to urge the manufacturer to respect the limits of that agreement. The retailer may communicate complaints about the provision of product to discounters, if that runs afoul of the promises in the distribution agreement. *Colgate* indicates that the retailer would also be within its rights to tell the manufacturer that it will no longer stock the manufacturer's product, if it is unhappy with the company it is keeping (*i.e.* if the manufacturer is sending too many goods to discounters, stores with a reputation for rude and sloppy service, or other undesirables).

Two facts distinguish these general rules from the situation in which TRU finds itself. First, unilateral actions of the sort protected by *Monsanto* and *Colgate* are not the same thing as a retailer's request to the manufacturer to change the latter's business practice. Under paragraph II(B) of the decree, TRU must not tell the manufacturer what to do; it is still permitted to decide which toys it wants to carry and which ones to drop, based on business considerations such as the expected popularity of the item. Second, to the extent paragraph II(B) might indirectly inhibit TRU from exercising its unilateral judgment, TRU must confront the fact that the FTC is not limited to restating the law in its remedial orders. Such orders can restrict the options for a company that has violated § 5, to ensure that the violation will cease and competition will be restored. *See National Lead Co., supra*, 352 U.S. at 430; *FTC v. Cement Institute*, 333 U.S. 683, 726-27 (1948); *Corning Glass Works v. FTC*, 509 F.2d 293, 303 (7th Cir.1975). *See also FTC v. Colgate-Palmolive Co.*, 380 U.S. 374, 392 (1965) (making the same point, in context of the Commission's deceptive practices authority).

The second point also applies to TRU's objections to paragraphs II(C) and II(D). In addition, we note that the retailer should not have any reason to obtain its suppliers' business records about shipments to the retailer's competitors. That is the supplier's concern. TRU is protected as long as it can ensure that it receives what was promised to it. Also, of course, the decree preserves TRU's right to enter into exclusive arrangements with respect to particular toys. In so doing, it also implicitly allows TRU to engage in communications that are necessary for the implementation and enforcement of such agreements. Paragraph II(D) directly addresses the Commission's finding of a horizontal agreement, and it orders TRU not to go out and create a new one. The Commission was certainly acting within the bounds of its discretion when it included these provisions.

Paragraph II(E) appears to be the one that causes the greatest concern to TRU. This strikes us as a closer call, but in this connection the standard of review becomes important. The Commission has represented in its brief to this court that the decree "leaves [TRU] free to make stocking decisions based on a wide range of business reasons; it must simply make those decisions—for a period of five years—independent of whether clubs or other discounters are carrying the same item." FTC Brief at 58. The attempt to use its market clout to harm the warehouse clubs lies at the heart of this case, and so it is easy to see why the Commission chose to prohibit reliance on the supplier's practices *vis-a-vis* the clubs as a reason for TRU's own purchasing decisions. At bottom, TRU is really just worried that it will be difficult to prove that any particular purchasing decision was free from the prohibited taint. It will be easy to refrain from announcements or communications about refusals to deal, which is what II(E)(1) prohibits. With respect to II(E)(2), if TRU implements adequate internal procedural safeguards, it should be possible to demonstrate that its buying decisions were not influenced by anything the manufacturers were doing with discounters like the clubs. These refusals to deal were the means TRU used to accomplish the unlawful result, and as such, they are subject to regulation by the Commission. *See National Lead*, 352 U.S. at 425. Under the abuse of discretion standard that governs our review of the Commission's choice of remedy, *see Siegel Co. v. FTC*, 327 U.S. 608, 612-13 (1946), this does not appear to be a remedy that "has no reasonable relation to the unlawful practices found to exist." We therefore have no warrant to set it aside. If, however, it becomes clear in practice that this provision is unworkable, TRU is free to return to the Commission to petition for a modification of the order.

III

We conclude that the Commission's decision is supported by substantial evidence on the record, and that its remedial decree falls within the broad discretion it has been granted under the FTC Act. The decision is hereby Affirmed.

COMMENTARY

1. Judge Wood cites *Klor's* and *NYNEX Corp. v. Discon, Inc.*, as well as referring to the arrangements by TRU as a boycott of the warehouse clubs, although she characterizes the Federal Trade Commission's use of the term, boycott, as pejorative. She also cites *Colgate*, a case noted as benchmark in non-price vertical restraint analysis. What are her criteria for distinguishing boycott analysis from vertical restraint analysis? Is the analysis of a *per se* violation the same for a boycott as for a non-price vertical restraint? Does Judge Wood hold that the arrangement was *per se* illegal or that it constituted an unreasonable restraint of trade?

2. Note the extension of antitrust analysis to the shifting modes of distribution. At the time of the *Dr. Miles* case, owner-operated pharmacies were predominant. *Parke-Davis* involved a pharmacy chain and a pharmaceutical manufacturer resisting a chain of discount pharmacies. After the single owner-operated stores gave way to the department store, came K-Mart, Target, and others as discount department stores. *Toy"R"Us* involved a large specialty retailer and the newest discount retailers, the wholesale clubs.

Can the antitrust laws adequately address these shifting structural arrangements? In the chapters that follow, consider whether the antitrust laws effectively address the more rapid changes in technology.

State Oil Company v. Khan

522 U.S. 3 (1997)

O'CONNOR, J., delivered the opinion for a unanimous Court.

Under § 1 of the Sherman Act, 26 Stat. 209, as amended, 15 U.S.C. § 1, "[e]very contract, combination . . . , or conspiracy, in restraint of trade" is illegal. In *Albrecht v. Herald Co.*, 390 U.S. 145 (1968), this Court held that vertical maximum price fixing is a *per se* violation of that statute. In this case, we are asked to reconsider that decision in light of subsequent decisions of this Court. We conclude that *Albrecht* should be overruled.

I

Respondents, Barkat U. Khan and his corporation, entered into an agreement with petitioner, State Oil Company, to lease and operate a gas station and convenience store owned by State Oil. The agreement provided that respondents would obtain the station's gasoline supply from State Oil at a price equal to a suggested retail price set by State Oil, less a margin of 3.25 cents per gallon. Under the agreement, respondents could charge any amount for gasoline sold to the station's customers, but if the price charged was higher than State Oil's suggested retail price, the excess was to be rebated to State Oil. Respondents could sell gasoline for less than State Oil's suggested retail price, but any such decrease would reduce their 3.25 cents-per-gallon margin.

About a year after respondents began operating the gas station, they fell behind in lease payments. State Oil then gave notice of its intent to terminate the agreement and commenced a state court proceeding to evict respondents. At State Oil's request, the state court appointed a receiver to operate the gas station. The receiver operated the station for several months without being subject to the price restraints in respondents' agreement with State Oil. According to respondents, the receiver obtained an overall profit margin in excess of 3.25 cents per gallon by lowering the price of regular-grade gasoline and raising the price of premium grades.

Respondents sued State Oil in the United States District Court for the Northern District of Illinois, alleging in part that State Oil had engaged in price fixing in violation of § 1 of the Sherman Act by preventing respondents from raising or lowering retail gas prices. According to the complaint, but for the agreement with State Oil, respondents could have charged different prices based on the grades of gasoline, in the same way that the receiver had, thereby achieving increased sales and profits. State Oil responded that the agreement did not actually prevent respondents from setting gasoline prices, and that, in substance, respondents did not allege a violation of antitrust laws by their claim that State Oil's suggested retail price was not optimal.

The District Court found that the allegations in the complaint did not state a *per se* violation of the Sherman Act because they did not establish the sort of "manifestly anticompetitive implications or pernicious effect on competition" that would justify *per se* prohibition of State Oil's conduct. Subsequently, in ruling on cross-motions for summary judgment, the District Court concluded that respondents had failed to demonstrate antitrust injury or harm to competition. The District Court held that respondents had not shown that a difference in gasoline pricing would have increased the station's sales; nor had they shown that State Oil had market power or that its pricing provisions affected competition in a relevant market. Accordingly, the District Court entered summary judgment for State Oil on respondents' Sherman Act claim.

The Court of Appeals for the Seventh Circuit reversed. 93 F.3d 1358 (1996). The court first noted that the agreement between respondents and State Oil did indeed fix maximum gasoline prices by making it "worthless" for respondents to exceed the suggested retail prices. After reviewing legal and economic aspects of price fixing, the court concluded that State Oil's pricing scheme was a *per se* antitrust violation under *Albrecht v. Herald Co.*, *supra.* Although the Court of Appeals characterized *Albrecht* as "unsound when decided" and "inconsistent with later decisions" of this Court, it felt constrained to follow that decision. In light of *Albrecht* and *Atlantic Richfield Co. v. USA Petroleum Co.*, 495 U.S. 328 (1990) (*ARCO*), the court found that respondents could have suffered antitrust injury from not being able to adjust gasoline prices.

We granted *certiorari* to consider two questions, whether State Oil's conduct constitutes a *per se* violation of the Sherman Act and whether respondents are entitled to recover damages based on that conduct. . . .

II

A

. . . .

A review of this Court's decisions leading up to and beyond *Albrecht* is relevant to our assessment of the continuing validity of the *per se* rule established in *Albrecht*. . . .

Albrecht . . . involved a newspaper publisher who had granted exclusive territories to independent carriers subject to their adherence to a maximum price on resale of the newspapers to the public. Influenced by its decisions in *Socony-Vacuum, Kiefer-Stewart*, and *Schwinn*, the Court concluded that it was *per se* unlawful for the publisher to fix the maximum resale price of its newspapers. 390 U.S. at 152-154. The Court acknowledged that "[m]aximum and minimum price fixing may have different consequences in many situations," but nonetheless condemned maximum price fixing for "substituting the perhaps erroneous judgment of a seller for the forces of the competitive market." . . .

Albrecht was animated in part by the fear that vertical maximum price fixing could allow suppliers to discriminate against certain dealers, restrict the services that dealers could afford to offer customers, or disguise minimum price fixing schemes. . . . The Court rejected the notion (both on the record of that case and in the abstract) that, because the newspaper publisher "granted exclusive territories, a price ceiling was necessary to protect the public from price gouging by dealers who had monopoly power in their own territories." . . .

In a vigorous dissent, Justice Harlan asserted that the majority had erred in equating the effects of maximum and minimum price fixing. . . . Justice Harlan pointed out that, because the majority was establishing a *per se* rule, the proper inquiry was "not whether dictation of maximum prices is ever illegal, but whether it is always illegal." . . . He also faulted the majority for conclusively listing "certain unfortunate consequences that maximum price dictation might have in other cases," even as it rejected evidence that the publisher's practice of fixing maximum prices counteracted potentially anticompetitive actions by its distributors. . . . Justice Stewart also dissented, asserting that the publisher's maximum price fixing scheme should be properly viewed as promoting competition, because it protected consumers from dealers such as Albrecht, who, as "the only person who could sell for home delivery the city's only daily morning newspaper," was "a monopolist within his own territory."

. . . .

Subsequent decisions of the Court, however, have hinted that the analytical underpinnings of *Albrecht* were substantially weakened by *GTE Sylvania*. We noted in *Maricopa County* that vertical restraints are generally more defensible than horizontal restraints. *See* 457 U.S. at 348, n.18. And we explained in *324 Liquor Corp. v. Duffy*, 479 U.S. 335, 341-342 (1987), that decisions such as *GTE Sylvania* "recognize the possibility that a vertical restraint imposed by a single manufacturer or wholesaler may stimulate interbrand competition even as it reduces intrabrand competition."

Most recently, in *ARCO*, 495 U.S. 328 (1990), although *Albrecht*'s continuing validity was not squarely before the Court, some disfavor with that decision was signaled by our statement that we would "assume, arguendo, that *Albrecht* correctly held that vertical, maximum price fixing is subject to the *per se* rule." 495 U.S. at 335, n.5. More significantly, we specifically acknowledged that vertical maximum price fixing "may have procompetitive interbrand effects," and pointed out that, in the wake of *GTE Sylvania*, "[t]he procompetitive potential of a vertical maximum price restraint is more evident . . . than it was when *Albrecht* was decided, because exclusive territorial arrangements and other nonprice restrictions were unlawful *per se* in 1968." 495 U.S. at 343, n.13 (citing several commentators identifying procompetitive effects of vertical maximum price fixing, including, *e.g.*, P. AREEDA & H. HOVENKAMP, ANTITRUST LAW ¶ 340.30b, p. 378, n.24 (1988 Supp.); Blair & Harrison, *Rethinking Antitrust Injury*, 42 VAND. L. REV. 1539, 1553 (1989); Easterbrook, *Maximum Price Fixing*, 48 U. CHI. L. REV. 886, 887-890 (1981)).

B

Thus, our reconsideration of *Albrecht*'s continuing validity is informed by several of our decisions, as well as a considerable body of scholarship discussing the effects of vertical restraints. Our analysis is also guided by our general view that the primary purpose of the antitrust laws is to protect interbrand competition. *See, e.g.*, *Business Electronics Corp. v. Sharp Electronics Corp.*, 485 U.S. 717, 726 (1988). "Low prices," we have explained, "benefit consumers regardless of how those prices are set, and so long as they are above predatory levels, they do not threaten competition." *ARCO, supra,* at 340. Our interpretation of the Sherman Act also incorporates the notion that condemnation of practices resulting in lower prices to consumers is "especially costly" because "cutting prices in order to increase business often is the very essence of competition." *Matsushita Elec. Industrial Co. v. Zenith Radio Corp.*, 475 U.S. 574, 594 (1986).

So informed, we find it difficult to maintain that vertically-imposed maximum prices could harm consumers or competition to the extent necessary to justify their *per se* invalidation. As Chief Judge Posner wrote for the Court of Appeals in this case:

> "As for maximum resale price fixing, unless the supplier is a monopsonist he cannot squeeze his dealers' margins below a competitive level; the attempt to do so would just drive the dealers into the arms of a competing supplier. A supplier might, however, fix a maximum resale price in order to prevent his dealers from exploiting a monopoly position. . . . [S]uppose that State Oil, perhaps to encourage . . . dealer services . . . has spaced its dealers sufficiently far apart to limit competition among them (or even given each of them an exclusive territory); and suppose further that Union 76 is a sufficiently distinctive and popular brand to give the dealers in it at least a modicum of monopoly power. Then State Oil might want to place a ceiling on the dealers' resale prices in order to prevent them from exploiting that monopoly power fully. It would do this not out of disinterested malice, but in its commercial self-interest. The higher the price at which gasoline is resold, the smaller the volume sold, and so the lower the profit to the supplier if the higher profit per gallon at the higher price is being snared by the dealer." 93 F.3d, at 1362. . . .

We recognize that the *Albrecht* decision presented a number of theoretical justifications for a *per se* rule against vertical maximum price fixing. But criticism of those premises abounds. The *Albrecht* decision was grounded in the fear that maximum price fixing by suppliers could interfere with dealer freedom. 390 U.S. at 152. In response, as one commentator has pointed out, "the ban on maximum resale price limitations declared in *Albrecht* in the name of 'dealer freedom' has actually prompted many suppliers to integrate forward into distribution, thus eliminating the very independent trader for whom *Albrecht* professed solicitude." 7 P. AREEDA, ANTITRUST LAW, ¶ 1635, p. 395 (1989). For example, integration in the newspaper industry since *Albrecht* has given rise to litigation between independent distributors and publishers. . . .

The *Albrecht* Court also expressed the concern that maximum prices may be set too low for dealers to offer consumers essential or desired services. . . . But such conduct, by driving away customers, would seem likely to harm manufacturers as well as dealers and consumers, making it unlikely that a supplier would set such a price as a matter of business judgment. . . . In addition, *Albrecht* noted that vertical maximum price fixing could effectively channel distribution through large or specially-advantaged dealers. . . . It is unclear, however, that a supplier would profit from limiting its market by excluding potential dealers. . . . Further, although vertical maximum price fixing might limit the viability of inefficient dealers, that consequence is not necessarily harmful to competition and consumers. . . .

Finally, *Albrecht* reflected the Court's fear that maximum price fixing could be used to disguise arrangements to fix minimum prices, . . . which remain illegal *per se*. Although we have acknowledged the possibility that maximum pricing might mask minimum pricing, *see Maricopa County*, 457 U.S. at 348, we believe that such conduct as with the other concerns articulated in *Albrecht* can be appropriately recognized and punished under the rule of reason. . . .

Not only are the potential injuries cited in *Albrecht* less serious than the Court imagined, the *per se* rule established therein could in fact exacerbate problems related to the unrestrained exercise of market power by monopolist-dealers. Indeed, both courts and antitrust scholars have noted that *Albrecht*' s rule may actually harm consumers and manufacturers. *See, e.g., Caribe BMW, Inc. v. Bayerische Motoren Werke Aktiengesellschaft,* 19 F.3d 745, 753 (1st Cir. 1994) (Breyer, C. J.). . . . Other commentators have also explained that *Albrecht*'s *per se* rule has even more potential for deleterious effect on competition after our decision in *GTE Sylvania*, because, now that vertical nonprice restrictions are not unlawful *per se*, the likelihood of dealer monopoly power is increased. . . . [*See*] *also ARCO*, 495 U.S. at 343, n.13. We do not intend to suggest that dealers generally possess sufficient market power to exploit a monopoly situation. Such retail market power may in fact be uncommon. *See, e.g., Business Electronics*, 485 U.S. at 727, n.2; *GTE Sylvania*, 433 U.S. at 54. Nor do we hold that a ban on vertical maximum price fixing inevitably has anticompetitive consequences in the exclusive dealer context.

After reconsidering *Albrecht*'s rationale and the substantial criticism the decision has received, however, we conclude that there is insufficient economic justification for *per se* invalidation of vertical maximum price fixing. That is so not only because it is difficult to accept the assumptions underlying *Albrecht*, but also because *Albrecht* has little or no relevance to ongoing enforcement of the Sherman Act. *See Copperweld Corp. v. Independence Tube Corp.*, 467 U.S. 752, 777, and n.25, (1984). Moreover, neither the parties nor any of the *amici curiae* have called our attention to any cases in which enforcement efforts have been directed solely against the conduct encompassed by *Albrecht*'s *per se* rule.

Respondents argue that reconsideration of *Albrecht* should require "persuasive, expert testimony establishing that the *per se* rule has distorted the market." Brief for Respondents 7. Their reasoning ignores the fact that *Albrecht* itself relied solely upon hypothetical effects of vertical maximum price fixing. Further, *Albrecht*'s dire predictions have not been borne out, even though manufacturers and suppliers appear to have fashioned schemes to get around the *per se* rule against vertical maximum price fixing. In these circumstances, it is the retention of the rule of *Albrecht*, and not, as respondents would have it, the rule's elimination, that lacks adequate justification. . . .

[The Court then considered (1) the significance of the Congressional failure to overrule *Albrecht* by legislation, and (2) the relevance of *stare decisis* in antitrust cases. It found that neither factor impeded its decision to overrule *Albrecht*—Eds.]

We . . . vacate the judgment of the Court of Appeals and remand the case for further proceedings consistent with this opinion.

It is so ordered.

COMMENTARY

1. In *Kahn*, the Court both subjected vertical maximum price agreements subject to evaluation under the rule of reason and overruled its earlier decision in *Albrecht v. Herald Co.* 390 U.S. 145 (1968). *Albrecht* had both (1) subjected vertical maximum price-fixing to *per se* condemnation and (2) elaborated the combination analysis of *Parke Davis*.

In the court of appeals decision in *State Oil*, Judge Posner invited the reversal of *Albrecht,* 93 F.3d 1358, 1363 (7th Cir. 1996). In the Supreme Court, the Federal Trade Commission and the Department of Justice jointly filed an *amicus* brief also urging the Court to abandon the *per se* treatment of maximum resale price constraints. Judge Posner and the *amicus* brief of the enforcement agencies viewed *Albrecht* as an anachronism which had been rendered obsolete by the economic reasoning of *GTE Sylvania* (page 202, *infra*).

A critic of the *State Oil* decision has noted that Justice O'Connor's opinion stressed consumer interests to the detriment of the freedom of dealers to price their product. *See* Alan J. Meese, *Economic Theory, Trader Freedom, and Consumer Welfare:* State Oil v. Khan *and the Continuing Incoherence of Antitrust Doctrine,* 84 CORNELL L. REV. 763 (1999). Does Justice O'Connor state that permitting a supplier to impose maximum resale price ceilings may constrain possible monopoly pricing by dealers? Barkat Khan, the dealer, went into bankruptcy during the pendency of this litigation. Was he likely to have had sufficient market power to engage in monopoly pricing?

2. *Albrecht* involved a vertical distribution system in which a St. Louis newspaper publisher set the maximum subscription price to be charged individual household subscribers by the newspaper carriers in the several territories assigned to them by the publisher. Carrier Albrecht, the plaintiff below, was terminated by the Herald Co. for failing to adhere to the stated maximum subscription price. Albrecht's territory was then divided between the Herald Co., which undertook to make home deliveries itself, and another carrier, Kroner. In order to assist it in dividing Albrecht's former territory, the Herald Co. enlisted a market intermediary, Milne Circulation Sales, Inc., to solicit Albrecht's customers for delivery by the Herald Co.

Justice White, writing for the majority, ruled that maximum price fixing was just as illegal as minimum price fixing:

> Maximum and minimum price fixing may have different consequences in many situations. But schemes to fix maximum prices, by substituting the perhaps erroneous judgment of a seller for the forces of the competitive market, may severely intrude upon the ability of buyers to compete and survive in that market. Competition, even in a single product, is not cast in a single mold. Maximum prices may be fixed too low for the dealer to furnish services essential to the value which goods have for the consumer or to furnish services and conveniences which consumers desire and for which they are willing to pay. Maximum price fixing may channel distribution through a few large or specifically advantaged dealers who otherwise would be subject to significant nonprice competition. Moreover, if the actual price charged under a maximum price scheme is nearly always the fixed maximum price, which is increasingly likely as the maximum price approaches the actual cost of the dealer, the scheme tends to acquire all the attributes of an arrangement fixing minimum prices. . . .

3. *Kahn* identifies each of the justifications set forth in *Albrecht* for condemning vertical maximum price fixing and rejects each of them. Moreover, *Kahn* points out how *Albrecht*'s application can create unconstrained monopoly power in a distributor (as it did for Albrecht himself).

4. Does *Kahn* provide any clues as to whether the Court ultimately may overrule *Dr. Miles*' subjection of vertical minimum price fixing to *per se* condemnation? After *Khan,* can a plaintiff rely on *Dr. Miles* by characterizing a specified maximum resale price as a minimum price? What criteria distinguish a maximum from a minimum vertically fixed price?

Overruling *Albrecht* opens up the task of identifying the circumstances in which vertical maximum price-fixing may be yet be illegal. Since Justice O'Connor stopped short of declaring all maximum vertical fixed prices lawful, what are the relevant factors in determining if and when such prices now may be illegal?

5. Justice Harlan dissented in *Albrecht*, on both the application of the *per se* rule to vertical maximum pricing arrangements and to the Court's determination that a combination had been shown. On the former issue Justice Harlan stated:

> The practice of setting genuine price "ceilings," that is maximum prices, differs from the practice of fixing minimum prices, and no accumulation of pronouncements from opinions of this Court can render the two economically equivalent.

390 U.S. at 156 (Harlan, J., dissenting).

6. The application of the *per se* rule to vertical maximum price-fixing, evoked widespread criticism. Hovenkamp, for example, wrote:

> . . . the Supreme Court misunderstood the economics of the newspaper industry. . . . The . . . [*per se*] rule as applied in *Albrecht* was particularly pernicious . . . because it effectively gave legal protection to the pricing activities of a natural monopolist.

Herbert Hovenkamp, *Vertical Integration by the Newspaper Monpolist*, 69 Iowa L. Rev. 451, 452 (1984). For further critical comment, see Milton Handler, *Reforming the Antitrust Laws*, 82 Colum. L. Rev. 1287, 1301 (1982); Frank Easterbrook, *Maximum Price Fixing*, 48 U. Chi. L. Rev. 886 (1981).

Hovenkamp's criticism is grounded on the premise that:

> A newspaper delivery route is often a natural monopoly . . . . An uncontrolled monopolist . . . has the power to reduce output and sell at a supercompetitive price. . . . These monopolistic practices, apparently used by Albrecht . . . adversely affect both the carrier's route customers and the publisher of the newspaper that the carrier distributes.
>
> * * *
>
> The *Albrecht* decision narrowed the means by which a newspaper can legally protect itself and its subscribers from the monopolistic pricing practices of carriers."

Hovenkamp, 69 Iowa L. Rev. at 452-56.

A minority of critics, however, supported the *Albrecht* rule. One commentator responded to Hovenkamp's comments as follows:

> Newspaper distribution is the only context in which even an arguable justification for maximum price fixing can be articulated. . . . Virtually all criticism of the *Albrecht* rule is based upon the "control of successive monopoly" paradigm . . . [when] monopoly exists at two stages of a product's distribution—manufacturing and distribution. . . . The effect of such an arrangement is a compound monopoly resulting in higher prices and lower output than if only the manufacturing stage is monopolized. If the monopoly pricing effects of the downstream monopolist can be eliminated . . . by vertical integration . . . or controlled . . . by maximum price fixing imposed by . . . [the manufacturer], prices, although still at a monopoly level, will be lower and output will be higher.

Mark E. Roszkowski, *Vertical Maximum Price Fixing: In Defense of* Albrecht, 23 Loyola U. Chi. L. Rev. 209, 227-28 (1992). This commentator points out that in *Albrecht* the Globe-Democrat was not the sole newspaper in St. Louis and that the distributor's monopoly existed only by the newspaper's grant of territorial exclusivity. He suggests that the distributors could have been given zones of influence and left to compete among themselves. How should a court apply § 1 to this issue arising in newspaper distribution, based on these differing economic characterizations of the practice?

These commentators on the *Albrecht* decision raise the issue of the whether the facts conform to the economic model of a natural monopoly, which has been defined as follows:

> Whether there is room for many firms in the market, each large enough to enjoy all scale economies, . . . [or] for only one firm (a *natural monopoly* situation) . . . depends upon the relevant technology and the size of the market, that is, the output that would be demanded at a price just sufficient to cover minimum unit cost.

F.M. SCHERER & DAVID ROSS, INDUSTRIAL MARKET STRUCTURE AND ECONOMIC PERFORMANCE 111 (3d ed. 1990). *See also* DONALD A. HAY & DEREK J. MORRIS, INDUSTRIAL ECONOMICS AND ORGANIZATION 622 (1991). Is the existence of the natural monopoly that Hovenkamp postulates a necessary condition for the application of Roszkowski's successive monopoly analysis?

7. In reversing the Eighth Circuit's affirmance of a jury verdict for the Herald Co., the *Albrecht* majority, writing through Justice White, elaborated on the analysis of a combination from *Parke, Davis* as follows:

> . . . Under *Parke, Davis* petitioner could have claimed a combination between respondent and himself, at least as of the day he unwillingly complied with respondent's advertised price. Likewise, he might successfully have claimed that respondent had combined with other carriers because the firmly enforced price policy applied to all carriers, most of whom acquiesced in it. . . . Petitioner's amended complaint did allege a combination between respondent and petitioner's customers. Because of our disposition of this case it is unnecessary to pass on this claim. It was not, however, a frivolous contention. . . .

390 U.S. at 150 n.6.

8. In *Perma Life Mufflers, Inc. v. International Parts Corp.*, 392 U.S. 134 (1968), a case contemporary with *Albrecht*, the Court employed the same theory of combination. In that case, certain Midas Muffler Shop dealers sued Midas, Inc., and its parent, International Parts Corp., for violating the antitrust laws in imposing certain restrictive provisions in their franchise contracts, such as provisions requiring the dealers to purchase their supplies exclusively from Midas, Inc. To the claim that the conspiracy element of a Sherman Act § 1 offense was missing, the Court replied:

> In any event each petitioner can clearly charge a combination between Midas and himself, as of the day he unwillingly complied with the restrictive franchise agreements, *Albrecht v. Herald Co.*, 390 U.S. 145,

> 150 n.6 (1968); *Simpson v. Union Oil Co., supra*, or between Midas and other franchise dealers, whose acquiescence in Midas' firmly enforced restraints was induced by "the communicated danger of termination," *United States v. Arnold, Schwinn & Co.*, 388 U.S. 365, 372 (1967); *United States v. Parke, Davis & Co.*, 362 U.S. 29 (1960).

Thereafter the Court referred to "these alternative theories of conspiracy." Was the Court being careless in its terminology? Was the Court more careful in the language quoted in the extract above and in the *Parke, Davis* and *Albrecht* opinions?

9. Another consequence of the reversal of *Albrecht* is the removal of its stricture on *Colgate*. However, it can be noted that in the immediate aftermath of the demise of *Albrecht,* the *Colgate* doctrine remains robust, to the extent that footnote 6 of the majority opinion in *Albrecht* cast a cloud over the scope and manner in which a seller could communicate terms of trading in that seller's product to customers and competitors in the channel of distribution. Footnote 6 stated that communication and acquiescence alone would identify members of an illegal combination. *See* Commentary 7, *supra*. That theory was undercut by the Court's vigorous confirmations of the continuing importance of *Colgate* in *Monsanto* (page 218, *infra*) and *Business Electronics* (page 226, *infra*). The end of *Albrecht* (and its footnote 6) helps further entrench *Colgate* in the caselaw. Yet the theory of *Albrecht*'s footnote 6 was reaffirmed in *Copperweld* (page 347, *infra*), a case decided in 1984, the same year that the Court began its rehabilitation of *Colgate* in *Monsanto*.

10. In his *Albrecht* dissent, Justice Harlan found the footnote 6 analysis of combination flawed. There can be no combination when a manufacturer dictates a maximum price to a retailer, Justice Harlan asserted, because the manufacturer is the only one interested in imposing the ceiling; hence, the concert of interests which underlies concerted behavior is absent. 390 U.S. at 163 (Harlan, J., dissenting). Harlan distinguished the situation in which a manufacturer compels a retailer to observe a minimum price, because in that case there is a concert of interest among all of the retailers in seeing that the minimum price is observed. A breach of the minimum by any one retailer undermines the ability of the others to maintain the minimum price. But a failure by one retailer to observe a price ceiling harms no other retailer.

C. The Rise and Fall of Fair Trade: Legislative Resale Price-Fixing

Consider the extent to which the following legislation provided a means of avoiding the holding of *Dr. Miles*.

Although the courts have been reluctant to make exceptions to the *per se* rule against price-fixing, Congress has not been. In 1937 Congress passed the Miller-Tydings Act, 50 Stat. 693. That Act amended the Sherman Act to create a limited exception to the prohibition of vertical price-fixing. The Miller-Tydings Act provided that a state could enact legislation permitting producers or distributors of commodities which were in free and open competition with other commodities of the same general class and which were marked with their trademarks, brands, or names to contract with dealers specifying minimum resale prices. Since state legislation was necessary to carve out the exception provided by the Miller-Tydings Act, the result was that a checkerboard pattern of the legality of vertical price-fixing agreements emerged. In those states which enacted legislation ("fair trade" acts) pursuant to the Miller-Tydings Act, conforming vertical price-fixing agreements were legal, while in those states which did not enact such legislation, vertical price-fixing agreements continued to be *per se* illegal under the *Dr. Miles* decision. What do you think was the theory behind the requirement that fair-traded commodities be marked with the trademark, brand or name of the producer or distributor? In *Dr. Miles* the manufacturer asserted a right to control resale prices on the basis of its ownership of the brand name, but the Court rejected that claim. Why do you think Congress was persuaded while the Court was not? Might there have been legislative facts relating to the hardships of the Great Depression presented to Congress, to which a court might not properly take judicial notice? Or perhaps Congress was merely capitulating to the lobbyists for associations of small retailers who wanted manufacturers to guarantee them freedom from competing with discounters. What do you think was the theory behind the requirement that the goods be in free and open competition with other goods of the same general class? Is this designed as a protection for the public?

Most state fair trade laws contained so-called "nonsigner" provisions. See example in § 369-b of the former New York fair trade law, *infra*. These provided that once the producer or distributor had contracted with one dealer about resale prices, all other dealers were bound by the price provisions stated in that contract, even though they had not signed it. Although the Miller-Tydings Act did not expressly authorize nonsigner provisions, it was generally thought that since § 1 of the Sherman Act prohibited contracts in restraint of trade, antitrust exemption was necessary only for vertical price-fixing contracts and not for state laws controlling the prices of nonsigners.

These expectations were upset, however, in *Schwegmann Bros. v. Calvert Distillers Corp.*, 341 U.S. 384 (1951), when the Supreme Court construed the Miller-Tydings Act as authorizing states to permit vertical price-fixing agreements, but as not authorizing state nonsigner provisions. Nonsigner provisions were held invalid as in conflict with the Sherman Act. As a reaction to the *Schwegmann Bros.* case, the Congress, in 1952, passed the McGuire Act as an amendment to the Federal Trade Commission Act. 66 Stat. 631-632. The McGuire Act restated the terms of the Miller-Tydings Act but added explicit permission to the states to adopt nonsigner provisions.

In 1975 Congress, as an anti-inflation measure, enacted a proposal of Congresswoman Barbara Jordan, repealing the Miller-Tydings and McGuire Acts. (Public Law 94-145 was signed by the President on December 12, 1975 and became effective on March 11, 1976.) So ended the period of "fair trade."

Another instance of a Congressional attempt to substitute legislative control over the market mechanism occurred in 1933. As a means of lifting the economy from the Great Depression, Congress enacted the National Industrial Recovery Act, 15 U.S.C. §§ 703-712 (repealed 1935). The Act permitted the President to establish an administrative agency to execute the legislative mandate to regulate the entire commercial sector. The National Recovery Administration enlisted the voluntary assistance of industry and labor representatives to adopt codes for every industry from handkerchief manufacture and the theater to the artificial flower and feather industry. The resulting codes when reviewed and approved, controlled wages, hours, prices, and all terms of trade. Some twenty two volumes of codes addressed not only retail prices, but advertising allowances, terms of consignment sales, the handling of merchandise returns, and described permissible discount practices.

Did this legislation accomplish an effective repeal of the Sherman Act during the two years of its operation?

In 1940 the legislature of the State of New York, acting in response to the Miller-Tydings Act, enacted the following legislation.

McKinney's Consolidated Laws of New York Annotated

Article XXIV-a—Fair Trade Law

§ 369-a. Price fixing of certain commodities permitted

1. No contract relating to the sale or resale of a commodity which bears, or the label or content of which bears, the trade mark, brand, or name of the producer or owner of such commodity and which is in fair and open competition with commodities of the same general class produced by others shall be deemed in violation of any law of the state of New York by reason of any of the following provisions which may be contained in such contracts:

- **(a)** That the buyer will not resell such commodity except at the price stipulated by the vendor;
- **(b)** That the vendee or producer require any dealer to whom he may resell such commodity to agree that he will not, in turn, resell except at the price stipulated by such vendor or by such vendees.

2. Such provisions in any contract shall be deemed to contain or imply conditions that such commodity may be resold without reference to such agreement in the following cases:

(a) In closing out the owner's stock for the purpose of discontinuing delivering any such commodity;

(b) When the goods are damaged or deteriorated in quality, and notice is given to the public thereof;

(c) By any officer acting under the orders of any court.

3. This article shall not be deemed or construed to apply to, or to fix or limit prices at which any commodity may be sold or offered for sale to the state of New York or to any administrative department of the state government, to any political subdivision of the state, to any municipality, to any public corporation or authority now or hereafter created by the legislature, to any college or university or any public library incorporated by an act of the legislature, or by the board of regents of the state education department or registered by the state education department, or to any nonprofit hospital maintained by a corporation organized under the religious corporations law or by a corporation organized for hospital purposes under the membership corporation law of this state or such other nonprofit hospital maintained by a corporation organized by special act of the legislature, or such other hospitals as shall have been approved for hospitalization contracts by the commissioner of health, pursuant to section two hundred fifty-four of the insurance law. Added L.1940, c. 195, § 3; amended L.1941, c. 39, § 38; L.1964, c. 69; L.1965m c. 331; L.1967, c. 492, § 2, eff. April 24, 1967.

§ 369-b. Unfair competition defined and made actionable

Wilfully and knowingly advertising, offering for sale or selling any commodity at less than the price stipulated in any contract entered into pursuant to the provision of section three hundred sixty-nine-a, whether the person so advertising, offering for sale or selling is or is not a party to such contract, is unfair competition and is actionable at the suit of any person damaged thereby. Added L. 1940, c. 195, § 3, eff. March 19, 1940.

D. The Consignment Device as a Method For Controlling Price to Consumers

Simpson v. Union Oil Co. of California

377 U.S. 13 (1964)

Mr. Justice Douglas delivered the opinion of the Court.

This is a suit for damages . . . for violation of §§ 1 and 2 of the Sherman Act. . . . [The suit was brought by Simpson, an operator of a retail gasoline station, after Union Oil Co. refused to renew his lease.]

. . . The complaint grows out of a so-called retail dealer "consignment" agreement. . . . The "consignment" agreement is for one year and thereafter until canceled, is terminable by either party at the end of any year and, by its terms, ceases upon any termination of the lease. The lease is also for one year; and it is alleged that it is used to police the retail prices charged by the consignees, renewals not being made if the conditions prescribed by the company are not met. The company, pursuant to the "consignment" agreement, sets the prices at which the retailer sells the gasoline. While "title" to the consigned gasoline "shall remain in Consignor until sold by Consignee," and while the company pays all property taxes on all gasoline in possession of Simpson, he must carry personal liability and property damage insurance by reason of the "consigned" gasoline and is responsible for all losses of the "consigned" gasoline in his possession, save for specified acts of God. Simpson is compensated by a minimum commission and pays all the costs of operation in the familiar manner.

The retail price fixed by the company for the gasoline during the period in question was 29.9 cents per gallon; and Simpson, despite the company's demand that he adhere to the authorized price, sold it at 27.9 cents, allegedly to meet a competitive price. Solely because Simpson sold gasoline below the fixed price, Union Oil refused to renew the lease; termination of the "consignment" agreement ensued; and this suit was filed. . . .

. . . The District Court granted the company's motion [for summary judgment]. . . . The Court of Appeals affirmed. . . .

We made clear in *United States v. Parke, Davis & Co.* . . . that a supplier may not use coercion on its retail outlets to achieve resale price maintenance. We reiterate that view, adding that it matters not what the coercive device is. . . . Here we have . . . an agreement; it is used coercively, and, it promises to be equally if not more effective in maintaining gasoline prices than were the *Parke, Davis* techniques in fixing monopoly prices on drugs.

Consignments perform an important function in trade and commerce, and their integrity has been recognized by many courts, including this one. . . . Yet consignments, though useful in allocating risks between the parties and determining their rights *inter se*, do not necessarily control the rights of others, whether they be creditors or sovereigns. . . .

One who sends a rug or a painting or other work of art to a merchant or a gallery for sale at a minimum price can, of course, hold the consignee to the bargain. A retail merchant may, indeed, have inventory on consignment, the terms of which bind the parties *inter se*. Yet the consignor does not always prevail over creditors in case of bankruptcy, where a recording statute or a "traders act" or a "sign statute" is in effect. . . . The interests of the Government also frequently override agreements that private parties make. Here we have an antitrust policy expressed in Acts of Congress. Accordingly, a consignment, no matter how lawful it might be as a matter of private contract law, must give way before the federal antitrust policy. . . .

Dealers, like Simpson, are independent businessmen; and they have all or most of the indicia of entrepreneurs, except for price fixing. The risk of loss of the gasoline is on them, apart from acts of God. Their return is affected by the rise and fall in the market price, their commissions declining as retail prices drop.[7] Practically the only power they have to be

---

[7] The basic agreement in force during most of the period when Simpson was a consignee provided that his commission was 1 1/2 cents per gallon more than the amount by which the price at which the company "authorized" him to sell exceeded a posted "tank wagon" price applicable to those gallons. However, if the "authorized" price fell below a posted "minimum retail" price, the commission was reduced by 50% of the difference between "minimum retail" and "authorized" retail. In no event could the commission be less than 5.95 cents for regular and 5.75 cents for ethyl. Shortly before Simpson ceased to be a consignee the program was changed. The guaranteed minimum was eliminated and the consignee absorbed 20% of the difference if "authorized" prices fell below "minimum retail." If the "authorized" price exceeded "minimum retail," the commission increased by 80% of the excess, as compared with 100% thereof under the former plan.

wholly independent businessmen, whose service depends on their own initiative and enterprise, is taken from them by the proviso that they must sell their gasoline at prices fixed by Union Oil. By reason of the lease and "consignment" agreement dealers are coercively laced into an arrangement under which their supplier is able to impose noncompetitive prices on thousands of persons whose prices otherwise might be competitive. The evil of this resale price maintenance program . . . is its inexorable potentiality for and even certainty in destroying competition in retail sales of gasoline by these nominal "consignees" who are in reality small struggling competitors seeking retail gas customers.

As we have said, an owner of an article may send it to a dealer who may in turn undertake to sell it only at a price determined by the owner. There is nothing illegal about that arrangement. When, however, a "consignment" device is used to cover a vast gasoline distribution system, fixing prices through many retail outlets, the antitrust laws prevent calling the "consignment" an agency, for then the end result of *United States v. Socony-Vacuum Oil Co.* . . . would be avoided merely by clever manipulation of words, not by differences in substance. The present, coercive "consignment" device, if successful against challenge under the antitrust laws, furnishes a wooden formula for administering prices on a vast scale.

Reliance is placed on *United States v. General Electric Co.* . . . where a consignment arrangement was utilized to market patented articles. . . . But whatever may be said of the *General Electric* case on its special facts, involving patents, it is not apposite to the special facts here.

. . . [W]e hold only that resale price maintenance through the present, coercive type of "consignment" agreement is illegal under the antitrust laws, and that petitioner suffered actionable wrong or damage. We reserve the question whether when all the facts are known, there may be any equities that would warrant only prospective application in damage suits of the rule governing price fixing by the "consignment" device which we announce today.

Reversed and remanded.

Mr. Justice STEWART, dissenting.

. . . .

In *United States v. General Electric*, . . . this Court held that a bona fide consignment agreement of this kind does not violate the Sherman Act. The . . . [majority] today concedes that "the consignment in that case somewhat parallels the one in the instant case." The fact of the matter is . . . [based on the record] the two agreements are virtually indistinguishable. Instead of expressly overruling *General Electric*, . . . the Court seeks to distinguish that case upon the specious ground that its underpinnings rest on patent law. . . . [U]ntil today no one has ever considered this fact relevant to the holding in that case.

COMMENTARY

1. It is generally accepted that Justice Stewart's interpretation of the *General Electric* case is accurate. A leading antitrust authority has criticized the majority opinion as "one of the most dishonest opinions of all time." William F. Baxter, *The Viability of Vertical Restraints Doctrine*, 75 CAL. L. REV. 933, 935 (1987).

2. Did the majority opinion consider the consignment contract alone coercive or was the threat of non-renewal of the short-term lease an essential ingredient of a finding of coercion? Can you reconcile *Simpson* with *Dr. Miles*, *Colgate* and *Parke-Davis* as statements of the antitrust law governing vertical restraints. Under each case, determine when coercion constitutes agreement. Does *Simpson* apply to a homeowner who signs a listing agreement with a real estate broker that permits the owner to refuse to pay the full contract commission if the broker finds a buyer for the house at 90% of the listed price? Do you agree with Judge Posner's characterization of *Simpson* as a case permitting use of consignments when ". . . the agency relationship has a function other than to circumvent the rule against price fixing." *Morrison v. Murray Biscuit Co.*, 797 F.2d 1430, 1436 (7th Cir. 1986). What are the indicia of a "bona fide" agency relationship? What criteria does the majority opinion in *Simpson* offer in finding "a so-called retail dealer 'consignment' agreement"? 377 U.S. at 14, or "a wooden formula for administering prices on a vast scale," *id.* at 22?

3. Note that *Simpson* involved a private party plaintiff suing under § 4 of the Clayton Act. The Ninth Circuit, affirming a dismissal of Simpson's claim by summary judgment below, in part because the parties were in *pari delicto*, noted that Simpson had the freedom ". . . to accept or reject the tendered lease and consignment contract. The record shows that he went into this deal with his eyes open and knew all the facts." 311 F.2d 764, 768 (9th Cir. 1963). Consider the nature of the record in a case decided on cross motions for summary judgment, when reversed by the Supreme Court. What was the evidentiary basis for Justice Douglas to conclude that the agency contract was a sham designed to coerce independent, retail gas station operators?

4. Does Justice Douglas suggest that price maintenance would be lawful if the arrangement were a *bona fide* consignment? A number of lower courts have distinguished *Simpson* on various grounds. In *Mesirow v. Pepperidge Farm, Inc.*, 703 F.2d 339 (9th Cir. 1983), *Simpson* was held inapplicable to wholesale prices. In *Hardwick v. Nu-Way Oil, Inc.*, 589 F.2d 806 (5th Cir. 1979), an oil company was permitted to set the retail price of gasoline of its consignee. *Simpson* was distinguished because its requirement of "indicia of entrepreneurship" were not present. *See also* Richard M. Steuer, *The Turning Points in Distribution Law*, 35 ANTITRUST BULL. 467, 471-72 (1990).

E. Nonprice Vertical Restrictions

By the late 1960s, the Court had also had some occasion to consider the application of a *per se* rule to other types of vertical agreements, those not involving price-fixing. In *White Motor Co. v. United States*, 372 U.S. 253 (1963), the Court considered the lawfulness of provisions in a distribution agreement limiting a truck distributor to making sales to customers located within a defined geographical territory and reserving government accounts to the manufacturer. The case reached the Supreme Court on review of the district court's grant of summary judgment to the government. Reversing the district court and refusing to apply the *per se* rule, Justice Douglas stated:

> This is the first case involving a territorial restriction in a vertical arrangement; and we know too little of the actual impact of both that restriction and the one respecting customers to reach a conclusion on the bare bones of the documentary evidence before us. . . . We do not know enough of the economic and business stuff out of which these arrangements emerge to be certain. They may be too dangerous to sanction or they may be allowable protections against aggressive competitors or the only practicable means a small company has for breaking into or staying in business . . . and within the "rule of reason." . . . We only hold that the legality of the territorial and customer limitations should be determined only after a trial.

Justice Brennan wrote a concurring opinion in which he characterized the contractual restrictions on the distributors' rights to resell "as a form of restraint upon alienation which is therefore historically and inherently suspect under the antitrust laws." Justice Brennan expressed an open mind, however, on the question of whether the territorial restrictions might be justified as a means of enhancing interbrand competition.

Prior to *White Motors*, a lower court had upheld the right of a manufacturer to establish an exclusive dealership by terminating a competing dealer, in the face of a declining market share for the product in that region. *See Packard Motor Car Co. v. Webster Motor Car Co.*, 243 F.2d 418 (D.C. Cir.), *cert. denied,* 355 U.S. 822 (1957). In *Packard*, however, the restraint was on the manufacturer, preventing the manufacturer from selling to a second dealer. No territorial restraints on dealers were involved.

The Supreme Court returned to the issue of territorial restraints imposed upon dealers by their suppliers in *United States v. Arnold, Schwinn & Co.*, 388 U.S. 365 (1967), the facts of which are as follows: Schwinn employed three methods to sell its bicycles: (1) sales to distributors, primarily cycle distributors, B.F. Goodrich and hardware jobbers; (2) sales to retailers by means of consignment or agency arrangements with distributors; and (3) sales to retailers under the so-called Schwinn Plan which involved direct shipment by Schwinn to the retailer with

Schwinn invoicing the dealers, extending credit, and paying a commission to the distributor taking the order.

Overcoming some of the doubts which troubled it in *White Motor Co.*, the Court held that "where a manufacturer *sells* products to his distributor subject to territorial restrictions upon resale, a *per se* violation of the Sherman Act results" as it also does when the manufacturer restricts the "outlets with which the distributors may deal" and when it places restraints upon the retailers to whom the goods are sold. On the other hand, the Court indicated that where the manufacturer retained "title, dominion, and risk" and "the position and function of the dealer . . . are . . . indistinguishable from those of an agent or salesman" such restrictions would be judged under a rule of reason approach:

> . . . If the manufacturer parts with dominion over his product or transfers risk of loss to another, he may not reserve control over its destiny or the conditions of its resale. To permit this would sanction franchising and confinement of distribution as the ordinary instead of the unusual method which may be permissible in an appropriate and impelling competitive setting, since most merchandise is distributed by means of purchase and sale. On the other hand, . . . we are not prepared to introduce the inflexibility which a *per se* rule might bring if it were applied to prohibit all vertical restrictions of territory and all franchising, in the sense of designating specified distributors and retailers as the chosen instruments through which the manufacturer, retaining ownership of the goods, will distribute them to the public. Such a rule might severely hamper smaller enterprises resorting to reasonable methods of meeting the competition of giants and of merchandising through independent dealers, and it might sharply accelerate the trend towards vertical integration of the distribution process. But to allow this freedom where the manufacturer has parted with dominion over the goods—the usual marketing situation—would violate the ancient rule against restraints on alienation and open the door to exclusivity of outlets and limitation of territory further than prudence permits.
>
> . . . Where the manufacturer retains title, dominion, and risk with respect to the product and the position and function of the dealer in question are, in fact, indistinguishable from those of an agent or salesman of the manufacturer, it is only if the impact of the confinement is "unreasonably" restrictive of competition that a violation of § 1 results from such confinement, unencumbered by culpable price fixing. . . . Schwinn adopted the challenged distribution programs in a competitive situation dominated by mass merchandisers which command access to large-scale advertising and promotion, choice of retail outlets, both owned and franchised, and adequate sources of supply. . . . [T]here is nothing in this record . . . to lead us to conclude that Schwinn's program exceeded the limits reasonably necessary to meet the competitive problems posed by

its more powerful competitors. In these circumstances, the rule of reason is satisfied.

We do not suggest that the unilateral adoption by a single manufacturer of an agency or consignment pattern and the Schwinn type of restrictive distribution system would be justified in any and all circumstances by the presence of the competition of mass merchandisers and by the demonstrated need of the franchise system to meet that competition. But certainly, in such circumstances, the vertically imposed distribution restraints—absent price fixing and in the presence of adequate sources of alternative products to meet the needs of the unfranchised—may not be held to be *per se* violations of the Sherman Act. The Government, in this Court, so concedes in this case.

. . . Critical in this respect are the facts: (1) that other competitive bicycles are available to distributors and retailers in the marketplace, and there is no showing that they are not in all respects reasonably interchangeable as articles of competitive commerce with the Schwinn product;[8] (2) that Schwinn distributors and retailers handle other brands of bicycles as well as Schwinn's; (3) in the present posture of the case we cannot rule that the vertical restraints are unreasonable because of their intermixture with price fixing; and (4) we cannot disagree with the findings of the trial court that competition made necessary the challenged program; that it was justified by, and went no further than required by, competitive pressures; and that its net effect is to preserve and not to damage competition in the bicycle market. . . .

388 U.S. at 381-82.

When the Court chose to make the *per se* rule applicable to territorial and customer restrictions imposed by a manufacturer who did not retain title and to make the rule of reason applicable to similar restrictions imposed by a manufacturer who did retain title, the Court adopted a distinction which proved to be untenable. It is true that this distinction incorporates the traditional common-law hostility to restraints upon alienation which Justice Brennan had described in his *White Motor Co.* concurrence and to which the *Dr. Miles* Court had referred. Yet the Court had just refused to make antitrust law turn on the same distinction three years earlier in *Simpson v. Union Oil Co.* The *Schwinn* rule was the subject of continuing criticism in the law journals and many of the lower courts viewed the rule with hostility and applied it only reluctantly. After ten years of life, *Schwinn* was finally overruled in 1977 by the case that follows.

One antitrust commentator criticized *Schwinn* as follows:

Schwinn [is] a mischievous precedent which rested on a nonexistent principle of ancient property law, and was historically incorrect, indefensi-

---

8 We do not regard Schwinn's claim of product excellence as establishing the contrary.

> ble as a matter of logic, and unjustifiable as a matter of economics. That case . . . [is] unique in the annals of antitrust for the volume of futile and costly litigation it generated . . . .

Milton Handler, *Changing Trends in Antitrust Doctrine: An Unprecedented Supreme Court Term—1977*, 77 COLUM. L. REV. 979, 980 (1977).

Continental T.V., Inc. v. GTE Sylvania, Inc.

433 U.S. 36 (1977)

Mr. Justice POWELL delivered the opinion of the Court.

Franchise agreements between manufacturers and retailers frequently include provisions barring the retailers from selling franchised products from locations other than those specified in the agreements. This case presents important questions concerning the appropriate antitrust analysis of these [nonprice] restrictions under § 1 of the Sherman Act . . . and the Court's decision in *United States v. Arnold, Schwinn & Co.*, 388 U.S. 365 (1967).

I

Respondent GTE Sylvania Inc. (Sylvania) manufactures and sells television sets through its Home Entertainment Products Division. Prior to 1962, like most other television manufacturers, Sylvania sold its televisions to independent or company-owned distributors who in turn resold to a large and diverse group of retailers. Prompted by a decline in its market share to a relatively insignificant 1% to 2% of national television sales, Sylvania conducted an intensive reassessment of its marketing strategy, and in 1962 adopted the franchise plan challenged here. Sylvania phased out its wholesale distributors and began to sell its televisions directly to a smaller and more select group of franchised retailers. An acknowledged purpose of the change was to decrease the number of competing Sylvania retailers in the hope of attracting the more aggressive and competent retailers thought necessary to the improvement of the company's market position. To this end, Sylvania limited the number of franchises granted for any given area and required each franchisee to sell his Sylvania products only from the location or locations at which he was franchised. A franchise did not constitute an exclusive territory, and Sylvania retained sole discretion to increase the number of retailers in an area in light of the success or failure of existing retailers in developing their market. The revised marketing strategy appears to have been successful during the period at issue here, for by 1965 Sylvania's share of national television sales had increased to approximately 5%, and the company ranked as the Nation's eighth largest manufacturer of color television sets.

This suit is the result of the rupture of a franchiser-franchisee relationship that had previously prospered under the revised Sylvania plan. Dissatisfied with its sales in the city of San Francisco, Sylvania decided in the spring of 1965 to franchise Young Brothers, an established San Francisco retailer of televisions, as an additional San Francisco retailer. The proposed location of the new franchise was approximately a mile from a retail outlet operated by petitioner Continental T.V., Inc. (Continental), one of the most successful Sylvania franchisees. Continental protested that the location of the new franchise violated Sylvania's marketing policy, but Sylvania persisted in its plans. Continental then canceled a large Sylvania order and placed a large order with Phillips, one of Sylvania's competitors.

During this same period, Continental expressed a desire to open a store in Sacramento, Cal., a desire Sylvania attributed at least in part to Continental's displeasure over the Young Brothers decision. Sylvania believed that the Sacramento market was adequately served by the existing Sylvania retailers and denied the request. In the face of this denial, Continental advised Sylvania in early September 1965, that it was in the process of moving Sylvania merchandise from its San Jose, Cal., warehouse to a new retail location that it had leased in Sacramento. Two weeks later, allegedly for unrelated reasons, Sylvania's credit department reduced Continental's credit line from $300,000 to $50,000. In response to the reduction in credit and the generally deteriorating relations with Sylvania, Continental withheld all payments owed to John P. Maguire & Co., Inc. (Maguire), the finance company that handled the credit arrangements between Sylvania and its retailers. Shortly thereafter, Sylvania terminated Continental's franchises . . . .

The antitrust issues before us originated in cross-claims brought by Continental against Sylvania and Maguire. Most important . . . was the claim that Sylvania had violated § 1 of the Sherman Act by entering into and enforcing franchise agreements that prohibited the sale of Sylvania products other than from specified locations. [The District Court entered judgment on the antitrust claim in favor of Continental; the Court of Appeals for the Ninth Circuit sitting en banc reversed by a divided vote.]

. . . .

The market impact of vertical restrictions is complex because of their potential for a simultaneous reduction of intrabrand competition and stimulation of interbrand competition. . . .

Vertical restrictions promote interbrand competition by allowing the manufacturer to achieve certain efficiencies in the distribution of his products. . . . Economists have identified a number of ways in which manufacturers can use such restrictions to compete more effectively against other manufacturers. . . . For example, new manufacturers and manufacturers entering new markets can use the restrictions in order to induce competent and aggressive retailers to make the kind of investment of capital and labor that is often required in the distribution of products unknown to the consumer. Established manufacturers can use them to induce retailers to engage in promotional activities or to provide service and repair facilities necessary to the efficient marketing of their products. Service and repair are vital for many products, such as automobiles and major household appliances. The availability and quality of such services affect a manufacturer's goodwill and the competitiveness of his product. Because of market imperfections such as the so-called "free rider" effect, these services might not be provided by retailers in a purely competitive situation, despite the fact that each retailer's benefit would be greater if all provided the services than if none did. . . .

. . . .

[T]o the extent that the form of the transaction is related to interbrand benefits, the Court's distinction is inconsistent with its articulated concern for the ability of smaller firms to compete effectively with larger ones. Capital requirements and administrative expenses may prevent smaller firms from using the exception for nonsale transactions. . . .

We conclude that the distinction drawn in *Schwinn* between sale and nonsale transactions is not sufficient to justify the application of a *per se* rule in one situation and a rule of reason in the other. The question remains whether the *per se* rule stated in *Schwinn* should be expanded to include non-sale transactions or abandoned in favor of a return to the rule of reason. We have found no persuasive support for expanding the *per se* rule. . . .[9] And even Continental does not urge us to hold that all such restrictions are *per se* illegal.

. . . [Vertical] restrictions, in varying forms, are widely used in our free market economy. . . . [T]here is substantial scholarly and judicial authority supporting their economic utility. There is relatively little authority to the contrary. . . . [W]e conclude that the *per se* rule stated in *Schwinn* must be overruled. In so holding we do not foreclose the possibility that particular applications of vertical restrictions might justify *per se* prohibition. . . . But we do make clear that departure from the rule-of-reason standard must be based upon demonstrable economic effect rather than as in *Schwinn* upon formalistic line drawing.

In sum, we conclude that the appropriate decision is to return to the rule of reason that governed vertical restrictions prior to *Schwinn*. When anticompetitive effects are shown to result from particular vertical restrictions they can be adequately policed under the rule of reason. . . . Accordingly, the decision of the Court of Appeals is affirmed.

Mr. Justice WHITE, concurring in the judgment.

Although I agree with the majority that the location clause at issue in this case is not a *per se* violation of the Sherman Act and should be judged under the rule of reason, I cannot agree that this result requires the overruling of *United States v. Arnold, Schwinn & Co.*, 388 U.S. 365 (1967). In my view this case is distinguishable from *Schwinn* because there is less potential for restraint of intrabrand competition and more potential for stimulating interbrand competition. As to intrabrand competition, Sylvania, unlike Schwinn, did not restrict the customers to whom or the territories where its purchasers could sell. As to interbrand competition, Sylvania, unlike Schwinn, had an insignificant market share at the time it adopted its challenged distribution practice and enjoyed no consumer preference that would allow its retailers to charge a premium over other brands. . . .

I have a further reservation about the majority's reliance on "relevant economic impact" as the test for retaining *per se* rules regarding vertical restraints. It is common ground among the leading advocates of a purely economic approach to the question of distribution restraints that the economic arguments in favor of allowing vertical nonprice restraints generally apply to vertical price restraints as well. Although the majority asserts that "the *per se* illegality of price restrictions . . . involves significantly different questions of analysis and policy," . . . I suspect this purported distinction may be as difficult to justify as that of *Schwinn* under the terms of the majority's analysis. Thus Professor Posner, in an article cited five times by the majority, concludes: "I believe that the law should treat price and nonprice restrictions the same and that it should make no distinction between the imposition of restrictions in a sale contract and their imposition in an agency contract." . . . Indeed, the Court has already recognized that resale price maintenance may increase output by inducing "demand-creating activity" by dealers (such as additional retail outlets, advertising and promotion, and product servicing) that outweighs the additional sales that would result from lower prices brought about by dealer price competition. . . . These same output-enhancing possibilities of nonprice vertical restraints are relied upon by the major-

---

[9] Continental's contention that balancing intrabrand and interbrand competitive effects of vertical restrictions is not a "proper part of the judicial function,". . . is refuted by *Schwinn* itself. *United States v. Topco Associates, Inc.*, 405 U.S. at 608, is not to the contrary, for it involved a horizontal restriction among ostensible competitors.

ity as evidence of their social utility and economic soundness . . . and as a justification for judging them under the rule of reason. The effect, if not the intention, of the Court's opinion is necessarily to call into question the firmly established *per se* rule against price restraints.

COMMENTARY

1. Compare the *Sylvania* opinion with *White Motor*, pages 199-200, *supra,* as offering guidance to lower courts in applying rule of reason analysis to vertical non-price restraints. *See* Note 3, below. Left with the task of determining when vertical nonprice restraints have an adverse competitive effect, lower court judges have tended to interpret the balancing test of *Sylvania* differently. *See* Note 2, below.

On remand in the *Sylvania* case itself, the District Court held that the territorial location clause was reasonable, since the location clause was likely to promote interbrand competition by more than it suppressed intrabrand competition. The opinion did not, however, set out its calculus of the balance between suppressed intrabrand competition and the advancement of interbrand competition. 461 F. Supp. 1046 (N.D. Cal. 1978). In affirming, the Court of Appeals stated its rationale for striking a balance between intrabrand restraint and interbrand enhancement as follows:

> We recognize . . . that . . . Sylvania did check intrabrand competition to some extent. This was an inevitable incident to Sylvania's attempt to promote and maintain interbrand competition. . . . [I]t is important to emphasize . . . that in a market dominated by a single company (RCA), Sylvania possessed only a minor fraction of the total market, that many other brands were available to the consumer . . ., [and] that Sylvania dealers could and did carry competing brands.

GTE Sylvania Inc. v. Continental T.V., Inc. 537 F.2d 980, 1000-01 (9th Cir. 1976).

In the cases that follow, consider the extent to which the *Sylvania* opinion has become a touchstone for all aspects of vertical restraint analysis, including resale price maintenance. In *Business Electronics Corp. v. Sharp Electronics Corp.*, 485 U.S. 717 (1988) (excerpted in Section E, *infra*), the Supreme Court defined as illegal *per se* only specific agreements to fix resale prices or price levels. Justice Scalia supported this conclusion as follows:

> . . . [T]here is a presumption in favor of a rule-of-reason standard; . . . departure from that standard must be justified by demonstrable economic effect . . . ; that interbrand competition is the primary concern of the antitrust laws; and that rules in this area should be formulated with a view toward protecting the doctrine of *GTE Sylvania.*

Id. at 726.

2. The antitrust treatment of distribution limitations by suppliers was in process of change when *Sylvania* announced a major shift. One commentator's writings document the development. Earlier in *Schwinn*, Judge Posner, then in the Solicitor General's office, briefed and argued the case, urging that a standard of presumptive illegality be applied. Under this standard, restriction of competition at the dealer level could be rebutted by a showing that interbrand competition had been enhanced. In that case, the Court rejected this approach. 388 U.S. 365 (1967).

Writing in response to *Sylvania*, Posner took the position that price and non-price vertical restraints be treated the same, but suggested that more experience was needed because: "[W]e don't yet know enough about restricted distribution to adopt a rule of *per se* legality." Richard A. Posner, *The Rule of Reason and the Economic Approach: Reflections on the* Sylvania *Decision*, 45 U. CHI. L. REV. 1, 2 (1977). Subsequently, Judge Posner took the position that all vertical restraints, including price restraints should be deemed legal *per se*. *See* Richard A. Posner, *The Next Step in the Antitrust Treatment of Restricted Distribution: Per Se Legality*, 48 U. CHI. L. REV. 6 (1981).

Other commentators laud the continuing differential analysis of price and non-price restraints:

> By overruling the *Schwinn* doctrine, the . . . Court moved antitrust analysis of vertical restrictions solidly forward. . . . [T]he Court's rationale in justifying the *per se* rule against vertical price fixing and the way in which it distinguished non-price vertical restrictions from vertical price fixing create a sound underpinning for future antitrust analysis. . . . [B]y offering only minimal guidance as to how a rule of reason will be applied, the Court has guaranteed many years of perplexing litigation.

Robert Pitofsky, *The* Sylvania *Case: Antitrust Analysis of Non-Price Vertical Restrictions*, 78 COLUM. L. REV. 1, 37-38 (1978).

3. Lower courts applying *Sylvania* have taken differing approaches to rule of reason analysis of nonprice vertical restraints. A recent review of some 45 court of appeals cases involving nonprice vertical restraints that were decided on the authority of *Sylvania*, concludes that the Supreme Court's test of balancing restriction of intrabrand competition against the enhancement of interbrand competition, is unworkable.

> Courts, and indeed economists, are ill equipped to carry out the Supreme Court's instruction to balance the conflicting effects that economic theory attributes to vertical restraints, much less to determine whether the net result of a particular restraint is on balance to impede or to promote competition.

Douglas H. Ginsburg, *Vertical Restraints: De Facto Legality Under the Rule of Reason*, 60 ANTITRUST L.J. 67, 68 (1991). Noting that defendants prevailed in 41 of the 45 cases, Judge Ginsburg found four different, alternative approaches to the

Supreme Court's balancing test being applied by courts of appeals. These tests are: First, the market power screen—where a manufacturer producing only a small share among several brands in a competitive market, uses a location clause, territorial or customer restriction, or selective dealing arrangement, the inquiry is ended; the defendant prevails. In these circumstances, it is deemed unnecessary to inquire further into the actual effects of the vertical restraint because it is deemed most unlikely that competition could be harmed. This is the approach of the Seventh Circuit in *Valley Liquors, Inc. v Renfield Importers, Ltd.*, 822 F.2d 656, 669 (7th Cir. 1987).

The second approach accepts any credible evidence of some gain in interbrand competition as a predicate for finding for the defendant manufacturer under a rule of reason analysis of the vertical restraint. In *Crane & Shovel Sales Corp. v. Bucyrus-Erie Co.*, 854 F.2d 802, 808 (6th Cir. 1988), the court upheld the elimination of all intrabrand competition on the statement that vertical restraints are "generally found to be potentially beneficial." Under this view, market share is irrelevant; any credible evidence of interbrand enhancement serves to uphold the restraint.

The third approach focuses solely on the possibility of harm to interbrand competition. Judge Ginsburg identifies this as the approach taken by the Ninth Circuit on the remand in the *Sylvania* case. *See* Note 1, above. He saw this opinion as an example of when:

> . . . the balancing test envisioned by the Supreme Court was limited to a one-sided search for any reason to fear that the location clause challenged . . . would harm interbrand competition.

Ginsburg, *supra,* at 75.

The final approach is characterized as one in which the court seems to balance the various consequences of the vertical restraint, but in effect yields to evidence of interbrand benefits. In *Three Movies of Tarzana v. Pacific Theatres*, 828 F.2d 1395 (9th Cir. 1987), the court reviewed the restraint and found it to be a minor factor in inhibiting intrabrand competition that, on balance, encouraged interbrand competition. The court did not weight the various factors, but merely stated them along with the conclusion.

Consider the distinctions made by each of these approaches. Under the market power test, what are the indicia of market power, how should they be applied, and over what period of time? How should the potential of new entrants be assessed or discounted? Who should have the burden of proof on these issues? Are the second and fourth approaches distinctly different or are they alternative formulations of the same characterization?

4. In *Sylvania*, the Court abandoned the distinction between (1) sales to dealers and distributors passing title to them and (2) shipment of goods on consignment to dealers and distributors with title reserved in the supplier until final sale to the ultimate customer as a basis for determining when the *per se* rule applied. Yet, as Justice White pointed out in his concurrence, the Court embraced another distinction which he feared might prove just as untenable. Under the *Sylvania* decision, vertical agreements between suppliers and dealers which control the dealer's price are illegal *per se*, whereas vertical agreements between suppliers and dealers which impose nonprice restrictions upon the dealers are evaluated under the rule of reason. Consider whether this distinction between vertical price and nonprice restrictions is a viable one. Consider whether it is based upon a solid rationale. Can you state that rationale?

5. Commentators since *Sylvania* have suggested various approaches to applying its rule of reason to nonprice vertical restraints. One view favors the application of market, product, and entry barrier criteria, as in a § 2 monopoly case. *See* Chapter 9. Eugene F. Zelek, Louis W. Stern & Thomas W. Dunfee, *A Rule of Reason Decision Model After* Sylvania, 68 CAL. L. REV. 13, 31-36 (1980). An alternative view urges an approach that places the burden of justifying the restraint on the manufacturer, *see* Note, *A Criticism of the Post-*Sylvania *Decisions and a Proposal to Make the Rule of Reason Reasonable Again*, 1980 UTAH L. REV. 795.

6. *Sylvania* allows vertical nonprice restrictions to be evaluated under the rule of reason because the Court relied on a body of economic and legal analysis holding that vertical nonprice restrictions stimulated interbrand competition, Note 7, page 163, *supra*. From this theoretical perspective, nonprice restrictions—such as limitations upon the territories in which a dealer is permitted to sell, or the customers to whom the dealer is permitted to sell, or the location at which the dealer must be located—force the dealers to exert all of their promotional and sales efforts within the geographical area and/or customer class allocated to them. They are thus forced to search out the marginal sale available within their assigned area and thus to cultivate that assigned area to the fullest.

Moreover, the manufacturer (or supplier), by confining each dealer to a specific area and/or customer class prevents the manufacturer's dealers from expending their sales efforts in competition with each other, and forces them to exert their efforts to take sales away from dealers handling rival brands. The interests of the White Motor Company, for example, are not furthered when its dealers struggle to take sales away from each other, since whichever dealer makes the sale, the White Motor Company only sells one more truck. But White does gain when one of its dealers takes a sale away from a dealer selling another brand. In the latter case, White (the manufacturer) has gained an additional sale.

Again, when there is only one dealer in a given area, that dealer profits from enhancements in the reputation of the brand, because that dealer is the only source from which that brand can be obtained. That dealer's incentive to promote the manufacturer's brand (through sales efforts, promotions, providing good service to customers, etc.) is maximized. Conversely, when there are several (or many) dealers in an area, the incentive of any one dealer to promote the particular brand is diminished, because that dealer will share only partially in any enhancement of the brand's reputation. The more dealers in the same brand who compete in the same area, the less benefit will any one dealer receive from its efforts in promoting the brand. The other dealers will capture the benefit of much of its effort, since they can offer the same brand to the same customers. In the situation described, the other dealers who benefit from the first dealer's efforts and expenditures in promoting the brand are often called "free riders," because they benefit from efforts and expenditures made by someone else. Indeed, the free-riding dealers are assisted in undercutting the dealer who engaged in brand-promoting activities, because they have not incurred the latter's promotional costs. The elimination of free-riding, therefore, carries the potential of stimulating the incentives of dealers to engage in brand promoting activities.

The factors identified above suggest that in many cases the elimination of competition among dealers carrying the same brand, *i.e.,* the elimination of intrabrand competition, is likely to enhance the effectiveness of a manufacturer's distribution system. The dealers are more likely to direct their efforts to taking sales away from sellers of rival brands and are more likely to engage in brand promotion. A distribution system restricted in the manner described, accordingly, is often a cost-effective (or efficient) way for a manufacturer to increase its sales.

Note that as a manufacturer becomes more effective in selling its brand, competition among manufacturers is intensified. Since the cost-effectiveness of a manufacturer's distribution system is one aspect of its overall efficiency, the more cost-effective is the manufacturer's distribution system, the more efficient is that manufacturer's entire operation. Since the goal of the antitrust laws is to further efficiency, there can be little doubt that enhancement of the cost-effectiveness of a manufacturer's distribution system furthers antitrust goals.

7. Given these factors favoring limited antitrust scrutiny under rule of reason analysis for nonprice vertical restraints, should the scope of the *per se* rule against vertical minimum and maximum resale price maintenance be revised or withdrawn? Should *Dr. Miles* be overruled? This issue remains disputed. Many of the same economic arguments are used to justify both vertical price and nonprice restraints. *See* Notes 2 and 6, *supra*. Turner notes that one material difference between price and nonprice restraints is that price restraints lack the efficiency enhancing possibility of scale economies. Donald F. Turner, *The Durability, Relevance, and Future of American Antitrust Policy*, 75 CAL. L. REV. 797, 804 (1987).

Recall that the majority opinion in *Sylvania* cites with approval Justice Brennan's concurring opinion in *White Motor* as follows:

> Resale price maintenance is not designed to, but almost invariably does in fact, reduce price competition not only *among* sellers of the affected product, but quite as much *between* that product and competing brands.

433 U.S. at 51, n.18.

Judge Bork, in his commentary on the *Sylvania* case also considers this quotation as follows:

> Mr. Justice Brennan's observation is an accurate description of resale price maintenance but does not distinguish that restraint from vertical

> market division. The purpose of both vertical price and nonprice restraints is to allow a higher price to induce additional activity and to compensate for its costs. Both . . . have an effect in the same direction on price competition with other brands. Nor is there reason to doubt that the net effect of each restraint is, despite formal differences, beneficial.
>
> Industry-wide use of resale price maintenance might facilitate cartelization, but it is not likely and is easily detected if it should occur.

Robert H. Bork, *Vertical Restraints:* Schwinn *Overruled*, 1977 SUP. CT. REV. 171, 190.

The *per se* treatment of vertical price restraints remains controversial. In the *Monsanto* case, below, the government filed an amicus brief that contended that resale price maintenance should no longer be treated as a *per se* offense. Congress responded just prior to oral argument by attaching a rider to the appropriation bill for the Department of Justice forbidding the Department from presenting this argument in open court. Departments of Commerce, Justice, and State, the Judiciary and Related Agencies Appropriation Act of 1984, Pub. L. No 98-166, § 510, 97 Stat. 1071, 1102-03 (1983). *See also* Robert A. Pitofsky, *In Defense of Discounters: The No-Frills Case for a Per Se Rule Against Vertical Price Fixing*, 71 GEO. L.J. 1487 (1983).

A former Antitrust Division head argues for retaining the *per se* rule for vertical price arrangements on practical, rather than theoretical grounds as follows:

> The basic reason the *per se* rule continues to be accepted is that those . . . who would argue against it, have not made their case outside of an economics laboratory. My concern is that most of what I have seen in the resale price fixing area are situations in which either initially or eventually most resale price maintenance schemes are hatched, nurtured, or preserved by the retailers in a cartel-like manner. That is the reality.

Sanford M. Litvack, *The Future Viability of the Current Antitrust Treatment of Vertical Restraints*, 75 CAL. L. REV. 955, 956-57 (1987). *See also* M.B. Lewis, *Restraints Under* Schwinn *and* Sylvania: *An Argument for the Continued Use of a Partial Per Se Approach*, 75 MICH. L. REV. 175 (1976).

Consider whether the shift in analytical emphasis to intrabrand competition set out below, tends to favor or undercut the argument over the reversal of *Dr. Miles*?

8. The determination of appropriate antitrust policy toward price and nonprice vertical restraints remains a contested issue as the doctrinal basis of *Sylvania* is reviewed and subjected to empirical testing. As the literature that is summarized below suggests, *Sylvania*'s emphasis on interbrand competition may incorporate implicit assumptions of perfect competition at the distributor level. When this assumption is addressed and imperfectly competitive modes of competition at the distributor level are considered as alternative possibilities, the scope of the conclusion reached by the analysis in Note 5, above, becomes an issue. The fragmentary empirical evidence that is available, also questions the conclusion of *Sylvania* that vertical restraints can never reduce allocative efficiency.

The *Sylvania* opinion is unequivocal in elevating interbrand competition as the central issue in vertical restraint analysis as follows:

> Interbrand competition . . . is the primary concern of antitrust law . . . when interbrand competition exists . . . it provides a significant check on the exploitation of intrabrand market power because of the ability of consumers to substitute a different brand of the same product.

433 U.S. at 52 n.19.

One theme of the current review is the reexamination of the relationship between a manufacturer and its distributors. This had led to the conclusion that it is one of substantially greater complexity than previously perceived. This perspective has led in turn to a reconsideration of the nature of intrabrand competition. As one commentator views the relationship: "Once we leave 'unilateral' action by the supplier, we encounter a seamless web of possible forms of interaction between the supplier and its resellers." Wesley J. Liebeler, *Intrabrand 'Cartels' under* GTE Sylvania, 30 UCLA L. REV. 1, 9 (1982). Another commentator has characterized this relationship as a:

> . . . subtle context in which the effects of alternative bargains between manufacturer and retailer are determined. A policy change . . . will have consequences for both intrabrand and interbrand competition—consequences that vary from product to product, depending on the cost structures of the retailers, the dimensions of nonprice rivalry available to them, and all structural conditions of the manufacturers' market that determine the extent and character of interbrand competition.

Richard E. Caves, *Vertical Restraints in Manufacturer-Distributor Relations, in* ANTITRUST AND REGULATION 29, 46 (R. Grieson ed. 1986).

A further consequence of this revised perception of the manufacturer-supplier relationship has been a refinement of the free rider analysis. Thus, a commentator identifies vertical restraints more broadly as a method of inducing service by retailers to manufacturers, instead of to retail customers, finds that the package of retailing services provides: ". . . [A] plausible efficiency rationale . . . *even broader* than the usual free-rider argument suggests." Victor P. Goldberg, *The Free Rider Problem, Imperfect Pricing, and the Economics of Retailing Services*, 79 NW. U. L. REV. 736, 756 (1984). Other commentators have added to the analysis by recognizing the existence of contracts in the implementation of vertical restraints. This work underscores the power of termination of that contract as a factor in its function, as follows:

> The standard economic analysis of vertical restraints is fundamentally flawed. Vertical restraints, by themselves, do not create a direct incentive for retailers to supply desired services. Consider the standard case of a retailer free riding on other retailers' product demonstrations. Even

> if the manufacturer fixes the retail price and does not permit price competition, retailers still have an incentive to free ride by providing non-price services that are not desired by the manufacturer, but are of value to consumers. . . . [F]ree-riding retailers of personal computers could encourage consumers to obtain a product demonstration from a full-service retailer before purchasing the product from them with, say, lower priced-tied accessories. . . . [R]etailers may merely take the additional money created by the vertical restraint and continue to free ride.
>
> * * *
>
> . . . In the real world . . . a manufacturer-dealer distribution agreement is made under . . . contracts, where . . . the dealer derive(s) at least part of their motivation by the threat of termination.

Benjamin Klein & Benjamin M. Murphy, *Vertical Restraints as Contract Enforcement Mechanisms*, 31 J.L. & ECON. 265, 266, 295 (1988). Both commentators, however, accept the conclusion of the standard *Sylvania*, analysis, namely that vertical restraints are, absent collusion, efficiency enhancing.

9. Footnote 19 of Justice Powell's majority opinion explains the economic assumptions about the relationship of intrabrand competition to interbrand competition as follows:

> The degree of intrabrand competition is wholly independent of the level of interbrand competition confronting the manufacturer. Thus, there may be fierce intrabrand competition among the distributors of a product produced by a monopolist and no intrabrand competition among the distributors of a product produced by a firm in a highly competitive industry. But when interbrand competition exists, as it does among television manufacturers, it provides a significant check on the exploitation of intrabrand market power because of the ability of consumers to substitute a different brand of the same product.

433 U.S. at 52, n.19. Can you reconcile the first sentence of this paragraph with the last sentence?

More recently a basic premise of the *Sylvania* analysis has been subjected to criticism as follows.

> It is the long standing but deeply flawed assumption that in the absence of a cartel the markets downstream from the manufacturer are close enough to being inert and perfectly competitive that they can be safely eliminated from economic models of consumer goods industries.

Robert L. Steiner, *Intrabrand Competition—Stepchild of Antitrust*, 36 ANTITRUST BULL. 155, 200 (1991). Steiner models circumstances that take account of the effect of vertical restraints on industry output, costs, and profit margins at both the manufacturing and distribution levels. His conclusion is as follows:

> If on the industry level inter- and intrabrand competition are negatively associated, the adoption of vertical restraints will stimulate interbrand competition among manufacturers and reduce average factory prices. But the restraints may produce an even greater increase in average dollar retail gross margins, leading to higher retail prices and a fall in consumer surplus and probably in . . . [industry] surplus, as well. Longer term, the restraints have often sheltered an anachronistic, high-cost group of retailers against the entry of new and more efficient types of distributors. They have also tended to delay the transition to a more efficient vertical allocation of functions in the industry. Hence, there is no a priori basis for the almost universal assumption by the courts and in the economics and legal literature that sacrificing interbrand competition is a welfare-enhancing trade-off.

Id. at 177.

Testing his hypothesis empirically, Steiner reports that in the toy industry as intrabrand competition became more vigorous, there were higher margins at the manufacturing level as well as reduced distribution costs that were passed along to the consumer in the form of lower prices. *Id.* at 185. In the blue jean industry, an FTC Consent Order generated increased intrabrand competition that led, in turn, to increased interbrand competition. *Id.* at 188. Steiner accepts the outcome in *Sylvania*, noting that the restraints did serve to enhance efficiency for a low market share manufacturer. *Id.* at 179.

Steiner has described the relationship between intrabrand and interbrand competition as follows:

> The strength of interbrand competition among manufacturers governs their margins. But even the most vigorous sort of interbrand competition among manufacturers does not discipline retailers' margins when intrabrand competition is free—much less when it is restrained. Generally, it is the onset of intrabrand competition that *first* forces down the margins and prices of well-known brands. *Then*, interbrand competition—primarily within stores rather than between them—depresses the price of competing goods.
>
> There is . . . often . . . a negative correlation between the vigor of interbrand competition in an industry's manufacturing segment and that of intrabrand competition in its retailing segment. The markets downstream from the final consumer goods manufacturer are sizeable. Consequently, when this inverse relationship holds, there is no basis for a sweeping generalization that the net welfare effect of stifling intrabrand competition and stimulating interbrand competition will be favorable.

Robert L. Steiner, Sylvania *Economics—A Critique*, 60 ANTITRUST L.J. 41, 44-45 (1991). To the extent there may be validity to Steiner's analysis, how should the antitrust scrutiny of vertical restraints be modified? What criteria would this analysis provide that would enable a court to distinguish an efficiency enhancing use from one that was not, under rule of reason analysis?

10. Early in the twentieth century syrup manufacturers, Coca Cola and others, licensed their trademarks to bottlers under related vertical restraint, territorial and customer restrictions. Such arrangements became standard in the industry. In two cases, *Coca Cola Co.*, 91 F.T.C. 517 and *Pepsico, Inc.*, 91 F.T.C. 680 (1978), *vacated and remanded for dismissal*, 642 F.2d 1387 (D.C. Cir. 1978), the FTC ordered the companies to cease imposing territorial restraints and customer restrictions. The FTC had begun that case under the assumptions of the *Schwinn* case. The Congress rejected the FTC position by enacting the Soft Drink and Interbrand Competition Act, now codified at 15 U.S.C. §§ 3501-03, which became effective in 1980.

A commentator has noted that changes in the technology of bottling and accompanying changes in the marketing of soft drinks had diminished the significance of territorial and customer restrictions as follows:

> Whatever the benefits of territorial restrictions to syrup manufacturers in an earlier era, they have certainly diminished with time.
>
> . . . [T]he coming of national advertising media . . . shifted much of the comparative advantage in sales promotion from the local bottler to the national franchisor.
>
> . . . [T]he costs resulting from territorial restrictions have increased over time. Economies of scale in soft drink bottling (and now canning) have become more important because of technological advances and improvements in the nation's transportation system since bottling territories were originally allocated. The result is that many bottlers are confined to territories in which demand is too small to enable them to produce at an efficient rate of output.
>
> . . . [I]t is clear that a large majority of soft drink bottlers are below minimum efficient size. And territorial restrictions . . . prevent bottlers from growing to minimum efficient size by expanding the size of . . . [their] market area.

Robert Larner, *The Economics of Territorial Restrictions in the Soft Drink Industry*, 22 ANTITRUST BULL. 145, 152-53 (1977). Other commentators supported the Commission's finding of illegality on economic grounds. *See* Louis Stern, Eugene F. Zelek & Thomas W. Dunfee, *A Rule of Reason Analysis of Territorial Restrictions in the Soft Drink Industry*, 27 ANTITRUST BULL. 481, 514 (1982).

An invalidation of the territorial provisions on antitrust grounds would, in the circumstances of the soft drink industry, have facilitated the reorganization of that industry on more efficient lines. To the extent that the soft drink syrup producers were bound by contractual provisions entered into in a time of different technology and which the bottlers were unwilling to alter, antitrust laws could have been the means for a needed restructuring.

11. The *Sylvania* price/nonprice distinction poses definitional problems in application. Most cases involving the validity of vertical restraints are brought by dealers or distributors who have been terminated by their suppliers. If an ex-dealer is able to make the claim that its termination was the result of a price-fixing agreement, the terminated dealer can prove its antitrust claim under a theory of *per se* liability. In such a case, the terminated dealer wins if it can show the existence of a price-fixing agreement and that its termination was due to the parties implementing that price-fixing agreement. In a typical case, the plaintiff terminated dealer would claim that its supplier had agreed with other dealers on the resale prices that dealers would charge. It would further allege that it, *viz.*, the terminated dealer, had been undercutting the fixed resale price—thereby undermining the price-fixing agreement—and as a result the supplier had agreed with one or more of the other dealers to terminate the plaintiff. In such circumstances, the supplier's termination of the plaintiff would be seen as part of a larger agreement to fix resale prices.

On the other hand, for a terminated dealer to prevail in the absence of a price-fixing agreement, it would have to prove a rule of reason case. Proof of a rule of reason case usually requires the plaintiff to establish that the restraints which it is challenging reduced output in the interbrand market. Output is almost never reduced when a manufacturer or supplier terminates a particular dealer, because the manufacturer is probably terminating the dealer in order to replace it with a more effective dealer, *i.e.*, one who shows promise of increasing the sales of the manufacturer's product. Also, the presence or absence of a single dealer of a particular manufacturer is generally unlikely to affect the amount of goods sold on the interbrand market in which the goods of all manufacturers are sold.

12. As indicated previously, because it is easier to prove a *per se* case than a rule of reason case, a terminated dealer has an incentive to characterize the events surrounding its termination in such a way as to bring it within a *per se* rule. *Sylvania* produced a spate of litigation in which disputes between manufacturers and dealers that had been terminated were brought as price-fixing cases. The Supreme Court ultimately addressed this issue in *Monsanto*, the case following. As an example of this problem, consider *Cernuto, Inc. v. United Cabinet Corp.*, 595 F.2d 164 (3d Cir. 1979), a case decided shortly after the Supreme Court's decision in *Sylvania*.

Although another panel of the Third Circuit repudiated the analysis of *Cernuto* the following year in *Edward J. Sweeney & Sons v. Texaco*, 637 F.2d 105, 111 (3d Cir. 1980), other circuits had already adopted it, *e.g.*, *Bostick Oil Co. v. Michelin Tire Corp.*, 702 F.2d 1207, 1213-15 (4th Cir. 1983), and the Seventh Circuit in the *Monsanto* case below, *Spray-Rite Service Corp. v. Monsanto Co.*, 684 F.2d 1226, 1238 (7th Cir. 1982). For a full listing of lower court cases, see footnote 5 in the *Monsanto* opinion below.

In *Cernuto, Inc. v. United Cabinet Corp.*, 595 F.2d 164 (3d Cir. 1979), plaintiff, Cernuto, Inc. (Cernuto) was a seller in Western Pennsylvania of kitchen cabinets. Beginning in March, 1974, United Cabinet Corporation (United) agreed to supply Cernuto with United cabinets for at least a two-year period. Three months after entering into this agreement United informed Cernuto that United would cease supplying the cabinets. Plaintiff Cernuto alleged that Famous Furnace & Supply Co. (Famous), a retail store selling United cabinets in the same competitive area as Cernuto, complained to United about Cernuto's low prices which were undercutting those of Famous.

Cernuto convinced the court to reverse the district court's entry of summary judgment for the defendant on the ground that Cernuto had adequate evidence to recover on a *per se* theory. Thus, under this view, Cernuto's inability to prove a lessening of competition in the general (interbrand) market was irrelevant. In so contending, Cernuto proceeded on two prongs: First, Cernuto successfully contended, when the manufacturer terminated Cernuto at the request of Famous, a rival, the agreement should be treated as a "horizontal" agreement (and therefore more suspect) than a "vertical" agreement, which under *Sylvania* is *prima facie* entitled to rule of reason evaluation. Second, Cernuto convinced the court that its termination should be viewed as having been done pursuant to a price-fixing agreement:

> Two of the most crucial differences between the conduct under consideration here and other accepted manufacturer actions are, upon analysis, readily apparent. When a manufacturer acts on its own, in pursuing its own market strategy, it is seeking to compete with other manufacturers by imposing what may be defended as reasonable vertical restraints. This would appear to be the rationale of the *GTE Sylvania* decision. However, if the action of a manufacturer or other supplier is taken at the direction of its customer, the restraint becomes primarily horizontal in nature in that one customer is seeking to suppress its competition by utilizing the power of a common supplier. Therefore, although the termination in such a situation is, itself, a vertical restraint, the desired impact is horizontal and on the dealer, not the manufacturer, level.
>
> . . . So here, if United . . . acted at Famous' direction, both the purpose and effect of the termination was to eliminate competition at the retail level, and not, as in *GTE Sylvania*, to promote competition at the manufacturer level. Accordingly, the pro-competitive redeeming virtues so critical in *GTE Sylvania* may not be present here.
>
> Equally important, the motivating factor in Famous' efforts and therefore the resulting conspiracy was, at least according to Cernuto's theory of the case, price. The pre-eminence of price considerations in antitrust law was summarized recently by Justice Stevens:

> "Price is the 'central nervous system of the economy,' and an agreement that 'interfere[s] with the setting of price by free market forces' is illegal on its face."

It is true that the alleged combination in the case at hand did not set prices at an exact level. But such a traditional conspiracy is not a *sine qua non* of a *per se* violation of the Act under the price-fixing rubric. If the purpose and effect of the challenged conduct is to restrain price movement and the free play of market forces, it is then illegal *per se*. As the Supreme Court stated in the celebrated price-fixing case, *United States v. Socony-Vacuum Oil Co.*:

> "Any combination which tampers with price structures is engaged in an unlawful activity. Even though the members of the price-fixing group were in no position to control the market, to the extent that they . . . stabilized prices they would be directly interfering with the free play of market forces."

Cernuto's pretrial narrative statement points to the centrality of price in the combination of Famous, . . . , and United to cut off plaintiff. The thrust of Famous' communication to United, it is alleged, was "that [Cernuto] was selling United products in Famous' territory and that [Cernuto] was a low price volume dealer." Cernuto is a "discount house," and, it must be presumed, was prepared to sell United cabinets at prices lower than those offered by Famous. Famous' concern, understandably, was that Cernuto's low prices would force Famous' own prices down if it were to compete effectively in selling United cabinets. By prevailing upon United . . . to terminate their contract with Cernuto, Famous effectively eliminated the threatened competition and was able to maintain prices at its own preferred levels. It is just this type of conduct that the antitrust laws were designed to reach.

595 F.2d at 168-69.

Do you agree with the Third Circuit's analysis in the *Cernuto* case? To what extent do you believe that the *Cernuto* decision undermines (or is consistent with) the policy goals of *Sylvania*? Certainly, *Cernuto* emphasizes the importance of the *Sylvania* distinction between price restraints and nonprice restraints. *Cernuto*—and cases like *Cernuto*—strengthened the incentive of terminated dealers to cast antitrust complaints in a form in which the termination is the result of a price-fixing agreement. As noted below, the success of such strategies, however, would turn on the way price-fixing behavior is understood.

When a manufacturer establishes a limited distribution system involving only one or a few dealers in a geographical area, the manufacturer is opting to eliminate or reduce intrabrand competition in order to stimulate brand-promoting behavior by its dealers. The elimination or reduction of intrabrand competition does reduce the downward pressure on the price of the brand offered to ultimate consumers. True, the brand is constrained by interbrand competition, but—within those constraints—any purely brand premium which consumers are willing to pay for the brand over other competing brands is captured in full or in part in the ultimate sales price. It is not eroded away, as it would be if intrabrand competition were permitted. Thus, an argument can be made that the maintenance of a restricted distribution system in itself helps to maintain (brand) prices. When a manufacturer terminates a dealer because the dealer's behavior has threatened in one way or another the integrity of a restricted distribution system, the termination could be viewed as incident to a system of price-maintenance or price-fixing, broadly defined.

Perhaps because decisions like *Cernuto* raised the possibility that many dealer terminations could be described as connected with price-fixing agreements under a broad definition of price-fixing, those decisions threatened the policy goal of *Sylvania*—which was to afford wide flexibility to manufacturers to establish restricted distribution systems, under the rationale (set forth above) that such flexibility furthered interbrand competition. Consider the extent to which the following cases can properly be understood as efforts by the Court to maintain the effectiveness of the *Sylvania* policies. Consider the extent to which these decisions undermine *Dr. Miles*.

Monsanto Co. v. Spray-Rite Service Corp.

465 U.S. 752 (1984)

Justice Powell delivered the opinion of the Court.

This case presents a question as to the standard of proof required to find a vertical price-fixing conspiracy in violation of Section 1 of the Sherman Act.

I

Petitioner Monsanto Company manufactures chemical products, including agricultural herbicides. By the late 1960s, the time at issue in this case, its sales accounted for approximately 15% of the corn herbicide market and 3% of the soybean herbicide market. In the corn herbicide market, the market leader commanded a 70% share. In the soybean herbicide market, two other competitors each had between 30% and 40% of the market. Respondent Spray-Rite Service Corporation was engaged in the wholesale distribution of agricultural chemicals from 1955 to 1972. . . . Spray-Rite was a discount operation, buying in large quantities and selling at a low margin.

Spray-Rite was an authorized distributor of Monsanto herbicides from 1957 to 1968. In October 1967, Monsanto announced that it would appoint distributors for one-year terms, and that it would renew distributorships according to several new criteria. Among the criteria were: (i) whether the distributor's primary activity was soliciting sales to retail dealers; (ii) whether the distributor employed trained salesmen capable of educating its customers on the technical aspects of Monsanto's herbicides; and (iii) whether the distributor could be expected "to exploit fully" the market in its geographical area of primary responsibility. Shortly thereafter, Monsanto also introduced a number of incentive programs, such as making cash payments to distributors that sent salesmen to training classes, and providing free deliveries of products to customers within a distributor's area of primary responsibility.

In October 1968, Monsanto declined to renew Spray-Rite's distributorship. At that time, Spray-Rite was the tenth largest out of approximately 100 distributors of Monsanto's primary corn herbicide. Ninety percent of Spray-Rite's sales volume was devoted to herbicide sales, and 16% of its sales were of Monsanto products. After Monsanto's termination, Spray-Rite continued as a herbicide dealer until 1972. It was able to purchase some of Monsanto's products from other distributors, but not as much as it desired or as early in the season as it needed. . . . Spray-Rite brought this action under Section 1 of the Sherman Act. . . . It alleged that Monsanto and some of its distributors conspired to fix the resale prices of Monsanto herbicides. Its complaint further alleged that Monsanto terminated Spray-Rite's distributorship, adopted compensation programs and shipping policies, and encouraged distributors to boycott Spray-Rite in furtherance of this conspiracy. Monsanto denied the allegations of conspiracy, and asserted that Spray-Rite's distributorship had been terminated because of its failure to hire trained salesmen and promote sales to dealers adequately.

The case was tried to a jury. The District Court instructed the jury that Monsanto's conduct was *per se* unlawful if it was in furtherance of a conspiracy to fix prices. In answers to special interrogatories, the jury found that (i) the termination of Spray-Rite was pursuant to a conspiracy between Monsanto and one or more of its distributors to set resale prices . . . . The jury awarded $3.5 million in damages, which was trebled to $10.5 million. Only the first of the jury's findings is before us today.

The Court of Appeals for the Seventh Circuit affirmed. . . . It held that there was sufficient evidence to satisfy Spray-Rite's burden of proving a conspiracy to set resale prices. The court stated that "proof of termination following competitor complaints is sufficient to support an inference of concerted action." . . . Canvassing the testimony and exhibits that were before the jury, the court found evidence of numerous complaints from competing Monsanto distributors about Spray-Rite's price-cutting practices. It also noted that there was testimony that a Monsanto official had said that Spray-Rite was terminated because of the price complaints.

In substance, the Court of Appeals held that an antitrust plaintiff can survive a motion for a directed verdict if it shows that a manufacturer terminated a price-cutting distributor in response to or following complaints by other distributors. This view brought the Seventh Circuit into direct conflict with a number of other Courts of Appeals. We granted *certiorari* to resolve the conflict. . . . We reject the statement by the Court of Appeals for the Seventh Circuit of the standard of proof required to submit a case to the jury in distributor-termination litigation, but affirm the judgment under the standard we announce today.

. . . .

II

This Court has drawn two important distinctions that are at the center of this and any other distributor-termination case. First, there is the basic distinction between concerted and independent action—a distinction not always clearly drawn by parties and courts. Section 1 of the Sherman Act requires that there be a "contract, combination . . . or conspiracy" between the manufacturer and other distributors in order to establish a violation. . . . Independent action is not proscribed. A manufacturer of course generally has a right to deal, or refuse to deal, with whomever it likes, as long as it does so independently. *United States v. Colgate & Co.*, 250 U.S. 300, 307 (1919); *cf.*, *United States v. Parke, Davis & Co.*, 362 U.S.

29 (1960). Under *Colgate*, the manufacturer can announce its resale prices in advance and refuse to deal with those who fail to comply. And a distributor is free to acquiesce in the manufacturer's demand in order to avoid termination.

The second important distinction in distributor-termination cases is that between concerted action to set prices and concerted action on nonprice restrictions. The former have been *per se* illegal since the early years of national antitrust enforcement. *See Dr. Miles Medical Co. v. John D. Park & Sons Co.*, 220 U.S. 373, 404-409 (1911). The latter are judged under the rule of reason, which requires a weighing of the relevant circumstances of a case to decide whether a restrictive practice constitutes an unreasonable restraint on competition. *See Continental T.V., Inc. v. GTE Sylvania Inc.*, 433 U.S. 36 (1977).[7]

While these distinctions in theory are reasonably clear, often they are difficult to apply in practice. In *Sylvania* we emphasized that the legality of arguably anticompetitive conduct should be judged primarily by its "market impact." . . . But the economic effect of all of the conduct described above—unilateral and concerted vertical price-setting, agreements on price and nonprice restrictions—is in many, but not all, cases similar or identical. *See, e.g., Parke, Davis, supra*, at 44; n.7 *supra*. And judged from a distance, the conduct of the parties in the various situations can be indistinguishable. For example, the fact that a manufacturer and its distributors are in constant communication about prices and marketing strategy does not alone show that the distributors are not making independent pricing decisions. A manufacturer and its distributors have legitimate reasons to exchange information about the prices and the reception of their products in the market. Moreover, it is precisely in cases in which the manufacturer attempts to further a particular marketing strategy by means of agreements on often costly nonprice restrictions that it will have the most interest in the distributors' resale prices. The manufacturer often will want to ensure that its distributors earn sufficient profit to pay for programs such as hiring and training additional salesmen or demonstrating the technical features of the product, and will want to see that "free-riders" do not interfere. . . . Thus, the manufacturer's strongly felt concern about resale prices does not necessarily mean that it has done more than the *Colgate* doctrine allows.

Nevertheless, it is of considerable importance that independent action by the manufacturer, and concerted action on nonprice restrictions, be distinguished from price-fixing agreements, since under present law the latter are subject to *per se* treatment and treble damages. On a claim of concerted price-fixing, the antitrust plaintiff must present evidence sufficient to carry its burden of proving that there was such an agreement. If an inference of such an agreement may be drawn from highly ambiguous evidence, there is a considerable danger that the doctrines enunciated in *Sylvania* and *Colgate* will be seriously eroded.

---

[7] The Solicitor General (by brief only) and several other *amici* suggest that we take this opportunity to reconsider whether "contract[s], combination[s] . . . or conspirac[ies]" to fix resale prices should always be unlawful. They argue that the economic effect of resale price maintenance is little different from agreements on nonprice restrictions. . . . They say that the economic objections to resale price maintenance that we discussed in *Sylvania*, . . .—such as that it facilitates horizontal cartels—can be met easily in the context of rule-of-reason analysis.

Certainly in this case we have no occasion to consider the merits of this argument. This case was tried on *per se* instructions to the jury. Neither party argued in the District Court that the rule of reason should apply to a vertical price-fixing conspiracy, nor raised the point on appeal. In fact, neither party before this Court presses the argument advanced by *amici*. We therefore decline to reach the question, and we decide the case in the context in which it was decided below and argued here.

The flaw in the evidentiary standard adopted by the Court of Appeals in this case is that it disregards this danger. Permitting an agreement to be inferred merely from the existence of complaints, or even from the fact that termination came about "in response to" complaints, could deter or penalize perfectly legitimate conduct. As Monsanto points out, complaints about price-cutters "are natural—and from the manufacturer's perspective, unavoidable—reactions by distributors to the activities of their rivals." Such complaints, particularly where the manufacturer has imposed a costly set of nonprice restrictions, "arise in the normal course of business and do not indicate illegal concerted action." . . . Moreover, distributors are an important source of information for manufacturers. In order to assure an efficient distribution system, manufacturers and distributors constantly must coordinate their activities to assure that their product will reach the consumer persuasively and efficiently. To bar a manufacturer from acting solely because the information upon which it acts originated as a price complaint would create an irrational dislocation in the market. . . .

Thus, something more than evidence of complaints is needed. There must be evidence that tends to exclude the possibility that the manufacturer and nonterminated distributors were acting independently. As Judge Aldisert has written, the antitrust plaintiff should present direct or circumstantial evidence that reasonably tends to prove that the manufacturer and others "had a conscious commitment to a common scheme designed to achieve an unlawful objective." *Edward J. Sweeney & Sons, supra*, at 111; *accord H.L. Moore Drug Exchange v. Eli Lilly & Co.*, 662 F.2d 935, 941 (2d Cir. 1981), *cert. denied*, 459 U.S. 880 (1982); *cf. American Tobacco Co. v. United States*, 328 U.S. 781, 810 (1946) (Circumstances must reveal "a unity of purpose or a common design and understanding, or a meeting of minds in an unlawful arrangement").[9]

III

A

Applying this standard to the facts of this case, we believe there was sufficient evidence for the jury reasonably to have concluded that Monsanto and some of its distributors were parties to an "agreement" or "conspiracy" to maintain resale prices and terminate price-cutters. In fact there was substantial direct evidence of agreements to maintain prices. There was testimony from a Monsanto district manager, for example, that Monsanto on at least two occasions in early 1969, about five months after Spray-Rite was terminated, approached price-cutting distributors and advised that if they did not maintain the suggested resale price, they would not receive adequate supplies of Monsanto's new corn herbicide. . . . When one of the distributors did not assent, this information was referred to the Monsanto regional office, and it complained to the distributor's parent company. There was evidence that the parent instructed its subsidiary to comply, and the distributor informed Monsanto that it would charge the suggested price. . . . Evidence of this kind plainly is relevant and persuasive as to a meeting of minds.

. . . .

[9] The concept of "a meeting of the minds" or "a common scheme" in a distributor-termination case includes more than a showing that the distributor conformed to the suggested price. It means as well that evidence must be presented both that the distributor communicated its acquiescence or agreement, and that this was sought by the manufacturer.

IV

We conclude that the Court of Appeals applied an incorrect standard to the evidence in this case. The correct standard is that there must be evidence that tends to exclude the possibility of independent action by the manufacturer and distributor. That is, there must be direct or circumstantial evidence that reasonably tends to prove that the manufacturer and others had a conscious commitment to a common scheme designed to achieve an unlawful objective. Under this standard, the evidence in this case created a jury issue as to whether Spray-Rite was terminated pursuant to a price-fixing conspiracy between Monsanto and its distributors. The judgment of the court below is affirmed.

It is so ordered.

COMMENTARY

1. Consider the expressed concerns underlying the Court's conspiracy ruling in *Monsanto*, particularly its reference to "highly ambiguous evidence" being presented to a jury. Was the Court concerned that significant nonmeritorious cases would reach juries under the approach of the court of appeals? Why could juries not be trusted to sort out the nonmeritorious cases from the meritorious ones? Are the manufacturer and the terminated dealer akin to warring spouses—in that truth is an early casualty?

Was the Court concerned that the approach of the court of appeals would inhibit socially beneficial communications between manufacturers and distributors, *e.g.*, limit access to distributors as a source of market information for manufacturers? Does the determination of what constitutes an agreement to fix prices under § 1 have the potential for creating causes of action grounded in garden variety differences between a manufacturer and a distributor that are only marginally related to price determination?

What standard of review of the evidence does *Monsanto* require of an appellate court reviewing a jury verdict in a dealer termination case? In *McCabe's Furniture, Inc. v. La-Z-Boy Chair Co.*, 798 F.2d 323 (8th Cir. 1986), the appellate court reversed a jury verdict for the plaintiff on insufficiency of the evidence. There was evidence in the record that manufacturer had discussions about price maintenance with the terminated dealer and others, but the manufacturer had also complained about low sales volume, failure to advertise and to properly display. In reversing, the majority stated:

> The distinction emphasized in *Monsanto* between *per se* and rule of reason legality . . . must turn ultimately on motive. . . . When faced with conflicting evidence, the jury must determine whether the nonprice justifications for the termination advanced by the defendant are legitimate or are mere pretext to disguise a *per se* illegal agreement with the nonterminated dealer to maintain resale prices. It is the court's duty under *Monsanto* to decide whether sufficient evidence was presented for a jury to make that determination.

Id. at 329. Is motive an element of a cause of action under § 1? Might the court better have written, "objective"?

2. Does *Monsanto* also address the definition of agreement for purposes of § 1? Did the Court in *Monsanto* consider the possible agreement to be a horizontal or a vertical agreement? Did the court in *Cernuto* consider a horizontal or vertical agreement? Given the perceived complexity of the manufacturer-dealer relationship noted in the recent literature, above, try to formulate a definition of "vertical" and of "horizontal" in this context. Was the court in the *Cernuto* case confused over the meanings of these terms?

Does the *Monsanto* decision unsettle *Colgate*? Commentators agree that the *Monsanto* decision reinvigorates the *Colgate* doctrine, *e.g.*, Terry Calvani & Michael L. Sibarium, *Antitrust Today; Maturity or Decline*, 35 ANTITRUST BULL. 123, 154 (1990). Note the language of the opinion that supports this conclusion. Should *Colgate* have been expressly overruled? One commentator who takes this position reasons as follows:

> . . . *Monsanto*'s preservation of the *Colgate* doctrine seems inappropriate. Wherever vertical restraints have undesirable economic effects suggesting illegality, there is no substantial reason for permitting a manufacturer to achieve the same results by threatening to terminate distributors who fail to comply with its announced restraint policy.

Donald F. Turner, *The Durability, Relevance, and Future of American Antitrust Policy*, 75 CAL. L. REV. 797, 804-5 (1987). Would overruling *Colgate* then shift the inquiry over the legality of a vertical restraint to a determination of whether acquiescence to a manufacturer's demand constituted an illegal agreement?

3. What effect does the *Monsanto* case have on the doctrine of combination (agreement) set forth in *Parke Davis* and *Albrecht*? Was a different view of the combination doctrine stated by the Eighth Circuit's opinion in *Russell Stover Candies*? Did the Supreme Court recently express a limit of the combination doctrine in its *Copperweld Corp. v. Independence Tube Corp.,* 467 U.S. 752 (1984), decision that withdrew coordinated activity between a parent and its wholly owned subsidiary from combination analysis? *See infra*, Chapter 8, page 347.

If you were to write a memorandum setting out the legal standard for a finding of agreement under § 1 in terms of *Colgate*, *Parke Davis*, footnote 6 of the now overruled *Albrecht* decision, and *Monsanto*, would you find these cases consistent? Explain.

What is a plaintiff's burden of proof when alleging agreement? Is it the same for an allegation of a horizontal and a vertical agreement? In *Matsushita Electric Industrial Co., Ltd. v. Zenith Radio Corp.*, 475 U.S. 574 (1986) (excerpted in Chapter 14), the Court seems to have adopted the *Monsanto* view for allegations of horizontal agreement when it stated:

> . . . [A]ntitrust law limits the range of permissible inferences from ambiguous evidence in a § 1 case. . . . To survive a motion for summary judgment . . . , a plaintiff must present evidence that tends to exclude the possibility that the alleged conspirators acted independently.

Id. at 588.

4. Can you explain how the doctrine announced in *Colgate* would be in danger of being seriously eroded under the approach of the court of appeals? Was the Court implying that unilateral behavior might be confused with vertical price-fixing agreements? Has unilateral behavior been so confused in past cases of which you have any knowledge? Does the *Albrecht* approach to combination create a danger of confusing unilateral behavior with concerted behavior? Was the Court sensitive to this danger in *Copperweld* (excerpted in Chapter 8)? Do you think that the Court's reaffirmation in *Copperweld* of the combination doctrine articulated in the now overruled *Albrecht* decision undercut its efforts in *Monsanto* to preserve the vigor of the *Colgate* doctrine?

5. What do you think would be the practical effects of the *Monsanto* opinion on the significance of the *Cernuto* case (Note 12, page 215, *supra*) as a precedent? Do you think that *Cernuto* was overruled by implication in *Monsanto*?

6. In the *Cernuto* case, was the manufacturer concerned about the level of distributor resale prices apart from its desire to keep one pre-existing distributor content? Was the manufacturer in *Colgate* so concerned? Does the phrasing of the Court's footnote 9 in *Monsanto* suggest that the manufacturer was concerned about the level of resale prices independently of the wishes of any particular distributor? Could the standard set forth in footnote 9 be used in a case like *Cernuto*? Does footnote 9 describe the evidence necessary to reach a jury on a claim of a price-fixing conspiracy when the contention is that a dissatisfied dealer has successfully persuaded a manufacturer to take action against a price-cutting distributor? How would you reword the evidentiary standard contained in footnote 9 so that it could be applied to a *Cernuto* type case where the impetus comes from a distributor?

7. In *Monsanto* the Court stated that the economic effects of *Colgate*-type unilateral action, nonprice vertical restraints, and vertical price-fixing agreements can be quite similar. Was the Court suggesting that the *per se* rule against vertical price-fixing agreements is an anomaly? In *Schwinn* (discussed on pages 199-202, *supra*) the court had distinguished between manufacturer-distributor agreements embodying territorial and customer restrictions, which were treated as *per se* illegal if the manufacturer sold its goods to distributors for resale, but were subjected to rule of reason evaluation if the manufacturer shipped its goods on consignment to the distributors. In *Sylvania* the Court ruled that this difference in legal treatment of transactions having similar economic effects could not be justified. Could the Court in *Monsanto* have been pointing to another set of legal distinctions which are not justified by the underlying economics. Has the Court laid the groundwork for the overruling of *Dr. Miles*, page 157, *supra*? Justice White had warned in his concurring opinion in *Sylvania*, page 204, *supra,* that the distinction between nonprice vertical restraints and vertical price-fixing might not be able to be maintained.

8. How radical a step would the overruling of *Dr. Miles* be? Would such an overruling give manufacturers a power which they have lacked since 1911? To what extent have manufacturers been able to control wholesale or retail prices since 1911? In answering this question, consider (i) the *Colgate* doctrine; (ii) the period of fair trade under the Miller-Tydings and McGuire Acts, pages 193-95, *supra* and (iii) the ability of manufacturers to control price to ultimate purchasers through consignment distribution, both before and after *Simpson v. Union Oil Co.*, page 195, *supra.*

Alvord-Polk, Inc. v. F. Schumacher & Co.

37 F.3d 996 (3d Cir. 1994)

[Consult the opinion set out in Chapter 4, page 144 and consider the following comments.]

COMMENTARY

1. Although the Court's ruling in *Monsanto* is designed to facilitate communication between a manufacturer and its distributors, *Alvord-Polk* indicates that it is still dangerous for a manufacturer to act upon information which it receives from its distributors when that information is communicated through a dealer organization.

2. The leading case involving a manufacturer joining a dealer conspiracy is *United States v. General Motors Corp.*, 384 U.S. 127 (1966). In that case, a number of so-called "discount houses" located in the Los Angeles area began offering to sell new cars to the public at allegedly bargain prices. Their sources of supply were franchised dealers. In meetings of the local Chevrolet Dealers Association, member dealers discussed the problem and resolved to bring it to the attention of General Motors officials. They flooded General Motors with hundreds of letters and telegrams. One General Motors official responded that the practices to which the dealers were objecting "in some instances represent the establishment of a second and unauthorized sales outlet or location contrary to the provisions of the General Motors Dealers Selling Agreements." General Motors officials then contacted the offending dealers and ordered them to terminate their relations with the discounters. Later General Motors cooperated with the Dealers Association in policing practices designed to ensure that all relations between dealers and the discounters had been terminated. Although the trial court ruled that General Motors had not participated in a conspiracy, the Supreme Court reversed. In sweeping language, the Court ruled that General Motors had, by cooperating with its dealers, engaged in a "classic conspiracy":

> We have here a classic conspiracy in restraint of trade: joint, collaborative action by dealers, the appellee associations, and General Motors to eliminate a class of competitors by terminating business dealings between them and a minority of Chevrolet dealers and to deprive franchised dealers of their freedom to deal through discounters if they so choose. Against this fact of unlawful combination, the "location clause" is of no avail. Whatever General Motors might or might not lawfully have done to enforce individual Dealer Selling Agreements by action within the borders of those agreements and the relationship which each defines, is beside the point. And, because the action taken constitutes a combination or conspiracy, it is not necessary to consider what might be the legitimate interest of a dealer in securing compliance by others with the "location clause," or the lawfulness of action a dealer might individually take to vindicate this interest.

384 U.S. at 140.

The *General Motors* case illustrates the difficulties faced by a manufacturer that wishes to police its distribution system and makes use of information supplied by dealers to do so.

3. In both *General Motors* and *Alvord-Polk*, the opinions suggest that the manufacturer could legitimately pursue its own economic interest, so long as it did not participate in a horizontal conspiracy established by its dealers. What are the criteria for determining when a manufacturer is merely using information furnished by or through a dealer association and when a manufacturer is participating in a dealer conspiracy? Is it a satisfactory answer to say that whether the manufacturer is acting unilaterally or has joined a dealer conspiracy is a question of fact for the jury?

Business Electronics Corp. v. Sharp Electronics Corp.

485 U.S. 717 (1988)

Justice SCALIA delivered the opinion of the Court.

Petitioner Business Electronics Corporation seeks review of a decision of the United States Court of Appeals for the Fifth Circuit holding that a vertical restraint is *per se* illegal under § 1 of the Sherman Act . . . only if there is an express or implied agreement to set resale prices at some level. . . . We granted *certiorari*, 482 U.S. ____ (1987), to resolve a conflict in the Courts of Appeals regarding the proper dividing line between the rule that vertical price restraints are illegal *per se* and the rule that vertical nonprice restraints are to be judged under the rule of reason.[1]

In 1968, petitioner became the exclusive retailer in the Houston, Texas area of electronic calculators manufactured by respondent Sharp Electronics Corporation. In 1972, respondent appointed Gilbert Hartwell as a second retailer in the Houston area. During the relevant period, electronic calculators were primarily sold to business customers for prices up to $1000. While much of the evidence in this case was conflicting—in particular, concerning whether petitioner was "free riding" on Hartwell's provision of presale educational and promotional services by providing inadequate services itself—a few facts are undisputed. Respondent published a list of suggested minimum retail prices, but its written dealership agreements with petitioner and Hartwell did not obligate either to observe them, or to charge any other specific price. Petitioner's retail prices were often below respondent's suggested retail prices and generally below Hartwell's retail prices, even though Hartwell too sometimes priced below respondent's suggested retail prices. Hartwell complained to respondent on a number of occasions about petitioner's prices. In June 1973, Hartwell gave respondent the ultimatum that Hartwell would terminate his dealership unless respondent ended its relationship with petitioner within 30 days. Respondent terminated petitioner's dealership in July 1973.

Petitioner brought suit in the United States District Court for the Southern District of Texas, alleging that respondent and Hartwell had conspired to terminate petitioner and that such conspiracy was illegal under § 1 of the Sherman Act. The case was tried to a jury. The District Court submitted a liability interrogatory to the jury that asked whether "there was an agreement or understanding between Sharp Electronics Corporation and Hartwell to terminate Business Electronics as a Sharp dealer because of Business Electronics' price cutting." Record, Doc. No. 241. The District Court instructed the jury at length about this question:

> "The Sherman Act is violated when a seller enters into an agreement or understanding with one of its dealers to terminate another dealer because of the other dealer's price cutting. Plaintiff contends that Sharp terminated Business Electronics in furtherance of Hartwell's desire to eliminate Business Electronics as a price-cutting rival.
>
> "If you find that there was an agreement between Sharp and Hartwell to terminate Business Electronics because of Business Electronics' price cutting, you should answer yes to Question Number 1.
>
> . . . .
>
> "A combination, agreement or understanding to terminate a dealer because of his price cutting unreasonably restrains trade and cannot be justified for any reason. Therefore, even though the combination, agreement or understanding may have been formed or engaged in . . . to eliminate any alleged evils of price cutting, it is still unlawful. . . .

---

[1] The Seventh, Eighth, and Tenth Circuits have agreed with the analysis of the Fifth. *See McCabe's Furniture, Inc. v. La-Z-Boy Chair Co.*, 798 F.2d 323, 329 (8th Cir. 1986), *cert. pending*, No. 86-1101; *Morrison v. Murray Biscuit Co.*, 797 F.2d 1430, 1440 (7th Cir. 1986); *Westman Comm'n Co. v. Hobart Int'l, Inc.*, 796 F.2d 1216, 1223-1224 (10th Cir. 1986), *cert. pending*, No. 86-484. Decisions of the Third and Ninth Circuits have disagreed. *See Cernuto, Inc. v. United Cabinet Corp.*, 595 F.2d 164, 168-170 (3rd Cir. 1979); *Zidell Explorations, Inc. v. Conval Int'l, Ltd.*, 719 F.2d 1465, 1469-1470 (9th Cir. 1983).

"If a dealer demands that a manufacturer terminate a price cutting dealer, and the manufacturer agrees to do so, the agreement is illegal if the manufacturer's purpose is to eliminate the price cutting." App. 18-19.

The jury answered Question 1 affirmatively and awarded $600,000 in damages. The District Court rejected respondent's motion for judgment notwithstanding the verdict or a new trial, holding that the jury interrogatory and instructions had properly stated the law. It entered judgment for petitioner for treble damages plus attorney's fees.

The Fifth Circuit reversed, holding that the jury interrogatory and instructions were erroneous, and remanded for a new trial. It held that, to render illegal *per se* a vertical agreement between a manufacturer and a dealer to terminate a second dealer, the first dealer "must expressly or impliedly agree to set its prices at some level, though not a specific one. The distributor cannot retain complete freedom to set whatever price it chooses."...

....

II

A

Section 1 of the Sherman Act provides that "[e]very contract, combination in the form of trust or otherwise, or conspiracy, in restraint of trade or commerce among the several States, or with foreign nations, is declared to be illegal." 15 U.S.C. § 1. Since the earliest decisions of this Court interpreting this provision, we have recognized that it was intended to prohibit only unreasonable restraints of trade.... Ordinarily, whether particular concerted action violates § 1 of the Sherman Act is determined through case-by-case application of the so-called rule of reason—that is, "the factfinder weighs all of the circumstances of a case in deciding whether a restrictive practice should be prohibited as imposing an unreasonable restraint on competition." ... Certain categories of agreements, however, have been held to be *per se* illegal, dispensing with the need for case-by-case evaluation. We have said that *per se* rules are appropriate only for "conduct that is manifestly anticompetitive," ... that is, conduct "that would always or almost always tend to restrict competition and decrease output." ...

Although vertical agreements on resale prices have been illegal *per se* since *Dr. Miles Medical Co. v. John D. Park & Sons Co.*, 220 U.S. 373 (1911), we have recognized that the scope of *per se* illegality should be narrow in the context of vertical restraints. In *Continental T.V., Inc. v. GTE Sylvania Inc.*, supra, we refused to extend *per se* illegality to vertical nonprice restraints, specifically to a manufacturer's termination of one dealer pursuant to an exclusive territory agreement with another. We noted that especially in the vertical restraint context "departure from the rule-of-reason standard must be based on demonstrable economic effect rather than ... upon formalistic line drawing." ... We concluded that vertical nonprice restraints had not been shown to have such a "'pernicious effect on competition'" and to be so "'lack[ing] [in] ... redeeming value'" as to justify *per se* illegality.... Rather, we found, they had real potential to stimulate interbrand competition, "the primary concern of antitrust law" ....

Moreover, we observed that a rule of *per se* illegality for vertical nonprice restraints was not needed or effective to protect intrabrand competition. First, so long as interbrand competition existed, that would provide a "significant check" on any attempt to exploit intrabrand market power.... In fact, in order to meet that interbrand competition, a manufacturer's dominant incentive is to lower resale prices.... Second, the *per se* illegality of vertical restraints would create a perverse incentive for manufacturers to integrate vertically into distribution, an outcome hardly conducive to fostering the creation and maintenance of small businesses. . . .

Finally, our opinion in *GTE Sylvania* noted a significant distinction between vertical nonprice and vertical price restraints. That is, there was support for the proposition that vertical price restraints reduce interbrand price competition because they "facilitate cartelizing." . . . The authorities cited by the Court suggested how vertical price agreements might assist horizontal price fixing at the manufacturer level (by reducing the manufacturer's incentive to cheat on a cartel, since its retailers could not pass on lower prices to consumers) or might be used to organize cartels at the retailer level. . . . Similar support for the cartel-facilitating effect of vertical nonprice restraints was and remains lacking.

We have been solicitous to assure that the market-freeing effect of our decision in *GTE Sylvania* is not frustrated by related legal rules. In *Monsanto Co. v. Spray-Rite Service Corp.*, 465 U.S. 752, 763 (1984), which addressed the evidentiary showing necessary to establish vertical concerted action, we expressed concern that "[i]f an inference of such an agreement may be drawn from highly ambiguous evidence, there is considerable danger that the doctrin[e] enunciated in *Sylvania* . . . will be seriously eroded." . . . We eschewed adoption of an evidentiary standard that "could deter or penalize perfectly legitimate conduct" or "would create an irrational dislocation in the market" by preventing legitimate communication between a manufacturer and its distributors. . . .

Our approach to the question presented in the present case is guided by the premises of *GTE Sylvania* and *Monsanto*: that there is a presumption in favor of a rule-of-reason standard; that departure from that standard must be justified by demonstrable economic effect, such as the facilitation of cartelizing, rather than formalistic distinctions; that interbrand competition is the primary concern of the antitrust laws; and that rules in this area should be formulated with a view towards protecting the doctrine of *GTE Sylvania*. These premises lead us to conclude that the line drawn by the Fifth Circuit is the most appropriate one.

There has been no showing here that an agreement between a manufacturer and a dealer to terminate a "price cutter," without a further agreement on the price or price levels to be charged by the remaining dealer, almost always tends to restrict competition and reduce output. Any assistance to cartelizing that such an agreement might provide cannot be distinguished from the sort of minimal assistance that might be provided by vertical nonprice agreements like the exclusive territory agreement in *GTE Sylvania*, and is insufficient to justify a *per se* rule. Cartels are neither easy to form nor easy to maintain. Uncertainty over the terms of the cartel, particularly the prices to be charged in the future, obstructs both formation and adherence by making cheating easier. . . . Without an agreement with the remaining dealer on price, the manufacturer both retains its incentive to cheat on any manufacturer-level cartel (since lower prices can still be passed on to consumers) and cannot as easily be used to organize and hold together a retailer-level cartel.[2]

The District Court's rule on the scope of *per se* illegality for vertical restraints would threaten to dismantle the doctrine of *GTE Sylvania*. Any agreement between a manufacturer

---

[2] The dissent's principal fear appears to be not cartelization at either level, but Hartwell's assertion of dominant retail power. This fear does not possibly justify adopting a rule of *per se* illegality. Retail market power is rare, because of the usual presence of interbrand competition and other dealers, *see Continental T.V., Inc. v. GTE Sylvania Inc.*, 433 U.S. 36 (1977), and it should therefore not be assumed but rather must be proved. *Cf.* Baxter, *The Viability of Vertical Restraints Doctrine*, 75 CALIF. L. REV. 933, 948-949 (1987). Of course this case was not prosecuted on the theory, and therefore the jury was not asked to find, that Hartwell possessed such market power.

and a dealer to terminate another dealer who happens to have charged lower prices can be alleged to have been directed against the terminated dealer's "price cutting." In the vast majority of cases, it will be extremely difficult for the manufacturer to convince a jury that its motivation was to ensure adequate services, since price cutting and some measure of service cutting usually go hand in hand. Accordingly, a manufacturer that agrees to give one dealer an exclusive territory and terminates another dealer pursuant to that agreement, or even a manufacturer that agrees with one dealer to terminate another for failure to provide contractually-obligated services, exposes itself to the highly plausible claim that its real motivation was to terminate a price cutter. Moreover, even vertical restraints that do not result in dealer termination, such as the initial granting of an exclusive territory or the requirement that certain services be provided, can be attacked as designed to allow existing dealers to charge higher prices. Manufacturers would be likely to forgo legitimate and competitively useful conduct rather than risk treble damages and perhaps even criminal penalties.

We cannot avoid this difficulty by invalidating as illegal *per se* only those agreements imposing vertical restraints that contain the word "price," or that affect the "prices" charged by dealers. Such formalism was explicitly rejected in *GTE Sylvania*. As the above discussion indicates, all vertical restraints, including the exclusive territory agreement held not to be *per se* illegal in *GTE Sylvania*, have the potential to allow dealers to increase "prices" and can be characterized as intended to achieve just that. In fact, vertical nonprice restraints only accomplish the benefits identified in *GTE Sylvania* because they reduce intrabrand price competition to the point where the dealer's profit margin permits provision of the desired services. As we described it in *Monsanto*: "The manufacturer often will want to ensure that its distributors earn sufficient profit to pay for programs such as hiring and training additional salesmen or demonstrating the technical features of the product, and will want to see that 'free-riders' do not interfere." 465 U.S. at 762-763. *See also GTE Sylvania*, 433 U.S. at 55.

. . . .

Finally, we do not agree with petitioner's contention that an agreement on the remaining dealer's price or price levels will so often follow from terminating another dealer "because of [its] price cutting" that prophylaxis against resale price maintenance warrants the District Court's *per se* rule. Petitioner has provided no support for the proposition that vertical price agreements generally underlie agreements to terminate a price cutter. That proposition is simply incompatible with the conclusion of *GTE Sylvania* and *Monsanto* that manufacturers are often motivated by a legitimate desire to have dealers provide services, combined with the reality that price cutting is frequently made possible by "free riding" on the services provided by other dealers. The District Court's *per se* rule would therefore discourage conduct recognized by *GTE Sylvania* and *Monsanto* as beneficial to consumers.

B

In resting our decision upon the foregoing economic analysis, we do not ignore common-law precedent concerning what constituted "restraint of trade" at the time the Sherman Act was adopted. But neither do we give that pre-1890 precedent the dispositive effect some would. The term "restraint of trade" in the statute, like the term at common law, refers not to a particular list of agreements, but to a particular economic consequence, which may be produced by quite different sorts of agreements in varying times and circumstances. The changing content of the term "restraint of trade" was well recognized at the time the Sherman Act was enacted. . . .

The Sherman Act adopted the term "restraint of trade" along with its dynamic potential. It invokes the common law itself, and not merely the static content that the common law had assigned to the term in 1890. . . . If it were otherwise, not only would the line of *per se* illegality have to be drawn today precisely where it was in 1890, but also case-by-case evaluation of legality (conducted where *per se* rules do not apply) would have to be governed by 19th-century notions of reasonableness. It would make no sense to create out of the single term "restraint of trade" a chronologically schizoid statute, in which a "rule of reason" evolves with new circumstances and new wisdom, but a line of *per se* illegality remains forever fixed where it was.

Of course the common law, both in general and as embodied in the Sherman Act, does not lightly assume that the economic realities underlying earlier decisions have changed, or that earlier judicial perceptions of those realities were in error. It is relevant, therefore, whether the common law of restraint of trade ever prohibited as illegal *per se* an agreement of the sort made here, and whether our decisions under § 1 of the Sherman Act have ever expressed or necessarily implied such a prohibition.

With respect to this Court's understanding of pre-Sherman Act common law, petitioner refers to our decision in *Dr. Miles Medical Co. v. John D. Park & Sons Co., supra*. Though that was an early Sherman Act case, its holding that a resale price maintenance agreement was *per se* illegal was based largely on the perception that such an agreement was categorically impermissible at common law. . . . As the opinion made plain, however, the basis for that common-law judgment was that the resale restriction was an unlawful restraint on alienation. . . . As we explained [in a prior case] . . . "*Dr. Miles* . . . decided that under the general law the owner of movables . . . could not sell the movables and lawfully by contract fix a price at which the product should afterwards be sold, because to do so would be at one and the same time to sell and retain, to part with and yet to hold, to project the will of the seller so as to cause it to control the movable parted with when it was not subject to his will because owned by another." In the present case, of course, no agreement on resale price or price level, and hence no restraint on alienation, was found by the jury, so the common-law rationale of *Dr. Miles* does not apply. . . .

Petitioner's principal contention has been that the District Court's rule on *per se* illegality is compelled not by the old common law, but by our more recent Sherman Act precedents. First, petitioner contends that since certain horizontal agreements have been held to constitute price fixing (and thus to be *per se* illegal) though they did not set prices or price levels . . . , it is improper to require that a vertical agreement set prices or price levels before it can suffer the same fate. This notion of equivalence between the scope of horizontal *per se* illegality and that of vertical *per se* illegality was explicitly rejected in *GTE Sylvania*. . . .

In sum, economic analysis supports the view, and no precedent opposes it, that a vertical restraint is not illegal *per se* unless it includes some agreement on price or price levels. Accordingly, the judgment of the Fifth Circuit is

Affirmed.

Justice STEVENS, with whom Justice WHITE joins, dissenting.

In its opinion the majority assumes, without analysis, that the question presented by this case concerns the legality of a "vertical nonprice restraint." . . . [However] the restraint that results when one or more dealers threaten to boycott a manufacturer unless it terminates its relationship with a price-cutting retailer is more properly viewed as a "horizontal" restraint. Moreover, an agreement to terminate a dealer because of its price cutting is more certainly not a "nonprice restraint."

. . . .

. . . [D]espite the contrary implications in the majority opinion, this is not a case in which the manufacturer is alleged to have imposed any vertical nonprice restraints on any of its dealers. . . .

. . . [I]t does not appear that respondent imposed any vertical nonprice restraints upon either petitioner or Hartwell. . . .

. . . [T]his is not a case in which the manufacturer acted independently. Indeed, given the jury's verdict, it is not even a case in which the termination can be explained as having been based on any distribution policy adopted by respondent. The termination was motivated by the ultimatum that respondent received from Hartwell and that ultimatum, in turn was the culmination of Hartwell's complaints about petitioner's competitive price cutting. This termination was plainly the product of coercion by the stronger of two dealers rather than an attempt to maintain an orderly and efficient system of distribution.

. . . .

In sum, this simply is not a case in which procompetitive vertical nonprice restraints have been imposed; in fact, it is not a case in which *any* procompetitive agreement is at issue. . . .

COMMENTARY

1. The approach of the district court was similar to the approach of the Third Circuit in *Cernuto*, was it not? The Supreme Court's decision in *Business Electronics*, therefore, effectively rejects the *Cernuto* approach.

2. The Fifth Circuit held that in order to constitute a *per se* violation of the Sherman Act the agreement to terminate a price-cutting dealer had to be accompanied by an agreement with the remaining dealer(s) on the maintenance of a specific price level. Does this standard effectively reduce the likelihood of success for terminated dealers? Did the Supreme Court adopt the position of the Fifth Circuit? on what rationale?

3. What is the legal status of vertical price-fixing agreements after *Business Electronics*? Has *Dr. Miles* been overruled? To what extent is *Dr. Miles* considered by the Court in *Business Electronics* to state a rule against restraints on alienation?

4. Justice Scalia's opinion for the Court reiterates the position—frequently found in the Court's antitrust opinions—that *per se* rules are appropriate only for conduct that would always or almost always tend to restrict competition and decrease output. Justice Scalia says that without a further agreement with the surviving dealers on resale price an agreement between a manufacturer and a dealer to terminate a price-cutting dealer would not bear the output-decreasing characteristics which would bring it within the *per se* rule.

Scalia also says that vertical price fixing agreements are likely to produce anticompetitive effects only in two identifiable situations: where there is a manufacturers' cartel or where there is a retailer cartel. Probably Scalia would include within the scope of a manufacturers' cartel an oligopolistically-structured industry as well. Why? In the case of a manfacturers' cartel, vertical price-fixing agreements could reinforce or otherwise aid the maintenance or operation of the cartel, as he explains. It is more difficult for a manufacturer to cheat on a horizontal price-fixing agreement when dealers are bound to a set resale price: the fixed dealer price level impedes dealers in disposing of the additional product routed to them by the cheating manufacturer. Moreover, dealer price-cutting is often more visible than manufacturer price-cutting. Does this analysis suggest that vertical price-fixing agreements can also strengthen the interdependence of pricing decisions by manufacturers in an oligopolistic industry? Was there evidence in the record of this case as to the market structure (competitive or oligopoly) either at the manufacturer or distributor level? Is it not apparent that vertical price-fixing agreements are anti-competitive only in the presence of a manufacturers' or retailers' cartel or an oligopoly?

The reinforcement which vertical price fixing agreements provide to a manufacturer cartel was noted in *Continental T.V., Inc. v. GTE Sylvania*, 433 U.S. at 51 n.18. *See also* Richard A. Posner, *Antitrust Policy and the Supreme Court: An Analysis of the Restricted Distribution, Horizontal Merger and Potential Competition Decisions*, 75 Colum. L. Rev. 282, 294 (1975); Lester Telser, *Why Should Manufacturers Want Fair Trade?,* 3 J.L. & Econ. 86, 96-99 (1960).

5. Under the analysis suggested in the preceding paragraph, a small manufacturer in an industry composed of many sellers could enter into a vertical price-fixing agreement with its dealers assured that its agreements would be evaluated under the rule of reason. Justice Scalia's opinion provides some substantial support for that view, does it not?

6. *Dr. Miles* can be read as recognizing the importance of intrabrand competition at the retail level. *Colgate* stresses the importance of a manufacturer's freedom to select and to dismiss its distributors. *Sylvania* reflects concern for the need of a manufacturer to build a reliable distributor network as a means of enabling competition among manufacturers. Does the analysis of *Sylvania* affect that of *Dr. Miles*? Were *Dr. Miles* to be overruled, what antitrust claims or interests, if any, of manufacturers, distributors, or consumers would be restricted?

7. Prior to the Supreme Court's decision in *State Oil Company v. Khan* (page 183, *supra*), two courts of appeals had held that the Supreme Court had not implicitly overruled *Albrecht*. *Caribe BMW, Inc. v. Bayerische Motoren Werke Aktiengesellschaft*, 19 F.3d 745, 752-54 (1st Cir. 1994); *Khan v. State Oil Co.*, 93 F.3d 1358 (7th Cir. 1996). Do those rulings imply that the Court has not overruled *Dr. Miles*?

8. The majority opinion in *Business Electronics* has been characterized by one commentator as ". . . a confusing and internally inconsistent decision. . . ." William

B. Slowey, *The Effect of* GTE Sylvania *on Antitrust Jurisprudence*, 60 ANTITRUST L.J. 11, 18 (1991).

How should the difference between the majority and the dissenters as to the definition of "vertical" and "horizontal" be resolved? Suppose the facts of this case had been that there were originally three distributors, Hartwell, Business Electronics, and X Co., and that both Hartwell and X were complaining to Sharp. Should the resulting termination of Business Electronics be characterized in terms of the relationship between Hartwell and X Co. as a horizontal case? Should the characterization be a function of the number of participants? How did the *Cernuto* court deal with this issue? the *Business Electronics* majority? Justice Stevens?

How should the antitrust rules governing dealer termination be structured to avoid burdening the federal courts with contractual disputes cast up as antitrust issues? Is the *Business Electronics* case an example of use of the Sherman Act to impose litigating costs on a rival, instead of competing aggressively in the marketplace?

Chapter 6
Tying Arrangements

A. Tying as a Troublesome Antitrust Issue

How antitrust law should treat "tying arrangements"—the conditioning of the sale or lease of one product or service to another—has troubled antitrust practitioners, enforcement officials, scholars, and observers for the better part of a century. Currently, the issue is one of the principal foci of the *Microsoft* antitrust litigation. In that case, as well as in a number of other current cases, the tying issue is sometimes cast in the form of a charge of monopolization.

B. Introduction and Historical Development

A tying arrangement is one in which a seller conditions a sale (or lease) of one product on the condition that the purchaser (or lessee) take a second product as well. This practice is possible when the buyer's intensity of demand for one product, the tying product, is significantly greater than the buyer's interest in the second product, the tied product. The seller makes the first product available only on condition that the second product is also purchased. The seller may announce the condition at the outset of dealing or may invoke it subsequently in an on-going transactional relationship. Like the arrangements considered in Chapter 5, tying arrangements are vertical restraints; unlike resale price maintenance or territorial limitations, however, tying arrangements usually involve the seller directly with the ultimate consumer, rather than involving the distributor as an intermediary. Bundling is a related practice that raises many of the same antitrust issues. Bundling involves the decision of a seller to associate one or more independent products as a package that constitutes the product as marketed. For exampIe, a restaurant may offer either an ala carte or complete dinner menu, a theater might offer tickets to individual performances or a package of season tickets, a personal computer may be offered for sale as a package including the CPU, a modem, keyboard, peripheral disk drives, a monitor, and a printer. A variant of bundling is full-line forcing, a practice in which a manufacturer requires its distributors to stock the manufacturer's entire line of products.

In the tying cases brought prior to 1970, the tying arrangements involved two products coupled by the seller under the terms of a contract. In industries of emerging technology, as demonstrated by the law suits filed against IBM in the 1970s, tying arrangements may also be implemented by product design. In a series of cases filed against IBM, rival component manufacturers alleged that IBM introduced design changes in successive generations of the IBM System 370 mainframe computer in order to make incompatible the disk drive and other peripheral components of rival manufacturers. The design changes, it was alleged, were timed to take place whenever a rival manufacturer of IBM System 370 peripherals achieved a significant market share. Given the dominance of IBM in the computer market at that time, many of these cases were brought alleging both illegal tying under § 1 and monopolization under § 2. *See Telex Corp. v. IBM Corp.*, 367 F. Supp. 258 (N.D. Okla. 1973), *rev'd*, 510 F.2d 894 (10th Cir. 1975); *California Computer Products v. IBM Corp.*, 613 F.2d 727 (9th Cir. 1979); *Transamerica Computer Co. v. IBM Corp.*, 481 F. Supp. 965 (N.D. Cal. 1979), *aff'd*, 698 F.2d 1377 (9th Cir. 1983). The application of tying analysis to products marked by rapid technological innovation required the courts to distinguish between design changes reflecting progressive innovation from design changes made to impede competitors. IBM won each of these cases by persuading the courts that technological improvement was the dominant feature of their design changes.

In contrast to the United States experience, when IBM was investigated by the European Commission for these same practices as an "abuse of a dominant position" under Article 86, it settled the case and agreed to operate under a set of Guidelines. The terms of this settlement required IBM (among other practices) "to disclose in a timely manner sufficient interface information to enable competing companies in the EEC to attach both hardware and software products to . . . [IBM's] System 370." EEC, IBM SETTLEMENT OF AUGUST 1984, FOURTEENTH REPORT ON COMPETITION POLICY 79 (1984).

In the materials that follow, consider the extent to which the courts have addressed the issue of distinguishing technological improvement changes from anti-competitive design changes masked as technological improvements. The cases in this Chapter do not involve patent, trademark, or copyright issues. Tying arrangements in the licensed use of such products pose additional antitrust issues as well as issues of patent misuse. *See* Chapter 15 and 35 U.S.C. § 271(d), cited in its 1952 version on pages 793-94 and in its current version on pages 811-12.

Given the nature of the practices of tying and bundling, courts have found it necessary to define a "product" in this context. In the recent past, a product or service has generally been deemed to constitute a separate item in a tying or bundling case if a separate consumer demand for the item has been demonstrated by a showing of an identifiable channel of distribution for that item. The Supreme Court has recently applied this definitional approach in *Eastman Kodak Co. v. Image Technical Services, Inc.*, 504 U.S. 451, 462 (1992). Given the meandering course of judicial treatment of tying and bundling arrangements, some courts have interpreted broadly the doctrine of tying and tied products. In *Faulkner Associates v. Nissan Motors Corp.*, 905 F.2d 769 (4th Cir. 1990), the court accepted a claim of tying between vehicles and the advertising services promoting their sale.

Public attention was focused upon tying arrangements early in this century when the United States sued the United Shoe Machinery Corp., charging that its practice (of leasing machinery only upon condition that the lessee also take all of its machinery needs from that supplier) violated the Sherman Act. The government claimed that a lease contract by which United Shoe Machinery secured the lessor's agreement to lease one machine only on condition that the lessor agreed to take a second machine was a contract in unreasonable restraint of trade in violation of § 1 of the Sherman Act; and that the act of compelling a lessor to take a second machine which it did not want constituted monopolization in violation of Sherman Act § 2. *See United States v. United Shoe Machinery Co.*, 247 U.S. 32, 59-67 (1918). Although the government failed in this case, it later succeeded when it again attacked the company's leases and succeeded with the help of the newly enacted Clayton Act. *United Shoe Machinery Co. v. United States,* 258 U.S. 451 (1922).

During the pendency of the *Shoe Machinery* litigation, Congress debated and enacted the Clayton Act of 1914 containing § 3, set out in Appendix A. The Shoe Machinery Company's tying leases had received sufficient public attention for Congress to take note of them when it enacted § 3 of the Clayton Act, a fact of which the trial judge also took notice. Citing the legislative history of § 3 of the Clayton Act, he wrote: "There can be no question but that the Act of Congress . . . [§ 3 of the Clayton Act] was aimed directly at the defendant the Shoe Machinery Company." *United States v. United Shoe Machinery Co.*, 227 F. 507, 510 (E.D. Mo. 1915). Accordingly, tying arrangements are subject to antitrust scrutiny under either § 3 of the Clayton Act or § 1 of the Sherman Act.

For an historical review of the antitrust law of tying arrangements, see Victor H. Kramer, *The Supreme Court and Tying Arrangements*, 69 MINN. L. REV. 1013 (1985).

C. The Economics of Tying Arrangements

1. In General

Until quite recently, the courts have viewed tying arrangements as trade restraints, an extension of the seller's power in the market for the tying product. A 1950 Supreme Court opinion stated: "The essence of illegality in tying arrangements is the wielding of monopolistic leverage; a seller exploits his dominant position in one market to expand his empire into the next." *Times-Picayune Publishing Co. v. United States*, 345 U.S. 594, 611 (1950). Ultimately, under this analysis, the supplier may foreclose large portions of the tied-product market to its rivals and may even acquire a monopoly in the tied-product market. Three years earlier, the Supreme Court, in its unanimous decision in *International Salt Co. v. United States*, 322 U.S. 392 (1947), had expressed the view that tying arrangements involving any substantial amount of commerce in the tied product were illegal *per se*. In addition, the absence of market power in the tying product has become a critical factor in most tying cases.

Scholars began to challenge the view that tying involves the leveraging of monopoly power in the late 1950s. Ward Bowman's article, *Tying Arrangements and the Leverage Problem,* 67 YALE L.J. 19 (1957), led the attack. Bowman identified two kinds of leverage, distinguishing leverage as a revenue-maximizing device from leverage as a monopoly-creating device. He pointed out that only the use of existing monopoly power as a lever need be the concern of antitrust enforcement. As he explained the benign consequences of the revenue-maximizing case:

> If the tying seller is maximizing his return on the tying product, and the same output of the tied product can still be produced under circumstances consistent with competitive production of the tied product, no additional or new monopoly effect should be assumed.

Id. at 19-20.

More recently, economists have shown that Bowman had described a special case, rather than a general rule. Bowman had assumed perfect competition, constant returns to scale, and a static model. Whinston describes the more realistic case as follows:

> Once one allows for scale economies and strategic interaction, tying can make continued operation by a monopolist's tied market rival unprofitable by leading to the foreclosure of tied goods sales . . . .

Michael D. Whinston, *Tying, Foreclosure, and Exclusion,* 80 AMER. ECON. REV. 837, 855 (1990). Whinston's models demonstrated that a tying arrangement could be used to induce the departure of a rival in the market for the tied product with the resulting increase in profits for the tying firm. This line of analysis has been extended by other economists to the case of tying complementary products in industries in which product innovation is material and product life cycles are short. Carlton and Waldman expressly addressed the use of tying to preserve and extend a monopoly position in the tying product market. They describe the anticompetitive effect of tying in these circumstances as follows:

> In each of our analyses, when the monopolist ties there is a direct reduction in the alternative producers' return . . . . In turn, because of the complementary links between the products, the alternative producer . . . [is deterred from] entering the primary market and related markets.

Dennis W. Carlton & Michael Waldman, *The Strategic Use of Tying to Preserve and Create Market Power in Evolving Industries*, 40 (WORKING PAPER # 145), STIGLER CENTER, U. OF CHICAGO (1998).

Scherer and Ross identify the potential for anticompetitive consequences when tying is coupled with market power in the following example.

> Tying is also used to increase the profits derived from monopoly power. In probably what is the most important and common case, tying permits

> a firm with monopoly power to discriminate in price according to the intensity of demand. Suppose . . . that one copying machine user makes 3,000 copies per month while another makes 20,000 copies per month. It would be difficult for a company selling only copying machines to price its machines in such a way as to extract more revenue from the more intensive user. But if the machine maker can tie the purchase of special ink (toner) to the purchase of the machine, and if it can price the . . . [toner] so as to realize a supra-normal profit margin . . ., it will be able to extract additional profits from the higher-volume user.

F.M. SCHERER & DAVID ROSS, INDUSTRIAL MARKET STRUCTURE AND ECONOMIC PERFORMANCE 565-56 (3d ed. 1990).

If the copying machine manufacturer has a 25 percent market share in that product and many active and innovative rivals, could the manufacturer price the copying machine at a level that would yield supra-normal profits? Could it price the toner so as to yield supra-normal profits? Were the toner to be priced to yield supra-normal profits, would consumers of copying machines be likely to consider the expensive toner as part of the costs of that brand of copying machine?

Suppose instead, the copying machine manufacturer had a 40% market share and had two rivals, each having a 30% share and the three firms, without conferring or agreeing watched each other, kept their selling prices about the same, each being content with its market position. Consider the consequences of the firm with the largest market share pricing the toner to yield supra-normal profits. Would the other two firms have an incentive to follow? Would increasing the price of the toner be different from increasing the price of the machine directly?

Tying arrangements have also been identified in connection with the avoidance of regulated prices, as for example during a period of legal price controls as during World War II or by regulation as in telecommunications. When legally imposed ceiling prices prevent a seller from setting a full profit-maximizing price, there is an incentive to use a tying arrangement. As the practice has been described:

> . . . [B]uyers could be coerced . . . to purchase under a tying arrangement an unregulated item. The portion of "lost profit" due to the ceiling on the tying good could be recouped by the higher price on the tied good. Analogously, a firm not wanting to upset an oligopoly price structure in one market might employ a tying arrangement as an alternative to changing its price.

EUGENE M. SINGER, ANTITRUST ECONOMICS AND LEGAL ANALYSIS 105 (1981). For further treatment of the economic analysis of these practices, see M.L. Burstein, *The Economics of Tie-In Sales*, 32 REV. ECON. & STAT. 68 (1960); *A Theory of Full-Line Forcing*, 55 NW. U. L. REV. 67 (1960); Roger D. Blair & David L. Kaserman, *Vertical Integration, Tying, and Antitrust Policy*, 68 AM. ECON. REV. 397 (1978); William J. Adams & Janet L. Yellen, *Commodity Bundling and the Burden of Monopoly*, 90 Q.J. ECON. 475 (1976); Robert E. Dansby & Cecilia Conrad, *Commodity Bundling*, 74 AM. ECON. REV. 377 (1984).

2. The *IBM* Case: Machines Plus Tabulating Cards

An example of judicial misapprehension of tying is *International Business Machines Corp. v. United States*, 298 U.S. 131 (1936). In that case, International Business Machines Corp. ("IBM") leased an early version of computers whose operation required the use of cards, perforations on which would contain numerical data entries. IBM leased its machines on condition that the lessees use only tabulating cards supplied by IBM. The government, fearing that IBM would drive out independent suppliers from the card market, successfully challenged the practice as a violation of the Sherman and Clayton Acts. In the view of the government and the Court, the case involved "leveraging": IBM was using its power in the market for tabulating machines to give it an unjustified advantage in selling cards.

It is unlikely that IBM was seeking to monopolize the tabulating card market. Unless IBM could produce tabulating cards at lower cost than it could purchase them, it would prefer to buy the tabulating cards it required from independent manufacturers on the open market for resale to its computing-machine lessees. Accordingly, it is unlikely that any independent producers of tabulating cards would have been foreclosed from the market as a result of IBM's tying practice.

An intellectually more satisfying explanation is that IBM believed that the market for tabulating machines could be segmented. Suppose that IBM believed that users of tabulating machines fell into two groups: high intensity users and low intensity users. The high-intensity users valued tabulating machines highly and, accordingly, were willing to pay a high price for them. Conversely, the low-intensity users valued tabulating machines less and would purchase—or lease—such machines only at comparatively low prices. In such circumstances, the challenge for IBM to meet would be this: How could IBM sell to the high intensity users at high prices and still profit from the demand of the low intensity users who were willing to pay only comparatively low prices for the machines?

First. Observe that if IBM sold the machines at two different prices, its price differential would soon be eroded by a process known as arbitrage: The low-price purchasers would resell to the high-price purchasers at a mark-up over the low price which they (the low-price purchasers) paid but at a price which undercut IBM's high price. Soon IBM would be forced to lower the level of its higher price and ultimately would be unable to maintain a two-price structure. If, however, IBM only leased the machines, users would not be able to resell. The arbitrage problem would be eliminated.

Second. How would IBM be able to differentiate between the high-intensity users who presumably would be willing to pay a high price and the low intensity users who would be willing only to pay a low price? IBM might offer the machines at a relatively low basic rental and impose a user charge which increased the total rent with use: the more that a lessee used a machine, the higher would be its total rent. Under such a system, the low intensity users would pay a low total rent and the high intensity users would pay a high total rent.

Use of the machines could be recorded by a meter attached to the machines. This method has been employed extensively in leases of copying machines. Alternatively, if it was impractical for any reason to attach meters to the tabulating machines, IBM might require that tabulating cards employed with the machines be purchased from IBM itself. IBM would then purchase the tabulating cards on the open market and resell them to its lessees at a mark-up equal to its user charge.

COMMENTARY

1. In this case, the Supreme Court rejected IBM's claim of quality control as justification for the tying arrangement. IBM argued that its commercial reputation would be injured by the use of inferior cards that might jam the machine. The Court stated that other manufacturers could meet IBM's specifications.

Subsequently, the Court accepted quality control as justification for a tying arrangement in a case involving cable television in its early commercial use. The trial court noted,

> A wave of system failures at the start would have greatly retarded, if not destroyed, this new industry and would have been disastrous for . . . [defendant company], who . . . did not have a diversified business to fall back on but had put all its eggs in one precarious basket. . . .
>
> . . . [T]his court concludes that . . . [defendant's] policy and practice of selling its community equipment only in conjunction with a service contract was reasonable and not in violation of § 1 of the Sherman Act.
>
> . . .

United States v. Jerrold Electronics Corp., 187 F. Supp. 545, 557 (E.D. Pa. 1960), *aff'd per curiam*, 363 U.S. 567 (1961).

2. Consider the effect on an industry of a government antitrust attack on tying practices. An industry study concludes that the 1936 *IBM* case had little, if any, long-term effect on the defendant. By 1956, IBM had a 90% share of an expanded tabulating card market. *See* William L. Baldwin, *The Feedback Effect of Business Conduct on Industry Structure*, 12 J.L. & Econ. 123 (1969). As the dominant firm in the industry, United Shoe Machinery and the government were involved in several antitrust cases, the effect of which overall, has not been perceived as markedly successful.

> . . . [t]he antitrust laws . . . as interpreted today . . . will give small competitors a somewhat better chance to expand their market, . . . and may possibly induce a faster rate of technological progress.

2 Simon N. Whitney, Antitrust Policies 144 (1958).

3. Commenting on the situation illustrated by the *IBM* case, Robert Bork said:

> [Some writers] think the *per se* ban on tying arrangements justified because it limits the potential gains from monopoly power. Indeed, it does, but that is to apply the wrong criterion to the problem. The objection to monopoly is not that it makes some people too rich but that it leaves consumers poorer than they need be. The question to be answered, then, is whether consumers are better or worse off if tying arrangements are allowed. Often, permitting a monopolist to maximize his gains will be better for consumers. Monopoly misallocates resources because the monopolist must restrict output to maximize net revenues—but that proposition holds only if the monopolist is confined to charging a single price. If he could charge the monopoly price to all who would pay it, and a series of lower prices to others, he would produce the same amount as a competitive industry. Under such circumstances, there would be no misallocation of resources. . . . [T]ying arrangements are often methods of approximating this result. When they are, they are both promonopolist and proconsumer, and it makes no particular sense to object to the promonopolist effect and overlook the proconsumer effect. Striking the tie-in such cases merely makes everybody worse off.

ROBERT H. BORK, THE ANTITRUST PARADOX 375 (1978).

Part of the problem of effective antitrust enforcement is the difficulty of crafting a suitable decree. Consider the treatment of leasing arrangements in the decree after the second *United Shoe Machinery* case. A student of this litigation explains that provision of the decree as follows.

> Judicial caution is not the only limitation which constrains the form of a decree. Anti-trust remedies affect others than defendants. . . . In the Shoe Machinery Case, the Court decided not to impose a requirement that United cease absolutely to lease on grounds of fairness.

CARL M. KAYSEN, UNITED STATES V. UNITED SHOE MACHINERY CORPORATION 342 (1956).

Greater success is perceived as a result of the government suits against tying arrangements in the metal container industry. Three-fourths of the tying arrangements requiring the leasing of patented can-closing machines as a condition of purchase of tin cans were converted to outright sales, price competition increased, and the market shares of the small firms in the industry rose from 20% to 50%. *See* James M. McKie, *The Decline of Monopoly in the Metal Container Industry*, 45 AM. ECON. REV. 499 (1955).

4. Tying arrangements under § 3 of the Clayton Act and under § 1 the Sherman Act:

a) *Coverage*. The phrasing of § 3 limits the Clayton Act to tying arrangements over commodities; it does not cover services or real estate. By contrast, the Sherman Act's broader language enables it to cover arrangements beyond the reach of the Clayton Act. Also the Clayton Act has a slightly more limited jurisdictional range than does the Sherman Act: while the Clayton Act extends to acts "in commerce," the Sherman Act extends to all arrangements "affecting commerce."

b) *Standards*. In *Times-Picayune Publishing Co. v. United States*, 345 U.S. 594 (1953), the Court set forth the prevailing view of the relation between the Sherman and Clayton Acts. In that case the government had attacked, as an unlawful tying arrangement, the policy of Times-Picayune, a publisher of a morning newspaper (the TIMES-PICAYUNE) and an evening newspaper (the STATES), which sold advertising only in both newspapers together as a package. In order to purchase advertising in the TIMES-PICAYUNE, an advertiser also had to take advertising in the STATES as well. Since advertising was not deemed to be a "commodity," the Court applied the Sherman Act. Summarizing the caselaw of the time, the Court had this to say about the relation between the Sherman, Clayton and Federal Trade Commission Acts as they applied to tying arrangements:

> From the "tying" cases a perceptible pattern of illegality emerges: When the seller enjoys a monopolistic position in the market for the "tying" product, or if a substantial volume of commerce in the "tied" product is restrained, a tying arrangement violates the narrower standards expressed in § 3 of the Clayton Act because from either factor the requisite potential lessening of competition is inferred. And because for even a lawful monopolist it is "unreasonable, per se, to foreclose competitors from any substantial market," a tying arrangement is banned by § 1 of the Sherman Act whenever both conditions are met. In either case, the arrangement transgresses § 5 of the Federal Trade Commission Act, since minimally that section registers violations of the Clayton and Sherman Acts.

345 U.S. at 608-09. Applying those standards, the Court resolved the case against the government, because the morning TIMES-PICAYUNE (which accounted for about one-third of newspaper advertising) lacked monopoly power in the market in which the tying product was sold. That market, the Court ruled, was not morning newspaper advertising but newspaper advertising. (If it had been the former, the TIMES-PICAYUNE would have held 100%.)

In a series of subsequent cases applying the Sherman Act to tying arrangements, the Court rephrased the standards set out in *Times Picayune* so as effectively to collapse the Sherman Act standards into the less stringent Clayton Act standards. Thus in *Northern Pacific Ry. v. United States*, 356 U.S. 1 (1958), Northern Pacific, whose predecessor had been granted large tracts of land by the government in the nineteenth century as a subsidy for building a transcontinental railroad, had sold or leased those lands under contracts containing "preferential routing" clauses. Those clauses required the purchasers or lessees to ship commodities produced or manufactured on the land on the Northern Pacific Railway, provided that its rates (and in some cases its services) were equal to competing carriers. The government's attack on these preferential routing clauses as unlawful tying arrangements was upheld by the Supreme Court in sweeping language which rephrased the language of *Times-Picayune* to make it easier to establish a violation of the Sherman Act:

> . . . "tying agreements serve hardly any purpose beyond the suppression of competition." . . . They deny competitors free access to the market for the tied product, not because the party imposing the tying requirements has a better product or a lower price but because of his power or leverage in another market. At the same time buyers are forced to forego their free choice between competing products. . . . They are unreasonable in and of themselves whenever a party has sufficient economic power with respect to the tying product to appreciably restrain free competition in the market for the tied product and a "not insubstantial" amount of interstate commerce is affected. . . .
>
> * * *
>
> . . . [T]he undisputed facts established beyond any genuine question that the defendant possessed substantial economic power by virtue of its extensive landholdings which it used as leverage to induce large numbers of purchasers and lessees to give it preference, to the exclusion of its competitors, in carrying goods or produce from the land transferred to them. . . . This land was strategically located in checkerboard fashion amid private holdings and within economic distance of transportation facilities. . . . [T]his particular land was often prized by those who purchased or leased it and was frequently essential to their business activities. In disposing of its holdings the defendant entered into contracts of sale or lease covering at least several million acres of land which included "preferential routing" clauses. The very existence of this host of tying arrangements is itself compelling evidence of the defendant's great power, at least where, as here, no other explanation has been offered for the existence of these restraints. The "preferential routing" clauses conferred no benefit on the purchasers or lessees. While they got the land they wanted by yielding their freedom to deal with competing carriers, the defendant makes no claim that it came any cheaper than if the restrictive clauses had been omitted. . . .
>
> * * *
>
> While there is some language in the *Times-Picayune* opinion which speaks of "monopoly power" or "dominance" over the tying product as a necessary precondition for application of the rule of *per se* unreasonableness to tying arrangements, we do not construe this general language as requiring anything more than sufficient economic power to impose an appreciable restraint on free competition in the tied product (assuming all the time, of course, that a "not insubstantial" amount of interstate commerce is affected). . . .

356 U.S. at 6, 7, 11.

One review of the record in *Northern Pacific* concludes that the contracts were improperly characterized as tying arrangements, but were instead the basis of a cartel among the railroads. F.J. Cummings & Wayne E. Ruhter, *The* Northern Pacific *Case*, 22 J.L. & ECON. 329 (1979).

In *United States v. Loew's, Inc.*, 371 U.S. 38 (1962), the Court further confused the analysis of tying arrangements by taking the special case of intellectual property rights as a basis for a broad pronouncement on market dominance. It upheld a government attack upon "block-booking" of motion pictures to television stations. The Court viewed the practice of motion picture companies distributing copyrighted motion picture films only in packages of several films as conditioning the sale or lease of one motion picture (the tying product) upon the sale or lease of another (the tied product). Again the Court rephrased the economic power required to be shown for a Sherman Act violation. Speaking for the Court, Justice Goldberg stated:

> . . . Market dominance—some power to control price and to exclude competition—is by no means the only test of whether the seller has the requisite economic power. Even absent a showing of market dominance, the crucial economic power may be inferred from the tying product's desirability to consumers or from uniqueness in its attributes. . . .

Here Justice Goldberg ruled that the copyrighted nature of the films established a uniqueness sufficient to satisfy this test. The fact that the films were to be shown on television did not eliminate their legal or economic uniqueness nor make the films fungible with other types of programming. The district court's findings that the films varied in theme, artistic performance, stars, audience appeal, etc., confirmed the presumption of uniqueness resulting from the copyright.

For an exposition of the incompleteness of the analysis in *Loew's*, see George J. Stigler, United States v. Loew's, Inc.: *A Note on Block Booking*, 1963 SUP. CT. REV. 152.

The unrefined leverage theory reached its apogee in the first of two Supreme Court decisions involving Fortner Enterprises, Inc. These cases involved a real estate developer, Fortner Enterprises, Inc., and its relations with its supplier, United States Steel Corp. Fortner, which was developing land outside of Louisville, Kentucky, was unable to obtain needed financing from any conventional lender. Finally, it was able to obtain financing from United States Steel Homes Credit Corp., a U.S. Steel subsidiary, on the condition that it erect a prefabricated house manufactured by U.S. Steel on each of the lots purchased with the loan proceeds. Fortner took the financing and erected the houses. Later, when a dispute broke out between Fortner and U.S. Steel over alleged defects in the houses, Fortner brought suit against its supplier—not under contract or warranty theories—but under the antitrust laws, alleging that the supply arrangements violated the Sherman Act as tying arrangements! Consider the following excerpt from *Fortner Enterprises, Inc. v. United States Steel Corp.*, 394 U.S. 495 (1969) (*Fortner I*):

The standard of "sufficient economic power" does not . . . require that the defendant have a monopoly or even a dominant position throughout the market for the tying product. Our tie-in cases have made unmistakably clear that the economic power over the tying product can be sufficient even though the power falls far short of dominance and even though the power exists only with respect to some of the buyers in the market. . . . As we said in the *Loew's* case, . . . "Even absent a showing of market dominance, the crucial economic power may be inferred from the tying product's desirability to consumers or from uniqueness in its attributes."

. . . [B]ecause tying arrangements generally serve no legitimate business purpose that cannot be achieved in some less restrictive way, the presence of any appreciable restraint on competition provides a sufficient reason for invalidating the tie. Such appreciable restraint results whenever the seller can exert some power over some of the buyers in the market, even if his power is not complete over them and over all other buyers in the market. In fact, complete dominance throughout the market . . . would never exist even under a pure monopoly. Market power is usually stated to be the ability of a single seller to raise price and restrict output, for reduced output is the almost inevitable result of higher prices. Even a complete monopolist can seldom raise his price without losing some sales; many buyers will cease to buy the product, or buy less, as the price rises. Market power is therefore a source of serious concern for essentially the same reason, regardless of whether the seller has the greatest economic power possible or merely some lesser degree of appreciable economic power. In both instances, despite the freedom of some or many buyers from the seller's power, other buyers—whether few or many, whether scattered throughout the market or part of some group within the market—can be forced to accept the higher price because of their stronger preferences for the product, and the seller could therefore choose instead to force them to accept a tying arrangement that would prevent free competition for their patronage in the market for the tied product. Accordingly, the proper focus of concern is whether the seller has the power to raise prices, or impose other burdensome terms such as a tie-in, with respect to any appreciable number of buyers within the market.

The affidavits put forward by petitioner clearly entitle it to its day in court under the standard. The construction company president stated that competitors of U.S. Steel sold prefabricated houses and built conventional homes for at least $400 less than U.S. Steel's price for comparable models. Since in a freely competitive situation buyers would not accept a tying arrangement obligating them to buy a tied product at a

> price higher than the going market rate, this substantial price differential with respect to the tied product (prefabricated houses) in itself may suggest that respondents had some special economic power in the credit market. In addition, petitioner's president, A. B. Fortner, stated that he accepted the tying condition on respondents' loan solely because the offer to provide 100% financing, lending an amount equal to the full purchase price of the land to be acquired, was unusually and uniquely advantageous to him. He found that no such financing was available to his corporation on any such cheap terms from any other source during the 1959-1962 period. . . .

Id. at 502-03. When the Court indicated that the requirement of the seller's power in the market for the tying product was the power to "raise prices . . . with respect to any appreciable number of buyers within the market," it appeared to be equating the power necessary for a tie-in violation with the power possessed by any seller of a differentiated product. At that point the first requirement for a Sherman Act violation set forth in *Times Picayune* seemed to have eroded into insignificance. The tests for a Sherman Act violation and a Clayton Act violation were apparently identical.

The Court began to revise its uncompromisingly hostile attitude towards tying arrangements in the second *Fortner* case, *United States Steel Corp. v. Fortner Enterprises, Inc.*, 429 U.S. 610 (1977) (*Fortner II*). After *Fortner I*, the case was remanded for trial. After the second trial, judgment was entered for Fortner and that judgment was affirmed by the court of appeals. This time, however, (in an opinion by Justice Stevens) the Supreme Court reversed on the ground that the record lacked evidence of U.S. Steel's power in the market for the tying product:

> The fact that Fortner and presumably other Home Division customers as well paid a noncompetitive price for houses also lends insufficient support to the judgment of the lower court. Proof that Fortner paid a higher price for the tied product is consistent with the possibility that the financing was unusually inexpensive and that the price for the entire package was equal to, or below, a competitive price. And this possibility is equally strong even though a number of Home Division customers made a package purchase of homes and financing.[10]

---

[10] Relying on *Advance Business Systems & Supply Co. v. SCM Corp.*, 415 F.2d 55 (4th Cir. 1969), *cert. denied*, 397 U.S. 920, Fortner contends that acceptance of the package by a significant number of customers is itself sufficient to prove the seller's economic power. But this approach depends on the absence of other explanations for the willingness of buyers to purchase the package. . . . In the *Northern Pacific* case, for instance, the Court explained: "The very existence of this host of tying arrangements is itself compelling evidence of the defendant's great power, at least where, as here, no other explanation has been offered for the existence of these restraints . . . ."

As this passage demonstrates, this case differs from *Northern Pacific* because use of the tie-in in this case can be explained as a form of price competition in the tied product, whereas that explanation was unavailable to the Northern Pacific Railway.

> The most significant finding made by the District Court related to the unique character of the credit extended to Fortner. This finding is particularly important because the unique character of the tying product has provided critical support for the finding of illegality in prior cases. . . .
>
> . . . [T]hese decisions do not require that the defendant have a monopoly or even a dominant position throughout the market for a tying product. . . . They do, however, focus attention on the question whether the seller has the power, within the market for the tying product, to raise prices or to require purchasers to accept burdensome terms that could not be exacted in a completely competitive market. In short, the question is whether the seller has some advantage not shared by his competitors in the market for the tying product.
>
> * * *
>
> Without any such advantage differentiating his product from that of his competitors, the seller's product does not have the kind of uniqueness considered relevant in prior tying-clause cases. . . .
>
> Quite clearly, if the evidence merely shows that credit terms are unique because the seller is willing to accept a lesser profit or to incur greater risks than its competitors, that kind of uniqueness will not give rise to any inference of economic power in the credit market. Yet this is, in substance, all that the record in this case indicates.
>
> The unusual credit bargain offered to Fortner proves nothing more than a willingness to provide cheap financing in order to sell expensive houses. Without any evidence that the Credit Corp. had some cost advantage over its competitors or could offer a form of financing that was significantly differentiated from that which other lenders could offer if they so elected the unique character of its financing does not support the conclusion that petitioners had the kind of economic power which Fortner had the burden of proving in order to prevail in this litigation.

429 U.S. at 618-22. In *Fortner II*, the Court was no longer so willing to infer market power from an unusually high price for the tied product. Indeed, if a product is a differentiated one, how can we determine whether the price is unusually high? But even if we are satisfied that the price is unusually high, that price may be offset by an unusually low price for the "tied" product. In *Fortner II* the Court articulated the position that if the package price is a competitive one, there is no evidence of power in any market. Had the Court embraced that position in *Fortner I,* it could not have written the opinion there that it did.

D. The Modern Case Law

1. *Jefferson Parish* to *Eastman Kodak*

Jefferson Parish Hospital District No. 2 v. Hyde
466 U.S. 2 (1984)

Justice STEVENS delivered the opinion of the Court.

At issue in this case is the validity of an exclusive contract between a hospital and a firm of anesthesiologists. We must decide whether the contract gives rise to a *per se* violation of § 1 of the Sherman Act because every patient undergoing surgery at the hospital must use the services of one firm of anesthesiologists, and, if not, whether the contract is nevertheless illegal because it unreasonably restrains competition among anesthesiologists.

In July 1977, respondent Edwin G. Hyde, a board certified anesthesiologist, applied for admission to the medical staff of East Jefferson Hospital. The credentials committee and the medical staff executive committee recommended approval, but the hospital board denied the application because the hospital was a party to a contract providing that all anesthesiological services required by the hospital's patients would be performed by Roux & Associates, a professional medical corporation. Respondent then commenced this action seeking a declaratory judgment that the contract is unlawful and an injunction ordering petitioners to appoint him to the hospital staff. After trial, the District Court denied relief, finding that the anticompetitive consequences of the Roux contract were minimal and outweighed by benefits in the form of improved patient care. . . . The Court of Appeals reversed because it was persuaded that the contract was illegal "*per se*." . . . We granted *certiorari* . . . and now reverse.

. . . .

The exclusive contract had an impact on two different segments of the economy: consumers of medical services, and providers of anesthesiological services. Any consumer of medical services who elects to have an operation performed at East Jefferson Hospital may not employ any anesthesiologist not associated with Roux. No anesthesiologists except those employed by Roux may practice at East Jefferson.

There are at least 20 hospitals in the New Orleans metropolitan area and about 70 per cent of the patients living in Jefferson Parish go to hospitals other than East Jefferson. Because it regarded the entire New Orleans metropolitan area as the relevant geographic market in which hospitals compete, this evidence convinced the District Court that East Jefferson does not possess any significant "market power"; therefore it concluded that petitioners could not use the Roux contract to anticompetitive ends. The same evidence led the Court of Appeals to draw a different conclusion. Noting that 30 percent of the residents of the Parish go to East Jefferson Hospital, and that in fact "patients tend to choose hospitals by location rather than price or quality," the Court of Appeals concluded that the relevant geographic market was the East Bank of Jefferson Parish. The conclusion that East Jefferson Hospital possessed market power in that area was buttressed by the facts that the prevalence of health insurance eliminates a patient's incentive to compare costs, that the patient is not sufficiently informed to compare quality, and that family convenience tends to magnify the importance of location.

The Court of Appeals held that the case involves a "tying arrangement" because the "users of the hospital's operating rooms (the tying product) are also compelled to purchase the hospital's chosen anesthesia service (the tied product)." 686 F.2d at 289. Having defined the relevant geographic market for the tying product as the East Bank of Jefferson Parish, the court held that the hospital possessed "sufficient market power in the tying market to coerce purchasers of the tied product." 686 F.2d at 291. Since the purchase of the tied product constituted a "not insubstantial amount of interstate commerce," under the Court of Appeals' reading of our decision in *Northern Pac. R. Co. v. United States*, 356 U.S. 1, 11 (1957), the tying arrangement was therefore illegal "*per se*."

II

Certain types of contractual arrangements are deemed unreasonable as a matter of law. . . . It is far too late in the history of our antitrust jurisprudence to question the proposition that certain tying arrangements pose an unacceptable risk of stifling competition and therefore are unreasonable "*per se*." . . .

It is clear, however, that every refusal to sell two products separately cannot be said to restrain competition. If each of the products may be purchased separately in a competitive market, one seller's decision to sell the two in a single package imposes no unreasonable restraint on either market, particularly if competing suppliers are free to sell either the entire package or its several parts. . . .

Our cases have concluded that the essential characteristic of an invalid tying arrangement lies in the seller's exploitation of its control over the tying product to force the buyer into the purchase of a tied product that the buyer either did not want at all, or might have preferred to purchase elsewhere on different terms. . . .

Thus, the law draws a distinction between the exploitation of market power by merely enhancing the price of the tying product, on the one hand, and by attempting to impose restraints on competition in the market for a tied product, on the other. When the seller's power is just used to maximize its return in the tying product market, where presumably its product enjoys some justifiable advantage over its competitors, the competitive ideal of the Sherman Act is not necessarily compromised. But if that power is used to impair competition on the merits in another market, a potentially inferior product may be insulated from competitive pressures. This impairment could either harm existing competitors or create barriers to entry of new competitors in the market for the tied product, *Fortner I*, 394 U.S. at 509, and can increase the social costs of market power by facilitating price discrimination, thereby increasing monopoly profits over what they would be absent the tie, *Fortner II*, 429 U.S. at 617. . . .

Per se condemnation—condemnation without inquiry into actual market conditions—is only appropriate if the existence of forcing is probable. . . . Of course, as a threshold matter there must be a substantial potential for impact on competition in order to justify *per se* condemnation. If only a single purchaser were "forced" with respect to the purchase of a tied item, the resultant impact on competition would not be sufficient to warrant the concern of antitrust law. It is for this reason that we have refused to condemn tying arrangements unless a substantial volume of commerce is foreclosed thereby. . . . Similarly, when a purchaser is "forced" to buy a product he would not have otherwise bought even from another seller in the tied product market, there can be no adverse impact on competition because no portion of the market which would otherwise have been available to other sellers has been foreclosed.

Once this threshold is surmounted, *per se* prohibition is appropriate if anticompetitive forcing is likely. . . .

Our cases indicate . . . that the answer to the question whether one or two products are involved turns not on the functional relation between them, but rather on the character of the demand for the two items. . . . Thus, in this case no tying arrangement can exist unless there is a sufficient demand for the purchase of anesthesiological services separate from hospital services to identify a distinct product market in which it is efficient to offer anesthesiological services separately from hospital services.

Unquestionably, the anesthesiological component of the package offered by the hospital could be provided separately and could be selected either by the individual patient or by one of the patient's doctors if the hospital did not insist on including anesthesiological services in the package it offers to its customers. . . . The record amply supports the conclusion that consumers differentiate between anesthesiological services and the other hospital services provided by petitioners.

Thus, the hospital's requirement that its patients obtain necessary anesthesiological services from Roux combined the purchase of two distinguishable services in a single transaction. . . .

. . . .

IV

The question remains whether this arrangement involves the use of market power to force patients to buy services they would not otherwise purchase. . . .

Seventy per cent of the patients residing in Jefferson Parish enter hospitals other than East Jefferson. . . . Thus East Jefferson's "dominance" over persons residing in Jefferson Parish is far from overwhelming. The fact that a substantial majority of the parish's residents elect not to enter East Jefferson means that the geographic data does not establish the kind of dominant market position that obviates the need for further inquiry into actual competitive conditions. The Court of Appeals acknowledged as much; it recognized that East Jefferson's market share alone was insufficient as a basis to infer market power, and buttressed its conclusion by relying on "market imperfections" that permit petitioners to charge noncompetitive prices for hospital services: the prevalence of third party payment for health care costs reduces price competition, and a lack of adequate information renders consumers unable to evaluate the quality of the medical care provided by competing hospitals. 686 F.2d at 290. While these factors may generate "market power" in some abstract sense, they do not generate the kind of market power that justifies condemnation of tying.

Tying arrangements need only be condemned if they restrain competition on the merits by forcing purchases that would not otherwise be made. A lack of price or quality competition does not create this type of forcing. If consumers lack price consciousness, that fact will not force them to take an anesthesiologist whose services they do not want—their indifference to price will have no impact on their willingness or ability to go to another hospital where they can utilize the services of the anesthesiologist of their choice. Similarly, if consumers cannot evaluate the quality of anesthesiological services, it follows that they are indifferent between certified anesthesiologists even in the absence of a tying arrangement—such an arrangement cannot be said to have foreclosed a choice that would have otherwise been made "on the merits."

. . . .

Thus, neither of the "market imperfections" relied upon by the Court of Appeals forces consumers to take anesthesiological services they would not select in the absence of a tie. It is safe to assume that every patient undergoing a surgical operation needs the services of an anesthesiologist; at least this record contains no evidence that the hospital "forced" any such services on unwilling patients. The record therefore does not provide a basis for applying the *per se* rule against tying to this arrangement.

V

In order to prevail in the absence of *per se* liability, respondent has the burden of proving that the Roux contract violated the Sherman Act because it unreasonably restrained competition. . . . There is, however, insufficient evidence in this record to provide a basis for finding that the Roux contract, as it actually operates in the market, has unreasonably restrained competition. . . . [T]here is no evidence that any patient who was sophisticated enough to know the difference between two anesthesiologists was not also able to go to a hospital that would provide him with the anesthesiologist of his choice.[50]

In sum, all that the record establishes is that the choice of anesthesiologists at East Jefferson has been limited to one of the four doctors who are associated with Roux and therefore have staff privileges. Even if Roux did not have an exclusive contract, the range of alternatives open to the patient would be severely limited by the nature of the transaction and the hospital's unquestioned right to exercise some control over the identity and the number of doctors to whom it accords staff privileges. If respondent is admitted to the staff of East Jefferson, the range of choice will be enlarged from four to five doctors, but the most significant restraints on the patient's freedom to select a specific anesthesiologist will nevertheless remain. Without a showing of actual adverse effect on competition, respondent cannot make out a case under the antitrust laws, and no such showing has been made.

VI

. . . There is no evidence that the price, the quality, or the supply or demand for either the "tying product" or the "tied product" involved in this case has been adversely affected by the exclusive contract between Roux and the hospital. . . . [T]here has been no showing that the market as a whole has been affected at all by the contract. Indeed . . . the record tells us very little about the market for the services of anesthesiologists. Yet that is the market in which the exclusive contract has had its principal impact. . . . Accordingly, the judgment of the Court of Appeals is reversed and the case is remanded to that court for further proceedings consistent with this opinion.

It is so ordered.

Justice BRENNAN, with whom Justice MARSHALL joins, concurring.

As the opinion for the Court demonstrates, we have long held that tying arrangements are subject to evaluation for *per se* illegality under § 1 of the Sherman Act. . . . I see no reason to depart from that principle in this case and therefore join the opinion and judgment of the Court.

Justice O'CONNOR, with whom Chief Justice BURGER, Justice POWELL, and Justice REHNQUIST join, concurring in the judgment.

. . . .

The "*per se*" doctrine in tying cases has thus always required an elaborate inquiry into the economic effects of the tying arrangement. As a result, tying doctrine incurs the costs of a Rule of Reason approach without achieving its benefits: the doctrine calls for the exten-

---

50 If, as is likely, it is the patient's doctor and not the patient who selects an anesthesiologist, the doctor can simply take the patient elsewhere if he is dissatisfied with Roux. The District Court found that most doctors in the area have staff privileges at more than one hospital. . . .

sive and time-consuming economic analysis characteristic of the Rule of Reason, but then may be interpreted to prohibit arrangements that economic analysis would show to be beneficial. Moreover, the *per se* label in the tying context has generated more confusion than coherent law because it appears to invite lower courts to omit the analysis of economic circumstances of the tie that has always been a necessary element of tying analysis.

The time has therefore come to abandon the "*per se*" label and refocus the inquiry on the adverse economic effects, and the potential economic benefits, that the tie may have. The law of tie-ins will thus be brought into accord with the law applicable to all other allegedly anticompetitive economic arrangements, except those few horizontal or quasi-horizontal restraints that can be said to have no economic justification whatsoever.

. . . [E]xploitation of consumers in the market for the tying product is a possibility that exists and that may be regulated under § 2 of the Sherman Act without reference to any tying arrangements that the seller may have developed. The existence of a tied product normally does not increase the profit that the seller with market power can extract from sales of the tying product. A seller with a monopoly on flour, for example, cannot increase the profit it can extract from flour consumers simply by forcing them to buy sugar along with their flour. Counterintuitive though that assertion may seem, it is easily demonstrated and widely accepted. . . .

Tying may be economically harmful primarily in the rare cases where power in the market for the tying product is used to create additional market power in the market for the tied product. The antitrust law is properly concerned with tying when, for example, the flour monopolist threatens to use its market power to acquire additional power in the sugar market, perhaps by driving out competing sellers of sugar, or by making it more difficult for new sellers to enter the sugar market. But such extension of market power is unlikely, or poses no threat of economic harm, unless the two markets in question and the nature of the two products tied satisfy three threshold criteria.

First, the seller must have power in the tying product market. . . .

Second, there must be a substantial threat that the tying seller will acquire market power in the tied-product market. No such threat exists if the tied-product market is occupied by many stable sellers who are not likely to be driven out by the tying, or if entry barriers in the tied-product market are low. . . .

Third, there must be a coherent economic basis for treating the tying and tied products as distinct. All but the simplest products can be broken down into two or more components that are "tied together" in the final sale. . . . For products to be treated as distinct, the tied product must, at a minimum, be one that some consumers might wish to purchase separately without also purchasing the tying product. When the tied product has no use other than in conjunction with the tying product, a seller of the tying product can acquire no additional market power by selling the two products together. . . .

Even when the tied product does have a use separate from the tying product, it makes little sense to label a package as two products without also considering the economic justifications for the sale of the package as a unit. When the economic advantages of joint packaging are substantial the package is not appropriately viewed as two products, and that should be the end of the tying inquiry. . . .

These three conditions—market power in the tying product, a substantial threat of market power in the tied product, and a coherent economic basis for treating the products as distinct—are only threshold requirements. Under the Rule of Reason a tie-in may prove acceptable even when all three are met. Tie-ins may entail economic benefits as well as economic harms, and if the threshold requirements are met these benefits should enter the Rule of Reason balance. . . .

The ultimate decision whether a tie-in is illegal under the antitrust laws should depend upon the demonstrated economic effects of the challenged agreement. . . . A tie-in should be condemned only when its anticompetitive impact outweighs its contribution to efficiency.

III

Application of these criteria to the case at hand is straightforward.

. . . [T]he third threshold condition for giving closer scrutiny to a tying arrangement is not satisfied here: there is no sound economic reason for treating surgery and anesthesia as separate services. Patients are interested in purchasing anesthesia only in conjunction with hospital services, so the Hospital can acquire no additional market power by selling the two services together. Accordingly, the link between the Hospital's services and anesthesia administered by Roux will affect neither the amount of anesthesia provided nor the combined price of anesthesia and surgery for those who choose to become the Hospital's patients. In these circumstances, anesthesia and surgical services should probably not be characterized as distinct products for tying purposes.

Even if they are, the tying should not be considered a violation of § 1 of the Sherman Act because tying here cannot increase the seller's already absolute power over the volume of production of the tied product, which is an inevitable consequence of the fact that very few patients will choose to undergo surgery without receiving anesthesia. The Hospital-Roux contract therefore has little potential to harm the patients. On the other side of the balance . . . the tie-in conferred significant benefits upon the hospital and the patients that it served.

The tie-in improves patient care and permits more efficient hospital operation in a number of ways. From the viewpoint of hospital management, the tie-in ensures 24 hour anesthesiology coverage, aids in standardization of procedures and efficient use of equipment, facilitates flexible scheduling of operations, and permits the hospital more effectively to monitor the quality of anesthesiological services. Further, the tying arrangement is advantageous to patients because . . . the closed anesthesiology department places upon the hospital . . . responsibility to select the physician who is to provide anesthesiological services. . . .

COMMENTARY

1. Consider the facts in transactional, supply and demand terms. Is the hospital a seller of specific services—room, board, operating rooms and equipment, medical supplies, nursing care, laboratories, and physicians of varying specialties? Are there two types of physicians connected with the hospital—those that admit and manage care and those that provide ancillary services to the admitting and care-giving physicians, *e.g.*, pathologists, radiologists, anesthesiologists, nurses, and physical therapists, among other services? Is the hospital the buyer of all these physician and ancillary services? As buyer does the hospital acquire these services under exclusive dealing contracts? Does it matter whether patients are billed separately by such ancillary suppliers? Might the above information describe the supply side of hospital operations?

Consider the demand side. Is the hospital a re-seller of these available services? Who is the buyer—the patient or the admitting physician? Is the admitting physician the patient's agent in the purchase? Was the *Hyde* case an application of antitrust scrutiny of an exclusive dealing contract between the hospital and a provider of ancillary surgical services? An economic analysis of the case suggests this. *See* William J. Lynk & Michael A. Morrissey, *The Economic Basis of* Hyde: *Are Market Power and Hospital Exclusive Contracts Related*, 30 J.L. & ECON. 399 (1987).

What is the likelihood that this suit would have been brought as a tying case had there not been a *per se* rule for tying arrangements? Might this issue alternatively be characterized as an exclusive dealing case? Another commentator has characterized the case as having: ". . . teetered on the brink between characterization as a tying case and characterization as an exclusive dealing case. . . ." Richard M. Steuer, *Exclusive Dealing After* Jefferson Parish, 54 ANTITRUST L.J. 1229 (1986). For treatment of exclusive dealing arrangements, see Chapter 7.

2. In his opinion for the Court, Justice Stevens has identified factors which he would employ as a basis for determining the applicability of the *per se* rule. In her concurrence, Justice O'Connor has identified factors which she would employ to dismiss tying claims. Consider whether these Justices employ any common factors in their respective analyses. Does Justice O'Connor employ the concept of "forcing" used by Justice Stevens?

Contrast the *per se* rule as defined in *Addyston Pipe* and *Socony-Vacuum* with the differing definitions invoked by Justices Stevens and O'Connor. Is Justice Stevens using the *per se* label in the same sense as it is applied in the price-fixing cases—*i.e.,* as a conclusive presumption of illegality? Does his concern with high market share of the tying product, uniqueness of the tied product, and forcing of the consumer go beyond the scope of the inquiry in price-fixing? Would the majority opinion better be cited as one invoking a "modified" rule of reason approach—*i.e.,* the modification being that the *per se* rule as Justice Stevens invokes it is no longer a substantive rule, but is rather an evidentiary rule. Would this also be a fair characterization of Justice O'Connor's rule of reason analysis? An antitrust scholar suggests such an approach:

> Courts should view the per se and rule of reason methods primarily as a single method of analysis, regarding them as evidentiary rules establishing presumptions and burdens of proof rather than as hard and fast substantive rules to be rigidly applied.
>
> . . . With this method courts use presumptions as tools for investigating the actual facts of cases and the assumptions underlying the relevant rules.

John J. Flynn, *The "Is" and "Ought" of Vertical Restraints After* Monsanto Co. v. Spray-Rite Service Corp., 71 CORNELL L. REV. 1095, 1143 (1986).

3. Can you describe the elements a of case which would meet O'Connor's criteria for dismissal but for which Stevens would apply a rule of *per se* liability?

4. What criteria would Justice Stevens apply in evaluating a tying arrangement which fell outside the *per se* category? Would he be receptive to employing the criteria identified by Justice O'Connor in a rule of reason evaluation?

5. Since four Justices wanted to abandon the *per se* rule for tying arrangements under the Sherman Act, many observers believed that it was only a matter of time until the *per se* rule would be abandoned. The *Kodak* case, *infra*, however, indicates that the overruling of the *per se* approach may not be imminent.

6. How should the Court's decision in *Hyde* affect the approach of the courts to the legality of tying arrangements under the Clayton Act? The Congressional policy set forth in § 3 of the Clayton Act cannot be abandoned by the courts, but there is substantial room for judicial interpretation of that section. Consider whether some of the language in *Hyde* could be used for construing § 3.

Eastman Kodak Co. v. Image Technical Services, Inc.

504 U.S. 451 (1992)

Justice BLACKMUN delivered the opinion of the Court.

. . . .

Petitioner Eastman Kodak Company manufactures and sells photocopiers and micrographic equipment. Kodak also sells service and replacement parts for its equipment. Respondents are 18 independent service organizations (ISOs) that in the early 1980s began servicing Kodak copying and micrographic equipment. Kodak subsequently adopted policies to limit the availability of parts to ISOs and to make it more difficult for ISOs to compete with Kodak in servicing Kodak equipment.

. . . .

Kodak provides service and parts for its machines to its customers. It produces some of the parts itself; the rest are made to order for Kodak by independent original equipment manufacturers (OEMs). . . . Kodak does not sell a complete system of original equipment, lifetime service, and lifetime parts for a single price. Instead, Kodak provides service after the initial warranty period either through annual service contracts, which include all necessary parts or on a per-call basis. . . . It charges, through negotiations and bidding, different prices for equipment, service, and parts for different customers. . . .

B

In 1987, the ISOs filed the present action in the District Court, alleging, *inter alia*, that Kodak had unlawfully tied the sale of service for Kodak machines to the sale of parts, in violation of § 1 of the Sherman Act, and had unlawfully monopolized and attempted to monopolize the sale of service for Kodak machines, in violation of § 2 of the Sherman Act.

. . . .

Kodak counters that even if it concedes monopoly *share* of the relevant parts market, it cannot actually exercise the necessary market *power* for a Sherman Act violation. This is so, according to Kodak, because competition exists in the equipment market. Kodak argues that it could not have the ability to raise prices of service and parts above the level that would be charged in a competitive market because any increase in profits from a higher price in the aftermarkets at least would be offset by a corresponding loss in profits from lower equipment sales as customers began purchasing equipment with more attractive service costs.

Kodak does not present any actual data on the equipment, service, or parts markets. Instead, it urges the adoption of a substantive legal rule that "equipment competition precludes any finding of monopoly power in derivative markets." . . . A legal presumption against a finding of market power is warranted in this situation, according to Kodak, because the existence of market power in the service and parts markets absent power in the equipment market "simply makes no economic sense." . . .

The extent to which one market prevents exploitation of another market depends on the extent to which consumers will change their consumption of one product in response to a price change in another, *i.e.*, the "cross-elasticity of demand." . . . Kodak's proposed rule rests on a factual assumption about the cross-elasticity of demand in the equipment and aftermarkets: "If Kodak raised its parts or service prices above competitive levels, potential customers would simply stop buying Kodak equipment. Perhaps Kodak would be able to increase short term profits through such a strategy, but at a devastating cost to its long term interests." Brief for Petitioner 12. Kodak argues that the Court should accept, as a matter of law, this "basic economic realit[y]," . . . that competition in the equipment market necessarily prevents market power in the aftermarkets.

. . . .

Respondents offer a forceful reason why Kodak's theory, although perhaps intuitively appealing, may not accurately explain the behavior of the primary and derivative markets for complex durable goods: the existence of significant information and switching costs. These costs could create a less responsive connection between service and parts prices and equipment sales.

For the service-market price to affect equipment demand, consumers must inform themselves of the total cost of the "package"—equipment, service and parts—at the time of purchase; that is, consumers must engage in accurate lifecycle pricing. Lifecycle pricing of complex, curable equipment is difficult and costly. . . .

Kodak acknowledges the cost of information, but suggests, again without evidentiary support, that customer information needs will be satisfied by competitors in the equipment markets. . . . It is a question of fact, however, whether competitors would provide the necessary information. A competitor in the equipment market may not have reliable information about the lifecycle costs of complex equipment it does not service or the needs of customers it does not serve. . . .

As Kodak notes, there likely will be some large-volume, sophisticated purchasers who will undertake the comparative studies and insist, in return for their patronage, that Kodak charge them competitive lifecycle prices. Kodak contends that these knowledgeable customers will hold down the package price for all other customers. . . . There are reasons, however, to doubt that sophisticated purchasers will ensure that competitive prices are charged to unsophisticated purchasers, too. As an initial matter, if the number of sophisticated customers is relatively small, the amount of profits to be gained by supracompetitive pricing in the service market could make it profitable to let the knowledgeable consumers take their business elsewhere. More importantly, if a company is able to price-discriminate between sophisticated and unsophisticated consumers, the sophisticated will be unable to prevent the exploitation of the uninformed. . . .

A second factor undermining Kodak's claim that supracompetitive prices in the service market lead to ruinous losses in equipment sales is the cost to current owners of switching to a different product. . . . If the cost of switching is high, consumers who already have purchased the equipment, and are thus "locked-in," will tolerate some level of service-price increases before changing equipment brands. Under this scenario, a seller profitably could maintain supracompetitive prices in the aftermarket if the switching costs were high relative to the increase in service prices, and the number of locked-in customers were high relative to the number of new purchasers.

Moreover, if the seller can price-discriminate between its locked-in customers and potential new customers, this strategy is even more likely to prove profitable. The seller could simply charge new customers below-marginal cost on the equipment and recoup the charges in service, or offer packages with life-time warranties or long-term service agreements that are not available to locked-in customers.

Respondents have offered evidence that the heavy initial outlay for Kodak equipment, combined with the required support material that works only with Kodak equipment, makes switching costs very high for existing Kodak customers. And Kodak's own evidence confirms that it varies the package price of equipment/parts/service for different customers.

We conclude, then, that Kodak has failed to demonstrate that respondents' inference of market power in the service and parts market is unreasonable, and that, consequently, Kodak is entitled to summary judgment. . . .

We need not decide whether Kodak's behavior has any procompetitive effects and, if so, whether they outweigh the anticompetitive effects. We note only that Kodak's service and parts policy is simply not one that appears always or almost always to enhance competition, and therefore to warrant a legal presumption without any evidence of its actual economic impact. In this case, when we weigh the risk of deterring procompetitive behavior by proceeding to trial against the risk that illegal behavior go unpunished, the balance tips against summary judgment.

IV

In the end, of course, Kodak's arguments may prove to be correct. It may be that its parts, service, and equipment are components of one unified market, or that the equipment market does discipline the aftermarkets so that all three are priced competitively overall, or that any anti-competitive effects of Kodak's behavior are outweighed by its competitive effects. But we cannot reach these conclusions as a matter of law on a record this sparse. Accordingly, the judgment of the Court of Appeals denying summary judgment is affirmed.

It is so ordered.

Justice SCALIA, with whom Justice O'CONNOR and Justice THOMAS join, dissenting.

This is not, as the Court describes it, just "another case that concerns the standard for summary judgment in an antitrust controversy." . . . Rather, the case presents a very narrow—but extremely important—question of substantive antitrust law: whether, for purposes of applying our *per se* rule condemning "ties," and for purposes of applying our exacting rules governing the behavior of would-be monopolists, a manufacturer's conceded lack of power in the interbrand market for its equipment is somehow consistent with its possession of "market," or even "monopoly," power in wholly derivative aftermarkets for that equipment. In my view, the Court supplies an erroneous answer to this question, and I dissent.

. . . .

The Court today finds in the typical manufacturer's inherent power over its own brand of equipment—over the sale of distinctive repair parts for that equipment, for example—the sort of "monopoly power" sufficient to bring the sledgehammer of § 2 into play. And, not surprisingly in the light of that insight, it readily labels single-brand power over aftermarket products "market power" sufficient to permit an antitrust plaintiff to invoke the *per se* rule against tying. In my opinion, this makes no economic sense. The holding that market power can be found on the present record causes these venerable rules of selective proscription to extend well beyond the point where the reasoning that supports them leaves off. Moreover, because the sort of power condemned by the Court today is possessed by every manufacturer of durable goods with distinctive parts, the Court's opinion threatens to release a torrent of litigation and a flood of commercial intimidation that will do much more harm than good to enforcement of the antitrust laws and to genuine competition. . . .

Had Kodak—from the date of its entry into the micrographics and photocopying markets—included a lifetime parts and service warranty with all original equipment, or required consumers to purchase a lifetime parts and service contract with each machine, that bundling of equipment, parts and service would no doubt constitute a tie under the tests enunciated in *Jefferson Parish Hospital Dist. No. 2 v. Hyde*. . . . Nevertheless, it would be immune from *per se* scrutiny under the antitrust laws because the *tying* product would be *equipment*, a market in which (we assume) Kodak has no power to influence price or quantity. . . . The same result would obtain, I think, had Kodak—from the date of its market entry—consistently pursued an announced policy of limiting parts sales in the manner alleged in this case, so that customers bought with the knowledge that aftermarket support could be obtained only from Kodak. The foreclosure of respondents from the business of servicing Kodak's micrographics and photocopying machines in these illustrations would be undeniably complete—as complete as the foreclosure described in respondents' complaint. Nonetheless, we would inquire no further than to ask whether Kodak's *market power* in the equipment market effectively forced consumers to purchase Kodak micrographics or photocopying machines subject to the company's restrictive aftermarket practices. If not, that would end the case insofar as the *per se* rule was concerned. . . . The evils against which the tying prohibition is directed would simply not be presented. Interbrand competition would render Kodak powerless to gain economic power over an additional class of consumers, to price discriminate by charging each customer a "system" price equal to the system's economic value to that customer, or to raise barriers to entry in the interbrand equipment markets. . . .

I have described these illustrations as hypothetical, but in fact they are not far removed from this case. . . . [A]t least all post-1985 purchasers of micrographics equipment, like all post-1985 purchasers of new Kodak copiers, could have been aware of Kodak's parts practices. The only thing lacking to bring all of these purchasers (accounting for the vast bulk of the commerce at issue here) squarely within the hypotheticals we have described is concrete evidence that the restrictive parts policy was announced or generally known. Thus, under the Court's approach the existence *vel non* of such evidence is determinative of the legal standard (the *per se* rule versus the rule of reason) under which the alleged tie is examined. It is quite simply anomalous that a manufacturer functioning in a competitive equipment market should be exempt from the *per se* rule when it bundles equipment with parts-and-service, but not when it bundles parts with service. This vast difference in the treatment of what will ordinarily be economically similar phenomena is alone enough to call today's decision into question.

B

In the Court of Appeals, respondents sought to sidestep the impediment posted by interbrand competition to their invocation of the *per se* tying rule by zeroing in on the parts and service "aftermarkets" for Kodak equipment. By alleging a tie of *parts* to service, rather than of *equipment* to parts-and-service, they identified a tying product in which Kodak unquestionably held a near-monopoly share: the parts uniquely associated with Kodak's brand of machines. . . . The Court today holds that such a facial showing of market share in a single-brand aftermarket is sufficient top invoke the *per se* rule. The existence of even vibrant interbrand competition is no defense. . . .

I find this a curious form of market power on which to premise the application of a *per se* proscription. It is enjoyed by virtually every manufacturer of durable goods requiring aftermarket support with unique, or relatively unique, goods. . . . Under the Court's analysis, the *per se* rule may now be applied to single-brand ties effected by the most insignificant players in fully competitive interbrand markets, as long as the arrangement forecloses aftermarket competitors from more than a *de minimis* amount of business. . . . This seems to me quite wrong. A tying arrangement "forced" through the exercise of such power no more implicates the leveraging and price discrimination concerns behind the *per se* tying prohibition than does a tie of the foremarket brand to its aftermarket derivatives, which—as I have explained—would not be subject to *per se* condemnation. . . .

In the absence of interbrand power, a seller's predominant or monopoly share of its single-brand derivative markets does not connote the power to raise derivative market prices *generally* by reducing quantity. As Kodak and its principal *amicus*, the United States, point out, a rational consumer considering the purchase of Kodak equipment will inevitably factor into his purchasing decision the expected cost of aftermarket support. . . . If Kodak set generally supracompetitive prices for either spare parts or repair services without making an offsetting reduction in the price of its machines, rational consumers would simply turn to Kodak's competitors for photocopying and micrographic systems. . . .

The Court attempts to counter this theoretical point with theory of its own. It says that there are "information costs"—the costs and inconvenience to the consumer of acquiring and processing life-cycle pricing data for Kodak machines—that "could create a less responsive connection between service and parts prices and equipment sales." . . . But this truism about the functioning of markets for sophisticated equipment cannot create "market power" of concern to the antitrust laws where otherwise there is none. "Information costs," or, more accurately, gaps in the availability and quality of consumer information, pervade real-world markets. . . . We have never suggested that the principal players in a market with such commonplace informational deficiencies (and, thus, bands of apparent consumer pricing indifference) exercise market power in any sense relevant to the antitrust laws. . . .

Respondents suggest that, even if the existence of interbrand competition prevents Kodak from raising prices *generally* in its single-brand aftermarkets, there remain certain consumers who are necessarily subject to abusive Kodak pricing behavior by reason of their being "locked in" to their investments in Kodak machines. The Court agrees; indeed, it goes further by suggesting that even a *general* policy of supracompetitive aftermarket prices might be profitable over the long run because of the "lock-in" phenomenon. "[A] seller profitably could maintain supracompetitive prices in the aftermarket," the Court explains, "if the switching costs were high relative to the increase in service prices, and the number of locked-in customers were high relative to the number of new purchasers." . . . In speculating about this latter possibility, the Court is essentially repudiating the assumption on which we are bound to decide this case, viz., Kodak's lack of any power whatsoever in the interbrand market. . . .

The Court's narrower point, however, is undeniably true. There will be consumers who, because of their capital investment in Kodak equipment, "will tolerate some level of service-price increases before changing equipment brands." . . . But this "circumstantial" leverage created by consumer investment regularly crops up in smoothly functioning, even perfectly competitive, markets, and in most—if not all—of its manifestations, it is of no concern to the antitrust laws. The leverage held by the manufacturer of a malfunctioning refrigerator (which is measured by the consumer's reluctance to walk away from his initial investment in that device) is no different in kind or degree from the leverage held by the swimming pool contractor when he discovers a 5-ton boulder in his customer's backyard and demands an additional sum of money to remove it. . . . Leverage, in the form of circumstantial power, plays a role in each of these relationships; but in none of them is the leverage attributable to the dominant party's *market* power in any relevant sense. Though that power can plainly work to the injury of certain consumers, it produces only "a brief perturbation in competitive conditions—not the sort of thing the antitrust laws do or should worry about." . . .

COMMENTARY

1. The primary issue in *Kodak* was whether servicing constituted a separable market. Kodak argued that the servicing market was not independent of the market for copiers. Therefore, although Kodak had excluded independents from the servicing market, no anticompetitive effects would follow because Kodak's prices in the servicing market would be constrained by competition in the copier market: if Kodak attempted to charge supracompetitive prices for servicing Kodak copiers, buyers would be deterred from buying Kodak copiers and would switch to other brands.

2. The difference between the majority and dissent is not a rejection of the possibility that the two markets are connected. Rather the majority and dissent differ on whether the connection between the two markets can be deduced on the basis of economic theory or whether the connection must be proved at trial.

3. Justice O'Connor's position in the dissent can be explained from her opinion in *Jefferson Parish*: Who, she would argue, would want a servicing for a Kodak copier other than a purchaser of a Kodak copier? When buyers purchase a Kodak copier, they commit themselves to buy the copier plus the servicing, just as a person requiring an operation takes the hospital plus the anesthesiology service. They are two parts of the same product in the sense that the buyers will pay less for the copiers if they anticipate that the servicing charges will be higher.

4. This case involves a claim that the persons who have already purchased a Kodak copier are "locked in" to that copier and now are at the mercy of Kodak who controls servicing. As to those persons, Kodak has a monopoly. Kodak responds, however, that the owners of Kodak copiers are protected by competition in the market for copying machines: Kodak dares not raise the price of servicing above competitive levels or it will suffer in the copier market as potential customers switch to other brands. Is Kodak's argument based on the effect of interbrand competition? Did Kodak make a quality control argument? Did it raise the "free rider" problem? Why did Justice Blackmum find that Kodak's argument failed to "mirror reality"?

5. There are many varieties of "lock in" situations not unlike like this one. The buyers of any physically differentiated product are locked in to their supplier for spare parts unless independents enter the market. Does *Kodak* mean that all manufacturers of physically differentiated products (for which no independent source of spare parts has emerged) will be vulnerable to charges of tying spare parts to the original equipment?

6. Does Justice Scalia's dissent emphasize the basic definitional issue in tying analysis by posing the issue of varying the outcome if Kodak had tied parts *and* service to equipment? Would the practice in this case better be illuminated for antitrust purposes if the practice had been characterized as bundling, rather than tying? Might the need for market information have underscored the absence of a record in the case?

7. Do you agree with the following summary of the majority position?

> *Kodak* can be read as raising a defendant's summary judgment burden by implying that a triable issue on market power in derivative markets is always present whenever plaintiffs present some evidence of nontrivial information imperfections and switching costs.

The Supreme Court, 1991 Term—Leading Cases, 106 HARV. L. REV. 334 (1992). Is the procedural burden properly allocated between the parties? Should a plaintiff so easily be permitted to shift the burden of justification to the defendant? Does the underlying economic analysis ratify the majority's burden allocation?

8. Consider the majority's reliance on the costs of obtaining information. What is the analytical basis for its assumptions about information costs? In the economic model of perfect competition the cost of market information is eliminated by the assumption of perfect knowledge of prices and supply. Textbook economics holds that:

> A market is perfectly competitive if the following conditions hold:
> (i) no buyer or seller is able to influence prices by his individual trading behavior;
> (ii) every economic agent is completely informed about his relevant production or consumption possibilities;
> (iii) economic agents always predict prices correctly; and
> (iv) act to maximize their gain . . .;
> (v) factors of production are perfectly mobile.

C.A. TISDELL, MICROECONOMICS: THE THEORY OF ECONOMIC ALLOCATION 45 (1974). However, when product differentiation occurs, markets combine elements of perfect competition with a degree of monopoly over differentiated products. In such markets, as Stigler showed in a pioneering article, lack of information on prices charged by various sellers of the same product enables some sellers to charge higher prices for the same product. However, when consumers actually search for the lowest price, the power of any seller to charge a higher price is reduced and this competition tends to drive the market price for that product toward equality. *See* George J. Stigler, *The Economics of Information*, 69 J. POL. ECON. 213 (1961); Joseph Stiglitz, *Imperfect Information in the Product Market*, in 1 HANDBOOK OF INDUSTRIAL ORGANIZATION 318 (Richard Schmalensee & Robert D. Willig eds. 1989).

Empirical evidence validates this analysis, showing that the larger the amount of the intended expenditure, the probability increases that the consumer will undertake the search for the best price with the consequence that prices will tend to equality. The function of advertising as a source of market information is also taken into account. *See* John W. Pratt, David A. Wise & Richard Zeckhauser, *Price Differences in Almost Competitive Markets*, 93 Q.J. ECON. 206 (1979); John Kwoka, *Advertising and the Price and Quality of Optometric Services*, 74 AM. ECON. REV. 211 (1984); John R. Schroeter, Scott Smith & Steven Cox, *Advertising and Competition in Routine Legal Services Markets*, 36 J. IND. ECON. 49 (1987).

9. How should antitrust doctrines of tying and bundling arrangements take account of this empirical data? Should the majority have sent the case back for trial to determine the extent to which buyers of Kodak copiers actually knew of the price of alternative machines? If a consumer is indifferent to price disparities, should antitrust law serve consumer protection interests? What would be the antitrust relevance of data showing that the brand name, Kodak, led consumers to pay more for that copier? Are the buyers of high-speed copiers and micrographics equipment typical consumers? Are the prices of such machines more likely to be influenced by the quality and physical characteristics of the machines than by the brand names attached to them?

10. The *Kodak* decision compelled a number of lower courts to examine issues about lock-ins and information costs in ongoing litigation. *See Allen-Myland v. International Bus. Mach. Corp.*, 33 F.3d 194, 205 (3d Cir. 1994); *Virtual Maintenance, Inc. v. Prime Computer, Inc.*, 11 F.3d 660, 666 (6th Cir. 1993).

PSI Repair Services, Inc. v. Honeywell Inc.

104 F.3d 811 (6th Cir. 1997)

[Honeywell manufactures and sells industrial control equipment, equipment used to control manufacturing processes in refineries and factories. The Honeywell equipment contains and depends heavily upon printed circuit boards. These boards, which range in price from $200 to $5000, are comprised of a thin rectangle of fiberglass that is laminated with copper foil. Placed on this fiberglass are numerous components, such as computer chips, that communicate with each other via the copper foil on the board. These components periodically fail, which in turn often causes the circuit board and the industrial control equipment also to fail. When a circuit board fails, Honeywell will replace it with a new or refurbished board, charging its customer fifty percent of the list price, so long as the customer returns the defective board.

[Roughly ninety-five percent of the components on the circuit boards ("generic components") can be purchased either from the component manufacturer or from a component distributor. The other five percent are designed specifically for Honeywell by third-party manufacturers, as Honeywell itself does not manufacture components. Honeywell has restrictive agreements with these manufacturers whereby the manufacturers agree not to sell these components to either Honeywell equipment owners or service organizations. Honeywell also has a stated policy of not selling its components to anyone. When a circuit board fails, equipment owners cannot usually identify which component caused the failure. Thus, as a result of Honeywell's restrictive policy, its equipment owners essentially must return to Honeywell to obtain an entire replacement board.

[PSI, a servicing organization, offers circuit-board repair services to owners of industrial control equipment. It does not manufacture industrial control equipment and it does not manufacture board components. PSI provides board services for customers who own systems manufactured by Honeywell's competitors by purchasing the necessary components from either the equipment or component manufacturer. Because PSI is unable to obtain any of the components manufactured exclusively for Honeywell, it is, for all practical purposes, unable to compete in the market for repair of Honeywell boards.

[In this case, PSI brought suit against Honeywell on tying and monopolization grounds. PSI claimed that Honeywell, like Kodak, forced owners of Honeywell brand equipment to purchase repair services from Honeywell, thereby foreclosing PSI from the market for servicing Honeywell-brand equipment. According to PSI, Honeywell used its control over parts to force customers to purchase repair service, a service which here consisted in the replacement of circuit boards. In the following extract, the court focuses upon PSI's tying claim in the light of the Supreme Court's decision in *Kodak*.]

MOORE, Circuit Judge.

. . . .

[Honeywell] . . . contends that while Kodak changed its service and parts policy to include the tie after many Kodak customers purchased their equipment, Honeywell has consistently maintained its policy of board replacement. While Honeywell does not clearly articulate why this distinction is important, we interpret Honeywell's argument to be that the *Kodak* Court's finding of a material issue of fact on the definition of the relevant market resulted from Kodak's change in policy. PSI, on the other hand, argues that even without a change in policy, significant information costs still exist. It points to deposition testimony by Honeywell's own personnel that it would be "very difficult" for customers to determine the life-cycle cost of its equipment. There is also evidence in the record that it would be difficult for Honeywell to predict the cost of parts down the road. And while Honeywell equipment owners may know that Honeywell's equipment is often capable of lasting for the lifetime of the plant, the owners are constantly upgrading and enhancing the equipment along the way, so that these costs are difficult to gauge.

The Court in *Kodak* did not explicitly state the extent to which Kodak's change in policy affected the Court's analysis. Nonetheless, it suggested that the outcome might have been different had Kodak presented evidence that its restrictive parts policy was consistently maintained and generally known. In responding to Justice Scalia's dissent, which argued, inter alia, that but for Kodak's change in policy, the Court would be faced with a traditional tie between copiers and aftermarket service, the majority responded:

> The dissent disagrees [with our conclusion in this case] based on its hypothetical case of a tie between equipment and service. "The only thing lacking" to bring this case within the hypothetical case, states the dissent, "is concrete evidence that the restrictive parts policy was . . . generally known." But the dissent's "only thing lacking" is the crucial thing lacking—evidence. Whether a tie between parts and service should be treated identically to a tie between equipment and service, as the dissent and Kodak argue, depends on whether the equipment market prevents the exertion of market power in the parts market. Far from being "anomalous," requiring Kodak to provide evidence on this factual question is completely consistent with our prior precedent.

504 U.S. at 477 n.24 (internal citations omitted). This passage can be read to imply that had Kodak presented undisputed evidence that it never changed its policy and that its policy was generally known, the Court would have considered Kodak copiers as the tying product and service and parts combined as the product being tied. *See* 10 PHILLIP E. AREEDA, ET AL., ANTITRUST LAW ¶ 1740c, at 150 (1996) ("The majority [in *Kodak*] apparently agreed with [the dissent] when it emphasized the absence of evidence that Kodak's policy was generally known."); *id.* at 157 ("[T]he *Kodak* majority indicated that it would assess the defendant's power in the interbrand machine market (where it had none) were it 'generally known' to machine buyers that the defendant supplied unique repair parts only in connection with its service, notwithstanding ignorance of life-cycle prices.").

Both the First and the Seventh Circuits have interpreted *Kodak* to be limited to situations in which the seller's policy was not generally known. *See Digital Equip. Corp. v. Uniq Digital Techs., Inc.*, 73 F.3d 756, 763 (7th Cir.1996) ("The Court did not doubt in *Kodak* that if spare parts had been bundled with Kodak's copiers from the outset, or Kodak had informed customers about its policies before they bought its machines, purchasers could have shopped around for competitive life-cycle prices. The material dispute that called for a trial was whether the change in policy enabled Kodak to extract supra-competitive prices from customers who had already purchased its machines."); *Lee v. Life Ins. Co. of North America*, 23 F.3d 14, 20 (1st Cir.), *cert. denied*, __ U.S.__ , 115 S. Ct. 427, 130 L. Ed. 2d 340 (1994) ("[T]he timing of the 'lock in' at issue in *Kodak* was central to the Supreme Court's decision. . . . Had previous customers known, at the time they bought their Kodak copiers, that Kodak would implement its restrictive parts-servicing policy, Kodak's 'market power,' i.e., its leverage to induce customers to purchase Kodak servicing, could only have been as significant as its [market power] in the copier market, which was stipulated to be inconsequential or nonexistent.").

We likewise agree that the change in policy in *Kodak* was the crucial factor in the Court's decision. By changing its policy after its customers were "locked in," Kodak took advantage of the fact that its customers lacked the information to anticipate this change. Therefore, it was Kodak's own actions that increased its customers' information costs. In our view, this was the evil condemned by the Court and the reason for the Court's extensive discussion of information costs. While PSI's argument seems to suggest that *Kodak* supports a finding of market power whenever information costs are present, such a position cannot be reconciled with *Jefferson Parish*. In *Jefferson Parish*, the plaintiff argued there were various "market imperfections" that enabled the hospital to charge noncompetitive prices and that saddled the consumers with inadequate information, which in turn "render[ed] consumers unable to evaluate the quality of the medical care provided by competing hospitals." 466 U.S. at 27. Dismissing this argument, the Court responded that "[w]hile these factors may generate 'market power' in some abstract sense, they do not generate the kind of market power that justifies condemnation of tying." *Id.* Put another way, the Court rejected the premise that imperfect consumer information resulting from basic market imperfections could be used as a basis to infer market power for purposes of the Sherman Act. We are unwilling to conclude that *Kodak* overruled this portion of *Jefferson Parish*, especially because the Court in *Kodak* cites *Jefferson Parish* with approval in its general discussion of market power. *Kodak*, 504 U.S. at 464.

In light of our reading of *Jefferson Parish* and *Kodak*, we thus hold that an antitrust plaintiff cannot succeed on a *Kodak*-type theory when the defendant has not changed its policy after locking-in some of its customers, and the defendant has been otherwise forthcoming about its pricing structure and service policies. This rule should encourage manufacturers to divulge all relevant information at the time of sale. While we recognize that some information costs will still exist even with full disclosure by a seller, *see* Mark R. Patterson, *Product Definition, Product Information, and Market Power:* Kodak *in Perspective*, 73 N.C. L. REV. 185, 215-216 (1994) ("The buyer's pre-purchase knowledge of a tie allows her only to anticipate those additional costs of the tie about which she knows prior to the purchase; it does not reduce the effects of the information costs that prevented buyers of Kodak equipment from accurately determining life-cycle prices."), these additional information costs stem from the fact that our economy is not one of perfect information, a factor that alone should not invoke antitrust condemnation. Accepting PSI's argument would expose many manufacturers of durable, expensive equipment to potential antitrust liability for having inherent power over the aftermarkets of their products, a result certainly not intended by *Kodak* and not consistent with *Jefferson Parish*.

The present dispute provides an ideal example as to how our reading of *Kodak* can be applied in practice. In this case, there are no allegations that Honeywell changed its parts-restrictive policy in order to lock-in customers, nor has PSI alleged that Honeywell's policy was not generally known. There also is evidence that Honeywell and its customers engage in lengthy negotiations before the sale of Honeywell equipment. This fact is hardly surprising in light of the substantial price of the equipment. The record also contains evidence that Honeywell will provide estimates of service costs and failure rates of various parts if asked by its customers, and that it offers various service plans to enable the customers more accurately to estimate the cost of the equipment. All of these actions by Honeywell reduce the information costs faced by its consumers. If there were any evidence in the record that Honeywell took advantage of its customers' imperfect information in order to reap supracompetitive profits in the aftermarkets for its equipment, we would not hesitate to allow a *Kodak*-type theory to be submitted to the jury. However, we can find nothing in the record or PSI's brief that alleges that Honeywell engaged in such activities. In this situation a *Kodak*-type theory is not applicable. Since PSI has not alleged or shown that Honeywell has market power in the relevant market—the primary equipment market—summary judgment is appropriate in favor of Honeywell on PSI's § 1 claim.

COMMENTARY

1. The Sixth Circuit correctly observed that the *Kodak* majority highlighted its differences with the dissent in a footnote that directed attention to the fact that Kodak changed its policy from one which made parts available to anyone to one which denied those parts to purchasers other than equipment owners which did their own repairs. If Kodak had changed its policy midstream, then purchasers who bought before the policy change might not have anticipated that change, as the court said. Yet the Second Circuit had stated in its opinion that "Kodak exempted micrographic equipment manufactured before 1985 from these new policies." 903 F.2d at 614. The First Circuit later asserted that Kodak's "later announced policy . . . was made applicable both to prospective and existing Kodak copier owners." *Lee v. Life Ins. Co.*, 23 F.3d 14, 20 (1st Cir. 1994). Are these statements consistent? Are these courts saying that Kodak exempted preexisting owners of micrographic equipment from its new policy but not preexisting owners of copiers?

2. If Kodak had made its new policy apply only to new purchasers, how would this aspect of its policy be relevant to antitrust tying analysis? Preexisting purchasers would then not be exploited by Kodak's monopoly on service, would they? Why did the Sixth Circuit not discuss the relevance of this aspect of the Kodak policy change? Why did the Supreme Court not discuss its relevance, if that Court viewed the change in policy as crucial? Perhaps the Supreme Court merely meant that Kodak should be required to prove that pre-1985 purchasers were treated differently from post-1985 purchasers. Was there a dispute about this? If there was no dispute about this, should not the matter have been handled by stipulation? Judge Easterbrook stated in *Digital Equip. Corp. v. Uniq Digital Technologies, Inc.*, 73 F.3d 757, 763 (7th Cir. 1996), that: "The material dispute that called for a trial was whether the change in policy enabled Kodak to extract supracompetitive prices from customers who had already purchased its machines."

3. *PSI Services* is not the only decision by the courts of appeals which has sought to limit the scope of the *Kodak* decision. *See Digital Equipment Corp. v. Uniq Digital Technologies, Inc.*, 73 F.3d 757, 763 (7th Cir. 1996).

4. To what extent does *Kodak* remain as a major precedent for antitrust analysis after the Sixth Circuit's opinion in *PSI Repair Services*? If the Sixth Circuit is correct in the way it has distinguished *Kodak*, why did the Supreme Court grant certiorari in the *Kodak* case in the first place?

5. In his opinion, Judge Moore stated the scope of *Kodak* as follows:

> We . . . agree that the change in policy in *Kodak* was the crucial factor in the Court's decision.
>
> . . . .
>
> If there were any evidence in the record that Honeywell took advantage of its customers' imperfect information in order to reap supra-competitive profits in the aftermarkets for its equipment, we would not hesitate to allow a *Kodak*-type theory to be submitted to the jury. However, we can find nothing in the record . . . that alleges Honeywell engaged in such activities.

104 F.3d at 820-21.

Does this narrowing of the *Kodak* holding in the Sixth Circuit effectively leave the *per se* rule in its pre-*Kodak* scope? What do you think is the likelihood that, as the lower courts narrow and refine tying analysis, these courts will ultimately follow Justice O'Connor's suggestion in *Jefferson Parish* that the *per se* rule for tying cases be abandoned?

2. The Aftermarket Issue and Intellectual Property Rights

After the Supreme Court decision in *Eastman Kodak*, the case went to trial. Prior to the closing arguments, the ISOs withdrew their § 1 tying and conspiracy claims, so the case went to the jury on monopolization and attempted monopolization claims only. The jury found against Kodak, awarding damages which, after trebling, amounted to $71.8 million. Kodak, which had contended at the trial that its intellectual property rights justified it in refusing to sell or license its patented parts and its copyrighted diagnostic and service software, reasserted those contentions on appeal. The Ninth Circuit accepted Kodak's view that an owner of intellectual property rights has no obligation to sell or license them. The court, however, upheld the judgment against Kodak on the ground that the jury had implicitly determined that Kodak's proffered intellectual property justifications for its behavior were pretextual.

In re Independent Service Organizations Antitrust Litigation, 203 F.3d 1322 (Fed. Cir. 2000), involved behavior which was virtually identical to Kodak's. In 1984, the Xerox Corporation decided to stop selling parts for its Series 10 copiers to independent servicing organizations, and, in 1987, extended that policy to its Series 9 copiers. Xerox also refused to sell independent servicing organizations copyrighted manuals and to license copyrighted software to them. The plaintiff, an independent servicing organization, was thereby disabled from competing with Xerox in the aftermarket for servicing Xerox Series 9 and 10 copiers. Asserting that Xerox had engaged in monopolization, the plaintiff sued under a theory of monopolization drawn from the *Eastman Kodak* case. Despite the close resemblance of Xerox's behavior to Kodak's, Xerox successfully defended on the ground that the parts manuals and software were protected under its patents and copyrights, and that under the patent and copyright laws Xerox was entitled to refuse to license its software. The Federal Circuit indicated its agreement with the Ninth Circuit that an owner of intellectual property has no duty to sell or to license protected material. The Federal Circuit, however, disagreed with that part of the Ninth Circuit's *Kodak* ruling which permitted the jury to treat a proffered intellectual-property justification as pretextual.

This decision illustrates the potential conflict between antitrust principles and intellectual property principles. *See* E. Thomas Sullivan, *The Confluence of Antitrust and Intellectual Property at the New Century,* 1 MINN. INTELL. PROP. REV. 1 (2000). The intersection of antitrust law and the patent and copyright regimes is further considered in Chapter 15, *infra.*

3. A Fragment of Computer Technology

Some distinctive features of computer technology illuminate the tying issue in the *Microsoft* litigation and in other software cases. Microsoft's principal product, Windows 2000, is a copyrighted software program for an operating system which directs the operation of the typical desktop computer. Unix and Linux are alternative operating systems. The operating system software provides the instructions that allow the computer and its internal microprocessors to manage their basic functions. The operating system provides for the transmission of commands and data at the direction of the human user via the mouse and the keyboard to the machine's internal memory and then to its external devices, *e.g.*, disk drives, printers, communications programs, and web browsers. Application programs are a second category of software programs that execute particular functions, *e.g.*, writing text, calculating compound interest, playing games, or managing spreadsheets, among other tasks. The vast and expanding array of application programs gives the personal computer its great versatility.

The making of software programs bears some resemblance to the making of many other commercial products. In common with many other products, software programs are works of industrial design in which computer programmers design and test the product. Like other products of industrial design, such as automobile tires, the would-be maker of an applications program needs to make the new program compatible with the related products with which it interacts. For example, to design a program that enables the preparation of an individual federal income tax return, the programmer would need to know the APIs (Application Program Interface) of the underlying operating system. The APIs are a set of software design routines or protocols for building software applications that are compatible with a given operating system. If the tire manufacturer does not make the tire to the exact specifications of the wheel of a given model automobile, the tire will not function. Similarly, if a new application program is not compatible with the operating system and other application programs, the computer will "crash" and become inoperative.

The difficulty of applying traditional antitrust tying analysis to computer programs is twofold. First, unlike automobile wheels, the Microsoft operating system is protected by copyright (and trademark). Contrariwise, the basic configuration of the automobile wheel is ineligible for patent or copyright protection, although some distinctive design features may receive limited copyright or trademark protection. Thus, any tire maker may freely acquire access to the wheel of any model of automobile and derive the specifications of that wheel in order to develop a line of tires for that vehicle. Like automobile tires, application programs must be tailored to the specifications of the operating system in order to function. Unlike the automobile wheel, however, operating system programs may be protected under the patent and copyright regimes. Obtaining access and taking the steps necessary (copying and using) to determine the specifications may be actionable as infringement under the patent and copyright regimes.

The second difficulty in applying traditional antitrust tying doctrines to computer programs arises from the very nature of computer technology. Because computer programs are functional, task-oriented products made up of lines of code in a computer language, there is great flexibility in their design. Software engineers are able to design and produce application programs in a great variety of packages and formats. Accordingly, it is possible for a software designer to incorporate a given computer task, such as an Internet browser, within an operating system program. Alternatively, if desired, the same Internet browser can be produced as a separate and distinct application program. *See* Pamela Samuelson, Randall Davis, Mitchell D. Kapor & J.H. Reichman, *A Manifesto Concerning the Legal Protection of Computer Programs,* 94 COLUM. L. REV. 2308, 2327 ff. (1994) (explaining the design of computer programs); BEN SCHNEIDERMAN, DESIGNING THE USER INTERFACE, Chap. 1 (3rd ed. 1998) (explaining the human factor in program design). The flexible nature of computer program design effectively blurs the traditional antitrust tying analysis which requires the unambiguous identification of two separate and distinct goods or services, *e.g.*, salt tablets and a salt-injecting machine or patented spare parts and the service of installing them. This difficulty of discerning a function embedded in an operating system from a function designed as a separate program has generated a new vocabulary. A function embedded in an operating system is said to constitute an "integrated product."

E. The Microsoft Antitrust Litigation

In 1994, the Department of Justice brought suit against the Microsoft Corporation, challenging its licensing practices.[1] Microsoft had been licensing computer manufacturers to install its operating system in ways that were equivalent to exclusive supply contracts. Microsoft obtained commitments from computer man-

---

1 The description of the litigation is drawn from Daniel J. Gifford, *Microsoft Corporation, the Justice Department, and Antitrust Theory*, 25 SW. U. L. REV. 621, 632 (1996).

ufacturers to purchase licenses for their estimated production capacity. Microsoft then negotiated a royalty charge equal to the licensee's estimated production multiplied by an agreed-upon fee per unit of that production. This arrangement was generally referred to as a "per processor" license, because it was measured by the number of microprocessors which the licensee shipped. This practice effectively excluded rival producers of operating systems from dealing with any personal computer manufacturer who entered into any such arrangement with Microsoft, because the manufacturer had already paid for a license for the Microsoft operating system for all of its output. To purchase a license from another source would effectively require the manufacturer to pay twice: once to Microsoft and once to the rival supplier.

The 1994 lawsuit was settled in 1995 in a consent decree. The consent decree prohibited the practice of "per processor" licensing arrangements just described. It also contained a provision (§ IV(E)) prohibiting tying but nonetheless specifically allowing Microsoft to develop integrated products.

When Microsoft required computer manufacturers who sought a license to install its Windows 95 operating system on their products to also install the Microsoft Internet Explorer browser as well, the Department of Justice instituted a contempt proceeding. The Department contended that Microsoft was violating § IV(E) of the consent decree. The district court ruled that the decree was ambiguous and, therefore, that Microsoft could not be held in contempt for its past behavior. The district court, however, resolved the ambiguity in favor of the Department's position, enjoining future bundling of the browser with Microsoft's operating system. Microsoft appealed this ruling to the Court of Appeals. In the following opinion, the U.S. Court of Appeals for the District of Columbia both construed the consent decree and expressed its views upon the law of tying:

United States v. Microsoft Corporation

147 F.3d 935 (D.C. Cir. 1998)

Stephen F. Williams, Circuit Judge:

The district court entered a preliminary injunction prohibiting Microsoft Corporation from requiring computer manufacturers who license its operating system software to license its internet browser as well. . . . Microsoft appeals the preliminary injunction . . . . We find that the district court erred procedurally in entering a preliminary injunction without notice to Microsoft and substantively in its implicit construction of the consent decree on which the preliminary injunction rested. . . .

I.

This case arises from Microsoft's practices in marketing its Windows 95 operating system. An operating system is, so to speak, the central nervous system of the computer, controlling the computer's interaction with peripherals such as keyboards and printers. Windows 95 is an operating system that integrates a DOS shell with a graphical user interface, *i.e.*, a technology by which the operator performs functions not by typing at the keyboard but by clicks of his mouse. Operating systems also serve as "platforms" for application software such as word processors. As the word "platform" suggests, the operating system provides a basic support structure for an application via "application programming interfaces" ("APIs"), which provide general functions on which applications can rely. Each operating system's APIs are unique; hence applications tend to be written for particular operating systems. The primary market for operating systems consists of original equipment manufacturers ("OEMs"), which make computers, install operating systems and other software that they have licensed from vendors such as Microsoft, and sell the package to end users. These may be either individual consumers or businesses.

In an earlier opinion, also arising from litigation generated by the Justice Department's 1994 antitrust suit against Microsoft, we briefly described Microsoft's role in the software industry and some of the industry's economics. *United States v. Microsoft Corp.*, 56 F.3d 1448, 1451-52 (D.C.Cir.1995). Because IBM chose to install Microsoft's operating system on its personal computers, Microsoft acquired an "installed base" on millions of IBM and IBM-compatible PCs. That base constituted an exceptional advantage, and created exceptional risks of monopoly, because of two characteristics of the software industry—increasing returns to scale and network externalities. First, because most of the costs of software lie in the design, marginal production costs are negligible. Production of additional units appears likely to lower average costs indefinitely. (*I.e.*, the average cost curve never turns upward.) Second, an increase in the number of users of a particular item of software increases the number of other people with whom any user can share work. As a result, Microsoft's large installed base increases the incentive for independent software vendors to write compatible applications and thereby increases the value of its operating system to consumers.

The Department's 1994 complaint alleged a variety of anticompetitive practices, chiefly in Microsoft's licensing agreements with OEMs. Along with it, the Department filed a proposed consent decree limiting Microsoft's behavior, the product of negotiations between Microsoft, the Department and European competition authorities. Most relevant here is § IV(E) of the decree:

> Microsoft shall not enter into any License Agreement in which the terms of that agreement are expressly or impliedly conditioned upon:
>
> (i) the licensing of any other Covered Product, Operating System Software product or other product (provided, however, that this provision in and of itself shall not be construed to prohibit Microsoft from developing integrated products); or
>
> (ii) the OEM not licensing, purchasing, using or distributing any non-Microsoft product.

The Department sees a violation of § IV(E)(i) in Microsoft's marketing of Windows 95 and its web browser, Internet Explorer ("IE").

The Internet is a global network that links smaller networks of computers. The World Wide Web ("the Web") is the fastest-growing part of the Internet, composed of multimedia "pages" written in Hypertext Markup Language ("HTML") and connected to other pages by hypertext links. Browsers enable users to navigate the Web and to access information.

Most browsers are designed according to a "multiplatform" approach, with different versions for each of a variety of different operating systems. Joint Appendix ("J.A.") 81. Browsers also have the potential to serve as user interfaces and as platforms for applications (which could then be written for the APIs of a particular browser rather than of a particular operating system[1]), providing some of the traditional functions of an operating system. Widespread use of multi-platform browsers as user interfaces has some potential to reduce any monopoly-increasing effects of network externalities in the operating system market. Browsers can enable the user to access applications stored on the Internet or local networks, or to operate applications that are independent of the operating system. J.A. 103-05.

Microsoft has developed successive versions of IE, the first of which was initially released with Windows 95 in July 1995. Microsoft's Windows 95 license agreements have required OEMs to accept and install the software package as sent to them by Microsoft, including IE, and have prohibited OEMs from removing any features or functionality, *i.e.*, capacity to perform functions such as browsing. J.A. 86-89.

The first three versions of IE were actually included on the Windows 95 "master" disk supplied to OEMs. Department Br. at 4; J.A. 1277-78. IE 4.0, by contrast, was initially distributed on a separate CD-ROM and OEMs were not required to install it. Microsoft intended to start requiring OEMs to preinstall IE 4.0 as part of Windows 95 in February 1998. On learning of Microsoft's plans, the Department became concerned that this practice violated § IV(E)(i) by effectively conditioning the license for Windows 95 on the license for IE 4.0, creating (in its view) what antitrust law terms a "tie- in" between the operating system and the browser. (It is not clear why extension of Microsoft's established IE policy to IE 4.0 aroused the Department's concern.) It filed a petition seeking to hold Microsoft in civil contempt for its practices with respect to IE 3.0, and requesting "further" that the court explicitly order Microsoft not to employ similar agreements with respect to any version of IE.

. . . .

IV.

Section IV(E) arose from a 1993 complaint filed with the Directorate General IV of the European Union ("DG IV") (the principal competition authority in Europe). Novell, a rival software vendor, alleged that Microsoft was tying its MS-DOS operating system to the graphical user interface provided by Windows 3.11. Before the introduction of Windows 95, which integrated the two, Microsoft marketed the DOS component and the Windows component of the operating system separately, and Windows 3.11 could be operated with other DOS products. But Novell, which marketed a competing DOS product, DR-DOS, complained that by means of specific marketing practices—particularly "per processor and per system licenses," J.A. 754—Microsoft was creating economic incentives for OEMs to preinstall MS-DOS as well as Windows 3.11, thereby using its power in the market for DOS-compatible graphical user interfaces (where it commanded a near 100% market share) to affect OEM choice in the DOS market.[8] J.A. 839-48.

During June 1994 negotiations with the Department, Microsoft proposed the possibility of a joint settlement, and representatives of DG IV participated in meetings in Brussels and later in Washington, D.C. On July 15, 1994, the three sides reached agreement and Microsoft and the Department signed a stipulation agreeing to entry of the consent decree,

---

[1] Similarly, Sun Microsystems's "Java" programming language allows programmers to write applications that will run on any computer, regardless of the operating system, as long as certain Java-related software (a Java "virtual machine" and Java "class libraries") is present. Internet browsers incorporate the necessary Java-related software, and hence allow Java programs to live up to their "write once, run anywhere" billing.

[8] The indirect nature of the alleged tie may explain why § IV(E)(i) bars an agreement whose terms are "expressly or impliedly conditioned upon . . . the licensing of any other Covered Product."

including § IV(E). Both Microsoft and the Department characterize § IV(E) as an "anti-tying" provision.

. . . .

We think it quite possible . . . to find a construction of § IV(E)(i) that is consistent with the antitrust laws and accomplishes the parties' evident desires on entering the decree. The Department and DG IV were concerned with the alleged anticompetitive effects of tie-ins. Microsoft's goal was to preserve its freedom to design products that consumers would like. Antitrust scholars have long recognized the undesirability of having courts oversee product design, and any dampening of technological innovation would be at cross-purposes with antitrust law. Thus, a simple way to harmonize the parties' desires is to read the integration proviso of § IV(E)(i) as permitting any genuine technological integration, regardless of whether elements of the integrated package are marketed separately.

This reading requires us, of course, to give substantive content to the concept of integration. We think that an "integrated product" is most reasonably understood as a product that combines functionalities (which may also be marketed separately and operated together) in a way that offers advantages unavailable if the functionalities are bought separately and combined by the purchaser.

The point of the test is twofold and may be illustrated by its application to the paradigm case of the Novell complaint and the subsequent release of Windows 95. First, "integration" suggests a degree of unity, something beyond merely placing disks in the same box. If an OEM or end user (referred to generally as "the purchaser") could buy separate products and combine them himself to produce the "integrated product," then the integration looks like a sham. If Microsoft had simply placed the disks for Windows 3.11 and MS-DOS in one package and covered it with a single license agreement, it would have offered purchasers nothing they could not get by buying the separate products and combining them on their own.[11]

Windows 95, by contrast, unites the two functionalities in a way that purchasers could not; it is not simply a graphical user interface running on top of MS-DOS. Windows 95 is integrated in the sense that the two functionalities—DOS and graphical interface—do not exist separately: the code that is required to produce one also produces the other. Of course one can imagine that code being sold on two different disks, one containing all the code necessary for an operating system, the other with all the code necessary for a graphical interface. But as the code in the two would largely overlap, it would be odd to speak of either containing a discrete functionality. Rather, each would represent a disabled version of Windows 95. The customer could then "repair" each by installing them both on a single computer, but in such a case it would not be meaningful to speak of the customer "combining" two products. Windows 95 is an example of what Professor Areeda calls "physical or technological interlinkage that the customer cannot perform." X AREEDA, ELHAUGE & HOVENKAMP, ANTITRUST LAW § 1746b at 227, 228 (1996).

---

[11] The same analysis would apply to peripherals. If, for example, Microsoft tried to bundle its mouse with the operating system, it would have to show that the mouse/operating system package worked better if combined by Microsoft than it would if combined by OEMs. This is quite different from showing that the mouse works better with the operating system than other mice do. *See* X AREEDA, ELHAUGE & HOVENKAMP, ANTITRUST LAW ¶ 1746b. Problems seem unlikely to arise with peripherals, because their physical existence makes it easier to identify the act of combination. It seems unlikely that a plausible claim could be made that a mouse and an operating system were integrated in the sense that neither could be said to exist separately. An operating system used with a different mouse does not seem like a different product. But Windows 95 without IE's code will not boot, J.A. 1623, and adding a rival browser will not fix this. If the add/remove utility is run to hide the IE 4 technologies, Windows 95 reverts to an earlier version, OEM service release ("OSR") 2.0. J.A. 1660-61.

So the combination offered by the manufacturer must be different from what the purchaser could create from the separate products on his own. The second point is that it must also be better in some respect; there should be some technological value to integration. Manufacturers can stick products together in ways that purchasers cannot without the link serving any purpose but an anticompetitive one. The concept of integration should exclude a case where the manufacturer has done nothing more than to metaphorically "bolt" two products together, as would be true if Windows 95 were artificially rigged to crash if IEXPLORE.EXE were deleted. *Cf. ILC Peripherals Leasing Corp. v. International Business Machines Corp.*, 448 F. Supp. 228, 233 (N.D.Cal.1978) ("If IBM had simply bolted a disk pack or data module into a drive and sold the two items as a unit for a single price, the 'aggregation' would clearly have been an illegal tying arrangement."), *aff'd per curiam sub nom. Memorex Corp. v. International Business Machines Corp.*, 636 F.2d 1188 (9th Cir.1980); X AREEDA, ELHAUGE & HOVENKAMP, ANTITRUST LAW ¶ 1746 at 227 (discussing literal bolting). Thus if there is no suggestion that the product is superior to the purchaser's combination in some respect, it cannot be deemed integrated.[12]

It might seem difficult to put the two elements discussed above together. If purchasers cannot combine the two functionalities to make Windows 95, it might seem that there is nothing to test Windows 95 against in search of the required superiority. But purchasers can combine the functionalities in their stand-alone incarnations. They can install MS-DOS and Windows 3.11. The test for the integration of Windows 95 then comes down to the question of whether its integrated design offers benefits when compared to a purchaser's combination of corresponding stand-alone functionalities. The decree's evident embrace of Windows 95 as a permissible single product can be taken as manifesting the parties' agreement that it met this test.

The short answer is thus that integration may be considered genuine if it is beneficial when compared to a purchaser combination. But we do not propose that in making this inquiry the court should embark on product design assessment. In antitrust law, from which this whole proceeding springs, the courts have recognized the limits of their institutional competence and have on that ground rejected theories of "technological tying." A court's evaluation of a claim of integration must be narrow and deferential.[13] As the Fifth Circuit put it, "[S]uch a violation must be limited to those instances where the technological factor tying the hardware to the software has been designed for the purpose of tying the products, rather than to achieve some technologically beneficial result. Any other conclusion would enmesh the courts in a technical inquiry into the justifiability of product innovations." *Response of Carolina, Inc. v. Leasco Response, Inc.*, 537 F.2d 1307, 1330 (5th Cir.1976).

In fact, Microsoft did, in negotiations, suggest such an understanding of "integrated." In response to the Department and DG IV's statement of concern about tying, it asserted its

---

12 Thus of course we agree with the separate opinion that "commingling of code . . . alone is not sufficient evidence of true integration." Commingling for an anticompetitive purpose (or for no purpose at all) is what we refer to as "bolting."

13 The separate opinion seems to take this reluctance to engage in the evaluation of product design as deference to Microsoft's interpretation of the consent decree. It is nothing of the sort. We defer to neither party in interpreting the consent decree; in fact, we reject both parties' readings. We suggest here only that the limited competence of courts to evaluate high-tech product designs and the high cost of error should make them wary of second-guessing the claimed benefits of a particular design decision.

right to "continue to develop integrated products like [Windows 95] *that provide technological benefits to end users.*" J.A. 756 (emphasis added). Microsoft later withdrew this qualifying phrase, J.A. 760, in order, it claims, to avoid the application of "vague or subjective criteria"—though why the absence of criteria should cure a vagueness problem is unclear. But we do not think that removing the phrase can drain the word "integrated" of all meaning, and we do not accept the suggestion that the Department and DG IV bargained for an "integrated products" proviso so boundless as to swallow § IV(E)(i). Significantly, Microsoft assured the Department and DG IV that the elimination of the qualifying phrase "did not represent a substantive change." J.A. 761.

We believe this understanding is consistent with tying law. The Court in *Eastman Kodak Co. v. Image Tech. Servs.*, 504 U.S. 451, 112 S. Ct. 2072, 119 L. Ed. 2d 265 (1992), for example, found parts and service separate products because sufficient consumer demand existed to make separate provision efficient. . . . But we doubt that it would have subjected a self-repairing copier to the same analysis; *i.e.*, the separate markets for parts and service would not suggest that such an innovation was really a tie-in. (The separate opinion, we take it, makes roughly the same point by its observation about digital cameras. Similarly, Professor Areeda argues that new products integrating functionalities in a useful way should be considered single products regardless of market structure. *See* X AREEDA, ELHAUGE & HOVENKAMP, ANTITRUST LAW ¶ 1746b.[14]

We emphasize that this analysis does not require a court to find that an integrated product is superior to its stand-alone rivals. *See ILC Peripherals Leasing Corp. v. International Business Machines Corp.*, 458 F. Supp. 423, 439 (N.D.Cal.1978) ("Where there is a difference of opinion as to the advantages of two alternatives which can both be defended from an engineering standpoint, the court will not allow itself to be enmeshed 'in a technical inquiry into the justifiability of product innovations.'") (quoting *Leasco*, 537 F.2d at 1330), *aff'd per curiam sub nom. Memorex Corp. v. IBM Corp.*, 636 F.2d 1188 (9th Cir.1980). We do not read § IV(E)(i) to "put[ ] judges and juries in the unwelcome position of designing computers." IX AREEDA, ANTITRUST LAW ¶ 1700j at 15 (1991). The question is not whether the integration is a *net* plus but merely whether there is a plausible claim that it brings some advantage. Whether or not this is the appropriate test for antitrust law generally, we believe it is the only sensible reading of § IV(E)(i).

On the facts before us, Microsoft has clearly met the burden of ascribing facially plausible benefits to its integrated design as compared to an operating system combined with a stand-alone browser such as Netscape's Navigator.[15] Incorporating browsing functionality into the operating system allows applications to avail themselves of that functionality without starting up a separate browser application. J.A. 944, 965.[16] Further, components of

---

14 The antitrust question is of course distinct. The parties agree that the consent decree does not bar a challenge under the Sherman Act.

15 This issue is peripheral on the Department's interpretation of § IV(E)(i), and the Department may not have contested it as vigorously as it might. The guidance this opinion seeks to provide is limited to setting out the legal framework for analysis. The ultimate sorting out of any factual disputes is a different question, and one we of course cannot resolve on the limited record before us.

16 It is possible, of course, for applications vendors to bring about this Microsoft-created integration by distributing IE with their applications, which is apparently a relatively common practice. *See* J.A. 953, 966. Distribution by application vendors does not affect the conclusion that the integrated design brings benefits, nor does it suggest that IE has an existence apart from Windows 95. The consequence of this practice is simply that such

IE 3.0 and even more IE 4—especially the HTML reader—provide system services not directly related to Web browsing, enhancing the functionality of a wide variety of applications. J.A. 607-22, 1646-48. Finally, IE 4 technologies are used to upgrade some aspects of the operating system unrelated to Web browsing. For example, they are used to let users customize their "Start" menus, making favored applications more readily available. J.A. 490-95; 1662-64. They also make possible "thumbnail" previews of files on the computer's hard drive, using the HTML reader to display a richer view of the files' contents. J.A. 1664-69. Even the Department apparently concedes that integration of functionality into the operating system can bring benefits; responding to a comment on the proposed 1994 consent decree (which the Department published in the Federal Register as required by the Tunney Act), it stated that "a broad injunction against such behavior generally would not be consistent with the public interest." 59 Fed. Reg. 59426, 59428 (Nov. 17, 1994).

The conclusion that integration brings benefits does not end the inquiry we have traced out. It is also necessary that there be some reason Microsoft, rather than the OEMs or end users, must bring the functionalities together. *See* X AREEDA, ELHAUGE & HOVENKAMP, ANTITRUST LAW ¶ 1746b at 227; ¶ 1747 at 229. Some more subtleties emerge at this stage, parallel to those encountered in determining the integrated status of Windows 95. Microsoft provides OEMs with IE 4 on a separate CD-ROM (a fact to which the Department attaches great significance). It might seem, superficially, that the OEM is just as capable as Microsoft of combining the browser and the operating system.

But the issue is not which firm's employees should run particular disks or CD-ROMs. A program may be provided on three disks—Windows 95 certainly could be—but it is not therefore three programs which the user combines. Software code by its nature is susceptible to division and combination in a way that physical products are not; if the feasibility of installation from multiple disks meant that the customer was doing the combination, no software product could ever count as integrated. The idea that in installing IE 4 an OEM is combining two stand-alone products is defective in the same way that it would be nonsensical to say that an OEM installing Windows 95 is itself "combining" DOS functionality and a graphical interface. As the discussion above indicates, IE 3 and IE 4 add to the operating system features that cannot be included without also including browsing functionality. *See* J.A. 1661-68. Thus, as was the case with Windows 95, the products—the full functionality of the operating system when upgraded by IE 4 and the "browser functionality" of IE 4—do not exist separately.[17] This strikes us as an essential point. If the prod-

---

applications upgrade the purchaser's operating system to the Windows 95/IE level. The customer's act of installing the application implements Microsoft's prior integration of IE into Windows 95.

The record also suggests that there are some inefficiencies associated with application vendors' redistribution of IE code. Application vendors' affidavits assert that if the browser is installed in computers before sale, "installation of our product is faster, we have reduced product support issues, the perceived footprint (memory use) of our product is smaller, and in general customer perception of our product is better." J.A. 953, 966. Although the drawbacks of installation by applications vendors can be alleviated by OEMs' preinstalling an integrated operating system containing IE technologies, the drawbacks are not necessary consequences of a stand-alone design, but rather incidental costs of a particular method of bringing about the benefits of integration, namely, distribution of code by applications vendors. Thus they are not relevant to our comparison of the stand-alone and integrated designs.

[17] Our colleague's separate opinion suggests that IE may be separated from Windows 95 by treating some or all of the code that supplies operating system functionality as part of the operating system. But apart from that code, there is nothing more to IE than the four lines of programming required to summon browsing functionality from code that also supplies operating system functionality. J.A. 1654. Those four lines look more like a key to opening IE than anything that could plausibly be considered IE itself.

ucts have no separate existence, it is incorrect to speak of the purchaser combining them. Purchasers who end up with the Windows 95/IE package may have installed code from more than one disk; they may have taken the browser out of hiding;[18] they may have upgraded their operating system—indeed, Netscape characterizes the installation of IE 4 as "really an OS [operating system] upgrade." J.A. 589. But they have not combined two distinct products.

What, then, counts as the combination that brings together the two functionalities? Since neither fully exists separately, we think the only sensible answer is that the act of combination is the creation of the design that knits the two together. OEMs cannot do this: if Microsoft presented them with an operating system and a stand-alone browser application, rather than with the interpenetrating design of Windows 95 and IE 4, the OEMs could not combine them in the way in which Microsoft has integrated IE 4 into Windows 95. They could not, for example, make the operating system use the browser's HTML reader to provide a richer view of information on the computer's hard drive, J.A. 1665—not without changing the code to create an integrated browser. This reprogramming would be absurdly inefficient. Consequently, it seems clear that there is a reason why the integration must take place at Microsoft's level. This analysis essentially replays our comparison of Windows 95 to a bundle of MS-DOS and Windows 3.11 and concludes that the Windows 95/IE package more closely resembles Windows 95 than it does the bundle. The factual conclusion is, of course, subject to reexamination on a more complete record. On the facts before us, however, we are inclined to conclude that the Windows 95/IE package is a genuine integration; consequently, § IV(E)(i) does not bar Microsoft from offering it as one product.

. . . .

A few words with respect to our colleague's separate opinion may clarify our position. Judge Wald suggests that "the prohibition and the proviso could reasonably be construed to state that Microsoft may offer an 'integrated' product to OEMs under one license only if the integrated product achieves synergies great enough to justify Microsoft's extension of its monopoly to an otherwise distinct market." We are at a loss to understand how a section that (1) articulates a prohibition and (2) sets a limit on the reach of the prohibition[19] can be read to state a balancing test. Apart from the lack of textual support, we think that a balancing test that requires courts to weigh the "synergies" of an integrated product against the "evidence of distinct markets" is not feasible in any predictable or useful way. Courts are ill equipped to evaluate the benefits of high-tech product design,[20] and even could they place such an evaluation on one side of the balance, the strength of the "evidence of distinct mar-

---

[18] The preliminary injunction, as construed by the parties' later stipulation, treats Microsoft as in compliance if it allows the options of (1) running the Add/Remove Programs utility with respect to IE 3.x and (2) removing the IE icon from the desktop and from the Programs list in the Start menu and marking the file IEXPLORE.EXE "hidden." *See* above. The injunction's evidently unique status as a remedy for a "tying" complaint, requiring the defendant merely to allow an intermediary to hide the allegedly tied product, suggests the oddity of treating as separate products functionalities that are integrated in the way that Windows 95 and IE are.

[19] The proviso may be read to do this either by clarifying the concepts of "Covered Product" and an "other product" to prevent an "integrated" product from constituting a forbidden duo, or by carving out an exception for integrated products even if they otherwise represent such a duo. We do not believe that the choice of approach makes a substantive difference.

[20] Our colleague seems to hint that one way to perform this evaluationis to examine whether the integrated product "overwhelm[s]" the separate market. But data on market performance will obviously not be available when the new product is introduced, and in any case, the overwhelming of the separate market is precisely what is feared and may simply indicate anticompetitive practices.

kets," proposed for the other side of the scale, seems quite incommensurable. Both *Jefferson Parish* and *Eastman Kodak* use their "distinct markets" analysis in a binary fashion: markets are distinct or they are not. *See* 466 U.S. at 21-22, 104 S. Ct. 1551; 504 U.S. at 462, 112 S. Ct. 2072. If, as the record suggests, Microsoft proposed modification of the integration proviso because of concern about "vague or subjective criteria," J.A. 760, an interpretation requiring courts to weigh evidence that establishes distinctness (or does not) against a sliding scale of net synergistic value looks like the most total transvaluation one can imagine.

Institutional competence may not have been foremost in the parties' minds in drafting the consent decree, and judicial inability to apply a test does not ipso facto mean that the parties did not intend it. But if they did intend a balancing test, they kept that intent well hidden. Nothing in their contemporaneous conduct (or in the conduct of anyone, at any time) suggests that they contemplated a balancing inquiry. Windows 95 was not subjected to any such analysis, though the markets it unified were substantial and obviously distinct. J.A. 790-96. Indeed, one might think that an especially compelling case would be required to "justify Microsoft's extension of its monopoly" via Windows 95. Windows 95 leveraged Microsoft's Windows 3.11 market power into the operating system market, where network externalities are most apparent. *See Microsoft*, 56 F.3d at 1451. According to the separate opinion, Windows 95 should have required the utmost justification. But nothing suggests that it was analyzed that way, and it seems more likely that it passed muster not because the synergies of its integration outweighed the evidence of distinct markets but because it was, simply, integrated.

The view expressed in the separate opinion seems sure to thwart Microsoft's legitimate desire to continue to integrate products that had been separate—and hence necessarily would have been provided in distinct markets. By its very nature "integration" represents a change from a state of affairs in which products were separate, to one in which they are no longer. By focusing on the historical fact of separate provision, the separate opinion puts a thumb on the scale and requires Microsoft to counterbalance with evidence courts are not equipped to evaluate. We do not think that this makes sense in terms of the text of the consent decree, the evidence of the parties' intents, the values the decree was presumably intended to promote, or the competence of the judiciary.

. . . .

At this stage, then, the Department has not shown a reasonable probability of success on the merits. Given this failure, there is no reason to allow the preliminary injunction to remain in effect pending a proper hearing, and we reverse the district court's grant.

. . . .

COMMENTARY

1. The issue involved here is often referred to as "technological tying." When a manufacturer redesigns a product to incorporate a previously separate component, has the manufacturer "tied" the component to the main product? During the 1970s, when the IBM Corporation sometimes incorporated disk drives or other peripheral devices into its mainframe computers, it was forced to defend its behavior against antitrust plaintiffs. The tying charge, however, was sometimes cast in the language of monopolization. *See, e.g.*, *California Computer Products, Inc. v. International Bus. Mach. Corp.*, 613 F.2d 727 (9th Cir. 1979), and pages 235-36, *supra*.

2. The Department of Justice brought a new lawsuit against Microsoft Corp. in 1998, attacking Microsoft's bundling of its browser and its operating system. In that lawsuit, the practice was challenged as both tying and as monopolization. A number of recent cases have challenged tying practices as monopolization. Tying practices which are challenged as monopolization are examind in Chapter 9. Some tying practices have involved products protected by patents or copyrights. We examine these cases in Chapter 15.

United States v. Microsoft Corporation

87 F. Supp. 2d 30 (D.D.C. 2000)

[The United States charged the Microsoft Corporation with violating §§ 1 and 2 of the Sherman Act. One of the Government's principal contentions was that by bundling its browser (the Microsoft Internet Explorer) with its operating system (Windows 95 and Windows 98), Microsoft was violating § 1 by unlawfully tying the browser to the operating system and was violating § 2 by using its effective monopoly in operating systems to expand its modest share of the browser market. Underlying the Government's tying and monopolization claims is the belief that Microsoft's attempts to expand the share of its browser are directed at forestalling a threat to its operating system monopoly from "middleware."

Microsoft's Windows operating systems presently accounts for well over 80% of personal computer operating systems. This practical monopoly is reinforced by the need of software vendors to write software first for Windows and only later, if at all, for Macintosh and other operating systems. Software vendors write first for Windows because Windows users are the largest market for new software. Thus most software is written for Windows. Computer users want the Windows operating system because more software applications are written for Windows than for other operating systems. These two effects feed on each other: Software vendors write applications programs for the Windows operating system because Windows users are the largest market. Users insist on Windows as their operating system because more software is available for Windows systems.

Middleware is software which can connect software applications to different operating systems. Sun Microsystem's Java, for example, is prime example of middleware. Java is a programming language that can be used to write software programs which can run on different operating systems. Java works as follows: Software written in Java programming language is compiled into Java byte code. Any computer on which is installed a "Java virtual machine" is able to run such software, regardless of its operating system. A Java virtual machine is software which converts Java byte code into the machine code appropriate for the operating system of the host computer.

Presently, most computer users obtain new software by purchase from computer stores and download the software on to their hard drives. The Government believes, however, that within the foreseeable future, software programs increasingly will be made available from Internet servers. Presently all browsers contain Java virtual machines. All users, regardless of their operating systems (whether they are Windows, Macintosh, Unix, etc.), accordingly, will be able to use software programs written in the Java programming language and made available from Internet servers. When and if this new software distribution system arrives, Microsoft's practical monopoly over personal computer operating systems would be destroyed.]

CONCLUSIONS OF LAW

JACKSON, District Judge.

The United States, nineteen individual states, and the District of Columbia ("the plaintiffs") . . . charge, in essence, that Microsoft has waged an unlawful campaign in defense of its monopoly position in the market for operating systems designed to run on Intel-compatible personal computers ("PCs"). Specifically, the plaintiffs contend that Microsoft violated § 2 of the Sherman Act by engaging in a series of exclusionary, anticompetitive, and predatory acts to maintain its monopoly power. They also assert that Microsoft attempted, albeit unsuccessfully to date, to monopolize the Web browser market, likewise in violation of § 2. Finally, they contend that certain steps taken by Microsoft as part of its campaign to protect its monopoly power, namely tying its browser to its operating system and entering into exclusive dealing arrangements, violated § 1 of the Act.

Upon consideration of the Court's Findings of Fact ("Findings"), filed herein on November 5, 1999, as amended on December 21, 1999, the proposed conclusions of law submitted by the parties, the briefs of *amici curiae*, and the argument of counsel thereon, the Court concludes that Microsoft maintained its monopoly power by anticompetitive means and attempted to monopolize the Web browser market, both in violation of § 2. Microsoft also violated § 1 of the Sherman Act by unlawfully tying its Web browser to its operating system. The facts found do not support the conclusion, however, that the effect of Microsoft's marketing arrangements with other companies constituted unlawful exclusive dealing under criteria established by leading decisions under § 1.

. . . .

II. SECTION ONE OF THE SHERMAN ACT

Section 1 of the Sherman Act prohibits "every contract, combination . . . , or conspiracy, in restraint of trade or commerce . . . ." 15 U.S.C. § 1. Pursuant to this statute, courts have condemned commercial stratagems that constitute unreasonable restraints on competition, *see Continental T.V., Inc. v. GTE Sylvania Inc.*, 433 U.S. 36, 49, 97 S. Ct. 2549, 53 L. Ed. 2d 568 (1977); *Chicago Board of Trade v. United States*, 246 U.S. 231, 238-39, 38 S. Ct. 242, 62 L. Ed. 683 (1918), among them "tying arrangements" and "exclusive dealing" contracts. Tying arrangements have been found unlawful where sellers exploit their market power over one product to force unwilling buyers into acquiring another. *See Jefferson Parish Hospital District No. 2 v. Hyde*, 466 U.S. 2, 12, 104 S. Ct. 1551, 80 L. Ed. 2d 2 (1984); *Northern Pac. Ry. Co. v. United States*, 356 U.S. 1, 6, 78 S. Ct. 514, 2 L. Ed. 2d 545 (1958); *Times-Picayune Pub. Co. v. United States*, 345 U.S. 594, 605, 73 S. Ct. 872, 97 L. Ed. 1277 (1953). Where agreements have been challenged as unlawful exclusive dealing, the courts have condemned only those contractual arrangements that substantially foreclose competition in a relevant market by significantly reducing the number of outlets available to a competitor to reach prospective consumers of the competitor's product. *See Tampa Electric Co. v. Nashville Coal Co.*, 365 U.S. 320, 327, 81 S. Ct. 623, 5 L. Ed. 2d 580 (1961); *Roland Machinery Co. v. Dresser Industries, Inc.*, 749 F.2d 380, 393 (7th Cir.1984).

A. Tying

Liability for tying under § 1 exists where (1) two separate "products" are involved; (2) the defendant affords its customers no choice but to take the tied product in order to obtain the tying product; (3) the arrangement affects a substantial volume of interstate commerce; and (4) the defendant has "market power" in the tying product market. *Jefferson Parish*, 466 U.S. at 12-18, 104 S. Ct. 1551. The Supreme Court has since reaffirmed this test in *Eastman Kodak Co. v. Image Technical Services, Inc.*, 504 U.S. 451, 461-62, 112 S. Ct. 2072, 119 L. Ed. 2d 265 (1992). All four elements are required, whether the arrangement is subjected to a *per se* or Rule of Reason analysis.

The plaintiffs allege that Microsoft's combination of Windows and Internet Explorer by contractual and technological artifices constitute unlawful tying to the extent that those actions forced Microsoft's customers and consumers to take Internet Explorer as a condition of obtaining Windows. While the Court agrees with plaintiffs, and thus holds that Microsoft is liable for illegal tying under § 1, this conclusion is arguably at variance with a decision of the U.S. Court of Appeals for the D.C. Circuit in a closely related case, and must therefore be explained in some detail. Whether the decisions are indeed inconsistent is not for this Court to say.

The decision of the D.C. Circuit in question is *United States v. Microsoft Corp.*, 147 F.3d 935 (D.C.Cir.1998) ("*Microsoft II*") which is itself related to an earlier decision of the same Circuit, *United States v. Microsoft Corp.*, 56 F.3d 1448 (D.C.Cir.1995) ("*Microsoft I*"). The history of the controversy is sufficiently set forth in the appellate opinions and need not be recapitulated here, except to state that those decisions anticipated the instant case, and that *Microsoft II* sought to guide this Court, insofar as practicable, in the further proceedings it fully expected to ensue on the tying issue. Nevertheless, upon reflection this Court does not believe the D.C. Circuit intended *Microsoft II* to state a controlling rule of law for purposes of this case. As the *Microsoft II* court itself acknowledged, the issue before it was the construction to be placed upon a single provision of a consent decree that, although animated by antitrust considerations, was nevertheless still primarily a matter of determining contractual intent. The court of appeals' observations on the extent to which software product design decisions may be subject to judicial scrutiny in the course of § 1 tying cases are in the strictest sense *obiter dicta*, and are thus not formally binding. Nevertheless, both prudence and the deference this Court owes to pronouncements of its own Circuit oblige that it follow in the direction it is pointed until the trail falters.

The majority opinion in *Microsoft II* evinces both an extraordinary degree of respect for changes (including "integration") instigated by designers of technological products, such as software, in the name of product "improvement," and a corresponding lack of confidence in the ability of the courts to distinguish between improvements in fact and improvements in name only, made for anticompetitive purposes. Read literally, the D.C. Circuit's opinion appears to immunize any product design (or, at least, software product design) from antitrust scrutiny, irrespective of its effect upon competition, if the software developer can postulate *any* "plausible claim" of advantage to its arrangement of code. 147 F.3d at 950.

This undemanding test appears to this Court to be inconsistent with the pertinent Supreme Court precedents in at least three respects. First, it views the market from the defendant's perspective, or, more precisely, as the defendant would like to have the market viewed. Second, it ignores reality: The claim of advantage need only be plausible; it need not be proved. Third, it dispenses with any balancing of the hypothetical advantages against any anticompetitive effects.

The two most recent Supreme Court cases to have addressed the issue of product and market definition in the context of Sherman Act tying claims are *Jefferson Parish, supra*, and *Eastman Kodak, supra*. In *Jefferson Parish*, the Supreme Court held that a hospital offering hospital services and anesthesiology services as a package could not be found to have violated the anti-tying rules unless the evidence established that *patients*, *i.e.* consumers, perceived the services as separate products for which they desired a choice, and that the package had the effect of forcing the patients to purchase an unwanted product. 466 U.S. at 21-24, 28-29, 104 S. Ct. 1551. In *Eastman Kodak* the Supreme Court held that a manufacturer of photocopying and micrographic equipment, in agreeing to sell replacement parts for its machines only to those customers who also agreed to purchase repair services from it as well, would be guilty of tying if the evidence at trial established the existence of consumer demand for parts and services separately. 504 U.S. at 463, 112 S. Ct. 2072.

Both defendants asserted, as Microsoft does here, that the tied and tying products were in reality only a single product, or that every item was traded in a single market.[3] In *Jefferson Parish*, the defendant contended that it offered a "functionally integrated package of services"—a single product—but the Supreme Court concluded that the "character of the demand" for the constituent components, not their functional relationship, determined whether separate "products" were actually involved. 466 U.S. at 19, 104 S. Ct. 1551. In *Eastman Kodak*, the defendant postulated that effective competition in the equipment market precluded the possibility of the use of market power anticompetitively in any after-markets for parts or services: Sales of machines, parts, and services were all responsive to the discipline of the larger equipment market. The Supreme Court declined to accept this premise in the absence of evidence of "actual market realities," 504 U.S. at 466-67, 112 S. Ct. 2072, ultimately holding that "the proper market definition in this case can be determined only after a factual inquiry into the 'commercial realities' faced by consumers." *Id.* at 482, 112 S. Ct. 2072 (quoting *United States v. Grinnell Corp.*, 384 U.S. 563, 572, 86 S. Ct. 1698, 16 L. Ed. 2d 778 (1966)).[4]

In both *Jefferson Parish* and *Eastman Kodak*, the Supreme Court also gave consideration to certain theoretical "valid business reasons" proffered by the defendants as to why the arrangements should be deemed benign. In *Jefferson Parish*, the hospital asserted that the combination of hospital and anesthesia services eliminated multiple problems of scheduling, supply, performance standards, and equipment maintenance. 466 U.S. at 43-44, 104 S. Ct. 1551. The manufacturer in *Eastman Kodak* contended that quality control, inventory management, and the prevention of free riding justified its decision to sell parts only in conjunction with service. 504 U.S. at 483, 112 S. Ct. 2072. In neither case did the Supreme Court find those justifications sufficient if anticompetitive effects were proved. *Id.* at 483-86, 112 S. Ct. 2072; *Jefferson Parish*, 466 U.S. at 25 n.42, 104 S. Ct. 1551. Thus, at a minimum, the admonition of the D.C. Circuit in *Microsoft II* to refrain from any product design assessment as to whether the "integration" of Windows and Internet Explorer is a "net plus," deferring to Microsoft's "plausible claim" that it is of "some advantage" to consumers, is at odds with the Supreme Court's own approach.

The significance of those cases, for this Court's purposes, is to teach that resolution of product and market definitional problems must depend upon proof of commercial real-

---

[3] Microsoft contends that Windows and Internet Explorer represent a single "integrated product," and that the relevant market is a unitary market of "platforms for software applications." Microsoft's Proposed Conclusions of Law at 49 n.28.

[4] In *Microsoft II* the D.C. Circuit acknowledged it was without benefit of a complete factual record which might alter its conclusion that the "Windows 95/IE package is a genuine integration." 147 F.3d at 952.

ity, as opposed to what might appear to be reasonable. In both cases the Supreme Court instructed that product and market definitions were to be ascertained by reference to evidence of consumers' perception of the nature of the products and the markets for them, rather than to abstract or metaphysical assumptions as to the configuration of the "product" and the "market." *Jefferson Parish*, 466 U.S. at 18, 104 S. Ct. 1551; *Eastman Kodak*, 504 U.S. at 481-82, 112 S. Ct. 2072. In the instant case, the commercial reality is that consumers today perceive operating systems and browsers as separate "products," for which there is separate demand. Findings ¶¶ 149-54. This is true notwithstanding the fact that the software code supplying their discrete functionalities can be commingled in virtually infinite combinations, rendering each indistinguishable from the whole in terms of files of code or any other taxonomy. *Id.* ¶¶ 149-50, 162-63, 187-91.

Proceeding in line with the Supreme Court cases, which are indisputably controlling, this Court first concludes that Microsoft possessed "appreciable economic power in the tying market," *Eastman Kodak*, 504 U.S. at 464, 112 S. Ct. 2072, which in this case is the market for Intel-compatible PC operating systems. *See Jefferson Parish*, 466 U.S. at 14, 104 S. Ct. 1551 (defining market power as ability to force purchaser to do something that he would not do in competitive market); *see also Fortner Enterprises, Inc. v. United States Steel Corp.*, 394 U.S. 495, 504, 89 S. Ct. 1252, 22 L. Ed. 2d 495 (1969) (ability to raise prices or to impose tie-ins on any appreciable number of buyers within the tying product market is sufficient). While courts typically have not specified a percentage of the market that creates the presumption of "market power," no court has ever found that the requisite degree of power exceeds the amount necessary for a finding of monopoly power. *See Eastman Kodak*, 504 U.S. at 481, 112 S. Ct. 2072. Because this Court has already found that Microsoft possesses monopoly power in the worldwide market for Intel-compatible PC operating systems (*i.e.*, the tying product market), Findings ¶¶ 18-67, the threshold element of "appreciable economic power" is *a fortiori* met.

Similarly, the Court's Findings strongly support a conclusion that a "not insubstantial" amount of commerce was foreclosed to competitors as a result of Microsoft's decision to bundle Internet Explorer with Windows. The controlling consideration under this element is "simply whether a total amount of business" that is "substantial enough in terms of dollar-volume so as not to be merely *de minimis*" is foreclosed. *Fortner*, 394 U.S. at 501, 89 S. Ct. 1252; *cf. International Salt Co. v. United States*, 332 U.S. 392, 396, 68 S. Ct. 12, 92 L. Ed. 20 (1947) (unreasonable *per se* to foreclose competitors from any substantial market by a tying arrangement).

Although the Court's Findings do not specify a dollar amount of business that has been foreclosed to any particular present or potential competitor of Microsoft in the relevant market,[5] including Netscape, the Court did find that Microsoft's bundling practices caused Navigator's usage share to drop substantially from 1995 to 1998, and that as a direct result Netscape suffered a severe drop in revenues from lost advertisers, Web traffic and purchases of server products. It is thus obvious that the foreclosure achieved by Microsoft's refusal to offer Internet Explorer separately from Windows exceeds the Supreme Court's *de minimis* threshold. *See Digidyne Corp. v. Data General Corp.*, 734 F.2d 1336, 1341 (9th Cir.1984) (citing *Fortner*).

The facts of this case also prove the elements of the forced bundling requirement. Indeed, the Supreme Court has stated that the "essential characteristic" of an illegal tying

---

[5] Most of the quantitative evidence was presented in units other than monetary, but numbered the units in millions, whatever their nature.

arrangement is a seller's decision to exploit its market power over the tying product "to force the buyer into the purchase of a tied product that the buyer either did not want at all, or might have preferred to purchase elsewhere on different terms." *Jefferson Parish*, 466 U.S. at 12, 104 S. Ct. 1551. In that regard, the Court has found that, beginning with the early agreements for Windows 95, Microsoft has conditioned the provision of a license to distribute Windows on the OEMs' purchase of Internet Explorer. Findings ¶¶ 158-65. The agreements prohibited the licensees from ever modifying or deleting any part of Windows, despite the OEMs' expressed desire to be allowed to do so. *Id.* ¶¶ 158, 164. As a result, OEMs were generally not permitted, with only one brief exception, to satisfy consumer demand for a browserless version of Windows 95 without Internet Explorer. *Id.* ¶¶ 158, 202. Similarly, Microsoft refused to license Windows 98 to OEMs unless they also agreed to abstain from removing the icons for Internet Explorer from the desktop. *Id.* ¶ 213. Consumers were also effectively compelled to purchase Internet Explorer along with Windows 98 by Microsoft's decision to stop including Internet Explorer on the list of programs subject to the Add/Remove function and by its decision not to respect their selection of another browser as their default. *Id.* ¶¶ 170-72.

The fact that Microsoft ostensibly priced Internet Explorer at zero does not detract from the conclusion that consumers were forced to pay, one way or another, for the browser along with Windows. Despite Microsoft's assertion that the Internet Explorer technologies are not "purchased" since they are included in a single royalty price paid by OEMs for Windows 98, *see* Microsoft's Proposed Conclusions of Law at 12-13, it is nevertheless clear that licensees, including consumers, are forced to take, and pay for, the entire package of software and that any value to be ascribed to Internet Explorer is built into this single price. *See United States v. Microsoft Corp.*, Nos. CIV. A. 98-1232, 98-1233, 1998 WL 614485, *12 (D.D.C., Sept. 14, 1998); IIIA Philip E. Areeda & Herbert Hovenkamp, Antitrust Law ¶ 760b6, at 51 (1996) ("[T]he tie may be obvious, as in the classic form, or somewhat more subtle, as when a machine is sold or leased at a price that covers 'free' servicing."). Moreover, the purpose of the Supreme Court's "forcing" inquiry is to expose those product bundles that raise the cost or difficulty of doing business for would-be competitors to prohibitively high levels, thereby depriving consumers of the opportunity to evaluate a competing product on its relative merits. It is not, as Microsoft suggests, simply to punish firms on the basis of an increment in price attributable to the tied product. *See Fortner*, 394 U.S. at 512-14, 89 S. Ct. 1252; *Jefferson Parish*, 466 U.S. at 12-13, 104 S. Ct. 1551.

As for the crucial requirement that Windows and Internet Explorer be deemed "separate products" for a finding of technological tying liability, this Court's Findings mandate such a conclusion. Considering the "character of demand" for the two products, as opposed to their "functional relation," *id.* at 19, Web browsers and operating systems are "distinguishable in the eyes of buyers." *Id.*; Findings ¶¶ 149-54. Consumers often base their choice of which browser should reside on their operating system on their individual demand for the specific functionalities or characteristics of a particular browser, separate and apart from the functionalities afforded by the operating system itself. *Id.* ¶¶ 149-51. Moreover, the behavior of other, lesser software vendors confirms that it is certainly efficient to provide an operating system and a browser separately, or at least in separable form. *Id.* ¶ 153. Microsoft is the only firm to refuse to license its operating system without a browser. *Id.*; *see Berkey Photo, Inc. v. Eastman Kodak Co.*, 603 F.2d 263, 287 (2d Cir.1979). This Court concludes that Microsoft's decision to offer only the bundled—"integrated"—version of Windows and Internet Explorer derived not from technical necessity or business efficiencies; rather, it was the result of a deliberate and purposeful choice to quell incipient competition before it reached truly minatory proportions.

The Court is fully mindful of the reasons for the admonition of the D.C. Circuit in *Microsoft II* of the perils associated with a rigid application of the traditional "separate products" test to computer software design. Given the virtually infinite malleability of software code, software upgrades and new application features, such as Web browsers, could virtually always be configured so as to be capable of separate and subsequent installation by an immediate licensee or end user. A court mechanically applying a strict "separate demand" test could improvidently wind up condemning "integrations" that represent genuine improvements to software that are benign from the standpoint of consumer welfare and a competitive market. Clearly, this is not a desirable outcome. Similar concerns have motivated other courts, as well as the D.C. Circuit, to resist a strict application of the "separate products" tests to similar questions of "technological tying." *See, e.g., Foremost Pro Color, Inc. v. Eastman Kodak Co.*, 703 F.2d 534, 542-43 (9th Cir.1983); *Response of Carolina, Inc. v. Leasco Response, Inc.*, 537 F.2d 1307, 1330 (5th Cir.1976); *Telex Corp. v. IBM Corp.*, 367 F. Supp. 258, 347 (N.D.Okla.1973).

To the extent that the Supreme Court has spoken authoritatively on these issues, however, this Court is bound to follow its guidance and is not at liberty to extrapolate a new rule governing the tying of software products. Nevertheless, the Court is confident that its conclusion, limited by the unique circumstances of this case, is consistent with the Supreme Court's teaching to date.[6]

ORDER

In accordance with the Conclusions of Law filed herein this date, it is, this 3rd day of April, 2000,

ORDERED, ADJUDGED, and DECLARED, that Microsoft has violated §§ 1 and 2 of the Sherman Act . . . .

COMMENTARY

In another portion of this *Microsoft* opinion, which appears in Chapter 9 *infra*, page 453, the government prevailed in a § 2 claim of monopolization. Microsoft appealed to the Court of Appeals for the District of Columbia; the government appealed directly to the Supreme Court under the Expediting Act, 15 U.S.C. § 29(b). On September 16, 2000, the Supreme Court, Justice Breyer dissenting, denied the government's petition for *certiorari* and remanded the case to the Court of Appeals for the District of Columbia. *Microsoft Corp. v. United States,* 530 U.S. 301 (2000). The decision of the Court of Appeals follows.

---

6 *Amicus curiae* Lawrence Lessig has suggested that a corollary concept relating to the bundling of "partial substitutes" in the context of software design may be apposite as a limiting principle for courts called upon to assess the compliance of these products with antitrust law. This Court has been at pains to point out that the true source of the threat posed to the competitive process by Microsoft's bundling decisions stems from the fact that a competitor to the tied product bore the potential, but had not yet matured sufficiently, to open up the tying product market to competition. Under these conditions, the anticompetitive harm from a software bundle is much more substantial and pernicious than the typical tie. *See* X PHILLIP E. AREEDA, EINER ELHAUGE & HERBERT HOVENKAMP, ANTITRUST LAW ¶ 1747 (1996). A company able to leverage its substantial power in the tying product market in order to force consumers to accept a tie of partial substitutes is thus able to spread inefficiency from one market to the next, *id.* at 232, and thereby "sabotage a nascent technology that might compete with the tying product but for its foreclosure from the market." III PHILLIP E. AREEDA & HERBERT HOVENKAMP, ANTITRUST LAW ¶ 1746.1d at 495 (Supp.1999).

United States v. Microsoft Corporation

253 F.3d 34 (D.C. Cir. 2001)

PER CURIAM.

Microsoft Corporation appeals from judgments of the District Court finding the company in violation of §§ 1 and 2 of the Sherman Act and ordering various remedies.

[The parts of this opinion that address monopolization, attempted monopolization, trial proceedings, and remedy are in Ch. 9, *infra*—Eds.]

. . . .

TYING

Microsoft . . . contests the District Court's determination of liability under § 1 of the Sherman Act. The District Court concluded that Microsoft's contractual and technological bundling of the IE web browser (the "tied" product) with its Windows operating system ("OS") (the "tying" product) resulted in a tying arrangement that was *per se* unlawful. . . . We hold that the rule of reason, rather than *per se* analysis, should govern the legality of tying arrangements involving platform software products. . . . Accordingly, we vacate the District Court's finding of a *per se* tying violation and remand the case. Plaintiffs may on remand pursue their tying claim under the rule of reason.

The facts underlying the tying allegation substantially overlap with those set forth . . . in connection with the § 2 monopoly maintenance claim. The key District Court findings are that (1) Microsoft required licensees of Windows 95 and 98 also to license IE as a bundle at a single price; . . . (2) Microsoft refused to allow OEMs to uninstall or remove IE from the Windows desktop; . . . (3) Microsoft designed Windows 98 in a way that withheld from consumers the ability to remove IE by use of the Add/Remove Programs utility; . . . and (4) Microsoft designed Windows 98 to override the user's choice of default web browser in certain circumstances. . . . The court found that these acts constituted a *per se* tying violation. . . . Although the District Court also found that Microsoft commingled operating system-only and browser-only routines in the same library files, . . . it did not include this as a basis for tying liability despite plaintiffs' request that it do so . . . .

. . . .

Microsoft does not dispute that it bound Windows and IE . . . . Instead it argues that Windows (the tying good) and IE browsers (the tied good) are not "separate products,". . . and that it did not substantially foreclose competing browsers from the tied product market . . . .

. . . .

The requirement that a practice involve two separate products before being condemned as an illegal tie started as a purely linguistic requirement: unless products are separate, one cannot be "tied" to the other. . . .

. . . .

The first case to give content to the separate-products test was *Jefferson Parish* . . . . That case addressed a tying arrangement in which a hospital conditioned surgical care at its facility on the purchase of anesthesiological services from an affiliated medical group. The facts were a challenge for casual separate-products analysis because the tied service—anesthesia—was neither intuitively distinct from nor intuitively contained within the tying service—surgical care. . . .

The *Jefferson Parish* Court resolved the matter in two steps. First, it clarified that "the answer to the question whether one or two products are involved" does not turn "on the functional relationship between them . . . ." . . . In other words, the mere fact that two items are complements, that "one . . . is useless without the other" . . . does not make them a single "product" for purposes of tying law. . . . Second, reasoning that the "definitional question [whether two distinguishable products are involved] depends on whether the arrangement may have the type of competitive consequences addressed by the rule [against tying]" . . . the Court decreed that "no tying arrangement can exist unless there is sufficient *demand* for the purchase of anesthesiological services separate from hospital services to identify a distinct product market in which it is *efficient* to offer anesthesiological services separately from hospital service." . . .

. . . .

To understand the logic behind the Court's consumer demand test, consider first the postulated harms from tying. The core concern is that tying prevents goods from competing directly for consumer choice on their merits. . . . With a tie, a buyer's "freedom to select the best bargain in the second market [could be] impaired by his need to purchase the tying product, and perhaps by an inability to evaluate the true cost of either product . . . ." Direct competition on the merits of the tied product is foreclosed when the tying product either is sold only in a bundle with the tied product or, though offered separately, is sold at a bundled price, so that the buyer pays the same price whether he takes the tied product or not. In both cases, a consumer buying the tying product becomes entitled to the tied product; he will therefore likely be unwilling to buy a competitor's version of the tied product even if, making his own price/quality assessment, that is what he would prefer.

But not all ties are bad. Bundling obviously saves distribution and consumer transaction costs. . . . This is likely to be true, to take . . . [an example] from the computer industry, with the integration of . . . spell checkers in word processors. . . . Bundling can also capitalize on certain economies of scope. A possible example is the "shared" library files that perform OS and browser functions with the same lines of code and thus may save drive space . . . .

Recognizing the potential benefits from tying, . . . the Court in *Jefferson Parish* forged a separate-products test that, like those of market power and substantial foreclosure, attempts to screen out false positives under *per se* analysis. The consumer demand test is a rough proxy for whether a tying arrangement may, on balance, be welfare-enhancing, and unsuited to *per se* condemnation. . . . Only when the efficiencies from bundling are dominated by the benefits to choice for enough consumers, however, will we actually observe consumers making independent purchases.

. . . On the supply side, firms without market power will bundle two goods only when the cost savings from joint sale outweigh the value consumers place on separate choice. So bundling by all competitive firms implies strong net efficiencies. If a court finds either that there is no noticeable separate demand for the tied product, or there being not direct evidence of separate demand, that the entire "competitive fringe" engages in the same behavior as the defendant, . . . then the tying and the tied products should be declared one product and *per se* liability should be rejected.

Before concluding our exegesis of *Jefferson Parish*'s separate-products test, we should clarify two things. First, *Jefferson Parish* does not endorse a direct inquiry into the efficiencies of a bundle. Rather it proposes easy-to administer proxies for net efficiency. In describing the separate-products test we discuss efficiencies only to explain the rationale behind the consumer demand inquiry. To allow the separate-products test to become a detailed inquiry into possible welfare consequences would turn a screening test into the very process it is expected to render unnecessary. . . .

Second, the separate-products test is not a one-sided inquiry into the cost savings from a bundle. Although *Jefferson Parish* acknowledged that prior lower court cases looked at cost-savings to decide separate products, . . . the Court conspicuously did not adopt that approach in its disposition of tying arrangements before it. Instead it chose proxies that balance cost savings against reduction in consumer choice.

With this background, we now turn to the separate products inquiry before us. The District Court found that many consumers, if given the option, would choose their browser separately from the OS. . . . Turning to industry custom, the court found that, although all major OS vendors bundled browsers with their OSs, these companies either sold versions without a browser, or allowed OEMs or end-users either not to install the bundled browser or in any event to "uninstall" it. . . .

. . . .

In light of the monopoly maintenance section, . . . we do not find that Microsoft's integration is welfare-enhancing or that it should be absolved of tying liability. . . .

. . . .

We now address directly the larger question as we see it: whether standard *per se* analysis should be applied "off the shelf" to evaluate the defendant's tying arrangement, one which involves software that serves as a platform for third party applications. . . . [T]here are strong reasons to doubt that the integration of additional software functionality into an OS falls among these arrangements. Applying *per se* analysis to such an amalgamation creates undue risks of error and of deterring welfare-enhancing innovation.

. . . .

There may also be a number of efficiencies that, although very real, have been ignored in the calculations underlying the adoption of a *per se* rule for tying. We fear that these efficiencies are common in technologically dynamic markets where product development is especially unlikely to follow an easily foreseen linear pattern. . . . We do not have enough empirical evidence regarding the effect of Microsoft's practice on the amount of consumer surplus created or consumer choice foreclosed by the integration of added functionality into platform software to exercise sensible judgment regarding that entire class of behavior. . . . [W]e vacate the District Court's finding of *per se* tying liability under Sherman Act § 1. We remand the case for evaluation of Microsoft's tying arrangements under the rule of reason. . . .

. . . .

Our judgment regarding the comparative merits of the *per se* rule and the rule of reason, is confined to the tying arrangement before us, where the tying product is software whose major purpose is to serve as a platform for third-party applications and the tied product is complementary software functionality. . . . [W]e do not have the confidence to speak to facts outside the record . . . . Nor should we be interpreted as setting a precedent for switching to the rule of reason every time a court identifies an efficiency justification for a tying arrangement. Our reading of the record suggests merely that integration of new functionality into platform software is a common practice and that wooden application of *per se* rules in this litigation may cast a cloud over platform innovation in the market for PCs, network computers and information appliances.

Should plaintiffs choose to pursue a tying claim under the rule of reason, we note the following for the benefit of the trial court:

First, on remand, plaintiffs must show that Microsoft's conduct unreasonably restrained competition. Meeting that burden "involves an inquiry into the actual effect" of Microsoft's conduct on competition in the tied good market, . . . the putative market for browsers. . . .

Second, the fact that we have already considered some of the behavior plaintiffs allege to constitute tying violations in the monopoly maintenance section does not resolve the

§ 1 inquiry. The two practices that plaintiffs have most ardently claimed as tying violations are, indeed, a basis for liability under plaintiffs' § 2 monopoly maintenance claim. . . .

Finally, the District Court must also consider an alleged tying violation that we did not consider under § 2 monopoly maintenance: price bundling. First, the court must determine if Microsoft indeed price bundled—that is, was Microsoft's charge for Windows and IE higher than its charge would have been for Windows alone?

. . . .

COMMENTARY

1. Subsequent to the decision in the *Microsoft* case by the Court of Appeals for the D.C. Circuit on June 28, 2001, there have been three significant developments relating to the remand. First, District Judge Colleen Kollar-Kotelly was selected to supervise this phase of the case. Second, the Department of Justice and the state attorneys-general agreed not to seek the dissolution of Microsoft into two companies in the remedy phase of the case. Third, the Department of Justice and the state attorneys-general further agreed to withdraw their claim that Microsoft had illegally tied its Internet Explorer to the Windows operating system from this phase of the litigation. N.Y. TIMES, Sept. 21, 2001, at C9, col. 1.

2. What is the meaning of the Court of Appeals' statement that "The facts underlying the tying allegation substantially overlap with those set forth . . . in connection with the § 2 monopoly maintenance claim"? How does the D.C. Circuit opinion express the relationship between §§ 1 and 2 of the Sherman Act with regard to the conduct of bundling the browser function with the operating system? Does the opinion suggest that the challenged conduct (*e.g.*, contractual tying) may support a monopoly maintenance claim under § 2 without also stating an illegal tying arrangement under § 1? Is the court stating that the conduct of a tying arrangement that contributed to the maintenance of the market power of the tying product is to be considered as part of a § 2 claim, but that a tying arrangement that affected the market for the tied product remained a tying claim under § 1? Consider this issue again in Chapter 9, *infra*.

3. Explain the reasons why the *per se* tying rule is rejected by the court. What are the perceived deficiencies of the *per se* rule that deprive it of relevance to the *Microsoft* case on remand? What is the plaintiff's burden under the rule of reason on remand? Under the exegesis of the *Jefferson Parish* analysis presented by the court of appeals, could Microsoft prevail on the tying issue if it introduces only evidence of substantial cost savings attributable to the bundling?

Does the D.C. Circuit's decision to apply a rule of reason approach to assess the bundling of new functionalities into platform software reinforce the position taken by Justice O'Connor in her concurring opinion in *Jefferson Parish*? *See* pages 252-54, *infra*. Is the *per se* rule suited to addressing tying claims involving the products of new technology?

Chapter 7
Other Vertical Restraints

A. Introduction

In Chapter 5, we examined (1) vertical price-fixing agreements, (2) vertical nonprice agreements which restricted the territories in which (or customers to whom) distributors and dealers were permitted to sell, and (3) exclusive dealing contracts: contracts in which a manufacturer or supplier agrees with a dealer not to supply other dealers in the same area. In Chapter 6, we examined the lawfulness of tying agreements. In this Chapter, we examine exclusive supply (or requirements) contracts pursuant to which a customer agrees to purchase its needs for a product exclusively from a single supplier.

B. Exclusive Supply Contracts

Like tying arrangements, the legality of exclusive supply contracts may be governed by §§ 1 and 2 of the Sherman Act, § 3 of the Clayton Act, or § 5 of the Federal Trade Commission Act. As in the case of tying contracts, the application of the Clayton Act turns upon whether the product being supplied is a "commodity" or something else (like an intangible asset, a service or real property), since the language of the Clayton Act limits its application to "goods, wares, merchandise . . . or other commodities." Unlike tying arrangements, the courts have not applied the *per se* characterization to exclusive dealing contracts. The U.S. Supreme Court has ruled upon the lawfulness of exclusive supply or requirements contracts in two cases, once in 1949 and again twelve years later in 1961. In 1949, the Court wrestled with the issue of whether the stringent standards that the Court had just adopted for the imposition of Clayton Act § 3 to tying arrangements should be also applied to requirements contracts evaluated under that same § 3, and, as we shall see, provided an ambiguous answer.

The antitrust treatment of exclusive supply arrangements has a lengthy caselaw history. After the enactment of the Clayton Act in 1914, the newly-established Federal Trade Commission undertook actively to enforce § 3 of the Clayton Act as absolutely barring exclusive supply contracts. *Standard Electric Manufacturing Co.*, 5 F.T.C. 376 (1923). The first Supreme Court review came in *Standard Fashion Co. v. Magrane-Houston Co.*, 258 U.S. 346 (1922), a case involving a dominant dress pattern manufacturer whose exclusive contracts extended to 40%

of the available outlets. In finding the requisite probability of a lessening of competition under § 3 of the Clayton Act, the Court noted that Congress had deemed the Sherman Act, as interpreted, limited to full-blown restraints of trade. In enacting § 3 of the Clayton Act, Congress intended earlier intervention under a different standard, which the court described as follows:

> The Clayton Act sought to reach the agreements embraced within its sphere in their incipiency. . . .
>
> . . . It was intended to prevent such agreements as would under the circumstances disclosed probably lessen competition, or create an actual tendency to monopoly. That it was not intended to reach every remote lessening of competition is shown in the requirement that such lessening must be substantial.

258 U.S. at 356-57. Unlike the *Standard Electric Manufacturing* litigation, the trial court in *Standard Fashion* admitted evidence of industry practice as well as testimony of the defendant on the basis of its decision to use exclusive supply contracts. When the Supreme Court came to consider *Standard Stations* in 1949 (set forth below), there was at that time the precedent of a "rule of reason" approach in *Standard Fashion* as well as the *per se* approach of the Court two years earlier in *International Salt Co. v. United States*, 332 U.S. 292 (1947), in which it was held that a tying arrangement that involved a "not insubstantial" amount of commerce measured in dollar terms, would be considered without more to violate § 3 of the Clayton Act. In bringing the *Standard Stations* case, the government sought to obtain a uniform, *per se* rule under § 3 for both tying arrangements and exclusive dealing.

In the excerpt of *Standard Stations* that follows, consider the extent to which the Court considered the precedents and the two practices. In reading the lengthy extract from that case, observe the Court's recognition of the procompetitive or efficiency-enhancing aspects of requirements contracts. Consider whether the Court gave a clear-cut and readily understandable answer to the question before it. Does the case invoke an inference of foreclosure from its definition of substantial commerce stated in terms of market share? Can you state the Court's definition of substantial?

Recall that the *Jefferson Parish* case in the prior Chapter involved a five-year exclusive contract for anesthesiology services with the hospital. Since the plaintiff had failed to make out a *per se* tying case, the majority opinion asserted that the plaintiff bore the burden of proving that the Roux contract unreasonably restrained competition, thus blurring the question of the type of analysis to which the Roux contract would be subjected. The four concurring justices did state the standard for determining the legality of an exclusive dealing arrangement under a rule of reason analysis as follows:

> In determining whether an exclusive-dealing contract is unreasonable, the proper focus is on the structure of the market for the products or services in question—the number of sellers and buyers

> in the market, the volume of their business, and the ease with which buyers and sellers can redirect their purchases or sales to others. Exclusive dealing is an unreasonable restraint on trade only when a significant fraction of buyers or sellers are frozen out of a market by the exclusive deal.

466 U.S. 2, 45 (1984).

In the materials that follow, consider whether the concurring justices have stated a fair summary of the current antitrust law governing exclusive dealing contracts. Consider how the rule of reason analysis may have been changed by the decision in *California Dental Association* (in Chapter 2, *supra*). Is the 30% benchmark of market power in *Jefferson Parish* applicable to an exclusive dealing contract?

Standard Oil Co. of California v. United States (Standard Stations)

337 U.S. 293 (1949)

[The Standard Oil Company of California, the largest seller of gasoline in the "Western Area" (composed of Arizona, California, Idaho, Nevada, Oregon, Utah and Washington) sold, inter alia, to the operators of independent service stations under exclusive supply contracts. Standard's sales under such contracts constituted 6.7% of the total gasoline sold in the Western Area. Retail service-station sales by Standard's six leading competitors absorbed 42.5% of the total taxable gallonage and those companies also employed exclusive supply contracts.

[Two years earlier, the Court had decided *International Salt Co. v. United States*, 332 U.S. 392 (1947), a case in which it considered how it should construe § 3 of the Clayton Act to tying contracts. In *International Salt* the Court adopted a "quantitative substantiality" approach to the application of § 3.]

Since § 3 of the Clayton Act was directed to prohibiting specific practices even though not covered by the broad terms of the Sherman Act,[1] it is appropriate to consider first whether the enjoined contracts fall within the prohibition of the narrower Act. . . .

Obviously the contracts here at issue would be proscribed if § 3 stopped short of the qualifying clause beginning, "where the effect of such lease, sale, or contract for sale. . . ." If effect is to be given that clause, however, it is by no means obvious, in view of Standard's minority share of the "line of commerce" involved, of the fact that share has not recently increased, and of the claims of these contracts to economic utility, that the effect of the contracts may be to lessen competition or tend to create a monopoly. It is the qualifying clause, therefore, which must be construed.

---

[1] After the Clayton Bill, H.R. 15657, had passed the House, the Senate struck § 4, the section prohibiting tying clauses and requirements contracts, on the ground that such practices were subject to condemnation by the Federal Trade Commission under the then pending Trade Commission Bill. In support of a motion to reconsider this vote, Senator Reed of Missouri argued that the Trade Commission would be unlikely to outlaw agreements of a type held by this Court, in *Henry v. A. B. Dick Co.,* 224 U.S. 1, not to be in violation of the Sherman Act. See 51 Cong. Rec. 14088, 14090–92. The motion was agreed to. Id. at 14223.

[This Court's decision in *International Salt Co. v. United States*, 332 U.S. 392 (1947)] . . . at least as to contracts tying the sale of a nonpatented to a patented product, rejected the necessity of demonstrating economic consequences once it has been established that "the volume of business affected" is not "insignificant or insubstantial" and that the effect of the contracts is to "foreclose competitors from [a] substantial market." . . . It is clear, therefore, that unless a distinction is to be drawn for purposes of the applicability of § 3 between requirements contracts and contracts tying the sale of a nonpatented to a patented product, the showing that Standard's requirements contracts affected a gross business of $58,000,000 comprising 6.7% of the total in the area goes far toward supporting the inference that competition has been or probably will be substantially lessened.

In favor of confining the standard laid down by the *International Salt* case to tying agreements, important economic differences may be noted. Tying agreements serve hardly any purpose beyond the suppression of competition. The justification most often advanced in their defense—the protection of the good will of the manufacturer of the tying device—fails in the usual situation because specification of the type and quality of the product to be used in connection with the tying device is protection enough. . . .

Requirements contracts, on the other hand, may well be of economic advantage to buyers as well as to sellers, and thus indirectly of advantage to the consuming public. In the case of the buyer, they may assure supply, afford protection against rises in price, enable long-term planning on the basis of known costs, and obviate the expense and risk of storage in the quantity necessary for a commodity having a fluctuating demand. From the seller's point of view, requirements contracts may make possible the substantial reduction of selling expenses, give protection against price fluctuations, and—of particular advantage to a newcomer to the field to whom it is important to know what capital expenditures are justified—offer the possibility of a predictable market. . . . They may be useful, moreover, to a seller trying to establish a foothold against the counterattacks of entrenched competitors. . . . Since these advantages of requirements contracts may often be sufficient to account for their use, the coverage by such contracts of a substantial amount of business affords a weaker basis for the inference that competition may be lessened than would similar coverage by tying clauses, especially where use of the latter is combined with market control of the tying device. A patent, moreover, although in fact there may be many competing substitutes for the patented article, is at least prima facie evidence of such control. And so we could not dispose of this case merely by citing *International Salt Co. v. United States*. . . .

Thus, even though the qualifying clause of § 3 is appended without distinction of terms equally to the prohibition of tying clauses and of requirements contracts, pertinent considerations support, certainly as a matter of economic reasoning, varying standards as to each for the proof necessary to fulfill the conditions of that clause. If this distinction were accepted, various tests of the economic usefulness or restrictive effect of requirements contracts would become relevant. Among them would be evidence that competition has flourished despite use of the contracts, and under this test much of the evidence tendered by appellant in this case would be important. . . . Likewise bearing on whether or not the contracts were being used to suppress competition, would be the conformity of the length of their term to the reasonable requirements of the field of commerce in which they were used. . . . Still another test would be the status of the defendant as a struggling newcomer or an established competitor. Perhaps most important, however, would be the defendant's degree of market control, for the greater the dominance of his position, the stronger the inference that an important factor in attaining and maintaining that position has been the use of requirements contracts to stifle competition rather than to serve legitimate economic needs. . . .

Yet serious difficulties would attend the attempt to apply these tests. We may assume, as did the court below, that no improvement of Standard's competitive position has coincided with the period during which the requirements-contract system of distribution has been in effect. We may assume further that the duration of the contracts is not excessive and that Standard does not by itself dominate the market. But Standard was a major competitor when the present system was adopted, and it is possible that its position would have deteriorated but for the adoption of that system. When it is remembered that all the other major suppliers have also been using requirements contracts, and when it is noted that the relative share of the business which fell to each has remained about the same during the period of their use, it would not be farfetched to infer that their effect has been to enable the established suppliers individually to maintain their own standing and at the same time collectively, even though not collusively, to prevent a late arrival from wresting away more than an insignificant portion of the market. If, indeed, this were a result of the system, it would seem unimportant that a short-run by-product of stability may have been greater efficiency and lower costs, for it is the theory of the antitrust laws that the long-run advantage of the community depends upon the removal of restraints upon competition. . . . It seems hardly likely that, having with one hand set up an express prohibition against a practice thought to be beyond the reach of the Sherman Act, Congress meant, with the other hand, to reestablish the necessity of meeting the same tests of detriment to the public interest as that Act had been interpreted as requiring. Yet the economic investigation which appellant would have us require is of the same broad scope as was adumbrated with reference to unreasonable restraints of trade in *Chicago Board of Trade v. United States*. . . . To insist upon such an investigation would be to stultify the force of Congress' declaration that requirements contracts are to be prohibited wherever their effect "may be" to substantially lessen competition. If in fact it is economically desirable for service stations to confine themselves to the sale of the petroleum products of a single supplier, they will continue to do so though not bound by contract, and if in fact it is important to retail dealers to assure the supply of their requirements by obtaining the commitment of a single supplier to fulfill them, competition for their patronage should enable them to insist upon such an arrangement without binding them to refrain from looking elsewhere.

We conclude, therefore, that the qualifying clause of § 3 is satisfied by proof that competition has been foreclosed in a substantial share of the line of commerce affected. It cannot be gainsaid that observance by a dealer of his requirements contract with Standard does effectively foreclose whatever opportunity there might be for competing suppliers to attract his patronage, and it is clear that the affected proportion of retail sales of petroleum products is substantial. In view of the widespread adoption of such contracts by Standard's competitors and the availability of alternative ways of obtaining an assured market, evidence that competitive activity has not actually declined is inconclusive. Standard's use of the contracts creates just such a potential clog on competition as it was the purpose of § 3 to remove wherever, were it to become actual, it would impede a substantial amount of competitive activity.

Since the decree below is sustained by our interpretation of § 3 of the Clayton Act, we need not go on to consider whether it might also be sustained by § 1 of the Sherman Act. . . .

The judgment below is affirmed.

Affirmed.

COMMENTARY

1. This case came to the Supreme Court from a district court opinion in which Judge Yankwich excluded evidence of the business justification for the exclusive supply contracts and refused to make findings from the admitted evidence of the decline in market share of the defendant. However, he expressly rejected *per se* treatment in favor of an inquiry into the "actual" economic effect of the contracts. *United States v. Standard Oil Co.*, 78 F. Supp. 850, 863 (S.D. Cal. 1948). Judge Yankwich considered the legislative history of § 3 of the Clayton Act, particularly the concern with tying arrangements and exclusive dealing, to foreclose a Sherman Act rule of reason approach. Accordingly, he developed a record in which he applied a legal yardstick of economic effect to a record that was bare of economic evidence.

It appears that the Supreme Court also groped for an appropriate legal standard, vacillating between Sherman Act and Clayton Act criteria in terms of the record below. Justice Jackson, in dissent, objected to the majority's acceptance of proof that the quantity of commerce covered by the contracts was sufficient to taint them with illegality. 337 U.S. at 322 (Jackson, J., dissenting). Justice Douglas' dissent expressed concern that the majority opinion would induce large oil companies to integrate forward and thus eliminate small, independent station operators. *Id.* at 320 (Douglas, J., dissenting).

The theory underlying the *Standard Oil* decision is that the outlets for the product were limited and Standard (together with its major rivals) had commitments from outlets representing such a large proportion of total purchasers that the efforts of other sellers and new entrants to sell their products would be impaired. Also, entry into production would be deterred (since new producers would be unable to compete for customers who were already locked-in to existing suppliers).

Do you think that the Court made its decision obscure in order to resolve the statutory dilemma that faced it? The question before it was whether it would apply the "quantitative substantiality" test which it had adopted to determine the lawfulness of tying contracts. Under that standard, if a "not insubstantial amount of commerce" were restrained by a tying contract, the contract was condemned by Clayton Act § 3. In *Standard Oil of California*, the Court first acknowledged the efficiencies of requirements contracts. Then it suggested that it would be too difficult to recognize these efficiencies in the process of administering the antitrust laws. But finally it adopted a test for evaluating the lawfulness of requirements contracts which differed from the test it used in tying contract cases. Do you think that the Court made it sufficiently clear that it was adopting a different test for requirements contracts than for tying contracts? The test adopted for evaluating requirements contracts focused on whether "competition has been foreclosed in a substantial share of the line of commerce affected," while the test used for evaluating tying contracts focused upon amount of commerce in the tied product which was restrained and thereby foreclosed to the seller's rivals. In short, the relevant foreclosure was assessed in percentage-of-the-market terms for requirements contracts but in absolute dollar terms for purposes of tying contracts.

Does the difference between tying arrangements and exclusive dealing contracts warrant this difference of approach? Might the major oil companies have adopted the exclusive dealer contracts as an alternative to dealing with employees and the consequent obligations of social security taxes, tort liability, and medical insurance? Does the "lessening of competition" language of § 3 of the Clayton Act support the distinction?

Do you agree with the following statement of the holding in the case: ". . . when competitors are foreclosed by . . . [exclusive] contracts from a substantial enough share of the market, it is not farfetched to infer a substantial lessening of competition." Friedrich Kessler & Richard H. Stern, *Competition, Contract, and Vertical Integration*, 69 YALE L.J. 1, 30 (1959). Contemporary commentators were critical of the majority's inarticulate reliance on quantitative substantiality without reference to the market conditions in which exclusive contracts were being used.

> Viewed as a problem of economic policy alone, it seems clear that the desirability of any exclusive dealing or use arrangement in the light of the national policy to preserve competition cannot be decided merely by reference to the quantity or share of commerce affected. . . . These economic factors . . . [should be] considered in relation to exclusive dealing . . . arrangements, independent of tying arrangements, since the latter involve special considerations that require separate treatment.

W.B. Lockhart & Howard R. Sacks, *The Relevance of Economic Factors in Determining Whether Exclusive Arrangements Violate Section 3 of the Clayton Act*, 65 HARV. L. REV. 913, 919 (1952). Another criticism of the case, stated that illegality under § 3 should be found:

> . . . only when supported by the "substantial evidence" to be drawn from a realistic economic investigation and the fair conclusion that a particular arrangement probably will unduly restrict competition.

R. McClaren, *Related Problems of "Requirements" Contracts and Acquisitions in Vertical Integration under the Antitrust Laws*, 45 ILL. L. REV. 141, 172 (1950). Might the paucity of the economic evidence in the record of this case have led the Court to decide it in the *per se* fashion of *International Salt*?

In 1961, the Court reconsidered the standards governing the lawfulness of requirements contracts in *Tampa Electric Co. v. Nashville Coal Co.*, 365 U.S. 320 (1961). The Nashville Coal Co. had entered into a contract to supply all of the coal required by the Tampa Electric Co.'s new Gannon Station electric generating plant for a period of 20 years. The case arose when the Nashville Coal Co. repudiated the contract, justifying its refusal on the ground that the contract was illegal under the antitrust laws.

The Supreme Court ruled that the contract was lawful. The issue, the Court said, was whether the coal committed under the requirements contract constituted a substantial share of the coal sold in the relevant market. The case thus turned on the identification of the relevant market, since the larger the market, the smaller would be the proportion of that market represented by the particular contract in issue. Tampa's 1959 requirements were approximately equal to the 700,000 tons of coal otherwise consumed in peninsular Florida. Thus if peninsular Florida were the relevant market, the coal sold under the contract would represent 50 percent of the market. The Court's analysis of this issue follows:

> Respondents contend that the coal tonnage covered by the contract must be weighed against either the total consumption of coal in peninsular Florida, or all of Florida, or the Bituminous Coal Act area comprising peninsular Florida and the Georgia "finger," or, at most, all of Florida and Georgia. If the latter area were considered the relevant market, Tampa Electric's proposed requirements would be 18% of the tonnage sold therein. . . .
>
> We are persuaded that on the record in this case, neither peninsular Florida, nor the entire State of Florida, nor Florida and Georgia combined constituted the relevant market of effective competition. We do not believe that the pie will slice so thinly. By far the bulk of the overwhelming tonnage marketed from the same producing area as serves Tampa is sold outside of Georgia and Florida, and the producers were "eager" to sell more coal in those States. While the relevant competitive market is not ordinarily susceptible to a "metes and bounds" definition, . . . it is of course the area in which respondents and the other 700 producers effectively compete. . . . The record shows that, like the respondents, they sold bituminous coal "suitable for [Tampa's] requirements," mined in parts of Pennsylvania, Virginia, West Virginia, Kentucky, Tennessee, Alabama, Ohio and Illinois. We take notice of the fact that the approximate total bituminous coal (and lignite) product in the year 1954 from the districts in which these 700 producers are located was 359,289,000 tons, of which some 290,567,000 tons were sold on the open market. . . . From these statistics it clearly appears that the proportionate volume of the total relevant coal product as to which the challenged contract pre-empted competition, less than 1%, is, conservatively speaking, quite insubstantial. A more accurate figure, even assuming pre-emption to the extent of the maximum anticipated total requirements, 2,250,000 tons a year, would be .77%.

Having concluded that the percentage of the coal market foreclosed to other suppliers was less than one percent, the Court then attempted to distinguish its earlier decision in *Standard Oil of California* and to recognize the advantages of the contract in issue:

> The remaining determination, therefore, is whether the pre-emption of competition to the extent of the tonnage involved tends to substantially foreclose competition in the relevant coal market. We think not. That market sees an annual trade in excess of 250,000,000 tons of coal and over a billion dollars—multiplied by 20 years it runs into astronomical

> figures. There is here neither a seller with a dominant position in the market as in *Standard Fashions* . . . nor myriad outlets with substantial sales volume, coupled with an industry-wide practice of relying upon exclusive contracts, as in *Standard Oil* . . . nor a plainly restrictive tying arrangement as in *International Salt*. . . . On the contrary, we seem to have only that type of contract which "may well be of economic advantage to buyers as well as to sellers." *Standard Oil Co. v. United States*. . . . In the case of the buyer it "may assure supply," while on the part of the seller it "may make possible the substantial reduction of selling expenses, give protection against price fluctuations, and . . . offer the possibility of a predictable market." . . . The 20-year period of the contract is singled out as the principal vice, but at least in the case of public utilities the assurance of a steady and ample supply of fuel is necessary in the public interest. Otherwise consumers are left unprotected against service failures owing to shutdowns; and increasingly unjustified costs might result in more burdensome rate structures eventually to be reflected in the consumer's bill. . . . This is not to say that utilities are immunized from Clayton Act proscriptions, but merely that, in judging the term of a requirements contract in relation to the substantiality of the foreclosure of competition, particularized considerations of the parties' operations are not irrelevant. In weighing the various factors, we have decided that in the competitive bituminous coal marketing area involved here the contract sued upon does not tend to foreclose a substantial volume of competition.
>
> We need not discuss the respondents' further contention that the contract also violates § 1 and § 2 of the Sherman Act, for if it does not fall within the broader proscription of § 3 of the Clayton Act it follows that it is not forbidden by those of the former. . . .
>
> The judgment is reversed and the case remanded. . . .

2. Note that the *Tampa Electric* opinion declines to address the application of § 1 (and § 2) of the Sherman Act. Note also the Court's reference to the "broader proscription of § 3 of the Clayton Act . . . ." Is the Court in *Tampa Electric* interpreting § 3 of the Clayton Act to outlaw a broader range of conduct than would be barred by § 1 of the Sherman Act? The lower courts have subsequently divided on the issue of whether § 3 requires a greater showing of anti-competitiveness than does § 1 of the Sherman Act. In *Barr Laboratories, Inc. v. Abbott Laboratories*, 978 F.2d 98, 110 (3d Cir. 1992), the court interpreted § 3 as imposing a stiffer standard. In *Roland Machinery Co. v. Dresser Industries, Inc.*, 749 F.2d 380, 393 (7th Cir. 1984), Judge Posner considered both sections to be subject to the same test. *See also Bepco, Inc. v. Allied-Signal, Inc.*, 106 F. Supp. 2d 814 (M.D.N.C. 2000) (noting the division on this issue).

3. State the differences in burden of proof and admissibility of evidence of business practices under the holdings of *Standard Stations* and *Tampa Electric*. The latter opinion has been cited as announcing a rule of "qualitative substantiality" in relaxation of the rule of *Standard Stations*. Richard M. Steuer, *Exclusive Dealing in Distribution*, 69 CORNELL L. REV. 101, 107 (1983). Can you identify the major qualitative factors in Justice Clark's opinion? Does the *Tampa* rule consider the likely effect on competition in a localized market of the exclusive contracts? *Tampa* has been criticized for the generality of the factors to be considered:

> The "relative strength of the parties" . . . is a treacherous concept, as one can understand all too readily by asking how one would decide whether the largest producer of shirts . . . is stronger than a leading department store to which . . . it sells.

Derek Bok, *The* Tampa Electric *Case and the Problem of Exclusive Arrangements Under the Clayton Act*, 1961 SUP. CT. REV. 267, 283. Does the *Tampa* opinion identify the factors to be weighed in applying the statutory standard of a lessening of competition?

The apogee of judicial hostility towards exclusive supply contracts may have been the Supreme Court's decision in *FTC v. Brown Shoe Co.*, 384 U.S. 316 (1966). In that case the FTC had challenged Brown's exclusive supply contracts with several hundred retailers. In that case the Court upheld the power of the FTC to condemn those contracts without proof of their effects:

> The record . . . shows beyond doubt that Brown, the country's second largest manufacturer of shoes, has a program, which requires shoe retailers, unless faithless to their contractual obligations with Brown, substantially to limit their trade with Brown's competitors. This program obviously conflicts with the central policy of both § 1 of the Sherman Act and § 3 of the Clayton Act against contracts which take away freedom of purchasers to buy in an open market.

384 U.S. at 321.

During the 1970s, the Court again focused its attention on long-term supply contracts. *United States v. General Dynamics Corp.*, 415 U.S. 486 (1974), involved § 7 of the Clayton Act, a provision containing the identical lessening competition language of § 3. The Court observed that:

> to an increasing degree, nearly all coal sold to utilities is transferred under long-term requirements contracts, under which coal producers promise to meet utilities' coal consumption requirements for a fixed period of time, and at predetermined prices. The court [below] described the mutual benefits accruing to both producers and consumers of coal from such long-term contracts in the following terms:
>
>> This major investment [in electric utility equipment] can be jeopardized by a disruption in the supply of coal. Utilities are, therefore, concerned with assuring the supply of coal to such

> a plant over its life. In addition, utilities desire to establish in advance, as closely as possible, what fuel costs will be for the life of the plant. For these reasons, utilities typically arrange long-term contracts for all or at least a major portion of the total fuel requirements for the life of the plant. . . .
>
> The long-term contractual commitments are not only required from the consumer's standpoint, but are also necessary from the viewpoint of the coal supplier. Such commitments may require the development of new mining capacity. . . . Coal producers have been reluctant to invest in new mining capacity in the absence of long-term contractual commitments for the major portion of the mine's capacity. Furthermore, such long-term contractual commitments are often required before financing for the development of new capacity can be obtained by the producer.

4. Over time, the Court has come to recognize procompetitive aspects of exclusive-supply contracts. In *General Dynamics*, the Court recognized their importance in financing: *i.e.,* that exclusive-supply contracts lowered the risks in committing capital to long-term projects. In *Tampa*, the Court recognized explicitly that exclusive-supply contracts were potentially capable of providing supplies to the end user at lower costs than would otherwise be available.

Although *General Dynamics* primarily involved the § 7 issue of the proper definition of the relevant product and geographic markets for measuring the lessening of competition, the Court took account of the quantitative substantiality formula for competitive impact, raised in *Standard Stations*. Here the Court relaxed further the approaches of *Standard Stations* and *Tampa*, which had been premised upon a presumption of illegality based upon the percentage of the market foreclosed. The Court stated: ". . . [S]tatistics concerning market share and concentration, while of great significance, were not conclusive indicators of anticompetitive effects." 415 U.S. at 498. Commentators have characterized this opinion as: ". . . reemphasizing . . . [its] central point that market share is not solely determinative of competitive impact." T.W. Dunfee, L.W. Stern & F.D. Sturdivant, *Bounding Markets in Merger Cases: Identifying Relevant Competitors*, 78 Nw. U. L. Rev. 733, 738 (1984).

5. On the academic front, Oliver Williamson in his Markets and Hierarchies, published in 1975, investigated the role of supply-contracts in achieving economies. Williamson pointed out, *inter alia,* that business firms (1) would integrate completely through merger of the input supplier with the output producer or (2) would integrate partially through supply contracts or (3) would avoid integration completely as when the output producer purchased its inputs on the open market, depending upon which course of action could be undertaken at the least cost. Williamson pointed out that savings in transactions costs, *i.e.*, the costs of actually getting together and making a deal through which the inputs were supplied to the output producer, are often the critical economies which can be achieved only in full or partial vertical integration.

Williamson's major analytical contribution takes transactions costs and strategic behavior into account. Williamson rejects the view of Posner (*see*, Note 2, page 206 in Chapter 5) that efficiency gains inherent in vertical restraints warrant the policy of making them legal *per se*. Of Posner's and like models, Williamson writes:

> . . . I submit that these are rather special cases and the main incentive for vertical integration is that integration serves to economize on transaction costs and/or is undertaken for the strategic purpose of impeding entry.
>
> * * *
>
> The two situations in which disadvantage to rivals may arise are dominant firm (or otherwise very concentrated) industries and moderately concentrated industries where collusion has been successfully effected.

Oliver Williamson, *The Economics of Antitrust: Transaction Cost Considerations*, 122 U. PA. L. REV. 1439, 1461 (1974). Williamson adds to the traditional model the costs of operating a firm, plus the possibility that its managers will adopt a strategy of injuring their competitors, instead of relying exclusively on a maximizing function. As he explains his approach:

> The transactions cost approach is concerned with the costs of running the economic system, especially the costs of adapting efficiently to uncertainty. It expressly makes allowance for elementary attributes of human decision makers. . . . Transaction cost analysis is more a complement to than a substitute for received microtheory.

Id. at 1494.

Strategic behavior by firm managers designed to use vertical restraints as the basis of exclusionary, anticompetitive policies is developed by Thomas G. Krattenmaker and Steven C. Salop in *Anticompetitive Exclusion: Raising Rivals' Costs to Achieve Power Over Price*, 96 YALE L.J. 209 (1986). They, too, reject the conclusion that vertical agreements may injure some competitors, but cannot diminish the vigor of competition. As they put it:

> . . . [N]one of the . . . [traditional] doctrines . . . requires . . . proof of a set of facts that are reasonably reliable indicators that the practice entrenches market power or facilitates its exercise.

Id. at 223.

6. A significant amount of contemporary economic analysis accepts the position that vertical restraints have the potential for anticompetitive effects. A leading economics text characterizes recent developments in this literature as follows:

> . . . [T]he debate over vertical restraints can be characterized . . . as a contest between the . . . "Chicago School" and the rest of the world. . . .

> . . . [A]s competition in the marketplace of ideas continued, serious weaknesses in the Chicago position materialized.
>
> * * *
>
> . . . Chicagoans . . . argue for letting upstream sellers impose restraints that enhance downstream monopoly power . . . [in the] belief that *whatever* upstream firms do in their efforts to maximize profits must be efficient, and hence not to be discouraged.
>
> * * *
>
> . . . [V]ertical restraints . . . can be either welfare-enhancing or welfare-reducing, depending upon the circumstances. Under plausible conditions, a tendency toward welfare reductions seems more likely than the opposite. The . . . [view] that *all* profitable vertical restraints are welfare-increasing is false.

F.M. SCHERER & DAVID ROSS, INDUSTRIAL MARKET STRUCTURE AND ECONOMIC PERFORMANCE 541, 548 (3d ed. 1990).

7. As with other issues of antitrust policy, differences of opinion are grounded in differences of premises and inferences. Williamson acknowledges the contributions of the Chicago School as follows:

> . . . [A]ntitrust specialists in law and economics owe an everlasting debt to this tradition, which has insisted that complex policy matters be assessed in a tough-minded economic fashion in which rudimentary issues are stated in stark microeconomic terms. . . . The principal problems that I find in this approach are that its proponents often disregard transaction costs and rarely concede that strategic considerations sometimes operate.
>
> * * *
>
> The possibility that vertical restraints and strategic objectives are linked is . . . resisted by . . . [this] tradition. Although Bork acknowledges that exclusionary purposes occasionally operate, his discussion of these matters reduces them to insignificance. A broader view in which transaction costs are expressly acknowledged demonstrates that strategic behavior may occur in a wider range of circumstances than his discussion discloses.
>
> * * *
>
> . . . Bork and I differ in a serious way only with respect to the use of exclusive dealing in dominant firm industries.

Oliver Williamson, *Assessing Vertical Market Restrictions: Antitrust Ramifications of the Transaction Cost Approach*, 127 U. PA. L. REV. 953, 990-91 (1979).

8. The differences between the so-called "Chicago School" and some of the "post-Chicago" approaches are examined at pages 312-14, *infra.*

C. An Insight Into Exclusive Supply Relationships From the Japanese Experience

Recently, and as a result of the dramatic successes of Japanese companies in the world markets, attention has been drawn to the ways the Japanese have organized their industries and in particular to the relations between input suppliers and output producers in that country.

1. The Japanese "Keiretsu"

Japanese industry tends to be organized in large groups called "keiretsu," and are generally centered on a bank.[1] The keiretsu are loose organizations of business firms, generally centered around a bank. In Japan there are six major keiretsu (the Sumitomo, Mitsui, Mitsubishi, Sanwa, Fuyo, and Dai Ichi Kango groups). Within each keiretsu, in addition to a bank, there is generally one producer active in each major segment of Japanese industry and a trading company (which oversees import and export operations). The firms within each keiretsu generally own significant amounts of stock in other firms within the keiretsu.

Smaller "enterprise" groups called "kigyo keiretsu" exist within the larger framework of a keiretsu dominated by a financial or trading company. These enterprise keiretsu are centered around a manufacturing company and involve its suppliers and distributors. In this form of organization, the manufacturing company maintains long-term relationships with its suppliers, working with them to help develop new input products adapted to changing requirements of the manufacturing company and to assist the suppliers in reducing their costs. Because the manufacturing company, in working with its suppliers in this manner, is likely to be making sensitive information available to those suppliers, it is essential that the suppliers work only with that particular manufacturer and not with its rivals. This close working relationship is also critical to the use of so-called "just-in-time" manufacturing in which an input supplier is expected to furnish zero-defect supplies at specified times.[2]

---

1 *See generally* T. ITO, THE JAPANESE ECONOMY 177-205 (1992); C.L. PRESTOWITZ, JR., TRADING PLACES 294-306 (1989); LESTER C. THUROW, HEAD TO HEAD 136 (1992).

2 PRESTOWITZ, *supra* note 1, at 305.

The close relationship between the manufacturing company and its suppliers dictates that the companies acknowledge a significant degree of loyalty to each other: *i.e.,* that the supplier will not supply rivals of the manufacturer and that the supplier can count on the manufacturer as a steady source of orders. At the same time, the suppliers and the manufacturing company remain autonomous, thereby retaining the advantages of a tight-knit organization and keeping managers closely in touch with operations.

Learning from Japan

BUSINESS WEEK (JAN. 27, 1992)

> Like countless suppliers before him, James J. Lohman was seething as he left a 1985 meeting in Detroit. Three years earlier he had mortgaged his company, Excel Industries Inc. in Elkhart, Ind., to develop a better way to make car windows. His innovations promised to help Ford Motor Co., Excel's top customer, slice inventory and assembly costs. Yet now, Ford was planning to bring the technology in-house—a move that would ravage Excel.
>
> Lohman still recalls with satisfaction what happened next: Ford couldn't master Excel's process. So, in a humbling rapprochement, America's No. 2 auto maker proposed a sweet deal. For $18 million, Excel would buy Ford's window factory in Fulton, Ky. Then, to keep some control, Ford would acquire 40% of Excel for $25 million. Ford also agreed to buy 70% of its windows from Excel through 1993. By last year, the smaller company's sales had hit $350 million, nearly four times its 1985 revenues, and Ford had saved millions. Today, it can equip new Ford models a year faster than before, helping Ford shorten its new-product cycle. Declares Dennin F. Wilke, general manager of Ford's glass division: "There's a spirit of trust. We're both trying to find the most efficient solutions."
>
> . . . In the past six years, hundreds of companies, from big IBM to little Excel, in industries as diverse as computers, semiconductors, autos, farm implements, and motorcycles, have shared Ford's revelation. They, too, are revamping their cultures and recasting their investment practices to form cooperative links both vertically, down their supply lines, and horizontally, with universities, research labs, and their peers. . . .

Does recent United States experience of labor strife over the practice of "outsourcing"—a major auto manufacturer ceasing the making of its own components—validate or limit the significance of the Japanese model?

2. Antitrust Law and Organizational Efficiency

Will the United States antitrust laws impede the efforts of American business firms to develop efficient relationships with their suppliers? The Supreme Court listed an array of ways in which long-term supply contracts promote efficiency in *Standard Stations*; yet still ruled the contracts of that company illegal. More recently, however, dicta in the Court's *General Dynamics* opinion suggests that the Court is now more likely to give increased weight to their efficiency effects in ruling upon their legality. In both *Standard Stations* and *General Dynamics*, however, the positive aspects of long-term supply contracts which the Court recognized have to do with the facilitation of planning and/or the raising of capital. The Court has not yet had the opportunity to recognize explicitly, in the context of long-term and exclusive supplier-customer relations, the dynamic efficiencies which arise from close cooperation in the design, development and production of low-cost, high-quality, specially tailored components.

A recent study contrasting the Japanese procurement system in the automobile industry with procurement practices in the United States automobile industry, suggests that quality control, rather than cost-savings, may govern the sources of inputs in Japan. *See* Curtis R. Taylor & Steven N. Wiggins, *Competition or Compensation: Supplier Incentives Under the American and Japanese Subcontracting Systems*, 87 AM. ECON. REV. 598 (1997). This study argues that because small lots are repeatedly ordered from the same supplier, quality control is assured, even though the price of that supplier may not be the lowest available. Under the Japanese system, deliveries of parts are rarely inspected by the buyer because it is understood that the delivery of poor quality products will end the relationship.

Accordingly, a higher price by the supplier reflects compensation to the supplier in the form of economic rent. This study also notes that Toyota and other Japanese manufacturers have adopted multiple-sourcing and parallel-sourcing procurement, which is the American system. *Id.* at 612. How should antitrust enforcement view a long-term, exclusive contract between a Japanese automobile manufacturer building cars in the United States, and the largest supplier of axles, for all of the output of the axle manufacturer? Does this study suggest there may be a significant trade-off between good quality and low-cost automobile parts?

3. The Keiretsu, Transplants, and Vertical Relationships: An Antitrust Problem?

United States auto parts suppliers had expected the establishment of Japanese auto plants in the United States (so-called "transplants") to provide them with new opportunities to sell their wares. It turns out, however, that the new production facilities purchase large amounts of their auto parts from Japanese suppliers, many of whom have also established plants in the United States. To a substantial extent, the keiretsu relationship between suppliers and manufacturers has been replicated in the

United States between Japanese manufacturers and their suppliers, to the detriment of United States parts manufacturers.

The United States parts manufacturers have complained that they have been shut out of potential business. Frequently they have complained that they have been victims of antitrust violations. In response to their complaints, the Federal Trade Commission began an investigation of the purchasing practices of the transplant manufacturers.

On the basis of your knowledge of antitrust law, consider whether there is, or might be, an antitrust problem. Can you describe the difficulties of which the United States parts manufacturers are complaining in antitrust terms? What standards would you employ to evaluate their complaint?

Suppose you were assigned the task of preparing a memorandum for the Federal Trade Commission or the Department of Justice, Antitrust Division setting out enforcement policy with regard to these arrangements. What criteria, derived from *Standard Stations*, *Tampa Electric*, *General Dynamics*, the Guidelines, and other authorities, including the material in Chapters 5 and 6, would you apply in determining when scarce enforcement resources would be committed? What measurement of market power or dominant firm would you invoke? What kind of strategic behavior would be of concern? By what criteria would you identify anticompetitive, exclusionary conduct?

D. The Vertical Guidelines of the U.S. Department of Justice

In 1985, the United States Department of Justice issued Guidelines on Vertical Restraints and revoked them in 1993. Earlier, in 1982 and in 1984, the Department had issued sets of Merger Guidelines, setting forth criteria which the Department said it would use in determining whether to challenge a corporate merger or acquisition.

In both the vertical restraints guidelines and the part of the merger guidelines which dealt with vertical mergers, the Department took an approach which reflected a growing appreciation of the potential of vertical arrangements to promote efficiency. The guidelines also were much more skeptical of the anticompetitive potential of vertical arrangements than was most of the Supreme Court caselaw of the time (with the possible exception of dicta in the *General Dynamics* opinion). The focus of the vertical restraints guidelines is on the extent to which vertical restraints exert either an exclusionary effect (by raising rivals' costs) or facilitate collusion or otherwise reinforce oligopolistic behavior.

The guidelines use two conceptual tools: a coverage ratio, which is the percentage of a supplier or dealer market restrained and a vertical restraints index. The vertical restraints index (VRI) is calculated by squaring the percentage of the market occupied by each firm adhering to the type of contract in question and adding the resulting numbers. Because the Department believed that the anticompetitive potential for vertical arrangements had been overemphasized in the past, the vertical restraints guidelines were designed in part to provide a safe haven for small firms or apparently innocuous restraints. The following excerpts from the vertical restraints guidelines show the Department's general approach towards the evaluation of vertical restraints and describe the market structure screen which provides the safe haven for unproblematic restraints:

> . . . vertical restraints are unlikely to facilitate collusion unless three market conditions are met:
>
> (1) Concentration is high in the primary market;
> (2) The firms in the secondary markets using the restraint account for a large portion of sales in that market; and
> (3) Entry into the primary market is difficult.
>
> * * *
>
> An exclusive dealing arrangement is unlikely to be used to exclude rivals unless it has two characteristics: (a) it must significantly raise rivals' costs of gaining access to an input or to distribution facilities, and (b) if the restraint raises a firm's own costs, the firm (or firms) employing this restraint must be able to collect a sufficiently large return from the practice to offset the increase in its (or their) costs caused by the restraint.
>
> In turn, for exclusive dealing to facilitate anticompetitive exclusion, the following market conditions normally must be met:
>
> (1) The "nonforeclosed market" is concentrated and the leading firms in the market use the restraint;
> (2) The firms subject to the restraint control a large share of the "foreclosed market"; and
> (3) Entry into the "foreclosed market" is difficult.

The Department then concluded that it would employ a market structure screen to identify restraints that would not be challenged. (Other restraints would then be evaluated under a structured rule of reason.) It described the screen as follows:

> The Department will employ the following screen in evaluating territorial and customer restrictions and exclusive dealing arrangements. The use of a vertical restraint by a particular firm will not be challenged if:
>
> (1) the firm employing the restraint has a share of the relevant market of 10 percent or less; or
> (2) the VRI is under 1,200 and the coverage ratio is below 60 percent in the same (*e.g.,* supplier or dealer) relevant market; or
> (3) the VRI is under 1,200 in both relevant markets; or
> (4) the coverage ratio is below 60 percent in both relevant markets.

> In short, this screen provides four alternative tests that can be applied by a firm considering using a restraint. If any one of the tests is satisfied, the Department will not challenge the use of the restraint in question.

It is generally understood that the Department hoped that the Vertical Restraints Guidelines would influence the courts in interpreting and applying the Sherman and Clayton Acts.

The DOJ Vertical Restraints Guidelines turned out to be politically sensitive. The National Association of [State] Attorneys General produced their own set of Vertical Restraints Guidelines in response to the DOJ Guidelines. The NAAG Guidelines reflected a somewhat more traditional approach than did the DOJ Guidelines in that the NAAG Guidelines tended to find a greater likelihood of antitrust problems in vertical arrangements than did the Department of Justice.

Probably the point at which the DOJ Guidelines differed most from the NAAG Guidelines is at their respective treatment of agreements among dealers carrying the same brand. The DOJ Guidelines (§ 2.1) subjected such agreements to rule of reason evaluation, while the NAAG Guidelines (§ 2.2) subject those agreements to the rule of *per se* illegality. The Department of Justice revoked the Vertical Restraints Guidelines in 1993.

E. Exclusive Dealing Contracts

1. In General

Exclusive dealing contracts are restrictions upon manufacturers or suppliers pursuant to which the manufacturer or supplier agrees with a dealer not to sell to any other dealer in the area served by that dealer. Generally, exclusive dealing contracts are treated as reasonable restraints of trade, at least if other manufacturers or suppliers are also selling to dealers in the same area, so that interbrand competition exists in the local market served by the dealer.

The leading case on exclusive dealing contracts is *Packard Motor Car Co. v. Webster Motor Car Co.*, 243 F.2d 418 (D.C. Cir.), *cert. denied*, 355 U.S. 822 (1957). In that case, Zell Motor Car Co., the largest of three Packard dealers in Baltimore, told Packard that it would quit unless Packard gave it an exclusive contract. Packard complied, terminating its other two dealers. Webster Motor Car Co., one of the terminated Packard dealers, brought suit, charging Packard with violating §§ 1 and 2 of the Sherman Act. A verdict for Webster was reversed by the court of appeals:

> When an exclusive dealership is "not part and parcel of a scheme to monopolize" and effective competition exists at both the seller and buyer levels, the arrangement has invariably been upheld as a reasonable restraint of trade. In short, the rule was virtually one of *per se* legality,

> until the District Court decided the present case. Of Packard's 1600 dealers, 1100 were the only Packard dealers in their cities, some of which were nearly as large as Baltimore, and such a ratio was typical in the automobile industry. . . . The fact that Zell asked for the arrangement does not make it illegal. Since the immediate object of an exclusive dealership is to protect the dealer from competition in the manufacturer's product, it is likely to be the dealer who asks for it.

Note that many of the same arguments made on behalf of territorial restrictions apply to exclusive dealerships. When there is only one dealer in an area offering the manufacturer's brand, that dealer receives the benefit of enhancements of the brand's reputation. That, in turn, provides an incentive to the dealer to provide services and to promote the brand.

Again, sometimes economies of scale may lend an additional justification to an exclusive dealership. If, for example, Zell experienced economies of scale in servicing or selling automobiles, the elimination of other Packard dealers would route the existing Packard customer base to it, enabling it to advance on a declining cost curve. It is not unlikely that Zell was in such a position, since auto dealerships require a heavy capital investment. Increased patronage would allow Zell to allocate those fixed expenditures over a greater number of units, thus reducing its unit or average costs.

Consider how the lower courts currently determine the illegality of exclusive dealing contracts. In *Minnesota Mining and Manufacturing Co. v. Appleton Papers, Inc.*, 35 F. Supp. 2d 1138, 1143 (D. Minn. 1999), the court described a two-step process as follows:

> . . . First, the court must determine the baseline foreclosure rate. . . . [A] foreclosure rate of at least 30 to 40 percent must be found to support a violation of the antitrust laws. . . . Second, unless the foreclosure rate is so great that it . . . [indicates] that competitors are frozen out of the relevant market, the court must weigh a number of factors in measuring the actual anticompetitive effect of the exclusivity arrangements. Perhaps most important among the factors is the duration and terminability of the arrangement: the shorter an agreement's term and the easier it is to terminate, the more likely that it will be upheld.
>
> . . . [T]he following factors should be considered in gauging whether an exclusive dealing restraint . . . "has a probable adverse effect on interbrand competition":
>
>> the willingness of consumers to comparison shop and their loyalty to existing distributors; the existence of entry barriers to new distributors; the availability of alternative methods of distribution; and any trend toward growth (or decline) in the level of competition at the supplier level. 823 F.2d at 1234 . . . . In addition to these specific factors, courts will also

> examine procompetitive effects that may justify exclusive dealing agreements in the relevant market, consistent with the rule of reason analysis conducted in other antitrust settings. . . .

Is the above analysis consistent with that of *Standard Stations*? Does the above analysis conform to the *Tampa Electric* opinion? *See also Bepco, Inc. v. Allied-Signal, Inc.*, 106 F. Supp. 2d 814, 827-28 (M.D.N.C. 2000) (rejecting distributor's claim that it was "forced" to maintain the full line of manufacturer's products):

> A plaintiff makes out a *prima facie* case of unlawful exclusive dealing by demonstrating first that a significant percentage of the market in question is foreclosed by the provision challenged.[3] Unless this percentage is so high as to be presumed substantial, the plaintiff must demonstrate its substantiality through an analysis of the nature of the market. . . . This test has been dubbed the "qualitative substantiality" test, and factors relevant to the analysis include the duration of the exclusive agreement, the ability of consumers to comparison shop and their propensity to switch products, the existence of barriers to entry, and the availability of alternative channels of distribution.

2. Other Aspects of Vertical Integration

In addition to the efficiencies connected with vertical integration, economists have long recognized that vertical integration (through exclusive supply contracts or merger) was a way of avoiding market restraints at the supplier level. Consider the case in which suppliers set supracompetitive prices because they have formed a cartel or because the oligopolistic structure of their industry has enabled them to tacitly cooperate on prices.

In a case such as the one described, a final product producer which merges with its supplier shortcuts the market restraint at the supplier level. The final product producer and its supplier become one enterprise, seeking to maximize the profits of the entire enterprise. The result is equivalent to the supplier providing supplies to the final product producer at a marginal-cost transfer price. Consumers benefit because the costs of the final-product producer are reduced and that reduction at least in part will be passed on to those consumers. Even without a merger, a supplier and a final product producer may be able to replicate the benefits of such a merger by a carefully drawn exclusive supply contract.

---

3 Courts and commentators have not settled on a magic percentage as constituting significant foreclosure: provisions involving foreclosure as low as twenty-four per cent . . . have been condemned while others involving foreclosure as high as fifty per cent . . . have been tolerated. . . . Professor Hovenkamp suggests twenty per cent . . . as an appropriate minimum foreclosure percentage.

3. Post-Chicago Antitrust Analysis

During most of the period from the mid-1970s, the use of microeconomic analysis (which had always been employed in antitrust law) assumed a heightened importance, as it was employed as a major tool for reform. Scholars were able to show how the existing antitrust caselaw had not only failed to serve as a guardian of competitive markets, but had even protected inefficient business firms from the rigors of competition. The approach which identified the furtherance of productive and allocative efficiency as the sole goal of the antitrust laws and which employed microeconomic analysis to further reform came to be referred to as the "Chicago School" antitrust approach.

Scholars who aligned themselves with the Chicago School emphasized the efficiencies which are often connected with vertical arrangements. In the case of requirements contracts, the Chicago School approach tends to focus upon the whole range of cost savings which such contracts make possible. (Many of these cost savings were identified in the *Standard Stations* and *General Dynamics* opinions.) The Chicago School tends to take issue with the foreclosure approach exemplified in both *Standard Stations* and *Tampa Electric*. Both of those cases endorsed a standard under which requirements contracts would be ruled illegal if they foreclosed a "substantial share" of the customer market from suppliers. Chicago School theorists tend to see requirements contracts such as the ones involved in those cases as, at the most, realigning the supply and customer relations among existing firms. Thus, for example, if Standard Stations entered into requirements contracts with independent retailers involving 6.7% of the gasoline sold in the relevant area (as it did), then the only effect upon Standard's competitors would be that they would have to sell to other retailers who had not made such a commitment. Conversely, Standard would not be able to sell to retailers who had contracted to purchase only from one of its rivals. While Standard's requirements contracts removed the purchases of the dealers contracting with it from the general market for short-term supplies, it correspondingly removed itself as a seller to that extent from the general market. Since both supply and demand in the general market were reduced, there is no reason to believe that Standard's contracts had any effect on competition there at all.

In the Justice Department's 1985 Vertical Restraints Guidelines (as well as in the part of its 1982 and 1984 merger guidelines which dealt with vertical mergers) the Justice Department took a more tolerant view of vertical arrangements than the caselaw had generally reflected.

By the mid 1980s, the tolerance of vertical arrangements reflected in the Chicago School approach and in the Justice Department's guidelines was being challenged by a group of scholars employing a "post-Chicago" approach.

Post-Chicago antitrust analysis tends to accept the contribution of the Chicago School as a positive one, but to emphasize its limitations. Generally, the criticism is that Chicago School analysis employs "static" analysis, *i.e.*, an analysis played out over the current period in which capital investment and other basic assumptions remain unchanged. As a result, these critics charge, the Chicago School theorists underemphasize "dynamic" analysis: what happens over several periods of time. In particular, these critics assert that Chicago School analysis pays insufficient attention to "strategic behavior" and market imperfections, especially those involving informational disparities among the actors. As with any intellectual movement, there are many contributors. Probably the most influential of the post-Chicago School movement, however, are Steven C. Salop, Thomas G. Krattenmaker, Louis Kaplow and Herbert Hovenkamp.

In 1987, one of the major blueprints of post-Chicago antitrust analysis was published by Georgetown University Professors Thomas G. Krattenmaker and Steven C. Salop, *Anticompetitive Exclusion: Raising Rivals' Costs to Achieve Power Over Price*, 96 YALE L.J. 209 (1986). These authors posit that a dominant firm can, by its purchasing power, prevail upon its suppliers of common industry inputs to cut off or discriminate against the rivals of the dominant firm. The effect of this strategy is to raise the marginal cost to the rival firms of the dominant firm. A corollary of this strategy, available where the supply of the common input is relatively inelastic, would permit the dominant firm to use its superior financial resources to purchase larger amounts of the input than needed in the short-run in order to increase the input price to rivals. Is such conduct a variant of the practice in *Lorain Journal* (excerpted in Chapter 10), in which the dominant newspaper refused to publish the advertisements of customers that patronized its rival?

The new institutional economics scholars have produced a substantial body of theoretical and empirical work devoted to exclusionary practices. *E.g.*, Eric B. Rasmusen, J. Mark Ramseyer & John S. Wiley, *Naked Exclusion*, 81 AM. ECON. REV. 1137 (1991) (showing a model in which a dominant firm could provide economic incentives for intermediary suppliers to adopt practices injurious to the rivals of the dominant firm); Elizabeth Granitz & Benjamin Klein, *Monopolization by "Raising Rivals' Costs": The* Standard Oil *Case,* 39 J.L. & ECON. 1 (1996) (Standard Oil effectively cartelized the petroleum transportation providers to punish Standard's rivals by the use of its own shipping orders); Victor Goldberg & John R. Erickson, *Quantity and Price Adjustment in Long-Term Contracts: A Case Study of* Petroleum Coke, 30 J.L. & ECON. 369 (1987) (an intensive study of actual contract terms serving to coordinate conduct, to accomplish some vertical restraints, and to permit strategic behavior); Keith B. Leffler & Randal Rucker, *Transaction Costs and Efficient Organization of Production: A Study of Timber-Harvesting Contracts,* 99 J. POL. ECON. 1060 (1991); Tim R. Sass & David S. Saurman, *Mandated Exclusive Territories and Economic Efficiency: An Empirical Analysis of the Malt Beverage Industry,* 36 J.L. & ECON. 153 (1993); Patrick J. Kaufmann & Francine Lafontaine, *Costs of Control: The Source of Economic Rents for McDonald's Franchises,* 37 J.L. & ECON. 417 (1994). For a review of this literature see Harold A. Shelanski & Peter G. Klein, *Empirical Research in Transaction Cost Economics: A Review and Assessment,* 11 J.L. ECON. & ORG. 335 (1995), and John Shepard Wiley, Jr., *Exclusionary Agreements*, in THE NEW PALGRAVE DICTIONARY OF ECONOMICS AND THE LAW (1997).

How should enforcement policy be directed in the face of contradictory economic models and an inconclusive body of empirical evidence? If a dominant firm has the capacity to raise rivals' costs, is the remedy to address its dominance and concentration in that market, rather than to extend the strained analysis of *Standard Stations* against exclusive dealing arrangements? Did then-Judge Breyer strike the proper note for enforcement when he wrote in *Interface Group, Inc. v. Massachusetts Port Authority*, 816 F.2d 9, 11 (1st Cir. 1987), "exclusive dealing arrangements may *sometimes* be found unreasonable under the antitrust law . . ."? Should enforcement agencies be sensitive to private solutions against abusive practices by a dominant firm? Consider *Sewell Plastics v. Coca-Cola Co.,* 720 F. Supp. 1186, 1196 (W.D.N.C. 1988), *aff'd mem.*, 912 F.2d 463 (4th Cir. 1990). Prior to 1986, the plaintiff, a manufacturer of 2-liter plastic bottles, had 90 percent of the market in the Southeast. After refusal of the request to Sewell by its customers for a price reduction, some 30 licensee-bottlers of Coca Cola, customers of Sewell, obtained financial assistance from Coca-Cola and formed a wholly-owned corporation to produce 2-liter bottles. In dismissing Sewell's antitrust claims of price-fixing, attempting to monopolize, boycott, and exclusive dealing, the trial court noted that the price of these bottles fell by about half after the advent of the new firm's production. 720 F. Supp. at 1199. Should exclusive dealing arrangements be the object of enforcement action only when there is demonstrable evidence of abuse?

Chapter 8

Conspiracy, Cooperation, and Integration

A. Conspiracy

1. The Contemporary Scene

Blomkest Fertilizer, Inc. v.
Potash Corporation of Saskatchewan, Inc.
203 F.3d 1028 (8th Cir. 2000)

Before: Wollman, Chief Judge, Heaney, McMillian, Richard S. Arnold, John R. Gibson, Bowman, Beam, Loken, Hansen, Morris Sheppard Arnold, and Murphy, Circuit Judges.

BEAM, Circuit J.

A certified class of potash consumers appeals the district court's[1] grant of summary judgment in favor of defendants (collectively "the producers") in this action for conspiracy in restraint of trade under section 1 of the Sherman Act. We affirm.

I. BACKGROUND

This case involves the production and sale of potash, a mineral essential to plant growth and therefore used in fertilizer. The certified class includes all of those persons who directly purchased potash from one of the producers between April 1987 and July 1994. The class named six Canadian potash companies and two American companies.[2]

Both parties agree that the North American potash industry is an oligopoly.[3] Prices in an oligopolistic market tend to be higher than those in purely competitive markets, and will fluctuate independently of supply and demand. . . . Furthermore, "price uniformity is normal in a market with few sellers and homogeneous products." . . . This is because all producers in an oligopoly must charge roughly the same price or risk losing market share.

---

1 The Honorable Richard H. Kyle, United States District Judge for the District of Minnesota, adopting the Report and Recommendation of the Honorable Raymond L. Erickson, United States Magistrate Judge for the District of Minnesota.

2 (1) Potash Corporation of Saskatchewan, Inc. and Potash Corporation of Saskatchewan Sales, Ltd. (collectively "PCS"); (2) Cominco, Ltd. and Cominco American, Inc. (collectively "Cominco"); (3) IMC Global, Inc.; (4) Kalium Chemicals, Ltd., Kalium Canada, Ltd. and its former owner and operator, PPG Industries, Inc. and PPG Canada, Ltd. (collectively "Kalium"); (5) Noranda Mineral, Inc., Noranda Sales Corporation Ltd. and Central Canada Potash Co. (collectively "Noranda"); (6) Potash Corporation of America, Inc. and its owner Rio Algom, Ltd. (collectively "PCA"); (7) New Mexico Potash Corporation (NMPC) and its affiliate; (8) Eddy Potash Inc. (Eddy).

3 An oligopoly is an "[e]conomic condition where only a few companies sell substantially similar or standardized products." BLACK'S LAW DICTIONARY 1086 (6th ed.1990).

The Canadian province of Saskatchewan is the source of most potash consumed in the United States. The province founded defendant Potash Corporation of Saskatchewan (PCS), which holds thirty-eight percent of the North American potash production capacity. As a governmental company, PCS had no mandate to maximize profits and was not accountable to private owners. Instead, the company was primarily concerned with maintaining employment and generating money for the local economy. Not surprisingly, PCS suffered huge losses as it mined potash in quantities that far outstripped global demand. These policies impacted the entire potash industry: during the 1980's, the price of potash fell to an historic low. In 1986, Saskatchewan voters elected a provincial government which had promised to privatize PCS. New management was appointed to PCS after the elections. Thereafter, PCS significantly reduced its output and raised its prices.

Also in 1986, New Mexico Potash Corporation (NMPC) and another American potash producer (who is not a named defendant) filed a complaint with the United States Department of Commerce. Frustrated with low potash prices, the petitioners alleged that Canadian producers had been dumping their product in the United States at prices below fair market value. In 1987, the Department issued a preliminary determination that the Canadian producers were dumping potash and ordered the companies to post bonds on all exports to the United States. These bonds were set according to each firm's calculated "dumping margin."[4] Eventually, the Department negotiated a Suspension Agreement with each of the Canadian producers. The agreement raised the price of Canadian potash in the United States by setting a minimum price at which each Canadian producer could sell in the United States.[5] That agreement remains in effect today. When the Canadian producers entered into the Suspension Agreement, PCS announced that it was raising its prices by eighteen dollars per ton. Other producers quickly followed suit. The price of potash has remained markedly higher after the Suspension Agreement, although prices have slowly but steadily declined for the most part since the agreement was signed by the producers on January 8, 1988.

The class alleges that between April 1987 and July 1994 the producers colluded to increase the price of potash. The producers, in turn, maintain that the price increase was the product of the interdependent nature of the industry and its reaction to the privatization of PCS and the Suspension Agreement. The district court granted the producers's motions for summary judgment and the class appeals.

II. DISCUSSION

The class asserts that if we affirm the district court, we will "stand alone in holding that circumstantial evidence, even if overwhelming, cannot be used to defeat a summary judgment motion in anti-trust cases." We make no such legal history here, however, because the class's proffered evidence, far from overwhelming, fails to establish the elements of a prima facie case.

Section 1 prohibits concerted action by two or more parties in restraint of trade. 15 U.S.C. § 1. The Supreme Court in *Monsanto Co. v. Spray-Rite Service Corp.*, 465 U.S. 752, 764 & 768, 104 S.Ct. 1464, 79 L.Ed.2d 775 (1984), and *Matsushita Electric Industrial Co. v. Zenith Radio Corp.*, 475 U.S. 574, 588, 106 S.Ct. 1348, 89 L.Ed.2d 538 (1986), provided

---

4 The dumping margin was calculated by the Department based on a comparison of the United States sale price, foreign market value, and cost of production for each producer.

5 Under the agreement, each firm could sell potash in the United States at less than fair market value by an amount equal to 15% of its preliminary dumping margin.

the standard used to determine whether the plaintiffs's evidence of a section 1 violation survives a summary judgment motion. In order to state a section 1 case, plaintiffs must present evidence that "tends to exclude the possibility of independent action" by the defendants. *Monsanto*, 465 U.S. at 768, 104 S.Ct. 1464. This means that conduct that is "as consistent with permissible [activity] as with illegal conspiracy does not, standing alone, support an inference of antitrust conspiracy." *Matsushita*, 475 U.S. at 588, 106 S.Ct. 1348. We are among the majority of circuits to apply *Monsanto* and *Matsushita*, broadly, and in both horizontal and vertical price fixing cases. . . . Applied in this case, the standard requires that if it is as reasonable to infer from the evidence a price-fixing conspiracy as it is to infer permissible activity, then the plaintiffs's claim, without more, fails on summary judgment.

The class's price-fixing claim is based on a theory of conscious parallelism. Conscious parallelism is the process "not in itself unlawful, by which firms in a concentrated market might in effect share monopoly power, setting their prices at a profit-maximizing, supracompetitive level by recognizing their shared economic interests." . . . The class points out that the producers' prices were roughly equivalent during the alleged conspiracy, despite differing production costs. It further points out that price changes by one producer were quickly met by the others. This establishes only that the producers consciously paralleled each other's prices.

Evidence that a business consciously met the pricing of its competitors does not prove a violation of the antitrust laws. *See Theatre Enter., Inc. v. Paramount Film Distrib. Corp.*, 346 U.S. 537, 540-41, 74 S.Ct. 257, 98 L.Ed. 273 (1954). Particularly when the product in question is fungible, as potash is, courts have noted that parallel pricing lacks probative significance. . . . An agreement is properly inferred from conscious parallelism only when certain "plus factors" exist. . . . A plus factor refers to "'the additional facts or factors required to be proved as a prerequisite to finding that parallel [price] action amounts to a conspiracy.'" *In re Baby Food*, 166 F.3d at 122 (quoting 6 PHILLIP E. AREEDA, ANTITRUST LAW § 1433(e) (1986)).

A plaintiff has the burden to present evidence of consciously paralleled pricing supplemented with one or more plus factors. . . . However, even if a plaintiff carries its initial burden, a court must still find, based upon all the evidence before it, that the plaintiff's evidence tends to exclude the possibility of independent action. *See Monsanto*, 465 U.S. at 764 & 768, 104 S.Ct. 1464; *Matsushita*, 475 U.S. at 588, 106 S.Ct. 1348; *see also In re Baby Food*, 166 F.3d at 122. As noted, the class identified parallel pricing. The class also asserts that it has established the existence of three plus factors: (1) interfirm communications between the producers; (2) the producers's acts against self-interest; and (3) econometric models which purport to prove that the price of potash would have been substantially lower in the absence of collusion. The evidence underlying these assertions, however, does not bear the weight the class places upon it.

A. Interfirm Communications

The class alleges a high level of interfirm communications between the producers and complains most vociferously about price verification information. Courts have held that a high level of communications among competitors can constitute a plus factor which, when combined with parallel behavior, supports an inference of conspiracy. . . . However, the evidence presented by the class here is far too ambiguous to support such an inference. Considering the proof as a whole, the evidence of interfirm communications does not tend to exclude the possibility of independent action, as required under *Monsanto* and *Matsushita*, since other significant events strongly suggest independent behavior. The fundamental difficulty with the class's argument regarding price verifications is that it assumes a conspiracy first, and then sets out to "prove" it. However, a litigant may not proceed by first assuming a conspiracy and then explaining the evidence accordingly.

The class's evidence shows that the communications include meetings at trade shows and conventions, price verification calls, discussions regarding a Canadian potash export association, and the like. Taking the class's evidence as true, roughly three dozen price verifications occurred between employees, including high-level sales employees, of different companies, over at least a seven-year period. In large part, these contacts involved the verification of prices the companies had already charged on particular sales. The impotence of this circumstantial evidence is that it bears no relationship to the price increases most in question because it lacks the logical link necessary to infer such a relationship.

The class alleges that the price-fixing conspiracy began "at least as early as April, 1987." . . . In 1987, the price for potash was at historically low levels, such that producers were losing millions of dollars. Then, a sudden and dramatic increase in price by PCS occurred on September 4, 1987, and approximately a week later the remaining producers followed suit.[6] The class argues that the large and parallel price increases together with nearly simultaneous price verifications create an inference sufficient to survive summary judgment.

The problem with this theory, as indicated, is that the price verification communications only concerned charges on particular completed sales, not future market prices. There is no evidence to support the inference that the verifications had an impact on price increases. The only evidence is that prices were possibly cut as a result. "[T]o survive summary judgment, there must be evidence that the exchanges of information had an impact on pricing decisions." *In re Baby Food*, 166 F.3d at 125 (citing *Krehl v. Baskin-Robbins Ice Cream Co.*, 664 F.2d 1348, 1357 (9th Cir.1982)). There is no evidence here that price increases resulted from any price verification or any specific communication of any kind. Subsequent price verification evidence on particular sales cannot support a conspiracy for the setting of a broad market price on September 4, 1987.

Even if we were to find the price verification evidence relevant, when considered with all the facts, it does not tend to exclude the possibility of independent action. To the contrary, there is strong evidence of independent action. Just before and concurrent with the suspect price increases, the following occurred: the price of potash was at historic lows and the producers were losing millions; potash companies in the United States complained to the United States Department of Commerce that the Canadian producers were dumping potash at well-below market value; the Department of Commerce made a preliminary determination that the Canadian producers were dumping and required expensive bonds for all imports; the industry leader, the government-founded PCS, hired new management and began privatization with the goal of becoming profitable; legislation was passed in the province of Saskatchewan—the source of nearly all United States potash—that provided for the setting and prorating of potash production; potash producers reached a Suspension Agreement with the Department of Commerce that set price floors for potash; and PCS was finally privatized and significantly reduced its output. In the face of these circumstances and

---

6 This price increase was rescinded in the wake of the Suspension Agreement. In its place came a much smaller increase by PCS on January 11, 1988—three days after the Suspension Agreement created a price floor—which pricing decision was followed thereafter by the remaining producers.

with the price leadership of PCS in this oligopolistic industry, it would have been ridiculous for the remaining companies to not also raise their prices in a parallel fashion. Thus, we find the class's weak circumstantial evidence that the dramatic increases were the result of a price-fixing agreement is not sufficient to survive summary judgment.

This leaves only the question whether there is sufficient evidence to support an agreement to stabilize and maintain prices in violation of section 1 of the Sherman Act. The class's evidence of an agreement to maintain the price of potash at an artificially high level after the initial price increases is again the parallel pricing and price verifications. Parallel pricing has been conceded, leaving the burden once again on the verifications. Common sense dictates that a conspiracy to fix a price would involve one company communicating with another company before the price quotation to the customer. Here, however, the class's evidence consists solely of communications to verify a price on a completed sale. The price verifications relied upon were sporadic and testimony suggests that price verifications were not always given. The fact that there were several dozen communications is not so significant considering the communications occurred over at least a seven-year period in which there would have been tens of thousands of transactions. Furthermore, one would expect companies to verify prices considering that this is an oligopolistic industry and accounts are often very large. We find the evidence falls far short of excluding the possibility of independent action.

. . . .

The class directs our attention to *In re Brand Name Prescription Drugs Antitrust Litigation*, 123 F.3d 599, 614 (7th Cir.), *cert. denied*, 522 U.S. 1153, 118 S.Ct. 1178, 140 L.Ed.2d 186 (1998), in which the plaintiffs, like the class, searched through an enormous quantity of discovery material and culled out a number of suspicious interfirm communications. The court in *Brand Name* described these documents produced as "smoking guns." *Id.* By contrast, the communications here are facially innocent contacts which are, at most, ambiguous on the question of whether the producers schemed to set prices.

The class argues that a memorandum issued by Canpotex, a lawful Canadian cartel that sets prices for potash sold outside of the United States, is the class's "smoking gun." This memorandum, dated January 8, 1988, and directed to its "agents and offices" reads in pertinent part:

> FYI Canadian potash producers have reached agreement with the United States Department of Commerce and all dumping action has been suspended for minimum 5 years. It is rumoured that the USD 35.00 per metric ton increase posted by Canadian producers in 1987 to cover possible tariff payments to the U.S. Govt will be refunded in full or part. In the meantime new price lists are being issued on Monday Jan. 11 at:
>
> | | |
> |---|---|
> | Standard Grade | USD 80.00 |
> | Coarse Grade | USD 84.00 |
> | Granular Grade | USD 86.00 |
>
> . . . .

The class asserts that this memorandum establishes an agreement to fix prices. The class argues that the people who received the January 8, 1988, memorandum were all high-ranking officials in the producers's companies who were on the Board of Directors of Canpotex, and therefore, the memorandum is evidence that tends to exclude an inference that the producers acted independently.

The magistrate judge disagreed that this memorandum was sufficient evidence to exclude the possibility that the producers acted independently. The magistrate judge first noted that PCS had also announced the same prices in a telex to its customers on January 8, 1988, and thus the possibility that Canpotex learned of the price list from a customer of PCS could not be excluded. . . . Further, the magistrate judge discovered that while most of the Canadian defendants had matched the prices in the memorandum by January 22, 1988, they did not uniformly issue price lists matching those prices on January 11, 1988, and one producer, Kalium, did not match those prices at all. *See id.* However, as the magistrate judge pointed out, "evidence that the alleged conspirators were aware of each other's prices, before announcing their own prices, 'is nothing more than a restatement of conscious parallelism,' which is not enough to show an antitrust conspiracy." . . .

We agree with the magistrate judge's finding that this document was not sufficient evidence to exclude an inference that the producers acted independently. First, the memorandum was written by R.J. Ford and directed to "agents and offices." . . . It is not at all clear who this memorandum was sent to or received by, and a thorough review of the appellants' voluminous joint appendix has not clarified this point. Dozens of these high ranking officials were deposed during pretrial discovery, and according to the documents submitted by the class in its joint appendix, only one person, Dave Benusa, was asked if he received "any document dated the 8th of January 1988 concerning pricing." . . . Benusa was manager of marketing for Cominco American in 1988. Benusa stated in his deposition that he did not receive any document dated January 8, 1988, concerning pricing. The class apparently did not depose the author of the memorandum, R.J. Ford, nor did they make any further attempt that we can find to identify who received this "smoking gun" piece of evidence. Another document produced by Canpotex, an inter-office memorandum dated September 8, 1993, is actually directed to "Members of the Board of Directors of Canpotex Limited." . . . We assume that had the January 8, 1988, memorandum been intended for the members of the board of directors, it likewise would have so stated.

Furthermore, even if, as the class asserts, the memorandum had been received by high-ranking officials in the producers's companies, we agree with the magistrate judge's reasoning that the memorandum does not assist the class in proving the existence of a conspiracy. As the magistrate judge pointed out, the producers did not uniformly increase prices to match the memorandum on January 11, 1988, and furthermore, one producer, Kalium, did not match the memorandum price at all. The fact that most of the producers did increase prices to match the PCS price increase of January 11, 1988, is not surprising in a market where conscious parallelism is the norm. Despite submitting a five-volume joint appendix, the class has failed to present evidence about this memorandum which tends to exclude the possibility of independent action by the producers. As it turns out, the "smoke" from this gun is barely, if at all, discernible.

Finally, the class asserts that the producers signaled pricing intentions to each other through advance price announcements and price lists. The Supreme Court has held, however, that "the dissemination of price information is not itself a *per se* violation of the Sherman Act." *United States v. Citizens & S. Nat'l Bank*, 422 U.S. 86, 113, 95 S.Ct. 2099, 45 L.Ed.2d 41 (1975).

As we noted at the outset, the class may not proceed by first assuming a conspiracy and then setting out to prove it. If the class were to present independent evidence tending to exclude an inference that the producers acted independently, then, and only then, could it use these communications for whatever additional evidence of conspiracy they may provide. As the record stands, we find these contacts far too ambiguous to defeat summary judgment. *See The Corner Pocket*, 123 F.3d at 1112.

B. Actions Against Self-Interest

Evidence that defendants have acted against their economic interest can also constitute a plus factor. . . . However, where there is an independent business justification for the defendants' behavior, no inference of conspiracy can be drawn. . . .

The only evidence of actions against interest that the class has identified is the producers' uniform participation in the Suspension Agreement.[7] The class argues that those producers with low dumping margins could have undercut other producers's prices and gained market share while still maintaining prices at profitable levels. Instead, the low tariff producers joined the Suspension Agreement. The class further posits that NMPC's[8] failure to object to the agreement was an action against self-interest.

In response, the producers point out that Department of Commerce investigations are unpredictable, and participation in the agreement reduced uncertainty. Furthermore, without the Suspension Agreement, even low tariff producers would have been required to post substantial bonds which would have caused considerable capital drain on corporate coffers. Like the Canadian producers, NMPC was uncertain about the ultimate outcome of the Department of Commerce's investigation. Under the Suspension Agreement, NMPC obtained certainty and a higher price for potash sold in the American market. This is the relief NMPC initially sought, and it is unsurprising that NMPC would not oppose such an outcome.

The class has thus failed to carry its burden to rebut the producers's independent business justification for their actions. . . . There is nothing in this record that contradicts the conclusion that ending the dumping investigation with a settlement that required unreasonably low potash prices to rise was a legitimate business decision for the low tariff producers. They benefitted from increased revenues, while avoiding the cost of litigation and the risk of penalties. This cannot be construed as an act against self-interest.

C. Expert Testimony

Finally, the class argues that its expert's econometric model provided crucial confirmation that the prevailing potash prices during the alleged conspiracy were above those expected in the absence of collusion. While their expert concedes that the prices have primarily steadily decreased[9] since January 8, 1988, he asserts that prices would have been much lower absent an agreement to fix prices. We need not decide whether such evidence,

---

[7] The class also asserts that PCS acted against its self-interest when it agreed to supply potash to PCA when PCA's mine flooded. This agreement occurred in February 1987, before the class contends the conspiracy ever began. It is, therefore, of little relevance to this case.

[8] The class also asserts that failure to object to the Suspension Agreement was contrary to Eddy's self-interest. This argument is puzzling because Eddy was not in existence at the time of the agreement and thus could hardly have objected to it.

[9] It has been suggested that in the context of a price-fixing agreement among several producers in an oligopoly, the price actually would decrease somewhat over time because individual producers would attempt to "cheat" on the agreement by slightly lowering prices. Our review of the learned treatises on oligopolies and antitrust law does not seem to bear this theory out. First, there is very little discussion of the phenomenon of steadily lowering prices in an alleged price-fixing conspiracy. Second, several commentators have suggested that the incentive to lower prices while other oligopolists maintain prices deters collusion in the first place. *See*

in a proper case, could constitute a plus factor, because we find the report in this case is not probative of collusion.

The class's expert evidence is lacking in two crucial respects. First, the expert admits that his model fails to take into account the dramatic events of 1986. In his deposition, the class's expert confirmed that his model considers neither the privatization of PCS nor the anti-dumping proceedings. It is beyond dispute that even without collusion, those events would have led to higher potash prices. A model that does no more than report that prices did, indeed, rise after these events tells us nothing about the existence of industry collusion.

A second flaw in the expert's report, as the magistrate judge noted, is that it relies almost exclusively on evidence (such as the producers' common membership in trade associations and their publication of price lists to customers) that is not probative of collusion as a matter of law. Under Federal Rule of Evidence 703, the facts underlying an expert's opinion need not be admissible if they are "of a type reasonably relied upon by experts in a particular field." The rule, however, contemplates that there will be "sufficient facts already in evidence or disclosed by the witness as a result of his or her investigation to take such expert opinion testimony out of the realm of guesswork and speculation." . . .

III. CONCLUSION

We have carefully considered each of the class's other arguments and find them to be without merit. The class has failed to present evidence of collusion sufficient to create a genuine issue of material fact. The producers are therefore entitled to summary judgment. For the foregoing reasons, the decision of the district court is affirmed.

John R. GIBSON, Circuit Judge, Dissenting, with whom HEANEY, MCMILLIAN, Richard S. ARNOLD, and MURPHY, Circuit Judges, Join.

I dissent.[1]

. . . .

According to accepted economic theory, oligopolies are characterized by interdependent behavior because each seller is a big enough player to affect the market by price cuts; as a result, in raising or lowering prices or output, each seller must take into account his competitors' responses to his action. . . .

Even though oligopoly pricing harms the consumer in the same way monopoly does, interdependent pricing that occurs *with no actual agreement* does not violate the Sherman Act, for the very good reason that we cannot order sellers to make their decisions without taking into account the reactions of their competitors. . . .

Jonathan B. Baker, *Two Sherman Act Section 1 Dilemmas: Parallel Pricing, the Oligopoly Problem, and Contemporary Economic Theory*, 38 ANTITRUST BULL. 143, 151 (1993) (analyzing George Stigler's 1964 article, *A Theory of Oligopoly*, 72 J. POL. ECON. 44 (1964), and recognizing that "the unilateral incentive to deviate on a cooperative arrangement to fix price . . . is the very market force by which competition insures low prices and high output"); *see also* Donald F. Turner, *The Definition of Agreement Under the Sherman Act: Conscious Parallelism and Refusals to Deal*, 75 HARV. LAW REV. 655, 660 (1962) (noting that without an agreement among oligopolists, the pressure to cut prices is irresistible).

[1] Four producers present special reasons entitling them to summary judgment. As to Noranda, New Mexico Potash Corporation, Eddy Potash and PPG, I concur in the judgment for the reasons discussed in the panel opinion at 176 F.3d 1055, 1071-72 (8th Cir.1999).

While the oligopoly market structure naturally facilitates supra-competitive pricing, that same market structure also makes cooperative arrangements unstable, for this reason: It is in the best interest of each individual competitor for his competitors to charge high prices, while he charges somewhat less when that will help him steal customers from his competitors. . . . The temptation to shade prices secretly is just as inherent in the oligopoly market structure as the temptation to collude to raise prices. . . .

If the oligopolists agree, either tacitly or expressly, to coordinate price increases, they have committed a *per se* violation of section 1 of the Sherman Act. . . .

In a rather primitive way, the "plus factors" test incorporates the economic principles outlined above as a way to distinguish between innocent interdependence and illegal conspiracy. Under this test, plaintiffs can establish a prima facie case of conspiracy by showing parallel prices together with "plus factors" that increase the likelihood that the parallel prices resulted from conspiracy. . . .

We must, of course, take care to interpret the "plus factors" test in a way that is consistent with *Monsanto.* With *Monsanto* in mind, it is useful to distinguish between "plus factors" that establish a background making conspiracy likely and "plus factors" that tend to exclude the possibility that the defendants acted without agreement. For instance, "motive to conspire" and "high level of interfirm communications," are often cited as "plus factors" because they make conspiracy possible. . . . Background facts showing a situation conducive to collusion do not tend to exclude the possibility of independent action, *see id.*, but they nevertheless form an essential foundation for a circumstantial case. In *Matsushita Electric Industrial Co. v. Zenith Radio Corp.*, 475 U.S. 574, 593-98, 106 S.Ct. 1348, 89 L.Ed.2d 538 (1986), the Supreme Court held that a conspiracy case based on circumstantial evidence must be economically plausible. The background "plus factors" of market structure, motivation and opportunity play an important role in establishing such plausibility. Generally, these background "plus factors" are necessary but not sufficient to prove conspiracy.[2]

On the other hand, acts that would be irrational or contrary to the defendant's economic interest if no conspiracy existed, but which would be rational if the alleged agreement existed, do tend to exclude the possibility of innocence. . . .

A.

Of the "plus factors" that merely make conspiracy possible, such as motive and opportunity to conspire, the class has adduced abundant evidence. . . .

B.

The stage was clearly set for conspiracy in this case. The question is whether the additional evidence tends to exclude the possibility that the producers acted independently. I believe that it does.

First, the class has produced evidence that the producers cooperated in disclosing prices they had charged on particular sales. The industry practice was that each producer published a price list stating its price, the dates for which that price would be available, and

---

[2] It is possible that some types of evidence not logically inconsistent with innocence, such as a high level of interfirm communications, could become so unusual that they suffice to make a prima facie case. *See City of Tuscaloosa v. Harcros Chems., Inc.*, 158 F.3d 548, 570-73 (11th Cir.1998) (incumbency rate on new contracts so high it was inconsistent with independent action), *cert. denied*, ___ U.S. ___, 120 S.Ct. 309, 145 L.Ed.2d 42 (1999).

any discounts that the producer would extend. The price lists were widely distributed to customers and certainly were no secret. However, actual prices sometimes deviated from the lists. When Childers and Doyle came to PCS, a key aspect of their program to raise industry prices was to insist on the list price. Doyle stated in an industry publication: "When I first came on board in the spring of 1987, the first word I put out to our sales force was that the price list was our price, stick to that price and no bending. Anybody who bends was out of here." Despite published price lists with the high follow-the-leader price, the producers continued to undercut each other in privately negotiated deals. (This is what one would expect even from a cartel operating under an illegal agreement . . . .) When word of the discounting got around to PCS, PCS executives, particularly sales chief Doyle, were quite active in contacting the discounter and asking for verification of the rumored price. Significantly, Doyle testified that he never made any such price verification calls before 1987. The number of these verification communications is difficult to pin down, but Doyle estimated he initiated or received three to four calls per year with PCA, five to six per year with IMC, three to four per year with Cominco, five to six total with Kalium, "a few" with NMPC, and one to two total with Noranda. Doyle was by no means the only person making such calls on behalf of PCS, and there is evidence that the other defendants called each other as well (except that there is no evidence of others calling Noranda).

. . . [A]cts that would be contrary to the actor's self-interest in the absence of a conspiracy, but which make economic sense as part of a conspiracy, provide the crucial type of "plus factor" evidence necessary to exclude the possibility of independent action. The class contends that "the price verification calls were inconsistent with the 'pricing secrecy' sought by participants in oligopolistic industries because in such industries 'each producer would like to secretly "shade" price[s], thereby gaining sales and avoiding retaliation.'" The class's argument finds support in the reasoning of *United States v. United States Gypsum Co.*, 438 U.S. 422, 98 S.Ct. 2864, 57 L.Ed.2d 854 (1978), which stated:

> Price concessions by oligopolists generally yield competitive advantages only if secrecy can be maintained; when the terms of the concession are made publicly known, other competitors are likely to follow and any advantage to the initiator is lost in the process. Thus, if one seller offers a price concession for the purpose of winning over one of his competitor's customers, it is unlikely that the same seller will freely inform its competitor of the details of the concession so that it can be promptly matched and diffused.

Id. at 456, 98 S.Ct. 2864 (citations omitted). Therefore, if there were no reciprocal agreement to share prices (and the producers certainly do not argue that there was), an individual seller who revealed to his competitors the amount of his privately negotiated discounts would have been shooting himself in the foot. On the other hand, if there were a cartel, it would be crucial for the cartel members to cooperate in telling each other about actual prices charged in order to prevent the sort of widespread discounting that would eventually sink the cartel.

. . . .

The Court's third reason for dismissing the price verifications is that the verifications were "sporadic." . . . The evidence indicates that the producers called each other when they had reason to think their competitors were cutting prices, and that they responded to each other's inquiries. The total number of such inquiries is difficult to set, but the defendants characterize it as "no more than several dozen"—surely more than a scintilla. *Cf. Container Corp.*, 393 U.S. at 335, 89 S.Ct. 510 (liability where "all that was present was a request by each defendant of its competitor[s] for information as to the most recent price charged or quoted, whenever it needed such information" . . . ; "[t]here was to be sure an infrequency and irregularity of price exchanges").

This "sporadic" argument seems to be directed to the quantum of proof, rather than the quality of it. In other words, it is an argument that more proof should exist, rather than an argument that the existing proof is not probative. If the plaintiff adduces evidence of the kind that tends to prove the existence of a conspiracy, I do not believe that *Monsanto* and *Matsushita* give a justification for rejecting it. *Monsanto* and *Matsushita* lay out a test for the kind of proof necessary in antitrust cases, not the quantity of it. *Compare Monsanto*, 465 U.S. at 764, 104 S.Ct. 1464; and *Matsushita*, 475 U.S. at 587-88, 106 S.Ct. 1348 ("antitrust law limits the range of permissible inferences from ambiguous evidence"; if claim makes no economic sense, plaintiff's evidence must be "more persuasive" than would otherwise be necessary), *with Anderson v. Liberty Lobby, Inc.*, 477 U.S. 242, 254-55, 106 S.Ct. 2505, 91 L.Ed.2d 202 (1986) (where substantive law imposes a heightened standard of proof, as in libel cases, a higher quantum of proof is required to survive summary judgment). *Cf. Merck-Medco Managed Care v. Rite Aid Corp.*, 201 F.3d 436 (4th Cir.1999) (unpublished per curiam) (holding that *Monsanto-Matsushita* inquiry requires higher quantum of probative evidence depending on relative strength of plaintiff and defendant's cases). There is no heightened "clear and convincing" standard of proof in civil antitrust conspiracy cases, requiring a greater quantum of proof than the ordinary "preponderance of the evidence" standard. *See In re Brand Name Prescription Drugs Antitrust Litig.*, 186 F.3d 781, 787-88 (7th Cir.1999), *cert. denied*, ___ U.S. ___, 120 S.Ct. 1220, 145 L.Ed.2d 1120 (2000). The plaintiff's evidence must amount to more than a scintilla, but the plaintiff does not have to outweigh the defendant's evidence item by item. *See Rossi v. Standard Roofing, Inc.*, 156 F.3d 452, 466 (3d Cir.1998).

. . . .

The producers have not made a showing that the governmental intervention so explains their actual behavior as to take away the probative power of the class's case. This case should therefore proceed to trial. Accordingly, I dissent.

COMMENTARY

Blomkest illustrates the difficulties plaintiffs face in attempting to prove conspiracy in oligopolistic industries. Because in such industries each seller provides a major segment of industry supply, it is aware that any change in its price/output policy is likely to provoke a reaction by its rivals, so it assesses the probable reaction in advance. The result is likely to be parallel pricing: each seller sells at the same prices as its rivals. Often in such circumstances, one firm becomes a "price leader," one whose pricing decisions are generally followed by the others.

A price-fixing agreement can be proved either by direct evidence or by circumstantial evidence. Sometimes documentary or other evidence is available as direct evidence of agreement. Such a memo may have been in the record in the *Prescription Drug* litigation and even though the document may have been ambiguous, the court would allow it to be interpreted by the jury.

> There is enough evidence of such an agreement to create a triable fact. For example, an internal memorandum of defendant Burroughs Wellcome, dated September 1993 and entitled "Price Escalation Proposal," states that "the industry has generally agreed to informally keep its prices in line with CPI or CPI plus 1 to 2 %." The document is subject to interpretation (as is the other evidence, unnecessary to describe, that also supports the claim), but the interpretation of ambiguous documentary evidence of collusion is for the jury.

In re Prescription Drugs Antitrust Litigation, 186 F.3d 781 (7th Cir. 1999). When circumstantial evidence is used to establish a conspiracy, however, that evidence must not be ambiguous. Then the courts are likely to apply the standard of *Monsanto* which requires that evidence must exclude the possibility of independent action. This is the standard applied in *Blomkest*.

Thus as *Blomkest* makes clear, in oligopoly situations, courts require the showing of factors in addition to parallel pricing to create an inference of conspiracy: so-called "plus factors." While it is sometimes relatively easy to produce evidence of motive and opportunity, it is generally more difficult to produce evidence that excludes the possibility that the defendants acted without agreement. The primary evidence that excludes that possibility is evidence showing behavior which would be against the self-interest of the defendants without an agreement but which would be in their self-interest with an agreement. Although the majority in *Blomkest* thought such evidence was lacking, the dissent disagreed. What do you think? The Third Circuit recently pointed out the ambiguities in the concept of action against self interest:

> The concept of "action against self-interest" is ambiguous and one of its meanings could merely constitute a restatement of interdependence. As the court pointed out in *Coleman v. Cannon Oil Company*, 849 F. Supp. 1458, 1467 (N.D. Ala. 1993), refusing to raise or lower prices unless rivals do the same could be against a firm's self-interest but nevertheless could spring from independent behavior.

In re Baby Food Antitrust Litigation, 166 F.3d 112, 122 (3d Cir. 1999). The *Baby Food* case also gave elaborate consideration to "plus factors." In that case the defendant companies had information in their files about the pricing plans of their rivals. The court rejected the contention that this showed conspiracy, however, because each company appeared independently to collect this kind of information through the efforts of low-level salespersons socializing with their counterparts in other companies. *Id.* at 133. The Ninth Circuit recently dealt with a question as to whether one particular company, Cargill, Inc., had participated in a conspiracy in which several of its rivals admittedly participated. Because Cargill had business explanations for its behavior, the plaintiff's evidence did not meet the standard of excluding the possibility of agreement. *In re Citric Acid Litigation*, 191 F.3d 1090 (9th Cir. 1999).

2. The Formation of Antitrust Conspiracy Theory in the Supreme Court

The present approach to antitrust conspiracy is an outgrowth of struggles in which the Supreme Court grappled with that subject during the period immediately preceding and immediately following World War II. In reviewing these cases, consider the pitfalls faced by the Court. In which aspects of these was the Court on solid ground? Where do you think it failed?

Interstate Circuit, Inc. v. United States

306 U.S. 208 (1939)

Mr. Justice STONE delivered the opinion of the Court.

. . . The case is . . . now before us on findings of the District Court specifically stating that appellants did in fact agree with each other to enter into and carry out the contracts, which the court found to result in unreasonable and therefore unlawful restraints of interstate commerce.

Appellants comprise the two groups of defendants in the District Court. . . . The distributor appellants are engaged in the business of distributing in interstate commerce motion picture films, copyrights on which they own or control, for exhibition in theatres throughout the United States. They distribute about 75 per cent. of all first-class feature films exhibited in the United States. . . . The exhibitor group of appellants consists of Interstate Circuit, Inc., and Texas Consolidated Theatres, Inc., and Hoblitzelle and O'Donnell, who are respectively president and general manager of both and in active charge of their business operations. The two corporations are affiliated with each other and with Paramount Pictures Distributing Co., Inc., one of the distributor appellants.

Interstate operates forty-three first-run and second-run motion picture theatres, located in six Texas cities. It has a complete monopoly of first-run theatres in these cities, except for one in Houston operated by one distributor's Texas agent. In most of these theatres the admission price for adults for the better seats at night is 40 cents or more. Interstate also operates several subsequent-run theatres in each of these cities, twenty-two in all, but in all but Galveston there are other subsequent-run theatres which compete with both its first- and subsequent-run theatres in those cities.

Texas Consolidated operates sixty-six theatres, some first- and some subsequent-run houses, in various cities and towns in the Rio Grande Valley and elsewhere in Texas and in New Mexico. In some of these cities there are no competing theatres, and in six leading cities there are no competing first-run theatres. It has no theatres in the six Texas cities in which Interstate operates. That Interstate and Texas Consolidated dominate the motion picture business in the cities where their theatres are located is indicated by the fact that at the time of the contracts in question Interstate and Consolidated each contributed more than 74 per cent of all the license fees paid by the motion picture theatres in their respective territories to the distributor appellants.

On July 11, 1934 . . . O'Donnell, the manager of Interstate and Consolidated, sent to each of . . . [the eight branch managers of the distributor appellants] a letter on the letterhead of Interstate, each letter naming all of them as addressees, in which he asked compliance with two demands as a condition of Interstate's continued exhibition of the distributors' films in its "A" or first-run theatres at a night admission of 40 cents or more. One demand was that the distributors "agree that in selling their product to subsequent runs, that this 'A' product will never be exhibited at any time or in any theatre at a smaller admission price than 25¢ for adults in the evening." The other was that "on 'A' pictures which are exhibited at a night admission of 40¢ or more—they shall never be exhibited in conjunction with another feature picture under the so-called policy of double features." The letter added that with respect to the "Rio Grande Valley situation," with which Consolidated alone was concerned, "We must insist that all pictures exhibited in our 'A' theatres at a maximum night admission price of 35¢ must also be restricted to subsequent runs in the Valley at 25¢."

The admission price customarily charged for preferred seats at night in independently operated subsequent-run theatres in Texas at the time of these letters was less than 25 cents. In seventeen of the eighteen independent theatres of this kind whose operations were described by witnesses the admission price was less than 25 cents. In one only was it 25 cents. In most of them the admission was 15 cents or less. It was also the general practice in those theatres to provide double bills either on certain days of the week or with any feature picture which was weak in drawing power. . . .

The local representatives of the distributors, having no authority to enter into the proposed agreements, communicated the proposal to their home offices. Conferences followed between Hoblitzelle and O'Donnell, acting for Interstate and Consolidated, and the representatives of the various distributors. In these conferences each distributor was represented by its local branch manager and by one or more superior officials from outside the state of Texas. In the course of them each distributor agreed with Interstate for the 1934-35 season to impose both the demanded restrictions upon their subsequent-run licensees in the six Texas cities served by Interstate, except Austin and Galveston. . . .

The O'Donnell letter named on its face as addressees the eight local representatives of the distributors, and so from the beginning each of the distributors knew that the proposals were under consideration by the others. Each was aware that all were in active competition and that without substantially unanimous action with respect to the restrictions for any given territory there was risk of a substantial loss of the business and good will of the subsequent-run and independent exhibitors, but that with it there was the prospect of increased profits. There was, therefore, strong motive for concerted action. . . .

There was risk, too, that without agreement diversity of action would follow. Compliance with the proposals involved a radical departure from the previous business practices of the industry and a drastic increase in admission prices of most of the subsequent-run theatres. . . . While as a result of independent negotiations either of the two restrictions without the other could have been put into effect by any one or more of the distributors and in any one or more of the Texas cities served by Interstate, the negotiations which ensued and which in fact did result in modifications of the proposals resulted in substantially unanimous action of the distributors, both as to the terms of the restrictions and in the selection of the four cities where they were to operate. . . . [W]e are unable to find in the record any persuasive explanation, other than agreed concert of action, of the singular unanimity of action on the part of the distributors by which the proposals were carried into effect as written in four Texas cities but not in a fifth or in the Rio Grande Valley. . . . It taxes credulity to believe that the several distributors would, in the circumstances, have accepted and put into operation with substantial unanimity such far-reaching changes in their business methods without some understanding that all were to join, and we reject as beyond the range of probability that it was the result of mere chance.

Appellants [urge] . . . that the rejection of Consolidated's proposal for the Rio Grande Valley may have been due to the fact that the demand with respect to that territory differed materially from that directed to the six Texas cities. . . . The record discloses no reason for the distinction taken between first-run theatres in the six cities charging an admission of 40 cents or more and those in the Valley served by Consolidated charging 35 cents, other than the fact that the cities there were smaller. . . . Taken together, the circumstances of the case which we have mentioned, when uncontradicted and with no more explanation than the record affords, justify the inference that the distributors acted in concert and in common agreement in imposing the restrictions upon their licensees in the four Texas cities.

This inference was supported and strengthened when the distributors, with like unanimity, failed to tender the testimony, at their command, of any officer or agent of a distributor who knew, or was in a position to know, whether in fact an agreement had been reached among them for concerted action. When the proof supported, as we think it did, the inference of such concert, the burden rested on appellants of going forward with the evidence to explain away or contradict it. They undertook to carry that burden by calling upon local managers of the distributors to testify that they had acted independently of the other distributors, and that they did not have conferences with or reach agreements with the other distributors or their representatives. The failure under the circumstances to call as witnesses those officers who did have authority to act for the distributors and who were in a position to know whether they had acted in pursuance of agreement is itself persuasive that their testimony, if given, would have been unfavorable to appellants. The production of weak evidence when strong is available can lead only to the conclusion that the strong would have been adverse. . . .

While the District Court's finding of an agreement of the distributors among themselves is supported by the evidence, we think that in the circumstances of this case such agreement for the imposition of the restrictions upon subsequent-run exhibitors was not a prerequisite to an unlawful conspiracy. It was enough that, knowing that concerted action was contemplated and invited, the distributors gave their adherence to the scheme and participated in it. Each distributor was advised that the others were asked to participate; each knew that cooperation was essential to successful operation of the plan. They knew that the plan, if carried out, would result in a restraint of commerce, which . . . was unreasonable . . . and knowing it, all participated in the plan. . . .

. . . [A]n unlawful conspiracy may be and often is formed without simultaneous action or agreement on the part of the conspirators. . . . Acceptance by competitors, without previous agreement, of an invitation to participate in a plan, the necessary consequence of which, if carried out, is restraint of interstate commerce, is sufficient to establish an unlawful conspiracy under the Sherman Act. . . .

Affirmed.

COMMENTARY

1. In speaking of the distributors' response to the Interstate proposal, the Court stated that "There was risk that without agreement diversity of action would follow." What adverse consequences would fall upon a distributor who followed the Interstate proposal when other distributors did not? The Court thought that unanimity of action by the distributors was necessary in each one's interest. Was this true? Consider the alternatives of each distributor set out in Notes 2 and 3 below.

2. Does it appear that the distributors earned more profit from doing business with the first-run or the subsequent-run theatres? Generally, distributors are paid a percentage of the exhibitor's gross receipts. If Interstate would not do business with a distributor who rejected its proposal, that distributor could only lease its new films to second-run theatres in all of those cities in which Interstate held a monopoly of first-run theatres. The result would be that the spurned distributor would be making one or more subsequent-run theatres into first-run theatres.

The latter alternative probably was not attractive to the distributor, because the second-run theatres tended to be smaller than the first-run theatres and located in neighborhoods, rather than situated in the center of the city. Thus the sizes and locations of the second-run theatres made them less desirable as marketing outlets for new films.

Perhaps a distributor would earn more profit by acceding to the Interstate proposal than by rejecting it, whether or not the other distributors acceded to it. Without Interstate, the distributor would be forced to use the small, neighborhood (second-run) theatres to market its new films. That prospect might have been sufficiently unattractive to induce acceptance of the Interstate proposal. If the distributors were compensated by a percentage of gross receipts, then the larger the theatre and the greater the audience the more profits would it earn.

If each distributor independently examined its own prospects with and without access to Interstate's first-run theatres, each may very well have independently concluded that acceptance of Interstate's proposal was in its best interest. True, accepting the Interstate proposal would have alienated the second-run theatres, but it might be better to alienate the second-run theatres than to alienate the owner of the first-run theatres. Thus the fact that all of the distributors accepted Interstate's proposal may very well be explained by the fact that acceptance was in each distributor's interest, regardless of how the other distributors responded. Professor Turner has said that "the identical response [of each of the distributors] might well have been accounted for by the hypothesis of independent responses by the distributors to an unwanted but a coerced choice, each choosing to risk the loss of twenty-five percent of his receipts rather than the loss of seventy-five." Donald F. Turner, *The Definition of Agreement Under the Sherman Act: Conscious Parallelism and Refusals to Deal*, 75 HARV. L. REV. 655, 701 (1962).

The Court assumed—perhaps erroneously—that it would have made no sense for any one distributor to accept the Interstate proposal unless it had assurance that all other distributors were also accepting it, *i.e.,* that the proposal would have increased the distributors' profits if and only if it was unanimously accepted and otherwise would have decreased the profits of any accepting distributor. Such an assumption by the Court would help to explain its decision.

3. The Interstate (O'Donnell) letter was designed to let each distributor know that identical proposals were being made to each of them. The Court said that "It was enough that, knowing that concerted action was contemplated and invited, the distributors gave their adherence to the scheme and participated in it." What was the "scheme"? a diversion of trade from the second-run theatres to the first-run theatres? Would a distributor be giving its adherence to such a scheme merely by choosing to deal with Interstate when it was given a choice by Interstate of accepting its proposals or not doing business with it? Would such a distributor be participating in the scheme if, given a choice between doing business with a large theatre or doing business with a small theatre, it chose the large one because of the greater revenues it could earn there? Suppose the distributor foresaw that other distributors would be making the same choice, because they, too, would earn greater revenues by doing business with the larger theatre. Would this foresight be relevant to the selection of its own course of action? How? Would this foresight be relevant to a court's evaluation of the lawfulness of its conduct?

4. Note the absence of any testimony by any officer of a distributor as to the reason why the Interstate proposal was accepted. Was the inference of agreement reinforced by this evidentiary gap?

5. *Theatre Enterprises, Inc. v. Paramount Film Distributing Corp.*, 346 U.S. 537, 540-41 (1954). The owners of a small suburban Baltimore motion-picture theatre (the "Crest"), brought suit against several motion picture producers and distributors for allegedly conspiring to restrict the exhibition of "first-run" motion pictures to downtown Baltimore theatres and thereby to confine the suburban theatre to subsequent runs and unreasonable clearances. The respondent-defendants (who prevailed below):

> asserted that day and date first-runs [*i.e.*, two theatres exhibiting a first-run picture at the same time] are normally granted only to noncompeting theatres. Since the Crest is in "substantial competition" with the downtown theatres, a day and date arrangement would be economically unfeasible. And even if respondents wished to grant petitioner such a license, no downtown exhibitor would waive his clearance rights over the Crest and agree to a simultaneous showing. As a result, if petitioner were to receive first-runs, the license would have to be an exclusive one. However, an exclusive license would be economically unsound because the Crest is a suburban theatre, located in a small shopping center, and served by limited public transportation facilities; and, with a drawing area of less than one-tenth that of a downtown theatre, it cannot compare with those easily accessible theatres in the power to draw patrons. Hence the downtown theatres offer far greater opportunities for the widespread advertisement and exploitation of newly released features, which is thought necessary to maximize the overall return from subsequent runs as well as first-runs. . . .

> The crucial question is whether respondents' conduct toward petitioner stemmed from independent decision or from an agreement, tacit or express. To be sure, business behavior is admissible circumstantial evidence from which the fact finder may infer agreement. . . . But this Court has never held that proof of parallel business behavior conclusively establishes agreement or, phrased differently, that such behavior itself constitutes a Sherman Act offense. Circumstantial evidence of consciously parallel behavior may have made heavy inroads into the traditional judicial attitude toward conspiracy; but "conscious parallelism" has not yet read conspiracy out of the Sherman Act entirely. . . .
>
> *Affirmed.*

6. Is *Theatre Enterprises* consistent with *Interstate Circuit*? How did the behavior of the defendants in the two cases differ? Does *Theatre Enterprises* merely avoid the misinterpretation of the facts pointed out by Professor Turner (*supra*, Note 2) while respecting *Interstate*'s approach towards inferring a conspiracy when knowing cooperation is essential to each participant's gain?

7. *In re Re/Max International, Inc.*, 173 F.3d 995 (6th Cir. 1999). Traditionally, when one real-estate agent brings a purchaser to another real-estate agent representing the seller, the two agents split the commission. The agents then usually split their respective shares with their employer-broker. Re/Max International operates a real-estate broker franchise system employing a different approach to agent compensation. Under the compensation system employed by Re/Max, sales agents keep 95% to 100% of their share of sales commissions instead of the traditional practice of splitting them 50-50 with their employer.

When Re/Max franchisees entered the real-estate brokerage market in Northeast Ohio, the dominance of two large brokers in that area, Realty One and Smythe Crammer Company, was threatened. Because of the attractiveness of the commission policies of Re/Max, these brokers feared that their most experienced sales agents would leave to join a Re/Max franchise. Both Realty One and Smythe Crammer adopted a so-called "adverse splits" policy under which the brokerage split would be 70/30 or 75/25 in their favor whenever a Re/Max agent was on the other side of the table. This adverse splits policy increased the commissions for their own agents, reducing the likelihood that their agents would defect to Re/Max.

Re/Max sued, alleging a conspiracy. In deposition testimony, plaintiff's expert contended that the adoption of an adverse splits policy simultaneously by both defendant brokers was evidence of a conspiracy. The court ruled that such testimony was sufficient to generate an issue of fact for trial:

> Dr. Martin testified that if Smythe Cramer had no assurance that Realty One would also adhere to adverse splits against Re/Max, the danger of unilateral imposition would have outweighed the potential loss of agents.

For example, a unilateral-splits policy against Re/Max adopted only by Smythe Cramer would keep Smythe Cramer's agents from leaving for Re/Max, but it would result in customers and sales agents leaving for Realty One. Dr. Martin clearly stated in different ways on a number of occasions that "without coordinated conduct, parallel imposition of adverse splits is implausible." He explained that, in a market with two dominant competitors, the risk of loss of sales agents to a third entrant offering more favorable employment terms is outweighed by the risk of loss of market share if a dominant competitor imposes adverse splits on the new market entrant. For example, one of two dominant competitors (Smythe Cramer) acting rationally will not independently impose adverse splits on a new competitor (Re/Max), because doing so will cause the new competitor to concentrate on supplying buyers to purchase properties listed by the other dominant competitor (Realty One). Thus, the dominant competitor who does not impose the adverse splits will sell more homes faster, while the other dominant competitor will lose agents and referral business in a downward cycle.

Furthermore, the best of both worlds for either dominant competitor is for the other to impose the adverse splits against the new entrant. In that situation, the non-imposing competitor obtains a "very high" increase in profits while the imposing competitor sinks to "very low." When both dominant competitors impose adverse splits, both increase their profits, but neither obtains a "very high" increase. Thus, even when one dominant competitor has already adopted adverse splits on its own (a "highly unlikely" event in the first place), the other dominant competitor has a strong incentive not to do likewise. Importantly, the defendants have not challenged Dr. Martin's qualifications or his data to support this analysis, but rather only his conclusions. Because his conclusions follow logically from his analysis, they cannot be rejected solely as a matter of law.

Dr. Martin's reasoned rejection of the defendants' proffered explanation for their common adverse-splits policy lends additional credence to the inference that Realty One's and Smythe Cramer's conduct was not independent. The defendants claim they were forced to impose adverse splits in order to recoup the costs they incurred in training new agents; Re/Max, on the other hand, incurs no such costs, but instead recruits experienced agents from other firms. To "level the playing field," the defendants were forced to penalize Re/Max for "appropriating" the value of their investments in their experienced agents.

Dr. Martin noted, however, that real-estate agents are usually at-will employees, and that the knowledge and skill they attain is easily transferrable to other firms. Thus, a real-estate agent could leave his brokerage at any time and take all the value of his training with him. Therefore, he said, "investments and training undertaken by the real estate firm will

> be designed to allow for the ever present risk of agent turnover that may occur before a return can be realized." If the risk of agent turnover is incorporated into the agent's commission rate (*i.e.*, an inexperienced agent, in effect, "pays" for his training by receiving lower commissions), then a brokerage cannot lose its "incubation expenses" when an experienced agent leaves. Thus, according to Dr. Martin, the defendants' proffered explanation for their actions is pretextual.

Note the double significance of the expert's testimony. First, his identification of behavior against self interest was adequate to create a factual issue for trial. Second, his testimony created an issue as to whether defendant's explanation was pretextual. Consider the extent to which an issue of pretext is itself evidence of a conspiracy.

American Tobacco Co. v. United States

328 U.S. 781 (1946)

Mr. Justice BURTON delivered the opinion of the Court.

The petitioners are The American Tobacco Company, Liggett & Myers Tobacco Company, R.J. Reynolds Tobacco Company, American Suppliers, Inc., a subsidiary of American, and certain officials of the respective companies who were convicted by a jury, in the District Court of the United States for the Eastern District of Kentucky, of violating §§ 1 and 2 of the Sherman Anti-Trust Act.

. . . .

II.

The verdicts show . . . that the jury found that the petitioners conspired to fix prices and to exclude undesired competition in the distribution and sale of their principal products. . . .

The following record of price changes is circumstantial evidence of the existence of a conspiracy and of a power and intent to exclude competition coming from cheaper grade cigarettes. During the two years preceding June, 1931, the petitioners produced 90% of the total cigarette production in the United States. In that month tobacco farmers were receiving the lowest prices for their crops since 1905. The costs to the petitioners for tobacco leaf, therefore, were lower than usual during the past 25 years, and their manufacturing costs had been declining. It was one of the worst years of financial and economic depression in the history of the country. On June 23, 1931, Reynolds, without previous notification or warning to the trade or public, raised the list price of Camel cigarettes, constituting its leading cigarette brand, from $6.40 to $6.85 a thousand. The same day, American increased the list price for Lucky Strike cigarettes, its leading brand, and Liggett the price for Chesterfield cigarettes, its leading brand, to the identical price of $6.85 a thousand. No economic justification for this raise was demonstrated. The president of Reynolds stated that it was "to express our own courage for the future and our own confidence in our industry." The president of American gave as his reason for the increase, "the opportunity of making some money." He further claimed that because Reynolds had raised its list price, Reynolds would therefore have additional funds for advertising and American had raised its price in order to have a similar amount for advertising. The officials of Liggett claimed that they thought the increase was a mistake as there did not seem to be any reason for making a price advance but they contended that unless they also raised their list price for Chesterfields, the other companies would have greater resources to spend in advertising and thus would put Chesterfield cigarettes at a competitive disadvantage. This general price increase soon resulted in higher retail prices and in a loss in volume of sales. Yet in 1932, in the midst of the national depression with the sales of the petitioners' cigarettes falling off greatly in number, the petitioners still were making tremendous profits as a result of the price increase. Their net profits in that year amounted to more than $100,000,000. This was one of the three biggest years in their history.

Before 1931, certain smaller companies had manufactured cigarettes retailing at 10 cents a package, which was several cents lower than the retail price for the leading brands of the petitioners. Up to that time, the sales of the 10 cent cigarettes were negligible. However, after the above described increase in list prices of the petitioners in 1931, the 10 cent brands made serious inroads upon the sales of the petitioners. These cheaper brands of cigarettes were sold at a list price of $4.75 a thousand and from 1931 to 1932, the sales of these cigarettes multiplied 30 times, rising from 0.28% of the total cigarette sales of the country in June, 1931, to 22.78% in November, 1932. In response to this threat of competition from the manufacturers of the 10 cent brands, the petitioners, in January, 1933, cut the list price of their three leading brands from $6.85 to $6 a thousand. In February, they cut again to $5.50 a thousand. . . . Following the first price cut by petitioners, the sales of the 10 cent brands fell off considerably. After the second cut they fell off to a much greater extent. When the sale of the 10 cent brands had dropped from 22.78% of the total cigarette sales in November, 1932, to 6.43% in May, 1933, the petitioners, in January, 1934, raised the list price of their leading brands from $5.50 back up to $6.10 a thousand. During the period that the list price of $5.50 a thousand was in effect, Camels and Lucky Strikes were being sold at a loss by Reynolds and American. Liggett at the same time was forced to curtail all of its normal business activities and cut its advertising to the bone in order to sell at this price. The petitioners, in 1937, again increased the list prices of their above named brands to $6.25 a thousand and in July, 1940, to $6.53 a thousand.

[The Court then described the efforts of the petitioners to ensure that retailers maintained a differential of not more than three cents between the retail prices of petitioners' brands and the retail prices of the so-called 10-cent brands.]

III.

It was on the basis of such evidence that the Circuit Court of Appeals found that the verdicts of the jury were sustained by sufficient evidence on each count. . . . A correct interpretation of the statute and of the authorities makes it the crime of monopolizing, under § 2 of the Sherman Act, for parties, as in these cases, to combine or conspire to acquire or maintain the power to exclude competitors from any part of the trade or commerce among the several states or with foreign nations, provided they also have such a power that they are able, as a group, to exclude actual or potential competition from the field and provided that they have the intent and purpose to exercise that power. . . .

. . . No formal agreement is necessary to constitute an unlawful conspiracy. . . . Where the conspiracy is proved, as here, from the evidence of the action taken in concert by the parties to it, it is all the more convincing proof of an intent to exercise the power of exclusion acquired through that conspiracy. The essential combination or conspiracy in violation of the Sherman Act may be found in a course of dealings or other circumstances as well as in any exchange of words. . . . Where the circumstances are such as to warrant a jury in finding that the conspirators had a unity of purpose or a common design and understanding, or a meeting of minds in an unlawful arrangement, the conclusion that a conspiracy is established is justified. . . .

In the present cases, the petitioners have been found to have conspired to establish a monopoly and also to have the power and intent to establish and maintain the monopoly. . . .

Affirmed.

COMMENTARY

1. This case was the second major antitrust case involving the tobacco industry. In *United States v. American Tobacco Co.*, 221 U.S. 106 (1911), the original Tobacco Trust was found to have violated § 2 of the Sherman Act and its dissolution into a number of separate companies was ordered by the court. 191 F. Supp. 371, 417 (S.D.N.Y. 1911). *See also* William H. Nichols, Price Problems in the Cigarette Industry 26-32 (1951). The 1946 ruling of the Supreme Court upheld a determination below that the major successor companies to the Trust ordered dissolved in 1911 were in violation of §§ 1 and 2 of the Sherman Act.

2. We are reading *American Tobacco* for its treatment of conspiracy in the context of a market structure that appears oligopolistic. What was the evidence of conspiracy in this case? Did that evidence partially consist of American and Liggett following Reynolds' price increase? of these companies reducing price at approximately the same time? Would it have been rational economic behavior for any of the three defendants to sell at a price different from its rivals? What would have happened to Reynolds' sales of Camels if American had held the price of Lucky Strikes steady in the face of Reynolds' June 1931 price increase? Do you think consumer brand loyalty would have been great enough to enable Reynolds to hold most of its customers despite American's lower prices? How do you know that consumer brand loyalty was not so strong? What course of action would be forced upon Reynolds when its sales volume was rapidly eroding as a result of American's lower prices? What would have happened if Reynolds did not reduce its prices at the same time that American and Liggett did? *See* Donald F. Turner, *The Definition of Agreement Under the Sherman Act*, 75 Harv. L. Rev. 655, 661 (1962), below.

3. When Reynolds announced a price increase, was it "contemplating and inviting" "concerted action" within the meaning of the *Interstate Circuit* opinion? If its price increase was followed by American and Liggett, were they "knowing that concerted action was contemplated and invited" giving "their adherence to the scheme and [participating] . . . in it"? If American held its prices steady in the face of Reynolds' price increase and Reynolds then withdrew its price increase, would Reynolds be adhering to a scheme proposed by American and so become a conspirator?

4. In commenting upon the *American Tobacco* case, Professor Turner had this to say about the June 1931 price increases by the three major cigarette companies:

> Any economist worthy of the name would immediately brand this price behavior as noncompetitive. One can hardly find clearer evidence of an absence of effective competition than in increases of prices in the face of declining costs and weakening demand. But neither would any economist worthy of the name conclude on the basis of these facts alone that there had been an actual price agreement among the three companies concerned. As we know, economic theory has suggested that this kind of noncompetitive behavior might well arise in an "oligopoly" situation (*i.e.*, where the sellers are "few") without overt communication or agreement, but solely through a rational calculation by each seller of what the consequences of his price decision would be, taking into account the probable or virtually certain reactions of his competitors.
>
> * * *
>
> Noncompetitive price levels are maintained [in oligopolistic markets], in some cases at or around what they would be if the various competitors actually agreed in the obvious ways. Here . . . the decisions of the individual competitors are interdependent rather than independent. The decision of an individual seller to forego immediate additional sales by lowering his price makes sense only if his competitors likewise abstain. Persistent price stability in the face of general excess capacity indicates confidence on the part of each seller that his competitors will hold the price line and that such confidence has not been misplaced. Finally . . . there may be no agreement in the traditional sense. But since each seller is fully aware of the interdependence and the consequences of his taking advantage of it, it is not at all preposterous, to say the least, to classify what transpires as a "tacit agreement," and to conclude, since "price fixing" is involved, that the agreement is unlawful.

Turner, *supra*, 75 HARV. L. REV. at 661-63. Yet Turner finds such a conclusion "repellant." What do you think about such a conclusion? What reasons could you give in support of Turner's position? Part of Turner's own reasons for rejecting this broad meaning of "agreement" is the difficulty of framing an injunctive remedy which would effectively prohibit the kind of oligopolistic pricing behavior found in *American Tobacco*.

5. Some commentators took the view that the 1946 *American Tobacco* opinion announced a new interpretation of § 1:

> Ruthless and predatory behavior need not be shown. The actual elimination of small competitors is unnecessary. Parallel action, price leadership, a reliance on advertising rather than price competition and, above all, size—the market advantage of a small number of large sellers

> or buyers—these are now the key points to be proved in a case of . . . combination in restraint of trade.

Eugene V. Rostow, *The New Sherman Act: A Positive Instrument of Progress*, 14 U. Chi. L. Rev. 567, 585 (1947). What role did Rostow contemplate for the element of conspiracy or combination in a § 1 case? How did he imply that these elements would be proved?

6. Was the Court equating oligopolistic pricing behavior with an unlawful conspiracy? Was Rostow, in the extract above? Was the Court able to avoid facing the consequences of such an equation only because the case before it was a criminal proceeding and therefore no injunction came before the Court for approval? Do you agree with Rostow? with Turner?

7. Oligopoly (*i.e.*, a market with a small number of sellers) has presented the antitrust laws with a perplexing problem of proving collusion by inference. Historically, many of the major industries have been oligopolistically structured. Because of the small number of sellers, each seller is aware that its own price/output decisions will have a substantial impact on its rivals. Furthermore, the impact will be great enough to provoke a response. In this circumstance, each seller assesses the likely reactions of its rivals to any change in its price or output.

As the *American Tobacco* case illustrates, in an oligopoly a seller can raise price successfully only if its rivals follow with price increases of their own. Otherwise, the first seller will have to retract its price increase. Should any seller be significantly undercut by a rival, it would lose a major part of its business to the rival. For these reasons, all sellers generally must follow price reductions by their rivals. The economic result of each seller recognizing its interdependence of its pricing with its rivals' pricing is the same as if there were an actual agreement among the sellers.

The law cannot practically prohibit sellers from following price moves by their rivals, because that is the only way that price can change. The courts could break up each of the oligopolists in an industry into a number of small companies. That would convert the industry into a competitively structured one, where the number of firms would be so large that the behavior of any one firm would not create a significant impact on the market. Then the price/output decisions of any one firm would not provoke a reaction from its rivals and each firm could make price/output decisions without taking into account its rivals' reactions. The problem with that solution to the oligopoly problem is that it would destroy the economies of scale which the large oligopolistic firms are likely to have attained. Courts generally have been unwilling to break up oligopolists, just because they did not want to destroy such economies.

Enforcement agencies, courts, and commentators have differed over the inferences of collusion or coordinated conduct to be drawn from the exchange of market information in oligopoly markets. Thus, "price leadership" has been identified as one means of accomplishing coordinated pricing among a group of few competitors without resorting to overt collusion. *See* Jesse W. Markham, *The Nature and Significance of Price Leadership*, 41 AM. ECON. REV. 891 (1951). Price leadership was identified in markets of few sellers characterized by close substitutability of products, similar cost curves, inelastic market demand, and barriers to entry. The leadership firm typically is first to announce a price, which is then followed by the other firms. Might the cigarette industry as it is today described in *American Tobacco v. United States*, above, be viewed as a price leadership case? The Federal Trade Commission proceeded against the leading firms in the breakfast food industry on a price leadership theory, *In the Matter of Kellogg Co.,* FTC Dkt. 8883 (1972). The case was brought on the allegation that Kellogg, the leader, General Mills, and General Foods were involved in a price leadership oligopoly. The offer of proof consisted of identifying 15 rounds of price increases between 1965 and 1970, twelve of which were initiated by Kellogg and followed by the others. General Foods followed Kellogg nine times and General Mills followed on ten occasions. Price leadership was also identified in such major industries as steel, automobiles, gasoline, and coal. *See* LEONARD W. WEISS, ECONOMICS AND AMERICAN INDUSTRY (1961); LAWRENCE J. WHITE, THE AUTOMOBILE INDUSTRY SINCE 1945 (1971); A.D.H. KAPLAN, JOEL B. DIRLAM & ROBERT F. LANZILLOTTI, PRICING IN BIG BUSINESS: A CASE APPROACH (1958).

What significance is to be attached to the absence of current enforcement activity based on price leadership? Might this theory be characterized as placing emphasis upon an intermediate step in market performance, rather than on the ultimate performance itself? A related economic doctrine, based on observation of the relative constancy of prices in a specific market, is that of "rigid" or "administered" prices. *See* Gardiner C. Means, INDUSTRIAL PRICES AND THEIR RELATIVE INFLEXIBILITY, S. DOC. NO. 13, 74th Cong. 1st Sess. 1 (1935); F.V. Waugh, *Does the Consumer Benefit from Price Instability?*, 58 Q.J. ECON. 602 (1944) (consumer welfare is higher with flexible prices); Walter Y. Oi, *The Desirability of Price Instability Under Perfect Competition*, 29 ECONOMETRICA 58 (1961) (a model showing flexible prices led to higher expected profits). Based on the studies of market performance as a contributing factor to the Great Depression, economists examined the changes in price in a given market over time. Finding relative stability of prices in major product markets led to the inference that price rigidity or inflexibility warranted a thesis of the collusive adoption of a joint profit maximization strategy among the few firms in an industry. The term, "shared monopoly" was also applied to this theory. This theory was initiated by Robert L. Hall and Charles J. Hitch in their article, *Price Theory and Business Behavior*, 2 OXFORD ECON. PAPERS 12 (1939). They postulated a kinked demand curve as characteristic of a market in which the few firms agreed on an "administered" price for their product, one in which changes in demand and cost conditions would, by agreement, not result in price adjustments, but would rather be managed by output and inventory adjustments to clear the market. This analysis was criticized by George J. Stigler, in *The Kinky Oligopoly Demand Curve and Rigid Prices*, 55 J. POL. ECON. 432 (1947). This analysis, like the inference of actionable collusive behavior from the existence of oligopolistic markets without more, has lapsed from significance as a basis of antitrust enforcement. The next case reflects two decades of concern with rigid prices which evolved from a formulary pricing practice known as basing-point pricing, described below. After a spate of contributions to the economics literature and this litigation, this topic, too, has receded from antitrust enforcement concern.

---

2. Basing-Point Pricing

Federal Trade Commission v. Cement Institute
333 U.S. 683 (1948)

Mr. Justice BLACK delivered the opinion of the Court.

We granted *certiorari* to review the decree of the Circuit Court of Appeals which, with one judge dissenting, vacated and set aside a cease and desist order issued by the Federal Trade Commission against the respondents. . . . Those respondents are: The Cement Institute, an unincorporated trade association composed of 74 corporations which manufacture, sell and distribute cement; the 74 corporate members of the Institute; and 21 individuals who are associated with the Institute. . . .

. . . The core of the charge [of engaging in an unfair method of competition in violation of § 5 of the Federal Trade Commission Act] was that the respondents had restrained and hindered competition in the sale and distribution of cement by means of a combination among themselves made effective through mutual understanding or agreement to employ a multiple basing point system of pricing. It was alleged that this system resulted in the quotation of identical terms of sale and identical prices for cement by the respondents at any given point in the United States. . . .

. . . .

The Multiple Basing Point Delivered Price System.—Since the multiple basing point delivered price system of fixing prices and terms of cement sales is the nub of this controversy, it will be helpful at this preliminary stage to point out in general what it is and how it works. A brief reference to the distinctive characteristics of "factory" or "mill prices" and "delivered prices" is of importance to an understanding of the basing point delivered price system here involved.

Goods may be sold and delivered to customers at the seller's mill or warehouse door or may be sold free on board (f.o.b.) trucks or railroad cars immediately adjacent to the seller's mill or warehouse. In either event the actual cost of the goods to the purchaser is, broadly speaking, the seller's "mill price" plus the purchaser's cost of transportation. However, if the seller fixes a price at which he undertakes to deliver goods to the purchaser where they are to be used, the cost to the purchaser is the "delivered price." A seller who makes the "mill price" identical for all purchasers of like amount and quality simply delivers his goods at the same place (his mill) and for the same price (price at the mill). He thus receives for all f.o.b. mill sales an identical net amount of money for like goods from all customers. But a "delivered price" system creates complications which may result in a seller's receiving different net returns from the sale of like goods. The cost of transporting 500 miles is almost always more than the cost of transporting 100 miles. Consequently if customers

100 and 500 miles away pay the same "delivered price," the seller's net return is less from the more distant customer. . . .

The best known early example of a basing point price system was called "Pittsburgh plus." It related to the price of steel. The Pittsburgh price was the base price, Pittsburgh being therefore called a price basing point. In order for the system to work, sales had to be made only at delivered prices. Under this system the delivered price of steel from anywhere in the United States to a point of delivery anywhere in the United States was in general the Pittsburgh price plus the railroad freight rate from Pittsburgh to the point of delivery. Take Chicago, Illinois, as an illustration of the operation and consequences of the system. A Chicago steel producer was not free to sell his steel at cost plus a reasonable profit. He must sell it at the Pittsburgh price plus the railroad freight rate from Pittsburgh to the point of delivery. Chicago steel customers were by this pricing plan thus arbitrarily required to pay for Chicago produced steel the Pittsburgh base price plus what it would have cost to ship the steel by rail from Pittsburgh to Chicago had it been shipped. The theoretical cost of this fictitious shipment became known as "phantom freight." But had it been economically possible under this plan for a Chicago producer to ship his steel to Pittsburgh, his "delivered price" would have been merely the Pittsburgh price, although he actually would have been required to pay the freight from Chicago to Pittsburgh. Thus the "delivered price" under these latter circumstances required a Chicago (non-basing point) producer to "absorb" freight costs. That is, such a seller's net returns became smaller and smaller as his deliveries approached closer and closer to the basing point.

Several results obviously flow from use of a single basing point system such as "Pittsburgh plus" originally was. One is that the "delivered prices" of all producers in every locality where deliveries are made are always the same regardless of the producers' different freight costs. Another is that sales made by a non-base mill for delivery at different localities result in net receipts to the seller which vary in amounts equivalent to the "phantom freight" included in, or the "freight absorption" taken from the "delivered price."

As commonly employed by respondents, the basing point system is not single but multiple. That is, instead of one basing point, like that in "Pittsburgh plus," a number of basing point localities are used. In the multiple basing point system, just as in the single basing point system, freight absorption or phantom freight is an element of the delivered price on all sales not governed by a basing point actually located at the seller's mill. And all sellers quote identical delivered prices in any given locality regardless of their different costs of production and their different freight expenses. Thus the multiple and single systems function in the same general manner and produce the same consequences—identity of prices and diversity of net returns. Such differences as there are in matters here pertinent are therefore differences of degree only.

. . . After having made . . . detailed findings of concerted action, the Commission followed them by a general finding that "the capacity, tendency, and effect of the combination maintained by the respondents herein in the manner aforesaid is to . . . promote and maintain their multiple basing point delivered-price system and obstruct and defeat any form of competition which threatens or tends to threaten the continued use and maintenance of said system and the uniformity of prices created and maintained by its use." . . .

. . . Thus . . . the Commission found that respondents, collectively maintained a multiple basing point delivered price system for the purpose of suppressing competition in cement sales. . . .

When the Commission rendered its decision there were about 80 cement manufacturing companies in the United States operating about 150 mills. Ten companies controlled more than half of the mills and there were substantial corporate affiliations among many of the others. This concentration of productive capacity made concerted action far less difficult than it would otherwise have been. The belief is prevalent in the industry that because of the standardized nature of cement, among other reasons, price competition is wholly unsuited to it. That belief is historic. . . . Evidence shows [the multiple basing point delivered price system] . . . to be a handy instrument to bring about elimination of any kind of price competition. The use of the multiple basing point delivered price system by the cement producers has been coincident with a situation whereby for many years, with rare exceptions, cement has been offered for sale in every given locality at identical prices and terms by all producers. Thousands of secret sealed bids have been received by public agencies which corresponded in prices of cement down to a fractional part of a penny.[15]

Occasionally foreign cement has been imported, and cement dealers have sold it below the delivered price of the domestic product. Dealers who persisted in selling foreign cement were boycotted by the domestic producers. Officers of the Institute took the lead in securing pledges by producers not to permit sales f.o.b. mill to purchasers who furnished their own trucks, a practice regarded as seriously disruptive of the entire delivered price structure of the industry.

During the depression in the 1930's, slow business prompted some producers to deviate from the prices fixed by the delivered price system. Meetings were held by other producers; an effective plan was devised to punish the recalcitrants and bring them into line. The plan was simple but successful. Other producers made the recalcitrant's plant an involuntary base point. The base price was driven down with relatively insignificant losses to the producers who imposed the punitive basing point, but with heavy losses to the recalcitrant who had to make all its sales on this basis. In one instance, where a producer had made a low public bid, a punitive base point price was put on its plant and cement was reduced 10¢ per barrel; further reductions quickly followed until the base price at which this recalcitrant had to sell its cement dropped to 75¢ per barrel, scarcely one-half of its former base price of $1.45. Within six weeks after the base price hit 75¢ capitulation occurred and the recalcitrant joined a Portland cement association. Cement in that locality then bounced back to $1.15, later to $1.35, and finally to $1.75.

---

15 The following is one among many of the Commission's findings as to the identity of sealed bids: An abstract of the bids for 6,000 barrels of cement to the United States Engineer Office at Tucumcari, New Mexico, opened April 23, 1936, shows the following:

Name of Bidder	Price per Bbl.	Name of Bidder	Price per Bbl.
Monarch	$3.286854	Oklahoma	$3.286854
Ash Grove	3.286854	Consolidated	3.286854
Lehigh	3.286854	Trinity	3.286854
Southwestern	3.286854	Lone Star	3.286854
U. S. Portland Cement Co	3.286854	Universal	3.286854
		Colorado	3.286854

All bids subject to 10 cents per barrel discount for payment in 15 days. (Com.Ex. 175-A.) *See* 157 F.2d at page 576.

. . . Respondents introduced the testimony of economists to the effect that competition alone could lead to the evolution of a multiple basing point system of uniform delivered prices and terms of sale for an industry with a standardized product and with relatively high freight costs. These economists testified that for the above reasons no inferences of collusion, agreement, or understanding could be drawn from the admitted fact that cement prices of all United States producers had for many years almost invariably been the same in every given locality in the country. There was also considerable testimony by other economic experts that the multiple basing point system of delivered prices as employed by respondents contravened accepted economic principles and could only have been maintained through collusion.

The Commission did not adopt the views of the economists produced by the respondents. It decided that even though competition might tend to drive the price of standardized products to a uniform level, such a tendency alone could not account for the almost perfect identity in prices, discounts, and cement containers which had prevailed for so long a time in the cement industry. The Commission held that the uniformity and absence of competition in the industry were the results of understandings or agreements entered into or carried out by concert of the Institute and the other respondents. It may possibly be true, as respondents' economists testified, that cement producers will, without agreement express or implied and without understanding explicit or tacit, always and at all times (for such has been substantially the case here) charge for their cement precisely, to the fractional part of a penny, the price their competitors charge. Certainly it runs counter to what many people have believed, namely, that without agreement, prices will vary—that the desire to sell will sometimes be so strong that a seller will be willing to lower his prices and take his chances. We therefore hold that the Commission was not compelled to accept the views of respondents' economist-witnesses that active competition was bound to produce uniform cement prices. The Commission was authorized to find understanding, express or implied, from evidence that the industry's Institute actively worked, in cooperation with various of its members, to maintain the multiple basing point delivered price system; that this pricing system is calculated to produce, and has produced, uniform prices and terms of sale throughout the country; and that all of the respondents have sold their cement substantially in accord with the pattern required by the multiple basing point system.

Unfair Methods of Competition.—We sustain the Commission's holding that concerted maintenance of the basing point delivered price system is an unfair method of competition prohibited by the Federal Trade Commission Act. . . .

COMMENTARY

1. This case involved § 5 of the Federal Trade Commission Act which prohibits "unfair methods of competition." Although the statute does not require the existence of an agreement as a component of a violation, the Commission held that "concerted" maintenance of the basing point delivered pricing system was an unfair method of competition. The respondents attempted to show that each firm could separately and independently decide to use the same multiple-basing-point pricing system, and that in such a case there would be no "concerted" maintenance of such a system.

2. The basing-point pricing system was a topic of debate among business managers, economists, antitrust enforcement officials, and members of Congress from the 1920s until 1948. In that year, the illegality of the basing-point pricing system was announced in the Supreme Court opinion in the *Cement Institute* case and the decision of the Seventh Circuit in *Triangle Conduit & Cable Co. v. Federal Trade Commission*, 168 F.2d 175 (7th Cir. 1948), *aff'd per curiam by an equally divided court, sub. nom., Clayton Mark & Co. v. Federal Trade Commission,* 366 U.S. 956 (1948) (concurrent use of basing-point pricing by several competitors established an unlawful agreement). *See* Frank A. Fetter, *Exit Basing Point Pricing,* 38 AM. ECON. REV. 815 (1948).

These victories in 1948 marked the end of the government's efforts over more than two decades. The government lost its initial challenge to the steel industry's use of basing-point pricing in *United States v. United States Steel Corp.*, 252 U.S. 417 (1920), in which the lower court had made a finding that the basing-point pricing practices of the steel company were the result of free and unfettered competition. *United States v. United States Steel Corp.*, 223 F. 55, 82 (1915). The government was then successful in *American Column & Lumber Co. v. United States,* 257 U.S. 377 (1921), and in *United States v. American Linseed Oil Co.*, 262 U.S. 371 (1923). Each of these cases involved a trade association operating "open price" programs incorporating a basing-point pricing system. *See* pages 360-62, *infra.* The Federal Trade Commission also prevailed in its attack on the basing-point system in the steel industry, issuing a Cease and Desist Order barring further use of a single-basing point pricing system. *In the Matter of United States Steel Corp.*, 8 F.T.C. 1, 59 (1924). This victory was short-lived. Although the steel corporation responded by filing a statement of compliance with the Order, promising to accept its directions "insofar as it is practible to do," the subsequent response of the corporation was to adopt a multiple-basing-point system. *See* FRITZ MACHLUP, THE BASING-POINT SYSTEM 67 (1949). As with the steel industry, the government's first attack on the basing-point system in the cement industry failed. The Supreme Court held in *Cement Manufacturers Protective Ass'n v. United States,* 268 U.S. 588 (1925), that the basing-point system reflected active, free, and unrestrained competition in an industry characterized by a standardized commodity traded among informed, professional buyers. *Id.* at 605-06.

The government's continuous opposition to basing-point pricing was grounded in the then-prevailing view among economists that such a system was an instrumentality of collusive and discriminatory pricing. Professor John R. Commons, who served as a expert witness in the Federal Trade Commission's *United States Steel Corporation* case of 1924, subsequently published an article noting the discriminatory feature of delivered pricing systems. *See* John R. Commons, *The Delivered Price Practice in the Steel Market,* 14 AM. ECON. REV. 505, 514 (1924). Professor Frank Fetter, another expert witness in this case, published his book, THE MASQUERADE OF MONOPOLY in 1931, referring to the basing-point system as ". . . the proof and exercise of monopoly power." THE MASQUERADE OF MONOPOLY 153, 158 (Kelly ed. 1931). *But see* John M. Clark, *Basing Point Methods of Price Quoting*,

4 CANADIAN J. ECON. 477 (1938). Clark voiced doubt that a legal requirement of f.o.b. mill pricing would be effective in bringing prices to the full competitive level, given the potential in markets of few sellers for a mutually profitable pricing structure to prevail without overt agreement. He also expressed a preference for the enforcement agencies and courts to restrict reliance on expert testimony because the experts tended to provide a theoretical explanation, rather than identifying actual market imperfections and suggesting appropriate remedial measures. Clark's later work anticipated some of the economic analysis with followed the *Cement Institute* decision. *E.g.*, John M. Clark, *The Law and Economics of Basing Points: Appraisal and Proposals,* 39 AM. ECON. REV. 430 (1949).

Despite the meandering course of the case law on the legality of basing-point pricing, the interest of economists in this practice remained relatively constant. During the 1930s, interest was sustained by the study of pricing practices as causal or contributing factors of the Great Depression. The Temporary National Economic Committee, which was established in 1938 and terminated in 1941, was directed to study the concentration of economic power (*see* Chapter 1, page 19), and thus directly addressed the significance of this practice. The Committee's conclusion about the function of basing-point systems supported its recommendation for legislation as follows:

> Extensive hearings on basing-point systems showed that they are used in many industries as an effective device for eliminating price competition. . . .
>
> * * *
>
> We . . . recommend that the Congress enact legislation declaring such pricing systems to be illegal.

FINAL REPORT AND RECOMMENDATIONS OF THE TEMPORARY NATIONAL ECONOMIC COMMITTEE 33 (1941). Similar legislation had been proposed as S. 4055, 74th Cong., 2d Sess. (1936), in the debate over the Robinson-Patman Act. See Chapter 13 for the treatment of freight absorption under a basing-point system as discriminatory pricing. However, no legislation expressly outlawing basing-point pricing was enacted as a result of these proposals. After the government's 1948 victories, legislation to reverse the decision in the *Cement Institute* case was discussed. Machlup notes that after this decision, the Senate Resolution authorized an inquiry by the Senate Committee on Interstate and Foreign Commerce into the effects of the *Cement Institute* decision on business. MACHLUP, THE BASING POINT SYSTEM, *supra,* at 55-56. The charge to the committee was to report its findings as well as its recommendations for legislation as it might deem advisable. In the discussion of the need for legislation, industry leaders were quoted in the press as warning that the removal of the basing-point system would lead to inflation, plant relocation and shortages of basic materials, as well as injury to small business. No such legislation was introduced, however. In July of 1948, the steel and cement industries announced their adoption of f.o.b. mill pricing. At the same time prices were raised, coupled with the explanation that the increase was required by the change in pricing method. *Id.* at 57.

The *Cement Institute* decision produced yet another round of economic analysis of basing-point pricing. This literature shifted the emphasis of the discourse from the previous concern with the collusive and discriminatory aspects of the system to a consideration of the economic conditions which fostered this pricing practice. Thus, Carl Kaysen identified the conditions common to industries in which basing-point pricing flourished. *See* Carl A. Kaysen, *Basing Point Pricing and Public Policy,* 63 Q.J. ECON. 289 (1949). Kaysen identified the following nurturing characteristics: a standardized commodity of low value per unit weight, for which the transportation cost is a substantial portion of the purchase price, an industry in which typical shipments are of substantial distances because of either: 1) economies of scale which make local producers uneconomical as in cement or 2) locational factors concentrating production in a few areas as in steel and hardwood. The need to make cyclical adjustments to capacity was the material determinant of basing-point pricing. As he put it,

> The essence of the cyclical problem in industries . . . [utilizing basing-point pricing] lies in the cyclical unadaptability of capacity to demand in the short run . . . and the high income elasticity and low price elasticity of demand for their products. . . . This means that a capacity just sufficient to meet the minimum level of demand at the cyclical trough would fall far short of what was required . . . in a boom. . . . The problem then is, how shall the costs of providing the peak load capacity be met.

Id. at 306. Kaysen then concludes that a policy of marginal cost pricing at all times would result in great fluctuations of prices over the business cycle. At output below full capacity, marginal cost would be below average cost; near full capacity marginal cost would rise sharply over a narrow range of output. Under this regime, producers would set capacity at a level to produce high returns during peak demand in order to cover shortfalls in revenue during slack demand. This analysis avoided the characterization of basing-point pricing as an arrangement initiated by motives of collusion. As a subsequent commentator has noted, the practice is now viewed as a rational response to the economic conditions noted by Kaysen. *See also* George J. Stigler, *A Theory of Delivered Price Systems*, 39 AM. ECON. REV. 1143 (Pt. 2 1949). Haddock thus concludes:

> The economic theory of basing-point prices enjoys an ancient . . . history. . . . [F]irms are sometimes attacked in the courts with no evidence of wrongdoing but basing-point prices. . . . Even the less mundane phenomena of freight absorption and cross hauling may arise benignly from noncollusive circumstances. Indeed, it has proven impossible to construct a believable example of an effective collusion or monopoly that could not do better by adopting some alternative strategy.

David D. Haddock, *Basing-Point Pricing: Competitive vs. Collusive Theories*, 72 AM. ECON. REV. 289, 303 (1982).

In the light of this analysis, it is not surprising that basing-point pricing is no longer a concern of the enforcement agencies.

3. Do you think the cement manufacturers involved in the FTC case separately adopted a multiple-basing-point pricing system or do you think they acted "in concert"? Suppose the dominant firm in the cement industry had devised the multiple-basing-point system as a mutually beneficial arrangement and published it in a trade paper. Subsequently, a majority of the managers of the other firms decided, without ever communicating with the dominant firm's management, that such a pricing system served the interests of all sellers by eliminating bargaining with buyers and all firms adhered to the system. Would these facts constitute agreement under the *Interstate Circuit* test? Under Professor Turner's test? Would these facts constitute an unfair method of competition under § 5 of the Federal Trade Commission Act, as interpreted by the *Cement Institute* case? Would these facts constitute an example of price leadership in an oligopoly market?

---

3. Intracorporate Conspiracy

Copperweld Corp. v. Independence Tube Corp.

467 U.S. 752 (1984)

Chief Justice BURGER delivered the opinion of the Court.

We granted *certiorari* to determine whether a parent corporation and its wholly owned subsidiary are legally capable of conspiring with each other under § 1 of the Sherman Act.

[Petitioner Copperweld Corp. had purchased the business of the Regal Tube Division of Lear Siegler, Inc. and had placed the assets of that business in a newly formed corporation, the Regal Tube Co., all of whose stock was owned by Copperweld. An employee of Lear Siegler, Inc. then formed respondent Independence Tube Co. and went into business in competition with Regal. Concerned that the owner of Independence Tube would be using know-how and trade secrets which Copperweld had purchased, Copperweld warned all of the business firms having dealings with Independence of its claims. As a result of Copperweld's warnings, the Yoder Co.—which had agreed to build Independence a tubing mill—withdrew its acceptance. As a result, Independence was delayed nine months in commencing operations.]

. . . .

In 1976 respondent filed this action in the District Court against petitioners and Yoder. The jury found that Copperweld and Regal had conspired to violate § 1 of the Sherman Act . . . but that Yoder was not part of the conspiracy. . . .

We granted *certiorari* to reexamine the intra-enterprise conspiracy doctrine . . . and we reverse.

II

Review of this case calls directly into question whether the coordinated acts of a parent and its wholly owned subsidiary can, in the legal sense contemplated by § 1 of the Sherman Act, constitute a combination or conspiracy. . . .

The problem began with *United States v. Yellow Cab Co.*, 332 U.S. 218 (1947). The controlling shareholder of the Checker Cab Manufacturing Corp., Morris Markin, also controlled numerous companies operating taxicabs in four cities. With few exceptions, the operating companies had once been independent and had come under Markin's control by acquisition or merger. The complaint alleged conspiracies under §§ 1 and 2 of the Sherman Act among Markin, Checker, and five corporations in the operating system. The Court stated that even restraints in a vertically integrated enterprise were not "necessarily" outside of the Sherman Act, observing that an unreasonable restraint

> "*may result as readily from a conspiracy among those who are affiliated or integrated under common ownership as from a conspiracy among those who are otherwise independent*. . . . The complaint charges that the restraint of interstate trade was not only effected by the combination of the appellees but was the primary object of the combination. The theory of the complaint . . . is that 'dominating power' over the cab operating companies 'was not obtained by normal expansion . . . but by deliberate, calculated purchase for control.'" . . .

It is the underscored language that later breathed life into the intra-enterprise conspiracy doctrine. The passage as a whole, however, more accurately stands for a quite different proposition. It has long been clear that a pattern of acquisitions may itself create a combination illegal under § 1, especially when an original anticompetitive purpose is evident from the affiliated corporations' subsequent conduct. The *Yellow Cab* passage is most fairly read in light of this settled rule. In *Yellow Cab*, the affiliation of the defendants was irrelevant because the original acquisitions were themselves illegal. . . .

The ambiguity of the *Yellow Cab* holding yielded the one case giving support to the intra-enterprise conspiracy doctrine. In *Kiefer-Stewart Co. v. Joseph E. Seagram & Sons, Inc.*, 340 U.S. 211 (1951), the Court held that two wholly owned subsidiaries of a liquor distiller were guilty under § 1 of the Sherman Act for jointly refusing to supply a wholesaler who declined to abide by a maximum resale pricing scheme. The Court off-handedly dismissed the defendants' argument that "their status as 'mere instrumentalities of a single manufacturing-merchandising unit' makes it impossible for them to have conspired in a manner forbidden by the Sherman Act." With only a citation to *Yellow Cab* and no further analysis, the Court stated that the "suggestion runs counter to our past decisions that common ownership and control does not liberate corporations from the impact of the antitrust laws" and stated that this rule was "especially applicable" when defendants "hold themselves out as competitors." . . .

Unlike the *Yellow Cab* passage, this language does not pertain to corporations whose initial affiliation was itself unlawful. In straying beyond *Yellow Cab*, the *Kiefer-Stewart* Court failed to confront the anomalies an intra-enterprise doctrine entails. It is relevant nonetheless that, were the case decided today, the same result probably could be justified on the ground that the subsidiaries conspired with wholesalers other than the plaintiff.[9] An

---

[9] Although the plaintiff apparently never acquiesced in the resale price maintenance scheme, . . . one of the subsidiaries did gain the compliance of other wholesalers after once terminating them for refusing to abide by the pricing scheme. . . . A theory of combination between the subsidiaries and the wholesalers could now support

intra-enterprise conspiracy doctrine thus would no longer be necessary to a finding of liability on the facts of *Kiefer-Stewart*.

. . . .

The same is true of *Perma Life Mufflers, Inc. v. International Parts Corp.*, 392 U.S. 134 (1968), which involved a conspiracy among a parent corporation and three subsidiaries to impose various illegal restrictions on plaintiff franchisees. The Court did suggest that, because the defendants

> "availed themselves of the privilege of doing business through separate corporations, the fact of common ownership could not save them from any of the obligations that the law imposes on separate entities. . . ."

But the Court noted immediately thereafter that "[i]n any event" each plaintiff could "clearly" charge a combination between itself and the defendants or between the defendants and other franchise dealers. *Ibid.* Thus, for the same reason that a finding of liability in *Kiefer-Stewart* could today be justified without reference to the intra-enterprise conspiracy doctrine, *see* n.9, *supra*, the doctrine was at most only an alternative holding in *Perma Life Mufflers*.

In short, while this Court has previously seemed to acquiesce in the intra-enterprise conspiracy doctrine, it has never explored or analyzed in detail the justifications for such a rule; the doctrine has played only a relatively minor role in the Court's Sherman Act holdings.

III

A

. . . .

We limit our inquiry to the narrow issue squarely presented: whether a parent and its wholly owned subsidiary are capable of conspiring in violation of § 1 of the Sherman Act. We do not consider under what circumstances, if any, a parent may be liable for conspiring with an affiliated corporation it does not completely own.

B

The distinction between unilateral and concerted conduct is necessary for a proper understanding of the terms "contract, combination . . . or conspiracy" in § 1. Nothing in the literal meaning of those terms excludes coordinated conduct among officers or employees of the same company. But it is perfectly plain that an internal "agreement" to implement a single, unitary firm's policies does not raise the antitrust dangers that § 1 was designed to police. The officers of a single firm are not separate economic actors pursuing separate economic interests, so agreements among them do not suddenly bring together economic power that was previously pursuing divergent goals. Coordination within a firm is as likely to result from an effort to compete as from an effort to stifle competition. In the marketplace, such coordination may be necessary if a business enterprise is to compete effectively. For these reasons, officers or employees of the same firm do not provide the plurality of actors imperative for a § 1 conspiracy.

. . . .

---

§ 1 relief, whether or not it could have when *Kiefer-Stewart* was decided. *See Albrecht v. Herald Co.*, 390 U.S. 145, 149-150, and n.6 (1968); *United States v. Parke, Davis & Co.*, 362 U.S. 29 (1960).

C

. . . [T]he coordinated activity of a parent and its wholly owned subsidiary must be viewed as that of a single enterprise for purposes of § 1 of the Sherman Act. A parent and its wholly owned subsidiary have a complete unity of interest. Their objectives are common, not disparate; their general corporate actions are guided or determined not by two separate corporate consciousnesses, but one. They are not unlike a multiple team of horses drawing a vehicle under the control of a single driver. With or without a formal "agreement," the subsidiary acts for the benefit of the parent, its sole shareholder. If a parent and a wholly owned subsidiary do "agree" to a course of action, there is no sudden joining of economic resources that had previously served different interests, and there is no justification for § 1 scrutiny.

Indeed, the very notion of an "agreement" in Sherman Act terms between a parent and a wholly owned subsidiary lacks meaning. A § 1 agreement may be found when "the conspirators had a unity of purpose or a common design and understanding, or a meeting of minds in an unlawful arrangement." *American Tobacco Co. v. United States*, 328 U.S. 781, 810 (1946). But in reality a parent and a wholly owned subsidiary always have a "unity of purpose or a common design." They share a common purpose whether or not the parent keeps a tight rein over the subsidiary; the parent may assert full control at any moment if the subsidiary fails to act in the parent's best interests.

The intra-enterprise conspiracy doctrine looks to the form of an enterprise's structure and ignores the reality. Antitrust liability should not depend on whether a corporate subunit is organized as an unincorporated division or a wholly owned subsidiary. A corporation has complete power to maintain a wholly owned subsidiary in either form. The economic, legal, or other considerations that lead corporate management to choose one structure over the other are not relevant to whether the enterprise's conduct seriously threatens competition. Rather, a corporation may adopt the subsidiary form of organization for valid management and related purposes. Separate incorporation may improve management, avoid special tax problems arising from multistate operations, or serve other legitimate interests. Especially in view of the increasing complexity of corporate operations, a business enterprise should be free to structure itself in ways that serve efficiency of control, economy of operations, and other factors dictated by business judgment without increasing its exposure to antitrust liability. . . .

If antitrust liability turned on the garb in which a corporate subunit was clothed, parent corporations would be encouraged to convert subsidiaries into unincorporated divisions. Indeed, this is precisely what the Seagram company did after this Court's decision in *Kiefer-Stewart Co. v. Joseph E. Seagram & Sons, Inc.* . . . Such an incentive serves no valid antitrust goals but merely deprives consumers and producers of the benefits that the subsidiary form may yield.

. . . .

IV

We hold that Copperweld and its wholly owned subsidiary Regal are incapable of conspiring with each other for purposes of § 1 of the Sherman Act. To the extent that prior decisions of this Court are to the contrary, they are disapproved and overruled. Accordingly, the judgment of the Court of Appeals is reversed.

It is so ordered.

COMMENTARY

1. *Copperweld* held that a parent and its wholly-owned subsidiaries were legally incapable of conspiring. Suppose that a parent company merely owns a majority interest in its subsidiaries. Would their capacity to conspire with each other be changed? In its 1988 Guidelines for International Operations, the Justice Department set forth its view of the scope of the *Copperweld* doctrine:

> In *Copperweld Corp v. Independence Tube Corp.*, the Supreme Court held that, because a parent corporation and its wholly-owned subsidiary have a "complete unity" of economic interests, they are not independent actors capable of conspiring to restrain trade within the meaning of section 1 of the Sherman Act. The Court declined to decide whether the same result would apply where a subsidiary is less than wholly-owned. In the Department's view, however, the policies underlying the Sherman Act (as discussed in *Copperweld*) support the conclusion that a parent corporation and any subsidiary corporation of which the parent owns more than 50 percent of the voting stock are a single economic unit under common control and are thus legally incapable of conspiring with one another within the meaning of section 1. If a parent company controlled a significant but less than majority share of the voting stock of a subsidiary, the Department would make a factual inquiry to determine whether the parent corporation actually had effective working control of the subsidiary.

The 1995 Enforcement Guidelines for International Operations, however, omits mention of the *Copperweld* issue. Stephen Calkins, Copperweld *in the Courts: The Road to* Caribe, 63 ANTITRUST L.J. 345, 351-52 (1995).

2. *Chicago Professional Sports Limited Partnership v. National Basketball Association*, 95 F.3d 593 (7th Cir. 1996). In this case, the court considered the question of whether the NBA engages in concerted action when it imposes rules governing broadcasts by individual teams:

> *Copperweld* does not hold that only conflict-free enterprises may be treated as single entities. Instead it asks why the antitrust laws distinguish between unilateral and concerted action, and then assigns a parent-subsidiary group to the "unilateral" side in light of those functions. Like a single firm, the parent-subsidiary combination cooperates internally to increase efficiency. Conduct that "deprives the marketplace of the independent centers of decisionmaking that competition assumes," 467 U.S. at 769, 104 S.Ct. at 2740, without the efficiencies that come with integration inside a firm, go on the "concerted" side of the line. And there are entities in the middle: "mergers, joint ventures, and various vertical agreements" (*id.* at 768, 104 S.Ct. at 2740) that reduce the number of independent decisionmakers yet may improve efficiency. These are

> assessed under the Rule of Reason. We see no reason why a sports league cannot be treated as a single firm in this typology. It produces a single product; cooperation is essential (a league with one team would be like one hand clapping); and a league need not deprive the market of independent centers of decisionmaking. The district court's legal standard was therefore incorrect, and a judgment resting on the application of that standard is flawed.
>
> Whether the NBA itself is more like a single firm, which would be analyzed only under § 2 of the Sherman Act, or like a joint venture, which would be subject to the Rule of Reason under § 1, is a tough question under *Copperweld*. It has characteristics of both. . . .

---

4. Combinations and Vertical Conspiracies

During the 1960s the Court developed a broad meaning for the term "combination" as it appears in § 1 of the Sherman Act. This elaboration occurred principally in *United States v. Parke, Davis & Co.*, 362 U.S. 29 (1960); *Albrecht v. Herald Co.*, 390 U.S. 145 (1968); and *Perma Life Mufflers, Inc. v. International Parts Corp.*, 392 U.S. 134 (1968). These cases were all concerned with vertical relations between suppliers and dealers and appear in Chapter 5, Section E. This caselaw development of "combination" was described and approved during the 1980s in *Copperweld Corp. v. Independence Tube Corp.*, 467 U.S. 752 (1984).

While the Supreme Court cases cited above have apparently made it easier to establish a vertical combination, other Supreme Court cases have articulated standards governing the proof of a vertical conspiracy and especially of a vertical price fixing conspiracy which, on balance, make such conspiracies more difficult to prove. *Monsanto Co. v. Spray-Rite Service Corp.*, 465 U.S. 752 (1984); *Business Electronics Corp. v. Sharp Electronics Corp.*, 485 U.S. 717 (1988). Currently, the law appears to be moving in the direction of imposing stricter requirements for proof of vertical conspiracies.

5. Integration as Negating Conspiracy, and Related Matters

Agreements—even those about selling prices entered into by firms which have formerly been competing with each other—will not run afoul of the Sherman Act if they are entered into incident to a legitimate integration of their operations. When two or more formerly independent firms integrate fully by merger, consolidation or otherwise, they become a single firm and conspiracy thereafter is legally impossible. Again, when two or more competing firms form an otherwise lawful joint venture, agreements incident to the venture will normally be evaluated under the rule of reason. Agreements will also necessarily form part of other attempts at lawful cooperation.

Arizona v. Maricopa County Medical Society, 457 U.S. 332, 356-57 (1982), emphasized the critical factor of integration or its absence. In this case two groups of physicians in Maricopa County, Arizona had established two "foundations" whose principal activity was to set maximum fees for their members under foundation-approved insurance plans. They also reviewed the medical necessity and appropriateness of treatment provided by their members under those plans and could draw checks on insurance company accounts to pay doctors for services performed for covered patients. The defendants argued that the foundations were procompetitive in that they identified to insurance companies and others low-cost providers of medical care in a marketplace where low-cost providers were hard to identify.

In holding that even maximum price-fixing agreements were illegal *per se*, the Court pointed out that the parties to the maximum price-fixing agreement had not integrated their businesses or done anything in common other than to agree on price:

> The foundations are not analogous to partnerships or other joint arrangements in which persons who would otherwise be competitors pool their capital and share the risks of loss as well as the opportunities for profit. In such joint ventures, the partnership is regarded as a single firm competing with other sellers in the market. The agreement under attack is an agreement among hundreds of competing doctors concerning the price at which each will offer his own services to a substantial number of consumers. It is true that some are surgeons, some anesthesiologists, and some psychiatrists, but the doctors do not sell a package of three kinds of services. If a clinic offered complete medical coverage for a flat fee, the cooperating doctors would have the type of partnership arrangement in which a price-fixing agreement among the doctors would be perfectly proper. But the fee agreements disclosed by the record in this case are among independent competing entrepreneurs. They fit squarely into the horizontal price-fixing mold.

Thus because the physicians had not integrated their operations, they were treated as participants in a price-fixing arrangement and subjected to the rule of *per se* illegality. *Maricopa* raises the tantalizing question of how much integration would take the physicians out of the scope of the *per se* rule and into the scope of the rule of reason.

6. Hub-and-Spoke Conspiracy

Impro Products, Inc. v. Herrick
715 F.2d 1267 (8th Cir. 1983)

HEANEY, Circuit Judge.

Impro Products, Inc., appeals from a district court order granting summary judgment in favor of the defendants on Impro's claims under Sections 1 and 2 of the Sherman Act. The court found no evidence that any of the defendants had conspired to suppress Impro as a competitor in the animal health field. We affirm.

. . . .

Impro Products, Inc. . . . produces and markets a variety of animal biologics containing whey antibodies. . . . Dr. John Herrick, during the events in question here, was a USDA extension veterinarian, and a tenured professor of veterinary science at Iowa State University. . . . Between 1966 and 1976, Dr. Herrick entered into consulting arrangements with each of the corporate defendants. None of them, however, knew that Dr. Herrick had similar consulting arrangements with the other corporate defendants until this lawsuit was filed. Between November, 1959, and the spring of 1962, Dr. Herrick also was in communication with Impro officials concerning the use, efficacy and commercial possibilities of Impro's products. . . .

According to Impro, its intrastate biological products are in competition with the antibiotic drugs produced by the corporate defendants. . . . Impro contends that its products are effective in increasing milk production, and in preventing or controlling infections, and that its products do not produce the adverse side effects—primarily the creation of resistant bacteria and the existence of antibiotic residues in meat and dairy products—caused by antibiotic drugs.

Impro further asserts that the corporate defendants entered into a single conspiracy or several conspiracies with Dr. Herrick—under the guise of consulting agreements—to destroy Impro or to limit its effectiveness as a competitor. Its theory is that in return for compensation from the corporate defendants, Dr. Herrick used his various positions to promote the products of the corporate defendants, to disparage Impro's products, and to influence various federal and state governmental officials to deny Impro necessary licensing for its products.

The corporate defendants deny that any of them entered into a conspiracy with Dr. Herrick to suppress Impro as an effective competitor in the animal health field. They contend that there would be no reason for any of them to enter into such an agreement because Impro's biologics do not compete with their products and because there is no adequate scientific data indicating that Impro's products are efficacious. They additionally assert that Dr. Herrick's comments with respect to the products of Impro and the corporate defendants were legitimately and independently made in the course of his duties as an extension veterinarian and professor.

. . . .

The plaintiff argues that it introduced evidence which reasonably supports an inference that Dr. Herrick and each of the corporate defendants entered into an agreement to suppress Impro as a viable competitor in the animal health industry, and that this evidence precludes summary judgment.

Impro relies primarily on three factors in support of this contention: First, the plaintiff's teat dips and biological products compete with the antibiotics, biologics and teat dips sold by the various corporate defendants (or in the case of RM & D, sold by its client American Cyanamid) in an overall animal health market. Impro urges that this competition provided the motive for the defendants to conspire against the plaintiff.

Second, each of the corporate defendants entered into an agreement with Dr. Herrick under which Herrick received a substantial consulting fee. Impro contends that these arrangements provide both circumstantial evidence of an opportunity to conspire and direct evidence of agreements between Dr. Herrick and each corporate defendant.

Third, the various defendants engaged in activities which were harmful to the plaintiff. Impro claims that these activities are consistent with the inference of concerted action to harm it which is raised by the evidence of motive and opportunity to conspire.

Impro introduced evidence indicating that the following activities may have occurred: First, Dr. Herrick . . . actively promote[d] the products of the corporate defendants and . . . disparage[d] those sold by Impro when speaking to or writing for farmers, veterinarians, academicians, and others in the animal health field. For example, Dr. Herrick's articles in Dairy Illustrated, a Babson publication, contained favorable comments about products sold by Babson, Philips Roxane, and RM & D's client, American Cyanamid. In addition, Dr. Herrick appeared at a Philips Roxane press conference at which it introduced a new product—Somnugen—and subsequently worked to promote this product, including publishing a favorable article in a farm-oriented magazine and helping Philips Roxane refute charges that Somnugen contributed to bovine respiratory disease. Dr. Herrick also prepared an article in 1977 for a publication entitled "Animal Nutrition and Health," which stressed the alleged hazards of intrastate biologic products.

Second, Dr. Herrick made various efforts to prevent the company from obtaining federal and state licenses to market its products. . . .

In 1976, Dr. Herrick worked on proposed state legislation in Iowa intended to restrict the use of intrastate biologics. Herrick also told an official from Grand Laboratories—a competing intrastate biologics producer—that the legislation was aimed at Impro, not Grand Laboratories. In addition, Dr. Herrick also provided information about Impro to officials from other states—including Minnesota, Michigan, Vermont and California—who were investigating the plaintiff's products.

Third, certain of the corporate defendants also engaged in conduct harmful to Impro by participating in trade associations and sponsoring university research which were generally hostile to the plaintiff's products. . . .

The consulting agreements between Dr. Herrick and the various corporate defendants obviously had a legitimate business purpose. Standing alone they do not evince knowing participation by any of the corporate defendants in an arrangement with Dr. Herrick to harm Impro. Notwithstanding extended discovery, however, Impro has not uncovered any evidence that any of the agreements, in fact, represented a *quid pro quo* for Dr. Herrick's disparaging comments about Impro.

Nor was the plaintiff able to introduce any other evidence showing a connection between Dr. Herrick's activities and any of the corporate defendants. Uncontradicted testimony established that no employees of the corporate defendants . . . ever discussed Impro or its products with Dr. Herrick before this litigation was commenced. . . .

The plaintiff alternatively contends that the record evinces a hub-and-spoke or rimless wheel conspiracy in which each corporate defendant entered into a separate agreement with Dr. Herrick to harm Impro and each was aware that it was part of a larger scheme, but there was no overall agreement among all of the defendants.

In *Elder-Beerman Stores Corp. v. Federated Department Stores, Inc.*, 459 F.2d 138, 146-147 (6th Cir. 1972), the Sixth Circuit articulated the following test for establishing a hub-and-spoke conspiracy in an antitrust context:[14]

> (1) that there is an *overall*-unlawful plan or "common design" in existence; (2) that knowledge that others must be involved is inferable to each member because of his knowledge of the unlawful nature of the subject of the conspiracy but knowledge on the part of each member of the exact scope of the operation or the number of people involved is not required, and (3) there must be a showing of each alleged member's participation. (Emphasis in original).

It is clear that the district court did not err in granting summary judgment in favor of the defendants on the plaintiff's hub-and-spoke conspiracy theory. First, the third requirement of the *Elder-Beerman* test is the existence of a separate unlawful agreement between each spoke conspirator and the hub conspirator. As we detailed above, the record shows that no agreement to harm Impro existed between any of the corporate defendants and Dr. Herrick.

Second, the record shows that none of the corporate defendants communicated with any of the others concerning Impro or its products until after the plaintiff commenced this lawsuit, and that none of the corporate defendants knew that Herrick had consulting agreements with any of the other corporate defendants. This evidence—combined with the district court's findings that none of the corporate defendants had entered into an agreement with Dr. Herrick to disparage Impro—precludes this Court from concluding, as required by the *Elder-Beerman* test, that there existed an overall plan to suppress the plaintiff as a competitor or that each defendant had knowledge that others were involved in the conspiracy. . . .

Because Impro failed to introduce evidence which at least raised a material question of fact as to whether it could satisfy the requirements of a hub-and-spoke conspiracy theory, the district court did not commit reversible error in granting summary judgment in favor of the defendants on this issue.

. . . .

---

[14] There is some question whether the conspiracy provisions of Sections 1 and 2 of the Sherman Act apply to a hub-and-spoke conspiracy. We believe that they do. Two federal courts addressing this question have recognized—at least implicitly—that such a conspiracy is cognizable under the Sherman Act if the plaintiff introduces sufficient evidence to demonstrate that one exists. *See Elder-Beerman Stores Corp. v. Federated Department Stores, Inc.*, 459 F.2d 138, 146-147 (6th Cir.1972); *Harlem River Consumer Cooperative, Inc. v. Associated Grocers of Harlem, Inc.*, 408 F. Supp. 1251, 1279 (S.D.N.Y. 1976). Moreover, in *Kotteakos v. United States*, 328 U.S. 750 (1946), when the Supreme Court first recognized that in certain circumstances criminal defendants can be jointly tried on a hub-and-spoke conspiracy theory, it indicated that such a theory might be used in a civil case even though it may not be appropriate in a criminal case. Because Impro's evidence is insufficient to sustain a hub-and-spoke conspiracy theory, we need not determine whether it properly could be utilized in this case. . . .

COMMENTARY

1. How does a hub-and-spoke conspiracy differ from conventional kinds of conspiracy such as those involved in *Trenton Potteries* or in *Socony-Vacuum*? Would the conspiracy involved in *Interstate Circuit* fit the criteria for establishing a hub-and-spoke conspiracy articulated in *Impro*? How do the criteria articulated here fit the concept of conspiracy as set forth in *Monsanto*?

2. In its GUIDELINES FOR INTERNATIONAL OPERATIONS (1988), the Justice Department suggested that a hub-and-spoke conspiracy might arise in circumstances in which a Government Minister in a foreign nation were coordinating the efforts of private companies based in that nation to restrict their sales in the United States. In that case the Government Minister would be the "hub" and the private companies would be the spokes.

B. Cooperation

1. Information Gathering

American Column & Lumber Co. v. United States
257 U.S. 377 (1921)

[Three hundred sixty-five firms, operating 465 mills, took part in an activity which they designated as the "Open Competition Plan." While the defendant firms operated only 5% of the mills engaged in hardwood manufacture in the United States, they produced one-third of the total national hardwood production in mills located chiefly in the hardwood producing territory of the Southwest. Pursuant to the Plan each member firm was required to submit six reports to the secretary: 1) a daily report of all sales actually made, with the name and address of the purchaser, the kind, grade and quality of lumber sold and all special agreements of every kind; 2) a daily shipping report, with exact copies of the invoices, all special agreements as to terms, grade, etc.; 3) a monthly production report, showing the production of the member reporting during the previous month, with the grades and thickness classified as prescribed in the Plan; 4) a monthly stock report by each member, showing the stock on hand on the first day of the month; 5) price-lists, f.o.b. shipping point to be filed at the beginning of each month; 6) inspection reports. The latter were prepared by the association upon the basis of inspections of each member carried out by the chief inspector of the Plan and his assistants. The Secretary of the Plan, in return, was required to send to each member: 1) a monthly summary showing the production of each member for the previous month; 2) a weekly report of all sales, giving each sale and the price, and the name of the purchaser; 3) a weekly report of each shipment by each member; 4) a monthly report, showing the individual stock on hand of each member and a summary of all stocks, sold and unsold; 5) a monthly summary of the price-lists of each member; 6) a market report letter "pointing out changes in conditions both in the producing and consuming sections, giving a comparison of production and sales and in general an analysis of the market conditions." The Plan also called for periodic meetings among members which should "afford opportunity for discussion of all subjects of interest to the members." The District Court granted the government a permanent injunction under section 1 of the Sherman Act and the defendants appealed.]

Mr. Justice CLARKE delivered the opinion of the Court.

. . . .

This elaborate plan for the interchange of reports does not simply supply to each member the amount of stock held, the sales made and the prices received, by every other member of the group, thereby furnishing the data for judging the market, on the basis of supply and demand and current prices. It goes much farther. It not only furnishes such information, with respect to stock, sales and prices, but also reports, giving the views of each member as to "market conditions for the next few months"; what the production of each will be for the next "two months"; frequent analysis of the reports by an expert [F.R. Gadd, the Manager of Statistics], with . . . significant suggestions as to both future prices and production; and opportunities for future meetings for the interchange of views. . . . It is plain that the only element lacking in this scheme to make it a familiar type of the competition suppressing organization is a definite agreement as to production and prices. But this is supplied: By the disposition of men "to follow their most intelligent competitors," especially when powerful; by the inherent disposition to make all the money possible, joined with the steady cultivation of the value of "harmony" of action; and by the system of reports, which makes the discovery of price reductions inevitable and immediate. The sanctions of the plan obviously are financial interest, intimate personal contact, and business honor, all operating under the restraint of exposure of what would be deemed bad faith and of trade punishment by powerful rivals.

. . . [Early in 1919] the members of the Plan began actively to co-operate . . . to suppress competition by restricting production. This is very clearly shown by the excerpts following from the minutes of meetings and from the market letters and sales reports distributed at them.

Thus, at the meeting held at Cincinnati, on January 21, 1919, in the discussion of business conditions, the chairman said:

> "If there is *no increase in production*, particularly in oak, there is going to be good business." "*No man is safe in increasing production.* If he does, he will be in bad shape, as the demand won't come."

. . . [I]n the stock report of March 8, 1919, after pointing out that the stock at the mills was only about three-fourths normal and that the production in the Memphis group of manufacturers was only 56 per cent. of normal, the letter of the Manager of Statistics continues:

> "There has been a long drawn out and desperate effort to break the hardwood market by withdrawal of demand; but, be it said to the eternal credit of the hardwood producers, *they have maintained a stout heart and stiff backbone*; with the result that there has been exhibited a strength in the market which has been little short of remarkable in the face of the light demand and the vigorous efforts which have been steadily made to hammer down prices. . . .

. . . [I]n the market letter of April 26th, this influential agent of the association, after pointing out that stocks were less than seventy-five per cent. of normal, that production was about sixty per cent. of normal and that the demand was far in excess of the supply, adds:

> "If ever there was a time when rich rewards awaited the producer of hardwood lumber, now is that time. *There are glorious opportunities ahead.* . . . Supply and demand must necessarily govern prices. The demand is with us, the supply inadequate, therefore *values must increase, as our competition in hardwood is only among ourselves.*"
>
> . . . .

These quotations are sufficient to show beyond discussion that the purpose of the organization, and especially of the frequent meetings, was to bring about a concerted effort to raise prices regardless of cost or merit, and so was unlawful. . . .

Such close cooperation, between many persons, firms, and corporations controlling a large volume of interstate commerce . . . is plainly in theory, as it proved to be in fact, inconsistent with that free and unrestricted trade which the statute contemplates shall be maintained. . . .

Genuine competitors do not make daily, weekly, and monthly reports of the minutest details of their business to their rivals, as the defendants did; they do not contract, as was done here, to submit their books to the discretionary audit, and their stocks to the discretionary inspection, of their rivals, for the purpose of successfully competing with them; and they do not submit the details of their business to the analysis of an expert, jointly employed, and obtain from him a "harmonized" estimate of the market as it is, and as, in his specially and confidentially informed judgment, it promises to be. This is not the conduct of competitors, but is so clearly that of men united in an agreement, express or implied, to act together and pursue a common purpose under a common guide that, if it did not stand confessed a combination to restrict production and increase prices in interstate commerce, and as, therefore, a direct restraint upon that commerce, as we have seen that it is, that conclusion must inevitably have been inferred from the facts which were proved. . . .

In the presence of this record it is futile to argue that the purpose of the "Plan" was simply to furnish those engaged in this industry, with widely scattered units, the equivalent of such information as is contained in the newspaper and government publications with respect to the market for commodities sold on Boards of Trade or Stock Exchanges. One distinguishing and sufficient difference is that the published reports go to both seller and buyer, but these reports go to the seller only; and another is that there is no skilled interpreter of the published reports, such as we have in this case, to insistently recommend harmony of action likely to prove profitable in proportion as it is unitedly pursued.

Convinced, as we are, that the purpose and effect of the activities of the Open Competition Plan . . . were to restrict competition . . . by concerted action in curtailing production and in increasing prices, we agree with the District Court that it constituted a combination and conspiracy in restraint of interstate commerce . . . and the decree of that court must be

Affirmed.

COMMENTARY

1. The use of the trade association as a forum for coordinating price determination among competitors has been attributed to a book written as a response to the *Standard Oil* decision of the Supreme Court in 1911. *See* George W. Stocking, *The Rule of Reason, Workable Competition, and the Legality of Trade Association Activities*, 21 U. CHI. L. REV. 527, 542 (1954). Stocking states that Arthur Eddy's book, THE NEW COMPETITION, provided the basis of the trade association as an "open-price association," with the objective of substituting cooperation for competition. Eddy clearly rejected competition as a desired mode of commerce, noting:

> . . . [F]ar from promoting progress, competition stays and hinders. . . . [T]here is not a single good result accomplished by man . . . [in commerce] . . . that should not be attained by intelligent and far-sighted cooperation.

ARTHUR EDDY, THE NEW COMPETITION 26 (1912).

Accordingly, Eddy proposed detailed arrangements to accomplish his objective of "open-prices" as follows:

> In industries where there are only a few companies or individuals, all that will be needed is a chairman and a secretary. . . . The two essential factors are, 1. A central office or bureau . . . 2. A secretary. . . .
>
> * * *
>
> With a central office in charge of a secretary the association is ready to establish the open-price by filing with the secretary: 1. All inquiries . . . [about prices] 2. All bids 3. All contracts.
>
> Upon receipt of the information the secretary proceeds as follows: The information in the reports . . . is *not* interchanged. Members are not furnished any information regarding prospective bids. There is no legal objection to giving such information *providing it does not lead to collusive bidding*; . . . From the reports of inquiries the secretary makes up a weekly bulletin containing statistical information.

ARTHUR EDDY, THE NEW COMPETITION 120-28 (1912).

Economic analysis recognizes that information about relevant price variables is obtained at a cost, can rarely be fully developed, yet remains central to the function of competitive markets. The nature of information and the means of gathering it limit the perfect access posited in the competitive model. As one commentator stated:

> . . . [A]n essential part of the phenomena with which we . . . [economists] have to deal . . . [is] the unavoidable imperfection of . . . knowledge and the consequent need for a process by which knowledge is constantly communicated and acquired.

F.A. Hayek, *The Use of Knowledge in Society*, 36 AM. ECON. REV. 519, 530 (1945). *See also* George J. Stigler, *The Economics of Information*, 69 J. POL. ECON. 213, 214 (1961) (price dispersion is a measure of ignorance in the market); Jacob Marschak, *The Economics of Inquiring, Communicating, and Deciding*, 58 AM. ECON. REV. 1 (Papers and Proceedings 1968); Sanford J. Grossman & Joseph E. Stiglitz, *On the Impossibility of Informationally Efficient Markets*, 70 AM. ECON. REV. 393 (1980) (the lack of information restricts the competitive performance of markets).

Since information can function either to enhance or to depress competition, how should enforcement activity deal with information-gathering entities, such as trade associations? Should the structure and performance of the market for a product or service be the touchstone of enforcement decisions? Or is the conduct of firm managers in obtaining and transmitting the information leading to the determination of prices the strategic variable in a competitive outcome? There has been no enforcement action against trade associations for decades. What factors might account for this posture of the enforcement agencies involved?

2. The Court observed that the Plan adherents consisted of "365 natural competitors, controlling one-third of the trade of the country." Does the statement by the Court indicate an awareness that control over a significant amount of the supply of a product is a necessary condition for the collective determination of price and output decisions?

3. A cartel provides an institutionalized mechanism among competitors, too numerous to coordinate decision-making by tacit understanding, in which price, output, and other relevant factors are collectively determined. (*See* pages 373-74, *infra*). In many cartels, an office or a committee serves as the means of coordination. Did the Association or its Secretary in *American Column & Lumber* perform the coordination function of a cartel?

4. Cartels are inherently unstable because each participant has an economic incentive covertly to make price and output decisions for its individual benefit. The most acute problem in maintaining a cartel is ensuring against cheating by cartel members on output limitations. To the extent that a cartel is successful, it brings about an increase in prices. As prices become higher and profit margins increase, the reward for selling more units by undercutting rivals increases. Once widespread cheating occurs, the cartel breaks down. *See* DONALD DEWEY, MONOPOLY IN ECONOMICS AND LAW 18-19 (1959). One way of strengthening a cartel is to set up a stringent system for discovering and identifying firms who cheat on the cartel agreement. Such a system then both discourages cheating and reassures the cartel members that no cheating is occurring other than that which the system discovers.

5. Note that the information collected and disseminated would have identified those firms who were "cheating" on an agreement to restrict production and to raise prices. Because information about the details of particular sales by particular firms was collected and disseminated, any seller who sought to make a sale by undercutting the prices of the others would be identified.

6. The preceding paragraphs show that one reason why the Plan collected and disseminated the details of particular transactions could have been to facilitate the operation of a cartel by the Plan's adherents.

7. There was no legitimate reason why the Plan had to disseminate details of particular transactions. If the members needed more information about the value of their lumber, that need would probably have been met by the dissemination of averages. Persons who trade on the stock or commodity markets do not need the details of particular transactions. They are well informed when they know the high, low, and closing amounts or bid and asked prices or the current running market levels.

8. The defendants should have been asked why they needed the details of particular transactions. Perhaps they could show that their situation is critically different from a trader on the stock or commodities markets. But when a group of business firms control a substantial part of the supply of goods in the market, they should be able to justify their need to collect and distribute this highly particularistic kind of information. If they cannot, the court should presume that it is being used to strengthen the operation of a cartel.

Maple Flooring Manufacturers Ass'n v. United States

268 U.S. 563 (1925)

[In a suit brought by the government under section 1 of the Sherman Act, the District Court granted an injunction and the defendants appealed.]

Mr. Justice Stone delivered the opinion of the Court.

. . . [B]ill in equity filed March 5, 1923 . . . .

The defendants are the Maple Flooring Manufacturers' Association, an unincorporated "trade association"; twenty-two corporate defendants, members of the association, engaged in the business of selling and shipping maple, beech, and birch flooring in interstate commerce, all but two of them having their principal places of business in Michigan, Minnesota, or Wisconsin. . . . Of the corporate defendants, approximately one-half own timber lands and sawmills and are producers of the rough lumber from which they manufacture finished flooring. . . . The other defendants purchase rough flooring lumber in the open market and manufacture it into finished flooring. . . . Estimates submitted in behalf of the government indicate that in the year 1922 the defendants produced 70% of the total production of . . . [maple, beech and birch] flooring, the percentage having been gradually diminished during the five years preceding, the average for the five years being 74.2%. . . . The activities . . . of the present association of which the government complains may be summarized as follows:

(1) The computation and distribution among the members of the Association of the average cost to Association members of all dimensions and grades of flooring.
(2) The compilation and distribution among members of a booklet showing freight rates on flooring from Cadillac, Mich., to between five and six thousand points of shipment in the United States.
(3) The gathering of statistics which at frequent intervals are supplied by each member of the Association to the secretary of the Association, giving complete information as to the quantity and kind of flooring sold and prices received by the reporting members, and the amount of stock on hand, which information is summarized by the secretary and transmitted to members without, however, revealing the identity of the members in connection with any specific information thus transmitted.
(4) Meetings at which the representatives of members congregate and discuss the industry and exchange views as to its problems.

. . . .

The contention of the Government is that there is a combination among the defendants, which is admitted; that the effect of the activities of the defendants carried on under the plan of the Association must necessarily be to bring about a concerted effort on the part of members of the Association to maintain prices at levels having a close relation to the average cost of flooring reported to members; and that consequently there is a necessary and inevitable restraint of interstate commerce; and that therefore the plan of the Association itself is a violation of § 1 of the Sherman Act, which should be enjoined regardless of its actual operation and effect so far as price maintenance is concerned. The case must turn, therefore, on the effect of the activity of the defendants in the gathering and dissemination of information as to the cost of flooring, since, without that, the other activities complained of could have no material bearing on price levels in the industry . . . .

Computation and distribution, among the members, of information as to the average cost of their product.

There are three principal elements which enter into the computation of the cost of finished flooring. They are the cost of raw material, manufacturing cost, and the percentage of waste in converting rough lumber into flooring. . . . Manufacturing costs were ascertained by questionnaires sent out to members by which members were requested to give information as to labor costs, cost of warehousing, insurance and taxes, interest at 6% on the value of the plant. . . . To this cost there was at one time added an estimated 5% for contingencies, which practice, however, was discontinued by resolution of the Association of July 19, 1923. . . .

In order to determine the cost of a given type or grade of flooring, it was necessary to distribute the total cost of the aggregate of the different types and grades of finished flooring produced from a given amount of rough lumber among the several types and grades thus produced. This distribution was made by the officials of the Association, and the estimated cost thus determined was tabulated and distributed among the members of the Association. There is no substantial claim made on the part of the Government that the preparation of these estimates of cost were not made with all practicable accuracy, or that they were in any respect not what they purported to be, an estimate of the actual cost of commercial grades of finished flooring fairly ascertained from the actual experience of members of the Association, except that the point is made by the Government that the distribution of cost among the several types and grades of finished flooring produced from a given amount of rough lumber was necessarily arbitrary and that it might be or become a cover for price fixing. Suffice it to say that neither the Government nor the defendants seem to have found it necessary to prove upon what principle of cost accounting this distribution of cost was made, and there are no data from which any inference can be drawn as to whether or not it conformed to accepted practices of cost accounting applied to the manufacture of a diversified product from a single type of raw material.

The compilation and distribution among members of information as to freight rates.

. . . It appears from the evidence to have been the usual practice, in the maple flooring trade, to quote flooring at a delivered price and that purchasers of flooring usually will not buy on any other basis. . . . It also appears that the mills of most of the members of the association are located in small towns in Michigan and Wisconsin and that the average freight rates from these principal producing points . . . to the principal centers of consumption . . . are approximately the same as the freight rate from Cadillac, Mich., to the same centers of consumption. . . . and that the freight rate book served a useful and legitimate purpose in enabling members to quote promptly a delivered price on their product by adding to their mill price a previously calculated freight rate which approximated closely to the actual rate from their own mill towns.

. . . .

The gathering and distributing among members of trade statistics.

. . . .

It was not the purpose or the intent of the Sherman Anti-Trust Law to inhibit the intelligent conduct of business operations. . . . Persons who unite in gathering and disseminating information in trade journals and statistical reports on industry, who gather and publish statistics as to the amount of production of commodities . . . and who report market prices, are not engaged in unlawful conspiracies in restraint of trade merely because the ultimate result of their efforts may be to stabilize prices or limit production through a better understanding of economic laws and a more general ability to conform to them. . . . Sellers of any commodity who guide the daily conduct of their business on the basis of market reports would hardly be deemed to be conspirators engaged in restraint of interstate commerce. They would not be any the more so merely because they became stockholders in a corporation or joint owners of a trade journal, engaged in the business of compiling and publishing such reports.

. . . .

The decree of the District Court is reversed.

COMMENTARY

1. As in *American Column & Lumber*, the trade association here was collecting highly specific information and disseminating it among its members. In his opinion, Justice Stone stated that: "from and after July 19, 1923, the identifying number of the mill making the report was omitted," but the case was brought on March 5, 1923! Thus the identifying number of the reporting mill was furnished, and continued to be furnished, to the members of the trade association until four months after the case began.

2. As in the previous case, information about the details of particular transactions would identify sellers who were departing from an underlying agreement to observe set prices. That data could also be used to determine whether any seller was departing from an output quota.

3. Should the Court not have inquired into why the defendants wanted average cost information? That kind of information is not very meaningful, especially when computed for the production of many companies, located in different states, with plants of different ages and producing differing proportions of several kinds of lumber. The costs include depreciation on plant which at the time that the case was litigated was not governed by strict accounting conventions and thus was subject to widely varying approaches. Moreover, even if depreciation was calculated on the historical cost of the plant, the varying ages of the different plants incorporating as they did the price levels as of the time that the respective plants were built detracted from the comparability of the resulting figures. Finally, allocating the resulting charges among differing types of lumber would involve matters of judgment which, again, would work against the meaningfulness of any resulting amount. In addition, taxes would be likely to vary from plant to plant. So would labor costs and advertising costs. Collecting all of these widely differing costs and averaging them would tell the companies almost nothing about their efficiencies of production. Even if it did, the only cost information relevant to any company in selling its flooring was its own costs, which it was in the best position to calculate for itself. In short, the information was not helpful for any legitimate purpose and was almost meaningless.

Why did the companies want this information? It would have been useful as a basis for a price-fixing agreement. The companies might take an average cost figure, add on a percentage mark up, and they would have a price to which they would all adhere. The average would tend to adjust to large changes in the economy, so that the companies would not have to renegotiate the price agreement every time there was some such major change.

4. In this case, there was strong evidence as to the terms of an underlying agreement. In another part of the Court's opinion, it is stated that the members of the trade association had entered into a an output restriction agreement in 1913 and thereafter followed it with a series of price-fixing agreements, all of which were predicated upon the sellers setting price at a set mark up over "average cost." It looks as if the arrangement provided the mechanism for a price-fixing agreement with prices which adjusted to major changes in the economic conditions of the industry.

Sugar Institute, Inc. v. United States

297 U.S. 553 (1936)

[In a suit brought by the government under section 1 of the Sherman Act, the District Court granted a permanent injunction and the defendants appealed.]

Mr. Chief Justice HUGHES delivered the opinion of the Court.

This suit was brought to dissolve the Sugar Institute, Inc., a trade association. . . .

First. The sugar industry and practices prior to the formation of The Sugar Institute.—Domestic refined sugar, beet sugar, and foreign and insular refined sugar . . . constitute about 99 per cent. of the nation's supply. . . . The fifteen defendant companies, members of the Institute, refine practically all the imported raw sugar processed in this country. . . . Prior to the organization of the Institute in 1927, they provided more than 80 per cent. of the sugar consumed in the United States, and they have since supplied from 70 to 80 per cent. . . .

The court found that the defendants' refined cane sugar "is a thoroughly standardized commodity in physical and chemical properties." . . . In sales by refiners to manufacturers of products containing sugar—about one-third of the sugar consumed—"price, not brand, was always the vital consideration." . . . The court found that, perhaps as early as 1921 and increasingly thereafter, the practice developed on the part of some, but not all, refiners of giving secret concessions. There were five refiners who never indulged in that practice, but the others, called "unethical" refiners, did so to such an extent that at least 30 per cent. of all the sugar sold by the refiners in 1927 carried secret concessions of some kind. The need of secrecy was urgent, for as soon as it was known that a specific concession was granted it would be generally demanded. That concessions were widely granted was generally known in the trade, and while each refiner was able to find out in a general way the approximate prices and terms of his competitors, it was impossible to know with any degree of accuracy the actual prices and terms granted in the innumerable transactions. The court also found that various causes contributed to the development of these selling methods on the part of the unethical refiners, chief among which was an overcapacity since the war of at least 50 per cent. Other probable causes were the lack of statistical information as to amount of production, deliveries and stocks on hand, leading to overproduction. . . . The concessions granted were largely, although not entirely, arbitrary. They were given principally to large buyers. . . . [T]he evidence and findings leave no doubt that the industry was in a demoralized state which called for remedial measures. The court summed up the facts in the following finding:

> "29. The industry was characterized by highly unfair and otherwise uneconomic competitive conditions, arbitrary, secret rebates and concessions were extensively granted by the majority of the companies in most of the important market areas and the widespread knowledge of the market conditions necessary for intelligent, fair competition were lacking. . . ."

. . . .

Third. The agreement and practices of the members of the Institute.—The evidence consists of the "Code of Ethics" and "Interpretations," oral testimony, the minutes of the Institute, and correspondence. . . . [T]he findings of restraints of trade rest upon the basic agreement of the refiners to sell only upon prices and terms openly announced, and upon certain supplementary restrictions.

1. The "basic agreement."—The "Code of Ethics" provided as follows:

> "All discriminations between customers should be abolished. To that end, sugar should be sold only upon open prices and terms publicly announced."

. . . .

These price announcements must be considered in the light of the trade practice known as "*Moves*." The great bulk of sugar, as the court found, "always was and is purchased on what is known in the trade as 'moves,' although very substantial quantities are sold from time to time apart from moves." A "move" takes place when the refiners make public announcements that at a fixed time they will advance their selling price to a named figure, either higher than the presently current selling price or higher than a reduced price which the announcements offer before the advance. Some period of grace was always allowed during which sugar could be bought at the price prevailing before the advance. And in order to obtain their sugar at the lower price, the trade, unless it was felt that the move occurred at too high a price, would then enter into contracts covering their needs for at least the next thirty days. Defendants point out that in actual practice the initial announcements might be made by any one of the refiners and that the move actually takes place only if all refiners follow a similar course. If any one fails to follow with a like announcement, the others must withdraw their advance, since sugar is a completely standardized commodity.

. . . .

The court further found that the refiners "did not consult with one another after an advance had been announced by one of them and that the grace period was not in fact used by them to persuade a reluctant member to follow the example set, despite the business necessity of withdrawing an advance unless it were followed by all." The court found "no agreement among defendants on basis prices in the sense of an agreement to adopt a certain basis price from time to time and to maintain it during any period. Frequently an announcement by one refiner of an advance would result in a series of announcements by others, ultimately leading to a decline. Often, too, the advance would be withdrawn because one refiner would refrain from following the announcement. Except in a few instances, a decline announcement was followed by all." . . .

The distinctive feature of the "basic agreement" was not the advance announcement of prices, or a concert to maintain any particular basis price for any period, but a requirement of adherence, without deviation, to the prices and terms publicly announced. Prior to the Institute, the list prices which many of the "unethical" refiners announced, "were merely nominal quotations and bore no relation to the actual 'selling bases' at which their sugar was sold. . . . The selling price was the price at which they purported to sell; the secret concessions were from this basis." And, in the case of some of the "unethical" refiners, changes in selling bases were made from time to time without formal public announcement in advance. The Institute sought to prevent such departures. . . . The court deemed it to be reasonably certain that "any unfair method of competition caused by the secret concession system" could have been prevented by "immediate publicity given to the prices, terms and conditions in all closed transactions," without an agreement to sell only on the basis "of open public announcement in advance of sales." A "purpose and effect" of that agreement, the court found, was to aid defendants in preventing and limiting "certain types of transactions in which private negotiations are essential." Its operation "tended in fact, as it naturally would tend, toward maintenance of price levels relatively high as compared with raws."

The court found that "the number of price changes for refined as compared to raw sugar" had been relatively less since the Institute than before. This was "too marked to be explained by the drop in raw prices." There was "a marked increase in margin and a substantial increase in profits despite a concededly large excess capacity." . . .

Defendants concede the correctness of the statement of the trial court that if immediate publicity had been given to prices and terms in all "closed transactions," competitive pressure would have been so great that the refiners "would either have had to abandon the discriminatory concessions or extend them to all." They concede that it is "*publicity*" that prevents such concessions and "not the sequence in time between the sale and the publicity." But they raise the fundamental objection that the proposal is not adaptable to the sugar industry. They say that in an industry which "has traditionally, and for good reason, sold its products on 'moves,' through the mechanism of announcing price changes in *advance* of sales in order that buyers may have an opportunity to buy before the price rises, it is not helpful to suggest a system of announcing price changes *after* sales."

Defendants' argument on this point is a forcible one, but we need not follow it through in detail. For the question, as we have seen, is not really with respect to the practice of making price announcements in advance of sales, but as to defendants' requirement of adherence to such announcements without the deviations which open and fair competition might require or justify. The court below did not condemn mere open price announcements in advance of sales. The court was careful to say in its opinion that it found it "unnecessary to pass upon the legality of the use of the Institute" for relaying such announcements, "if each refiner entirely independently of the others voluntarily made his own announcements without obligation to adhere thereto."

. . . The unreasonable restraints which defendants imposed lay not in advance announcements, but in the steps taken to secure adherence, without deviation, to prices and terms thus announced. It was that concerted undertaking which cut off opportunities for variation in the course of competition however fair and appropriate they might be. But, in ending that restraint, the beneficial and curative agency of publicity should not be unnecessarily hampered. The trial court left defendants free to provide for immediate publicity as to prices and terms in all closed transactions. We think that a limitation to that sort of publicity fails to take proper account of the practice of the trade in selling on "moves," as already described, a practice in accordance with which the court found that "the great bulk of sugar always was and is purchased." That custom involves advance announcements, and it does not appear that arrangements merely to circulate or relay such announcements threaten competitive opportunities. On the other hand, such provision for publicity may be helpful in promoting fair competition. If the requirement that there must be adherence to prices and terms openly announced in advance is abrogated and the restraints which followed that requirement are removed, the just interests of competition will be safeguarded and the trade will still be left with whatever advantage may be incidental to its established practice.

The decree.—The court below did not dissolve the Institute. The practices which had been found to constitute unreasonable restraints were comprehensively enjoined. . . . [The defendants were enjoined from:]

. . . .

> "2. Selling only upon or adhering to prices, terms, conditions or freight applications announced, reported or relayed in advance of sale or refraining from deviating therefrom."

. . . .

[Paragraph 5 of the lower court's decree was removed by the Supreme Court. Paragraph 5 thus eliminated had forbidden the defendants, pursuant to any agreement, from:]

> "5. Giving any prior notice of any change or contemplated change in prices, terms, conditions or freight applications, or relaying, reporting or announcing any such change in advance thereof."

Such reporting or relaying, as we have said, permits voluntary price announcements by individual refiners, in accordance with trade usage, to be circulated, and subject to the restrictions imposed by the decree does not appear to involve any unreasonable restraint of competition.

. . . .

The decree is modified in the particulars above stated and, as thus modified, is affirmed.

It is so ordered.

COMMENTARY

1. Observe the use of language by the sugar producers. The price cutters were termed "unethical." By what standard is price-cutting unethical? The price cuts were negotiated in secret bargaining. Why? Perhaps it was only through secret negotiation that price cuts were feasible means of assuring a sale. Suppose a large buyer would not commit itself until the seller reduced price. If the seller reduces price publicly, then other sellers are likely to follow immediately. (Remember the dynamics of the cigarette industry from the *American Tobacco* case. In the sugar industry, each seller seems to be a significant enough supply factor to produce a reaction from rivals.) If the other sellers follow the first seller's price reduction immediately, the first seller has no price advantage over its rivals. Thus in order to use price reduction as a means of making a sale, the reduction has to take place in private—and secret—negotiation.

2. The *American Column and Lumber* and *Maple Flooring* cases involved industries with many sellers, industries which but for the agreements would have operated competitively. Sellers in that environment have a genuine need for market information, but that need is likely to be met with generalized information: high, low, close, bid, asked, etc., information which does not provide the terms of particular transactions with identified parties. In those cases, the dissemination of information providing highly particularized data on the terms of particular transactions indicated that the information could have been used to reinforce a price-fixing or output-limiting cartel.

By contrast, the sugar industry seems to be operating like an oligopoly: the pricing decisions of each seller have such a significant impact that rivals are compelled by market factors to respond immediately to any change. In that context, each seller's pricing decisions are interdependent with those of its rivals in the way that the cigarette companies' were in the *American Tobacco* case. A seller is inhibited from reducing price, unless it can negotiate the price reduction in exchange for a sale. As observed in Note 1, this negotiation process must be done in private.

3. Although some of the Court's language may be obscure, it is clear that the Court recognized a need for sellers and buyers to negotiate in secret, is it not? By prohibiting the Institute from requiring adherence to prices publicly announced in advance, sellers were assured of room to negotiate price reductions with buyers in secret. The Court allowed the Institute to require immediate publicity for any price changes, but that would still permit a seller to clinch a new sale in return for the reduction before it was announced. Moreover a requirement of immediate publicity would force the general—public—price down to the level of the privately negotiated reduction!

4. The *Sugar Institute* decision is the earliest authority which recognizes that secret negotiation is the primary means by which oligopoly prices are eroded. See the discussion of this matter in Chief Justice Burger's opinion in *United States Gypsum Co.*, page 384, *infra.*

United States v. Container Corporation of America

393 U.S. 333 (1969)

[On appeal from the dismissal of the complaint by the District Court.]

Mr. Justice DOUGLAS delivered the opinion of the Court.

This is a civil antitrust action charging a price-fixing agreement in violation of § 1 of the Sherman Act. . . . The District Court dismissed the complaint. . . .

Here all that was present was a request by each defendant of its competitor for information as to the most recent price charged or quoted, whenever it needed such information and whenever it was not available from another source. Each defendant on receiving that request usually furnished the data with the expectation that it would be furnished reciprocal information when it wanted it. That concerted action is of course sufficient to establish the combination or conspiracy, the initial ingredient of a violation of § 1 of the Sherman Act. . . .

The defendants account for about 90% of the shipment of corrugated containers from plants in the Southeastern United States. While containers vary as to dimensions, weight, color, and so on, they are substantially identical, no matter who produces them, when made to particular specifications. The prices paid depend on price alternatives. Suppliers when seeking new or additional business or keeping old customers, do not exceed a competitor's price. It is common for purchasers to buy from two or more suppliers concurrently. A defendant supplying a customer with containers would usually quote the same price on additional orders, unless costs had changed. Yet where a competitor was charging a particular price, a defendant would normally quote the same price or even a lower price.

The exchange of price information seemed to have the effect of keeping prices within a fairly narrow ambit. Capacity has exceeded the demand from 1955 to 1963, the period covered by the complaint, and the trend of corrugated container prices has been downward. Yet despite this excess capacity and the downward trend of prices, the industry has expanded in the Southeast from 30 manufacturers with 49 plants to 51 manufacturers with 98 plants. An abundance of raw materials and machinery makes entry into the industry easy with an investment of $50,000 to $75,000.

The result of this reciprocal exchange of prices was to stabilize prices though at a downward level. Knowledge of a competitor's price usually meant matching that price. . . . [A]s we held in *United States v. Socony-Vacuum Oil Co.* . . . interference with the setting of price by free market forces is unlawful *per se*. Price information exchanged in some markets may have no effect on a truly competitive price. But the corrugated container industry is dominated by relatively few sellers. The product is fungible and the competition for sales is price. The demand is inelastic, as buyers place orders only for immediate, short-run needs. The exchange of price data tends toward price uniformity. For a lower price does not mean a larger share of the available business but a sharing of the existing business at a lower return. Stabilizing prices as well as raising them is within the ban of § 1 of the Sherman Act. . . .

Price is too critical, too sensitive a control to allow it to be used even in an informal manner to restrain competition.

Reversed.

COMMENTARY

1. Justice Fortas filed a separate concurring opinion in this case; Justices Marshall, Harlan, and Stewart dissented. Justice Fortas stated:

> I do not understand the Court's opinion to hold that the exchange of specific information among sellers as to prices charged to individual customers, pursuant to mutual arrangement, is a *per se* violation of the Sherman Act. . . . In this case, the probability that the exchanges of specific price information led to an unlawful effect upon prices is adequately buttressed by evidence in the record.

393 U.S. at 338-39 (Fortas, J., dissenting). The District Court had dismissed the government's Complaint so that the record in the case consisted almost entirely of the pleadings.

The dissent drew different inferences from the information about the structure of the market:

> Complete market knowledge is certainly not an evil in perfectly competitive markets. This is not . . . such a market, and there is admittedly

> some danger that price information will be used for anticompetitive purposes, particularly the maintenance of prices at a high level. . . .
>
> I do not think the danger is sufficiently high in the present case. Defendants are only 18 of the 51 producers of corrugated containers in the Southeastern United States. Together, they do make up 90% of the market and the six largest defendants do control 60% of the market. But entry is easy; an investment of $50,000 to $75,000 is ordinarily all that is necessary. In fact, the number of sellers has increased from 30 to the present 51 in the eight-year period covered by the complaint. The size of the market has almost doubled because of increased demand for corrugated containers. . . . [S]ome excess capacity is present. The products produced by defendants are undifferentiated. Industry demand is inelastic. . . .
>
> . . . Given the uncertainty about the probable effect of an exchange of price information in this context, I would require that the Government prove that the exchange was entered into for the purpose of, or that it had the effect of, restraining price competition.

393 U.S. at 342-43 (Marshall, J., dissenting).

2. Did the majority opinion in *Container Corporation* condemn the exchange of price information in all circumstances? How would you describe the limits of *Container Corporation* as a precedent? Is the case's application limited to certain market structures?

3. Can you describe the market structure of the container industry in the Southeastern United States at the time of the relevant events involved in the case? Note that the Court described in detail that market structure. Was the Court suggesting that the market structure made exchanges of price information particularly suspect?

4. Note that capacity exceeded demand and that entry was continuing. If there was already more than enough capacity to meet demand, then in a competitive market, price would be expected to fall. Yet prices were high enough to attract new entry! This suggests that the firms already in the market were restricting production in an effort to keep prices above competitive levels.

2. Cartels

a. An Economic Analysis of Cartel Operations

i. Background

A monopoly exists when a firm has sole control over the supply of an industry's product. This control over supply enables it to choose the point on the industry demand curve at which it will operate. It thus normally would possess the power to sell fewer units at high prices or larger numbers of units at lower prices.[1] Since a profit-maximizing monopolist would choose that price-output policy which—taking into account its own cost conditions—would maximize its profits, such a monopolist normally would be expected to restrict industry production to a level somewhat less than it would be if production were in the hands of many independent producers. Prices in a market controlled by a monopoly supplier, accordingly, would tend to be somewhat higher than they would be in an industry composed of many independent producers.

In a competitive industry in which there exist a large number of sellers, price is normally set by the marketplace and is independent of the power of any one seller to control it. Thus market price is the result of the independent decisions of each of the many sellers responding to the market conditions as it perceives them: those conditions being the prices at which its rivals are offering their goods and the continuing willingness of buyers to pay those prices. If a firm wishes to sell, it must meet the prices of its rivals, which become for it the going market price. In a perfectly competitive market, a firm would expand production until marginal cost rose to the level of market price.

If the many producers in a competitively-structured industry wish to make pricing and output decisions in the manner of a monopolist, *i.e.,* to set the price at which they will sell or to restrict production so as to influence market price upwards, they can do so only if they act in concert. If all the producers of a given product act in concert, the group will itself become a monopolist. The group, acting together as a unit, will then be able to determine the total amount of the product which will be produced, to whom it will be sold, and the price at which the product will be sold. With less than complete industry participation, the group may nonetheless be able to control or to influence market price. The greater the proportion of total industry production which the group controls, the greater will be its control of, or influence upon, price.

---

1 Because the monopolist's power is over industry supply, it is constrained by the demand for the industry product: it can sell no more units at any price level than buyers are willing to purchase at that price. Thus its power consists in its ability to choose the point on the industry demand curve at which it will operate, but it cannot sell greater quantities than are represented on that curve.

ii. A Simple Output-Restriction Cartel in an Industry of Many Sellers

In an industry of many sellers, a collusive restriction of output will require the cooperation of a large number of firms. This cooperation presents a number of difficulties. If the firms in such an industry were to decide that they would like to replicate collectively the behavior which would be followed by a hypothetical monopolist which owned all of the production capacity in the industry, the firms would first have to establish some mechanism for collective decision-making and for determining the price-output behavior of this hypothetical monopolist. Second, after the firms determined their optimum collective price-output policy, they would have to decide upon a method for allocating responsibilities among themselves for achieving that collective price-output policy. Thus, for example, if the firms decided to focus upon restricting industry production as a way of forcing prices upwards, then they would necessarily have to devise a formula for allocating the limited industry production into quotas assignable to the various participating firms. Third, the firms would have to establish some mechanism for revising their agreed-upon output quotas or agreed-upon prices as market conditions changed. Fourth, the firms would have to establish some mechanism for detecting cheating on their agreement and for encouraging compliance.

If the firms determined that their joint interests would be served by a 25% cutback in industry production, the simplest way to allocate this industry production cutback among themselves would be to impose on each firm a duty to decrease its own production by 25% from the previous year.

The firm which has cut back its own production and has thereby contributed to the aggregate reduction of supply is increasingly tempted to expand its own output as the collusive activity of the cartel becomes successful. As the cartel succeeds in decreasing industry supply (and if other factors remain the same), market price increases. Each individual firm which has cut back its own production now finds that it has increasing unused capacity to produce at prices producing supracompetitive profits. Moreover, because each such firm is of insignificant size in relation to the industry as a whole, its own failure to conform to the output restriction will not have any significant impact on market price. Thus the temptation for each firm to cheat on the cartel's quota assignments grows stronger as the cartel becomes increasingly successful in raising price. Yet while cheating by any one firm will not affect the success of the cartel, cheating by many firms will produce an oversupply of goods at the then-going price and will force market price downwards. Such a cartel thus tends to create the potential for its own destruction.

b. Beyond the Obvious Restrictions: The Theoretically-Optimum Goals of a Comprehensive Cartel

i. A "Pooling" Cartel

A simple cartel might be satisfied with distributing a production cutback among its members on a straight-percentage basis, such as the 25% reduction from last year's output employed in the example. But this method of assigning quotas would not produce the highest producer profits attainable. The cartel could further increase the aggregate profits of its members if the industry production which was decided upon were produced by the more efficient firms in the industry and if each of those firms were producing at a level at which its marginal cost was equal to the marginal cost of every other producing firm. Profit-maximization would be attained when the industry production level chosen by the cartel equated industry marginal revenue with the marginal cost of each producing firm. This degree of fine-tuning of industry production would be impractical, however, so long as the Sherman Act is effectively enforced.

Such fine-tuning of industry production, if it were carried out, would require the closing of some plants, *i.e.,* the least efficient ones, and the assignment of differing quotas among the plants which remained in operation. Quotas would be set so that each of the producing firms was operating at a marginal cost equal to each of the other producing firms. Thus the more efficient plants would receive the proportionately larger quotas while the less efficient plants of those that remained in operation would receive the proportionately smaller quotas. At these assigned outputs, production costs would be minimized.

Since under this arrangement the aggregate producer profits would be the largest possible, the potential would exist for distributing those profits in ways that would make every firm better off. Aggregate industry profits would be great enough to compensate those firms whose plants were ordered closed an amount which would be greater than the profits which such firms could earn without the cartel and under competitive market conditions. Similarly, firms which were assigned a proportionately smaller production quota could be compensated in an amount which would be greater than the amount which they could earn under competitive conditions unrestrained by a production quota. In the absence of external constraints such as the antitrust laws, the owners of each firm (if they were rational profit-maximizers) might ultimately agree on a formula for distribution of aggregate cartel profits that would make each of them better off than they were prior to the formation of the profit-pooling cartel.

ii. Economies in Centralizing Production Decisions: "Rationalization" of Cartel Production

Even if all member firms of a cartel had identical plants and operated under identical cost conditions, economies would be achievable by closing some plants in order to operate the remainder at more efficient levels. Thus in an industry composed of many producers each operating equally efficient plants under conditions of competitive equilibrium, a reduction in industry output decreed by a newly organized cartel would necessitate the imposition of quotas upon member firms. But if the cutback in industry production were borne equally by each firm through the assignment of equal quotas to each firm, each firm would be producing at unduly high cost.

iii. Long Run Cartel Policy and Problems of Plant Replacement

Should the cartel remain in existence for a period long enough to embrace the replacement of the present plant, then the cartel members will be forced to confront the issue of whether to adopt a policy of profit pooling and the production of industry output with optimum scale plants, even though this means that some cartel members may be left without plants; or whether to structure industry production in less than optimum scale plants. Alternatively, if the cartel itself does not adjust production quotas so as to facilitate production in plants of optimum scale, the member firms may buy and sell quotas among themselves so as to facilitate production in optimum scale plants. If, however, production quotas are not adjusted to accommodate the construction of optimum scale plants by order of the cartel administration or as a result of the buying and selling of quotas among the cartel members themselves, then the cartel arrangement will tend to encourage the construction of replacement plants which will be of an optimum scale for the production of each firm's quota, but which will tend not to possess the economies attainable through larger scale production. *See* DONALD DEWEY, MONOPOLY IN ECONOMICS AND LAW Chs. II, III (1959); DONALD DEWEY, THE THEORY OF IMPERFECT COMPETITION: A RADICAL RECONSTRUCTION Chs. III, IV (1969).

c. The Mechanisms of Cartel Operations

i. In General

First. Any group of sellers which wishes to curtail their collective production or fix price must select a mechanism for arriving at industry price or output goals (and in the latter case, assigning output quotas among the group of participating firms), and for revising these decisions from time to time as demand and cost conditions change. As the number of sellers acting in concert increases, it becomes increasingly inconvenient for these decisions to be reached through a process of negotiation involving each of the cooperating firms. Moreover, because periodic meetings among representatives of all of the member firms of an industry would tend to be highly visible to the officials in the Antitrust Division who would be likely to investigate such activities, the cooperating firms would find it dangerous to engage in full-scale negotiations for every revision of cartel price-output policy. Second, as noted earlier, a successful cartel creates a temptation among its members to cheat. When cheating on the cartel price-output policies becomes widespread, the cartel will break down. In order to ensure the successful operation of a cartel, methods must be devised to detect and to deter cheating by firms on cartel-assigned quotas or on cartel-specified prices. Both the need to avoid periodic meetings involving large numbers of people and the need to detect and deter cheating by cartel members will tend to influence the operational mechanics of cartel administration.

ii. An Executive Committee

One mechanism for dealing with the need periodically to revise prices and production for the group is an executive committee which spends its full time evaluating cost and demand conditions for widgets. It could then determine the appropriate prices at which widgets should be sold and the volume of production consonant with that price, could allocate production quotas among the various members of the group (which would, of course, be revised with each revision of prices) and could forward that information to the members of the group. A group executive committee, however, would be a highly visible violation of the Sherman Act. Accordingly, we can probably expect that if, and when, members of an industry attempt to agree on prices and production, they will do so under some guise which is not so apparently a price and production fixing agreement.

iii. A Self-Adjusting Formula

In the *Maple Flooring* case, there were suggestions that in the past the producers had agreed that each would charge a price which was equal to (average) cost plus 5 percent. Such an agreement would not effect revisions of the group price in response to changes in consumer demand, but it might revise group prices in response to changes in average costs.[2] Thus an increase in the cost of raw materials would be likely to affect all members of the group equally, and an upward revision of group prices in response to the increase in raw material costs would occur automatically if each producer understood that when a new average-cost figure was circulated by a central information center, it was to increase its own prices to the level of the new average cost plus 5%. Increases in wage and other costs would induce an automatic revision of the agreed-upon prices when they are incorporated into an average cost figure and the group understanding is that prices should equal average cost plus 5%.

Even in a competitive market where no concerted action takes place, any increase in production costs is likely to produce an increase in prices. The average-cost-plus-a-stated-percentage formula provides a workable means, however, by

---

[2] The usefulness of an average-cost formula is diminished by the elements in the average which are not common to all of the group members. An average plant depreciation cost component, for example, might lessen the usefulness of the average cost figure if plant construction costs (and hence depreciation costs) varied substantially in the different times and places in which the group members built their plants.

which cooperating firms can maintain a higher than competitive price and to work a continual revision in that price, so that throughout changes in costs, the group prices remain continually above the level at which they would be were they set competitively and without agreement.

iv. A Central Interpreter

What function could a central interpreter, *cf., American Column & Lumber Co. v. United States*, page 357, *supra,* of data serve to effect a curtailment of production or a setting of prices that is not served by trade journal editorials lamenting the current high volume of industry production? The central interpreter's recommendations may have a force that newspaper editorials do not have if there is an understanding among the group members that they will follow the recommendations of the central interpreter. Normally there would be no such understanding about newspaper editorials; and since it is to no one's advantage to curtail its own production unless others are also curtailing their production, a firm owner reading a trade newspaper editorial complaining about the large size of industry production which is exerting a depressing effect on price would be likely to sympathize with the editorial but to take no action upon it. What action could the firm take? Restricting its own production would be senseless without some assurance that others are acting in a similar manner. It is possible that a central interpreter could serve as a symbol which each of the firms would understand and to which it would relate its production and/or pricing decisions. Even so, a central interpreter which did no more than utter platitudes about the desirability of holding back production would not tell industry members anything more than they could get from a trade journal editorial. Effective communication from the central interpreter would require either i) specific directions as to how much each firm was to produce or the (currently revised) prices at which goods were to be sold or ii) (assuming that each firm has been provided with specific directions on prices and quotas) credible assurances that significant cheating was not occurring or the disclosure of the identities of cheaters.

v. Sales Information About the Identity of Particular Sellers and Buyers

Traders in corporate stocks can make intelligent decisions about buying or selling particular stocks on the basis of information contained in the financial pages of the daily newspapers, perhaps aided by such other information about a particular company which they obtain from the financial press and/or their brokers. But they might consider information that John Jones from Topeka, Kansas sold 100 shares of General Motors and that Sally Smith from Augusta, Maine purchased 100 shares of AT&T irrelevant in deciding whether to buy or sell those stocks. Their principal interest in transaction information would be market price, and perhaps volume traded. In some of the trade association cases, a central agency collected information about particular transactions including the identity of buyers and sellers and the terms of the respective transactions and relayed that information to the association's members. The interesting question thus arises, what useful purpose does information about the identity of particular buyers and sellers serve? Most pricing and production decisions could be made on the basis of generalized price information and information about total quantities sold.

One purpose which could be served by collecting information about which seller sold how much to which buyer at what price would be the uncovering of cheaters: the exposure of those who violated the group agreement about prices or output. The distribution of information containing the details of particular transactions, therefore, has been characteristic of many output-restricting cartels.

vi. Base Prices

The *Maple Flooring* case refers to the distribution of freight-rate information from Cadillac, Michigan to many other points of the United States. Since most of the flooring manufacturers were grouped in the Midwest not terribly far from Cadillac, the information probably served (as the Court found) a purpose of making the quotation of delivered prices easier and more convenient. But let us consider the use of "basing points" in other situations. (The analysis of basing points can become quite complex. Here the simpler aspects of the mechanism are sketched.) Suppose manufacturer A makes widgets in New York City, manufacturer B makes widgets in Buffalo, N.Y., manufacturer C makes widgets in Binghamton, N.Y., manufacturer D makes widgets in Watertown, N.Y., manufacturer E makes widgets in Syracuse, N.Y., *etc.* If the group wishes to eliminate or to reduce competition among themselves, there are a number of ways to go about it. One way would be for each company to adhere to a schedule of delivered prices. At each place, under such a system, a buyer would find that its total outlay for widgets would be the same regardless of from whom it purchased. Since the widget manufacturers might not want to take the trouble to set a delivered price for every hamlet in New York state, they might select one or more "basing points," say New York City, Syracuse, and Buffalo. Each manufacturer selling to a purchaser would quote a delivered price composed of (1) a factory price component plus (2) transportation costs (calculated from a transportation cost table adopted by the group of widget manufacturers) from the basing point nearest to the purchaser to the business place of the purchaser. Under such a system any purchaser would be quoted exactly the same price on widgets by every manufacturer; price competition among the widget manufacturers would be entirely eliminated. One advantage of a basing-point system as a price-fixing device is that it makes deviations from the system highly visible; deviations cannot be hidden in partially absorbed transportation costs by the sellers which might be obscured by the actual or claimed use of varying types or routes of transportation.

It should be noted, however, that if manufacturer B wishes to compete for sales with manufacturer A in any given city, say Albany, manufacturer B cannot offer widgets in Albany at a higher price than manufacturer A. If manufacturer A offers widgets in Albany at a price equal to its New York City factory price plus transportation from New York to Albany, manufacturer B, if it is to sell widgets in

Albany must sell at a price which is not higher than manufacturer A's factory price plus transportation from New York to Albany. In so calculating its delivered price, it begins to look as if manufacturer B is adopting New York City as its basing point.

In short, the use by a group of manufacturers of the same basing points is one method of facilitating a price-fixing plan. But the use of identical basing points by several manufacturers can result from the independent decision of each manufacturer as to what is in its own (as opposed to the group's) best interest. One must be cautious, therefore, in evaluating a situation in which the same basing points are used by several manufacturers. It may evidence a price-fixing conspiracy or agreement; but it may evidence only the result of the independent determination of each manufacturer as to what is in its own individual best interest.

A NOTE ON THE ROBINSON-PATMAN ACT AND THE EXCHANGE OF PRICE INFORMATION

1. *The Origins of the Robinson-Patman Act.*[3] The Robinson-Patman Act[4] was enacted in 1936 as an amendment to § 2 of the Clayton Act. Both the Robinson-Patman Act and its predecessor were designed to combat price discriminations

---

[3] Extract (edited) from Daniel J. Gifford, *Assessing Secondary-Line Injury Under the Robinson-Patman Act: The Concept of "Competitive Advantage,"* 44 GEO. WASH. L. REV. 48-52 (1975).

[4] Act of June 19, 1936, ch. 592, §§ 1-4, 49 Stat. 1526 (codified at 15 U.S.C. §§ 13-13b, 21a (1988)). This article is concerned, almost exclusively, with §§ 2(a) and 2(b) of the Robinson-Patman Act, 15 U.S.C. §§ 13(a), (b) (1988). Section 2(a) provides:

> It shall be unlawful for any person engaged in commerce, in the course of such commerce, either directly or indirectly, to discriminate in price between different purchasers of commodities of like grade and quality, where either or any of the purchasers involved in such discrimination are in commerce, where such commodities are sold for use, consumption, or resale within the United States or any Territory thereof or the District of Columbia or any insular possession or other place under the jurisdiction of the United States, and where the effect of such discrimination may be substantially to lessen competition or tend to create a monopoly in any line of commerce, or to injure, destroy, or prevent competition with any person who either grants or knowingly receives the benefit of such discrimination, or with customers of either of them: *Provided*, That nothing herein contained shall prevent differentials which make only due allowance for differences in the cost of manufacture, sale, or delivery resulting from the differing methods or quantities in which such commodities are to such purchasers sold or delivered: *Provided, however*, That the Federal Trade Commission may, after due investigation and hearing to all interested parties, fix and establish quantity limits, and revise the same as it finds necessary, as to particular commodities or classes of commodities, where it finds that available purchasers in greater quantities are so few as to render differentials on account thereof unjustly discriminatory or promotive of monopoly in any line of commerce; and the foregoing shall then not be construed to permit differentials based on differences in quantities greater than those so fixed and established: *And provided further*, That nothing herein contained shall prevent persons engaged in selling goods, wares, or merchandise in commerce from selecting their own customers in bona fide transactions and not in restraint of trade: *And provided further*, That nothing herein contained shall prevent price changes from time to time where in response to changing conditions affecting the market for or the marketability of the goods concerned, such as but not limited to actual or imminent deterioration of perishable goods,

that would be likely to produce anticompetitive effects. The older § 2[5] had been enacted in 1914 primarily as a means of preventing predatory geographical price discrimination believed to be practiced by multimarket firms[6] such as the Standard Oil Company and the American Tobacco Company. In the mid-1930s Congress shared a widespread concern that the chain stores were a major threat to small wholesale and retail businesses.[7] It was believed that excess capacity among suppliers was a common phenomenon and that, as a result, many suppliers could be induced to accept cutrate prices on orders that were large enough to employ significant amounts of otherwise idle plant facilities.[8] Large buyers thus would demand and receive "marginal cost" prices, prices that compensated the supplier for the extra costs it incurred in producing the goods, but which failed to compensate

---

> obsolescence of seasonal goods, distress sales under court process, or sales in good faith in discontinuance of business in the goods concerned.

15 U.S.C. § 13(a) (1988). Section 2(b) provides:

> Upon proof being made, at any hearing on a complaint under this section, that there has been discrimination in price or services or facilities furnished, the burden of rebutting the prima-facie case thus made by showing justification shall be upon the person charged with a violation of this section, and unless justification shall be affirmatively shown, the Commission is authorized to issue an order terminating the discrimination: *Provided, however*, That nothing herein contained shall prevent a seller rebutting the prima-facie case thus made by showing that his lower price or the furnishing of services or facilities to any purchaser or purchasers was made in good faith to meet an equally low price of a competitor, or the services or facilities furnished by a competitor.

15 U.S.C. § 13(b) (1988).

[5] The predecessor to the Robinson-Patman Act was § 2 of the Clayton Act, ch. 323, § 2, 38 Stat. 730 (1914), which provided:

> [I]t shall be unlawful for any person engaged in commerce, in the course of such commerce, either directly or indirectly, to discriminate in price between different purchasers of commodities, which commodities are sold for use, consumption, or resale within the United States or any Territory thereof or the District of Columbia, or any insular possession, or any other place under the jurisdiction of the United States where the effect of such discrimination may be to substantially lessen competition or tend to create a monopoly in any line of commerce: *Provided*,
>
> That nothing herein contained shall prevent discrimination in price between purchasers of commodities on account of differences in the grade, quality, or quantity of the commodity sold, or that makes only due allowance for difference in the cost of selling or transportation, or discrimination in price in the same or different communities made in good faith to meet competition: And provided further, That nothing herein contained shall prevent persons engaged in selling goods, wares, or merchandise in commerce from selecting their own customers in bona fide transactions and not in restraint of trade.

[6] *See* H.R. Rep. No. 627, 63d Cong., 2d Sess. 8-9 (1914). The 63rd Congress believed that firms such as Standard Oil and American Tobacco would sell their products at unprofitable or below-cost prices in target markets in order to drive out their rivals there while recouping their losses by charging higher prices in other markets over which they possessed monopoly power.

[7] *See, e.g.*, H.R. Rep. No. 2287, 74th Cong., 2d Sess. 3 (1936); 80 Cong. Rec. 7324, 8104 (1936). *Cf.* FTC, Final Report on the Chain Store Investigation, S. Doc. No. 4, 74th Cong., 1st Sess. (1935).

[8] *See, e.g.*, 80 Cong. Rec. 6621, 7324, 7887, 8104 (1936). It was believed that suppliers would be influenced by the need to generate revenues with their unused plants in order to meet fixed charges on those plants.

it for proportionate overhead, depreciation, and other fixed expenses allocated to the production of these goods.[9] At the same time, it was believed that producers had certain "earnings requirements"[10] which would in fact be met so long as they stayed in business. When pro rata earnings requirements were not met from the marginal-cost sales to large buyers, it was believed that suppliers would recoup the deficit by charging higher prices to their smaller customers.[11] These customers, generally wholesalers, and the retailers supplied by those wholesalers, would thus be in a position of competing with chains and other large buyers who had access to lower supply prices.

It was in this situation that Congress perceived a threat to the continued existence of smaller businesses. It saw the chains triumphing, not because of superior efficiency but because of the unfair use of their purchasing power to obtain their inventories at lower supply prices than their smaller rivals. The Congressional response was the enactment of the Robinson-Patman Act, designed to preserve and to strengthen the old § 2 and to expand its application to discrimination that operated vertically through the distribution system to create anticompetitive

---

[9] The technical meaning of "marginal cost" is the incremental cost of the last unit of output. In the text above, the phrase "marginal cost prices" refers to prices that cover the incremental cost to a seller of supplying an order, but do not cover all of his fully allocated costs, including overhead, depreciation, and other fixed charges.

[10] The "earnings requirements" argument was best articulated in the congressional debates by Congressman Miller. *See* 80 Cong. Rec. 6621, 6622 (1936). The Congressman intimated that for a firm to remain in business, it must earn a sufficient amount to cover its overhead and other fixed charges, to cover its operating expenses, and to earn a reasonable profit on its operations. These earnings requirements enunciated by the Congressman are similar, although not identical, to the earnings that an economist would posit as essential to a firm's longrun survival. The principal difference is that for longrun survival the firm need not necessarily cover its fixed costs, but merely earn enough to make economically feasible the replacement of existing capital as the latter wears out. This is not the same as earnings covering fixed charges on existing equipment, both because the price level for the relevant kind of capital equipment may have changed since the time of the original investment and because at capital replacement time the prospect of profitable future earnings may make replacement investment advisable despite unprofitable operations during the immediately prior period. Also, the economist, to be in agreement with Congressman Miller, would refer to a "normal" rather than to a "reasonable" profit. Allowing for a degree of imprecision expected when technical concepts are restated by lay persons, the Congressman stated with reasonable accuracy the longrun survival requirements of a firm. By expressing longrun survival requirements in terms of a minimum earnings requirement, however, he also gave a superficially plausible explanation for why a firm "needed" or "required" a certain level of earnings. Once he had established a requirement for a certain level of earnings, the step to the recoupment or subsidy analysis was obvious: Income deficits would result from sales at prices below the firm's aggregate income requirements averaged over all of the units that it sold. These deficits would have to be offset by sales at prices above the firm's average per-unit earnings requirements.

Where Congressman Miller's analysis fails, however, is in his usage of the "earnings requirements" phrase. In his usage two meanings blend imperceptibly but erroneously. With the technical corrections suggested above, he has correctly stated the earnings that a firm would require to stay in business over the long run. Here "requirements" is used in the sense of a condition of survival. But there is no assurance that any firm will obtain the earnings that it needs to survive. Yet the sense of "requirements" as a condition of survival is shifted subtly to "requirements" as a course of action that the firm imposes on others, *viz.*, requiring of its customers that in the aggregate they pay to the firm an amount equal to the earnings necessary for its survival. In this latter usage, it is assumed that the firm has the power to make this imposition.

[11] *See, e.g.*, S. Rep. No. 1502, 74th Cong., 2d Sess. 4 (1936); H.R. Rep. No. 2287, 74th Cong., 2d Sess. 8 (1936).

effects.[12] Yet Congress was careful both in 1914 and in 1936 not to outlaw discrimination *per se.* It wished to prevent competition from being distorted by the buying power of the chains but not to discourage efficiencies or to interfere with the pricing flexibility that is a necessary part of competitive behavior. Thus, it prohibited price discrimination only where the effects of the discrimination "may" lessen competition or tend to create a monopoly or injure competition with the grantor or recipient of the discrimination.[13] Congress provided, moreover, that a discrimination can be cost-justified where the difference in the prices that a supplier charges two groups of purchasers reflects no more than the difference in the supplier's costs of serving those two groups.[14] Additionally, regardless of the supplier's costs, it may, under the Act, meet the "equally low price of a competitor."[15]

It is not clear whether all of these provisions are entirely consistent with each other. They pose difficult questions of application. Their lack of clarity and the conservative manner in which they have been interpreted, moreover, have sometimes tended to introduce rigidities into pricing behavior that are incompatible with a truly competitive marketplace.[16] It appears, however, that Congress was attempting to establish a marketplace in which large and small businesses could compete on the basis of efficiency and service and in which competition would not be threatened because one group of dealers had privileged access to favorable supply prices.

2. As suggested in the preceding extract, a major objection to the Robinson-Patman Act lies in the rigidities which it probably introduces into the pricing decisions of business firms, often strengthening existing tendencies towards oligopolistic pricing and inhibiting the breakdown of such pricing. Because of this (and other features) of the Robinson-Patman Act, it is not at all easy to reconcile that Act with the procompetitive policies embodied in the other antitrust laws.

3. Section 2(b) of the Robinson-Patman Act provides a defense to price discrimination which might otherwise be prohibited by that Act when the discriminating seller lowers price selectively to one or more buyers "in good faith to meet the equally low price of a competitor." Prior decisions construing this provision of the Robinson-Patman Act have raised the question of the extent to which a seller (in order to be in "good faith") must investigate to determine whether the discriminatorily-low price it is contemplating offering a buyer actually does meet the equally low price of a competing seller. Can a seller take a prospective buyer's word that a particular price has been offered to that buyer by another seller, or must the seller investigate? If it must investigate, how much should be required of it? Must

---

[12] *Federal Trade Commission v. Anheuser-Busch, Inc.,* 363 U.S. 536, 544 (1960).

[13] Robinson-Patman Act § 2(a), 15 U.S.C. § 13(a) (1970).

[14] *Id.*

[15] *Id.* § 2(b), 15 U.S.C. § 13(b) (1988).

[16] *See e.g., Automatic Canteen Co. v. Federal Trade Commission,* 346 U.S. 61, 65, 68-69 (1953). *See generally* M. ADELMAN, A&P: A STUDY IN PRICE-COST BEHAVIOR AND PUBLIC POLICY Ch. 8 (1959).

it actually inquire of the rival seller whose price it is seeking to meet? If it inquires of the rival seller as to the latter's prices, is it not in danger of violating the Sherman Act as construed in *Container*?

These questions were most recently addressed in *United States v. United States Gypsum Co.*, 438 U.S. 422 (1978), a criminal price-fixing case in which a defense was raised that exchanges of price information among competing firms were justified by the need to establish a § 2(b) defense to possible Robinson-Patman Act liability. An extract from Chief Justice Burger's opinion for the Court follows.

United States v. United States Gypsum Co.

438 U.S. 422 (1978)

[The defendants were convicted of violating § 1 of the Sherman Act by engaging in a price-fixing conspiracy involving the practice of inter-seller price verification. Their conviction was reversed by the U.S. Court of Appeals for the Third Circuit on the ground that the jury had not been properly instructed that § 2(b) of the Robinson-Patman Act will, in some circumstances, constitute a "controlling circumstance" excusing such conduct. The Supreme Court granted *certiorari*.]

Mr. Chief Justice BURGER delivered the opinion of the Court.

. . .

Section 2(a) of the Clayton Act, as amended by the Robinson-Patman Act . . . embodies a general prohibition of price discrimination between buyers when an injury to competition is the consequence. The primary exception to the § 2(a) bar is the meeting-competition defense which is incorporated as a proviso to the burden-of-proof requirements set out in § 2(b):

> "*Provided, however*, That nothing herein contained shall prevent a seller rebutting the prima facie case thus made by showing that his lower price or the furnishing of services or facilities to any purchaser or purchasers was made in good faith to meet an equally low price of a competitor, or the services or facilities furnished by a competitor."

. . . .

In *FTC v. A. E. Staley Mfg. Co.*, 324 U.S. 746 (1945), the Court provided the first and still the most complete explanation of the kind of showing which a seller must make in order to satisfy the good-faith requirement of the § 2(b) defense:

> "Section 2(b) does not require the seller to justify price discriminations by showing that in fact they met a competitor's price. But it does place on the seller the burden of showing that the price was made in good faith to meet a competitor's. . . . We agree with the Commission that the statute at least requires the seller, who has knowingly discriminated in price, to show the existence of facts which would lead a reasonable and prudent person to believe that the granting of a lower price would in fact meet the equally low price of a competitor."
>
> . . .

Application of these standards to the facts in *Staley* led to the conclusion that the § 2(b) defense had not been made out. The record revealed that the lower price had been based simply on reports of salesmen, brokers, or purchasers with no efforts having been made by the seller "to investigate or verify" the reports or the character and reliability of the informants. . . . Similarly, in *Corn Products Co. v. FTC*, 324 U.S. 726 (1945), decided the same day, the § 2(b) defense was not allowed because "[t]he only evidence said to rebut the *prima facie* case . . . of the price discriminations was given by witnesses who had no personal knowledge of the transactions, and was limited to statements of each witness's assumption or conclusion that the price discriminations were justified by competition." . . .

Staley's "investigate or verify" language coupled with *Corn Products*' focus on "personal knowledge of the transactions" have apparently suggested to a number of courts that, at least in certain circumstances, direct verification of discounts between competitors may be necessary to meet the burden-of-proof requirements of the § 2(b) defense. . . .

A good-faith belief, rather than absolute certainty, that a price concession is being offered to meet an equally low price offered by a competitor is sufficient to satisfy the § 2(b) defense. While casual reliance on uncorroborated reports of buyers or sales representatives without further investigation may not . . . be sufficient to make the requisite showing of good faith, nothing in the language of § 2(b) or the gloss on that language in *Staley* and *Corn Products* indicates that direct discussions of price between competitors are required. . . .

The so-called problem of the untruthful buyer which concerned the Court of Appeals does not in our view call for a different approach to the § 2(b) defense. The good-faith standard remains the benchmark . . . and we agree with the Government and the FTC that this standard can be satisfied by efforts falling short of interseller verification in most circumstances where the seller has only vague, generalized doubts about the reliability of its commercial adversary—the buyer. . . . Certainly, evidence that a seller had received reports of similar discounts from other customers . . . or was threatened with a termination of purchases if the discount were not met . . . would be relevant in this regard. Efforts to corroborate the reported discount by seeking documentary evidence or by appraising its reasonableness in terms of available market data would also be probative as would the seller's past experience with the particular buyer in question.

There remains the possibility that in a limited number of situations a seller may have substantial reasons to doubt the accuracy of reports of a competing offer and may be unable to corroborate such reports in any of the generally accepted ways. Thus the defense may be rendered unavailable since unanswered questions about the reliability of a buyer's representations may well be inconsistent with a good-faith belief that a competing offer had in fact been made. As an abstract proposition, resort to interseller verification as a means of checking the buyer's reliability seems a possible solution to the seller's plight, but careful examination reveals serious problems with the practice.

Both economic theory and common human experience suggest that interseller verification—if undertaken on an isolated and infrequent basis with no provision for reciprocity or cooperation—will not serve its putative function of corroborating the representations of unreliable buyers regarding the existence of competing offers. Price concessions by oligopolists generally yield competitive advantages only if secrecy can be maintained; when the terms of the concession are made publicly known, other competitors are likely to follow and any advantage to the initiator is lost in the process. . . . Thus, if one seller offers a price concession for the purpose of winning over one of his competitor's customers, it is unlikely that the same seller will freely inform its competitor of the details of the concession so that it can be promptly matched and diffused. Instead, such a seller would appear to have at least as great an incentive to misrepresent the existence or size of the discount as would the buyer who received it. Thus verification, if undertaken on a one-shot basis for the sole purpose of complying with the § 2(b) defense, does not hold out much promise as a means of shoring up buyers' representations.

The other variety of interseller verification is, like the conduct charged in the instant case, undertaken pursuant to an agreement, either tacit or express, providing for reciprocity among competitors in the exchange of price information. Such an agreement would make little economic sense, in our view, if its sole purpose were to guarantee all participants the opportunity to match the secret price concessions of other participants under § 2(b). For in such circumstances, each seller would know that his price concession could not be kept from his competitors and no seller participating in the information-exchange arrangement would, therefore, have any incentive for deviating from the prevailing price level in the industry. . . . Regardless of its putative purpose, the most likely consequence of any such agreement to exchange price information would be the stabilization of industry prices. . . . Instead of facilitating use of the § 2(b) defense, such an agreement would have the effect of eliminating the very price concessions which provide the main element of competition in oligopolistic industries and the primary occasion for resort to the meeting-competition defense.

Especially in oligopolistic industries such as the gypsum board industry, the exchange of price information among competitors carries with it the added potential for the development of concerted price-fixing arrangements which lie at the core of the Sherman Act's prohibitions. . . .

We are left, therefore, on the one hand, with doubts about both the need for and the efficacy of interseller verification as a means of facilitating compliance with § 2(b), and, on the other, with recognition of the tendency for price discussions between competitors to contribute to the stability of oligopolistic prices and open the way for the growth of prohibited anticompetitive activity. To recognize even a limited "controlling circumstance" exception for interseller verification in such circumstances would be to remove from scrutiny under the Sherman Act conduct falling near its core with no assurance, and indeed with serious doubts, that competing antitrust policies would be served thereby. . . . [A]s a general rule the Robinson-Patman Act should be construed so as to insure its coherence with "the broader antitrust policies that have been laid down by Congress." . . . [E]xchanges of price information—even when putatively for purposes of Robinson-Patman Act compliance—must remain subject to close scrutiny under the Sherman Act.

[The Court then affirmed the decision of the Court of Appeals on grounds unrelated to the price-verification issue.]

COMMENTARY

In a circumstance like the one in *Gypsum*, would a buyer who had contrived to make a supplier believe that it should rebid at a lower price in order to avoid being underbid by a rival for a large supply contract be liable under § 2(f) of the Robinson-Patman Act for inducing an unlawful discrimination? Or would the seller's reasonable belief that its rebid was necessary in order not to lose out to the rival and the seller's consequent entitlement to the § 2(b) meeting-competition defense exonerate the buyer from liability under § 2(f)? Compare *Kroger Co. v. Federal Trade Commission*, 438 F.2d 1372 (6th Cir. 1971), with *Great Atlantic & Pacific Tea Co. v. Federal Trade Commission*, 440 U.S. 69 (1979). *See infra*, Chapter 13, page 690.

Alvord-Polk, Inc. v. F. Schumacher & Co.

37 F.3d 996 (3d Cir. 1994)

[The facts of this case were set out in Chapter 2, above. The case involved a claim by the plaintiff discount wallpaper dealers (referred to in the case as "800-number" dealers because of the method they generally employed to solicit orders) that the defendant manufacturer had conspired with the members of a retailer trade association to exclude the 800-number members from handling its brand of wallpaper. In the extract below, the court considers the issue of whether action by an executive of the trade association is tantamount to concerted action by all members of the association.]

LEWIS, Circuit Judge.

. . . .

IV.

At Count I, in which plaintiffs named only NDPA as a defendant, they alleged that conventional retailers, acting through the NDPA, conspired to pressure manufacturers to eliminate them from the marketplace. The district court examined the record for evidence of "officially sanctioned NDPA activity," found none, and ruled that plaintiffs could not meet the "concerted action" requirement because "[t]he NDPA can only act pursuant to a resolution from its board and no such resolution has been identified." . . . We will reverse.

A.

. . . .

Here, plaintiffs rely on *American Society of Mechanical Engineers, Inc. v. Hydrolevel Corp.*, 456 U.S. 556, 102 S. Ct. 1935, 72 L. Ed. 2d 330 (1982), to argue that NDPA took concerted action when its officers spoke out in protest against the 800-number dealers' business methods and when NDPA publications included letters complaining about 800-number dealers. In *Hydrolevel*, the Supreme Court, relying on general principles of agency law, determined that the American Society of Mechanical Engineers ("ASME") could be held liable for the actions of its officers and agents taken with apparent authority. Writing for the majority, Justice Blackmun held that imposing liability based upon apparent authority comported with the intent of the antitrust laws because ASME possessed great power and the codes and standards it issued influenced policies and affected entities' abilities to do business. *Hydrolevel*, 456 U.S. at 570, 102 S. Ct. at 1945. "When it cloaks its subcommittee officials with the authority of its reputation, ASME permits those agents to affect the destinies of businesses and thus gives them the power to frustrate competition in the marketplace." *Id.* at 570-71, 102 S. Ct. at 1945. Imposing antitrust liability on the association for the actions of its agents would encourage ASME to police its ranks and prevent the use of associations by one or more competitors to injure another. . . .

The issue presented here, however, is markedly different. In *Hydrolevel*, the plaintiff had named three defendants in its conspiracy claim. Although it is difficult to discern the exact contours of the alleged conspiracy from the *Hydrolevel* opinion, it is quite clear that the plaintiff there was not seeking to hold ASME liable for concerted action solely on the basis of actions taken by one official with apparent authority. The conspiracy alleged apparently was between the chairman of an ASME standards committee and the plaintiff's primary competitor; the question before the Court was whether ASME could be held liable for its agent's anticompetitive activity in participating in the conspiracy even though no one else at ASME had authorized the violation. Because a conspiracy was alleged to have taken place between the ASME official and another conspirator, the Court did not address the question of whether an agent with apparent authority can cause a trade association to be held liable for violating the antitrust laws by taking action on behalf of the association which would have amounted to such a violation if the association itself, as a combination of competitors, had undertaken it.

We believe that the *Hydrolevel* rule that an association's economic power may justify its being held liable for the actions of its agents cannot be extended to defeat the "concerted action" requirement of section 1. Imposing liability on an association, as we did in *Weiss*, does not abolish or diminish the first element of section 1 liability; it merely recognizes that a group of competitors with a unity of purpose are engaged in concerted action, whether or not they act under one name. As we explained in *Nanavati*, in the absence of a co-conspirator, an association's actions satisfy the concerted action requirement only when taken in a group capacity. The potential for antitrust liability arising from the concerted action of a group such as a trade association, as that liability may be established by the apparent authority of an agent to speak on behalf of and bind that association, has not yet been fully explored in a trade restraint case.[11] In *Hydrolevel*, for example, the Court described the concept of apparent authority as one which results in liability on a principal's part for an agent's torts. *Hydrolevel*, 456 U.S. at 565-66, 102 S. Ct. at 1942. Thus, if an agent commits fraud, his or her principal is liable if he or she acted with apparent authority to act on behalf of that principal. . . . Applying that general principle to the antitrust area leads us to conclude that a principal will be liable for an antitrust violation if an agent acting with apparent authority violates the antitrust laws, as one did in *Hydrolevel* by conspiring with another person. . . .

We are dealing here, however, with a trade association which is charged with violating the antitrust laws by constituting a horizontal conspiracy to eliminate the 800-number dealers. Clearly, an association, as a combination of its members, can violate the antitrust laws through such a conspiracy. This was the nature of the claim which prompted the FTC to initiate its complaint against the NDPA in 1985. The singular characteristic of plaintiffs' allegations here is that the association is now charged with acting through agents whom it has imbued with apparent authority. It is uncontested that the NDPA is highly sophisticated and possesses significant market power; it is unrealistic to think that such a sophisticated trade association, wary of the antitrust laws, would ingenuously act as an association in endorsing the type of activity forbidden by the consent decree.

In considering the antitrust implications of this situation, though, our first concern must be whether plaintiffs' allegations demonstrate an antitrust violation. Specifically, we must determine whether statements by NDPA officers demonstrate that NDPA recommended that its members refuse to deal with any seller of wallcoverings on account of the prices or distribution methods of that seller. We must also determine whether the evidence

---

11 There is, however, authority for the proposition that a trade association, in and of itself, is a unit of joint action sufficient to constitute a section 1 combination. *See* G.D. WEBSTER, THE LAW OF ASSOCIATIONS § 9a.01[1], 9A3-4 (1991) ("There is no question that an association is a 'combination' within the meaning of Section 1 of the Sherman Act. Although a conspiracy requires more than one person, an association, by its very nature a group, satisfies the requirement of joint action. Thus, any association activity which restrains interstate commerce can be violative of Section 1 even if no one acts in concert with the association."); Stephanie W. Kanwit, *FTC Enforcement Efforts Involving Trade and Professional Associations*, 46 ANTITRUST L.J. 640, 640 (1977) ("Because trade associations are, by definition, organizations of competitors, they automatically satisfy the combination requirements of § 1 of the Sherman Act.")

could show that the NDPA officers' statements were made with the apparent authority of the membership of the NDPA for those officers to act as the NDPA's agents. This method of analysis is consistent with *Hydrolevel*, which instructs that a court must find an antitrust violation before deciding whether to hold an association liable for that violation by virtue of the perpetrator's apparent authority.[12]

B.

Having focused our inquiry not just upon whether Petit or other NDPA agents might have acted with apparent authority but also upon whether their actions could constitute an antitrust violation in the absence of that authority, we believe that a rational jury could find for the plaintiffs if the evidence presented to us is proven at trial. As noted previously, Petit has acknowledged that since the entry of the FTC consent decree he has continued to urge manufacturers to take steps to hinder 800-number dealers in the conduct of their business. . . . He described himself as conveying "the concerns of NDPA," . . . and he stated that he views it as part of his job to convey those concerns. . . .

Moreover, the record contains evidence from which a rational juror could also infer that Petit's actions represented concerted action. That is, a jury could find that, while representing NDPA, Petit went beyond merely voicing complaints to manufacturers to actually coercing (or attempting to coerce) them into cooperating in eliminating 800-number dealers. There is some evidence that Petit emphasized to manufacturers with whom he met "the anger felt by the retailers in [the] lack of support from the wallcovering industry." . . . Such evidence, when viewed against the existing backdrop of urgings from NDPA officers and editors that retailers should support only those manufacturers who supported them, could imply a threat of a retailers' boycott if manufacturers did not take steps to help eliminate 800-number dealers from the marketplace.

In sum, nothing in either the antitrust laws or the FTC consent decree prohibits NDPA from voicing complaints. Granting all reasonable inferences to the plaintiffs, however, a rational jury could find that NDPA did more than serve as a conduit for members' complaints in this case. It could, for example, find that NDPA, acting through its officers, threatened a retailers' boycott of manufacturers and thus could hold NDPA liable for a section 1 violation. For these reasons, we will reverse the district court's grant of summary judgment at Count I.

COMMENTARY

1. What do use understand, from the court's opinion, to have been the ruling in *Hydrolevel*? Was the ruling in *Hydrolevel* merely the acceptance, for antitrust purposes, of the common-law rule governing the responsibility of a principal for its acts of its agent? Or, did *Hydrolevel* involve something more like *respondeat superior*, *i.e.*, the responsibility of a master for the acts of a servant? Do you

---

12 We do not, however, require that members of NDPA actually ratify an agent's actions before NDPA may be held liable for them. Such a rule not only would be unrealistic . . . , but it also would contravene the Court's admonition that agents of trade associations acting with apparent authority exercise the associations' economic power regardless of whether they are acting to benefit the associations. *Hydrolevel*, 456 U.S. at 573-74.

remember the difference from your studies of tort law and agency? Does the liability of a principal for the acts of its agent extend solely to matters of contract? Are there circumstances in which an agent's action may subject the principal to liability in tort?

2. Would a parent corporation be liable for the anticompetitive acts of its subsidiary? Under *Hydrolevel*? Under *Copperweld*?

3. Who were the alleged conspirators in *Hydrolevel*? What was plaintiff's theory of conspiracy in *Alvord-Polk* which the court rejected? Do you agree with that rejection? Would a contrary ruling have imperiled the existence of trade associations? Does *Alvord-Polk* nonetheless show that trade associations are peculiarly vulnerable to antitrust claims? What was the conspiracy contention in *Alvord-Polk* which the court held would, if proved, constitute a Sherman Act violation?

Chapter 9
Monopolization

A. Introduction

The central theme of this chapter is "market power." This phrase, which is central to antitrust law, generally describes the ability of a firm to raise the price of its product or service above the competitive price without experiencing unsustainable losses. A violation of § 2 of the Sherman Act by monopolization requires a finding that the defendant firm possesses substantial market power. A charge of attempted monopolization requires a showing of an intent coupled with conduct seeking to achieve market power under market conditions in which there is a high probability of success (and a high probability of success normally requires market power). Moreover, market power is also applied in the interpretation of §7 of the Clayton Act, since the objective of this provision is to prevent mergers which result in a firm's being able to exercise market power. Section 1 analysis has also relied on market power considerations in the analysis of tying arrangements, as well as in reviewing patent and copyright licensing practices.

The phrase, "market power," is not a phrase of art in economics. Economists tend to use the phrase, "monopoly power" to convey departures from the competitive model. The distinction between these two phrases has been blurred sufficiently so that they may be used interchangeably. Economists utilize two basic approaches in defining monopoly power: one is performance-based; the other is derived from the structure of markets. Both measures rest on the economic theory which teaches that the vigor of competition is a function of both the number of firms and their size distribution in a defined market. The model of perfect competition is stated in terms of many sellers facing many buyers with a fungible commodity or service under circumstances in which no one seller has control of sufficient supply of the product or service to determine the price for that product or service in that market. At the other end of the economist's analytical spectrum predicting the vigor of competition is the case of the monopolist. A monopolist, so the theory goes, has complete or virtually complete control of the supply of a good or service and will be a rational economic maximizer by limiting output and raising price. In this model, by definition, there is little, if any competition.

Economists have developed two performance-based criteria to assess market arrangements between these models of perfect competition and complete monopoly. One, the Lerner index, measures a seller's price against that seller's marginal cost. The Lerner index may be stated as: M = (price – marginal cost) / price. The essence of Lerner's index is that the monopoly model is the one in which there is an inefficient allocation of resources shown by the increase of price above marginal cost, by the restriction of output, and by blocked entry. Thus, M will be a positive number when monopoly power exists. Conversely, when M = 0, there is no exercise of monopoly power because price is equal to marginal cost. *See* Abba P. Lerner, *The Concept of Monopoly and the Measurement of Monopoly Power,* 1 REV. ECON. STUD. 157 (1934); William M. Landes & Richard A. Posner, *Market Power in Antitrust Cases,* 94 HARV. L. REV. 937, 939 (1981).

The economists' second performance-based criterion of the existence of monopoly power is profitability—the rate of return to a firm over its invested capital and other costs. Unlike the Lerner index, which rests on the theory of competition, profitability is grounded in an empirical analysis of a firm's performance. The measurement of profitability is the product of the industrial organization literature. The rationale for measuring profitability as an index of market power rests on the paradigm developed by early industrial organization scholars which holds that the structure of a market—that is the number of firms and their distribution by size—affects the conduct of the decision-makers of the firms in that market. From this paradigm, it is reasoned, a testable hypothesis emerges. If there are 100 firms in a market, each with 1% market share, this market conforms to the model of perfect competition. Accordingly, price will equal marginal cost and the rate of profit will be a "normal" rate of return. However, if four firms in this market account for 90% of the assets and sales revenue in that industry, and the other 96 firms share the remaining 10% of the business, this configuration approaches the monopoly model. In the latter example, theory would provide a testable hypothesis. Deriving the requisite data to determine the validity of the structure-performance paradigm required the development of a methodology for classifying the structure of markets in the economy. Economists began to address this problem. *See* N.R. Collins & L.E. Preston, *The Size Structure of the Largest Industrial Firms,* 51 AM. ECON. REV. 986 (1961); RALPH L. NELSON, CONCENTRATION IN THE MANUFACTURING INDUSTRIES OF THE UNITED STATES (1963).

The measurement of market structures in terms relevant to the paradigm became standardized and published by the United States Department of Commerce in its publication, U.S. CENSUS OF MANUFACTURES. This data, referred to as concentration ratios, is organized by a standard classification of industries in terms of the percentage of total industry sales accounted for by the largest four firms and the largest eight firms ranked in terms of total shipments, sales, employment, or physical shipments. Interpreting and applying this data poses many problems, *e.g.,* it has been pointed out that the census data do not necessarily correspond to actual markets, such as regional or local markets. Also, some products such as beet sugar and cane sugar may be substitutes in the actual market, but they are recorded as separate industries in the census. *See* CARL KAYSEN & DONALD F. TURNER, ANTITRUST POLICY 297 (1959). Based on the conceptual and statistical difficulties both in generating as well as in using this data, it is not surprising that there is substantial divergence in the conclusions. *See* James L. Bothwell, Thomas F. Cooley

& Thomas E. Hall, *A New View of the Market Performance-Structure Debate,* 32 J. IND. ECON. 397 (1984). It seems clear from the empirical studies of profitability that market shares alone are less significant than an analysis which takes account of the elasticities of supply and of demand—the availability of near substitutes for the products at issue. It also seems clear that while economists have established some positive correlation between concentration and profitability, it is understood that this correlation does not establish causation. An earlier commentator has summarized the profitability-concentration literature in this vein as follows:

> Dominant firms are expected to have especially high margins in virtually everyone's theory and my . . . tabulation . . . suggests that they generally do. This may be due to economies of scale or superior business acumen or to a valid patent, or it may derive from long dead patents or from ancient mergers plus high barriers to entry. Monopolization cases may or may not be in the public's interest depending on what the mix of these causes may be. Each case should be examined separately to determine the source of the market power.

Leonard W. Weiss, *The Concentration-Profits Relationship and Antitrust,* in INDUSTRIAL CONCENTRATION: THE NEW LEARNING 184, 232-33 (Harvey J. Goldschmid, H. Michael Mann & J. Fred Weston eds. 1974).

Other economists have noted the relationship between concentration in an industry and the conditions of entry. The inference is that concentration reflects the fact that new resources are not entering that industry. Recognition of this fact imposes a cautionary perspective on drawing conclusions of market or monopoly power from high profit returns in concentrated industries. Another economist expresses this view as follows:

> Standing alone, a persistently high rate of profit (however defined) for a high concentration industry merely indicates that "something" is discouraging the inflow of resources. But such profitability tells us nothing about the nature of this something; it could be public policy, fear of "predatory" competition, recognition that the industry would not profitably support another firm, scarcity of raw materials, an imperfect capital market, and no doubt many other things as well. To ascribe . . . a high rate of profit in a high concentration industry to its "monopoly power" or "market power" is to evade the investigation of an empirical question by failing to recognize that it exists.

Donald Dewey, *Industrial Concentration and the Rate of Profit: Some Neglected Theory,* 19 J.L. & ECON. 67, 78 (1976). *See also* F.M. SCHERER, INDUSTRIAL MARKET STRUCTURE AND ECONOMIC PERFORMANCE 411-12 (1990).

Economists have set out some relevant variables for assessing market or monopoly power. In the cases which follow, consider the extent to which the courts rely on these variables; consider also the efficacy of the antitrust remedies applied in reducing monopoly power. See also the Note on the various measures of concentration employed by the enforcement agencies, below at pages 415-20.

In addition to the technical issues set out above, there is a larger public policy question relating to the size of firms. In addition to the competition issues posed by the existence of large firms and by the dominance in some markets of relatively few large firms, there are distributional and political issues. The distributional issues arise when large, dominant firms serve to transfer revenue from consumers to corporate managers and to the shareholders of such corporations. Similarly, there is the controversy over the contributions of major corporations to financing state and federal candidates seeking election to public office. The implication here is that the size of these enterprises permits them to generate large revenue flows and the collateral inference is that these enterprises unduly influence elected officials by the size of their campaign contributions. There is, however, no consensus that the antitrust laws can or should address such concerns.

An industrial organization economist has put the case for vigorous enforcement of § 2 of the Sherman Act in terms of "competitive parity." As he put it:

> It is important to begin with the essential nature of competition. Effective competition involves a mutual striving among comparable rivals on a basis of *competitive parity*. . . . If parity is maintained . . . then effective competition continues to . . . constrain all firms' prices toward costs.
>
> * * *
>
> Whenever parity is absent and firms are not comparable, then competition is not effective. In the standard situation of market dominance, the leading firm has over 40%-50% of the market and there is no close rival. The dominant firm is capable of eliminating any small rival it chooses at any given time or possibly all of its rivals. . . . The dominant firm is able to deploy competitive weapons unavailable to the little rivals, particularly the strong use of selective pricing and promotions. Its costs of capital are commonly lower and its profits are usually more stable . . . .

William G. Shepard, *Section 2 and the Problem of Market Dominance,* 35 ANTITRUST BULL. 833, 835-38 (1990).

On the issue of the significance of size, there is an opposing view among industrial organization economists. This group of economists points out that it is equally persuasive to posit that:

> . . . [S]ome products are more efficiently produced by firms possessing a large share of the market. . . . Those firms that first act on the belief that large scale is an advantage, and that invest in the marketing and production techniques prerequisite to executing the move to large scale, will possess a competitively secured advantage in timing and in obtaining early consumer acceptance. . . . The market may not have grown large enough to accommodate more than a handful of such firms. These firms can produce at lower unit cost than smaller firms. They are superior in this respect, and they command an economic rent for achieving primacy.

Harold Demsetz, *Two Systems of Belief About Monopoly, in* INDUSTRIAL CONCENTRATION: THE NEW LEARNING 164, 176-77 (Harvey J. Goldschmid, H. Michael

Mann & J. Fred Weston eds. 1974). For further development of this perspective see John S. McGee, *Efficiency and Economies of Scale,* in *id.* at 55.

This difference of opinion persists. Enforcement policy since the 1980s has tended to follow the Demsetz-McGee position. As the cases in this chapter indicate, there have been relatively few § 2 cases brought by the agencies against dominant firms. In Chap. 12, dealing with mergers, note the settlement by consent decree of a recent § 2 case against Microsoft, a dominant firm in its industry. Note the terms of the consent decree. Do the terms of that decree (discussed in Chapter 12, pages 609-11, *infra.*) reflect a concern with Microsoft's dominant market position or with some of its practices? If you were asked by the Assistant Attorney General in charge of the Antitrust Division to write a recommendation of the enforcement policy for § 2, what would be your principal points?

United States v. E.I. du Pont de Nemours & Co.

351 U.S. 377 (1956)

[The United States charged du Pont with monopolizing, attempting to monopolize and conspiracy to monopolize interstate commerce in cellophane and cellulosic caps and bands in violation of § 2 of the Sherman Act. After a lengthy trial, judgment was entered for du Pont on all issues. The Government appealed, attacking "only the ruling that du Pont had not monopolized trade in cellophane."]

Mr. Justice REED delivered the opinion of the Court.

....

During the period that is relevant to this action, du Pont produced almost 75% of the cellophane sold in the United States, and cellophane constituted less than 20% of all "flexible packaging material" sales....

The Government contends that, by so dominating cellophane production, du Pont monopolized a "part of the trade or commerce" in violation of § 2. Respondent agrees that cellophane is a product which constitutes "a 'part' of commerce within the meaning of Section 2." ... But it contends that the prohibition of § 2 against monopolization is not violated because it does not have the power to control the price of cellophane or to exclude competitors from the market in which cellophane is sold. The court below found that the "relevant market for determining the extent of du Pont's market control is the market for flexible packaging materials," and that competition from those other materials prevented du Pont from possessing monopoly powers in its sales of cellophane....

The Government asserts that cellophane and other wrapping materials are neither substantially fungible nor like priced. For these reasons, it argues that the market for other wrappings is distinct from the market for cellophane and that the competition afforded cellophane by other wrappings is not strong enough to be considered in determining whether du Pont has monopoly powers....

The burden of proof, of course, was upon the Government to establish monopoly....

If cellophane is the "market" that du Pont is found to dominate, it may be assumed it does have monopoly power over that "market." Monopoly power is the power to control prices or exclude competition. It seems apparent that du Pont's power to set the price of cellophane has been limited only by the competition afforded by other flexible packaging materials. Moreover, it may be practically impossible for anyone to commence manufacturing cellophane without full access to du Pont's technique. However, du Pont has no power to prevent competition from other wrapping materials. The trial court consequently had to determine whether competition from the other wrappings prevented du Pont from possessing monopoly power in violation of § 2. Price and competition are so intimately entwined that any discussion of theory must treat them as one. It is inconceivable that price could be controlled without power over competition or vice versa. . . .

. . . [W]here there are market alternatives that buyers may readily use for their purposes, illegal monopoly does not exist merely because the product said to be monopolized differs from others. . . . What is called for is an appraisal of the "cross-elasticity" of demand in the trade. . . . In considering what is the relevant market for determining the control of price and competition, no more definite rule can be declared than that commodities reasonably interchangeable by consumers for the same purposes make up that "part of the trade or commerce," monopolization of which may be illegal. . . . In determining the market under the Sherman Act, it is the use or uses to which the commodity is put that control. The selling price between commodities with similar uses and different characteristics may vary, so that the cheaper product can drive out the more expensive. Or, the superior quality of higher priced articles may make dominant the more desirable. Cellophane costs more than many competing products and less than a few. . . .

It may be admitted that cellophane combines the desirable elements of transparency, strength and cheapness more definitely than any of the [other wrapping materials]. . . .

But, despite cellophane's advantages it has to meet competition from other materials in every one of its uses. . . . Food products are the chief outlet [for cellophane], with cigarettes next. . . . [C]ellophane furnishes less than 7% of wrappings for bakery products, 25% for candy, 32% for snacks, 35% for meats and poultry, 27% for crackers and biscuits, 47% for fresh produce, and 34% for frozen foods. Seventy-five to eighty percent of cigarettes are wrapped in cellophane. . . . Thus, cellophane shares the packaging market with others. The over-all result is that cellophane accounts for 17.9% of flexible wrapping materials, measured by the wrapping surface. . . .

An element for consideration as to cross-elasticity of demand between products is the responsiveness of the sales of one product to price changes of the other. If a slight decrease in the price of cellophane causes a considerable number of customers of other flexible wrappings to switch to cellophane, it would be an indication that a high cross-elasticity of demand exists between them; that the products compete in the same market. The court below held that the "[g]reat sensitivity of customers in the flexible packaging markets to price or quality changes" prevented du Pont from possessing monopoly control over price. . . . The record sustains these findings. . . .

We conclude that cellophane's interchangeability with the other materials mentioned suffices to make it a part of this flexible packaging material market.

. . . .

The "market" which one must study to determine when a producer has monopoly power will vary with the part of commerce under consideration. The tests are constant. That market is composed of products that have reasonable interchangeability for the purposes for which they are produced—price, use and qualities considered. While the application of the tests remains uncertain, it seems to us that du Pont should not be found to monopolize cellophane when that product has the competition and interchangeability with other wrappings that this record shows.

On the findings of the District Court, its judgment is affirmed.

Affirmed.

United States v. Syufy Enterprises

903 F.2d 659 (9th Cir. 1990)

KOZINSKI, Circuit Judge

Suspecting that giant film distributors like Columbia, Paramount and Twentieth Century-Fox had fallen prey to Raymond Syufy, the canny operator of a chain of Las Vegas, Nevada, movie theatres, the United States Department of Justice brought this civil antitrust action to force Syufy to disgorge the theatres he had purchased in 1982-84 from his former competitors. The case is unusual in a number of respects: The Department of Justice concedes that moviegoers in Las Vegas suffered no direct injury as a result of the allegedly illegal transactions; nor does the record reflect complaints from Syufy's bought-out competitors, as the sales were made at fair prices and not precipitated by any monkey business; and the supposedly oppressed movie companies have weighed in on Syufy's side. The Justice Department nevertheless remains intent on rescuing this platoon of Goliaths from a single David.

. . . [In 1981] Raymond Syufy . . . entered the Las Vegas market with a splash by opening a six-screen theatre. Newly constructed and luxuriously furnished, it put existing facilities to shame. Syufy's entry into the Las Vegas market caused a stir, precipitating a titanic bidding war.[1] Soon, theatres in Las Vegas were paying some of the highest license fees in the nation, while distributors sat back and watched the easy money roll in.

It is the nature of free enterprise that fierce, no holds barred competition will drive out the least effective participants in the market, providing the most efficient allocation of productive resources. And so it was in the Las Vegas movie market in 1982. After a hard fought battle among several contenders, Syufy gained the upper hand. Two of his rivals, Mann Theatres and Plitt Theatres, saw their future as rocky and decided to sell out to Syufy. While Mann and Plitt are major exhibitors nationwide, neither had a large presence in Las Vegas. Mann operated two indoor theatres with a total of three screens; Plitt operated a single theatre with three screens. Things were relatively quiet until September 1984; in September, Syufy entered into earnest negotiations with Cragin Industries, his largest remaining competitor.[2] Cragin sold out to Syufy midway through October, leaving Roberts Company, a small exhibitor of mostly second-run films, as Syufy's only competitor for first-run films in Las Vegas.

---

1 Film distributors do not hand out prints for free; they sell exhibition licenses. These licenses normally specify a percentage of weekly house receipts, known as license fees, payable by the theatre owner to the distributor. Where more than one theatre in a given area volunteers to pay the license fee for a particular film, the distributor has several options: It can license the film to more than one theatre in the area; it can award the film to a particular theatre with which it has an ongoing relationship; or it can let them all bid for exclusive exhibition rights. Where the distributor adopts the competitive bidding approach, as virtually all distributors did in Las Vegas prior to October 1984, the high bid usually includes a guarantee—a minimum fee payable to the distributor even if the film bombs. As bidding in Las Vegas grew more fierce, guarantee amounts went over the top. Too often, the bids were so high that theatre owners ran up substantial losses. The industry refers to these as busted guarantees, meaning that because the film did less business than was expected, the theatre was trapped into paying the higher guarantee amount instead of the percentage of box office it had negotiated. Occasionally, guarantees in Las Vegas were so high that they exceeded the gate at a particular theatre.

2 Cragin's Redrock Theatre was an 11-screen multiplex. It was sold to Syufy when the enterprise fell upon hard times because of a dispute between partners Lucille Cragin and Horst Schmidt.

It is these three transactions—Syufy's purchases of the Mann, Plitt and Cragin theatres—that the Justice Department claims amount to antitrust violations.[3] As government counsel explained at oral argument, the thrust of its case is that "you may not get monopoly power by buying out your competitors." . . .

Discussion

. . . [O]f significance is the government's concession that Syufy was only a monopsonist, not a monopolist.[4] Thus, the government argues that Syufy had market power, but that it exercised this power only against its suppliers (film distributors), not against its consumers (moviegoers). This is consistent with the record, which demonstrates that Syufy always treated moviegoers fairly: The movie tickets, popcorn, nuts and the Seven-Ups cost about the same in Las Vegas as in other, comparable markets. While it is theoretically possible to have a middleman who is a monopolist upstream but not downstream, this is a somewhat counterintuitive scenario. Why, if he truly had significant market power, would Raymond Syufy have chosen to take advantage of the big movie distributors while giving a fair shake to ordinary people? And why do the distributors, the alleged victims of the monopolization scheme, think that Raymond Syufy is the best thing that ever happened to the Las Vegas movie market?

The answers to these questions are significant because, like all antitrust cases, this one must make economic sense. . . . Keeping in mind that competition, not government intervention, is the touchstone of a healthy, vigorous economy, we proceed to examine whether the district court erred in concluding that Syufy does not, in fact, hold monopoly power. There is universal agreement that monopoly power is the power to exclude competition or control prices. . . . The district court determined that Syufy possessed neither power. As the government's case stands or falls with these propositions, the parties have devoted much of their analysis to these findings. So do we.

1. Power to Exclude Competition

It is true, of course, that when Syufy acquired Mann's, Plitt's and Cragin's theatres he temporarily diminished the number of competitors in the Las Vegas first-run film market. But this does not necessarily indicate foul play; many legitimate market arrangements diminish the number of competitors. It would be odd if they did not, as the nature of competition is to make winners and losers.[5] If there are no significant barriers to entry, however, eliminating competitors will not enable the survivors to reap a monopoly profit; any attempt to raise prices above the competitive level will lure into the market new competitors able and willing to offer their commercial goods or personal services for less. *See Metro Mobile CTS, Inc. v. New Vector Commun., Inc.*, 892 F.2d 62, 63 (9th Cir.1989).

---

3 Specifically, the government's complaint alleges monopolization and/or attempted monopolization of a part of commerce in violation of Section 2 of the Sherman Act, 15 U.S.C. § 2 (1988), and substantial lessening of competition by acquisition within a line of commerce in violation of Section 7 of the Clayton Act, 15 U.S.C. § 18 (1988).

4 Monopsony is defined as a "market situation in which there is a single buyer or a group of buyers making joint decisions. Monopsony and monopsony power are the equivalent on the buying side of monopoly and monopoly power on the selling side." R. Lipsey, P. Steiner & D. Purvis, *Economics* 976 (7th ed. 1984).

5 *See* 3 P. Areeda & D. Turner, *Antitrust Law* ¶ 608e, at 20-21 (1978); L. Sullivan, HANDBOOK OF THE LAW OF ANTITRUST § 34, at 96 (1977). Given this reality, it would be perverse to expect rivals engaged in head on competition to act like best friends; indeed, it would be cause for suspicion if they did.

Time after time, we have recognized this basic fact of economic life:

> A high market share, though it may ordinarily raise an inference of monopoly power, will not do so in a market with low entry barriers or other evidence of a defendant's inability to control prices or exclude competitors.

. . . There is nothing magic about this proposition; it is simple common sense, embodied in the Antitrust Division's own Merger Guidelines:

> If entry into a market is so easy that existing competitors could not succeed in raising price for any significant period of time, the Department is unlikely to challenge mergers in that market. Antitrust Policies and Guidelines, U.S. Dep't of Justice, Merger Guidelines § 3.3, reprinted in 4 Trade Reg. Rep. (CCH) P 13,103 at 20,562 (1988).

The district court, after taking testimony from a dozen and a half witnesses and examining innumerable graphs, charts, statistics and other exhibits, found that there were no barriers to entry in the Las Vegas movie market. Our function is narrow: we must determine whether that finding is clearly erroneous. *See Oahu Gas*, 838 F.2d at 363, 367. Our review of the record discloses that the district court's finding is amply supported by the record.

We bypass as surplusage the hundreds of pages of expert and lay testimony that support the district court's finding, and focus instead only on a single—to our minds conclusive—item. Immediately after Syufy bought out the last of his three competitors in October 1984, he was riding high, having captured 100% of the first-run film market in Las Vegas. But this utopia proved to be only a mirage. That same month, a major movie distributor, Orion, stopped doing business with Syufy, sending all of its first-run films to Roberts Company, a dark horse competitor previously relegated to the second-run market.[6] Roberts Company took this as an invitation to step into the major league and, against all odds, began giving Syufy serious competition in the first-run market. Fighting fire with fire, Roberts opened three multiplexes within a 13-month period, each having six or more screens. By December 1986, Roberts was operating 28 screens, trading places with Syufy, who had only 23. At the same time, Roberts was displaying a healthy portion of all first-run films. In fact, Roberts got exclusive exhibition rights to many of its films, meaning that Syufy could not show them at all.

. . . .

The Justice Department correctly points out that Syufy still has a large market share, but attributes far too much importance to this fact.[9] In evaluating monopoly power, it is not market share that counts, but the ability to maintain market share. . . . Syufy seems unable

---

[6] Second-run films are the same as first-run films, only older. When a film is initially released for public exhibition, it is in its first run. Once public demand for the film has fallen off (but usually before it is reduced to a dead calm), the first-run theatre will ship it out to make room for something more recent. The film may then open elsewhere in the same area, usually at a lower ticket price, this being the film's second run.

[9] The government also challenges the district court's definition of the relevant upstream product market in Las Vegas. The court defined the market broadly to include not only first-run theatrical exhibition, but also "exhibition on home video, cable television, and pay-per-view television." 712 F. Supp. at 1389. We agree with the government that this is not the proper market definition in examining Syufy's power over film distributors. While moviegoers may well view these alternative methods of film exhibition as readily substitutable, film

to do this. In 1985, Syufy managed to lock up exclusive exhibition rights to 91% of all the first-run films in Las Vegas. By the first quarter of 1988, that percentage had fallen to 39%; United Artists had exclusive rights to another 25%, with the remaining 36% being played on both Syufy and UA screens.

. . . .

The government concedes that there are no structural barriers to entry into the market: Syufy does not operate a bank or similar enterprise where entry is limited by government regulation or licensing requirements. Nor is this the type of industry, like heavy manufacturing or mining, which requires onerous front-end investments that might deter competition from all but the hardiest and most financially secure investors.[12] . . . Nor do we have here a business dependent on a scarce commodity, control over which might give the incumbent a substantial structural advantage. Nor is there a network of exclusive contracts or distribution arrangements designed to lock out potential competitors. To the contrary, the record discloses a rough-and-tumble industry, marked by easy market access, fluid relationships with distributors, an ample and continuous supply of product, and a healthy and growing demand.[13] It would be difficult to design a market less susceptible to monopolization.

---

distributors do not. Distributors use first-run theatrical exhibition to make sure that audiences are exposed to a film so that, even if it gets bad reviews and fails to turn a profit in theatres, people switching channels or checking out videos will recognize the title and be induced by its fame to watch it. That first-run theatrical exhibition enhances a film's performance in auxiliary markets does not mean that auxiliary markets can substitute for theatrical release. The district court was therefore mistaken in relying on testimony that "of the 578 films produced in 1987, 214 were released on home video and not in the theatres," *id.* at 1400, as there was no suggestion that any of these 214 films were suitable for theatrical release, or that any film has ever been released first on home video and then later played in first-run theaters. Jane Fonda's Low Impact Aerobic Workout may be a best-selling videocassette, but it is unlikely to be the hit at a local movie theatre. The district court's erroneous definition of the relevant upstream product market does not warrant reversal, however. The district court repeatedly made alternative findings using the government's narrower market definition limited solely to first-run exhibition. Our review of the record convinces us that these alternative findings are supported by substantial evidence.

[12] The Justice Department argues that it is expensive to build a multiplex, but the district court was rightly unimpressed by this contention. Syufy was neither the first nor the last to open a multiplex in Las Vegas: Cragin's 11-screen Redrock was there before Syufy came into the market and, soon thereafter, Roberts opened three multiplexes in quick succession. In fact, Roberts was spared the expense of construction, as several of its theatres were financed by shopping center developers from whom Roberts later leased space. . . .

[13] The Justice Department claims that the district court misunderstood the evidence on this point. It argues that Las Vegas is "overscreened," *i.e.*, that potential competitors declined to enter the market because there was not enough business to go around. The district court made detailed contrary findings: The rule of thumb in the film industry is that it takes 10,000 people to support one screen. Las Vegas is populated by approximately 600,000 residents and 100,000 tourists at any given time, leaving room for as many as 70 screens. Yet, at the time of trial, there were only 50 first-run screens in the city, meaning that the Las Vegas market offered ample opportunities to potential entrants. In addition, Las Vegas is a boom town, growing at the rate of 30,000 people a year. Thus, the potential for new entry into the first-run film market will continue. RT 2:300, 3:338, 6:989. "Because untapped potential provides a mouth-watering incentive for vigorous competition, it is axiomatic that monopoly power is unlikely to arise in dynamic industries marked by a rapidly expanding volume of demand and low barriers to entry." *Metro Mobile CTS, Inc. v. New Vector Commun., Inc.*, 892 F.2d 62, 63 (9th Cir.1989).

More fundamentally, the government's static model, which assumes that there is only so much demand for a particular product, is alien to modern economic theory, as well as common sense, which teach us that things change. The demand for movie tickets can fluctuate with a variety of factors such as price, quality of the movie theatre, cost of related goods such as concession stand products, and quality of films shown. Even assuming that the Las Vegas movie market was, in some static sense, operating at capacity, the entry of a new competitor might, as the district court found, simply result in "the exit of some of the less attractive and less efficient theatres in Las Vegas." 712 F. Supp. at 1396. Or, a new competitor with high hopes might price movie tickets lower, increase

Confronted with this record and the district court's clear findings, the government trots out a shopworn argument we had thought long abandoned: that efficient, aggressive competition is itself a structural barrier to entry. According to the government, competitors will be deterred from entering the market because they could not hope to turn a profit competing against Syufy. In the words of government counsel:

> There is no legal barrier. There is no law that says you can't come into this market, it's not that kind of barrier. . . . But, the fact of mere possibility in the literal sense, is not the appropriate test. Entry, after all, must, to be effective to dissipate the monopoly power that Syufy has, entry must hold some reasonable prospect of profitability for the entrant, or else the entrant will say, as Mann Theatres said . . . this is not an attractive market to enter. There will be shelter. And the reason is very clear. You have to compete effectively in this market. And witness after witness testified you would need to build anywhere from 12 to 24 theatres, which is a very expensive and time consuming proposition. *And, you would then find yourself in a bidding war against Syufy.*

Tr. of Oral Arg. at 5 (emphasis added).

The notion that the supplier of a good or service can monopolize the market simply by being efficient reached high tide in the law 44 years ago in Judge Learned Hand's opinion in *United States v. Aluminum Co. of Am.*, 148 F.2d 416 (2d Cir.1945).[14] In the intervening decades the wisdom of this notion has been questioned by just about everyone who has taken a close look at it. . . .

The argument government counsel presses here is a close variant of *Alcoa*: The government is not claiming that Syufy monopolized the market by being too efficient, but that Syufy's effectiveness as a competitor creates a structural barrier to entry, rendering illicit Syufy's acquisition of its competitors' screens. We hasten to sever this new branch that the government has caused to sprout from the moribund *Alcoa* trunk.

. . . .

---

advertising, provide more convenient parking facilities, or otherwise induce people to go to the movies more often. Or, a theatre operator might hit the jackpot by catering to parents of small children who might be more likely to patronize drive-in theatres. We cannot and should not speculate as to the details of a potential competitor's performance; we need only determine whether there were barriers to the entry of new faces into the market. As we discuss in greater detail below, in making that determination we are not concerned with whether, once in the market, the competitor will wind up doing well. The thing to remember is that doing business in the crucible of free enterprise is inherently unpredictable.

[14] In *Alcoa*, Judge Hand concluded that defendant corporation violated the antitrust laws simply by making all the right moves, in particular, by filling the demand of which it was the creator:

> True, it stimulated demand and opened new uses for the metal, but not without making sure that it could supply what it had evoked. . . . "Alcoa" avows it as evidence of the skill, energy and initiative with which it has always conducted its business; as a reason why, having won its way by fair means, it should be commended, and not dismembered. . . . [W]e may assume that all it claims for itself is true. . . . [But i]t was not inevitable that it should always anticipate increases in the demand for ingot and be prepared to supply them. Nothing compelled it to keep doubling and redoubling its capacity before others entered the field. It insists that it never excluded competitors; but we can think of no more effective exclusion than progressively to embrace each new opportunity as it opened, and to face every newcomer with new capacity already geared into a great organization, having the advantage of experience, trade connections and the elite of personnel. . . . That was to "monopolize" that market, however innocently it otherwise proceeded.

148 F.2d at 430-32.

The Supreme Court has accordingly distanced itself from the *Alcoa* legacy, taking care to distinguish unlawful monopoly power from "growth or development as a consequence of a superior product, business acumen, or historic accident," *United States v. Grinnell Corp.*, 384 U.S. 563, 571 (1966), which is off limits to the enforcer of our antitrust laws. If a dominant supplier acts consistent with a competitive market—out of fear perhaps that potential competitors are ready and able to step in—the purpose of the antitrust laws is amply served. We make it clear today, if it was not before, that an efficient, vigorous, aggressive competitor is not the villain antitrust laws are aimed at eliminating. Fostering an environment where businesses fight it out using the weapon of efficiency and consumer goodwill is what the antitrust laws are meant to champion. . . .

But we need not rely on theory alone in rejecting the government's argument. The record here conclusively demonstrates that neither acquiring the screens of his competitors nor working hard at better serving the public gave Syufy deliverance from competition. Immediately following the disappearance of Mann, Plitt and Cragin, Roberts took up the challenge, aggressively competing with Syufy for first-run films—and with considerable success. United Artists, with substantial resources at its disposal and nationwide experience in running movie theatres, considered the market sufficiently open that it bought out Roberts in 1987. We see no indication that competition suffered in the Las Vegas movie market as a result of Syufy's challenged acquisitions.[15] The district court certainly had ample basis in the record for its finding that Syufy lacked the power to exclude competitors. Indeed, on this voluminous record we are hard-pressed to see how the district court could have come to the other conclusion.

2. Power to Control Prices

The crux of the Justice Department's case is that Syufy, top gun in the Las Vegas movie market, had the power to push around Hollywood's biggest players, dictating to them what prices they could charge for their movies. The district court found otherwise. This finding too has substantial support in the record.

Perhaps the most telling evidence of Syufy's inability to set prices came from movie distributors, Syufy's supposed victims. At the trial, distributors uniformly proclaimed their satisfaction with the way the Las Vegas first-run film market operates; none complained about the license fees paid by Syufy. Columbia's President of Domestic Distribution testified that "Syufy paid a fair amount of film rental" that compared favorably with other markets. . . .

While successful, Syufy is in no position to put the squeeze on distributors. The one time he tried there was an immediate backlash. In 1984, about seven days after allegedly acquiring its monopoly, Syufy informed Orion Releasing Group that he had cold feet about The Cotton Club and would not honor the large guarantees he had contracted for, only

---

[15] The government points out that the interiors of United Artists' theatres were not as luxurious as those of Syufy. We have no clue what sinister inference the government would have us draw from this fact. As the district court noted, "No one stopped United Artists from remodeling Roberts' theatres after it acquired them. As the largest exhibitor in the nation, it certainly has the resources to do so." 712 F. Supp. at 1402. Competitors need not provide a perfectly undifferentiated product in order to be competitive; it is a strength of our free market economy that competitors often provide products that cater to the varied tastes and preferences of consumers. Syufy made a business decision to invest in luxury theatres while Roberts and United Artists apparently decided to dispose of their profits in some other fashions. It remains to be seen which strategy will ultimately prevail. Indeed, it is not a winner take all situation; in a free market, any number can play and any number can win. We therefore agree with the district court's refusal to conclude that this difference in business strategies was an indication of market failure.

to see his gambit backfire. Orion sued Syufy for breach of contract, *see Orion Pictures Distrib. Corp. v. Syufy Enters.*, 829 F.2d 946 (9th Cir.1987), licensed the film to Roberts and cut Syufy off cold turkey. To this day, Orion refuses to play its films in any Syufy theatre, in Las Vegas or elsewhere. 712 F. Supp. at 1393. Accordingly, Syufy lost the opportunity to exhibit top moneymakers like Robocop, Platoon, Hannah and Her Sisters and No Way Out.[17] The district court found no evidence that Orion considered Roberts/UA's theatres a less than adequate substitute for Syufy's. *Id.*

. . . .

Conclusion.

The judgment of the district court is affirmed.

COMMENTARY

The *du Pont* and *Syufy* cases raise the issue of anticompetitive conduct associated with market power. In *Syufy,* the court also considers whether the defendant created a barrier to entry. In each of these cases, what evidence does the opinion discuss relating to the cause of the defendant's large market share? In each case, was profitability a factor in the decision? In the *du Pont* case did the Court begin its inquiry into the defendant's market power by defining a relevant market? Was the defendant's market share then determined for that market? What was the inference that led to the conclusion that there was no exercise of market power by the defendant? Consider the discussion of cross-elasticity in defining the relevant market. Did flexible wrapping materials become part of the relevant market on evidence that there was high cross-elasticity of demand between cellophane and flexible wrapping materials? Does this mean that the court considered that consumers substituted other flexible wrapping materials for cellophane? If so, would it follow that du Pont had little market power over flexible wrapping materials? This analysis by the Court has been criticized as being ambiguous. If the Court meant by the use of the phrase, cross-elasticity, merely that many consumers viewed other flexible wrapping materials as substitutes for cellophane, this was a reference which would support a finding of no market power. If, however, the Court was applying the phrase as would an economist—namely, that there was substitution for cellophane at the current price of cellophane, that would be consistent with a firm which was exercising market power because economic theory holds that a monopolist always faces an elastic demand at the price and output which a monopolist is maximizing its profit. This use of the phrase would be consistent with a finding of substantial market power. *See* Donald F. Turner, *Antitrust Policy and the Cellophane Case,* 70 HARV. L. REV. 281, 302 (1956). If the definition of the relevant market is flawed is the decision left without a foundation? Two economists who reviewed the case

---

[17] The list of Orion films that played exclusively at Roberts theaters also includes such popular fare as Amadeus, Back to School, Bull Durham, Colors, Hoosiers, Married to the Mob, Radio Days and the unforgettable Throw Momma From the Train.

found the decision unfounded on the basis of their profitability calculations. *See* George W. Stocking & Willard F. Mueller, *The Cellophane Case and the New Competition,* 45 AM. ECON. REV. 29, 62 (1955). If the Lerner index could be calculated, despite the difficulty of determining marginal cost from standard accounting records, and it showed that cellophane was a high priced item produced cheaply, would that be sufficient to support a finding that § 2 had been violated?

The economic analysis underlying the definition of a market is the predicate on which the courts have developed the concept of the relevant market—the arena in which there is effective competition—for purposes of § 2 of the Sherman Act and § 7 of the Clayton Act. The opinion in the *Cellophane* case discusses "reasonable interchangeability" as one part of the economist's definition as adapted to defining the relevant market for purpose of § 2, namely the product/price component. There is also a geographic component to defining the market, which is set out in Note 1 following the opinion in *Aspen*, on page 443, *infra.* The Supreme Court has recognized these two components of the definition of the relevant market in *Spectrum Sports, Inc. v. McQuillan,* 506 U.S. 447, 448 (1993). The product component involves both the actual product (or service) in which the litigants trade, *e.g.,* cellophane, as well as those products that are reasonably interchangeable or are near substitutes for the actual product (or service). In *United States v. Grinnell*, 384 U.S. 563, 561(1966), page 423, *infra*, the Supreme Court recognized the link between product definition and price as follows.

> In the case of a product it may be of such a character that substitute products must also be considered, as customers may turn to them if there is a slight increase in the price of the main product. . . . [C]ommodities reasonably interchangeable make up that "part" of the trade or commerce which § 2 protects against monopoly power.

Although the cases cited above were concerned with consumers—*i.e.,*the demand side of market analysis, the fact of reasonable interchangeability is also an element of the relevant market calculus when the supply side of the market is involved. *Twin City Sportservices, Inc. v. Charles O. Finley & Co.,* 512 F.2d 1264, 1271 (9th Cir. 1975). Because of the differences between the legal issues framed by § 2 of the Sherman Act from those raised by § 7 of the Clayton Act, supply side considerations arise rarely in monopolization cases under § 2, but are more often significant in merger cases under § 7 of the Clayton Act through the analysis of barriers to entry that is required by the Merger Guidelines. *See* Chapter 12.

B. Monopolistic Behavior: The Classic Statements

United States v. Aluminum Co. of America

148 F.2d 416 (2d Cir. 1945)

[The United States charged the Aluminum Company of America (Alcoa) with monopolizing commerce, particularly in the manufacture and sale of "virgin" aluminum ingot and sought Alcoa's dissolution. After taking extensive testimony and other evidence, the district judge dismissed the complaint. The United States appealed to the Supreme Court which was unable to entertain the appeal because of an absence of a quorum of qualified justices. That Court then referred the case to the United States Court of Appeals for the Second Circuit under 15 U.S.C.A. § 29 to hear the case as a court of last resort.]

L. HAND, Circuit Judge.

It is undisputed that [from 1912 to the present] . . . "Alcoa" continued to be the single producer of "virgin" ingot in the United States; and the plaintiff argues that this without more was enough to make it an unlawful monopoly. It also takes an alternative position; that in any event during this period "Alcoa" consistently pursued unlawful exclusionary practices, which made its dominant position certainly unlawful.

There are various ways of computing "Alcoa's" control of the aluminum market. . . . The percentage we have already mentioned—over ninety—results only if we both include all "Alcoa's" production and exclude secondary [*i.e.*, ingot made from scrap]. That percentage is enough to constitute a monopoly; it is doubtful whether sixty or sixty-four percent would be enough; and certainly thirty three per cent is not.

We conclude therefore that "Alcoa's" control over the ingot market must be reckoned at over ninety per cent; that being the proportion which its production bears to imported "virgin" ingot. If the fraction which it did not supply were the produce of domestic manufacture there could be no doubt that this percentage gave it a monopoly. . . . The producer of so large a proportion of the supply has complete control within certain limits. It is true that, if by raising the price he reduces the amount which can be marketed—as always, or almost always, happens—he may invite the expansion of the small producers who will try to fill the place left open; nevertheless, not only is there an inevitable lag in this, but the large producer is in a strong position to check such competition; and, indeed, if he has retained his old plant and personnel, he can inevitably do so.

The case at bar is however different, because, for aught that appears there may well have been a practically unlimited supply of imports as the price of ingot rose. . . . [W]e may . . . assume . . . that, had "Alcoa" raised its prices, more ingot would have been imported. Thus there is a distinction between domestic and foreign competition: the first is limited in quantity, and can increase only by an increase in plant and personnel; the second is of producers who, we must assume, produce much more than they import, and whom a rise in price will presumably induce immediately to divert to the American market what they have been selling elsewhere. It is entirely consistent with the evidence that it was the threat of greater foreign imports which kept "Alcoa's" prices where they were, and prevented it from exploiting its advantage as sole domestic producer; indeed, it is hard to resist the conclusion that potential imports did put a "ceiling" upon those prices. Nevertheless, within the limits afforded by the tariff and the cost of transportation, "Alcoa" was free to raise its prices as it chose.

. . . Having proved that "Alcoa" had a monopoly of the domestic ingot market, the plaintiff had gone far enough; if it was an excuse, that "Alcoa" had not abused its power, it lay upon "Alcoa" to prove that it had not. But the whole issue is irrelevant anyway, for it is no excuse for "monopolizing" a market that the monopoly has not been used to extract from the consumer more than a "fair" profit. The Act has wider purposes. Indeed, even though we disregarded all but economic considerations, it would by no means follow that such concentration of producing power is to be desired, when it has not been used extortionately. Many people believe that possession of unchallenged economic power deadens initiative, discourages thrift and depresses energy; that immunity from competition is a narcotic, and rivalry is a stimulant, to industrial progress; that the spur of constant stress is necessary to counteract an inevitable disposition to let well enough alone. Such people believe that competitors, versed in the craft as no consumer can be, will be quick to detect opportunities for saving and new shifts in production, and be eager to profit by them.

. . . [I]t might have been thought adequate to condemn only those monopolies which could not show that they had exercised the highest possible ingenuity, had adopted every possible economy, had anticipated every conceivable improvement, stimulated every possible demand. No doubt, that would be one way of dealing with the matter, although it would imply constant scrutiny and constant supervision, such as courts are unable to provide. Be that as it may, that was not the way that Congress chose; it did not condone "good trusts" and condemn "bad" ones; it forbade all. Moreover, in so doing it was not necessarily actuated by economic motives alone. It is possible, because of its indirect social or moral effect, to prefer a system of small producers, each dependent for his success upon his own skill and character, to one in which the great mass of those engaged must accept the direction of a few.

. . . Starting . . . with the authoritative premise that all contracts fixing prices are unconditionally prohibited, the only possible difference between them and a monopoly is that while a monopoly necessarily involves an equal, or even greater, power to fix prices, its mere existence might be thought not to constitute an exercise of that power. That distinction is nevertheless purely formal; it would be valid only so long as the monopoly remained wholly inert; it would disappear as soon as the monopoly began to operate; for, when it did—that is, as soon as it began to sell at all—it must sell at some price and the only price at which it could sell is a price which it itself fixed. Thereafter the power and its exercise must need coalesce. Indeed it would be absurd to condemn such contracts unconditionally, and not to extend the condemnation to monopolies; for the contracts are only steps toward that entire control which monopoly confers. . . .

We have been speaking only of the economic reasons which forbid monopoly; but, as we have already implied, there are others, based upon the belief that great industrial consolidations are inherently undesirable, regardless of their economic results. . . . Throughout the history of these [antitrust and related] statutes it has been constantly assumed that one of their purposes was to perpetuate and preserve, for its own sake and in spite of possible cost, an organization of industry in small units which can effectively compete with each other. We hold that "Alcoa's" monopoly of ingot was of the kind covered by § 2.

It does not follow because "Alcoa" had such a monopoly, that it "monopolized" the ingot market: it may not have achieved monopoly; monopoly may have been thrust upon it. . . . A market may, for example, be so limited that it is impossible to produce at all and meet the cost of production except by a plant large enough to supply the whole demand. Or there may be changes in taste or in cost which drive out all but one purveyor. A single producer may be the survivor out of a group of active competitors, merely by virtue of his superior skill, foresight and industry. In such cases a strong argument can be made that, although, the result may expose the public to the evils of monopoly, the Act does not mean to condemn the resultant of those very forces which is its prime object to foster: finis opus coronat. The successful competitor, having been urged to compete, must not be turned upon when he wins.

It would completely misconstrue "Alcoa's" position in 1940 to hold that it was the passive beneficiary of a monopoly, following upon an involuntary elimination of competitors by automatically operative economic forces. . . . We need charge it with no moral derelictions after 1912. . . . The only question is whether it falls within the exception established in favor of those who do not seek, but cannot avoid, the control of a market. It seems to us that that question scarcely survives its statement. It was not inevitable that it should always anticipate increases in the demand for ingot and be prepared to supply them. Nothing compelled it to keep doubling and redoubling its capacity before others entered the field. It insists that it never excluded competitors; but we can think of no more effective exclusion than progressively to embrace each new opportunity as it opened, and to face every newcomer with new capacity already geared into a great organization, having the advantage of experience, trade connections and the elite of personnel. . . .

COMMENTARY

1. Should foreign-produced aluminum have been included in the relevant market? How did foreign aluminum affect Alcoa's control over the price of aluminum ingot? How much power, therefore, did Alcoa possess? Did foreign aluminum set a ceiling to Alcoa's power over price? How is the impact of foreign aluminum prices on Alcoa's pricing power distinguishable from the impact that the prices of any competitor have upon the prices of a rival? Do not a rival's prices almost always establish a ceiling over the prices that a firm can effectively charge?

2. Why, according to Hand, is there no real distinction between Alcoa's monopoly power and the exercise of that power? Do you agree with his analysis? Why or why not? Does that analysis make all monopolies unlawful? *i.e.*, do all monopolies "monopolize"? What exception does Hand allow?

3. Explain Hand's statement that:

> . . . we can think of no more effective exclusion than progressively to embrace each new opportunity as it opened, and to face every newcomer with new capacity already geared into a great organization, having the advantage of experience, trade connections and the elite of personnel.

Is this kind of behavior one would expect of a firm in a competitive market? Explain. Judge Hand's assertion that Alcoa acted in an exclusionary way by building new plants ahead of demand ignored the Government's contention that Alcoa was blameworthy for not expanding more rapidly. The Government "argued that Alcoa's failure to expand faster was responsible for the lack of aluminum capacity to meet the government's 1940 airplane building program." 2 SIMON N. WHITNEY,

ANTITRUST POLICIES 112 (1958). In fact, there is ground for believing that capacity expansion in the aluminum industry was elicited by substantial increases in aluminum consumption during the decades preceding the litigation. Aluminum consumption increased twenty-five times between 1907 and 1940 while copper, lead and zinc taken together only doubled. *Id.* at 112-13.

Other companies expand ahead of demand. Intel, for example, in the highly competitive microprocessor business, builds new semiconductor plants ahead of demand. Its president-elect says: "We build factories two years in advance of needing them, before we have the products to run in them, and before we know the industry's going to grow." FORTUNE, February 17, 1997, at 63. Does it matter that Intel has aggressive competitors such as Advanced Micro Devices and Cyrix? Does the same behavior carry different implications when performed by a firm in a competitive industry as when performed in a monopoly? Or was Judge Hand just wrong?

4. Judge Hand observed that because conduct falling short of monopoly "is not illegal unless it is part of a plan to monopolize, or to gain such other control of a market as is equally forbidden," the plaintiff in an attempt-to-monopolize case must prove "'specific intent'; an intent which goes beyond the mere intent to do the act." But in the case before him, Hand ruled that "no intent is relevant except that which is relevant to any liability, criminal or civil: *i.e.,* an intent to bring about the forbidden act. . . . [N]o monopolist monopolizes unconscious of what he is doing. So here, 'Alcoa' meant to keep, and did keep, that complete and exclusive hold upon the ingot market with which it started. That was to 'monopolize' that market, however innocently it otherwise proceeded. . . ." 148 F.2d at 431-32. Do you understand the difference between "specific" intent and the kind of "intent" which Hand attributed to Alcoa? Alcoa had the kind of intent which is frequently referred to as "general" intent. What is "general" intent in this context?

5. Would Judge Hand consider it be evidence of either "general" or "specific" intent that management met each year, reviewed actual and projected increases in ingot sales, and decided to increase the square footage of floor space devoted to the production of ingots by ten percent more than in the most favorable projection of anticipated sales for the next year? Suppose the increase in sales was projected to be twelve percent and management voted to increase the production capacity for ingots by sixty percent? Could such conduct be appropriately described as "predatory investment"? What standards would properly distinguish predatory from non-predatory investment? Would an increase in capacity of one hundred percent constitute predatory investment if it took place during a period when there was substantial unemployment in the local construction industry and it was anticipated that the new plant could be built cheaply? Messrs. Areeda and Turner think that the concept of predatory investment makes sense in theory but is so unlikely a possibility that antitrust law should ignore it. *See* 3 PHILLIP E. AREEDA & DONALD F. TURNER, ANTITRUST LAW 180 (1978). For an evaluation (under § 5 of the Federal Trade Commission Act) of preemptive investment, see *E.I. du Pont de Nemours & Co.*, 96 F.T.C. 653 (1980).

6. What is the legal significance of Judge Hand's "thrust upon" defense? Can this defense serve as a guideline for the decisions of a firm's managers as to price, output, and expansion? Can it be grounded in an economic maxim incorporating marginal cost pricing? Explain.

7. Do you agree with Hand's catalogue of the evils of monopoly? Does a monopolist have an incentive to reduce costs? Explain. How is its incentive to reduce costs different from that of a firm operating in a competitive market?

8. What are the implications of Hand's concern with the sociological structure of society? Is his concern solely related to the connection he perceives between monopoly and inefficiency? Note Hand's assertion that one of the purposes of the antitrust laws "was to perpetuate and preserve, for its own sake and in spite of possible cost, an organization of industry in small units which can effectively compete with each other." Is this concern compatible with the concern, also expressed by Judge Hand, to avoid the evils of monopoly? If one of the evils of monopoly is lethargy, is lethargy not also an evil connected with the maintenance of an industrial structure "in spite of [its] possible cost"? Is Hand suggesting that society should maintain a class of lethargic (and inefficient) entrepreneurs by subsidizing their inefficiencies through high prices?

9. The *Alcoa* case is representative both of the protracted trials associated with antitrust litigation and of the complexity of fashioning a remedy. The trial consumed three hundred and fifty-eight days from 1938 to 1941. Oral delivery of the trial court's opinion began on September 30 and ended on October 9, 1941. *United States v. Aluminum Co. of America*, 44 F. Supp. 97 (S.D.N.Y. 1942). *See* 2 WHITNEY, ANTITRUST POLICIES 89 (1958). In reversing the trial court, which had found for the defendant on all issues, Judge L. Hand took notice of the changes in the aluminum industry brought about by the construction of nine aluminum smelters by the Defense Plant Corporation as part of the war effort. He remanded the case to the District Court for the fashioning of a remedy appropriate to the changed circumstances brought about by the disposition of these plants by the Surplus Property Administration between 1945 and 1947. As this point, government construction accounted for sixty-two percent of total ingot capacity. The Surplus Property Act of 1944, 58 Stat. 765, directed that these plants be disposed of in a manner, *inter alia,* which would discourage monopolistic practices. The Act also required the Attorney General to rule on whether the disposition of any government-owned plant would be to a buyer whose acquisition would be violative of the antitrust laws. Accordingly, Reynolds and Kaiser were permitted to acquire government-surplus alumina plants, smelting plants, and fabricating plants. Alcoa was permitted to acquire only an extrusion plant and a smelter, contiguous to an existing Alcoa facility. The effect of this disposal program was to introduce two fully-integrated competitors into the market with Alcoa.

Based on these changes, Alcoa petitioned the District Court in March of 1947 to be relieved of the monopolizing holding since there was now effective competition in the market The government opposed this motion on the grounds that it was too soon to determine the competitiveness of the aluminum market, and petitioned the court to divest Alcoa of several plants in order to assure effective competition. Judge Knox denied the request for divestiture

> . . . because there is little guarantee that the creation of one new aluminum company, in the presence of a still strong Alcoa, would materially change the competitive situation that now exists.

United States v. Aluminum Co. of America, 91 F. Supp. 333, 418 (S.D.N.Y. 1950). In order to insure the survival of Reynolds and Kaiser, the court retained jurisdiction of the case for five years. Finally, the court ordered large shareholders (including some officers and directors) to divest themselves of their Alcoa shares or the shares of Aluminium, Ltd. within ten years. The purpose of this divestiture was to prevent Alcoa and Aluminium Ltd. from combining to the detriment of Reynolds and Kaiser and to provide competition from an independent Canadian firm. As the five year period of retained jurisdiction neared an end, the government moved for an extension of the period on grounds that some doubts remained as to the viability of Reynolds and Kaiser. This motion was denied after an extended review of sales and market position data. *United States v. Aluminum Co. of America*, 153 F. Supp. 132 (S.D.N.Y. 1957).

NOTE: THE SIGNIFICANCE OF MARKET SHARES IN THE CASELAW

1. Courts generally treat market share as highly relevant to the determination of market power. The most famous statement about market share in the context of a monopolization case is probably Judge Hand's in *Alcoa*, where he stated:

> The percentage we have already mentioned—over ninety . . . is enough to constitute a monopoly; it is doubtful whether sixty or sixty-four percent would be enough; and certainly thirty-three per cent is not.

148 F.2d at 424. Yet, as *Syufy Enterprises*, *supra* page 397, illustrates, evidence of a high market share alone will not establish the existence of market power when entry is easy. Moreover, a recurring question is specifying the minimum share which will give rise to an inference of market power. *See, e.g.*, *Reazin v. Blue Cross & Blue Shield of Kansas*, 899 F.2d 951 (10th Cir. 1990):

> Market share is relevant to the determination of the existence of market or monopoly power, but "market share alone is insufficient to establish market power." *Bright*, 824 F.2d at 824; *see also Colorado Interstate Gas Co. v. Natural Gas Pipeline Co.*, 885 F.2d 683, 695 (10th Cir.1989);

> *Shoppin' Bag*, 783 F.2d at 162; Landes & Posner, *Market Power in Antitrust Cases*, 94 HARV. L. REV. 937, 947 (1981). It may or may not reflect actual power to control price or exclude competition. *See generally Ball Memorial Hosp.*, 784 F.2d at 1335. Courts have not completely agreed on whether a particular market share should be given conclusive or merely presumptive effect in determining market or monopoly power, or whether market share is only a starting point in the inquiry into market or monopoly power. *Compare Valley Liquors, Inc. v. Renfield Importers, Ltd.*, 822 F.2d 656, 667 (7th Cir.) ("Without a showing of special market conditions or other compelling evidence of market power, the lowest possible market share legally sufficient to sustain a finding of monopolization is between 17% and 25%."), *cert. denied*, 484 U.S. 977 (1987), and *Dimmitt Agri Indus., Inc. v. CPC Int'l, Inc.*, 679 F.2d 516, 529 (5th Cir.1982) ("market shares in the range of 16 to 25 percent, such as those held by [defendant] are insufficient—at least absent other compelling structural evidence—as a matter of law to support monopolization"), *cert. denied*, 460 U.S. 1082 (1983), *with Hayden Publishing Co. v. Cox Broadcasting Corp.*, 730 F.2d 64, 69 n.7 (2d Cir.1984) ("a party may have monopoly power in a particular market, even though its market share is less than 50%") *and Broadway Delivery Corp. v. United Parcel Serv. of America*, 651 F.2d 122, 128 (2d Cir.) ("The trend of guidance from the Supreme Court and the practice of most courts endeavoring to follow that guidance has been to give only weight and not conclusiveness to market share evidence."), *cert. denied*, 454 U.S. 968 (1981). *See also* Areeda & Turner, *Antitrust Law*, ¶ 518.3c ("there is a substantial merit in a *presumption* that market shares below 50 or 60 percent do not constitute monopoly power") (emphasis added). This court recently stated in dicta:
>
> > "While the Supreme Court has refused to specify a minimum market share necessary to indicate a defendant has monopoly power, lower courts generally require a minimum market share of between 70% and 80%."
>
> *Colorado Interstate Gas Co.*, 885 F.2d at 694 n.18 (citing 2 E. KINTNER, FEDERAL ANTITRUST LAW, § 12.6 (1980); AREEDA & TURNER, ANTITRUST LAW, ¶ 803). We do not view *Colorado Interstate Gas* as establishing a firm market share percentage required before a finding of monopoly power can ever be sustained. We prefer the view that market share percentages may give rise to presumptions, but will rarely conclusively establish or eliminate market or monopoly power.

In *Reazin*, the Tenth Circuit upheld a jury finding of market and monopoly power on evidence which indicated that the market share of Blue Cross was between 47% and 62%. 899 F.2d at 970. In so holding, the court remarked that: "Blue Cross' market share is such that there could be at most a presumption of a lack of monopoly or market power. We disagree with Blue Cross that such a market share prohibits, as a matter of law, a conclusion of market or monopoly power."

2. In *Broadway Delivery Corp. v. United Parcel Service of America, Inc.*, 651 F.2d 122 (2d Cir.), *cert. denied*, 351 U.S. 968 (1981), the court held erroneous a jury instruction precluding a finding of monopoly power if the defendant's share was less than 50%:

> We do not doubt the significance of market share evidence as an indicator of either the presence or absence of monopoly power. As the cases and commentators have cautioned, however, the true significance of market share data can be determined only after careful analysis of the particular market. Formulas can express the pertinent relationships between market power, market share, and demand and supply elasticities . . . but the data required for sophisticated analysis of a particular market are not always available, and their comprehension by jurors is uncertain at best.
>
> In ruling on a motion for summary judgment or directed verdict, a trial judge should recognize that determining the existence of monopoly power often does not require resolution of the sharp factual disputes associated with issues as agreement, intent, preparedness, or damages, issues frequently involving credibility disputes that ordinarily require jury resolution. . . . Undisputed facts may enable the trial judge to rule on a claim of monopoly power as a matter of law, employing economic analysis to the extent the data permit. . . . [A conclusion that the defendant lacks monopoly power] may be reached if the defendant's share is less than 50%, or even somewhat above that figure, and the record contains no significant evidence concerning the market structure to show that the defendant's share of that market gives it monopoly power. In the absence of such evidence and any other evidence from which the power to control prices or exclude competition can reasonably be inferred, a monopolization claim may be withdrawn from a jury.
>
> . . . It usually will be helpful to advise a jury that the higher a market share, the stronger is the inference of monopoly power. . . . Sometimes, but not inevitably, it will be useful to suggest that a market share below 50% is rarely evidence of monopoly power, a share between 50% and 70% can occasionally show monopoly power, and a share above 70% is usually strong evidence of monopoly power. But when the evidence presents a fair jury issue of monopoly power, the jury should not be told that it must find monopoly power lacking below a specified share or existing above a specified share. . . . We do not suggest that, evidence of market share is invariably a requirement of a monopolization claim, but when such a traditional form of proof is lacking, the plaintiff must produce unambiguous evidence that the defendant has the power to control prices or exclude competition. . . .

See also Domed Stadium Hotel, Inc. v. Holiday Inns, Inc., 732 F.2d 480, 489-90 (5th Cir. 1984) (citing Judge Hand's discussion of market shares in *Alcoa* and suggesting that normally a 50% market share is the minimum which would support a charge of monopolization).

3. Market share alone is not always dispositive in establishing monopolization. External constraints on the ability of a defendant's power to raise prices, may preclude a finding of monopolization. Thus, for example, in *Metro Mobile CTS, Inc. v. New Vector Communications, Inc.*, 892 F.2d 62 (9th Cir. 1989), the Ninth Circuit reversed a finding of monopolization where the defendant mobile phone service had a 100% market share, but its prices were regulated by the Federal Communications Commission. In *Humboldt Bay Municipal Water District v. Louisiana-Pacific Corp.,* 608 F. Supp. 562 (D.C. Cal.), *aff'd mem.,* 787 F.2d 597 (9th Cir. 1985), summary judgment was granted defendant water company since the power to control the price and the duration of the supply contract, lay with the Water District, rather than with the distributor-water company. Similarly, in *National Reporting Co. v. Alderson Reporting Co.,* 763 F.2d 1020, 1022 (8th Cir. 1985), the Eighth Circuit reversed the trial court in a monopolization case involving a sole court reporter under contract, because under the court's rules, an existing contract could only be renewed at the existing contract price; if the reporter sought to raise the price, the work was required to be put out for competitive bids.

4. In *Broadway Delivery*, the court, in ruling that the jury instruction was error, held that a defendant could possess monopoly power even though it possessed a market share of less than 50 percent. The court in *Reazin* stated that evidence about "the existence and intensity of entry barriers, elasticity of supply and demand, the number of firms in the market and market trends" is relevant on the issue of market power. 899 F.2d at 967. What about the converse? Should it be possible for a plaintiff to prevail in a monopolization case without presenting evidence of the defendant's market share? Is structural data generally essential? Can it be dispositive? Is it always dispositive?

5. The minimum market share which will support an attempted monopolization case is generally believed to be lower than the minimum share necessary to support a monopolization case. *See Rebel Oil Co. v. Atlantic Richfield Co.*, 51 F.3d 1421 (9th Cir. 1995):

> We agree with Rebel that the minimum showing of market share required in an attempt case is a lower quantum than the minimum showing required in an actual monopolization case. It is true, as the district court stated, that numerous cases hold that a market share of less than 50 percent is presumptively insufficient to establish market power. However, these cases and others cited by the district court involve claims of *actual* monopolization. When the claim involves attempted monopolization,

> most cases hold that a market share of 30 percent is presumptively insufficient to establish the power to control price. . . . ARCO's market share of 44 percent is sufficient as a matter of law to support a finding of market power, if entry barriers are high and competitors are unable to expand their output in response to supracompetitive pricing.

6. Consider the following remarks from *In re IBM Peripheral EDP Devices Antitrust Litigation*, 481 F. Supp. 965, 975 (N.D. Cal. 1979):

> A relatively small market share would lead to the inference that monopoly power was not present since the ready availability of substitutes would defeat attempts to use that power. The larger defendant's market share, the stronger is the inference that competitors would be unable to effectively check exercises of monopoly power.
>
> The distribution of the share of the market not supplied by defendant is also telling. Defendant's share is more likely to indicate monopoly power if the rest of the market is widely distributed among many small competing suppliers than it would be if the size of competitors and the market share held by them approached defendant's size and share.

7. Consider the following extract from EUGENE M. SINGER, ANTITRUST ECONOMICS 125 (1968):

> Absolute measures of concentration refer to the percentage of assets, employees, or value of shipments accounted for by a given number of leading firms in an industry. Relative measures of concentration, which are less frequently employed, consider the size of competitors in relationship to each other. An industry with sales fairly evenly divided among a few firms may simultaneously possess a high degree of absolute concentration but a low degree of relative concentration. For example, an industry including four firms each with 25 per cent of total sales has a high degree of absolute concentration since the top three firms account for 75 per cent of sales, but the relative concentration in this industry is nil since each competitor is equal in size as measured by their respective sales.

Was the court, in the quoted passage from *In re IBM Peripheral EDP Devices Antitrust Litigation*, employing the concept of relative concentration in its analysis? Was the court suggesting that a high relative concentration might tend to magnify the market power that might be inferred from the defendant's market share? Consider the following passage from *Pacific Coast Agricultural Export Association v. Sunkist Growers, Inc.*, 526 F.2d 1196, 1204 (9th Cir. 1975), *cert. denied*, 425 U.S. 959 (1976):

> Sunkist's control of the Hong Kong export market ranged from 45 to 70% during the period 1967 to 1971. . . . Here Sunkist's competitors,

> although organized into a trade association, were relatively small, with no single competitor controlling over 18% of the market before, or 12% of the market after, Sunkist's entry.

As the note below points out, courts in the past often employed measures of absolute concentration in performing antitrust analysis. During the 1980s and 1990s, however, the courts have given increasing attention to the Herfindahl-Hirshman Index, a measure of market concentration which also reflects the relative differences in size among market participants.

NOTE: CONCENTRATION, MONOPOLY POWER, AND THEIR MEASUREMENT

Given the historical concern with structure and its characteristics, the record of a typical § 2 case is replete with detailed information about the number of firms in the industry involved and with data about the total sales revenue, value of assets, and number of employees of each firm. This information provides a basis for judicial inferences about the character of competition in the industry. The rationale for collecting this data is derived from the economic theory of markets, which by its categories, pure or perfect competition, oligopoly, and monopoly, implies a positive causal linkage between the number of firms in a market and the vigor of competition. Thus, the purely competitive category posits a model of a market in which there are many sellers, homogeneous (*i.e.*, undifferentiated) products, and ease of entry. Here competition among firms dominates behavior: a slight reduction in price by one seller will cause all buyers to buy only from that one seller. Oligopoly, by definition, is descriptive of few sellers and is associated with an assumption of consciously interdependent behavior by the sellers. Monopoly is the category in which a sole seller undertakes to maximize its own net returns, mindful only of the existence of substitutes of varying degrees of proximity.

Concentration Ratios. There have been several approaches to discerning and predicting the character of competition in actual markets from empirical observations of their structure. Counting the firms is the starting point; data about relative market position is the next step. The most common method of describing the number and size distribution of firms in a given market (industry) is to list each firm in terms of a uniform set of indicators and to note its share of the total value of those indicators. Such a listing provides a measure of the significance of size distribution and is often referred to as a "concentration ratio." In its Census of Manufacturers, the United States Census Bureau includes concentration ratios which utilize sales revenue as the base. According to a complex classification system known as the Standard Industrial Classification, the sales revenue of each establishment (plant or retail store) is compiled by industries. The concentration ratio is then expressed as follows: If, say, in classification 3211, flat glass, there were a total of 11 firms in that industry. One column, headed 4-firm ratio, might show the number 94, indicating that four firms account for 94% of total sales revenue in the flat glass industry; the next column, headed 8-firm ratio, shows the number 99, indicating that eight firms account for 99% of sales in that industry. Thus, the concentration ratio for the flat glass industry would be 94% among four firms and 99% among eight firms. Similarly, if for classification number 2851, paints and allied products, the total number of firms were 1,579, the 4-firm ratio is 23 and the 8-firm ratio is 34. In the examples given, the flat glass industry is relatively concentrated; the paint and allied products industry is relatively unconcentrated. *See* U.S. Department of Commerce, Bureau of the Census, *1982 Census of Manufactures: Concentration Ratios in Manufacturing* (Washington, D.C.; U.S. Government Printing Office, 1986). *See also* Report, Concentration Ratios in Manufacturing Industry: 1963, Part I, U.S. Senate, Committee on the Judiciary, Subcommittee on Antitrust and Monopoly (1966).

More information than is provided by concentration ratios is generally required in resolving monopolization cases. On the issue of monopoly power, the concentration ratios are relevant only so far as market structure provides a basis for inferring power. When the defendant attempts to show that the plaintiff is employing the wrong market definition or that power is otherwise lacking, the case may rapidly expand to embrace a variety of issues. Similarly, whether a defendant possessing monopoly power has abused that power may raise a host of sub-issues. The existence of entry barriers, the history of the industry, the technological features of the relevant product, the existence of patents, patent licenses and grant-backs, product differentiation, and a variety of industry practices may become relevant on the issue of monopoly power or on issues connected with abuse of that power. Recall the *Trenton Potteries* case discussed in Chapter 1, page 18, *supra*. Did the Court take account of the fact that the defendant firms accounted for 82% of the supply of sanitary pottery? What inferences were drawn for purposes of § 1? What structural data did the government rely upon in the *du Pont Cellophane* case? How did the defendant meet that data?

A number of problems of interpretation arise in the use of concentration ratios. The use of sales revenue as a base has the infirmity of understating the significance of a vertically integrated firm, since its intra-firm sales are omitted in the Census reporting system. Moreover, there are substantial definitional problems underlying the classification system resulting from the difficulty of stating the degree of proximity of near substitutes for any product. Thus, the classification 3411, metal cans, may be too narrowly defined since, for many products, glass containers are effective substitutes for metal cans. For further application of this measure in merger cases, see pages 565-70, *infra*. *See generally* G. Rosenbluth, *Measures of Concentration, in* BUSINESS CONCENTRATION AND PRICE POLICY 57-100 (1955). The several indices of market power that economists have developed are set out below.

The Herfindahl Index. This index, also known as the Herfindahl-Hirshman Index, has two advantages over the concentration ratios themselves. First, it uses information about the market shares of all the firms in an industry, rather than the shares of the top four. Second, it displays dramatically the departure from perfect equality of market shares among firms in an industry. The Herfindahl index is an alternative measure of concentration which combines in a single figure the number of firms in an industry and the size inequality among them. (HHI is a customary designation for this index, reflecting the association of Professor Albert Hirschman with this measure.) In formulary terms, the Herfindahl index may be stated as:

$$HHI = \sum_{i=1}^{n} [S_i^2]$$

where S represents the percentage size of firm i expressed in terms of sales revenues or other indicator. The Herfindahl index is thus the sum of the squares of the percentage shares of each firm in the industry. An industry entirely occupied by a single firm causes the index to reach its maximum value of 1.0 or 10,000. An industry with two equal sized firms would produce a Herfindahl index of $(50\%)^2 + (50\%)^2$ or $(.5)^2 + (.5)^2$ or (.25) + (.25) or .5. An industry with five equal sized firms (each accounting for 20% of the industry) would produce a Herfindahl index of $(.2)^2 + (.2)^2 + (.2)^2 + (.2)^2 + (.2)^2 = .04 + .04 + .04 + .04 + .04 = .2$. As the examples make evident, in a market composed of a number of sellers of equal size, the Herfindahl index is 1.00 over the number (n) of firms in the industry, or 1.00/n. Thus the Herfindahl index produces lower readings as the number of equal-sized firms composing an industry increases.

When the firms composing the industry are of differing sizes, the Herfindahl index provides a measure which weighs more heavily the larger than the smaller firms. Thus, for example, when an industry consists of two identical firms, the Herfindahl index is .5. When, however, an industry is composed of two firms, one of which occupies 60% of the industry and the other the remaining 40%, the Herfindahl index is .52 $[(.6)^2 + (.4)^2 = (.36) + (.16) = .52]$. Again, when an industry is composed of five identical firms, the Herfindahl index is .2. When, however, an industry is composed of five firms which occupy, respectively 40%, 30%, 10%, 10%, and 10% of the industry, the Herfindahl index is .28 $[(.4)^2 + (.3)^2 + (.1)^2 + (.1)^2 + (.1)^2 = (.16) + (.09) + (.01) + (.01) + (.01) = .28]$. This index may also be expressed as a four-digit number, *e.g.*, in the instant example, .28 may be stated as 2800. Thus, in general, with industries involving the same number of firms, the Herfindahl index increases as the disproportion among firm sizes increases.

The Lerner Index. While concentration ratios are most widely used to lay a foundation for assessing market power and changes in market power, they are not the only measure of monopoly power. The Lerner index is an alternative measure which rests upon the concept of price elasticity of demand. It measures monopoly by the divergence of price from marginal cost;

$$\frac{\text{price} - \text{marginal cost}}{\text{price}}$$

is a formulary expression of the Lerner index. In the case of pure competition, price is equal to marginal cost, so that the index is zero. The zero index indicates the absence of monopoly power. Although the Lerner index would show the proportion by which a firm's price differed from the competitive price in a case in which a firm's marginal cost was constant, the index provides only an upper limit of the proportional deviation of the firm's price from the competitive price in cases in which marginal cost is rising. Should marginal cost be falling, the Lerner index would understate this deviation. The Lerner index has not come into wide use because of the difficulty of constructing actual demand and marginal cost curves for existing firms. *See* P. ASCH, ECONOMIC THEORY AND THE ANTITRUST DILEMMA 141-42 (1970); William Landes & Richard A. Posner, *Market Power in Antitrust Cases*, 94 HARV. L. REV. 937, 941-43 (1981).

Although the Lerner index depicts fewness and inequality, the resolution of a § 2 monopolization case almost invariably requires a fact-intensive survey of the relationships among firms. Even though, in a given case, the Lerner index is low, if investigation discloses that the firms are colluding on pricing policy and raising artificial barriers to the entry of rivals, a § 2 violation could be found. If, instead, the firms are not colluding nor excluding rivals and enjoy their position as the result of their efficient methods of operation, there would be no basis for a § 2 violation. *See* P. ASCH, ECONOMIC THEORY AND THE ANTITRUST DILEMMA 155-56 (1970); TERRY CALVANI & SIEGFRIED, ECONOMIC ANALYSIS AND ANTITRUST LAW 108-09 (1979).

Measures of the number of firms in an industry and the inequality of size among them, serve only to describe the structure of that industry. Without more, the indices are not dispositive of the issue of monopolizing in a § 2 case. Inferences about actual and predictable behavior may in varying degrees be supported by these structural descriptions. A trier of fact is required to make a determination about whether the defendant's behavior is effectively or workably competitive or essentially monopolistic. To this task concentration ratios and related index criteria are relevant, but not dispositive of the legal issue. *See* Morris A. Adelman, *Comment on the "H" Concentration Measure as a Numbers-Equivalent*, 51 REV. ECON. & STAT. 99 (1969).

An alternative measure of market power is the "q ratio," derived from the macroeconomic work of Nobel Laureate, James Tobin. *See* James Tobin, *A Monetary Approach to General Equilibrium Theory*, 1 J. MONEY, CREDIT & BANKING 15 (1969). Tobin's q ratio, as applied to an individual firm, measures the market value of the firm's assets against the replacement cost of those assets. The significance of this relationship to market power is the thesis that the q ratio should approximate unity if the firm is operating in a competitive market. When this ration is greater than 1, there is an incentive for new firms to purchase assets relevant to that line of production or for existing firms to expand capacity by buying new assets. This incentive arises from the potential return to be derived from these assets, given their lower cost price. However, if entry is restricted, a firm can raise price and earn returns on invested capital above "ordinary" return to such assets.

Another such indicator seeks to determine the exercise of market power from the rate of profit of a firm measured over time. Like the Tobin q, Bain's profit index probes the return on invested capital. *See* Joe S. Bain, *The Profit Rate as a Measure of Monopoly Power*, 55 Q.J. ECON. 293 (1951). The "Bain Index" identifies monopoly power in a firm or industry that persistently earns profits in excess of a "normal" rate of return on invested capital.

All of these measures have been subjected to critical review and found to be limited in their descriptive and predictive power. The Lerner Index is limited by the need to measure marginal cost at some rate of output. Critics have pointed out that determining a firm's actual marginal cost begins with accounting data. Given the difficulty associated with determining marginal cost from such data, average variable cost is often used as an approximation. *See* Chapter 11, pages 509-16, *infra*. Such measurements pose problems of interpretation, as the discussion on pages 403-04, *supra*, shows. Caution is required in evaluating time-series data of prices in the application of the Lerner Index. A disparity between marginal cost and price at two different time periods could be explained either as evidence of market power or as a change in demand. The ultimate function of the Lerner and other indices is to indicate the existence and exercise of market power over some significant period of time. Selecting the time period over which time-series data is relevant poses the difficult task of empirically distinguishing the short-run from the long-run in the productive cycle of a particular firm—a task which is said to have evoked the response from John Maynard Keynes, "In the long-run we are all dead."

Related difficulties have been identified with implementing the Tobin q index. Undertaking to value a firm's assets from its balance sheet figures, immediately requires adjusting for the firm's selection of depreciation and inventory valuation methods, choices made by firm managers on the basis of federal income tax considerations rather than valuation concerns. Further adjustment is required when the firm's balance sheet asset values are shown at historical cost, rather than current market value. Another complexity is introduced when valuing the intangible assets such as goodwill, patents, trade secrets, trademarks, and copyrights. Valuing these assets involves adjustments based on advertising outlays and research and development expenses which may have contributed to the value of a trademark or a patent.

These indices have been applied and have been found to be less than determinative. The overall conclusion that can be drawn from this literature is that there is no formula for the resolution of market power issues. Applications of both the Lerner and Tobin q indices, produce results that require further interpretation. The most valid conclusion to be drawn from this literature is that these indices can be relevant and illuminating, but that their results must be received with caution, given their conceptual infirmities. For example, one application of the Lerner and Tobin q indices determined that the Tobin q values for the 246 industries surveyed ranged from .045 to 8.53. Eric B. Lindenberg & Stephen A. Ross, *Tobin's q Ratio and Industrial Organization*, 54 J. BUS. 1, 18-21 (1981). These authors point out that some of the firms with high q ratios sell products that have valuable trademarks. Other firms in the high q ratio group engaged in specialized production, such as pharmaceutical drugs. They also found that the firms with low q ratios included aluminum, steel, and cement.

Interpreting Bain's Profit Index illustrates the substantial statistical problems raised in the application of these indices. In his 1951 study, Bain found substantiation of his thesis that profits were higher in industries with high concentration ratios and substantial barriers to entry. However, a 1971 reviewer of the same data pointed out that Bain had failed to take account of business cycle fluctuations. When Bain's data base was extended to a longer time period, most of the firms that Bain had identified as high profit receivers suffered a decline in profits in the subsequent period, while many of Bain's low profit firms subsequently enjoyed an improvement in their profits. By thus extending Bain's data to the longer time period, Brozen reduced Bain's profit differential from 4.3 percent between concentrated/high entry barrier industries and unconcentrated/low entry barrier industries, to 1.1 percent. Brozen further reduced the statistical significance of Bain's profit differential by noting that Bain had taken the profit margin of the leading firm in some industries and the profit margin of the entire industry in others as the basis of his comparison. *See* Yale Brozen, *Bain's Concentration and Rates of Return Revisited*, 14 J.L. & ECON. 351 (1971). The vast empirical literature devoted to the analysis of actual markets is summarized in DENNIS W. CARLTON & JEFFREY M. PERLOFF, MODERN INDUSTRIAL ORGANIZATION 331-72 (2d ed. 1994).

In the cases which follow, consider the extent to which economic analysis portrays the context of the market and conduct of the defendant firm. Consider the extent to which the courts rely on any of the above indices.

United States v. Griffith
334 U.S. 100 (1948)

Mr. Justice DOUGLAS delivered the opinion of the Court.

This is a suit brought by the United States in the District Court to prevent and restrain appellees from violating §§ 1 and 2 of the Sherman Act. . . . The District Court, finding there was no violation of the Act in any of the respects charged in the complaint, dismissed the complaint on the merits. The case is here by appeal under § 2 of the Expediting Act. . . .

The appellees are four affiliated corporations and two individuals who are associated with them as stockholders and officers. The corporations operate (or own stock in corporations which operate) moving picture theatres in Oklahoma, Texas, and New Mexico. With minor exceptions, the theatres which each corporation owns do not compete with those of its affiliates but are in separate towns. In April, 1939, when the complaint was filed, the corporate appellees had interests in theatres in 85 towns. In 32 of those towns there were competing theatres.

Prior to the 1938-1939 season these exhibitors used a common agent to negotiate with the distributors for films for the entire circuit. Beginning with the 1938-1939 season one agent negotiated for the circuit represented by two of the corporate appellees, and another agent negotiated for the circuit represented by the other two corporate appellees. A master agreement was usually executed with each distributor covering films to be released by the distributor during an entire season. There were variations among the master agreements. But in the main they provided as follows: (a) They lumped together towns in which the appellees had no competition and towns in which there were competing theatres. (b) They generally licensed the first run exhibition in practically all of the theatres in which appellees had a substantial interest of substantially all of the films to be released by the distributor during the period of a year. (c) They specified the towns for which second runs were licensed for exhibition by appellees, the second-run rental sometimes being included in the first-run rental. (d) The rental specified often was the total minimum required to be paid (in equal weekly or quarterly installments) by the circuit as a whole for use of the films throughout the circuit, the appellees subsequently allocating the rental among the theatres where the films were exhibited. (e) Films could be played out of the order of their release, so that a specified film need not be played in a particular theatre at any specified time.

The complaint charged that certain exclusive privileges which these agreements granted the appellee exhibitors over their competitors unreasonably restrained competition by preventing their competitors from obtaining enough first- or second-run films from the distributors to operate successfully. The exclusive privileges charged as violations were preemption in the selection of films and the receipt of clearances over competing theatres. It also charged that the use of the buying power of the entire circuit in acquiring those exclusive privileges violated the Act.

. . . .

In *United States v. Crescent Amusement Co.*, 323 U.S. 173, a group of affiliated exhibitors, such as we have in the present case, were found to have violated §§ 1 and 2 of the Sherman Act by the pooling of their buying power and the negotiation of master agreements similar to those we have here. A difference between that case and the present one, which the District Court deemed to be vital, was that in the former the buying power was used for the avowed purpose of eliminating competition and of acquiring a monopoly of theatres in the several towns, while no such purpose was found to exist here. To be more specific, the defendants in the former case through the pooling of their buying power increased their leverage over their competitive situations by insisting that they be given monopoly rights in towns where they had competition, else they would give a distributor no business in their closed [*i.e.,* monopoly] towns.

It is, however, not always necessary to find a specific intent to restrain trade or to build a monopoly in order to find that the antitrust laws have been violated. It is sufficient that a restraint of trade or monopoly results as the consequence of a defendant's conduct or business arrangements. . . . To require a greater showing would cripple the Act. As stated in *United States v. Aluminum Co. of America* . . . "no monopolist monopolizes unconscious of what he is doing." Specific intent in the sense in which the common law used the term is necessary only where the acts fall short of the results condemned by the Act. . . . The antitrust laws are as much violated by the prevention of competition as by its destruction. . . . It follows *a fortiori* that the use of monopoly power, however lawfully acquired, to foreclose competition, to gain a competitive advantage, or to destroy a competitor, is unlawful.

A man with a monopoly of theatres in any one town commands the entrance for all films into that area. If he uses that strategic position to acquire exclusive privileges in a city where he has competitors, he is employing his monopoly power as a trade weapon against his competitors. It may be a feeble, ineffective weapon where he has only one closed or monopoly town. But as those towns increase in number throughout a region, his monopoly power in them may be used with crushing effect on competitors in other places. He need not be as crass as the exhibitors in *United States v. Crescent Amusement Co.*, *supra*, in order to make his monopoly power effective in his competitive situations. Though he makes no threat to withhold the business of his closed or monopoly towns unless the distributors give him the exclusive film rights in the towns where he has competitors, the effect is likely to be the same where the two are joined. When the buying power of the entire circuit is used to negotiate films for his competitive as well as his closed towns, he is using monopoly power to expand his empire. And even if we assume that a specific intent to accomplish that result is absent, he is chargeable in legal contemplation with that purpose since the end result is the necessary and direct consequence of what he did. . . .

The consequence of such a use of monopoly power is that films are licensed on a non-competitive basis in what would otherwise be competitive situations. That is the effect whether one exhibitor makes the bargain with the distributor or whether two or more exhibitors lump together their buying power, as appellees did here. It is in either case a misuse of monopoly power under the Sherman Act. If monopoly power can be used to beget monopoly, the Act becomes a feeble instrument indeed. Large scale buying is not, of course, unlawful *per se*. It may yield price or other lawful advantages to the buyer. It may not, however, be used to monopolize or to attempt to monopolize interstate trade or commerce. Nor . . . may it be used to stifle competition by denying competitors less favorably situated access to the market.

Appellees were concededly using their circuit buying power to obtain films. Their closed towns were linked with their competitive towns. No effort of concealment was made as evidenced by the fact that the rental specified was at times the total minimum amount required to be paid by the circuit as a whole. Monopoly rights in the form of certain exclusive privileges were bargained for and obtained. These exclusive privileges, being acquired by the use of monopoly power, were unlawfully acquired. The appellees, having combined with each other and with the distributors to obtain those monopoly rights, formed a conspiracy in violation of §§ 1 and 2 of the Act. . . . On the record as we read it, it cannot be doubted that the monopoly power of appellees had some effect on their competitors and on the growth of the Griffith circuit. Its extent must be determined on a remand of the cause. We remit to the District Court not only that problem but also the fashioning of a decree which will undo as near as may be the wrongs that were done and prevent their recurrence in the future.

Reversed.

COMMENTARY

1. Is *Griffith* a monopoly case? What was the relevant market in which Griffith had a monopoly? Was Griffith's monopoly (in the "closed" towns) a monopoly vis-à-vis movie patrons only? Did Griffith have monopsony buying power vis-à-vis motion picture distributors?

2. Did Griffith have a different kind of "power" than Broadway-Hale had in the *Klor's* case? than Theatre Enterprises had? than Zell (Packard's Baltimore dealer) had?

3. Was Griffith using monopoly revenues from one market to gain an advantage in another market? Does this depend upon whether Griffith had monopoly (or monopsony) power vis-à-vis the film distributors with whom it dealt? Did Griffith have such power?

4. If Griffith paid the distributor a percentage of its net revenues as rent for a film, would not the distributor then be sharing in monopoly revenues generated in the closed towns? Could Griffith then be said to be purchasing favorable terms for its operations in the open towns with monopoly revenues from the closed towns? Would this constitute the use of monopoly power in one market to gain an advantage in a different market? Was the Court thinking in these terms? Was the Court confused?

5. Does *Griffith* mean that specific intent will no longer be required in many cases that previously were treated as attempts to monopolize? Is *Lorain Journal*, under a *Griffith* analysis, really a monopolization case? Explain. Why were *Lorain Journal* and *Otter Tail* decided as attempt cases? *See* pages 482-84, *infra*. If so, did they overrule *Griffith* sub silentio? Explain.

United States v. Grinnell Corp.

384 U.S. 563 (1966)

[Grinnell Corporation manufactures and supplies fire sprinkler systems. It also had acquired at various times 76% of the stock of American District Telegraph Co. (ADT), 89% of the stock of Automatic Fire Alarm Co. of Delaware (AFA) and 100% of the stock of Holmes Electric Protective Co. (Holmes). Pursuant to various agreements among these companies dating back to the early part of the present century, AFA provided central station sprinkler and waterflow alarm and automatic fire alarm service in New York City, Boston and Philadelphia; Automatic Fire Protection Co. provided central station sprinkler supervisory and waterflow alarm service throughout the United States except in New York, Boston and Philadelphia; ADT provided burglar alarm and nightwatch service throughout the United States except for burglar alarm service in a major part of the Middle Atlantic States; Holmes provided burglar alarm services in the Middle Atlantic States area not served by ADT; and Grinnell agreed to furnish and install all sprinkler supervisory and waterflow alarm actuating devices used in systems that AFA and Automatic would install, and otherwise not to engage in the central station protection business. AFA and Automatic received 25% of the revenue produced by the sprinkler supervisory waterflow alarm service which they provided in their respective territories; ADT and Grinnell received 50% and 25%, respectively, of the revenue which resulted from such service. In 1954 Grinnell and ADT renewed an agreement with a Rhode Island company which received the exclusive right to render central station service within Rhode Island at prices no lower than those of ADT and which agreed to use certain equipment supplied by Grinnell and ADT and to share its revenues with those companies. ADT over the years reduced its minimum basic rates to meet competition and renewed contracts at substantially increased rates in cities where it had a monopoly of accredited central station service. ADT threatened retaliation against firms that contemplated inaugurating central station service. And the record indicated that, in contemplating opening a new central station, ADT officials frequently stressed that such action would deter their competitors from opening a new station in that area. In the past ADT and Holmes had between them acquired 30 competitor firms. The District Court found that the affiliated defendants had violated §§ 1 and 2 of the Sherman Act.]

Mr. Justice DOUGLAS delivered the opinion of the Court.

The offense of monopoly under § 2 of the Sherman Act has two elements: (1) the possession of monopoly power in the relevant market and (2) the willful acquisition or maintenance of that power as distinguished from growth or development as a consequence of a superior product, business acumen, or historic accident. . . . In *United States v. du Pont & Co.* . . . we defined monopoly power as "the power to control prices or exclude competition." The existence of such power ordinarily may be inferred from the predominant share of the market. . . . In the present case, 87% of the accredited central station service business leaves no doubt that the congeries of these defendants have monopoly power—power which, as our discussion of the record indicates, they did not hesitate to wield—if that business is the relevant market.

The District Court treated the entire accredited central station service business as a single market and we think it was justified in so doing. Defendants argue that the different central station services offered are so diverse that they cannot under *du Pont* be lumped together to make up the relevant market. For example, burglar alarm services are not interchangeable with fire alarm services. They further urge that *du Pont* requires that protective services other than those of the central station variety be included in the market definition.

. . . .

But there is here a single use, *i.e.*, the protection of property, through a central station that receives signals. It is that service, accredited, that is unique and that competes with all the other forms of property protection. We see no barrier to combining in a single market a number of different products or services where that combination reflects commercial realities. . . .

In § 2 cases under the Sherman Act, as in § 7 cases under the Clayton Act (*Brown Shoe Co. v. United States* . . .) there may be submarkets that are separate economic entities. We do not pursue that question here. First, we deal with services, not with products; and second, we conclude that the accredited central station is a type of service that makes up a relevant market and that domination or control of it makes out a monopoly of a "part" of trade or commerce within the meaning of § 2 of the Sherman Act. The defendants have not made out a case for fragmentizing the types of services into lesser units.

. . . .

We have said enough about the great hold that the defendants have on this market. The percentage is so high as to justify the finding of monopoly. And, as the facts already related indicate, this monopoly was achieved in large part by unlawful and exclusionary practices. The restrictive agreements that pre-empted for each company a segment of the market where it was free of competition of the others were one device. Pricing practices that contained competitors were another. The acquisitions by Grinnell of ADT, AFA, and Holmes were still another. Grinnell long faced a problem of competing with ADT. That was one reason it acquired AFA and Holmes. Prior to settlement of its dispute and controversy with ADT, Grinnell prepared to go into the central station service business. By acquiring ADT in 1953, Grinnell eliminated that alternative. Its control of the three other defendants eliminated any possibility of an outbreak of competition that might have occurred when the

1907 agreements terminated. By those acquisitions it perfected the monopoly power to exclude competitors and fix prices.

. . . .

The judgment below is affirmed. . . .

COMMENTARY

1. Did the Court in *Grinnell* redefine monopolization or merely restate Judge Hand's *Alcoa* definition? Does Justice Douglas in *Grinnell* shift the burden of justifying a monopoly from the defendant to the plaintiff? Explain. Under the *Grinnell* approach, who bears the burden of proof on the question of willful acquisition or maintenance of monopoly power? How did Judge Hand allocate the burden of proof on the issue of whether the monopoly was "thrust upon" the defendant?

2. When Douglas stated that the defendants "have not made out a case for fragmentizing the types of services into lesser units," he was allocating the burden of persuasion on further fragmentizing of the market to the defendants, was he not? Who bore the burden of persuasion on establishing the market as the "entire central station service business?" The plaintiff? Why? Why did not the carrying of that burden necessarily negate the propriety of using component parts of that market as relevant markets for the purposes of deciding the § 2 issue? If it did then the burden on the fragmentizing issue was borne by the plaintiff, was it not? But Douglas was suggesting that the defendants bear that burden. Explain.

3. In selecting as the relevant product market "the entire accredited central station service business," did the district court follow the approach employed in the *du Pont Cellophane* case? Explain.

C. *Berkey Photo*: *Alcoa* Revisited and Monopoly Leveraging

Berkey Photo, Inc. v. Eastman Kodak Co.

603 F.2d 263 (2d Cir. 1979), *cert. denied*, 444 U.S. 1093 (1980)

[The District Court entered judgment for the plaintiff; the defendant appealed, and the plaintiff cross-appealed.]

IRVING R. KAUFMAN, Chief Judge:

This action, one of the largest and most significant private antitrust suits in history, was brought by Berkey Photo, Inc., a far smaller but still prominent participant in the industry. Berkey competes with Kodak in providing photofinishing services—the conversion of exposed film into finished prints, slides, or movies. Until 1978, Berkey sold cameras as well. It does not manufacture film, but it does purchase Kodak film for resale to its customers, and it also buys photofinishing equipment and supplies, including color print paper, from Kodak.

The two firms thus stand in a complex, multifaceted relationship, for Kodak has been Berkey's competitor in some markets and its supplier in others. In this action, Berkey claims that every aspect of the association has been infected by Kodak's monopoly power in the film, color print paper, and camera markets, willfully acquired, maintained, and exercised in violation of § 2 of the Sherman Act. . . . A number of the charges arise from Kodak's 1972 introduction of the 110 photographic system, featuring a "Pocket Instamatic" camera and a new color print film, Kodacolor II. . . .

Despite the generally recognized evils of monopoly power, it is "well settled," . . . that § 2 does not prohibit monopoly simpliciter. . . .

Thus, while proclaiming vigorously that monopoly power is the evil at which § 2 is aimed, courts have declined to take what would have appeared to be the next logical step—declaring monopolies unlawful *per se* unless specifically authorized by law. To understand the reason for this, one must comprehend the fundamental tension—one might almost say the paradox—that is near the heart of § 2. This tension creates much of the confusion surrounding § 2. It makes the cryptic *Alcoa* opinion a litigant's wishing well, into which, it sometimes seems, one may peer and find nearly anything he wishes.

The conundrum was indicated in characteristically striking prose by Judge Hand, who was not able to resolve it. Having stated that Congress "did not condone 'good trusts' and condemn 'bad' ones; it forbade all," *Alcoa, supra,* 148 F.2d at 427, he declared with equal force, "The successful competitor, having been urged to compete, must not be turned upon when he wins," *id.* at 430. Hand, therefore, told us that it would be inherently unfair to condemn success when the Sherman Act itself mandates competition. Such a wooden rule, it was feared, might also deprive the leading firm in an industry of the incentive to exert its best efforts. Further success would yield not rewards but legal castigation. The antitrust laws would thus compel the very sloth they were intended to prevent. We must always be mindful lest the Sherman Act be invoked perversely in favor of those who seek protection against the rigors of competition.

In *Alcoa* the crosscurrents and tugs of § 2 law were reconciled by noting that, although the firm controlled the aluminum ingot market, "it may not have achieved monopoly; monopoly may have been thrust upon it." 148 F.2d at 429. In examining this language, which would condemn a monopolist unless it is "the passive beneficiary of a monopoly," *id.* at 430, we perceive Hand the philosopher. As an operative rule of law, however, the "thrust upon" phrase does not suffice. It has been criticized by scholars . . . and the Supreme Court appears to have abandoned it. . . . *Grinnell* instructs that after possession of monopoly power is found, the second element of the § 2 offense is "the willful acquisition or maintenance of that power as distinguished from growth or development as a consequence of a superior product, business acumen, or historic accident."

. . . Thus the statement in *Alcoa* that even well-behaved monopolies are forbidden by § 2 must be read carefully in context. Its rightful meaning is that, if monopoly power has been acquired or maintained through improper means, the fact that the power has not been used to extract improper benefits provides no succor to the monopolist. . . .

Even if the origin of the monopoly power was innocent, therefore, the *Grinnell* rule recognizes that maintaining or extending market control by the exercise of that power is sufficient to complete a violation of § 2. . . . Thus the rule of *Grinnell* must be read together with the teaching of *Griffith*, that the mere existence of monopoly power "whether lawfully or unlawfully acquired," is in itself violative of § 2, "provided it is coupled with the purpose or intent to exercise that power."

The key to analysis, it must be stressed, is the concept of market power. Although power may be derived from size, . . . the two are not identical. . . . A firm that has lawfully acquired a monopoly position is not barred from taking advantage of scale economies by constructing, for example, a large and efficient factory. These benefits are a consequence of size and not an exercise of power over the market. . . .

. . . .

C. Monopoly Power as a Lever in Other Markets

It is clear that a firm may not employ its market position as a lever to create—or attempt to create a monopoly in another market. . . . Kodak, in the period relevant to this suit, was never close to gaining control of the markets for photofinishing equipment or services and could not be held to have attempted to monopolize them. Berkey nevertheless contends that Kodak illicitly gained an advantage in these areas by leveraging its power over film and cameras. Accordingly, we must determine whether a firm violates § 2 by using its monopoly power in one market to gain a competitive advantage in another, albeit without an attempt to monopolize the second market. We hold, as did the lower court, that it does. . . . It is the use of economic power that creates the liability. But, as we have indicated, a large firm does not violate § 2 simply by reaping the competitive rewards attributable to its efficient size, nor does an integrated business offend the Sherman Act whenever one of its departments benefits from association with a division possessing a monopoly in its own market. So long as we allow a firm to compete in several fields, we must expect it to seek the competitive advantages of its broad-based activity—more efficient production, greater ability to develop complementary products, reduced transaction costs, and so forth. These are gains that accrue to any integrated firm, regardless of its market share, and they cannot by themselves be considered uses of monopoly power. . . .

. . . .

A. Attempt to Monopolize and Monopolization of the Camera Market

There is little doubt that the evidence supports the jury's implicit finding that Kodak had monopoly power in cameras. The principal issues presented to us regarding the effect of the 110 introduction in the camera market are whether Kodak engaged in anticompetitive conduct and, if so, whether that conduct caused injury to Berkey.

It will be useful at the outset to present the arguments on which Berkey asks us to uphold its verdict:

> (1) Kodak, a film and camera monopolist, was in a position to set industry standards. Rivals could not compete effectively without offering products similar to Kodak's. Moreover, Kodak persistently refused to make film available for most formats other than those in which it made cameras. Since cameras are worthless without film, this policy effectively prevented other manufacturers from introducing cameras in new formats. Because of its dominant position astride two markets, and by use of its film monopoly to distort the camera market, Kodak forfeited its own right to reap profits from such innovations without providing its rivals with sufficient advance information to enable them to enter the market with copies of the new product on the day of Kodak's introduction.

This is one of several "predisclosure" arguments Berkey had advanced in the course of this litigation. . . .

For the reasons explained below, we do not believe any of these contentions is sufficient on the facts of this case to justify an award of damages to Berkey. We therefore reverse this portion of the judgment.

. . . .

As Judge Frankel indicated, and as Berkey concedes, a firm may normally keep its innovations secret from its rivals as long as it wishes, forcing them to catch up on the strength of their own efforts after the new product is introduced. *See, e.g.*, *Kewanee Oil Co. v. Bicron Corp.*, 416 U.S. 470, 481 (1974). It is the possibility of success in the marketplace, attributable to superior performance, that provides the incentives on which the proper functioning of our competitive economy rests. If a firm that has engaged in the risks and expenses of research and development were required in all circumstances to share with its rivals the benefits of those endeavors, this incentive would very likely be vitiated.

Withholding from others advance knowledge of one's new products, therefore, ordinarily constitutes valid competitive conduct. Because as we have already indicated, a monopolist is permitted, and indeed encouraged, by § 2 to compete aggressively on the merits, any success that it may achieve through "the process of invention and innovation" is clearly tolerated by the antitrust laws. . . .

An antitrust plaintiff urging a predisclosure rule, therefore, bears a heavy burden in justifying his request. Berkey recognizes the weight of this burden. It contends that it has been met. Kodak is not a monolithic monopolist, acting in a single market. Rather, its camera monopoly was supported by its activity as a film manufacturer. Berkey therefore argues that by not disclosing the new format in which it was manufacturing film, Kodak unlawfully enhanced its power in the camera market. Indeed, Kodak not only participates in but monopolizes the film industry. The jury could easily have found that, when Kodak introduced a new film format, rival camera makers would be foreclosed from a substantial segment of the market until they were able to manufacture cameras in the new format. Accordingly, Berkey contended that Kodak illegitimately used its monopoly power in film to gain a competitive advantage in cameras. Thus Berkey insists that the jury was properly permitted to consider whether, on balance, the failure to predisclose the new format was exclusionary. We disagree. . . .

Clearly . . . the policy considerations militating against predisclosure requirements for monolithic monopolists are equally applicable here. The first firm, even a monopolist, to design a new camera format has a right to the lead time that follows from its success. The mere fact that Kodak manufactured film in the new format as well, so that its customers would not be offered worthless cameras, could not deprive it of that reward. Nor is this conclusion altered because Kodak not only participated in but dominated the film market. Kodak's ability to pioneer formats does not depend on its possessing a film monopoly. Had the firm possessed a much smaller share of the film market, it would nevertheless have been able to manufacture sufficient quantities of 110-size film—either Kodacolor X or Kodacolor II—to bring the new camera to market. It is apparent, therefore, that the ability to introduce the new format without predisclosure was solely a benefit of integration and not, without more, a use of Kodak's power in the film market to gain a competitive advantage in cameras. . . .

IV. FILM AND COLOR PAPER CLAIMS

. . . .

It is clear that Kodak possessed a monopoly in the film and color paper markets during the period relevant to this suit. Berkey contends that this power, which enabled Kodak to overcharge its customers, was acquired and maintained, at least in part, by anticompetitive conduct.

. . . .

Excessive prices, maintained through exercise of a monopolist's control of the market, constituted one of the primary evils that the Sherman Act was intended to correct. . . . Where a monopolist has acquired or maintained its power by anticompetitive conduct, therefore, a direct purchaser may recover the overcharge caused by the violation of § 2. . . .

But unless the monopoly has bolstered its power by wrongful actions, it will not be required to pay damages merely because its prices may later be found excessive. Setting a high price may be a use of monopoly power, but it is not in itself anticompetitive. Indeed, although a monopolist may be expected to charge a somewhat higher price than would prevail in a competitive market, there is probably no better way for it to guarantee that its dominance will be challenged than by greedily extracting the highest price it can. . . . If a firm has taken no action to destroy competition, it may be unfair to deprive it of the ordinary opportunity to set prices at a profit-maximizing level. Thus, no court has required a lawful monopolist to forfeit to a purchaser three times the increment of its price over that which would prevail in a competitive market. . . . Indeed, as one commentator who might favor such a rule concedes, such judicial oversight of pricing policies would place the courts in a role akin to that of a public regulatory commission. . . . We would be wise to decline that function unless Congress clearly bestows it upon us.

For a purchaser to recover damages under § 2, therefore, it must demonstrate that the monopolist has engaged in some anticompetitive conduct. Two further questions must be resolved, however, to give shape to the purchaser's treble damage suit:

1. If an overcharge paid during the limitations period was caused by the defendant's monopoly power, may a plaintiff satisfy the conduct element of the § 2 offense by proving anticompetitive actions that occurred more than four years prior to the commencement of suit?
2. If a defendant has violated § 2, may a purchaser recover the excess of its price over a competitive price, or merely the increment attributable to its anticompetitive conduct?

. . . .

We hold . . . that a purchaser suing a monopolist for overcharges paid within the previous four years may satisfy the conduct prerequisite to recovery by pointing to anticompetitive actions taken before the limitations period. . . . [But a] trial court in its discretion may always "set a reasonable cutoff date, evidence before which point is considered too remote to have sufficient probative value to justify burdening a record with it." . . .

Assuming that a purchaser establishes a monopolist's liability for an unlawful price, two potential rules of damages come into view. Judge Frankel apparently stated, and in any event the jury clearly acted upon, what may be called the competitive price theory—that a purchaser may recover for the entire excess of the monopolist's price over that which would prevail in a competitive market. We believe that this was error, and that the true measure of damages, which we shall refer to as the wrongful conduct rule, is the price increment caused by the anticompetitive conduct that originated or augmented the monopolist's control over the market.

. . . .

The two issues we have discussed above established the framework for a purchaser's action under § 2 of the Sherman Act. We believe this structure is not only compelled by law but sensible as well. The wrongful conduct rule indicates that a purchaser can recover for an overcharge paid to a violator of § 2 only to the extent that the price he paid exceeds that which would have been charged in the absence of anticompetitive action. An intermediate step in the analysis may be an attempt to estimate what the monopolist's market share would likely have been but for the illegitimate conduct; it would then be possible to gauge approximately what price the defendant would have been able to charge with that degree of market control. In any event, courts applying this rule must be aware of the practical limits of the burden of proof that may be demanded of treble damage plaintiffs. . . .

[The judgment of the District Court was reversed in part.]

COMMENTARY

1. Was Berkey alleging in part, that Kodak was using its capability of innovation in film as a strategic move to injure it? Can innovation be used as a tool of predation? This is suggested by Janusz Ordover & Robert Willig, *An Economic Definition of Predation: Pricing and Product Innovation,* 91 YALE L.J. 8 (1981). These economists suggest that by innovation a firm may forego short-run profits in order to impose costs on market rivals. John Sidak rejects this assertion as an untenable theory based on principles unsuited for courts to administer, in his *Debunking Predatory Innovation*, 83 COLUM. L. REV. 1121 (1983). If General Motors changes the look of its cars each year are they imposing costs on their rivals or are they competing by differentiating their products?

2. *Berkey* clarifies the passage in *Grinnell* condemning the "willful acquisition or maintenance of that [monopoly] power as distinguished from growth or development as a consequence of a superior product, business acumen, or historic accident." Under *Berkey*, in order to violate the monopolization clause, a firm would have to "use" its monopoly power to disadvantage its rivals. Such use of its power appears to require conduct which is objectively anticompetitive. *See, e.g., Olympia Equip. Leasing Co. v. Western Union Tel. Co.*, 797 F.2d 370, 379 (7th Cir. 1986). ("[It] has become an antitrust commonplace, that if conduct is not objectively anticompetitive the fact that it was motivated by hostility to competitors . . . is irrelevant."). Would a motion picture exhibitor like Griffith be "using" monopoly power when it used its control over access to cities in which it possessed the only theaters to bargain with its distributor for "unreasonable" clearance rights over its rivals in cities where competitive theaters existed? *See Syufy Enterprises v. American Multicinema, Inc.*, 793 F.2d 990, 997 (9th Cir. 1986).

3. To what extent does *Alcoa* remain a viable precedent after *Berkey*? Do you agree that *Grinnell* is inconsistent with *Alcoa*? Is the "thrust upon" exception formulated by Judge Hand in *Alcoa* equatable with an absence of a "purpose or intent to exercise that [monopoly] power" referred to in *Grinnell*? Explain. Does *Grinnell* allocate the burden of proof differently than *Alcoa*? How is the burden allocated in *Berkey*?

4. How do you think Judge Hand would have formulated a measure of damages for monopoly pricing? Would he have accepted the "wrongful conduct rule"? Why or why not?

5. Did the Second Circuit employ the *Griffith* formulation of monopolization? Do you agree with the court that Kodak did not use its film monopoly to gain an advantage in the camera market? Explain. Kodak's policy of refusing to make film for most formats other than those in which it made cameras did not prevent other manufacturers from developing new types of cameras which used existing film formats, did it?

6. Kodak's policy of refusing to make film for most formats other than those in which it made cameras effectively prevented rival camera manufacturers from developing new cameras which required special film formats, did it not? Did that policy therefore not guarantee that Kodak would be the first firm to introduce a product like the 110 Pocket Instamatic camera? What is the likelihood of a camera manufacturer which does not also produce film developing a new camera requiring special film? Explain.

7. Because Kodak was both a producer of film and a manufacturer of cameras, Kodak was able to employ technology which it had developed through its film operations to its advantage in the camera market. Was the resulting advantage which Kodak acquired in the camera market analytically comparable to the advantage which the Southern New England Telephone Company (SNET) had in the telephone equipment market by virtue of its being a diversified seller? *See Northeastern Telephone Co. v. American Telephone & Telegraph Co.*, 651 F.2d 76 (2d Cir. 1981), Note 11, below, and page 529, *infra*. In the latter case, the plaintiff complained that SNET was able to sell equipment at marginal cost because its fixed costs were covered by its other operations. How do the advantages of diversification differ in the two cases?

8. If the court had viewed Kodak as having employed its film monopoly to gain an advantage in the camera market, might the court have imposed a "predisclosure" obligation upon Kodak? Such an obligation would have been met only if Kodak had notified rival camera manufacturers of its plans to market the 110 camera sufficiently in advance to enable them to introduce competing products at the same time, would it not? Since any such predisclosure obligation created after the fact by the court would not have been complied with, what liability would Kodak have incurred in having failed to fulfill such an obligation? How would Berkey's damages from Kodak's failure to predisclose have been calculated?

9. If such a predisclosure obligation had been imposed, would it have effectively offset the advantage Kodak would have been deemed to have obtained from its film monopoly? Explain. Would such predisclosure have divested Kodak of a significant amount of the returns it expected from the development of the 110 camera? Would such an imposition of a predisclosure obligation upon Kodak constitute a precedent deterring research and development of new products? To what extent was the court influenced against imposing a predisclosure obligation on Kodak by its concern to maintain incentives for new product development? Does the treble-damage liability imposed upon antitrust violators magnify the adverse impact which a predisclosure precedent would have upon new product development?

10. Might Berkey have decided to bring its action because Kodak had previously entered into a consent decree in the government's § 2 case alleging monopolization of the color film processing market? In that consent decree, Kodak agreed to unbundle processing services from the price of film and agreed to license its patents and know-how on processing at reasonable royalties. *See United States v. Eastman Kodak Co.*, CCH 1954 Trade Cases ¶67,920; CCH 1961 Trade Cases ¶70,100.

11. In *Northeastern Telephone Co. v. American Telephone & Telegraph Co.*, 651 F.2d 76 (2d Cir. 1981), an independent supplier of telephone equipment challenged, *inter alia,* a two-tier pricing system employed by Southern New England Telephone Company (SNET), an AT&T affiliate. Under the two tier system, customers would agree to pay for capital equipment costs (Tier A) in equal monthly installments over a fixed period of time; and would pay SNET's operating costs (Tier B) for as long as they used the equipment. Should any customers decide to end the agreement before the due date, they would be required to pay a termination charge equal to the discounted present value of their remaining Tier A payments, but would receive a "termination credit" if SNET could use the equipment in providing service to other customers. The plaintiff contended that the pricing system was an "economic lock-in" because "once a SNET customer began making Tier A payments, he would not switch to a competitor's product, since to do so he would not only incur a termination charge but would also duplicate the capital charges he had already paid to SNET." Although SNET's two-tier pricing system was similar to payment plans offered by many independent suppliers of telephone equipment (including the plaintiff), the plaintiff argued that SNET should be precluded from the use of such a pricing system because of its dominant position in the market and its possession of monopoly power. The court of appeals reversed a lower court ruling for the plaintiff: "Just as a SNET customer is unlikely to purchase Northeastern's product, the latter is unlikely to switch to SNET's terminal equipment. Thus, SNET's use of the two-tier plan is no more anticompetitive than Northeastern's practice of selling PBXs. Neither one is an action that is 'possible or effective only if taken by a firm that dominates its smaller rivals.' [citing *Berkey*]. . . . On the contrary, both are 'ordinary marketing methods available to all in the market.' *Telex Corp. v. International Bus. Mach. Corp.*, 510 F.2d 894, 926 (10th Cir.), *cert. dismissed*, 123 U.S. 802 (1975). . . ."

12. Does the decision in *Northeastern Telephone Co.* that SNET could lawfully employ its two-tier pricing system (despite its obvious effect of discouraging customers from switching to rival equipment suppliers) follow from the *Berkey* case? Was SNET "using" its monopoly power when it employed its two-tier pricing system? Under *Berkey* and *Telex*, is a monopolist always permitted to employ the same marketing methods as its smaller rivals?

13. When the plaintiff asserted that the two-tier pricing system was an "economic lock-in," was the plaintiff asserting that the two-tier pricing system produced anticompetitive consequences? Were these consequences the foreclosure of SNET's present customers from buying equipment from the plaintiff? Did the two-tier pricing system employed by SNET produce foreclosure effects similar to requirements contracts? Explain. Under the rationale of *Northeastern Telephone Co.*, would it be permissible for a dominant firm to employ a distribution system making extensive use of requirements contracts whenever it would be lawful for smaller firms to do so? Would it be precluded from doing so by § 3 of the Clayton Act? Does *Northeastern Tel. Co.* implicitly suggest a revision of the substantial share test employed in *Standard Oil Co. of California* and *Tampa*? Is the analogy to requirements contracts an inappropriate one? Why?

MONOPOLY LEVERAGING IN THE NINTH CIRCUIT: THE *ALASKA AIRLINES* CASE

Alaska Airlines, Inc. v. United Airlines, Inc., 948 F.2d 536 (9th Cir. 1991). In this case rival airlines brought suit against United Airlines and American Airlines, claiming a violation of the monopolization clause based upon the way that United and American operated their respective computerized reservation systems ("CRS") named, respectively, Apollo and SABRE. The underlying facts as well as the plaintiffs antitrust claims were described by the court as follows:

> [The Court of Appeals affirmed the grant of partial summary judgment against plaintiffs, Alaska Airlines, Muse Air, Midway, and Northwest Airlines.]
>
> The CRS works as follows. The airlines pass flight information to the CRSs, and the CRSs then provide this information to their subscribers, the travel agents. The travel agents in turn use the information to serve consumers, who naturally desire the lowest airfares and the most convenient flights. The CRSs charge travel agents only a nominal fee, or no fee, for the CRSs' services. In contrast, the CRSs charge airlines a substantial amount for such services, in the form of a per booking fee. For example, since the Civil Aeronautics Board ("the Board") ruled in 1984 that each CRS owner must charge its airline customers a uniform rate, American has charged a uniform fee of $1.75 for each booking made through SABRE.

> The CRS market's triangular structure makes the market unusually resistant to normal disciplinary mechanisms. A CRS's market share (the proportion of flights that are booked through a given CRS) might ordinarily be thought to depend on both how many travel agents and how many airlines subscribe to the CRS. However, because each and every airline subscribes to each and every viable CRS, the market share of a given CRS depends solely on the number of travel agents who subscribe to that CRS. Airlines generally subscribe to every CRS because the CRSs charge the airline per booking. The $1.75 fee to secure a booking is of little consequence because a $300 or $400 fare may otherwise be lost. This is not to say that a CRS can charge its airline subscribers any fee that it desires, no matter how high. Basic economic theory tells us that an airline will withdraw from the CRS if the cost of using it causes the marginal cost of providing a flight booked on the CRS to exceed the marginal revenue gained by the booking. . . . However, since CRS fees are a relatively small part of the total costs incurred by a "booked" airline when it provides air transportation to a paying passenger, the CRSs have leeway to charge substantial booking fees.
>
> The plaintiffs, each previous subscribers to Apollo and SABRE, were unhappy about the ability of their largest competitors to extract substantial booking fees from them. Accordingly, plaintiffs brought suit under the Sherman Act. Plaintiffs argued that United and American had individually violated Section 2 of the Sherman Act by, among other things: (1) denying plaintiffs reasonable access to their CRS services, which were alleged to be "essential facilities;" and (2) "leveraging" their dominance in the CRS market to gain a competitive advantage in the downstream air transportation market. The district court granted summary judgment in favor of defendants on both claims. Plaintiffs have appealed.

When the Ninth Circuit considered the "monopoly leveraging" part of the plaintiffs' claim, it explicitly rejected the Second Circuit's *Berkey* analysis:

> The origin of the notion that a single firm may be liable for "monopoly leveraging," even in the absence of a threat that the "leveraged" market will be monopolized, is *Berkey Photo, Inc. v. Eastman Kodak Co.*, 603 F.2d 263 (2d Cir.1979), *cert. denied*, 444 U.S. 1093 (1980). In *Berkey Photo*, Kodak possessed a monopoly in the film and camera markets. Berkey Photo argued that Kodak had "leveraged" its dominant position in these areas to gain a "competitive advantage" in the photofinishing equipment and services markets. Berkey Photo conceded that there was no dangerous probability that Kodak could monopolize either of these markets. *Id.* at 275.

The *Berkey Photo* court announced and applied the rule that "a firm violates § 2 by using its monopoly power in one market to gain a competitive advantage in another, albeit without an attempt to monopolize the second market." *Id.* In contrast to the traditional actions for monopoly and attempted monopoly, *Berkey Photo's* "monopoly leveraging" doctrine has only two rather loose elements: 1) there must be monopoly power in some market, and 2) such power must be "exercise[d] . . . to the detriment of competition" in another market. The *Berkey Photo* court slighted the functions performed by the elements of the traditional Section 2 offenses, stating: "There is no reason to allow the exercise of [monopoly] power to the detriment of competition, in either the controlled market or any other. That the competition in the leveraged market may not be destroyed but merely distorted does not make it more palatable." *Id.* at 275.

We now reject *Berkey*'s monopoly leveraging doctrine as an independent theory of liability under Section 2. Even in the two-market situation, a plaintiff cannot establish a violation of Section 2 without proving that the defendant used its monopoly power in one market to obtain, or attempt to attain, a monopoly in the downstream, or leveraged, market. We believe that *Berkey Photo* misapplied the elements of Section 2 by concluding that a firm violates Section 2 merely by obtaining a competitive advantage in the second market, even in the absence of an attempt to monopolize the leveraged market.[17]

As traditionally interpreted, the Sherman Act punishes any individual or entity that uses "predatory" means to attain a monopoly, or to perpetuate a monopoly after the competitive superiority that originally gave rise to the monopoly has faded. *See Aspen Skiing Co.*, 472 U.S. at 602, 610-11 (upholding liability of a monopolist that had used predatory conduct to attain or preserve monopoly power); *Grinnell Corp.*, 384 U.S. at 570-71. A monopoly attained or perpetuated by such means unnecessarily raises the cost of the relevant product or service, with the ultimate victim being the consumer. *See United States v. Syufy Enterprises*, 903 F.2d 659, 663 (9th Cir.1990); *United States v. Aluminum Co. of Am.*, 148 F.2d 416, 427 (2d Cir.1945).

---

[17] Plaintiffs also rely on two other cases, neither of which need be addressed at length. First, although *United States v. Griffith*, 334 U.S. 100 (1948), does contain some broad language, it is not controlling since it is a Section 1 case involving concerted action. *See Copperweld*, 467 U.S. at 774-77 (noting the difference between Section 1's focus on concerted activity and Section 2's focus on unilateral activity). Plaintiffs also cite *Kerasotes Mich. Theatres, Inc. v. National Amusements, Inc.*, 854 F.2d 135 (6th Cir.1988), *cert. dismissed sub nom., G.K.C. Mich. Theatres, Inc. v. National Amusements, Inc.*, 490 U.S. 1087 (1989). In *Kerasotes*, the Sixth Circuit held that the use of monopoly power in one market to gain a competitive advantage in a second market is forbidden, even when there is no danger of monopolization in the second market. *Id.* at 137-38. *Kerasotes* is in error for the same reasons that *Berkey Photo* is in error.

COMMENTARY

1. The doctrine which the Ninth Circuit calls "monopoly leveraging" was taken by the Second Circuit in *Berkey* from the Supreme Court's decision in *Griffith*, was it not? The Ninth Circuit cannot be rejecting the Supreme Court's *Griffith* decision as a precedent, can it? Although the Ninth Circuit does refer to the *Griffith* decision in its opinion, it could have done a much better job in explaining how its decision could reject the *Berkey* approach and still remain faithful to *Griffith* as a binding precedent.

2. The Ninth Circuit's opinion suggests that monopoly leveraging should not be considered any more unlawful than monopoly pricing. Do you agree? Are there reasons for not treating monopoly pricing as an offense which do not apply to monopoly leveraging? What views have been expressed on the Supreme Court about leveraging in a tying context? See Chapter 6, *supra*.

3. How does the Ninth Circuit read *Griffith*'s prohibition against a monopolist using its monopoly to gain a competitive advantage over a rival? The opinion suggests that when the advantage is so great as to afford a firm the opportunity of acquiring a second monopoly, a violation occurs. Would a firm which held a monopoly in one market, thereby enabling it to earn revenues from that market alone which covered all of its fixed costs, and which then charged marginal-cost prices in a second market be in violation of § 2? Not even the Second Circuit thinks so. *See Northeastern Tel. Co. v. American Tel. & Tel. Co.*, 651 F.2d 76 (2d Cir. 1981), *cert. denied*, 455 U.S. 943 (1982).

4. Is the Ninth Circuit saying that in order to violate § 2 a firm must act in a predatory way?

D. New Directions in Monopolization: The "Business Justification" Requirement and Other Matters

1. In General

Aspen Skiing Co. v. Aspen Highlands Skiing Corp.

472 U.S. 585 (1985)

Justice STEVENS delivered the opinion of the Court.

In a private treble-damages action, the jury found that petitioner Aspen Skiing Company (Ski Co.) had monopolized the market for downhill skiing services in Aspen, Colorado. The question presented is whether that finding is erroneous as a matter of law because it rests on an assumption that a firm with monopoly power has a duty to cooperate with its smaller rivals in a marketing arrangement in order to avoid violating § 2 of the Sherman Act.

I

Aspen is a destination ski resort with a reputation for "super powder," "a wide range of runs," and an "active night life," including "some of the best restaurants in North America." . . . Between 1945 and 1960, private investors independently developed three major facilities for downhill skiing: Aspen Mountain (Ajax), Aspen Highlands (Highlands), and Buttermilk. A fourth mountain, Snowmass, opened in 1967.

The development of any major additional facilities is hindered by practical considerations and regulatory obstacles. The identification of appropriate topographical conditions for a new site and substantial financing are both essential. Most of the terrain in the vicinity of Aspen that is suitable for downhill skiing cannot be used for that purpose without the approval of the United States Forest Service. That approval is contingent, in part, on environmental concerns. Moreover, the county government must also approve the project, and in recent years it has followed a policy of limiting growth.

Between 1958 and 1964, three independent companies operated Ajax, Highlands, and Buttermilk. In the early years, each company offered its own day or half-day tickets for use of its mountain. . . . In 1962, however, the three competitors also introduced an interchangeable ticket. . . . The 6-day, all-Aspen ticket provided convenience to the vast majority of skiers who visited the resort for weekly periods, but preferred to remain flexible about what mountain they might ski each day during the visit. . . . It also emphasized the unusual variety in ski mountains available in Aspen.

As initially designed, the all-Aspen ticket program consisted of booklets containing six coupons, each redeemable for a daily lift ticket at Ajax, Highlands, or Buttermilk. The price of the booklet was often discounted from the price of six daily tickets, but all six coupons had to be used within a limited period of time—seven days, for example. The revenues from the sale of the 3-area coupon books were distributed in accordance with the number of coupons collected at each mountain. . . .

In 1964, Buttermilk was purchased by Ski Co., but the interchangeable ticket program continued. In most seasons after it acquired Buttermilk, Ski Co. offered 2-area, 6- or 7-day tickets featuring Ajax and Buttermilk in competition with the 3-area, 6-coupon booklet. Although it sold briskly, the all-Aspen ticket did not sell as well as Ski Co.'s multiarea ticket until Ski Co. opened Snowmass in 1967. Thereafter, the all-Aspen coupon booklet began to outsell Ski Co.'s ticket featuring only its mountains. . . .

[The four-area pass was discontinued for the 1972-73 season, but reappeared the following year.] In the next four seasons, Ski Co. and Highlands used . . . surveys to allocate the revenues from the 4-area, 6-day ticket. Highlands' share of the revenues from the ticket was 17.5% in 1973-1974, 18.5% in 1974-1975, 16.8% in 1975-1976, and 13.2% in 1976-1977. During these four seasons, Ski Co. did not offer its own 3-area, multi-day ticket in competition with the all-Aspen ticket. By 1977, multiarea tickets accounted for nearly 35% of the total market. . . . Holders of multiarea passes also accounted for additional daily ticket sales to persons skiing with them.

Between 1962 and 1977, Ski Co. and Highlands had independently offered various mixes of 1-day, 3-day, and 6-day passes at their own mountains. In every season except one, however, they had also offered some form of all-Aspen, 6-day ticket, and divided the revenues from those sales on the basis of usage. Nevertheless, for the 1977-1978 season, Ski Co. offered to continue the all-Aspen ticket only if Highlands would accept a 13.2% fixed share of the ticket's revenues.

Although that had been Highlands' share of the ticket revenues in 1976-1977, Highlands contended that season was an inaccurate measure of its market performance since it had been marked by unfavorable weather and an unusually low number of visiting skiers. Moreover, Highlands wanted to continue to divide revenues on the basis of actual usage, as that method of distribution allowed it to compete for the daily loyalties of the skiers who had purchased the tickets. . . . Fearing that the alternative might be no interchangeable ticket at all, and hoping to persuade Ski Co. to reinstate the usage division of revenues, Highlands eventually accepted a fixed percentage of 15% for the 1977-1978 season. . . . No survey was made during that season of actual usage of the 4-area ticket at the two competitors' mountains. . . .

In March 1978, the Ski Co. management recommended to the board of directors that the 4-area ticket be discontinued for the 1978-1979 season. The board decided to offer Highlands a 4-area ticket provided that Highlands would agree to receive a 12.5% fixed percentage of the revenue—considerably below Highlands' historical average based on usage. . . . Later in the 1978-1979 season, a member of Ski Co.'s board of directors candidly informed a Highlands official that he had advocated making Highlands "an offer that [it] could not accept." . . .

Finding the proposal unacceptable, Highlands suggested a distribution of the revenues based on usage to be monitored by coupons, electronic counting, or random sample surveys. . . . If Ski Co. was concerned about who was to conduct the survey, Highlands proposed to hire disinterested ticket counters at its own expense—"somebody like Price Waterhouse"—to count or survey usage of the 4-area ticket at Highlands. . . . Ski Co. refused to consider any counterproposals, and Highlands finally rejected the offer of the fixed percentage.

As far as Ski Co. was concerned, the all-Aspen ticket was dead. In its place Ski Co. offered the 3-area, 6-day ticket featuring only its mountains. In an effort to promote this ticket, Ski Co. embarked on a national advertising campaign that strongly implied to people who were unfamiliar with Aspen that Ajax, Buttermilk, and Snowmass were the only ski mountains in the area. For example, Ski Co. had a sign changed in the Aspen Airways waiting room at Stapleton Airport in Denver. The old sign had a picture of the four mountains in Aspen touting "Four Big Mountains" whereas the new sign retained the picture but referred only to three. . . .

Ski Co. took additional actions that made it extremely difficult for Highlands to market its own multiarea package to replace the joint offering. Ski Co. discontinued the 3-day, 3-area pass for the 1978-1979 season,[13] and also refused to sell Highlands any lift tickets, either at the tour operator's discount or at retail. . . . Highlands finally developed an alternative product, the "Adventure Pack," which consisted of a 3-day pass at Highlands and three vouchers, each equal to the price of a daily lift ticket at a Ski Co. mountain. The vouchers were guaranteed by funds on deposit in an Aspen bank, and were redeemed by Aspen merchants at full value. . . . Ski Co., however, refused to accept them.

Later, Highlands redesigned the Adventure Pack to contain American Express Traveler's Checks or money orders instead of vouchers. Ski Co. eventually accepted these nego-

---

[13] Highlands' owner explained that there was a key difference between the 3-day, 3-area ticket and the 6-day, 3-area ticket: "with the three day ticket, a person could ski on the . . . Aspen Skiing Corporation mountains for three days and then there would be three days in which he could ski on our mountain; but with the six-day ticket, we are absolutely locked out of those people." . . . As a result of "tremendous consumer demand" for a 3-day ticket, Ski Co. reinstated it late in the 1978-1979 season, but without publicity or a discount off the daily rate. . . .

tiable instruments in exchange for daily lift tickets.[15] . . . Despite some strengths of the product, the Adventure Pack met considerable resistance from tour operators and consumers who had grown accustomed to the convenience and flexibility provided by the all-Aspen ticket. . . .

Without a convenient all-Aspen ticket, Highlands basically "becomes a day ski area in a destination resort." . . . Highlands' share of the market for downhill skiing services in Aspen declined steadily after the 4-area ticket based on usage was abolished in 1977: from 20.5% in 1976-1977, to 15.7% in 1977-1978, to 13.1% in 1978-1979, to 12.5% in 1979-1980, to 11% in 1980-1981. . . . Highlands' revenues from associated skiing services like the ski school, ski rentals, amateur racing events, and restaurant facilities declined sharply as well.

II

In 1979, Highlands filed a complaint in the United States District Court for the District of Colorado naming Ski Co. as a defendant. Among various claims, the complaint alleged that Ski Co. had monopolized the market for downhill skiing services at Aspen in violation of § 2 of the Sherman Act, and prayed for treble damages. The case was tried to a jury which rendered a verdict finding Ski Co. guilty of the § 2 violation and calculating Highlands' actual damages at $2.5 million. . . .

. . . .

III

In this Court, Ski Co. contends that even a firm with monopoly power has no duty to engage in joint marketing with a competitor, that a violation of § 2 cannot be established without evidence of substantial exclusionary conduct, and that none of its activities can be characterized as exclusionary. It also contends that the Court of Appeals incorrectly relied on the "essential facilities" doctrine and that an "anticompetitive intent" does not transform nonexclusionary conduct into monopolization. In response, Highlands submits that, given the evidence in the record, it is not necessary to rely on the "essential facilities" doctrine in order to affirm the judgment. . . .

"The central message of the Sherman Act is that a business entity must find new customers and higher profits through internal expansion—that is, by competing successfully rather than by arranging treaties with its competitors." *United States v. Citizens & Southern National Bank*, 422 U.S. 86, 116 (1975). Ski Co., therefore, is surely correct in submitting that even a firm with monopoly power has no general duty to engage in a joint marketing program with a competitor. Ski Co. is quite wrong, however, in suggesting that the judgment in this case rests on any such proposition of law. For the trial court unambiguously instructed the jury that a firm possessing monopoly power has no duty to cooperate with its business rivals. . . .

The absence of an unqualified duty to cooperate does not mean that every time a firm declines to participate in a particular cooperative venture, that decision may not have evidentiary significance, or that it may not give rise to liability in certain circumstances. The absence of a duty to transact business with another firm is, in some respects, merely the

---

[15] Of course, there was nothing to identify Highlands as the source of these instruments, unless someone saw the skier "taking it out of an Adventure Pack envelope." . . . For the 1981-1982 season, Ski Co. set its single ticket price at $22 and discounted the 3-area, 6-day ticket to $114. According to Highlands, this price structure made the Adventure Pack unprofitable. . . .

counterpart of the independent businessman's cherished right to select his customers and his associates. The high value that we have placed on the right to refuse to deal with other firms does not mean that the right is unqualified.

. . . .

The qualification on the right of a monopolist to deal with whom he pleases is not so narrow that it encompasses no more than the circumstances of *Lorain Journal*. In the actual case that we must decide, the monopolist did not merely reject a novel offer to participate in a cooperative venture that had been proposed by a competitor. Rather, the monopolist elected to make an important change in a pattern of distribution that had originated in a competitive market and had persisted for several years. The all-Aspen, 6-day ticket with revenues allocated on the basis of usage was first developed when three independent companies operated three different ski mountains in the Aspen area. . . . It continued to provide a desirable option for skiers when the market was enlarged to include four mountains, and when the character of the market was changed by Ski Co.'s acquisition of monopoly power. Moreover, since the record discloses that interchangeable tickets are used in other multimountain areas which apparently are competitive,[30] it seems appropriate to infer that such tickets satisfy consumer demand in free competitive markets.

Ski Co.'s decision to terminate the all-Aspen ticket was thus a decision by a monopolist to make an important change in the character of the market.[31] Such a decision is not necessarily anticompetitive, and Ski Co. contends that neither its decision, nor the conduct in which it engaged to implement that decision, can fairly be characterized as exclusionary in this case. It recognizes, however, that as the case is presented to us, we must interpret the entire record in the light most favorable to Highlands and give to it the benefit of all inferences which the evidence fairly supports, even though contrary inferences might reasonably be drawn. *Continental Ore Co. v. Union Carbide & Carbon Corp.*, 370 U.S. 690, 696 (1962).

. . . .

IV

The question whether Ski Co.'s conduct may properly be characterized as exclusionary cannot be answered by simply considering its effect on Highlands. In addition, it is relevant to consider its impact on consumers and whether it has impaired competition in an

---

30 Ski Co. itself participates in interchangeable ticket programs in at least two other markets. For example, since 1970, Ski Co. has operated the Breckenridge resort in Summit County, Colorado. Breckenridge participates in the "Ski the Summit" 4-area interchangeable coupon booklet which allows the skier to ski at any of the four mountains in the region: Breckenridge, Copper Mountain, Keystone, and Arapahoe Basin. . . . In the 1979-1980 season Keystone and Arapahoe Basin—which are jointly operated—had about 40% of the Summit County market, and the other two ski mountains each had a market share of about 30%. . . . During the relevant period of time, Ski Co. also operated Blackcomb Mountain, northeast of Vancouver, British Columbia, which has an interchangeable ticket arrangement with nearby Whistler Mountain, an independently operated facility. . . . Interchangeable lift tickets apparently are also available in some European skiing areas. . . .

31 "In any business, patterns of distribution develop over time; these may reasonably be thought to be more efficient than alternative patterns of distribution that do not develop. The patterns that do develop and persist we may call the optimal patterns. By disturbing optimal distribution patterns one rival can impose costs upon another, that is, force the other to accept higher costs." [R. Bork, THE ANTITRUST PARADOX 156 (1978).] In § 1 cases where this Court has applied the per se approach to invalidity to concerted refusals to deal, "the boycott often cut off access to a supply, facility or market necessary to enable the boycotted firm to compete, . . . and frequently the boycotting firms possessed a dominant position in the relevant market." *Northwest Wholesale Stationers, Inc. v. Pacific Stationery & Printing Co.* . . .

unnecessarily restrictive way. If a firm has been "attempting to exclude rivals on some basis other than efficiency," it is fair to characterize its behavior as predatory. It is, accordingly, appropriate to examine the effect of the challenged pattern of conduct on consumers, on Ski Co.'s smaller rival, and on Ski Co. itself.

Superior Quality of the All-Aspen Ticket

The average Aspen visitor "is a well-educated, relatively affluent, experienced skier who has skied a number of times in the past. . . ." . . . Over 80% of the skiers visiting the resort each year have been there before—40% of these repeat visitors have skied Aspen at least five times. . . . Over the years, they developed a strong demand for the 6-day, all-Aspen ticket in its various refinements. Most experienced skiers quite logically prefer to purchase their tickets at once for the whole period that they will spend at the resort; they can then spend more time on the slopes and enjoying apres-ski amenities and less time standing in ticket lines. The 4-area attribute of the ticket allowed the skier to purchase his 6-day ticket in advance while reserving the right to decide in his own time and for his own reasons which mountain he would ski on each day. It provided convenience and flexibility, and expanded the vistas and the number of challenging runs available to him during the week's vacation.

While the 3-area, 6-day ticket offered by Ski Co. possessed some of these attributes, the evidence supports a conclusion that consumers were adversely affected by the elimination of the 4-area ticket. In the first place, the actual record of competition between a 3-area ticket and the all-Aspen ticket in the years after 1967 indicated that skiers demonstrably preferred four mountains to three. . . . Highlands' expert marketing witness testified that many of the skiers who come to Aspen want to ski the four mountains, and the abolition of the 4-area pass made it more difficult to satisfy that ambition. . . . A consumer survey undertaken in the 1979-1980 season indicated that 53.7% of the respondents wanted to ski Highlands, but would not; 39.9% said that they would not be skiing at the mountain of their choice because their ticket would not permit it. . . .

Expert testimony and anecdotal evidence supported these statistical measures of consumer preference. A major wholesale tour operator asserted that he would not even consider marketing a 3-area ticket if a 4-area ticket were available. During the 1977-1978 and 1978-1979 seasons, people with Ski Co.'s 3-area ticket came to Highlands "on a very regular basis" and attempted to board the lifts or join the ski school. Highlands officials were left to explain to angry skiers that they could only ski at Highlands or join its ski school by paying for a 1-day lift ticket. Even for the affluent, this was an irritating situation because it left the skier the option of either wasting 1 day of the 6-day, 3-area pass or obtaining a refund which could take all morning and entailed the forfeit of the 6-day discount. An active officer in the Atlanta Ski Club testified that the elimination of the 4-area pass "infuriated" him. . . .

Highlands' Ability to Compete

The adverse impact of Ski Co.'s pattern of conduct on Highlands is not disputed in this Court. Expert testimony described the extent of its pecuniary injury. The evidence concerning its attempt to develop a substitute product either by buying Ski Co.'s daily tickets in bulk, or by marketing its own Adventure Pack, demonstrates that it tried to protect itself from the loss of its share of the patrons of the all-Aspen ticket. The development of a new distribution system for providing the experience that skiers had learned to expect in Aspen proved to be prohibitively expensive. As a result, Highlands' share of the relevant market steadily declined after the 4-area ticket was terminated. The size of the damages award also confirms the substantial character of the effect of Ski Co.'s conduct upon Highlands.[38]

Ski Co.'s Business Justification

Perhaps most significant, however, is the evidence relating to Ski Co. itself, for Ski Co. did not persuade the jury that its conduct was justified by any normal business purpose. Ski Co. was apparently willing to forgo daily ticket sales both to skiers who sought to exchange the coupons contained in Highlands' Adventure Pack, and to those who would have purchased Ski Co. daily lift tickets from Highlands if Highlands had been permitted to purchase them in bulk. The jury may well have concluded that Ski Co. elected to forgo these short-run benefits because it was more interested in reducing competition in the Aspen market over the long run by harming its smaller competitor.

That conclusion is strongly supported by Ski Co.'s failure to offer any efficiency justification whatever for its pattern of conduct.[39] In defending the decision to terminate the jointly offered ticket, Ski Co. claimed that usage could not be properly monitored. The evidence, however, established that Ski Co. itself monitored the use of the 3-area passes based on a count taken by lift operators, and distributed the revenues among its mountains on that basis. Ski Co. contended that coupons were administratively cumbersome, and that the survey takers had been disruptive and their work inaccurate. Coupons, however, were no more burdensome than the credit cards accepted at Ski Co. ticket windows. . . . Moreover, in other markets Ski Co. itself participated in interchangeable lift tickets using coupons, n. 30, *supra*. As for the survey, its own manager testified that the problems were much overemphasized by Ski Co. officials, and were mostly resolved as they arose. . . . Ski Co.'s explanation for the rejection of Highlands' offer to hire—at its own expense—a reputable national accounting firm to audit usage of the 4-area tickets at Highlands' mountain, was that there was no way to "control" the audit. . . .

In the end, Ski Co. was pressed to justify its pattern of conduct on a desire to disassociate itself from what it considered the inferior skiing services offered at Highlands. . . . The all-Aspen ticket based on usage, however, allowed consumers to make their own choice on these matters of quality. Ski Co.'s purported concern for the relative quality of Highlands' product was supported in the record by little more than vague insinuations, and was sharply contested by numerous witnesses. Moreover, Ski Co. admitted that it was willing to associate with what it considered to be inferior products in other markets. . . .

Although Ski Co.'s pattern of conduct may not have been as "bold, relentless, and predatory" as the publisher's actions in *Lorain Journal*, the record in this case comfortably supports an inference that the monopolist made a deliberate effort to discourage its cus-

---

[38] In considering the competitive effect of Ski Co.'s refusal to deal or cooperate with Highlands, it is not irrelevant to note that similar conduct carried out by the concerted action of three independent rivals with a similar share of the market would constitute a per se violation of § 1 of the Sherman Act. *See Northwest Wholesale Stationers, Inc. v. Pacific Stationery & Printing Co., ante*, at 294. Cf. *Lorain Journal Co. v. United States*, 342 U.S. 143, 154 (1951).

[39] "The law can usefully attack this form of predation only when there is evidence of specific intent to drive others from the market by means other than superior efficiency and when the predator has overwhelming market size, perhaps 80 or 90 percent. Proof of specific intent to engage in predation may be in the form of statements made by the officers or agents of the company, evidence that the conduct was used threateningly and did not continue when a rival capitulated, or *evidence that the conduct was not related to any apparent efficiency.* These matters are not so difficult of proof as to render the test overly hard to meet." Bork 157 (emphasis added).

tomers from doing business with its smaller rival. The sale of its 3-area, 6-day ticket, particularly when it was discounted below the daily ticket price, deterred the ticket holders from skiing at Highlands. The refusal to accept the Adventure Pack coupons in exchange for daily tickets was apparently motivated entirely by a decision to avoid providing any benefit to Highlands even though accepting the coupons would have entailed no cost to Ski Co. itself, would have provided it with immediate benefits, and would have satisfied its potential customers. Thus the evidence supports an inference that Ski Co. was not motivated by efficiency concerns and that it was willing to sacrifice short-run benefits and consumer goodwill in exchange for a perceived long-run impact on its smaller rival.

Because we are satisfied that the evidence in the record,[44] construed most favorably in support of Highlands' position, is adequate to support the verdict under the instructions given by the trial court, the judgment of the Court of Appeals is

Affirmed.

COMMENTARY

1. Two economists, Kenneth Elzinga & Thomas F. Hogarty, have proposed using physical shipment data, rather than data on prices, to depict the functional geographic boundaries of a market. Two tests utilizing shipment data flesh out the supply and demand sides of a market as follows. The supply side component is treated under the acronym, LOFI—little out from inside. This is computed as a ratio of the sales of sellers in the putative market area to customers in that area divided by the total sales of these firms to all geographic destinations. The demand side, LIFO—little in from outside, accounts for the demand side by a calculation that takes the sales of firms within the identified producing area to customers within that geographic area, divided by the total purchases these customers make from all sellers without reference to seller location. Suppose State X is a major producer of peaches and the purchases of peaches in State X consist of 98% home grown peaches. Is State X the relevant market for peaches? Suppose also that there is data showing that 25% of the total peach production of all growers in State X is sold in contiguous States, B and C. What is the relevant market for this grade of peaches? See the articles by Kenneth G. Elzinga and Thomas F. Hogarty, *The Problem of Geographic Market Delineation in Antimerger Suits,* 18 ANTITRUST BULL. 45 (1973); *The Problem of Geographic Market Delineation Revisited*, 23 ANTITRUST BULL. 1 (1978).

The Elzinga-Hogarty test is a refinement in the application of the traditional economist's definition of a market, which is:

---

44 Given our conclusion that the evidence amply supports the verdict under the instructions as given by the trial court, we find it unnecessary to consider the possible relevance of the "essential facilities" doctrine, or the somewhat hypothetical question whether nonexclusionary conduct could ever constitute an abuse of monopoly power if motivated by an anticompetitive purpose. If, as we have assumed, no monopolist monopolizes unconscious of what he is doing, that case is unlikely to arise.

> The area in which the price of a commodity tends to uniformity, allowance being made for transportation cost. . . . Since the market is defined by uniformity of price, its area will be at least as large as the larger of the areas of seller' competition and buyers' competition, or the sum of the areas when they partially overlap.

GEORGE J. STIGLER, THE THEORY OF PRICE 85 (1966). Under Stigler's definition, if all the peaches in the United States were produced in State X under the control of one seller—a monopolist, the expectation would be that competition among buyers would result in a uniform f.o.b. price at the seller's distribution point in State X. If, however, the seller is able to discern that there were particular demand characteristics by consumers of peaches in State M, the seller could discriminate among the buyers and charge more to State M buyers.

Consider how these economist's definitions of a market might have been applied in *Aspen.* If Aspen is a "destination ski resort," as the Court says, then it is in competition with other destination ski resorts throughout the Rocky Mountains, as well as with ski resorts in eastern North America and in Europe, is it not? For further discussion of market definition in the merger context, see Chapter 12. Because the case reached the Court in a procedural form in which the relevant market issue was no longer open, the Court was forced to decide the case as if Aspen, Colorado were the relevant market. One town, however, cannot possibly be a plausible relevant geographic market for downhill skiing services provided by destination ski resorts.

2. How does the Court characterize Ski Co.'s pattern of conduct toward Highland? Are "predatory," "anticompetitive," and "exclusionary" used interchangeably by courts in their characterization of the conduct which is a probative of monopolization under § 2? See, however, Chapter 11 for the analysis of predatory pricing, a different antitrust issue.

3. The cases stress scrutiny of a defendant's business practices in a monopolization case to distinguish active, vigorous, if not aggressive, competition from anticompetitive or exclusionary conduct. Does § 2 require a monopolist to cooperate with its rivals? The Court asserted that "even a firm with monopoly power has no general duty to engage in a joint marketing program with a competitor." Yet, in context, Ski Co. was held to have violated § 2 because of its failure to cooperate with its rival in a marketing program. Does the Court in *Aspen* qualify *Colgate* and *Grinnell* by imposing a burden of justification for refusal to deal on a defendant? Recall that the Supreme Court in *United States v. Colgate,* 250 U.S. 300, 307 (1919), stated:

> In the absence of any purpose to create or maintain a monopoly, the act does not restrict the long-recognized right of trader or manufacturer . . . freely to exercise his own independent discretion as to parties with whom he will deal.

How does the Court in *Aspen* qualify *Colgate* and *Grinnell* when the issue is whether the defendant's conduct is designed to maintain monopoly power? In *Oahu Gas Services, Inc. v. Pacific Resources, Inc.*, 838 F.2d 360, 368 (9th Cir. 1988), the defendant, the sole producer of propane gas in Hawaii at the time, refused to expand production to accommodate the entry of a new competitor. In reversing a finding of exclusionary conduct, the court stated:

> Where a monopolist's refusal to aid a competitor is based partly on a desire to restrict competition, we determine antitrust liability by asking whether there was a legitimate business justification for the monopolist's conduct. [citing *Aspen*] . . .
>
> The investment required of . . . [the defendant] to produce propane would have resulted in a negative return. In the light of the then-existing price controls, it was not economically efficient . . . to invest its resources in propane production. . . . The economic rationale, even if not the only rationale for the decision . . . distinguished this conduct from "willful maintenance of monopoly power." [citing *Grinnell*]

4. In *Aspen*, the Court was careful to point out the joint marketing program had originated when three rivals (each with its own mountain) were contending for customers, a market which the Court referred to as a "competitive" one. As the Court put it, "the monopolist elected to make an important change in a pattern of distribution that had originated in a competitive market and had persisted for several years." Is the Court in this case imposing the burden of justification on a defendant to explain changed joint arrangements?

5. Does *Aspen* hold that anticompetitive harm can be inferred in a § 2 case from the refusal of a dominant firm to deal with a rival? In *Rural Telephone Service v. Feist Publications,* 957 F.2d 765 (10th Cir.), *cert. denied,* 506 U.S. 984 (1992), the court held that the refusal of the dominant firm to permit its rival to copy its copyrighted white page listings was not, without more, sufficient to establish an anticompetitive effect. The court distinguished injury to the rival from injury to competition, noting that the rival's market share had increased, the price for telephone book advertising had remained competitive, and that the rival's prices were higher than those of the dominant, refusing firm. In other post-*Aspen* cases, courts have permitted a business justification defense. A monopolization claim based on refusal to deal was rejected on a showing that the refusal was based on grounds of protection of a trademark and of product image in *Trans Sport, Inc. v. Starter Sportswear, Inc.*, 964 F.2d 186 (2d Cir. 1992). In accord is *City of Chanute, Kansas v. Williams Natural Gas Co.*, 955 F.2d 641 (10th Cir. 1992), where refusal to sell gas was justified on grounds of limiting liability. For a further discussion of the business justification defense, see Patrick J. Ahern, *Refusals to Deal After* Aspen, 63 ANTITRUST L.J. 153, 172 (1994).

6. A major unanswered question raised by *Aspen* is on what terms Ski Co. would be required to cooperate in the joint marketing arrangement with Highlands. Ski Co. had offered Highlands a 13.2% share of the revenue from the all-Aspen ticket for the 1977-78 season, which was Highland's share from the preceding season as determined by surveys. Highland held out for a 15% share of the 1977-78 season but rejected an offer of 13.2% for the following season.

If Ski Co. is required to cooperate with Highland in the joint marketing of an all-Aspen ticket, what share of the total revenue is to be allocated to Highland? Just as some proposed revenue allocations were found unacceptable by Highland, so Ski Co. would probably find other proposed revenue allocations unacceptable to it. Is the Court to be the judge of a "reasonable" allocation of revenues from the all-Aspen ticket? Is Ski Co.'s refusal to participate in joint marketing to be lawful or unlawful, depending upon whether or not a court finds a proposed revenue allocation reasonable?

7. In the latter part of its opinion, the Court states that "the evidence supports an inference that Ski Co. was not motivated by efficiency concerns and that it was willing to sacrifice short-run benefits and consumer goodwill in exchange for a perceived long-run impact on its smaller rival." This language suggests that Ski Co. was acting predatorily, *i.e.,* surrendering short-run profits in order to destroy its rival and obtain a monopoly for itself.

In this case the Court based its opinion on a characterization of the facts in the record that may not have accurately reflected the business decision of the defendant. Might the Court not have inferred from the record that Ski Co. had concluded that it would earn greater profits from a three-mountain pass whose revenues did not have to be shared than it would earn from a four-mountain pass whose revenues would have to be shared? In such a case, Ski Co. would be maximizing its short-run profits by declining to participate in marketing a four-mountain pass.

The surveys indicated that Highland's share of the all-Aspen ticket was 13.2% during the 1976-77 season and declining. Yet Ski Co. agreed to allocate 15% of the revenues from that ticket during the 1977-78 season to Highland. Ski Co. would lose revenue on an all-Aspen ticket which was used only 13.2% of the time on Highland mountain and yet for which Highland received 15% of the revenue, would it not? In such circumstances, Ski Co. would maximize its short-run profits by withdrawing from the joint marketing arrangement.

The legal rules embodied in the decision are binding, of course, whether or not the Court had mischaracterized the facts. Instances of mischaracterizing facts or evidence—if they occur and are identified—merely erode public confidence in the judicial system as a source of antitrust law. For further discussion of predatory pricing, see Chapter 11. Consider whether the case which follows deals with a dominant seller refusing to deal with competitors.

Eastman Kodak Co. v. Image Technical Services, Inc.

504 U.S. 451 (1992)

Justice BLACKMUN delivered the opinion of the Court.

[The facts are set out in the edited version of this case appearing in Chapter 6, page 256.]

. . . .

III

Respondents also claim that they have presented genuine issues for trial as to whether Kodak has monopolized or attempted to monopolize the service and parts markets in violation of § 2 of the Sherman Act. "The offense of monopoly under § 2 of the Sherman Act has two elements: (1) the possession of monopoly power in the relevant market and (2) the willful acquisition or maintenance of that power as distinguished from growth or development as a consequence of a superior product, business acumen, or historic accident." *United States v. Grinnell Corp.*, 384 U.S. at 570-571.

A

The existence of the first element, possession of monopoly power, is easily resolved. As has been noted, respondents have presented a triable claim that service and parts are separate markets, and that Kodak has the "power to control prices or exclude competition" in service and parts. *du Pont,* 351 U.S. at 391. Monopoly power under § 2 requires, of course, something greater than market power under § 1. . . . Respondents' evidence that Kodak controls nearly 100% of the parts market and 80% to 95% of the service market, with no readily available substitutes, is, however, sufficient to survive summary judgment under the more stringent monopoly standard of § 2. . . .

Kodak also contends that, as a matter of law, a single brand of a product or service can never be a relevant market under the Sherman Act. We disagree. The relevant market for antitrust purposes is determined by the choices available to Kodak equipment owners. . . . Because service and parts for Kodak equipment are not interchangeable with other manufacturers' service and parts, the relevant market from the Kodak-equipment owner's perspective is composed of only those companies that service Kodak machines. . . . This Court's prior cases support the proposition that in some instances one brand of a product can constitute a separate market. . . . The proper market definition in this case can be determined only after a factual inquiry into the "commercial realities" faced by consumers. . . .

B

The second element of a § 2 claim is the use of monopoly power "to foreclose competition, to gain a competitive advantage, or to destroy a competitor." *United States v. Griffith*, 334 U.S. 100, 107 (1948). If Kodak adopted its parts and service policies as part of a scheme of willful acquisition or maintenance of monopoly power, it will have violated § 2. *Grinnell Corp.*, 384 U.S. at 570-571; *United States v. Aluminum Co. of America*, 148 F.2d 416, 432 (2nd Cir. 1945); *Aspen Skiing Co. v. Aspen Highlands Skiing Corp.*, 472 U.S. 585, 600-605 (1985).[32]

---

[32] It is true that as a general matter a firm can refuse to deal with its competitors. But such a right is not absolute; it exists only if there are legitimate competitive reasons for the refusal. *See Aspen Skiing Co. v. Aspen Highlands Skiing Corp.*, 472 U.S. 585, 602-05 (1985).

As recounted at length above, respondents have presented evidence that Kodak took exclusionary action to maintain its parts monopoly and used its control over parts to strengthen its monopoly share of the Kodak service market. Liability turns, then, on whether "valid business reasons" can explain Kodak's actions. *Aspen Skiing Co.*, 472 U.S. at 605; *United States v. Aluminum Co. of America*, 148 F.2d, at 432. Kodak contends that it has three valid business justifications for its actions: "(1) to promote interbrand equipment competition by allowing Kodak to stress the quality of its service; (2) to improve asset management by reducing Kodak's inventory costs; and (3) to prevent ISOs from free riding on Kodak's capital investment in equipment, parts and service.". . . Factual questions exist, however, about the validity and sufficiency of each claimed justification, making summary judgment inappropriate.

Kodak first asserts that by preventing customers from using ISOs, "it [can] best maintain high quality service for its sophisticated equipment" and avoid being "blamed for an equipment malfunction, even if the problem is the result of improper diagnosis, maintenance or repair by an ISO.". . . Respondents have offered evidence that ISOs provide quality service and are preferred by some Kodak equipment owners. This is sufficient to raise a genuine issue of fact. . . .

Moreover, there are other reasons to question Kodak's proffered motive of commitment to quality service; its quality justification appears inconsistent with its thesis that consumers are knowledgeable enough to lifecycle price, and its self-service policy. Kodak claims the exclusive-service contract is warranted because customers would otherwise blame Kodak equipment for breakdowns resulting from inferior ISO service. Thus, Kodak simultaneously claims that its customers are sophisticated enough to make complex and subtle lifecycle-pricing decisions, and yet too obtuse to distinguish which breakdowns are due to bad equipment and which are due to bad service. Kodak has failed to offer any reason why informational sophistication should be present in one circumstance and absent in the other. In addition, because self-service customers are just as likely as others to blame Kodak equipment for breakdowns resulting from (their own) inferior service, Kodak's willingness to allow self-service casts doubt on its quality claim. In sum, we agree with the Court of Appeals that respondents "have presented evidence from which a reasonable trier of fact could conclude that Kodak's first reason is pretextual." . . .

There is also a triable issue of fact on Kodak's second justification—controlling inventory costs. As respondents argue, Kodak's actions appear inconsistent with any need to control inventory costs. Presumably, the inventory of parts needed to repair Kodak machines turns only on breakdown rates, and those rates should be the same whether Kodak or ISOs perform the repair. More importantly, the justification fails to explain respondents' evidence that Kodak forced OEMs, equipment owners, and parts brokers not to sell parts to ISOs, actions that would have no effect on Kodak's inventory costs.

Nor does Kodak's final justification entitle it to summary judgment on respondents' § 2 claim. Kodak claims that its policies prevent ISOs from "exploit[ing] the investment Kodak has made in product development, manufacturing and equipment sales in order to take away Kodak's service revenues." . . . Kodak does not dispute that respondents invest substantially in the service market, with training of repair workers and investment in parts inventory. Instead, according to Kodak, the ISOs are free-riding because they have failed to enter the equipment and parts markets. This understanding of free-riding has no support in our caselaw.[33] To the contrary, as the Court of Appeals noted, one of the evils proscribed

---

[33] Kodak claims that both *Continental T.V.*, and *Monsanto* support its free-rider argument. Neither is applicable. In both *Continental T.V.*, 433 U.S. at 55, and *Monsanto*, 465 U.S. at 762-763, the Court accepted

by the antitrust laws is the creation of entry barriers to potential competitors by requiring them to enter two markets simultaneously. . . .

None of Kodak's asserted business justifications, then, are sufficient to prove that Kodak is "entitled to a judgment as a matter of law" on respondents' § 2 claim. Fed. Rule Civ. Proc. 56(c).

. . . .

Justice SCALIA, with whom Justice O'CONNOR and Justice THOMAS join, dissenting.

. . . .

III

. . . Without even so much as asking whether the purposes of § 2 are implicated here, the Court points to Kodak's control of "100% of the parts market and 80% to 95% of the service market," markets with "no readily available substitutes," . . . and finds that the proffer of such statistics is sufficient to fend off summary judgment. But this showing could easily be made, as I have explained, with respect to virtually any manufacturer of differentiated products requiring aftermarket support. By permitting antitrust plaintiffs to invoke § 2 simply upon the unexceptional demonstration that a manufacturer controls the supplies of its single-branded merchandise, the Court transforms § 2 from a specialized mechanism for responding to extraordinary agglomerations (or threatened agglomerations) of economic power to an all-purpose remedy against run-of-the-mill business torts.

In my view, if the interbrand market is vibrant, it is simply not necessary to enlist § 2's machinery to police a seller's intrabrand restraints. In such circumstances, the interbrand market functions as an infinitely more efficient and more precise corrective to such behavior, rewarding the seller whose intrabrand restraints enhance consumer welfare while punishing the seller whose control of the aftermarkets is viewed unfavorably by interbrand consumers. . . . Because this case comes to us on the assumption that Kodak is without such interbrand power, I believe we are compelled to reverse the judgment of the Court of Appeals. I respectfully dissent.

A NOTE ON BUSINESS JUSTIFICATION

1. The substance of the business justification requirement.

If Ski Co. could have prevailed by persuading the jury that its conduct was justified by "any normal business purpose," then it apparently could have prevailed if it could have shown that it would have maximized its short-run profits by withdrawing from the joint marketing arrangement. If its short-run profits would be increased by such a withdrawal, then its withdrawal could not be attacked as predatory.

---

free-riding as a justification because without restrictions a manufacturer would not be able to induce competent and aggressive retailers to make the kind of investment of capital and labor necessary to distribute the product. In *Continental T.V.* the relevant market level was retail sale of televisions and in *Monsanto* retail sales of herbicides. Some retailers were investing in those markets; others were not, relying, instead, on the investment of the other retailers. To be applicable to this case, the ISOs would have to be relying on Kodak's investment in the service market; that, however, is not Kodak's argument.

The test of lawfulness under § 2 then largely equates with a test of predatory behavior: Is the behavior of the monopolist consistent with short-run profit maximization? This is the approach to § 2 taken by the Ninth Circuit in *Alaska Airlines*. This approach also can be used to elucidate the classic definitions of monopolization employed by the Court in such cases as *Griffith*, *Grinnell*, and *Alcoa*. The "use" of monopoly power referred to in *Griffith* "to foreclose competition, to gain a competitive advantage, or to destroy a competitor" would involve predatory behavior. The "willful acquisition or development of . . . [monopoly] power as distinguished from growth or development as a consequence of a superior product, business acumen, or historic accident" similarly would imply predatory behavior. A monopoly, in the terminology employed by Judge Hand in *Alcoa*, would be "thrust upon" the recipient so long as it was not acquired through predatory means.

Formulating even a working definition of "predatory" behavior, however, is a complicated matter. Predatory conduct is taken up in detail in Chapter 11.

2. The procedural consequences of the business justification requirement.

When, in its *Aspen* opinion, the Court indicated that Ski Co. could have prevailed had it persuaded the jury that its conduct was justified by a normal business purpose, the Court effectively drew new procedural rules for the litigation of a monopolization case. Judge Hand's *Alcoa* opinion appears to place the burden of establishing a justification in a monopolization case on the defendant: It is the defendant who must establish that the monopoly was "thrust upon" it. Justice Douglas' opinion in *Grinnell* seems to offer a different version of the burdens upon the parties. By the way in which he there set forth the elements of the monopolization offense, Douglas' opinion suggests that the absence of a justification is part of the offense rather than an affirmative defense. Under such an approach, proof of the absence of a justification would fall upon the plaintiff.

Justice Stevens' opinion for the Court in *Aspen* makes justification an affirmative defense. If the precedential effect of *Aspen* is narrow, Stevens' opinion will be perhaps be taken to place the burden on justification on the defendant only in joint marketing cases where the defendant withdraws from a joint marketing practice which had originated in a more competitive period—as in the *Aspen* case. The ramifications of attributing a broad precedential effect to the *Aspen* case, however, are profound, since the *Aspen* approach effectively forces all monopolization cases (in which the defendant possesses a market share large enough to be treated as a monopoly) to trial on the issue of justification for the defendant's monopoly.

When the burden of justification is placed on the defendant, the role played by summary judgment is diminished. If the defendant bears the burden of proving that its behavior is justified, justification will always raise a factual issue for trial. By contrast, if the plaintiff has the burden of proving lack of justification, then the plaintiff's case would be vulnerable to a motion for summary judgment if, after discovery, the plaintiff lacked evidence on that issue.

The Supreme Court's recent *Eastman Kodak* decision is complicated by the relevant market issue. Whether the aftermarket in replacement parts is properly conceived as a separate relevant market is obviously critical to the monopolization issue. Justice Scalia, who believes that no manufacturer should be treated as possessing a "monopoly" in its own brand of replacement parts, thinks that the Court has radically transformed § 2 into a mechanism for presuming § 2 liability. By requiring manufacturers to justify their behavior, the Court has effectively forced large numbers of meritless § 2 cases to trial. Do you agree?

In many areas of antitrust law, summary judgment has become an effective means for courts to dispose of nonmeritorious cases prior to trial. To what extent do *Aspen Skiing* and *Eastman Kodak* carry the opposite potential for forcing nonmeritorious cases to trial? How would you fashion the burden of proof in monopolization cases?

---

2. Tying as Monopolization

In the aftermath of the *Eastman Kodak* decision, the courts have confronted numerous monopolization claims based upon the tying of a product or service to another. Consider, *e.g.*, the following cases:

SMS Systems Maintenance Services, Inc. v. Digital Equipment Corp., 188 F.3d 11 (1st Cir. 1999). In 1994, Digital Equipment Corp. (DEC), a computer manufacturer, introduced its "Alpha" line of mid-range servers. Although one-year warranties were the norm for mid-range computers in 1994, DEC included a three-year warranty in the Alpha package. SMS Systems Maintenance Corp., an independent servicing organization, unsuccessfully attacked the warranty as foreclosing the servicing aftermarket from SMS, in violation of § 2. In discussing the relevance of *Eastman Kodak*, the court observed:

> . . . [In *Kodak*,] a group of ISOs complained that a copy-machine manufacturer which competed with ISOs in servicing its brand of copiers had engaged in exclusionary behavior in its parts and services aftermarket (Kodak had stopped supplying the ISOs with the parts required to service Kodak copy machines, while at the same time entering into pacts with independent parts manufacturers that prohibited them from supplying the ISOs with copier parts). *See Kodak*, 504 U.S. at 455-56, 112 S. Ct. 2072. Then, the manufacturer told its customers that they could not purchase parts unless they agreed to use the manufacturer's aftermarket services. *See id.* at 456-58, 112 S. Ct. 2072. Coupling evidence of this scheme with evidence that Kodak was charging supracompetitive prices in the aftermarket, the ISOs accused Kodak of improperly expanding its monopoly in the services aftermarket. *See id.*, 112 S. Ct. 2072.
>
> Kodak countered that, as a matter of law, a manufacturer cannot wield monopoly power in a derivative market because competitive primary markets, by definition, always check aftermarket behavior. The Court

> granted certiorari to consider the bona fides of this argument. *See id.* at 454-55, 112 S. Ct. 2072. Ultimately, it rejected Kodak's contention as a matter of law and affirmed the remand for further proceedings because data in the record suggested that Kodak might in fact have been exacting monopoly prices in its derivative market and there was no sign that competition in the primary market deterred it from doing so. *See id.* at 477-78, 112 S. Ct. 2072.
>
> *Kodak*, then, stands for the proposition that the foremarket does not always exert sufficient competitive pressure to insulate the aftermarket from monopolistic practices. It does not hold, as SMS entreats, that the foremarket never exerts sufficient competitive pressure to keep the aftermarket pristine. And the fact that the primary market at times may fail to discipline a derivative market does not mean that the latter necessarily constitutes the relevant market for antitrust analysis. Rather, a litigant who envisions the aftermarket as the relevant market must advance hard evidence dissociating the competitive situation in the aftermarket from activities occurring in the primary market. *Cf. id.* at 477, 112 S. Ct. 2072 (noting that the plaintiff adduced evidence that the defendants were able to—and did—charge supracompetitive prices in the aftermarket). Put another way, a court may conclude that the aftermarket is the relevant market for antitrust analysis only if the evidence supports an inference of monopoly power in the aftermarket that competition in the primary market appears unable to check. *See id.* at 481-82, 112 S. Ct. 2072; *see also* 10 AREEDA & HOVENKAMP, *supra*, ¶ 1740, at 170-71.

In re Independent Service Organizations Antitrust Litigation, 203 F.3d 1322 (Fed. Cir. 2000). In this case, the Xerox Corporation decided in 1984 to stop selling parts for its Series 10 copiers to independent servicing organizations. In 1987, that policy was extended to its Series 9 copiers. Xerox also refused to sell independent servicing organizations copyrighted manuals and to license copyrighted software to them. The plaintiff, an independent servicing organization, was thereby disabled from competing with Xerox in the aftermarket for servicing Series 9 and 10 copiers. Asserting that Xerox had engaged in monopolization, the plaintiff sued under a theory of monopolization drawn from the *Eastman Kodak* case. Although Xerox's behavior closely resembled that of Kodak, Xerox successfully defended on the ground that the parts were protected under its patents, and that under the patent and copyright laws Xerox was entitled to refuse to sell its patented parts and copyrighted manuals and it was entitled to refuse to license its copyrighted software. This case is furthered considered in Chapter 15.

United States v. Microsoft Corporation

87 F. Supp. 2d 30 (D.D.C. 2000)

[The Microsoft litigation involves an array of issues. In Chapter 6, we examined part of the District Court's decision dealing with the Government's contention that Microsoft's bundling of its browser with its operating system constituted an illegal tie under § 1 of the Sherman Act. Here is an excerpt from the District Court's opinion which considers that bundle as unlawful monopolization:]

CONCLUSIONS OF LAW

JACKSON, District Judge.

The United States, nineteen individual states, and the District of Columbia ("the plaintiffs") bring these consolidated civil enforcement actions against defendant Microsoft Corporation ("Microsoft") under the Sherman Antitrust Act, 15 U.S.C. §§ 1 and 2. The plaintiffs charge, in essence, that Microsoft has waged an unlawful campaign in defense of its monopoly position in the market for operating systems designed to run on Intel-compatible personal computers ("PCs"). Specifically, the plaintiffs contend that Microsoft violated § 2 of the Sherman Act by engaging in a series of exclusionary, anticompetitive, and predatory acts to maintain its monopoly power. . . .

I. SECTION TWO OF THE SHERMAN ACT

A. Maintenance of Monopoly Power by Anticompetitive Means

Section 2 of the Sherman Act declares that it is unlawful for a person or firm to "monopolize . . . any part of the trade or commerce among the several States, or with foreign nations . . . ." 15 U.S.C. § 2. This language operates to limit the means by which a firm may lawfully either acquire or perpetuate monopoly power. Specifically, a firm violates § 2 if it attains or preserves monopoly power through anticompetitive acts. *See United States v. Grinnell Corp.*, 384 U.S. 563, 570-71, 86 S.Ct. 1698, 16 L.Ed.2d 778 (1966) ("The offense of monopoly power under § 2 of the Sherman Act has two elements: (1) the possession of monopoly power in the relevant market and (2) the willful acquisition or maintenance of that power as distinguished from growth or development as a consequence of a superior product, business acumen, or historic accident."); *Eastman Kodak Co. v. Image Technical Services, Inc.*, 504 U.S. 451, 488, 112 S.Ct. 2072, 119 L.Ed.2d 265 (1992) (Scalia, J., dissenting) ("Our § 2 monopolization doctrines are . . . directed to discrete situations in which a defendant's possession of substantial market power, combined with his exclusionary or anticompetitive behavior, threatens to defeat or forestall the corrective forces of competition and thereby sustain or extend the defendant's agglomeration of power.").

. . . .

2. Maintenance of Monopoly Power by Anticompetitive Means

In a § 2 case, once it is proved that the defendant possesses monopoly power in a relevant market, liability for monopolization depends on a showing that the defendant used anticompetitive methods to achieve or maintain its position. *See United States v. Grinnell*, 384 U.S. 563, 570-71, 86 S.Ct. 1698, 16 L.Ed.2d 778 (1966); *Eastman Kodak Co. v. Image Technical Services, Inc.*, 504 U.S. 451, 488, 112 S.Ct. 2072, 119 L.Ed.2d 265 (1992) (Scalia, J., dissenting); *Intergraph Corp. v. Intel Corp.*, 195 F.3d 1346, 1353 (Fed.Cir.1999). Prior cases have established an analytical approach to determining whether challenged conduct should be deemed anticompetitive in the context of a monopoly maintenance claim. The threshold question in this analysis is whether the defendant's conduct is "exclusionary"—that is, whether it has restricted significantly, or threatens to restrict significantly, the ability of other firms to compete in the relevant market on the merits of what they offer customers. *See Eastman Kodak*, 504 U.S. at 488, 112 S.Ct. 2072 (Scalia, J., dissenting) (§ 2 is "directed to discrete situations" in which the behavior of firms with monopoly power "threatens to defeat or forestall the corrective forces of competition").[1]

If the evidence reveals a significant exclusionary impact in the relevant market, the defendant's conduct will be labeled "anticompetitive"—and liability will attach—unless the defendant comes forward with specific, procompetitive business motivations that explain the full extent of its exclusionary conduct. *See Eastman Kodak*, 504 U.S. at 483, 112 S.Ct. 2072 (declining to grant defendant's motion for summary judgment because factual questions remained as to whether defendant's asserted justifications were sufficient to explain the exclusionary conduct or were instead merely pretextual); *see also Aspen Skiing Co. v. Aspen Highlands Skiing Corp.*, 472 U.S. 585, 605 n.32, 105 S.Ct. 2847, 86 L.Ed.2d 467 (1985) (holding that the second element of a monopoly maintenance claim is satisfied by proof of "'behavior that not only (1) tends to impair the opportunities of rivals, but also (2) either does not further competition on the merits or does so in an unnecessarily restrictive way'") (quoting III PHILLIP E. AREEDA & DONALD F. TURNER, ANTITRUST LAW ¶ 626b, at 78 (1978)).

If the defendant with monopoly power consciously antagonized its customers by making its products less attractive to them—or if it incurred other costs, such as large outlays of development capital and forfeited opportunities to derive revenue from it—with no prospect of compensation other than the erection or preservation of barriers against competition by equally efficient firms, the Court may deem the defendant's conduct "predatory." As the D.C. Circuit stated in *Neumann v. Reinforced Earth Co.*,

> [P]redation involves aggression against business rivals through the use of business practices that would not be considered profit maximizing except for the expectation that (1) actual rivals will be driven from the market, or the entry of potential rivals blocked or delayed, so that the predator will gain or retain a market share sufficient to command monopoly profits, or (2) rivals will be chastened sufficiently to abandon competitive behavior the predator finds threatening to its realization of monopoly profits.

786 F.2d 424, 427 (D.C.Cir.1986).

Proof that a profit-maximizing firm took predatory action should suffice to demonstrate the threat of substantial exclusionary effect; to hold otherwise would be to ascribe irrational behavior to the defendant. Moreover, predatory conduct, by definition as well as by nature, lacks procompetitive business motivation. *See Aspen Skiing*, 472 U.S. at 610-11, 105 S.Ct. 2847 (evidence indicating that defendant's conduct was "motivated entirely by a decision to avoid providing any benefits" to a rival supported the inference that defendant's conduct "was not motivated by efficiency concerns"). In other words, predatory behavior is

---

1 Proof that the defendant's conduct was motivated by a desire to prevent other firms from competing on the merits can contribute to a finding that the conduct has had, or will have, the intended, exclusionary effect. *See United States v. United States Gypsum Co.*, 438 U.S. 422, 436 n.13, 98 S.Ct. 2864, 57 L.Ed.2d 854 (1978) ("consideration of intent may play an important role in divining the actual nature and effect of the alleged anticompetitive conduct").

patently anticompetitive. Proof that a firm with monopoly power engaged in such behavior thus necessitates a finding of liability under § 2.

In this case, Microsoft early on recognized middleware as the Trojan horse that, once having, in effect, infiltrated the applications barrier, could enable rival operating systems to enter the market for Intel-compatible PC operating systems unimpeded. Simply put, middleware threatened to demolish Microsoft's coveted monopoly power. Alerted to the threat, Microsoft strove over a period of approximately four years to prevent middleware technologies from fostering the development of enough full-featured, cross-platform applications to erode the applications barrier. In pursuit of this goal, Microsoft sought to convince developers to concentrate on Windows-specific APIs and ignore interfaces exposed by the two incarnations of middleware that posed the greatest threat, namely, Netscape's Navigator Web browser and Sun's implementation of the Java technology. [*See* Chapter 6, Part D, § 3, page 269—Eds.] Microsoft's campaign succeeded in preventing—for several years, and perhaps permanently—Navigator and Java from fulfilling their potential to open the market for Intel-compatible PC operating systems to competition on the merits. Findings ¶¶ 133, 378. Because Microsoft achieved this result through exclusionary acts that lacked procompetitive justification, the Court deems Microsoft's conduct the maintenance of monopoly power by anticompetitive means.

a. Combating the Browser Threat

. . . Microsoft focused its efforts on minimizing the extent to which developers would avail themselves of interfaces exposed by that nascent platform. Microsoft realized that the extent of developers' reliance on Netscape's browser platform would depend largely on the size and trajectory of Navigator's share of browser usage. Microsoft thus set out to maximize Internet Explorer's share of browser usage at Navigator's expense. *Id.* ¶¶ 133, 359-61. The core of this strategy was ensuring that the firms comprising the most effective channels for the generation of browser usage would devote their distributional and promotional efforts to Internet Explorer rather than Navigator. Recognizing that pre-installation by OEMs and bundling with the proprietary software of IAPs led more directly and efficiently to browser usage than any other practices in the industry, Microsoft devoted major efforts to usurping those two channels. *Id.* ¶ 143.

i. The OEM Channel

. . . The Court has already found that no quality-related or technical justifications fully explain Microsoft's refusal to license Windows 95 to OEMs without version 1.0 through 4.0 of Internet Explorer, or its refusal to permit them to uninstall versions 3.0 and 4.0. *Id.* ¶¶ 175-76. The same lack of justification applies to Microsoft's decision not to offer a browserless version of Windows 98 to consumers and OEMs, *id.* ¶ 177, as well as to its claim that it could offer "best of breed" implementations of functionalities in Web browsers. With respect to the latter assertion, Internet Explorer is not demonstrably the current "best of breed" Web browser, nor is it likely to be so at any time in the immediate future. The fact that Microsoft itself was aware of this reality only further strengthens the conclusion that Microsoft's decision to tie Internet Explorer to Windows cannot truly be explained as an attempt to benefit consumers and improve the efficiency of the software market generally, but rather as part of a larger campaign to quash innovation that threatened its monopoly position. *Id.* ¶¶ 195, 198.

To the extent that Microsoft still asserts a copyright defense, relying upon federal copyright law as a justification for its various restrictions on OEMs, that defense neither explains nor operates to immunize Microsoft's conduct under the Sherman Act. As a general proposition, Microsoft argues that the federal Copyright Act, 17 U.S.C. § 101 *et seq.*, endows the holder of a valid copyright in software with an absolute right to prevent licensees, in this case the OEMs, from shipping modified versions of its product without its express permission. In truth, Windows 95 and Windows 98 are covered by copyright registrations, Findings ¶ 228, that "constitute *prima facie* evidence of the validity of the copyright." 17 U.S.C. § 410(c). But the *validity* of Microsoft's copyrights has never been in doubt; the issue is what, precisely, they protect.

Microsoft has presented no evidence that the contractual (or the technological) restrictions it placed on OEMs' ability to alter Windows derive from any of the enumerated rights explicitly granted to a copyright holder under the Copyright Act. Instead, Microsoft argues that the restrictions "simply restate" an expansive right to preserve the "integrity" of its copyrighted software against any "distortion," "truncation," or "alteration," a right nowhere mentioned among the Copyright Act's list of exclusive rights, 17 U.S.C. § 106, thus raising some doubt as to its existence. *See Twentieth Century Music Corp. v. Aiken*, 422 U.S. 151, 155, 95 S.Ct. 2040, 45 L.Ed.2d 84 (1975) (not all uses of a work are within copyright holder's control; rights limited to specifically granted "exclusive rights"); *cf.* 17 U.S.C. § 501(a) (infringement means violating specifically enumerated rights).[2]

It is also well settled that a copyright holder is not by reason thereof entitled to employ the perquisites in ways that directly threaten competition. *See, e.g., Eastman Kodak*, 504 U.S. at 479 n.29, 112 S.Ct. 2072 ("The Court has held many times that power gained through some natural and legal advantage such as a . . . copyright, . . . can give rise to liability if 'a seller exploits his dominant position in one market to expand his empire into the next.'") (quoting *Times-Picayune Pub. Co. v. United States*, 345 U.S. 594, 611, 73 S.Ct. 872, 97 L.Ed. 1277 (1953)); *Square D Co. v. Niagara Frontier Tariff Bureau, Inc.*, 476 U.S. 409, 421, 106 S.Ct. 1922, 90 L.Ed.2d 413 (1986); *Data General Corp. v. Grumman Systems Support Corp.*, 36 F.3d 1147, 1186 n.63 (1st Cir.1994) (a copyright does not exempt its holder from antitrust inquiry where the copyright is used as part of a scheme to monopolize); *see also Image Technical Services, Inc. v. Eastman Kodak Co.*, 125 F.3d 1195, 1219 (9th Cir.1997), *cert. denied*, 523 U.S. 1094, 118 S.Ct. 1560, 140 L.Ed.2d 792 (1998) ("Neither the aims of intellectual property law, nor the antitrust laws justify allowing a monopolist to rely upon a pretextual business justification to mask anticompetitive conduct."). Even constitutional privileges confer no immunity when they are abused for anticompetitive purposes. *See Lorain Journal Co. v. United States*, 342 U.S. 143, 155-56, 72 S.Ct. 181, 96 L.Ed. 162 (1951).

The Court has already found that the true impetus behind Microsoft's restrictions on OEMs was not its desire to maintain a somewhat amorphous quality it refers to as the "integrity" of the Windows platform, nor even to ensure that Windows afforded a uniform and stable platform for applications development. Microsoft itself engendered, or at least countenanced, instability and inconsistency by permitting Microsoft-friendly modifications to the desktop and boot sequence, and by releasing updates to Internet Explorer more fre-

---

[2] While Microsoft is correct that some courts have also recognized the right of a copyright holder to preserve the "integrity" of artistic works in addition to those rights enumerated in the Copyright Act, the Court nevertheless concludes that those cases, being actions for infringement without antitrust implications, are inapposite to the one currently before it. *See, e.g., WGN Continental Broadcasting Co. v. United Video, Inc.*, 693 F.2d 622 (7th Cir.1982); *Gilliam v. ABC, Inc.*, 538a F.2d 14 (2d Cir.1976).

quently than it released new versions of Windows. Findings ¶ 226. Add to this the fact that the modifications OEMs desired to make would not have removed or altered any Windows APIs, and thus would not have disrupted any of Windows' functionalities, and it is apparent that Microsoft's conduct is effectively explained by its foreboding that OEMs would preinstall and give prominent placement to middleware like Navigator that could attract enough developer attention to weaken the applications barrier to entry. *Id.* ¶ 227. In short, if Microsoft was truly inspired by a genuine concern for maximizing consumer satisfaction, as well as preserving its substantial investment in a worthy product, then it would have relied more on the power of the very competitive PC market, and less on its own market power, to prevent OEMs from making modifications that consumers did not want. *Id.* ¶¶ 225, 228-29.

ORDER

In accordance with the Conclusions of Law filed herein this date, it is, this 3rd day of April, 2000,

ORDERED, ADJUDGED, and DECLARED, that Microsoft has violated §§ 1 and 2 of the Sherman Act, 15 U.S.C. §§ 1, 2, as well as . . . [certain] state law provisions . . . .

COMMENTARY

1. The court views Microsoft's bundling of its browser with its operating system as a means by which Microsoft was perpetuating its monopoly over its Windows operating system. Now most software applications programs are written to interface with the Windows operating system, because most personal computers are equipped with the Windows operating system. In the language of the computer industry, the Windows operating system is a "platform" to which software is written. The court, however, believes that browsers might emerge as an alternative platform to which software applications would be written. Software written to interface with browsers could be used by all computer users, regardless of the operating system which they employed.

In the future, computer users may obtain their software applications from an internet server, rather then buying packages of software at computer stores and installing the software on their hard drives. In that world browsers might very well become the new platform. In that case, operating systems such as Windows would be selected for their technical merits alone. No longer would a particular operating system, such as Windows, also be the dominant "platform" to which all applications programs would be written.

2. Java is a programming language, developed by Sun Microsystems. Both the Netscape browser and the Microsoft browser are equipped with Java capability. It is possible that someday software applications developers will write their programs in Java. Java programs delivered from an internet server would be read by software carried by the browser (a so-called "java virtual machine") and translated into the machine code appropriate for the user's operating system. The java-capable browser might emerge as a possible alternative platform.

3. In the light of the foregoing, do you understand why the court believes that Microsoft's bundling of its browser (the Internet Explorer) with its Windows operating system is preventing the emergence of this new platform? Why could not Microsoft's own browser provide the base for a Java-resident browser platform?

In answering that question consider the following: Sun's goal is to make Java fully interoperable, *i.e.*, to provide Java with the capability of carrying a fully articulated program. But that goal has not yet been attained. Most large programs written in Java still must still make some "native calls," *i.e.*, invoke directly (rather than through the Java virtual machine) calls to the recipient machine's operating system. At the time of the events underlying the litigation, Microsoft's browser would not transmit native calls through Java Native Interface (JNI) or Remote Method Invocation (RMI), methods employed in the official version of Java. Microsoft's browser is designed to transmit native calls employing Raw Native Interface (RNI), a technique incorporated in Microsoft's unofficial version of Java.

Some commentators have expressed the concern that Microsoft's version of Java might have anticompetitive consequences. Lemley and McGowan state:

> If Microsoft could alter the Java technology to disrupt platform independence, it could short-circuit the promise of Java insofar as operating systems competition is concerned.

See Mark A. Lemley & David McGowan, *Could Java Change Everything? The Competitive Propriety of a Proprietary Standard*, 43 ANTITRUST BULL. 715, 765 (1998).

4. Java is a powerful technology through which internet servers can communicate with personal computers. Microsoft has been promoting an alternative set of technologies (sometimes referred to as ActiveX) which can facilitate such communication. While both the Netscape and Microsoft browsers are Java capable, Netscape considered but rejected the option of equipping its browser with ActiveX technology.

5. Could Netscape's rejection of the ActiveX technology constitute a justification for Microsoft's bundling of its browser with its operating system?

6. When the court ruled that Microsoft maintained its Windows monopoly by bundling its browser with its operating system, was it implicitly finding that in the absence of the bundle, the Netscape browser would have been likely to emerge as an alternative platform? In a monopoly-maintenance case, should the government be required to prove that the defendant's behavior actually prevented its monopoly from being eroded? that the defendant's behavior probably prevented such an erosion? that it created a substantial threat to the defendant's monopoly?

United States v. Microsoft Corporation
253 F.3d 34 (D.C. Cir. 2001)

Before: EDWARDS, Chief Judge, WILLIAMS, GINSBURG, SENTELLE, RANDOLPH, ROGERS and TATEL, Circuit Judges.

[For the part of this opinion dealing with the tying issue as a § 1 claim see Chapter 6, *supra.*]

I. INTRODUCTION

A. Background

In July 1994, officials at the Department of Justice ("DOJ"), on behalf of the United States, filed suit against Microsoft, charging the company with, among other things, unlawfully maintaining a monopoly in the operating system market through anticompetitive terms in its licensing and software developer agreements. The parties subsequently entered into a consent decree, thus avoiding a trial on the merits. . . . ("*Microsoft I*"). Three years later, the Justice Department filed a civil contempt action against Microsoft for allegedly violating one of the decree's provisions. On appeal from a grant of a preliminary injunction, this court held that Microsoft's technological bundling of IE 3.0 and 4.0 with Windows 95 did not violate the relevant provision of the consent decree. . . . ("*Microsoft II*"). We expressly reserved the question whether such bundling might independently violate §§ 1 or 2 of the Sherman Act. . . .

. . . .

Relying almost exclusively on Microsoft's varied efforts to unseat Netscape Navigator as the preeminent internet browser, plaintiffs charged four distinct violations of the Sherman Act: (1) unlawful exclusive dealing arrangements in violation of § 1; (2) unlawful tying of IE to Windows 95 and Windows 98 in violation of § 1; (3) unlawful maintenance of a monopoly in the PC operating system market in violation of § 2; and (4) unlawful attempted monopolization of the internet browser market in violation of § 2. The States also brought pendent claims charging Microsoft with violations of various State antitrust laws.

. . . .

What is somewhat problematic, however, is that just over six years have passed since Microsoft engaged in the first conduct plaintiffs allege to be anticompetitive. As the record in this case indicates, six years seems like an eternity in the computer industry. By the time a court can assess liability, firms, products, and the marketplace are likely to have changed dramatically. This, in turn, threatens enormous practical difficulties for courts considering the appropriate measure of relief in equitable enforcement actions, both in crafting injunctive remedies in the first instance and reviewing those remedies in the second. Conduct remedies may be unavailing in such cases, because innovation to a large degree has already rendered the anticompetitive conduct obsolete (although by no means harmless). And broader structural remedies present their own set of problems, including how a court goes about *restoring* competition to a dramatically changed, and constantly changing, marketplace. . . .

We do not mean to say that enforcement actions will no longer play an important role in curbing infringements of the antitrust laws in technologically dynamic markets, nor do we assume this in assessing the merits of this case. Even in those cases where forward-looking remedies appear limited, the Government will continue to have an interest in defining the contours of the antitrust laws so that law-abiding firms will have a clear sense of what is permissible and what is not. And the threat of private damage actions will remain to deter those firms inclined to test the limits of the law.

. . . We decide this case against a backdrop of significant debate amongst academics and practitioners over the extent to which "old economy" § 2 monopolization doctrines should apply to firms competing in dynamic technological markets characterized by network effects. . . .

In technologically dynamic markets, however, such entrenchment may be temporary, because innovation may alter the field altogether. . . . Rapid technological change leads to markets in which "firms compete through innovation for temporary market dominance, from which they may be displaced by the next wave of product advancements." ([Some] . . . competition, . . . proceeds "sequentially over time rather than simultaneously across a market"). Microsoft argues that the operating system market is just such a market.

. . . .

II. MONOPOLIZATION

. . . The District Court . . . found that Microsoft possesses monopoly power in the market for Intel-compatible PC operating systems. . . .

We begin by considering whether Microsoft possesses monopoly power, *see infra* Section II.A, and finding that it does, we turn to the question whether it maintained this power through anticompetitive means. Agreeing with the District Court that the company behaved anticompetitively . . . . and that these actions contributed to the maintenance of its monopoly power . . . we affirm the court's finding of liability for monopolization.

A. Monopoly Power

. . . .

The District Court considered these structural factors and concluded that Microsoft possesses monopoly power in a relevant market. Defining the market as Intel-compatible PC operating systems, the District Court found that Microsoft has a greater than 95% share. It also found the company's market position protected by a substantial entry barrier. . . .

Microsoft argues that the District Court incorrectly defined the relevant market. It also claims that there is no barrier to entry in that market. Alternatively, Microsoft argues that because the software industry is uniquely dynamic, direct proof, rather than circumstantial evidence, more appropriately indicates whether it possesses monopoly power. Rejecting each argument, we uphold the District Court's finding of monopoly power in its entirety.

1. Market Structure

a. Market definition

. . . Microsoft's main challenge to the District Court's market definition . . . [is] the exclusion of middleware.

. . . .

Because market definition is meant to identify products "reasonably interchangeable by consumers" . . ., and because middleware is not now interchangeable with Windows, the District Court had good reason for excluding middleware from the relevant market.

b. Market power

Having thus properly defined the relevant market, the District Court found that Windows accounts for a greater than 95% share. . . .

. . . Microsoft claims that even a predominant market share does not by itself indicate monopoly power. . . . [T]he court focused not only on Microsoft's present market share, but also on the structural barrier that protects the company's future position. . . . That barrier—the "applications barrier to entry"—stems from two characteristics of the software market: (1) most consumers prefer operating systems for which a large number of applications have already been written; and (2) most developers prefer to write for operating systems that already have a substantial consumer base. . . . This "chicken-and-egg" situation ensures that applications will continue to be written for the already dominant Windows, which in turn ensures that consumers will continue to prefer it over other operating systems. . . .

. . . .

Thus, despite the limited success of its rivals, Microsoft benefits from the applications barrier to entry.

. . . .

2. Direct Proof

Having sustained the District Court's conclusion that circumstantial evidence proves that Microsoft possesses monopoly power, we turn to Microsoft's alternative argument that it does not behave like a monopolist. . . .

Microsoft's argument fails because, even assuming that the software market is uniquely dynamic in the long term, the District Court correctly applied the structural approach to determine if the company faces competition in the short term. Structural market power analyses are meant to determine whether potential substitutes constrain a firm's ability to raise prices above the competitive level; only threats that are likely to materialize in the relatively near future perform this function to any significant degree. . . .

The structural approach, as applied by the District Court, is thus capable of fulfilling its purpose even in a changing market. Microsoft cites no case, nor are we aware of one, requiring direct evidence to show monopoly power in any market. We decline to adopt such a rule now. . . . More telling, the District Court found that some aspects of Microsoft's behavior are difficult to explain unless Windows is a monopoly product. For instance, according to the District Court, the company set the price of Windows without considering rivals' prices . . . something a firm without a monopoly would have been unable to do. The District Court also found that Microsoft's pattern of exclusionary conduct could only be rational "if the firm knew that it possessed monopoly power." . . .

B. Anticompetitive Conduct

. . . A firm violates § 2 only when it acquires or maintains, or attempts to acquire or maintain, a monopoly by engaging in exclusionary conduct "as distinguished from growth or development as a consequence of a superior product, business acumen, or historic accident." . . . Specifically, the District Court held Microsoft liable for: (1) the way in which it integrated IE into Windows; (2) its various dealings with Original Equipment Manufacturers ("OEMs"), Internet Access Providers ("IAPs"), Internet Content Providers ("ICPs"), Independent Software Vendors ("ISVs"), and Apple Computer; (3) its efforts to contain and to subvert Java technologies; and (4) its course of conduct as a whole. Upon appeal, Microsoft argues that it did not engage in any exclusionary conduct.

. . . .

. . . First, to be condemned as exclusionary, a monopolist's act must have an "anticompetitive effect." That is, it must harm the competitive *process* and thereby harm consumers. In contrast, harm to one or more *competitors* will not suffice. . . .

Second, the plaintiff, on whom the burden of proof of course rests . . . must demonstrate that the monopolist's conduct indeed has the requisite anticompetitive effect. . . .

Third, if a plaintiff successfully establishes a *prima facie* case under § 2 by demonstrating anticompetitive effect, then the monopolist may proffer a "procompetitive justification" for its conduct. . . . If the monopolist asserts a procompetitive justification—a nonpretextual claim that its conduct is indeed a form of competition on the merits because it involves, for example, greater efficiency or enhanced consumer appeal—then the burden shifts back to the plaintiff to rebut that claim. . . .

Fourth, if the monopolist's procompetitive justification stands unrebutted, then the plaintiff must demonstrate that the anticompetitive harm of the conduct outweighs the procompetitive benefit. In cases arising under § 1 of the Sherman Act, the courts routinely apply a similar balancing approach under the rubric of the "rule of reason." . . .

Finally, in considering whether the monopolist's conduct on balance harms competition and is therefore condemned as exclusionary for purposes of § 2, our focus is upon the effect of that conduct, not upon the intent behind it. Evidence of the intent behind the conduct of a monopolist is relevant only to the extent it helps us understand the likely effect of the monopolist's conduct. . . .

1. Licenses Issued to Original Equipment Manufacturers

The District Court condemned a number of provisions in Microsoft's agreements licensing Windows to OEMs, because it found that Microsoft's imposition of those provisions (like many of Microsoft's other actions at issue in this case) serves to reduce usage share of Netscape's browser and, hence, protect Microsoft's operating system monopoly. The reason market share in the browser market affects market power in the operating system market is complex, and warrants some explanation.

. . . .

. . . Microsoft's efforts to gain market share in one market (browsers) served to meet the threat to Microsoft's monopoly in another market (operating systems) by keeping rival browsers from gaining the critical mass of users necessary to attract developer attention away from Windows as the platform for software development. . . .

. . . .

a. *Anticompetitive effect of the license restrictions*

The restrictions Microsoft places upon Original Equipment Manufacturers are of particular importance in determining browser usage share because having an OEM pre-install a browser on a computer is one of the two most cost-effective methods by far of distributing browsing software. (The other is bundling the browser with internet access software distributed by an IAP.) . . .

. . . .

. . . [T]he OEM channel is one of the two primary channels for distribution of browsers. By preventing OEMs from removing visible means of user access to IE, the license restriction prevents many OEMs from pre-installing a rival browser and, therefore, protects Microsoft's monopoly from the competition that middleware might otherwise present. Therefore, we conclude that the license restriction at issue is anticompetitive. . . .

The second license provision at issue prohibits OEMs from modifying the initial boot sequence—the process that occurs the first time a consumer turns on the computer. . . . Microsoft's prohibition on any alteration of the boot sequence thus prevents OEMs from using that process to promote the services of IAPs, many of which—at least at the time

Microsoft imposed the restriction—used Navigator rather than IE in their internet access software. . . . Because this prohibition has a substantial effect in protecting Microsoft's market power, and does so through a means other than competition on the merits, it is anticompetitive. . . .

Finally, Microsoft imposes several additional provisions that, like the prohibition on removal of icons, prevent OEMs from making various alterations to the desktop: Microsoft prohibits OEMs from causing any user interface other than the Windows desktop to launch automatically, from adding icons or folders different in size or shape from those supplied by Microsoft, and from using the "Active Desktop" feature to promote third-party brands. These restrictions impose significant costs upon the OEMs; prior to Microsoft's prohibiting the practice, many OEMs would change the appearance of the desktop in ways they found beneficial. . . . The anticompetitive effect of the license restrictions is, as Microsoft itself recognizes, that OEMs are not able to promote rival browsers, which keeps developers focused upon the APIs in Windows. . . .

b. *Microsoft's justifications for the license restrictions*

Microsoft argues that the license restrictions are legally justified because, in imposing them, Microsoft is simply "exercising its rights as the holder of valid copyrights." . . . Microsoft also argues that the licenses "do not unduly restrict the opportunities of Netscape to distribute Navigator in any event."

Microsoft's primary copyright argument borders upon the frivolous. The company claims an absolute and unfettered right to use its intellectual property as it wishes: "[I]f intellectual property rights have been lawfully acquired," it says, then "their subsequent exercise cannot give rise to antitrust liability." . . . That is no more correct than the proposition that use of one's personal property, such as a baseball bat, cannot give rise to tort liability. . . .

. . . .

Apart from copyright, Microsoft raises one other defense of the OEM license agreements: It argues that, despite the restrictions in the OEM license, Netscape is not completely blocked from distributing its product. That claim is insufficient to shield Microsoft from liability for those restrictions because, although Microsoft did not bar its rivals from all means of distribution, it did bar them from the cost-efficient ones.

In sum, we hold that with the exception of the one restriction prohibiting automatically launched alternative interfaces, all the OEM license restrictions at issue represent uses of Microsoft's market power to protect its monopoly, unredeemed by any legitimate justification. The restrictions therefore violate § 2 of the Sherman Act.

2. Integration of IE and Windows

". . . [I]n late 1995 or early 1996, Microsoft set out to bind [IE] more tightly to Windows 95 as a technical matter."

Technologically binding IE to Windows, the District Court found, both prevented OEMs from pre-installing other browsers and deterred consumers from using them. In particular, having the IE software code as an irremovable part of Windows meant that pre-installing a second browser would "increase an OEM's product testing costs," because an OEM must test and train its support staff to answer calls related to every software product preinstalled on the machine; moreover, pre-installing a browser in addition to IE would to many OEMs be "a questionable use of the scarce and valuable space on a PC's hard drive." . . .

. . . Microsoft took . . . [three specific actions] to weld IE to Windows: excluding IE from the "Add/Remove Programs" utility; designing Windows so as in certain circumstances to override the user's choice of a default browser other than IE; and commingling code related to browsing and other code in the same files, so that any attempt to delete the files containing IE would, at the same time, cripple the operating system. . . .

a. *Anticompetitive effect of integration*

. . . .

The District Court first condemned as anticompetitive Microsoft's decision to exclude IE from the "Add/Remove Programs" utility in Windows 98. . . . Microsoft had included IE in the Add/Remove Programs utility in Windows 95 . . . but when it modified Windows 95 to produce Windows 98, it took IE out of the Add/Remove Programs utility. This change reduces the usage share of rival browsers not by making Microsoft's own browser more attractive to consumers but, rather, by discouraging OEMs from distributing rival products. . . . Because Microsoft's conduct, through something other than competition on the merits, has the effect of significantly reducing usage of rivals' products and hence protecting its own operating system monopoly, it is anticompetitive . . . .

Second, the District Court found that Microsoft designed Windows 98 "so that using Navigator on Windows 98 would have unpleasant consequences for users" by, in some circumstances, overriding the user's choice of a browser other than IE as his or her default browser. . . . Microsoft does not deny . . . that overriding the user's preference prevents some people from using other browsers. Because the override reduces rivals' usage share and protects Microsoft's monopoly, it too is anticompetitive.

Finally, the District Court condemned Microsoft's decision to bind IE to Windows 98 "by placing code specific to Web browsing in the same files as code that provided operating system functions." Putting code supplying browsing functionality into a file with code supplying operating system functionality "ensure[s] that the deletion of any file containing browsing-specific routines would also delete vital operating system routines and thus cripple Windows . . . ." . . . As noted above, preventing an OEM from removing IE deters it from installing a second browser because doing so increases the OEM's product testing and support costs; by contrast, had OEMs been able to remove IE, they might have chosen to pre-install Navigator alone. . . .

. . . .

. . . [W]e conclude that such commingling has an anticompetitive effect; . . . the commingling deters OEMs from pre-installing rival browsers, thereby reducing the rivals' usage share and, hence, developers' interest in rivals' APIs as an alternative to the API set exposed by Microsoft's operating system.

b. *Microsoft's justifications for integration*

. . . Microsoft failed to meet its burden of showing that its conduct serves a purpose other than protecting its operating system monopoly. Accordingly, we hold that Microsoft's exclusion of IE from the Add/Remove Programs utility and its commingling of browser and operating system code constitute exclusionary conduct, in violation of § 2.

As for the other challenged act that Microsoft took in integrating IE into Windows—causing Windows to override the user's choice of a default browser in certain circumstances—Microsoft argues that it has "valid technical reasons." Specifically, Microsoft claims that it was necessary to design Windows to override the user's preferences when he or she invokes one of "a few" out "of the nearly 30 means of accessing the Internet." . . . According to Microsoft:

> The Windows 98 Help system and Windows Update feature depend on ActiveX controls not supported by Navigator, and the now-discontinued Channel Bar utilized Microsoft's Channel Definition Format, which Navigator also did not support. Lastly, Windows 98 does not invoke Navigator if a user accesses the Internet through "My Computer" or "Windows Explorer" because doing so would defeat one of the purposes of those features—enabling users to move seamlessly from local storage devices to the Web *in the same browsing window*.

. . . The plaintiff bears the burden not only of rebutting a proffered justification but also of demonstrating that the anticompetitive effect of the challenged action outweighs it. In the District Court, plaintiffs appear to have done neither, let alone both; in any event, upon appeal, plaintiffs offer no rebuttal whatsoever. Accordingly, Microsoft may not be held liable for this aspect of its product design.

3. Agreements with Internet Access Providers

. . . .

. . . [W]e agree with plaintiffs that a monopolist's use of exclusive contracts, in certain circumstances, may give rise to a § 2 violation even though the contracts foreclose less than the roughly 40% or 50% share usually required in order to establish a § 1 violation. . . .

In this case, plaintiffs allege that, by closing to rivals a substantial percentage of the available opportunities for browser distribution, Microsoft managed to preserve its monopoly in the market for operating systems. The IAPs constitute one of the two major channels by which browsers can be distributed. . . .

Plaintiffs having demonstrated a harm to competition, the burden falls upon Microsoft to defend its exclusive dealing contracts with IAPs by providing a procompetitive justification for them. Significantly, Microsoft's only explanation for its exclusive dealing is that it wants to keep developers focused upon its APIs—which is to say, it wants to preserve its power in the operating system market. . . . That is not an unlawful end, but neither is it a procompetitive justification for the specific means here in question, namely exclusive dealing contracts with IAPs. Accordingly, we affirm the District Court's decision holding that Microsoft's exclusive contracts with IAPs are exclusionary devices, in violation of § 2 of the Sherman Act.

4. Dealings with Internet Content Providers, Independent Software Vendors, and Apple Computer

. . . .

. . . On appeal Microsoft likewise does not claim that the exclusivity required by the deals serves any legitimate purpose; instead, it states only that its ISV agreements reflect an attempt "to persuade ISVs to utilize Internet-related system services in Windows rather than Navigator." . . . [K]eeping developers focused upon Windows—that is, preserving the Windows monopoly—is a competitively neutral goal. Microsoft having offered no procompetitive justification for its exclusive dealing arrangements with the ISVs, we hold that those arrangements violate § 2 of the Sherman Act.

. . . .

. . . [In July of 1997] Apple and Microsoft had reached an agreement pursuant to which Microsoft's primary obligation is to continue releasing up-to-date versions of Mac Office for at least five years . . . [and] Apple has agreed . . . to "bundle the most current version of [IE] . . . with [Mac OS]" . . . [and to] "make [IE] the default [browser]" . . . . The agreement also prohibits Apple from encouraging users to substitute another browser for IE, and states that Apple will "encourage its employees to use [IE]." . . .

. . . .

Microsoft offers no procompetitive justification for the exclusive dealing arrangement. It makes only the irrelevant claim that the IE-for-Mac Office deal is part of a multifaceted set of agreements between itself and Apple . . . . Accordingly, we hold that the exclusive deal with Apple is exclusionary, in violation of § 2 of the Sherman Act.

5. Java

Java, a set of technologies developed by Sun Microsystems, is another type of middleware posing a potential threat to Windows' position as the ubiquitous platform for software development. . . . The Java technologies include: (1) a programming language; (2) a set of programs written in that language, called the "Java class libraries," which expose APIs; (3) a compiler, which translates code written by a developer into "bytecode"; and (4) a Java Virtual Machine ("JVM"), which translates bytecode into the instructions to the operating system. . . .

In May 1995 Netscape agreed with Sun to distribute a copy of the Java runtime environment with every copy of Navigator . . . . Microsoft, too, agreed to promote the Java technologies—or so it seemed. . . . [T]he District Court found that Microsoft took four steps to exclude Java from developing as a viable cross-platform threat: (a) designing a JVM incompatible with the one developed by Sun; (b) entering into contracts, the so-called "First Wave Agreements," requiring major ISVs to promote Microsoft's JVM exclusively; (c) deceiving Java developers about the Windows-specific nature of the tools it distributed to them; and (d) coercing Intel to stop aiding Sun in improving the Java technologies.

a. *The incompatible JVM*

. . . The JVM developed by Microsoft allows Java applications to run faster on Windows than does Sun's JVM . . . . [A] monopolist does not violate the antitrust laws simply by developing a product that is incompatible with those of its rivals. . . . The JVM, however, does allow applications to run more swiftly and does not itself have any anticompetitive effect. Therefore, we reverse the District Court's imposition of liability for Microsoft's development and promotion of its JVM.

b. *The First Wave Agreements*

The District Court also found that Microsoft entered into First Wave Agreements with dozens of ISVs to use Microsoft's JVM. . . .

To the extent Microsoft's First Wave Agreements with the ISVs conditioned receipt of Windows technical information upon the ISVs' agreement to promote Microsoft's JVM exclusively, they raise a . . . competitive concern. . . .

. . . Because Microsoft's agreements foreclosed a substantial portion of the field for JVM distribution and because, in so doing, they protected Microsoft's monopoly from a middleware threat, they are anticompetitive.

Microsoft offered no procompetitive justification for the default clause that made the First Wave Agreements exclusive as a practical matter. . . . Because the cumulative effect of the deals is anticompetitive and because Microsoft has no procompetitive justification for them, we hold that the provisions in the First Wave Agreements requiring use of Microsoft's JVM as the default are exclusionary, in violation of the Sherman Act.

c. *Deception of Java developers*

Microsoft's "Java implementation" included, in addition to a JVM, a set of software development tools it created to assist ISVs in designing Java applications. . . . Microsoft's tools included "certain 'keywords' and 'compiler directives' that could only be executed properly by Microsoft's version of the Java runtime environment for Windows." . . . As a result, even Java "developers who were opting for portability over performance . . . unwittingly [wrote] Java applications that [ran] only on Windows." . . . That is, developers who relied upon Microsoft's public commitment to cooperate with Sun and who used Microsoft's tools to develop what Microsoft led them to believe were cross-platform applications ended up producing applications that would run only on the Windows operating system.

. . . .

. . . [O]ther Microsoft documents confirm that Microsoft intended to deceive Java developers, and predicted that the effect of its actions would be to generate Windows-dependent Java applications that their developers believed would be cross-platform; these documents also indicate that Microsoft's ultimate objective was to thwart Java's threat to Microsoft's monopoly in the market for operating systems. One Microsoft document, for example, states as a strategic goal: "Kill cross-platform Java by grow[ing] the polluted Java market." . . .

Microsoft's conduct related to its Java developer tools served to protect its monopoly of the operating system in a manner not attributable either to the superiority of the operating system or to the acumen of its makers, and therefore was anticompetitive. Unsurprisingly, Microsoft offers no procompetitive explanation for its campaign to deceive developers. Accordingly, we conclude this conduct is exclusionary, in violation of § 2 of the Sherman Act.

d. *The threat to Intel*

. . . In 1995 Intel was in the process of developing a highperformance, Windows-compatible JVM. Microsoft wanted Intel to abandon that effort because a fast, cross-platform JVM would threaten Microsoft's monopoly in the operating system market. At an August 1995 meeting, Microsoft's Gates told Intel that its "cooperation with Sun and Netscape to develop a Java runtime environment . . . was one of the issues threatening to undermine cooperation between Intel and Microsoft." . . .

. . . By 1996 "Intel had developed a JVM designed to run well . . . while complying with Sun's cross-platform standards." . . . Microsoft threatened Intel that if it did not stop aiding Sun on the multimedia front, then Microsoft would refuse to distribute Intel technologies bundled with Windows. . . .

Intel finally capitulated in 1997. . . .

Microsoft's internal documents and deposition testimony confirm both the anticompetitive effect and intent of its actions. . . .

Microsoft does not deny the facts found by the District Court, nor does it offer any procompetitive justification for pressuring Intel not to support cross-platform Java. Microsoft lamely characterizes its threat to Intel as "advice." The District Court, however, found that Microsoft's "advice" to Intel to stop aiding cross-platform Java was backed by the threat of retaliation, and this conclusion is supported by the evidence cited above. Therefore we affirm the conclusion that Microsoft's threats to Intel were exclusionary, in violation of § 2 of the Sherman Act.

. . . .

C. Causation

As a final parry, Microsoft urges this court to reverse on the monopoly maintenance claim, because plaintiffs never established a causal link between Microsoft's anticompetitive conduct, in particular its foreclosure of Netscape's and Java's distribution channels, and the maintenance of Microsoft's operating system monopoly. . . .

. . . .

We may infer causation when exclusionary conduct is aimed at producers of nascent competitive technologies as well as when it is aimed at producers of established substitutes. . . .

. . . .

. . . [T]he question in this case is not whether Java or Navigator would actually have developed into viable platform substitutes, but (1) whether as a general matter the exclusion of nascent threats is the type of conduct that is reasonably capable of contributing significantly to a defendant's continued monopoly power and (2) whether Java and Navigator reasonably constituted nascent threats at the time Microsoft engaged in the anticompetitive conduct at issue. As to the first, suffice it to say that it would be inimical to the purpose of the Sherman Act to allow monopolists free reign to squash nascent, albeit unproven, competitors at will—particularly in industries marked by rapid technological advance and frequent paradigm shifts. . . . As to the second, the District Court made ample findings that both Navigator and Java showed potential as middleware platform threats.

V. TRIAL PROCEEDINGS AND REMEDY

. . . .

Over Microsoft's objections, the District Court proceeded to consider the merits of the remedy and on June 7, 2000 entered its final judgment. The court explained that it would not conduct "extended proceedings on the form a remedy should take" . . . .

The decree's centerpiece . . . [of the District Court's Final Judgment] is the requirement that Microsoft submit a proposed plan of divestiture, with the company to be split into an "Operating Systems Business," or "OpsCo," and an "Applications Business," or "AppsCo." . . . OpsCo would receive all of Microsoft's operating systems, such as Windows 98 and Windows 2000, while AppsCo would receive the remainder of Microsoft's businesses, including IE and Office. The District Court identified four reasons for its "reluctant[ ]" conclusion that "a structural remedy has become imperative." . . . First, Microsoft "does not yet concede that any of its business practices violated the Sherman Act." *Id.* Second, the company consequently "continues to do business as it has in the past." . . . Third, Microsoft "has proved untrustworthy in the past." And fourth, the Government, whose officials "are by reason of office obliged and expected to consider—and to act in—the public interest," won the case, "and for that reason alone have some entitlement to a remedy of their choice."

The decree also contains a number of interim restrictions on Microsoft's conduct. For instance, Decree § 3.b requires Microsoft to disclose to third-party developers the APIs and other technical information necessary to ensure that software effectively interoperates with Windows. . . . "To facilitate compliance," § 3.b further requires that Microsoft establish "a secure facility" at which third-party representatives may "study, interrogate and interact with relevant and necessary portions of [Microsoft platform software] source code." . . . Section 3.e, entitled "Ban on Exclusive Dealing," forbids Microsoft from entering contracts which oblige third parties to restrict their "development, production, distribution, promotion or use of, or payment for" non-Microsoft platform-level software. Under Decree

§ 3.f—"Ban on Contractual Tying"—the company may not condition its grant of a Windows license on a party's agreement "to license, promote, or distribute any other Microsoft software product." . . . And § 3.g imposes a "Restriction on Binding Middleware Products to Operating System Products" unless Microsoft also offers consumers "an otherwise identical version" of the operating system without the middleware. . . .

. . . .

. . . [T]he District Court erred when it resolved the parties' remedies-phase factual disputes by consulting only the evidence introduced during trial and plaintiffs' remedies-phase submissions, without considering the evidence Microsoft sought to introduce. We therefore vacate the District Court's final judgment, and remand with instructions to conduct a remedies-specific evidentiary hearing.

D. Failure to Provide an Adequate Explanation

We vacate the District Court's remedies decree for the additional reason that the court has failed to provide an adequate explanation for the relief it ordered. The Supreme Court has explained that a remedies decree in an antitrust case must seek to "unfetter a market from anticompetitive conduct," . . . [and] to "terminate the illegal monopoly, deny to the defendant the fruits of its statutory violation, and ensure that there remain no practices likely to result in monopolization in the future" . . . .

The District Court has not explained how its remedies decree would accomplish those objectives. . . .

E. Modification of Liability

Quite apart from its procedural difficulties, we vacate the District Court's final judgment in its entirety for the additional, independent reason that we have modified the underlying bases of liability. Of the three antitrust violations originally identified by the District Court, one is no longer viable: attempted monopolization of the browser market in violation of Sherman Act § 2. One will be remanded for liability proceedings under a different legal standard: unlawful tying in violation of § 1. Only liability for the § 2 monopoly-maintenance violation has been affirmed—and even that we have revised. . . .

. . . .

In short, we must vacate the remedies decree in its entirety and remand the case for a new determination. . . .

F. On Remand

. . . .

On remand, the District Court must reconsider whether the use of the structural remedy of divestiture is appropriate with respect to Microsoft, which argues that it is a unitary company. By and large, cases upon which plaintiffs rely in arguing for the split of Microsoft have involved the dissolution of entities formed by mergers and acquisitions. . . .

. . . .

VI. JUDICIAL MISCONDUCT

Canon 3A(6) of the Code of Conduct for United States Judges requires federal judges to "avoid public comment on the merits of [ ] pending or impending" cases. Canon 2 tells judges to "avoid impropriety and the appearance of impropriety in all activities," on the bench and off. Canon 3A(4) forbids judges to initiate or consider *ex parte* communications on the merits of pending or impending proceedings. Section 455(a) of the Judicial Code requires judges to recuse themselves when their "impartiality might reasonably be questioned." 28 U.S.C. § 455(a).

All indications are that the District Judge violated each of these ethical precepts by talking about the case with reporters. The violations were deliberate, repeated, egregious, and flagrant.

. . . .

. . . [We] conclude that the appropriate remedy for the violations of § 455(a) is disqualification of the District Judge retroactive only to the date he entered the order breaking up Microsoft. We therefore will vacate that order in its entirety and remand this case to a different District Judge, but will not set aside the existing Findings of Fact or Conclusions of Law . . . .

. . . .

COMMENTARY

1. On the remand, how should the district court implement the recognition by the Court of Appeals of the unique requirements for antitrust analysis involving technology-driven markets such as those for computer software?

2. In affirming the District Court's findings of "anticompetitive effect" by Microsoft through its OEM licensing restrictions, excluding IE from the add/remove program utility, and commingling browser code with other code, did the Court of Appeals consider effects which it measured objectively in the marketplace? Or, did the Court of Appeals consider effects in which the questioned conduct could reasonably be assumed to significantly contribute to maintaining monopoly power?

3. The Court of Appeals opinion frequently refers to the fact that Microsoft failed to offer a procompetitive justification for a given practice. Explain the court's analysis of monopolization under § 2 and state when the burden of presenting such a justification devolves on a defendant.

4. Microsoft argued that its license restrictions were justified because it was a holder of valid copyrights. In dismissing this justification, consider whether the Court of Appeals was implying that when there is a conflict between copyright (and patent rights) and antitrust claims, the antitrust claim prevails. Consider this issue again when you read *In re Independent Service Organization Antitrust Litigation*, in Chapter 15, page 794, *infra*.

5. The Court of Appeals reversed the District Court's finding that Microsoft's development of its JVM violated § 2. Does this suggest that technological improvement of a dominant product—*e.g.*, allowing applications to run faster—may justify some anticompetitive effect such as incompatibility with a competing product?

6. Trade papers report that the new Windows operating system, WindowsXP will contain new Internet software for listening to music, shopping, and instant messaging. As Windows XP is about to be released, the market for the software for media players is dominated by a Microsoft rival, RealNetworks, and the instant messaging market is dominated by AOL Time Warner. Would you advise Microsoft that it can design Windows XP so that it only permits Windows Media Player to run on Windows XP? What terms restricting the RealNetworks and AOL instant messaging icons would you advise in a WindowsXP license to an OEM ?

7. As to divestiture as a remedy for anticompetitive conduct, the history of the enforcement of the antitrust laws records the use of divestiture as a means of ending such conduct. In *Standard Oil Co. of New Jersey v. United States*, 221 U.S. 1 (1911), the Standard Oil Trust, consisting of 37 subsidiary corporations was dissolved. Similarly the Tobacco Trust was dissolved into 3 companies in *United States v. American Tobacco Co.*, 221 U.S. 106 (1911). In *United States v. A.T.&T. Co.*, 552 F. Supp. 131 (D.D.C. 1982), *aff'd sub nom., Maryland v. United States*, 400 U.S. 1001 (1982), the American Telephone and Telegraph Co. was reorganized as a group of regional Bell telephone companies. *See* Chapter 1, *supra*, page 21ff., for a discussion of the structure of firms and industries with reference to antitrust law. As to mergers, the Supreme Court has described divestiture as "the most important of antitrust remedies. It is simple, relatively easy to administer, and sure." *United States v. E.I. du Pont de Nemours & Co.*, 366 U.S. 316, 330-31 (1961).

See also Stephen C. Fraidin, *Dissolution and Reconstruction: A Structural Remedy and Alternatives,* 33 GEO. WASH. L. REV. 693 (1965); Kevin J. O'Connor, *The Divestiture Remedy in Sherman Act § 2 Cases*, 13 HARV. J. ON LEGIS. 687 (1976); William E. Kovacic, *Designing Antitrust Remedies for Dominant Firm Misconduct,* 31 CONN. L. REV. 1285 (1999); Howard A. Shelanski & J. Gregory Sidak, *Antitrust Divestiture in Network Industries,* 68 U. CHI. L. REV. 1 (2001).

8. As the dominant antitrust case of the 1990s, the Microsoft litigation has attracted the attention of journalists. *See* KEN AULETTA, WORLD WAR 3.0: MICROSOFT AND ITS ENEMIES (2001). In this book, the journalist records his interviews with the principal participants in this litigation including the trial judge. Auletta describes his conversations with Judge Jackson that took place during the trial and after the verdict (but before the appeals process had been exhausted) as follows:

> We met for several hours on October 6, 1999, and began talking about the case. . . . [We met] on April 9, 2000, and our . . . final session was on July 9, 2000. All our sessions were taped and on the record.

Id. at 405. Note the grounds on which the Court of Appeals remanded this case to different district court judge.

3. The Essential Facilities Doctrine

The origins of the essential facilities doctrine, on which the court of appeals in *Aspen* relied (and which reliance was rejected by the Supreme Court in its affirmance), originated in *United States v. Terminal Railroad Ass'n of St. Louis*, 224 U.S. 383 (1912). St. Louis, Missouri is situated on the western bank of the Mississippi River. Twenty four railways converged at that point, approximately half terminating in Illinois on the eastern bank of the river and the remainder at St. Louis on the western bank. Led by the famous robber baron Jay Gould, six railroads had formed the Terminal Railroad Association. (Subsequently other railroads were admitted to membership; the membership, however, never embraced all of the railroads terminating at St. Louis.) The Association acquired the union station, the Eads or St. Louis Bridge, and every connecting or terminal company by means of which that bridge could be used by railroads terminating on either side of the River. The Association subsequently acquired the Merchants Bridge and the Wiggins Ferry Company, giving it control over every means by which rail traffic could cross the River at that point.

The government sought dissolution of the Association under the antitrust laws. When the case reached the Supreme Court, the Court took a different approach. It held that the combination of all terminal facilities in a single system would not be unlawful, if the system were operated as the agent of each of the railroads and thus accorded equal treatment to all of them. Accordingly, the Court held that dissolution would not be ordered if membership in the Terminal Association were made open to all railroads and if those railroads not wishing to become members were nonetheless provided with access to the terminal facilities on reasonable terms.

Two things were clear to the Court: (1) it would be both wasteful and impractical for each railroad to build its own bridge across the River; and (2) the antitrust law would not permit some railroads to acquire the only means of crossing the river and to exploit that monopoly by denying passage to other railroads or to impose unreasonable charges on them.

In 1945, the Supreme Court took a slightly different position in *Associated Press v. United States*, 326 U.S. 1 (1945). In that case the issue concerned access to the pool of news possessed by the Associated Press ("AP"), a cooperative venture formed by newspapers located in most of the major U.S. cities. Each newspaper member of the AP contributed the local news which it routinely collected for its own local operations to the AP news pool. That aggregate pool of news was made available to each newspaper member, thus providing each member with access to a huge pool of news. Although it was easy for a newspaper from an uncovered area to become a member, the Associated Press bylaws made it exceedingly difficult for newspapers located in areas served by an existing member (and therefore competing with an existing member) to join. Since the bylaws also prohibited members from selling news to nonmembers, nonmembers were effectively denied access to a valuable pool of news.

Although there were other news gathering organizations competing with the Associated Press in selling news to newspapers (such as United Press and International News Service), the Court believed that access to the Associated Press pool of news was important: "It is apparent that the exclusive right to publish news in a given field, furnished by AP and all of its members, gives many newspapers a competitive advantage over their rivals. Conversely, a newspaper without AP service is more than likely to be at a competitive disadvantage."

The Court agreed with the government that the AP news pool was competitively significant, but did not order AP membership be made open to all applicants. Rather, the district court ruled that competition with an existing member could not be taken into account when the Association determined whether or not to admit a new applicant for membership. On appeal of the district court's ruling, the Court affirmed: "Interpreting the decree to mean that AP news is to be furnished to competitors of old members without discrimination through By-Laws controlling membership or otherwise, we approve it." Aside from a passing reference to *Associated Press* in *Otter Tail Power,* 410 U.S. 366, 377 (1973), the Supreme Court has not elaborated on the doctrine contained in that case.

In 1977, the Court of Appeals for the District of Columbia described the *Terminal Railroad* case as applying the "essential facilities" doctrine. *Hecht v. Pro-Football, Inc.*, 570 F.2d 982 (D.C. Cir. 1977). The lower courts, however, have applied that doctrine to the limitation of use or access to a natural monopoly or "bottleneck facility" that restricts horizontal competition. As the late Professor Areeda wrote of this doctrine in 1989:

> . . . [M]ost Supreme Court cases invoked in support do not speak of it and can be explained without reference to it. . . . It is less a doctrine than an epithet, indicating some exception to the right to keep one's creations to oneself, but not telling us what those exceptions are.

Essential Facilities: An Epithet in Need of Limiting Principles, 58 ANTITRUST L.J. 841 (1989). Another recent commentator has stated that:

> The essential facilities concept . . . is not currently a coherent antitrust doctrine. . . . [P]erhaps courts should abandon the doctrine. Denials . . . [of access] that increase or maintain market power are already subject to attack . . . [as a] group boycott, monopolization, or attempt to monopolize.

James R. Ratner, *Should There Be an Essential Facility Doctrine?,* 21 U.C. DAVIS L. REV. 327, 382 (1988). Economists are equally critical of the doctrine. *See* David Reiffen & Andrew N. Kleit, Terminal Railroad *Revisited: Foreclosure of an Essential Facility or Simple Horizontal Monopoly?,* 33 J.L. & ECON. 419, 437 (1990) (The essential facilities doctrine . . . may discourage efficient behavior without a corresponding benefit in . . . deterring anticompetitive conduct.). Many lower courts have invoked the doctrine both in the regulated and unregulated sectors of the economy. *E.g.,* in *Fishman v. Wirtz,* 807 F.2d 520 (7th Cir. 1986), the court of appeals applied the doctrine to a sports stadium and held (over a dissent by Judge

Easterbrook that questioned whether there was an issue of antitrust injury) that the refusal to lease constituted monopolization as well as an illegal boycott. In the regulated sector, MCI prevailed, on essential facility principles, in requiring AT&T to grant it access to local telephone exchanges, as required by federal regulatory policy. *See MCI Communications Co. v. American Telephone and Telegraph Co.,* 708 F.2d 1801 (7th Cir.), *cert. denied,* 464 U.S. 891 (1983). Similarly, the divestiture of AT&T by Judge Greene in *United States v. American Telephone and Telegraph Co.,* 552 F. Supp. 131 (D.C. 1982); *aff'd sub nom., Maryland v. United States*, 460 U.S. 1001 (1983), was based on the theory that AT&T, having acquired control of all long-distance telephone lines, was required to grant access to them by competitors.

In the case that follows, was the essential facility doctrine a tool of analysis or an epithet, as Professor Areeda characterized it above?

City of Anaheim v. Southern California Edison Co.

955 F.2d 1373 (9th Cir. 1992)

FERNANDEZ, Circuit Judge.

The Cities of Anaheim, Riverside, Banning, Colton and Azusa (the Cities) brought this action against Southern California Edison Company (Edison) and alleged that Edison had violated section 2 of the Sherman Act, 15 U.S.C. § 2 (§ 2) by engaging in a regulatory price squeeze and by denying access to an essential facility. After a court trial, the district court found in favor of Edison and entered judgment accordingly. The Cities appeal. We affirm.

BACKGROUND

Edison is an investor-owned fully integrated public utility, which generates, transmits, and distributes electric power within its service area, an area which includes much of Central and Southern California. The Cities are located in Edison's service area, but each has its own electrical distribution system and is the sole provider of retail electric service within its own boundaries. Edison provides retail service to all customers who are within its area and not within the boundaries of the Cities.

Although the Cities distribute power at retail within their boundaries, they do not generate their own electricity. Thus, they obtain their power in bulk elsewhere and receive it over Edison's transmission lines. That wholesale power is purchased from Edison or from other electrical utilities. It is Edison's responsibility to see to it that the Cities receive all of the power that they need. Edison also purchases power from and sells it to other utilities.

. . . .

Among the facilities which Edison has access to are certain high-power transmission lines (the Pacific Intertie) which bring hydroelectric power to Edison's control area from the Pacific Northwest. That power is generated by various entities in the Pacific Northwest, including the Bonneville Power Administration (BPA). When conditions are favorable, that power becomes available for export and is significantly cheaper than bulk power generated in California and the other Western states. Edison shares access to the Pacific Intertie with certain other utilities, which means that it is entitled to only a portion of the lines' total capacity.

Two of the cities, Anaheim and Riverside, asked for firm access to the Pacific Intertie, but Edison rejected that on grounds that it expected to use its full capacity rights in the Intertie to bring power into its service area for the benefit of all of its customers. It did offer interruptible access, however. The Cities assert that they cannot purchase the BPA and other Pacific Northwest power if access is interruptible. They assign this as another § 2 violation. . . .

B. The Essential Facility Claim.

In order to consider the Cities' claim that the Pacific Intertie is an essential facility to which they have improperly been denied access, we must first consider the scope of that doctrine. We will then apply it to the facts found by the district court.

1. The Theory.

The essential facility doctrine has a long history, although its contours are still far from clear. In *United States v. Terminal R.R. Ass'n*, 224 U.S. 383 (1912), the Court found an antitrust violation where virtually all terminal facilities through which railroad traffic could enter the City of St. Louis were controlled by a monopolist. The Court required that access to the terminal be allowed to others on nondiscriminatory terms. Stated thus, in the simplest and rawest of terms, it would seem that a company in a monopoly position is required to aid its competitors at all costs. That is not true. *See Aspen Skiing Co. v. Aspen Highlands Skiing Corp.*, 472 U.S. 585, 600-01 (1985); *Oahu*, 838 F.2d at 368. Neither is it true that a refusal to deal can be issued for no good business reason whatever. *Aspen*, 472 U.S. at 608-11; *Oahu*, 838 F.2d at 368.

The essential facility doctrine is a facet of this overarching concept. A company which has monopoly power over an essential facility may not refuse to make the facility available to others where there is no legitimate business reason for the refusal. The wrong perpetrated by that misuse of the facility is that a monopolist "can extend monopoly power from one stage of production to another, and from one market into another." *MCI Communications Corp. v. American Tel. & Tel. Co.*, 708 F.2d 1081, 1132 (7th Cir.), *cert. denied*, 464 U.S. 891 (1983). In *MCI*, for example, AT & T refused to allow MCI use of AT & T's local facilities and did so for no good reason. . . . Nevertheless, unless [a facility] . . . can be and is used to improperly interfere with competition, it cannot be called essential. For example, it seems clear that Edison's local transmission system, without which the Cities cannot feasibly obtain power at all, is essential. *See Otter Tail* [*Power Co. v. United States*], 410 U.S. at 378. As the district court recognized, the Pacific Intertie is a different matter entirely.

Once it is decided that a facility is essential, we must still determine whether the monopolist is liable for refusing to allow use of the facility. In *MCI*, the court identified four necessary elements:

> (1) control of the essential facility by a monopolist; (2) a competitor's inability practically or reasonably to duplicate the essential facility; (3) the denial of the use of the facility to a competitor; and (4) the feasibility of providing the facility.

708 F.2d at 1132-33 (citations omitted).

We do not disagree with that listing, but must point out that the second element is effectively part of the definition of what is an essential facility in the first place. That is to say, if the facility can be reasonably or practically duplicated it is highly unlikely, even impossible, that it will be found to be essential at all. . . .

It should also be pointed out that the fourth element basically raises the familiar question of whether there is a legitimate business justification for the refusal to provide the facility, as application of the doctrine in *MCI* itself demonstrates. . . .

2. Application of the Theory.

The district court found that the Pacific Intertie is not, standing alone, an essential facility at all. It so held because, as a matter of fact, the Cities could obtain power from many other sources. One of those sources was Edison itself. If they obtained power from that source, they would have ready access to a fair proportion of all power that could be brought in over the Pacific Intertie. That is so because Edison's reason for denying firm access was simply that when Northwest Power was available and inexpensive Edison was fully using its capacity to import that power into its whole system. Furthermore, if the Cities wished to obtain power elsewhere, Edison would still wheel it to them.

In short, there was no dearth of available power. Nor, as a matter of fact, did inability to obtain Pacific Northwest Power preclude the Cities from obtaining power at reasonable rates to meet their needs and the needs of their customers. As the district judge recognized, "the Cities' whole argument asks the Court to turn the essential facility doctrine on its head. Rather than seeking to impose a duty to deal based on the harm that would result to competition from the monopolist's refusal, the Cities seek to impose a duty to deal based on the extent to which a competitor might benefit if it had unlimited access to the monopolist's facility." In short, the fact that the Cities could achieve savings at the expense of Edison and its other customers is not enough to turn the Pacific Intertie into an essential facility. That being so, the district court did not err.

If the Pacific Intertie were an essential facility, Edison could still deny access if it had legitimate business reasons for that denial. The district court properly found that Edison did.

As we have already stated, Edison had a limited right to use the capacity of the Pacific Intertie, and it desired to use that capacity to the limit when it could get inexpensive power from the Pacific Northwest. Thus, it refused to give the Cities firm access because it could not transmit all of the power it wanted if a portion of its capacity rights were being used by the Cities at the same time.

When Edison obtains less expensive power, that is rolled into its other costs and results in a savings to all of its customers. In this sort of regulated industry, it is certainly to the benefit of the monopolist's customers if its rates are kept as low as possible. Indeed, that is a major reason for the existence of regulatory commissions such as CPUC and FERC. In other words, the public interest is well served when that happens, and that gives even more weight to the propriety of the refusal. . . .

This is not a situation where the capacity is not being used (*MCI*) or the sole reason for the denial of access is to maintain a monopoly (*Otter Tail*). It is a situation where Edison can use its own facility in full to obtain the inexpensive power. The Cities seem to contend that Edison has to disable itself so that they can get cheap power. The law requires no such thing.

Put bluntly, the Cities desired to benefit their customers at the expense of all of the other customers of Edison. We cannot express surprise at the Cities' single-minded desire to benefit their own—it is much like Edison's single-minded attention to its rate demands. However, we also cannot say that Edison's refusal lacked a reasonable business justification.

. . . .

4. Epilogue

Over the years since the decisions in *du Pont* and *Griffith,* there has been a decline in the number of cases brought by the government under § 2. In 1959, Carl Kaysen and Donald F. Turner published an important book reflecting the collaboration of an economist and a lawyer, ANTITRUST POLICY, in which they expressed concern over the abusive potential of concentration and advocated an antitrust policy of deconcentration. In the interim, economic analysis had produced new insights into the significance of structure as a predictor of the behavior of market actors. Accordingly, the central role assigned by economists to the structure of markets that was characteristic of the writing of the 1940s (described in Chapter 1 at pages 21-23), was reduced. In place of structure, by the 1970s considerations of consumer welfare and allocative efficiency were added to the criteria for assessing the performance of markets. In 1986, Judge Richard Posner described this shift in doctrinal emphasis as it is reflected in the case law as follows:

> Opinion about the offense of monopolization has undergone an evolution. Forty years ago it was thought that even a firm with a lawful monopoly . . . would not be allowed to defend its monopoly against would-be competitors by tactics otherwise legitimate; it had to exercise special restraint. . . . So Alcoa was condemned as a monopolist because it had assiduously created enough productive capacity to supply all new increments of demand for aluminum; it would not have been condemned if by keeping its prices high it had kept demand down to a level it could supply without increasing its capacity. . . . Later, as the emphasis of antitrust policy shifted from the protection of competition as a process of rivalry to the protection of competition as a means of promoting allocative efficiency, . . . it became recognized that the lawful monopolist should be free to compete like everyone else.
>
> * * *
>
> Today it is clear that a firm with lawful monopoly power has no general duty to help its competitors. . . .

Olympia Equipment Leasing Co. v. Western Union Telegraph Co., 797 F.2d 370, 375 (7th Cir. 1986).

Returning to the historical perspective, it became apparent by the mid-1970s that criteria other than structure were relevant. In 1974, the publication of a joint lawyer-economist volume containing the results of a conference on the role of concentration in antitrust policy convened at Columbia Law School drew attention to the issue. That book, entitled INDUSTRIAL CONCENTRATION: THE NEW LEARNING (Harvey Goldschmid, H. Michael Mann & J. Fred Weston eds.), was in part a reaction to a legislative proposal by Senator Philip Hart (S. 1167, 93rd Cong., 2d Sess. (1974)), a measure that was premised upon the concept that concentration was a condition requiring correction. The introduction conveys the tone of the Bill:

> The Congress finds and declares that (1) . . . [we are] committed to a . . . free market economy, in the belief that competition spurs innovation, promotes productivity, preserves a democratic society; and provides an opportunity for an equitable distribution of wealth while avoiding the undue concentration of economic, social, and political power; (2) the decline of competition in industries with oligopoly or monopoly power has contributed to unemployment, inflation, inefficiency, and underutilization of economic capacity, and the decline of exports, thereby rendering monetary and fiscal policies inadequate. . . .

To address the concerns expressed, Bill § 101(a) provided:

> It is hereby declared to be unlawful for any corporation or two or more corporations, whether by agreement or not, to possess monopoly power in any line of commerce. . . .
>
> (b) There shall be a rebuttable presumption that monopoly power is possessed—
>
> (1) by any corporation if the average rate of return on net worth after taxes is in excess of 15 percentum over a period of five consecutive years out of the most recent seven years preceding the filing of the complaint, or
>
> (2) if there has been no substantial price competition among two or more corporations . . . for a period of three consecutive years out of the most recent five years preceding the filing of the complaint.

This emphasis on structure stated in S. 1167 was also reflected in enforcement policy. In 1972, the Federal Trade Commission filed a complaint against the four major manufacturers of ready to eat cereal, Kellogg, General Mills, General Food, and Quaker Oats. This complaint was based on the novel theory that these few, dominant firms were maintaining a "shared monopoly" by artificial differentiation of products, unfair methods of competition in advertising and promotion, restrictive retail shelf space programs, and acquisition of competitors. ANTITRUST & TRADE REG. REP., (BNA) July 11, 1952, No. 571, A-5. The underlying premise of the complaint was that the anticompetitive behavior was fostered by the oligopolistic structure of the market in which the firms operated. This action was dismissed in *In the Matter of Kellogg*, 99 F.T.C. 8, 16 (1982), after critical comment by economists and others. BRIAN HARRIS, SHARED MONOPOLY AND THE CEREAL INDUSTRY (1979); Yale Brozen, *Entry Barriers: Advertising and Product Differentiation,* in INDUSTRIAL CONCENTRATION: THE NEW LEARNING 115 (Goldschmid, Mann & Weston eds. 1974).

The Antitrust Division's acceptance of the importance of structure was reflected in the two major cases it brought against IBM and AT&T in 1969 and in 1974. The complaint against IBM detailed antitcompetitive conduct designed to maintain its dominance in the industry amounting to illegal monopolization. The

AT&T case rested on a theory of monopolization of both the communications services and equipment markets. Ultimately, the IBM case was abandoned by the Antitrust Division in 1982 and on the same day, the AT&T case was settled by the divestiture of some twenty local operating companies, leaving the parent company with control of the long distance business. *See* NEW YORK TIMES, Saturday, January 9, 1982, p. 1, col. 6, p. C1, col. 4.

COMMENTARY

1. See Chapter 11 on Predatory Pricing. Do the cases and literature on this topic rest on structural or on conduct considerations? The shift away from emphasis on structure was described by F. M. Scherer in his pioneering 1970 review of the structural literature, INDUSTRIAL MARKET STRUCTURE AND ECONOMIC PERFORMANCE 6, as follows:

> Bain [Joe Bain was a pioneer in the study of market structure] stresses the formulation of direct empirical links between market structure and economic performance, deemphasizing intermediate conduct. . . . In this volume, by contrast, much of the analysis . . . attacks the question of structure . . . by focusing intensely on the business conduct which spans those phenomena. . . . [I]t could be said that Bain is predominantly a structuralist, while the author of the present work is a behaviorist.

Later critics of Bain's approach were: John S. McGee, *Efficiency and Economies of Size,* and Harold Demsetz, *Two Systems of Belief About Monopoly, in* INDUSTRIAL CONCENTRATION: THE NEW LEARNING 55.

2. Given the current conception of the role of antitrust law described in Chapter 1, how should antitrust enforcement policy be focused? Note the significance of structure in the enforcement of merger policy in Chapter 12, *infra.* See the discussion in Chapter 12 of the judicial review of the consent decree in *United States v. Microsoft,* a § 2 case. Note that the government did not seek divestiture in that case, a structural remedy, but rather addressed certain business practices. To what extent is structure a reliable indicator of business practices? Might the government's position in *Microsoft* reflect a change in the significance that was given to structure when the § 2 case, noted above, was brought against IBM in 1974? Should enforcement policy be focused primarily on conduct? What are the best indicators of the kind of anticompetitive conduct that should be inhibited or punished?

Chapter 10
Attempt to Monopolize

A. The Origins and Contours of the Attempt Offense: An Historical Note

In interpreting the phrase in § 2 of the Sherman Act, "attempt to monopolize," courts again have had to characterize business practices, as they were required to do in the § 2 monopolization cases. Here the task is more complex since by definition, the defendant lacks the requisite degree of market power to warrant a charge of monopolizing. Courts have filled this evidentiary gap with a requirement of a finding of intent. Courts apply a three-part test in determining liability for attempted monopolization: 1) proof of specific intent to monopolize, 2) proof of a dangerous probability that the attempt will succeed, and 3) anticompetitive or exclusionary conduct. As the following material shows, courts have increasingly been enmeshed in seeking to distinguish "predatory," "anticompetitive,"or "exclusionary" business practices from vigorous competition, often in circumstances involving a single firm with less than a dominant share of the market. Over two decades ago an antitrust scholar, having reviewed the "attempt to monopolize" cases, warned against the dangers inherent in judicial evaluation of business behavior:

> Judicial competence to evaluate competitive behavior is limited. The predominant lines of present law confine judicial intrusion to areas in which the dangers of anticompetitive behavior are enhanced by substantial elements of market power, in which there is a correspondingly increased probability that a judicial decision to intervene will not upset desirable competitive arrangements, and in which mistakenly depriving a major firm of desirable competitive freedom may not be as grave as imposing the same limitations on a lesser firm. Once the invitation to intrude in areas of lesser market power is accepted, it is difficult to resist the seductive temptation to pass adverse judgment on neutral or even desirable forms of competition. If the attempt offense is given an independent life of its own, free from any requirement of a close approach to completed monopolization, the dangers of mistaken judgment seem too great to be borne.

Edward H. Cooper, *Attempts and Monopolization: A Mildly Expansionary Answer to the Prophylactic Riddle of Section Two,* 72 MICH. L. REV. 375, 378 (1974).

The contours of the attempt offense can be seen in the following decisions of the U.S. Supreme Court: *Swift & Co. v. United States*, 196 U.S. 375 (1905); *Lorain Journal Co. v. United States*, 342 U.S. 143 (1951); and *Otter Tail Power Co. v. United States*, 410 U.S. 366 (1973). These decisions must be read in the light of the Court's decision in *United States v. Griffith*, 334 U.S. 100 (1948), a monopolization case, which forms part of the background essential to an understanding of the attempt clause.

1. *Swift & Co. v. United States*, 196 U.S. 375 (1905)

The government alleged that several large meat packers, controlling 60% of the meat packing business in the United States, were acting in combination, *inter alia*, to maintain prices on meat. In upholding the government's complaint, Justice Holmes, writing for the Court, included the following remarks:

> It is suggested that the several acts charged are lawful, and that intent can make no difference. But they are bound together as the parts of a single plan. The plan may make the parts unlawful. . . . Intent is almost essential to such a combination, and is essential to such an attempt. Where acts are not sufficient in themselves to produce a result which the law seeks to prevent,—for instance, the monopoly,—but requires further acts in addition to the mere forces of nature to bring that result to pass, an intent to bring it to pass is necessary in order to produce a dangerous probability that it will happen. But when the intent and the consequent dangerous probability exist, this statute, like many others, and like the common law in some cases, directs itself against that dangerous probability as well as against the completed result.

2. *Lorain Journal Co. v. United States*, 342 U.S. 143 (1951)

The defendant published the only daily newspaper in Lorain, Ohio. After the Elyria-Lorain Broadcasting Company established a local radio station (WEOL) serving Lorain and two smaller neighboring communities, the publisher refused to accept advertising from any Lorain County advertiser who advertised over WEOL. The trial court found that "the purpose and intent of this procedure was to destroy the broadcasting company" by discouraging advertisers from patronizing the station. The Supreme Court affirmed an injunction prohibiting the publisher from continuing to reject advertising from advertisers who patronized the station. Justice Burton's opinion states:

> 1. *The conduct complained of was an attempt to monopolize interstate commerce.* It consisted of the publisher's practice of refusing to accept local Lorain advertising from parties using WEOL for local advertising. Because of the Journal's complete daily newspaper monopoly of local

advertising in Lorain and its practically indispensable coverage of 99% of the Lorain families, this practice forced numerous advertisers to refrain from using WEOL for local advertising. That result not only reduced the number of customers available to WEOL in the field of local Lorain advertising and strengthened the Journal's monopoly in that field, but more significantly tended to destroy and eliminate WEOL altogether. Attainment of that sought-for elimination would automatically restore to the publisher of the Journal its substantial monopoly in Lorain of the mass dissemination of all news and advertising, interstate and national, as well as local.

* * *

2. *The publisher's attempt to regain its monopoly of interstate commerce by forcing advertisers to boycott a competing radio station violated § 2.* . . .

WEOL's greatest potential source of income was local Lorain advertising. Loss of that was a major threat to its existence. The court below found unequivocally that appellants' conduct amounted to an attempt by the publisher to destroy WEOL and, at the same time, to regain the publisher's pre-1948 substantial monopoly over the mass dissemination of all news and advertising.

. . . While appellants' attempt to monopolize did succeed insofar as it deprived WEOL of income, WEOL has not yet been eliminated. The injunction may save it. "[W]hen that intent [to monopolize] and the consequent dangerous probability exist, this statute [the Sherman Act], like many others and like the common law in some cases, directs itself against that dangerous probability as well as against the completed result." *Swift & Co. v. United States*, 196 U.S. 375, 396. . . .

Assuming the interstate character of the commerce involved, it seems clear that if all the newspapers in a city, in order to monopolize the dissemination of news and advertising by eliminating a competing radio station, conspired to accept no advertisements from anyone who advertised over that station, they would violate §§ 1 and 2 of the Sherman Act. . . . It is consistent with that result to hold here that a single newspaper, already enjoying a substantial monopoly in its area, violates the "attempt to monopolize" clause of § 2 when it uses its monopoly to destroy threatened competition.

The publisher claims a right as a private business concern to select its customers and to refuse to accept advertisements from whomever it pleases. We do not dispute that general right. . . . The right claimed by the publisher is neither absolute nor exempt from regulation. Its exercise as a purposeful means of monopolizing interstate commerce is prohibited by the Sherman Act. . . . "*In the absence of any purpose to create or*

> *maintain a monopoly*, the act does not restrict the long recognized right of a trader or manufacturer engaged in an entirely private business, freely to exercise his own independent discretion as to parties with whom he will deal." (Emphasis supplied.) *United States v. Colgate & Co.*, 250 U.S. 300, 307. . . .

3. *Otter Tail Power Co. v. United States*, 410 U.S. 366 (1973)

The Otter Tail Power Company was an electric utility selling electric power at retail in 465 towns in Minnesota, North Dakota, and South Dakota (where it controlled available transmission lines). The district court had found that Otter Tail had attempted to prevent communities in which its retail distribution franchise had expired from replacing it with a municipal distribution system by refusing to "wheel" power to such systems, *i.e.*, transfer by direct transmission or displacement electric power from one utility to another over the facilities of an intermediate utility, by instituting litigation designed to prevent or delay the establishment of those systems and by invoking provisions in its transmission contracts with other suppliers to deny municipal systems access to those suppliers. The district court then entered judgment for the United States. The Supreme Court (through Justice Douglas) affirmed:

> The record makes abundantly clear that Otter Tail used its monopoly power in the towns in its service area to foreclose competition or gain a competitive advantage, or to destroy a competitor, all in violation of the antitrust laws. *See United States v. Griffith*, 334 U.S. 100, 107. The District Court determined that Otter Tail has "a strategic dominance in the transmission of power in most of its service area" and that it used this dominance to foreclose potential entrants into the retail area from obtaining electric power from outside sources of supply. . . . Use of monopoly power "to destroy threatened competition" is a violation of the "attempt to monopolize clause" of § 2 of the Sherman Act. *Lorain Journal v. United States*, 342 U.S. 143, 154; *Eastman Kodak Co. v. Southern Photo Materials Co.*, 273 U.S. 359, 375.

Justice Holmes' description in *Swift & Co.* remains the classic definition of the attempt offense. What is necessary is (1) intent, (2) a dangerous probability the intended goal will be achieved, and (3) (implicitly) the identification and proof of the market which is intended to be monopolized. *Lorain Journal* appears to be a routine application of Holmes' formulation of the offense in *Swift & Co. Otter Tail* is similar to *Lorain Journal* in that the defendants in both cases employed their dominant position in one area of business activity (newspaper advertising, power transmission) as a means of excluding rivals.

B. A Modern Application of the Attempt Clause

In the cases which follow consider whether Professor Cooper's comments (at the beginning of this Chapter) regarding the ability of courts to distinguish competitive from anticompetitive conduct are valid. Based on the cases below, would you advocate a very limited application of the attempt offense?

United States v. American Airlines, Inc.

743 F.2d 1114 (5th Cir. 1984)

W. EUGENE DAVIS, Circuit Judge

The question presented in this antitrust case is whether the government's complaint states a claim of attempted monopolization under section 2 of the Sherman Act against the defendants, American Airlines, and its president Robert L. Crandall, for Crandall's proposal to the president of Braniff Airlines that the two airlines control the market and set prices. The district court dismissed the complaint for failure to state a claim under Federal Rule of Civil Procedure 12(b)(6) on the grounds that the failure to allege an agreement to monopolize was a fatal defect in the complaint and that more than an allegation of solicitation to monopolize was required to state a claim for attempted monopolization. We disagree and reverse.

I.

In February 1982, American Airlines (American) and Braniff Airlines (Braniff) each had a major passenger airline complex, or "hub" at the Dallas-Fort Worth International Airport (DFW).[1] These hubs enabled American and Braniff to gather passengers from many cities, concentrate them at DFW, and then arrange connections for them on American and Braniff flights to other cities. The hub systems gave American and Braniff a marked competitive advantage over other airlines that served or might wish to serve DFW. In addition, the limitations on arrivals imposed by the Federal Aviation Administration (FAA) after the 1981 air traffic controllers' strike impeded any significant expansion or new entry by airlines into service at DFW. These limitations helped enable American and Braniff to maintain their high market shares in relation to other competitors.

In February 1982, American and Braniff together enjoyed a market share of more than ninety percent of the passengers on non-stop flights between DFW and eight major cities, and more than sixty percent of the passengers on flights between DFW and seven other cities. The two airlines had more than ninety percent of the passengers on many flights connecting at DFW, when no non-stop service was available between the cities in question. Overall, American and Braniff accounted for seventy-six percent of monthly enplanements at DFW.

For some time before February 1982, American and Braniff were competing fiercely for passengers flying to, from and through DFW, by offering lower fares and better service.

---

[1] Many airlines structure their services around major airports in network complexes termed hubs. The term derives from the fact that the routes of an airline maintaining a hub operation resemble the hub and spokes of a wheel, with the major airport, for example, DFW, as the hub and the routes to other cities radiating like spokes.

During a telephone conversation between Robert Crandall, American's president, and Howard Putnam, Braniff's president, the following exchange occurred:

Crandall:	I think it's dumb as hell for Christ's sake, all right, to sit here and pound the . . . out of each other and neither one of us making a . . . dime.
Putnam:	Well—
Crandall:	I mean, you know, goddamn, what the . . . is the point of it?
Putnam:	Nobody asked American to serve Harlingen. Nobody asked American to serve Kansas City, and there were low fares in there, you know, before. So—
Crandall:	You better believe it, Howard. But, you, you, you know, the complex is here—ain't gonna change a goddamn thing, all right. We can, we can both live here and there ain't no room for Delta. But there's, ah, no reason that I can see, all right, to put both companies out of business.
. . . .	
Putnam:	Do you have a suggestion for me?
Crandall:	Yes. I have a suggestion for you. Raise your goddamn fares twenty percent. I'll raise mine the next morning.
Putnam:	Robert, we—
Crandall:	You'll make more money and I will too.
Putnam:	We can't talk about pricing.
Crandall:	Oh bull . . . , Howard. We can talk about any goddamn thing we want to talk about.

Putnam did not raise Braniff's fares in response to Crandall's proposal; instead he presented the government with a tape recording of the conversation.

The United States subsequently sought an injunction . . . against American Airlines and Crandall based on an alleged violation of section 2 of the act which forbids an attempted monopolization. On a motion by the defendants, the district court dismissed the government's complaint for failure to state a claim under Fed. R. Civ. P. 12(b)(6).

The government asserts that the district court erred in holding that (1) an agreement is required for the offense of attempted monopolization; and (2) an attempt must amount to more than a solicitation to commit a crime.

II.

The language of the Sherman Act, its legislative history, the general criminal law relating to attempt and the jurisprudence relating to attempt specifically under the Sherman Act, lead us to the same conclusion: the government need not allege or prove an agreement to monopolize in order to establish an attempted joint monopolization under section 2 of the Sherman Act.

Our first step in the analysis of the requisites of attempted monopolization is a consideration of the elements of the completed offense of monopolization.

To establish illegal monopolization two elements must be shown: (1) the possession of monopoly power in the relevant market, and (2) "the willful acquisition or maintenance of that power as distinguished from growth or development as a consequence of a superior product, business acumen, or historic accident." *United States v. Grinnell Corp.*, 384 U.S.

563, 570-71 (1966). Monopoly power is "the power to control price or exclude competition." *United States v. E.I. du Pont de Nemours & Co.*, 351 U.S. 377, 391 (1956). . . .

Applying these principles to the case at hand, we conclude that if Putnam had accepted Crandall's offer, the two airlines, at the moment of acceptance, would have acquired monopoly power. At that same moment, the offense of joint monopolization would have been complete.

Since the Act does not list or define the activities which may constitute the offense of attempted monopolization, we must examine the facts of each case, mindful that the determination of what constitutes an attempt, as Justice Holmes explained, "is a question of proximity and degree." *Swift & Company v. United States*, 196 U.S. 375, 402 (1904).[8] In *Swift*, the Court stated further that "when that intent and the consequent dangerous probability exist, this statute, like many others, and like the common law in some cases, directs itself against that dangerous probability as well as against the completed result." *Swift*, 196 U.S. at 396. The offense of attempted monopolization thus has two elements: (1) specific intent to accomplish the illegal result; and (2) a dangerous probability that the attempt to monopolize will be successful. . . . When evaluating the element of dangerous probability of success, we do not rely on hindsight but examine the probability of success at the time the acts occur. . . .

The government unequivocally alleged that Crandall proposed to enlist his chief competitor in a cartel so that American and Braniff, acting together, could control prices and exclude competition at DFW; as Crandall explained to Putnam, "we can both live here and there ain't no room for Delta." As a result of the monopolization, Braniff would "make more money and I will too."

Both Crandall and Putnam were the chief executive officers of their airlines; each arguably had the power to implement Crandall's plan. The airlines jointly had a high market share in a market with high barriers to entry. American and Braniff, at the moment of Putnam's acceptance, would have monopolized the market. Under the facts alleged, it follows that Crandall's proposal was an act that was the most proximate to the commission of the completed offense that Crandall was capable of committing. Considering the alleged market share of American and Braniff, the barriers to entry by other airlines, and the authority of Crandall and Putnam, the complaint sufficiently alleged that Crandall's proposal had a dangerous probability of success.

The requirement that an accused's conduct have a dangerous probability of success expresses a significant antitrust principle that the antitrust laws protect competition, not

---

[8] Justice Holmes, a leading authority on the law of attempt, had more than one occasion to explain the principles of attempt. In THE COMMON LAW (1881), he observed that "[e]minent judges have been puzzled where to draw the line [between what constitutes attempt and what does not], or even to state the principle on which it should be drawn. . . . But the principle is . . . similar to that on which all other lines are drawn by the law. Public policy, that is to say, legislative considerations, are at the bottom of the matter; the considerations in this case being the nearness of the danger, the greatness of the harm, and the degree of apprehension felt." O. HOLMES, JR., THE COMMON LAW 68 (1881).

In *Commonwealth v. Peaslee*, 177 Mass. 267, 59 N.E. 55 (1901), Justice Holmes, writing for the Massachusetts Supreme Judicial Court, held that "if the preparation comes very near to the accomplishment of the act, the intent to complete it renders the crime so probable" that the act will constitute an attempt. 177 Mass. at 272, 59 N.E. 55. "Every question of proximity," Justice Holmes stated, "must be determined by its own circumstances . . . analogy is too imperfect to give much help." *Commonwealth v. Kennedy*, 170 Mass. 18, 48 N.E. 770, 771 (1897).

competitors, and its related principle that the Sherman Act does not reach practices only unfair, impolite, or unethical. *Dimmitt Agri Industries, Inc. v. CPC International, Inc.*, 679 F.2d 516 (5th Cir. 1982), *cert. denied*, 460 U.S. 1082 (1983); *Kearney & Trecker Corp. v. Giddings & Lewis, Inc.*, 452 F.2d 579 (7th Cir. 1971) (Stevens, J.).

In *United States v. Mandujano*, 499 F.2d 370 (5th Cir. 1974), *cert. denied*, 419 U.S. 1114 (1975), we set forth the general requirements for criminal attempt. The defendant (1) "must have been acting with the kind of culpability otherwise required for the commission of the crime which he is charged with attempting," and (2) "must have engaged in conduct which constitutes a substantial step toward commission of the crime." 499 F.2d at 376. While similar, the common law requirement of a substantial step toward commission and dangerous probability of success are not the same. While both exact a relationship between an attempt and the offense, they differ in important ways. The focus of dangerous probability of success is upon the likelihood of the prohibited result, whereas the focus of the substantial step toward commission is upon a defendant's intent. The move along the increasing scale of proximity of attempt to offense carries with it a corresponding shift in focus from intent alone to substantive result. The inquiry is by necessity into the defendant's intent but under the Sherman Act that inquiry also includes a predictive examination of the results if the intent were accomplished. As Justice Stevens, then Judge, put it in *Kearney:* "[w]e must consider the firm's capacity to commit the offense, the scope of its objective, and the character of its conduct. The ultimate concern is the firm's actual or threatened impact on competition in the relevant market." 452 F.2d at 598. . . . We see Crandall's alleged conduct as uniquely unequivocal and its potential, given the alleged market conditions, as being uniquely consequential. In sum, our decision that the government has stated a claim does not add attempt to violations of Section 1 of the Sherman Act or lower the incipiency gate of Section 2.

Finally, we note one final consequence of our reasoning. If a defendant had the requisite intent and capacity, and his plan if executed would have had the prohibited market result, it is no defense that the plan proved to be impossible to execute. As applied here, if Putnam from the beginning never intended to agree such fact would be of no aid to Crandall and American.

. . .

In an alternate ground for its dismissal of the complaint, the district court concluded that Crandall's proposal was a solicitation and that the common law, at the time of the enactment of the Sherman Act, required proof of more than a solicitation to establish an attempt.

Appellees argue that in 1890 the common law so clearly held that an attempt required more than a mere solicitation, that Congress intended to incorporate that well-accepted principle into section 2 of the Sherman Act. Our study of the authorities, however, leads us to the conclusion that there was no clear consensus among the pre-1890 cases on the issue. Less than half of the forty-two state jurisdictions had addressed the issue, even peripherally, by 1890. The jurisdictions which had confronted the question were evenly split. These cases demonstrate that the answer to the question of whether a solicitation could be an attempt at common law was neither old nor well-recognized; to the contrary it was unsettled and still evolving. It follows that in enacting the Sherman Act, Congress could not have supposed that a solicitation could never be an attempt. *See Associated Gen. Contractors v. Carpenters*, 459 U.S. 519, at 533 n.28 (1983).

The district court also cited a number of modern cases in support of its conclusion that an attempt can never encompass a solicitation, and appellees refer us to others. These cases involving murder, sodomy, and other crimes, however, are not instructive in determining the requirements for attempted monopolization. In the cited cases, an agreement to the solicitation would not result in the completion of the substantive offense at the moment of agreement; other physical acts were required for the completed offense.

The federal courts have generally rejected a rigid or formalistic approach to the attempt offense. Instead they commonly recognize that "[t]he determination whether particular conduct constitutes . . . [an attempt] is so dependent on the particular facts of each case that, of necessity, there can be no litmus test to guide the reviewing courts." *United States v. Ivic*, 700 F.2d 51, 66 (2d Cir. 1983). Following this analysis, which we consider the better reasoned approach, several federal courts have concluded that a solicitation accompanied by the requisite intent may constitute an attempt.

In *United States v. May*, 625 F.2d 186 (8th Cir. 1980), a defendant challenged his conviction for "unlawfully attempt[ing] to cause to have concealed, obliterated, or destroyed" government records in violation of 18 U.S.C. § 2071, on the grounds that his telephone call to the person who controlled certain relevant records constituted only a solicitation and was not an attempt. The Eighth Circuit affirmed his attempt conviction.

> May also argues that his . . . conviction must fall because his conduct constituted only a solicitation, not an attempt to commit a crime. Specifically, he contends that the evidence showed only preparation and that no overt act constituting a substantial step in the attempt was shown. We disagree. When May called General Miller, he engaged in a course of conduct designed to culminate in the unlawful concealment of government records.

In *United States v. Robles*, 185 F. Supp. 82, 85 (N.D. Cal. 1960), a solicitation by letter was held to be an attempt to unlawfully import a narcotic.

In sum, we reject appellee's contention that the law in 1890 clearly required more than a solicitation to constitute an attempt. We also conclude that the better reasoned authorities support the view that a highly verbal crime such as attempted monopolization may be established by proof of a solicitation along with the requisite intent.

III.

Our decision that the government's complaint states a claim of attempted monopolization is consistent with the Act's language and purpose. The application of section 2 principles to defendants' conduct will deter the formation of monopolies at their outset when the unlawful schemes are proposed, and thus, will strengthen the Act.

Under appellees' construction of the Act, an individual is given a strong incentive to propose the formation of cartels. If the proposal is accepted, monopoly power is achieved; if the proposal is declined, no antitrust liability attaches. If section 2 liability attaches to conduct such as that alleged against Crandall, naked proposals for the formation of cartels are discouraged and competition is promoted.

Appellees argue that price fixing is an offense under section 1 of the Sherman Act and since the government charges that Crandall sought to have American and Braniff fix prices, the government's complaint in reality seeks to have us write an attempt provision into section 1. This argument is meritless. Appellees confuse the section 1 offense of price fixing with the power to control price following acquisition of monopoly power under section 2. Under the facts alleged in the complaint, Crandall wanted both to obtain joint monopoly power and to engage in price fixing. That he was not able to price fix and thus, has no liability under section 1, has no effect on whether his unsuccessful efforts to monopolize constitute attempted monopolization. *See Multiflex*, 709 F.2d at 992.

Nor do we agree with appellees' suggestion that firms or executives will be subject to liability for ambiguous or "intemperate words." We first note that under the allegations of the complaint Crandall's statements are not ambiguous. Second, a person must specifically intend to monopolize for his conduct to violate section 2; without the requisite intent, no liability attaches.

CONCLUSION

We hold that an agreement is not an absolute prerequisite for the offense of attempted joint monopolization and that the government's complaint sufficiently alleged facts that if proved would permit a finding of attempted monopolization by defendants. We therefore vacate the dismissal of the complaint and remand for further proceedings consistent with this opinion.

REVERSED AND REMANDED.

COMMENTARY

1. Section 2 contains a third offense, "combine or conspire to monopolize." Can you speculate on why the case was not brought under the combine or conspire part of § 2 or under § 1 as a conspiracy to fix prices? Do either of these provisions make illegal an attempt to combine or to conspire?

2. Given the hub operations of American and Braniff and the constraints on entry and expansion in the DFW airport described by the court, did American by itself have monopoly power when it made the price-fixing offer to Braniff? Viewed in terms of § 2, was American's offer one jointly to monopolize? Would there be power to set price in this market if American had acted alone? Since Braniff rejected the price-fixing offer, wasn't the trial court correctly interpreting the attempt phrase in dismissing the complaint? Or can a persuasive case be made that such clearly anticompetitive conduct as that of American is precisely the circumstance for invoking the attempt offense? In *United States v. Empire Gas Corp.*, 537 F.2d 296, 301 (8th Cir. 1976), the trial court dismissed the government's complaint in an attempt case involving repeated invitations to competitors to fix prices by a seller of liquid petroleum with a 50% market share. The court of appeals affirmed the dismissal for failure to establish dangerous probability, but noted in *dictum* that defendant's threats to competitors refusing to fix prices, followed by drastic price cuts in that market, established specific intent.

C. Specific Intent as an Element of the Offense

In his opinion in *Swift & Co.*, Justice Holmes made "intent" an element of the attempt offense. The criminal law often treats an attempt to commit a crime as criminal in itself. Generally to be guilty of an attempt to commit a criminal offense (*viz.*, attempted murder, attempted robbery, etc.) a person must have intended to perform the complete offense and to have performed an overt act directed to its accomplishment. Perhaps Justice Holmes was drawing from the law of criminal attempt when he listed the components of an attempt to monopolize.

The intent required to prove a person attempted to monopolize is commonly referred to as "specific intent." This "specific intent" differs from the "general intent" which is a part of the monopolization offense. The latter is merely an intent by an actor to perform the act which the actor performs. The proof of the specific intent element in the attempt offense has traditionally been understood to require proof of something more than an intent to do the act. Specific intent could be understood as an instrumental intent: an intent to bring about an objective. Under such a view, the specific intent involved in the attempt offense would be an intent to bring about the forbidden result of monopolization. So understood, specific intent would perform the function of resolving ambiguity in behavior which might be a step leading to either an anticompetitive or procompetitive result. Employing "specific intent" as a means to resolve an ambiguity in an actor's behavior, however, poses a number of problems. As the discussion below suggests, the evidence which litigants use to prove specific intent is itself highly likely to be ambiguous. Furthermore, an emphasis upon an actor's subjective intent carries the danger of shifting the focus of litigation from antitrust policy to morality.

D. The Relation of an "Intent" Requirement to the Monopolization and Attempt Clauses

Judge Davis, in *American Airlines*, discusses the relation between the "intent" component of the attempt offense and the "dangerous probability of success" component. In his discussion, he explains how the attempt offense differs from the completed offense of monopolization. Judge Davis also explains that while the specific intent element shows the direction in which the defendant is heading, the proof of the dangerous probability element is meant to show that the defendant has in fact moved significantly towards its ultimate goal of monopolization.

Cases like *American Airlines* show the function of the attempt clause: to render unlawful behavior which, unless stopped, possesses a high likelihood of creating a monopoly. Yet other cases to which the attempt clause has been applied may be more easily reached under the monopolization clause. Thus the behavior of the defendants in the *Lorain Journal* and *Otter Tail* cases resembles the behavior involved in *United States v. Griffith*, 334 U.S. 100 (1948), a monopolization case. Note further that in *Otter Tail*, the Court cites *Griffith* as authority for its determination that Otter Tail had violated the attempt clause. Consider *Griffith* (below) and then try to state how the attempt clause relates to the monopolization clause:

United States v. Griffith
334 U.S. 100 (1948)

[The affiliated owners of motion picture theaters negotiated with motion-picture distributors for exhibition rights. The owners controlled theaters located in 85 towns, in only 32 of which did competing theaters exist. The owners negotiated for the entire circuit (and later negotiated separately for each of two subcircuits composing the entire circuit) and as a result obtained certain exclusive privileges which, the government charged, prevented their competitors from obtaining enough first- or second-run films from the distributors to operate successfully. Reversing a judgment for the defendants, the Court (through Justice Douglas) ruled that:]

Specific intent in the sense in which the common law used the term is necessary only where the acts fall short of the results condemned by the Act. . . . The anti-trust laws are as much violated by the prevention of competition as by its destruction. . . . It follows *a fortiori* that the use of monopoly power, however lawfully acquired, to foreclose competition, to gain a competitive advantage, or to destroy a competitor, is unlawful.

A man with a monopoly of theaters in any one town commands the entrance for all films into that area. If he uses that strategic position to acquire exclusive privileges in a city where he has competitors, he is employing his monopoly power as a trade weapon against his competitors. It may be a feeble, ineffective weapon where he has only one closed or monopoly town. But as those towns increase in number throughout a region, his monopoly power in them may be used with crushing effect on competitors in other places.

[*Griffith* makes clear that while "specific intent" to monopolize must be shown to prove an attempt to monopolize, only "general intent" or intent to do the act is required to prove monopolization.]

E. The Relation Between Sections 1 and 2 of the Sherman Act

The relation between §§ 1 and 2 of the Sherman Act has often troubled the courts. At its most superficial level, the relationship appears straightforward: Section 1 is directed at concerted actions and § 2 is directed at single-firm monopolization. The role of § 1 is, in effect, derived from § 2's prohibition of monopolization. In this view, § 1 is needed to forbid several firms (each of which would be powerless acting alone) from joining together to impose market restraints similar to those which a monopolist would be able to impose.

The relation becomes more complex, however, when the role of the attempt clause is considered. Justice Holmes seems to have viewed the attempt clause of § 2 as performing a role analogous to the laws making the attempted commission of a crime in itself criminal. In this view, the attempt clause would play a prophylactic role, forestalling behavior which, if not stopped beforehand, would ultimately result in monopolization. Because the behavior which might ultimately result in monopolization might itself be ambiguous, Justice Holmes required specific intent to be included as an element of the attempt offense in order to help resolve any such ambiguity. Holmes further required that dangerous probability of success be shown in order to identify those attempts which, if left unchallenged, would present a realistic threat of achieving monopolization.

This view of the attempt clause, however, was undermined when the Supreme Court decided the *Griffith* case. *Griffith*—which is the foundation of the so-called "monopoly leveraging" offense—held that a firm violates the monopolization clause when it uses a monopoly in one market to gain a monopoly or a competitive advantage in that or another market. Many attempt cases have involved the use of a monopoly in one market to gain a monopoly in another market. *Lorain Journal* is a case in point, where the defendant used a monopoly in daily newspapers to try to achieve a monopoly in all media. Under the reasoning of *Griffith,* such cases could be litigated as monopolization cases, thus dispensing with the need to prove specific intent. *Griffith* thus appeared to have made the attempt clause redundant in those cases in which a firm with a share close to monopoly in one market seeks to consolidate its hold on that market or to acquire a monopoly in another market.

F. The Struggles of the Ninth Circuit With the Attempt Clause

1. The Ill-Fated Approach of *Lessig v. Tidewater Oil Co.*

In *Lessig v. Tidewater Oil Co.*, 327 F.2d 459 (9th Cir.), *cert. denied*, 377 U.S. 993 (1964), the Ninth Circuit began an assault upon the traditional understanding of the attempt offense, an assault whose ramifications are still being felt. The Supreme Court ultimately rejected the *Lessig* approach, but not until almost three decades afterwards. *See Spectrum Sports, Inc. v. McQuillan*, 506 U.S. 447 (1993) (page 500, *infra*). Throughout the intervening era, *Lessig* and its progeny raised havoc with the law of attempted monopolization. Although the *Lessig* approach has now been repudiated, antitrust lawyers need to understand the problem which gave rise to that decision and its rationale, because of the wide impact which *Lessig* has had on the caselaw, both in the Ninth Circuit and elsewhere.

Lessig, a former lessee and operator of a Tidewater (brand) gasoline station charged Tidewater, *inter alia,* with an attempt to monopolize as a result of the latter's setting the resale price of gasoline in Tidewater stations and excluding other suppliers from those stations. On Lessig's appeal from an adverse judgment, the Ninth Circuit reversed:

> We think the court erred in withdrawing from the jury the charge that Tidewater attempted to monopolize. . . . We reject the premise that probability of actual monopolization is an essential element of proof of attempt to monopolize. Of course, such a probability may be relevant circumstantial evidence of intent, but the specific intent itself is the only

> evidence of dangerous probability the statute requires—perhaps on the not unreasonable assumption that the actor is better able than others to judge the practical possibility of achieving his illegal objective.
>
> When the charge is attempt (or conspiracy) to monopolize . . . the relevant market is "not in issue." . . . Section 2 prohibits attempts to monopolize "any part" of commerce, and a dominant position in the business of distributing petroleum products and TBA [tires, batteries, accessories] was not necessarily prerequisite to ability to attempt to monopolize an appreciable segment of interstate sales in such products. If the jury found that Tidewater intended to fix the price at which 2,700 independent service station operators resold gasoline, and to exclude other suppliers of petroleum products and sponsored TBA items from competing for the patronage of these operators, and took steps to accomplish that purpose, it could properly conclude that Tidewater attempted to monopolize a part of interstate commerce in violation of section 2 of the Sherman Act.

Lessig, 327 F.2d at 474-75.

Consider the "part" of interstate commerce that—under this reasoning—Tidewater was attempting to monopolize: Tidewater was attempting to monopolize the retail sale of Tidewater-brand gasoline! There was no possibility of Tidewater actually "monopolizing," however, because Tidewater gasoline was in intense competition with other brands of gasoline. In this circumstance, Tidewater had no power to exert any realistic control over the price of even Tidewater-brand gasoline.

It is not surprising that the court excluded the relevant market from consideration, as it did, because a relevant market analysis would have shown that Tidewater-brand gasoline is only a part of a relevant market composed of all competing brands of gasoline, *i.e.,* the interbrand gasoline market. In this circumstance, it would have been impossible to show that Tidewater possessed any "dangerous probability" of monopolizing this interbrand gasoline market.

The logic of *Lessig* leads to the view that a producer can violate the attempt-to-monopolize clause by taking over distribution of its own brand of product. When the cases forced that issue, the Ninth Circuit retreated. Eight years after its revolutionary decision in *Lessig*, that is exactly what happened in *Bushie v. Stenocord Corp.*, 460 F.2d 116 (9th Cir. 1972).

In *Bushie*, the plaintiffs were local distributors of Stenocord office dictating machines in the Phoenix, Arizona area. When Stenocord decided to sell its machines in that area directly through its own company-operated outlet and canceled the distributorship of the plaintiffs, the plaintiffs charged Stenocord with monopolizing and attempting to monopolize. Under the traditional analysis enunciated in *Swift & Co.*, no attempt case would lie, because there was no realistic possibility that Stenocord could monopolize (within Phoenix, Arizona) the distribution of all brands of dictating machines. According to *Lessig,* however, there is no need to prove a relevant market or dangerous possibility of success: All a plaintiff need do is to prove "specific intent" to monopolize "a part" (or "an appreciable segment") of commerce. Despite its earlier language in *Lessig*, the Ninth Circuit employed a relevant-market analysis to reject the plaintiffs' contentions.

2. The Ninth Circuit's "Gap" Approach

The misguided analysis of *Lessig* has its roots in the Supreme Court's formulation of the monopolization offense in *Griffith*. Apparently impressed with the new breadth of application of the monopolization clause under *Griffith*, the Ninth Circuit began to suggest that the attempt clause—as traditionally interpreted—had become redundant.

Under the impression that anticompetitive behavior by any firm with a market share large enough to satisfy the traditional "dangerous probability" requirement of the attempt offense could usually be dealt with under the monopolization clause (under *Griffith*), the Ninth Circuit pondered (in cases like *Greyhound Computer Corp. v. IBM Corp.*, 559 F.2d 488 (9th Cir. 1977), *cert. denied*, 434 U.S. 1040 (1978)) whether there was any role for the attempt clause at all.

In an attempt to restore the attempt clause to usefulness, the Ninth Circuit focused upon a potential "gap" in the Sherman Act's coverage and determined that the proper role for the attempt clause would be to cover this gap. The gap was "anticompetitive" behavior by a single firm which possessed only a small market share. Because the behavior was unilateral, it was not covered by § 1. The behavior was of a firm with a small market share, and would not be covered by the monopolization clause. Thus, the new role for the attempt clause would be to cover anticompetitive behavior by a single firm with a small market share. Compare the following extract from the Supreme Court's opinion in *Copperweld Corp. v. Independence Tube Corp.*, 467 U.S. 752, 774-775 (1984):

> Any reading of the Sherman Act that remains true to the Act's distinction between unilateral and concerted conduct will necessarily disappoint those who find that distinction arbitrary. It cannot be denied that § 1's focus on concerted behavior leaves a "gap" in the Act's proscription against unreasonable restraints of trade. . . . An unreasonable restraint of trade may be effected not only by two independent firms acting in concert; a single firm may restrain trade to precisely the same extent if it alone possesses the combined market power of those same two firms. Because the Sherman Act does not prohibit unreasonable restraints of trade as such—but only restraints effected by a contract, combination, or conspiracy—it leaves untouched a single firm's anticompetitive conduct (short of threatened monopolization) that may be indistinguishable in economic effect from the conduct of two firms subject to § 1 liability.
>
> We have already noted that Congress left this "gap" for eminently sound reasons. Subjecting a single firm's every action to judicial scrutiny . . .

> would threaten to discourage the competitive enthusiasm that the antitrust laws seek to promote.

In *Copperweld*, the Supreme Court thus both acknowledged a gap in the Sherman Act, and, without reference to the Ninth Circuit cases like *Lessig* and *Greyhound*, saw no need to expand the interpretation of the Sherman Act to reach single-firm behavior. Prior to *Copperweld*, however, the Ninth Circuit sought to close the gap by construing the attempt clause in an expansionary manner. Thus in *Greyhound Computer Corp. v. IBM Corp.*, 559 F.2d 488 (9th Cir. 1977), *cert. denied*, 434 U.S. 1040 (1978), the Ninth Circuit suggested that because of a need to prohibit anticompetitive conduct unilaterally performed by a single firm with a small market share, the court would construe the attempt clause to reach anticompetitive conduct by such a small firm. (In adopting this expansionary approach to the attempt clause, the Ninth Circuit also was influenced by its belief that the Supreme Court's *Griffith* decision had effectively made the attempt clause redundant.)

Rejecting the extension of the attempt clause in § 2 of the Sherman Act to close the perceived "gap" is soundly grounded in the structure of the Sherman Act. The flawed analysis of cases such as *Lessig* and *Greyhound* would necessitate dispensing with some of the traditional elements of an attempt-to-monopolize case. Consistent with the Ninth Circuit's view in *Lessig* and *Greyhound*, there could be no requirement of proof of an economically-defined relevant market nor could there be a requirement that the defendant's behavior had put it in a position where it was dangerously probable of succeeding in a quest for monopoly. This, of course, was exactly the approach which the Ninth Circuit had adopted in *Lessig* and which had proved troublesome in cases like *Bushie*. Nonetheless, more than twenty years after its *Lessig* decision, the Ninth Circuit was asserting in *Greyhound* that:

> If proof of an economic market, technically defined, and proof of a dangerous probability of monopolization of such a market were made essential elements of an attempt to monopolize, as a practical matter the attempt offense would cease to have independent significance. A single firm that did not control something close to 50 percent of the entire market . . . would be free to indulge in any activity however unreasonable, predatory, or destructive of competition and without business justification.

This revisionist approach to the attempt clause was surely unwise: It expanded the potential coverage of the attempt clause and yet failed to provide safeguards against its abuse. Moreover, the court ignored several important considerations: First, firms without market power cannot act anticompetitively by themselves. Second, firms with market shares of less than 50% may possess some market power, but they generally are unlikely to pose a threat of acquiring an actual monopoly. The principal kind of anticompetitive behavior in which these firms could engage would be oligopolistic pricing or even coercion of maverick firms into conformity with an oligopolistic price structure. As we will see, these behaviors do not violate either the attempt clause or the monopolization clause.

The attempt clause, therefore, has no role to play vis-à-vis the behavior of a single firm with a small market share. Rather, the traditional function—identified by Justice Holmes—of dealing with behavior by a firm with sufficient market power to threaten full-fledged monopolization is the role of the attempt clause. The attempt clause, therefore, will reach firms with some market power which the monopolization clause might embrace only marginally, if at all.

After the decision of the United States Supreme Court in *Spectrum Sports, Inc. v. McQuillan*, 506 U.S. 447 (1993), the Ninth Circuit adopted a new position on the attempt clause. In *Rebel Oil Co. v. Atlantic Richfield Co.*, 51 F.3d 1421, 1443 (9th Cir. 1995) (discussed *infra*, at page 506), the Ninth Circuit rejected a contention that a single firm could violate the attempt clause by trying to impose oligopoly pricing. Since such a firm would pose a threat of oligopolistic pricing rather than a threat of actual monopolization, it would not violate either the attempt clause or the monopolization clause.

G. Proof of Subjective Intent

Justice Holmes required proof of specific intent as an element in proof of an attempt to monopolize offense. Justice Holmes, however, required proof of dangerous probability of success as a further element in the proof of such a case. To the extent that the Ninth Circuit would permit an inference of dangerous probability of success—and relevant market as well—to be drawn from proof of specific intent, that court made proof of specific intent the critical element.

The problem posed by permitting proof of intent to play a critical role in the proof of an attempt case is that the files of most businesses are replete with memos from sales executives which use military metaphors to describe relations with rivals. "Our new sales campaign will drive our rivals from the market." Such language, although meant only as an expression of aggressive competition, is vulnerable to misunderstanding when it is read to a jury in an antitrust case. Richard Posner has pointed out this danger:

> It is extraordinarily difficult to ascertain the intent of a large corporation by the methods of litigation. What juries (and many judges) do not understand is that the availability of evidence of improper intent is often a function of luck and of the defendant's legal sophistication, not of the underlying reality. A firm with executives sensitized to antitrust problems will not leave any documentary trail of improper intent; one whose executives lack this sensitivity will often create rich evidence of such intent simply by the clumsy choice of words to describe innocent behavior. Especially misleading here is the inveterate tendency of sales executives to brag to their superiors about their competitive prowess, often using metaphors of coercion that are compelling evidence of predatory intent to the naive.

RICHARD A. POSNER, ANTITRUST LAW 189-90 (1976). Since the mid-1970s many courts have become increasingly disposed to treat evidence of subjective intent with skepticism. Many courts now disallow evidence of subjective intent unless it is corroborated with evidence of predatory behavior.

H. Use of a Double Inference to Prove an Attempt to Monopolize Case

Although the double inference method is employed in a number of Circuits, it has received the most judicial attention in the opinions of the Ninth Circuit. The Ninth Circuit has been willing to permit an inference of dangerous probability (and perhaps the existence of a relevant market) from a specific intent to monopolize. The Ninth Circuit took that approach at the time of *Lessig*, and as the preceding discussion makes clear, has been following in that path (more or less) since the time of *Lessig*. The Ninth Circuit, however, besides emphasizing the importance of specific intent, has also placed a powerful gloss upon the specific intent factor: That court has been willing to permit an inference of specific intent to be drawn from predatory conduct. This is the double-inference method of proving an attempt to monopolize case: The plaintiff presents evidence of predatory conduct. If the jury believes that predatory conduct has occurred, it is permitted to infer specific intent and from specific intent, it is permitted to infer dangerous probability of success and thus an attempt to monopolize.

This approach again can be traced back to that Circuit's ill-advised 1964 decision in *Lessig v. Tidewater Oil Co.*, 327 F.2d 459 (9th Cir.), *cert. denied*, 377 U.S. 993 (1964). Although the *Lessig* opinion emphasized the importance of specific intent, it permitted that specific intent to be inferred from "predatory" conduct, thus adopting the double-inference method of proof.

The critical element in applying the double-inference is the identification and proof of "predatory" conduct. If it can be shown that the defendant's conduct is a type which would only be performed by a firm possessing market power and then only if that firm is using that market power to drive its rivals out of the marketplace, then the inference of specific intent is appropriate and the further inference regarding the defendant's dangerous probability of success in achieving monopoly may also be appropriate. That is to say, the drawing of such inferences would not conflict with the underlying policy of the Sherman Act. The Supreme Court, however, has recently abrogated the double-inference approach in its *Spectrum Sports* decision, thus at least temporarily ending speculation about the appropriate and inappropriate uses of that approach.

Historically, the double-inference test had a shaky history. In *Lessig* and many of the cases following it, the defendant's conduct was not unambiguously predatory. As a result, the double-inference approach did not always produce trustworthy results. Beginning in the late 1970s, however, the Areeda-Turner approach to predatory pricing (taken up in Chapter 11) helped the courts to define predatory behavior in a more rigorous way. At least when the double-inference approach is employed in predatory pricing cases, therefore, its reliability has been substantially improved.

I. The Current Status of the Double-Inference Test

The Ninth Circuit has found it difficult over the years to confine application of the double-inference test to cases involving truly predatory behavior. For a time that court described the conduct giving rise to the double inference as "anticompetitive or predatory." In *McQuillan v. Sorbothane, Inc.*, 1990 WL 92599 (9th Cir.), reversed by the Supreme Court in the opinion which follows, the court of appeals described the conduct giving rise to a double inference as "unfair or predatory conduct." The switch from "anticompetitive" to "unfair" changes the focus from the conditions of the marketplace to the ethics of business behavior and, thus, away from the underlying concern of the antitrust laws with the maintenance of marketplace competition.

In *Sorbothane*, the Ninth Circuit upheld an attempt to monopolize ruling reached through the double-inference method of proof. In that case, a producer of sorbothane (a shock resistant material) terminated the plaintiff who had distributed the product (for athletic and equestrian uses) in the southwestern United States. The plaintiff claimed that by replacing her with another distributor, the supplier and that other distributor had attempted to monopolize the athletic-shoe-insert market, the polymer-athletic-shoe submarket or the sorbothane-athletic-shoe-insert market.

The opinion gives little or no indication of evidence of any anticompetitive constraint on competition in the marketplace. There was evidence of pressure exerted against the plaintiff to sell one of the product lines of her distributorship or be terminated entirely. There was also evidence that her customer list had been turned over to the successor distributor by her supplier. While the plaintiff may have been badly treated, there is no reference in the opinion to evidence of a constraint on competition in the general marketplace.

Nonetheless, by employing the double-inference approach, the Ninth Circuit upheld a judgment for the plaintiff, holding that there was evidence of "unfair or predatory conduct":

> There is sufficient evidence from which the jury could conclude that the S.I. Group and Spectrum Group engaged in unfair or predatory conduct and thus inferred that they had the specific intent and the dangerous probability of success and, therefore, McQuillan did not have to prove relevant market or the defendant's marketing power.

> . . . There is sufficient evidence in the record to sustain the attempt to monopolize claim.

Whether or not the plaintiff was treated "unfairly," the recited evidence does not show "predatory" conduct. A judgment rendered on this evidence, accordingly, makes the attempt clause a weapon to be used against overreaching, rather than against anticompetitive behavior. The Ninth Circuit's double-inference method of proof appears finally to have been halted by the Supreme Court, as the following opinion shows.

Spectrum Sports, Inc. v. McQuillan

506 U.S. 447 (1993)

JUSTICE WHITE delivered the opinion of the Court.

Section 2 of the Sherman Act, 26 Stat. 209, as amended, 15 U.S.C. § 2, makes it an offense for any person to "monopolize, or attempt to monopolize, or combine or conspire with any other person or persons, to monopolize any part of the trade or commerce among the several States." The jury in this case returned a verdict finding that petitioners had monopolized, attempted to monopolize, and/or conspired to monopolize. The District Court entered a judgment ruling that petitioners had violated § 2, and the Court of Appeals affirmed on the ground that petitioners had attempted to monopolize. The issue we have before us is whether the District Court and the Court of Appeals correctly defined the elements of that offense.

I

Sorbothane is a patented elastic polymer whose shock-absorbing characteristics make it useful in a variety of medical, athletic, and equestrian products. BTR, Inc. (BTR), owns the patent rights to sorbothane, and its wholly owned subsidiaries manufacture the product in the United States and Britain. Hamilton-Kent Manufacturing Company (Hamilton-Kent) and Sorbothane, Inc. (S. I.) were at all relevant times owned by BTR. S. I. was formed in 1982 to take over Hamilton-Kent's sorbothane business. . . . Respondents Shirley and Larry McQuillan, doing business as Sorboturf Enterprises, were regional distributors of sorbothane products from 1981 to 1983. Petitioner Spectrum Sports, Inc. (Spectrum), was also a distributor of sorbothane products. Petitioner Kenneth B. Leighton, Jr., is a co-owner of Spectrum. . . . Kenneth Leighton, Jr., is the son of Kenneth Leighton, Sr., the president of Hamilton-Kent and S. I. at all relevant times.

In 1980, respondents Shirley and Larry McQuillan signed a letter of intent with Hamilton-Kent, which then owned all manufacturing and distribution rights to sorbothane. The letter of intent granted the McQuillans exclusive rights to purchase sorbothane for use in equestrian products. Respondents were designing a horseshoe pad using sorbothane.

In 1981, Hamilton-Kent decided to establish five regional distributorships for sorbothane. Respondents were selected to be distributors of all sorbothane products, including medical products and shoe inserts, in the Southwest. Spectrum was selected as distributor for another region. . . .

In January 1982, Hamilton-Kent shifted responsibility for selling medical products from five regional distributors to a single national distributor. In April 1982, Hamilton-Kent told respondents that it wanted them to relinquish their athletic shoe distributorship as a condition for retaining the right to develop and distribute equestrian products. As of May 1982, BTR had moved the sorbothane business from Hamilton-Kent to S. I. . . . In May, the marketing manager of S. I. again made clear that respondents had to sell their athletic distributorship to keep their equestrian distribution rights. At a meeting scheduled to discuss the sale of respondents' athletic distributorship to petitioner Leighton, Jr., Leighton, Jr., informed Shirley McQuillan that if she did not come to agreement with him she would be "looking for work." . . . Respondents refused to sell and continued to distribute athletic shoe inserts.

In the fall of 1982, Leighton, Sr., informed respondents that another concern had been appointed as the national equestrian distributor, and that they were "no longer involved in equestrian products." . . . In January 1983, S. I. began marketing through a national distributor a sorbothane horseshoe pad allegedly indistinguishable from the one designed by respondents. *Ibid.* In August 1983, S. I. informed respondents that it would no longer accept their orders. . . . Spectrum thereupon became national distributor of sorbothane athletic shoe inserts. . . . Respondents sought to obtain sorbothane from the BTR's British subsidiary, but were informed by that subsidiary that it would not sell sorbothane in the United States. Respondents' business failed. . . .

Respondents sued petitioners seeking damages for alleged violations of §§ 1 and 2 of the Sherman Act . . . and § 2[2] and § 3 of the Clayton Act . . . the Racketeer Influenced and Corrupt Organizations Act . . . and two provisions of California business law. Respondents also alleged fraud, breach of oral contract, interference with prospective business advantage, bad faith denial of the existence of an oral contract, and conversion.

The case was tried to a jury, which returned a verdict against one or more of the defendants on each of the 11 alleged violations on which it was to return a verdict. All of the defendants were found to have violated § 2 by, in the words of the verdict sheet, "monopolizing, attempting to monopolize, and/or conspiring to monopolize." . . . Petitioners were also found to have violated civil RICO and the California unfair practices law, but not § 1 of the Sherman Act. The jury awarded $1,743,000 in compensatory damages on each of the violations found to have occurred. This amount was trebled under § 4 of the Clayton Act. The District Court also awarded nearly $1 million in attorneys' fees and denied motions for judgment notwithstanding the verdict and for a new trial.

The Court of Appeals for the Ninth Circuit affirmed the judgment in an unpublished opinion. The court . . . conclude[d] that a case of attempted monopolization had been established.[4] The court rejected petitioners' argument that attempted monopolization had not been established because respondents had failed to prove that petitioners had a specific intent to monopolize a relevant market. The court also held that in order to show that respondents' attempt to monopolize was likely to succeed it was not necessary to present evidence of the

---

[2] Two violations of § 1 were alleged, resale price maintenance and division of territories. Attempted monopolization, monopolization, and conspiracy to monopolize were charged under § 2. All in all, four alleged violations of federal law and seven alleged violations of state law were sent to the jury.

[4] The District Court's jury instructions were transcribed as follows:

"In order to win on the claim of attempted monopoly, the Plaintiff must prove each of the following elements by a preponderance of the evidence: first, that the Defendants had a specific intent to achieve monopoly power in the relevant market; second, that the Defendants engaged in exclusionary or restrictive conduct in furtherance of its specific intent; third, that there was a dangerous probability that Defendants could sooner or later achieve [their] goal of monopoly power in the relevant market; fourth, relevant market or of the defendants' market power. In so doing, the Ninth Circuit relied on *Lessig v. Tidewater Oil Co.*, 327 F. 2d 459 (9th Cir.), *cert. denied*, 377 U.S. 993 (1964), and its progeny. . . . The Court of Appeals noted that these cases, in dealing with attempt to monopolize claims, had ruled that "if evidence of unfair or predatory conduct is presented, it may satisfy both the specific intent and dangerous probability elements of the offense, without any proof of relevant market or the defendant's marketpower [sic]." . . . If, however, there is insufficient evidence of unfair or predatory conduct, there must be a showing of "relevant market or the defendant's marketpower [sic]." *Ibid.* The court went on to find:

> "There is sufficient evidence from which the jury could conclude that the S. I. Group and Spectrum Group engaged in unfair or predatory conduct and thus inferred that they had the specific intent and the dangerous probability of success and, therefore, McQuillan did not have to prove relevant market or the defendant's marketing power." *Id.* at A21.

The decision below, and the *Lessig* line of decisions on which it relies, conflicts with holdings of courts in other Circuits. Every other Court of Appeals has indicated that proving an attempt to monopolize requires proof of a dangerous probability of monopolization of a relevant market.[5] We granted *certiorari* . . . to resolve this conflict among the Circuits.[6] We reverse.

II

. . . .

The Court's decisions since *Swift* have reflected the view that the plaintiff charging attempted monopolization must prove a dangerous probability of actual monopolization, which has generally required a definition of the relevant market and examination of market power. In *Walker Process Equipment, Inc. v. Food Machinery & Chemical Corp.*, 382

> that the Defendants' conduct occurred in or affected interstate commerce; and, fifth, that the Plaintiff was injured in their business or property by the Defendants' exclusionary or restrictive conduct.
>
> . . . .
>
> "If the Plaintiff has shown that the Defendant engaged in predatory conduct, you may infer from that evidence the specific intent and the dangerous probability element of the offense without any proof of the relevant market or the Defendants' marketing [sic] power." . . .

Id. at 251-252. See also App. to Pet. for Cert. A16, A20.

[5] *See, e.g., CVD, Inc. v. Raytheon Co.*, 769 F.2d 842, 851 (1st Cir. 1985), *cert. denied*, 475 U.S. 1016 (1986); *Twin Laboratories, Inc. v. Weider Health & Fitness*, 900 F.2d 566, 570 (2d Cir. 1990); *Harold Friedman, Inc. v. Kroger Co.*, 581 F.2d 1068, 1079 (3d Cir. 1978); *Abcor Corp. v. AM Int'l, Inc.*, 916 F.2d 924, 926, 931 (4th Cir. 1990); *C.A.T. Industrial Disposal, Inc. v. Browning-Ferris Industries, Inc.*, 884 F.2d 209, 210 (5th Cir. 1989); *Arthur S. Langenderfer, Inc. v. S. E. Johnson Co.*, 917 F.2d 1413, 1431-32 (6th Cir. 1990), *cert. denied*, 502 U.S. ___, ___ (1991); *Indiana Grocery, Inc. v. Super Valu Stores, Inc.*, 864 F.2d 1409, 1413-16 (7th Cir. 1989); *General Industries Corp. v. Hartz Mountain Corp.*, 810 F.2d 795, 804 (8th Cir. 1987); *Colorado Interstate Gas Co. v. Natural Gas Pipeline Co. of America*, 885 F.2d 683, 693 (10th Cir. 1989), *cert. denied*, 498 U.S. 972 (1990); *Key Enterprises of Delaware, Inc. v. Venice Hospital*, 919 F.2d 1550, 1565 (11th Cir. 1990); *Neumann v. Reinforced Earth Co.*, 252 U.S. App. D.C. 11, 15-16, 786 F.2d 424, 428-29, *cert. denied*, 479 U.S. 851 (1986); *Abbott Laboratories v. Brennan*, 952 F.2d 1346, 1354 (Fed. Cir. 1991), *cert. denied*, 505 U.S. ___ (1992).

[6] Our grant of *certiorari* was limited to the first question presented in the petition: "Whether a manufacturer's distributor expressly absolved of violating Section 1 of the Sherman Act can, without any evidence of market power or specific intent, be found liable for attempting to monopolize solely by virtue of a unique Ninth Circuit rule?" Pet for Cert. i.

U.S. 172, 177 (1965), we found that enforcement of a fraudulently obtained patent claim could violate the Sherman Act. We stated that, to establish monopolization or attempt to monopolize under § 2 of the Sherman Act, it would be necessary to appraise the exclusionary power of the illegal patent claim in terms of the relevant market for the product involved. . . . The reason was that "[w]ithout a definition of that market there is no way to measure [the defendant's] ability to lessen or destroy competition." . . .

Similarly, this Court reaffirmed in *Copperweld Corp. v. Independence Tube Corp.*, 467 U.S. 752 (1984), that "Congress authorized Sherman Act scrutiny of single firms only when they pose a danger of monopolization. Judging unilateral conduct in this manner reduces the risk that the antitrust laws will dampen the competitive zeal of a single aggressive entrepreneur." . . . Thus, the conduct of a single firm, governed by § 2, "is unlawful only when it threatens actual monopolization." . . .

The Courts of Appeals other than the Ninth Circuit have followed this approach. Consistent with our cases, it is generally required that to demonstrate attempted monopolization a plaintiff must prove (1) that the defendant has engaged in predatory or anticompetitive conduct with (2) a specific intent to monopolize and (3) a dangerous probability of achieving monopoly power. . . . In order to determine whether there is a dangerous probability of monopolization, courts have found it necessary to consider the relevant market and the defendant's ability to lessen or destroy competition in that market.

Notwithstanding the array of authority contrary to *Lessig*, the Court of Appeals in this case reaffirmed its prior holdings; indeed, it did not mention either this Court's decisions discussed above or the many decisions of other Courts of Appeals reaching contrary results. Respondents urge us to affirm the decision below. We are not at all inclined, however, to embrace *Lessig*'s interpretation of § 2, for there is little if any support for it in the statute or the case law, and the notion that proof of unfair or predatory conduct alone is sufficient to make out the offense of attempted monopolization is contrary to the purpose and policy of the Sherman Act.

The *Lessig* opinion claimed support from the language of § 2, which prohibits attempts to monopolize "any part" of commerce, and therefore forbids attempts to monopolize any appreciable segment of interstate sales of the relevant product. . . . The "any part" clause, however, applies to charges of monopolization as well as to attempts to monopolize, and it is beyond doubt that the former requires proof of market power in a relevant market. *United States v. Grinnell Corp.*, 384 U.S. 563, 570-571 (1966); *United States v. E. I. du Pont de Nemours & Co.*, 351 U.S. 377, 404 (1956).[9]

In support of its determination that an inference of dangerous probability was permissible from a showing of intent, the *Lessig* opinion cited, and added emphasis to, this Court's reference in its opinion in *Swift* to "intent and the *consequent* dangerous probability." 327 F.2d at 474, n.46, quoting 196 U.S. at 396. But any question whether dangerous probability of success requires proof of more than intent alone should have been removed by the subsequent passage in *Swift* which stated that "not every act that may be done with an intent to produce an unlawful result . . . constitutes an attempt. It is a question of proximity and degree." . . .

---

[9] *Lessig* cited *United States v. Yellow Cab Co.*, 332 U.S. at 226, in support of its interpretation, but *Yellow Cab* relied on the "any part" language to support the proposition that it is immaterial how large an amount of interstate trade is affected, or how important that part of commerce is in relation to the entire amount of that type of commerce in the Nation.

The *Lessig* court also relied on a footnote in *du Pont & Co., supra*, 351 U.S. at 395, n.23, for the proposition that when the charge is attempt to monopolize, the relevant market is "not in issue." That footnote, which appeared in analysis of the relevant market issue in *du Pont*, rejected the Government's reliance on several cases, noting that "the scope of the market was not in issue" in *Story Parchment Co. v. Paterson Parchment Paper Co.*, 282 U.S. 555 (1931). That reference merely reflected the fact that, in *Story Parchment*, which was not an attempt to monopolize case, the parties did not challenge the definition of the market adopted by the lower courts. Nor was *du Pont* itself concerned with the issue in this case.

It is also our view that *Lessig* and later Ninth Circuit decisions refining and applying it are inconsistent with the policy of the Sherman Act. The purpose of the Act is not to protect businesses from the working of the market; it is to protect the public from the failure of the market. The law directs itself not against conduct which is competitive, even severely so, but against conduct which unfairly tends to destroy competition itself. It does so not out of solicitude for private concerns but out of concern for the public interest. . . . Thus, this Court and other courts have been careful to avoid constructions of § 2 which might chill competition, rather than foster it. It is sometimes difficult to distinguish robust competition from conduct with long-term anticompetitive effects; moreover, single-firm activity is unlike concerted activity covered by § 1, which "inherently is fraught with anticompetitive risk." *Copperweld*, 467 U.S. at 767-769. For these reasons, § 2 makes the conduct of a single firm unlawful only when it actually monopolizes or dangerously threatens to do so. . . . The concern that § 2 might be applied so as to further anticompetitive ends is plainly not met by inquiring only whether the defendant has engaged in "unfair" or "predatory" tactics. Such conduct may be sufficient to prove the necessary intent to monopolize, which is something more than an intent to compete vigorously, but demonstrating the dangerous probability of monopolization in an attempt case also requires inquiry into the relevant product and geographic market and the defendant's economic power in that market.

III

We hold that petitioners may not be liable for attempted monopolization under § 2 of the Sherman Act absent proof of a dangerous probability that they would monopolize a particular market and specific intent to monopolize. In this case, the trial instructions allowed the jury to infer specific intent and dangerous probability of success from the defendants' predatory conduct, without any proof of the relevant market or of a realistic probability that the defendants could achieve monopoly power in that market. In this respect, the instructions misconstrued § 2, as did the Court of Appeals in affirming the judgment of the District Court. Since the affirmance of the § 2 judgment against petitioners rested solely on the legally erroneous conclusion that petitioners had attempted to monopolize in violation of § 2 and since the jury's verdict did not negate the possibility that the § 2 verdict rested on the attempt to monopolize ground alone, the judgment of the Court of Appeals is reversed . . . and the case is remanded for further proceedings consistent with this opinion.[10]

So ordered.

---

[10] Respondents conceded in their brief that the case should be remanded to the Court of Appeals if we found error in the instruction on attempt to monopolize. . . .

COMMENTARY

1. What is the status of the double-inference method of proof after the Supreme Court's decision in *Spectrum Sports*? Does the Court purport to end the double-inference method? Is it permissible, after *Spectrum Sports*, to infer specific intent from conduct?

2. Many courts (including both the Ninth and other Circuits) have allowed a plaintiff to establish an attempted monopolization case by proving predatory pricing. As we will see in the next chapter, a plaintiff is often permitted to present a prima facie case by proof that the defendant has priced at a level below average variable cost. Proof of this conduct raises an inference of specific intent and the intent raises an inference of dangerous probability of monopolization. This is the double-inference method of proof. Will this approach to predatory pricing have to be changed in the light of *Spectrum Sports*? Is it ever permissible to infer dangerous probability of monopolization from specific intent or conduct?

3. If the double-inference method of proving attempted monopolization was erroneous, why did the Supreme Court wait for twenty-nine years to repudiate the Ninth Circuit's decision in the *Lessig* case? (*Lessig*, the origin of the double-inference method of proof, was decided in 1964.)

4. What did the Court have to say about the need to prove a relevant market in an attempted monopolization case? What would a plaintiff have to prove to establish "dangerous probability of success"?

5. Does the decision in *Spectrum Sports* move the law of monopolization back to where it was before the decision in *Lessig*?

6. Consider whether there is a minimum market share below which a defendant cannot pose a "dangerous probability" of monopolizing. In *Rebel Oil Co. v. Atlantic Richfield Co.*, 51 F.3d 1421, 1438 (9th Cir. 1995), the Ninth Circuit said that "most cases hold that a market share of 30 percent is presumptively insufficient to establish the power to control price." In that case the court stated that a market share of 44% would be sufficient to support a jury finding of market power in an attempt case, but only "if entry barriers are high and competitors are unable to expand their output in response to surracompetitive pricing."

It is generally believed that the minimum market share necessary to establish the completed offense of monopolization is higher than the share necessary to establish attempted monopolization. *See* Chapter 9, page 410, *supra*.

J. Attempted Monopolization, Monopolization, and Oligopoly

As observed above, the Ninth Circuit was not the only court to conclude that there was a "gap" in the Sherman Act. The Supreme Court, in *Copperweld*, also noted the existence of a gap in the Act. The Court, however, observed both that the gap was intentional and that there were reasons why the gap was desirable:

> We have already noted that Congress left this "gap" for eminently sound reasons. Subjecting a single firm's every action to judicial scrutiny for reasonableness would threaten to discourage the competitive enthusiasm that the antitrust laws seek to promote. . . . Moreover, whatever the wisdom of the distinction, the Act's plain language leaves no doubt that Congress made a purposeful choice to accord different treatment to unilateral and concerted conduct. Had Congress intended to outlaw unreasonable restraints of trade as such, § 1's requirement of a contract, combination, or conspiracy would be superfluous, as would the entirety of § 2.

467 U.S. at 775-76.

Thus the behavior of a single firm aimed at creating or reinforcing an oligopoly would not, under this reasoning, constitute a Sherman Act offense. Consider the following cases.

1. *Indiana Grocery, Inc. v. Super Valu Stores, Inc.*, 864 F.2d 1147 (7th Cir. 1989)

Indiana Stores charged that Kroger engaged in predatory pricing in order to discipline its principal rival into following an oligopolistic pricing scheme. The Seventh Circuit rejected this allegation as legally insufficient:

> Unfortunately, Indiana Grocery's theory does not implicate section 2 of the Sherman Act. At best, it poses the danger that Kroger's allegedly anticompetitive conduct could result in diminished price competition in an oligopolistic, or, at worst, a duopolistic market. Section 2, however, does not govern single-firm anticompetitive conduct aimed only at creating an oligopoly.

864 F.2d at 1416.

2. *Rebel Oil Co. v. Atlantic Richfield Co.*, 51 F.3d 1421 (9th Cir. 1995)

Rebel charged that Atlantic Richfield (ARCO) attempted to monopolize the retail gasoline market in Las Vegas, Nevada. Rebel alleged that ARCO set prices at predatory levels, forcing out many rival retail stations, and thereby acquired a 54% market share for itself. Rebel further alleged that ARCO then raised its prices to supracompetitive levels, recouping the losses which it incurred during the predatory period. Although 54% is not a monopoly, Rebel theorized that ARCO was able to set supracompetitive prices because all of the refiner-suppliers which supply gasoline to Las Vegas are oligopolists who would raise their wholesale prices in tandem with ARCO's increase in retail prices, thus preventing any independent retailer from challenging ARCO's pricing. The Ninth Circuit rejected Rebel's claim on the basis that it rested upon an asserted goal of oligopoly pricing rather than monopolization:

> To pose a threat of monopolization, one firm *alone* must have the power to control market output and exclude competition. . . . An oligopolist lacks this unilateral power. By definition, oligopolists are interdependent. An oligopolist can increase market price, but only if the others go along. . . . We recognize that a gap in the Sherman Act allows oligopolies to slip past its prohibitions, . . . but filling that gap is the concern of Congress, not the judiciary.

51 F.3d at 1443 (emphasis in the original).

COMMENTARY

1. Note that the courts recognize that unilateral behavior directed at establishing or reinforcing an oligopoly is anticompetitive but nonetheless find it lawful. The rationale is the absence of language in the Sherman Act targeting unilateral behavior seeking to bring about an oligopoly.

2. Observe that the Ninth Circuit in *Rebel Oil* continues to recognize the existence of a "gap" in the Sherman Act, but that it no longer employs an expansionary construction of the attempt clause in order to eliminate that gap. That court is now willing to live with the "gap."

3. Should the Sherman Act be amended to prohibit attempts to "oligopolize"?

Chapter 11
Predatory Pricing

A. Predatory Pricing in General: An Historical Note

Section 3 of the Robinson-Patman Act of 1936, 15 U.S.C. § 13a (1994), expressly forbids "any person engaged in commerce, in the course of such commerce . . . to sell, or contract to sell, goods at unreasonably low prices for the purpose of destroying competition or eliminating a competitor." In enacting this legislation in 1936, Congress extended its earlier concern with predatory and discriminatory pricing practices which originated with the disclosure of such practices in the early Sherman Act cases against the great combinations, *Standard Oil Co. of New Jersey v. United States*, 221 U.S. 1 (1911), and *American Tobacco Co. v. United States*, 221 U.S. 106 (1911). The legislative history described the concern of the sponsors of the Clayton Act of 1914, 38 Stat. 740, with predatory pricing as follows:

> The necessity for legislation to prevent unfair . . . [practices] in prices with a view to destroying competition needs little argument to sustain the wisdom of it. In the past it has been a common practice of great and powerful combinations . . . —notably the Standard Oil Co., and the American Tobacco Co., and others of less notoriety, but of great influence—to lower prices of their commodities, oftentimes below the cost of production in certain communities and sections where they had competition, with the intent to destroy . . . the business of their competitors, and with the ultimate purpose in view of thereby acquiring a monopoly in the particular locality or section. . . .

H. REP. NO. 63-627, at 8 (1914); S. REP. NO. 63-698, at 3 (1914). For the cases concerned with discriminatory pricing between and among a seller's customers under § 2 of the Clayton Act, as amended by the Robinson-Patman Act of 1936, 15 U.S.C. § 13a (1994), see Chapter 13, *infra*.

When courts review pricing practices with a view to distinguishing vigorous competition from "predatory" pricing, economic analysis is invoked. The conventional economic wisdom from the turn of the century until the 1930s, characterized predatory pricing—sales below costs—as a short-run aberration from the theoretical competitive norm. This analysis posited that such pricing would indicate a quest for monopoly power because a potential monopolist might adopt a short-term strategy of drastic price cuts in order to deter entry of a new competitor or to dispatch a small rival with limited financial resources. *See* ALFRED MARSHALL, PRINCIPLES OF ECONOMICS 339 (1890); E.A.G. ROBINSON, MONOPOLY 74 (1941). However, were monopoly to be achieved, then that would be considered an unstable condition because the monopoly profits would attract new entrants to erode the monopoly position. This process would eliminate the incentive to achieve monopoly by reliance on drastic pricing practices.

In the 1950s, economists revisited the classical theory of predatory pricing. John McGee challenged the classical view that there existed even a short-run incentive for drastic price cutting in his study of the *Standard Oil* case of 1911, one of the cases that drew congressional attention to this practice, as reflected in the debates over the Clayton Act in 1914. McGee's review of the record in *Standard Oil* led him to the conclusion that the classical view of injurious pricing as a short-run phenomenon was flawed. He argued that predatory pricing was never rational, profit-maximizing economic behavior for a monopolist because monopoly power could more efficiently be acquired by alternative means, such as mergers. *See* John S. McGee, *Predatory Price Cutting: The* Standard Oil (N.J.) *Case*, 1 J.L. & ECON. 137 (1958).[1] McGee's thesis was endorsed by Lester Telser in a subsequent article, *Abusive Trade Practices: An Economic Analysis*, 30 LAW & CONTEMP. PROBS. 488 (1965), in which Telser also identified collusion as a more efficient tool than predatory pricing to achieve monopoly power. Telser also accepted McGee's position regarding mergers as a tool to monopoly status as follows:

> Price wars between the two [predator and target] is equivalent to forming a coalition between each firm and the consumers, such that the consumers gain from the conflict between the firms. Since both firms can benefit by agreeing on a merger price, and both stand to lose by sales below cost, one would think that rational men would prefer merger.

Lester Telser, *Cutthroat Competition and the Long Purse*, 9 J.L. & ECON. 259, 265 (1966).

These articles precipitated a number of theoretical and empirical works supporting these conclusions. The empirical studies found, moreover, that predation was not widespread. *See* Terry Calvani & James M. Lynch, *Predatory Pricing Under the Robinson-Patman and Sherman Acts: An Introduction*, 51 ANTITRUST L.J. 375, 377 (1982) (summarizing this literature); *see also* Richard Zerbe, *The American Sugar Refining Company, 1887-1914: The Story of a Monopoly*, 12 J.L. & ECON. 339 (1969), Kenneth G. Elzinga, *Predatory Pricing: The Case of the Gunpowder Trust*, 13 J.L. & ECON. 223 (1970).

---

1 A more recent review by economists of the same case attributes Standard Oil's success in achieving a monopoly position in the petroleum industry, not to mergers, collusion, or predatory pricing, but to the company's ability to impose higher transportation costs on its rivals. *See* Elizabeth Granitz & Benjamin Klein, *Monopolization by "Raising Rivals' Costs": The* Standard Oil *Case*, 39 J.L. & ECON. 1 (1996).

The consensus surrounding the McGee-Telser analysis of predatory pricing began to dissolve after the publication of Basil Yamey's 1972 article, *Predatory Price Cutting: Notes and Comments*, 15 J.L. & ECON. 129 (1972). Yamey questioned McGee's assumption that predatory prices were limited to prices below long-run marginal or average cost. Instead, Yamey posited a motive for a temporary price reduction as a statement by a dominant seller to a competitor of an intention to make further cuts as needed to compel compliant behavior.

". . . [A]ll that is necessary is that the price be taken to a level lower than that which would otherwise prevail," wrote Yamey. This article then cited the operation of the shipowners' cartel analyzed in the House of Lords decision in *Mogul Steamship Co. v. McGregor, Gow & Co.* (1892) A.C. 25, as an example of the use of temporary low prices that were not below cost, but had the effect of deterring entry of a competitor. This example led to the conclusion that ". . . predatory pricing or the threat of its use, *may* itself operate as an effective hindrance to new entry even in situations where the conventional barriers to entry are weak or absent." 15 J.L. & ECON. at 142.

Is the McGee-Telser position distinguished from Yamey's by a difference in an underlying assumption? Does Yamey consider predatory pricing as part of the analysis of the conditions of entry and do McGee-Telser view this practice as an independent attribute of profit-maximizing conduct? Judge Posner suggested another limiting condition of the McGee premise by pointing out that it is rational economic behavior for a dominant seller to sell below cost in one geographic market, if it is possible to generate offsetting monopoly profits in another geographic market. *See* Richard A. Posner, *Exclusionary Practices and the Antitrust Laws,* 41 U. CHI. L. REV. 506, 516 (1974). Predatory pricing as plausible anticompetitive conduct by a single firm with less than full-blown monopoly power was recognized by Edward H. Cooper, in *Attempts and Monopolization: A Mildly Expansionary Answer to the Prophylactic Riddle of Section Two*, 72 MICH. L. REV. 373 (1974).

As courts were increasingly presented with claims of below cost pricing, under § 2 of the Sherman Act and § 2(a) of the Robinson-Patman Act, lawyers and economists addressed the problem of formulating a legal rule of predatory pricing. The 1975 article of Areeda and Turner, *Predatory Pricing and Related Practices Under Section 2 of the Sherman Act*, 88 HARV. L. REV. 697 (1975), undertook to supply such a rule. In the early-1970s, Harvard Law School Professors Phillip Areeda and Donald Turner became concerned about a possible misuse of the antitrust laws by business firms who faced intense price competition. The managers of such firms might seek refuge under the antitrust laws from the rigor of price competition in the marketplace by making claims based upon allegedly predatory pricing by their rivals, when the rivals were in fact engaged in competitive pricing. What the courts needed, Areeda and Turner concluded, was an easily applicable test for distinguishing legitimate claims of predatory pricing from the unmeritorious claims against price reductions to obtain more sales, the essence of competition. They, accordingly, set out to develop such a test.

Areeda and Turner argued that "A firm which drives out or excludes rivals by selling at unremunerative prices is not competing on the merits, but engaging in behavior that may properly be called predatory." They asserted, therefore, that there is "good reason for including a 'predatory pricing' antitrust offense within the proscription of monopolization or attempts to monopolize in section 2 of the Sherman Act." Areeda and Turner thought, however, that "predatory intent" ought not to be a component of such an offense. They reached this conclusion primarily because they feared that a subjective component of this offense would encourage the bringing of frivolous lawsuits. Instead, they developed an "objective" measure of predatory conduct: They argued that a firm ought to be deemed to have acted in a predatory fashion if it priced its goods at a level below short-run marginal cost. In such a case, the firm would be worsening its position with each additional sale. Its conduct could not be explained as a rational attempt to maximize its short-run profits or to minimize its short-term losses. Therefore, it must be seeking a longer-term goal, such as increased market dominance or a further entrenchment of its present dominance by warding off potential rivals. Areeda and Turner argued, conversely, that so long as a firm set its prices at or above marginal costs it would not be discouraging entry by equally efficient firms. Therefore, prices at or above marginal cost ought to be considered lawful ones.

The professors added several qualifications and modifications to this basic approach. When marginal cost exceeded average cost, they would not find a firm's prices predatory unless they also fell below average cost. And because it is very difficult to ascertain marginal cost in practice, Areeda and Turner would permit the use of the easier-to-calculate average variable cost as a "surrogate" for marginal cost in the determination of predatory behavior. Since average variable cost is always below average total cost, a firm would be held to have acted in a predatory manner when it prices its goods below average variable cost. Consider why Areeda and Turner would wish to condemn a firm which priced below average variable cost, but above marginal cost.

Areeda and Turner thus undertook to state when price cutting by an established firm with market power is illegal as predatory pricing under the Sherman Act in terms of a cost-based rule. The basic premise of their article is derived from static, short-run, microeconomic analysis, which teaches that marginal cost is the proper standard for efficient pricing. If, in the above examples, a dominant firm sets the price of its product(s) at least equal to marginal cost, there can be no deleterious consequence. When a competitor cannot meet the efficient price, consumers will not patronize it and society is well-served by the departure of a high-cost producer from the market. Thus, meeting the condition of pricing at or above marginal cost begins the definition of a non-predatory price. Areeda and Turner made two adjustments to this standard in order to facilitate its implementation. First, as noted above, they shifted from reliance on marginal cost because of the accounting difficulties involved in its computation, a circumstance which would materially detract from its evidentiary reliability. Second, they took account of the fact that the relationship of price to marginal cost was always determined for some level of output and once output varied, the relationship among the cost functions, short-run marginal cost, average variable cost, and average total cost also varied. See the diagram, below. Also they sought to give some dynamic content to their analysis by relying on "reasonably anticipated costs" rather than actual costs. 88 HARV. L. REV. at 715.

For these reasons, they concluded that average variable cost ". . . is a useful surrogate for predatory pricing analysis." *Id.* at 718. Areeda and Turner recognized that their formulation omitted fixed costs from their rule. They explained the omission of fixed costs from their formulation as follows:

> To conclude that there should be a rule against predatory pricing but not against predatory investment requires that a workable line be drawn between the short run and the long run. In theory this is difficult since fixed costs become variable over . . . [a long enough period], but we think the issue is practically resolvable. Since the offense is limited to predatory pricing, the relevant question is which costs were variable during the period of alleged predation. Normal accounting procedures will usually supply the answer: costs charged as a direct expense should be treated as variable; costs charged as an investment for depreciation and tax purposes should be treated as fixed.

Id. at 720. They relied on the following functions:

Areeda-Turner Pricing Floors

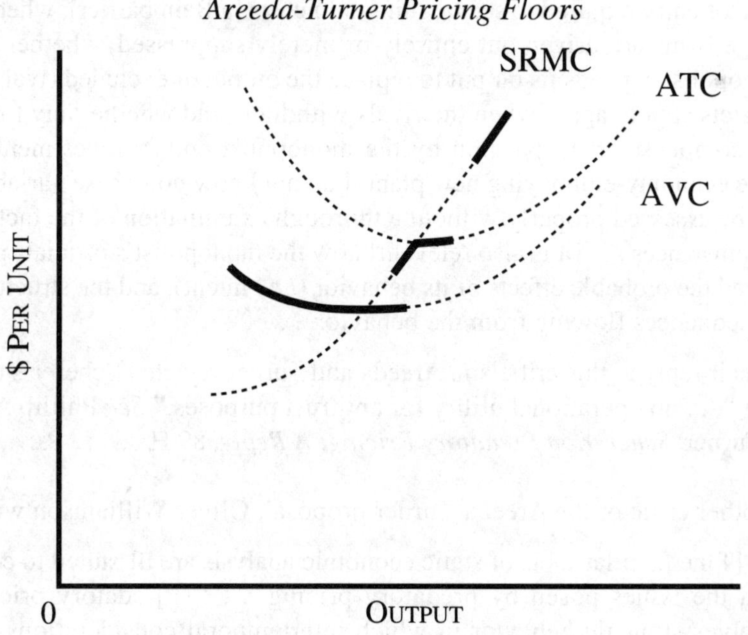

This article precipitated several lively responses, primarily from economists, who pointed out that although Areeda and Turner had suggested longer term applications of their analysis, they were limited by the short-run assumptions of their static model. The critics of Areeda and Turner differed over whether a short-run or a long-run perspective was relevant. To many of the critics, the Areeda-Turner standard was no more than mechanical reliance on cost/price relationships based on a short-term model, whereas the essence of predatory pricing was as a form of long-run strategic behavior whose objective was communicating to an actual or prospective competitor that the long-run prospects of recovering any investment there were remote, if not nonexistent. See, for example, F.M. Scherer, *Predatory Pricing and the Sherman Act: A Comment*, 89 HARV. L. REV. 869, 890 (1976), who wrote,

> The Areeda-Turner article goes astray by stressing unimportant exclusionary scenarios, by giving short shrift to the problems posed by deterrence of large-scale entry, and by failing to develop a correct economic analysis of how exclusionary pricing affects long-run allocative efficiency.
>
> . . . Courts that attempt to substitute simple cost rules for such analyses of effect and intent in alleged predation cases are likely to reach economically unsound decisions.

Scherer's analysis led him to advocate a full review of market conditions to determine the conditions that would maximize long-term economic welfare, the key variables of which are:

> . . . the relative cost positions of the monopolist and fringe firms, the scale of entry required to secure minimum costs [a Bain barrier], whether fringe firms are driven out entirely or merely suppressed, whether the monopolist expands its output to replace the output of excluded rivals or restricts supply again when the rivals withdraw, and whether any long-run compensatory expansion by the monopolist entails investment in scale economy-embodying new plant. I do not know how these variables can be assessed properly without a thorough examination of the factual circumstances . . . [it is also relevant] how the monopolist's officials perceived the probable effects of its behavior (*i.e.*, intent), and the structural consequences flowing from the behavior. . . .

In their reply to this criticism, Areeda and Turner rejected Scherer's approach as having ". . . no operational utility for antitrust purposes." *See* Phillip Areeda & Donald Turner, *Scherer on Predatory Pricing: A Reply*, 89 HARV. L. REV. 891, 897 (1976).

Another critic of the Areeda-Turner proposal, Oliver Williamson wrote,

> . . . [T]he familiar tools of static economic analysis are ill-suited to cope with the issues posed by predatory pricing. . . . [P]redatory pricing involves strategic behavior in which intertemporal considerations are central. Static economic models that fail to capture these attributes miss crucial features of the predatory pricing issue.

Predatory Pricing: A Strategic and Welfare Analysis, 87 YALE L.J. 284 (1977). Williamson perceived that the Areeda-Turner rule would not inhibit predatory behavior because a dominant firm could manipulate its output to avoid it by building a plant that is larger than needed. According to Williamson, the dominant firm would then maintain a level of output below that of its optimum and have excess capacity. At such level of output, the marginal cost curve is below short-run average cost. When the dominant firm increases its output, its short-run average cost will decrease. If entry by another firm is threatened or occurs at that point, the dominant firm can eliminate the entrant by either maintaining that price or by expanding output to a level that will cause price to fall in response to the increased output. This will force price below the entrant's average cost, but not below the dominant firm's marginal cost. Williams's policy recommendation was to bar a dominant firm from expanding output when faced with new entry for an eighteen month period and from selling below average total cost for the longer term. His recommendation would consider price/output responses as predatory when made in response to new entrants but not when made toward existing rivals.

William Baumol, also critical of the Areeda-Turner model for its static cost-price emphasis, wrote,

> . . . [A] firm, seeking to prevent entry by others need not confine itself to a single price move. Instead, it may chose to cut price temporarily when entry occurs, raising price again after the threat recedes, or it may take a more complex sequence of price changes, responding step by step to each change in an entrant's decisions. The resulting threat to competition and to the general welfare is not a function of the relationship between price and costs, but rather a matter of the responsiveness of pricing to changing competitive developments. Thus, it seems appropriate to look beyond the Areeda-Turner test, which evaluates matters solely in terms of the relation between the established firm's prices and its marginal . . . or average variable costs.

Quasi-Permanence of Price Reductions: A Policy for the Prevention of Predatory Pricing, 89 YALE L.J. 1, 3 (1979). Baumol proposes an arbitrary rule to address the problem. He would allow a dominant firm to reduce price without review or restriction in the face of competition or a new entrant, but once this reduced price had the result either of discouraging a prospective entrant or of causing a smaller firm to leave the market, the dominant firm would be required to adhere to that price for several years, unless the firm could demonstrate increased costs or other relevant changes. What evidence would be probative of the discouragement of a prospective entrant?

Like Baumol, Paul Joskow and Alvin Klevorick reviewed the economic literature of predatory pricing and agreed with Baumol's characterization of the problem as posing the difficult task ". . . of inferring long-run market outcomes from observable short-run behavior . . . and market conditions." In their article, *A Framework for Analyzing Predatory Pricing Policy* 89 YALE L.J. 213, 255 (1979), these economists proposed a two-tier policy. The first tier requires a finding that monopolistic conditions exist in the relevant market based on a review of concentration, entry conditions, profit margins, innovation, and related factors. Absent a finding of monopoly conditions, the inquiry is ended. If the first-tier conditions are met, the second tier relies on speculative conditions that are beyond the Areeda-Turner formulation. The second tier review of the alleged predatory conduct is governed by rules as follows: A price below average variable cost establishes predation. A price between average variable cost and average total cost is presumptive evidence of predation, but the presumption can be rebutted by a showing that the alleged predator has substantial excess capacity, which was not the result of exclusionary conduct. Finally, a price reduction to a point above average total cost, unless reversed by a significant price increase within two years, is presumed legal.

The articles summarized above are discussed in further detail by Joseph F. Brodley & George A. Hay, *Predatory Pricing: Competing Economic Theories and the Evolution of Legal Standards,* 66 CORNELL L. REV. 738 (1981); *see also* ABA ANTITRUST SECTION, MONOGRAPH NO. 22, PREDATORY PRICING 7-9 (1996). Consider the application of the predatory price rules in the cases that follow and consider also the following questions. Which of the economists' rule for establishing "below cost" pricing do you favor? Should the standard for Sherman Act and Robinson-Patman Act predatory price claims be the same? To what extent have courts adopted an economic analysis of predatory pricing?

Based on the writings of these economists, what evidence would you marshal to draft a complaint alleging predatory pricing? Assume you engage cost accountants as expert witnesses. What data would you instruct them to gather? Should the accountants gather data on fixed, variable, and opportunity costs? What approach would you instruct them to take on the allocation of costs in a multi-product firm? What problems would a court encounter in applying Joskow and Klevorick's two-tier rules?

B. Sherman Act Claims of Predatory Pricing

United States v. AMR Corporation

140 F. Supp. 2d 1141 (D. Kan. 2001)

J. Thomas MARTEN, Judge.

The present action arises from competition between American Airlines and several smaller low cost carriers on various airline routes centered on Dallas-Fort Worth Airport (DFW) from 1995 to 1997. During this period, these low cost carriers created a new market dynamic, charging markedly lower fares on certain routes. For a certain period (of differing length in each market) consumers of air travel on these routes enjoyed lower prices. The number of passengers also substantially increased. American responded to the low cost carriers by reducing some of its own fares, and increasing the number of flights serving the routes. In each instance, the low fare carrier failed to establish itself as a durable market presence, and eventually moved its operations, or ceased its separate existence entirely. After the low fare carrier ceased operations, American generally resumed its prior marketing strategy, and in certain markets reduced the number of flights and raised its prices, roughly to levels comparable to those prior to the period of low fare competition.

In the present action the plaintiff United States alleges that the defendants AMR Corporation, American Airlines, Inc., and AMR Eagle Holding Company, (all hereafter "American"), participated in a scheme of predatory pricing against the low cost carriers in violation of Section 2 of the Sherman Act. The government alleges that American's pricing and capacity decisions on the routes in question resulted in pricing its product below cost, and that it intended to subsequently recoup these costs by supra-competitive pricing by monopolizing or attempting to monopolize these routes. It further alleges that, in addition to these routes, American has violated Section 2 in a large number of additional airline routes, contending that American has monopolized or attempted to monopolize by means of the "reputation for predation" it allegedly gained in its successful competition against low fare carriers in the core markets.

American has moved for summary judgment on the outstanding claims, arguing that its competition against the low cost carriers was competition on the merits, and not conduct unlawful within the terms of the Sherman Act. Having reviewed the arguments of the parties and the evidence submitted in connection with the motion for summary judgment, the court finds that summary judgment is appropriate.

. . . .

The government's expert, Professor Stiglitz, states:

> First, one must determine whether the incumbent had clear alternatives that the incumbent knew or could reasonably be expected to have known would have made it more money absent any predation profits. Importantly, it is not necessary to compare the alleged predator's actual behavior with its *most* profitable alternative. The key is whether the alleged predator clearly passed up a *more* profitable alternative. . . . If there is clear evidence that the predator had available one or more alternative actions that—but for the anti-competitive effect—would have yielded higher profits, then a suspicious sacrifice has occurred. . . . Note that anytime we evaluate the costs and benefits of a firm's conduct in this way, we are necessarily comparing the conduct actually undertaken to *some* alternative conduct, in this case, the alternative of *not* adding capacity, *i.e.*, leaving capacity at its pre-entry level.

Professor Stiglitz testified that

> . . . price cost tests focus on the narrow question of [whether there] . . . was a sacrifice, did the firm experience a loss relative to what it could have otherwise done in the short run. . . . They say in the short run today did I produce more than was profit maximizing. In the short run. Very narrow question.

Professor Stiglitz concedes that his proposed "sacrifice" test would condemn output expansions that leave American's revenues above average variable cost.

. . . .

. . . The court holds that the government's claims against American in the present action must meet the standards of proof set forth in *Brooke Group*: the plaintiff must prove both that the defendant priced its product below an appropriate measure of cost, and that the defendant enjoyed a realistic prospect of recouping its losses by supra-competitive pricing. Under that standard, the government's claims fail.

. . . The Supreme Court . . . expressed skepticism [about predatory pricing claims] in *Brooke Group*:

> These prerequisites to recovery [proof of below-cost pricing and recoupment] are not easy to establish, but they are not artificial obstacles to recovery; rather, they are essential components of real market injury. As we have said in the Sherman Act context, predatory pricing schemes are rarely tried, and even more rarely successful, and the costs of an erroneous finding of liability are high. The mechanism by which a firm engages in predatory pricing—lowering prices—is the same mechanism by which a firm stimulates competition. . . . It would be ironic indeed if the standards for predatory pricing liability were so low that antitrust suits themselves became a tool for keeping prices high.

509 U.S. at 226, 113 S. Ct. 2578 (citations and internal quotations omitted).[9]

The rationale for cost-based analysis rests in the limited ability of courts to accurately separate real-world predation from vigorous but lawful competition, and the inherent threat to competition that a failure to make such a recognition creates. There has been no shortage of non-cost measures under which courts would supposedly detect and police unlawful predatory pricing.

The problem with all such strategies is not that we doubt their existence or even their anticompetitive consequences. Rather, identifying them in the particular case without chilling aggressive, competitive pricing is far beyond the capacity of any antitrust tribunal. Once we cross the threshold and permit prices above cost to be condemned as predatory, we throw the doors open to all kinds of speculation about the pricing strategies of large firms—speculation that judges ordinarily address by opening discovery, including evidence of presumed anticompetitive intent, and making a jury the final decision-maker. *Antitrust begins with the premise that all firms, even dominant firms, are permitted to compete aggressively, and that hard competition is a desideratum rather than an evil. Thus prices above the relevant measure of cost become an absolute safe harbor*. Dicta in the Supreme Court's *Brooke* decision commanded as much. . . . .

. . . .

In addition, the court must note that evidence of below-cost pricing is an *essential* element of the government's claim. Under *Brooke Group*, the government must show pricing below an appropriate level of costs. This is an objective standard. Other, non-objective evi-

---

[9] Another authority has also urged caution:

> An argument that a practice is "predatory" is likely to point to exactly those things that ordinarily signify efficient conduct. A plaintiff charging predation will classify a reduction in price, an expansion in output, the building of a new plant, and so on as proof of the defendant's villainy. Unless we have some powerful tools to separate predation from its cousin, hard competition, any legal inquiry is apt to lead to more harm than good. Given the general agreement that almost all price reductions, sales increases, additions to capacity, and so on are beneficial, we need a very good ground indeed to treat a particular instance of such conduct as unlawful.

F. Easterbrook, *Predatory Strategies and Counterstrategies,* 48 U. Chi. L. Rev. 263, 266-67 (1981) (footnotes omitted).

dence will not transform above-cost pricing into illegal predatory conduct. Above-cost pricing, whether or not it is combined with other conduct, does not "inflict injury to competition cognizable under the antitrust laws." *Brooke Group*, 509 U.S. at 223, 113 S. Ct. 2578. Areeda and Hovenkamp also discuss the effect of this conclusion, stating: "the Supreme Court's *Brooke* holds that no matter how strong and unambiguous the evidence of the defendant's anti-competitive intent, unlawful predation cannot be established without a determination from objective market factors that predation will yield profitable recoupment. Further forceful dicta in that decision indicates that a predatory price requires objective evidence of prices that are below 'some measure of incremental cost.'" 3 AREEDA & HOVENKAMP, ¶ 738a at p. 359-60.[10]

. . . .

The court finds that, in reality, the government's two proposed incremental cost tests focus on whether the defendant, in the short run, failed to maximize its profits. Such tests are inappropriate as a matter of law to determine the existence of predatory conduct in the present case.

As discussed above [the internal accounting cost measure asserted by the government as a proper measure of American's costs] . . . includes essentially all (at least 97% and upwards of 99%) of American's total costs. It includes variable expenses, the costs of aircraft ownership, fixed overhead, interest, return on equity and income taxes. The court finds that the use of [this accounting measure] . . . is the functional equivalent of applying an average total cost test to assess predation. Such an approach clearly is against prevailing law. *See* 3 AREEDA & HOVENKAMP, ¶ 741c at p. 398 ("Average total cost tests appear to be ruled out by forceful dicta in the Supreme Court's *Brooke* opinion that a price must be shown to be lower than some measure of 'incremental' cost."). Accordingly, the court finds that tests of alleged predation based on [the asserted measure] are legally insufficient because such tests ultimately rest on American's total costs.

. . . [D]efendant American's Motion for Summary Judgment . . . is hereby granted.

---

[10] The objective nature of this inquiry was also stressed by the Seventh Circuit in *A.A. Poultry Farms, Inc. v. Rose Acre Farms, Inc.*, 881 F.2d 1396, 1401-02 (7th Cir.1989), where the court observed that subjective measures may be inherently misleading:

> Firms "intend" to do all the business they can, to crush their rivals if they can. "'Intent to harm' without more offers too vague a standard in a world where executives may think no further than 'Let's get more business,'" *Barry Wright* [*v. ITT Grinnell Corp.*], 724 F.2d [227,] 232 [(1st Cir.1983)]. Rivalry is harsh, and consumers gain the most when firms slash costs to the bone and pare price down to cost, all in pursuit of more business. Few firms cut price unaware of what they are doing; price reductions are carried out in pursuit of sales, at others' expense. Entrepreneurs who work hardest to cut their prices will do the most damage to their rivals, and they will see good in it. You cannot be a sensible business executive without understanding the link among prices, your firm's success, and other firms' distress.
>
> . . . .

COMMENTARY

1. Despite rejecting the government's claim, does the court approve of government-expert Stiglitz's "sacrifice" test in stating the court's test for predatory pricing?

2. From reading this opinion, do you conclude that the doctrine of predatory pricing is an objective concept in antitrust analysis or does it require inferences of subjective intent?

3. Do you think this case was rightly decided? If you were an attorney in the Antitrust Division, would you recommend an appeal? Are you surprised to learn that the government announced that it will appeal? *See* NEW YORK TIMES, June 27, 2001, C1 col. 5.

William Inglis & Sons Baking Co. v. ITT Continental Baking Co.

668 F.2d 1014 (9th Cir. 1981)
as amended on denial of rehearing
and rehearing en banc (1982)

SNEED, Circuit Judge

I

. . . .

Inglis' complaint . . . was founded on charges that Continental sought to eliminate competition in the northern California market for wholesale bread by charging discriminatory and below-cost prices for its private label bread. . . . The theory on which Inglis structured its case was that the growth of private label bread, which began in northern California in 1967 or 1968, began to weaken Continental's market for Wonder bread. In response to this challenge Continental also began selling private label bread, but the price gap between private label and Wonder bread persisted. Inglis argues that Continental then decided to pursue a strategy of predatory pricing in its sales of private label bread, with the intent of eliminating independent wholesalers like Inglis who were financially less capable of withstanding a price war. The ultimate goal, Inglis asserts, was to acquire a large share of the private label market and then to use the enhanced market power to raise private label prices, which would diminish the competitive disadvantage of Wonder bread. . . .

II

THE SECTION 2 ATTEMPT TO MONOPOLIZE CLAIM—PREDATORY PRICING

A. . . .

1. . . .

. . . .

Although the law of this circuit on attempted monopolization has not been static, its current state recognizes three elements of an attempt claim under section 2 of the Sherman

Act: (1) specific intent to control prices or destroy competition in some part of commerce; (2) predatory or anticompetitive conduct directed to accomplishing the unlawful purpose; and (3) a dangerous probability of success. . . . To state these elements, however, is merely to begin the process of understanding the legal standards of conduct under an attempt claim. Each element interacts with the others in significant and unexpected ways. . . .

2. *Dangerous Probability of Success*

. . . .

Part of the uncertainty results . . . from the tendency to treat the element of dangerous probability of success and proof of market power as equivalent. Although related, they are not equivalent. . . .

These more recent decisions . . . establish that the dangerous probability of success requirement is not designed as a means of screening out cases of minimal concern to antitrust policy but is instead a way of gauging more accurately the purpose of a defendant's actions. Accordingly, the level of the probability of success appropriately may be raised by the defendant . . . even if the plaintiff has made his case without direct proof of dangerous probability. Thus, if market conditions are such that a course of conduct described by the plaintiff would be unlikely to succeed in monopolizing the market, it is less likely that the defendant actually attempted to monopolize the market. Conversely, a firm with substantial market power may find it more rational to engage in a monopolistic course of conduct than would a smaller firm in a less concentrated market.

. . . .

3. *Conduct*

. . . In the absence of direct and probative evidence of specific intent to monopolize . . . a plaintiff must introduce evidence of conduct amounting to a substantial claim of restraint of trade or conduct clearly threatening to competition or clearly exclusionary. Direct evidence of intent, on the other hand, may permit reliance on a broader range of conduct, simply because the purpose of ambiguous conduct may be more clearly understood. But, in general, conduct that will support a claim of attempted monopolization must be such that its anticipated benefits were dependent upon its tendency to discipline or eliminate competition and thereby enhance the firm's long-term ability to reap the benefits of monopoly power. . . .

B. *Predatory Pricing*

. . . .

1. *When Is a Price Predatory?*

Much of the dispute on appeal concerns the proper relationship between direct evidence of intent and evidence concerning the relationship between the cost and price of Continental's products. . . .

2. *The Areeda-Turner Test*

One such economic test that has found favor in this and other circuits was developed by Professors Areeda and Turner. *See* Areeda & Turner, *Predatory Pricing and Related Practices Under Section 2 of the Sherman Act,* 88 HARV. L. REV. 697 (1975). In their view a price should not be considered predatory if it equals or exceeds the marginal cost of producing the product. When a firm prices at marginal cost, they argue, only less efficient firms will suffer larger losses per unit of output at that price. Moreover, such pricing enables resources to be properly allocated because the price accurately "signals" to the consumer the true social cost of the product. Therefore, "pricing at marginal cost is the competitive and socially optimal result." *Id.* at 711. In contrast, pricing below marginal cost should be conclusively presumed illegal. Recognizing that business records rarely reflect marginal costs of production, Areeda and Turner suggest the use of average variable cost as an evidentiary surrogate.

3. *This Court's Approach to Establishing Predation*

. . . .

Our approach to proof of intent through use of conduct is to focus on what a rational firm would have expected its prices to accomplish. . . . [A] price should be considered predatory if its anticipated benefits depended on its tendency to eliminate competition. If the justification for a price reduction did not depend upon this anticipated effect, then it does not support a claim of attempted monopolization, even if it had the actual effect of taking sales from competitors. . . .

In this case Continental has conceded that some of the prices challenged by Inglis were below average total cost. Taken alone this does not brand Continental's prices as predatory. Pricing below average total cost may be a legitimate means of minimizing losses, particularly when the firm is "temporarily" experiencing "excess capacity" in its productive facilities. When this is the case, the firm's average variable cost—the sum of those costs that vary with output divided by the total units of output—generally will be less than the firm's marginal cost—the variable cost associated with producing the last unit of output. . . .

. . . [W]e hold that to establish predatory pricing a plaintiff must prove that the anticipated benefits of defendant's price depended on its tendency to discipline or eliminate competition and thereby enhance the firm's long-term ability to reap the benefits of monopoly power. If the defendant's prices were below average total cost but above average variable cost, the plaintiff bears the burden of showing defendant's pricing was predatory. If, however, the plaintiff proves that the defendant's prices were below average variable cost, the plaintiff has established a *prima facie* case of predatory pricing and the burden shifts to the defendant to prove that the prices were justified without regard to any anticipated destructive effect they might have on competitors.

. . . Although Inglis' expert testified that during the period examined in his study Continental's prices were below average variable cost, the district court concluded that because excess capacity existed in the relevant market, only proof of prices below marginal cost could establish predatory pricing. The district court erred. The jury reasonably could have concluded that prices below average variable cost were predatory. Even when excess capacity exists, pricing below average variable cost, to repeat, is sufficiently questionable to support the inference that the prices were designed to eliminate competition. . . .

4. *How to Determine Which Costs Are Fixed and Which Are Variable*

. . . [T]o determine whether particular costs are variable, one must evaluate the relationship of the prospective change in output to that level of output which presently exists. For example, some production decisions of great magnitude may entail the substantial retirement or expansion . . . of productive capacity, in which case costs typically considered fixed become variable. At the other extreme, small expansions of output may entail no change in costs, such as labor or transportation, that are considered typically variable.[37]

. . . .

. . . It follows that the determination of which costs are variable and which fixed will vary with the facts of each case. . . . In this case a new trial is warranted because the evidence upon which Inglis depended to prove predatory conduct was not based upon a calculation of which costs were fixed and which variable that was rooted in the particular facts of this case. . . .

For all the reasons set forth in this opinion, we reverse the entry of JNOV by the trial court and remand this case to the district court for a new trial in accordance with the views expressed in this opinion. . . .

COMMENTARY

1. The Ninth Circuit had employed the Areeda-Turner standard several times prior to its decision in *Inglis*. *See* Daniel J. Gifford, *The Role of the Ninth Circuit in the Development of the Law of Attempt to Monopolize*, 61 NOTRE DAME L. REV. 1021 (1986). In *Inglis*, that Circuit, in an extensive opinion, carefully incorporated the Areeda-Turner standard into the caselaw which that Circuit had been developing on the attempt clause. *Inglis* probably represents the most thoughtful and thorough circuit court consideration and evaluation of the Areeda-Turner standard. As the opinion makes clear, the court, while adopting the basic outlines of the Areeda-Turner approach, *i.e.,* the employment of a marginal-cost/average-variable-cost standard, rejected other parts of the Areeda-Turner recommendations. The court refused to make the definition of fixed cost a question of law as those authors had recommended. Moreover, the court made the marginal-cost/average-variable-cost standard more rebuttable than Areeda and Turner thought proper. The Ninth Circuit also permits the use of an average-total-cost standard in a limited number of circumstances.

---

[37] The principal dispute in the trial court was whether expenses such as truck rental and wages for workers and drivers committed to the production and distribution of private label bread should be considered variable. Such costs were among those typically considered variable in *Janich.* [*Janich Bros, Inc. v. American Distilling Co.*, 570 F.2d 848 (9th Cir. 1977), *cert. denied*, 439 U.S. 829 (1978)]. Continental argued, however, that increased production of private label bread merely filled excess oven time and truck space already available and that the only cost items that properly could be considered variable were ingredients, wrappers, fuel, and salesmen's commissions. If these costs were the only ones that actually increased as a result of the price reduction, and if the prices were sufficient to recover them, then there is less reason to infer predation than Inglis maintains. Of course . . . it may be that Continental avoided other commercially reasonable means of minimizing losses that would have been more effective, and this fact would strengthen the inference of predation. . . .

Some modified version of the Areeda-Turner standard is now accepted in most of the Circuits.[2] The First Circuit has opted for an objective cost-based standard, but has as yet not indicated whether that standard is the Areeda-Turner one.[3]

Although most circuits now follow some version of the Areeda-Turner approach to predatory pricing, there are a few anomalies. The Eleventh Circuit has insisted upon the use of evidence of subjective intent in the determination of predatory pricing. And, in Chapter 13, we will observe that Judge Easterbrook in the Seventh Circuit had suggested (prior to the Supreme Court's decision in *Brooke Group*, *infra*) that the Areeda-Turner standard not apply to primary-line claims under the Robinson-Patman Act's § 2(a). The decision in *Brooke Group* makes moot Judge Easterbrook's suggestion.

The Eleventh Circuit approach to the determination of predatory pricing was set forth in *McGahee v. Northern Propane Gas Co.*, 858 F.2d 1487 (11th Cir. 1988) (citing legislative history of the Robinson-Patman Act that Congress intended to bar pricing below average total cost). Contrary to the "objective" approach taken by most circuits, the Eleventh Circuit attributes importance to evidence of subjective intent. Moreover, in *McGahee* the Eleventh Circuit drew from the Supreme Court's now-repudiated *Utah Pie* opinion (pages 525, 638, *infra*) to shape its own approach to predatory pricing under the Sherman Act. Excerpts from the *McGahee* opinion follow:

> The Areeda and Turner test is like the Venus de Milo: it is much admired and often discussed, but rarely embraced. Perhaps this reluctance to embrace is due to the substance from which it is formed. The Areeda and Turner test is carved from economic assumptions, not from antitrust statutes and judicial precedents. Perhaps this reluctance is due to attacks upon it. The Areeda and Turner test has been criticized for being impractical, for using static short-run analysis, and for being too permissive of predatory activity; these criticisms break any notion that economists agree that the Areeda and Turner test is best. We, like our sister circuits other than the Second Circuit and the Fifth Circuit, our Siamese twin, decline to embrace the Areeda and Turner test.

McGahee, 858 F.2d at 1495-96.

---

[2] *Kelco Disposal, Inc. v. Browning Ferris Indus.*, 845 F.2d 404, 407 (2d Cir. 1988), *aff'd*, 492 U.S. 257 (1989); *Bayou Bottling, Inc. v. S.E. Johnson Co.*, 725 F.2d 300 (5th Cir. 1984), *cert. denied*, 469 U.S. 833 (1984); *Arthur S. Langenderfer, Inc. v. S.E. Johnson Co.*, 729 F.2d 1050, 1060 (6th Cir.), *cert. denied*, 469 U.S. 1036 (1984); *Chillicothe Sand & Gravel Co. v. Martin Marietta Corp.*, 615 F.2d 427, 431 (7th Cir. 1980); *Morgan v. Ponder*, 892 F.2d 1355, 1360 (8th Cir. 1989); *Marsann Co. v. Brammall, Inc.*, 788 F.2d 611, 616 (9th Cir. 1986); *Instructional Systems Dev. Corp. v. Aetna Cas. & Sur. Co.*, 817 F.2d 639, 649 (10th Cir. 1987). *See also Barr Laboratories, Inc. v. Abbott Laboratories*, 978 F.2d 98 (3d Cir. 1992).

[3] In *Barry Wright Corp. v. ITT Grinnell Corp.*, 724 F.2d 227 (1st Cir. 1983), the First Circuit spoke approvingly of incremental cost as the ordinary standard for evaluating predatory pricing claims, but it refused to decide whether the Areeda-Turner average-variable-cost test should be incorporated into the law of that Circuit. The use of an incremental cost standard was also approved in *Clamp-All Corp. v. Cast Iron Soil Pipe Institute*, 851 F.2d 478, 483 (1st Cir. 1988), *cert. denied*, 488 U.S. 1007 (1989).

Many states have enacted statutes prohibiting sales below cost, often called unfair practices acts. *E.g.*, ARK CODE ANN. §§ 4-75-201 to -214. In *Wal-Mart Stores v. American Drugs, Inc.*, 891 S.W.2d 30 (Ark. 1995), the Arkansas Supreme court held that sales below cost as a "loss leader" did not violate the Arkansas statute.

2. Recall the criticism of the Areeda-Turner 1975 article by F.M. Scherer (page 514, *supra*) and note his formulation of a predatory pricing rule of illegality. Scherer would include intent as a factor to be considered. However, intent may become material at two levels of a predatory price inquiry. At one level, legislative intent is material; at the other, the intent of the "below cost" seller is material under some formulations of a rule.

Discerning Congressional intent and attributing it to a legislative body in the interpretation of statutory language is a large topic that has generated a continuing debate. *See* Felix Frankfurter, *Some Reflections on the Reading of Statutes*, 47 COLUM. L. REV. 527, 528 (1947) (statutory words are not empty vessels to be filled by predilections of judges); HENRY HART & ALBERT SACHS, THE LEGAL PROCESS 1172 (1994 ed.) (all the circumstances surrounding the legislative decisional process, including the "facts" the legislature considered, may be taken into account); Antonin Scalia, *The Rule of Law as a Law of Rules*, 56 U. CHI. L. REV 1175 (1989) (legislation is in the nature of a contract with judges, who are obliged to interpret the statutory language quite literally). As noted earlier in these materials, courts have generally interpreted the Sherman Act as a broad charter, drafted in terms of near-Constitutional breadth. See Chief Justice Hughes' opinion in *Appalachian Coals*, 288 U.S. at 359-60. Given the Congressional concerns with trusts in the last decades of the nineteenth century, the absence of any direct legislative guidance regarding the practice of predatory pricing is surprising. The existence of this gap is underscored by the fact that courts in predatory pricing cases under the Sherman Act have looked primarily to the economics literature for guidance in interpretation. The legislative history of § 2 of the Clayton Act as enacted in 1914, however, acknowledges the practice of predatory pricing. *See* Chapter 13, pages 633-635, *infra.*

3. The Supreme Court addressed the proper definition of cost and the admissibility of evidence relevant to its proof, in four cases under both the Sherman and Robinson-Patman Acts. In *Utah Pie Co. v. Continental Baking Co.,* 386 U.S. 685 (1967), brought under both statutes, the evidence at the trial below showed that defendants, three large national companies, had sold frozen pies in the Salt Lake City marketing area for more than three years, at prices below their cost and below their prices in other markets that were closer to their plants. The jury found for the national sellers on the Sherman Act conspiracy count and for the plaintiff on the price discrimination charge. The court of appeals reversed on the single issue of the sufficiency of the evidence to support a claim of price discrimination under § 2(a) of the Clayton Act. The Supreme Court held this evidence was sufficient to support a finding of injury to competition despite the increasing sales volume of plaintiff, a local company, and the fact that plaintiff continued to make a profit. *Id.* at 702-03. The Court's opinion dealt with the conduct of each defendant separately, concluding that "there was some evidence of predatory intent with respect to each of these [defendants]." *Utah Pie*, 386 U.S. at 702. The Court said the first defendant "suffered substantial losses on its frozen pie sales," *id.* at 697, the second defendant had a price in Salt Lake City that "was less than its direct cost plus an allocation for overhead," *id.* at 698, and the third defendant had prices that were "admittedly well below its costs," *id.* at 701. In addition, as to the first defendant, the Court held that the jury could rely on statements by the first defendant's management that plaintiff was "an unfavorable factor" that "d[u]g holes in our operation" in concluding that the first defendant's discriminatory pricing was aimed at injuring plaintiff. *Id.* at 696-97. Relying on this evidence to show predatory intent, the Court then relied on this predatory intent to show injury to competition.

Subsequent to *Utah Pie* some lower courts viewed the test for "primary line"[4] Robinson-Patman violations to be less stringent than that for a predatory pricing claim under § 2. *See A.A. Poultry Farms v. Rose Acre Farms*, 881 F.2d 1396 (7th Cir. 1989). Does the opinion in *Brooke Group,* below, address this issue? What is the burden of proof on a claimant of predatory pricing under § 2(a) of the Clayton Act? How, if at all, is it different for a claimant under § 2 of the Sherman Act?

Utah Pie was severely criticized for confusing price competition with predatory pricing. *See* Ward S. Bowman, *Restraint of Trade by the Supreme Court: The* Utah Pie *Case*, 77 YALE L.J. 70 (1967) ("Prior to *Utah Pie*, the Supreme Court never unequivocally required a restraint of trade."); Kenneth G. Elzinga & Thomas F. Hogarty, Utah Pie *and the Consequences of Robinson-Patman,* 21 J.L. & ECON. 427 (1978); United States Department of Justice, REPORT ON THE ROBINSON-PATMAN ACT (1977) (expressing doubt as to the efficacy of the Robinson-Patman Act). The critics noted that the defendants had but a small share of the Salt Lake City market. Moreover, when the other sellers in the market met the defendants' price, total sales increased, including the plaintiff's market share, and the plaintiff's operation was profitable. Justices Harlan and Stewart in dissent underscored the competitive performance of the market. *Utah Pie,* 386 U.S. at 705 (Harlan, J., dissenting). *See generally* E. KINTNER & J. BAUER, 3 FEDERAL ANTITRUST LAW § 22.8 at 285 & nn.165 & 166 (1983).

Cargill Inc. v. Monfort of Colorado, Inc. 479 U.S. 104 (1989), page 538, *infra*, was a private action to enjoin a merger on the theory that the combined firm would engage in predatory pricing. There the Court considered objective evidence other than prices and costs, which does not necessarily support the use of subjective evidence, but is inconsistent with Areeda and Turner's predatory pricing test used by the district court, which relies solely on objective evidence of prices and costs. The government had asked the Court to announce a *per se* rule denying stand-

---

[4] Primary and secondary line are Robinson-Patman Act phrases of art which designate the level of distribution at which a seller's liability for discriminatory pricing is assessed. *See* Chapter 13, pages 637, 641.

ing to a party in opposition to a merger on predatory pricing grounds. Justice Brennan, writing for a 6-2 majority, rejected this suggestion.

In *Matsushita Electric Industrial Co. v. Zenith Radio Corp.,* 475 U.S. 574 (1986), two U.S. competitor manufacturers sued 21 Japanese owned or controlled corporations alleging a conspiracy to engage in predatory pricing. The trial court dismissed the complaint on the grounds that the evidence on pricing showed only competition, not predation. The appeals court, in reversing, held that a jury could infer the existence of a conspiracy. In the Supreme Court, a majority of five reversed on the ground that the plaintiffs' theory lacked economic plausibility, so that the conclusions that could be drawn from the ambiguous evidence were limited. Because the alleged conduct had no rational economic basis, the majority concluded that a plaintiff would have to offer unambiguous evidence and remanded to the trial court with instructions that "The evidence must tend to exclude the possibility that the petitioners underpriced . . . to compete for business rather than to implement an economically senseless conspiracy." 475 U.S. at 598-99. The majority accepted a variant of the Areeda-Turner formulation, noting in dictum that " . . . 'predatory pricing' means pricing below some appropriate measure of cost." *Id.* at 584.

Justices White, Brennan, Blackmun, and Stevens in dissent stated that the majority had distorted the summary judgment standard. They would have affirmed the appeals court on grounds that the lower court had made the finding of conspiracy which was supported by the evidence, including expert testimony, from which a trier of fact could infer a strategy on the part of the defendant other than long-run recoupment. Expert testimony had stated that the defendants exchanged proprietary information, had sought to avoid intragroup competition, and had acted in concert to depress the price of the product in the U.S. market.

4. In addition to *Matsushita,* many, but not all lower courts accepted some variant of the Areeda-Turner formulation. *See Henry v. Chloride, Inc.,* 809 F.2d 1334, 1344 (8th Cir. 1987); *O. Hommel Co. v. Ferro Corp.,* 659 F.2d 340, 345 (3d Cir. 1981); *Chillocothe Sand & Gravel v. Martin Marietta Corp.,* 615 F.2d 427, 431 (7th Cir. 1980); *Pacific Engineering & Production Co. of Nevada v. Kerr-McGee Corp.,* 551 F.2d 790, 797 (10th Cir. 1977).

Recall the discussion (pages 511-16, *supra*) of the Areeda-Turner proposal that average variable cost was the appropriate standard of predation. In part, this departure from marginal cost was justified on grounds both of the difficulty of computing marginal costs and the possibility of average variable costs being calculated from ordinary business accounting records, once it had been determined which costs were properly counted as fixed and which were variable. Judge Easterbrook has noted the difficulty posed by price/cost tests generally as follows:

> Trying to infer (or refute) predatory conduct from the relation between price and cost is difficult business. Often price below cost reflects only the sacrifice necessary to establish a presence in a competitive market (for example, . . . [a] new magazine. . .). . . . Measuring costs creates

> additional problems. Are advertising and research costs expensed or capitalized? How does one allocate the cost of activities that have joint products? Agencies engaged in ratemaking struggle with these problems for years . . . without producing clear answers. If we could measure costs, what would be the right benchmark? Short-run variable cost? Long-run variable cost? Average total cost? Any of these (and there are more measures) might be best in a given case, depending on the strategy the aggressor has selected and the length of time it will take to succeed. *A.A. Poultry Farms, Inc. v. Rose Acre Farms, Inc.*, 881 F.2d 1396, 1404 (7th Cir. 1989) (predatory pricing claim rejected).

How valid is the Areeda-Turner assumption that the accounting treatment of disbursements readily defines a cost as fixed or variable? Is this distinction best made by the court or by a jury? In *Kelco Disposal v. Browning-Ferris Industries of Vermont, Inc.,* 845 F.2d 404, 408 (2d Cir. 1988), the court stated:

> The characterization of certain costs as either variable or fixed frequently becomes a battleground . . . [in] predatory [price litigation]. The reason is obvious: the higher a party's average variable cost, the more likely it is that the party has priced below that cost.
>
> Defendants argue that equipment depreciation should have been considered a fixed cost because defendants' accountants have always treated it so. . . . [T]he general legal rule is that depreciation caused by use is a variable cost while depreciation through obsolescence is a fixed cost. The characterization of legitimately disputed costs is a question of fact for the jury."

Some courts resolve the question of whether advertising expenses are fixed or variable by reference to § 2. They characterize advertising expenses as capital expenditures because they serve as a barrier to entry. *U.S. Philips Corp. v. Windermere Corp.,* 861 F.2d 695, 701 (Fed. Cir. 1988). Other courts consider advertising expenses as presumptively fixed, placing the burden on the claimant to show they vary with output. *Lomar Wholesale Grocery, Inc. v. Dieter's Gourmet Foods, Inc.*, 824 F.2d 582, 598 (8th Cir. 1987) (rejecting a claim of predatory pricing as to 4 of 180 items). How should fixed costs be allocated among 180 items? *See also* Richard A. Posner, *The Chicago School of Antitrust Analysis*, 127 U. PA. L. REV. 925, 930 (1979) (advertising is a capital expenditure).

Some commentators have noted that reliance on accounting data fails to include an item of economic cost—opportunity cost. Recall Judge Kaufman's opinion in *Northeastern Telephone,* below. Suppose a shoe wholesaler, operating as a sole proprietor, is defending a predatory pricing action. In addition to the actual money outlays for clerical assistance and accounting services, this proprietor, whose hobby is writing computer software programs, saves the $3,000 that a consultant quoted to prepare a program this business, by preparing the program unassisted. Under tax and accounting conventions, the $3,000, not having been disbursed, could not be expensed. Should it be included in variable cost accurately to compute a benchmark for "below cost" pricing? The ABA Antitrust Section, Monograph No. 22, PREDATORY PRICING 64 (1996), notes that little attention has been given to this issue and poses this question: "The reluctance to consider opportunity costs may reflect the considerable practical obstacles to quantifying those costs and the courts' lack of familiarity with the concept."

Should this question be put to the jury? Would the defendant in a predatory pricing case argue that depreciation and certain overhead costs were fixed or were variable? Is it to the defendant's advantage to increase or to reduce the amount of variable costs? Explain.

5. Does the above cursory review of the judicial approach to the cost accounting of predation suggest that the Areeda-Turner approach is superior to that of Baumol, Scherer, or Williamson discussed on pages 513-16, *supra*? Explain. Which of the latter commentators would require an "all facts and circumstances" review of alleged predatory conduct and what facts, other than cost/price relationships would become material under the approach of Baumol, Scherer, or Williamson?

C. Predatory Pricing as Monopolization

The courts which have adopted a version of the Areeda-Turner test for evaluating allegedly predatory pricing in an attempt-to-monopolize context generally also apply that test to evaluate predatory pricing claims when the charge is monopolization. *See, e.g., Irvin Industries, Inc. v. Goodyear Aerospace Corp.*, 974 F.2d 241 (2d Cir. 1992); *H.J. Inc. v. International Tel. & Tel. Corp.*, 867 F.2d 1531 (8th Cir. 1989); *Northeastern Tel. Co. v. American Tel. & Tel. Co.*, 651 F.2d 76 (2d Cir. 1981), *cert. denied*, 455 U.S. 943 (1982).

Northeastern Telephone Co. v. American Telephone and Telegraph Co.

651 F.2d 76 (2d Cir. 1981)

[Northeastern, an independent supplier of telephone equipment, sued alleging that Southern New England Telephone Company (SNET), an AT&T affiliate, was attempting to monopolize and monopolizing the market for telephone equipment by pricing its telephone equipment in a predatory manner. The lower court awarded judgment to Northeastern and SNET appeals.]

IRVING R. KAUFMAN, Circuit Judge

. . . .

That SNET is a multi-product firm seems to enhance the likelihood that it would profit from a policy of predatory pricing. One might assume that while SNET leased its PBXs at unremunerative rates, it would subsidize its losses with profits earned in other areas of its business. But although subsidization may stave off bankruptcy, it does not appreciably reduce the short-run costs of predation. In terms of lost profits, or in economic jargon "opportunity costs," unremunerative prices will be as expensive to a diversified monopolist as to a single-product firm. Furthermore, the subsidization theory ignores an important prerequisite of a successful predatory campaign. For unremunerative pricing to make economic sense, the predator must be assured that he will be able to recoup his short term losses in the future. . . . [H]e must be reasonably certain that once his prey has fallen, he will be able to reap supranormal returns. . . . Such profits, of course, will invite new entry. . . . As Northeastern's own experience indicates, the barriers to entry into the business telephone equipment market were relatively low. This . . . shows that this market was not conducive to a policy of unremunerative pricing. Therefore, we need not adopt a more stringent test of predation [than the Areeda-Turner marginal cost/average variable cost standard] merely because SNET is a diversified firm.[19] . . .

Northeastern pins its last hopes for an average or fully-distributed cost test on the second distinguishing characteristic of this case that SNET is subject to the authority of a state regulatory agency. Northeastern contends that even if the market can be relied upon to apportion the joint expenses of an unregulated firm,[21] a regulated utility can allocate all of its joint costs to the monopoly aspects of its business, thereby giving it a permanent advantage over its unregulated competitors.[22] Judge Eginton accepted this argument, reasoning that:

> [t]o permit SNET to allocate all or a disproportionate percentage of its unattributable cost to the noncompetitive sector of its business . . . is to give defendants an improper pricing advantage over Northeastern and other single market competitors who must allocate all costs directly to their terminal equipment rates. A fully distributed cost standard, on the other hand, would . . . substantially curtai[l] potential subsidization.

This analysis is seriously flawed. *First,* it proves too much. The advantage Judge Eginton identifies may be enjoyed by all diversified firms, whether regulated or unregulated. But . . . allowing a diversified firm to maintain an artificial pricing floor above marginal cost is impractical and provides a haven for inefficient competitors.

Second, this approach emphasizes the interests of single-market rivals over those of consumers and the competitive process. Marginal cost pricing maximizes short run consumer welfare. . . . Fully distributed cost pricing, in contrast, requires some consumers to pay a higher price for the desired product, and forces others to do without that product entirely, although they are willing to pay the costs of its production. Moreover, a fully distributed cost rule would have perverse consequences when the dominant firm's rival was itself diversified. In that case, presumably, both firms would have to set their prices above their fully distributed costs. So high a price floor might prevent the diversified rival from ever entering the market, thereby curtailing competition rather than promoting it.

---

[19] Moreover, the more demanding average cost test of predatory pricing gives rise to serious problems when applied to a diversified enterprise. This is because the accounting conventions used to allocate joint costs, i.e., those costs that are not directly attributable to a particular product, are all arbitrary to a degree. *See* 3 P. Areeda & D. Turner, *supra*, ¶ 719, at 183. Even Northeastern's expert witness, who testified that appellants should have allocated a portion of their joint expenditures to the cost of their PBXs, did not explain how those costs should be apportioned. . . .

[21] *See* note 19 *supra*.

[22] If an unregulated, diversified monopolist were to try this tactic, its high price on the product bearing all of the firm's joint costs would come under heavy competitive attack. To remain competitive, the monopolist would have to lower that product's price, thereby reallocating common expenditures.

Third, Northeastern's argument in favor of the fully distributed cost test is based on a misunderstanding of the economic notion of subsidization. Northeastern seems to believe that whenever a product's price fails to cover fully distributed costs, the enterprise must subsidize that product's revenues with revenues earned elsewhere. But when the price of an item exceeds the costs directly attributable to its production, that is, when price exceeds marginal or average variable cost, no subsidy is necessary. On the contrary, any surplus can be used to defray the firm's non-allocable expenses.

Finally, Northeastern's fear that SNET will be able to allocate all of its overhead to its monopoly services rests on the premise that the DPUC [*i.e.*, the (Connecticut) Division of Public Utilities Control] is either asleep or incompetent. . . . If comity and federalism mean anything in this context, they require that we not create an exception to the general rule of marginal cost pricing on the basis of plaintiff's bald assertion that the DPUC cannot perform the duties delegated to it by the state.

. . . .

[The court, accordingly, reversed the district court's judgment.]

COMMENTARY

Is Judge Kaufman's assumption of rational economic behavior also an implicit premise of the Areeda-Turner rule? In the view of those commentators who subscribe to the premise that predatory pricing is a two-step process, the first step is discouraging of a competitor by "below-cost" pricing and the second step is recoupment of the losses thus incurred by charging a supra-normal price after the departure of the discouraged competitor. Since incurring losses in this way is not profit-maximizing conduct, commentators who subscribe to this view deem predatory pricing as a problem not needing an antitrust solution. Thus, Judge Bork rejects the Areeda-Turner rule as unnecessary and urges that below-cost pricing be deemed as *per se* legal. ROBERT H. BORK, THE ANTITRUST PARADOX 148 (1978). This approach has recently been summarized as follows:

> The position, advocated by Bork and Easterbook, . . . that predatory pricing does not pose a serious problem is based on the premise that rational profit maximizing firms do not have any incentive to engage in predatory pricing. Stated otherwise, the Bork-Easterbrook position is based on an economic analysis that concludes that predatory pricing is unprofitable.

ABA Antitrust Section, Monograph No. 22, PREDATORY PRICING 41-42 (1996). Consider whether this premise was the basis of the majority opinions in *Matsushita,* above, and in *Brooke*, which follows.

In the cases that follow, consider which of these opposing views of predation have found favor in the courts.

D. The U.S. Supreme Court on Predatory Pricing

Brooke Group Ltd. v. Brown & Williamson Tobacco Corp.

509 U.S. 209 (1993)

Justice KENNEDY delivered the opinion of the Court.

This case stems from a market struggle that erupted in the domestic cigarette industry in the mid-1980's. Petitioner Brooke Group, Ltd., whom we, like the parties to the case, refer to as Liggett because of its former corporate name, charges that to counter its innovative development of generic cigarettes, respondent Brown & Williamson Tobacco Corporation introduced its own line of generic cigarettes in an unlawful effort to stifle price competition in the economy segment of the national cigarette market. Liggett contends that Brown & Williamson cut prices on generic cigarettes below cost and offered discriminatory volume rebates to wholesalers to force Liggett to raise its own generic cigarette prices and introduce oligopoly pricing in the economy segment. We hold that Brown & Williamson is entitled to judgment as a matter of law.

I

In 1980, Liggett pioneered the development of the economy segment of the national cigarette market by introducing a line of "black and white" generic cigarettes. The economy segment of the market, sometimes called the generic segment, is characterized by its bargain prices and comprises a variety of different products: black and whites, which are true generics sold in plain white packages with simple black lettering describing their contents; private label generics, which carry the trade dress of a specific purchaser, usually a retail chain; branded generics, which carry a brand name but which, like black and whites and private label generics, are sold at a deep discount and with little or no advertising; and "Value-25s," packages of 25 cigarettes that are sold to the consumer some 12.5% below the cost of a normal 20-cigarette pack. By 1984, when Brown & Williamson entered the generic segment and set in motion the series of events giving rise to this suit, Liggett's black and whites represented 97% of the generic segment, which in turn accounted for a little more than 4% of domestic cigarette sales. Prior to Liggett's introduction of black and whites in 1980, sales of generic cigarettes amounted to less than 1% of the domestic cigarette market.

. . . .

By 1980 . . . broad market trends were working against the industry. Overall demand for cigarettes in the United States was declining, and no immediate prospect of recovery existed. As industry volume shrank, all firms developed substantial excess capacity. This decline in demand, coupled with the effects of nonprice competition, had a severe negative impact on Liggett. Once a major force in the industry, with market shares in excess of 20%, Liggett's market share had declined by 1980 to a little over 2%. With this meager share of the market, Liggett was on the verge of going out of business.

At the urging of a distributor, Liggett took an unusual step to revive its prospects: It developed a line of black and white generic cigarettes. When introduced in 1980, black and whites were offered to consumers at a list price roughly 30% lower than the list price of full-priced, branded cigarettes. They were also promoted at the wholesale level by means of rebates that increased with the volume of cigarettes ordered. Black and white cigarettes thus represented a new marketing category. The category's principal competitive characteristic was low price. Liggett's black and whites were an immediate and considerable success, growing from a fraction of a percent of the market at their introduction to over 4% of the total cigarette market by early 1984.

As the market for Liggett's generic cigarettes expanded, the other cigarette companies found themselves unable to ignore the economy segment. In general, the growth of generics came at the expense of the other firms' profitable sales of branded cigarettes. Brown & Williamson was hardest hit, because many of Brown & Williamson's brands were favored by consumers who were sensitive to changes in cigarette prices. Although Brown & Williamson sold only 11.4% of the market's branded cigarettes, 20% of the converts to Liggett's black and whites had switched from a Brown & Williamson brand. Losing volume and profits in its branded products, Brown & Williamson determined to enter the generic segment of the cigarette market. In July 1983, Brown & Williamson had begun selling Value-25s, and in the spring of 1984, it introduced its own black and white cigarette.

Brown & Williamson was neither the first nor the only cigarette company to recognize the threat posed by Liggett's black and whites and to respond in the economy segment. R.J. Reynolds had also introduced a Value-25 in 1983. And before Brown & Williamson introduced its own black and whites, R.J. Reynolds had repriced its "Doral" branded cigarette at generic levels. To compete with Liggett's black and whites, R.J. Reynolds dropped its list price on Doral about 30% and used volume rebates to wholesalers as an incentive to spur orders. Doral was the first competition at Liggett's price level.

Brown & Williamson's entry was an even graver threat to Liggett's dominance of the generic category. Unlike R.J. Reynolds' Doral, Brown & Williamson's product was also a black and white and so would be in direct competition with Liggett's product at the wholesale level and on the retail shelf. Because Liggett's and Brown & Williamson's black and whites were more or less fungible, wholesalers had little incentive to carry more than one line. And unlike R.J. Reynolds, Brown & Williamson not only matched Liggett's prices but beat them. At the retail level, the suggested list price of Brown & Williamson's black and whites was the same as Liggett's, but Brown & Williamson's volume discounts to wholesalers were larger. Brown & Williamson's rebate structure also encompassed a greater number of volume categories than Liggett's, with the highest categories carrying special rebates for orders of very substantial size. Brown & Williamson marketed its black and whites to Liggett's existing distributors as well as to its own full list of buyers, which included a thousand wholesalers who had not yet carried any generic products.

Liggett responded to Brown & Williamson's introduction of black and whites in two ways. First, Liggett increased its own wholesale rebates. This precipitated a price war at the wholesale level, in which Liggett five times attempted to beat the rebates offered by Brown & Williamson. At the end of each round, Brown & Williamson maintained a real advantage over Liggett's prices. Although it is undisputed that Brown & Williamson's original net price for its black and whites was above its costs, Liggett contends that by the end of the rebate war, Brown & Williamson was selling its black and whites at a loss. This rebate war occurred before Brown & Williamson had sold a single black and white cigarette.

Liggett's second response was to file a lawsuit . . . [containing a] Robinson-Patman Act claim, which is the subject of the present controversy. Liggett alleged that Brown & Williamson's volume rebates to wholesalers amounted to price discrimination that had a reasonable possibility of injuring competition, in violation of § 2(a). Liggett claimed that Brown & Williamson's discriminatory volume rebates were integral to a scheme of predatory pricing, in which Brown & Williamson reduced its net prices for generic cigarettes below average variable costs. According to Liggett, these below-cost prices were not promotional but were intended to pressure it to raise its list prices on generic cigarettes, so that the percentage price difference between generic and branded cigarettes would narrow. Liggett explained that it would have been unable to reduce its wholesale rebates without losing substantial market share to Brown & Williamson; its only choice, if it wished to avoid prolonged losses on its principal product line, was to raise retail prices. The resulting reduction in the list price gap, it was said, would restrain the growth of the economy segment and preserve Brown & Williamson's supracompetitive profits on its branded cigarettes.

. . . .

II

A

Liggett contends that Brown & Williamson's discriminatory volume rebates to wholesalers threatened substantial competitive injury by furthering a predatory pricing scheme designed to purge competition from the economy segment of the cigarette market. This type of injury, which harms direct competitors of the discriminating seller, is known as primary-line injury. . . . We last addressed primary line injury over 25 years ago, in *Utah Pie Co. v. Continental Baking Co.*, 386 U.S. 685 (1967). In *Utah Pie*, we reviewed the sufficiency of the evidence supporting jury verdicts against three national pie companies that had engaged in a variety of predatory practices in the market for frozen pies in Salt Lake City, with the intent to drive a local pie manufacturer out of business. We reversed the Court of Appeals and held that the evidence presented was adequate to permit a jury to find a likelihood of injury to competition. . . .

Utah Pie has often been interpreted to permit liability for primary-line price discrimination on a mere showing that the defendant intended to harm competition or produced a declining price structure. The case has been criticized on the grounds that such low standards of competitive injury are at odds with the antitrust laws' traditional concern for consumer welfare and price competition. . . . We do not regard the *Utah Pie* case itself as having the full significance attributed to it by its detractors. *Utah Pie* was an early judicial inquiry in this area and did not purport to set forth explicit, general standards for establishing a violation of the Robinson-Patman Act. As the law has been explored since *Utah Pie*, it has become evident that primary-line competitive injury under the Robinson-Patman Act is of the same general character as the injury inflicted by predatory pricing schemes actionable under § 2 of the Sherman Act. . . . There are, to be sure, differences between the two statutes. For example, we interpret § 2 of the Sherman Act to condemn predatory pricing when it poses "a dangerous probability of actual monopolization," *Spectrum Sports, Inc. v. McQuillan*, 506 U.S. 447, 452 (1993), whereas the Robinson-Patman Act requires only that there be "a reasonable possibility" of substantial injury to competition before its protections are triggered. . . . But whatever additional flexibility the Robinson-Patman Act standard may imply, the essence of the claim under either statute is the same: A business rival has priced its products in an unfair manner with an object to eliminate or retard competition and thereby gain and exercise control over prices in the relevant market.

Accordingly, whether the claim alleges predatory pricing under § 2 of the Sherman Act or primary-line price discrimination under the Robinson-Patman Act, two prerequisites to recovery remain the same. First, a plaintiff seeking to establish competitive injury resulting from a rival's low prices must prove that the prices complained of are below an appropriate measure of its rival's costs. . . .

Even in an oligopolistic market, when a firm drops its prices to a competitive level to demonstrate to a maverick the unprofitability of straying from the group, it would be illogical to condemn the price cut: The antitrust laws then would be an obstacle to the chain of events most conducive to a breakdown of oligopoly pricing and the onset of competition. Even if the ultimate effect of the cut is to induce or reestablish supracompetitive pricing, discouraging a price cut and forcing firms to maintain supracompetitive prices, thus depriving consumers of the benefits of lower prices in the interim, does not constitute sound antitrust policy. . . .

The second prerequisite to holding a competitor liable under the antitrust laws for charging low prices is a demonstration that the competitor had a reasonable prospect, or, under § 2 of the Sherman Act, a dangerous probability, of recouping its investment in below-cost prices. . . .

B

Liggett does not allege that Brown & Williamson sought to drive it from the market but that Brown & Williamson sought to preserve supracompetitive profits on branded cigarettes by pressuring Liggett to raise its generic cigarette prices through a process of tacit collusion with the other cigarette companies. Tacit collusion, sometimes called oligopolistic price coordination or conscious parallelism, describes the process, not in itself unlawful, by which firms in a concentrated market might in effect share monopoly power, setting their prices at a profit-maximizing, supracompetitive level by recognizing their shared economic interests and their interdependence with respect to price and output decisions. . . .

III

Although Liggett's theory of liability, as an abstract matter, is within the reach of the statute, we agree with the Court of Appeals and the District Court that Liggett was not entitled to submit its case to the jury. . . .

A

Liggett's theory of competitive injury through oligopolistic price coordination depends upon a complex chain of cause and effect: Brown & Williamson would enter the generic segment with list prices matching Liggett's but with massive, discriminatory volume rebates directed at Liggett's biggest wholesalers; as a result, the net price of Brown & Williamson's generics would be below its costs; Liggett would suffer losses trying to defend its market share and wholesale customer base by matching Brown & Williamson's rebates; to avoid further losses, Liggett would raise its list prices on generics or acquiesce in price leadership by Brown & Williamson; higher list prices to consumers would shrink the percentage gap in retail price between generic and branded cigarettes; and this narrowing of the gap would make generics less appealing to the consumer, thus slowing the growth of the economy segment and reducing cannibalization of branded sales and their associated supracompetitive profits.

Although Brown & Williamson's entry into the generic segment could be regarded as procompetitive in intent as well as effect, the record contains sufficient evidence from which a reasonable jury could conclude that Brown & Williamson envisioned or intended this anticompetitive course of events. . . . There is also sufficient evidence in the record from which a reasonable jury could conclude that for a period of approximately 18 months, Brown & Williamson's prices on its generic cigarettes were below its costs . . . and that this below-cost pricing imposed losses on Liggett that Liggett was unwilling to sustain, given its corporate parent's effort to locate a buyer for the company. . . . Liggett has failed to demonstrate competitive injury as a matter of law, however, because its proof is flawed in a critical respect: The evidence is inadequate to show that in pursuing this scheme, Brown &

Williamson had a reasonable prospect of recovering its losses from below-cost pricing through slowing the growth of generics. As we have noted, "[t]he success of any predatory scheme depends on maintaining monopoly power for long enough both to recoup the predator's losses and to harvest some additional gain." *Matsushita*, 475 U.S. at 589 (emphasis omitted).

No inference of recoupment is sustainable on this record, because no evidence suggests that Brown & Williamson—whatever its intent in introducing black and whites may have been—was likely to obtain the power to raise the prices for generic cigarettes above a competitive level. Recoupment through supracompetitive pricing in the economy segment of the cigarette market is an indispensable aspect of Liggett's own proffered theory, because a slowing of growth in the economy segment, even if it results from an increase in generic prices, is not itself anticompetitive. Only if those higher prices are a product of nonmarket forces has competition suffered. If prices rise in response to an excess of demand over supply, or segment growth slows as patterns of consumer preference become stable, the market is functioning in a competitive manner. Consumers are not injured from the perspective of the antitrust laws by the price increases; they are in fact causing them. Thus, the linchpin of the predatory scheme alleged by Liggett is Brown & Williamson's ability, with the other oligopolists, to raise prices above a competitive level in the generic segment of the market. Because relying on tacit coordination among oligopolists as a means of recouping losses from predatory pricing is "highly speculative," . . . competent evidence is necessary to allow a reasonable inference that it poses an authentic threat to competition. The evidence in this case is insufficient to demonstrate the danger of Brown & Williamson's alleged scheme.

. . . .

IV

We understand that the chain of reasoning by which we have concluded that Brown & Williamson is entitled to judgment as a matter of law is demanding. But a reasonable jury is presumed to know and understand the law, the facts of the case, and the realities of the market. We hold that the evidence cannot support a finding that Brown & Williamson's alleged scheme was likely to result in oligopolistic price coordination and sustained supracompetitive pricing in the generic segment of the national cigarette market. Without this, Brown & Williamson had no reasonable prospect of recouping its predatory losses and could not inflict the injury to competition the antitrust laws prohibit. The judgment of the Court of Appeals is

Affirmed.

[Justices Stevens, Blackmun, and White in dissent considered the evidence sufficient to sustain a finding of injury to competition.]

COMMENTARY

1. Recall the discussion of *Matsushita Electric Industrial Co. v. Zenith Radio Corp.*, 475 U.S. 574 (1985), on page 527, above. There the Court effectively rejected a predatory pricing claim brought by Zenith against competing Japanese producers of television sets. Zenith claimed that the Japanese companies were selling their products at predatory levels in the United States. Because Zenith was claiming that the Japanese producers had been pricing predatorily for a number of years, the Court found the claim implausible. The Court thought that the longer the period involved, the less likely was predatory pricing on the ground that the predators are incurring losses on each sale and those losses have ultimately to be recouped if the predatory pricing is to be economically rational. Moreover, Zenith was claiming a conspiracy to monopolize and the Court thought that it was even more unlikely that a predatory pricing conspiracy—involving, as it would, several actors—could be maintained over a substantial period. Without adopting either the Areeda/Turner or any other specific test of predatoriness, the majority stated its reliance on one branch of predatory price theory:

> Finally, if predatory pricing conspiracies are generally unlikely to occur, they are especially so where, as here, the prospects of attaining monopoly power seem slight. In order to recoup their losses, petitioners must obtain enough market power to set higher than competitive prices, and then must sustain those prices long enough to earn in excess profits what they earlier gave up in below-cost prices. . . . Two decades after their conspiracy is alleged to have commenced, petitioners appear to be far from achieving this goal: the two largest shares of the retail market in television sets are held by RCA and respondent Zenith, not by any of petitioners. . . . Moreover, those shares, which together approximate 40% of sales, did not decline appreciably during the 1970s. . . . Petitioners' collective share rose rapidly during this period, from one-fifth or less of the relevant markets to close to 50%. . . . Neither the District Court nor the Court of Appeals found, however, that petitioners' share presently allows them to charge monopoly prices; to the contrary, respondents contend that the conspiracy is ongoing—that petitioners are still artificially *depressing* the market price in order to drive Zenith out of the market. The data in the record strongly suggest that that goal is yet far distant.
>
> The alleged conspiracy's failure to achieve its ends in the two decades of its asserted operation is strong evidence that the conspiracy does not in fact exist. Since the losses in such a conspiracy accrue before the gains, they must be "repaid" with interest. And because the alleged losses have accrued over the course of two decades, the conspirators could well require a correspondingly long time to recoup. Maintaining supracompetitive prices in turn depends on the continued cooperation of the conspirators, on the inability of other would-be competitors to enter the market, and (not incidentally) on the conspirators' ability to escape antitrust liability for their *minimum* price-fixing cartel. Each of these factors weighs more heavily as the time needed to recoup losses grows. If the losses have been substantial—as would likely be necessary in order to drive out the competition—petitioners would most likely have to sustain their cartel for years simply to break even.

475 U.S. at 590-93. In the *Matsushita* case, after observing that normally the term "predatory pricing" means "pricing below some appropriate measure of cost," the Court declined to endorse any particular definition of predatoriness:

> Throughout this opinion, we refer to the asserted conspiracy as one to price "predatorily." This term has been used chiefly in cases in which a single firm, having a dominant share of the relevant market, cuts its prices in order to force competitors out of the market, or perhaps to deter potential entrants from coming in. . . . In such cases, "predatory pricing" means pricing below some appropriate measure of cost. . . .
>
> There is a good deal of debate, both in the cases and in the law reviews, about what "cost" is relevant in such cases. We need not resolve this debate here, because unlike the cases cited above, this is a Sherman Act § 1 case. For purposes of this case, it is enough to note that respondents have not suffered an antitrust injury unless petitioners conspired to drive respondents out of the relevant markets by (i) pricing below the level necessary to sell their products, or (ii) pricing below some appropriate measure of cost. An agreement without these features would either leave respondents in the same position as would market forces or would actually benefit respondents by raising market prices. Respondents therefore may not complain of conspiracies that, for example, set maximum prices above market levels, or that set minimum prices at *any* level.

Id. at 584-85, n.8.

The Court also avoided adopting any particular cost-based standard of "below cost" pricing in several other cases in which it discussed predatory pricing. In *Cargill, Inc. v. Montfort of Colorado, Inc.*, 479 U.S. 104 (1986), and *Atlantic Richfield Co. v. USA Petroleum Co.*, 495 U.S. 328 (1990), the Court indicated that for pricing to be predatory, it would have to fall below some level of cost, but the Court declined to be more specific. In *Aspen Skiing Co. v. Aspen Highlands Skiing Corp.*, 472 U.S. 585 (1985), the Court used the language of predation to describe the defendant's behavior, but it entirely avoided performing any type of economic analysis of that behavior. Rather, in *Aspen Skiing* the Court cast the burden on the defendant of establishing a "business justification" for its behavior. In context, this meant that the defendant was required to prove that it had not sacrificed short-run benefits in order to secure supracompetitive profits in the future.

As the Court observed, because the principal case involved a predatory pricing conspiracy, it bordered on the implausible. Any agreement to price below the competitive level requires the conspirators to forgo profits that free competition would offer them. The forgone profits may be considered an investment in the future. For the investment to be rational, the conspirators must have a reasonable expectation of recovering, in the form of later monopoly profits, more than the losses suffered. As then-Professor Bork, discussing predatory pricing by a single firm, explained:

> Any realistic theory of predation recognizes that the predator as well as his victims will incur losses during the fighting, but such a theory supposes it may be a rational calculation for the predator to view the losses as an investment in future monopoly profits (where rivals are to be killed) or in future undisturbed profits (where rivals are to be disciplined). The future flow of profits, appropriately discounted, must then exceed the present size of the losses.

ROBERT H. BORK, THE ANTITRUST PARADOX 145 (1978). *See also* McGee, *Predatory Pricing Revisited,* 23 J.L. & ECON. 289, 295-97 (1980).

As this explanation shows, the success of such schemes is inherently uncertain: the short-run loss is definite, but the long-run gain depends on successfully neutralizing the competition. Moreover, it is not enough simply to achieve monopoly power, as monopoly pricing may breed quick entry by new competitors eager to share in the excess profits. The success of any predatory scheme depends on *maintaining* monopoly power for long enough both to recoup the predator's losses and to harvest some additional gain. Absent some assurance that the hoped-for monopoly will materialize, *and* that it can be sustained for a significant period of time, "[t]he predator must make a substantial investment with no assurance that it will pay off." Easterbrook, *Predatory Strategies and Counterstrategies*, 48 U. CHI. L. REV. 263, 268 (1981). For this reason, there is a consensus among commentators that predatory pricing schemes are rarely tried, and even more rarely successful. *See, e.g.*, BORK, *supra*, at 149-55; Areeda & Turner, *Predatory Pricing and Related Practices Under Section 2 of the Sherman Act*, 88 HARV. L. REV. 697, 699 (1975); Easterbrook, *supra*; Koller, *The Myth of Predatory Pricing—An Empirical Study*, 4 ANTITRUST LAW & ECON. REV. 105 (1971); McGee, *Predatory Price Cutting: The* Standard Oil (N.J.) *Case*, 1 J.L. & ECON. 137 (1958); McGee, *Predatory Pricing Revisited*, 23 J.L. & ECON. at 292-94. *See also Northeastern Telephone Co. v. American Telephone & Telegraph Co.*, 651 F.2d 76, 88 (2d Cir. 1981) ("[N]owhere in the recent outpouring of literature on the subject do commentators suggest that [predatory] pricing is either common or likely to increase"), *cert. denied*, 455 U.S. 943 (1982).

In the predatory pricing analysis debate, as elsewhere in antitrust law, the fundamental assumptions about rational economic behavior shape approaches to interpretation and to enforcement. Critics of the Bork-Easterbrook view rely on the concept of "strategic behavior," a course of conduct that may seek to maximize various economic incentives that vary with time and circumstance. Thus, Judge Richard A. Posner criticizes the premise that predation is insignificant because it is a departure from rational economic behavior,

> . . . [This argument] neglects strategic considerations. Assume it is lawful to buy a rival. It does not follow that a firm will never resort to predatory pricing. After all, it wants to minimize the price at which it buys its rivals, and that price will be lower if it can convince them of its willingness to drive them out of business unless they sell out on its terms.

Richard A. Posner, *The Chicago School of Antitrust Analysis,* 127 U. PA. L. REV. 925, 939 (1979).

Judge Posner gave as another example of a rational economic incentive to predation, a dominant seller operating in two geographic markets, one in which there was a competitor and other in which that seller enjoyed complete dominance. For such a seller, he pointed out, it would be profit-maximizing to price below cost in the competitive market and to recoup the loss by a supra-competitive price in the other. Judge Posner also recognized that limited access to information and to capital markets, may constitute a strategic advantage. *Id.* at 939-40. Is Judge Posner's reference to strategic behavior consistent with the behavioral assumptions of either Salop or Simon? *See* Chapter 1, pages 10-11.

Other economists, theorizing about the nature of price competition have identified other strategic reasons for "below-cost" pricing. One model expands on Judge Posner's example of a dominant seller in at least two markets, noting that a rational seller might benefit from the reputation of a "below-cost" seller because that reputation would inhibit competitors in other markets both from entry, as well as from vigorous price competition. Others have applied game theory to model firms with superior resources and better access to information and to capital markets, suggesting an economic incentive to drive a weaker rival from the market. Others have developed models of predation as signaling lower costs, as well as an intention to inhibit entrants by giving notice of an intention to drive rivals from the market. *See* Janusz Ordover & Garth Saloner, *Predation, Monopolization, and Antitrust*, *in* 1 HANDBOOK OF INDUSTRIAL ORGANIZATION 545 (Richard Schmalensee & Robert Willig eds. 1989) (reviewing the strategic behavior literature); *see also* William Comanor & H.E. Frech III, *Predatory Pricing and the Meaning of Intent*, 38 ANTITRUST BULL. 293 (1993); Malcolm Burns, *Predatory Pricing and the Acquisition Costs of Competitors*, 94 J. POL. ECON. 266 (1986) (recognizing the signaling effect of below-cost pricing); Richard O. Zerbe & Donald S. Cooper, *An Empirical and Theoretical Comparison of Predation Rules*, 61 TEX. L. REV. 655 (1982) (finding successful predation and reduction of consumer welfare in 27 of 39 case studies). Zerbe and Cooper recommend a modification of the Areeda-Turner rule to rely on average total cost at high levels of output and on average variable cost at low levels of output.

2. How many of the cases in this chapter have been brought by private litigants who were competitors, as compared to cases brought by the government? In how many cases has the competitor prevailed? Would it be rational economic behavior for a competitor to undertake to inhibit vigorous competition from a hypothetical Microsoft, for example, by imposing litigation costs on a rival? It is reported that when American Airlines defended itself against predatory pricing charges by Continental and Northwest airlines, the cost of legal fees was $20 million. There is speculation that Brown and Williamson spent a substantial multiple of that amount in legal fees in the *Brooke Group* litigation. *See* Michael L. Denger & John A. Herfort, *Predatory Pricing Claims after* Brooke Group, 62 ANTITRUST L.J. 541, n.2 (1994);

see also William J. Baumol & Januscz Ordover, *Uses of Antitrust to Subvert Competition*, 28 J.L. & ECON. 247, 252 (1985).

Is the potential for abusive litigation a more significant basis for constricting predatory pricing claims than the possible economic irrationality of such behavior? Were a future court to adopt the analysis of Scherer, Williamson, or any of the strategic behavior economists, would the potential for abusive litigation be lessened? Would a court applying Williamson's criteria instead of Areeda-Turner's have to review the business strategy of the enterprise and then speculate about the long-run effects of that strategy in the market directly affected and other markets? Would this also be true of Scherer's proposal?

3. How does the *Brooke Group* opinion allocate the burden of proof of a predatory pricing claimant under the Clayton Act and under the Sherman Act? Did this opinion resolve the differences among the lower courts on the formulation of the Areeda-Turner test? Does the opinion address the definition of fixed and variable costs?

4. What specific acts of predatory conduct did Liggett allege—signaling, attempt to bankrupt, maintain oligopoly pricing, or others? Does the standard of recoupment adopted in the opinion invite or discourage courts to dispose of predatory price cases by summary judgment? State the recoupment standard. Does this standard require evidence of oligopoly pricing, significant entry barriers, and sufficient financial resources of the alleged predator? To the extent that the recoupment prospect is stressed in *Brooke Group,* is the Areeda-Turner test made less significant? Explain. *See* Kenneth G. Elzinga & David E. Mills, *Trumping the Areeda-Turner Test: The Recoupment Standard in* Brooke Group, 62 ANTITRUST L.J. 559, 560 (1994) (exercise of monopoly power in recoupment of losses as central issue).

E. Predatory Behavior Other than Predatory Pricing

In *Alcoa*, Judge Hand thought that he had identified predatory investment. Now that you are familiar with predatory pricing analysis, would you be able to formulate a test for distinguishing between normal investment and predatory investment?

A more recent case in which a defendant's actions have appeared predatory to a court has been *Aspen Skiing Company v. Aspen Highlands Skiing Corp.*, 472 U.S. 585 (1985) (page 436, *supra*). In that case, the Supreme Court suggested that the Ski Company's behavior was predatory:

> . . . Ski Co. was apparently willing to forgo daily ticket sales both to skiers who sought to exchange the coupons contained in Highlands' Adventure Pack, and to those who would have purchased Ski Co. daily lift tickets from Highlands if Highlands had been permitted to purchase them in bulk. The jury may well have concluded that Ski Co. elected to

> forgo these short-run benefits because it was more interested in reducing competition in the Aspen market over the long run by harming its smaller competitor.
>
> . . . The refusal to accept the Adventure Pack coupons in exchange for daily tickets was apparently motivated entirely by a decision to avoid providing any benefit to Highlands even though accepting the coupons would have entailed no cost to Ski Co. itself, would have provided it with immediate benefits, and would have satisfied its potential customers. Thus the evidence supports an inference that Ski Co. was not motivated by efficiency concerns and that it was willing to sacrifice short-run benefits and consumer goodwill in exchange for a perceived long-run impact on its smaller rival.

Because the Ski Co.'s behavior appeared predatory to the Court, it was required to justify its refusal to accept some form of joint selling arrangement with its competitor. Do you agree with the Court that Ski Co.'s probable motivation was a predatory one?

In *Universal Analytics v. MacNeal-Schwendler Corp.*, 914 F.2d 1256 (9th Cir. 1990), the court had to evaluate the plaintiff's claim that the defendant engaged in "predatory hiring." The defendant, which held 90% of the market for NASTRAN computer software programs used in aerospace technology, allegedly hired five key employees of the plaintiff, its only competitor. On these facts, the court was willing to rule that the defendant possessed monopoly power and that the hiring adversely impacted the plaintiff's ability to compete. In the court's view, the relevant issue was whether the defendant "willfully maintained its monopoly power" by illegally raiding the plaintiff's employees. The court relied upon the Areeda and Turner treatise to hold that the plaintiff had not presented a prima facie case of predatory hiring.

> So far as we have been able to determine, this is the first reported case of a claimed violation of section 2 as a result of alleged employee raiding or predatory hiring. . . . We agree with the district court that the allegations of predatory hiring stated a claim capable of surviving a motion to dismiss . . . and that the case therefore turned on whether there were any genuine issues of material fact concerning UAI's allegations that the hirings were predatory. The most helpful and comprehensive discussion of the concept of predatory hiring is in Areeda and Turner, *supra*. Unlawful predatory hiring occurs when talent is acquired not for purposes of using that talent but for purposes of denying it to a competitor. Such cases can be proved by showing the hiring was made with such predatory intent, i.e. to harm the competition without helping the monopolist, or by showing a clear nonuse in fact. Absent either of those circumstances, according to Professors Areeda and Turner, employment should not be held exclusionary.

The only evidence that the plaintiff possessed a predatory motivation was a memorandum from the executive vice president. It read as follows:

> Do not put this in personnel folder—throw out.
> Joe:
>
> This guy came through some months ago, and we turned him down because he didn't give us a warm feeling. In your case, he made reference to Stuttgart connection, which you found implausible.
>
> Since then, Nima B. [an earlier UAI employee] has given him a strong endorsement. As Nima is a winner, this is important. Also *we wound UAI again*, and Layfield has shown that he is hard-nosed enough to fire someone who does not work out.
>
> I recommend a hire.
>
> MG

In evaluating the memo, the court stated:

> The "wound memo" evidence was insufficient for a jury to find the requisite elements of predatory conduct on the part of MSC. The memo at most shows that a secondary motivation of the hiring was to disadvantage the competition. The memo does not undermine MSC's legitimate business reasons for hiring much needed and competent computer programmers, or permit a jury to find that any of MSC's reasons for hiring the programmers was pretextual. . . .

As a result, the court affirmed summary judgment for the defendant.

COMMENTARY

Does the *Universal Analytics* decision help the courts to deal with allegations of predatory behavior other than predatory pricing? Can the Areeda/Turner standards be translated into the nonprice context? Or do different standards remain to be developed? Expansion of routes was dismissed as a claim of monopolizing by a small airline when a large airline, that had initially given passengers to the small airline for short mile destinations, decided to expand its service to those points. *Pacific Express Inc. v. United Airlines, Inc.,* 959 F.2d 814 (9th Cir. 1992). Similarly claims of monopolization and attempted monopolization were dismissed in a suit by a radio station against a competitor which allegedly hired away some of its employees and charged below cost advertising rates. *Midwest Radio Co. Inc. v. Forum Publishing Co.,* 942 F.2d 1294 (8th Cir. 1991). In granting summary judgment for the defendant, the court gave weight to the defendant's evidence of promotional activity as a business justification.

Chapter 12

Mergers and Acquisitions

A. Introduction

Antitrust scrutiny of mergers has had a meandering history. The Sherman Act as enacted in 1890 made no reference to them. This omission provided an opportunity to avoid the full force of the sanctions of §§ 1 and 2 of the Sherman Act, 15 U.S.C. §§ 1, 2 (1994), by permitting a merger to serve as a means of engaging in coordinated conduct within a single corporate shell as, for example, the merger which followed the judgment in *Addyston Pipe* noted in Chapter 1, page 16, above. The initial version of § 7 of the Clayton Act, enacted in 1914, restricted only one form of executing a merger of corporations, those made by acquisition of corporate stock. The 1950 amendment of § 7 finally brought mergers, whether by stock or by asset acquisition, under full antitrust scrutiny. Subsequently, enforcement activity relied on market structure as measured by concentration data as the primary indicator of competitive behavior. Accordingly, as the cases that follow illustrate, there was diminished concern with efficiency gains and with other indicia of competition. The May 1996 REPORT OF THE FEDERAL TRADE COMMISSION STAFF, ANTICIPATING THE 21ST CENTURY: COMPETITION POLICY IN THE NEW HIGH-TECH, GLOBAL MARKETPLACE seems to concede these omissions by suggesting a new approach as follows:

> . . . [W]hen firms resort increasingly to mergers, joint ventures, and other strategic alliances to cut costs and to compete in today's global, innovation-based markets, antitrust must take special care to weed out actions that harm competition while not discouraging others that are procompetitive. For mergers, this means antitrust must give more attention to efficiencies claims than it may have previously done. Even when firms struggle or entire industries erode, preserving competition should prevail over special dispensation for the distressed firm, but increased attention to efficiencies should avoid unnecessarily harsh effects of enforcement.

Id. at 35.

Section 7 invites a judgment of the likelihood of an adverse impact on competition. Because the statutory test of an illegal merger is the determination of whether its effect "may be substantially to lessen competition or tend to create a monopoly"—the incipiency test—many factors are involved in assessing the legality of a particular merger. The determination of a restraint of trade under the Sherman Act directs the inquiry to conduct during a specific, bounded time period. The review of the legality of a merger under § 7 of the Clayton Act imposes the statutory task of assessing the probability of a lessening of competition both immediately, as well as for a relevant period in the future. Moreover, the determination of a probable lessening of competition is complicated by the case law requirement that the likelihood of the entry of firms not presently in that market be taken into account. Accordingly the ultimate issue under § 7, the possibility of a lessening of competition, looks to existing and future states of competition including the likelihood of potential competition. The statute requires that the potential competitive impact of a proposed merger be assessed, although the statutory provision offers little guidance as to the factors to be weighed in this process. As a means of focusing this broad inquiry into the potential anticompetitive impact, the Department of Justice and the Federal Trade Commission have issued Merger Guidelines setting out the agencies' views as to how this determination should be made. These Guidelines inform the merger clearance procedure that rests on basic transactional information required by Congress prior to the consummation of a merger. The primary function of the Guidelines, however, is to provide the framework on which the agencies, as well as the proponents of a merger, may assess the information presented. The authoritative weight of the Guidelines is as an interpretive statement of merger policy by the agencies. Guidelines are to be distinguished from Regulations (or "legislative" rules), which must conform to certain requirements of the Federal Administrative Procedure Act, 5 U.S.C. §§ 551-559. (1996). Agency Regulations are subject to the "notice and comment" procedure when proposed, and are published in the Code of Federal Regulations when promulgated in final form. *See* DANIEL J. GIFFORD, ADMINISTRATIVE LAW 201-02 (1992).

As the analysis of the Guidelines in this chapter shows, the static economic models, which have dominated antitrust analysis, are currently being modified by the introduction of some dynamic considerations. For example, the concept of innovation market analysis, which was introduced by the Antitrust Guidelines for the Licensing of Intellectual Property in 1995, further refines the analysis of markets. 4 TRADE REG. REP. (CCH) ¶ 13,132.

The function of this analytical construct has been described as follows:

> Innovation market analysis is the latest step in the enforcement agencies' realignment of merger review from static structural models toward an examination of the effect of a transaction on future competition. . . . Today, examination of a merger encompasses more than merely defining a relevant product and geographic market and crunching concentration numbers. Merger analysis now looks to whether future entry is likely, whether there are likely anticompetitive effects resulting from the merger. . . .
>
> . . . [I]nnovation market analysis takes a future-oriented direction, recognizing the possibility that future competition can be harmed by mergers that result in a reduction of research and development.

Thomas N. Dahdough & James F. Mongoven, *The Shape of Things to Come*: *Innovation Market Analysis in Merger Cases,* 64 ANTITRUST L.J. 405 (1996).

The introduction of innovation market analysis has, however, been subject to substantial criticism on both theoretical and empirical grounds. The theoretical basis of the criticism is that innovation market analysis reopens the controversial topic of the relationship between the concentration in a market and the innovation that will be undertaken. It was the Schumpeterian thesis that concentration in markets is necessary and desirable in order to provide an incentive for firms to undertake the costs of research and development. (Schumpeter's theory is discussed further in Chapter 15, which deals with patents and other forms of intellectual property.) Innovation market analysis not only rejects Schumpeter's thesis that concentration nurtures innovation, it holds that concentration tends to limit research and development. As is frequently the case in antitrust analysis, definitive empirical validation of either position is unavailable. Proponents of innovation market analysis maintain that the concept is a useful tool of merger analysis. For example, Gilbert and Sunshine advocate the benefit of innovative market analysis as follows:

> We propose that delineating innovation markets can be a valuable instrument for evaluating the effects of merger-induced structural changes on the incentives for research and development and the resulting force of industrial innovation.

Richard J. Gilbert & Steven C. Sunshine, *Incorporating Dynamic Efficiency Concerns in Merger Analysis: The Use of Innovation Markets*, 63 ANTITRUST L.J. 569, 570 (1995). *See also* Richard J. Gilbert & Steven C. Sunshine, *The Use of Innovation Markets: A Reply to Hay, Rapp, and Hoerner,* 64 ANTITRUST L.J. 75, 77 (1995).

The dispute over the validity and utility of innovative market analysis illustrates the difficulty of discerning the strategic variables in making the determination of whether a combination of firms will lessen competition in a relevant market. Thus, one of the critics of innovation market analysis perceives a lack of content in the concept, as follows:

> Innovation is intangible, uncertain, unmeasurable, and often even unobservable, except in retrospect. There are no market transactions in innovation. . . . Thus, R&D expenditure is an *input* to the process of innovation. When we use the term, "innovation market," but measure market shares in terms of R&D expenditures or R&D capacity, we are making either an error or a leap in faith The error would be to suppose that innovation and R&D are the same thing. The leap of faith is to believe that there is a positive functional relationship between the rate of R&D expenditure (or the amount of R&D capacity) and the quantum of innovation produced by a firm.

Richard T. Rapp, *The Misapplication of the Innovation Market Approach to Merger Analysis,* 64 ANTITRUST L.J. 19, 27 (1995).

Nonetheless, the dominant issue of merger analysis for both agency and proponents remains the prediction of the likely impact of the proposed joinder of firms on the prices of products in a relevant market. In a recent revision of the efficiency criteria of the Horizontal Merger Guidelines, a prediction of the ultimate impact on prices is required.

> The Agency will not challenge a merger if cognizable efficiencies are of a character and magnitude such that the merger is not likely to result in price increases in any relevant market.
>
> To make the requisite determination, the Agency considers whether cognizable efficiencies likely would be sufficient to reverse the merger's potential to harm consumers in the relevant market, e.g. by preventing price increases in that market.

In the detailed analysis required by these Guidelines, three factors control: 1) substantial increases in concentration, 2) the impact on the conditions of entry, and 3) the achievement of demonstrable efficiencies in research and development, in production, and in management and distribution. U.S. Department of Justice & Federal Trade Commission, REVISION TO THE HORIZONTAL MERGER GUIDELINES 2 (1997). In reading the horizontal merger cases which follow, consider how they might have been decided under the current Guidelines.

As to actual enforcement of § 7 of the Clayton Act, both the Antitrust Division of the Department of Justice and the Federal Trade Commission have enforcement jurisdiction. Conflicting overlapping actions are avoided by inter-agency coordination procedures. Beginning in 1968, with revisions in 1982, 1984, 1992 and 1997, the Department of Justice has established a series of antimerger Guidelines to sketch the framework of analysis in applying § 7. (The current Horizontal Merger Guidelines are set out in Appendix C). As will be noted below, the successive editions of the Guidelines reflect the evolution of a different weighting of such factors as increased concentration, the increased prospects of collusive conduct, and of efficiency concerns. In the course of these successive editions of Merger Guidelines, the enforcement focus has moved away from the initial emphasis on structural tests toward a more flexible, multi-factor approach. Absent recent Supreme Court review of § 7 cases, merger analysis has been in some disarray. The enforcement agencies, various commentators, and lower court judges differ in their emphasis on structure, efficiency, methods of proof, and the application of presumptions. The various factors set out in the Guidelines are viewed by some as opaque and ambiguous, while others view them as providing the requisite flexibility for a case by case determination. The existence of differences in policy and analysis is reflected in the separate HORIZONTAL MERGER GUIDELINES ADOPTED BY THE NATIONAL ASSOCIATION OF ATTORNEYS GENERAL, SPECIAL SUPP., 64 ANTITRUST & TRADE REG. REP. April 1, 1993. For a review of merger policy and analysis, see William Blumenthal, *Thirty-One Merger Policy Questions Still Lingering After the 1992 Guidelines*, 38 ANTITRUST BULL. 593 (1993); Robert Pitofsky, *Proposals for Revised United States Enforcement in a Global Economy,* 81 GEO. L.J. 195 (1992).

This chapter is designed to set out the caselaw, Guidelines, and enforcement agencies' analysis of mergers. It will become apparent that, compared to caselaw, the Guidelines and enforcement agency policy have increasingly risen in significance in the more than twenty years since the Supreme Court last heard merger cases such as *United States v. Citizens & Southern National Bank,* 422 U.S. 86 (1975), *United States v. Marine Bancorporation*, 418 U.S. 602 (1974), and *United States v. General Dynamics Corp*., 415 U.S. 486 (1974). *See* Guidelines § 0.1 for a statement of the objectives of the agencies in enforcing § 7.

The decade of the 1990s was one of a rising volume of mergers. Starting in 1991, the annual number of filings of premerger notifications required by Hart-Scott-Rodino had risen overall. In 1998, there were 4,728 filings for the fiscal year; for fiscal 1999 there was a drop to 4,642 filings, and in 2000 the number of filings was 4,926.[1] Because most of these mergers are strategically driven by such considerations as acquiring technical talent, entering new markets, or obtaining new products, among others, such mergers pose complex analytical and remedial issues. Moreover, given the rising volume of global commerce, many mergers such as the Boeing/McDonnell Douglas,[2] MCI/WorldCom, and General Electric/ Honeywell, pose international issues. In these mergers foreign parties or assets are involved or the proposed merger may have a material impact on a foreign market, so that the competition laws of a foreign jurisdiction are invoked.

When more than one set of merger rules are applicable to a single merger transaction, conflict and increased transaction costs may ensue. At the outset, one jurisdiction may not be aware of the data submitted to the other jurisdiction. Moreover, the sharing of proprietary information may be complicated, if not entirely foreclosed by rules of confidentiality. Procedures to minimize such outcomes were initially addressed in 1994 by the Organization for Economic Cooperation and Development (OECD). In that year, the OECD's Committee on Competition Law and Policy published a report prepared by Professor Richard Whish and then-Professor Diane Wood entitled, *Merger Cases in the Real World—A Study of Merger Control Procedures*.[3] Subsequently, the OECD Committee, adopting a recommendation of the Whish/Wood Report, published a suggested uniform Notification and Report form for the use of parties in multi-jurisdictional mergers.[4] These initiatives

---

1 Antitrust Division, Workload Statistics FY 1991-2000, <http://www.usdoj.gov/atr/public/7344.htm>.

2 The conflict generated by differences in national substantive standards and enforcement procedures has been noted. *See* Daniel J. Gifford & E. Thomas Sullivan, *Can International Antitrust Be Saved for the Post-Boeing Merger World? A Proposal to Minimize International Conflict and to Rescue Antitrust from Misuse*, 45 Antitrust Bull. 55 (2000); William E. Kovacic, *Transatlantic Turbulence: The Boeing-McDonnell Douglas Merger and International Competition Policy*, 68 Antitrust L.J. 805 (2001). *See also* Thomas E. Kauper, *Merger Control in the United States and the European Union*, 74 St. John's L. Rev. 305 (2000).

3 Cited in OECD Report on Notification of Transnational Mergers 2, <www.oecd.org/daf/clp/reports.htm>.

4 *See* Note 2, *supra*.

were followed by informal discussions among the merger staffs of the Antitrust Division and the FTC with their foreign counterparts. Subsequently, the United States merger enforcement agencies have entered into bilateral antitrust cooperation agreements with eight countries. Although these agreements deal with a variety of other antitrust issues, such as transnational cartel arrangements, coordination of merger notification data is also addressed.[5] The most significant coordination framework rests on the EU/U.S. Agreement which was executed in final form in 1995.[6] This agreement imposes mutual obligations on the signatory parties to notify of enforcement activity affecting the other party, to exchange basic information about the investigation of a specific proposed transaction subject to the constraints of confidentiality, to coordinate enforcement activities, and to undertake enforcement activities with a view to the important interests of the other party.

One result of the substantive and procedural differences in the review of proposed mergers between the United States and the European Union is the practice by American competitors of making appearances before the European Competition Commission to urge disapproval of pending mergers between rivals. When the General Electric/Honeywell merger was pending before the Commission, two of General Electric's domestic rivals, United Technologies and Rockwell International, sought to block EU Commission approval. Commentators have noted that these European avionic manufacturers expressed their concern that General Electric's aircraft leasing company, the dominant firm in aircraft leasing, would buy only Honeywell avionic equipment or that General Electric would use its jet engine business to bolster Honeywell sales of avionic products.[7] Ultimately, the European Competition Commission disapproved the merger.

Antitrust officials on both sides of the Atlantic have recognized the potential for adverse outcomes inherent in multi-jurisdictional review of mergers. The former general counsel of one United States enforcement agency has stated as the objective of reviewing multi-jurisdictional mergers, "[that] we reach . . . solutions . . . that neither conflict nor force firms to choose between complying with U.S. or EC law."[8] Alexander Schaub, the EU Director General for Competition has cautioned that lack of effective coordination between antitrust enforcement agencies could impede competition. He noted that the multi-jurisdictional review process,

---

5 These countries include: Australia, Brazil, Canada, Germany, European Community, Israel, Japan, and Mexico. *See* <www.usdoj.gov/atr/public/international/int_arrangements.htm>.

6 Agreement Between the Government of the United States of America and The Commission of European Communities regarding the application of their competition laws, 1995 O.J. L95/47. *See also* VALENTINE KORAH, 2 COMPETITION LAW OF THE EUROPEAN COMMUNITY Ch. 8 (2000).

7 NEW YORK TIMES, June 19, 2001, p. 1, col. 2.

8 FTC General Counsel Debra A. Valentine, *Building A Co-operative Framework for Oversight in Mergers: The Answer to Extraterritorial Issues in Merger Review*, 6 GEO. MASON L. REV. 525, 527-28 (1998).

> [G]ives private parties the opportunity to pit antitrust authorities against each other. There is also the risk of treating companies in an inefficient manner or making them suffer fragmentary and incoherent solutions. . . .[9]

B. The Rationale for Merging

Although the substantial literature addressing the reasons for the decision of firm managers to merge is diffuse, there is consensus that analysis of cost, price, and output consequences that illuminate the interpretation of §§ 1 and 2 of the Sherman Act, are inadequate fully to explain mergers. The decision of one firm to acquire the stock or assets of another firm engaged in interstate commerce not only initiates the enforcement agency review and clearance procedures but poses the question of an economic rationale for the decision to merge. Ultimately an understanding of the economic basis of a merger serves also to infuse and guide the enforcement approach to it. Often, the justification of the proposed merger becomes "the story" associated with the merger and shapes the approach of the agencies. The importance of a careful analysis and explanation of the reasons for the merger is underscored by the attention given by the Guidelines to predicted behavior and to business practices.

The persistence of merger cycles has drawn scholarly attention to them. The economic history of the United States has been marked by four documented episodes of marked merger activity—their ending dates being noted as 1904, 1929, 1968, and 1985. The 1990s brought a spate of mergers in banking, communication, and technology, the full significance of which remains be determined. The merger movement of the 1980s coincided with a shift in economic analysis employed in antitrust law, and resulted in reduced enforcement activity toward mergers. In the period from 1960 to 1980, the Department of Justice and the Federal Trade Commission challenged about 20 mergers per year. Between 1981 and 1984, about 10 challenges each year were brought. *See* F.M. Scherer, *Merger Policies in the 1970s and 1980s*, *in* ECONOMICS AND ANTITRUST POLICY, 84 (Robert J. Larner ed. 1988); NAOMI R. LAMOREAUX, THE GREAT MERGER MOVEMENT IN AMERICAN BUSINESS, 1895-1904 (1985); F.M. SCHERER, INDUSTRIAL MARKET STRUCTURE AND ECONOMIC PERFORMANCE (2d ed. 1980); Jesse W. Markham, *Survey of the Evidence and Findings on Mergers, in* BUSINESS CONCENTRATION AND PRICE POLICY (1955).

Among the motives that have been identified as relevant to explain the decision of enterprise managers and shareholders to merge are control and coordination, the quest of market power, and speculation in share and asset prices. Control and

---

[9] Alexander Schaub, *International Co-operation in Antitrust Matters: Making the Point in the Wake of the Boeing/MDD Proceedings*, 1 COMPETITION POLICY NEWSLETTER 2-6 (1998).

coordination of facilities frequently accomplishes material cost saving and related efficiency gains. However, mergers may also be the means by which a dominant firm in an industry can eliminate a small, efficient rival. The primary historical examples of achieving market dominance by mergers resulted in two famous antitrust cases. The Standard Oil Company achieved a 90 percent market share of refining capacity by more than 100 mergers. The United States Steel Corporation achieved dominance by mergers with some 200 independent iron and steel producers. Where a merger improves the acquiring firm's market position and profit prospects, higher share prices are likely to result. There is also historical evidence that a speculative environment may foster the activities of "merger marketers," market intermediaries—investment bankers, lawyers, and accountants—who may derive large fees for professional services in arranging and executing mergers. More than one or all of these motives may by present in any given decision to merge. PETER O. STEINER, MERGERS, MOTIVES, EFFECTS, POLICIES (1975). Commentators have noted a change in motivation for mergers in the 1990s:

> In the 1980s there was a plethora of 'financial plays' . . . entrepreneurs and speculators would put a company 'in play' (as a takeover target) and often reap financial rewards through the run-up in stock value. . . . The market and people have just matured a lot. . . . Even the terminology suggests it. Talk of cowboys and pirates has given way to words like 'synergy' and 'strategic alliance.' Corporations now want to merge with or acquire companies with activities that will complement or enhance their own.

Lisa Stansky, *M&A Is Back*, 83 ABA J. 61 (1997).

Analysis of the success of mergers is also complicated and equivocal. One study of 329 mergers accomplished between 1888 and 1905 found that 53 collapsed soon after and that 141 were financial failures. *See* Shaw Livermore, *The Success of Industrial Mergers,* 49 Q.J. ECON. 68 (1935). It is not clear from this study which mergers represented mistakes in judgment as to the value of assets of essentially failing firms and which achieved efficiencies by prosperous firms. Another study of the 1926-1929 merger movement found that mergers arranged by bankers rather than corporate managers, failed more frequently. *See* Jesse W. Markham, *Survey of the Evidence and Findings on Mergers, in* NBER, BUSINESS CONCENTRATION AND PRICE POLICY 141 (1955).

The decision to acquire corporate assets, stock, or control by a merger, rather than by purchase, may be shaped by the federal income tax provisions permitting nonrecognition of gain to merging corporations and their shareholders. Sections 354, 355, 358, and 368 of the Internal Revenue Code (26 U.S.C.) provide for nonrecognition transactions in corporate reorganizations (including mergers). Accordingly, a corporation with appreciated assets may transfer the ownership of those assets by merger without having to recognize the gain inherent in those assets at that time. An outright sale of the assets would be a taxable transaction. Mergers may also offer access to loss carryovers and other tax attributes. For a recognition of the tax incentives to mergers, see Federal Trade Commission Staff Report On Corporate Mergers to the Antitrust Subcommittee of the Senate Judiciary Committee (Nov. 3, 1969). *See also* Alan J. Auerbach & David Reishus, *The Impact of Taxation on Mergers and Acquisitions, in* MERGERS AND ACQUISITIONS 69 (Alan J. Auerbach ed. 1988).

Since any merger or acquisition requires an agreement between the acquiring and acquired entities, merger transactions also fall under the purview of § 1 of the Sherman Act. In addition, an acquisition or merger which threatened to create a monopoly would fall within the scope of § 2 of the Sherman Act as well. Prior to 1950, when § 7 of the Clayton Act, which deals directly with mergers, was amended to reach mergers by acquisition of assets, the Sherman Act was used against asset acquisition mergers. *E.g., United States v. Columbia Steel Co.,* 334 U.S. 495 (1948).

In functional terms, mergers accomplish the coordination of various stages of production and distribution by transactions under state laws permitting enterprises organized in the corporate form to acquire other corporations. In Chapter 5 on vertical arrangements, it was noted that contracts may serve also as a means of accomplishing such coordination. Many of the economic criticisms of the antitrust analysis of vertical restraints by contract are also applicable to vertical mergers. Recall, for example, the material on agency and franchise arrangements, as well as on contracts establishing exclusive dealing, territorial limitations, and providing for a constant supply of materials. *See* Friedrich Kessler & Richard H. Stern, *Competition, Contract, and Vertical Integration,* 69 YALE L.J. 1 (1959). Mergers offer a transactional alternative to some of these contractual arrangements.

Mergers are designated by their transactional format. A vertical merger, one that may serve the coordination and control objectives of a franchise agreement, involves an amalgamation of enterprises functioning on different levels of production and distribution, *e.g.*, a manufacturer may acquire a retail outlet or a supplier of raw materials may acquire a manufacturer. A horizontal merger is one in which the parties are engaged at the same level of production or distribution (and are in direct competition). The term conglomerate identifies a merger in which the parties were not related functionally and may have been in different industries.

C. Statutory History

1. In General

Paradoxically, the concern with the concentration of assets and with economic power which dominated the congressional debates over the Sherman Act, did not produce an express statutory reference to corporate acquisitions. Despite the various formal devices available for concentrating corporate control, the Sherman Act expressly addressed only the use of the trust, the prevalent mode of corporate combination employed as early as 1879 when the Standard Oil Trust was formed. *See*

D. MARTIN, MERGERS AND THE CLAYTON ACT 4 (1959). The enactment of the Sherman Act did not halt the progress of corporate amalgamation. The large number of corporate acquisitions and combinations which took place between 1895 and 1905 has been characterized as accomplishing a major change in the technology and organization of manufacturing in the United States. *See* Jesse W. Markham, *Survey of the Evidence and Findings on Mergers, in* BUSINESS CONCENTRATION AND PRICE POLICY 141 (1955). It was during that period that firms such as General Electric, Westinghouse, United States Steel, American Tobacco, and du Pont were formed. This process brought about substantial concentration in the manufacturing sector. By 1904, more than 130 different industries were dominated by a single firm. *See* G.W. NUTTER, THE EXTENT OF ENTERPRISE MONOPOLY IN THE UNITED STATES: 1899-1939, App. B. (1951).

Enacted without explicit language designed to limit corporate combinations (by acquisitions or otherwise), the Sherman Act was invoked only against the resultant combination. It remained for the Clayton Act, 38 Stat. 730 (1914), to provide a weapon directed specifically against acquisitions. However, the Supreme Court did apply § 1 of the Sherman Act to dissolve the merger of the Great Northern and the Northern Pacific railroads. In *Northern Securities Co. v. United States*, 193 U.S. 197 (1904), it was held that the use of a holding company for the stock of both railroad corporations constituted an illegal combination in restraint of trade. Subsequently, the Supreme Court relied on §§ 1 and 2 of the Sherman Act to dissolve the oil and the tobacco trusts. *See* page 17, *supra*. In each case the trust had long since brought about the corporate combination of former competitors that became the basis of the illegal conduct.

But it was neither public nor congressional concern with corporate combinations which led to the passage of the Clayton Act, and its express provision dealing with corporate acquisitions. Rather, the Clayton Act owes its passage primarily to Congressional outrage over the announcement by the Supreme Court of the rule of reason in the *Standard Oil* case of 1911. *See* page 17, *supra*. The chairman of the Senate Committee on Interstate Commerce stated:

> The committee . . . is unwilling to repose in . . . [the Supreme] court, or any other court, the vast and undefined power which it must exercise in the administration of the statute under the rule which it has promulgated. It substitutes the court in the place of Congress. . . . [T]he court does not administer the law, but makes the law. . . .
>
> The people of this country will not permit the courts to declare a policy for them with respect to this subject.

Report of Senate Committee on Interstate Commerce xii (1913), quoted in GERALD HENDERSON, THE FEDERAL TRADE COMMISSION 16 (1924).

The passage of the Clayton Act ended the exclusive reliance upon the Sherman Act to control corporate combinations. Unfortunately, § 7, the anti-acquisition provision, 38 Stat. 731 (1914), was flawed in that it addressed only stock acquisitions, while omitting entirely any reference to an equally functional method of corporate acquisition by assets. The original § 7 provided in relevant part:

> . . . no corporation engaged in commerce shall acquire . . . the whole or any part of the stock . . . of another corporation . . . where the effect of such acquisition may be to substantially lessen competition between the corporation whose stock is so acquired and the corporation making the acquisition, or to restrain such commerce in any section or community, or tend to create a monopoly of any line of commerce.

38 Stat. 731 (1914).

Compare the original version of § 7 with the current, amended version, Appendix A. Could the original provision be applied to a vertical merger? How? Could it reach a conglomerate merger?

The pressure to remedy the gaps in the scope of the original § 7 of the Clayton Act began with judicial recognition of their existence. Crucial was the decision in *Federal Trade Commission v. Western Meat Co.*, 272 U.S. 554 (1926), where the Court held that the Commission lacked the authority to order the distribution of acquired assets, since § 7 addressed only stock acquisitions. Two factors coalesced in bringing about the amendment of § 7 in 1950.

First was the heightened concern with economic concentration which accompanied the Great Depression. The economic boom of the 1920s had fostered a rapid increase in the number of corporate combinations. One study showed that nearly 5,000 firms were acquired in the period from 1926 until 1930. *See* J. WESTON, THE ROLE OF MERGERS IN THE GROWTH OF LARGE FIRMS 31 (1953). The Depression widened the concern with the potential for anti-social conduct by large, dominant corporations. *See* ADOLF BERLE & GARDINER MEANS, THE MODERN CORPORATION AND PRIVATE PROPERTY 18 (1932).

Second was the demonstrated inadequacy of the existing antitrust statutes in the first major merger case after the Second World War. The government moved against the acquisition by Columbia Steel, a wholly-owned subsidiary of the United States Steel Corporation, of the assets of Consolidated Steel, a regional fabricator of steel plates and pressure vessels. Since § 7 of the Clayton Act was inapplicable to an asset acquisition, the government brought this case under the Sherman Act. The complaint alleged restraints of trade under § 1 by the elimination of competition between the acquired and the acquiring firm. A separate count alleged an attempt to monopolize the fabricated steel market in violation of § 2. The trial court found against the government on all counts in *United States v. Columbia Steel Co.*, 74 F. Supp. 671 (D. Del. 1947). The government lost also in the Supreme Court, a 5 to 4 decision in *United States v. Columbia Steel Co.*, 334 U.S. 495 (1948).

The final impetus for the amendment of § 7 in 1950 was provided by a controversial Report of the Federal Trade Commission entitled: REPORT ON THE MERGER MOVEMENT: A SUMMARY REPORT (1948). Citing the disappearance of about 2,500 firms through combinations in the period from 1940 to 1947, the Report concluded on a note of urgency:

> . . . [I]f nothing is done to check the growth in concentration, either the giant corporations will ultimately take over the country, or the Government will be impelled to step in and impose some form of direct regulation in the public interest.

Id. at 68. This Report was accorded substantial weight by Congress in its deliberations on the amendment to § 7. *See* S. REPT. NO. 81-1775, at 5 (1950). *See also* 95 CONG. REC. 11485 (1949) (Remarks of Rep. Celler).

Controversy soon developed over the methodology and conclusions of this Report as the result of an article by two Harvard Business School economists. *See* John Lintner & James Butters, *Effect of Mergers on Industrial Concentration, 1940-47,* 32 REV. OF ECON. & STAT. 30 (1950). Subsequently, two government economists who had participated in the preparation of the Report conceded that the mergers of that period had not materially increased concentration in the manufacturing sector of the economy. *See* J. Blair & Houghton, *The Lintner-Butters Analysis of the Effect of Mergers on Industrial Concentration, 1940-44,* 33 REV. OF ECON. & STAT. 61, 63 (1951). Further analysis of this data by others has corroborated the findings of Lintner and Butters that this period was not one in which there was a significant increase in concentration in the economy overall. *See* Morris A. Adelman, *The Measurement of Industrial Concentration,* 33 REV. OF ECON. & STAT. 269 (1951).

In its *Brown Shoe* opinion (summarized page 559, *infra*) the Court relied upon legislative history for its interpretation of the amended § 7. To what extent should a federal judge rely upon legislative history which incorporates flawed analysis? *See* Derek Bok, *Section 7 of the Clayton Act and the Merging of Law and Economics,* 74 HARV. L. REV. 226, 233-37 (1960).

Consider whether the cases which follow were instrumental as precedents in making the traditional horizontal merger more likely to come under antitrust attack. Could the difficulty of engaging in lawful horizontal mergers serve as an incentive to diversify in corporate acquisitions? One commentator has concluded that the rise in conglomerate mergers in the period from 1960 through 1965 was a measure of the difficulty in accomplishing a horizontal or a vertical merger which would survive challenge under § 7 as then interpreted. *See* PETER O.. STEINER, MERGERS, MOTIVES, EFFECTS, POLICIES 157 (1975).

In 1976 Congress made an additional change in § 7 by the addition of § 7A (15 U.S.C. § 18a), providing for premerger notice by the parties to a merger and for an automatic delay in the execution of the merger for an initial maximum period of thirty days for a stock tender offer and fifteen days for a cash tender offer. The Federal Trade Commission or the Assistant Attorney General (Antitrust Division, Department of Justice) may extend the waiting period for an additional twenty days in the case of a stock tender offer and ten days for a cash tender offer. Denial of the automatic delay period requires a showing by the Federal Trade Commission or the Assistant Attorney General before a United States district court of substantial non-compliance by a party to the notice requirement or failure fully to submit requested additional information concerning the merger. These notice requirements apply to mergers in which the acquiring firm has total assets or net annual sales of $100 million or more and in which the acquired firm has net annual sales of $10 million or more.

This amendment is described in the House Report as leaving unchanged the existing substantive criteria of § 7, being concerned with improvement of its enforcement by:

> . . . giving the government antitrust agencies a fair and reasonable opportunity to detect and investigate large mergers of questionable legality before they are consummated. The government will thus have a meaningful chance to win a premerger injunction—which is often the only effective and realistic remedy against large, illegal mergers—before the assets, technology, and management of the merging firms are hopelessly and irreversibly scrambled together, and before competition is substantially and perhaps irremediably lessened. . . .

H. Rep. No. 94-1373, at 5 (1976).

Consider the effect of a temporary injunction on a cash tender offer of $12 million to be financed by a clearance loan for three days at 15% interest. Or consider a tender offer by an acquiring firm, involving a block of newly-issued stock, which will be held in an escrow account pending the hearing on the government's motion for an injunction. Some of the circuit courts have held the government to a showing of irreparable injury and probable success on the merits. *See Federal Trade Commission v. National Tea Co.*, 603 F.2d 694 (8th Cir. 1979). The Second Circuit, however, affords the government a presumption of irreparable injury in a § 7 case. *See United States v. Siemens Corp.*, 621 F.2d 499 (2d Cir. 1980).

2. After 1950

From 1957 through the 1960s, a series of Supreme Court decisions indicated that the new amendment would treat a wide range of vertical and horizontal mergers and acquisitions as suspect and presumptively illegal. This period began with the *du Pont-General Motors* and *Brown Shoe* cases scrutinizing vertical acquisitions harshly, analogizing them to tying contracts (which were then viewed as lacking any redeeming social value). *Brown Shoe* indicated that vertical mergers and acquisitions would be subjected to this strict scrutiny even when the so-called "foreclosure" aspects of a merger or acquisition were small and the merger or acquisition produced distributional efficiencies. Starting with *Brown Shoe* and continuing through a series of subsequent cases, the Court further indicated that the new amendment would condemn horizontal mergers and acquisitions of any significant size.

Note the absence of enforcement activity against mergers since the 1980s. Although the cases that follow remain part of § 7 analysis, their current precedential value must be considered as diminished in the light of the most recent Merger Guidelines.

a. The Prelude: *DuPont-General Motors*

The first case under the 1950 Amendment, *Brown Shoe Co. v. United States*, 370 U.S. 294, did not reach the Supreme Court until 1962. A hint of things to come was provided in 1957 when the Supreme Court decided in *United States v. E.I. du Pont de Nemours & Co.*, 353 U.S. 586, that the DuPont Company's gradual acquisition of a 23% stock interest in General Motors during the period from 1917 to 1919 violated the original version of § 7.

The Court reached this result as a result of DuPont's supplying large amounts of automobile finishes and fabrics to General Motors, DuPont at the time being the largest chemical company in the world and General Motors then being the largest automobile manufacturer in the world. (The Court noted that DuPont supplied 67% of G.M.'s requirements for finishes in 1946 and 68% in 1948. In fabrics, DuPont supplied 52.3% of G.M.'s requirements in 1946 and 38.5% in 1947.) The Justice Department's Complaint alleged that DuPont's large market share in supplying G.M. with paints and fabrics resulted from DuPont's ownership stake in G.M., rather than from the competitive merits of the DuPont products. Because G.M. then accounted for almost one-half of the automobile industry's sales, the Complaint further alleged a §7 lessening of competition from other suppliers of paints and fabrics. The Court ruled that there was a danger that G.M.'s purchasing decisions (and hence DuPont's market position) might have been influenced by DuPont's shareholdings in its major customer. On this reasoning, the Court ruled DuPont's acquisition of those shares illegal under § 7, since this provision barred acquisitions which "tend to create a monopoly of any line of commerce."

One major difficulty with the Court's reasoning was that the Clayton Act was directed against stock acquisitions, not stock holdings as an investment. (Section 7 then stated, "No corporation . . . shall acquire . . . the whole or any part of the stock . . . of another corporation. . . .") DuPont had acquired 23% of General Motor's stock in the 1917-1919 period, when General Motors occupied only about an 11% share of the automobile industry, and hence posed no likelihood of providing DuPont with special access to a major part of the automobile industry's purchases. Brushing aside this difficulty, the Court asserted that the "aim (of the Clayton Act) was primarily to arrest apprehended consequences of intercorporate relationships before those relationships could work their evil, *which may be at or any time after the acquisition*, depending upon the circumstances of the particular case." 353 U.S. at 597. (Emphasis supplied).

Although the district court, after a detailed review of the evidence on the conduct of DuPont officials after 1917 on the matter of exercising influence over G.M. officials to purchase DuPont paint and fabrics, found no such influence, the Supreme Court's majority considered this finding irrelevant under its interpretation of § 7. For the majority, § 7 required a determination of whether the likelihood of a lessening of competition might arise at any time after the acquisition and the fact that no actual lessening of competition did materialize was not dispositive under the incipiency standard of § 7. In dissent, Justices Burton and Frankfurter pointed out that the pre-1950 version of § 7 did not apply to vertical mergers, but, they urged, that even if it did, the time to test the lessening of competition was at the time of the acquisition, rather than at the time of the litigation.

The Court also demonstrated its willingness to undo corporate acquisitions under the Clayton Act by taking a different approach to the definition of a relevant product market than it had taken the preceding year in *United States v. E.I. du Pont de Nemours & Co.*, 351 U.S. 377 (1956), involving cellophane. There, the Court had adopted substitutability (cross-elasticity of demand or of production facilities) as the principal determinant of the relevant market. In *DuPont-General Motors*, the Court ignored the possibility that automobile finishes and fabrics compete with other finishes and fabrics or that suppliers could readily convert from nonautomotive finishes and fabrics to automobile finishes and fabrics. Accepting a contention which it had rejected in *Cellophane*, the Court ruled that because automotive finishes and fabrics have "peculiar characteristics and uses" they constituted a product market separate from all other finishes and fabrics. As a result of the Court's decision, DuPont was forced to divest its shares in General Motors. DuPont's potential federal income tax liability on the substantial appreciation in the value of the General Motors shares was ameliorated by an amendment to the Internal Revenue Code, Pub. L. 87-403, 76 Stat. 4 (1962), which was repealed by Pub. L. 94-455, 90 Stat. 1786 (1976).

b. *Brown Shoe Co. v. United States*, 370 U.S. 294 (1962)

In this case the government attacked the acquisition by the Brown Shoe Company of the G.R. Kinney Company, basing its attack on the amended version of § 7. There were both horizontal and vertical aspects to the merger, as both Brown and Kinney sold shoes at retail and Kinney also was purchasing shoes from Brown.

(i) *Markets and submarkets.*—The Court took the occasion to reconcile the approaches to relevant market definition which it had taken in *Cellophane* (cross-elasticity of demand) and in *DuPont-General Motors* (peculiar characteristics and uses). In *Brown Shoe*, the Court asserted:

> The outer boundaries of a product market are determined by the reasonable interchangeability of use or the cross-elasticity of demand between the product itself and substitutes for it. However, within this broad market, well-defined submarkets may exist which, in themselves, constitute product markets for antitrust purposes. . . . The boundaries of such a submarket may be determined by examining such practical indicia as industry or public recognition of the submarket as a separate economic entity, the product's peculiar characteristics and uses, unique production facilities, distinct customers, distinct prices, sensitivity to price changes, and specialized vendors.

The common contemporary reading of this passage was that merger analysis could legitimately make use of submarkets which were narrower in scope than a market defined on the basis of cross-elasticity of demand. It is now probably correct to say that *Brown Shoe*'s submarkets are treated as shortcuts to identifying economically viable markets. And that if it can be shown (using a cross-elasticity-of-demand analysis) that use of the practical indicia of *Brown Shoe* do not in fact identify an economically viable market, then the purported submarket cannot be used for merger analysis.

(ii) Brown Shoe*'s horizontal merger analysis.*—The Court took as relevant geographic markets those cities and with a population exceeding 10,000 and their environs in which both Brown and Kinney retailed shoes through their own outlets. It then concluded that in any such market in which the combined sales of Brown and Kinney exceeded 5% of total sales, the merger should be condemned. It reached that conclusion partly because it believed that if it approved a merger resulting in a 5% combined market share, it would be required to approve other mergers producing 5% market shares and thus ultimately to transform a highly competitive industry into an oligopoly. (The opinion did not address the possibility of evaluating each merger in context.)

(iii) Brown Shoe*'s vertical merger analysis.*—Brown, the fourth largest shoe manufacturer in the United States, produced about 4% of U.S. production. Kinney was the twelfth largest producer, producing .5% of U.S. production. Kinney owned and operated the largest independent chain of shoe retailers in the country, accounting for about 1.2% of U.S. shoe sales (measured by dollar volume). At the time of the merger, Kinney was purchasing about 7.9% of its supplies from Brown. As it had in *DuPont-General Motors*, the Court analogized Brown's stock ownership in Kinney to a tying arrangement, facilitating Brown's sales to Kinney. (The stock was the tying product; the shoes sold to Kinney constitute the tied product.) This analogy strengthened the Court's belief that a merger between the fourth largest manufacturer and the largest retail chain involved an unacceptably high potential market foreclosure. The Court, accordingly, disapproved the vertical aspects of the merger. (Note the "foreclosure" was 7.9% of 1.2%, or a foreclosure of .0948% at the time of the merger!)

The Court capped its evaluation of the merger by perversely deciding that efficiencies which the merger may have created were reasons for invalidating the merger, rather than reasons for upholding it. It reached this conclusion by adopting Judge Hand's view that the antitrust laws incorporate a concern for protecting and preserving small businesses, regardless of whether they operate at higher costs:

> A . . . significant aspect of this merger is that it creates a large national chain which is integrated with a manufacturing operation. The retail outlets of integrated companies, by eliminating wholesalers and by increasing the volume of purchases from the manufacturing division of the enterprise, can market their own brands at prices below those of competing independent retailers. Of course, some of the results of large integrated or chain operations are beneficial to consumers. Their expansion is not rendered unlawful by the mere fact that small independent stores may be adversely affected. It is competition, not competitors, which the Act protects. But we cannot fail to recognize Congress' desire

> to promote competition through the protection of viable, small, locally owned businesses. Congress appreciated that occasional higher costs and prices might result from the maintenance of fragmented industries and markets. It resolved these competing considerations in favor of decentralization.

370 U.S. at 344.

c. *United States v. Philadelphia National Bank*, 374 U.S. 321 (1963)

The year after its decision in *Brown Shoe*, the Court again reviewed the application of § 7 to horizontal acquisitions. In this case the Philadelphia National Bank (the second largest bank in Philadelphia) had acquired a rival bank, the Girard Trust Company. In that case, the Court adopted a presumptive rule of thumb with which to evaluate such mergers:

> . . . we think that a merger which produces a firm controlling an undue percentage share of the relevant market, and results in a significant increase in the concentration of firms in that market, is so inherently likely to lessen competition substantially that it must be enjoined in the absence of evidence clearly showing that the merger is not likely to have such anticompetitive effects. . . .
>
> The merger of appellees will result in a single bank's controlling at least 30% of the commercial banking business in the four-county Philadelphia metropolitan area. Without attempting to specify the smallest market share which would still be considered to threaten undue concentration, we are clear that 30% represents that threat. Further, whereas presently the two largest banks in the area (First Pennsylvania and PNB) control between them approximately 44% of the area's commercial banking business, the two largest after the merger (PNB-Girard and First Pennsylvania) will control 59%. Plainly, we think, this increase of more than 33% in concentration must be regarded as significant.

COMMENTARY

1. Banks, as supervised entities, have had a unique history of antitrust enforcement. Until the Supreme Court's decision in *United States v. South-Eastern Underwriters Ass'n*, 322 U.S. 533 (1944), banking, like the business of insurance, was not considered as "commerce" for Sherman Act purposes. Accordingly, banks were effectively exempted from the Sherman and Clayton Acts until the bank merger litigation that began with *Philadelphia National Bank.* The authority for this interpretation of exempt status for banks was in part statutory. For example, the Clayton Act, as amended in 1950, § 11, 15 U.S.C. § 21, delegates enforcement authority of its provisions as applied to banks, to the Federal Reserve Board. This effective immunity of banks from antitrust scrutiny was reinforced by the wording of the original § 7, which was applicable only to stock acquisitions. Accordingly, this version of § 7 was effectively inapplicable to bank mergers, which were traditionally asset acquisition transactions. Moreover, the 1950 amendment of § 7 further suggests an immunity of banks from antitrust scrutiny, since the scope of the amendment was expressly made applicable to corporations under the jurisdiction of the Federal Trade Commission. As a supervised industry, banking activities are subject to review by their Chartering authorities. State banks are reviewed at the state agency, national banks are accountable to the United States Comptroller of the Currency, and banks which are members of the Federal Reserve System are accountable to the Federal Reserve Bank. Because of this diverse regulatory scheme, it was assumed that banks were not subject to the jurisdiction of the antitrust authorities. Practical circumstances also contributed to the exemption of banks from antitrust scrutiny. Throughout most of the history of banking in the United States, solvency rather than competition was the primary public policy concern about the banking system, a view that was underscored by the Great Depression of the 1930s. *See* Bernard Shull, *The Origins of Antitrust in Banking: An Historical Perspective,* 41 ANTITRUST BULL. 255 (1996).

After 1950, concerns with the trend toward concentration of the banking system, as well some clearly antitcompetitive practices, such as the joint fixing of service charges by competing banks, led the Federal Reserve Board to exercise its antitrust enforcement authority under § 7. The Board, concerned by the rapid acquisition by Transamerica, a holding company of the Bank of America, of some forty banks in five western states, an arrangement which effectively permitted the Bank of America to operate branch banks outside its home state of California, obtained an order under § 7 of the Clayton Act for divestiture of these acquisitions. On appeal by the bank from a divestiture order, however, the court of appeals set aside the order on the ground that the Board had failed to show the antitcompetitive effects in a relevant market. *Board of Governors v. Transamerica Corp.,* 206 F.2d 163 (3d Cir. 1953). However, the general perception of increased concentration of the economy that led to the amending of § 7 of the Clayton Act, was reflected in Congressional concern over a rising concentration in the banking industry. The perceived abuse of bank holding companies to aggregate multi-state ownership of banks led to the enactment of the Bank Holding Company Act of 1956, c. 240, 70 Stat. 133, 12 U.S.C. §§ 1841 *et seq* (1994). This legislation requires a corporation owning two or more banks to register with the Federal Reserve Board and to avoid the acquisition of banks other than those in the state of their principal office. In addition to limiting the use of holding companies by banks, Congress also addressed bank mergers. The Bank Merger Act of 1960, Pub. L. No. 86-463, 74 Stat. 129, 12 U.S.C. §§ 1828 *et seq* (1994), as amended in 1966, P.L. 89-356, 80 Stat. 7, provided for limited antitrust scrutiny of banks by a complex administrative procedure. Under the Bank Merger Act, pre-merger approval was required from the Comptroller of the Currency for national banks, from the Federal Reserve Board for state-chartered Federal Reserve member banks, and from the Federal Deposit Insurance Corporation for state-chartered, nonmember, insured banks. The statute directed each reviewing agency to balance bank solvency and stability considerations against competitive factors, but the Act did not make competitive factors paramount. Subsequently, in the 1966 amendments to the Bank Merger Act, Congress expressly added Sherman and Clayton Act criteria to the approval standards imposed on each administrative agency. *See, e.g.*, 12 U.S.C. §§ 1828(c)(5)(A) & (B) (1994) (barring approval by the Federal Deposit Insurance Corporation of a merger "(A) . . . which would be in furtherance of any combination or conspiracy to monopolize or attempt to monopolize" or "(B) . . . may . . . substantially . . . lessen competition."). The addition of these competitive criteria marked the end of a long Congressional debate over the proper balance of bank solvency with antitrust concerns.

However, the problem remained of achieving administrative finality among the several authorities required by the Bank Merger Act to review a proposed bank merger. The 1960 statute provided that each reviewing agency was required to seek an advisory opinion from the Attorney General in each case. But the 1960 statutory scheme did not address the procedure to be followed if the reviewing agency rejected the opinion of the Attorney General. This gap in the statutory scheme led to the *Philadelphia National Bank* litigation. The *Philadelphia National Bank*, in compliance with the 1960 Bank Merger Act, sought and obtained the approval of the Comptroller of the Currency to acquire Girard Trust, an insured state bank. However, the other participants in the review process, the Attorney General, the Federal Reserve Board, and the Federal Deposit Insurance Corporation were unanimous in their disapproval of the merger. The Comptroller gave his final consent on February 24, 1961; the Attorney General responded by filing the complaint on the next day. The district court dismissed the complaint on the grounds that § 7 was inapplicable to bank mergers and that, moreover, the government had failed to show anticompetitive effects. On appeal, the Supreme Court reversed, holding that § 7 controlled and that there was sufficient evidence to show the requisite lessening of competition. The clear break with the historical exemption of banking from antitrust scrutiny was noted by the dissenting Justices, Harlan and Stewart, who wrote at the outset of their dissenting opinion: ". . . [N]o one will be more surprised than the Government to find that the Clayton Act has carried the day for its case in this Court." 374 U.S. at 373 (Harlan, J., dissenting). *See* William T. Lifland, *The Supreme Court, Congress, and Bank Mergers,* 32 LAW & CONTEMP. PROBS. 15 (1967).

The year following the decision in *Philadelphia National Bank*, the government challenged the merger of the largest of six banks in Fayette County, Kentucky with the fourth largest, under § 1 of the Sherman Act. Again, the Comptroller of the Currency was the alone in approving the merger. The Supreme Court again reversed the dismissal of the complaint by the district court, and limiting the *Columbia Steel* case to its facts, held for the government on the § 1 count, which was that the merger restrained trade by removing major competitors from the relevant market,

United States v. First National Bank & Trust Co. of Lexington, 376 U.S. 665, 672 (1964).

This historical experience with separate antitrust treatment of bank mergers leaves the larger question of defining an appropriate merger policy for banks. The rise of electronic payments systems and credit card markets, coupled with the spread of automatic teller networks, and the global use of banking facilities, pose questions of the adequacy of existing merger criteria. Commentators have questioned whether the narrow, metropolitan area definition of the relevant market for banking services stated in *Philadelphia National Bank* remains valid. Bank merger policy is of increased significance, given the merger movement which began in 1995. *See* Lawrence J. White, *Banking, Mergers, and Antitrust: Historical Perspectives and the Research Tasks Ahead,* 41 ANTITRUST BULL. 323, 332 (1996). The widened geographic scope of banking operations is further underscored by the passage of the Riegle-Neal Interstate Banking and Branching Efficiency Act of 1994, Pub. L. 103-328, 108 Stat. 2338, 12 U.S.C. §§ 1842 *et seq* (1994), which permits bank holding companies to hold multi-state banks, and thereby to achieve interstate branch banking, a practice barred in 1956. *See* Mark D. Rollinger, *Interstate Banking and Branching Under The Riegle-Neal Act,* 33 HARV. J. LEGIS. 183 (1996). For further discussion of antitrust enforcement in regulated industries, see E. THOMAS SULLIVAN & JEFFREY L. HARRISON, UNDERSTANDING ANTITRUST AND ITS ECONOMIC IMPLICATIONS § 3.05 (2d ed. 1994).

Consider how the framework of the Merger Guidelines, which follow, should be brought to bear on bank mergers in the light of the distinctive supervision of banks.

2. Outside the arena of banking, after the decision in *Philadelphia National Bank,* courts continued to struggle with defining a "trip wire" of concentration to determine illegal mergers. After ostensibly adopting a presumption of unlawfulness applicable to mergers resulting in a post-merger market share of 30%, the Court decided a series of merger cases during the next several years which upheld every governmental challenge. In *United States v. Aluminum Co. of America*, 377 U.S. 271 (1964), Alcoa's acquisition of Rome Cable Company was upheld on the ground that the merged companies together controlled 27.8% of the "aluminum conductor" market. The decision was controversial because there was no recognized aluminum conductor market. There were separate markets for insulated aluminum conductor and for bare aluminum conductor, but the facts would not have supported a condemnation of the merger in either of the recognized product markets: In the insulated aluminum market the combination would have produced a market share of 4.7% + 11.6% = 16.3%, vastly short of the 30% presumptively illegal standard of *Philadelphia Bank*. In the bare aluminum market Alcoa's preexisting share of 32.5% would be augmented only by a de minimis .3% by the acquisition of Rome.

The Court then decided *United States v. Continental Can Co.*, 378 U.S. 441 (1964), in which it condemned the acquisition by Continental Can Company (a producer of metal containers) of the Hazel-Atlas Glass Company (a producer of glass containers). That decision broke new ground because there was no short-run cross-elasticity of demand between metal and glass container markets. Although the Court opted to use long-run cross-elasticity between those two markets, its decision lost some persuasiveness when it chose to omit plastic containers from its long-run construct involving metal and glass containers.

In *United States v. Pabst Brewing Co.*, 384 U.S. 546 (1966), the Court condemned the acquisition by the Pabst Brewing Co. of the Blatz Brewing Company. Although the district court had dismissed the case on the ground that the government "failed to prove either Wisconsin or the three-state area of Wisconsin, Illinois and Michigan constituted 'a relevant section of the country within the meaning of Section 7,'" the Supreme Court, through Justice Black, reversed:

> Apparently the District Court thought that in order to show a violation of § 7 it was essential for the Government to show a "relevant geographic market" in the same way the *corpus delicti* must be proved to establish a crime.

Justice Black then went on to say:

> The merger of Pabst and Blatz brought together two very large brewers competing against each other in 40 States. In 1957 these two companies had combined sales which accounted for 23.95% of the beer sales in Wisconsin, 11.32% of the sales in the three-state area of Wisconsin, Illinois, and Michigan, and 4.49% of the sales throughout the country. In accord with our prior cases, we hold that the evidence as to the probable effect of the merger on competition in Wisconsin, the three-state area, and in the entire country was sufficient to show a violation of § 7 in each and all of these three areas.

Read literally, Justice Black was condemning a merger which resulted in a post-merger combined market share of 4.49%!

In that same year, the Court decided *United States v. Von's Grocery Co.*, 384 U.S. 270 (1966), which condemned a merger between two supermarket chains which resulted in a combined post-merger share of the Los Angeles grocery market of 7.9%. *Pabst* and *Von's* were understood to erect an antitrust prohibition barring all but de minimis horizontal mergers.

---

3. After 1980: The Guidelines

Recall the discussion about measuring market power by concentration ratios and the Herfindahl-Hirschman Index in Chapter 9. Those measures, when combined with other factors such as the height of entry barriers, persistent price discrimination, and persistent supra-normal profits, provide an objective basis for determining the vigor of competition in terms of the number of firms in an industry. The HH Index was described as a measure of the number of firms and inequality among them stated in terms of market shares. So, if there were one firm in an industry, the

HH Index would be 1.0 or 10,000. As more firms exist in the industry, the Index declines, but as the inequality among them rises, the index rises; compare the cases under the HH Index in which four firms have equal market shares with the case in which one of the four firms has a 99% and the other three firms have the remainder.

COMMENTARY

Consult the current Horizontal Merger Guidelines in Appendix C, and consider the following questions.

1. Recall the debate over the policy objectives of the antitrust laws in Chapter 1, page 29, *infra*. Do the Guidelines state as their objectives both efficiency and distributional effects, such as wealth transfer from consumers to producers? *See* § 0.1.

2. How does evidence of price discrimination figure in the assessment of the legality of a merger under §§ 1.0 and 1.12?

3. Recall the discussion in Chapter 1, pages 10-12, *supra,* about the behavioral assumptions underlying the economic analysis of markets. As Judge Posner puts it:

> . . . [E]conomics is the science of rational choice in a world . . . in which resources are limited in relation to human wants. . . . The task of economics . . . is to explore the implications of assuming that is a rational maximizer of . . . ends. . . .

RICHARD A. POSNER, ECONOMIC ANALYSIS OF LAW 3 (4th ed. 1992). Since the focus of § 7 requires a prediction of an economic response to the hypothetical structural change, the behavioral premise is underscored. Does § 0.1 of the Guidelines fully adopt Judge Posner's statement?

4. Section 0.1 of the Horizontal Merger Guidelines of 1992 states: "Throughout the Guidelines, the analysis is focused on whether consumers or producers 'likely would' take certain actions, that is, whether the action is in the actor's economic interest."

5. How should the "likely would" standard of this section be modified in the light of recent economic analysis asserting that in corporate hierarchies, the individual decision-maker may act in his/her short-run interest rather than in the interest of the corporate entity? How would the strategic, bounded rationality of game theory, a branch of economic analysis that studies the interaction of rational individuals, be brought to bear on the "likely would"standard? *See* DONALD M. KREPS, GAME THEORY AND ECONOMIC MODELING 5 (1990). Nobel laurelate Herbert A. Simon urges a view of rational economic behavior that is linked to ". . . a procedural theory of rationality. . . ." He writes,

> The rational person . . . goes about making his or her decisions in a way that is procedurally reasonable in the light of the available knowledge and means of computation.
>
> * * *
>
> To move . . . to procedural rationality requires a major extension of the empirical foundations of economics. It is not enough to add theoretical postulates about the shape of the utility function, or about the way in which actors form expectations about the future, or about their attention or inattention to particular environmental variables. These are assumptions about matters of fact, and the whole ethos of science requires such assumptions to be supported by publicly repeatable observations that are obtained and analyzed objectively.

Herbert A. Simon, *Rationality in Psychology and Economics,* 59 J. BUSINESS 209 (1986).

6. Recall the discussion of market definition in Chapter 9, in which the cases differed as to which criteria should dominate the definition of a relevant market. *Cellophane* and *Brown Shoe* stressed cross-elasticity of demand, while *Philadelphia National Bank* and *Tampa Electric* emphasized that a geographic market is to be defined as the market area in which a seller operates, a position that looks to shipping and purchase patterns—an analysis that encompasses supply substitution and production flexibility. Do the Guidelines adopt both demand and supply substitution criteria in §§ 1.0, 1.31 & 1.321?

7. Note the standard in § 1.1 of an assumed "small but significant non-transitory price increase" to be applied in the determination of the substitution effect on buyers. Do the Guidelines apply a constant 5% price increase? Note also that under this provision the ". . . hypothetical monopolist will be assumed to pursue maximum profits in deciding whether to raise the price of any or all . . . products under its control." Given a hypothetical monopolist operating in several geographic markets, some in which there is less competition, others in which there is more, how would a rise of 4% in the former market affect the analysis?

8. How do the Guidelines identify participants in a relevant market and measure their significance under § 1.31? State how the Guidelines proceed from beginning with all currently producing or selling firms to include other participants? Does the output of a vertically integrated firm selling its entire output to its parent or subsidiary count? In *Aluminum Co. of America*, Judge Hand excluded scrap aluminum from the relevant aluminum market. Under this provision, do the Guidelines reject the Hand analysis and include firms that recycle or recondition? What is the significance of the distinction in footnote 14 to § 1.321 between product and process? How are "sunk costs" relevant to possible entry under § 1.322?

9. By what statistical data should market shares be measured under Guidelines § 1.41? Identify an industry described by footnote 15 to this section of the Guidelines. Does the last paragraph of § 1.41 codify the result in *General Dynamics*? Since § 7 is forward-looking, for what duration should a requirements contract be written in order for the supply to be considered "committed capacity"? Should the two year period applied for testing entry in § 3.2 be applied here? How should foreign competition be treated under this provision? Consider the discretion granted to the enforcement agencies under Guidelines § 1.521 to take account of changing circumstances in the determination of market shares. Would an enforcement agency take "judicial notice" of a statutory change such as the Telecommunication Act of 1996 and consider the telephone companies as likely entrants into the cable market? Do Guidelines §§ 1.52 & 1.522 permit adjustment of actual market share data?

10. When should adverse competitive effects warrant enforcement action against a horizontal merger under the Guidelines? *See* § 0.2. In § 1.5, the Guidelines rely on the HHI notation as the measure of post-merger concentration as well as the increase in concentration resulting from the merger. See § 1.5, footnote 18 for examples of the calculations. The general standards governing enforcement action are set out in § 1.5 and describe a three-tier decision tree. The first tier states a safe harbor in which no enforcement activity will occur when the post merger HHI is below 1000. The second tier is measured by a post-merger HHI ranging from 1000 to 1800. If, within this range, the increase in concentration as measured according to footnote 18, is 100 or less, no enforcement action will be contemplated. However, if the increase in concentration is more than 100, for mergers in this range, further review will be made, to consider the increase in the light of the potential for coordinated activity, entry conditions, efficiency considerations, and related factors set out in § 2. The third tier addresses mergers in which the post-merger concentration exceeds 1800, considered by the agencies to describe highly concentrated markets. Here an increase in the HHI of less than 50 is deemed to have no adverse competitive consequences. But if the increase in the HHI is 100 or greater, there is a presumption of adverse competitive effect, subject to being rebutted by a showing based on conditions of entry, enhanced efficiency, and other factors that the merger will be unlikely to create or enhance market power or facilitate its exercise. See Guidelines §§ 1.52, 1.521, and 1.522 for factors to be considered in assessing the significance of the numbers in determining enforcement action. (Consult the discussion of the HHI and other measures of market power in Chapter 9, above.)

The relationship, if any, between concentration measures and anticompetitive behavior is the topic of a long-running debate among economists. Judge Posner and Harold Demsetz argue that the link between high market shares by a firm or a few firms in a market and supra-competitive prices has not been empirically validated. In *United States v. Rockford Memorial Corp.*, 898 F.2d 1278 (7th Cir. 1990), a horizontal merger case, Judge Posner held that the government had made out a *prima facie* case of a violation of § 7 by showing that the merger would create a market share of around 66%, the *Alcoa* test of Judge Hand. Judge Posner precipitated a debate by his dictum that:

> It is regrettable that antitrust cases are decided on the basis of theoretical guesses as to what particular market-structure characteristics portend for competition.
>
> * * *
>
> This is a studiable hypothesis by modern methods of multivariate statistical analysis. . . . Unfortunately, this literature is at an early and inconclusive stage.

Id. at 1286.

Professor Demsetz had written in 1974 that: "[T]heoretical support of the market concentration doctrine . . . is weak or nonexistent. . . . [T]he policy-maker ought not suppose that conclusive evidence of the statistical relationship exists." Harold A. Demsetz, *Two Systems of Belief About Monopoly, in* INDUSTRIAL CONCENTRATION: THE NEW LEARNING 164, 174 (Harvey Goldschmid, H. Michael Mann & J. Fred Weston eds. 1974). Various commentators have differed as to the inferences to be drawn from concentration data in making the prediction required by § 7. *See* Samuel C. Thompson, Jr., *A Proposal for Antitrust Merger Enforcement Reform: Repudiating Judge Bork in Favor of Current Economic Learning,* 41 ANTITRUST BULL. 79, 111 (1996). Dean Thompson ratifies, but modifies, Nobel laureate Stigler's position that concentration data serve as presumptions in assessing mergers in violation of § 7. *See* George J. Stigler, *Mergers and Preventive Antitrust Policy,* 104 U. PA. L. REV. 176, 181 (1955) (mergers resulting in firms with market shares of 20% or more presumptively violate § 7).

Dean Thompson proposes an "effects test" of § 7 illegality which would subject to further scrutiny any merger resulting in a post-merger market with a four-firm concentration ratio of at least 50% or an HHI of at least 1250 (41 ANTITRUST BULL. at 190). This approach would give little, if any, weight to conditions of entry or to efficiency defenses. The rationale is:

> . . . [F]inance theory teaches that acquisitions should not be made unless they produce positive net present values, that is, economic rents. Thus, it can be expected that acquiring firms are on rent seeking missions. Any such rent seeking involving substantial firms in concentrated markets should be prohibited.

Thompson, *supra,* at 133. For further discussion of the economic literature on structure and concentration, see Chapter 9 on Monopoly and Monopolization.

Calculate the likelihood of enforcement action under these Guidelines if the facts of *Brown Shoe*, *Von's Grocery*, and *Philadelphia National Bank* arose in 1997. Would Dean Thompson's test produce different results than the Guidelines?

William Blumenthal points out that the enforcement agencies differ as to the evidentiary weight accorded to concentration numbers in determining adverse competitive consequences. He notes that the Antitrust Division accords no weight to higher concentration numbers, once the benchmarks are reached or exceeded. However, the Federal Trade Commission applies a sliding scale perspective, giving greater weight to the possibility of adverse competitive effect from higher numbers in the HHI. *See* William Blumenthal, *Thirty-One Merger Policy Questions Still Lingering After the 1992 Guidelines,* 38 ANTITRUST BULL. 593, 622-23 (1993).

11. See Guidelines § 2.1 for the factors to be considered in assessing the potential adverse competitive effects of a merger by leading to coordinated or collusive interaction detrimental to consumers. Consider the coordinated activity described in the following cases, assuming the facts to be the result of a merger: *Interstate Circuit, American Column & Lumber*, and *Sugar Institute.*

12. Note the factors of unilateral anticompetitive effects in § 2.2. Is the availability of near substitutes linked to the ability of the combined firm to raise prices and maintain them? Are advertising expenditures a factor in product differentiation? Would *Procter & Gamble* (page 576, *infra*) be accorded a negative factor on account of its strong brand for bleach? Would the savings in advertising costs be a positive factor under § 4 of the Guidelines? How should these two factors be balanced, if at all? Consider the discussion of differentiated products in § 2.21 and footnote 21. Is this discussion of grouping consumers a reference to the reliance in *Brown Shoe* of sub-markets?

Is the distinction made between coordinated action in §§ 2.1 and 2.11 and unilateral action an innovation of the Guidelines or is this a traditional Sherman Act distinction? What weight do the Guidelines § 2.12 give to the size and buying practices of buyers in a market in assessing the likelihood of effective price and output coordination post-merger? *See* Guidelines § 5.4, dealing with powerful buyers.

13. Consider the achievement of efficiency as justification for a merger under § 4 of the Guidelines. Who has the burden of proof of this justification under § 0.1, footnote 5? Where a merger poses the prospect of the creation or enhancement of market power, how does proof of some cost-saving offset market power? One commentator suggests that the enforcement agencies "limit significantly the ability of parties to justify the transaction on efficiency grounds," in cases in which there is enhanced market power. *See* Kevin J. Arquit, *Perspectives on the 1992 U.S. Government Horizontal Merger Guidelines*, 61 ANTITRUST L.J. 121, 135 (1992) (Arquit was the Director of the FTC's Bureau of Competition at the time of publication; a footnote contains the usual disclaimer that he is not speaking for the Commission). In order to prevail in establishing efficiencies, does the proponent have to show that the claimed efficiency would benefit consumers? Kevin Arquit suggests this by stating the Guidelines treatment of efficiencies are "consistent with precedent," citing *Federal Trade Commission v. University Health, Inc*, 938 F.2d 1206, 1223 (11th Cir. 1991) (page 601, *infra*), which states that the proponent of a merger asserting efficiencies ". . . must demonstrate significant economies . . . that . . . ultimately would benefit competition and hence, consumers."

Is there a statutory basis for including consumer welfare in the merger analysis? If Mr. Arquit's reference to consumers as the ultimate beneficiaries of efficiencies is interpreted as invoking the conception of consumer welfare, is he adopting Judge Bork's view of the goal of the antitrust laws, which is:

> Whether one looks at the texts of the antitrust statutes, the legislative intent behind them, or the requirements of proper judicial behavior, . . . the case is overwhelming for judicial adherence to the single goal of consumer welfare in the interpretation of the antitrust laws.

ROBERT H. BORK, THE ANTITRUST PARADOX 89 (1978). Bork uses the phrase, "consumer welfare" as equivalent to the combination of consumer and producer surplus.

If Mr. Arquit intends to use the phrase, "consumer welfare" as a requirement of merger clearance does he intend the phrase to mean the net of producer and consumer surplus? Would Judge Bork's definition require a merger proponent to show that the combined firm was capable of increased output? What would be probative of an alternative definition which considered only increases in consumer surplus as indicative of consumer welfare enhancement? *See* Gary L. Roberts & Steven C. Salop, *Efficiencies in Dynamic Merger Analysis,* 19 WORLD COMPETITION 5 (1996).

Note § 4 provides that enforcement agencies will reject efficiency arguments, if the savings can reasonably be achieved by other means. Does this require merger proponents to show at the outset that all other alternative means of lowering costs are unavailable or ineffective? Do the proponents have to make an offer of proof that a reduction in work force, cheaper sources of inputs, and other efficiencies can only be accomplished by a merger?

Does the analysis of efficiencies in the revised § 4 of the Guidelines take account of the recognized distinction between production efficiency, allocative efficiency, and innovation efficiency? Should these categories of efficiencies be included in merger analysis? Some commentators doubt they are applicable. *See* Alan A. Fisher & Robert H. Lande, *Efficiencies Considerations in Merger Enforcement*, 71 CAL. L. REV. 1580 (1983). Another point of view is that efficiency analysis is essential in mergers, but that a balance must be struck between efficiency gains and anticompetitive losses in each instance. *See* Oliver E. Williamson, *Economies as an Antitrust Defense: Efficiency, Consumer Welfare and Technological Progress,* 58 AM. ECON. REV. 18 (1968).

Given the predictive and necessarily speculative nature of the analysis and proof of efficiencies in a merger, a procedural remedy of a two-step clearance has been suggested. The nub of this proposal is that an initial request for clearance in a merger under 15 U.S.C. § 18a, in which efficiencies are a material factor in the claimed justification, be granted, as a conditional clearance, subject to becoming final on a post-merger presentation of proof of realization of the those claimed efficiencies. This proposal was made by Robert Pitofsky and others prior to his becoming chairman of the FTC in *Proposals for Revised United States Merger Enforcement in a Global Economy*, 81 GEO. L.J. 195, 218 (1992). *See also* F.M. Scherer, *R&D Cooperation and Competition, in* BROOKINGS PAPERS ON ECONOMIC ACTIVITY (MICROECONOMICS) (1990). This procedural change has recently been endorsed and refined by Joseph Brodley, who advocates narrowing the definition of efficiency concerns to exclude from submission in the first stage procedure for clearance, such factors as passing on cost savings to consumers, loss of employment, managerial economies, as well as economies in acquiring capital. Brodley would limit the definition of efficiencies in this context to economies associated with production and innovation—*i.e.*, scale and scope economies, plus efficiencies in research and development. The second stage requires a backward look at the merger within three to five years after its execution. How would the enterprise be managed during the second phase? Would separate records be kept? Would the enforcement agency make interim inspections or provide advisory guidance on some transactions? Would such a regime be likely to promote efficiency?

In this second stage, three basic criteria, each having its own limitations, would be applied. First, an enforcement agency would apply a survivorship test, a review of product improvement and of increase in market share. The theory of the survivor test is that where a merger has not enhanced market share, it should be taken as one element of no improvement in output. Contrariwise, a loss of market share would yield the conclusion that no efficiencies had been realized by the merger. The second criterion of Brodley's backward look is cost-saving. This test would measure the cost data of the merged firms against comparable data of other firms in that industry for a three to five year post-merger period. The third criteria, the stock market test, is considered as supplemental to the firsts two criteria. This test would look to the value of the stock relative to the subsequent behavior of the stock prices of comparable firms. This criterion would serve to refine the conclusion of the other two insofar as enhanced stock price might be attributable to higher earnings achieved by production and innovation efficiencies. In addition to this supplemental test, two confirming tests are proposed. One relies on engineering studies; the other employs statistical analysis. Engineering data of plant design and operation may offer proof of plant economies. The statistical test would employ multiple regression analysis to data of cost and productivity against such inputs as capacity, operations, and customer density. Analysis at the firm level could identify the effect of change in each input. Such data would permit comparison of the merged firm with industry cross-sectional studies.

Aside from the formidable statistical problems this approach requires are the equally difficult problems of assigning causality to change in any of these criteria. This recommendation does, however, serve to illuminate the difficult, if not speculative, nature of the prediction required by § 7 generally and to efficiencies in particular. *See* Joseph F. Brodley, *Proof of Efficiencies in Mergers and Joint Ventures*, 64 ANTITRUST L.J. 575 (1996). *See also* Gary J. Roberts & Steven C. Salop, *Efficiencies in Dynamic Merger Analysis,* 19 WORLD COMPETITON 5, 13-14 (1996). In this article, prepared while the senior author was Associate Director of the Bureau of Economics of the Federal Trade Commission, a sliding scale standard is proposed for judging the prospects of achieving efficiencies by a proposed merger. As they put it:

> This dynamic framework thus provides a method for evaluating efficiencies that . . . could make efficiencies dispositive in a larger number of cases. . . . Markets in which concentration and market shares are higher, market demand elasticity is lower, entry is more difficult, and anticompetitive effects are more likely, would require greater efficiency benefits to offset the higher likelihood of anticompetitive harm. Any expected short-run price increases would be balanced against longer-run consumer benefits from lower prices and enhanced competition.

What time period would be appropriate to judge the realization of cost-saving benefits?

14. Consider efficiency arguments under the Sherman Act and some early merger cases. In *Sylvania,* does the Court's conclusion of enhanced interbrand competition rest on the premise that the manufacturer can achieve efficiencies in distribution? Does the opinion in *Broadcast Music* take note of the reduction in transactions costs by centralizing licensing? Find the efficiency reference in *Northwest Wholesalers*. Contrast an earlier merger case in which the efficiency argument was rejected by the Court, *e.g., FTC v. Procter & Gamble*, 386 U.S. 568, 597 (1967) (concurring opinion). Do the Guidelines adopt the definition of potential competition in the cases that follow?

D. Potential Competition and Conglomerate Mergers and Acquisitions

1. The Judicial Origins of the Potential Competition Doctrine

As the amended § 7 was interpreted to restrict traditional horizontal and vertical mergers during the 1960s, corporate managers began to diversify by acquiring the stock and assets of companies which were neither competitors, suppliers, nor customers. These transactions came to be known as conglomerate or market extension mergers. The administrative and judicial responses to these mergers are set out below. Consider the introductory discussion of the motives for mergers on pages 551-53, *supra*. Note the reasons given for acquiring an unrelated enterprise in the cases that follow.

In *United States v. El Paso Natural Gas Co.*, 376 U.S. 651 (1964), and *United States v. Penn-Olin Chemical Co.*, 378 U.S. 158 (1964), the Court began to develop its "potential competition" doctrine. The *El Paso* case concerned the acquisition of Pacific Northwest Pipeline Corp. by El Paso, a supplier of natural gas. Prior to the acquisition, Pacific Northwest had unsuccessfully sought to supply gas to Southern California Edison Co., an industrial user which was dissatisfied with the "interruptible" service which it was then receiving from El Paso. As a result of Pacific Northwest's attempt to supply Southern California Edison, El Paso responded with a 25% price reduction to Southern California Edison and noninterruptible service. The Court viewed these events as indicating that Pacific Northwest's competitive presence was felt in the California market, even though it had not been successful in its attempts to sell to any California buyer. This was the beginning of the judicially developed potential competition doctrine.

In the *Penn-Olin* case, the Court was confronted with a joint venture between the Pennsalt Chemicals Corporation and the Olin Mathieson Chemical Corporation. These two companies formed a third company, Penn-Olin Chemical Co., in which they each owned 50% of the stock. Penn-Olin was formed to produce sodium chlorate in the southeastern part of the United States, a product used in the manufacture of paper. The district court concluded that the joint venture would be unlawful only if, absent the joint venture, both parents would independently have entered the sodium chlorate market in the southeastern United States. If both companies would have entered, then the joint venture replaced two new companies with one company, and competition would have been lessened. On review, the Supreme Court ruled that a proper evaluation of the lawfulness of the joint venture required consideration of the possibility that, in the absence of the joint venture, one company would have entered and the other would have exerted a competitive impact as a result of its potential for entering the market:

> Certainly the sole test would not be the probability that both companies would have entered the market. Nor would the consideration be limited to the probability that one entered alone. There still remained for consideration the fact that Penn-Olin eliminated the potential competition of the corporation that might have remained at the edge of the market continually threatening to enter. . . . Potential competition . . . as a substitute for . . . [actual competition] may restrain producers from overcharging those to whom they sell or underpaying those from whom they buy. . . .

Is the concept of potential competition implied by the use of the term, "competition," in § 7 of the Clayton Act? Could the prospect of entry by a geographically contiguous competitor be incorporated as well into the definition of a relevant market? How is that issue treated in the Merger Guidelines? For further application of the potential competition doctrine, see pages 575-76, *infra*.

---

2. Conglomerate Mergers

Conglomerate mergers and acquisitions involve companies which are neither in a competitive relationship nor a customer/supplier relationship with each other. The Court has dealt with one conglomerate acquisition which raised the issue of whether it would increase the probabilities of inducing reciprocal buying patterns. The remainder of the Court's conglomerate cases have involved market-extension mergers or acquisitions. A market extension acquisition takes place when a firm acquires a second firm in a related business or acquires a second firm in the same business, but in a different geographic market. Conglomerate mergers seem to have been something of a fad of the 1960s. An empirical study of mergers of that period concludes:

> Accounting and profitability studies show that many mergers and acquisitions were not efficient. . . . [M]any business decisions (including . . . the 1960s conglomerate merger trend) appear incorrect after the fact.

Paul A. Pautler & Robert P. O'Quinn, *Recent Empirical Evidence on Mergers and Acquisitions*, 38 Antitrust Bull. 741, 779 (1993).

a. Acquisitions Raising the Issue of Reciprocity

In *Federal Trade Commission v. Consolidated Foods Corp.*, 380 U.S. 592 (1965), Consolidated Foods Corp. operated food processing plants and a network of wholesale and retail grocery stores. In 1951, Consolidated acquired Gentry, Inc., a manufacturer of dehydrated onion and garlic. Gentry, Inc. and its principal rival, Basic Vegetable Products, Inc., accounted for 90% of the sales of dehydrated onion and garlic. The Commission ruled the acquisition unlawful because of the potential for reciprocal buying which it believed was generated by the acquisition. The Commission believed that food processors would be likely to skew their purchases of dehydrated onion and garlic towards Gentry (rather than Basic) in order to curry favor with Consolidated, since these food processors (who were purchasing dehydrated onion and garlic from Consolidated) wanted to sell their own processed food products to Consolidated's grocery stores. On review the Supreme Court upheld the Commission: ". . . where, as here, the acquisition is of a small company that commands a substantial share of a market, a finding of probability of reciprocal buying by the Commission whose expertise the Congress trusts, should be honored, if there is substantial evidence to support it."

Reciprocity as a basis for challenging conglomerate mergers enjoyed a brief tenure. An experienced enforcement official has described its defects and demise as follows:

> For a while it was fashionable to challenge conglomerate mergers under a theory which placed a combined firm in a strengthened position to engage in "reciprocity"—if you want to sell to my newly acquired Division A, you must buy raw material from my Division B. . . . It was almost immediately recognized that the theory raised exceptionally elusive issues of proof—would coercive pressure be applied and would the coerced firm be likely to cave in—and therefore was soon discarded as a viable enforcement approach.

Robert Pitofsky, *Proposals for Revised United States Merger Enforcement in a Global Economy,* 81 GEO. L.J. 195, 204, n.39 (1992).

b. Market Extension Acquisitions

A market extension acquisition occurs when a business firm acquires another firm performing the same or analogous functions as itself, but in another market not previously occupied by the acquiring firm. When the market in which the acquired firm is operating is geographically distinct, the acquisition is referred to as a geographic market extension acquisition. When the acquired firm is selling a different but related product from the one sold by the acquiring firm, the acquisition is referred to as a product market extension acquisition.

1. *Federal Trade Commission v. Procter & Gamble Co.*, 386 U.S. 568 (1967). The Federal Trade Commission attacked the acquisition by Procter & Gamble, a large manufacturer of soaps and detergents, of Clorox Chemical Co., a bleach manufacturer. When the case reached the Supreme Court, that Court upheld the Commission's condemnation of the acquisition on three grounds:

> (i) *Entrenchment*: The acquisition entrenched Clorox as the dominant bleach manufacturer, because Clorox would now have the immense resources of Procter & Gamble behind it. Also, Clorox could now get increased advertising exposure and at reduced costs. As an independent company, Clorox would have to pay standard television rates for advertising and as a single-product company would have to allocate the entire cost of a three-minute time slot to bleach. Because P&G was a multi-product company, it could present a Clorox ad together with P&G detergent ads in the same television time slots, thus reducing the cost allocated to bleach.
>
> (ii) *Perceived potential competition*: The acquisition eliminated P&G as a potential entrant into the bleach business, thus removing the constraint of its potential entry on bleach producers' pricing decisions. The concept here was one of "limit pricing." Clorox was the largest bleach producer. Purex was the next largest. The Court thought that Clorox and Purex may have been operating as oligopolists, maintaining supracompetitive prices for bleach. P&G, however, was a likely entrant into the bleach industry, because bleach is a complementary product to detergent and is marketed through the same distribution systems and to the same target consumers. The possibility that P&G might enter the bleach industry would have upset the Clorox/Purex oligopoly, forcing those producers to share their market with P&G. To discourage P&G from entering, Clorox and Purex would keep their prices just low enough to discourage P&G's entry. This is the concept generally known as "limit pricing." While their prices would continue to be above the competitive level, they would nonetheless be lower than they would in the absence of the possibility that P&G might enter. The acquisition of

Clorox by P&G then eliminated this moderating effect that P&G's potential entry exerted on the pricing of Clorox and Purex.

[Actually, this may have been a flawed analysis, because there were many small producers of bleach and entry into the bleach industry was easy. Clorox and Purex, therefore, should not have been viewed as oligopolists—Eds.]

(iii) *Actual potential competition*. If the acquisition were prohibited, then P&G might enter the bleach industry independently, either by building its own bleach plants (*de novo* entry) or by acquiring a small bleach producer and expanding (a toe-hold acquisition). Then the industry structure would change from two large companies (Clorox and Purex) to three large companies (Clorox, Purex and P&G), thus lowering the level of concentration in the industry.

2. *United States v. Falstaff Brewing Corp.*, 410 U.S. 526 (1973). Falstaff sold beer in 32 states, but not in the northeast. Because certain competitive advantages (principally national advertising and product prestige) are possessed by brewers selling their products over the entire nation, Falstaff had publicly expressed its determination to achieve "national" status. In 1965 Falstaff acquired the Narragansett Brewing Co., the largest seller of beer in New England which supplied 20% of the beer sold in that area. The government's suit under § 7 of the Clayton Act was unsuccessful in the district court.

The Supreme Court reversed and remanded to the district court for a finding as to whether Falstaff exerted a restraining influence upon existing firms in the New England beer market. Because it remanded the case, the Court declined to decide whether a merger could be condemned solely on the basis of a deconcentration analysis. Thus the Court left open the question:

> of whether § 7 bars a market-extension merger by a company whose entry into the market would have no influence whatsoever on the present state of competition in the market—that is, the entrant will not be a dominant force in the market and has no current influence in the marketplace. We leave for another day the question of the applicability of § 7 to a merger that will leave competition in the marketplace exactly as it was, neither hurt nor helped, and that is challengeable under § 7 only on grounds that the company could, but did not, enter *de novo* or through "toe-hold" acquisition and that there is less competition than there would have been had entry been in such a manner. . . .

A NOTE ON "LIMIT PRICING" AND "ENTRY BARRIERS"

Limit pricing is said to occur when an existing monopolist or group of oligopolists decide against pursuing the maximum short-run monopoly profit or oligopoly profits available so as not to encourage entry by outsiders. Rather, the existing monopolist or oligopolists decide to set price at a level higher than the competitive level, but low enough to discourage entry. By this strategy, the existing firms both preserve their monopoly or oligopoly for the long run and still extract some (lesser) degree of supracompetitive profits. *See, e.g.*, JOE S. BAIN, PRICE THEORY 213-218 (1952). Professor Bain explains limit pricing with reference to "entry barriers." Thus, according to Bain:

> . . . [T]he barrier to entry—or advantage which the monopolist enjoys over potential entrant firms—may be high enough that the monopolist can set a price sufficient to earn some supernormal profits without inducing other firms to enter, but low enough that if he were to set a higher price, sufficient to maximize industry profits, other firms would enter and share the market with him. When we recognize that much monopoly may be based on patent or resource control which confers a significant, but not indefinitely large, cost advantage on the monopolist, or may be based on a limited transport-cost advantage, as in the case of regional monopoly, we see that this sort of situation is quite conceivable. A monopoly might be protected by such a limited barrier to entry from the outset. Or it might arrive in this situation, after previously enjoying a complete barricade of entry, because of technological developments or other changes which reduced the effectiveness of its barriers to entry.

Thus, in the absence of entry barriers, any supracompetitive profits would attract entry. When outside firms are impeded from entering the industry by entry barriers, then the existing monopolist or oligopolists are enabled to raise price above the competitive level to some extent without attracting entry, because barriers are impeding entry. When prices (and profits) are raised to sufficiently high levels, however, entry becomes sufficiently attractive to outside firms to overcome the deterrent effect of the entry barriers. Under such an analysis, the level of the limit price is a function of the "height" of the entry barriers, is it not?

What does Professor Bain visualize as constituting "entry barriers"? Might Bain's entry barriers include such conditions as high initial capital investment for plant and equipment, lack of availability of patented technology, absence of managerial skill, lack of access to distribution channels, as well as cost advantages? Compare the following extract from Professor Harold Demsetz:

> The lack of a theoretical justification for identifying certain types of expenditures as "barriers to entry" is . . . glaring. . . . The costliness of producing commodities does, of course, limit the amounts that will be made available at particular prices; in this sense cost does create a "barrier" to production, but no pejorative interpretation can be given to such a "barrier to entry." Indeed, it would be wasteful to produce addi-

> tional units when the cost of doing so exceeds the value of these units to prospective purchasers. Cost, whether incurred to acquire labor or capital or to inform prospective buyers, sets proper limits on the production and marketing of commodities.
>
> What does it mean to say that advertising expenditures and capital outlays constitute barriers to entry? One meaning is that firms must make such expenditures if they are to produce and communicate about the commodities they hope to sell. Such expenditures are no more barriers than are expenditures on labor and material. A second meaning is that existing firms are more efficient in the employment of inputs than are firms not yet in the industry. If this is so, the existing firms deserve applause, not divestiture. A third meaning is that existing firms have an *undesirable* advantage in the use of these inputs. Since all firms can borrow in the capital markets and can purchase advertising campaigns, it is difficult to see wherein the unfair advantage lies. If large firms are better risks to lenders and, therefore, if they can borrow at lower rates (internally or externally) than can small or new firms, then this element of superiority for the large-scale, older firm is properly recognized by capital markets. Similarly, if buyers have more confidence in, and are more knowledgeable about, well-established products, then this also is a real efficiency not to be denied to firms that have invested in building substantial reputations. Nor should buyers who do not desire to bear the risk of consuming and the cost of searching for *possibly* equally good but less well-known alternatives be denied the advantage of trading with older, larger firms.

Harold Demsetz, *Two Systems of Belief About Monopoly*, *in* INDUSTRIAL CONCENTRATION: THE NEW LEARNING 164, 173 (Goldschmid, Mann & Weston eds. 1974). Is Demsetz complaining that the concept of "entry barriers" lacks a useful definition and that many alleged entry barriers are merely cost advantages possessed by existing firms? And that the use of the term "entry barriers" is really a way of referring to the relative efficiencies of existing firms over potential entrants? Does Bain agree that entry barriers describe cost advantages of existing firms over their potential rivals?

The definition of the phrase, "entry barrier," has been the subject of debate among economists; the opposing views have been summarized as follows:

> Among alternative definitions, the most prominent are those advanced by Stigler and Bain. Stigler defines an entry barrier as "a cost of producing (at some or every rate of output) which must be borne by a firm which seeks to enter an industry but is not borne by firms already in the industry." This definition is generally recognized to include such conditions as limited access to a necessary resource, tariffs, patents and licensing and other regulatory restrictions. Bain, by contrast, defines an entry barrier as the "extent to which, in the long run, established firms

> can elevate their selling prices above the minimal average costs of production and distribution . . . without inducing potential entrants to enter the industry."
>
> This definition is generally regarded as broader than Stigler's and includes such additional considerations as economies of scale, capital requirements, and product differentiation. Other definitions have been advanced by Ferguson and Demsetz. Ferguson defines entry barriers as "factors that make entry unprofitable while permitting established firms to set prices above marginal cost, and to persistently earn monopoly return." This definition includes economies of scale, but does not include capital requirements and product differentiation (unless they are a source of economies of scale).
>
> Demsetz disputes the Stigler, Bain, and Ferguson definitions because they "focus attention on different opportunities facing insiders and outsiders. This not only diverts attention from other types of barriers, but also hides the value judgments implicit in the barriers notion." Although not entirely explicit on the point, Demsetz apparently would define an entry barrier as any condition that "keeps some types of resources out of the . . . industry." This definition is potentially broader than those of the other commentators.

ABA ANTITRUST SECTION, MONOGRAPH NO. 12, HORIZONTAL MERGERS: LAW AND POLICY 211-13 (1986).

Do the Guidelines adopt a definition of entry barriers closer to that of Bain or of Stigler in § 3.0? Is the use of a "small but significant and nontransitory price" in §§ 1.11 & 1.21 consistent with the Bain definition? Explain.

---

3. Predicting Potential Competition and Market Extension

United States v. Marine Bancorporation, Inc.
418 U.S. 602 (1974)

Mr. Justice POWELL delivered the opinion of the Court.

The United States brought this civil antitrust action under § 7 of the Clayton Act . . . to challenge a proposed merger between two commercial banks. The acquiring bank is a large, nationally chartered bank based in Seattle, Washington, and the acquired bank is a medium-size, state-chartered bank located at the opposite end of the State in Spokane. The banks are not direct competitors to any significant degree in Spokane or any other part of the State. They have no banking offices in each other's home cities. The merger agreement would substitute the acquiring bank for the acquired bank in Spokane and would permit the former for the first time to operate as a direct participant in the Spokane market.

. . . .

After a full trial, the District Court held against the Government on all aspects of the case. We affirm that court's judgment. . . .

The acquiring bank, National Bank of Commerce (NBC), is a national banking association with its principal office in Seattle, Washington. Located in the northwest corner of the State, Seattle is the largest city in Washington. NBC is a wholly owned subsidiary of a registered bank holding company, Marine Bancorporation, Inc. (Marine), and in terms of assets, deposits, and loans is the second largest banking organization with headquarters in the State of Washington. At the end of 1971, NBC had total assets of $1.8 billion, total deposits of $1.6 billion, and total loans of $881.3 million. It operates 107 branch banking offices within the State, 59 of which are located in the Seattle metropolitan area and 31 of which are in lesser developed sections of eastern Washington. In order of population, the four major metropolitan areas in Washington are Seattle, Tacoma, Spokane, and Everett. NBC has no branch offices in the latter three areas.

The target bank, Washington Trust Bank (WTB), founded in 1902, is a state bank with headquarters in Spokane. Spokane is located in the extreme eastern part of the State, approximately 280 road miles from Seattle. It is the largest city in eastern Washington, with a population of 170,000 within the corporate limits and of approximately 200,000 in the overall metropolitan area. The city has a substantial commercial and industrial base. The surrounding region is sparsely populated and is devoted largely to agriculture, mining, and timber. Spokane serves as a trade center for this region. NBC, the acquiring bank, has had a longstanding interest in securing entry into Spokane.

WTB has seven branch offices, six in the city of Spokane and one in Opportunity, a Spokane suburb. WTB is the eighth largest banking organization with headquarters in Washington and the ninth largest banking organization in the State. At the end of 1971, it had assets of $112 million, total deposits of $95.6 million, and loans of $57.6 million. It controls 17.4% of the 46 commercial banking offices in the Spokane metropolitan area. . . .

. . . There are six banking organizations operating in the Spokane metropolitan area. One organization, Washington Bancshares, Inc., controls two separate banks and their respective branch offices. As of midyear 1972, this organization in the aggregate held 42.1% of total deposits in the area. Seattle-First National Bank, by comparison, held 31.6%. The target bank held 18.6% of total deposits at that time, placing it third in the Spokane area. . . . Thus, taken together, Washington Bancshares, Seattle-First National Bank, and WTB hold approximately 92% of total deposits in the Spokane area. . . .

The degree of concentration of the commercial banking business in Spokane may well reflect the severity of Washington's statutory restraints on *de novo* geographic expansion by banks. Although Washington permits branching, the restrictions placed on that method of internal growth are stringent. Subject to the approval of the state supervisor of banking, Washington banks with sufficient paid-in capital may open branches in the city or town in which their headquarters are located, the unincorporated areas of the county in which their headquarters are located, and incorporated communities which have no banking office. WASH. REV. CODE ANN. § 30.40.020 (Supp. 1973). But under state law, no state-chartered bank "shall establish or operate any branch . . . in any city or town outside the city or town in which its principal place of business is located in which any bank, trust company or national banking association regularly transacts a banking or trust business, except by taking over or acquiring an existing bank, trust company or national banking association. . . ." *Id.* Since federal law subjects nationally chartered banks to the branching limitations imposed on their state counterparts, national and state banks in Washington are restricted to mergers or acquisitions in order to expand into cities and towns with pre-existing banking organizations.

The ability to acquire existing banks is also limited by a provision of state law requiring that banks incorporating in Washington include in their articles of incorporation a clause forbidding a new bank from merging with or permitting its assets to be acquired by another bank for a period of at least 10 years, without the consent of the state supervisor of banking. WASH. REV. CODE ANN. § 30.08.020(7) (1961 and Supp. 1973). In addition, once a bank acquires or takes over one of the banks operating in a city or town other than the acquiring bank's principal place of business, it cannot branch from the acquired bank. WASH. REV. CODE ANN. § 30.40.020 (Supp. 1973). Thus, an acquiring bank that enters a new city or town containing banks other than the acquired bank is restricted to the number of bank offices obtained at the time of the acquisition. Moreover, multibank holding companies are prohibited in Washington. WASH. REV. CODE ANN. § 30.04.230 (Supp. 1973). Under state law, no corporation in Washington may own, hold, or control more than 25% of the capital stock of more than one bank. *Id.* . . . Accordingly, it is not possible in Washington to achieve the rough equivalent of free branching by aggregating a number of unit banks under a bank holding company.

. . . .

The District Court found that the relevant geographic market is the Spokane metropolitan area. . . . Prior to trial the Government stipulated that the Spokane area is a relevant geographic market in the instant case, and there is no dispute that it is the only banking market in which WTB is a significant participant. Nevertheless, the Government contends that the entire State is also an appropriate "section of the country" in this case. It is conceded that the State is not a banking market. But the Government asserts that the State is an economically differentiated region, because its boundaries delineate an area within which Washington banks are insulated from most forms of competition by out-of-state banking organizations. The Government further argues that this merger, and others it allegedly will trigger, may lead eventually to the domination of all banking in the State by a few large banks, facing each other in a network of local, oligopolistic banking markets. This assumed eventual statewide linkage of local markets, it is argued, will enhance statewide the possibility of parallel, standardized, anticompetitive behavior. This concern for the possible statewide consequences of geographic market extension mergers by commercial banks appears to be an important reason for the Government's recent efforts to block such mergers through an application of the potential-competition doctrine under § 7.

The Government's proposed reading of the "any section of the country" phrase of § 7 is at variance with this Court's § 7 cases, and we reject it. Without exception the Court has treated "section of the country" and "relevant geographic market" as identical, and it has defined the latter concept as the area in which the goods or services at issue are marketed to a significant degree by the acquired firm. *E.g., Philadelphia National Bank, supra*. . . . In cases in which the acquired firm markets its products or services on a local, regional, and national basis, the Court has acknowledged the existence of more than one relevant geographic market. But in no previous § 7 case has the Court determined the legality of a merger by measuring its effects on areas where the acquired firm is not a direct competitor. . . . We hold that in a potential-competition case like this one, the relevant geographic market or appropriate section of the country is the area in which the acquired firm is an actual, direct competitor.

Apart from the fact that the Government's statewide approach is not supported by the precedents, it is simply too speculative on this record. . . .

. . . Unequivocal proof that an acquiring firm actually would have entered *de novo* but for a merger is rarely available. Thus, as *Falstaff* indicates, the principal focus of the doctrine is on the likely effects of the premerger position of the acquiring firm on the fringe of the target market. In developing and applying the doctrine, the Court has recognized that a market extension merger may be unlawful if the target market is substantially concentrated, if the acquiring firm has the characteristics, capabilities, and economic incentive to render it a perceived potential *de novo* entrant, and if the acquiring firm's premerger presence on the fringe of the target market in fact tempered oligopolistic behavior on the part of existing participants in that market. . . . [T]he Court has interpreted § 7 as encompassing what is commonly known as the "wings effect"—the probability that the acquiring firm prompted premerger competitive effects within the target market by being perceived by the existing firms in that market as likely to enter *de novo*.

The Government's potential-competition argument in the instant case proceeds in five steps. First, it argues that the potential-competition doctrine applies with full force to commercial banks. Second, it submits that the Spokane commercial banking market is sufficiently concentrated to invoke that doctrine. Third, it urges us to resolve in its favor the question left open in *Falstaff*. [*See* page 577, *supra.*] Fourth, it contends that, without regard to the possibility of future deconcentration of the Spokane market, the challenged merger is illegal under established doctrine because it eliminates NBC as a perceived potential entrant. Finally, it asserts that the merger will eliminate WTB's potential for growth outside Spokane. . . .

Since *United States v. Philadelphia National Bank* . . . the Court has taken the view that, as a general rule, standard § 7 principles applicable to unregulated industries apply as well to mergers between commercial banks. . . . [W]e hold that geographic market extension mergers by commercial banks must pass muster under the potential-competition doctrine. We further hold, however, that the application of the doctrine to commercial banking must take into account the unique federal and state regulatory restraints on entry into that line of commerce. . . . The conceptual difficulty with the Government's approach . . . is that it fails to accord full weight to the extensive federal and state regulatory barriers to entry into commercial banking. This omission is of great importance, because ease of entry on the part of the acquiring firm is a central premise of the potential-competition doctrine.

. . . .

In *Philadelphia National Bank, supra*, the Court relied on regulatory barriers to entry to support its conclusion that mergers between banks in direct competition in the same market must be scrutinized with particular care under § 7. . . . But the same restrictions on new entry render it difficult to hold that a geographic market extension merger by a commercial bank is unlawful under the potential-competition doctrine. Such limitations often significantly reduce, if they do not eliminate, the likelihood that the acquiring bank is either a perceived potential *de novo* entrant or a source of future competitive benefits through *de novo* or foothold entry. . . .

. . . The potential-competition doctrine has meaning only as applied to concentrated markets. That is, the doctrine comes into play only where there are dominant participants in the target market engaging in interdependent or parallel behavior and with the capacity effectively to determine price and total output of goods or services. If the target market performs as a competitive market in traditional antitrust terms, the participants in the market will have no occasion to fashion their behavior to take into account the presence of a potential entrant. The present procompetitive effects that a perceived potential entrant may produce in an oligopolistic market will already have been accomplished if the target market is performing competitively. Likewise, there would be no need for concern about the prospects of long-term deconcentration of a market which is in fact genuinely competitive.

In an effort to establish that the Spokane commercial banking market is oligopolistic, the Government relied primarily on concentration ratios indicating that three banking organizations (including WTB) control approximately 92% of total deposits in Spokane. . . . We conclude that by introducing evidence of concentration ratios of the magnitude of those present here the Government established a prima facie case that the Spokane market was a candidate for the potential-competition doctrine. On this aspect of the case, the burden was then upon appellees to show that the concentration ratios, which can be unreliable indicators of actual market behavior, *see United States v. General Dynamics Corp.*, 415 U.S. 486 (1974), did not accurately depict the economic characteristics of the Spokane market. In our view, appellees did not carry this burden. . . .

We note that it is hardly surprising that the Spokane commercial banking market is structurally concentrated. As the Government's expert witness conceded, *all* banking markets in the country are likely to be concentrated. This is so because as a country we have made the policy judgment to restrict entry into commercial banking in order to promote bank safety. Thus, most banking markets in theory will be subject to the potential-competition doctrine. But the same factor that usually renders such markets concentrated and theoretical prospects for potential-competition § 7 cases—regulatory barriers to new entry—will also make it difficult to establish that the doctrine invalidates a particular geographic market extension merger.

. . . [R]esolution of the question reserved in *Falstaff,* was the primary basis on which the case was presented to the District Court and to us. . . . Two essential preconditions must exist before it is possible to resolve whether the Government's theory, if proved, establishes a violation of § 7. It must be determined: (i) that in fact NBC has available feasible means for entering the Spokane market other than by acquiring WTB; and (ii) that those means offer a substantial likelihood of ultimately producing deconcentration of that market or other significant procompetitive effects. . . .

It is undisputed that under state law NBC cannot establish *de novo* branches in Spokane and that its parent holding company cannot hold more than 25% of the stock of any other bank. Entry for NBC into Spokane therefore must be by acquisition of an existing bank. The Government contends that NBC has two distinct alternatives for acquisition of banks smaller than WTB and that either alternative would be likely to benefit the Spokane commercial banking market.

First, the Government contends that NBC could arrange for the formation of a new bank (a concept known as "sponsorship"), insure that the stock for such a new bank is placed in friendly hands, and then ultimately acquire that bank. Appellees respond that this approach would violate the spirit if not the letter of state-law restrictions on bank branching. . . . Although we note that the intricate procedure for entry by sponsorship espoused by the Government can scarcely be compared to the *de novo* entry opportunities available to unregulated enterprises such as beer producers, *see Falstaff, supra*, we will assume, *arguendo,* that NBC conceivably could succeed in sponsoring and then acquiring a new bank in Spokane at some indefinite time in the future. It does not follow from this assumption, however, that this method of entry would be reasonably likely to produce any significant procompetitive benefits in the Spokane commercial banking market. To the contrary, it appears likely that such a method of entry would not significantly affect that market.

State law would not allow NBC to branch from a sponsored bank after it was acquired. NBC's entry into Spokane therefore would be frozen at the level of its initial acquisition. Thus, if NBC were to enter Spokane by sponsoring and acquiring a small bank, it would be trapped into a position of operating a single branch office in a large metropolitan area with no reasonable likelihood of developing a significant share of that market. This assumed method of entry therefore would offer little realistic hope of ultimately producing deconcentration of the Spokane market. Moreover, it is unlikely that a single new bank in Spokane with a small market share, and forbidden to branch, would have any other significant procompetitive effect on that market. . . .

As a second alternative method of entry, the Government proposed that NBC could enter by a foothold acquisition of one of two small, state-chartered commercial banks that operate in the Spokane metropolitan area. . . . Granting the Government the benefit of the doubt that these two small banks were available merger partners for NBC, or were available at some not too distant time, it again does not follow that an acquisition of either would produce the long-term market-structure benefits predicted by the Government. Once NBC acquired either of these banks, it could not branch from the acquired bank. This limitation strongly suggests that NBC would not develop into a significant participant in the Spokane market. . . .

In sum, with regard to either of its proposed alternative methods of entry, the Government has offered an unpersuasive case on the first precondition of the question reserved in *Falstaff*—that feasible alternative methods of entry in fact existed. Putting these difficulties aside, the Government simply did not establish the second precondition. It failed to demonstrate that the alternative means offer a reasonable prospect of long-term structural improvement or other benefits in the target market. In fact, insofar as competitive benefits are concerned, the Government is in the anomalous position of opposing a geographic market extension merger that will introduce a third full-service banking organization to the Spokane market, where only two are now operating, in reliance on alternative means of entry that appear unlikely to have any significant procompetitive effect. Accordingly, we cannot hold for the Government on its principal potential-competition theory. Indeed, since the preconditions for that theory are not present, we do not reach it, and therefore we express no view on the appropriate resolution of the question reserved in *Falstaff*. . . .

The Government's failure to establish that NBC has alternative methods of entry that offer a reasonable likelihood of producing procompetitive effects is determinative of the fourth step of its argument. Rational commercial bankers in Spokane, it must be assumed, are aware of the regulatory barriers that render NBC an unlikely or an insignificant potential entrant except by merger with WTB. In light of those barriers, it is improbable that NBC exerts any meaningful procompetitive influence over Spokane banks by "standing in the wings."

. . . .

In the final step of its argument, the Government challenges the merger on the ground that it will eliminate the prospect that WTB may expand outside its base in Spokane and eventually develop into a direct competitor with large Washington banks in other areas of the State. The District Court found, however, that the Government had "failed to establish . . . that there is any reasonable probability that WTB will expand into other banking markets . . . ."

. . . .

The judgment is

Affirmed

COMMENTARY

1. In *Marine Bancorporation*, the court employed a "wings effect" analysis on the issue of perceived potential entry. That analysis, you recall, was derived from the Court's *El Paso* decision and was elaborated somewhat in its *Penn-Olin* and *Falstaff* opinions. In *Marine Bancorporation* the Court makes explicit what its earlier opinions had assumed—the wings effect analysis requires the following conditions: the relevant market itself be operating in a noncompetitive way; that market manifests oligopolistic interdependence in pricing and output decisions; and that the acquiring firm has the character and capability of being perceived as a *de novo* potential entrant. Does potential competition theory require that evidence of fairly concrete plans to enter the target market be submitted to a court or an enforcement agency? Is this the standard required by the Guidelines in §§ 3.0 and 3.3? Must the existing firms in that market perceive the acquiring firm as a potential entrant? Or would expert testimony be sufficient to establish that the acquiring firm had the "character and capability" of being objectively identified as a potential entrant? Does the entry analysis of § 4 of the current Horizontal Merger Guidelines supplant the analysis of these cases?

2. If the plaintiff must establish that the target market is oligopolistically structured, must it not first establish the existence of an economically meaningful target market? In the companion case of *United States v. Connecticut National Bank*, 418 U.S. 656 (1974), the Court, through Justice Powell, stated that in a § 7 market-extension case, the government bears the burden of producing evidence on the relevant geographic market as follows:

> The difficulty of the responsibility imposed on the District Court with regard to defining the geographic markets of the two banks is ameliorated by several considerations. First, the burden of producing evidence on this subject is on the Government. The Government repeatedly notes that it is not required to define the geographic market "by metes and bounds," citing *United States v. Pabst Brewing Co.* . . . To the extent that this means that such markets need not—indeed cannot—be defined with scientific precision, it is accurate. But it is nevertheless the Government's role to come forward with evidence delineating the rough approximation of localized banking markets mandated by *Philadelphia National Bank* . . . and *Phillipsburg National Bank*. . . .

Justice Powell also indicated that in the absence of other supporting evidence the government could not employ Standard Metropolitan Statistical Areas (*i.e.*, areas defined by the Office of Management and Budget to determine areas of economic and social integration) or political boundaries such as those of towns for defining relevant markets. Was the Court's position in *Connecticut Bank* as to the burden borne by the government on the relevant market issue consistent with its earlier *Pabst* position?

Do the market definition criteria of Guidelines §§ 1.11 and 1.21 adopt Justice Powell's approach?

In § 2.212, the Guidelines address "repositioning of product lines" as a means of bringing a near substitute into a market. How is the likelihood of repositioning to be determined? How is ease of entry defined by Guidelines § 3? What is "committed entry" and what are its criteria under the Guidelines entry analysis? Is the likelihood of entry assessed in response to a hypothetical, nontrivial, nontransitory price increase? Is this because the Guidelines relate the conditions of entry to the exercise of market power? The concept of "committed entry" is derived from the analysis of contestable markets noted in Chapter 1, pages 30-31. This theory posits industries in which the conditions of entry are virtually without cost or restriction so that no firm can exercise market power, free of the prospect that competition for that market will attract a competitor. *See* WILLIAM J. BAUMOL, JOHN C. PANZAR & ROBERT D. WILLIG, CONTESTABLE MARKETS AND THE THEORY OF INDUSTRY STRUCTURE, Ch. 1 (1982). The reliance on the theory of contestable market analysis in the entry provisions of the 1982 and 1992 Merger Guidelines is noted by Janusz Ordover and Robert D. Willig in *The 1982 Department of Justice Merger Guidelines: An Economic Assessment,* 71 CAL. L. REV. 535, 563 (1983). *See also* Janusz Ordover & Jonathan Baker, *Entry Analysis Under the 1992 Horizontal Merger Guidelines,* 61 ANTITRUST L.J. 139, 141 (1992). See the 1992 Guidelines §§ 1.32 and 3.0 *et seq.* The limited application of contestable market analysis to actual markets is noted by William G. Shepard, *Contestability vs. Competition,* 74 AM. ECON. REV. 572 (1984).

Assume that a firm that manufactures steel or aluminum mailboxes by a process of stamping, adapts its machinery to make hubcaps. Does that constitute uncommitted entry because it is a response on the supply side of the market (requiring little or no added capital investment)? Is a committed entrant by definition one that cannot quickly shift production to supply a near-substitute product? Characterize in terms of committed or uncommitted entry the decision of a soap and cosmetics manufacturer to add non-leaded hair dye to its trademarked line.

Recall the discussion of entry barriers, pages 578-79, *supra.* State the three part test of § 3 of committed entry. Does § 3.2 employ a sliding-scale definition of timeliness that is a function of sunk costs? Does application of this section of the Guidelines necessarily have an impact on the definition of a relevant market in § 1.1 in both product terms and in geographic terms? Suppose the merging firms produce identical manual transmissions for four-wheel drive passenger vehicles serving a national market, and suppose further a third, unrelated firm in another geographic region produces a transmission that is lighter in weight and more durable than the product of the merging firms. The third firm acquires a vacant factory in the market area of the merging firms and announces it willingness to sell its transmissions at the prevailing, pre-merger price. How is this event to be analyzed in assessing the merger of the two firms already in the same market? *See* Janusz A. Ordover & Jonathan B. Baker, *Entry Analysis Under the 1992 Horizontal Merger Guidelines*, 61 ANTITRUST L.J. 139 (1992). How does the three-part test determine whether that entry would "would deter or counteract" the anticompetitive effects of the merger?

4. The Failing Company Defense and Related Matters

Consider the failing company defense in the wider context of alternative governmental responses to the decline of a large firm or of an industry. Government bailout, high tariffs, direct subsidies, voluntary import quotas, and exemption from antitrust scrutiny have also been governmental policy regarding industrial decline. Recall the discussion in the *Appalachian Coals* (page 18) opinion of the significance of voluntary action in reviving competition in a distressed industry. None of these other responses, however, directly address the issue of inefficiency. Indeed, tariff and other means of protection may nurture inefficiency by shielding a domestic firm from foreign competition. The inquiry required by § 7 is primarily on a firm, rather than on an industry, and the economic distress is examined against competitive norms and prospects. In the materials that follow, consider the extent to which the cases and Guidelines address the issue of excess capacity and inefficient use of assets in these terms.

The failing company defense entered merger analysis as *dictum* in the Supreme Court opinion in *International Shoe Co. v. FTC*, 280 U.S. 291 (1930), but was initially considered as a formal defense in the Senate Committee Report concerning the amending of § 7 of the Clayton Act in 1950. *See* S. Rep. No. 81-1775, at 7 (1950). The *dictum* in the *International Shoe* opinion merely stated that the likelihood of failure might be considered in evaluating the consequences of a merger; there was no suggestion how that prospect should figure in merger analysis. The failing company defense was refined in Justice Douglas' opinion in *Citizen Publishing Co. v. United States*, 394 U.S. 131 (1969), which drew on that Senate Report.

What is the policy underlying the failing company defense? If the merger is disallowed and those assets and persons leave that market, the remaining firms have an increased share and there are fewer firms in the market by one—hence, more concentration. If the merger is allowed, there is one fewer firm in the market and the acquired firm is larger—also, increased concentration. In the cases that follow, consider how the policy of the failing company defense is articulated.

Citizen Publishing Company v. United States
394 U.S. 131 (1969)

[The government's complaint alleged violations of §§ 1 & 2 of the Sherman Act and § 7 of the Clayton Act. The government asserted that the latter provision was triggered as a result of the acquisition by one newspaper's shareholders of the stock of a rival newspaper corporation. The district court granted the government summary judgment on the § 1 count based on *per se* violations in the agreement, which is described below. The case went to trial on the remaining counts in which the Court found violations of both §§ 2 & 7.]

Mr. Justice Douglas delivered the opinion of the Court.

Tucson, Arizona, has only two daily newspapers of general circulation, the Star and the Citizen. . . . Prior to 1940 the two papers vigorously competed with each other. While their circulation was about equal, the Star sold 50% more advertising space than the Citizen and operated at a profit, while the Citizen sustained losses. . . .

In 1936 the stock of the Citizen was purchased by one Small and one Johnson for $100,000 and they invested an additional $25,000 of working capital. . . . It does not appear that Small and Johnson sought to sell the Citizen; nor was the Citizen about to go out of business. The owners did, however, negotiate a joint operating agreement between the two papers which was to run for 25 years from March 1940, a term that was extended in 1953 until 1990. By its terms the agreement may be canceled only by mutual consent of the parties.

The agreement provided that each paper should retain its own news and editorial department, as well as its corporate identity. It provided for the formation of Tucson Newspapers, Inc. (TNI), which was to be owned in equal shares by the Star and Citizen and which was to manage all departments of their business except the news and editorial units. The production and distribution equipment of each paper was transferred to TNI. The latter had five directors—two named by the Star, two by the Citizen, and the fifth chosen by the Citizen out of three named by the Star.

The purpose of the agreement was to end any business or commercial competition between the two papers and to that end three types of controls were imposed. First was *price fixing*. The newspapers were sold and distributed by the circulation department of TNI; commercial advertising placed in the papers was sold only by the advertising department of TNI; the subscription and advertising rates were set jointly. Second was *profit pooling*. All profits realized were pooled and distributed to the Star and the Citizen by TNI pursuant to an agreed ratio. Third was a *market control*. It was agreed that neither the Star nor the Citizen nor any of their stockholders, officers, and executives would engage in any other business in Pima County—the metropolitan area of Tucson—in conflict with the agreement. Thus competing publishing operations were foreclosed.

All commercial rivalry between the papers ceased. Combined profits before taxes rose from $27,531 in 1940 to $1,727,217 in 1964.

At the end of the trial the District Court found that the joint operating agreement in purpose and effect monopolized the only newspaper business in Tucson in violation of § 2 of the Sherman Act [and that] . . . in Pima County, the appropriate geographic market, the Citizen's acquisition of the Star stock had the effect of continuing in a more permanent form a substantial lessening of competition in daily newspaper publishing that is condemned by § 7.

The decree does not prevent all forms of joint operation. It requires, however, appellants to submit a plan for divestiture and re-establishment of the Star as an independent competitor and for modification of the joint operating agreement so as to eliminate the price-fixing, market control, and profit-pooling provisions. . . .

We affirm the judgment. . . .

The only real defense of appellants was the "failing company" defense—a judicially created doctrine. The facts tendered were excluded on the § 1 charge but were admitted on the § 2 charge as well as on the § 7 charge under the Clayton Act. So whether or not the District Court was correct in excluding the evidence under the § 1 charge, it is now before us; and a consideration of it makes plain that the requirements of the failing company doctrine were not met. That defense was before the Court in *International Shoe Co. v. FTC*, 280 U.S. 291, where § 7 of the Clayton Act was in issue. The evidence showed that the resources of one company were so depleted and the prospect of rehabilitation so remote that "it faced the grave probability of a business failure." . . . There was, moreover, "no other prospective purchaser." . . . It was in that setting that the Court held that the acquisition of that company by another did not substantially lessen competition within the meaning of § 7. . . .

In the present case the District Court found:

> "At the time Star Publishing and Citizen Publishing entered into the operating agreement, and at the time the agreement became effective, Citizen Publishing was not then on the verge of going out of business, nor was there a serious probability at that time that Citizen Publishing would terminate its business and liquidate its assets unless Star Publishing and Citizen Publishing entered into the operating agreement." . . .

The evidence sustains that finding. There is no indication that the owners of the Citizen were contemplating a liquidation. They never sought to sell the Citizen and there is no evidence that the joint operating agreement was the last straw at which the Citizen grasped. Indeed the Citizen continued to be a significant threat to the Star. How otherwise is one to explain the Star's willingness to enter into an agreement to share its profits with the Citizen? Would that be true if as now claimed the Citizen was on the brink of collapse?

The failing company doctrine plainly cannot be applied in a merger or in any other case unless it is established that the company that acquires the failing company or brings it under dominion is the only available purchaser. For if another person or group could be interested, a unit in the competitive system would be preserved and not lost to monopoly power. So even if we assume, *arguendo*, that in 1940 the then owners of the Citizen could not long keep the enterprise afloat, no effort was made to sell the Citizen; its properties and franchise were not put in the hands of a broker; and the record is silent on what the market, if any, for the Citizen might have been. . . .

Moreover, we know from the broad experience of the business community since 1930, the year when the *International Shoe* case was decided, that companies reorganized through receivership, or through Chapter X or Chapter XI of the Bankruptcy Act often emerged as strong competitive companies. The prospects of reorganization of the Citizen in 1940 would have had to be dim or nonexistent to make the failing company doctrine applicable to this case.

The burden of proving that the conditions of the failing company doctrine have been satisfied is on those who seek refuge under it. That burden has not been satisfied in this case.

We confine the failing company doctrine to its present narrow scope.

. . . .

Affirmed.

COMMENTARY

1. Was a joint venture present in *Citizen Publishing?* Did the decision affect the terms of the agreement between the parties?

2. What were the relevant dates for the court to employ in assessing the economic condition of the Star for purposes of applying the failing company doctrine? 1940, when the Citizen and Star first executed their operating agreement? 1953, when the operating agreement was extended from an original expiration date of

1965 to a new expiration date of 1990? or 1965, when the Citizen acquired ownership of the Star through the acquisition of Star stock by Arden Publishing Company? Does your answer depend upon whether you are considering the charges under § 1 or § 2 of the Sherman Act or § 7 of the Clayton Act? Are the combined before tax profits in 1964 dispositive? See Justice Harlan's concurring opinion in the *Citizen Publishing Co.* case, 394 U.S. at 140-43, where he states that the failing company exception was barred by the finding of the District Court that in 1964, the profits of the joint venture were $1.7 million. Accordingly, Justice Harlan would require the papers to make a ". . . conscientious effort to operate independently before they could properly contend that their operating agreement was a business necessity."

3. Justice Douglas and the majority viewing this transaction as of 1940, took the occasion to provide some criteria for lower courts to consider in applying the failing company exception under § 7. Consider the application of these criteria. Is the depletion of resources to be determined by the bankruptcy standard? What evidence is probative of a "grave possibility of a business failure"? How is a court to determine when the prospects of reorganization through receivership or bankruptcy are "dim or nonexistent"? Is the test of the majority essentially one of balancing loss of assets in that market and the resultant social harm against increased concentration—or are these criteria an unconditional requirement for application of the failing company exception under § 7?

4. Compare the majority's criteria with § 5 of the current Horizontal Merger Guidelines, entitled, "Failure and Exiting Assets." Have the Guidelines refined the solvency criterion of the majority in *Citizen Publishing* by substituting ". . . inability to meet financial obligations in the near future" for "facing grave probability of business failure"? Would a six month record of payables ten times in excess of assets and receivables be dispositive under the Guidelines? What evidence is relevant under the case criterion? Do the Guidelines add precision by focusing on eligible reorganizations under Chapter 11 to the exclusion of state and informal work-outs of insolvency? Under Guidelines § 5.1(2), a claimant company could only claim the defense by showing that "it would not be able to reorganize successfully under Chapter 11 of the Bankruptcy Act." A commentator suggests elimination of this criterion entirely from the Guidelines because it only indirectly addresses the ultimate § 7 issue—maintaining those assets in the market. Note that § 5.1(3) of the Guidelines requires an "unsuccessful good-faith effort to elicit alternative offers . . . that would keep its . . . assets in the relevant market." *See* Edward O. Correia, *Reexamining the Failing Company Defense*, 64 ANTITRUST L.J. 683, 691-93 (1996). Correia would redraft Guidelines § 5 as follows:

> A merger is not likely to create or enhance market power or facilitate its exercise if the following conditions are met: (1) the allegedly failing firm would be unable to meet its financial obligations in the near future; (2)

> it has made unsuccessful good-faith efforts to elicit reasonable alternative offers of acquisition of the failing firm that would both keep its tangible and intangible assets in the relevant market and pose a less severe danger to competition than does the proposed merger; and (3) absent the acquisition, there is a high probability that the assets of the failing firm would exit the relevant market. In assessing the significance of the risk that the assets will exit the relevant market, the Agency will consider the degree to which the merger, if allowed to proceed, is likely to enhance market power or to facilitate its exercise.

Correia, *supra,* at 701. What benefits can you attribute to this version?

5. Congress responded to the *Citizen Publishing* decision by enacting the Newspaper Preservation Act, Pub. L. 91-353, 84 Stat. 466, 15 U.S.C. §§ 1801 *et seq*. (1970), stating a Congressional declaration of policy: ". . . to preserve the publication of newspapers in any city where a joint operating arrangement has been heretofore entered into because of economic distress. . . ." This Act grants exemption from any antitrust law for any joint newspaper operating arrangement that has been cleared by the Attorney General of the United States. Section 1802(5) of this statute defines a "failing newspaper" as ". . . a newspaper publication which . . . is in probable danger of financial failure." Does this definition of a failing company offer an easier burden on the claimant than is required by the Guideline § 5.1? In *Michigan Citizens for an Independent Press v. Thornburg,* 868 F.2d 1285 (D.C. Cir. 1989), the court upheld a determination by the Attorney General where the claimant newspaper had suffered irreversable losses, but had not yet entered into a condition of financial stringency. Does shifting the determination from the judicial arena to the Attorney General invite political considerations to enter? Is the office of the Attorney General an appropriate forum for consideration of the loss of jobs and of a municipal tax base in the consideration of a proposed merger?

6. Note that Guidelines § 5.2 permits failing company analysis to apply to divisions within a corporation. Is this view of the corporation consistent with the usual treatment of the corporation as a single actor under the Sherman Act? Consider *Copperweld* on page 347.

7. The failing company defense rekindles the basic issue addressed in Chapter 1; the ultimate objective of the antitrust laws. There is recognition of hardship by courts, usually as *dicta*, in cases permitting a merger under the failing company defense. *Union Leader Corp. v. Newspapers of New England, Inc.*, 284 F.2d 582 (1st Cir. 1960). Some commentators urge express consideration of the hardship to shareholders, creditors, employees, and community. *See* Richard D. Friedman, *Untangling the Failing Company Doctrine*, 64 TEXAS L. REV. 1375, 1412 (1983); Wesley A. Conn, Jr., *Section 7 of the Clayton Act and the Pursuit of Economic 'Objectivity': Is There Any Role for Social and Political Values in Merger Policy?,*

60 NOTRE DAME L. REV. 273 (1985). One premise of this view is that the enforcement agencies rather than courts are better able to take these social policy considerations into account. In 1994, Senator Kennedy introduced S. 1668, 103rd Cong., 2d Sess., which was not enacted, as an amendment to § 7 which would require courts to take account of the impact of a merger on employees and the relevant communities. *See also* Note 5, above, for the treatment of these interests under the Newspaper Preservation Act.

8. Certain foreign antitrust laws do expressly consider wider social and political consequences of failing firms as exceptions to the full application of competitive norms. Spencer Waller cites the interpretation of EEC Treaty Article 85(3), which provides an exception to the prior parts of this Article by exempting certain coordinated conduct and anticompetitive agreements from the competitive norms stated in Article 85(1). The application of Art. 85(3) is conditioned, in part, on a finding by the Commission that such conduct or agreement contributes to "... promoting technical or economic progress" and "allows consumers a fair share of the resulting benefits." Waller recommends against transferring such concerns to our merger analysis. *See* Spencer Weber Waller, *A Comparative Look at Failing Firms and Failing Industries,* 64 ANTITRUST L.J. 703 (1996).

United States v. General Dynamics Corporation

415 U.S. 486 (1974)

Mr. Justice STEWART delivered the opinion of the Court.

On September 22, 1967, the Government commenced this suit in the United States District Court for the Northern District of Illinois, challenging as violative of § 7 of the Clayton Act . . . the acquisition of the stock of United Electric Coal Companies by Material Service Corp. and its successor, General Dynamics Corp. After . . . trial . . . the District Court issued an opinion and judgment finding no violation of the Clayton Act. . . .

At the time of the acquisition involved here, Material Service Corp. was a large midwest producer and supplier of building materials, concrete, limestone, and coal. All of its coal production was from deep-shaft mines operated by it or its affiliate, appellee Freeman Coal Mining Corp., and production from these operations amounted to 6.9 million tons of coal in 1959 and 8.4 million tons in 1967. In 1954, Material Service began to acquire the stock of United Electric Coal Companies. United Electric at all relevant times operated only strip or open-pit mines in Illinois and Kentucky; at the time of trial in 1970 a number of its mines had closed and its operations had been reduced to four mines in Illinois and none in Kentucky. In 1959, it produced 3.6 million tons of coal, and by 1967, it had increased this output to 5.7 million tons. Material Service's purchase of United Electric stock continued until 1959. At this point Material's holdings amounted to more than 34% of United Electric's outstanding shares and—all parties are now agreed on this point—Material had effective control of United Electric. . . .

Some months after this takeover, Material Service was itself acquired by the appellee General Dynamics Corp. . . . As a result of the purchase of Material Service, and through it, of Freeman and United Electric, General Dynamics became the Nation's fifth largest commercial coal producer. During the early 1960s General Dynamics increased its equity in United Electric by direct purchases of United Electric stock, and by 1966 it held or controlled 66.15% of United Electric's outstanding shares. . . . [After a successful tender offer in that year] United Electric . . . became a wholly owned subsidiary of General Dynamics.

The thrust of the Government's complaint was that the acquisition of United Electric by Material Service in 1959 violated § 7 of the Clayton Act because the takeover substantially lessened competition in the production and sale of coal in [the State of Illinois or the Eastern Interior Coal Province Sales Area, comprising Illinois, Indiana, and parts of Kentucky, Tennessee, Iowa, Minnesota, Wisconsin, and Missouri]. . . .

The Government sought to prove a violation of § 7 of the Clayton Act principally through statistics showing that within certain geographic markets the coal industry was concentrated among a small number of large producers; that this concentration was increasing; and that the acquisition of United Electric would materially enlarge the market share of the acquiring company and thereby contribute to the trend toward concentration.

The concentration of the coal market in Illinois and, alternatively, in the Eastern Interior Coal Province, was demonstrated by a table of the shares of the largest two, four, and 10 coal-producing firms in each of these areas for both 1957 and 1967 that revealed the following:

	Eastern Interior Coal Province		Illinois	
	1957	1967	1957	1967
Top 2 Firms	29.6	48.6	37.8	52.9
Top 4 Firms	43.0	62.9	54.5	75.2
Top 10 Firms	65.5	91.4	84.0	98.0

These statistics, the Government argued, showed not only that the coal industry was concentrated among a small number of leading producers, but that the trend had been toward increasing concentration. Furthermore, the undisputed fact that the number of coal-producing firms in Illinois decreased almost 73% during the period of 1957 to 1967 from 144 to 39 was claimed to be indicative of the same trend. The acquisition of United Electric by Material Service resulted in increased concentration of coal sales among the leading producers in the areas chosen by the Government, as shown by the following table:

	1959			1967		
	Share of top 2 but for merger	Share of top 2 given merger	Percent Increase	Share of top 2 but for merger	Share of top 2 given merger	Percent Increase
Province	33.1	37.9	14.5	45.0	48.6	8.0
Illinois	36.6	44.3	22.4	44.0	52.9	20.2

Finally, the Government's statistics indicated that the acquisition increased the share of the merged company in the Illinois and Eastern Interior Coal Province coal markets by significant degrees:

	Province		Illinois	
	Rank	Share (percent)	Rank	Share (percent)
1959				
Freeman	2	7.6	2	15.1
United Electric	6	4.8	5	8.1
Combined	2	12.4	1	23.2
	Province		Illinois	
	Rank	Share (percent)	Rank	Share (percent)
1967				
Freeman	5	6.5	2	12.9
United Electric	9	4.4	6	8.9
Combined	2	10.9	2	21.8

In prior decisions involving horizontal mergers between competitors, this Court has found *prima facie* violations of § 7 of the Clayton Act from aggregate statistics of the sort relied on by the United States in this case. . . .

While the statistical showing proffered by the Government in this case, the accuracy of which was not discredited by the District Court or contested by the appellees, would under this approach have sufficed to support a finding of "undue concentration" in the absence of other considerations, the question before us is whether the District Court was justified in finding that other pertinent factors affecting the coal industry and the business of the appellees mandated a conclusion that no substantial lessening of competition occurred or was threatened by the acquisition of United Electric. We are satisfied that the court's ultimate finding was not in error.

In *Brown Shoe v. United States* . . . we cautioned that statistics concerning market share and concentration, while of great significance, were not conclusive indicators of anticompetitive effects . . . .

. . . [T]he [district] court found that to an increasing degree, nearly all coal sold to utilities is transferred under long-term requirements contracts, under which coal producers promise to meet utilities' coal consumption requirements for a fixed period of time, and at predetermined prices. The court described the mutual benefits accruing to both producers and consumers of coal from such long-term contracts in the following terms:

> "This major investment (in electric utility equipment) can be jeopardized by a disruption in the supply of coal. Utilities are, therefore, concerned with assuring the supply of coal to such a plant over its life. In addition, utilities desire to establish in advance, as closely as possible, what fuel costs will be for the life of the plant. For these reasons, utilities typically arrange long-term contracts for all or at least a major portion of the total fuel requirements for the life of the plant. . . .
>
> "The long-term contractual commitments are not only required from the consumer's standpoint, but are also necessary from the viewpoint of the coal sup-

> plier. Such commitments may require the development of new mining capacity. . . . Coal producers have been reluctant to invest in new mining capacity in the absence of long-term contractual commitments for the major portion of the mine's capacity. Furthermore, such long-term contractual commitments are often required before financing for the development of new capacity can be obtained by the producer."

341 F. Supp. at 543 (footnote omitted). These developments in the patterns of coal distribution and consumption, the District Court found, have limited the amounts of coal immediately available for "spot" purchases on the open market, since "[t]he growing practice by coal producers of expanding mine capacity only to meet long-term contractual commitments and the gradual disappearance of the small truck mines has tended to limit the production capacity available for spot sales." *Ibid.*

Because of these fundamental changes in the structure of the market for coal, the District Court was justified in viewing the statistics relied on by the Government as insufficient to sustain its case. Evidence of past production does not, as a matter of logic, necessarily give a proper picture of a company's future ability to compete. In most situations, of course, the unstated assumption is that a company that has maintained a certain share of a market in the recent past will be in a position to do so in the immediate future. . . .

In the coal market, as analyzed by the District Court, however, statistical evidence of coal *production* was of considerably less significance. The bulk of the coal produced is delivered under long-term requirements contracts, and such sales thus do not represent the exercise of competitive power but rather the obligation to fulfill previously negotiated contracts at a previously fixed price. The focus of competition in a given time frame is not on the disposition of coal already produced but on the procurement of new long-term supply contracts. In this situation, a company's past ability to produce is of limited significance, since it is in a position to offer for sale neither its past production nor the bulk of the coal it is presently capable of producing, which is typically already committed under a long-term supply contract. A more significant indicator of a company's power effectively to compete with other companies lies in the state of a company's uncommitted reserves of recoverable coal. A company with relatively large supplies of coal which are not already under contract to a consumer will have a more important influence upon competition in the contemporaneous negotiation of supply contracts than a firm with small reserves, even though the latter may presently produce a greater tonnage of coal. In a market where the availability and price of coal are set by long-term contracts rather than immediate or short-term purchases and sales, reserves rather than past production are the best measure of a company's ability to compete.

The testimony and exhibits in the District Court revealed that United Electric's coal reserve prospects were "unpromising." . . . While United ranked fifth among Illinois coal producers in terms of annual production, it was 10th in reserve holdings, and controlled less than 1% of the reserves held by coal producers in Illinois, Indiana, and western Kentucky. . . . [T]he District Court found that of the 52,033,304 tons of currently minable reserves in Illinois, Indiana, and Kentucky controlled by United, only four million tons had not already been committed under long-term contracts. . . .

Viewed in terms of present and future reserve prospects—and thus in terms of probable future ability to compete—rather than in terms of past production, the District Court held that United Electric was a far less significant factor in the coal market than the Government contended or the production statistics seemed to indicate. While the company had been and remained a "highly profitable" and efficient producer of relatively large amounts of coal, its current and future power to compete for subsequent long-term contracts was severely limited by its scarce uncommitted resources. Irrespective of the company's size when viewed as a producer, its weakness as a competitor was properly analyzed by the District Court and fully substantiated that court's conclusion that its acquisition by Material Service would not "substantially . . . lessen competition" . . . .

. . . [T]he Government contends that reliance on depleted and committed resources is essentially a "failing company" defense which must meet the strict limits placed on that defense by this Court's decisions. . . . A company invoking the defense has the burden of showing that its "resources (were) so depleted and the prospect of rehabilitation so remote that it faced the grave probability of a business failure . . ." and further that it tried and failed to merge with a company other than the acquiring one. . . . [B]ut the District Court's conclusion was not, as the Government suggests, identical with or even analogous to . . . a finding [that United was a failing company]. The failing-company defense presupposes that the effect on competition and the "loss to [the company's] stockholders and injury to the communities where its plants were operated," . . . will be less if a company continues to exist even as a party to a merger than if it disappears entirely from the market. It is, in a sense, a "lesser of two evils" approach, in which the possible threat to competition resulting from an acquisition is deemed preferable to the adverse impact on competition and other losses if the company goes out of business. The appellees' demonstration of United's weak reserves position, however, proved an entirely different point. Rather than showing that United would have gone out of business but for the merger with Material Service, the finding of inadequate reserves went to the heart of the Government's statistical *prima facie* case based on production figures and substantiated the District Court's conclusion that United Electric, even if it remained in the market, did not have sufficient reserves to compete effectively for long-term contracts. The failing-company defense is simply inapposite to this finding and the failure of the appellees to meet the prerequisites of that doctrine did not detract from the validity of the court's analysis.

. . . The Government asserts that the paucity of United Electric's coal reserves could not have the significance perceived by the District Court, since all companies engaged in extracting minerals at some point deplete their reserves and then acquire new reserves or the new technology required to extract more minerals from their existing holdings. United Electric, the Government suggests, could at any point either purchase new strip reserves or acquire the expertise to recover currently held deep reserves.

But the District Court specifically found new strip reserves not to be available. . . .

Moreover, the hypothetical possibility that United Electric might in the future acquire the expertise to mine deep reserves proves nothing—or too much. As the Government pointed out in its brief and at oral argument, in recent years a number of companies with no prior experience in extracting coal have purchased coal reserves and entered the coal production business in order to diversify and complement their current operations. The mere possibility that United Electric, in common with all other companies with the inclination and the corporate treasury to do so, could some day expand into an essentially new line of business does not depreciate the validity of the conclusion that United Electric at the time of the trial did not have the power to compete on a significant scale for the procurement of future long-term contracts, nor does it vest in the production statistics relied on by the Government more significance than ascribed to them by the District Court.

. . . .

The judgment of the District Court is affirmed.

It is so ordered.

COMMENTARY

1. Did the government establish a *prima facie* case against the acquisition of United Electric by Material Service Corp. when it submitted the statistics set forth in the Court's opinion? What else besides these statistics would the government have to offer into evidence to avoid a directed verdict for the defendant at the end of its case? Do the Court's opinions in *Marine Bancorporation* and *Connecticut National Bank* provide assistance in answering these questions?

2. Why is not the "failing company" doctrine a version of the principle embodied in *General Dynamics*? Would not a "failing company" be an entity which would not survive in the marketplace? Is its competitive potential, therefore, insignificant? Why should the strict requirements set forth in *Citizen Publishing Co.* limit the applicability of the failing company doctrine when no comparable requirements limit the applicability of the *General Dynamics* type of defense?

3. In *Federal Trade Commission v. National Tea Co.,* 603 F.2d 694 (8th Cir. 1979), the district court had refused an FTC request temporarily to enjoin National Tea Company, a large grocery chain operating stores in the Minneapolis-St. Paul metropolitan area, from acquiring Applebaum's Food Markets, Inc., another grocery chain operating in the same area. In denying the injunction, the district court found that National would leave the Minneapolis-St. Paul market if the merger were enjoined. On appeal, held: affirmed: "[I]f National had experienced such serious marketing problems in the Minneapolis-St. Paul area that it was leaving the area, its present market share was an inaccurate reflection of its future competitive strength. . . . The prospective loss of National from the relevant market if the merger is enjoined is a relevant factor. . . ."

4. Does the *General Dynamics* opinion provide a more searching examination of the economic conditions that would affect a firm's ability to exercise market power than does the failing company doctrine? Might Guidelines §§ 2.1 & 2.12 dealing with the conditions of coordinated behavior be characterized as reflecting this mode of analysis? Since 1990, there have been a spate of lower court cases, most of which permitted a proposed merger, in which the proponents pointed out the presence of a large, strong, sophisticated buyer in the market. The argument of the proponents is based on the presence of monopsony and the doctrine of "countervailing power," made fashionable in the 1950s by John Kenneth Gailbraith, which states that the existence of large sophisticated buyers in a market will impede the coordinated conduct of oligopolists and tend to make a market competitive, despite its high concentration. This theory holds that a large buyer is able to approach the members of an oligopoly individually offering each its exclusive purchases in exchange for a price below that set by the coordinated action of the group, perhaps obtaining a secret rebate. In this way, the large buyer provides a group member an opportunity to surrender the quiet life of coordination for the prospect of increased profit. Alternatively, a large buyer may have the resources to enter upstream into the production of the product or to induce another to do so. In this way the large buyer becomes a factor in the merger analysis as a likely, timely entrant. Similarly, a large buyer may have a purchasing department that is able to analyze costs of its suppliers and thus can identify instances of supra-competitive prices.

Some merger cases have recognized this analysis and the label, "power-buyer" defense has been coined by the commentators to describe it. *See* Mary Lou Steptoe, *The Power-Buyer Defense in Merger Cases*, 61 ANTITRUST L.J. 493 (1990). *United States v. Syufy*, 903 F.2d 659 (9th Cir. 1990) (reproduced in Chapter 9, page 397), raised analogous issues in a context in which countervailing power came from sellers. In *Syufy,* the Justice Department proceeded against a motion picture exhibitor, who had acquired by mergers over a two-year period all of the first-run theatres in Las Vegas. The government's complaint alleged monpolization and attempted monopolization under § 2 and a substantial lessening of competition under § 7. Judge Kozinski's opinion affirmed the district court's dismissal of the complaint, noting that there were no barriers to entry into the theatre market and that competition for films had not been lessened. The significant market power of buyers was also noted by the court in *United States v. Country Lake Foods*, 754 F. Supp. 669 (D. Minn. 1990), a case which permitted a merger of fluid milk processors where the concentration of the buyers exceeded that of the post-merger suppliers. This reasoning also prevailed in *United States v. Baker Hughes*, 908 F.2d 981 (D.C. Cir. 1990), and in *FTC v. Donnelley & Sons,* 1990-2 Trade Cas. (CCH) ¶ 64,852 (D.C. Cir. 1990).

Both *Syufy* and *Baker Hughes* also raised the issue of interpreting the entry provisions of the Guidelines. In each of these cases, the resolution of the ultimate § 7 issue, the likely lessening of competition, depended on the court's assessment of the impact of likely entrants on the ability of the combined firm to raise price. Earlier, in *United States v. Waste Management Co.,* 743 F.2d 976 (2d Cir. 1984), the Second Circuit had interpreted the entry provisions of the 1982 Guidelines as according dispositive weight to a finding of easy entry. This finding would conclusively negate a finding of anticompetitive effect of a merger. As the *Waste Management* opinion put it:

> . . . [T]he *Merger Guidelines* issued by the government itself not only recognize the economic principle that ease of entry is relevant to appraising the impact upon competition of a merger but also state that it may override all other factors.

743 F.2d at 982. Does § 3.0 of the 1992 Guidelines codify the *Waste Management* holding by stating that a finding that entry is timely, likely, and sufficient, would require a finding of no likely lessening of competition? The *Syufy* and *Baker Hughes* opinions show the difficulty of defining and applying the concept of "committed entry" under the Guidelines. In *Baker Hughes*, the government had unsuccessfully sought to enjoin the merger of two firms producing custom-made

hydraulic underground drilling equipment, arguing that the merger would result in a significant increase in concentration. In denying the injunction, the district court noted, among other factors, that while entry into this rather small, albeit growing market was costly, there were several foreign "edge" firms which might be induced to enter by the exercise of "buyer power." As the trial court found:

> It appears likely to the Court that if . . . [the merger is executed], one or two of these . . . [edge] companies will enter successfully sometime in the future, because major United States customers, who are quite sophisticated and financially strong, will insist on receiving alternative bids.

United States v. *Baker Hughes, Inc.,* 731 F. Supp. 3, 11 (D.D.C. 1990). The district court assumed, without so stating, that the existing firms were committed entrants, having noted earlier that "a considerable commitment of time and capital" was necessary for entry. The appellate court found adequate evidence to support the finding of ease of entry and affirmed without any discussion of committed entry conditions. 908 F.2d 981, 987 (D.C. Cir. 1991).

In *Syufy*, the government argued in the Ninth Circuit that the defendant, to prevail, needed to establish easy entry. In this context, would this not mean "committed entry," as used in the Guidelines? For only committed entry would be relevant to meet the capital investment of the combined firms. The opinion cites the government's argument:

> . . . [E]ntry must hold some reasonable prospect of profitability for the entrant. . . . You have to compete effectively in this market. And witness[es] . . . testified that you would need to build anywhere from 12 to 24 theaters. . . . *And then you would find yourself in a bidding war against Syufy.*

United States v. Syufy Enterprises, 903 F.2d 659, 667-68 (9th Cir. 1990). *See* Jonathan B. Baker, *The Problem with* Baker Hughes *and* Syufy*: On the Role of Entry in Merger Analysis,* 65 ANTITRUST L.J. 353 (1997). However, the court of appeals declined to consider the committed entry argument, noting that absent proof by a plaintiff of structural barriers to entry, ease of entry is presumed and considerations of the entrant's profitability were dismissed as speculative and irrelevant. *Syufy,* 903 F.2d at 667, n.13.

Consider drafting a memorandum describing the burden of proof of a defendant establishing ease of entry in the Ninth Circuit.

Like *Baker Hughes,* the pro-competitive effect of large-volume buyers trading with large producers has also been recognized under § 1 of the Sherman Act. In *Balmoral Cinema v. Allied Artists Pictures Corp*., 885 F.2d 313 (6th Cir. 1989), the court affirmed rule of reason analysis of an alleged group boycott, reasoning that the aggregation of local motion picture exhibitors was not actionable by the excluded exhibitor, because,

> Exhibitors, as purchasers of films, may be justified in combating the market power of film suppliers by group action. Such action may lower

> prices to moviegoers at the box office and may serve rather than undermine consumer welfare.

Id. at 316-17.

Review the material on the economics of vertical integration in Chapter 5, suggesting that vertical arrangements may in some circumstances induce collusion. In writing about the *Syufy* case, Herbert Hovenkamp suggests this possibility as follows:

> If the distributor enters into the exhibiting market itself, or encourages other independent theaters to do so, the exhibition market will become competitive, and the exhibitor will lose its monopoly profits. But if the two firms maintain the exhibition monopoly and share in the proceeds, both firms will retain a portion of the monopoly profits.

Herbert Hovenkamp, *Mergers and Buyers*, 77 VA. L. REV. 1369, 1377 (1991). The exercise of market power by buyers is also an element of analysis under §1 tying analysis and under § 2 attempt and monopolizing cases. For a review of these cases, see ROGER D. BLAIR & JEFFREY L. HARRISON, MONOPSONY (1993).

Federal Trade Commission v. University Health, Inc.

938 F.2d 1206 (11th Cir. 1991)

[In this case, the FTC challenged a proposed acquisition by University Health, Inc. (UHI), University Health Services, Inc. (UHS), and University Health Resources, Inc. (UHR) (collectively, University). UHS operated University Hospital, a nonprofit facility that it leased from the Richmond County (Georgia) Hospital Authority. University planned to acquire the assets of St. Joseph Hospital, Augusta, Georgia, Inc. (St. Joseph), a nonprofit entity owned by the Health Care Corporation of Sisters of St. Joseph of Carondelet (HCC), a Missouri nonprofit corporation run by the Roman Catholic Church. The district court denied the FTC's request for a preliminary injunction. The Court of Appeals reversed. Part of the Court of Appeals opinion addressed the issue of whether efficiency is a legitimate defense to an antitrust challenge to the acquisition. That part of the opinion is set forth below.]

b.

The appellees argue that the proposed acquisition would generate significant efficiencies and, therefore, would not substantially lessen competition. The FTC responds that the law recognizes no such efficiency defense in any form. We conclude that in certain circumstances, a defendant may rebut the government's *prima facie* case with evidence showing that the intended merger would create significant efficiencies in the relevant market. Here, however, the appellees have failed to introduce sufficient evidence to demonstrate that their transaction would yield any efficiencies, and the district court's factual finding to the contrary is clearly erroneous. Accordingly, the appellees may not rely on an efficiency defense.

The Supreme Court stated in *FTC v. Procter & Gamble Co.*, 386 U.S. 568 (1967) (*Clorox*), that "[p]ossible economies cannot be used as a defense to illegality" in section 7 merger cases. *Id.* at 579; *see also Philadelphia Nat'l Bank*, 374 U.S. at 371 ("We are clear

. . . that a merger the effect of which 'may be substantially to lessen competition' is not saved because, on some ultimate reckoning of social or economic debits and credits, it may be deemed beneficial."); *Brown Shoe Co. v. United States*, 370 U.S. 294, 344 (1962). Courts and scholars have debated the meaning of this precedent. Some argue that the Court completely rejected the use of efficiency evidence by defendants in section 7 cases. *See RSR Corp. v. FTC*, 602 F.2d 1317, 1325 (9th Cir.1979) ("RSR argues that the merger can be justified because it allows greater efficiency of operation. This argument has been rejected repeatedly."), *cert. denied*, 445 U.S. 927 (1980); Fisher & Lande, *Efficiency Considerations in Merger Enforcement*, 71 CAL. L. REV. 1580, 1595 (1983). Others posit that the Court merely rejected the use of insufficient or speculative evidence to demonstrate efficiencies; a limited efficiency defense to the government's *prima facie* case, they argue, remains available. *See* P. Areeda & D. Turner, *supra* p. 22, ¶ 941b, at 154 ("To reject an economies defense based on mere possibilities does not mean that one should reject such a defense based on more convincing proof."); Murris, *The Efficiency Defense Under Section 7 of the Clayton Act*, 30 CASE W. RES. L. REV. 381, 412-13 (1980).

It is clear that whether an acquisition would yield significant efficiencies in the relevant market is an important consideration in predicting whether the acquisition would substantially lessen competition.[29] Market share statistics, which the government uses to make out a *prima facie* case under section 7, are not an end in themselves; rather, they are used to estimate the effect an intended transaction would have on competition. Thus, evidence that a proposed acquisition would create significant efficiencies benefitting consumers is useful in evaluating the ultimate issue—the acquisition's overall effect on competition. We think, therefore, that an efficiency defense to the government's *prima facie* case in section 7 challenges is appropriate in certain circumstances.[30]

---

[29] Of course, once it is determined that a merger *would* substantially lessen competition, expected economies, however great, will not insulate the merger from a section 7 challenge. *See Clorox*, 386 U.S. at 579 ("Congress was aware [when it enacted section 7] that some mergers which lessen competition may also result in economies but it struck the balance in favor of protecting competition."); *Philadelphia Nat'l Bank*, 374 U.S. at 371 ("Congress determined to preserve our traditionally competitive economy. It therefore proscribed anticompetitive mergers, the benign and the malignant alike, fully aware, we must assume, that some price might have to be paid.").

[30] It is unnecessary for us to define the parameters of this defense now; as we explain *infra*, the appellees failed to demonstrate that the proposed acquisition would generate significant efficiencies. We note, however, that it may further the goals of antitrust law to limit the availability of an efficiency defense, even when a defendant can demonstrate that its proposed acquisition would produce significant efficiencies. For example, it might be proper to require proof that the efficiencies to be gained by the acquisition cannot be secured by means that inflict less damage to competition, such as internal expansion or merger with smaller firms. For various suggestions on the proper scope of an efficiency defense, see Murris, *supra* p. 26, 426-31 (advocating absolute efficiency defense); P. AREEDA & D. TURNER, *supra* p. 1221, ¶¶ 939-62 (advocating partial defense limited to types of efficiencies); L. SULLIVAN, HANDBOOK OF THE LAW OF ANTITRUST § 204, at 631 (1977) (advocating partial defense limited only by evidentiary standard); Rogers, *The Limited Case for an Efficiency Defense in Horizontal Mergers*, 58 TUL. L. REV. 503, 521-25, 528 (1983) (advocating partial defense for merger between two small firms in market dominated by large firms). Some scholars advocate placing the efficiency issue before enforcement agencies rather than courts. *See, e.g.*, Williamson, *Economies as an Antitrust Defense Revisited*, 125 U. PA. L. REV. 699, 729-31 (1977) (proposing that the Justice Department and the FTC consider efficiencies but not the courts). Others have suggested that enforcement agencies simply take efficiencies into account by increasing the level of market concentration at which a merger is challenged, rather than engaging in case-by-case weighing of efficiencies. Fisher & Lande, *supra* p. 1222, at 1670-77; R. BORK, THE ANTITRUST PARADOX: A POLICY AT WAR WITH ITSELF 129 (1978); R. POSNER, ANTITRUST LAW: AN ECONOMIC PERSPECTIVE 112-13 (1976).

We recognize, however, that it is difficult to measure the efficiencies a proposed transaction would yield and the extent to which these efficiencies would be passed on to consumers. *See* R. Bork, *supra* note 30, at 127; R. Posner, *supra* note 30, at 112 ("The measurement of efficiency . . . [is] an intractable subject for litigation."); Fisher & Lande, *supra* p. 26, 1670-77; *see also* U.S. Dep't of Justice, Merger Guidelines § V.A., 4 Trade Reg. Rep. (CCH) ¶ 13,102, at 20,542 (1982) (claims about expected efficiency gains are "easier to allege than to prove"); *cf.* L. Sullivan, *supra* note 30, § 204, at 631. Moreover, it is difficult to calculate the anticompetitive costs of an acquisition against which to compare the gains realized through greater efficiency; such a comparison is necessary, though, to evaluate the acquisition's total competitive effect. Because of these difficulties, we hold that a defendant who seeks to overcome a presumption that a proposed acquisition would substantially lessen competition must demonstrate that the intended acquisition would result in significant economies and that these economies ultimately would benefit competition and, hence, consumers.[31] As Justice Harlan, concurring in *Clorox*, explained: "Economies cannot be premised solely on dollar figures, lest accounting controversies dominate § 7 proceedings. Economies employed in defense of a merger must be shown in what economists label 'real' terms." 386 U.S. at 604. To hold otherwise would permit a defendant to overcome a presumption of illegality based solely on speculative, self-serving assertions.

The appellees here have not presented sufficient evidence to support their claim that the intended acquisition would generate efficiencies benefitting consumers. The district court, in finding that the proposed acquisition would result in a "number of efficiencies," admitted that its finding was based on the appellees' "speculation." The appellees simply concluded that the intended acquisition would reduce "unnecessary duplication" between University Hospital and St. Joseph; they then approximated, in dollars, the savings these efficiencies would produce. They did not specifically explain, however, how these efficiencies would be created and maintained. In the end, the court conceded that "no one can tell at this point what all of [the efficiencies] are or are not." Clearly, the district court's conclusion is not well grounded *in fact*; while the proposed acquisition *may* produce significant economies, the appellees simply failed to demonstrate this.[32] Therefore, although we hold that an efficiency defense (the scope of which we do not discuss here, *see supra* note 30) may be used in certain cases to rebut the government's prima facie showing in a section 7 challenge, the appellees may not rely on this defense because they failed to demonstrate that their proposed acquisition would yield significant economies.

[See Chapter 19 for further treatment of hospital mergers under separate health industry Guidelines.]

---

[31] The Department of Justice and the FTC, in deciding whether to challenge a merger, require the same threshold showing. *See* Merger Guidelines, . . . § 3.5, ¶ 13,103, at 20,564.

[32] Nor did the appellees compare the benefits they expect to realize from the alleged efficiencies with the costs the intended acquisition may exact on competition. It is difficult, then, to conclude with any reliability that the acquisition ultimately would aid, rather than hinder, competition and consumers.

E. Non-Horizontal Mergers

Antitrust scrutiny of vertical mergers by the enforcement agencies has been more limited than that of horizontal mergers. The enforcement agencies consider the lessening of competition that may result from purely vertical mergers to remain governed by the analysis of the Vertical Guidelines of 1985. *See* Wayne D. Collins & James R. Loftis III, ABA Antitrust Section Monograph No. 14, *Non-Horizontal Mergers: Law and Policy* 38 (1988). The 1972 Supreme Court decision in *Ford Motor Co. v. United States*, 405 U.S. 562 (1972), applied the analysis of vertical mergers which the Court had begun in the *DuPont* and the *Brown Shoe* cases, which were set out at pages 558-61, *supra*. Since this decision, merger enforcement has embraced the objective of enhancing economic efficiency of firms and markets. The Guidelines not only shifted the emphasis away from reliance on structural features of markets, but stressed efficient performance of firms by examining the ability of the combined firm to raise price and to impede entry.

In 1961, the Justice Department brought an action under § 7 seeking divestitute by the Ford Motor Company of its asset acquisition of Autolite, a manufacturer of automobile spark plugs and batteries. The district court held that the acquisition violated § 7 with regard to automotive spark plugs on two grounds. First, Ford was a major customer of the acquired firm in a concentrated oligopoly market. Given that Ford's purchases accounted for 10% of the national output of spark plugs, the court reasoned that Ford exercised bargaining leverage on the pricing practices of the independent companies in the spark plug market. The second ground of the district court's decision rested on the foreclosure principle as stated in *Brown Shoe.* The district court, noting that the total output of the Autolite plant would satisfy all of Ford's (10%) national demand for spark plugs, referred to this foreclosure as a "blatant Clayton Act violation according to the teaching of *Brown Shoe*" and ordered divestiture of all acquired assets. *United States v. Ford Motor Co.*, 286 F. Supp. 407, 441 (E.D. Mich. 1968).

The Supreme Court affirmed the district court in *Ford Motor Co. v. United States*, 405 U.S. 562 (1974), on the rationale of *Brown Shoe.* Like *Brown Shoe,* the Supreme Court expressed a concern for competitors, particularly small firms. Justice Douglas, referring to the "letter and the spirit" of § 7 in the majority opinion, cited the statement of a sponsor of the 1950 amendment to § 7, in the hearings, "[W]e must see to it that that the basic materials and resources . . . are available to any little fellow . . . ." 405 U.S. at 569, n.5. Moreover, the opinion overall takes a mechanistic, formulary approach to interpreting § 7. The decision was based on such factors as: the percentage of commerce involved and foreclosed, the increase in concentration, the likely effect on entry barriers, and the existence of a trend toward concentration. Some lower courts accepted such an interpretation of § 7, *e.g.*, *Mississippi River Corp. v. FTC,* 454 F.2d 1083 (8th Cir. 1972) (probable vertical foreclosure in excess of the 1.5% in *Brown Shoe*)*; Ash Grove Cement Co. v. FTC,* 577 F.2d 1368 (9th Cir. 1978) (FTC study of trend toward vertical mergers sufficient for a finding of violation of § 7). However, some lower courts have rejected the mechanistic emphasis on foreclosure numbers, as well as the interpretation of § 7 as a protector of small competitors. *See Fruehauf Corp. v. FTC,* 603 F.2d 345 (2d Cir. 1979) (no evidence to support findings of foreclosure based entirely on percentages).

F. Current Merger Law

In the 1980s, relatively few cases were brought. The enforcement agencies espoused the view that enterprise managers were rational economic actors seeking efficiency gains. From this perspective, mergers were presumptively efficiency-enhancing transactions, which required little, if any, antitrust scrutiny. In the 1990s, the enforcement agencies have undertaken to fine-tune enforcement by utilizing the clearance procedure to identify the anticompetitive elements in a proposed merger. The basic premise of the 1980s was not rejected. Increased concentration as such, is not considered dispositive. And the significance of fostering efficiency gains is recognized. The current policy appears to be to permit the merger if efficiency gains are shown and the anticompetitive factors are eliminated by the consent of the proponents. In this process, the Guidelines have become the substantive framework for negotiations between the enforcement agencies and merger proponents.

In a 1996 Report of the Antitrust Division, the agency characterizes the present volume of mergers as "... a record-breaking merger wave." The Report notes that in fiscal year 1995, there were 8,956 mergers, of which 2,816 were formally reported to the Department, a marked increase over fiscal year 1993, when only 1,846 mergers were reported to the Department. The Report states the Department's merger policy as follows:

> ... [T]oday's mergers have been described as *strategic* mergers—in which one company buys another in the same or in a related industry. These strategic mergers may promote significant efficiencies that should be taken into account in enforcement decisions, but they also require close scrutiny to ensure that the parties do not foreclose entry to other competitors and lessen competition.
>
> * * *
>
> At the same time, the Division recognizes that the vast majority of mergers are competitively neutral, or even beneficial, for competition and consumers.

DOJ, Antitrust Divison, Opening Markets and Protecting Competition for America's Businesses and Consumers (1996). This stated policy objective is a continuation of the policy expressed by Deputy Assistant Attorney General Charles F. Rule in testimony before Congress a decade earlier. Rule stated the Division's policy toward mergers as one that distinguishes between procompetitive, efficiency-enhancing mergers and mergers that create a significant probability of increasing prices to consumers. *Mergers and Competition in the Airline Industry, Hearings Before Subcomm. on Monopolies and Commercial Law of the House Committee on the Judiciary,* 99th Cong., 2d Sess. 74-75 (1986).

G. Consent Decrees and Judicial Review

Since 1976, proposed mergers are subject to an agency clearance and review procedure enabled by the information collecting procedures under § 18 of the Clayton Act, enacted by the Hart-Scott-Rodino Antitrust Improvements Act of 1976, Pub. L. 94-435, 90 Stat. 1383 (1976) (codified also in Titles 18 & 28 U.S.C.). This legislation was enacted in response to the complaints of the enforcement agency officials about the lack of a systematic availability of information about proposed and executed merger transactions in sufficient time to study and review them. The thrust of this legislation is to require disclosure by the merger proponents of all relevant information, in accordance with the Notification Report Form provided in 16 C.F.R. § 803.1 (1996). Two conditions are imposed on a large corporation desiring to acquire the voting securities or the assets of certain other corporations. First, § 18 requires both parties to the merger to provide the two merger enforcement agencies with notice, and second, there is a mandatory waiting period after the filing before the acquisition may be executed. Sections 18(a)(2)(A), (B), and (C) restrict the obligation to provide notice to those mergers in which the acquiring firm has total assets or net annual sales of $100 million and the acquired company has total assets or net annual sales of $10 million. A third condition for giving notice of a merger is that of § 18(a)(3), which requires notice from an acquiring firm that will end up holding 15% or more of the voting securities or assets of the acquired firm or an aggregate amount of more than $15 million of the acquired firm's voting securities and assets. Section 18(c) provides for exemption from these requirements for corporations subject to regulation of mergers by other federal legislation, such as banks which are supervised under Title 12, U.S.C.

In § 18(d), Congress delegated the authority jointly to issue regulations controlling the rules of preacquisition notice to the FTC and to the Antitrust Division of the Department of Justice. These regulations, 16 C.F.R. §§ 801 *et seq.* (1996), provide for further refinements of the review process. Based on the information submitted, the agency may initiate an investigation. This investigation may lead to a request for supplemental information. Reg. § 803.10. However, if the agency is satisfied by the initial submission, it may shorten the waiting period. Section 18(b)(2). If, however, an agency determines that there is likely to be a lessening of competition, it is entitled to an expedited hearing for a preliminary injunction to stop the transaction. Section 18(f). Under § 18(2)(b), the waiting period begins to run from the date of the receipt of the *completed* notice by both enforcement agencies. The 30-day waiting period for stock tender offers and 15 days for cash tender offers is often extended either by the request of the agencies for additional information to complete the notice or, in the discretion of the agencies, for an additional 20 days for stock tenders or 10 days for cash tenders. Sections 18(b) and (e). The effective duration of the review of a merger may continue over several months, since the 30 day period begins when the agency determines that all required filings have been supplied to it. The agencies may respond to the Notice, when the filing is completed, by a formal statement of the agency's enforcement intention. According to 28 C.F.R. § 50.6 (1996), the Department of Justice may issue a Business Review Letter, giving the details upon which it rests its conclusions regarding the legality of the merger in the form in which it was disclosed by the Notice. The Federal Trade Commission may respond to the Notice in a formal interpretation of § 7, in accordance with 16 C.F.R. § 803.30 (1996). If the agency review has not identified any antitrust issues, the response may state that there is no present intention to take enforcement action. If the agency does identify some anticompetitive practices from the Notice, it may so notify the parties. In these circumstances, the agencies follow the policy of "fix it first," under which the agency and the merger proponents negotiate conditions and terms for the removal of the anticompetitve element. The agency and the merger proponents may reach an agreement incorporating the terms of the transaction in a consent decree which is then published in the Federal Register to invite comment from any interested party. If the agency does not request further change in the terms of the merger based on public comment, the consent decree is submitted for approval to the district court. Alternatively, the agency may consider the merger clearly to violate the statute with no prospect for any conforming modification. In that case, the agency will advise the parties that it will seek an injunction to block the merger.

There are substantial sanctions for failure to comply with all the notice requirements. In *United States v. Honickman,* 1992 WL 350620 (D.D.C.), an acquisition of assets of the value requiring notice was executed by the use of a series of sham entities which divided the acquired assets of each sham entity into amounts below the statutory sums that trigger the notice requirement. The officer responsible ultimately entered into a consent decree to pay $1,976,000 as a civil penalty under 15 U.S.C. § 18a(g)(1), which authorizes a civil penalty of $10,000 for each day of failure to comply with any provision of the Hart-Scott-Rodino notification procedure. Recently, the FTC fined one acquiring firm $5.1 million for failing to file notice of a $40 million stock purchase and fined another $3.1 million for failure to file notice of a $26 million acquisition. The Commission also fined an acquiring firm $2.97 million for filing an incomplete and misleading notice. 1997 WL-WSJ 2411345.

The clearance procedure enabled by § 18 has reinforced the consent decree, a traditional tool of antitrust enforcement. Since the clearance process brings about scrutiny of the potentially competition-lessening features of a merger, cases arise in which the agency would permit the merger, if certain elements of an acquisition are modified. In the Thomson-West merger noted below, for example, the resulting company did not end up with complete control over the publication of annotated codes. In this way, the clearance process offers a means of resolving issues in a manner consistent with § 7 criteria. The origin of the antitrust consent decree can be traced to *United States v. Otis Elevator*, 1 Decrees and Judgments in Fed. Antitrust Cas. 107 (N.D. Cal. 1907). There the court described the consent decree as follows:

> . . . an order of the court agreed upon by the representative of the Attorney General and of the defendant, without trial of the conduct challenged by the Attorney General, in proceedings instituted under the Sherman Act, Clayton Act, or related statutes.

ANTITRUST SUBCOMM., HOUSE COMM. ON THE JUDICIARY, 86TH CONG., 1ST SESS., REPORT ON THE CONSENT DECREE PROGRAM OF THE DEPT. OF JUSTICE ix (1959).

Although there is no statutory basis for the consent decree, the Supreme Court in *United States v. Swift,* 286 U.S. 106, 115 (1932), granted the status of judgment to the negotiated settlement reflected in the decree. Once the negotiated judgment was accorded equal status with a litigated judgment, controversy arose over the extent to which a judge should scrutinize the background of the negotiated settlement prior to accepting the consent decree. There was no agreement as to the standard of review or as to the circumstances in which a third-party intervenor could have standing to contest the decree. *See* H. Kalodner, *Consent Decrees as an Antitrust Enforcement Device,* 23 ANTITRUST BULL. 277 (1978). Congress addressed these issues by enacting the Antitrust Procedures and Penalties Act of 1974, Pub. L. No. 93-528, 88 Stat. 1706 (1974) (codified at 15 U.S.C. §§ 16(b)-(h) (1988)), also known as the Tunney Act. Under § 16(b), a submission for entry of a consent decree to a district court initiates a 60-day waiting period during which the United States is required to publish in the Federal Register and to make available to the public a copy of the proposed decree, a competitive impact statement, public comments on the proposed decree, and other relevant data. Section 16(c) requires the United States to publish summaries of these documents in newspapers of general circulation. The continuing controversy that hovers over consent decrees is the requirement of § 16(e) that prior to entering a decree, the district court is required to find that the entry is in "the public interest." This provision gives only general guidance as to the determination of the "public interest." It states that the court may take into account the competitive impact, termination of alleged violations, the impact on the public generally, and may also consider allegations of injury attributable to the alleged violations in the complaint from individuals. Areeda and Hovenkamp conclude that this provision, ". . . does not tell a judge how he is to appraise" a proposed consent decree. PHILLIP E. AREEDA & HERBERT HOVENKAMP, ANTITRUST LAW ¶ 348g (rev. ed. 1995). Two Ninth Circuit opinions have described the difficulty that judges face in assessing the public interest in a Tunney Act review. In *United States v. Bechtel Corp.,* 648 F.2d 660, 666 (9th Cir. 1981), the court stated:

> The statute suggests that a court may, and perhaps should look beyond the strict relationship between complaint and remedy in evaluating the

> public interest. We cannot agree that a district court should engage in an unrestricted evaluation of what relief would best serve the public.

There is no judicial consensus about the scope of a Tunney Act review. Judicial disagreement over Tunney Act standards recently led to a clash between an agency official and a reviewing district court judge. The Department of Justice filed a complaint charging violations of §§ 1 & 2 of the Sherman Act by Microsoft, the dominant producer of operating systems software for IBM compatible personal computers. This complaint was filed by the Department of Justice after the Antitrust Division took up the investigation of licensing and marketing practices, following an impasse at the Federal Trade Commission after four years of investigation. Within six months, the Division took up the case and within six months entered into settlement negotiations after Judge Sporkin held that the proposed consent decree was not in the public interest and rejected it. *See United States v. Microsoft,* 159 F.R.D. 318, 334-35.

In reversing Judge Sporkin, the court of appeals stated the Tunney Act review standard is: ". . . not to determine whether the . . . [proposed decree] is the one that will best serve society . . . [but only to confirm that it] is within the reaches of the public interest." *United States v. Microsoft*, 56 F.3d 1448, 1460 (D.C. Cir. 1995). The appeals court held that the proposed decree met this narrower standard. This litigation raises a basic issue in the use of the consent decree as well as the scope of its judicial review.

Judge Sporkin, the district court judge, gave his interpretation of the scope of review as follows: "The Tunney Act envisioned that the courts were to be an 'independent force' rather than a 'rubber stamp' in reviewing consent decrees." 159 F.R.D. at 325, n.13. Judge Sporkin noted his objection to the decree, in part, on the practice of pre-announcing forthcoming new operating system software before it was actually in existence, a practice not challenged in the complaint. This practice was known in the industry as "vaporware" and was alleged to have a chilling effect on potential competitors. His opinion states:

> The Government has pressed for the adoption of its decree on that grounds that it will open up competition. . . . [W]hy does it not want to take on the vaporware issue? When the Court gave Microsoft the opportunity to disavow this practice by an undertaking, it declined to do so. . . . The Court cannot sign off on a decree knowing that the defendant intends to continue to engage in an anticompetitive practice without the Government providing a full explanation of its "no action" stance.

Id. at 336.

In reversing Judge Sporkin, the Court of Appeals also addressed the vaporware issue, noting the manner in which it arose below. Judge Silberman wrote,

> At the first substantive status conference . . . , the district judge informed the parties that . . . he had read a book about Microsoft [JAMES WALLACE & JIM ERICKSON, HARD DRIVE: BILL GATES AND THE MAKING OF THE

> MICROSOFT EMPIRE (1992)]. . . . In particular, the judge focused on the allegation that Microsoft engages in "vaporware." . . . At a subsequent status hearing . . . , the district judge again referred to Hard Drive and its "vaporware" allegations . . . and [*sic*] telling the government that he wanted to be satisfied that the allegations in the book were not true.
>
> * * *
>
> To be sure, the Act . . . authorizes the district judge to "take testimony of Government officials . . . as the court may deem appropriate." 15 U.S.C. § 16(f)(1) (1988). We do not read this language, however, to authorize the district judge to seek the kind of information concerning the government's investigation and settlement negotiations that he wished to obtain here. . . . Here, the district court is not empowered to review the actions or behavior of the Department of Justice; the court is only authorized to review the decree itself. It is unnecessary to consider whether the district court might have broader authority to inquire into the Department's deliberations . . . if there were a credible showing of bad faith.

56 F.3d at 1452-53, 1459.

Assume that Microsoft had undertaken to acquire a competitor and that the above dispute over the standard of judicial review arose with regard to the agency's assessment of the likelihood of a 5% price increase under the Merger Guidelines. What is the effect of the appeals court's standard? If the district court judge considers the comments of interested parties to raise an issue not addressed in the proposed decree, must the judge reject the decree? May he ask the agency to explain its analysis? May the judge consider an issue not raised in the government's complaint? To what extent may a judicial inquiry be made into the investigative or deliberative activities of an agency, without raising a Separation of Powers issue? Suppose there is a perceived factual discrepancy in the record, may the court ask about the methodology of the investigation? If Judge Silberman's statement is taken literally, will a Tunney Act review tend to be either complete acceptance or complete rejection of a proposed decree? To what extent does the procedural issue of the standard of review mask the underlying substantive antitrust issue of how to characterize an aggressive innovator such as Microsoft?

The consent decree in a merger involving the two largest publishers of legal materials is illustrative of the negotiation process described above. In entering final judgment accepting the proposed consent decree, the district court in *United States v. Thomson Corp.*, 1997 WL 90992 (D.D.C.), the district court, stating it was bound by the standard of the court of appeals opinion in *Microsoft*, above, expressed the following concern over the bulk sale of some items to a competitor.

> Since the issuance . . . [of an interim opinion in this case], the Court has been informed that all of the Divestiture Products will be sold to LEXIS-NEXIS, West's main competitor in the online services market and its one-time fierce opponent in these proceedings. At a status conference . . . [earlier], the Court voiced its concern that this new development—

> which had not previously been discussed in any filings or public proceedings before the Court—might alter the competitive landscape in various legal product markets. The Court also lamented the loss in this litigation of the most powerful and vocal private sector opponent of the Thomson/West merger and indicated that LEXIS-NEXIS's new support for the merger might militate in favor of allowing the intervention of other more disinterested parties for the purpose of ensuring a vigorous appeal.
>
> * * *
>
> . . . While the fact that the parties now contemplate such a bulk sale is of some surprise, the Court has already decided that divestiture is an acceptable remedy for the anticompetitive effects of the . . . merger. . . . The fact that all of Divestiture products will be sold to LEXIS-NEXIS does not am [sic] [harm?] that conclusion. This is particularly true in view of the Justice Department assurances that it will maintain its vigilance pursuant to its duties as the primary enforcer of the antitrust laws, *a responsibility that goes beyond the specific terms of the consent decree*.

Id. (emphasis added). Is this decision within the rule of *Microsoft,* above? Is the district court going into matter outside the decree? Does the above excerpt suggest that the court sought and received a promise from the Department as to its future investigative conduct? If so, is this a judicial intrusion into the domain of an executive branch agency?

Given the facts of the Thomson/West Publishing Company merger as set out below, how would the case have been decided under the analysis of *Brown Shoe* and *Philadelphia National Bank*? The merger of the West Publishing Co. and Thomson Corp. was attacked by the Justice Department and seven state attorneys general as lessening competition in three relevant markets—enhanced primary law markets (an enhanced product consists of public domain judicial opinions plus head notes, case synopses, and annotated codes), 47 secondary law products (treatises, practice materials such as form books), and the comprehensive on-line legal research market. West also claimed copyright protection in its Star Pagination, a system whereby a judicial decision not published by West, can also be cited to the page in West's National Reporter system, a notation which is commonly required by courts. Thomson owns programs that search law and other electronic data bases permitting case histories and commentaries on data base material. The court approved the proposed consent order and entered final judgment after a Tunney Act review. 1997 WL 90992 (D.D.C.). The court approved the following changes required by the plaintiffs: 1) Thomson/West must divest itself of one enhanced code product for the U.S., California, Michigan, and New York, plus the Lawyers' Edition of the Supreme Court Reports, 2) Thomson agreed to permit California, Washington, and Wisconsin early termination of their current long-term contracts with Thomson for the publication of the official state reporter, in order to permit the states to invite competitive bids for the publication of the these reports, 3) divestiture would also be required of one secondary law product in each of the secondary law markets, 4) West/Thomson is required to license Star Pagination to any law publisher on request and Thomson is further required to divest itself of Auto-Cite and to extend the term of the existing license to use Thomson's non-legal data bases to LEXIS-NEXIS, West's only competitor to Westlaw.

By this merger, West Publishing is now part of the Thomson publishing conglomerate which already owned such law publishers as Bancroft-Whitney, Lawyers Co-Operative Publishing (ALR and Am.Jur.), and Research Institute of America, publisher of federal income tax material, plus recently-acquired Prentice-Hall, another major publisher of tax materials. Reed-Elsevier, a Dutch publishing conglomerate, owns LEXIS-NEXIS, Butterworth's, a major British publisher, and half of Shepard's Citations. The other half of Shepard's is owned by the Times-Mirror Corporation, the publisher of the Los Angeles Times and Matthew Bender. Kluwer, another Dutch publisher, has recently acquired Little, Brown & Co. and Commerce Clearing House. Should size and concentration become of second order antitrust significance? Is the merger enforcement policy one of permitting strategic, efficiency-enhancing mergers and implicitly leaving to the firm's managers the decision of divesting acquired assets if inefficiencies subsequently arise?

Given the shifts in the treatment of mergers described above, consider an appropriate contemporary merger policy for the global economy. What weight should be given to increased concentration resulting from the acquisition by Time-Warner of Turner Broadcasting, by CVS of Revco, and Morgan Stanley's acquisition of Dean Witter? Each of these mergers has initiated speculation that further mergers in each industry would follow. For example, a newspaper article reporting the Morgan Stanley merger states,

> Even as the directors of the Morgan Stanley Group met on Tuesday night to approve an $8.8 billion dollar merger with Dean Witter . . . that would shake Wall Street, the investment bankers were bombarded with telephone calls asking about their rumored takeover of Paine Webber.
>
> There was good reason for speculation. The Paine Webber Group, like Lehman Brothers and Salomon Brothers, is the kind of second-tier competitor that Wall Street now believes must find a partner if it wants to stay in the game with the full-service giants that are coming to dominate a swiftly changing financial services industry.

NY TIMES, February 6, 1997, C1. If there is an antitrust concern about these changes, what is it and what kind of antitrust scrutiny is warranted? Consider the conditions required by the enforcement agency in the following mergers.

In the Time-Warner/Turner Broadcasting merger, the FTC noted that Time-Warner, the nation's largest cable television distributor with a 17% market share, also owned Warner Bros. movie studios. Turner, operating both cable networks and film studios by ownership and by long-term contracts, together with Time-Warner would control 40% of all cable programming. The Commission's majority considered the relevant market to be cable television distribution; their principal concern was the ability of the new entity, by controlling access to cable distribution systems, to raise its prices unilaterally for all of its own programming. Approval was granted subject to changes that would limit the new firm's ability to bundle Time-Warner and Turner's programs and which would require Time-Warner to carry new programs that would compete with Turner's CNN. ANTITRUST AND TRADE REG. REP. (BNA) 266 (1996).

A dissenting opinion by Commissioner Azcuenaga stated that the definition of relevant market by the majority was not supported by caselaw, efficiency considerations were totally ignored, and the finding of barriers to entry was contrary to the evidence.

The FTC filed a complaint seeking a temporary restraining order and a preliminary injunction to halt the merger of the two largest office supply retailers in the United States. In the initial clearance process, Staples, the acquiring firm, offered to dispose of 63 stores in cities in which both it and the acquired firm, Office Depot, presently operated, to the third largest competitor in the industry, Office Max. FINANCIAL TIMES 1 (April 7, 1997). The Commission rejected this proposal and filed suit on April 10, 1997, alleging violation of § 7 in the relevant product market for "consumable office supplies" in 42 existing markets and by eliminating potential competition in 4 other metropolitan markets.

Federal Trade Commission v. Staples, Inc.

970 F. Supp. 1066 (D.D.C. 1997)

REDACTED MEMORANDUM OPINION

THOMAS F. HOGAN, District Judge.

Plaintiff, the Federal Trade Commission ("FTC" or "Commission"), seeks a preliminary injunction pursuant to Section 13(b) of the Federal Trade Commission Act, 15 U.S.C. § 53(b), to enjoin the consummation of any acquisition by defendant Staples, Inc., of defendant Office Depot, Inc., pending final disposition before the Commission of administrative proceedings to determine whether such acquisition may substantially lessen competition in violation of Section 7 of the Clayton Act, 15 U.S.C. § 18, and Section 5 of the Federal Trade Commission Act, 15 U.S.C. § 45. . . .

I. . . .

Defendants are both corporations which sell office products—including office supplies, business machines, computers and furniture—through retail stores, commonly described as office supply superstores, as well as through direct mail delivery and contract stationer operations. Staples is the second largest office superstore chain in the United States with approximately 550 retail stores located in 28 states and the District of Columbia, primarily in the Northeast and California. In 1996 Staples' revenues from those stores were approximately $4 billion through all operations. Office Depot, the largest office superstore chain, operates over 500 retail office supply superstores that are located in 38 states and the District of Columbia, primarily in the South and Midwest. Office Depot's 1996 sales were approximately $6.1 billion. OfficeMax, Inc., is the only other office supply superstore firm in the United States.

On September 4, 1996, defendants Staples and Office Depot, and Marlin Acquisition Corp. ("Marlin"), a wholly-owned subsidiary of Staples, entered into an "Agreement and Plan of Merger." . . . [Subsequently] the defendants and the FTC staff negotiated a consent decree that would have authorized the merger to proceed on the condition that Staples and Office Depot sell 63 stores to OfficeMax. However, the Commission voted 3-2 to reject the proposed consent decree on April 4, 1997. The FTC then filed this suit on April 9, 1997, seeking a temporary retraining order and preliminary injunction against the merger. . . .

II. The Geographic Market

One of the few issue about which the parties to this case do not disagree is that metropolitan areas are the appropriate geographic markets for analyzing the competitive effects of the proposed merger. A geographic market is that geographic area "to which consumers can practically turn for alternative sources of the product and in which the antitrust defendant faces competition." *Morgenstern v. Wilson,* 29 F.3d 1291, 1296 (8th Cir. 1994), *cert. denied*, 513 U.S. 1150 (1995). In its first amended complaint, the FTC identified forty-two such metropolitan areas[5] as well as future areas which could suffer anti-competitive effects from the proposed merger.[6] Defendants have not challenged the FTC's geographic market definition in this proceeding. Therefore, the Court will accept the relevant geographic markets identified by the Commission.

III. The Relevant Product Market

In contrast to the parties' agreement with respect to the relevant geographic market, the Commission and the defendants sharply disagree with respect to the appropriate definition of the relevant product market or line of commerce. As with many antitrust cases, the definition of the relevant product market in this case is crucial. In fact, to a great extent, this case hinges on the proper definition of the relevant product market.

---

[5] According to the FTC, the proposed merger would have an anti-competitive effect in the following geographic markets:

(1) in Salinas, California, San Diego, California, Visalia-Tulare-Porterville, California, Lakeland-Winter Haven, Florida, Ocala, Florida, Tampa-St. Petersburg-Clearwater, Florida, Fort Pierce-Port St. Lucie, Florida, Champaign-Urbana, Illinois, Louisville, Kentucky, Baltimore, Maryland, Greenville, North Carolina, Florence, South Carolina, Charlottesville, Virginia, Washington, D.C., and Spokane, Washington, where the number of office superstore firms would drop from two to one.

(2) in Los Angeles, California, Sacramento, California, San Francisco-Oakland-San Jose, California, Stockton-Lodi, California, Orlando, Florida, Sarasota-Bradenton, Florida, West Palm Beach-Boca Raton, Florida, Evansville, Indiana, Indianapolis, Indiana, South Bend, Indiana, Springfield, Illinois, Kalamazoo-Battle Creek, Michigan, Detroit-Ann Arbor-Flint, Michigan, Grand Rapids-Muskegon-Holland, Michigan, Middlesex County, New Jersey, Passaic County, New Jersey, Nassau-Suffolk, New York, Greensborough-Winston Salem-High Point, North Carolina, Raleigh-Durham, North Carolina, Cleveland, Ohio, Cincinnati-Hamilton, Ohio, Portland-Vancouver, Oregon-Washington, Pittsburgh, Pennsylvania, Columbia, South Carolina, Chattanooga, Tennessee, Nashville, Tennessee, and Salt Lake City-Ogden, Utah, where the number of superstore firms will be reduced from three to two.

[6] Metropolitan areas where Staples and Office Depot would have competed in the future include Bergen County, New Jersey, Fayetteville, North Carolina, Albany-Schenectady-Troy, New York, and Fredericksburg, Virginia, where Office Depot plans to open stores in Staples markets before the end of 1997. In addition, Staples predicted that it would face competition from Office Depot in 76% of its markets by the year 2000, compared to the 46% overlap between the two companies in 1996.

The Commission defines the relevant product market as "the sale of consumable office supplies through office superstores,"[7] with "consumable" meaning products that consumers buy recurrently, *i.e.*, items which "get used up" or discarded. For example, under the Commission's definition, "consumable office supplies" would not include capital goods such as computers, fax machines, and other business machines or office furniture, but does include such products as paper, pens, file folders, post-it notes, computer disks, and toner cartridges. The defendants characterize the FTC's product market definition as "contrived" with no basis in law or fact, and counter that the appropriate product market within which to assess the likely competitive consequences of a Staples-Office Depot combination is simply the overall sale of office products, of which a combined Staples-Office Depot accounted for 5.5% of total sales in North America in 1996. In addition, the defendants argue that the challenged combination is not likely "substantially to lessen competition" however the product market is defined. After considering the arguments on both sides and all of the evidence in this case and making evaluations of each witness's credibility as well as the weight that the Court should give certain evidence and testimony, the Court finds that the appropriate relevant product market definition in this case is, as the Commission has argued, the sale of consumable office supplies through office supply superstores.

The general rule when determining a relevant product market is that "[t]he outer boundaries of a product market are determined by the reasonable interchangeability of use [by consumers] or the cross-elasticity of demand between the product itself and substitutes for it." *Brown Shoe v. United States*, 370 U.S. 294, 325 (1962); *see also United States v. E.I. du Pont de Nemours and Co.*, 351 U.S. 377, 395 (1956). Interchangeability of use and cross-elasticity of demand look to the availability of substitute commodities, *i.e.*, whether there are other products offered to consumers which are similar in character or use to the product or products in question, as well as how far buyers will go to substitute one commodity for another. *E.I. du Pont de Nemours,* 351 U.S. at 393. In other words, the general question is "whether two products can be used for the same purpose, and if so, whether and to what extent purchasers are willing to substitute one for the other." *Hayden Pub. Co. v. Cox Broadcasting Corp.*, 730 F.2d 64, 70 n.8 (2d Cir. 1984).

Whether there are other products available to consumers which are similar in character or use to the products in question may be termed "functional interchangeability." *See, e.g., E.I. du Pont de Nemours,* 351 U.S. at 399 (recognizing "functional interchangeability" between cellophane and other flexible wrappings); *United States v. Archer-Daniels-Midland,* 866 F.2d 242, 246 (8th Cir. 1988) (discussing "functional interchangeability" between sugar and high fructose corn syrup), *cert. denied*, 493 U.S. 809 (1989). This case, of course, is an example of perfect "functional interchangeability." The consumable office products at issue here are identical whether they are sold by Staples or Office Depot or another seller of office supplies. A legal pad sold by Staples or Office Depot is "functionally interchangeable" with a legal pad sold by Wal-Mart. A post-it note sold by Staples or Office Depot is "functionally interchangeable" with a post-it note sold by Viking or Quill. A computer disk sold by Staples-Office Depot is "functionally interchangeable" with a computer disk sold by CompUSA. No one disputes the functional interchangeability of con-

---

7 The Commission also offered an alternative product market, that of the sale of consumable office supplies through retail stores to small businesses and individuals with home offices.

sumable office supplies. However, as the government has argued, functional interchangeability should not end the Court's analysis.

The Supreme Court did not stop after finding a high degree of functional interchangeability between cellophane and other wrapping materials in the *E.I. du Pont de Nemours* case. Instead, the Court also found that "an element for consideration as to cross-elasticity of demand between products is the responsiveness of the sales of one product to price changes of the other." *Id.* at 400. For example, in that case, the Court explained, "[i]f a slight decrease in the price of cellophane causes a considerable number of customers of other flexible wrappings to switch to cellophane, it would be an indication that a high cross-elasticity of demand exists between [cellophane and other flexible wrappings], [and therefore] that the products compete in the same market." *Id.* Following that reasoning in this case, the Commission has argued that a slight but significant increase in Staples-Office Depot's prices will not cause a considerable number of Staples-Office Depot's customers to purchase consumable office supplies from other non-superstore alternatives such as Wal-Mart, Best Buy, Quill, or Viking. On the other hand, the Commission has argued that an increase in price by Staples would result in consumers turning to another office superstore, especially Office Depot, if the consumers had that option. Therefore, the Commission concludes that the sale of consumable office supplies by office supply superstores is the appropriate relevant product market in this case, and products sold by competitors such as Wal-Mart, Best Buy, Viking, Quill, and others should be excluded.

The Court recognizes that it is difficult to overcome the first blush or initial gut reaction of many people to the definition of the relevant product market as the sale of consumable office supplies through office supply superstores. The products in question are undeniably the same no matter who sells them, and no one denies that many different types of retailers sell these products. After all, a combined Staples-Office Depot would only have a 5.5% share of the overall market in consumable office supplies. Therefore, it is logical to conclude that, of course, all these retailers compete, and that if a combined Staples-Office Depot raised prices after the merger, or at least did not lower them as much as they would have as separate companies, that consumers, with such a plethora of options, would shop elsewhere.

The Court acknowledges that there is, in fact, a broad market encompassing the sale of consumable office supplies by all sellers of such supplies, and that those sellers must, at some level, compete with one another. However, the mere fact that a firm may be termed a competitor in the overall marketplace does not necessarily require that it be included in the relevant product market for antitrust purposes. The Supreme Court has recognized that within a broad market, "well-defined submarkets may exist which, in themselves, constitute product markets for antitrust purposes." *Brown Shoe Co. v. United States*, 370 U.S. 294, 325 (1962), *see also Rothery Storage & Van Co. v. Atlas Van Lines, Inc.*, 792 F.2d 210, 218 (D.C.C. 1986) (Bork, J.), *cert. denied*, 479 U.S. 1033 (1987). With respect to such submarkets, the Court explained "[b]ecause Section 7 of the Clayton Act prohibits any merger which may substantially lessen competition 'in any line of commerce,' it is necessary to examine the effects of a merger in each such economically significant submarket to determine if there is a reasonable probability that the merger will substantially lessen competition. If such a probability is found to exist, the merger is proscribed." *Id.* There is a possibility, therefore, that the sale of consumable office supplies by office superstores may qualify as a submarket within a larger market of retailers of office supplies in general.

The Court in *Brown Shoe* provided a series of factors or "practical indicia" for determining whether a submarket exists including "industry or public recognition of the submarket as a separate economic entity, the product's peculiar characteristics and uses, unique production facilities, distinct customers, distinct prices, sensitivity to price changes, and specialized vendors." *Id.* Since the Court described these factors as "practical indicia" rather than requirements, subsequent cases have found that submarkets can exist even if only some of these factors are present. *See, e.g., Beatrice Foods Co. v. FTC*, 540 F.2d 303 (7th Cir. 1976) (finding submarket based on industry recognition, peculiar characteristics of the product, and differences in production methods and prices). *International Telephone and Telegraph Corp. v. General Telephone & Electronics Corp.*, 518 F.2d 913, 932 (9th Cir. 1975) (explaining that *Brown Shoe*'s practical indicia were meant as "practical aids rather than with the view that their presence or absence would dispose, in talismanic fashion, of the submarket issue").

The Commission discussed several of the *Brown Shoe* "practical indicia" in its case, such as industry recognition, and the special characteristics of superstores which make them different from other sellers of office supplies, including distinct formats, customers, and prices. Primarily, however, the FTC focused on what it termed the "pricing evidence," which the Court finds corresponds with *Brown Shoe*'s "sensitivity to price changes" factor. First, the FTC presented evidence comparing Staples' prices in geographic markets where Staples is the only office superstore, to markets where Staples competes with Office Depot or OfficeMax, or both. Based on the FTC's calculations, in markets where Staples faces no office superstore competition at all, something which was termed a one firm market during the hearing, prices are 13% higher than in three firm markets where it competes with both Office Depot and OfficeMax. The data which underlie this conclusion make it compelling evidence. Prices were compared as of January 1997, which, admittedly, only provides data for one specific point in time. However, rather than comparing prices from only a small sampling or "basket" of goods, the FTC used an office supply sample accounting for 90% of Staples' sales and comprised of both price sensitive and non price sensitive items. The FTC presented similar evidence based on Office Depot's prices of a sample of 500 items, also as of January 1997. Similarly, the evidence showed that Office Depot's prices are significantly higher—well over 5% higher,[8] in Depot-only markets than they are in three firm markets.

Other pricing evidence presented by the FTC is less convincing on its own, due to limitations in the underlying data. For example, relatively small samplings or "baskets" of goods may have been used or it may not be clear how many stock keeping units ("SKUs") of supplies were included. For example, the FTC also presented evidence comparing Staples' prices in Staples-only markets with Staples' prices in three-firm markets for four different time periods, August 1994, January 1995, August 1995, and May 1996. The result is startlingly similar to that found in the first two examples. Where Staples does not compete with other office superstores, it charges prices well over 5% higher than where it does so compete. While having the advantage of showing a trend over time, the Court recognizes that this evidence has some problems. These particular calculations were made based on a "basket" or sample of supplies comprised of supplies used by Staples to price check

---

[8] The analytical framework set forth in the Merger Guidelines approaches the inquiry regarding the reasonable interchangeability of use or cross-elasticity of demand by asking whether a "hypothetical monopolist would profitably impose at least a 'small but significant and nontransitory' [price] increase." Merger Guidelines at § 111. The Merger Guidelines use 5% of the usual approximation of a "small but significant and nontransatory price increase." *Id.* For this reason, the Court's analysis will often refer to this 5% number.

against Office Depot. The number of SKUs in the sample was not provided to the Court, and it appears that the components of the baskets may have changed over time. Therefore, the Court would not give much weight to this evidence standing alone. However, since additional evidence supports the same conclusion, the Court credits this evidence as confirmation of the general pricing trend.

The FTC also pointed to internal Staples documents which present price comparisons between Staples' prices and Office Depot's prices and Staples' prices and OfficeMax's prices within different price zones.[9] The comparisons between Staples and Office Depot were made in August 1994, January 1995, August 1995, and May 1996. Staples' prices were compared with OfficeMax's prices in August 1994, July 1995, and January 1996. For each comparison, Staples' calculations were based on a fairly large "basket" or sample of goods, approximately 2000 SKUs containing both price sensitive and non-price sensitive items. Using Staples' data, but organizing it differently to show which of those zones were one, two, or three firm markets, the FTC showed once again that Staples charges significantly higher prices, more than 5% higher, where it has no office superstore competition than where it competes with the two other superstores.

The FTC offered similar price comparison evidence for Office Depot, comparing Office Depot's prices across Staples' zones. The comparisons were made in August 1994, January 1995, August 1995, and May 1996. Again, a large sample, approximately 2000 SKUs, was considered. The results of this analysis are slightly less favorable to the FTC's position. Price differentials are significantly smaller and there are even a few instances where Office Depot's prices appear to be higher in one of its three firm markets than prices in its two firm markets and at least one point where prices in one of the Depot-only zones were lower than prices in one of the three firm markets. On average, however, this evidence shows that Office Depot's prices are highest in its one firm markets, and lowest in its three firm markets.

This evidence all suggests that office superstore prices are affected primarily by other office superstores and not by non-superstore competitors such as mass merchandisers like Wal-Mart, Kmart, or Target, wholesale clubs such as BJ's, Sam's, and Price Costco, computer or electronic stores such as Computer City and Best Buy, independent retail office supply stores, mail orders firms like Quill and Viking, and contract stationers. Though the FTC did not present the Court with evidence regarding the precise amount of non-superstore competition in each of Staples' and Office Depot's one, two, and three firm markets, it is clear to the Court that these competitors, albeit in different combinations and concentrations, are present in every one of these markets. For example, it is a certainty that the mail order competitors compete in all of the geographic markets at issue in this case. Office products are available through the mail in all 50 states, and have been for approximately 30 years. Despite this mail order competition, however, Staples and Office Depot are still able to charge higher prices in their one firm markets than they do in the two firm markets and the three firm markets without losing a significant number of customers to the mail order firms. The same appears to be true with respect to Wal-Mart. Bill Long, Vice President for Merchandising at Wal-Mart Stores, testifying through declaration, explained that price-checking by Wal-Mart of Staples' prices in areas where both Staples and Wal-Mart exist showed

---

[9] It was established at the hearing that Staples and Office Depot do not maintain nationally uniform prices in their stores. Instead, both companies currently organize their stores into price zones which are simply groups of one or more stores that have common prices.

that, on average, Staples' prices were higher where there was a Staples and a Wal-Mart but no other superstore than where there was a Staples, a Wal-Mart, and another superstore.[10]

The evidence with respect to the wholesale club stores is consistent. Mike Atkinson, Vice President, Division Merchandise Manager of BJ's Wholesale Club, testified at the hearing regarding BJ's price checking of Staples and Office Depot in areas where BJ's competes with one or both of those superstores. Though his sample was small—he testified that less than 10% of BJ's 80 stores are located in the same area as a Staples and/or Office Depot—BJ's price checking found that, in general, office supply superstore prices were lowest where there was both a Staples and an Office Depot. In addition, Staples' own pricing information shows that warehouse clubs have very little effect on Staples' prices. For example, Staples' maintains a "warehouse club only" price zone, which indicates a zone where Staples exists with a warehouse club but without another office superstore. The data presented by the Commission on Staples' pricing shows only a slight variation in prices (1%-2%) between "warehouse club only" zones and one superstore markets without a warehouse club. Additionally, in May 1996, two price comparison studies done by Staples, first using 2,084 SKUs including both price sensitive and non-price sensitive items and then using only 244 SKUs of price sensitive items, showed that prices in the "club only" zones, on average, were over 10% higher than in zones where Staples competes with Office Depot and/or OfficeMax.

There is also consistent evidence with respect to computer and/or consumer electronics stores such as Best Buy. For example, Office Depot maintains a separate price zone, which it calls "zone 30," for areas with Best Buy locations but no other office supply superstores. However, the FTC introduced evidence, based on a January 1997 market basket of "top 500 items by velocity," that prices in Office Depot's "zone 30" price zone are almost as high as in its "non-competitive" price zone, the zone where it does not compete with another office superstore.

There is similar evidence with respect to the defendants' behavior when faced with entry of another competitor. The evidence shows that the defendants change their price zones when faced with entry of another superstore, but do not do so for other retailers. For example, Staples changed its price zone for Cincinnati to a lower priced zone when Office Depot and OfficeMax entered that area. New entry by Staples and OfficeMax caused a decline in prices at Office Depot's Greensboro stores. In July 1996, after OfficeMax entered Jackson, Michigan, Staples moved its Jackson store to a new zone, cutting prices by 6%. There are numerous additional examples of zones being changed and prices falling as a result of superstore entry. There is no evidence that zones change and prices fall when another non-superstore retailer enters a geographic market.

Though individually the FTC's evidence can be criticized for looking at only brief snapshots in time or for considering only a limited number of SKUs, taken together, however, the Court finds this evidence a compelling showing that a small but significant increase in Staples' prices will not cause a significant number of consumers to turn to non-superstore alternatives for purchasing their consumable office supplies. Despite the high degree of functional interchangeability between consumable office supplies sold by the office superstores and other retailers of office supplies, the evidence presented by the

---

10 As the defendants pointed out and criticized during the hearing, Mr. Long submitted several declarations and/or revised declarations in which he modified portions of his declaration. However, his testimony remained unchanged on this particular issue. Therefore, the Court credited this particular testimony.

Commission shows that even where Staples and Office Depot charge higher prices, certain consumers do not go elsewhere for their supplies. This further demonstrates that the sale of office supplies by non-superstore retailers are not responsive to the higher prices charged by Staples and Office Depot in the one firm markets. This indicates a low cross-elasticity of demand between the consumable office supplies sold by the superstores and those sold by other sellers.

Turning back to the other *Brown Shoe* "practical indicia" of submarkets that the Commission offered in this case, the Commission presented and the Court heard a great deal of testimony at the hearing and through declarations about the uniqueness of office superstores and the differences between the office superstores and other sellers of office supplies such as mass merchandisers, wholesale clubs, and mail order firms as well as the special characteristics of office superstore customers. In addition, the Court was asked to go and view many of the different types of retail formats. That evidence shows that office superstores are, in fact, very different in appearance, physical size, format, the number and variety of SKU's offered, and the type of customers targeted and served than other sellers of office supplies.

The Court has observed that office supply superstores look far different from other sellers of office supplies. Office supply superstores are high volume, discount office supply chain stores averaging in excess of 20,000 square feet, with over 11,000 of those square feet devoted to traditional office supplies, and carrying over 5,000 SKUs of consumable office supplies in addition to computers, office furniture, and other non-consumables. In contrast, stores such as Kmart devote approximately 210 square feet to the sale of approximately 250 SKUs of consumable office supplies. Kinko's devotes approximately 50 square feet to the sale of 150 SKUs. Target sells only 400 SKUs. Both Sam's Club and Computer City each sell approximately 200 SKUs. Even if these SKU totals are low estimates as the defendants have argued, there is still a huge difference between the superstores and the rest of the office supply sellers.

In addition to the differences in SKU numbers and variety, the superstores are different from many other sellers of office supplies due to the type of customer they target and attract. The superstores' customer base overwhelmingly consists of small businesses with fewer than 20 employees and consumers with home offices. In contrast, mail order customers are typically mid-sized companies with more than 20 employees. Another example is contract stationers who focus on serving customers with more than 100 employees. While the Court accepts that some small businesses with fewer than 20 employees as well as home office customers do choose other sellers of office supplies, the superstores' customers are different from those of many of the purported competitors.

It is difficult to fully articulate and explain all of the ways in which superstores are unique. As the plaintiff and defendant requested, the Court viewed some of the various sellers of office supplies located in the Rockville, Maryland area, including Staples, Office Depot, CompUSA, Best Buy, CVS, Kmart, Giant Food, and Wal-Mart. Based on the Court's observations, the Court finds that the unique combination of size, selection, depth and breadth of inventory offered by the superstores distinguishes them from other retailers. Other retailers devote only a fraction of their square footage to office supplies as opposed to Staples or Office Depot. The evidence shows that the typical club, mass merchant, or computer store offers only 210 to 2000 square feet of office supplies, compared to over 11,182 square feet at a typical Staples. This was evident to the Court when visiting the various stores. Superstores are simply different in scale and appearance from the other retailers. No one entering a Wal-Mart would mistake it for an office superstore. No one entering

Staples or Office Depot would mistakenly think he or she was in Best Buy or CompUSA. You certainly know an office superstore when you see one. *Cf., Bon-Ton Stores, Inc. v. May Department Stores,* 881 F. Supp. 860, 870 (W.D.N.Y. 1994) ("Customers know a department store when they see it.").

Another of the "practical indicia" for determining the presence of a submarket suggested by *Brown Shoe* is "industry or public recognition of the submarket as a separate economic entity." *See also Rothery Storage & Van Co. v. Atlas Van Lines,* 792 F.2d 210, 219 (D.C. Cir. 1986) (Bork, J.) ("The industry or public recognition of the submarket as a separate economic unit matters because we assume that economic actors usually have accurate perceptions of economic realities."), *cert. denied,* 479 U.S. 1033, 107 S. Ct. 880, 93 L. Ed. 2d 834 (1987); *FTC v. Coca-Cola Co.,* 641 F. Supp. 1128, 1132 (D.D.C. 1986) ("Analysis of the market is a matter of business reality—a matter of how the market is perceived by those who strive for profit in it"), *vacated as moot,* 829 F.2d 191 (D.C. Cir. 1987). The Commission offered abundant evidence on this factor from Staples' and Office Depot's documents which shows that both Staples and Office Depot focus primarily on competition from other superstores. The documents reviewed by the Court show that the merging parties evaluate their "competition" as the other office superstore firms, without reference to other retailers, mail order firms, or independent stationers. In document after document, the parties refer to, discuss, and make business decisions based upon the assumption that "competition" refers to other office superstores only. For example, Staples uses the phrase "office superstore industry" in strategic planning documents. PX 15 at 3186. Staples' 1996 Strategy Update refers to the "Big Three" and "improved relative competitive position" since 1993 and states that Staples is "increasingly recognized as [the] industry leader." PX 15 at 3153. A document analyzing a possible acquisition of OfficeMax referenced the "[b]enefits from pricing in [newly] noncompetitive markets," and also the fact that there was "a potential margin lift overall as the industry moves to 2 players." . . .

When assessing key trends and making long range plans, Staples and Office Depot focus on the plans of other superstores. In addition, when determining whether to enter a new metropolitan area, both Staples and Office Depot evaluate the extent of office superstore competition in the market and the number of office superstores the market can support. When selecting sites and markets for new store openings, defendants repeatedly refer to markets without office superstores as "non-competitive," even when the new store is adjacent to or near a warehouse club, consumer electronics store, or a mass merchandiser such as Wal-Mart. In a monthly report entitled "Competitor Store Opening/Closing Report" which Office Depot circulates to its Executive Committee, Office Depot notes all competitor store closings and openings, but the only competitors referred to for its United States stores are Staples and OfficeMax. . . .

While it is clear to the Court that Staples and Office Depot do not ignore sellers such as warehouse clubs, Best Buy, or Wal-Mart, the evidence clearly shows that Staples and Office Depot each consider the other superstores as the primary competition. For example, Office Depot has a Best Buy zone and Staples has a warehouse club zone. However, each still refers to its one firm markets with no other office superstore as "non-competitive" zones or markets. In addition, it is clear from the evidence that Staples and Office Depot price check the other office superstores much more frequently and extensively than they price check other retailers such as BJ's or Best Buy, and that Staples and Office Depot are more concerned with keeping their prices in parity with the other office superstores in their geographic areas than in undercutting Best Buy or a warehouse club.

For the reasons set forth in the above analysis, the Court finds that the sale of consumable office supplies through office supply superstores is the appropriate relevant product market for purposes of considering the possible anti-competitive effects of the proposed merger between Staples and Office Depot. The pricing evidence indicates a low cross-elasticity of demand between consumable office products sold by Staples or Office Depot and those same products sold by other sellers of office supplies. This same evidence indicates that non-superstore sellers of office supplies are not able to effectively constrain the superstores' prices, because a significant number of superstore customers do not turn to a non-superstore alternative when faced with higher prices in the one firm markets. In addition, the factors or "practical indicia" of *Brown Shoe* support a finding of a "submarket" under the facts of this case, and "submarkets," as *Brown Shoe* established, may themselves be appropriate product markets for antitrust purposes. 370 U.S. at 325, 82 S. Ct. at 1523-24.[11]

IV. Probable Effect on Competition

After accepting the Commission's definition of the relevant product market, the Court next must consider the probable effect of a merger between Staples and Office Depot in the geographic markets previously identified. One way to do this is to examine the concentration statistics and HHIs within the geographic markets.[12] If the relevant product market is defined as the sale of consumable office supplies through office supply superstores, the HHIs in many of the geographic markets are at problematic levels even before the merger. Currently, the least concentrated market is that of Grand Rapids-Muskegon-Holland, Michigan, with an HHI of 3,597, while the most concentrated is Washington, D.C. with an HHI of 6,944. In contrast, after a merger of Staples and Office Depot, the least concentrated area would be Kalamazoo-Battle Creek, Michigan, with an HHI of 5,003, and many areas would have HHIs of 10,000. The average increase in HHI caused by the merger would be 2,715 points. The concentration statistics show that a merged Staples-Office Depot would have a dominant market share in 42 geographic markets across the country. The combined shares of Staples and Office Depot in the office superstore market would be 100% in 15 metropolitan areas. It is in these markets the post-merger HHI would be 10,000. In 27 other metropolitan areas, where the number of office superstore competitors would drop from three to two, the post-merger market shares would range from 45% to 94%, with post-merger HHIs ranging from 5,003 to 9,049. Even the lowest of these HHIs indicates a "highly concentrated" market.

According to the Department of Justice Merger Guidelines, a market with an HHI of less than 1000 is "unconcentrated." An HHI between 1000 and 1800 indicates a "moderately concentrated" market, and any market with an HHI over 1800 qualifies as "highly concentrated." *See FTC v. PPG Indus., Inc.*, 798 F.2d 1500, 1503 (D.C. Cir. 1986) (citing the

---

[11] As other courts have noted, use of the term "submarket" may be confusing. *See Allen-Myland v. IBM Corp.*, 33 F.3d 194, 208 n.16 (3rd Cir. 1994) (finding it less confusing to speak in terms of the relevant product market rather than the submarket), *cert. denied*, 513 U.S. 106 (1994); *Olin Corp. v. FTC*, 986 F.2d 1295, 1299 (9th Cir. 1993) ("[E]very market that encompasses less than all products is, in a sense, a submarket"), *cert. denied*, 510 U.S. 1110 (1994). Whatever term is used—market, submarket, relevant product market—the analysis is the same.

[12] Market power or the lack of it is often determined by the Herfindahl-Hirschmann Index ("HHI"). The HHI is calculated by squaring the individual market shares of all the firms in the market and adding up the squares. The HHI takes into account the relative size and distribution of the firms in a market, increasing both as the number of firms in the market decreases and as the disparity in size among those firms increases.

U.S. Department of Justice and Federal Trade Commission Horizontal Merger Guidelines) (hereinafter "Merger Guidelines"). Further, according to the Merger Guidelines, unless mitigated by other factors which lead to the conclusion that the merger is not likely to lessen competition, an increase in the HHI in excess of 50 points in a post-merger highly concentrated market may raise significant competitive concerns. In cases where the post-merger HHI is less than 1,800, but greater than 1,000, the Merger Guidelines presume that a 100 point increase in the HHI is evidence that the merger will create or enhance market power. The Merger Guidelines, of course, are not binding on the Court, but, as this Circuit has stated, they do provide "a useful illustration of the application of the HHI," *id.* at 1503 n.4, and the Court will use that guidance here. In addition, though the Supreme Court has established that there is no fixed threshold at which an increase in market concentration triggers the antitrust laws, *see, e.g., United States v. Philadelphia National Bank,* 374 U.S. 321, 363-65 (1963), this is clearly not a borderline case. The pre-merger markets are already in the "highly concentrated" range, and the post-merger HHIs show an average increase of 2,715 points. Therefore, the Court finds that the plaintiff's have shown a likelihood of success on the merits. With HHIs of this level, the Commission certainly has shown a "reasonable probability" that the proposed merger would have an anti-competitive effect.[13]

The HHI calculations and market concentration evidence, however, are not the only indications that a merger between Staples and Office Depot may substantially lessen competition. Much of the evidence already discussed with respect to defining the relevant product market also indicates that the merger would likely have an anti-competitive effect. The evidence of the defendants' own current pricing practices, for example, shows that an office superstore chain facing no competition from other superstores has the ability to profitably raise prices for consumable office supplies above competitive levels. The fact that Staples and Office Depot both charge higher prices where they face no superstore competition demonstrates that an office superstore can raise prices above competitive levels. The evidence also shows that defendants also change their price zones when faced with entry of another office superstore, but do not do so for other retailers. Since prices are significantly lower in markets where Staples and Office Depot compete, eliminating this competition with one another would free the parties to charge higher prices in those markets, especially those in which the combined entity would be the sole office superstore. In addition, allowing the defendants to merge would eliminate significant future competition. Absent the merger, the firms are likely, and in fact have planned, to enter more of each other's markets, leading to a deconcentration of the market and, therefore, increased competition between the superstores.

---

[13] The Court is also persuaded by the Commission's HHI calculations for its alternate relevant product market, that of the sale of consumable office supplies through retail stores to small businesses and individuals with home offices. In response to the defendants' arguments regarding the variety of competition in this larger office supply market, the Commission presented HHI calculations which included additional competitors. Besides Staples, Office Depot, and OfficeMax, the Commission included Price Costco, Sam's Club, BJ's, Best Buy, Wal-Mart, Kmart, Target, Circuit City, Computer City, CompUSA, and independent office supply dealers in this alternate HHI calculation. The result showed Sacramento, California as the least concentrated market post-merger with an HHI of 1,793, and Greenville, North Carolina as the most concentrated market post-merger with an HHI of 5,047. Overall, the HHIs increased by an average of 861 points post-merger, an increase that is still problematic according to the Merger Guidelines given that all the post-merger markets were in the "moderately" or "highly concentrated" range. Therefore, for this reason as well, the Court finds that the Commission has shown a "reasonable probability" that the merger would have an anti-competitive effect.

In addition, direct evidence shows that by eliminating Staples' most significant, and in many markets only, rival, this merger would allow Staples to increase prices or otherwise maintain prices at an anti-competitive level.[14] The merger would eliminate significant head-to-head competition between the two lowest cost and lowest priced firms in the superstore market. Thus, the merger would result in the elimination of a particularly aggressive competitor in a highly concentrated market, a factor which is certainly an important consideration when analyzing possible anti-competitive effects. *See, e.g., FTC v. Food Town Stores, Inc.,* 539 F.2d 1339, 1345 (4th Cir. 1976) (enjoining merger when merging firms had been "aggressive competitors in the past," by opening stores in each other's markets and increasing sales by greater than the industry's sales average). It is based on all of this evidence as well that the Court finds that the Commission has shown a likelihood of success on the merits and a "reasonable probability" that the proposed transaction will have an anti-competitive effect.

. . . .

V. Entry Into the Market

"The existence and significance of barriers to entry are frequently, of course, crucial considerations in a rebuttal analysis [because] [i]n the absence of significant barriers, a company probably cannot maintain supra-competitive pricing for any length of time." *Baker Hughes, Inc.,* 908 F.2d at 987. Thus, the Court must consider whether, in this case, "entry into the market would likely avert anticompetitive effects from [Staples'] acquisition of [Office Depot]." *Id.* at 989. If the defendants' evidence regarding entry showed that the Commission's market-share statistics give an incorrect prediction of the proposed acquisition's probable effect on competition because entry into the market would likely avert any anti-competitive effect by acting as a constraint on Staples-Office Depot's prices, the Court would deny the FTC's motion. The Court, however, cannot make such a finding in this case.

The defendants argued during the hearing and in their briefs that the rapid growth in overall office supply sales has encouraged and will continue to encourage expansion and entry. One reason for this, according to Dr. Hausman's declaration, is that entry is more attractive when an industry is growing, because new entrants can establish themselves without having to take all of their sales away from existing competitors. In addition, the defendants' impressive retailing expert, Professor Maurice Segall, testified at the hearing that there are "no barriers to entry in retailing," and defendants pointed to the fact that all office superstore entrants have entered within the last 11 years.

---

14 There has been tremendous argument regarding whether the FTC actually contends that prices will go up after the merger. The Court understands that is not precisely the Commission's contention. Rather, the Commission argues that the merger will have an anti-competitive effect such that the combined firm's prices will be higher after the merger than they would be absent the merger. This does not necessarily mean that prices would rise from the levels they are now. Instead, according to the Commission, prices would simply not decrease as much as they would have on their own absent the merger. It is only in this sense that the Commission has contended that prices would go up—prices would go up compared to where they would have been absent the merger. It is only in this sense that consumers would be faced with "higher" prices. Therefore, when the Court discusses "raising" prices it is also with respect to raising prices with respect to where prices would have been absent the merger, not actually an increase from present price levels.

In addition to this general testimony regarding entry, defendants emphasized specific examples of recent or planned entry. For example, defendants offered testimony from John Ledecky, Chairman and CEO of U.S. Office Products, regarding U.S. Office Products' acquisition of Mailboxes, Etc., an acquisition that was coincidentally announced the night before Mr. Ledecky's testimony in this case. Through this acquisition, U.S. Office Products, an organization or co-op of approximately 165 contract stationers located throughout the country, will acquire the 3300-unit Mailboxes, Etc. franchise operation. Defendants also offered testimony regarding Wal-Mart's plans to revamp and expand the office supply section in its stores. According to the deposition testimony of William Long, Vice President for Merchandizing at Wal-Mart, and David Glass, President and CEO of Wal-Mart, Wal-Mart will modify its office supplies department, called "Department 3," beginning in May 1997 and continuing through the summer. Though Mr. Long was not certain of the exact number of SKUs of office supplies Wal-Mart's new Department 3 will offer, he estimated the range to be 2,600 to 3,000 SKUs. Finally, defendants offered testimony regarding the general ability of mass merchandisers, computer superstores, and warehouse clubs to change store configurations and shift shelf space to accommodate new demands or popular products.

There are problems with the defendants' evidence, however, that prevent the Court from finding in this case that entry into the market by new competitors or expansion into the market by existing firms would likely avert the anti-competitive effects from Staples' acquisition of Office Depot. For example, while it is true that all office superstore entrants have entered within the last 11 years, the recent trend for office superstores has actually been toward exiting the market rather than entering. Over the past few years, the number of office superstore chains has dramatically dropped from twenty-three to three. All but Staples, Office Depot, and OfficeMax have either closed or been acquired. The failed office superstore entrants include very large, well-known retail establishments such as Kmart, Montgomery Ward, Ames, and Zayres. A new office superstore would need to open a large number of stores nationally in order to achieve the purchasing and distribution economies of scale enjoyed by the three existing firms. Sunk costs would be extremely high. Economies of scale at the local level, such as in the costs of advertizing and distribution, would also be difficult for a new superstore entrant to achieve since the three existing firms have saturated many important local markets. For example, according to the defendants' own saturation analyses, Staples estimates that there is room for less than two additional superstores in the Washington, D.C. area and Office Depot estimates that there is room for only two more superstores in Tampa, Florida.

The Commission offered Office 1 as a specific example of the difficulty of entering the office superstore arena. Office 1 opened its first two stores in 1991. By the end of 1994, Office 1 had 17 stores, and grew to 35 stores operating in 11 Midwestern states as of October 11, 1996. As of that date, Office 1 was the fourth largest office supply superstore chain in the United States. Unfortunately, also as of that date, Office 1 filed for Chapter 11 bankruptcy protection. Brad Zenner, President of Office 1, testified through declaration, that Office 1 failed because it was severely undercapitalized in comparison with the industry leaders, Staples, Office Depot, and OfficeMax. In addition, Mr. Zenner testified that when the three leaders ultimately expanded into the smaller markets where Office 1 stores were located, they seriously undercut Office 1's retail prices and profit margins. Because Office 1 lacked the capitalization of the three leaders and lacked the economies of scale enjoyed by those competitors, Office 1 could not remain profitable.

For the reasons discussed above, the Court finds it extremely unlikely that a new office superstore will enter the market and thereby avert the anti-competitive effects from

Staples' acquisition of Office Depot. The defendants, of course, focused their entry argument on more than just the entry of additional superstores, pointing also to the expansion of existing companies such as U.S. Office Products and Wal-Mart. The Court also finds it unlikely that the expansions by U.S. Office Products and Wal-Mart would avert the anti-competitive effects which would result from the merger.

. . . .

VI. Efficiencies

Whether an efficiencies defense showing that the intended merger would create significant efficiencies in the relevant market, thereby offsetting any anti-competitive effects, may be used by a defendant to rebut the government's *prima facie* case is not entirely clear. The newly revised efficiencies section of the Merger Guidelines recognizes that, "mergers have the potential to generate significant efficiencies by permitting a better utilization of existing assets, enabling the combined firm to achieve lower costs in producing a given quality and quantity than either firm could have achieved without the proposed transaction." *See* Merger Guidelines § 4. This coincides with the view of some courts that "whether an acquisition would yield significant efficiencies in the relevant market is an important consideration in predicting whether the acquisition would substantially lessen competition. . . . [T]herefore, . . . an efficiency defense to the government's *prima facie* case in section 7 challenges is appropriate in certain circumstances." *FTC v. University Health,* 938 F.2d 1206, 1222 (11th Cir. 1991). The Supreme Court, however, in *FTC v. Procter & Gamble Co.*, 386 U.S. 568, 579 (1967), stated that "[p]ossible economies cannot be used as a defense to illegality in section 7 merger cases." There has been great disagreement regarding the meaning of this precedent and whether an efficiencies defense is permitted. Compare *RSR Corp. v. FTC*, 602 F.2d 1317, 1325 (9th Cir. 1979) (finding that the efficiencies argument has been rejected repeatedly), *cert. denied*, 445 U.S. 927 (1980), with *University Health*, 938 F.2d at 1222 (recognizing the defense). Neither the Commission or the defendants could point to a case in which this Circuit has spoken on the issue. *But see FTC v. Coca-Cola Co.*, 641 F. Supp. 1128, 1141 (D.D.C. 1986) (Gesell) (finding that Congress recognized as desirable efficiencies that benefit consumers, but that they were to be "developed by dominant concerns using their brains, not their money by buying out troubling competitors. The Court has no authority to move in a direction neither Congress nor the Supreme Court has accepted"), vacated as moot, 829 F.2d 191 (D.C. Cir. 1987). Assuming that it is a viable defense, however, the Court cannot find in this case that the defendants' efficiencies evidence rebuts the presumption that the merger may substantially lessen competition or shows that the Commission's evidence gives an inaccurate prediction of the proposed acquisition's probable effect.

The Court agrees with the defendants that where, as here, the merger has not yet been consummated, it is impossible to quantify precisely the efficiencies that it will generate. In addition, the Court recognizes a difference between efficiencies which are merely speculative and those which are based on a prediction backed by sound business judgment. Nor does the Court believe that the defendants must prove their efficiencies by "clear and convincing evidence" in order for those efficiencies to be considered by the Court. That would saddle Section 7 defendants with the nearly impossible task of rebutting a possibility with a certainty, a burden which was rejected in *United States v. Baker Hughes, Inc.*, 908 F.2d 981, 992 (D.C. Cir. 1990). Instead, like all rebuttal evidence in Section 7 cases, the defendants must simply rebut the presumption that the merger will substantially lessen competition by showing that the Commission's evidence gives an inaccurate prediction of the proposed acquisition's probable effect. *See id.* at 991. Defendants, however, must do this with credible evidence, and the Court with respect to this issue did not find the defendants' evidence to be credible.

Defendants' submitted an "Efficiencies Analysis" which predicted that the combined company would achieve savings of between $4.9 and $6.5 billion over the next five years. In addition, the defendants argued that the merger would also generate dynamic efficiencies. For example, defendants argued that as suppliers become more efficient due to their increased sales volume to the combined Staples-Office Depot, they would be able to lower prices to their other retailers. Moreover, defendants argued that two-thirds of the savings realized by the combined company would be passed along to consumers.

Evaluating credibility, as the Court must do, the Court credits the testimony and Report of the Commission's expert, David Painter, over the testimony and Efficiencies Study of the defendants' efficiencies witness, Shira Goodman, Senior Vice President of Integration at Staples. Mr. Painter's testimony was compelling, and the Court finds, based primarily on Mr. Painter's testimony, that the defendants' cost savings estimates are unreliable. First, the Court notes that the cost savings estimate of $4.947 billion over five years which was submitted to the Court exceeds by almost 500% the figures presented to the two Boards of Directors in September 1996, when the Boards approved the transaction. The cost savings claims submitted to the Court are also substantially greater than those represented in the defendants' Joint Proxy Statement/Prospectus "reflecting the best currently available estimate of management," and filed with the Securities and Exchange Commission on January 23, 1997, or referenced in the "fairness opinions" rendered by the defendants' investment bankers which are contained in the Proxy Statement.

Therefore, the Court finds that the Commission has shown a likelihood that it will succeed in proving, after a full administrative trial on the merits, that the effect of the proposed merger between Staples and Office Depot "may be substantially to lessen competition" in violation of Section 7 of the Clayton Act. In addition, the Court has weighed the equities and finds that they tip in favor of granting a preliminary injunction. A preliminary injunction is, therefore, found to be in the public interest. The FTC's motion for a preliminary injunction shall be granted.

COMMENTARY

1. As a recent opinion applying the Merger Guidelines, consider the court's reliance upon "practical indicia" in its definition of the relevant product market. Does the court's conclusion that the product market was "the sale of consumable office supplies through office superstores," contain an implicit assumption that the physical environment in which a product is sold is as significant as its price? Are the physical premises of a seller an element of the definition of a geographic market under the Guidelines? In assessing the probable impact of the merger on competition for these products, in your opinion, did the court properly weigh the likelihood of consumers turning to K-Mart, Walmart, and other sellers for file folders, perforated pads, manila folders, and computer supplies? Were the merger permitted, and the price of these items rose on the average of 30%, would a consumer be deterred from seeking such alternative sellers? In considering the entry factors, is it valid to assume that K-Mart, Walmart, and other discounting retailers would only enter with physical sales areas like that of the merger proponents? Would you be willing to save 30% on your office supplies if you bought them in a small space in the K-Mart store in the same shopping mall as Staples? If you purchased them by e-mail from Walmart, would you be concerned about the space? Were the Guidelines properly applied by the court in rejecting the efficiency defense given by the merger proponents?

Note Judge Hogan's several references in the *Staples* opinion to the evidence presented by the FTC. The record in the case shows that the economists, who appeared as expert witnesses for each side, presented the court with sophisticated econometric analysis of the competitive impact of the proposed merger. These analytical techniques are increasingly being employed, *see, e.g., State v. Kraft Foods, Inc.,* 926 F. Supp. 321 (S.D.N.Y. 1995). The economist who appeared on behalf of the defendant in the *Kraft* case became the Deputy Assistant Attorney General in the Economic Analysis Section of the Antitrust Division in 1997. Is it a fair inference that Judge Hogan found the FTC's evidence persuasive, notwithstanding that the products at issue were ordinary, garden variety items available from several alternate sources in most cities of the United States? If, as appears to be the trend, the use of econometric analysis in merger cases increases, should this development be viewed as material improvement to the enforcement process? Given the material assumptions that are often required in the preparation and in the interpretation of such data, should there also be a concern that such data may convey an appearance of greater precision than is warranted in some circumstances?

2. After this decision, the parties decided to end their merger plans. A recent review of the office supply industry, with particular reference to the assumptions underlying Judge Hogan's opinion, has concluded that the defenders of the merger were correct in their assertions that new entrants would provide effective competition. In support of his conclusion that the case was wrongly decided, Christopher M. Grengs writes, in *The "Best Ever"* Staples *Antitrust Suit: Hoisted With Their Own Petards, a Case of* Hamlet *Without the Danish Prince,* <http://www.mises.org/journals/scholar/grengs.pdf>.

> *Staples* should not be viewed as a clear victory for the FTC. Quite to the contrary, it should be seen as a provocative and cautionary case study in the application of orthodox, fragmented, static, industrial organization and antitrust paradigms to the dynamic industries of the real world. Instead, industrial organization and the legal and public policies related to it should adopt the . . . coherent, dynamic, process-oriented paradigm articulated by . . . Joseph A. Schumpeter in his famous description of capitalism as a "continual process of creative destruction."
>
> . . . .
>
> Subsequent events in the office supply industry provide compelling empirical evidence that the FTC's exceedingly narrow "submarket" definition was incorrect. The . . . recent history of the office supply

> industry is overwhelming, self-explanatory evidence that the broader office supply industry—a much larger marketplace—with its numerous overlapping bundles of goods and services and frequent cross-shopping was the proper relevant market. In particular, the FTC had argued that discounters were not effective competition . . . and could not constrain their behavior. The reality is that discounters are genuine competitors for OSSs, and have the ability to constrain their prices and share of the broader office supply industry . . . .

Id. at 2, 83. For a statement of Schumpeter's thesis see page 766, *infra.* The application of various paradigms of antitrust enforcement are set out in Chapter 1, *supra.*

Some post-decision studies of market impact have supported the enforcement action. In 1975, the FTC entered into a consent order with the Xerox Corp. in an action charging monopolization based on its dry ink photocopying technology. The FTC order required a limited compulsory royalty-free license to three basic patents, *In re Xerox Corp.*, 86 F.T.C. 364, 373 (1975). In post-decision reviews of that relevant market, it was found that new entry was enhanced. *See* Timothy Bresnahan, *Post-Entry Competition in the Plain Paper Copier Market*, 75 AM. ECON. REV. 15 (1985); Fredric M. Scherer, *Antitrust, Efficiency, and Progress*, 62 N.Y.U. L. REV. 998, 1016 (1987).

Do you think it would be desirable to require a post-decision review of the consequences in every antitrust enforcement case? Do you agree with Grengs' statement that antitrust analysis in *Staples* rested on fragmented and static paradigms? How might a more dynamic, Schumpeterian approach be introduced? Could Judge Hogan have permitted the merger subject to the condition that there be significant entry of competitors within three years after the merger? Do the Merger Guidelines support such an approach?

3. Note that the FTC staff had proposed a consent decree in the Staples merger, a procedure which was rejected by the Commission. Consider the following discussion of the consent decree as an enforcement tool.

The rising volume of consent decrees has re-started a discussion about the increasingly regulatory nature of antitrust enforcement. William Baxter, head of the Antitrust Division in the Reagan administration, recently stated that merger review ". . . is becoming more and more regulatory." John R. Wilke & Brian Gruley, *Merger Monitors: Acquisitions Can Mean Long-Lasting Scrutiny by Antitrust Agencies,* WALL ST. J., March 4, 1997, at A1. This same article noted,

> Increasingly, the FTC and the Justice Department, reluctant to take big cases to court, are instead fashioning intrusive settlements that let big

> deals go ahead but leave the government with a continuing role in monitoring the business.

More than a decade earlier, an antitrust scholar identified this trend in the operation of the Antitrust Division as follows:

> . . . [T]he Antitrust Division has changed from a traditional, litigation-oriented enforcement agency to a regulatory agency. . . . [I]t has adopted a negotiational rather than an adversarial posture. . . . The change is not merely procedural. It has important implications for enforcement policy, compliance incentives, and substantive law. For example the present administration uses the review process to favor market deregulation. Another administration . . . may decide that the review process also permits a pervasive industrial policy. . . .

E. Thomas Sullivan, *The Antitrust Division as a Regulatory Agency: An Enforcement Policy in Transition,* 64 WASH. U. L.Q. 997 (1986).

In assessing the efficacy of antitrust enforcement policy regarding mergers, as with other substantive areas of antitrust law, the basic goals of the antitrust laws are an appropriate benchmark. Viewing merger transactions as one means of optimizing the use of resources, the public policy question arises of whether the Guidelines/Regulatory approach is an efficient procedure to bar non-optimizing mergers. A calculus of the relative social costs of litigation as compared with the regulatory approach is warranted. A substantial amount of data collection would be required at the outset. It seems clear that as prosecutors, the agencies were able to impose substantial legal expenses on merger proponents who contested an agency determination. In those proposed mergers which might have ultimately resulted in enhanced output and the availability of improved products at lower prices, which were abandoned at the prospect of protracted litigation costs, there is the social cost of these foregone benefits. However, the case for the regulatory approach is strengthened by those studies showing that most litigation ultimately ends in settlement. George L. Priest & Benjamin Klein, *The Selection of Disputes for Litigation,* 13 J. LEGAL STUD. 1 (1984).

Recent experience under the regulatory enforcement process in current merger law suggest various concerns with this regulatory system. The potential for distortions of the merits of a merger case presented to an agency is noted by an FTC economist as follows:

> Antitrust enforcement is a repeated game, so the agency could consider reputation effects in both the benefits . . . and the costs . . . . Thus, cases which do not benefit competition may have some value to the agency.

Malcolm B. Coate, *Winners and Losers in the Settlement of Merger Litigation, in* THE ECONOMICS OF THE ANTITRUST PROCESS 155 (Malcolm B. Coate & Andrew N. Kleit eds. 1996).

Another ground for concern is the involvement of the agency in post-merger management. In *FTC v. Promodes, S.A.,* 1989-2 TRADE CASES ¶ 68,688 (N.D. Ga.

1989), the Commission conditioned a merger on divestiture by the acquiring grocery chain within nine months of the acquisition of six supermarkets in Chattanooga, Tennessee. The divestiture could only be accomplished by sale to purchasers approved by the Commission and on authorized terms. 55 Fed. Reg. 7567 (March 2, 1990); 55 Fed. Reg. 23,138 (June 6, 1990). As part of the Consent Order, the Commission exercised its authority under 15 U.S.C. § 45(1) and required the acquiring firm to consent to the appointment of a trustee, with authorization to dispose of those properties not disposed of by the acquiring firm within the original nine month period. When divestiture of the six stores was not accomplished within the nine month period, a trustee was appointed. However, the trustee was unable to sell the stores either and subsequently, the Commission withdrew the requirement. By this time, three years had elapsed. *See* NAT'L L.J., June 2, 1995, at 1. The Department of Justice also conditions mergers on compliance with divestiture of certain assets within a stated time, either by the acquiring firm or an appointed trustee, as in the Walt Disney/Capital Cities merger. The Department required Disney to enter into a "definitive agreement" to sell KCAL-TV within nine months or to complete the sale within twelve months or to have a trustee appointed to accomplish the sale. 1996 WL 14876 (D.O.J.).

Given the rising volume of such negotiated merger transactions, the issue remains of the efficacy of this means of restricting anticompetitive outcomes. Would you advocate periodic oversight hearings by a congressional committee to review agency conduct and performance?

Chapter 13

Price Discrimination and the Robinson-Patman Act

A. The Price Discrimination Provisions of the Original (1914) Clayton Act and its (1936) Robinson-Patman Amendments

1. The Legislation of 1914

Section 2 of the Clayton Act, 38 Stat. 740, enacted in 1914, provided as follows:

> [I]t shall be unlawful for any person engaged in commerce, in the course of such commerce, either directly or indirectly, to discriminate in price between different purchasers of commodities, which commodities are sold for use, consumption, or resale within the United States or any Territory thereof or the District of Columbia, or any insular possession, or any other place under the jurisdiction of the United States, where the effect of such discrimination may be to substantially lessen competition or tend to create a monopoly in any line of commerce: Provided, That nothing herein contained shall prevent discrimination in price between purchasers of commodities on account of differences in the grade, quality, or quantity of the commodity sold, or that makes only due allowance for difference in the cost of selling or transportation, or discrimination in price in the same or different communities made in good faith to meet competition: And Provided further, That nothing herein contained shall prevent persons engaged in selling goods, wares, or merchandise in commerce from selecting their own customers in bona fide transactions and not in restraint of trade.

In enacting this legislation, the Congress was concerned primarily with the use of price discrimination as a predatory weapon directed at rivals of the discriminating sellers. The Committee reports describe behavior of the Standard Oil Company and the American Tobacco Company as the kind at which the Act is directed. According to the Committee reports, it had been a common practice of those companies:

> . . . to lower prices of their commodities, oftentimes below the cost of production in certain communities and sections where they had compe-

> tition, with the intent to destroy and make unprofitable the business of their competitors, and with the ultimate purpose in view of thereby acquiring a monopoly in the particular locality or section in which the discriminating price is made. Every concern that engages in this evil practice must of necessity recoup its losses in the particular communities or sections where their commodities are sold below cost or without a fair profit by raising the price of this same class of commodities above their fair market value in other sections of communities.

H.R. Rep. No. 63-627, at 8-9 (1914); S. Rep. No. 63-698, at 2-4 (1914).

The analysis of the Committee Report assumes that a firm which sells at below-cost prices must recoup its losses from monopoly revenues earned in other locations. This is incomplete, is it not? The monopoly revenues from other markets are not the only source of financing for the losses incurred through predatory pricing. There are other sources of financing. Indeed, a firm's own "deep pockets" could well be the principal source of such financing.

The Committee's focus on the financing (or subsidizing) of predatory pricing from monopoly revenues in other markets diverts the focus from the principal calculation which underlies all predatory pricing: Is the discounted present value of expected future monopoly revenues *from the market which is the subject of predatory pricing* sufficient (i) to recoup present losses incurred there through predatory pricing and (ii) to provide a profit for the predatory endeavor? Thus the more revealing focus is upon recoupment from future monopoly profits. If there is a likelihood that a firm can generate monopoly profits in the future more than sufficient to compensate it for losses incurred during a temporary period of predatory pricing, then predatory pricing is rational behavior. This inquiry is a powerful analytical tool, as explained below.

If there is no likely prospect that a firm's low prices will, by driving its rivals from the market or by coercing them into compliance with oligopoly or cartel prices, bring about some form of future monopoly or oligopoly pricing, then no such predatory scenario is possible. Whatever goal the managers of the firm charging the low prices had in mind cannot be a predatory one, since we have determined that in these circumstances the predatory scenario is not credible. As a presumably rational actor, the firm must have some other goal than a predatory one. This kind of analysis enables courts to dismiss many unmeritorious cases alleging predatory pricing. The Supreme Court's recent decision in *Brooke Group* has enthusiastically embraced this kind of "recoupment" analysis for all forms of predatory pricing claims, including predatory pricing under section two of the Clayton Act, as amended by the Robinson-Patman Act.

Finally, a word about terminology. In the 1914 legislation, Congress was (as we have seen) concerned with prohibiting the predatory pricing of the kind practiced by the Standard Oil and American Tobacco companies. The effects of that pricing took place on the same level of the distribution chain as Standard and American were operating: the victims were the competitors of Standard and American.

Business firms engaged in predatory pricing, therefore, produce effects on the market on the "primary line," *i.e.*, at the same level of the distribution chain as they (the predators) are operating.

2. The Robinson-Patman Act of 1936[1]

While § 2 of the Clayton Act was directed against the predatory pricing activities of firms like Standard Oil, Congress was concerned with an entirely different problem in 1936 when it amended § 2's provisions in the Robinson-Patman Act. The villains in 1936 were the chain stores, and in particular, the Great Atlantic and Pacific Tea Company (the "A&P"). The perceived problem was that the chain stores were able to purchase their supplies at lower prices than their smaller rivals, thus jeopardizing the existence of small, family-owned retail stores.

In the mid-1930s, Congress shared a widespread concern that the expansion of chain stores was a major threat to small wholesale and retail businesses. It was believed that excess capacity among suppliers was a common phenomenon and that, as a result, many suppliers could be induced to accept cut-rate prices on orders that were large enough to employ significant amounts of otherwise idle plant facilities. Large buyers thus would demand and receive "marginal cost" prices, prices that compensated the supplier for the extra costs it incurred in producing the goods, but which failed to compensate it for proportionate overhead, depreciation, and other fixed expenses allocated to the production of these goods. At the same time, it was believed that producers had certain "earnings requirements" which would in fact be met so long as they stayed in business. When *pro rata* earnings requirements were not met from the marginal cost sales to large buyers, it was believed that suppliers would recoup the deficit by charging higher prices to their smaller customers. These customers, generally wholesalers, and the retailers supplied by those wholesalers, would thus be in a position of having to compete with chains and other large buyers which had access to lower supply prices.

It was in this situation that Congress perceived a threat to the continued existence of smaller businesses. It saw the chains triumphing, not because of superior efficiency, but because of the "unfair use" of their purchasing power to obtain their inventories at lower supply prices than their smaller rivals. The congressional response was the enactment of the Robinson-Patman Act, designed to preserve and to strengthen the old § 2 and to expand its application to discrimination that operated vertically through the distribution system to create anticompetitive effects. Yet Congress was careful both in 1914 and in 1936 not to outlaw price discrimination *per se*. It wished to prevent competition from being distorted by the buying power of the chains, but not to discourage efficiencies or to interfere with the pricing flexibility that is a necessary part of competitive behavior. Thus, it prohibited price dis-

---

1 The following material draws heavily from Daniel J. Gifford, *Assessing Secondary-Line Injury Under the Robinson-Patman Act: The Concept of "Competitive Advantage,"* 44 GEO. WASH. L. REV. 48-52 (1975).

crimination only where the effects of the discrimination "may" lessen competition or tend to create a monopoly or (in the Robinson-Patman amendments) injure competition with the grantor or recipient of the discrimination. Congress provided, moreover, that a discrimination can be cost-justified where the difference in the prices that a supplier charges two groups of purchasers reflects no more than the difference in the supplier's costs of serving those two groups. Additionally, regardless of the supplier's costs, it may, under the Act, meet the "equally low price of a competitor."

The legislation which Congress adopted in 1936 thus had an entirely different objective from the 1914 legislation which it amended. In 1936 Congress wanted to protect small business. The legislation it enacted to achieve this objective is phrased in terms of protecting "competition." Yet, in fact, the buying power of the chains was almost always a reflection, not of monopoly or monopsony power, but of the efficiencies which inhere in large-scale production and distribution: the parties' transactions costs are reduced when a single sale accounts for the same volume as many smaller sales; planning in production and delivery is often facilitated by large volume transactions; and transportation costs are often reduced. Prices which reflect these efficiencies are fully consistent with competition in the sense in which an economist would use that term, but proof of these efficiencies sufficient to support the cost-justification defense is often unavailable. We must be careful, however, to remember that when dealing with the Robinson-Patman Act, Congress has misused the term "competition," or used it in a peculiar sense. The legislation speaks of protecting competition, but the legislation often means protecting small competitors from supply-cost advantages possessed by large-volume rivals.

Again, a terminology note. The effects of the discrimination that were the focus of Congressional concern in the Robinson-Patman legislation occurred on the secondary or tertiary lines: *i.e.,* the effects of the discrimination by the manufacturer disadvantaged the disfavored buyer or the customer of the disfavored buyer. These firms operated, respectively, at the one and two levels of the distribution chain below the level of the discriminating seller. Thus the discriminating seller was operating on the primary line but its customers were operating on the secondary line and their customers were operating on the tertiary line.

B. Discrimination Whose Effects Are on the Primary Line

Brooke Group Ltd. v. Brown & Williamson Tobacco Corp.
509 U.S. 209 (1993)

[The opinion is printed in Chapter 11, page 532.]

COMMENTARY

1. Section 2(a) does not make all price discrimination unlawful. Price discrimination becomes unlawful only where "the effect . . . may be substantially to lessen competition or tend to create a monopoly in any line of commerce. . . ." At least those were the words employed in the original § 2 and which have been carried over in the Robinson-Patman Amendments.

2. Besides retaining the language quoted in Note 1 from the original version of § 2, the Robinson-Patman Amendment amended the prohibition against discrimination to add additional italicized language to the prohibition. As amended the prohibition now makes price discrimination unlawful where:

> "the effect . . . may be substantially to lessen competition or tend to create a monopoly in any line of commerce or tend *to injure, destroy, or prevent competition with any person who either grants or knowingly receives the benefit of such discrimination, or with customers of either of them* . . ." (emphasis supplied).

The Robinson-Patman Amendments were directed primarily at circumstances in which discriminatorily-low pricing imposed a competitive disadvantage upon purchasers from the discriminating seller vis-à-vis other purchasers who were able to buy from that seller at lower prices. The Great Atlantic and Pacific Tea Company (the "A&P") which, in 1936, was the largest grocery chain store in the United States, was a principal target of the legislation. The Congress believed that the A&P exploited its bargaining power as a large purchaser to obtain supply prices which were significantly lower than those available to its smaller rivals in grocery retailing.

Some of the additional language quoted above can be explained by the desire of Congress to protect small retailers against price discrimination by suppliers benefitting the A&P. Some of the additional language, however, seems to be concerned with primary-line effects, *i.e.,* the effects of discrimination on rivals of the discriminating seller. Read the language quoted above carefully. Identify the language which is concerned with secondary-line effects. Identify the language which is concerned with primary-line effects.

Areeda and Turner have argued that because Congress was primarily concerned with secondary line effects in the 1936 Robinson-Patman Amendments, the interpretation of the revised § 2 should be guided by the legislative intent manifested by the Congress of 1914 which was clearly concerned with primary line effects. That is, the revised § 2 carries over the concern of the original § 2 with regard to predatory pricing and then adds prohibitions designed to protect commercial customers from the disadvantages of discriminatory supply prices. New language added in 1936 which is directed to primary line effects refers to injury, destruction or prevention of "competition" with the discriminating seller. This language, it is contended, requires us to examine the effects on competition in the market affected by the discrimination. This approach would attribute a normal market-oriented meaning to the term "competition." (However, where the legislation refers to injuring, destroying or preventing competition with the recipient of a discrimination, the prevailing construction attributes a peculiar meaning to "competition," referring to the effects of the supply-cost advantage possessed by the recipient of the discrimination.) An examination of competition in the market affected by the discriminator's low prices is furthered by employing the Areeda-Turner standard to determine whether those prices are predatory. If they are not predatory, then competition is not endangered in that market.

3. In *Brooke Group*, the Supreme Court adopted the Areeda-Turner approach to interpreting the Robinson-Patman Act: as it applies to price discrimination having effects on the primary line, it is directed only against predatory pricing. The rationale for this approach is that Congress was concerned with predatory pricing when it enacted the original provision in 1914. And its concerns incorporated into the Robinson-Patman Amendments have nothing to do with primary-line effects.

4. In *Brooke Group*, the Supreme Court essentially repudiated the position it took in the now-infamous *Utah Pie* case. *Utah Pie Co. v. Continental Baking Co.*, 386 U.S. 685 (1967).

NOTE: THE *UTAH PIE* CASE

Utah Pie was a local seller of frozen pies in the Salt Lake City area. Also selling in the Salt Lake area were three companies which sold frozen pies throughout the nation: Continental Baking Company, Carnation Company and Pet Milk Company. The Salt Lake frozen pie market was expanding rapidly and Utah Pie was aggressively marketing its pies. A price war developed in which prices fell substantially and sales expanded. Since Utah Pie sold only in Salt Lake, it could not discriminate geographically. But because the three national companies sold in other markets, they necessarily discriminated geographically when they sold at lower prices in Salt Lake than in other areas. The question, then, was whether their discrimination might have lessened competition or tended to create a monopoly within the meaning of the Robinson-Patman Act. In upholding a jury verdict for the plaintiff Utah Pie Company, the Court (through Justice White) stated:

> . . . This case concerns the sellers' market. In this context, the Court of Appeals placed heavy emphasis on the fact that Utah Pie constantly increased its sales volume and continued to make a profit. But we disagree with its apparent view that there is no reasonably possible injury to competition as long as the volume of sales in a particular market is expanding and at least some of the competitors in the market continue to operate at a profit. . . . We believe that the Act reaches price discrimination that erodes competition as much as it does price discrimination that is intended to have immediate destructive impact. In this case, the evidence shows a drastically declining price structure which the jury could rationally attribute to continued or sporadic price discrimination.
> . . .

386 U.S. at 702-03. In a footnote, Justice White added other (somewhat delphic) language: "It might be argued that the respondents' conduct displayed only fierce competitive instincts. Actual intent to injure another competitor does not, however, fall into that category, and neither, when viewed in the context of the Robinson-Patman Act, do persistent sales below cost and radical price cuts themselves discriminatory. . . ." 386 U.S. at 702.

At the beginning of the period of intense competition, Utah Pie occupied 66.5% of the market. Subsequently its share fell to 45.3%. It continuously expanded the absolute volume of its sales and continued throughout to make a profit. By common measures, the market had become more competitive and the activities of all of the parties constituted exactly the kind of price competition that the Sherman Act seeks to encourage.

When the *Utah Pie* case was decided, the Areeda-Turner standards had not yet been formulated. The Court, moreover, did not use anything remotely resembling those standards. Consider whether you can identify the standards which the Court employed to determine whether the defendant companies' discrimination violated § 2(a).

The Court pointed out that the evidence showed "a drastically declining price structure." Yet it is extremely hard to believe that the Court equated "a drastically declining price structure" with a lessening of competition. After all, competition is supposed to exert a depressing effect on price. In a footnote, the Court added that some of the defendant companies had been engaging in "persistent sales below cost and radical price cuts themselves discriminatory." This additional language suggests that a multi-market seller is precluded from making "radical" price cuts, *i.e.,* large ones, in a regional market when it is already selling at prices below its average total costs.

Perhaps the Court thought this approach would help to protect small competitors from intense price competition from multi-market rivals. But so interpreted, the Robinson-Patman Act would impose a stifling rigidity on pricing, inconsistent with the purposes of the Sherman Act.

NOTE: THE SUBSEQUENT HISTORY OF *UTAH PIE*

Utah Pie was widely criticized as inconsistent with the basic goals of the Sherman Act. Ward Bowman began the academic assault in an article in the Yale Law Journal entitled *Restraint of Trade by the Supreme Court: The Utah Pie Case.*[2] More influential in undermining the authority of that decision than direct critiques, however, was the seminal article by Professors Areeda and Turner on predatory pricing,[3] discussed in Chapter 11 *supra.* Areeda and Turner, who were primarily concerned with predatory pricing as an offense under the Sherman Act, developed an approach under which pricing which fell below marginal cost (or its surrogate, average variable cost) would be presumed predatory. Pricing above marginal cost (or its surrogate, average variable cost) would be presumed lawful. After developing that analysis, they argued that, in addition to using their approach to evaluate claims of predatory pricing under the Sherman Act, their marginal cost/average variable cost standard should also be used to evaluate claims of price discrimination with primary line effects under the Robinson-Patman Act.

We saw in Chapter 11, *supra*, that most circuit courts have adopted some version of the Areeda-Turner standard for use in evaluating claims of predatory pricing under the attempt and monopolization clauses of the Sherman Act's § 2. Most of the circuits which have considered the issue have also taken the view that the only primary-line cases with which the Robinson-Patman Act's § 2(a) is concerned are those that involve predatory pricing. And these courts generally have employed a version of the Areeda-Turner standard to evaluate such claims. As a result, the standard used by the U.S. Supreme Court in *Utah Pie* to evaluate primary-line § 2(a) cases have not been generally used by the circuit courts.

Just about the only voice expressing concern about this little-known revolt of the circuit courts was Judge Easterbrook of the Seventh Circuit. *See A.A. Poultry Farms, Inc. v. Rose Acre Farms, Inc.*, 881 F.2d 1396 (7th Cir. 1989). While recognizing *Utah Pie*'s anticompetitive policy implications, Easterbrook suggested that lower federal courts were nonetheless obliged to follow governing Supreme Court precedent. The subject of Judge Easterbrook's concern has now been eliminated as a result of the Supreme Court's decision in *Brooke Group*. In that decision, the Supreme Court has finally repudiated the approach which it took in the *Utah Pie* case.

---

2 Ward Bowman, *Restraint of Trade by the Supreme Court: The* Utah Pie *Case*, 77 YALE L.J. 70 (1967).

3 Phillip Areeda & Donald Turner, *Predatory Pricing, and Related Practices Under Section 2 of the Sherman Act*, 88 HARV. L. REV. 697 (1975).

C. Discrimination Whose Effects Are on the Secondary Lines and Below

1. The *Morton Salt* Presumption

Federal Trade Commission v. Morton Salt Co.
334 U.S. 37 (1948)

[The Federal Trade Commission, after a hearing, found that the respondent had discriminated in price in violation of the Robinson-Patman Act. The Court of Appeals for the Seventh Circuit set aside the Commission's order and the Supreme Court granted certiorari.]

Mr. Justice BLACK delivered the opinion of the Court.

. . . .

Respondent manufactures several different brands of table salt and sells them directly to (1) wholesalers or jobbers, who in turn resell to the retail trade, and (2) large retailers, including chain store retailers. Respondent sells its finest brand of table salt, known as Blue Label, on what it terms a standard quantity discount system available to all customers. Under this system the purchasers pay a delivered price and the cost to both wholesale and retail purchasers of this brand differs according to the quantities bought. These prices are as follows, after making allowance for rebates and discounts:

	Per Case
Less-than-carload purchases	1.60
Carload purchases	1.50
5,000-case purchases in any consecutive 12 months	1.40
50,000-case purchases in any consecutive 12 months	1.35

Only five companies have ever bought sufficient quantities of respondent's salt to obtain the $1.35 per case price. These companies could buy in such quantities because they operate large chains of retail stores in various parts of the country. As a result of this low price these five companies have been able to sell Blue Label salt at retail cheaper than wholesale purchasers from respondent could reasonably sell the same brand of salt to independently operated retail stores, many of whom competed with the local outlets of the five chain stores.

. . . It is argued that the findings fail to show that respondent's discriminatory discounts had in fact caused injury to competition. . . . After a careful consideration of this provision of the Robinson-Patman Act, we have said that "the statute does not require that the discriminations must in fact have harmed competition, but only that there is a reasonable possibility that they 'may' have such an effect." . . . Here the Commission found what would appear to be obvious, that the competitive opportunities of certain merchants were injured when they had to pay respondent substantially more for their goods than their competitors had to pay. . . .

. . . That respondent's quantity discounts did result in price differentials between competing purchasers sufficient in amount to influence their resale price of salt was shown by evidence. This showing in itself is adequate to support the Commission's appropriate findings that the effect of such price discriminations "may be substantially to lessen competition . . . and to injure, destroy and prevent competition."

The adequacy of the evidence to support the Commission's findings of reasonably possible injury to competition from respondent's price differentials between competing carload and less-than-carload purchasers is singled out for special attacks here. . . . The argument is that there is an obvious saving to a seller who delivers goods in carload lots. Assuming this to be true, that fact would not tend to disprove injury to the merchant compelled to pay the less-than-carload price. For a ten-cent carload price differential against a merchant would injure him competitively just as much as a ten-cent differential under any other name. However relevant the separate carload argument might be to the question of justifying a differential by cost savings, it has no relevancy in determining whether the differential works an injury to a competitor. Since Congress has not seen fit to give carload discounts any favored classification we cannot do so. Such discounts, like all others, can be justified by a seller who proves that the full amount of the discount is based on his actual savings in cost. The trouble with this phase of respondent's case is that it has thus far failed to make such proof.

It is also argued that respondent's less-than-carload sales are very small in comparison with the total volume of its business and for that reason we should reject the Commission's finding that the effect of the carload discrimination may substantially lessen competition and may injure competition between purchasers who are granted and those who are denied this discriminatory discount. To support this argument, reference is made to the fact that salt is a small item in most wholesale and retail businesses and in consumers' budgets. For several reasons we cannot accept this contention.

There are many articles in a grocery store that, considered separately, are comparatively small parts of a merchant's stock. Congress intended to protect a merchant from competitive injury attributable to discriminatory prices on any or all goods sold in interstate commerce, whether the particular goods constituted a major or minor portion of his stock. Since a grocery store consists of many comparatively small articles, there is no possible way effectively to protect a grocer from discriminatory prices except by applying the prohibitions of the Act to each individual article in the store.

Furthermore, in enacting the Robinson-Patman Act, Congress was especially concerned with protecting small businesses which were unable to buy in quantities, such as the merchants here who purchased in less-than-carload lots. . . . The committee reports on the Robinson-Patman Act emphasized a belief that § 2 of the Clayton Act had "been too restrictive in requiring a showing of general injury to competitive conditions. . . ." The new provision . . . was intended to justify a finding of injury to competition by a showing of "injury to the competitor victimized by the discrimination." . . .

. . . The evidence covers about two thousand pages, largely devoted to this single issue—injury to competition. It would greatly handicap effective enforcement of the Act to require testimony to show that which we believe to be self-evident, namely, that there is a "reasonable possibility" that competition may be adversely affected by a practice under which manufacturers and producers sell their goods to some customers substantially cheaper than they sell like goods to the competitors of these customers. This showing in itself is sufficient to justify our conclusion that the Commission's findings of injury to competition were adequately supported by evidence.

. . . .

Reversed.

NOTE: THE *MORTON SALT* PRESUMPTION

1. In *Morton Salt*, the Supreme Court effectively adopted a presumption that the Act is violated when a supplier sells goods to competing dealers at prices which are "substantially" different. The Court twice indicates that the government need only prove that the seller sold to two competing dealers at prices which differed "substantially" in amount. Identify these passages. Does the Court's language appear to be carefully chosen? Thus a "substantial" difference in price to competing dealers is equivalent to a showing that "competition" has been lessened.

2. Do you think that the presumption which the Court adopted here is rebuttable? *See Falls City Industries, Inc. v. Vanco Beverage, Inc.*, 460 U.S. 428 (1983) (indicating the presumption to be rebuttable). Do you think that the presumption is equally applicable to sales of inputs to competing manufacturers as well as to dealers purchasing for resale? *See Minneapolis-Honeywell Regulator Co. v. FTC*, 191 F.2d 786 (7th Cir. 1951), *cert. dismissed*, 344 U.S. 206 (1952) (less applicable to manufacturers).

3. Consider how the "substantiality" of a price difference might be measured. The Court implied that the differences in price were substantial because they were "sufficient in amount to influence . . . [purchasing dealers'] resale prices." Each case of salt purchased by a retailer contained 24 packages of salt. Simple arithmetic indicates that the per-package price differential between cases selling for $1.35 and $1.60 was approximately $.01, an amount which could be passed on by the favored retailer to its customers. The difference in per-package cost of salt contained in cases selling to one retailer at $1.60 and to a competing retailer at $1.50 was approximately $.0042. That discount could have been passed on to those buyers who purchased two packages of salt.

4. During the decades subsequent to *Morton Salt*, the Commission frequently employed a "narrow profit margin" test to demonstrate the anticompetitive potential of a supplier's price discrimination at the customer level. The Commission thus focused upon the amount of the supplier's price differential to competing dealers in relation to the amount of the generally prevalent dealer margins. When the prevailing profit margins were narrow and when the discrimination was large in relation to them, the Commission tended to find the requisite anticompetitive potential for a violation. *See* Daniel J. Gifford, *Assessing Secondary-Line Injury Under the Robinson-Patman Act: The Concept of "Competitive Advantage,"* 44 GEO. WASH. L. REV. 48, 62-65 (1975).

5. Consider why Justice Black was not persuaded by the argument that salt constitutes a very small portion of a grocery store's inventory and that therefore the supply cost of salt is not of serious concern to the store. Justice Black could not have been receptive to that kind of argument in the case, because the discrimination involved was keyed to the quantities purchased. It would be the large purchasers who were entitled to the quantity or volume discount. If quantity or volume discounts were held to be lawful on salt, they would be lawful on all other grocery items, no single one of which is of crucial concern to an average retailer. But the aggregate effect of quantity discounts on most inventory items would be important. Smaller stores would be disadvantaged in competing with larger stores which had access to quantity discounts. Since the Act was passed to protect small grocery stores from the A&P's access to lower supply costs, the acceptance of such an argument would have undermined the application of the Act to exactly the area in which Congress was most concerned.

6. Consider why Justice Black was not receptive to the argument that the price of salt in full railroad-car-loads should be lower than in smaller-sized shipments because it is cheaper to ship in full railroad-car-loads. The reason Justice Black did not listen to that argument was that it was out of place. The Act provides a "cost justification" defense. But the cost justification defense is not purely a matter of argument. The respondent must establish by evidence that the difference in price did not exceed the savings in cost attributable to the lower-priced sales.

7. *Morton Salt* was an action brought by the government. The government always has standing to enforce the law. When a private party brings an action, the party must establish its standing to bring suit. Consider what a private may have to show to establish standing to complain of a Robinson-Patman Act violation. Consider the difference in what must be shown to establish standing in a primary line case from what has to be shown in a secondary line case.

CAVEATS TO—AND LIMITS UPON—THE *MORTON SALT* PRESUMPTION

1. The *Morton Salt* presumption reinforces the stifling effect of the Robinson-Patman Act upon marketplace competition, exacerbating the conflict between the Robinson-Patman Act and the rest of the antitrust laws. *See* page 713, *infra*. As a result, some courts have recently attempted to construe the Act as condemning price discrimination only where the discrimination produces an adverse impact upon competition generally. These courts are then at least open to rebutting the presumption by evidence showing that competition in the market generally remains healthy in spite of the defendant's discriminatory pricing. This approach has been followed in *Boise Cascade Corp. v. FTC*, 837 F.2d 1127 (D.C. Cir. 1988), and in *Richard Short Oil Co. v. Texaco, Inc.*, 799 F.2d 415, 420 (8th Cir. 1986), which follow.

a. *Boise Cascade Corp. v. FTC*, 837 F.2d 1127 (D.C. Cir. 1988).

Boise Cascade was an integrated wholesaler-retailer of office supply products. The company sold large amounts at wholesale and also was a major retailer.

Because it met supplier criteria of a "wholesaler," it received the wholesale discount on all of its purchases from its several suppliers, including discounts on purchases which it resold as a retailer. Competing retailers paid between 5% and 33% more for their purchases from manufacturers than did Boise.

Under classic Robinson-Patman analysis, courts in the past would have said that the lower prices which Boise's suppliers charged it than they charged Boise's retailer rivals was the kind of price discrimination which would trigger the *Morton Salt* presumption. They would have reached that conclusion because the discounts accorded to Boise were systematic and continuous, producing a permanent supply-cost advantage in Boise over its rivals.

In *Boise*, however, the District of Columbia Court of Appeals was impressed with the evidence showing that the office-supply industry was thriving and that few, if any retailers, could be shown to have left the market for any reason traceable to Boise's supply cost advantage.

> It is clear that *Morton Salt*'s inference of competitive injury "may be overcome by evidence breaking the causal connection between a price differential and lost sales or profits," *Falls City*, 460 U.S. at 435. . . . In reason, *the inference can also be overcome by evidence showing an absence of competitive injury within the meaning of Robinson-Patman*. That is to say, a sustained and substantial price discrimination raises an inference, but it manifestly does not create an irrebuttable presumption of competitive injury. Specific, substantial evidence of absence of competitive injury . . . [is] in our view, sufficient to rebut what is, after all, only an inference. The Commission, in effect, employed the *Morton Salt* inference to presume competitive injury conclusively in this case, and would only treat as relevant evidence "breaking the causal connection" between that assumed injury and the price discrimination to rebut the inference. This approach defies both logic and the import of *Morton Salt* that the inference of injury is rebuttable; for if the respondent's evidence demonstrates that there is no competitive injury (or reasonable possibility of competitive injury) to begin with, then evidence breaking the causal connection is obviously impossible to adduce. There is, under those circumstances, no causal connection to break.
>
> * * *
>
> First. Important among the salient facts that the Commission chose to ignore was the ALJ's finding that the selected dealers were not wallowing in a hopeless or deteriorating environment. Quite to the contrary, as we have already recounted, the ALJ found that all selected dealers for which data was available enjoyed an increase in sales and gross profits in excess of 22% annually during the period in question, despite the recessionary condition of the economy. . . . Indeed, Judge Parker observed that various indicators showed high profitability and financial

health on the part of the selected dealers. . . . Although we need not decide the matter, this tends, if anything, to point to an absence of "lost profits" of the sort described in *Falls City* as one possible manifestation of injury to competition; accordingly, this evidence merited consideration by the Commission rather than the out-of-hand dismissal that it received.

There is yet another portion of the record relating to profitability left unexamined by the Commission and, in our view, deserving of attention in reaching a reasoned result. As computed by the Commission's accounting expert, Mr. Rowe, the selected dealers' median net profit before taxes as a percent of sales over the years 1976 to 1981 ranged from 2.3% to 3.5%. . . . Their net profit was thus apparently lower than those of dealer-members of NOPA [Office Products Dealer's Trade Association], whose net profit ranged from 3.0% to 3.9% from 1967 to 1980. . . . Although these statistics pose obvious comparative problems (in light of the fact that they are spread across different years and were computed by different entities), this *apparent* discrepancy in profitability obviously deserved consideration. But it received none. Likewise, the Commission failed to analyze the relationship of Boise's higher net profit (which, of course, reflected both its sales as a wholesaler and a dealer) to that of the selected dealers. . . .

In addition, the evidence . . . failed to demonstrate "displaced sales," another form the *Falls City* Court indicated injury could take. The ALJ found that switches of accounts from one supplier to another were "not uncommon"; to the contrary, they were the order of the day. . . . While on the one hand twenty-one of the twenty-three dealers testified that they had lost accounts to Boise's lower prices or better service in recent years, . . . the phenomenon of lost accounts was very much a two-way street. As the ALJ extensively recounted, Boise also lost accounts and it too was unable to meet competitors' prices in some instances. . . . Indeed, considered together, the number of accounts that switched from the selected dealers to Boise was quite small. . . . And the proportion of switched accounts to a dealer's total accounts was strikingly low. Whereas a typical dealer might have a thousand accounts (or more), only a handful of accounts were shown to have switched. On top of that, the reasons for the switches were manifold. The following finding by Judge Parker makes the key point:

> None of the selected dealers who lost accounts in whole or in part to Boise were able to conclude that the losses were due to the different prices charged them and Boise by the six manufacturers (citations omitted).

> . . . In short, the *switches to Boise apparently cannot be explained as sales diverted through operation of the wholesale discount*.[4]

837 F.2d at 1144-45.

b. *Richard Short Oil Co. v. Texaco, Inc.*, 799 F.2d 415 (8th Cir. 1986)

Short, a Texaco wholesale distributor, claimed that Texaco violated the Robinson-Patman Act by selling at lower prices to retailers than Texaco sold to Short. The Eighth Circuit upheld summary judgment for Texaco largely on the ground that competition in the general market appeared to be thriving:

> In order to set out a prima facie case of a § 2(a) injury, Short had the burden to prove that the price discrimination produced a reasonable possibility of financial injury to competition. The Act refers not to the effect upon competitors, but to the effect upon competition in general. That is, analysis of the injury to competition focuses on whether there has been a substantial impairment to the vigor or health of the contest for business, regardless of which competitor wins or loses. *See Brunswick Corp. v. Pueblo Bowl-0-Mat, Inc.*, 429 U.S. 477, 488 (1977).
>
> The record in this case indicates that there was little, if any, injury to competition in the Little Rock area by virtue of the discrimination in prices. On the contrary, the evidence at trial indicated that Texaco was only one of many sellers in the market and that the market was highly competitive and remained so after the changes in its rebate program.
>
> Nor has Short shown any substantial injury to its competitive position. Injury to competition is established by proof "of a substantial price discrimination between competing purchasers over time." *Falls City Industries v. Vanco Beverage, Inc.*, 460 U.S. at 435. Short's exhibits 4 and 13, which form the basis of its proof of competitive injury, were constructed so that the volume of the discriminatory sales and the duration of any

---

[4] Notwithstanding this welter of dealer-specific evidence marshalled by Boise and painstakingly sifted by Judge Parker, the Commission apparently viewed Boise's efforts as an attempt to muddy the Robinson-Patman waters by implanting market-structure analyses in alien legal soil. To be sure, Judge Parker made pertinent and seemingly well-founded observations as to the competitive health and vibrancy of the office products industry at large. Here is one such point: The battle between dealers in the office-products industry is highly competitive and it is inevitable that when Boise competes with the selected dealers it will lose accounts to them. . . . And it is also clear that Boise argued in favor of a market-structure analysis under Robinson-Patman. But that is not to say that Judge Parker found only evidence going broadly to the structure of the industry and the competitive health of that industry overall. There was in this respect no commingling of market-structure analysis appropriate under other provisions of the Clayton Act, such as section 7, 15 U.S.C. § 18 (1982), but, as the Commission claims, off-target as to Robinson-Patman's less global perspective. The ALJ's findings . . . are replete with the most specific, detailed facts about the twenty-three selected dealers and the six representative manufacturers, not just the structure of the entire industry. In short, Judge Parker did not lose sight of the trees in the midst of this vast forest. It seems to us, therefore, that the Commission mischaracterizes Boise's evidence as going to market structure, rather than to the twenty-three selected dealers themselves, when Boise, in fairness, adduced evidence as to both. . . .

price differences could not be ascertained. Moreover, the fact that Short's exhibits rely solely on end of the month sales rather than examining sales throughout the entire month, would have forced the jury to speculate as to whether there had been substantial injury over time.

In the final analysis, to sustain its prima facie case of injury to competition, Short would have had to present evidence of the amount and percentage of the discrimination and the degree of competition it faced in the market, as well as sustained price differentials which are more than *de minimus*. *See* E. KINTNER & J. BAUER, FEDERAL ANTITRUST LAW III § 22.6, at 270-71 (1983). The evidence presented by Short in this case as to the nature of the competitive market, the duration of the discriminatory sales, and the volume of the difference in price would have made it impossible for the jury to draw any reasonable conclusions. We conclude, therefore, that the district court properly found Short's injury to competition evidence insufficient to establish a *prima facie* case.

2. The *Morton Salt* Presumption in Earlier Decisions.

a. *Minneapolis-Honeywell Regulator Co. v. FTC,* 191 F.2d 786 (7th Cir. 1951), *cert. dismissed*, 344 U.S. 206 (1952).

Honeywell sold automatic temperature controls to oil burner manufacturers at standard volume discounts as follows:

bracket	annual volume	net price
1	50— 349	$17.35
2	350— 999	16.45
3	1,000—2,499	15.90
3A	2,500—4,999	15.35
4	5,000—7,499	14.90
4A	7,500—9,999	13.75
5	10,000—up	14.25

The FTC held that the Honeywell pricing system violated the Robinson-Patman Act. On review, the Seventh Circuit reversed:

> . . . The Commission based its conclusion that M-H's practices injured . . . [customer] competition on the general finding that because the price of the control represented the largest single item of cost among the various parts of the finished burner, changes in the price of controls to manufacturers resulted in corresponding changes in the price of completed burners and necessarily affected sales and profits. It further found generally that "oil-burner manufacturers testified that the question of price was important in the purchase of automatic temperature controls and that they had lost business to certain competitors, including Quiet-Heet, who enjoyed lower control prices from respondent, although the exact volume of such lost business could not be calculated."

The absence of causal connection between the price of controls and the price of the finished products generally is demonstrated by the stipulation entered into prior to the hearing:

> "Some manufacturers paying higher prices for respondent's automatic temperature controls were able to, and often did, sell their oil burners complete with controls at prices below those which other similar manufacturers paying lower prices for respondent's . . . controls sold their oil burners. . . ."

. . . [Some] manufacturers who paid the higher prices testified that they did not lose business as a result of paying such higher control prices, and that they considered other factors of far greater importance in determining the price of the completed burner. They referred to such matters as manufacturing methods, overhead, distribution costs, service, advertising, as having an important bearing on comparative prices in addition to the costs of the component parts.

In further proof of its contention that the price of controls was not the vital factor in arriving at burner prices and in fact had very little relation to it, M-H submitted a table derived from the findings of a nationwide survey showing the range of prices charged by its customers in each price bracket for the year 1941. From this survey, it will be noted that the highest price charged for burners, $114.50, was by a customer having the advantage of the lowest price bracket for M-H controls, and that a customer in the next-to-highest price bracket sold its burner for the lowest price, $45. Many variations can be made from these facts. All seem to add up to the one fact that there is little, if any, relationship between the prices of the controls and the prices of the burners into which the controls are built, hence that the evidence does not support the Commission's finding that "changes in the price of . . . controls resulted in corresponding changes in the price of completed burners."

Reference was made in the general finding . . . to Quiet-Heet as one of the manufacturers enjoying lower control prices to which other manufacturers lost an undetermined volume of business. . . . There is no question on this record but that Quiet-Heet, entering the field in 1936, very soon became the largest producer in the industry, and by 1941 was able to sell its burners at the lowest price. The Commission attributed this to the fact that it bought its controls from M-H for the lowest price. We think this is to ignore the vast discrepancy between the range of prices for controls and that for the finished burners. The fact was, as established by the evidence, that Quiet-Heet entered the field with entirely different theories of production and distribution from those of its already established competitors. Its proprietor testified that he "started out to merchandise it on a volume basis, effecting certain economies, making a few shortcuts here and there and trimming down my overhead

> and operating costs to the minimum." Among those economies were the elimination of all field service which was one of the heavy items of expense of the higher price manufacturers, reduction of advertising costs to a minimum by its own use of printed postcards to the trade and by charging dealers for all advertising matter furnished to them, and adoption of cheaper packaging methods and materials. It was this type of economies that enabled Quiet-Heet to sell its burner in 1941 for $68.50 less than its highest price competitor who paid the same price for the control, and for $66 less than its next highest price competitor who paid only $3.60 more for its controls . . . .
>
> Part of the fallacy of the Commission's position lies in its analysis of the competitive situation between the various manufacturers. This is reflected in its order where it refers to manufacturers "who in fact compete in the sale and distribution of such furnace controls," as if the controls themselves were the article of merchandise they dealt in instead of the burners of which the controls were only one part. It may be true that if the manufacturers were generally selling controls as such, a differential of two or three dollars in the price they paid for them would have a substantial effect on the price obtained. Under such circumstances a finding that a competitive advantage in purchase price paid would necessarily give rise to a competitive advantage in sale price would perhaps be justified. But where the controls were used in the manufacture of burners, the cost of which was determined by many other factors—cost of other materials and parts, service, advertising, to mention only a few—it cannot be said that discriminatory price differentials substantially injure competition or that there is any reasonable probability or even possibility that they will do so. . . . And a mere possibility of such injury is insufficient to sustain a charge of violation of the Act. *Corn Products Refining Co. v. Federal Trade Commission*, 324 U.S. 726, 742. . . .

191 F.2d at 792.

b. *Fred Bronner, Inc.*, 57 F.T.C. 771 (1960).

The respondent corporation, an importer of toys, granted a 3% discount to certain wholesalers, all but one of whom were members of an association known as March of Toys, Inc., which operated as a buying corporation for a group of toy wholesalers located throughout the country. The respondent did not extend this discount to other wholesalers competing with the favored ones. In ordering the complaint against the respondent dismissed, the Commission remarked:

> While in effect conceding that the dollar amount of the price discrimination is not substantial, counsel supporting the complaint rely on the Supreme Court's holding in the *Morton Salt* case to support their argument that the 3% price discount granted by respondents is illegal for the

> reason that if discounts at the same rate were granted to respondents' favored customers by all of their suppliers, the effect on competition would be substantial. In the *Morton Salt* case, there was sufficient evidence to show that in the respondent's sale of salt, less-than-carload purchasers might have been handicapped in competing with the more favored carload purchasers by the differential in price established by the respondent. The court ruled that this competitive handicap could not be minimized by reason of the fact that salt is only a small item in the non-favored purchasers' businesses. In effect, the court held that it was not necessary for the Commission to consider sales in other merchandise categories in determining injury to the purchaser victimized by respondent's price differential. The contention of counsel supporting the complaint that we project the discount to other merchandise purchased by the favored customers is clearly beyond the holding in the *Morton Salt* case and must be rejected.

57 F.T.C. at 783.

c. Does the *Minneapolis-Honeywell* decision provide a basis for limiting the application of the *Morton Salt* presumption to sales to dealers and distributors who purchase for resale? Or, would it be more accurate to say that the *Minneapolis-Honeywell* case provides a basis for rebutting the *Morton Salt* presumption? Perhaps the latter explanation is more apt today because we now know (from *Falls City Industries, Inc. v. Vanco Beverage, Inc.*, 460 U.S. 42 (1983) (page 657, *infra*) that that presumption is rebuttable. Does *Bronner* deal with the same issue as *Minneapolis-Honeywell*? Does *Bronner* show that the *Morton Salt* presumption is inapplicable when the discrimination is limited to one item out of many inventory items which are purchased by the favored and disfavored buyers and when the discrimination is not systematically replicated by other suppliers? Do these cases prefigure *Boise Cascade*?

---

2. The Cost Justification Defense

Allied Accessories & Auto Parts Co. v. General Motors Corp.

825 F.2d 971 (6th Cir. 1987)

NATHANIEL R. JONES, Circuit Judge.

. . . .

II.

. . . .

Allied is a wholesale distributor of automobile parts and accessories to mass merchandiser retailers. During the years 1972 to 1979, one of Allied's largest retail customers was the K Mart Corporation ("K Mart"). However, Allied had only once, for a few months, sold oil filters to K Mart. Prior to 1978, Campbell Filter Company ("Campbell") had supplied to K Mart oil filters manufactured by Campbell and sold under the K Mart name. Campbell also manufactured the Fram oil filters that K Mart sold.

In 1978, K Mart decided to change its marketing of oil filters. It switched to a policy of selling Original Equipment Manufacturer ("OEM") filters, *i.e.*, oil filters manufactured by automobile companies for the cars they build. K Mart had a policy of buying direct from the manufacturer whenever possible, since that was usually the best way to get the lowest price. . . . GM [General Motors Corp.] signed a contract with Campbell allowing Campbell to purchase [GM-produced] AC-Delco oil filters for the sole purpose of supplying K Mart. This agreement provided Campbell with a price discount 10 percent below warehouse distributor prices. This discount was not made available to Allied.

Several companies submitted bids to K Mart for supplying AC-Delco oil filters. The lowest bid was submitted by Campbell, and the second-lowest bid was submitted by Allied. The bid that was submitted by Campbell was 10 percent lower than plaintiff's bid. K Mart subsequently chose Campbell as its supplier for AC-Delco oil filters.

Allied brought suit in federal district court, alleging that GM's discount to Campbell violated the Robinson-Patman Act. The district court agreed with plaintiff that GM charged different prices for the same goods. It also agreed that Allied and Campbell were competitors, "since Campbell was stepping outside of its prior posture as a manufacturer and becoming a supplier, and offering to supply the same product to K Mart as was plaintiff." . . .

III.

. . . [B]ecause the defendant's cost justification analysis is virtually a textbook example of the analysis prohibited by *United States v. Borden Co.*, 370 U.S. 460 (1962), we reverse the district court's holding on this issue. In *Borden Co.*, the Supreme Court noted that the cost justification proviso of the Robinson-Patman Act, along with its legislative history, could support a requirement that "any discrepancy in price between any two purchasers . . . be individually justified. . . ." . . . Nevertheless, in light of the burden that such a requirement would impose on sellers with large numbers of customers, the Court chose not "to completely renounce class pricing." . . . However, the Court cautioned that:

> [t]his is not to say that price differentials can be justified on the basis of arbitrary classifications or even classifications which are representative of a numerical majority of the individual members. At some point practical considerations shade into a circumvention of the proviso. A balance is struck by the use of classes for cost justification which are composed of members of such selfsameness as to make the averaging of the cost of dealing with the group a valid and reasonable indicium of the cost of dealing with any specific group member.
>
> . . . .

In the case before us, GM created two classes in order to determine what price discount to Campbell could be cost justified. One class was composed of all 2,000 of its regular customers. According to defendant's witness, Van Hollenbeke, this class included warehouse distributor/feeders like plaintiff, retailer/manufacturers like Firestone and Goodyear, and warehouse distributors who sold through jobbers and affiliated jobbers. . . . This class was not broken down by geographic areas, by volume of purchases, or in any other way. The other class was composed of Campbell alone. The apparent rationale behind this classification was that all of GM's regular customers had an agreement with GM that entitled them to request advertising reimbursements, catalogues, the services of field representatives, and the benefits of GM incentive programs. Campbell, on the other hand, was offered a special contract wherein rights to incentive programs and cooperative advertising were waived. Furthermore, the services of field representatives and the provision of free catalogues would not be available to Campbell under this contract. This individualized contract provided that Campbell would buy oil filters only for sale to K Mart.

In order to determine the cost savings of selling to the "Campbell class," as compared to the class of all other customers, GM isolated six areas of expenses which affected GM's costs in distributing oil filters. With respect to its volume incentive program, cataloging, and field selling, GM totaled its actual national annual expenses and divided that by the number of oil filters it manufactured in order to arrive at the average per filter cost of providing those services to its class of 2,000 customers. Because GM did not intend to provide those three services to Campbell, it deducted that average cost per filter from its normal warehouse distributor price in order to determine part of Campbell's price discount. With respect to freight costs, GM figured the national average cost of shipping a filter by truck and compared that national average to the cost of using "piggyback" shipping to send filters to Campbell in Dexter, Missouri. The difference between the national average shipping cost per filter and Campbell's projected cost per filter was further deducted from the normal warehouse distributor price. Finally, with respect to its "T'n'P Incentive Program" and Co-op advertising, GM did not use figures derived from its 2,000 customers' actual use of those programs in order to determine the cost per unit of those services. Instead, GM assumed that all 2,000 customers used the maximum available amount of those services, and upon that assumption it calculated the average cost per unit for those services. Since those services would not be available to Campbell, that average cost per unit was also subtracted from the normal warehouse distributor price.

As noted at the outset, this method of justifying a price discount violates a number of the principles set forth by the Supreme Court in *Borden*. First, defendant never offered to the class of 2,000 the option of giving up the additional GM services which Campbell was permitted to forego. *See Borden*, 370 U.S. at 471 n.13 (suspect feature of defendant's cost justification was that services to be received by independents were "frozen"); *In re Mueller Co.*, 60 F.T.C. 120, 130 (1962) (unless right to perform additional services made available to all wholesalers, price discount to one who performed additional services illegal), *order enforced*, 323 F.2d 44 (7th Cir.1963), *cert. denied*, 377 U.S. 923 (1964). Although GM did have a previous agreement with its 2,000 customers, nothing in that agreement would seem to prohibit the formation of a new agreement, and GM offers "no justifiable business reason" for refusing to give its regular customers the opportunity to elect not to receive the cost-determinative services. . . .

Turning to the classifications used by GM for its cost justification, we find that GM, like the defendant in *Borden*, "not only failed to show that the economics relied upon were isolated within the favored class but affirmatively revealed that members of the classes utilized were substantially unlike in the cost saving aspects considered." . . . In regard to the cost savings allegedly peculiar to Campbell as a distributor of oil filters, plaintiff correctly notes that several of the services not provided to Campbell would have been unnecessary for any distributor selling to K Mart. For instance, Van Hollenbeke testified that K Mart refused to deal with sales people. Therefore, any distributor purchasing oil filters for eventual sale to K Mart would save GM its field selling costs for those filters. A contract entitling a distributor to GM's field selling services would not alter the fact that the distributor could not use those services for any sale to K Mart. Thus, some of the cost savings attributed to a sale to Campbell would have been garnered in any sale of oil filters for eventual distribution to K Mart. If GM wished to pass on this cost savings, it should have passed it on to all of its customers, not just to Campbell. *See generally* 3 E. KINTNER & J. BAUER, FEDERAL ANTITRUST LAW § 23.12 (1983).

Even more troublesome is GM's grouping of all its customers into a single 2,000 member class for the purposes of determining that Campbell was entitled to a price 10 percent lower than any other buyer. To say that all 2,000 had a contract entitling them to certain services by GM is not to prove that all of GM's customers possessed "such selfsameness as to make the averaging of the cost of dealing with the group a reasonable indicium of the cost of dealing with any specific group member." . . . The defendant in *Borden*, like GM here, attempted to rely on the costs of "optional customer service" generally provided to independent stores as costs attributable to all independent stores. The Court held that since *Borden* had been able to show only that a majority of the independent stores took advantage of the optional services, not that all independent stores used the services, it was impermissible to allocate those optional service costs to all the independent stores. . . .

Similarly, in the instant case GM has not demonstrated that even a majority of its 2,000 customers take any advantage of services like cooperative advertising or the provision of catalogues. Even if all of its customers do use such available services, GM has given no affirmative indication of the similarity in the degree to which such services are used by various types of customers. For instance, on cross-examination, Van Hollenbeke indicated that buyers who also retail would be more likely to use co-op advertising and admitted that a warehouse distributor/feeder might use up less field selling time than a jobber. But GM never attempted to demonstrate that any such differences were insignificant.

In light of the widely varying characteristics of GM's 2,000 customers, it is not self-evident that the average cost of dealing with all 2,000 is a reasonable indication of the cost of dealing with any one particular buyer. For example, plaintiff points out that as a large warehouse distributor selling primarily to large discount retailers, it neither needs nor uses many of GM's optional services, whereas a jobber or a retailer might use as many of GM's services as possible. Especially telling is GM's use of a national average for comparing shipping costs. While shipping to Campbell in Missouri cost less than the national average, Van Hollenbeke admitted that since GM's plant was in Michigan and plaintiff was also located in Michigan, shipping to plaintiff was "potentially" cheaper than shipping to Campbell.

Altogether, GM's comparison of Campbell to a single class of 2,000 is justifiable only on the assumption that all of GM's customers consistently used similar amounts of the services to which they were entitled. We do not believe that *Borden* permits such an assumption. . . . We therefore hold that defendant has failed to prove that its price differential was cost justified.

Accordingly, we REVERSE the district court's judgment for defendant and REMAND for further proceedings consistent with this opinion.

Uniroyal, Inc. v. Hoff and Thames, Inc.

511 F. Supp. 1060 (S.D. Miss. 1981)

MEMORANDUM OPINION

NIXON, District Judge.

. . . .

[Hoff and Thames, Inc., d/b/a Case Tire and Supply Company ("Case") claimed that Uniroyal had granted Otasco favorable prices which discriminated against Case, in violation of the Robinson-Patman Act. According to Case, Uniroyal violated the Robinson-Patman Act (a) by transferring tires to its company-owned stores at a price less than the price at which Case purchased; (b) by selling tires to other dealers in Mississippi at a lower price than the price at which Case purchased; and (c) by selling tires to Otasco at a lower price than the price at which Case purchased.]

This case is now before the Court on a Motion for Summary Judgment filed by Uniroyal . . . on Motion for Summary Judgment filed by Case with respect to cost justification studies prepared by Uniroyal in support of the functional discount granted by Uniroyal to Otasco. Extensive discovery has been undertaken which includes numerous depositions, extensive interrogatories, and the production of voluminous documents and the Court now finds this matter ripe for decision.

. . . .

CONCLUSIONS OF LAW

. . . .

III. THE ROBINSON-PATMAN ACT CLAIMS

. . . .

2. Cost Justification

Section 2(a) of the Robinson-Patman Act (15 U.S.C. § 13) provides that it is unlawful for a seller to discriminate in price between different purchasers of commodities of like grade and quality. The same section, however, creates an exception in favor of cost differentials that are justified by cost savings realized on sales to some customers, but not to others. Thus the statutory exception states that "nothing herein contained shall prevent differentials which make only due allowance for differences in the cost of manufacture, sale or delivery resulting from differing methods or quantities in which such commodities are to such purchasers sold or delivered."

As a second and alternate basis for summary judgment on the complaint concerning its sales to Otasco, Uniroyal contends that any price differentials granted by it to Otasco with respect to tires of like grade or quality sold by it to both Otasco and Case are the result of such savings to Uniroyal in its sales to Otasco. Otasco is a large company which markets products, including tires, in a wide geographic area to its company-owned outlets and to "associate," or privately owned, retail stores that it franchises.

Uniroyal perceived from its experience with other large accounts that it could realize substantial cost savings by dealing with a customer that would relieve Uniroyal of the cost of performing certain functions that, in sales to smaller, independent purchasers, it was required to perform. . . . For example, Otasco functions much like a wholesaler, purchasing tires in bulk, storing them in its warehouse and redistributing them to its various stores, which allowed Uniroyal to reduce its freight and handling costs by shipping tires in carload lots to the four Otasco warehouses, rather than making small shipments to Uniroyal's more than 6000 dealers. Again, by selling to Otasco, Uniroyal was relieved of credit and bad debt concerns that it would necessarily have with respect to sales to smaller, independent outlets, such as Case. The counter-defendant was also specifically relieved of its cost of the cooperative advertising campaign available to all dealers, including Case, whereby 50-60% of the cost of certain dealer advertising was borne by Uniroyal. Not only was Uniroyal relieved of the direct cost of such advertising, but it was also relieved of administrative cost relating thereto. Although it made no formal study specifically quantifying such apparent cost savings prior to its contract with Otasco, it has subsequently done so. A study performed by Mr. Ken Anderson, Divisional Plant Coordinator of Uniroyal's Detroit Tire Plant, has been introduced . . . and Mr. Anderson's testimony has been taken by deposition. The thrust of his study is that the total savings attributable to sales to Otasco was no less than 17.28%, compared to its tire sales to dealers such as Case. It is undisputed that the discount granted to Otasco by Uniroyal, while syled a "15% functional discount," actually resulted in a price reduction to Otasco of only 11.7%, because the base price to which the discount is applied is reduced by other discounts available to Case and Otasco. Accordingly, it appears that Uniroyal's prices to Otasco were justified by its cost savings with respect to such sales. On the record, the testimony of Mr. Anderson stands uncontradicted. Case has pointed to no errors or omissions in Mr. Anderson's study. Case has offered no cost study of its own, but argues instead that a Section 2(a) "cost justification" study is an affirmative defense, the burden of proof of which rests upon Uniroyal, and that Anderson's conclusions are "subject to test on cross-examination."

It is firmly established that the burden of proof on a Section 2(a) cost justification defense rests upon the party raising that defense. The difficulty with Case's argument here is that, in the Court's opinion, Uniroyal has assumed that burden and has sustained it. Case has in fact cross-examined Mr. Anderson, yet suggests no factors, such as inherent implausibility or contradiction by other evidence, that would negate the effect of his testimony for summary judgment purposes. . . . Case has offered no evidence to contradict the Anderson study, nor to render it suspect. Consequently, it stands unimpeached, and justifies the price differentials granted to Otasco by Uniroyal.

Case argues, based on *United States v. Borden Co.*, 370 U.S. 460 (1962), that the Uniroyal cost justification study is invalid because it compares costs to one large customer with costs to other customers. That argument is misplaced. *Borden* does not condemn all cost studies based on classifications of customers. 370 U.S. at 468-70. The Anderson comparisons are not, as in *Borden*, "like comparing one horse and one rabbit" 370 U.S. at 470. Mr. Anderson compared Uniroyal's costs to Otasco with certain of its costs to various other customers, including large Uniroyal dealers, all Uniroyal dealers, and company-owned stores.

Case's argument appears to suggest that it is impermissible to group or classify customers for cost study purposes. But that is not the law. Reasonable and proper classifications made for purposes of cost comparisons are clearly permissible, as the Fifth Circuit recognized in *Thomasville Chair Company v. FTC*, 306 F.2d 541, 544 (5th Cir. 1962). Moreover, it is firmly established "that individual cost justification is not required," *FTS v. Standard Motor Products, Inc.*, 371 F.2d 613, 619 (2d Cir. 1967).

Case does not point to any specific comparisons that it contends are unreasonable or improper; it relies instead upon its broad-brush assertion that Uniroyal's classifications for cost study purposes vitiate the entire study, an approach rejected in *Thomasville Chair*, *supra*, 306 F.2d at 544. Nor has Case suggested any alternative means of classifying customers, and to uphold its broadside attack would mean that Uniroyal "has left (to) it no practicable means of cost justification" . . . , a result clearly "at war with Congress' language and purpose." . . .

Absent any evidence to the contrary, Uniroyal's cost study, and the comparisons that comprise it, are reasonable. Accordingly, Uniroyal's sales to Otasco did not violate Section 2(a), and Uniroyal's motion for summary judgment relating to this claim will be granted. The same reasons discussed above that warrant summary judgment in favor of Uniroyal on its cost justification defense mandate denial of Case's cross-motion for summary judgment on that same defense.

. . . .

COMMENTARY

1. The cases show some of the difficulties involved in establishing the cost-justification defense. Many cost savings cannot be proved, although business executives are confident that they exist. The *General Motors* case illustrates the difficulties inherent in establishing, to the satisfaction of a court, the classifications which are necessary to show cost savings incurred in serving particular customers.

2. In some situations, it may be advisable for a business to justify its price differences as functional discounts. One of the traditional rationales of a functional discount is that the discount reflects the seller's cost savings as a result of the buyer's performance of services which the seller would otherwise have to perform. It is thus a way of compensating a buyer when the seller saves certain costs on the sale. Yet the standards of proof for establishing functional discounts are more flexible than the standards for establishing the cost-justification defense. Compare the functional discount upheld in *Edward J. Sweeney & Sons, Inc. v. Texaco*, 637 F.2d 105, 119-120 (3d Cir. 1980), *cert. denied*, 451 U.S. 911 (1981), with the cost justification rejected in the *General Motors* case, *supra*. *See Texaco Inc. v. Hasbrouck*, 496 U.S. 543 (1990), page 664, *infra*.

---

3. The Meeting Competition Defense

Falls City Industries, Inc. v. Vanco Beverage, Inc.

460 U.S. 428 (1983)

Justice BLACKMUN delivered the opinion of the Court.

. . . .

I

From July 1, 1972, through Nov. 30, 1978, petitioner Falls City Industries, Inc., sold beer f.o.b. its Louisville, Ky., brewery to wholesalers throughout Indiana, Kentucky, and 11 other States. Respondent Vanco Beverage, Inc., was the sole wholesale distributor of Falls City beer in Vanderburgh County, Ind. That county includes the city of Evansville. Directly across the state line from Vanderburgh County is Henderson County, Ky., where Falls City's only wholesale distributor was Dawson Springs, Inc. The city of Henderson, Ky., located in Henderson County, is less than 10 miles from Evansville. The two cities are connected by a four-lane interstate highway. The two counties generally are considered to be a single metropolitan area. . . . Vanco and Dawson Springs each purchased beer from Falls City and other brewers and resold it to retailers in Vanderburgh County and Henderson County, respectively. The two distributors did not compete for sales to the same retailers. This was because Indiana wholesalers were prohibited by state law from selling to out-of-state retailers, Ind. Code § 7.1-3-3-5 (1982), and Indiana retailers were not permitted to purchase beer from out-of-state wholesalers. *See* § 7.1-3-4-6. Indiana law also affected beer sales in two other ways relevant to this case. First, Indiana required brewers to sell to all Indiana wholesalers at a single price. § 7.1-5-5-7. Second, although it was ignored and virtually unenforced . . . state law prohibited consumers from importing alcoholic beverages without a permit. § 7.1-5-11-1.

In December 1976, Vanco sued Falls City in the United States District Court for the Southern District of Indiana, alleging, among other things, that Falls City had discriminated in price against Vanco, in violation of § 2(a) of the Clayton Act . . . as amended by the Robinson-Patman Act by charging Vanco a higher price than it charged Dawson Springs. . . .

[After trial, the district court entered judgment for Vanco.] The United States Court of Appeals for the Seventh Circuit, by a divided vote, affirmed the finding of liability. 654 F.2d 1224 (1981). The court held that Vanco had established a *prima facie* case of illegal price discrimination and that Falls City had not demonstrated that the discrimination "was a good faith effort to defend against competitors." *Id.* at 1230. We granted *certiorari* to review the Court of Appeals' holdings respecting injury to competition and the "meeting-competition" defense. . . .

To establish a *prima facie* violation of § 2(a), one of the elements a plaintiff must show is a reasonable possibility that a price difference may harm competition. . . . This reasonable possibility of harm is often referred to as competitive injury. Unless rebutted by one of the Robinson-Patman Act's affirmative defenses, a showing of competitive injury as part of a *prima facie* case is sufficient to support injunctive relief, and to authorize further inquiry by the courts into whether the plaintiff is entitled to treble damages under § 4 of the Clayton Act. . . .

Falls City contends that the Court of Appeals erred in relying on *FTC v. Morton Salt Co.* . . . to uphold the District Court's finding of competitive injury. In *Morton Salt* this Court held that, for the purposes of § 2(a), injury to competition is established *prima facie* by proof of a substantial price discrimination between competing purchasers over time. . . . In the absence of direct evidence of displaced sales, this inference may be overcome by evidence breaking the causal connection between a price differential and lost sales or profits. . . .

According to Falls City, the *Morton Salt* rule should be applied only in cases involving "large buyer preference or seller predation." . . . Falls City does not, however, suggest any economic reason why *Morton Salt*'s "self-evident" inference . . . should not apply when the favored competitor is not extraordinarily large. Although concerns about the excessive market power of large purchasers were primarily responsible for passage of the Robinson-Patman Act . . . the Act "is of general applicability and prohibits discriminations generally." . . . The determination whether to alter the scope of the Act must be made by Congress, not this Court . . . .

The *Morton Salt* rule was not misapplied in this case. In a strictly literal sense, this case differs from *Morton Salt* because Vanco and Dawson Springs did not compete with each other at the wholesale level; Vanco sold only to Indiana retailers and Dawson Springs sold only to Kentucky retailers. But the competitive injury component of a Robinson-Patman Act violation is not limited to the injury to competition between the favored and the disfavored purchaser; it also encompasses the injury to competition between their customers—in this case the competition between Kentucky retailers and Indiana retailers who, under a District Court finding not challenged in this Court, were selling in a single, interstate retail market.[7]

---

[7] The Court of Appeals upheld the District Court's findings that the sale of Falls City beer to Vanco was in interstate commerce and that Henderson County and Vanderburgh County constituted a unified retail market for beer. . . . These holdings are not before us. Falls City does not argue, and never has argued, "that Indiana's con-

After observing that Falls City had maintained a substantial price difference between Vanco and Dawson Springs over a significant period of time, the Court of Appeals, like the District Court, considered the evidence that Vanco's loss of Falls City beer sales was attributable to factors other than the price difference, particularly the marketwide decline of Falls City beer. Both courts found it likely that this overall decline accounted for some—or even most—of Vanco's lost sales. Nevertheless, if some of Vanco's injury was attributable to the price discrimination, Falls City is responsible to that extent. . . .

The Court of Appeals agreed with the District Court's findings that "the major reason for the higher Indiana retail beer prices was the higher prices charged Indiana distributors," and "the lower retail prices in Henderson County attracted Indiana customers away from Indiana retailers, thereby causing the retailers to curtail purchases from Vanco." . . . These findings were supported by direct evidence of diverted sales,[8] and more than established the competitive injury required for a *prima facie* case under § 2(a).

III

When proved, the meeting-competition defense of § 2(b) exonerates a seller from Robinson-Patman Act liability. . . . This Court consistently has held that the meeting-competition defense "at least requires the seller, who has knowingly discriminated in price, to show the existence of facts which would lead a reasonable and prudent person to believe that the granting of a lower price would in fact meet the equally low price of a competitor." . . .

. . . .

B

Vanco attempts to [argue] . . . that the existence of industry-wide price discrimination within the single geographic retail market itself indicates "tacit or explicit collusion, or . . . market power" inconsistent with a good faith response. . . . By its terms, however, the meeting-competition defense requires a seller to justify only its *lower* price. . . . Thus, although the Sherman Act would provide a remedy if Falls City's higher Indiana price were set collusively, collusion is relevant to Vanco's Robinson-Patman Act claim only if it affected Falls City's lower Kentucky price. If Falls City set its lower price in good faith to meet an equally low price of a competitor, it did not violate the Robinson-Patman Act.

Moreover, the collusion argument founders on a complete lack of proof. Persistent, industry-wide price discrimination within a geographic market should certainly alert a court to a substantial possibility of collusion. . . . Here, however, the persistent interstate price dif-

---

sumer-level nonimportation law compels a finding that Evansville and Henderson are separate retail beer markets." . . . Indeed, Falls City's counsel affirmatively waived this argument in a letter written to the District Court before trial . . . . Nor is the broader question whether Indiana and Kentucky constitute separate markets fairly included within the scope of the questions presented in Falls City's petition for *certiorari*. Counsel for Falls City made this very clear at oral argument, stating that "I'm not asking this Court to delve into the record to second guess that determination by the lower courts."

[8] Falls City's own sales agent reported that the different prices charged in the two States accounted—at least in part—for the substantial difference in Vanco's and Dawson Spring's sales performances. . . . The local press reported substantial purchases of beer in Kentucky by Indiana residents. . . . Kentucky retailers located just south of the Indiana state line on the four-lane highway between Evansville and Henderson advertised their low prices extensively in the Evansville media and utilized "drive-in windows" at which customers could purchase beer without leaving their cars. . . . Witnesses testified that they observed cars with Indiana license plates parked at Henderson County carry-out retailers, to which drivers would return carrying cases of beer. . . . One Indiana resident testified that he purchased beer in Kentucky because of lower prices there. . . . The District Court also relied on the differing rates of decline. . . .

ference could well have been attributable, not to Falls City, but to extensive state regulation of the sale of beer. Indiana required each brewer to charge a single price for its beer throughout the State, and barred direct competition between Indiana and Kentucky distributors for sales to retailers. In these unusual circumstances, the prices charged to Vanco and other wholesalers in Vanderburgh County may have been influenced more by market conditions in distant Gary and Fort Wayne than by conditions in nearby Henderson County, Ky. Moreover, wholesalers in Henderson County competed directly, and attempted to price competitively, with wholesalers in neighboring Kentucky counties. . . . . A separate pricing structure might well have evolved in the two States without collusion, notwithstanding the existence of a common retail market along the border. Thus, the sustained price discrimination does not itself demonstrate that Falls City's Kentucky prices were not a good faith response to competitors' prices there.

C

The Court of Appeals explicitly relied on two other factors in rejecting Falls City's meeting-competition defense: the price discrimination was created by raising rather than lowering prices, and Falls City raised its prices in order to increase its profits. Neither of these factors is controlling. Nothing in § 2(b) requires a seller to *lower* its price in order to meet competition. On the contrary, § 2(b) requires the defendant to show only that its "lower price . . . was made in good faith to meet an equally low price of a competitor." A seller is required to justify a price difference by showing that it reasonably believed that an equally low price was available to the purchaser and that it offered the lower price for that reason; the seller is not required to show that the difference resulted from subtraction rather than addition.

A different rule would not only be contrary to the language of the statute, but also might stifle the only kind of legitimate price competition reasonably available in particular industries. In a period of generally rising prices, vigorous price competition for a particular customer or customers may take the form of smaller price increases rather than price cuts. Thus, a price discrimination created by selective price increases can result from a good-faith effort to meet a competitor's low price.

Nor is the good faith with which the lower price is offered impugned if the prices raised, like those kept lower, respond to competitors' prices and are set with the goal of increasing the seller's profits. A seller need not choose between "ruinously cutting its prices to all its customers to match the price offered to one, [and] refusing to meet the competition and then ruinously raising its prices to its remaining customers to cover increased unit costs." . . . Nor need a seller choose between keeping all its prices ruinously low to meet the price offered to one, and ruinously raising its prices to all customers to a level significantly above that charged by its competitors. A seller is permitted "to retain a customer by realistically meeting in good faith the price offered to that customer, without necessarily changing the seller's price to its other customers." . . . The plain language of § 2(b) also permits a seller to retain a customer by realistically meeting in good faith the price offered to that customer, without necessarily freezing his price to his other customers.

Section 2(b) does not require a seller, meeting in good faith a competitor's lower price to certain customers, to forgo the profits that otherwise would be available in sales to its remaining customers. The very purpose of the defense is to permit a seller to treat different competitive situations differently. The prudent businessman responding fairly to what he believes in good faith is a situation of competitive necessity might well raise his prices to some customers to increase his profits, while meeting competitors' prices by keeping his prices to other customers low.

. . . .

D

Vanco also contends that Falls City did not satisfy § 2(b) because its price discrimination "was not a defensive response to competition." . . . According to Vanco, the Robinson-Patman Act permits price discrimination only if its purpose is to retain a customer. . . . We agree that a seller's response must be defensive, in the sense that the lower price must be calculated and offered in good faith to "meet not beat" the competitor's low price. Section 2(b), however, does not distinguish between one who meets a competitor's lower price to retain an old customer and one who meets a competitor's lower price in an attempt to gain new customers. . . . Such a distinction would be inconsistent with that section's language and logic . . . "would not be in keeping with elementary principles of competition, and would in fact foster tight and rigid commercial relationships by insulating them from market forces." 1955 Report [Report of the Attorney General's National Committee to Study the Antitrust Laws (1955)] at 184; *see* 1977 Report, at 26, 265.[13]

IV

. . . .

[Contrary to the view of the Court of Appeals], [t]here is no evidence that Congress intended to limit the availability of § 2(b) to customer-specific responses. Section 2(b)'s predecessor, § 2 of the original Clayton Act, stated that "nothing herein contained shall prevent . . . discrimination in price in the same or different communities made in good faith to meet competition." . . . The Judiciary Committee of the House of Representatives, which drafted the clause that became the current § 2(b) . . . explained the new section's anticipated function: "It should be noted that while the seller is permitted to meet *local* competition, [§ 2(b)] does not permit him to cut *local* prices until his competitor has first offered lower prices, and then he can go no further than to meet those prices." H.R. Rep. No. 2287, 74th Cong., 2d Sess., 16 (1936) (emphasis supplied). Congress intended to allow reasonable pricing responses on an area-specific basis where competitive circumstances warrant them. The purpose of the amendment was to "restric[t] the proviso to price differentials occurring in actual competition." . . . We conclude that Congress did not intend to bar territorial price differences that are in fact responses to competitive conditions.

. . . .

A seller may have good reason to believe that a competitor or competitors are charging lower prices throughout a particular region. . . . In such circumstances, customer-by-customer negotiations would be unlikely to result in prices different from those set according to information relating to competitors' territorial prices. A customer-by-customer requirement might also make meaningful price competition unrealistically expensive for smaller firms such as Falls City, which was attempting to compete with larger national breweries in 13 separate States.

. . . Territorial pricing . . . can be a perfectly reasonable method—sometimes the most reasonable method—of responding to rivals' low prices.[16] We choose not to read into § 2(b)

[13] *Standard Oil Co. v. FTC*, 340 U.S. 231 (1951), is not to the contrary. The Court there referred to the defense's being available to a seller seeking to "retain" customers . . . simply because the petitioner had so framed its defense in that particular case. . . .

[16] *See* [F. Rowe, Price Discrimination Under the Robinson-Patman Act (ed. 1962)] at 240 ("a seller's area-wide and blanket lower prices, if made in good faith to meet competitors' lower prices, may be justified . . . as responsive to an 'individual competitive situation'"). *Cf. Maryland Baking Co. v. FTC*, 243 F.2d 716, 719 (4th Cir. 1957) (FTC permits competitive area price variations to avert placing "prices in a straightjacket throughout

a restriction that would deny the meeting-competition defense to one whose area-wide price is a well tailored response to competitors' low prices.

Of course, a seller must limit its lower price to that group of customers reasonably believed to have the lower price available to it from competitors. A response that is not reasonably tailored to the competitive situation as known to the seller, or one that is based on inadequate verification, would not meet the standard of good faith. Similarly, the response may continue only as long as the competitive circumstances justifying it, as reasonably known by the seller, persist. One choosing to price on a territorial basis, rather than on a customer-by-customer basis, must show that this decision was a genuine, reasonable response to prevailing competitive circumstances. Unless the circumstances call into question the seller's good faith, this burden will be discharged by showing that a reasonable and prudent businessman would believe that the lower price he charged was generally available from his competitors throughout the territory and throughout the period in which he made the lower price available. . . .

Accordingly, the judgment of the Court of Appeals is vacated and the case is remanded. . . .

NOTE ON THE "MEETING COMPETITION" DEFENSE

1. Staley *and the limitation of the defense to "individual competitive situations."*—The Supreme Court gave the "meeting competition" defense a narrow scope in *FTC v. A.E. Staley Mfg. Co.*, 324 U.S. 746 (1945). The Court's opinion in *Staley* is best understood in the light of its ruling in a companion case, *Corn Products Refining Co. v. FTC*, 324 U.S. 726 (1945).

In *Corn Products*, the Court held that the respondent company had violated § 2(a) by employing a single basing point system in selling glucose (corn syrup) to candy manufacturers. The company had two plants, one at Argo, Illinois (within the Chicago switching district) and the other at Kansas City, and used Chicago as a basing point from which to compute the delivered price of its glucose. This system resulted in a delivered price which differed by transportation costs from Chicago. As a result, the differences in all of the delivered prices out of the Argo plant were cost justified. The problem arose from sales out of the Kansas City plant. Since the delivered prices of sales from that plant were also calculated on a Chicago basing point but the transportation to the buyer was from Kansas City (rather than from Argo or Chicago), the difference in price had no relation to differences in cost. Hence the differences in price could not be cost justified.

In a companion case, *FTC v. A.E. Staley Mfg. Co.*, 324 U.S. 746 (1945), the respondent raised the "meeting competition" defense. In that case the company had

---

the country"); *Anheuser-Busch, Inc.*, 54 F.T.C. 277, 301 (1957) (suggesting that offer of lower price throughout particular area might be responsive to "individual competitive situation"); *C.E. Niehoff & Co.*, 51 F.T.C. 1114, 1130, 1146 (1955) (rejecting position that "showing that the seller's discriminations were temporary and localized in area is an indispensible prerequisite" to defense).

glucose plants in Chicago and Decatur, Illinois and charged the buyer a delivered price equal to the Chicago price plus transportation from Chicago to the buyer, regardless of whether the glucose was actually produced in Chicago or in Decatur. The company claimed that since its rivals had used Chicago as a basing point, its delivered prices would meet those of its rivals and hence be justified under the § 2(b) "meeting competition" defense. Having already held that the delivered pricing system involved in the *Corn Products* case violated § 2(a), the Court was not willing to permit Staley to justify its own identical pricing system on the ground that it replicated the unlawful pricing system of a rival:

> . . . [R]espondents argue that they have sustained their burden of proof, as prescribed by 2(b), by showing that they have adopted and followed the basing point system of their competitors. In the *Corn Products Refining Company* case we hold that this price system of respondents' competitor in part involves unlawful price discriminations, to the extent that freight differentials enter into the computation of price, as a result of the selection as a basing point of a place distant from the point of production and shipment. Thus it is the contention that a seller may justify a basing point delivered price system, which is otherwise outlawed by § 2, because other competitors are in part violating the law by maintaining a like system. If respondents' argument is sound, it would seem to follow that even if the competitor's pricing system were wholly in violation of § 2 of the Clayton Act, respondents could adopt and follow it with impunity.

In thus holding that Staley was not entitled to the "meeting competition" defense, the Court included in its opinion some unfortunate language: Focusing upon the use of the singular case in § 2(b), the Court stated that "the Act . . . places emphasis on individual competitive situations, rather than upon a general system of competition." *Staley*, accordingly, generated a belief that § 2(b) was unavailable to justify a broad across-the-board reduction of prices in a particular area in order to meet the prices of one or more rivals selling there. It was available only to meet particular prices in particular transactions. *Staley*'s reading of § 2(b) effectively limited the "meeting competition" defense to those sellers who sold to buyers at individually negotiated prices.

Staley's narrow reading of § 2(b) was finally repudiated in *Vanco, supra.* Prior to *Vanco*, some lower courts had taken a broader reading of the "meeting competition" defense. *See, e.g., Calloway Mills Co. v. FTC*, 362 F.2d 435 (5th Cir. 1966).

2. *The* Staley *approach to the "meeting competition" defense and incentives to enter the market.*—Assume that most glucose manufacturers operated from plants based in Chicago. Since the transportation costs of glucose are significant, the costs of glucose to a candy manufacturer located at Kansas City would be higher than the costs of glucose to a candy manufacturer located in Chicago by the amount of the transportation costs incurred in shipping glucose from Chicago to

Kansas City. If glucose was selling for $5 a gallon in Chicago and it cost $2 to ship it to Kansas City, the Kansas City candy manufacturer would incur costs of $7 in acquiring a gallon of glucose.

Suppose that an independent company was contemplating building a glucose manufacturing plant at Kansas City. Under the market conditions described, it could sell glucose in Kansas City for $7, since the only alternative sources available to buyers would cost them $7.

Although a new company could establish a plant at Kansas City and charge $7 for a gallon of glucose, the *Corn Products* and *Staley* opinions suggest that a company with a Chicago plant (and which was charging buyers a delivered price calculated on a Chicago basing point) could not build a new plant in Kansas City and charge the $7 price for its product. If it did so, it might be treated as charging "phantom freight" to its Kansas City customers, *i.e.,* the increment to the Chicago price equal to the transportation from Chicago to the buyer.

It is clear, is it not, that an interpretation of §§ 2(a) and (b) which would diminish the incentive of sellers to respond to market demand is an incorrect one? Consider why it took thirty-eight years to correct *Staley*'s misconstruction of the Act. Why did not the FTC attempt to correct the Supreme Court's error?

---

4. Functional Discounts

The Robinson-Patman Act makes no mention of anything called a "functional discount." Nonetheless, functional discounts are an important part of Robinson-Patman jurisprudence. A functional discount, as that term is used in the Robinson-Patman context, is a discount from the normal supply price provided to a distributor who performs more services than its rivals as a means by which the supplier pays the distributor for those services. Such services encompass such matters as stocking, providing catalogues and other marketing activities. Functional discounts are governed by § 2(a) and generally come before the Commission and the courts for review when a supplier charged with a violation of § 2(a) defends upon the ground that the lower price accorded to some customers did not produce a competitive injury because it was a "functional discount" paid in exchange for distribution services.

Texaco Inc. v. Hasbrouck

496 U.S. 543 (1990)

Justice STEVENS delivered the opinion of the Court.

Petitioner (Texaco) sold gasoline directly to respondents and several other retailers in Spokane, Washington, at its retail tank wagon prices (RTW) while it granted substantial discounts to two distributors. During the period between 1972 and 1981, the stations supplied by the two distributors increased their sales volume dramatically, while respondents' sales suffered a corresponding decline. Respondents filed an action against Texaco under the

Robinson-Patman Amendment to the Clayton Act (Act). . . . Respondents recovered treble damages, and the Court of Appeals for the Ninth Circuit affirmed the judgment. We granted *certiorari*. . . .

I

. . . .

Respondents are 12 independent Texaco retailers. They displayed the Texaco trademark, accepted Texaco credit cards, and bought their gasoline products directly from Texaco. Texaco delivered the gasoline to respondents' stations.

The retail gasoline market in Spokane was highly competitive throughout the damages period, which ran from 1972 to 1981. Stations marketing the nationally advertised Texaco gasoline competed with other major brands as well as with stations featuring independent brands. Moreover, although discounted prices at a nearby Texaco station would have the most obvious impact on a respondent's trade, the cross-city traffic patterns and relatively small size of Spokane produced a city-wide competitive market. . . .

The respondents tried unsuccessfully to increase their ability to compete with lower priced stations. Some tried converting from full service to self-service stations. . . . Two of the respondents sought to buy their own tank trucks and haul their gasoline from Texaco's supply point, but Texaco vetoed that proposal. . . .

While the independent retailers struggled, two Spokane gasoline distributors supplied by Texaco prospered. Gull Oil Company (Gull) . . . purchased its gas from Texaco at prices that ranged from six to four cents below Texaco's RTW price. . . . Gull resold that product under its own name; the fact that it was being supplied by Texaco was not known by either the public or the respondents. . . . In Spokane, Gull supplied about 15 stations; some were "consignment stations" and some were "commission stations." In both situations Gull retained title to the gasoline until it was pumped into a motorist's tank. In the consignment stations, the station operator set the retail prices, but in the commission stations Gull set the prices and paid the operator a commission. Its policy was to price its gasoline at a penny less than the prevailing price for major brands. Gull employed two truck drivers in Spokane who picked up product at Texaco's bulk plant and delivered it to the Gull stations. It also employed one supervisor in Spokane. Apart from its trucks and investment in retail facilities, Gull apparently owned no assets in that market. . . . At least with respect to the commission stations, Gull is fairly characterized as a retailer of gasoline throughout the relevant period.

The Dompier Oil Company (Dompier) . . . became a full line distributor of Texaco products [in 1960], and by the mid-1970's its sales of gasoline represented over three-quarters of its business. . . . Dompier purchased Texaco gasoline at prices of 3.95 cents to 3.65 cents below the RTW price. Dompier thus paid a higher price than Gull, but Dompier, unlike Gull, resold its gas under the Texaco brand names. . . . It supplied about eight to ten Spokane retail stations. In the period prior to October 1974, two of those stations were owned by the president of Dompier but the others were independently operated. . . . In the early 1970's, Texaco representatives encouraged Dompier to enter the retail business directly, and in 1974 and 1975 it acquired four stations. . . . Dompier's president estimated at trial that the share of its total gasoline sales made at retail during the middle 1970's was "probably 84 to 90 percent." . . .

Like Gull, Dompier picked up Texaco's product at the Texaco bulk plant and delivered directly to retail outlets. Unlike Gull, Dompier owned a bulk storage facility, but it was seldom used because its capacity was less than that of many retail stations. Again unlike Gull, Dompier received from Texaco the equivalent of the common carrier rate for delivering the gasoline product to the retail outlets. Thus, in addition to its discount from the RTW price, Dompier made a profit on its hauling function.

The stations supplied by Dompier regularly sold at retail at lower prices than respondents'. Even before Dompier directly entered the retail business in 1974, its customers were selling to consumers at prices barely above the RTW price. . . . Dompier's sales volume increased continuously and substantially throughout the relevant period. Between 1970 and 1975 its monthly sales volume increased from 155,152 gallons to 462,956 gallons; this represented an increase from 20.7% to almost 50% of Texaco's sales in Spokane. . . .

. . . .

III

. . . .

It is appropriate to begin our consideration of the legal status of functional discounts[11] by examining the language of the Act. . . .

The Act contains no express reference to functional discounts. It does contain two affirmative defenses that provide protection for two categories of discounts—those that are justified by savings in the seller's cost of manufacture, delivery or sale, and those that represent a good faith response to the equally low prices of a competitor. . . . As the case comes to us, neither of those defenses is available to Texaco.

. . . .

V

. . . .

In *FTC v. Morton Salt Co.* . . . we held that an injury to competition may be inferred from evidence that some purchasers had to pay their supplier "substantially more for their goods than their competitors had to pay." . . . Texaco, supported by the United States and the Federal Trade Commission as *amici curiae*, (the Government), argues that this presumption should not apply to differences between prices charged to wholesalers and those charged to retailers. Moreover, they argue that it would be inconsistent with fundamental antitrust policies to construe the Act as requiring a seller to control his customers' resale prices. The seller should not be held liable for the independent pricing decisions of his customers. As the Government correctly notes . . . this argument endorses the position advocated 35 years ago in the Report of the Attorney General's National Committee to Study the Antitrust Laws (1955).

After observing that suppliers ought not to be held liable for the independent pricing decisions of their buyers, and that without functional discounts distributors might go uncompensated for services they performed, the Committee wrote:

> "The Committee recommends, therefore, that suppliers granting functional discounts either to single-function or to integrated buyers should not be held responsible for any consequences of their customers' pricing tactics. Price cutting at the resale level is not in fact, and should not be held in law, 'the effect of' a differential that merely accords due recognition and reimbursement for actual marketing functions. The price cutting of a customer who receives this

---

[11] In their brief filed as *amici curiae*, the United States and the Federal Trade Commission suggest the following definition of "functional discount," which is adequate for our discussion: "A functional discount is one given to a purchaser based on its role in the supplier's distributive system, reflecting, at least in a generalized sense, the services performed by the purchaser for the supplier." . . .

type of differential results from his own independent decision to lower price and operate at a lower profit margin per unit. The legality or illegality of this price cutting must be judged by the usual legal tests. In any event, consequent injury or lack of injury should not be the supplier's legal concern.

"On the other hand, the law should tolerate no subterfuge. For instance, where a wholesaler-retailer buys only part of his goods as a wholesaler, he must not claim a functional discount on all. Only to the extent that a buyer *actually* performs certain functions, assuming all the risk, investment, and costs involved, should he legally qualify for a functional discount. Hence a distributor should be eligible for a discount corresponding to any part of the function he actually performs on that part of the goods for which he performs it." . . .

We generally agree with this description of the legal status of functional discounts. A supplier need not satisfy the rigorous requirements of the cost justification defense in order to prove that a particular functional discount is reasonable and accordingly did not cause any substantial lessening of competition between a wholesaler's customers and the supplier's direct customers.[18] The record in this case, however, adequately supports the finding that Texaco violated the Act.

The hypothetical predicate for the Committee's entire discussion of functional discounts is a price differential "that merely accords due recognition and reimbursement for actual marketing functions." Such a discount is not illegal. In this case, however, both the District Court and the Court of Appeals concluded that . . . there was no substantial evidence indicating that the discounts to Gull and Dompier constituted a reasonable reimbursement for the value to Texaco of their actual marketing functions. . . . Indeed, Dompier was separately compensated for its hauling function, and neither Gull nor Dompier maintained any significant storage facilities.

. . . .

As we have already observed, the "due recognition and reimbursement" concept endorsed in the Attorney General's Committee's study would not countenance a functional discount completely untethered to either the supplier's savings or the wholesaler's costs. The

---

18 In theory, a supplier could try to defend a functional discount by invoking the Act's cost justification defense, but the burden of proof with respect to the defense is upon the supplier, and interposing the defense "has proven difficult, expensive, and often unsuccessful." 3 E. KINTNER & J. BAUER, FEDERAL ANTITRUST LAW § 23.19, pp. 366-367 (1983). Moreover, to establish the defense a "seller must show that the price reductions given did not exceed the actual cost savings," *id.* § 23.10, p. 345, and this requirement of exactitude is ill-suited to the defense of discounts set by reference to legitimate, but less precisely measured, market factors. . . .

Discounters will therefore likely find it more useful to defend against claims under the Act by negating the causation element in the case against them: a legitimate functional discount will not cause any substantial lessening of competition. . . . We thus find ourselves in substantial agreement with the view that:

> "Conceived as a vehicle for allowing differential pricing to reward distributive efficiencies among customers operating at the same level, the cost justification defense focuses on narrowly defined savings to the seller derived from the different method or quantities in which goods are sold or delivered to different buyers. . . . Moreover, the burden of proof as to the cost justification defense is on the seller charged with violating the Act, whereas the burden of proof remains with the enforcement agency or plaintiff in circumstances involving functional discounts since functional pricing negates the probability of competitive injury, an element of a prima facie case of violation."

Rill, *Availability and Functional Discounts Justifying Discriminatory Pricing*, 53 ANTITRUST L.J. 929, 935 (1985) (footnotes omitted).

longstanding principle that functional discounts provide no safe harbor from the Act is likewise evident from the practice of the Federal Trade Commission, which has, while permitting legitimate functional discounts, proceeded against those discounts which appeared to be subterfuges to avoid the Act's restrictions. . . .

Most of these cases involve discounts made questionable because offered to "complex types of distributors" whose "functions became scrambled." . . . This fact is predictable: manufacturers will more likely be able to effectuate tertiary line price discrimination through functional discounts to a secondary line buyer when the favored distributor is vertically integrated. Nevertheless, this general tendency does not preclude the possibility that a seller may pursue a price discrimination strategy despite the absence of any discrete mechanism for allocating the favorable price discrepancy between secondary and tertiary line recipients.

. . . Both Gull and Dompier received the full discount on all their purchases even though most of their volume was resold directly to consumers. The extra margin on those sales obviously enabled them to price aggressively in both their retail and their wholesale marketing. To the extent that Dompier and Gull competed with respondents in the retail market, the presumption of adverse effect on competition recognized in the *Morton Salt* case becomes all the more appropriate. Their competitive advantage in that market also constitutes evidence tending to rebut any presumption of legality that would otherwise apply to their wholesale sales.

The evidence indicates, moreover, that Texaco affirmatively encouraged Dompier to expand its retail business and that Texaco was fully informed about the persistent and marketwide consequences of its own pricing policies. Indeed, its own executives recognized that the dramatic impact on the market was almost entirely attributable to the magnitude of the distributor discount and the hauling allowance. Yet at the same time that Texaco was encouraging Dompier to integrate downward, and supplying Dompier with a generous discount useful to such integration, Texaco was inhibiting upward integration by the respondents: two of the respondents sought permission from Texaco to haul their own fuel using their own tankwagons, but Texaco refused. The special facts of this case thus make it peculiarly difficult for Texaco to claim that it is being held liable for the independent pricing decisions of Gull or Dompier.

. . . [O]ne would expect that most functional discounts will be legitimate discounts which do not cause harm to competition. At the least, a functional discount that constitutes a reasonable reimbursement for the purchasers' actual marketing functions will not violate the Act. When a functional discount is legitimate, the inference of injury to competition recognized in the *Morton Salt* case will simply not arise. Yet it is also true that not every functional discount is entitled to a judgment of legitimacy, and that it will sometimes be possible to produce evidence showing that a particular functional discount caused a price discrimination of the sort the Act prohibits. When such anticompetitive effects are proved—as we believe they were in this case—they are covered by the Act.

. . . .

The judgment is affirmed.

It is so ordered.

COMMENTARY

One classic debate involving functional discounts is the criteria by which they should be measured in order to ensure that they do not create a competitive injury within the meaning of the Robinson-Patman Act. The classic alternative ways to assess the lawfulness of a functional discount are to view it as reimbursement for the extra expenses incurred by the purchaser in performing distribution services, in which case the discount would be limited by the purchaser's expenses, or, alternatively, to view the discount as payment to the purchaser for performing services which would otherwise have to be performed by the supplier, in which case the discount would be limited by the savings to the seller as a result of the purchaser's having performed the services. These two ways of approaching a functional discount have caselaw references. Measuring a functional discount by the costs incurred by the dealer was the approach which the Commission took in *Doubleday & Co.*, 52 F.T.C. 169 (1955), and measuring the discount by the costs saved by the supplier was the approach which the Commission took a few years later in *Mueller Co.*, 60 F.T.C. 120 (1962), where it repudiated its *Doubleday* position. The controversy over the two alternative approaches was rekindled a few years ago when the Commission reconsidered both approaches and again chose the *Mueller* approach in *Boise Cascade*.

When *Boise Cascade* reached the U.S. Court of Appeals for the District of Columbia Circuit, however, that court reversed the Commission without reaching the *Doubleday-Mueller* issue. (*See Boise Cascade Corp. v. FTC*, 837 F.2d 1127 (D.C. Cir. 1988), page 644, *supra*). In its *Hasbrouck* decision, the Supreme Court declined to resolve the *Doubleday-Mueller* issue. Although it rejected a functional discount defense in the case before it on the ground that the discount was tethered neither to the supplier's savings or to the wholesaler's costs, the Court nonetheless spoke in tolerant terms about functional discounts generally. Although it stated that functional discounts would not provide an automatic "safe harbor," it also indicated that functional discounts would not be treated as presumptively unlawful:

> . . . one would expect that most functional discounts will be legitimate discounts which do not cause harm to competition. At the least, a functional discount that constitutes a reasonable reimbursement for the purchasers' actual marketing functions will not violate the Act. When a functional discount is legitimate, the inference of injury to competition recognized in the *Morton Salt* case will simply not arise.

496 U.S.at 571. The analogy between the *Mueller-Doubleday* criteria for the legitimacy of a functional discount and the cost-justification defense is apparent, because under either *Mueller* or *Doubleday* the discount is evaluated in relation to costs (incurred by the dealer or saved by the seller). In *Hasbrouk*, however, the Court indicated that "a causation defense in a functional discount case does not demand the rigorous accounting associated with a cost justification defense." 496 U.S. at 571.

D. Price Discrimination Involving Brands or Labels

Not infrequently a producer will market some of its products under a brand name which it advertises heavily and, at the same time, market other physically identical goods which bear a different and usually unadvertised brand at a lower price. One well-publicized example of such a practice occurred during the period in which the Robinson-Patman Act was pending before Congress. In a proceeding brought by the Federal Trade Commission under the original § 2, the Goodyear Tire & Rubber Company conceded that automotive tires which it had sold to Sears, Roebuck & Co. marked with the Sears house brand were "comparable in quality" to Goodyear-brand tires which it had sold to its own dealers at higher prices. *Goodyear Tire & Rubber Co.*, 22 F.T.C. 323 (1936).

Since § 2(a) of the Robinson-Patman Act applies only to discriminations in price between purchasers of commodities "of like grade and quality," the question arises as to whether a difference in brand identification should be deemed to affect the "grade and quality" of those goods. Second, if physically identical goods are deemed to be "of like grade and quality" despite differences in brand identification, it may still be necessary in instances in which the same seller is selling the goods bearing the advertised brand at a higher price than the goods bearing the unadvertised brand to consider how differences in brand identification may affect the application of the Act.

Borden Co. v. Federal Trade Commission

381 F.2d 175 (5th Cir. 1967)

HUTCHSON, Circuit Judge.

We consider for the second time a petition by the Borden Company to review and set aside a cease-and-desist order of the Federal Trade Commission based on its decision that Borden violated Section 2(a) of the Clayton Act as amended by the Robinson-Patman Act. . . . The order directs Borden to cease and desist from discriminating in price between purchasers of its Borden brand evaporated milk and purchasers of its private label evaporated milk, which is packaged under a brand owned by the purchaser. The only distinguishing feature in the manufacture of the milk is the label placed upon the can: otherwise, the milk is of the same chemical composition and is packed in the identical way. But because Borden is a nationally advertised brand which commands a consumer preference, reflected in the willingness to pay a premium price, the milk bearing the Borden label is sold by Borden, and at all levels of distribution, at a substantially higher price than the lesser known private label milk.[2] It is this price difference initiated by Borden and its effect which the Commission held violated Sec. 2(a).

---

2 The price differential may be illustrated by the range of prices in effect in July, 1957. Since the standard case contains 48 14-ounce cans, the data has been converted to a "tall 48" basis. Borden label milk was sold at a uniform delivered price of $6.45 per case from all plants, whereas the private label milk was sold f.o.b. at prices ranging from $5.01 to $5.59 per case. The average price differential between the differently labeled milk was $1.19 per case.

The threshold inquiry concerning a violation of Sec. 2(a) is whether the goods are "of like grade and quality." In our previous decision, we held that the marked consumer preference for the Borden brand was sufficient to differentiate the products and to place the price difference beyond the reach of Sec. 2(a). The Supreme Court reversed, holding that the economic factors inherent in brand names should not be considered in the jurisdictional inquiry under the "like grade and quality" test but rather under the more flexible "injury" and "cost justification" provisions of the statute. For that purpose, the case was remanded for a resolution of the remaining issues which had been raised before us by Borden. . . .

Evidence on the issue of injury in the secondary line was supplied by wholesalers and retailers from North Carolina and South Carolina. They had purchased from Borden the premium brand milk but not the private brand milk. Their testimony as to competitive injury was meager. In substance, it was that they would have been interested in buying the private brand milk in addition to the premium brand milk. The record shows, however, that wholesalers who did try to sell private label milk in the Carolinas met with minimal success. Many retailers never inquired about private label milk, and others who received specific offers from wholesalers either declined the offer or often waited as long as a year before accepting. And it is to be remembered that no customer who requested private brand milk from Borden was denied the right to purchase it at the same price being charged to other customers.[14]

It is easily understood why the private label milk is sold at all levels of distribution for substantially less than Borden brand milk. By increased advertising and promotional efforts over the years, Borden has created a decided consumer preference for milk bearing a Borden label. The label has come to represent a value in itself. Thus it was not surprising that the testifying wholesalers and retailers admitted that the private label milk was interesting to them only at a price $1.50 to $2.00 less per case than the Borden brand milk.[16] This position reflects their knowledge that they would have had to sell the private label milk for a correspondingly lower price.[17]

There has been no doubt that the economic factors associated with a premium brand would receive recognition under Sec. 2(a), the only question being the appropriate provision. Upon reversing this case, the Supreme Court made it clear that these factors should be taken into consideration under the injury and cost provisions.

The Commission apparently ignored completely the bearing which the value attached to the Borden label might have upon competitive injury. Relying upon *FTC v. Morton Salt Co.*, *supra*, the Commission declared that in order to justify a finding of the prescribed harmful competitive effect in the secondary line, it was sufficient that some merchants paid more for Borden brand than their competitors paid for like goods packaged under a private label. Aside from the total failure to consider, or even mention, the commercial significance

---

[14] *See Tri-Valley Packing Ass'n v. FTC*, 329 F.2d 694, 703-704 (9th Cir. 1964), which indicates that in such circumstances injury may not be the result of price discrimination but of the buyer's failure to take advantage of the opportunity available to him to buy at the same prices as other customers. *See also* Rowe [PRICE DISCRIMINATION UNDER THE ROBINSON-PATMAN ACT ACT (1962 ed.)], 97.

[16] This differential is greater than that actually established by Borden's average prices.

[17] "The purchaser of the unbranded version of the seller's product naturally pays less because he gets less. Either he buys cheaper what he must resell cheaper—under its own private brand at a corresponding price spread below the manufacturer's nationally promoted product which enjoys greater consumer appeal. Or he may have to offset the initial price quotation in his favor by his expenditures in promoting *his* own private brand to match the supplier's appeal in the market." Rowe, 72-73.

of the consumer appeal of the Borden label, Morton Salt used a standard volume discount to create a price differential, whose effects are so different from those involved here as to make that decision inapposite to the one before us.

We are of the firm view that where a price differential between a premium and non-premium brand reflects no more than a consumer preference for the premium brand, the price difference creates no competitive advantage to the recipient of the cheaper private brand product on which injury could be predicated. "Rather it represents merely a rough equivalent of the benefit by way of the seller's national advertising and promotion which the purchaser of the more expensive branded product enjoys."[18] The record discloses no evidence tending to show that Borden's price differential exceeds the recognized consumer appeal of the Borden label. Nor has it been suggested that the prices are unreasonably high for Borden brand milk on the one hand, or unrealistically low for the private label milk on the other.

We conclude that there is not substantial evidence to support a finding that Borden has violated Sec. 2(a). The price difference does not create a competitive advantage by which competition could be injured, and, furthermore, no customer has been favored over another.

. . . .

Petition to set aside the cease-and-desist order is

Granted.

COMMENTARY

1. The Federal Trade Commission had charged Borden with violating the Robinson-Patman Act by causing competitive harm on both the primary and secondary levels. Since *Brooke Group* has now made clear that predatory-pricing standards govern the assessment of harm on the primary level, the part of the opinion dealing with that issue is now obsolete and has been omitted.

2. As the opinion makes clear this was the second time that the Fifth Circuit issued a decision in the case. The first time around, that court had ruled that because of the differences in demand for the product, Borden-label milk was of a different "grade" than the private label milk. Hence the Act did not apply.

3. The Supreme Court reversed, holding that physically identical products sold by the same seller are of the same grade and quality for Robinson-Patman Act purposes. *FTC v. Borden Co.*, 383 U.S. 637 (1966). In so ruling, the Court followed the 1955 REPORT OF THE ATTORNEY GENERAL'S COMMITTEE. The Attorney General's Committee had recommended that economic differences between brands applied to physically identical products should be recognized in applying the cost-justification defense and in assessing the impact on competition. THE ATTORNEY GENERAL'S NATIONAL COMMITTEE TO STUDY THE ANTITRUST LAWS 158-59 (1955).

---

[18] Report on the Antitrust Laws, 159. This was the view of the Committee majority and the then FTC Chairman Kintner, see Rowe, 74 n.126. *Accord*, Rowe, 72-73.

4. The Attorney General's Committee had asserted: "that abandonment of a physical test of grade and quality in favor of a marketing comparison of intrinsically identical goods might not only enmesh the administrators of the statute in complex economic investigations for every price discrimination charge, but also could encourage easy evasion of the statute through artificial variations in the packaging, advertising or design of goods which the seller wishes to distribute at differential prices."

5. What do you think of the recommendation of the Attorney General's Committee—which was quoted with approval by the Supreme Court in its *Borden* opinion—that commercial differences resulting from the use of different brands be considered, *inter alia*, under the cost-justification provision? How would this work? Were the Committee and the Court suggesting that in cases like *Borden*, the price differential would be justified only so long as the difference in price between the Borden label milk and the private label milk did not exceed the allocated per-unit amount spent on advertising? Do you perceive any problems in such a suggestion? What criteria would a rational seller employ to decide how much to spend on advertising? Would a rational seller expend money on advertising unless the advertising increased the "value" of the goods more than its expenditure on advertising?

6. In the opinion of the Fifth Circuit on remand, the court easily disposes of the problem by ruling that no competitive injury can result unless the price differential between the Borden label milk and the private label milk exceeds the value of the brand. So long as both the Borden label and the private label milk are available to all buyers, the price difference must reflect the value of the brand, must it not?

7. In footnote 14 the court referred to the so-called availability defense: So long as the lower-priced item is realistically available to all who wish to buy it, there can be no harm to competitors cognizable under the Robinson-Patman Act. The facts giving rise to the availability defense also provide the basis for establishing that the price difference does not exceed the value of the brand. *See* Note 6 above.

E. Clauses (c) Through (f) of The Robinson-Patman Act: Brokerage; Promotional Allowances; Services or Facilities; and Inducing Discrimination

1. Clause (c): The Brokerage Allowance

When home owners wish to sell their house, they often employ a real estate broker. The function of the broker in this case is to locate a buyer. When the house is sold to a buyer found by the broker, the broker is paid a commission on the sale, usually a percentage of the sales price.

Business firms often employ brokers for the same reason: producers wish to find buyers for their products. Sometimes buyers employ brokers to find sellers. The reason that parties need brokers is because they lack information about the other firms interested in trading. The broker's task is to overcome this informational deficiency of the parties. The basic role of the broker thus is to bring buyers and sellers together so that they can trade with each other.

At the time that it enacted the Robinson-Patman Act, Congress had focused considerable attention on the food industry. In that industry it was common for manufacturers of processed food to employ brokers to find buyers. Generally the brokers would be paid commissions amounting to a percentage of the sales price.

Some buyers, however, were large enough to collect the information necessary to transact business themselves. The A&P (a large national integrated chain of supermarkets), for example, operated a buying subsidiary, the Atlantic Commission Company (ACCO), which scoured the marketplace for sellers wishing to dispose of supplies desired by the A&P. Indeed, ACCO also found it useful and profitable to buy and resell or otherwise arrange for the sale of some goods for resale to other grocery firms.[4] ACCO thus performed the brokerage function for A&P and others.

Although small firms generally require brokers' services to locate other small firms which wish to trade, very large firms (like the A&P of the 1930s) do not. The A&P's buying operations, for example, were so extensive that it acquired an excellent command of available sources of supply and found it efficient to contact sellers directly rather than to await the approach of sellers' brokers.

As a result, the A&P frequently asked sellers to pay the brokerage fee which the sellers would normally pay to their own brokers either to itself or to ACCO, its buying subsidiary, on the rationale that the A&P, through ACCO, really performed the brokerage function. Alternatively, the A&P would ask sellers to reduce their sales prices to the A&P by the amount of the brokerage fee. For a discussion of brokerage practices in the grocery industry at this time, see MORRIS ADELMAN, A&P: A STUDY IN PRICE-COST BEHAVIOR AND PUBLIC POLICY, Chs. 23-25 (1959).

---

4 *See, e.g.*, M. ADELMAN, A&P: A STUDY IN PRICE-COST BEHAVIOR AND PUBLIC POLICY 304, 470 (1959).

Congress, however, did not appreciate the fact that large buyers like the A&P were performing the brokerage function. Instead, Congress took the view that when the A&P and other large buyers were paid brokerage fees (either directly or through their own brokers), the payments were in effect disguised price discriminations. Section 2(c) was designed to thwart attempts to avoid § 2(a) by disguising discriminations as payments to buyers' brokers.

Federal Trade Commission v. Henry Broch & Co.

363 U.S. 166 (1960)

Mr. Justice DOUGLAS delivered the opinion of the Court.

. . . .

Respondent is a broker or sales representative for a number of principals who sell food products. One of the principals is Canada Foods Ltd., a processor of apple concentrate and other products. Respondent agreed to act for Canada Foods for a 5% commission. Other brokers working for the same principal were promised a 4% commission. Respondent's commission was higher because it stocked merchandise in advance of sales. Canada Foods established a price for its 1954 pack of apple concentrate at $1.30 per gallon in 50-gallon drums and authorized its brokers to negotiate sales at that price.

The J. M. Smucker Co., a buyer, negotiated with another broker, Phipps, also working for Canada Foods, for apple concentrate. Smucker wanted a lower price than $1.30 but Canada Foods would not agree. Smucker finally offered $1.25 for a 500-gallon purchase. That was turned down by Canada Foods, acting through Phipps. Canada Foods took the position that the only way the price could be lowered would be through reduction in brokerage. About the same time respondent was negotiating with Smucker. Canada Foods told respondent what it had told Phipps, that the price to the buyer could be reduced only if the brokerage were cut; and it added that it would make the sale at $1.25—the buyer's bid—if respondent would agree to reduce its brokerage from 5% to 3%. Respondent agreed and the sale was consummated at that price and for that brokerage. The reduced price of $1.25 was thereafter granted Smucker on subsequent sales. But on sales to all other customers, whether through respondent or other brokers, the price continued to be $1.30 and in each instance respondent received the full 5% commission. Only on sales through respondent to Smucker were the selling price and the brokerage reduced.

The customary brokerage fee of 5% to respondent would have been $2,036.84. The actual brokerage of 3% received by respondent was $1,222.11. The reduction of brokerage was $814.73 which is 50% of the total price reduction of $1,629.47 granted by Canada Foods to Smucker.

The Commission charged respondent with violating § 2(c) of the Act, and after a hearing and the making of findings entered a cease-and-desist order against respondent. The Court of Appeals . . . reversed. . . .

The Robinson-Patman Act was enacted in 1936 to curb and prohibit all devices by which large buyers gained discriminatory preferences over smaller ones by virtue of their greater purchasing power. A lengthy investigation revealed that large chain buyers were obtaining competitive advantages in several ways other than direct price concessions and were thus avoiding the impact of the Clayton Act. One of the favorite means of obtaining an indirect price concession was by setting up "dummy" brokers who were employed by the buyer and who, in many cases, rendered no services. The large buyers demanded that the seller pay "brokerage" to these fictitious brokers who then turned it over to their employer. This practice was one of the chief targets of § 2(c) of the Act. But it was not the only means by which the brokerage function was abused[5] and Congress in its wisdom phrased § 2(c) broadly, not only to cover the other methods then in existence but all other means by which brokerage could be used to effect price discrimination.

The particular evil at which § 2(c) is aimed can be as easily perpetrated by a seller's broker as by the seller himself. The seller and his broker can of course agree on any brokerage fee that they wish. Yet when they agree upon one, only to reduce it when necessary to meet the demands of a favored buyer, they use the reduction in brokerage to undermine the policy of § 2(c). The seller's broker is clearly "any person" as the words are used in § 2(c)—as clearly such as a buyer's broker.

It is urged that the seller is free to pass on to the buyer in the form of a price reduction any differential between his ordinary brokerage expense and the brokerage commission which he pays on a particular sale because § 2(a) of the Act permits price differentials based on savings in selling costs resulting from differing methods of distribution. From this premise it is reasoned that a seller's broker should not be held to have violated § 2(c) for having done that which is permitted under § 2(a). We need not decide the validity of that premise, because the fact that a transaction may not violate one section of the Act does not answer the question whether another section has been violated. Section 2(c), with which we are here concerned, is independent of § 2(a) and was enacted by Congress because § 2(a) was not considered adequate to deal with abuses of the brokerage function.

Before the Act was passed the large buyers, who maintained their own elaborate purchasing departments and therefore did not need the services of a seller's broker because they bought their merchandise directly from the seller, demanded and received allowances reflecting these savings in the cost of distribution. In many cases they required that "brokerage" be paid to their own purchasing agents. After the Act was passed they discarded the facade of "brokerage" and merely received a price reduction equivalent to the seller's ordinary brokerage expenses in sales to other customers. When haled before the Commission, they protested that the transaction was not covered by § 2(c) but, since it was a price reduction, was governed by § 2(a). They also argued that because no brokerage services were needed or used in sales to them, they were entitled to a price differential reflecting this cost saving. Congress had anticipated such a contention by the "in lieu thereof" provision.[9] Accordingly, the Commission and the courts early rejected the contention that such a price

---

[5] In the Final Report on the Chain-Store Investigation . . . Congress had before it examples not only of large buyers demanding the payment of brokerage to their agents but also instances where buyers demanded discounts, allowances, or outright price reductions based on the theory that fewer brokerage services were needed in sales to these particular buyers, or that no brokerage services were necessary at all. *Id.* at 25, 63. These transactions were described in the report as the giving of "allowances in lieu of brokerage" (*id.* at 62) or "discount(s) in lieu of brokerage." *Id.* at 27.

[9] The brokerage clause in the bill was originally directed only at outright commission payments by sellers to buyers' agents. The Senate added the phrases "or any allowance or discount in lieu thereof," and "either to the other party to such transaction (or his intermediary)." S. Rep. No. 1502, 74th Cong., 2d Sess., p. 7. "This phrasing of the law was obviously designed to prevent evasion of the restriction through a mere modification of the form of the sales contract. It was assumed that large buyers would seek to convert the brokerage which they had hitherto received into an outright price reduction." ZORN AND FELDMAN, BUSINESS UNDER THE NEW PRICE LAWS (1937), 219.

reduction was lawful because the buyer's purchasing organization had saved the seller the amount of his ordinary brokerage expense.

In *Great Atlantic & Pacific Tea Co. v. Federal Trade Comm.*, 3 Cir., 1939, 106 F.2d 667, a buyer sought to evade § 2(c) by accepting price reductions equivalent to the seller's normal brokerage payments. The court upheld the Commission's view that the price reduction was an allowance in lieu of brokerage under § 2(c) and was prohibited even though, in fact, the seller had "saved" his brokerage expense by dealing directly with the select buyer. The buyer also sought to justify its price reduction on the ground that it had rendered valuable services to the seller. The court rejected this argument also. Although that court's interpretation of the "services rendered" exception in § 2(c) has been criticized, its conclusion that the price reduction was an allowance in lieu of brokerage within the meaning of § 2(c) has been followed and accepted.

We are asked to distinguish these precedents on the ground that there is no claim by the present buyer that the price reduction, concededly based in part on a saving to the seller of part of his regular brokerage cost on the particular sale, was justified by the elimination of services normally performed by the seller or his broker. There is no evidence that the buyer rendered any services to the seller or to the respondent nor that anything in its method of dealing justified its getting a discriminatory price by means of a reduced brokerage charge. We would have quite a different case if there were such evidence and we need not explore the applicability of § 2(c) to such circumstances. One thing is clear—the absence of such evidence and the absence of a claim that the rendition of services or savings in distribution costs justified the allowance does not support the view that § 2(c) has not been violated.

The fact that the buyer was not aware that its favored price was based in part on a discriminatory reduction in respondent's brokerage commission is immaterial. The Act is aimed at price discrimination, not conspiracy. The buyer's intent might be relevant were he charged with receiving an allowance in violation of § 2(c). But certainly it has no bearing on whether the respondent has violated the law. The powerful buyer who demands a price concession is concerned only with getting it. He does not care whether it comes from the seller, the seller's broker, or both.

Congress enacted the Robinson-Patman Act to prevent sellers and sellers' brokers from yielding to the economic pressures of a large buying organization by granting unfair preferences in connection with the sale of goods. The form in which the buyer pressure is exerted is immaterial and proof of its existence is not required. It is rare that the motive in yielding to a buyer's demands is not the "necessity" for making the sale. An "independent" broker is not likely to be independent of the buyer's coercive bargaining power. He, like the seller, is constrained to favor the buyers with the most purchasing power. If respondent merely paid over part of his commission to the buyer, he clearly would have violated the Act. We see no distinction of substance between the two transactions. In each case the seller and his broker make a concession to the buyer as a consequence of his economic power. In both cases the result is that the buyer has received a discriminatory price. In both cases the seller's broker reduces his usual brokerage fee to get a particular contract. There is no difference in economic effect between the seller's broker splitting his brokerage commission with the buyer and his yielding part of the brokerage to the seller to be passed on to the buyer in the form of a lower price.

We conclude that the statute clearly applies to payments or allowances by a seller's broker to the buyer, whether made directly to the buyer, or indirectly, through the seller. The allowances proscribed by § 2(c) are those made by "any person" which, as we have said, clearly encompasses a seller's broker. The respondent was a necessary party to the price reduction granted the buyer. His yielding of part of his brokerage to be passed on to the buyer was a *sine qua non* of the price reduction. This is not to say that every reduction in price, coupled with a reduction in brokerage, automatically compels the conclusion that an allowance "in lieu" of brokerage has been granted. As the Commission itself has made clear, whether such a reduction is tantamount to a discriminatory payment of brokerage depends on the circumstances of each case. . . . Nor does this "fuse" provisions of § 2(a), which permits the defense of cost justification, with those of § 2(c) which does not; it but realistically interprets the prohibitions of § 2(c) as including an independent broker's allowance of a reduced brokerage to obtain a particular order.

Reversed.

COMMENTARY

Does the brokerage clause inhibit the pricing flexibility that a truly competitive market requires? What would be the likely market effects of the broker absorbing some of the discount which the buyer demanded?

Consider the case of the buyer's broker. A seller which pays brokerage to the buyer's broker is likely to be ruled in violation of § 2(c) in a proceeding brought by the FTC. But rivals may have difficulty establishing standing to complain. *See* Chapter 17, pages 922-27, *infra*.

---

2. The Brokerage Clause as Applied to Commercial Bribery

Stephen Jay Photography, Ltd. v. Olan Mills, Inc.

903 F.2d 988 (4th Cir. 1989)

WILKINS, Circuit Judge:

. . . .

Appellants are commercial photographers operating in cities in the Norfolk, Virginia, area. Appellees are also commercial photographers who operate in the Norfolk area, but are large national corporations with corporate headquarters in other states. Appellees contracted with all 22 high schools in the Norfolk area to photograph students for school yearbooks, Olan Mills contracting with 20 percent of the schools and Kinder-Care with 80 percent. Appellees obtained the contracts through competitive negotiation, a process whereby school officials contacted photographers (including photographers other than appellees) whom they believed would be interested in obtaining yearbook contracts. After negotiation, appellees contracted to take student yearbook pictures and pay the schools a percentage of the profits they earned from sales of optional portrait photographs (portraits) of the students.[10] In exchange, the schools designated the contract photographer as the "official pho-

---

10 Appellees agreed to pay the schools either 40 or 50 percent of their profits from portraits sold to underclassmen and 20 percent of their profits from portraits sold to seniors.

tographer," provided a location on school grounds where photographs could be taken, supplied a list of the students' names and addresses, and scheduled the students for their photographs.

While the students' yearbook pictures were being taken, appellees also took portraits. Both the schools and appellees sent letters to the students and their parents encouraging the purchase of a portrait from the "official photographer." The letters disclosed that an unspecified portion of the portrait photograph price would be given to the school to support various school activities. This marketing system of coordinating the yearbook pictures and portraits, coupled with the endorsement of the school, gave appellees a competitive advantage in selling portraits.

. . . .

III.

Appellants contend that the payment of the profits from the portrait sales by appellees to the schools constitutes commercial bribery in violation of section 2(c) of the Robinson-Patman Act. The issue of whether commercial bribery violates this section has not yet been addressed by this circuit.

The Robinson-Patman Act was enacted in 1936 to prohibit tactics used by large buyers or sellers to circumvent the discriminatory price prohibitions of the Clayton Act. Congress determined that rather than forcing direct price concessions, which violated the Clayton Act, monopolists were insisting on indirect price concessions. One method employed to circumvent the Clayton Act was through the use of "dummy brokerages." For example, a large buyer with economic clout might insist that in order to do business sellers must pay a fee to a designated "broker." The broker would then turn the money over to the large buyer.

Although dummy brokerages were the chief target of section 2(c), it also covers other means by which brokerages could be used to effect price discrimination. *See FTC v. Henry Broch & Co.*, 363 U.S. 166, 168-69 (1960). In *Henry Broch & Co.* the Court noted, in dicta, that the legislative history of the Robinson-Patman Act supports the proposition that section 2(c) might also "proscribe other practices such as the 'bribing' of a seller's broker by the buyer." *Henry Broch & Co.*, 363 U.S. at 169-70 n.6. *See also California Motor Transp. Co. v. Trucking Unlimited*, 404 U.S. 508, 513 (1972) ("bribery of a public purchasing agent" could violate section 2(c)) (dictum). The Senate Report discussing section 2(c) states in part:

> The relation of the broker to his client is a fiduciary one. To collect from a client for services rendered in the interest of a party adverse to him, is a violation of that relationship; and to protect those who deal in the streams of commerce against breaches of faith in its relations of trust, is to foster confidence in its processes and promote its wholesomeness and volume.

S. Rep. No. 1502, 74th Cong., 2d Sess. 7 (1936). Four circuits have applied a commercial bribery analysis in section 2(c) cases.[11]

---

[11] *See Environmental Tectonics v. W.S. Kirkpatrick, Inc.*, 847 F.2d 1052, 1066 (3d Cir.1988), *aff'd on other grounds*, 493 U.S. 400, 110 S. Ct. 701, 107 L. Ed. 2d 816 (1990); *Grace v. E.J. Kozin Co.*, 538 F.2d 170 (7th Cir.1976), *abrogation on other grounds recognized, Federal Paper Bd. Co. v. Amata*, 693 F. Supp. 1376 (D. Conn. 1988); *Rangen, Inc. v. Sterling Nelson & Sons, Inc.*, 351 F.2d 851 (9th Cir.1965), *cert. denied*, 383 U.S. 936 (1966); *Fitch v. Kentucky-Tennessee Light & Power*, 136 F.2d 12 (6th Cir.1943). *But see Seaboard Supply Co. v. Congoleum Corp.*, 770 F.2d 367, 371-72 (3d Cir.1985) (questioning the proposition that Congress intended to include commercial bribery within the ambit of section 2(c)).

The Third Circuit, when considering allegations that a scheme of commercial bribery between an employee of a manufacturer and the manufacturer's sales agent constituted a violation of section 2(c), held that although the conduct was reprehensible, it did not come within the scope of the antitrust laws. *Seaboard Supply Co.*, 770 F.2d at 372. In so ruling the court stated: "In the appellate decisions which have found commercial bribery within the ambit of section 2(c) the common thread has been the passing of illegal payments from seller to buyer or vice versa." *Id.* The court reasoned that by restricting liability to situations "when the seller-buyer line has been passed," courts have narrowed the scope of section 2(c) and upheld Congress' intent to leave the relationships of legitimate brokerages unaffected by section 2(c). *Id.*

Appellants contend that the "seller-buyer line" was crossed here because the schools acted as intermediaries in behalf of the students when they contracted to have appellees take the yearbook pictures. Thus, the issue is whether, as a matter of law, the payments made from appellees to the schools from profits on portrait sales crossed the seller-buyer line. In other words, was the school an intermediary acting in behalf of the students (the buyers) when the portrait sales were made to them by the appellees (the sellers)? The legislative history and the cases which address commercial bribery under section 2(c) are helpful in determining the answer.

Discussing the commercial bribery aspect of section 2(c), the Court in *Henry Broch & Co.*, 363 U.S. at 169-70 n.6, cited portions of two statements from the Congressional Record to support the proposition that Congress intended to bring commercial bribery within the ambit of section 2(c):

> A practice has grown up whereby large mass buyers bribe representatives of the seller, oftentimes the seller representing groups of farmers, under the guise of a brokerage allowance. It is not a brokerage allowance at all; it is a bribe. This bill will not compel the use of a broker but it will prohibit one party from bribing the representative of the other under the guise of brokerage allowances or commissions.

74 Cong. Rec. 7759-60 (1936) (statement of Sen. Patman). The second statement cited by the Court reads:

> There is a merchant in Virginia representing potato growers. He sells thousands of cars of potatoes a year, and our investigation has disclosed that he had a secret contract with a large mass corporate chain buyer by which he obligated himself to sell every car of those potatoes of those farmers to this large buyer. . . . This man representing the farmers sold those potatoes to that mass buyer, fixing the price himself, and what did he get out of it? He got a secret rebate of $2.50 to $5 on every car that the farmers knew nothing about. . . . That is the kind of dummy-brokerage arrangement we are trying to prohibit in this bill.

74 Cong. Rec. 8111-12 (1936) (statement of Sen. Patman). These statements refer to the corruption of an agency relationship. In Senator Patman's example the farmers' representative had the actual authority to bind the farmers in the sale of potatoes. Here, the schools did not have the authority to bind the students to purchase portraits. Instead the students were free to purchase portraits from appellees or from a photographer of their choice, or to purchase no portraits from anyone.

In harmony with these examples from the Congressional Record, circuit court cases finding commercial bribery in violation of section 2(c) all involve the corruption of an agency or employment relationship. *See E.J. Kozin Co.*, 538 F.2d 170 (sales manager and executive vice president of buyer received payments from seller to facilitate sales); *Rangen, Inc.*, 351 F.2d 851 (fish food seller bribed a state official so that the official, who was responsible for the nutritional value of fish food, would use his expertise to influence state purchasing officials to buy the seller's fish food); *Fitch*, 136 F.2d 12 (holding that a coal company which paid bribes to the president of a power company, for his personal use, to obtain sales of coal to the power company, was guilty of commercial bribery in violation of section 2(c)). Unlike these relationships, the relationship between the students and the schools does not rise to one akin to that of agency or employment. Without such a relationship to connect the students' purchasing decisions to the schools, the payments from the appellees to the schools do not cross the seller-buyer line.

Therefore, even assuming section 2(c) proscribes commercial bribery, we conclude that no violation occurred here. Unquestionably, the schools and the students enjoy a special relationship of trust. And it is true that the schools arranged to have yearbook photographs taken by appellees and encouraged students to purchase portraits from them. However, letters encouraging the students to purchase these photographs either expressly or implicitly indicated that their decision to purchase portraits was optional. From this correspondence it is abundantly clear that the schools did not assume a position resembling that of a portrait purchasing agent for the students.

. . . .

Based on the foregoing, we affirm the summary judgment granted by the district court in favor of appellees.

AFFIRMED.

COMMENTARY

1. Do the considerations underlying the brokerage provision properly extend to commercial bribery? What is the paradigm case of commercial bribery to which the brokerage provision would apply? Is a seller's payment to an employee of the buyer different in kind from the seller's payment of a brokerage fee to the buyer or to the buyer's broker? How? Is it significant that in the latter case the payment goes to the buyer whereas in the former case the payment goes (not to the buyer but) to the buyer's employee and is the quid pro quo for the diversion of the employee's loyalty from the buyer to the seller?

2. Do you agree with the court that the situation in the *Stephan Jay Photography* case did not involve commercial bribery? Was there a diversion of a duty of loyalty owed by the school to the students? Was the problem solved by full disclosure? Who was complaining? the students? a rival of the "official" photographer?

3. Would the purposes of the Robinson-Patman Act be served by finding liability in the instant case? Why or why not? What behavior does the court's ruling encourage? Is this kind of behavior consistent with the policies of the Robinson-Patman Act? of the other antitrust laws?

3. Clauses (d) and (e)

Eastern Auto Distributors, Inc. v. Peugeot Motors of America, Inc.

795 F.2d 329 (4th Cir. 1986)

SPROUSE, Circuit Judge:

Eastern Auto Distributors, Inc. (EAD) brought this action against Peugeot Motors of America, Inc. (PMA) and Automobiles Peugeot, S.A. asserting numerous breach of contract, civil conspiracy, antitrust, Robinson-Patman Act and Automobile Dealers Day in Court Act claims. . . . EAD and PMA are parties to a Peugeot distribution agreement, and this dispute arises out of that relationship. . . . At the close of EAD's evidence, the court directed a verdict in favor of Automobiles Peugeot, S.A. on all of EAD's claims and directed a verdict in favor of PMA on EAD's Robinson-Patman Act claims. . . .

I. Facts

This dispute revolves around the distribution of Peugeot vehicles and products in the United States. Automobiles Peugeot, S.A. (AP), a French corporation, manufactures the automobiles in France and sells them to various importers throughout the world. PMA, a Delaware corporation, is the exclusive importer of Peugeot products into the United States. For many years, PMA sold the vehicles it had purchased from AP to several intermediate distributors. Pursuant to an agreement with PMA, each of these distributors had the exclusive right to supply Peugeot vehicles to retail Peugeot dealers in a different section of this country. EAD was and still is the exclusive distributor for the southeastern United States. PMA gradually acquired the other intermediate distributors, however, and merged them into PMA. As a result, EAD has been the sole remaining independent distributor of Peugeot products in the United States since 1974. This consolidation has forced PMA to "wear two hats": it is both the sole importer of Peugeot products into the United States and the sole distributor of Peugeot products throughout all of the United States with the exception of the southeast region maintained by EAD.

. . . .

II. Robinson-Patman Act

EAD contends that PMA violated sections 2(d) and 2(e) of the Robinson-Patman Act (the Act), 15 U.S.C. § 13(d), (e) (1982), by providing cash incentives, parts repurchase programs and training facilities to PMA's dealers but not to EAD's dealers. At the close of EAD's evidence, the district court directed a verdict in favor of PMA on the grounds that (1) EAD failed to prove the existence of competition between its dealers and PMA's dealers, and (2) EAD failed to prove damages.

Sections 2(d) and 2(e) of the Act prohibit the providing of "anything of value" or the "furnishing [of] any services or facilities," respectively, unless the thing of value, service or facility is available on "proportionally equal terms" to, respectively, all other competing customers or all other purchasers. An essential element to a claim under these provisions is the existence of competition between the favored customers and the disfavored customers. *See FTC v. Simplicity Pattern Co.*, 360 U.S. 55, 62-64 (1959). Thus, discrimination by a seller in the provision of services to retail customers and wholesale customers would typically not be actionable since retailers and wholesalers do not normally compete with each other. *TriValley Packing Association v. FTC*, 329 F.2d 694, 708-10 (9th Cir. 1964). Similarly, a seller may lawfully discriminate in the provision of services to two retail customers located in separate geographic markets since they do not compete for the same consumers. *Id.*

To establish violations of sections 2(d) and 2(e), EAD had to prove that its dealers competed with PMA's dealers. As retail dealers of Peugeot automobiles, the two sets of dealers obviously competed at the same functional level. EAD had to prove, however, that its dealers and PMA's dealers also competed in the same geographic market, i.e., that the two sets of dealers competed for the same customers. This task was made difficult by the fact that EAD's dealers are located exclusively within EAD's southeastern territory, while PMA's dealers are located throughout the rest of the country. *See, e.g., Lupia v. Stella D'oro Biscuit Co.*, 586 F.2d 1163, 1171 (7th Cir. 1978), *cert. denied*, 440 U.S. 982 (1979); *Carlo C. Gelardi Corp. v. Miller Brewing Co.*, 421 F. Supp. 237, 245-46 (D.N.J. 1976). At the close of EAD's evidence, the district court ruled that EAD had failed to establish the necessary degree of competition and directed a verdict in favor of PMA.

EAD contends that there is evidence of significant competition between the two sets of dealers on the fringes of EAD's territory and that this degree of competition is sufficient to maintain its claim under sections 2(d) and 2(e) of the Act. The evidence consists of a report by PMA that of the 81,000 Peugeots sold in the United States between 1976 and 1982, 800, or less than one percent, were cross-border sales.[7] Of the 800 cross-border sales, the report indicates that approximately 260, or one-third, occurred in the Memphis, Tennessee area. The greater Memphis area is the only place where a PMA dealer and an EAD dealer are located within fifty miles of each other. Although EAD asserts that the two sets of dealers compete in other areas along the fringes of EAD's territory,[8] it offered no evidence other than the PMA report to support the existence of such competition.

. . . .

With the exception of the Memphis area, EAD simply failed to present sufficient evidence which would allow a jury to conclude that its dealers and PMA's dealers compete for the same customers. EAD presented no evidence of the relevant geographic markets for Peugeot vehicles. EAD instead relied solely upon the PMA report that less than one percent of total Peugeot sales were cross-border sales. EAD's president testified, however, that he did not know the reasons behind any of the cross-border sales in the report, and he acknowledged that such sales occurred for a variety of reasons other than competition between the two sets of dealers.[9] Unsupported by evidence of the relevant geographic markets or other evidence of actual competition, we find that the small number of unexplained cross-border sales in the PMA report could not reasonably support a finding of competition between

---

[7] A cross-border sale is a sale by a PMA dealer to a customer who registers the vehicle in EAD's territory or vice versa.

[8] EAD contends that competition occurred between PMA's dealer in Savannah, Georgia and EAD's dealer in Atlanta, Georgia and that there was competition between a PMA dealer and an EAD dealer along the Ohio-Kentucky border.

[9] For example: Q. And it could have been that a large number were made by military personnel who titled their car in their home states for tax purposes; is that correct? [EAD President]: That's a small part of it, I guess, yes. Q. But we do know in Norfolk that happens a great deal, don't we? [EAD President]: Yes.

PMA's dealers and EAD's dealers. *See Lupia*, 586 F.2d at 1171 ("de minimis" or sporadic competition insufficient to state a claim under the Act).

. . . .

COMMENTARY

1. The reported case focuses upon the interplay of the requirements of proportionally equal terms and a competitive relation between the disfavored dealer and other dealers. When the dealers are geographically distant from each other, the likelihood that they are in a competitive relationship is diminished. In some circumstances, territorial restrictions imposed by the supplier upon its dealers would also tend to diminish the likelihood that the dealers would stand in a competitive relationship with each other. Perhaps customer restrictions would be even more effective.

2. Sections 2(d) and (e) are concerned with different things. Section 2(d) is concerned with payments from the seller to the buyer, ostensibly in payment for services rendered by the buyer. Section 2(e) is concerned with the seller's provision of services or facilities to the buyer. Both are designed to prevent sellers from avoiding the proscriptions of § 2(a) by disguising price discounts in other forms.

Section 2(d) focuses upon the situation in which a seller disguises payments to the buyer as payments for promotional activity performed by the buyer. The paradigm case is one in which the payment is made for services which the buyer either does not perform at all or in which the payment substantially exceeds the costs incurred by the buyer in performing the services. Section 2(e) focuses upon the situation in which the seller itself provides services or furnishes facilities as a means of favoring particular buyers. Both sections require that the seller treat all competing buyers in proportionally equal terms.

Federal Trade Commission v. Fred Meyer, Inc.

390 U.S. 341 (1968)

[Respondent Fred Meyer, Inc. operated a chain of 13 supermarkets in the Portland, Oregon area which engaged in the retail sale of groceries, drugs, variety items, and a limited line of clothing. Since 1936 Meyer had conducted annually a four-week promotional campaign based on the distribution of coupon books to consumers. The books usually contained 72 pages, each page featuring a single product being sold by Meyer at a substantially reduced price. Consumers purchased the books for ten cents and surrendered the appropriate coupons when making purchases of goods. Meyer financed the promotion in large part by charging the suppliers of each featured product fees of at least $350 per supplier for each coupon-page advertising its product.

The Federal Trade Commission found that certain suppliers of Meyer, Tri-Valley Packing Association and Idaho Canning Company, which made such payments to Meyer also sold to certain wholesalers, Hudson House and Wadhams & Co., which, in turn, sold to retailers which competed with Meyer. No payments were made by Tri-Valley or Idaho Canning either to Hudson House or Wadhams or to the retailers to whom these wholesalers resold. On these facts, the Federal Trade Commission ruled that the payments made to Meyer by certain suppliers, including Tri-Valley and Idaho Canning, represented promotional allowances paid in violation of § 2(d) of the Robinson-Patman Act because similar allowances were not made available on proportionally equal terms to competing customers. The Court of Appeals for the Ninth Circuit reversed in part the Commission's ruling and the Supreme Court granted *certiorari*.]

Mr. Chief Justice WARREN delivered the opinion of the Court.

. . . Respondents argued that, purely as a matter of statutory construction, Tri-Valley and Idaho Canning could not have violated the requirement of proportional equality among "customers competing in the distribution" of their products because (1) Meyer, a retailer, was not "competing" in the distribution of canned corn and peaches with the disfavored wholesalers, Hudson House and Wadhams, and (2) the retailers found by the Commission to be competing with Meyer in the resale of these products were not "customers" of Tri-Valley and Idaho Canning but were customers of Hudson House and Wadhams.

The Commission rejected this reading of § 2(d), noting that, if respondents' view prevailed, a retailer buying from a wholesaler and having no direct dealings with his supplier would receive no protection against discriminatory promotional allowances given his competitor who purchased directly from the supplier. The Commission held that § 2(d) prohibits a supplier from granting promotional allowances to a direct-buying retailer, such as Meyer, unless the allowances are also made available to wholesalers who purchase from the supplier and resell to the direct-buying retailer's competitors. . . .

We agree with the Commission that the proscription of § 2(d) reaches the kind of discriminatory promotional allowances granted Meyer by Tri-Valley and Idaho Canning. . . . However, . . . we have concluded that Meyer's retail competitors, rather than the two wholesalers, were competing customers under the statute . . . .

IV.

The Commission's view of the impact of respondents' argument in no way conflicts with our own. . . . But rather than concluding, as we have, that retailers who purchased through Hudson House and Wadhams and competed with Meyer in resales were disfavored customers of Tri-Valley and Idaho Canning, a majority of the Commission held that the wholesalers, Hudson House and Wadhams, were the customers entitled to promotional allowances on proportionately equal terms with Meyer. . . . [W]e hold that, at least on the facts before us, § 2(d) does not require proportional equality between Meyer and the two wholesalers. . . . We cannot assume without a clear indication from Congress that § 2(d) was intended to compel the supplier to pay the allowances to a reseller further up the distributive chain who might or might not pass them on to the level where the impact would be felt directly. We conclude that the most reasonable construction of § 2(d) is one which places on the supplier the responsibility for making promotional allowances available to those resellers who compete directly with the favored buyer.

The Commission argues here that the view we take of § 2(d) is impracticable because suppliers will not always find it feasible to bypass their wholesalers and grant promotional allowances directly to their numerous retail outlets. Our decision does not necessitate such bypassing. We hold only that, when a supplier gives allowances to a direct-buying retailer, he must also make them available on comparable terms to those who buy his products through wholesalers and compete with the direct buyer in resales. Nothing we have said bars a supplier, consistently with other provisions of the antitrust laws, from utilizing his wholesalers to distribute payments or administer a promotional program, so long as the supplier takes responsibility, under rules and guides promulgated by the Commission for the regulation of such practices, for seeing that the allowances are made available to all who compete in the resale of his product.

The judgment of the Court of Appeals, insofar as it held that the promotional allowances granted Meyer by Tri-Valley and Idaho Canning did not violate §2(d), is reversed. The case is remanded to the Court of Appeals with directions to remand to the Commission for further proceedings consistent with this opinion.

It is so ordered.

COMMENTARY

1. When the respondents contended that Meyer was not "competing" in the distribution of canned corn and peaches with the disfavored wholesalers and that the retailers which were competing with Meyer were not "customers" of the canners which had paid promotional allowances to Meyer, they were contending that under the literal terms of § 2(d) no violation had occurred, were they not? How did the Supreme Court deal with that contention? Did the Court deny that under the literal terms of the Act no violation had occurred? On what grounds did the Court overlook the literal terms of § 2(d)? How did the Court's reading of the section differ from the Commission's? Was the Court correct? What problems do you see in the Court's approach? in the Commission's approach?

2. Assume that you have as a client, a producer which sells both to wholesalers and to direct-buying retailers. Your client has just informed you that it has paid significant amounts in promotional allowances to several direct-buying retailers. What steps would you advise your client to take to avoid § 2(d) liability? Would you seek the advice of the FTC? *See* Note 5 below.

3. Do the difficulties which the Commission and the courts encountered in applying § 2(d) in the *Meyer* case suggest that the structure of the Act is substantially flawed? Is this flawed structure the result of an unrealistically simplistic assumption employed by the Act's drafters that manufacturers always sell to wholesalers who always resell to retailers who always resell to consumers? When steps are added or eliminated from this three-tier distribution chain, the difficulties of applying the Act increase, do they not?

4. *Meyer* is a case in which the wholesale step was eliminated from Meyer's supply-chain but not from the supply-chain of Meyer's rivals. Can you think of other situations in which actual business behavior does not fit the Act's assumptions? How many of these other situations involve some form of vertical integration? Is the three-tier distribution system an assumption underlying the meeting-competition defense in § 2(b)? *See FTC v. Sun Oil Co.*, page 695, *infra.* What assumptions of standard business behavior underlie the brokerage provision in § 2(c)? *See* page 674, *supra.*

5. In *Meyer*, the Supreme Court held that the producers were responsible for ensuring that proportionally equal payments were available to Meyer's rivals. The Commission then stepped in and issued guides specifying the means through which producers could meet their obligations under § 2(d) in a *Fred Meyer* type situation. The guides were initially issued in 1969 and were amended in 1973. In 1990, the Commission further revised the *Fred Meyer* guides.[5] Under the revised guides, to fall under § 2(d), promotional allowances are required to be closely connected to resales of goods. Making contributions to a trade show, for example fall outside of their scope. The new guides also broaden the scope of the meeting-competition defense in accordance with the caselaw that now recognizes application of that defense on an area-wide, as opposed to a customer-specific, basis.

Federal Trade Commission v. Simplicity Pattern Co.
360 U.S. 55 (1959)

Mr. Justice CLARK delivered the opinion of the Court.

This case presents, for the first time in this Court, issues relating to the availability of certain defenses to a prima facie violation of § 2(e) of the Clayton Act. . . . The Federal Trade Commission has found that Simplicity Pattern Co., Inc., one of the Nation's largest dress pattern manufacturers, discriminated in favor of its larger customers by furnishing to them services and facilities not accorded to competing smaller customers on proportionally equal terms. The Commission held that neither the presence of "cost justification" nor the absence of competitive injury may constitute a defense to a § 2(e) violation. [The Court of Appeals for the District of Columbia Circuit remanded the case on the "cost justification" defense.]

Simplicity manufactures and sells tissue patterns which are used in the home for making women's and children's wearing apparel. Its volume of pattern sales, in terms of sales units, is greater than that resulting from the combined effort of all other major producers. . . . [Simplicity's] customers can be divided roughly into two categories. One, consisting largely of department and variety stores, comprises only 18% of the total number of customers, but accounts for 70% of the total sales volume. The remaining 82% of the customers are small stores whose primary business is the sale of yard-good fabrics.

. . . .

The variety stores handle and sell a multitude of relatively low-priced articles. Each article, including dress patterns, is sold for the purpose of returning a profit and would be

---

[5] 16 C.F.R. §§ 240.1-240.15 (1991).

dropped if it failed to do so. The fabric stores, on the other hand, are primarily interested in selling yard goods; they handle patterns at no profit or even at a loss as an accommodation to their fabric customers and for the purpose of stimulating fabric sales. These differences in motive are reflected in the manner in which each type of store handles its patterns. The variety stores devote the minimum amount of display space consistent with adequate merchandising—consisting usually of nothing more than a place on the counter for the catalogues, with the patterns themselves stored underneath the counter in the steel cabinets furnished by Simplicity. In contrast, the fabric stores usually provide tables and chairs where the customers may peruse the catalogues in comfort and at their leisure.

. . . Simplicity charges a uniform price, to all its customers. . . . However, in the furnishing of certain services and facilities Simplicity does not follow this uniformity. It furnishes patterns to the variety stores on a consignment basis, requiring payment only as and when patterns are sold—thus affording them an investment-free inventory. The fabric stores are required to pay cash for their patterns in regular course. In addition, the cabinets and the catalogues are furnished to variety stores free while the fabric stores are charged therefor, the catalogues averaging from $2 to $3 each. Finally, all transportation costs in connection with its business with variety stores are paid by Simplicity but none is paid on fabric-store transactions.

. . . .

1. Existence of Competition.

The unanimous conclusion of the Examiner, the Commission, and the Court of Appeals on this point was . . . that the variety and fabric stores, "operating in the same cities and in the same shopping area, often side by side, were competitors, purchasing from Simplicity at the same price and then at like prices retailing the identical product to substantially the same segment of the public." . . . Simplicity argues that "motivation" controls and that since the variety store sells for a profit and the fabric store for accommodation that the competition is minuscule. But the existence of competition does not depend on such motives. Regardless of the necessity the fabric stores find in the handling of patterns it does not remove their incentive to sell those on hand, especially when cash is tied up in keeping patterns on the shelves. The discriminatory terms under which they are obliged to handle them increase their losses. Furthermore, Simplicity not only takes advantage of the captive nature of the fabric stores in not granting them these advantages but compounds the damage by creating a sales outlet in the variety stores through the granting of these substantial incentives to engage in the pattern business. Without such partial subsidization the variety stores might not enter into the pattern trade at all.

Nor does it follow that the failure here to show specific injury to competition in patterns is inconsistent with a finding that competition in fact exists. It may be, as Simplicity argues, that the sale of patterns is minuscule in the overall business of a variety store, but the same is true of thousands of other items. While the giving of discriminatory concessions to a variety store on any one isolated item might cause no injury to competition with a fabric store in its overall operation, that fact does not render nonexistent the actual competition between them in patterns. . . .

2. Application of the Justification Defenses of § 2(b).

Simplicity contends that an absence of competitive injury constitutes a defense under the justification provisions of § 2(b) and further that it should have been permitted, under that subsection, to dispel its discrimination in services and facilities by a showing of lower costs in its transactions with the variety stores. . . .

In terms, the proscriptions of these three subsections are absolute. Unlike § 2(a), none of them requires, as proof of a *prima facie* violation, a showing that the illicit practice has had an injurious or destructive effect on competition. Similarly, none has any built-in defensive matter, as does § 2(a). Simplicity's contentions boil down to an argument that the exculpatory provisions which Congress has made expressly applicable only to price discriminations are somehow included as "justifications" for discriminations in services or facilities by § 2(b). . . .

We hold that the key word "justification" [in § 2(b)] can be read no more broadly than to allow rebuttal of the respective offenses in one of the ways expressly made available by Congress. Thus, a discrimination in prices may be rebutted by a showing under any of the § 2(a) provisos, or under the § 2(b) proviso—all of which by their terms apply to price discriminations. On the other hand, the only escape Congress has provided for discriminations in services or facilities is the permission to meet competition as found in the § 2(b) proviso. We cannot supply what Congress has studiously omitted.

. . . .

We hold, therefore, that neither "cost-justification" nor an absence of competitive injury may constitute "justification" of a prima facie § 2(e) violation. The judgment of the Court of Appeals must accordingly be reversed insofar as it set aside and remanded the Commission's order. . . .

It is so ordered.

COMMENTARY

1. In order for § 2(e) to be violated, the customer disfavored in the receipt of services or facilities must be in competition with the favored customer. This requirement applies to § 2(d) as well, does it not? A violation may be established under either section without showing that any specific injury to competition has occurred as a result of the proportionally unequal treatment. Why would it be necessary to show a competitive relationship between the favored and disfavored customers if it is unnecessary to show an injury to competition? The extent and kind of competition-related injury which must be shown is significantly different in a private actions and FTC proceedings. *See* Note 5 below and pages 922-27, *infra*.

2. Do you agree that the fabric stores competed with the variety stores? Did they compete in the sale of patterns? In their overall business?

3. Why did Simplicity discriminate in favor of the variety stores? Will the decision in the principal case increase or lessen competition in the sale of patterns? Will more patterns be sold? Fewer patterns? Does the decision in the principal case render significant assistance to fabric stores? Will they be aided by the decision? How?

4. Why would Congress have intended to allow the meeting-competition defense to apply to § 2(c), § 2(d), and § 2(e), but to disallow defenses based on cost justification rationales and lack of injury to competition?

5. In a private suit under § 2(e), must the plaintiff show injury? Must that injury be connected to the competitive relation between himself and the favored customer of the defendant supplier?

---

4. Clause (f): Inducing Discrimination

Great Atlantic & Pacific Tea Co. v. Federal Trade Commission
440 U.S. 69 (1979)

Mr. Justice STEWART delivered the opinion of the Court.

The question presented in this case is whether the petitioner, the Great Atlantic & Pacific Tea Co. (A&P), violated § 2(f) of the Clayton Act . . . as amended by the Robinson-Patman Act . . . by knowingly inducing or receiving illegal price discriminations from the Borden Co. (Borden).

The alleged violation was reflected in a 1965 agreement between A&P and Borden under which Borden undertook to supply "private label" milk to more than 200 A&P stores in a Chicago area that included portions of Illinois and Indiana. This agreement resulted from an effort by A&P to achieve cost savings by switching from the sale of "brand label" milk (milk sold under the brand name of the supplying dairy) to the sale of "private label" milk (milk sold under the A&P label).

To implement this plan, A&P asked Borden, its longtime supplier, to submit an offer to supply under private label certain of A&P's milk and other dairy product requirements. After prolonged negotiations, Borden offered to grant A&P a discount for switching to private-label milk provided A&P would accept limited delivery service. Borden claimed that this offer would save A&P $410,000 a year compared to what it had been paying for its dairy products. A&P, however, was not satisfied with this offer and solicited offers from other dairies. A competitor of Borden, Bowman Dairy, then submitted an offer which was lower than Borden's.[2]

At this point, A&P's Chicago buyer contacted Borden's chain store sales manager and stated: "I have a bid in my pocket. You [Borden] people are so far out of line it is not even funny. You are not even in the ball park." When the Borden representative asked for more details, he was told nothing except that a $50,000 improvement in Borden's bid "would not be a drop in the bucket."

Borden was thus faced with the problem of deciding whether to rebid. A&P at the time was one of Borden's largest customers in the Chicago area. Moreover, Borden had just invested more than $5 million in a new dairy facility in Illinois. The loss of the A&P account

---

2 The Bowman bid would have produced estimated annual savings of approximately $737,000 for A&P as compared with the first Borden bid, which would have produced estimated annual savings of $410,000.

would result in underutilization of this new plant. Under these circumstances, Borden decided to submit a new bid which doubled the estimated annual savings to A&P, from $410,000 to $820,000. In presenting its offer, Borden emphasized to A&P that it needed to keep A&P's business and was making the new offer in order to meet Bowman's bid. A&P then accepted Borden's bid after concluding that it was substantially better than Bowman's.

I

Based on these facts, the Federal Trade Commission filed a three-count complaint against A&P. . . . [T]he Commission held . . . that . . . A&P had violated § 2(f), finding that Borden had discriminated in price between A&P and its competitors, that the discrimination had been injurious to competition, and that A&P had known or should have known that it was the beneficiary of unlawful price discrimination. . . .

A&P filed a petition for review of the Commission's order in the Court of Appeals for the Second Circuit. The court held that substantial evidence supported the findings of the Commission and that as a matter of law A&P could not successfully assert a meeting-competition defense because it, unlike Borden, had known that Borden's offer was better than Bowman's. . . .

II

The Robinson-Patman Act was passed in response to the problem perceived in the increased market power and coercive practices of chainstores and other big buyers that threatened the existence of small independent retailers. Notwithstanding this concern with buyers, however, the emphasis of the Act is in § 2(a), which prohibits price discriminations by sellers. Indeed, the original Patman bill as reported by Committees of both Houses prohibited only seller activity, with no mention of buyer liability. Section 2(f), making buyers liable for inducing or receiving price discriminations by sellers, was the product of a belated floor amendment near the conclusion of the Senate debates.

As finally enacted, § 2(f) provides:

> That it shall be unlawful for any person engaged in commerce, in the course of such commerce, knowingly to induce or receive a discrimination in price *which is prohibited by this section*. (Emphasis added.)

Liability under § 2(f) thus is limited to situations where the price discrimination is one "which is prohibited by this section." While the phrase "this section" refers to the entire § 2 of the Act, only subsections (a) and (b) dealing with seller liability involve discriminations in price. Under the plain meaning of § 2(f), therefore, a buyer cannot be liable if a *prima facie* case could not be established against a seller or if the seller has an affirmative defense. In either situation, there is no price discrimination "prohibited by this section." The legislative history of § 2(f) fully confirms the conclusion that buyer liability under § 2(f) is dependent on seller liability under § 2(a).

. . . .

III

The petitioner, relying on this plain meaning of § 2(f) . . . argues that it cannot be liable under § 2(f) if Borden had a valid meeting-competition defense. The respondent, on the other hand, argues that the petitioner may be liable even assuming that Borden had such a defense. The meeting-competition defense, the respondent contends, must in these circumstances be judged from the point of view of the buyer. Since A&P knew for a fact that the final Borden bid beat the Bowman bid, it was not entitled to assert the meeting-competition defense even though Borden may have honestly believed that it was simply meeting competition. Recognition of a meeting-competition defense for the buyer in this situation, the respondent argues, would be contrary to the basic purpose of the Robinson-Patman Act to curtail abuses by large buyers.

A

The short answer to these contentions of the respondent is that Congress did not provide in § 2(f) that a buyer can be liable even if the seller has a valid defense. The clear language of § 2(f) states that a buyer can be liable only if he receives a price discrimination "prohibited by this section." If a seller has a valid meeting-competition defense, there is simply no prohibited price discrimination.

. . . .

B

. . . .

In a competitive market, uncertainty among sellers will cause them to compete for business by offering buyers lower prices. Because of the evils of collusive action, the Court has held that the exchange of price information by competitors violates the Sherman Act. *United States v. Container Corp.*, 393 U.S. 333. Under the view advanced by the respondent, however, a buyer, to avoid liability, must either refuse a seller's bid or at least inform him that his bid has beaten competition. Such a duty of affirmative disclosure would almost inevitably frustrate competitive bidding and, by reducing uncertainty, lead to price matching and anticompetitive cooperation among sellers.

Ironically, the Commission itself, in dismissing the charge under § 5 of the Federal Trade Commission Act in this case, recognized the dangers inherent in a duty of affirmative disclosure:

> The imposition of a duty of affirmative disclosure, applicable to a buyer whenever a seller states that his offer is intended to meet competition, is contrary to normal business practice and, we think, contrary to the public interest.
>
> . . . .
>
> We fear a scenario where the seller automatically attaches a meeting competition caveat to every bid. The buyer would then state whether such bid meets, beats, or loses to another bid. The seller would then submit a second, a third, and perhaps a fourth bid until finally he is able to ascertain his competitor's bid.

87 F.T.C. 1047, 1050-1051. The effect of the finding that the same conduct of the petitioner violated § 2(f), however, is to impose the same duty of affirmative disclosure which the Commission condemned as anticompetitive, "contrary to the public interest," and "contrary to normal business practice," in dismissing the charge under § 5 of the Federal Trade Commission Act. Neither the Commission nor the Court of Appeals offered any explanation for this apparent anomaly.

. . . [W]e decline to adopt a construction of § 2(f) that is contrary to its plain meaning and would lead to anticompetitive results. Accordingly, we hold that a buyer who has done no more than accept the lower of two prices competitively offered does not violate § 2(f) provided the seller has a meeting-competition defense.[15]

---

15 In *Kroger Co. v. FTC*, 438 F.2d 1372, the Court of Appeals for the Sixth Circuit held that a buyer who induced price concessions by a seller by making deliberate misrepresentations could be liable under § 2(f) even

IV

A

. . . Since good faith, rather than absolute certainty, is the touchstone of the meeting-competition defense, a seller can assert the defense even if it has unknowingly made a bid that in fact not only met but beat his competition. . . .

B

. . . .

Borden was unable to ascertain the details of the Bowman bid. It requested more information about the bid from the petitioner, but this request was refused. It could not then attempt to verify the existence and terms of the competing offer from Bowman without risking Sherman Act liability. *United States v. United States Gypsum Co.* [438 U.S. 422 (1978)]. . . . Faced with a substantial loss of business and unable to find out the precise details of the competing bid, Borden made another offer stating that it was doing so in order to meet competition. Under these circumstances, the conclusion is virtually inescapable that in making that offer Borden acted in a reasonable and good-faith effort to meet its competition, and therefore was entitled to a meeting-competition defense.

Since Borden had a meeting-competition defense and thus could not be liable under § 2(b), the petitioner who did no more than accept that offer cannot be liable under § 2(f).

Accordingly, the judgment is reversed.

It is so ordered.

COMMENTARY

1. When A&P's Chicago buyer told Borden's chain store sales manager that he had "a bid in my pocket," and that Borden was "not even in the ball park," was that statement true? Misleading? False? How did the A&P situation differ from the "lying buyer" situation involved in the *Kroger* case (cited by the Court in footnote 15)?

2. If, pursuant to the holding in the *Kroger* case, a "lying buyer" can violate § 2(f) even though the seller is entitled to a § 2(b) defense, then the provisions of § 2(f) are not being applied literally in all cases, are they? What policies embodied

---

if the seller has a meeting-competition defense.

This case does not involve a "lying buyer" situation. The complaint issued by the FTC alleged that "A&P accepted the said offer of Borden with knowledge that Borden had granted a substantially lower price than that offered by the only other competitive bidder and without notifying Borden of this fact." The complaint did not allege that Borden's second bid was induced by any misrepresentation. The Court of Appeals recognized that the *Kroger* case involved a "lying buyer," but stated that there was no meaningful distinction between the situation where "the buyer lies or merely keeps quiet about the nature of the competing bid." . . .

Because A&P was not a "lying buyer," we need not decide whether such a buyer could be liable under § 2(f) even if the seller has a meeting-competition defense.

in the Act exonerate the "misleading" buyer but not the "lying" buyer? Do these policies have anything to do with the preservation or enhancement of competition?

3. Was the Court in *A&P* employing Sherman Act policies as a guide to the interpretation of the Robinson-Patman Act? Is this a new development? Where have you seen this done before?

4. Was the Court in *A&P* trying to lessen the inhibiting effect of the Robinson-Patman Act on the bargaining which is necessary to make the marketplace operate in a competitive way? Is the Court showing an awareness of the anticompetitive nature of the Robinson-Patman Act?

5. Is the *A&P* case one like *Gypsum* and *Container Corp.* where the court sees informational uncertainty as conducive to competitive-market-like behavior?

F. Complex Distribution

Because the patterns of business behavior tend to change in response to shifts in demand, production and transportation costs, and the development of more efficient distributional techniques, similar or identical products may reach ultimate consumers through various (and asymmetrical) distributional modes. The Robinson-Patman Act, however, often seems to have been premised upon a static view of channels of distribution in which all competing products reach ultimate consumers through similar distributional systems involving the same number of sale-and-resale stages. It should not be surprising, therefore, that difficulties often arise in applying the Act when charges of unlawful discrimination involve competition between asymmetrical distribution systems.

We have already experienced, in the *Fred Meyer* case, an extreme awkwardness in fitting the Act's provisions requiring proportional equality in the payment of promotional allowances to a competitive situation involving both direct-buying retailers and non-direct-buying retailers. In the following materials, we will consider the availability of the § 2(b) meeting competition defense to a supplier selling directly to dealers. Is such a seller entitled to that defense when it drops its price to one or more (but less than all) of its dealers to enable them to meet the low prices of an integrated supplier-retailer? When a manufacturer sells both to wholesalers and to direct-buying retailers, is a retailer-customer of one of the purchasing wholesalers entitled to complain of discriminatory practices against the wholesaler from whom it obtains its supplies? Conversely, is a direct-buying retailer entitled to complain of a manufacturer's favoritism towards wholesalers who pass along their favored supply prices to their retailer customers who are thereby advantaged vis-a-vis the direct-buying retailer? Can a direct-buying retailer complain that his supplier charges it higher prices than the supplier itself charges large customers, thereby disabling the direct-buying retailer from competing with its supplier for those large-customer accounts?

Federal Trade Commission v. Sun Oil Co.

371 U.S. 505 (1963)

[McLean was a retail seller of Sunoco brand gasoline in Jacksonville, Florida. When McLean commenced operations, he was buying gasoline from Sun at 24.1 cents per gallon and reselling it at 28.9 cents per gallon. Four months after McLean opened his gasoline station, the Super Test Oil Company opened a Super Test station diagonally across the street from McLean and began selling its "regular" grade of gasoline at 26.9 cents per gallon. This 2-cent per gallon differential was the "normal" differential then prevailing between "major" and "non-major" brands of gasoline. Thereafter, Super Test dropped its price sporadically below 26.9 cents, later dropped it to 24.9 cents, then to 23.9 cents and finally to 22.9 cents.]

Mr. Justice GOLDBERG delivered the opinion of the Court.

This case grows out of a gasoline "price war" in Jacksonville, Florida. The question presented is whether a refiner-supplier of gasoline charged with the granting of a price discrimination in violation of § 2(a) of the Clayton Act, as amended by the Robinson-Patman Act, has available to it, under § 2(b) of the Act, the defense that the discriminatory lower price was given "in good faith to meet an equally low price of a competitor," when the gasoline refiner-supplier shows that it gave the discriminatory price to only one of a number of its independently owned retail station customers in a particular region in order to enable that station to meet price reductions of a competing service station owned and operated by a retail chain selling a different brand of gasoline.

The Federal Trade Commission held the § 2(b) defense to be unavailable under such circumstances. . . . The Court of Appeals for the Fifth Circuit reversed . . . and this Court granted *certiorari* . . . to review this difficult and important question concerning the scope and application of the § 2(b) defense.

. . . When . . . Super Test dropped its price for "regular" gasoline to 24.9 cents per gallon, McLean told Sun that he would have to post a price of 25.9 cents in order to meet the competition. On the same day, Sun gave McLean a price allowance or discount of 1.7 cents per gallon. McLean accordingly dropped his retail price three cents per gallon, from 28.9 cents to 25.9 cents, thus reducing his gross margin from the prior 4.8 cents per gallon to 3.5 cents per gallon, the amount regarded by Sun as the minimum gross margin which should be earned by its retail dealers. In lowering his price to within one cent of Super Test's, McLean absorbed 1.3 cents and Sun 1.7 cents of the per gallon price reduction. No corresponding price reduction was given by Sun to any of its other dealers in the area.

. . . .

During the period [in which Sun was extending a differential discount to McLean] . . . a number of Sun dealers located at distances varying from less than a mile (about 11 blocks) to about three and one-half miles from McLean's station suffered substantial declines in sales of Sunoco gasoline. . . .

. . . [T]he Court of Appeals assumed . . . that Super Test was an integrated supplier-retailer of gasoline. The record does not support this conclusion, however, and therefore, as the case comes to us, availability of the § 2(b) defense to Sun is determined on the assumption that Super Test was engaged solely in retail operations; similarly, since there is in the record no evidence as to Super Test's source of supply or the price at which it bought gasoline, we assume that Super Test was not the beneficiary of any enabling price cut from its own supplier.[7]

. . . .

Section 2(b) of the Act contains a proviso permitting a seller to rebut a prima facie case of discrimination in violation of § 2(a) by "showing that his lower price or the furnishing of services or facilities to any purchaser or purchasers was made in good faith to meet an equally low price of a competitor, or the services or facilities furnished by a competitor." This proviso is usually referred to as the "good faith meeting competition" defense. The seller has the burden of bringing himself within the exculpating provision of § 2(b), which has been interpreted to afford an absolute defense to a charge of violating § 2(a), notwithstanding the existence of the statutorily prohibited anticompetitive effect. . . .

Reading the words to have "their normal and customary meaning," . . . the § 2(b) phrase "equally low price of a competitor" would seem to refer to the price of a competitor of the seller who grants, and not of the buyer who receives, the discriminatory price cut. (In this case, this would mean a competitor of Sun, the refiner-supplier, and not a competitor of McLean, the retail dealer.) Were something more intended by Congress, we would have expected a more explicit recitation as, for example, is the case in § 2(a) in which the intent to give broader scope was expressly effected by the prohibition of price discriminations which *inter alia*, adversely affected competition not only with the seller (in this case Sun) who grants the favored price, but with the knowing recipient thereof (in this case McLean) and "with customers of either of them." Thus, since Congress expressly demonstrated in the immediately preceding provision of the Act that it knew how to expand the applicable concept of competition beyond the sole level of the seller granting the discriminatory price, it is reasonable to conclude that like clarity of expression would be present in § 2(b) if the defense available thereunder were similarly intended to be broadly read to encompass, as is urged, the meeting of lower prices set not only by the offending seller's competitor, but also by the purchaser's competitor. . . .

The fact that § 2(b) permits a seller to meet the competitor's "equally low" price is similarly suggestive of an interpretation which limits application of the proviso to situations in which the seller's reduction in price is made in response to a price cut by its own competitor rather than by a competitor of its customer. Linguistically and practically, it makes but little sense to talk, for example, of a wholesaler's meeting of the "equally low" price of one of his purchaser's retail competitors. The reduced retail price of the purchaser's competitor will almost invariably be higher than the supplier's wholesale price; even in those instances in which this is not so, it cannot seriously be suggested that under § 2(b) the wholesaler is entitled to reduce discriminatorily his wholesale price to the lower retail level. Such a result is not only economically unrealistic, but strains normal language use. Moreover, it is difficult to see what appropriately cognizable competitive interest Congress might be thought to have been serving in enacting a statute productive of such an anomalous result.

Recognizing the incongruity of such an interpretation, and having no need to go quite so far, respondent argues merely that as a wholesaler it is protected under § 2(b) when it lowers its own price sufficiently to allow its retail dealer, in turn, to reduce his retail price

---

7 Were it otherwise, *i.e.*, if it appeared either that Super Test were an integrated supplier-retailer, or that it had received a price cut from its own supplier—presumably a competitor of Sun—we would be presented with a different case, as to which we herein neither express nor intimate any opinion.

to meet a competitive retail offer. But this too extends the statute beyond its immediately apparent meaning; the language of the section contains no implication that it comprehends a two-stage price reduction effected by two separate economic units at different levels of distribution as the measure of setting the "equally low" price.

. . . .

Reversed.

COMMENTARY

1. Do you think that Sun should have been entitled to the § 2(b) defense on the facts as the Court understood them? Should Sun be protected by the § 2(b) defense if it lowered its price to the level at which Super Test's supplier was selling to Super Test?

2. How should the fact that Sun sells an advertised brand ("Sunoco") and that Super Test does not affect the application of the § 2(b) defense?

3. How should the § 2(b) defense have been applied if Super Test had been shown to be an integrated supplier-retailer? Did Congress give any thought to the application of the § 2(b) defense to a supplier whose customers are competing with an integrated supplier-retailer? Was the Act drafted without adequate attention to the variety of possible distribution methods?

4. According to the opinion, when McLean began retail operations, it was buying gasoline from Sun at 24.1 cents per gallon and reselling it for 28.9 cents per gallon, a gross margin of 4.8 cents per gallon. Suppose that when Super Test dropped its price to 24.9 cents, it was purchasing its supplies from its supplier at 19 cents per gallon. That would give Super Test a gross margin of 5.9 cents. To what level should the § 2(b) defense protect Sun in dropping its price to McLean? Would it affect your answer if Super Test's supplier had been selling to Super Test all along at 19 cents? Would it be legally significant if Super Test's supplier dropped its price to Super Test from 21 cents to 19 cents when Super Test dropped its retail price from 26.9 cents to 24.9 cents?

5. After its victory in the Supreme Court, the Commission dismissed its proceeding against Sun. *Sun Oil Co.*, 67 F.T.C. 341 (1965). Why would the Commission expend its limited resources to seek Supreme Court review of a case which it would later voluntarily dismiss? *See Eine Kleine Juristische Schlummergeschichte*, 79 HARV. L. REV. 921, 923 (1966).

Caribe BMW, Inc. v. Bayerische Motoren Werke Aktiengesellschaft

19 F.3d 745 (1st Cir. 1994)

BREYER, Chief Judge.

. . . [D]o a firm's wholly owned subsidiary and the firm itself amount to a "single seller" under the Robinson-Patman Act? . . . We answer . . . in the affirmative. . . .

I

Background

From 1981 through 1990, Caribe BMW, Inc. ("Caribe"), through contracts with the German BMW manufacturer, Bayerische Motoren Werke Aktiengesellschaft ("BMW AG"), bought BMW automobiles from BMW AG in Germany, imported them into Puerto Rico, and sold them at retail. In February 1991, Caribe (the appellant here) brought this lawsuit against (the appellees) BMW AG and BMW's wholly owned North American subsidiary, BMW of North America, Inc. ("BMW NA"). . . .

Count I charged a violation of the Robinson-Patman Act. 15 U.S.C. § 13. It said that BMW AG sold cars to BMW NA, which resold those cars to other retailers who competed with Caribe, at prices lower than, or on terms more favorable than, those at which BMW AG sold similar cars to Caribe. Count II charged a violation of § 1 of the Sherman Act. 15 U.S.C. § 1. It said that BMW AG had set maximum resale prices for the cars that it sold to Caribe by "threaten[ing] to terminate Caribe's contracts" unless Caribe would agree, in effect, to maintain low resale prices. . . .

II

The Robinson-Patman Act Claim

The Robinson-Patman Act forbids "any person"

> to discriminate in price between different purchasers of commodities of like grade and quality . . . where the effect of such discrimination may be . . . to injure . . . competition with any person who . . . grants . . . the . . . discrimination, or with [that granting person's] customers. . . .

15 U.S.C. § 13(a). Caribe's complaint alleges most of the essentials of a violation. It says that a "person" has "discriminate[d] in price between different purchasers" (namely, Caribe and other retailers in competition with Caribe) of cars, with the effect that "competition with" that person's "customer" (namely, Caribe) is "injure[d]." *See FTC v. Morton Salt Co.*, 334 U.S. 37 (1948). But, it embodies an ambiguity in respect to the "person " who did the discriminating. It says that BMW AG sold cars directly to Caribe, which resold them at retail. It then says that BMW NA sold cars to other retailers, who compete with Caribe, at lower prices than BMW AG sold its cars to Caribe. At this point, there appear to be two "persons" selling BMWs to retailers, namely, BMW AG (selling them to Caribe) and BMW NA (selling them to Caribe's competitors). The complaint adds, however, that BMW NA is the wholly owned subsidiary of BMW AG. Thus, we must face the legal question of whether or not this last mentioned fact is sufficient to make of the two separately incorporated companies a single "person" for Robinson-Patman Act purposes. If so, the complaint properly alleges that a single "person" has sold similar goods at two different prices (allegedly with the required statutory effect). If not, there may be no "person" who has "dis-

criminate[d]." *See id.* ("discrimination" requires at least two sales by a single person at different prices to different customers in competition with each other); *see also* PHILLIP AREEDA & LOUIS KAPLOW, ANTITRUST ANALYSIS ¶ 601(c) (4th ed. 1988); 3 EARL W. KINTNER & JOSEPH P. BAUER, FEDERAL ANTITRUST LAW § 21.11, at 192-93 (1983).

So far, when courts have faced this question—whether or not a firm and its subsidiary amount to a single "person" (or a "single seller")—they have answered it by examining the extent of common ownership and the degree of control over pricing and distribution policies that the one exercises over the other. . . . In this case, the extent of ownership is 100%; Caribe's complaint alleges nothing about actual control. Thus, we must ask whether 100% ownership, by itself, amounts to a sufficient allegation that the "firm plus subsidiary" are a single Robinson-Patman Act "person." We conclude, for reasons that we shall now explain, that it does.

For purposes of clarity, we shall refer in our explanation to hypothetical entities whom we shall call 1) the Manufacturer (M), 2) its wholly owned Distributor (D), 3) the Retailer (R1) who buys from D, and 4) the Direct Buying Retailer (DBR), who buys directly from M and who resells in competition with R1. The distribution arrangement looks like the following:

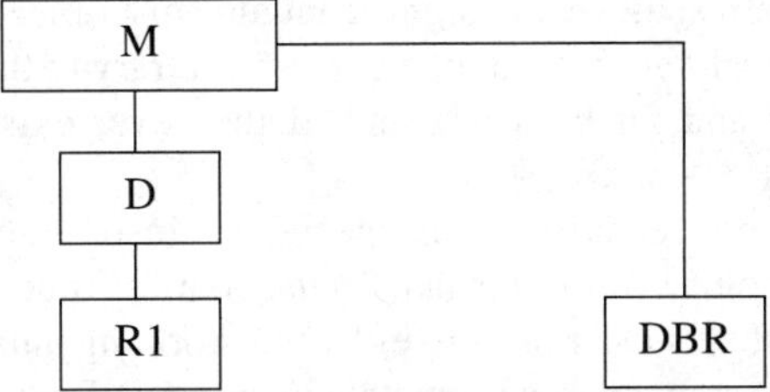

In our case, BMW AG holds the position of M; BMW NA, the position of D; Caribe, the position of DBR; and Caribe's unspecified retail competitors, the position of R1. The legal question, put in terms of the diagram, is whether or not M's 100% ownership of D makes M and D, together, a "single seller," say "MD." If so, a single "person" (allegedly) "discriminates" in price.

We now return to the reasons for our affirmative answer, which are three. First, in 1984, after many of the above-cited "single seller" cases were decided, the Supreme Court decided *Copperweld Corp. v. Independence Tube Corp.*, 467 U.S. 752 (1984). The Court there considered the scope of Sherman Act § 1's word "conspiracy." It held that the word did not cover an agreement between a wholly owned subsidiary and its parent, because a wholly owned subsidiary could not "conspire" with the parent. That, the Court said, is because they have

> a complete unity of interest. Their objectives are common, not disparate; their general corporate actions are guided or determined not by two separate corporate consciousnesses, but one. . . . [And] [t]hey share a common purpose whether or not the parent keeps a tight rein over the subsidiary. . . .

Id. at 771. The Court added that a "corporation has complete power to maintain" a portion of the enterprise either in the form of an unincorporated division, or in the form of a separately incorporated subsidiary. But, the

> economic, legal, or other considerations that lead corporate management to choose one structure over the other are not relevant to whether the enterprise's conduct seriously threatens competition.

Id. at 772. For these reasons, the Court held,

> the coordinated activity of a parent and its wholly owned subsidiary must be viewed as that of a single enterprise for purposes of § 1 of the Sherman Act.

Id. at 771.

Although the Court spoke of Sherman Act § 1 and of "coordinated activity," its reasoning applies here. *See* AREEDA & KAPLOW, *supra*, ¶ 601(c), at 929. In essence, the Court saw an identity of economic interest between parent and wholly owned subsidiary that, considered in terms of the economically oriented antitrust laws, warrants regarding them as one. *See generally* 7 PHILLIP E. AREEDA, ANTITRUST LAW ¶ 1464 (1986). Any claimed instance of truly "independent," owner-hostile, subsidiary decisionmaking would meet with the skeptical question, "But, if the subsidiary acts contrary to its parent's economic interest, why does the parent not replace the subsidiary's management?" Given the strength of that joint economic interest, we do not see how a case-specific judicial examination of "actual" parental control would help achieve any significant antitrust objective. Those instances in which a wholly owned subsidiary would intend to act contrary to the economic interests of its owner are likely few and far between, and, if they ever exist, would seem hard to prove. *Cf.* AREEDA & KAPLOW, *supra*, ¶ 215.

Second, there does not seem to be any special Robinson-Patman Act purpose that a case-specific "control" inquiry would further. To the contrary, one would not want a seller to be able to defeat the statute's clear objectives by transforming unlawful, into lawful, price discrimination through the creation of a separately incorporated subsidiary "distributor" that sells to the disfavored customers, whether or not the parent retained "control" over the pricing decisions of the subsidiary. Suppose, for example, that M violates the Act by selling to one retailer (DBR) at $10 and another competing retailer (R1) at $12. M should not be able to avoid the law simply by creating a wholly owned, but "independent" D, to whom it sells at $10, knowing that "independent" D will (say, for profit-maximizing reasons) "independently" resell to R1 at the same $12 price.

We are aware that this area of the law is filled with difficulty. For example, should Robinson-Patman Act liability attach in the example just given if (contrary to our assumption) the wholly owned distributor, D, really fulfills an important distribution function, necessary to supply R1, but not needed in the case of sales to DBR, such that DBR "ought" to receive a lower price? Or, suppose M (perhaps as here) sets a higher price to direct buyers in order to discourage direct sales and thereby to encourage the creation of an independent distribution network? These problems arise, however, in part, because it is difficult to reconcile the Robinson-Patman Act's strictures with traditional practices of corporations that seem to make sense from a practical viewpoint. *See, e.g., Texaco Inc. v. Hasbrouck*, 496 U.S. 543, 559-62 (1990); KINTNER & BAUER, *supra*, § 22.14; James F. Rill, *Availability and Functional Discounts Justifying Discriminatory Pricing*, 53 ANTITRUST L.J. 929 (1985). And the complexity of Robinson-Patman Act law has increased as courts have tried to introduce a degree of flexibility into the Act as applied. *See, e.g.*, KINTNER & BAUER, *supra*, § 25.7, at 454-460 (discussing the availability defense); *Hasbrouck*, 496 U.S. at 561 (discussing functional discounts); 15 U.S.C. § 13(a) (cost justification defense); *see also* Rill, *supra*.

For present purposes, however, we need only note that these same problems exist, in one form or another, regardless of our holding in this case. That is to say, a contrary holding would nonetheless produce the same problems wherever M does "control" the pricing policies of its wholly-owned subsidiary D (*i.e.,* in most cases). And, in the remaining cases (where wholly-owned D is somehow nonetheless "independent"), various other, related, Robinson-Patman Act problems would often arise if DBR complained about differences in price between M's price to D and M's price to DBR. . . . Thus, we find nothing special in the Robinson-Patman Act context that militates against *Copperweld*'s reasoning or result.

Third, applying *Copperweld* avoids a potential anomaly. A majority of courts, using a *Copperweld*-type analysis, have held that a firm M's sale of a good to a wholly owned subsidiary D is not a "sale" for Robinson-Patman Act purposes; rather, it is simply a transfer; and that is so whether D is, or D is not, somehow "independent" in reality. *See City of Mt. Pleasant v. Associated Elec. Coop., Inc.*, 838 F.2d 268, 278 (8th Cir.1988); *Russ' Kwik Car Wash, Inc. v. Marathon Petroleum Co.*, 772 F.2d 214, 221 (6th Cir.1985) (*per curiam*) (quoting *Copperweld*, 467 U.S. at 772 n.18; *O'Byrne v. Checker Oil Co.*, 727 F.2d 159, 164 (7th Cir.1984); *Security Tire & Rubber Co. v. Gates Rubber Co.*, 598 F.2d 962, 965-67 (5th Cir.), *cert. denied*, 444 U.S. 942 (1979). These holdings mean that D, the transferee, is not a "purchaser" from M, and, for that reason, M does not violate the Act even if he sells the same good to a direct buying retailer (DBR), or even a direct competitor of D, at a higher price than the price at which he "transfers" the good to D. Our holding today means that when the wholly-owned subsidiary D resells the good to R1, it must do so at a "nondiscriminatory" price, *i.e.*, at a price that would be permissible under the Act had D's sale to R1 been made by M. Thus, if M sells to DBR at 14, D cannot sell to R1 for less than 14 (assuming, of course, that all other Robinson-Patman Act liability conditions are met and no defenses are available).

But, suppose we were to hold the contrary. Suppose that we were to hold that a wholly-owned subsidiary D and its owner M were not a "single seller" where D was somehow nonetheless "independent." Then, an anomalous difficulty might well prevent DBR from bringing an action where M "transfers" to D at 10, D resells to R1 at 12, but M insists on charging DBR 14 (*i.e.*, approximately the allegations before us). The doctrine just mentioned—in effect finding that M and D are a single entity for purposes of the transfer between them—would prevent DBR from complaining about the effect of the M-D "transfer." *Cf. Hasbrouck*, 496 U.S. at 569-71. At the same time, our (imagined) holding (the opposite of our actual holding) that M and D were not a single entity for purposes of D's sale to R1 would likely prevent DBR from complaining about the effect of that sale because of its inability to find a single "person" who discriminated (because M does not sell to R1, while D does not sell to DBR . . .).

Perhaps one could somehow avoid this anomaly in other ways, but it seems undesirable to invent epicycles in an already too complex area of the law. It is simpler to hold in parallel fashion that ownership alone makes a "single seller" of a firm and its wholly owned distributor, just as ownership alone eliminates the possibility of a Robinson-Patman Act "sale" between them.

We therefore find it appropriate to apply *Copperweld*'s reasoning outside Sherman Act § 1. . . . We hold that BMW AG's ownership of BMW NA makes of those two entities, for Robinson-Patman Act purposes, a single seller.

We now turn to a second, independent reason the district court gave for concluding that the complaint did not adequately state a Robinson-Patman Act claim. The court correctly noted that if a seller makes its favorable prices and terms available to an otherwise disfavored customer, that customer has no legal right to complain. . . . The district court then concluded that Caribe, in a portion of its complaint, in effect conceded that BMW made its favorable prices and terms available to Caribe. That complaint portion says that in 1987

> despite Caribe's remarkable success, BMW attempted to convert Caribe from being an importer-retailer purchasing directly from the factory to being a mere retail dealer purchasing from BMW N.A.

We do not believe, however, that one can draw from this statement the "availability" concession that the district court found. The complaint also says that

> [*u*]*nbeknownst to Caribe*, and beginning by at least 1987, BMW began lowering its prices for BMWs sold to Caribe's competitors and offering those competitors other economic advantages while maintaining its prices to Caribe at a discriminatorily high level and not making the other economic advantages available to Caribe on proportionately equal terms.

The emphasized language says that Caribe did not know that its competitors were receiving favored treatment. And, we do not see how ordinarily one could say that a seller has made favored treatment "available" to a disfavored customer if the disfavored customer does not know about the favored treatment. . . .

Caribe also argues that the favored treatment, as a practical matter, was not "available" because BMW AG insisted that it give up various advantages of its importer's contract in order to obtain it. We cannot tell from the complaint, however, just what those advantages were and how they related to the practical "availability" of the favorable treatment given other retailers. Thus, we cannot say, at this time, whether or not Caribe will be able to prove that the favorable price and terms, as a practical matter, were not available. . . .

The judgment of the district court is vacated. . . .

COMMENTARY

1. In *Caribe*, the First Circuit followed several other circuits in holding that a sale to a wholly-owned subsidiary is not a sale for purposes of the Robinson-Patman Act. In so holding the courts are applying the single-enterprise theory of *Copperweld*.

2. Recall that the Justice Department takes the position that a single-enterprise exists when a parent owns more than 50% of the stock of a subsidiary and, even when the parent owns a lesser percentage but exercises effective control of the subsidiary. Do you think that these extensions of *Copperweld* should also be read into the Robinson-Patman Act?

3. Instead of having one distributor for North America, suppose that BMW AG sold to BMW USA for resale to U.S. dealers and also sold to BMW Canada for resale to Canadian dealers. Suppose further than BMW Canada was an independently owned company while BMW USA was a wholly-owned subsidiary of BMW AG. Under these suppositions, consider the following sets of facts:

(a) BMW AG sells standard sedans to BMW USA and to BMW Canada at $20,000. BMW USA sells these sedans to U.S. dealers for $25,000. BMW Canada sells most of these sedans to Canadian dealers for $25,000, but sells a few to selected U.S. dealers at $23,000.

(b) Facts are the same as in (a) above, except that BMW AG sells to BMW Canada at $19,000.

(c) Facts are the same as in (a) above, except that BMW USA responds to the cross-border sales of BMW Canada by selling at $23,000 to a few dealers who compete with the dealers to whom BMW Canada has sold sedans at $23,000.

What are the legalities of the various sales in the above examples?

Conoco Inc. v. Inman Oil Co.

774 F.2d 895 (8th Cir. 1985)

NICHOL, Senior District Judge.

Conoco brought this diversity action against Inman Oil Company (Inman Oil) and Ronald C. Inman, individually, for recovery of monies due Conoco for petroleum products delivered to the defendants. At trial Inman Oil asserted eight counterclaims, including allegations of federal and state antitrust violations, tortious interference with business relationships, breach of contract and misrepresentations. The magistrate ruled in favor of Conoco on all claims.

On appeal, Inman Oil contends the magistrate erred in holding (1) that Conoco did not violate the Robinson-Patman Act. . . .

BACKGROUND

For many years, the State of Missouri has been the leading lead producer in the United States. An area known as the Viburnum Trend, located in the remote Ozark Mountain region of the State, contains one of the largest and most productive belts of lead ore. Four major lead mining companies operate in the Viburnum Trend—St. Joe Minerals Corp. (St. Joe), the Amax Lead Company of Missouri (Amax), Cominco-American, Inc. (Cominco), and the Ozark Lead Company (Ozark Lead). The lead mining industry has large and specialized requirements for petroleum products, especially machinery lubricants. The central disputes in this case revolve around the market for these lubricants.

Inman Oil is a distributor of petroleum products, head-quartered in Salem, Missouri. Commonly known as a "jobber," Inman Oil purchases petroleum products from suppliers such as Conoco and resells them to users either directly or indirectly through retail outlets such as service stations. Jobbers in the oil industry customarily distribute products of more than one supplier.

Conoco markets its petroleum products through two unincorporated groups within the company. The Branded Division Operations (Branded Division) markets Conoco products through intermediate jobbers or distributors such as Inman Oil. The Wholesale and Commercial Operations (WCO) sells petroleum products directly to large commercial and industrial users. Since at least 1967, these two Conoco divisions have been under separate administrative control and have competed against each other for many of the same commercial accounts. Products sold by WCO to Viburnum Trend customers are delivered to the site by Conoco's consignment delivery agent, Consolidated Industrial Equipment Company (Consolidated).

. . . Since 1956, Inman Oil has supplied St. Joe with all of its petroleum products except bulk lubricants. Conoco during this period was competing as a supplier for Viburnum Trend business, with intermittent success. Competition was stiff—some seven oil suppliers were vying for the business of the four lead mining companies. By 1972, Conoco's WCO had at least a portion of the business at Amax and Cominco. Since the lead mining companies generally solicited bids each year, there were no long-term contracts between the mining companies and either oil suppliers or jobbers.

On October 18, 1972, Inman Oil entered into a Jobber Franchise Agreement (JFA) with Conoco. Under the agreement, Inman Oil received the right to obtain from Conoco and sell to its customers certain Conoco petroleum and nonpetroleum products. The jobber was given the right to display Conoco's trade names and trademarks. Conoco was obligated to deliver a certain annual volume of products in accordance with pricing and credit terms set forth in . . . the agreement. . . .

In 1972, Conoco's WCO was selling substantial amounts of petroleum products to Cominco and Amax but had yet to obtain any business with St. Joe, the largest of the lead mining companies, or with Ozark Lead. Inman Oil, on the other hand, was supplying all of St. Joe's packaged lubricant needs with Sinclair products. Subsequent to the execution of the 1972 JFA, in a series of meetings between Inman Oil and Conoco personnel, Inman Oil agreed to cooperate in Conoco's attempt to persuade St. Joe to switch from Sinclair to Conoco as its source of packaged lubricants. This effort was successful; St. Joe became an indirect Branded Division customer and Inman Oil began supplying St. Joe with Conoco packaged lubricants.

. . . From 1976 on, Conoco's WCO bid on lubricants in the Viburnum Trend at prices equal to or below Inman Oil's cost for the same products. WCO was able to do this because it absorbed the $0.12 per gallon cost of having its consignee, Consolidated, deliver and maintain a standing inventory of Conoco products. This cost would normally have been included in the delivered price.

It appears, however, that this pricing policy met with little success until 1980. From 1976 to 1980, Conoco's WCO, bidding for direct sales to the lead mining companies, competed with Conoco's Branded Division, bidding with Inman Oil for the same customers. . . .

Like the other lead mining companies, St. Joe actively solicited bids every year from all the oil suppliers in the area for all its petroleum needs. Evidently, however, 1980 was the first time that WCO bid against Inman Oil for the St. Joe packaged lubricant contract then held by Inman Oil in conjunction with the Branded Division. Before submitting this bid, WCO wrote to Branded advising the latter of its plan and acknowledging the potential for conflict. The record reveals no protest by Branded.

. . . In 1981, WCO bid low for the 1982 St. Joe packaged lubricant contract, and this time was successful. WCO again gave the delivery business to Consolidated rather than Inman Oil. WCO lost the 1982 Amax business to Mobil Oil and lost its bid for the St. Joe hydraulic oil contract to Sun Oil with Inman Oil as the delivery agent.

However, despite Inman Oil's contract to deliver Sun hydraulic oil to St. Joe, the loss of its lucrative, long-time St. Joe packaged lubricant account was a significant blow. Inman Oil went out of business on February 28, 1982.

. . . .

DISCUSSION

The conduct of Conoco about which Inman Oil complains the most in this appeal may be condensed as follows: From 1976 on, Conoco's WCO bypassed Inman Oil in its capacity as a Conoco jobber and solicited Viburnum Trend customers for direct sales of petroleum products; WCO did this by setting its base price for these customers at or below the base price of the same products for Inman Oil and in some instances by absorbing certain costs; this effort succeeded to the extent that WCO eventually obtained Inman Oil's plum long-term customer, St. Joe. These facts, Inman Oil argues, constitute proof that Conoco engaged in price discrimination in violation of section 2(a) of the Clayton Act, as amended by the Robinson-Patman Act, 15 U.S.C. section 13(a). . . .

The Robinson-Patman Act Claim

. . . .

The magistrate's opinion relates two specific instances of alleged price discrimination by Conoco, one involving St. Joe and the other involving Amax. In the fall of 1980, Conoco's WCO bid for and was awarded the St. Joe bulk hydraulic oil contract for 1981. WCO sold the oil to St. Joe at $1.80 per gallon delivered to the St. Joe mine in the Viburnum Trend. During the same period, Conoco sold the same product to Inman Oil at $1.70 per gallon f.o.b. the supply point. Since it cost Inman Oil $0.10 per gallon to transport the product from the supply point to the Viburnum Trend, the "actual delivered" price to both parties was the same. However, because Conoco delivered the St. Joe oil to the mine site, it incurred additional costs of $0.12 per gallon to store and maintain an inventory of the product with its on-site agent, Consolidated. These costs were absorbed by Conoco and were not reflected in its $1.80 price to St. Joe. Thus, the "net price" received by Conoco from St. Joe was $0.12 per gallon less, or $1.68 per gallon. The Amax incident entailed substantially the same facts.

Inman Oil contends that price, for purposes of the Robinson-Patman Act, means net price; otherwise, price discrimination may occur in subtle forms such as discounts, freight allowances, or credit terms and yet never be reachable by the Act. Conoco argues that the $0.12 per gallon represented internal operating costs which are irrelevant in determining price discrimination. The magistrate found that the relevant figure was "the amount actually paid by the buyer, *i.e.* invoice price less any discounts or allowances not reflected in the invoice price." . . . We agree and hold that price under the Robinson-Patman Act is the "net price" received by the seller.

. . . .

The Act does not prohibit mere price discrimination, however. To amount to a violation, the discrimination must be shown to have caused the requisite injury to competition. . . . The statute is concerned with the protection of competition on three levels: (1) competition with the seller who granted the discriminatory prices (primary line); (2) competition with the seller's purchaser who received the favorable lower price (secondary line); and (3) competition with a customer of the favored purchaser (tertiary line). . . .

In the case at bar, Inman Oil alleges only a primary line injury. Specifically, Inman Oil argues that because St. Joe, the customer receiving the favored price from Conoco, was also a customer of Inman Oil, Inman Oil was in competition with Conoco, the seller granting the favored price. It was this primary line competition, according to Inman Oil, which was injured by Conoco's price discrimination. Conoco asserts, and the magistrate ruled, that Inman Oil has not shown the required adverse effect on competition because Inman Oil and Conoco were not competitors. Under this theory, even if Conoco had charged the same price to Inman Oil that it charged to St. Joe and the other lead mining companies, Inman Oil would have had to raise its price on resale to make any profit. And, as the magistrate observed, because competition in the Viburnum Trend was such that price level was the determinative factor in the awarding of contracts, Inman Oil could not have made any sales at the higher price it would have had to charge. Thus, Conoco argues there was no real competition between it and Inman Oil and therefore no injury to competition resulting from Conoco's price discrimination.

Conoco relies for this argument primarily on *Secatore's, Inc. v. Esso Standard Oil Co.*, 171 F. Supp. 665 (D. Mass.1959). In *Secatore's*, the plaintiff operated two retail gasoline stations. Its customers drove their vehicles to the stations and had gasoline pumped into the tanks. The plaintiff had no facilities for delivering gasoline off its premises. The defendant was a refiner and distributor of petroleum products. It sold gasoline to customers who took delivery in their own tank trucks at defendant's refinery and also delivered gasoline in its tank trucks to customers, including the plaintiff, who had storage tanks and pumps on their premises. The plaintiff alleged that the defendant had violated the Robinson-Patman Act by selling to large commercial consumer customers at prices lower than it charged the plaintiff. The plaintiff had never sold or tried to sell to these customers and did not have the ability to deliver gasoline to them as defendant did.

The *Secatore's* court rejected the plaintiff's contention that this price differential injured the competition between plaintiff and defendant. Assuming that there was any actual or potential competition between them, the court observed that there would of course be no illegal price discrimination if defendant had sold to the plaintiff at the same price at which it sold to the customers in question. Yet even then the plaintiff could not have successfully competed with the defendant for these customers. As a matter of economics, it would have had to charge more for the gasoline than it paid defendant in order to cover expenses and make a profit. The customers would naturally have chosen the lower price offered by defendant. "If plaintiff cannot successfully compete with defendant for these customers when there is no differential, it is not harmed by any further reduction which defendant may make in the price it charges to them." *Id.* at 667 (citations omitted).

In response, Inman Oil relies on *Guyott Co. v. Texaco, Inc.*, 261 F. Supp. 942 (D. Conn. 1966), for its proposition that a distributor can be in primary line competition with its supplier, at least when they have customers in common. The defendant in *Guyott* was a refiner and supplier of petroleum products, including paving asphalt. The plaintiff was a distributor of paving asphalt who sold to customers known as "mixers." The mixers blended the paving asphalt with other ingredients and then either applied the mixture to road beds or sold it to construction contractors. The plaintiff alleged the defendant had violated the Robinson-Patman Act by selling directly to a long-time mixer customer of the plaintiff's at a net price lower than it charged the plaintiff.

In ruling on the defendant's motion for summary judgment, the *Guyott* court acknowledged that "'the existence of some competitive relationship' between 'sellers of the same product'" was essential to a primary line injury. . . . The court went on to hold, however, apparently on the basis of the common customer, that the plaintiff had not failed as a matter of law to establish a primary line case. . . . The court distinguished *Secatore's* on the grounds that the customers of the disfavored purchaser there were not in competition with either the favored purchaser or his customers, and that the favored purchaser there had never been a customer of the disfavored purchaser. . . .

Inman Oil asserts here that the existence of primary line competition between it and Conoco was proven by the fact that St. Joe, the favored purchaser, was previously a customer of Inman Oil, the disfavored purchaser. We think, however, that this fact simply illustrates the precarious position of the "middleman" in our system of market distribution. So long as it is profitable for the supplier of a product to utilize a distributor, business opportunities exist for those companies that wish to pursue them. It strains credulity, however, to suggest that the Robinson-Patman Act was intended to force a supplier to "support" a distributor's business even when it becomes unprofitable to do so. We are not persuaded by the rationale of the *Guyott* decision, and we find no other authority to support such a proposition. We hold that, for purposes of the Robinson-Patman Act, the distributor in this case was not in primary line competition with its supplier. *See Universal Lite Distributors, Inc. v. Northwest Industries, Inc.*, 452 F. Supp. 1206 (D. Md. 1978), *aff'd in relevant part*, 602 F.2d 1173 (4th Cir.1979); *Sano Petroleum Corp. v. American Oil Co.*, 187 F. Supp. 345 (E.D.N.Y. 1960).

CONCLUSION

In sum, we affirm the magistrate with respect to Inman Oil's claims of a Robinson-Patman Act violation . . . .

COMMENTARY

1. Why did the Court find it necessary to discuss "primary line" competition? What are the standards for proving a primary-line violation? *See Brooke Group Ltd. v. Brown & Williamson Tobacco Co.*, 509 U.S. 209 (1993), Chapter 11, *supra*. If the standards articulated in *Brooke Group* apply, then it would be difficult for the plaintiff to prevail, would it not?

2. What does *Conoco* suggest about the standards governing a supplier's sales to a direct-buying retailer at a price below the price at which the supplier sells to a wholesaler seeking to supply that and other retailers? Are those sales to be tested by primary or secondary line standards? or both? See the following cases for further complications.

Klein v. The Lionel Corp.

237 F.2d 13 (3d Cir. 1956)

BIGGS, Chief Judge.

The plaintiff, Klein, brought suit against The Lionel Corporation and others for treble damages alleging price discrimination under the Robinson-Patman Act of 1936. . . . The court below gave summary judgment in favor of The Lionel Corporation and other defendants. . . .

Lionel sells toy electric trains and accessories to jobbers, middlemen and to some retailers at a reasonable discount which is determined by the nature of the purchaser's organization, whether jobber, middleman or retailer. Klein is a retailer in Wilmington, Delaware, but he is not one of the retailers to whom Lionel sells directly. Klein purchases Lionel's products for resale from jobbers or middlemen. Klein's purchases are made at a discount smaller than that given to retailers to whom Lionel sells directly. Klein is in competition with the retailers to whom Lionel sells directly and therefore contends that he should receive as a discount a sum equivalent to the largest discount given to any of them.

. . . .

The decisions of many cases have crystallized the rule that an individual can have no cause of action under Section 2(a) of the Clayton Act unless he is an actual purchaser from the person charged with the discrimination. . . . Klein did purchase Lionel products, but not from Lionel. It follows that the necessary requisite of two purchasers from the same vendor is not met and Klein therefore can claim no protection under the Act as a direct purchaser.

. . . .

While Klein cannot claim to be a direct purchaser from Lionel, he hopes to obtain relief under the Act by other means. He argues that as a customer of a purchaser he falls within the language of Section 2(a), ". . . or with customers of either of them." These words do not include customers of purchasers within the category of a purchaser required by the Act. . . . The words merely indicate the level on which the discrimination practiced on a purchaser might be felt in order for it to be actionable. . . .

[T]he judgment of the court below will be affirmed.

COMMENTARY

1. Is the *Klein* decision consistent with *Perkins* below? Is it consistent with *Morton Salt*? Does not *Morton Salt* suggest that Robinson-Patman is concerned with protecting small retailers against larger ones who obtain favorable supply prices unavailable to the small retailers? Is it not the small retailers who are generally unable to buy directly from the manufacturer? Was it not the retailers who purchased from wholesalers who were the class which the FTC successfully protected in *Morton Salt*? How then can the court hold that Klein lacks standing to assert a Robinson-Patman claim against the supplier of its supplier?

2. Did Lionel sell to direct-buying retailers with whom Klein was competing at a lower price than Lionel sold to Klein's supplier?

3. Under what theory was Klein asserting that the supply-price which it received from the wholesaler from which it purchased was the responsibility of Lionel? Was Klein asserting that Lionel had an obligation not to undersell its wholesale customers? Was Klein asserting that Lionel charged a higher price to wholesalers than to direct-buying retailers? What position would Klein have been in if Lionel charged wholesalers and direct-buying retailers the same price?

4. If Lionel in fact charged the same price to the wholesaler supplying Klein as it charged the direct-buying retailer, then Klein would be disadvantaged, but there would be no price discrimination by Lionel, would there? Is this situation similar to *Conoco*? to *Secatore's*?

5. If Lionel sold to the direct-buying retailer at a lower price than it sold to the wholesaler supplying Klein, could Lionel defend on the ground that its discrimination did no harm, because Klein could not compete on price with the direct-buying retailer, even if there was no discrimination? Hence—the argument would run—the actual discrimination did no harm.

6. The argument set out in Note 5 is a powerful one, but only in circumstances where competition is entirely on the basis of price. That was the case in *Secatore's*. In circumstances like *Klein*, the disadvantaged retailer still can compete by making up for the price disadvantage with service competition. So long as there is actual or potential competition, the supply-cost disadvantage resulting from price discrimination causes harm.

7. Would a direct-buying retailer be protected by the Robinson-Patman Act against the manufacturer's selling to wholesalers at a lower price than the direct-buying retailer received from the manufacturer? Would it matter whether the wholesaler passed on its favorable supply price to retailer customers who were in competition with the direct-buying retailer?

Perkins v. Standard Oil Co. of California

395 U.S. 642 (1969)

Mr. Justice Black delivered the opinion of the Court.

In 1959 petitioner, Clyde A. Perkins, brought this civil antitrust action against the Standard Oil Company of California seeking treble damages under § 2 of the Clayton Act, as amended by the Robinson-Patman Act, for injuries alleged to have resulted from Standard's price discriminations in the sale of gasoline and oil during a period of over two years from 1955 to 1957. [After a jury verdict for the petitioner, the Court of Appeals for the Ninth Circuit ruled that the assessment of damages included injuries to Perkins that were not recoverable under the Act and therefore ordered a new trial.] . . . We granted *certiorari* to determine whether the Court of Appeals, in reversing the judgment, had correctly construed the Robinson-Patman Act.

Petitioner Perkins . . . was both a wholesaler, operating storage plants and trucking equipment, and a retailer through his own Perkins stations. From 1945 until 1957, Perkins purchased substantially all of his gasoline requirements from Standard. From 1955 to 1957 Standard charged Perkins a higher price for its gasoline and oil than Standard charged to its own Branded Dealers, who competed with Perkins, and to Signal Oil & Gas Co., a wholesaler whose gas eventually reached the pumps of a major competitor of Perkins. Perkins contends that Standard's price and price-related discriminations against him seriously harmed his competitive position and forced him, in 1957, to sacrifice by sale what remained of his once independent business to one of the major companies in the gasoline business, Union Oil.

. . . Standard admittedly sold gasoline to Signal at a lower price than it sold to Perkins. Signal sold this Standard gasoline to Western Hyway, which in turn sold the

Standard gasoline to Regal Stations Co., Perkins' competitor. Perkins alleged that the lower price charged Signal by Standard was passed on to Signal's subsidiary Western Hyway, and then to Western's subsidiary, Regal. Regal's stations were thus able to undersell Perkins' stations and, according to Perkins, the resulting competitive harm, along with that he suffered at the hands of Standard's favored Branded Dealers, destroyed his ability to compete and eventually forced him to sell what was left of his business. The Court of Appeals held, however, that any harm suffered by Perkins from impaired competition with Regal stations was beyond the scope of the Robinson-Patman Act because Regal was too far removed from Standard in the chain of distribution. . . .

We disagree with the Court of Appeals' conclusion that § 2 of the Clayton Act, as amended by the Robinson-Patman Act, does not apply to the damages suffered by Perkins as a result of the price advantage granted by Standard to Signal, then by Signal to Western, then by Western to Regal. The Act, in pertinent part, provides:

> "(a) It shall be unlawful for any person engaged in commerce, . . . either directly or indirectly, to discriminate in price between different purchasers of commodities of like grade and quality, . . . where the effect of such discrimination may be substantially to lessen competition or tend to create a monopoly in any line of commerce, or to injure, destroy, or prevent competition with any person who either grants or knowingly receives the benefit of such discrimination, or with customers of either of them. . . ."

The Court of Appeals read this language as limiting "the distributing levels on which a supplier's price discrimination will be recognized as potentially injurious to competition." . . . According to that court, the coverage of the Act is restricted to injuries caused by an impairment of competition with (1) the seller ("any person who . . . grants . . . such discrimination"), (2) the favored purchaser ("any person who . . . knowingly receives the benefit of such discrimination"), and (3) customers of the discriminating seller or favored purchaser ("customers of either of them"). Here, Perkins' injuries resulted in part from impaired competition with a customer (Regal) of a customer (Western Hyway) of the favored purchaser (Signal). The Court of Appeals termed these injuries "fourth level" and held that they were not protected by the Robinson-Patman Act. We conclude that this limitation is wholly an artificial one and is completely unwarranted by the language or purpose of the Act.

In *FTC v. Fred Meyer, Inc.*, 390 U.S. 341 (1968), we held that a retailer who buys through a wholesaler could be considered a "customer" of the original supplier within the meaning of § 2(d) of the Clayton Act, as amended by the Robinson-Patman Act, a section dealing with discrimination in promotional allowances which is closely analogous to § 2(a) involved in this case. In *Meyer*, the Court stated that to read "customer" narrowly would be wholly untenable when viewed in light of the purposes of the Robinson-Patman Act. Similarly, to read "customer" more narrowly in this section than we did in the section involved in *Meyer* would allow price discriminators to avoid the sanctions of the Act by the simple expedient of adding an additional link to the distribution chain. . . . Had Signal . . . sold its gas directly to the Regal stations, giving Regal stations a competitive advantage, there would be no question . . . that a clear violation of the Robinson-Patman Act had been committed. Instead of selling directly to the retailer Regal, however, Signal transferred the gasoline first to its subsidiary, Western Hyway, which in turn supplied the Regal stations. Signal owned 60% of the stock of Western Hyway; Western in turn owned 55% of the stock of the Regal stations. We find no basis in the language or purpose of the Act for immunizing Standard's price discriminations simply because the product in question passed through an additional formal exchange before reaching the level of Perkins' actual competitor. From Perkins' point of view, the competitive harm done him by Standard is certainly no less because of the presence of an additional link in this particular distribution chain from the producer to the retailer. Here Standard discriminated in price between Perkins and Signal, and there was evidence from which the jury could conclude that Perkins was harmed competitively when Signal's price advantage was passed on to Perkins' retail competitor Regal. These facts are sufficient to give rise to recoverable damages under the Robinson-Patman Act.

[The Court then concluded that there was sufficient evidence in the record from which the jury might have inferred that Perkins' injuries were "caused" by the price discrimination in violation of the Act.]

. . . The jury's verdict and judgment should be reinstated.

It is so ordered.

COMMENTARY

1. In *Perkins,* it is the direct-buying retailer who is complaining of discrimination. Where does the discrimination occur? Who is the favored purchaser?

2. Does a literal reading of the Act support the view of the lower court that the Act is not concerned with discrimination producing a cost advantage in the Regal stations vis-à-vis the competing Perkins stations? How did the Supreme Court deal with this literalist construction?

3. Is it crucial to the *Perkins* holding that Signal owned 60% of the stock of Western Hyway? That Western Hyway owned 55% of the stock of Regal? How would the court which decided the *Caribe* case approach these questions? *Perkins,* of course, was decided many years before *Copperweld* originated the single enterprise approach to corporate affiliations, an approach which has found application in the Robinson-Patman context in cases like *Caribe*. Remember that (in the conspiracy context) the Justice Department takes the view that less-than wholly owned subsidiaries are part of a single enterprise with the parent so long as the parent owns more than half of the subsidiary's stock or otherwise exercises effective control.

4. Would the Act protect the Regal stations against price favoritism which Standard might extend to Perkins over Signal (the supplier of Regal's supplier)? Does your answer depend upon whether or not account is taken of the stock ownership? If the Act would have protected the Regal stations even before *Copperweld* was decided, would the Act then protect Klein (an indirect purchaser) against favoritism extended by Lionel to a direct-buying retailer?

5. If Signal had not passed on its supply-price advantage to Western Hyway which in turn passed it on to Regal, would the Act have been violated? Could Standard have avoided violating the Act by policing the resale prices of Signal? How could Standard police those resale prices? What techniques would it use? Would the use of any of these techniques by Standard involve it in a violation of the Sherman Act?

6. The difficulties of applying the Act to protect a direct-buying retailer from the cost advantage enjoyed by competing retailers which are supplied by a favored wholesaler are illustrated in *Standard Oil Co.*, 43 F.T.C. 56 (1946), *modified and aff'd, Standard Oil Co. v. FTC*, 173 F.2d 210 (7th Cir. 1949), *rev'd on other grounds,* 340 U.S. 231 (1951). In that case Standard had been selling both directly to retailers and to jobbers or wholesalers who resold to retailers. In an attempt to protect Standard's direct-buying retailers from the competition of retailers who obtained their gasoline supplies from wholesalers who obtained favored supply prices from Standard and who passed the benefit of their low supply prices on to their own retailer-customers, the Federal Trade Commission's order forbade Standard from discriminating:

> By selling . . . gasoline to any jobber or wholesaler at a price lower than the price which the respondent charges its retailer-customers who in fact compete in the sale and distribution of such gasoline with the retailer-customers of such jobbers or wholesalers, where such jobber or wholesaler resells such gasoline to any of its said retailer customers at less than the respondent's posted tank-wagon price. . . .

7. On review of the Commission's *Standard Oil* order, the Seventh Circuit commented:

> . . . the petitioner may under the right to choose its customers refuse to sell to wholesalers who sell to retailers below the price the petitioner makes to its own retailers. The petitioner does not have to make price control agreements with anyone. It has only to govern its own conduct to avoid the impact of an unlawful discrimination. To govern its conduct, the order makes the petitioner deal with its wholesalers at its peril as to what they might do with the gasoline in the future. The petitioner has no control and can have no control over the price of the gasoline after it is sold to the wholesalers. The latter may put any price on it they may choose. They may give it away if they like. The petitioner should not be required to police its wholesalers and to sell to them at the petitioner's peril.

Standard Oil Co. v. FTC, 173 F.2d 210 (7th Cir. 1949), *rev'd on other grounds,* 340 U.S. 231 (1951). The court then rewrote the Commission's order to forbid Standard from discriminating:

> By selling such gasoline to any jobber or wholesaler at a price lower than the price which the respondent charges its retailer-customers who in fact compete in the sale and distribution of such gasoline with the retailer-

> customers of such jobbers or wholesalers, where such jobber or wholesaler, to the knowledge of the respondent or under such circumstances as are reasonably calculated to impute knowledge to the respondent, resells such gasoline or intends to sell the same to any of its said retailer-customers at less than respondent's posted tank-wagon price . . . .

Is the court's order an improvement over the Commission's? Do any problems inhere in the court's order?

EPILOGUE

1. The Robinson-Patman Act has been a topic of continuous controversy. A presidential task force appointed by President Johnson in 1967 explained its reasons for recommending a major revision of the statute as follows:

> . . . [A] thorough revision of the Robinson-Patman Act to remove features that unduly restrict the free play of competitive forces . . . [is needed]. . . . Many aspects of the Robinson-Patman Act in its present form have serious anticompetitive effects. The course of enforcement and interpretation of the Act have in many instances aggravated those effects. . . . Experience with the Act and the extensive criticism to which it has been subjected provide the basis for a general revision that will make it consistent with the major aims of antitrust policy. In our view such a revision is long overdue.

REPORT OF THE WHITE HOUSE TASK FORCE ON ANTITRUST POLICY (1967), *reprinted in* 2 J. ANTITRUST & ECON. 11, 17-18 (1968). No legislation followed this report, but concern over the prospect of modifying or repealing the Robinson-Patman Act generated congressional hearings during the administration of President Ford.

In his opening remarks, the chair of the House Subcommittee stated the position of the supporters of the Act as follows:

> This special Subcommittee was established as a result of widespread concern regarding alleged efforts to repeal or weaken the Robinson-Patman Act. . . . The Robinson-Patman Act, known as the "Magna Carta of small business," is vital and important to assure small businessmen of needed protection in the marketplace in such areas as volume sales by large manufacturers. . . .
>
> This landmark Act should be retained, continued, and enforced.

HEARINGS, AD HOC COMMITTEE ON ANTITRUST, THE ROBINSON-PATMAN ACT, AND RELATED MATTERS, HOUSE COMMITTEE ON SMALL BUSINESS-PART 1, 94th Cong., 1st Sess. 1 (1975).

The opposition to the Robinson-Patman Act that precipitated these hearings was expressed in a series of proposals by the Antitrust Division. In testimony,

Thomas Kauper, the Assistant Attorney General in charge of the Antitrust Division, explained his opposition as follows:

> . . . [T]he Department was satisfied that there was a need for some reform of the Robinson-Patman Act. I had . . . indicated my own view that I was not happy with the various reform proposals, and perhaps the best thing would be outright repeal; or, perhaps we should substitute a much more specific predatory pricing statute for Robinson-Patman. . . . As antitrust prosecutors we are persistently aware that the Robinson-Patman Act is used from time to time as a defense in various of our price-fixing proceedings.

HEARINGS, 587-88.

No legislative change resulted from these hearings. In the interim, the critics continue their opposition. Thus, one commentator concluded, "Although it has an antitrust facade, the Act to a large degree protects competitors from competition." Hugh C. Hansen, *Robinson-Patman Law: A Review and Analysis,* 51 FORDHAM L. REV. 1113, 1213 (1983). *See also* William Baxter, *A Parable,* 23 STAN L. REV. 973 (1971). A more recent commentator has noted:

> . . . [C]riticism of the Robinson-Act focuses on two things. First, although the Act was designed to protect small businesses, it has not done so very well. Often small businesses have run afoul of the Act. . . . Secondly, . . . the . . . Act is quite hostile toward economic competition. . . . The . . . Act has done an extraordinarily poor job of identifying those forms of price discrimination that . . . [are] consider[ed] . . . inefficient. At the same time, it has often been used to condemn efficient practices that were really evidence of healthy competition.

HERBERT HOVENKAMP, FEDERAL ANTITRUST POLICY 523 (1994).

2. From the cases in this chapter, it is clear that the Antitrust Division has brought no cases in two decades and that the Federal Trade Commission has drastically reduced, if not ended, its enforcement of the Act. Current litigation is largely among private parties, often competitors. Is this an adequate response to the criticisms of the Act? If the Robinson-Patman Act is validly characterized as a misguided, Depression-based statute for the protection of competitors, should it be repealed? Might its continued existence provide an inappropriate basis for private litigants to punish their competitors to the detriment of competition? Were the Act to be repealed, would the Sherman and Clayton Acts suffice to protect the public interest in competition?

Chapter 14

The Trade/Antitrust Interface

A. The Relation Between the Antitrust and Antidumping Laws[1]

1. An Overview

Congress enacted the antitrust laws—the Sherman, Clayton, and Federal Trade Commission Acts—to further marketplace competition and to prevent collusive or monopolistic and exclusionary behavior. Monopolistic behavior seeks to restrict the amount of goods and services entering the market, and exclusionary behavior attempts to handicap rivals or expel them from the market entirely.

Conversely, Congress designed several trade laws to protect domestic producers from the competition of foreign rivals. First, sales in the United States at prices below the foreign producers' home-market prices constitute international price discrimination, which is generally referred to as "dumping." Antidumping laws impose duties on foreign producers who sell their goods in the United States at a lower price than in their home markets (or who sell their goods in the United States at below-cost prices) whenever those low priced sales in the American market threaten to produce a material injury to an American industry. Second, countervailing duty laws discourage foreign government subsidies by authorizing offsetting duties whenever foreign subsidies produce a similar impact upon an American industry. Both antidumping and countervailing duty laws have been widely criticized as anticompetitive, in that they protect American producers from the pressures of foreign competition. From this perspective, the policies embodied in the antitrust laws (*i.e.*, the preservation of competition) and the policies in the trade laws (*i.e.*, the protection of domestic producers from "unfair" foreign competition) are in conflict.

2. History

Four years after enacting the Sherman Act in 1890, Congress, in the Wilson Tariff Act of 1894, 28 Stat. 570 (1894), 15 U.S.C. §§ 8-11 (1994), enacted antitrust legislation directed at restraints in the import trade. Phrased in the same kind of broad language which characterizes the Sherman Act, the Wilson Tariff Act provided in part:

---

[1] This Note draws heavily from Daniel J. Gifford, *Rethinking the Relationship Between Antidumping and Antitrust Laws*, 6 AM. U. J. INT'L. L. & POL'Y 277 (1991).

> Every combination, conspiracy, trust, agreement, or contract is declared to be contrary to public policy, illegal, and void when the same is made by or between two or more persons or corporations, either of whom, as agent or principal, is engaged in importing any article from any foreign country into the United States, and when such combination, conspiracy, trust, agreement, or contract is intended to operate in restraint of lawful trade, or free competition in lawful trade or commerce, or to increase the market price in any part of the United States of any article or articles imported or intended to be imported into the United States, or of any manufacture into which such imported article enters or is intended to enter. . . .

Congress returned to domestic antitrust concerns when, in 1914, it enacted the Clayton and the Federal Trade Commission Acts. Section two of the Clayton Act is directed against domestic price discrimination. Two years after passage of the Clayton Act, the Congress enacted the Antidumping Act of 1916, 39 Stat. 798 (1916), 15 U.S.C. § 72 (1994), which provided in part:

> It shall be unlawful for any person importing or assisting in importing any articles from any foreign country into the United States, commonly and systematically to import, sell or cause to be imported or sold such articles within the United States at a price substantially less than the actual market value or wholesale price of such articles, at the time of exportation to the United States, in the principal markets of the country of their production, or of other foreign countries to which they are commonly exported after adding to such market value or wholesale price, freight, duty, and other charges and expenses necessarily incident to the importation and sale thereof in the United States: Provided, That such act or acts be done with the intent of destroying or injuring an industry in the United States, or of preventing the establishment of an industry in the United States, or of restraining or monopolizing any part of trade and commerce in such articles in the United States.
>
> Any person who violates or combines or conspires with any other person to violate this section is guilty of a misdemeanor, and, on conviction thereof, shall be punished by a fine not exceeding $5,000, or imprisonment not exceeding one year, or both, in the discretion of the court.
>
> Any person injured in his business or property by reason of any violation of, or combination or conspiracy to violate, this section, may sue therefor in the district court of the United States for the district in which the defendant resides or is found or has an agent, without respect to the amount in controversy, and shall recover threefold the damages sustained, and the cost of the suit, including a reasonable attorney's fee.
>
> The foregoing provisions shall not be construed to deprive the proper State courts of jurisdiction in actions for damages thereunder.

42 Stat. 11 (1921), repealed by Trade Agreements Act of 1979, 93 Stat. 162 (1979), and substantially reenacted by 19 U.S.C. § 1673 (1994).

In 1921, Congress again enacted antidumping legislation. Responding to critics of the 1916 legislation who had asserted that injured business firms were unable to muster evidence sufficient to meet the demands of litigation (and especially unable to collect evidence about intent), Congress made the new antidumping legislation enforceable through administrative machinery and omitted any intent requirement. The 1921 legislation did, however, contain an injury requirement which largely tracked the intent to injure requirements of the 1916 legislation.

Dumping has always consisted (and continues to consist) of sales in the United States below fair value, fair value being defined in terms of the sales prices of the commodity in the foreign seller's home market. In 1974, Congress amended the Act to include below-cost sales in the United States within the rubric of dumping. The 1921 Act remained the primary antidumping law until the enactment of the Trade Agreements Act in 1979. Congress intended the 1979 Act to bring the United States law into conformity with the then recently negotiated GATT antidumping and countervailing duty codes. Congress formally repealed the provisions of the 1921 Act, but substantially reenacted them as an amendment adding Title VII to the Tariff Act of 1930.

3. The Subsidy Model of Dumping

Dumping—in the common understanding of the term—involves the sale of goods in the target market at prices lower than the prices prevailing in the seller's home market. That definition has been effectively incorporated into U.S. law and was—until 1974—the exclusive definition. Since 1974, dumping under U.S. law consists in sales in the United States at prices below the seller's home market prices or below the seller's costs. Under the classic definition, dumping involves price discrimination in international sales transactions.

The history of U.S. antidumping legislation suggests that Congress believed that a relationship exists between a dumping firm's high home market prices and its low American prices: that the dumping firm's higher home market prices in some way subsidize its lower export prices. The close relationship (in time of enactment and in statutory structure) between the 1916 Act and the Clayton Act suggests that this subsidy model of price discrimination underlay both Acts. The original version of Clayton Act § 2 is generally understood to be directed against price discrimination involving predatory pricing, as discussed in Chapters 11 and 13. The legislative history of the Clayton Act reveals a congressional belief that the price discrimination against which Congress was legislating involved the subsidization of predatorily low prices with monopoly revenues earned in different markets. It is not unlikely that a similar understanding underlay Congress' enactment of the 1916 Antidumping Act.

If the 1916 Antidumping Act is directed against predatory pricing, then that Act can be construed as broadly consistent with the antitrust laws. To the extent that the 1921 Act and its successor legislative embodiments are directed at nonpredatory dumping, then the prospect of substantial policy conflict between these laws and the antitrust laws arises.

4. The 1921 Antidumping Act

If the 1921 Act is viewed as crassly protective legislation, then no further analysis is required. The 1921 legislation, however, is directed at the specific practice of dumping: a practice which was widely viewed as unfair behavior. An understanding of just why Congress saw nonpredatory dumping as unfair would be helpful in construing the surviving provisions of that legislation. Such an understanding might also help in working out the policy conflicts between the trade and antitrust laws.

Congressional concern that in the aftermath of World War I foreign cartels would be seeking to dispose of excess production in the United States underlay the 1921 Act. Concerns about the likely impact of foreign cartel pricing suggest that some congressional backers of antidumping legislation perceived a relationship between the high and low prices significantly different from that embodied in the subsidy model underlying the 1916 Act. That relationship involved the use of dumping as a device to lower unit costs in industries with heavy fixed costs by producing in volume without eroding away high foreign home-market prices established through cartel behavior. Although foreign sellers might not possess predatory motives, they could, nonetheless, be viewed as drawing upon protected home-market positions to subject American rivals to persistent competition by marginal-cost pricing. The monopoly revenues in the home market would thus be essential to marginal-cost pricing in the American market. The monopoly prices in their protected home markets would provide coverage for fixed costs and generate profits, thereby facilitating the foreign sellers' ability to price at marginal-cost levels abroad. There is no subsidy in the sense that the export sales are incurring losses. Indeed, the export sales may be reducing the unit costs of the dumping firm by increasing sales volume in an industry with scale economies. Yet, higher revenues in a protected home market would provide the revenues that are a *sine qua non* for persistent (long-term) marginal-cost export pricing. A focus upon this kind of connection between the high home-market prices and the low American prices might explain some of the congressional references to dumping as unfair, monopolistic, or anticompetitive, even when the dumping is being carried out without predatory motives.

5. Reinterpreting the 1921 Antidumping Act and Successor Legislation

It is possible to construct a plausible argument that the 1921 Antidumping Act should be construed as directed solely against predatory dumping, *i.e.*, dumping which is designed to destroy an American industry and to replace it with a foreign monopoly. Although such an argument would be vulnerable to the contention that the Act has never been administered on that understanding, it could draw some support from the historical context of its enactment. Thus the argument in behalf of such a limited construction of the 1921 Act would draw from the close relationship between the 1916 Antidumping Act and the price discrimination provisions of the original Clayton Act. The Clayton Act was directed against predatory price discrimination. The 1916 Antidumping Act was closely modeled on the Clayton Act, indicating that the 1916 Act was also directed against predatory price discrimination, albeit in the international context. The 1921 Antidumping Act would then be explained as an attempt to attack the same problem which was the subject of the 1916 legislation, but in a more effective manner. The omission of an intent component of the dumping offense in the 1921 Act may be explained as an attempt by Congress to avoid the practical problems of proof which impeded the effectiveness of the 1916 legislation. But while the scope of the 1921 legislation may have been enlarged by the omission of the intent requirement, Congress may have been simultaneously limiting its application by entrusting its administration to a Cabinet officer.[2] A contention that the successor legislation to the 1921 Act reaches only predatory dumping was embraced by Commissioner Susan Liebler of the U.S. International Trade Commission. Commissioner Liebler's position was considered in the case set forth below:

USX Corporation v. United States
682 F. Supp. 60 (Ct. Int'l Trade 1988)

RESTANI, Judge:

Plaintiff, USX Corporation, brings this action challenging the final determination of the United States International Trade Commission (ITC) that an industry in the United States was neither materially injured nor threatened with material injury by reason of imports of cold-rolled carbon steel plates and sheets from Argentina that were sold at less than fair value. . . .

A. The Five Factor Causation Analysis

Plaintiff challenges the approach to causation analysis offered by one commissioner which would require ITC to consider five factors when determining whether the factual setting of a particular case merits an affirmative finding. According to the commissioner,

---

[2] The 1921 Act was administered by the Secretary of the Treasury. The successor antidumping provisions are presently administered by the Secretary of Commerce.

"[T]he stronger the evidence of the following . . . the more likely that an affirmative determination will be made: (1) large and increasing market share, (2) high dumping margins, (3) homogenous products, (4) declining prices and (5) barriers to entry to other foreign producers (low elasticity of supply of other imports)." Remand Determination at 14 (citing *Certain Red Raspberries from Canada*, USITC Pub. 1707, at 16, Inv. No. 731-TA-196 (June 1985)).

Applying these factors in the present case, the existence of relatively high dumping margins was acknowledged along with substitutable imported and domestic product and downward pricing trends, all consistent with an affirmative finding, but it was concluded [by the ITC Commissioner] that "these factors are outweighed by the absence of barriers to entry, and the fact that cumulated import penetration is very low, which strongly suggests the absence of unfair price discrimination." . . .

An attempt is made in the [ITC Commissioner's] determination to justify use of the five factor test and reliance on barriers to entry, in particular, as the determinative factor, by equating unlawful dumping with a particular form of "unfair price discrimination." In *Red Raspberries*, cited in this determination in support of the five factor analysis, it is more specifically explained that the antidumping statute is intended to protect U.S. industry only from unfair price discrimination in the form of predatory pricing, as that term is defined in the determination. . . . The *Red Raspberries* determination goes on to state that:

> Price discrimination can take several forms. The fact that Congress referred to unfair price discrimination suggests . . . that Congress meant some type of predatory pricing. Predatory pricing is a form of strategic behavior in which a firm lowers the price of its product below the marginal cost of production. Such behavior is only rational if the firm expects to be able to raise its prices in the future to a level at which it can more than recoup the losses it suffers in the present. Thus, predatory pricing can only be practiced by firms that have or expect to have market power.

Red Raspberries, USITC Pub. 1707, at 14-15 (footnote omitted) (citing R. POSNER & F. EASTERBROOK, ANTITRUST, 98-99, 680 (2d ed. 1981)). The problem with this position is twofold. One flaw is that this view necessarily makes the intent of a foreign producer the focus of the ITC causation inquiry. Another, but not unrelated flaw, is that this view seems to assume that the purpose of the antidumping statute is to prevent a particular type of "injury to competition" rather than merely material "injury to industry."

The "injury to industry" versus "injury to competition" distinction in international trade laws dates back to the early part of this century. The Antidumping Act of 1916 (codified at 15 U.S.C. §§ 71-77 (1982)) was enacted by Congress as an unfair competition law focusing specifically on the practice of predatory dumping. . . . Although the Act mentions injury to industry, the entire thrust of the statute, including the intent requirement, cause it to be recognized as a particular type of antitrust statute. . . .

In the Antidumping Act of 1921, however, Congress inserted an injury test considerably more sensitive to conditions in the domestic industry. Antidumping Act of 1921, ch. 14, § 201, 42 Stat. 11 (repealed 1979). . . . Likewise, the Trade Agreements Act of 1979 (1979 Act), which repealed the 1921 Act and re-enacted its provisions, as amended, into the Tariff Act of 1930, states that antidumping duties are to be imposed only upon a showing that a domestic industry is materially injured, threatened with material injury or that the establishment of a domestic industry is materially retarded by reason of less than fair value imports. 19 U.S.C. § 1673 (1982).

As indicated, the interpretation under discussion of the antidumping statute reflects a belief that despite the lack of express limitation in the statutes, Congress intended that dumping duties be enforced only if [a foreign seller is engaged in discriminatory pricing which is also predatory]. . . . The analysis begins with the assumption that foreign firms behave as rational profit maximizers. . . . [I]t is important to note the additional comments that unfair price discrimination is predatory pricing in the form of pricing below the marginal cost of production and that no gain can be had by such price discrimination unless an exporting firm ultimately is able to raise its prices in the U.S. market to take advantage of its increased market share. . . . It is further stated that a firm will be unable to raise prices if other nations are capable of exporting to the U.S. at competitive prices. Under this analysis, gainful dumping cannot be accomplished and, therefore, proof of causation of injury by dumped imports will not exist, unless there are barriers to entry of other imports. Thus, . . . this fifth factor is not just one of many relevant factors, but its absence likely will produce a negative determination in all cases relying solely upon the five factor test.

The view reflected in the determination rests upon the principle that pricing that is above the marginal cost of production cannot be said to be contrary to acceptable profit maximizing behavior, as a general matter. *See* R. POSNER & F. EASTERBROOK, ANTITRUST, 680-686 (2d ed. 1981);[9] Barcelo, *Antidumping Laws as Barriers to Trade—The United States and the International Antidumping Code*, 57 Cornell L. Rev. 491, 504-06 (1972). Under this view, only pricing below the marginal cost of production can be said, with any certainty, to be uneconomic and anticompetitive. Thus, by asking whether, rationally, goods would be priced below the marginal cost of production, the commissioner asks whether the pricing is unacceptably anticompetitive, not whether it is injurious to the industry in some other material way.

In international trade it is the object of an "injury to competition" causation test to protect the competitive process itself and not necessarily individual competitors. . . . Under the view expressed in the determination, only predation of the type described furnishes the requisite causation of injury to competition. The "injury to industry" causation standard, however, focuses explicitly upon conditions in the U.S. industry. *Id.* In effect, Congress has made a judgment that causally related injury to the domestic industry may be severe enough to justify relief from less than fair value imports even if from another viewpoint the economy could be said to be better served by providing no relief. . . .

As indicated, the commissioner has expressly cited ITC's *Red Raspberries* determination as a fuller statement of the views expressed here. There it is stated that statutory causation factors such as volume and pricing data are nothing more than "useful proxies" for a "direct inquiry into the intent of a foreign producer [which] would be difficult at best." *Red Raspberries*, USITC Pub. 1707, at 16. As stated, it is the 1916 Act which focuses on intent. In applying the antidumping law under which this action is brought it is improper for ITC to place at the center of its causation analysis the intent of a foreign producer. This inquiry is unavoidable, however, if one equates unlawful dumping with unfair price discrimination in the form of predatory pricing. Unlike the 1916 Act, there is neither a scienter requirement to be found in the statute relevant here, nor evidence in the relevant

---

[9] This work is relied upon in *Red Raspberries* which has been cited as a fuller statement of the views expressed here, thus the court assumes that the definition of marginal cost of production contained therein is also accepted. It is "change in total costs brought about by increasing (or decreasing) output by one unit." POSNER & EASTERBROOK, *supra*, at 684.

legislative history that Congress intended such a requirement. Thus, contrary to the suggestion in defendants' brief, what occurred in this case is not the mere incorporation of another relevant economic factor into a causation analysis as is clearly permissible under 19 U.S.C. § 1677(7)(B)-(C) (1982). Instead, the nature of the reliance on the barrier to entry factor has worked to change the focus of the injury investigation in a manner not permitted by Congress.

. . . .

This matter is hereby remanded to the ITC for further consideration consistent with this opinion. . . .

SO ORDERED.

COMMENTARY

1. When Congress enacted antidumping legislation, it appears to have been operating on an understanding that international price discrimination was, in some way, "unfair." Indeed, the histories of antidumping legislation are replete with assertions about the unfairness of selling goods in the United States at prices which are substantially lower than the prices at which the goods are sold in the seller's home market.

As the preceding material shows, the 1916 Antidumping Act is probably best construed as directed against "predatory" dumping, *i.e.*, dumping which is designed to destroy an American industry for the long term benefit of the seller. Such a construction of the 1916 Act would be consistent with the way § 2 of the Clayton Act treats domestic price discrimination directed at competitors. Since the two provisions appear historically linked, there are grounds for construing these provisions in similar ways.

The 1921 Act—which is the basis for almost all of today's antidumping activity—appears to be directed at more than predatory dumping. Indeed, that was the holding of the *USX* case above. The question then arises as under what rationale did Congress consider nonpredatory dumping to be "unfair," as it clearly indicated. In a prominent Tariff Commission Report issued in 1919,[3] the Commission had pointed out that selling goods abroad at lower than home market prices helps the seller to expand volume and thereby—in an industry with scale economies—to attain lower unit costs. In so doing the seller both helps itself to lower costs and benefits the buyers of its exports who are able to purchase their supplies cheaply.

The prevalent view in Congress, however, appears to have focused upon the use of dumping abroad by foreign firms as a means of facilitating cartel pricing at home. By selling abroad at marginal cost prices the foreign seller was able to reduce

---

3 United States Tariff Comm'n, Information Concerning Dumping and Unfair Foreign Competition in the United States and Canada's Anti-Dumping Law 19 & n.2 (1919).

its unit costs without lowering its home market prices. So viewed, dumping was an adjunct of a home-market cartel. When American producers were hurt by marginal-cost prices of imports, therefore, they could (and did) say that they were hurt by the monopolistic practices of foreign cartels. Congress largely accepted this view as the underlying rationale for its antidumping legislation.

The public rationale for the antidumping legislation could be supported by the existence and behavior of chemical and steel cartels in Germany in the period prior to World War I and by fears of a resumption of that type of behavior in the post-war world. Yet antidumping legislation did not (and does not) expressly limit its application to cartelized industries. Moreover, other factors undermine this public rationale for antidumping legislation: in the present world, exchange rates of currencies float freely and are subject to significant fluctuation. Swings in exchange rates may create situations where the U.S. prices of the goods of foreign firms suddenly become lower than their home market prices solely because the dollar has temporarily fallen in value.

Since the 1974 amendments, dumping now consists of sales below cost, even if the goods are sold below cost in the seller's home market as well. The rationale for such legislation may be a belief that goods cannot be sold indefinitely at below-cost prices, so that the below-cost prices mask a concealed subsidy. Such a rationale might be defended if it applied to below-cost selling for sustained periods. Because the present law contains no such requirement, it tends to be triggered when demand slacks in high-fixed cost industries. In such industries, sellers (both domestic and foreign) tend to produce at lower volume and hence at higher unit costs and to sell, during the slack-demand period, at prices which are below their temporarily high average total cost. The present law then treats this temporary circumstance as "dumping" by foreign sellers.

Despite these criticisms of the antidumping laws, it is nonetheless true that in the absence of trade barriers, dumping in its classic form of international price discrimination—apart from shipping cost margins—would be impossible for traded goods (as opposed to services). Any firm which attempted to sell goods abroad for less than it was selling the same goods for at home would create a situation in which arbitrageurs would rapidly end the discrimination by buying in the lower priced market and reselling in the higher priced market. Sustained and substantial dumping, therefore, could be probative of trade barriers in the home market of the dumping firms.

Again, while marginal cost prices benefit consumers, a foreign seller which is selling at marginal cost prices in the U.S. while selling at higher prices at home in a protected market makes it impossible for its equally efficient American rivals to compete in the long term. That is because in the long run a seller needs earnings sufficient to replace its capital. This situation is exacerbated the more capital intensive is the industry concerned. The competitive process—which selects the most efficient firms to survive in the long run—is distorted when one set of firms can operate behind a wall of protection where those protected firms earn capital replacement funds while subjecting a rival set of firms to long-run competition at short-run marginal cost prices.

The references by the Congress in the post World War I period to foreign cartels selling abroad at below home market prices were not precise. But the model underlying these congressional statements can be stated more precisely: it is a model of foreign firms (1) selling in protected home markets (whose revenues supply their capital) and (2) selling abroad indefinitely at short-run marginal cost prices. Such behavior appears to distort the competitive process because one group of producers possesses a market-barrier advantage not possessed by their rivals. Looked at from the perspective of competition policy, pricing advantage based on a protected home market appears objectionable. Yet the trade laws—at least in the form of the antidumping laws—do not appear to be well designed to deal with these distortions to competition. And the antitrust laws are not well designed to deal with these problems either, because they have tended to focus primarily upon the American market and the impact upon American consumers. While the antitrust laws guarantee American business firms the opportunity to compete with each other under the same competitive rules, they have not been able to help American producers overcome disadvantages imposed upon them when their rivals operate from foreign markets which are closed to them.

2. Complaints about the fairness of international competition were asserted by American television producers in *Matsushita Electric Industrial Co. v. Zenith Radio Corporation*, excerpted below. Consider the complaints and their resolution by the Supreme Court. The Japanese companies had previously been found to have been in violation of the antidumping laws. Do you agree with the Court that a decades-long conspiracy to maintain predatory prices is improbable? Could you have presented Zenith's case better than it was presented?

Matsushita Electric Industrial Co. v. Zenith Radio Corp.

475 U.S. 574 (1986)

Justice Powell delivered the opinion of the Court.

. . . .

Petitioners, defendants below, are 21 corporations that manufacture or sell "consumer electronic products" (CEPs)—for the most part, television sets. Petitioners include both Japanese manufacturers of CEPs and American firms, controlled by Japanese parents, that sell the Japanese-manufactured products. Respondents, plaintiffs below, are Zenith Radio Corporation (Zenith) and National Union Electric Corporation (NUE). Zenith is an American firm that manufactures and sells television sets. NUE is the corporate successor to Emerson Radio Company, an American firm that manufactured and sold television sets until 1970, when it withdrew from the market after sustaining substantial losses. Zenith and NUE began this lawsuit in 1974, claiming that petitioners had illegally conspired to drive American firms from the American CEP market. According to respondents, the gist of this conspiracy was a "'scheme to raise, fix and maintain artificially high prices for television receivers sold by [petitioners] in Japan and, at the same time, to fix and maintain low prices for television receivers exported to and sold in the United States.'" . . . These "low prices" were allegedly at levels that produced substantial losses for petitioners. . . . The conspiracy allegedly began as early as 1953, and according to respondents was in full operation by sometime in the late 1960's. Respondents claimed that various portions of this scheme violated §§ 1 and 2 of the Sherman Act, § 2(a) of the Robinson-Patman Act, § 73 of the Wilson Tariff Act, and the Antidumping Act of 1916.

. . . .

IV

A

A predatory pricing conspiracy is by nature speculative. Any agreement to price below the competitive level requires the conspirators to forego profits that free competition would offer them. The foregone profits may be considered an investment in the future. For the investment to be rational, the conspirators must have a reasonable expectation of recovering, in the form of later monopoly profits, more than the losses suffered. As then-Professor Bork, discussing predatory pricing by a single firm, explained:

> Any realistic theory of predation recognizes that the predator as well as his victims will incur losses during the fighting, but such a theory supposes it may be a rational calculation for the predator to view the losses as an investment in future monopoly profits (where rivals are to be killed) or in future undisturbed profits (where rivals are to be disciplined). The future flow of profits, appropriately discounted, must then exceed the present size of the losses. R. Bork, The Antitrust Paradox 145 (1978).

See also McGee, *Predatory Pricing Revisited*, 23 J. LAW & ECON. 289, 295-297 (1980). As this explanation shows, the success of such schemes is inherently uncertain: the short-run loss is definite, but the long-run gain depends on successfully neutralizing the competition. Moreover, it is not enough simply to achieve monopoly power, as monopoly pricing may breed quick entry by new competitors eager to share in the excess profits. The success of any predatory scheme depends on *maintaining* monopoly power for long enough both to recoup the predator's losses and to harvest some additional gain. Absent some assurance that the hoped-for monopoly will materialize, *and* that it can be sustained for a significant period of time, "[t]he predator must make a substantial investment with no assurance that it will pay off." Easterbrook, *Predatory Strategies and Counterstrategies*, 48 U. CHI. L. REV. 263, 268 (1981). For this reason, there is a consensus among commentators that predatory pricing schemes are rarely tried, and even more rarely successful. *See, e.g.*, R. Bork, *supra*, at 149-155; Areeda & Turner, *Predatory Pricing and Related Practices Under Section 2 of the Sherman Act,* 88 HARV. L. REV. 697, 699 (1975); Easterbrook, *supra*; Koller, *The Myth of Predatory Pricing—An Empirical Study*, 4 ANTITRUST LAW & ECON. REV. 105 (1971); McGee, *Predatory Price Cutting: The* Standard Oil (N.J.) *Case*, 1 J. LAW & ECON. 137 (1958); McGee, *Predatory Pricing Revisited,* 23 J. LAW & ECON. at 292-294. *See also Northeastern Telephone Co. v. American Telephone & Telegraph Co.*, 651 F.2d 76, 88 (2d Cir. 1981) ("[N]owhere in the recent outpouring of literature on the subject do commentators suggest that [predatory] pricing is either common or likely to increase"), *cert. denied*, 455 U.S. 943 (1982).

These observations apply even to predatory pricing by a *single firm* seeking monopoly power. In this case, respondents allege that a large number of firms have conspired over a period of many years to charge below-market prices in order to stifle competition. Such a conspiracy is incalculably more difficult to execute than an analogous plan undertaken by a single predator. The conspirators must allocate the losses to be sustained during the conspiracy's operation, and must also allocate any gains to be realized from its success. Precisely because success is speculative and depends on a willingness to endure losses for an indefinite period, each conspirator has a strong incentive to cheat, letting its partners suffer the losses necessary to destroy the competition while sharing in any gains if the conspiracy succeeds. The necessary allocation is therefore difficult to accomplish. Yet if conspirators cheat to any substantial extent, the conspiracy must fail, because its success depends on depressing the market price for *all* buyers of CEPs. If there are too few goods at the artificially low price to satisfy demand, the would-be victims of the conspiracy can continue to sell at the "real" market price, and the conspirators suffer losses to little purpose.

Finally, if predatory pricing conspiracies are generally unlikely to occur, they are especially so where, as here, the prospects of attaining monopoly power seem slight. In order to recoup their losses, petitioners must obtain enough market power to set higher than competitive prices, and then must sustain those prices long enough to earn in excess profits what they earlier gave up in below-cost prices. *See Northeastern Telephone Co. v. American Telephone & Telegraph Co.*, *supra*, at 89; Areeda & Turner, 88 HARV. L. REV. at 698. Two decades after their conspiracy is alleged to have commenced,[13] petitioners appear to be far from achieving this goal: the two largest shares of the retail market in television sets are held by RCA and respondent Zenith, not by any of the petitioners. . . . Moreover, those shares, which together approximate 40% of sales, did not decline appreciably during the 1970's. . . . Petitioners' collective share rose rapidly during this period, from one-fifth or less of the relevant markets to close to 50%. . . .[14] Neither the District Court nor the Court of Appeals found, however, that petitioners' share presently allows them to charge monopoly prices; to the contrary, respondents contend that the conspiracy is ongoing— that petitioners are still artificially *depressing* the market price in order to drive Zenith out of the market. The data in the record strongly suggests that that goal is yet far distant.[15]

The alleged conspiracy's failure to achieve its ends in the two decades of its asserted operation is strong evidence that the conspiracy does not in fact exist. Since the losses in such a conspiracy accrue before the gains, they must be "repaid" with interest. And because the alleged losses have accrued over the course of two decades, the conspirators could well require a correspondingly long time to recoup. Maintaining supracompetitive prices in turn

---

13 NUE's complaint alleges that petitioners' conspiracy began as early as 1960; the starting date used in Zenith's complaint is 1953. . . .

14 During the same period, the number of American firms manufacturing television sets declined from 19 to 13. . . . This decline continued a trend that began at least by 1960, when petitioner's sales in the United States market were negligible. . . .

15 Respondents offer no reason to suppose that entry into the relevant market is especially difficult, yet without barriers to entry it would presumably be impossible to maintain supracompetitive prices for an extended time. Judge Easterbrook, commenting on this case in a law review article, offers the following sensible assessment: "The plaintiffs [in this case] maintain that for the last fifteen years or more at least ten Japanese manufacturers have sold TV sets at less than cost in order to drive United States firms out of business. Such conduct cannot possibly produce profits by harming competition, however. If the Japanese firms drive some United States firms out of business, they could not recoup. Fifteen years of losses could be made up only by very high prices for the indefinite future. (The losses are like investments, which must be recovered with compound interest.) If the defendants should try to raise prices to such a level, they would attract new competition. There are no barriers to entry into electronics, as the proliferation of computer and audio firms shows. The competition would come from resurgent United States firms, from other foreign firms (Korea and many other nations make TV sets), and from defendants

depends on the continued cooperation of the conspirators, on the inability of other would-be competitors to enter the market, and (not incidentally) on the conspirators' ability to escape antitrust liability for their *minimum* price-fixing cartel.[16] Each of these factors weighs more heavily as the time needed to recoup losses grows. If the losses have been substantial—as would likely be necessary in order to drive out the competition[17]—petitioners would most likely have to sustain their cartel for years simply to break even.

. . . Whether or not petitioners have the means to sustain substantial losses in this country over a long period of time, they have no *motive* to sustain such losses absent some strong likelihood that the alleged conspiracy in this country will eventually pay off. The courts below found no evidence of any such success, and—as indicated above—the facts actually are to the contrary: RCA and Zenith, not any of the petitioners, continue to hold the largest share of the American retail market in color television sets. . . .

B

In *Monsanto*, we emphasized that courts should not permit factfinders to infer conspiracies when such inferences are implausible, because the effect of such practices is often to deter pro-competitive conduct. . . . [C]utting price in order to increase business often is the very essence of competition. Thus, mistaken inferences in cases such as this one are especially costly, because they chill the very conduct the antitrust laws are designed to protect. . . .

. . . [P]redatory pricing schemes require conspirators to suffer losses in order eventually to realize their illegal gains; moreover, the gains depend on a host of uncertainties, making such schemes more likely to fail than to succeed. These economic realities tend to make predatory pricing conspiracies self-deterring: unlike most other conduct that violates the antitrust laws, failed predatory pricing schemes are costly to the conspirators. . . . Finally, unlike predatory pricing by a single firm, *successful* predatory pricing conspiracies involving a large number of firms can be identified and punished once they succeed, since some form of minimum price-fixing agreement would be necessary in order to reap the benefits of predation. Thus, there is little reason to be concerned that by granting summary judgment in cases where the evidence of conspiracy is speculative or ambiguous, courts will encourage such conspiracies.

---

themselves. In order to recoup, the Japanese firms would need to suppress competition among themselves. On plaintiffs' theory, the cartel would last at least thirty years, far longer than any in history, even when cartels were not illegal. None should be sanguine about the prospects of such a cartel, given each firm's incentive to shave price and expand its share of sales. The predation-recoupment story therefore does not make sense, and we are left with the more plausible inference that the Japanese firms did not sell below cost in the first place. They were just engaged in hard competition." Easterbrook, *The Limits of Antitrust*, 63 TEXAS L. REV. 1, 26-27 (1984) (footnotes omitted).

[16] The alleged predatory scheme makes sense only if petitioners can recoup their losses. In light of the large number of firms involved here, petitioners can achieve this only by engaging in some form of price-fixing *after* they have succeeded in driving competitors from the market. Such price-fixing would, of course, be an independent violation of § 1 of the Sherman Act. *United States v. Socony-Vacuum Oil Co.*, 310 U.S. 150 (1940).

[17] The predators' losses must actually increase as the conspiracy nears its objective: the greater the predators' market share, the more products the predators sell; but since every sale brings with it a loss, an increase in market share also means an increase in predatory losses.

V

. . . [P]etitioners had no motive to enter into the alleged conspiracy. To the contrary, as presumably rational businesses, petitioners had every incentive *not* to engage in the conduct with which they are charged, for its likely effect would be to generate losses for petitioners with no corresponding gains. . . . [T]he absence of any plausible motive to engage in the conduct charged is highly relevant to whether a "genuine issue for trial" exists within the meaning of Rule 56(e). Lack of motive bears on the range of permissible conclusions that might be drawn from ambiguous evidence: if petitioners had no rational economic motive to conspire, and if their conduct is consistent with other, equally plausible explanations, the conduct does not give rise to an inference of conspiracy. . . .

The decision of the Court of Appeals is reversed. . . .

COMMENTARY

1. *Matsushita* is very important for what it says about summary judgment. It is widely considered to belong to a trio of Supreme Court rulings in the mid 1980s which increased the effectiveness of summary judgment: Besides *Matsushita*, those cases are *Celotex Corp. v. Catrett*, 477 U.S. 317 (1986), and *Anderson v. Liberty Lobby, Inc.*, 477 U.S. 242 (1986). *Celotex* and *Liberty Lobby* emphasized that when the plaintiff lacks the evidence needed to support a jury verdict in its favor, the other party is entitled to summary judgment. And *Matsushita* made clear that antitrust claims which are economically implausible must be supported by strong evidence to withstand such a motion.

2. What was the rationale on which the Supreme Court found Zenith's claims to be economically implausible? Was Zenith claiming that its Japanese rivals were pricing in the American market at predatory levels? Do you think that Zenith was claiming that the Japanese television sets were being sold at prices which were below average variable cost? Would such a claim be credible?

3. Suppose the Japanese producers were selling in the U.S. market at prices which were below average total cost. As counsel for Zenith, would such a fact be useful in constructing an antitrust case for your client?

4. The Court dismissed the relevance of the five-company rule and the evidence on check pricing on the ground that these were devices to keep prices up rather than to diminish them. The check prices were minimums which the Japanese producers allegedly agreed to respect. The five-company rule was a device for dividing American customers among the Japanese sellers. Why do you think the Japanese producers might have been conspiring to raise (rather than reduce) prices during the period when they were attempting to increase their share of the American market?

5. Clyde Prestowitz, Jr., a former Commerce Department official and critic of U.S. trade policy states that the check prices were widely disregarded by the

Japanese producers but that the five-company rule "was vigorously maintained," thus ensuring "that the full impact of the price cutting in the U.S. market would fall only on U.S. producers." CLYDE.V. PRESTOWITZ, JR., TRADING PLACES 355 (1989 ed.).

6. While the Court said that the U.S. antitrust laws were not concerned with restrictive practices in Japan, it also said that the plaintiffs had not connected restrictive practices in Japan with an impact in the American market. If the Japanese producers had gained an ability to undercut Zenith in the U.S. market as a result of cartel restrictions in their home market, should not Zenith have been able to able to point this out to the Court?

B. The Geographical Scope of U.S. Antitrust Laws

1. Introduction

We now consider the extent to which the United States antitrust laws reach activities taking place abroad. As early as 1909 the Supreme Court dealt with a contention that the Sherman Act had been violated as a result of behavior occurring in Central America. In *American Banana Co. v. United Fruit Co.*, 213 U.S. 347 (1909), Justice Holmes, speaking for the Court, rejected a claim that the United Fruit Co. had monopolized in violation of the Sherman Act by instigating the government of Costa Rica to seize the plaintiff's banana plantation and thereby to prevent the plaintiff from entering the banana market. Justice Holmes took a territorial view of the Sherman Act, presuming that its application was intended to be confined "to the territorial limits over which the lawmaker has general and legitimate power." By 1945, however, Judge Hand was taking a much more flexible approach to the Act's application. In *United States v. Aluminum Co. of America*, 148 F.2d 416, 444 (2d Cir. 1945), he ruled that the Sherman Act extended to conduct taking place abroad which was intended to, and did in fact, restrain American commerce.

Besides the question of whether the antitrust laws apply to behavior abroad, other related questions involve the discretion of the courts to adjudicate antitrust claims involving behavior abroad ("comity") and special defenses which sometimes arise in cases involving activity which occurs abroad such as sovereign compulsion and sovereign immunity. Frequently, issues involving the substantive application of the U.S. antitrust laws overlap issues involving comity, and the courts do not always keep their resolutions of these issues fully separate. To add to the complexity of these matters, Congress entered the arena in 1982 with the enactment of the Foreign Trade Antitrust Improvement Act of 1982, and the Department of Justice has addressed its enforcement policies over extraterritorial activity in policy statements.

There is often tension between the competitive conduct required of domestic firms engaged in domestic commerce and the conduct of domestic firms engaged in foreign commerce. Congress initially recognized this issue in enacting the

Webb-Pomerene Act, 40 Stat. 517 (1918), 15 U.S.C. §§ 61-65 (1994). At the end of the First World War, United States firms engaged in exporting to Europe complained of the need to adopt cartel-like conduct in order effectively to deal with the cartelized economies of their buyers. United States exporters stated the need to coordinate pricing, among other practices, in dealing with these buyers. Accordingly, 15 U.S.C. § 62 (§ 2 of the 1918 Act) provided for immunity from the Sherman Act of export associations as follows:

> Nothing contained in the Sherman Act shall be construed as declaring to be illegal an association entered into for the sole purpose of engaging in export trade and actually engaged solely in such export trade, or an agreement made or act done in the course of export trade by such trade association, provided such association, agreement or act is not in restraint of trade within the United States, and is not in restraint of trade of any domestic competitor of such association.

This statute permitted combination or agreement among firms organized as an association so long as domestic competition was not affected or the opportunity of a domestic competitor to compete abroad was untouched. The Webb-Pomerene exemption was often raised as a defense to anticompetitive conduct which did not clearly meet these statutory conditions, *e.g., United States v. Concentrated Phosphate Ass'n, Inc.,* 393 U.S. 199 (1968) (rejected on ground that the export consideration was insubstantial). Lower court decisions were criticized for their inadequate and inconsistent analyses of the foreign and domestic elements. *See* SPENCER WEBER WALLER, 1 ANTITRUST AND AMERICAN BUSINESS ABROAD § 9.5 (1997).

In 1982, Congress enacted the Foreign Trade Antitrust Improvements Act, 96 Stat. 1233 (1982), 15 U.S.C. §§ 4001 *et seq.* (1994), which undertook: 1) to restate the jurisdictional scope of the Sherman Act, 2) to establish an Office of Export Trade in the Department of Commerce, and 3) to provide for a new antitrust certification procedure to be administered in that Department. Under this certification procedure, an export trading company seeking antitrust immunity must apply for a certificate, for which the applicant need only be engaged in the export of goods or services, either as an individual firm or through an export trading company. The issuance of a certificate is subject to four conditions of § 4013 as follows: 1) that the export activities not lessen competition or restrain trade in the United States or constitute a substantial restraint on the export trade of a competitor of the applicant, 2) the export trade activities will not unreasonably enhance, stabilize, or depress prices in the United States of the goods or services exported by the applicant, 3) the export activities will not constitute unfair methods of competition against competitors engaged in the export of that class of goods or services, and 4) the export activity shall not include any act that may reasonably be expected to result in the sale for consumption or resale within the United States of the exported items. The Secretary of Commerce may not issue a certificate until 30 days after publication of notice in the Federal Register, and then only with the concurrence of the Attorney General under § 4013. Section 4013(b)(3) authorizes the Assistant Attorney General in charge of the Antitrust Division to conduct investigations of the activities of the certificate applicant. For a further review of this legislation, see Thomas

A. Piraino, *Reconciling Competition and Cooperation: A New Antitrust Standard for Joint Ventures,* 35 WM. & MARY L. REV. 971 (1994). For a recent interpretation of exemption from the Sherman Act, involving exempt entities acting together with nonexempt foreign entities, see *Hartford Fire Insurance,* page 738, *infra. See* JAMES R. ATWOOD, KINGMAN BREWSTER & SPENCER WEBER WALLER, ANTITRUST AND AMERICAN BUSINESS ABROAD Ch. 6 (3d ed. 1997).

2. Legislation and Policy Statements

a. The Foreign Trade Antitrust Improvement Act of 1982

UNITED STATES CODE
TITLE 15. COMMERCE AND TRADE
CHAPTER 1—MONOPOLIES AND COMBINATIONS IN RESTRAINT OF TRADE

§ 6a. Conduct involving trade or commerce with foreign nations

Sections 1 to 7 of this title shall not apply to conduct involving trade or commerce (other than import trade or import commerce) with foreign nations unless—

(1) such conduct has a direct, substantial, and reasonably foreseeable effect—

(A) on trade or commerce which is not trade or commerce with foreign nations, or on import trade or import commerce with foreign nations; or

(B) on export trade or export commerce with foreign nations, of a person engaged in such trade or commerce in the United States; and

(2) such effect gives rise to a claim under the provisions of sections 1 to 7 of this title, other than this section.

If sections 1 to 7 of this title apply to such conduct only because of the operation of paragraph (1)(B), then sections 1 to 7 of this title shall apply to such conduct only for injury to export business in the United States.

* * *

b. Excerpt from Department of Justice, Antitrust Guidelines for International Operations (June 8, 1988):

The Department of Justice (the "Department") focuses its antitrust enforcement efforts on anticompetitive conduct that affects U.S. consumer welfare. To be effective, of course, U.S. antitrust enforcement must reach some conduct that occurs outside the United States and that involves foreign actors. For example, an international cartel of private producers cannot impose higher prices on U.S. consumers with impunity simply by holding its cartel meetings outside the United States. On the other hand, U.S. antitrust enforcement does not reach conduct that has only a remote effect on U.S. consumer welfare. . . .

. . . The Department focuses its antitrust enforcement efforts against private restraints of trade that reduce U.S. consumer welfare by artificially restricting output and/or raising prices. The Department is not concerned with conduct that solely affects competition in foreign markets and could have no direct, substantial, and reasonably foreseeable effect on competition and consumers in the United States. Nor is the Department concerned with the export conduct of U.S. firms except where that conduct has a direct, substantial, and reasonably foreseeable anti-competitive effect on price and/or output in the United States. . . .

* * *

c. Department of Justice Policy Regarding Anticompetitive Conduct that Restricts U.S. Exports (April 9, 1992):

The Department of Justice will, in appropriate cases, take antitrust enforcement action against conduct occurring overseas that restrains United States exports, whether or not there is direct harm to U.S. consumers, where it is clear that:

(1) the conduct has a direct, substantial, and reasonably foreseeable effect on exports of goods or services from the United States;

(2) the conduct involves anticompetitive activities which violate the U.S. antitrust laws—in most cases, group boycotts, collusive pricing, and other exclusionary activities; and

(3) U.S. courts have jurisdiction over foreign persons or corporations engaged in such conduct.

This policy statement in no way affects existing laws or established principles of personal jurisdiction.

This enforcement policy is one of general application and is not aimed at any particular foreign country. The Department of Justice will continue its longstanding policy of considering principles of international comity when making antitrust enforcement decisions that may significantly affect another government's legitimate interests. The Department also will continue its practice of notifying and consulting with foreign governments, where appropriate.

This statement of enforcement policy supersedes a footnote in the Department of Justice's 1988 Antitrust Guidelines for International Operations that generally had been interpreted as foreclosing Department of Justice enforcement actions against anticompetitive conduct in foreign markets unless the conduct resulted in indirect harm to U.S. consumers. The new policy represents a return to the Department's pre-1988 position on such matters.

If the conduct is also unlawful under the importing country's antitrust laws, the Department of Justice is prepared to work with that country if that country is better situated to remedy the conduct and is prepared to take action against such conduct pursuant to its antitrust laws.

d. Department of Justice and Federal Trade Commission, Antitrust Enforcement Guidelines for International Operations (April 5, 1995):

Section 3.122 of the 1995 Guidelines repeats, essentially verbatim, the above quoted language from the 1992 Policy Statement. 4 TRADE REG. REP. (CCH) ¶ 13,107 (1995).

* * *

COMMENTARY

1. The emphasis of the 1988 Guidelines for International Operations on the welfare of domestic consumers to the exclusion of U.S. exporters does not appear to be consistent with the view that the objective of the antitrust laws is the furtherance of efficiency (or U.S. wealth maximization). This neglect of the interests of U.S. exporters was removed by the 1992 Policy Statement and the 1995 revision of the Guidelines.

2. The problem raised by the 1988 Guidelines, the 1992 Policy Statement, and the 1995 Guidelines highlights the ambiguity of the phrase "consumer welfare" as employed by Robert Bork in THE ANTITRUST PARADOX (1978) and the courts employing his terminology to identify the goals and purposes of the antitrust laws. Bork uses the phrase "consumer welfare" to mean the combination of producer surplus and consumer surplus. *See* THE ANTITRUST PARADOX, Chapter 5. Note that the extent of extraterritorial enforcement of the antitrust laws is related to the controversy surrounding the meaning attributed to consumer welfare by Bork. If the antitrust laws are deemed to embrace the furtherance of consumer welfare in the broad meaning attributed to that term by Bork, then extraterritorial enforcement which protects U.S. producers is called for. If, however, the purpose of the antitrust laws is deemed to be restricted to furtherance of the welfare of consumers in the strict sense, then there is no room for extraterritorial enforcement for the benefit of U.S. producers. Is it possible that the drafters of the 1988 Guidelines were confused by this ambiguous phrase, attributing to it a literal meaning (consumer surplus) when the antitrust context called for the broader Borkian meaning (consumer surplus plus producer surplus)? Or do you think that the drafters of the 1988 Guidelines intentionally chose the narrower meaning?

3. Do the 1992 Policy Statement and the 1995 Guidelines (which incorporate the 1992 Policy Statement) make the antitrust laws a device for opening foreign markets to U.S. firms which have been excluded by foreign cartels? Should the use of the antitrust laws against foreign cartels operating abroad be confined to the Department of Justice or should they be available to private plaintiffs as well? Can you think of reasons why the courts should entertain actions brought by the U.S. government against foreign companies for their activities abroad which would not apply to actions brought by private plaintiffs?

---

3. Comity

Laker Airways Ltd. v. Sabena, Belgian World Airlines
731 F.2d 909 (D.C. Cir. 1984)

[Laker Airways Ltd. had provided transatlantic air service at very low rates but ultimately terminated its service when it entered into bankruptcy. Claiming that its demise was brought about by a conspiracy of competing higher-priced carriers, Laker brought antitrust actions against several of its former competitors. As the opinion shows, some of these defendants procured an order of a British court commanding Laker to drop its suit against them. Laker then sought an order from the United States court in which its antitrust case was pending forbidding the remaining defendants from following the same course.]

WILKEY, Circuit Judge:

. . . Three months after Laker Airways, Ltd. ("Laker") filed an antitrust action in United States District Court for the District of Columbia against several defendants, including domestic, British, and other foreign airlines, the foreign airlines filed suits in the High Court of Justice of the United Kingdom seeking an injunction forbidding Laker from prosecuting its American antitrust action against the foreign defendants. After the High Court of Justice entered interim injunctions against Laker, the Court of Appeal issued a permanent injunction ordering Laker to take action to dismiss its suit against the British airlines. In the meantime, Laker responded by requesting injunctive relief in the United States District Court, arguing that a restraining order was necessary to prevent the remaining American defendants and the additional foreign defendants Laker had named in a subsequent antitrust claim from duplicating the foreign defendants' successful request for an English injunction compelling Laker to dismiss its suit against the defendants.

If these defendants had been permitted to file foreign injunctive actions, the United States District Court would have been effectively stripped of control over the claims—based on United States law—which it was in the process of adjudicating. Faced with no alternative but acquiescence in the termination of this jurisdiction by a foreign court's order, United States District Judge Harold H. Greene granted Laker's motion for a preliminary injunction restraining the remaining defendants from taking part in the foreign action designed to prevent the district court from hearing Laker's antitrust claims.

. . . .

Our review of the limited available facts strongly suggests that both the United States and Great Britain share concurrent prescriptive jurisdiction over the transactions giving rise to Laker's claim. Ordinarily antisuit injunctions are not properly invoked to preempt parallel proceedings on the same in personam claim in foreign tribunals. However, KLM and Sabena do not qualify under this general rule because the foreign action they seek to join is interdictory and not parallel. It was instituted by the foreign defendants for the sole purpose of terminating the United States claim. The only conceivable benefit that KLM and Sabena would reap if the district court's injunction were overturned would be the right to attack the pending United States action in a foreign court. This would permit the appellants to avoid potential liability under the United States laws to which their business operations and treaty obligations have long subjected them. In these circumstances there is ample precedent justifying the defensive use of an antisuit injunction.

. . . .

II. Analysis

. . . .

D. International Comity

Appellants and amici curiae argue strenuously that the district court's injunction violates the crucial principles of comity that regulate and moderate the social and economic intercourse between independent nations. We approach their claims seriously, recognizing that comity serves our international system like the mortar which cements together a brick house. No one would willingly permit the mortar to crumble or be chipped away for fear of compromising the entire structure.

. . . .

E. Judicial Reconciliation of Conflicting Assertion of Jurisdiction

. . . .

2. Judicial Interest Balancing

. . . .

b. Promotion of International Comity

However, there are limitations to the application of comity. When the foreign act is inherently inconsistent with the policies underlying comity, domestic recognition could tend either to legitimize the aberration or to encourage retaliation, undercutting the realization of the goals served by comity. No nation is under an unremitting obligation to enforce foreign interests which are fundamentally prejudicial to those of the domestic forum. Thus, from the earliest times, authorities have recognized that the obligation of comity expires when the strong public policies of the forum are vitiated by the foreign act. Case law on the subject is extensive and recognizes the current validity of this exception to comity.

. . . .

Despite the real obligation of courts to apply international law and foster comity, domestic courts do not sit as internationally constituted tribunals. Domestic courts are created by national constitutions and statutes to enforce primarily national laws. The courts of most developed countries follow international law only to the extent it is not overridden by national law. Thus, courts inherently find it difficult neutrally to balance competing foreign interests. When there is any doubt, national interests will tend to be favored over foreign interests. This partially explains why there have been few times when courts have found foreign interests to prevail.

The inherent noncorrelation between the interest balancing formula and the economic realities of modern commerce is an additional reason which may underlie the reluctance of most courts to strike a balance in favor of nonapplication of domestic law. An assertion of prescriptive jurisdiction should ultimately be based on shared assessments that jurisdiction is reasonable. Thus, international law prohibits the assertion of prescriptive jurisdiction unsupported by reasonable links between the forum and the controversy.

However, it does not necessarily follow, as the use of interest balancing as a method of choosing between competing jurisdictions assumes, that there is a line of reasonableness which separates jurisdiction to prescribe into neatly adjoining compartments of national jurisdiction. There is no principle of international law which abolishes concurrent jurisdiction. Since prescriptive jurisdiction is based on well recognized state contacts with controversies, the reality of our interlocked international economic network guarantees that overlapping, concurrent jurisdiction will often be present. There is, therefore, no rule of international law holding that a "more reasonable" assertion of jurisdiction mandatorily displaces a "less reasonable" assertion of jurisdiction as long as both are, in fact, consistent with the limitations on jurisdiction imposed by international law. That is the situation faced in this case: the territoriality and nationality bases of jurisdiction of the United Kingdom and the United States are both unimpeached.

. . . .

3. Political Compromise

The district court could capitulate to the British attacking law, at the cost of losing its jurisdiction to implement the substantive policies established by Congress. Alternatively it can act to preserve its jurisdiction, running the risk that counterinjunctions or other sanctions will eventually preclude Laker from achieving any remedy, if it is ultimately entitled to one under United States law. In either case the policies of both countries are likely to be frustrated at the cost of substantial prejudice to the litigants' rights.

We unhesitatingly conclude that United States jurisdiction to prescribe its antitrust laws must go forward and was therefore properly protected by the district court. Despite the contrary assertions of the British government, there is no indication in this case that the limits of international law are exceeded by either country's exercise of prescriptive jurisdiction. But even so, application of national law may go forward despite a conflict with international law. Both Britain and the United States recognize this rule. It follows *a fortiori* that national laws do not evaporate when counteracted by the legislation of another sovereign.

Although, in the interest of amicable relations, we might be tempted to defuse unilaterally the confrontation by jettisoning our jurisdiction, we could not, for this is not our proper judicial role. The problem in this case is essentially a political one, arising from the vast difference in the political-economic theories of the two governments which has existed for many years. Both nations have jurisdiction to prescribe and adjudicate. Both have asserted that jurisdiction. However, this conflict alone does not place the court in a position to initiate a political compromise based on its decision that United States laws should not be enforced when a foreign jurisdiction, contrary to the domestic court's statutory duty, attempts to eradicate the domestic jurisdiction. Judges are not politicians. The courts are not organs of political compromise. It is impossible in this case, with all the good will manifested by the English Justices and ourselves, to negotiate an extraordinarily long arms-length agreement on the respective impact of our countries' policies regulating anti-competitive business practices.

It is permissible for courts to disengage when judicial scrutiny would implicate inherently unreviewable actions, such as conduct falling within the act of state or sovereign immunity doctrines. But both institutional limitations on the judicial process and Constitutional restrictions on the exercise of judicial power make it unacceptable for the Judiciary to seize the political initiative and determine that legitimate application of American laws must evaporate when challenged by a foreign jurisdiction.

Unilateral abandonment by the Judiciary of legitimately prescribed national law in response to foreign counter-legislation would not materially advance the principles of comity and international accommodation which must form the foundation of any international system comprised of coequal nation states. The British Government's invocation of the Protection of Trading Interests Act to foreclose any proceeding in a non-English forum brought to recover damages for trade injuries caused by unlawful conspiracies is a naked attempt exclusively to reserve by confrontation an area of prescriptive jurisdiction shared concurrently by other nations. This assertion of interdictory jurisdiction propels into the courts a controversy whose eventual termination is restricted to two unsatisfactory alternatives: (1) either one state or the other will eventually capitulate, sacrificing its legitimate interests, or (2) a deadlock will occur to the eventual frustration of both the states' and the litigants' interests. The underlying goal of the legislation is apparently to compel the United States to cede its claims to regulate those aspects of its domestic economy deemed objectionable by the United Kingdom. However, the possibility of a cooperative, mutually profitable compromise by all affected countries is greatly restricted. Granting recognition to this form of coercion will only retard the growth of international mechanisms necessary to resolve satisfactorily the problems generated when radically divergent national policies intersect in an area of concurrent jurisdiction.

Rather than legitimizing the interference and stultifying effects that would follow widespread acceptance of interdictory jurisdiction, we prefer to permit Laker's suit, based as it is on well recognized prescriptive jurisdiction, to go forward as free as possible from the interference caused by foreign antisuit injunctions.

III. Conclusion

The conflict in jurisdiction we confront today has been precipitated by the attempts of another country to insulate its own business entities from the necessity of complying with legislation of our country designed to protect this country's domestic policies. At the root of the conflict are the fundamentally opposed policies of the United States and Great Britain regarding the desirability, scope, and implementation of legislation controlling anticompetitive and restrictive business practices.

No conceivable judicial disposition of this appeal would remove that underlying conflict. Because of the potential deadlock that appears to be developing, the ultimate question is not whether conflicting assertions of national interest must be reconciled, but the proper forum of reconciliation. The resources of the Judiciary are inherently limited when faced with an affirmative decision by the political branches of the government to prescribe specific policies. Absent an explicit directive from Congress, this court has neither the authority nor the institutional resources to weigh the policy and political factors that must be evaluated when resolving competing claims of jurisdiction. In contrast, diplomatic and executive channels are, by definition, designed to exchange, negotiate, and reconcile the problems which accompany the realization of national interests within the sphere of international association. These forums should and, we hope, will be utilized to avoid or resolve conflicts caused by contradictory assertions of concurrent prescriptive jurisdiction.

However, in the absence of some emanation from the Executive Branch, Laker's suit may go forward against appellants. Laker seeks to recover for injuries it allegedly sustained as a result of the defendants' conduct in violation of United States antitrust laws. The complaint alleges a conspiracy to drive out of business a corporation permitted by United States treaty to operate within the United States and conducting substantial business here. If Laker's allegations are proved, the intended and actual effects in the United States are clear since Laker, which was carrying up to one out of every seven transatlantic passengers, was subsequently forced into liquidation. Resolution of Laker's lawsuit would further the interests protected under United States law, since American creditors' interests in open forums, and consumers' interests in free competition may be vindicated.

Under these circumstances, judicial precedent construing the prescriptive jurisdiction of the United States antitrust laws unequivocally holds that the antitrust laws should be applied. That jurisdiction is well within the bounds of reason imposed by international law. Because the factual circumstances of this case made a preliminary injunction imperative to preserve the court's jurisdiction, and because that injunction is not proscribed by the principles of international comity, the district court acted within its discretion.

The decision of the district court is therefore

Affirmed.

COMMENTARY

1. Laker had carried passengers between the United Kingdom and the United States, two nations whose competition policies were in conflict as applied to the events in question.

2. In this case, the U.S. court was confronted with a direct challenge: an injunction by the British court ordering Laker (the plaintiff in the U.S. action) to dismiss the U.S. suit against the parties to the British suit. The policies of the United States and the United Kingdom were in direct conflict and there were no means for the U.S. court to resolve that conflict. In favor of permitting the case to go forward was the United States law which clearly applied, the clear impact upon American consumers, and the court's concern to maintain control over cases pending before it.

Had the impact upon American commerce been less or had the parties had available to them another forum for the resolution of their dispute, the court might have been more inclined to dismiss the action in the interests of comity. *See, e.g.*, *Timberlane Lumber Co. v. Bank of America Nat'l Trust and Savings Ass'n*, 549 F.2d 597 (9th Cir. 1976), excerpted at page 749, *infra*.

3. What kinds of jurisdictional issues were raised in the case? What is prescriptive jusisdiction? What other type of jurisdictional issue was involved in the *Laker* case? Would it be correct to describe the *Laker* case as merely involving a choice of law question? How, if at all, do the questions of comity differ from questions of jurisdiction? Justice Scalia discussed these questions extensively in his dissenting opinion in *Hartford Fire Ins. Co. v. California*, 509 U.S. 764 (1993), below.

4. Would the Foreign Trade Antitrust Improvement Act of 1982, 15 U.S.C. § 6a, reproduced at page 731, *supra*, apply to the events in the *Laker* case? Would that Act require a different result from the one which the court reached? Did the dispute involve the "export trade" or the "import trade"? Do you think that the Act was intended to affect results in cases involving international air transport? What position would the Department of Justice have taken under the 1988 Guidelines if they had then been in effect? Would the 1992 Policy Statement and/or the 1995 Guidelines affect the Department's position as applied to a dispute like the one in *Laker*?

Hartford Fire Insurance Co. v. California

509 U.S. 764 (1993)

Justice SOUTER announced the judgment of the Court and delivered the opinion of the Court with respect to Parts I, II(A), III, and IV, and an opinion with respect to Part II(B) in which Justice WHITE, Justice BLACKMUN and Justice STEVENS join.

The Sherman Act makes every contract, combination, or conspiracy in unreasonable restraint of interstate or foreign commerce illegal. . . . These consolidated cases present questions about the application of that Act to the insurance industry, both here and abroad.

The plaintiffs (respondents here) allege that both domestic and foreign defendants (petitioners here) violated the Sherman Act by engaging in various conspiracies to affect the American insurance market. A group of . . . foreign defendants argues that the principle of international comity requires the District Court to refrain from exercising jurisdiction over certain claims against it. We hold that . . . the principle of international comity does not preclude District Court jurisdiction over the foreign conduct alleged.

I

The two petitions before us stem from consolidated litigation comprising the complaints of 19 States and many private plaintiffs alleging that the defendants, members of the insurance industry, conspired in violation of § 1 of the Sherman Act to restrict the terms of coverage of commercial general liability (CGL) insurance[1] available in the United States. Because the cases come to us on motions to dismiss, we take the allegations of the complaints as true.

A

According to the complaints, the object of the conspiracies was to force certain primary insurers (insurers who sell insurance directly to consumers) to change the terms of their standard CGL insurance policies to conform with the policies the defendant insurers wanted to sell. The defendants wanted four changes.

First, CGL insurance has traditionally been sold in the United States on an "occurrence" basis, through a policy obligating the insurer "to pay or defend claims, whenever made, resulting from an accident or 'injurious exposure to conditions' that occurred during the [specific time] period the policy was in effect." . . . In place of this traditional "occurrence" trigger of coverage, the defendants wanted a "claims-made" trigger, obligating the insurer to pay or defend only those claims made during the policy period. Such a policy has the distinct advantage for the insurer that when the policy period ends without a claim having been made, the insurer can be certain that the policy will not expose it to any further liability. Second, the defendants wanted the "claims-made" policy to have a "retroactive date" provision, which would further restrict coverage to claims based on incidents that occurred after a certain date. Such a provision eliminates the risk that an insurer, by issuing a claims-made policy, would assume liability arising from incidents that occurred before the policy's effective date, but remained undiscovered or caused no immediate harm. Third, CGL insurance has traditionally covered "sudden and accidental" pollution; the defendants wanted to eliminate that coverage. Finally, CGL insurance has traditionally provided that the insurer would bear the legal costs of defending covered claims against the insured without regard to the policy's stated limits of coverage; the defendants wanted legal defense costs to be counted against the stated limits (providing a "legal defense cost cap").

To understand how the defendants are alleged to have pressured the targeted primary insurers to make these changes, one must be aware of two important features of the insurance industry. First, most primary insurers rely on certain outside support services for the type of insurance coverage they wish to sell. Defendant Insurance Services Office, Inc. (ISO), an association of approximately 1,400 domestic property and casualty insurers (including the primary insurer defendants, Hartford Fire Insurance Company, Allstate

[1] CGL insurance provides "coverage for third party casualty damage claims against a purchaser of insurance (the 'insured')." . . .

Insurance Company, CIGNA Corporation, and Aetna Casualty and Surety Company), is the almost exclusive source of support services in this country for CGL insurance. . . . ISO develops standard policy forms and files or lodges them with each State's insurance regulators; most CGL insurance written in the United States is written on these forms. . . . All of the "traditional" features of CGL insurance relevant to this case were embodied in the ISO standard CGL insurance form that had been in use since 1973 (1973 ISO CGL form). . . . For each of its standard policy forms, ISO also supplies actuarial and rating information: it collects, aggregates, interprets, and distributes data on the premiums charged, claims filed and paid, and defense costs expended with respect to each form . . . and on the basis of this data it predicts future loss trends and calculates advisory premium rates. . . . Most ISO members cannot afford to continue to use a form if ISO withdraws these support services. . . .

Second, primary insurers themselves usually purchase insurance to cover a portion of the risk they assume from the consumer. This so-called "reinsurance" may serve at least two purposes, protecting the primary insurer from catastrophic loss, and allowing the primary insurer to sell more insurance than its own financial capacity might otherwise permit. . . . Thus, "[t]he availability of reinsurance affects the ability and willingness of primary insurers to provide insurance to their customers." . . . Insurers who sell reinsurance themselves often purchase insurance to cover part of the risk they assume from the primary insurer; such "retrocessional reinsurance" does for reinsurers what reinsurance does for primary insurers. . . . Many of the defendants here are reinsurers or reinsurance brokers, or play some other specialized role in the reinsurance business; defendant Reinsurance Association of America (RAA) is a trade association of domestic reinsurers.

B

The prehistory of events claimed to give rise to liability starts in 1977, when ISO began the process of revising its 1973 CGL form. . . . For the first time, it proposed two CGL forms (1984 ISO CGL forms), one the traditional "occurrence" type, the other "with a new 'claims-made' trigger." . . . The "claims-made" form did not have a retroactive date provision, however, and both 1984 forms covered "'sudden and accidental' pollution" damage and provided for unlimited coverage of legal defense costs by the insurer. . . . Within the ISO, defendant Hartford Fire Insurance Company objected to the proposed 1984 forms; it desired elimination of the "occurrence" form, a retroactive date provision on the "claims-made" form, elimination of sudden and accidental pollution coverage, and a legal defense cost cap. Defendant Allstate Insurance Company also expressed its desire for a retroactive date provision on the "claims-made" form. . . . Majorities in the relevant ISO committees, however, supported the proposed 1984 CGL forms and rejected the changes proposed by Hartford and Allstate. In December 1983, the ISO Board of Directors approved the proposed 1984 forms, and ISO filed or lodged the forms with state regulators in March 1984. . . .

Dissatisfied with this state of affairs, the defendants began to take other steps to force a change in the terms of coverage of CGL insurance generally available, steps that, the plaintiffs allege, implemented a series of conspiracies in violation of § 1 of the Sherman Act. The plaintiffs recount these steps as a number of separate episodes corresponding to different Claims for Relief in their complaints; because it will become important to distinguish among these counts and the acts and defendants associated with them, we will note these correspondences.

. . . .

The Fifth Claim . . . charge[s] a conspiracy among a group of London reinsurers and brokers to coerce primary insurers in the United States to offer CGL coverage only on a claims-made basis. The reinsurers collectively refused to write new reinsurance contracts for, or to renew long-standing contracts with, "primary . . . insurers unless they were prepared to switch from the occurrence to the claims-made form," . . . ; they also amended their reinsurance contracts to cover only claims made before a "sunset date," thus eliminating reinsurance for claims made on occurrence policies after that date. . . .

The Sixth Claim . . . charge[s] another conspiracy among a somewhat different group of London reinsurers to withhold reinsurance for pollution coverage. The London reinsurers met and agreed that all reinsurance contracts covering North American casualty risks, including CGL risks, would be written with a complete exclusion for pollution liability coverage. . . . In accordance with this agreement, the parties have in fact excluded pollution liability coverage from CGL reinsurance contracts since at least late 1985. . . .

Finally, the Eighth Claim . . . charge[s] a group of London and domestic retrocessional reinsurers[5] with conspiring to withhold retrocessional reinsurance for North American seepage, pollution, and property contamination risks. Those retrocessional reinsurers signed, and have implemented, an agreement to use their "'best endeavors'" to ensure that they would provide such reinsurance for North American risks "only . . . where the original business includes a seepage and pollution exclusion wherever legal and applicable." . . .

. . . .

C

Nineteen States and a number of private plaintiffs filed 36 complaints against the insurers involved in this course of events, charging that the conspiracies described above violated § 1 of the Sherman Act . . . . After the actions had been consolidated . . . the defendants moved to dismiss for failure to state a cause of action, or, in the alternative, for summary judgment. The District Court granted the motions to dismiss . . . [on the ground that the conduct alleged was protected by the McCarran-Ferguson Act]. . . . The District Court also dismissed the three claims that named only certain London-based defendants,[7] invoking international comity and applying the Ninth Circuit's decision in *Timberlane Lumber Co. v. Bank of America, N.T. & S.A.*, 549 F.2d 597 (9th Cir. 1976).

The Court of Appeals reversed. . . . [A]s to the three claims brought solely against foreign defendants, the court applied its *Timberlane* analysis, but concluded that the principle of international comity was no bar to exercising Sherman Act jurisdiction.

We granted *certiorari* in . . . No. 91-1128 to address the application of the Sherman Act to the foreign conduct at issue.[9] . . . We now affirm in part, reverse in part, and remand.

. . . .

---

[5] The California and Connecticut Complaints' Statements of Facts describe this conspiracy as involving "[s]pecialized reinsurers in London and the United States." . . . The Claims for Relief, however, name only London reinsurers; they do not name any of the domestic defendants who are the petitioners in No. 91-1111. . . . Thus, we assume that the domestic reinsurers alleged to be involved in this conspiracy are among the "unnamed co-conspirators" mentioned in the complaints. . . .

[7] These are the Fifth, Sixth, and Eighth Claims for Relief of the California Complaint, and the corresponding Third, Fourth, and Fifth Claims for Relief of the Connecticut Complaint.

[9] The question presented in No. 91-1128 is: "Did the court of appeals properly assess the extraterritorial reach of the U.S. antitrust laws in light of this Court's teachings and contemporary understanding of international law when it held that a U.S. district court may apply U.S. law to the conduct of a foreign insurance market regulated abroad?" Pet. for Cert. in No. 91-1128, p. i.

III

Finally, we take up the question presented by No. 91-1128, whether certain claims against the London reinsurers should have been dismissed as improper applications of the Sherman Act to foreign conduct. The Fifth Claim . . . alleges a violation of § 1 of the Sherman Act by certain London reinsurers who conspired to coerce primary insurers in the United States to offer CGL coverage on a claims-made basis, thereby making "occurrence CGL coverage . . . unavailable in the State of California for many risks." . . . The Sixth Claim . . . alleges that the London reinsurers violated § 1 by a conspiracy to limit coverage of pollution risks in North America, thereby rendering "pollution liability coverage . . . almost entirely unavailable for the vast majority of casualty insurance purchasers in the State of California." . . . The Eighth Claim . . . alleges a further § 1 violation by the London reinsurers who, along with domestic retrocessional reinsurers, conspired to limit coverage of seepage, pollution, and property contamination risks in North America, thereby eliminating such coverage in the State of California. . . .

At the outset, we note that the District Court undoubtedly had jurisdiction of these Sherman Act claims, as the London reinsurers apparently concede. . . . ("Our position is not that the Sherman Act does not apply in the sense that a minimal basis for the exercise of jurisdiction doesn't exist here. Our position is that there are certain circumstances, and that this is one of them, in which the interests of another State are sufficient that the exercise of that jurisdiction should be restrained"). Although the proposition was perhaps not always free from doubt, *see American Banana Co. v. United Fruit Co.*, 213 U.S. 347 (1909), it is well established by now that the Sherman Act applies to foreign conduct that was meant to produce and did in fact produce some substantial effect in the United States. *See Matsushita Elec. Industrial Co. v. Zenith Radio Corp.*, 475 U.S. 574, 582, n.6 (1986); *United States v. Aluminum Co. of America*, 148 F.2d 416, 444 (2d Cir. 1945) (L. Hand, J.); RESTATEMENT (THIRD) OF FOREIGN RELATIONS LAW OF THE UNITED STATES § 415, and Reporters' Note 3 (1987) (hereinafter RESTATEMENT (THIRD) FOREIGN RELATIONS LAW); 1 P. AREEDA & D. TURNER, ANTITRUST LAW ¶ 236 (1978); *cf., Continental Ore Co. v. Union Carbide & Carbon Corp.*, 370 U.S. 690, 704 (1962); *Steele v. Bulova Watch Co.*, 344 U.S. 280, 288 (1952); *United States v. Sisal Sales Corp.*, 274 U.S. 268, 275-276 (1927).[22] Such is the conduct alleged here: that the London reinsurers engaged in unlawful conspiracies to affect the market for insurance in the United States and that their conduct in fact produced substantial effect.[23] *See* 938 F.2d at 933.

---

[22] Justice SCALIA believes that what is at issue in this case is prescriptive, as opposed to subject-matter, jurisdiction. The parties do not question prescriptive jurisdiction, however, and for good reason: it is well established that Congress has exercised such jurisdiction under the Sherman Act. *See* G. BORN & D. WESTIN, INTERNATIONAL CIVIL LITIGATION IN UNITED STATES COURTS 542, n.5 (2d ed. 1992) (Sherman Act is a "prime exampl[e] of the simultaneous exercise of prescriptive jurisdiction and grant of subject matter jurisdiction").

[23] Under § 402 of the Foreign Trade Antitrust Improvements Act of 1982 (FTAIA), . . . the Sherman Act does not apply to conduct involving foreign trade or commerce, other than import trade or import commerce, unless "such conduct has a direct, substantial, and reasonably foreseeable effect" on domestic or import commerce. . . . The FTAIA was intended to exempt from the Sherman Act export transactions that did not injure the United States economy, *see* H.R. Rep. No. 97-686, pp. 2-3, 9-10 (1982); P. AREEDA & H. HOVENKAMP, ANTITRUST LAW ¶ 236a, pp. 296-297 (Supp.1992), and it is unclear how it might apply to the conduct alleged here. Also unclear is whether the Act's "direct, substantial, and reasonably foreseeable effect" standard amends existing law or merely codifies it. *See id.*, ¶ 236a, p. 297. We need not address these questions here. Assuming that the FTAIA's standard affects this case, and assuming further that that standard differs from the prior law, the conduct alleged plainly meets its requirements.

According to the London reinsurers, the District Court should have declined to exercise such jurisdiction under the principle of international comity.[24] The Court of Appeals agreed that courts should look to that principle in deciding whether to exercise jurisdiction under the Sherman Act. . . . This availed the London reinsurers nothing, however. To be sure, the Court of Appeals believed that "application of [American] antitrust laws to the London reinsurance market 'would lead to significant conflict with English law and policy,'" and that "[s]uch a conflict, unless outweighed by other factors, would by itself be reason to decline exercise of jurisdiction." . . . But other factors, in the court's view, including the London reinsurers' express purpose to affect United States commerce and the substantial nature of the effect produced, outweighed the supposed conflict and required the exercise of jurisdiction in this case. . . .

When it enacted the Foreign Trade Antitrust Improvements Act of 1982 (FTAIA), . . . Congress expressed no view on the question whether a court with Sherman Act jurisdiction should ever decline to exercise such jurisdiction on grounds of international comity. *See* H.R. Rep. No. 97-686, p. 13 (1982) ("If a court determines that the requirements for subject matter jurisdiction are met, [the FTAIA] would have no effect on the court['s] ability to employ notions of comity . . . or otherwise to take account of the international character of the transaction") (citing *Timberlane*). We need not decide that question here, however, for even assuming that in a proper case a court may decline to exercise Sherman Act jurisdiction over foreign conduct (or, as Justice SCALIA would put it, may conclude by the employment of comity analysis in the first instance that there is no jurisdiction), international comity would not counsel against exercising jurisdiction in the circumstances alleged here.

The only substantial question in this case is whether "there is in fact a true conflict between domestic and foreign law." . . . The London reinsurers contend that applying the Act to their conduct would conflict significantly with British law, and the British Government, appearing before us as *amicus curiae*, concurs. . . . They assert that Parliament has established a comprehensive regulatory regime over the London reinsurance market and that the conduct alleged here was perfectly consistent with British law and policy. But this is not to state a conflict. "[T]he fact that conduct is lawful in the state in which it took place will not, of itself, bar application of the United States antitrust laws," even where the foreign state has a strong policy to permit or encourage such conduct. RESTATEMENT (THIRD) FOREIGN RELATIONS LAW § 415, Comment j; *see Continental Ore Co.*, *supra*, 370 U.S. at 706-707. No conflict exists, for these purposes, "where a person subject to regulation by two states can comply with the laws of both." RESTATEMENT (THIRD) FOREIGN RELATIONS LAW § 403, Comment e.[25]

---

[24] Justice SCALIA contends that comity concerns figure into the prior analysis whether jurisdiction exists under the Sherman Act. This contention is inconsistent with the general understanding that the Sherman Act covers foreign conduct producing a substantial intended effect in the United States, and that concerns of comity come into play, if at all, only after a court has determined that the acts complained of are subject to Sherman Act jurisdiction. *See United States v. Aluminum Co. of America*, 148 F.2d 416, 444 (2nd Cir. 1945) ("it follows from what we have . . . said that [the agreements at issue] were unlawful [under the Sherman Act], though made abroad, if they were intended to affect imports and did affect them"); *Mannington Mills, Inc. v. Congoleum Corp.*, 595 F.2d 1287, 1294 (3d Cir. 1979) (once court determines that jurisdiction exists under the Sherman Act, question remains whether comity precludes its exercise); H.R. Rep. No. 97-686, p. 13 (1982). *But cf.*, *Timberlane Lumber Co. v. Bank of America, N.T. & S.A.*, 549 F.2d 597, 613 (9th Cir. 1976); 1 J. ATWOOD & K. BREWSTER, ANTITRUST AND AMERICAN BUSINESS ABROAD 166 (1981). In any event, the parties conceded jurisdiction at oral argument . . . and we see no need to address this contention here.

[25] Justice SCALIA says that we put the cart before the horse in citing this authority, for he argues it may be apposite only after a determination that jurisdiction over the foreign acts is reasonable. . . . But whatever the order of cart and horse, conflict in this sense is the only substantial issue before the Court.

Since the London reinsurers do not argue that British law requires them to act in some fashion prohibited by the law of the United States, . . . or claim that their compliance with the laws of both countries is otherwise impossible, we see no conflict with British law. *See* RESTATEMENT (THIRD) FOREIGN RELATIONS LAW § 403, Comment e, § 415, Comment j. We have no need in this case to address other considerations that might inform a decision to refrain from the exercise of jurisdiction on grounds of international comity.

IV

The judgment of the Court of Appeals is affirmed in part and reversed in part, and the case is remanded for further proceedings consistent with this opinion.

It is so ordered.

Justice SCALIA delivered the opinion of the Court with respect to Part I, and delivered a dissenting opinion with respect to Part II, in which Justice O'CONNOR, Justice KENNEDY, and Justice THOMAS have joined.

. . . .

II

The petitioners in No. 91-1128, various British corporations and other British subjects, argue that certain of the claims against them constitute an inappropriate extraterritorial application of the Sherman Act.[8] It is important to distinguish two distinct questions raised by this petition: whether the District Court had jurisdiction, and whether the Sherman Act reaches the extraterritorial conduct alleged here. On the first question, I believe that the District Court had subject-matter jurisdiction over the Sherman Act claims against all the defendants (personal jurisdiction is not contested). The respondents asserted nonfrivolous claims under the Sherman Act, and 28 U.S.C. § 1331 vests district courts with subject-matter jurisdiction over cases "arising under" federal statutes. As precedents such as *Lauritzen v. Larsen*, 345 U.S. 571 (1953), make clear, that is sufficient to establish the District Court's jurisdiction over these claims. *Lauritzen* involved a Jones Act claim brought by a foreign sailor against a foreign shipowner. The shipowner contested the District Court's jurisdiction . . . , apparently on the grounds that the Jones Act did not govern the dispute between the foreign parties to the action. Though ultimately agreeing with the shipowner that the Jones Act did not apply . . . , the Court held that the District Court had jurisdiction.

> "As frequently happens, a contention that there is some barrier to granting plaintiff's claim is cast in terms of an exception to jurisdiction of subject matter. A cause of action under our law was asserted here, and the court had power to determine whether it was or was not founded in law and in fact." 345 U.S. at 575.

See also Romero v. International Terminal Operating Co., 358 U.S. 354, 359 (1959).

The second question—the extraterritorial reach of the Sherman Act—has nothing to do with the jurisdiction of the courts. It is a question of substantive law turning on whether, in enacting the Sherman Act, Congress asserted regulatory power over the challenged conduct. . . . If a plaintiff fails to prevail on this issue, the court does not dismiss the claim for want of subject-matter jurisdiction—want of power to adjudicate; rather, it decides the

---

8 The counts at issue in this case are the Fifth, Sixth and Eighth Claims for Relief in the California Complaint. . . .

claim, ruling on the merits that the plaintiff has failed to state a cause of action under the relevant statute. . . .

There is, however, a type of "jurisdiction" relevant to determining the extraterritorial reach of a statute; it is known as "legislative jurisdiction," . . . or "jurisdiction to prescribe," 1 RESTATEMENT (THIRD) OF FOREIGN RELATIONS LAW OF THE UNITED STATES 235 (1987) (hereinafter RESTATEMENT (THIRD)). This refers to "the authority of a state to make its law applicable to persons or activities," and is quite a separate matter from "jurisdiction to adjudicate." . . . There is no doubt, of course, that Congress possesses legislative jurisdiction over the acts alleged in this complaint: Congress has broad power under Article I, § 8, cl. 3 "[t]o regulate Commerce with foreign Nations," and this Court has repeatedly upheld its power to make laws applicable to persons or activities beyond our territorial boundaries where United States interests are affected. . . . But the question in this case is whether, and to what extent, Congress has exercised that undoubted legislative jurisdiction in enacting the Sherman Act.

Two canons of statutory construction are relevant in this inquiry. The first is the "long-standing principle of American law 'that legislation of Congress, unless a contrary intent appears, is meant to apply only within the territorial jurisdiction of the United States.'" . . . Applying that canon in *Aramco* [*EEOC v. Arabian American Oil Co.*, 499 U.S. 244 (1991)], we held that the version of Title VII of the Civil Rights Act of 1964 then in force, 42 U.S.C. §§ 2000e-2000e-17 (1988 ed.), did not extend outside the territory of the United States even though the statute contained broad provisions extending its prohibitions to, for example, "any activity, business, or industry in commerce." . . . We held such "boilerplate language" to be an insufficient indication to override the presumption against extraterritoriality. . . . The Sherman Act contains similar "boilerplate language," and if the question were not governed by precedent, it would be worth considering whether that presumption controls the outcome here. We have, however, found the presumption to be overcome with respect to our antitrust laws; it is now well established that the Sherman Act applies extraterritorially. *See Matsushita Elec. Industrial Co. v. Zenith Radio Corp.*, 475 U.S. 574, 582, n.6 (1986); *Continental Ore Co. v. Union Carbide & Carbon Corp.*, 370 U.S. 690, 704 (1962); *see also United States v. Aluminum Co. of America*, 148 F.2d 416 (2d Cir. 1945).

But if the presumption against extraterritoriality has been overcome or is otherwise inapplicable, a second canon of statutory construction becomes relevant: "[A]n act of congress ought never to be construed to violate the law of nations if any other possible construction remains." *Murray v. The Charming Betsy*, 2 Cranch 64, 118 (1804) (Marshall, C.J.). This canon is "wholly independent" of the presumption against extraterritoriality. . . . It is relevant to determining the substantive reach of a statute because "the law of nations," or customary international law, includes limitations on a nation's exercise of its jurisdiction to prescribe. *See* RESTATEMENT (THIRD) §§ 401-416. Though it clearly has constitutional authority to do so, Congress is generally presumed not to have exceeded those customary international-law limits on jurisdiction to prescribe.

Consistent with that presumption, this and other courts have frequently recognized that, even where the presumption against extraterritoriality does not apply, statutes should not be interpreted to regulate foreign persons or conduct if that regulation would conflict with principles of international law. For example, in *Romero v. International Terminal Operating Co.*, 358 U.S. 354 (1959), the plaintiff, a Spanish sailor who had been injured while working aboard a Spanish-flag and Spanish-owned vessel, filed a Jones Act claim against his Spanish employer. The presumption against extraterritorial application of federal statutes was inapplicable to the case, as the actionable tort had occurred in American waters. . . . The Court nonetheless stated that, "in the absence of contrary congressional direction," it would apply "principles of choice of law that are consonant with the needs of a general federal maritime law and with due recognition of our self-regarding respect for the relevant interests of foreign nations in the regulation of maritime commerce as part of the legitimate concern of the international community." . . . "The controlling considerations" in this choice-of-law analysis were "the interacting interests of the United States and of foreign countries." . . .

Romero referred to, and followed, the choice-of-law analysis set forth in *Lauritzen v. Larsen*, 345 U.S. 571 (1953). As previously mentioned, *Lauritzen* also involved a Jones Act claim brought by a foreign sailor against a foreign employer. The *Lauritzen* Court recognized the basic problem: "If [the Jones Act were] read literally, Congress has conferred an American right of action which requires nothing more than that plaintiff be 'any seaman who shall suffer personal injury in the course of his employment.'" . . . The solution it adopted was to construe the statute "to apply only to areas and transactions in which *American law would be considered operative under prevalent doctrines of international law*.". . . (emphasis added). To support application of international law to limit the facial breadth of the statute, the Court relied upon—of course—Chief Justice Marshall's statement in *The Charming Betsy* quoted *supra* . . . . It then set forth "several factors which, alone or in combination, are generally conceded to influence choice of law to govern a tort claim." . . .

Lauritzen, *Romero*, and *McCulloch* [*McCulloch v. Sociedad Nacional de Marineros de Honduras*, 372 U.S. 10 (1963)] were maritime cases, but we have recognized the principle that the scope of generally worded statutes must be construed in light of international law in other areas as well. . . . More specifically, the principle was expressed in *United States v. Aluminum Co. of America*, 148 F.2d 416 (2d Cir. 1945), the decision that established the extraterritorial reach of the Sherman Act. In his opinion for the court, Judge Learned Hand cautioned "we are not to read general words, such as those in [the Sherman] Act, without regard to the limitations customarily observed by nations upon the exercise of their powers; limitations which generally correspond to those fixed by the 'Conflict of Laws.'" . . .

More recent lower court precedent has also tempered the extraterritorial application of the Sherman Act with considerations of "international comity." *See Timberlane Lumber Co. v. Bank of America, N.T. & S.A.*, 549 F.2d 597, 608-615 (9th Cir. 1976); *Mannington Mills, Inc. v. Congoleum Corp.*, 595 F.2d 1287, 1294-1298 (3d Cir. 1979); *Montreal Trading Ltd. v. Amax Inc.*, 661 F.2d 864, 869-871 (10th Cir. 1981); *Laker Airways v. Sabena, Belgian World Airlines*, 235 U.S. App. D.C. 207, 236, and n.109, 731 F.2d 909, 938, and n.109 (1984); *see also Pacific Seafarers, Inc. v. Pacific Far East Line, Inc.*, 131 U.S. App. D.C. 226, 236, and n.31, 404 F.2d 804, 814, and n.31 (1968). The "comity" they refer to is not the comity of courts, whereby judges decline to exercise jurisdiction over matters more appropriately adjudged elsewhere, but rather what might be termed "prescriptive comity": the respect sovereign nations afford each other by limiting the reach of their laws. That comity is exercised by legislatures when they enact laws, and courts assume it has been exercised when they come to interpreting the scope of laws their legislatures have enacted. It is a traditional component of choice-of-law theory. *See* J. STORY, COMMENTARIES ON THE CONFLICT OF LAWS § 38 (1834) (distinguishing between the "comity of the courts" and the "comity of nations," and defining the latter as "the true foundation and extent of the obligation of the laws of one nation within the territories of another"). Comity in this sense includes the choice-of-law principles that, "in the absence of contrary congressional direction," are assumed to be incorporated into our substantive laws having extraterritorial reach. [citing *Romero*, *Lauritzen*, and *Hilton v. Guyot*, 159 U.S. 113, 162-166 (1895).] Considering comity in this way is just part of determining whether the Sherman Act prohibits the conduct at issue.[9]

In sum, the practice of using international law to limit the extraterritorial reach of statutes is firmly established in our jurisprudence. In proceeding to apply that practice to the present case, I shall rely on the RESTATEMENT (THIRD) OF FOREIGN RELATIONS LAW for the relevant principles of international law. Its standards appear fairly supported in the decisions of this Court construing international choice-of-law principles (*Lauritzen*, *Romero*, and *McCulloch*) and in the decisions of other federal courts, especially *Timberlane*. Whether the RESTATEMENT precisely reflects international law in every detail matters little here, as I believe this case would be resolved the same way under virtually any conceivable test that takes account of foreign regulatory interests.

Under the RESTATEMENT, a nation having some "basis" for jurisdiction to prescribe law should nonetheless refrain from exercising that jurisdiction "with respect to a person or activity having connections with another state when the exercise of such jurisdiction is unreasonable." RESTATEMENT (THIRD) § 403(1). The "reasonableness" inquiry turns on a number of factors including, but not limited to: "the extent to which the activity takes place within the territory [of the regulating state]," *id.* § 403(2)(a); "the connections, such as nationality, residence, or economic activity, between the regulating state and the person principally responsible for the activity to be regulated," *id.* § 403(2)(b); "the character of the activity to be regulated, the importance of regulation to the regulating state, the extent to which other states regulate such activities, and the degree to which the desirability of such regulation is generally accepted," *id.* § 403(2)(c); "the extent to which another state may have an interest in regulating the activity," *id.* § 403(2)(g); and "the likelihood of conflict with regulation by another state," *id.* § 403(2)(h). Rarely would these factors point more clearly against application of United States law. The activity relevant to the counts at issue here took place primarily in the United Kingdom, and the defendants in these counts are British corporations and British subjects having their principal place of business or residence outside the United States.[10] Great Britain has established a comprehensive regulatory scheme governing the London reinsurance markets, and clearly has a heavy "interest in regulating the activity," *id.* § 403(2)(g). *See* 938 F.2d at 932-933; *In re Insurance Antitrust Litigation*, 723 F. Supp. 464, 487-488 (N.D. Cal. 1989); *see also* J. BUTLER & R. MERKIN, REINSURANCE LAW A.1.1-02 (1992). Finally, § 2(b) of the McCarran-Ferguson Act allows state regulatory statutes to override the Sherman Act in the insurance field, subject only to the narrow "boycott" exception set forth in § 3(b)—suggesting that "the importance

---

9 Some antitrust courts, including the Court of Appeals in the present case, have mistaken the comity at issue for the "comity of courts," which has led them to characterize the question presented as one of "abstention," that is, whether they should "exercise or decline jurisdiction." *Mannington Mills, Inc. v. Congoleum Corp.*, 595 F.2d 1287, 1294, 1296 (3d Cir. 1979); *see also In re Insurance Antitrust Litigation*, 938 F.2d 919, 932 (9th Cir. 1991). As I shall discuss, that seems to be the error the Court has fallen into today. Because courts are generally reluctant to refuse the exercise of conferred jurisdiction, confusion on this seemingly theoretical point can have the very practical consequence of greatly expanding the extraterritorial reach of the Sherman Act.

10 Some of the British corporations are subsidiaries of American corporations, and the Court of Appeals held that "[t]he interests of Britain are at least diminished where the parties are subsidiaries of American corporations." 938 F.2d at 933. In effect, the Court of Appeals pierced the corporate veil in weighing the interests at stake. I do not think that was proper.

of regulation to the [United States]," *id.* § 403(2)(c), is slight. Considering these factors, I think it unimaginable that an assertion of legislative jurisdiction by the United States would be considered reasonable, and therefore it is inappropriate to assume, in the absence of statutory indication to the contrary, that Congress has made such an assertion.

It is evident from what I have said that the Court's comity analysis, which proceeds as though the issue is whether the courts should "decline to exercise . . . jurisdiction," . . . rather than whether the Sherman Act covers this conduct, is simply misdirected. I do not at all agree, moreover, with the Court's conclusion that the issue of the substantive scope of the Sherman Act is not in the case. . . . To be sure, the parties did not make a clear distinction between adjudicative jurisdiction and the scope of the statute. Parties often do not, as we have observed (and have declined to punish with procedural default) before. . . . It is not realistic, and also not helpful, to pretend that the only really relevant issue in this case is not before us. In any event, if one erroneously chooses, as the Court does, to make adjudicative jurisdiction (or, more precisely, abstention) the vehicle for taking account of the needs of prescriptive comity, the Court still gets it wrong. It concludes that no "true conflict" counseling nonapplication of United States law (or rather, as it thinks, United States judicial jurisdiction) exists unless compliance with United States law would constitute a *violation* of another country's law. . . . That breathtakingly broad proposition, which contradicts the many cases discussed earlier, will bring the Sherman Act and other laws into sharp and unnecessary conflict with the legitimate interests of other countries—particularly our closest trading partners.

In the sense in which the term "conflic[t]" was used in *Lauritzen* . . . , and is generally understood in the field of conflicts of laws, there is clearly a conflict in this case. The petitioners here, like the defendant in *Lauritzen*, were not compelled by any foreign law to take their allegedly wrongful actions, but that no more precludes a conflict-of-laws analysis here than it did there. . . . Where applicable foreign and domestic law provide different substantive rules of decision to govern the parties' dispute, a conflict-of-laws analysis is necessary. *See generally* R. WEINTRAUB, COMMENTARY ON CONFLICT OF LAWS 2-3 (1980); RESTATEMENT (FIRST) OF CONFLICT OF LAWS § 1, Comment *c* and Illustrations (1934).

Literally the *only* support that the Court adduces for its position is § 403 of the RESTATEMENT (THIRD) OF FOREIGN RELATIONS LAW—or more precisely Comment *e* to that provision, which states:

> "Subsection (3) [which says that a state should defer to another state if that state's interest is clearly greater] applies only when one state requires what another prohibits, or where compliance with the regulations of two states exercising jurisdiction consistently with this section is otherwise impossible. It does not apply where a person subject to regulation by two states can comply with the laws of both. . . ."

The Court has completely misinterpreted this provision. Subsection (3) of § 403 (requiring one State to defer to another in the limited circumstances just described) comes into play only after subsection (1) of § 403 has been complied with—*i.e.*, after it has been determined that the exercise of jurisdiction by *both* of the two states is not "unreasonable." That prior question is answered by applying the factors (inter alia) set forth in subsection (2) of § 403, that is, precisely the factors that I have discussed in text and that the Court rejects.[11]

---

[11] The Court skips directly to subsection (3) of § 403, apparently on the authority of Comment *j* to § 415 of the RESTATEMENT (THIRD). . . . But the preceding commentary to § 415 makes clear that "[a]ny exercise of [leg-

. . . .

I would reverse the judgment of the Court of Appeals on this issue, and remand to the District Court with instructions to dismiss for failure to state a claim on the three counts at issue in No. 91-1128.

COMMENTARY

1. In the Ninth Circuit, Judge Noonan had decided that comity did not require dismissal of the action against the British defendants. In so doing, he employed an analysis which he found in *Timberlane Lumber Co. v. Bank of America Nat'l Trust & Savings Ass'n*, 549 F.2d 597 (9th Cir. 1976), an earlier decision of the Ninth Circuit. *Timberlane* and *Mannington Mills, Inc. v. Congoleum Corp.*, 595 F.2d 1287 (3d Cir. 1979), both employed extensive balancing tests to resolve the issue of comity. These decisions are reviewed below.

a. *Timberlane Lumber Co. v. Bank of America Nat'l Trust & Savings Ass'n*, 549 F.2d 597 (9th Cir. 1976). In *Hartford Fire Insurance*, the Ninth Circuit followed the approach which it had adopted fifteen years earlier in *Timberlane*, although with the caveat that its use of the *Timberlane* analysis would necessarily be affected by the enactment of the Foreign Trade Antitrust Improvements Act in the intervening years.

In *Timberlane*, the plaintiff was an Oregon partnership involved, *inter alia*, in the wholesale distribution of lumber in the United States. Timberlane alleged that the Bank of America had conspired (through its Honduran subsidiaries) to prevent Timberlane from milling lumber in Honduras and exporting it to the United States. In that case, the Ninth Circuit held that the U.S. antitrust laws should not necessarily be applied to activities abroad, even though those activities produced "a direct and substantial effect" on American commerce.

> An effect on United States commerce, although necessary to the exercise of jurisdiction under the antitrust laws, is alone not a sufficient basis on which to determine whether American authority should be asserted in a given case as a matter of international comity and fairness. In some cases, the application of the direct and substantial test in the international context might open the door too widely by sanctioning jurisdiction over an action when these considerations would indicate dismissal. At other times, it may fail in the other direction, dismissing a case for which comity and fairness do not require forebearance, thus closing the jurisdictional door too tightly, for the Sherman Act does reach some restraints

---

islative] jurisdiction under this section is subject to the requirement of reasonableness" set forth in § 403(2). RESTATEMENT (THIRD) § 415, Comment *a*. Comment *j* refers back to the conflict analysis set forth in § 403(3) which, as noted above, comes after the reasonableness analysis of § 403(2).

> which do not have both a direct and substantial effect on the foreign commerce of the United States.

549 F.2d at 613.

The court, accordingly, adopted a "jurisdictional rule of reason," the components of which were discussed and applied by the Court of Appeals in the *Hartford Fire Insurance* case. According to the *Timberlane* court:

> The elements to be weighed include the degree of conflict with foreign law or policy, the nationality or allegiance of the parties and the locations or principal places of business of corporations, the extent to which enforcement by either state can be expected to achieve compliance, the relative significance of effects on the United States as compared with those elsewhere, the extent to which there is explicit purpose to harm or affect American commerce, the foreseeability of such effect, and the relative importance to the violations charged of conduct within the United States as compared with conduct abroad.

Id. at 614.

b. *Mannington Mills, Inc. v. Congoleum Corp.*, 595 F.2d 1287 (3d Cir. 1979). In this case, the plaintiff Mannington Mills charged that Congoleum had obtained foreign patents by fraud and enforced them abroad. Mannington alleged that these activities constituted a violation of the U.S. antitrust laws, on the theory that similar activities performed in the United States would be antitrust violations. Influenced by the Ninth Circuit's decision in *Timberlane*, the Third Circuit indicated that a broad inquiry into a number of factors would be required to determine whether a U.S. court should apply the U.S. antitrust laws to the conflict before it:

> In *Timberlane Lumber Co. v. Bank of America* . . . the Court of Appeals for the Ninth Circuit adopted a balancing process in determining whether extraterritorial jurisdiction should be exercised, an approach with which we find ourselves in substantial agreement. The factors we believe should be considered include:
>
> 1. Degree of conflict with foreign law or policy;
> 2. Nationality of the parties;
> 3. Relative importance of the alleged violation of conduct here compared to that abroad;
> 4. Availability of a remedy abroad and the pendency of litigation there;
> 5. Existence of intent to harm or affect American commerce and its foreseeability;
> 6. Possible effect upon foreign relations if the court exercises jurisdiction and grants relief;
> 7. If relief is granted, whether a party will be placed in the position of being forced to perform an act illegal in either country or be under conflicting requirements by both countries;

8. Whether the court can make its order effective;
9. Whether an order for relief would be acceptable in this country if made by the foreign nation under similar circumstances;
10. Whether a treaty with the affected nation has addressed the issue.

The Court of Appeals remanded for evidence on these factors. *Id.* at 1297-98.

2. How did the majority view the issues posed by Justice Scalia? What was the majority's position on the prescriptive jurisdiction issue? Did the majority believe that the substantive application of the Sherman Act to the British reinsurers was clear?

3. Did the majority understand the "comity" issue raised by the British reinsurers as involving the "comity of courts" as opposed to "prescriptive comity"? How did Justice Scalia characterize the British reinsurers' contention?

4. Under which approach—that of the majority or of Justice Scalia—would the courts become more involved in balancing the interests of foreign states against those of the United States? What standards did Justice Scalia suggest that the courts use in this balancing? To what extent is it appropriate for the courts to balance the interest of the United States in promoting competition against the interest of other nations in restraining it?

5. How, if at all, has *Hartford Fire Insurance* changed the law involving comity considerations in antitrust cases from the understandings expressed in *Timberlane* and *Mannington Mills*? Was Judge Noonan correct (in his opinion for the Ninth Circuit in *Hartford Fire Insurance*) that *Timberlane* had to be deemed modified by the Foreign Antitrust Improvements Act? How did the Foreign Antitrust Improvements Act modify *Timberlane*?

6. In its Antitrust Guidelines for International Operations, the Department of Justice has expressed its views on how policy conflicts with foreign nations should be resolved in the context of government antitrust enforcement actions. The Guidelines suggest certain constraints on the judicial role in resolving these matters. See the excerpt from the Guidelines below.

7. The majority opinion has been criticized for its emphasis on subject matter jurisdiction as a guide for judicial determination of when extraterritorial conduct is within the scope of the antitrust laws. *See* John A. Trenor, *Jurisdiction and the Extraterritorial Application of Antitrust Laws after* Hartford Fire, 62 U. CHI. L. REV. 1583, 1606 (1995). Trenor writes:

> ... [T]he subject matter jurisdiction characterization is inherently overly discretionary, and its analytic framework offers little guidance to courts. Under this analysis, the requirement of subject matter jurisdiction is

> solely within the court's discretion, guided only by notions of international comity. . . . Courts are told to balance U.S. and foreign interests to determine whether extraterritorial application would promote both "fairness" and . . . international "comity."

8. Are the Department's views consistent with those expressed by Justice Souter for the majority in the *Hartford Fire Insurance* case? With those of Justice Scalia? With the court in *Laker*? in *Timberlane*? in *Mannington Mills*?

9. The above excerpt should be read in conjunction with the Department's 1992 Policy Statement (page 732, *supra*) and § 3.122 of the 1995 Guidelines which state that the Department will also enforce the antitrust laws to protect U.S. exporters.

10. In which kinds of cases does the Department believe that its own weighing of the interests of a foreign sovereign against those of the United States ought to be determinative? What is the Department's rationale for this belief?

Department of Justice and Federal Trade Commission, Antitrust Guidelines for International Operations (April 5, 1995)

. . . .

In performing a comity analysis, the Agencies take into account all relevant factors. Among others, these may include (1) the relative significance to the alleged violation of conduct within the United States, as compared to conduct abroad; (2) the nationality of the persons involved in or affected by the conduct; (3) the presence or absence of a purpose to affect U.S. consumers, markets, or exporters; (4) the relative significance and foreseeability of the effects of the conduct on the United States as compared to the effects abroad; (5) the existence of reasonable expectations that would be furthered or defeated by the action; (6) the degree of conflict with foreign law or articulated foreign economic policies; (7) the extent to which the enforcement authorities of another country with respect to the same persons, including remedies resulting from those activities, may be affected; and (8) the effectiveness of foreign enforcement as compared to U.S. enforcement action.

The relative weight that each factor should be given depends on the facts and circumstances of each case. With respect to the factor concerning conflict with foreign law, the Supreme Court made clear in *Hartford Fire* that no conflict exists for purposes of an international comity analysis in the courts if the person subject to regulation by two states can comply with the laws of both. . . .

The Agencies also take full account of comity factors beyond whether there is a conflict with foreign law. In deciding whether or not to challenge an alleged antitrust violation, the Agencies would, as part of a comity analysis, consider whether one country encourages a certain course of conduct, leaves parties free to choose among different strategies or prohibits some of those strategies. In addition, the Agencies take into account the effect of their enforcement activities on related enforcement activities of a foreign antitrust authority. For example, the Agencies would consider whether their activities would interfere with or reinforce the objectives of the foreign proceeding, including any remedies contemplated or obtained by the foreign antitrust authority.

. . . In cases where the United States decides to prosecute an antitrust action, such a decision represents a determination by the Executive Branch that the importance of antitrust enforcement outweighs any relevant foreign policy concerns. The Department does not believe that it is the role of the courts to "second-guess the executive branch's judgment as to the proper role of comity concerns under these circumstances." To date, no Commission cases have presented the issue of the degree of deference that courts should give to the Commission's comity decisions. It is important also to note that in disputes between private parties, many courts are willing to undertake a comity analysis.[79]

4. The Act of State and Related Doctrines

O.N.E. Shipping Ltd. v. Flota Mercante Grancolombiana, S.A.

830 F.2d 449 (2d Cir. 1987)

MILTON POLLACK, Senior District Judge:

This appeal invokes the judicially created act of state doctrine on the anti-competitive effect of a foreign sovereign's cargo reservation laws—the laws of the Republic of Colombia—which require that 50% of licensed imports of liquid bulk cargo ("LBC") be transported on Colombian owned vessels, or on vessels chartered by a Colombian company.

The district court dismissed this suit brought under the Sherman Antitrust Act, 15 U.S.C. Sections 1, 2 (1982), on the ground that a federal court should not exercise jurisdiction hereof because "Colombian interests outweigh whatever antitrust enforcement interests the United States may have in this case as a matter of law." We affirm the dismissal.

. . . .

BACKGROUND

In the late 1960s, Colombia passed a series of "Cargo Reservation Laws." The purpose of these laws was to favor Colombian shipping companies and the Colombian economy by requiring that imports and exports of certain types of cargo be transported exclusively by Colombian carriers. After 1969, those laws required that the first 50% of each licensed shipment imported into Colombia on trade routes served by Colombian carriers be transported on Colombian-owned vessels or on vessels chartered by a Colombian company. As the result of a delicate compromise between the United States and Colombia, U.S. flag lines were not subject to the protection laws.

Appellant O.N.E. Shipping Ltd. ("O.N.E."), a Bermuda corporation, and its predecessor in interest, Overseas Liquid Gas, Inc., a U.S. corporation, had offered regular liquid bulk cargo tanker service from U.S. gulf ports to Central and South America. Before 1973 there were no Colombian vessels capable of carrying LBC, so shipping to Colombia of this product was unaffected by the Colombia cargo reservation laws. This situation changed in 1973 and thereafter.

Appellee Flota Mercante Grancolombiana, S.A. ("Flota"), a Colombia shipping line substantially owned by the National Federation of Coffee Growers of Colombia, is a public organization and is "an agency or instrumentality" of the Colombian Government within the meaning of the Foreign Sovereign Immunities Act of 1976, 28 U.S.C. Section

[79] *See, e.g., Timberlane Lumber Co. v. Bank of America*, 549 F.2d 597 (9th Cir. 1976).

1603(b). Flota is Colombia's national line. Flota had no specially equipped LBC tankers of its own.

In 1973, to accommodate the needs of Colombian importers, Flota entered into a chartering agreement (revised in 1976) with appellee Andino Chemical Shipping, Inc., a Panamanian corporation and carrier of LBC, to handle Colombia's Atlantic coast trade.

In 1976, Flota entered into a similar chartering agreement with appellee Maritima Transligra, S.A. ("Transligra"), an Ecuadoran corporation, to charter the latter's tankers for use in Colombia's Pacific coast trade.

As required by Colombian law, Flota's chartering agreements were filed with and approved by the Colombian Government, enabling the non-Colombian tankers to receive the preferences accorded to Colombian flag vessels under the cargo reservation laws. Together, the three appellees have captured up to 89% of the shipping imports of LBC into Colombia and O.N.E. has been virtually shut out therefrom.

As mentioned above, following a bilateral negotiation, no restrictions were placed by Colombia on the carriage of products imported from the United States if carried on United States flag vessels.

In April 1977, Flota, Andino and Transligra sought approval of their chartering agreements from the United States Federal Maritime Commission ("FMC") which would provide an exemption from U.S. antitrust laws. The FMC conditionally disapproved the agreements and subsequently conducted an investigation and a hearing. On May 23, 1983, the Administrative Law Judge ("ALJ") also disapproved the agreements. The ALJ found that Flota had attained near monopoly control over the LBC service to Colombia and that the agreements were prospectively unlawful. On appeal, the FMC affirmed the ALJ's order of disapproval and ruled that the agreements were anticompetitive, detrimental to United States commerce, contrary to the public interest and artificially increased transportation rates. The FMC ordered appellees to cease and desist. With these rulings in hand O.N.E. brought this antitrust action in the district court below.

O.N.E. charges appellees with unlawful concerted refusal to deal, conspiracy to exclude competitors, unlawful exclusive dealing, conspiracy to fix prices, conspiracy to divide markets and allocate customers, and attempt and conspiracy to monopolize.

DISCUSSION

O.N.E.'s antitrust suit represents a direct challenge to Colombia's cargo reservation laws and to the legality of appellees' space chartering agreements under those laws. The laws were designed to promote the development of a strong Colombian merchant marine and to assist Colombia's economic development.

Among other purposes, the cargo reservation laws enable the Colombian Government to monitor the allocation of the resources of Colombian shipping companies, to determine whether particular trade routes could prove harmful to the country's economy and to consider whether an applicant would provide effective, regular and continuous service.

The Colombian Government has repeatedly made known to the United States Department of State, as well as to the Federal Maritime Commission, its strong support for the cargo reservation laws and the chartering agreements thereunder among the appellees.

Applying the balancing tests of *Timberlane Lumber Co. v. Bank of America, N.T. & S.A.*, 549 F.2d 597 (9th Cir.1976) and *Mannington Mills, Inc. v. Congoleum Corp.*, 595 F.2d 1287 (3d Cir.1979) the district court concluded that because of Colombia's strong interest in its protectionist legislation and because of the Colombian government's ownership interest in Flota through the National Federation of Coffee Growers, there would be probable adverse effects upon our foreign relations were it to assert jurisdiction over this suit. The comity balancing test has been explicitly used in this Court. *See Joseph Muller Corp. Zurich v. Societe Anonyme de Gerance et D'Armament*, 451 F.2d 727 (2d Cir.1971) (per curiam), *cert. denied*, 406 U.S. 906 (1972).

In an effort to provide a single standard to determine whether American antitrust laws apply to a given extraterritorial transaction, Congress enacted the Foreign Trade Antitrust Improvements Act of 1982, Pub. L. No. 97-290, 96 Stat. 1246 (codified at 15 U.S.C. Section 6a) [hereinafter referred to as the "Act"].

Given the dismissal on comity grounds, the district judge did not decide whether the complaint should be dismissed under the "Act," although he did state that the Act "would not appear to provide a basis for refusing to exercise jurisdiction over this action."

Congress left it to the courts to decide when to employ notions of abstention from exercising jurisdiction in extraterritorial antitrust cases. Ninety years ago, the United States Supreme Court enunciated the American version of the act of state doctrine as follows:

> Every sovereign State is bound to respect the independence of every other sovereign State, and the courts of one country will not sit in judgment on the acts of government of another done within its own territory. Redress of grievances by reason of such acts must be obtained through the means open to be availed of by sovereign powers as between themselves.

Underhill v. Hernandez, 168 U.S. 250, 252 (1897).

In the landmark case of *Banco Nacional de Cuba v. Sabbatino*, 376 U.S. 398 (1964), the Supreme Court analyzed the significant policy considerations and "constitutional underpinnings" of the doctrine, noting that no case subsequent to *Underhill* had manifested any retreat therefrom. 376 U.S. at 416, 421-23. . . .

In essence, the act of state doctrine is a principle of law designed primarily to avoid judicial inquiry into the acts and conduct of the officials of the foreign state, its affairs and its policies and the underlying reasons and motivations for the actions of the foreign government. Such an inquiry is foreclosed under the act of state doctrine . . . and this is true regardless of whether the foreign government is named as a party to the suit or whether the validity of its actions are directly challenged in the pleadings. . . .

Although the district court engaged in the broader analysis of the possible adverse effects upon foreign relations were jurisdiction to be asserted, the long established act of state doctrine calls upon courts to make a preliminary assessment, on the record before it, of "the likely impact on international relations that would result from judicial consideration of the sovereign's act." . . . This Court has made it clear that this is a legitimate exercise of an Article III court, not to be controlled by the expressed view of the executive branch in a given case. . . .

O.N.E. contends that the cargo reservation laws were "implemented [by Colombia] under the manipulative guidance of Flota"; that "commercially determined carrier relationships" should not be replaced by "Colombian-government dictated relationships"; that its "challenge in this proceeding does not so much address Colombia's cargo reservation laws per se as it does appellees' manipulation of these laws"; and that Flota has "manipulate[d] the cargo reservation laws so as to carve out a monopoly for itself and exclude all competition."

O.N.E.'s allegations make clear that its antitrust suit is premised on contentions that it was harmed by acts and motivations of a foreign sovereign which the district court would be called on to examine and pass judgment on. . . .

When the causal chain between a defendant's alleged conduct and plaintiff's injury cannot be determined without an inquiry into the motives of the foreign government, claims made under the antitrust laws are dismissed. . . . Furthermore, where as here the conduct of the appellees has been compelled by the foreign government they are entitled to assert the defense of foreign government compulsion and the act of state doctrine is applicable.[4]

Colombia's interest in this action has not been confined to Flota itself; the liquid bulk cargo service of Flota, Andino and Transligra has been important to Colombia's economy, and the Colombian government has so represented.

O.N.E.'s "antitrust" claims reflect dissatisfaction with Colombia's cargo reservation laws, not with appellees' space chartering agreements. . . .

The dismissal of the complaint is affirmed. . . .

. . . .

COMMENTARY

1. Besides the question of comity, with which you are already familiar, what new antitrust defenses are discussed in the preceding case? What is the "act of state" doctrine? How is that doctrine related to the question of comity? Did the application of the act of state doctrine here render the comity question moot?

2. What is the doctrine of "foreign sovereign compulsion"? Was the doctrine of foreign sovereign compulsion involved in the *Flota* case? How is the doctrine of foreign sovereign compulsion related to the act of state doctrine?

3. Was the defendant Flota immune from suit under the Foreign Sovereign Immunities Act of 1976? As the court pointed out, Flota fit the definition of an agency or instrumentality of a foreign government under that Act, 28 U.S.C. § 1603(b). Did it fall within any exception in 28 U.S.C. § 1605? The relevant provisions of the Foreign Sovereign Immunities Act are set forth in Appendix A.

4. What antitrust defenses were available to the defendants Andino and Transligra? Did they have an "act of state" defense? Did they have a "foreign sovereign compulsion" defense? Were these defendants compelled to do anything against their will?

5. The doctrines referred to in the preceding paragraphs are conceptually related to (but different from) the domestic state action doctrine and related issues taken up in Chapter 18, *infra*.

---

4 The agreements in question were entered into by foreign parties, approved by the government of Colombia, and relate to commerce into Colombia. The two Supreme Court cases relied on by Judge Cardamone in his dissent, on the other hand, both related to alleged conspiracies entered into in the United States by United States citizens which sought to monopolize trade in the United States. *See United States v. Sisal Sales Corp.*, 274 U.S. 268, 276 (1927); *Continental Ore Co. v. Union Carbide & Carbon Corp.*, 370 U.S. 690, 698-99, 704 (1962). Furthermore, the Court noted in *Continental Ore* that there was no indication of foreign government approval of the actions in question. 370 U.S. at 706.

6. What would be the position of the Department of Justice on the issue of whether the interests of Columbia superceded the interest of the United States in antitrust enforcement in this case?

Department of Justice and Federal Trade Commission, Antitrust Guidelines for International Operations (April 5, 1995)

. . . Under *Hartford Fire,* if it is possible for the party to comply both with the foreign law and the U.S. antitrust laws, the existence of the foreign law does not provide any legal excuse for actions that do not comply with U.S. law. However, a direct conflict may arise when the facts demonstrate that the foreign sovereign has compelled the very conduct that the U.S. antitrust law prohibits.

In these circumstances, at least one court has recognized a defense under the U.S. antitrust laws, and the Agencies will also recognize it. There are two rationales underlying the defense of foreign sovereign compulsion. First, Congress enacted the U.S. antitrust laws against the background of well recognized principles of international law and comity among nations, pursuant to which U.S. authorities give due deference to the official acts of foreign governments. A defense for actions taken under the circumstances spelled out below serves to accomodate two equal sovereigns. Second, important considerations of fairness to the defendant require some mechanism that provides a predictable rule of decision for those seeking to conform their behavior to all pertinent laws.

Because of the limited scope of the defense, the Agencies will refrain from enforcement actions on the ground of foreign sovereign compulsion only when certain criteria are satisfied. First, the foreign government must have compelled the anticompetitive conduct under circumstances in which a refusal to comply with the foreign government's command would give rise to the imposition of penal or other severe sanctions. As a general matter, the Agencies regard the foreign government's formal representation that refusal to comply with its command would have such a result as being sufficient to establish that the conduct in question has been compelled, as long as that representation contains sufficient detail to enable the Agencies to see precisely how the compulsion would be accomplished under local law. Foreign government measures short of compulsion do not suffice for this defense, although they can be relevant in a comity analysis.

Second, although there can be no strict territorial test for this defense, the defense normally applies only when the foreign government compels conduct which can be accomplished entirely within its own territory. If the compelled conduct occurs in the United States, the Agencies will not recognize the defense. . . .

Third, . . . the order must come from the foreign government acting in its governmental capacity. . . .

COMMENTARY

1. The standards employed by the Justice Department for recognizing the defense of foreign sovereign compulsion are close to the standards that a court would employ. As in the case of comity generally, however, the Department would deny the courts the right to accept such a defense in an action brought by the government.

2. Foreign governments sometimes induce action by business firms through persuasion or suggestion rather than through compulsion. Thus, for example, the Japanese government extensively employs "administrative guidance." Professor Mitsuo Matsushita discussed administrative guidance extensively in his book INTERNATIONAL TRADE AND COMPETITION LAW IN JAPAN (1993). In his book Professor Matsushita quotes a widely accepted definition of administrative guidance:

> "[Administrative guidance] is not legal compulsion restricting the rights of individuals and imposing obligations on citizens. It is a request or guidance on the part of the government within the limit of the task and administrative responsibility of each agency as provided for in the establishment laws, asking for a specific action or inaction for the purpose of achieving some administrative objective through cooperation on the part of the parties who are the object of the administration."

MITSUO MATSUSHITA, INTERNATIONAL TRADE AND COMPETITION LAW IN JAPAN 60 (1993).

Under this definition, administrative guidance by the Japanese government would not meet the compulsion test. However, a government's pressure upon a business firm to conform to its policies may sometimes embody so much pressure as to be tantamount to coercion. Further blurring may occur when the government pressure is exerted in favor of a course of action which is profitable to the business firm.

C. The Use of United States Antitrust Law to Open Foreign Markets to American Exporters

1. Trade and Foreign Cartels

Almost all of the world's trading nations adhere to the World Trade Organization (WTO), the successor to the General Agreement on Tariffs and Trade (GATT). Participants in the GATT have agreed to eliminate all nontariff barriers (such as, for example, import quotas), leaving only tariffs as trade barriers. Over the many years since the establishment of the GATT in 1947, the GATT members have agreed in several rounds of negotiation to a series of progressive tariff reductions. GATT is widely regarded as responsible for the vast expanse in international trade since the end of World War II.

In a number of instances—many of which involve Japan—the United States has asserted that although official government barriers have been appropriately removed in accordance with GATT requirements, nonetheless outside companies have been unable to enter a national market. If entry is not blocked by a foreign government, but entry barriers nonetheless exist, those barriers may have been erected by a foreign cartel.

2. Proposals for International Competition Codes

It is widely recognized that progress towards free trade in the world is dependent not only upon governments reducing trade barriers, but also upon governments ensuring that barriers erected by private cartels do not supplant the barriers that governments remove. For that reason, the international community has addressed competition law issues periodically over the years.

The provisions of the GATT itself originally a component of a larger text, the Charter for the International Trade Organization (or Havana Charter) worked out at a conference in Havana, Cuba in the winter of 1947-48. The Havana Charter contained a restrictive business practices code, thus evidencing the understanding of the conferees that effective competition law was an integral part of an effective world trading system.

In 1980 the United Nations General Assembly adopted a set of principles on restrictive business practices.[4] Over the years the Organization for Economic Cooperation and Development (OECD) also has attempted to encourage the adoption and enforcement of effective competition laws. In 1976 the OECD issued a Declaration on International Investment and Multinational Enterprises which contained a section on competition policy, albeit a highly abstract and general one.

In 1991, the American Bar Association's Special Committee on International Antitrust considered the question of whether worldwide competition standards are feasible. While the Committee expressed the view that cartel behavior ought to be treated as criminal by all nations, it observed that many nations either do not enforce their anti-cartel policies or explicitly exempt many cartels from their competition laws. As a result, the Committee concluded that it was not practical at the present time for the world's nations to reach agreement on common anti-cartel provisions.

Most recently twelve scholars meeting in Munich in 1993 (the "Munich group") has proposed a competition code as the basis for a new trade agreement. The code drafted by the Munich group, however, has been criticized as overinclusive by sources within the OECD and the U.S. Department of Justice. *See* Daniel J. Gifford & Mitsuo Matsushita, *Antitrust or Competition Laws Viewed in a Trading Context, Harmony or Dissonance?, in* 2 FAIR TRADE & HARMONIZATION: PREREQUISITES FOR FREE TRADE? 269, 275 (Jagdish N. Bhaqwaiti & Robert E. Hudec ed. 1996).

---

[4] UNCTAD, The Set of Multilaterally Agreed Equitable Principles and Rules of the Control of Restrictive Business Practices, TD/RBP/Conf/10 (2 May 1980), adopted by U.N. General Assembly, 12 November 1980, A/C.2/35/L.75. The UNCTAD principles are extensively reviewed in 2 BARRY E. HAWK, UNITED STATES, COMMON MARKET AND INTERNATIONAL ANTITRUST 990-1003 (Supp. 1990).

3. U.S. Antitrust Policy on Foreign Cartels

The issuance, by the Department of Justice, of its 1992 Policy Statement (page 732, *supra*) signaled the determination of the Department to use the antitrust laws to assist American exporters against exclusionary practices of foreign cartels. How the Department would obtain jurisdiction over foreign companies which did not do business in the United States was a major problem in this approach. The answer, it appears, is provided by the ramifications of *Copperweld*: if parent and subsidiary are treated as a "single enterprise" so that it is impossible for them to conspire together, then the implication is that parent and subsidiary are a single enterprise for purpose of service of process. As this book goes to press, the Department has just begun to employ this theory. Its first attempt in this direction was against Pilkington PLC, a British glass manufacturer. See the Note immediately following.

NOTE: THE PILKINGTON CONSENT ORDER

In June 1994 the Department of Justice entered into a consent decree with Pilkington PLC, a British Company, that appears to have important ramifications upon the use of U.S. antitrust law against market-restrictive activity abroad.

Pilkington, the world's largest flat-glass maker, developed a process for making defect-free flat glass.[5] Essentially the Pilkington process invovles the pouring of molten glass upon a bed of molten metal. Since the molten metal is perfectly flat, the glass which congeals on its surface is also perfectly flat. Pilkington obtained patent protection, its U.S. patent having been issued in 1969.

Pilkington then issued licenses to various glass producers around the world. These licenses contained territorial restrictions, usually confining the licensee to selling the glass produced under the license to its home country. By 1994, however, Pilkington's patents had expired. Nonetheless, the license agreements continued, and every producer of flat glass was operating under a Pilkington license. This series of licenses thus operated as a means of allocating the world glass market among the world's glass producers.

The European Commission recently permitted Pilkington to acquire (jointly with Techint, an Italian company) SIV, an Italian glass manufacturer, thereby further increasing Pilkington's share of the European market. As a result of this acquisition the European Community has five float glass manufacturers: Pilkington/SIV, Glaverbel (majority owned by the Japanese Group Asahi) and the US-owned companies PPG and Guardian.[6]

---

5 *See Application of Pilkington,* 411 F.2d 1345 (Cust. & Pat. App. 1969).

6 *See* 66 Antitrust & Trade Reg. Rep. (BNA) No. 1646 (Jan. 13, 1994).

Because the license restrictions were means of excluding U.S. manufacturers from foreign markets, the Department of Justice wanted to have them declared invalid under the antitrust laws. This would, of course, be employing the U.S. antitrust laws extraterritorially to invalidate agreements between Pilkington and its foreign licensees, all of which had been executed and were being applied abroad. As the material above makes clear, however, the United States has long asserted some extraterritorial reach for its antitrust laws.

A major problem faced by the Justice Department in proceeding on this course was that Pilkington did not itself do business in the United States. If Pilkington was not here, how could it be served? The Department solved this problem by serving Libby-Owens-Ford Co., an 80%-owned Pilkington subsidiary, asserting jurisdiction over Pilkington through the subsidiary. Pilkington made it easy for the Justice Department: It accepted the jurisdiction of the U.S. courts and a consent decree holding that the license restrictions as they applied to U.S. firms (but only U.S. firms) were invalid. 59 Fed. Reg. 30,604 (D. Ariz. 1994); *PPG Industries, Inc. v. Pilkington*, 825 F. Supp. 1465 (D. Ariz. 1993).

Chapter 15

The Interface of Antitrust Law and the Intellectual Property Regimes

A. Introduction

The intellectual property laws and the antitrust laws share a common goal of seeking optimum allocation of talent and of resources. However, utilization of intellectual property rights, which are granted for limited times to the expressions of creative efforts, may conflict with the competitive norms of the antitrust laws. The tension between the patent and copyright, the principal federal intellectual property regimes, and the antitrust laws may arise from the terms of licensing agreements, the traditional contracts by which patent and copyright owners undertake to capture the economic reward granted them by the patent and copyright statutes for their creative endeavors. Other market consequences of intellectual property protection have been noted as follows,

> Patents, which give the inventor of a new product an exclusive right to sell it, have both desirable and undesirable effects. The chief benefit is that the possibility of obtaining monopoly profits encourages more inventive activity. The chief disadvantage is that new products may be sold at excessively high (monopoly) prices. [Of course] . . . a patented product may face competition from other products. Just because a product is protected by a patent does not guarantee that it is sold for more than the competitive price.

DENNIS W. CARLTON & JEFFREY M. PERLOFF, MODERN INDUSTRIAL ORGANIZATION 653 (1990).

The phrase "intellectual property" refers to various modes of federal and state statutory systems of protection for the product of creative activity. Although referred to as a form of property, this characterization is of limited use in describing the nature of patent, copyright, trademark, trade secret, know-how, and unfair competition laws. A more useful definition for present purposes is derived from an economic analysis of property rights that identifies the exclusionary powers associated with intellectual (and other) property rights. From this perspective, the grant of property rights affords an incentive for creative intellectual activity, as well as an incentive for efficient allocation of resources. RICHARD A. POSNER, ECONOMIC ANALYSIS OF LAW, 10 (4th ed. 1992). Thus, a patent holder may exclude all others, including one who has independently discovered the protected method or apparatus, from "making, using, or selling," the protected subject matter. 35 U.S.C. § 154(a)(1) (1994). Similarly, the copyright holder may bar another from reproducing, distributing, performing, or displaying the actual protected work. 17 U.S.C. § 106. The commercial exploitation of these intellectual property rights is reflected in the practice of licensing others to use the protected subject matter. In this way, a patent holder may obtain a royalty from a licensee in exchange for permitting the manufacture of a patented apparatus. Similarly, a copyright owner may obtain revenue by licensing the reproduction, distribution, performance, or display of copyrighted materials. For an overview of the several intellectual property regimes, see Stanley M. Besen & Leo J. Raskind, *An Introduction to the Law and Economics of Intellectual Property*, 5 J. ECON. PERSP. 1 (1991); *see also* Leo J. Raskind, *Licensing Under United States Antitrust Law*, 20 BROOK. J. INT'L. L. 49 (1993).

Economists agree that technological improvement, that is, improvement in production practices and equipment, has contributed materially to increased productivity per worker for the economy as a whole. Robert M. Solow received the Nobel prize for his pioneering work in identifying this relationship. See his *Technical Change and the Aggregate Production Function*, 39 REV. OF ECON. & STAT. 312 (1957). However, quantifying in monetary terms the incentive to be accorded the creative individual by patent and copyright law is difficult, if not impossible, since it involves interpersonal comparisons of valuation. The Supreme Court has, however, identified in general terms the incentive offered by the copyright (and patent) regimes in *Twentieth Century Music Corp. v. Aiken*, 422 U.S. 151 (1975):

> The limited scope of the copyright holder's statutory monopoly, like the limited copyright duration required by the Constitution, reflects a balance of competing claims upon the public interest: Creative work is to be encouraged and rewarded, but private motivation must ultimately serve the cause of providing public availability of literature, music, and the other arts. The immediate effect of our copyright law is to secure a fair return for an "author's" creative labor. But the ultimate aim is . . . to stimulate artistic creativity for the general public good.

Id. at 157.

Since neither case law nor independent economic analysis has articulated workable quantitative criteria for determining in monetary terms the incentive needed to stimulate creative activity, the courts are left to determine the appropriate balance of interests in specific cases involving patent and copyright licenses. Accordingly, two lines of judicial analysis have emerged. Some courts look to antitrust principles for guidance to determine the proper balance between the public interest and private arrangements which may have antitcompetitve effects—as for example, a license which grants exclusive rights to distribute copyrighted material on condition that an unprotected product also be purchased. Other courts have developed their own criteria under the general rubric of "misuse" of intellectual property rights. Both lines of cases are developed in this Chapter. Antitrust concerns are involved in both lines of case law. Since a license to manufacture a patented item is a contract that may condition the right to manufacture on a requirement which may raise antitrust concerns (such as setting the licensee's resale price of the manufactured item), the exploitation of intellectual property rights is subject to antitrust scrutiny under § 1 of the Sherman Act. Other terms in such licenses have been subjected to scrutiny under both the Sherman and Clayton Acts. Thus, the terms of the license may condition the production and distribution of the protected item in ways that constitute vertical or horizontal restraints under § 1 of the Sherman Act. Similarly, the acquisition of patent rights and the pooled use of them among competitors may raise an issue of monopolization under § 2. Alternatively, the terms of a license may require purchase of a non-patented product as a condition of use of the patented article, thus raising a tying arrangement issue under § 1 of the Sherman Act or § 3 of the Clayton Act. And patents and copyrights, although intangible property, are assets whose acquisition by merger may raise concerns under § 7 of the Clayton Act.

The difficult task for antitrust analysis is to permit the full exploitation of patents and copyrights as an incentive to creative activity, without also permitting arrangements that have anticompetitive consequence. *See* Donald F. Turner, *Basic Principles in Formulating Antitrust and Misuse Constraints on the Exploitation of Intellectual Property Rights*, 53 ANTITRUST L.J. 485 (1984). The difficulty of achieving an appropriate resolution of the tension between these two objectives is described by Richard C. Levin, an industrial organization economist, as follows,

> . . . [T]he treatment of patent practices under antitrust law raises very difficult issues in both law and economics. The issues are particularly complicated because there can be no presumption that the patent system creates the ideal level of incentives for innovation. Our research confirms systematically older impressions that the patent system is highly imperfect, providing powerful incentives to innovate in some markets but relatively weak incentives in others. This finding suggests that any rule of reason deliberation ought to consider at least, the efficacy of patent protection in the particular industrial setting. Indeed, any attempt to establish a per se rule in the area of patent use ought to consider whether the rule makes sense in industries where patents are weak, as well as in industries where patents in practice approach the theoretical ideal. . . . We economists have a considerable distance yet to travel before we can provide very clear guidance on how—via patent or antitrust policy, or both—the incentives for dynamically efficient industrial performance can be optimized.

Richard C. Levin, *Patents in Perspective*, 53 ANTITRUST L.J. 519, 522 (1984). In reading the cases that follow, consider how the balance is struck between the restrictions providing needed incentives and the preservation of competitive norms.

Technological advances have implications for antitrust law beyond the exploitation of intellectual property rights. As Chapter 14 on trade illustrates, much of the comparative advantage of the United States in the global economy comes from our high rate of innovation in pharmaceuticals, computers, computer software, machine tools, and aircraft. Many of these products are the subject matter of patent and copyright protection. A further consequence of technological innovation relates to the Chapters 9, 10, and 12 dealing with market structure. One body of economic analysis identified with the late Joseph Schumpeter holds that some degree of monopoly power is needed as an incentive for firms to invest in the research and development that generates new technology. According to this view, public policy ought not set the purely competitive model as the societal norm of competition policy. *See* FREDRIC M. SCHERER, INNOVATION AND GROWTH: SCHUMPETERIAN PERSPECTIVES Ch. 1 (1984); WILLIAM D. NORDHAUS, INVENTIONS, GROWTH AND WELFARE Ch. 1 (1969). While this position is controversial, it is clear that technology has an impact on market structure. The development of powerful desktop computer workstations and networking capabilities, for example, has drastically altered the market power previously exercised by IBM in the mainframe segment of the computer industry. The new technology has, in turn, fostered the growth of Microsoft and Hewlett-Packard.

A model relating market structure to the function of the patent system is provided by Edmund W. Kitch, in *The Nature and Function of the Patent System*, 20 J.L. & ECON. 265 (1977). Kitch points out that in a competitive market environment there is little incentive for firms to incur research and development costs in the absence of patent protection, because competitors would capture the economic benefit of the innovating firm's product or process before the innovator had an opportunity to do so. In this case, there is the perverse result that the competing firms would appropriate the innovation without cost, leaving the innovating firm the worse for the research expenditures and the likely prospect of a lower market price for the product or process reduced by competition from the non-innovating firms that had incurred no research costs.

The patent regime, which gives the patent holder the right to exclude others from making, using, or selling the protected subject matter, permits the innovating patent holder to command royalties for the period of twenty years from the date of the filing of the patent. Since the patent is granted on condition of full disclosure of the nature of the invention and the manner of practicing it, anyone may use the invention at the end of the period of protection.

Kitch points out that when the patent holder has significant market share, either as a monopoly or in an oligopoly situation, the prospects for full recovery of the economic value of the invention are optimum. This model further posits that the patent system serves in these circumstances also to promote commercial development of inventions. The protection of the patent provides an incentive to incur the expenses of development for commercial exploitation after the patent has issued. Patent protection then provides an opportunity to recoup the development costs as well.

A 1958 study of the patent system by the late Fritz Machlup, AN ECONOMIC REVIEW OF THE PATENT SYSTEM, Study No. 15, Sen. Comm. on the Judiciary (1958), had concluded that the empirical evidence to validate the Shumpeterian model was lacking. Subsequently, economists have produced a substantial literature of empirical investigation of the Schumpeterian-Kitch thesis that a less than fully competitive market structure was necessary to fund research and development expenditures. This literature is reviewed by Scherer and Ross in their INDUSTRIAL MARKET STRUCTURE AND ECONOMIC PERFORMANCE 660 (3d ed. 1990) as follows:

> Viewed in their entirety, the theory and evidence suggest a threshold concept of the most favorable climate for rapid technological change. A bit of monopoly power in the form of structural concentration is conducive to innovation, particularly when advances in the relevant knowledge base occur slowly. But very high concentration has a positive effect only in rare cases, and more often is apt to retard progress by restricting the number of independent sources of initiative and by dampening firms' incentive to gain market position by accelerated R&D. Likewise, given the important role that technically audacious newcomers play in making radical innovations, it seems important that barriers to new entry be kept at modest levels. Schumpeter was right in asserting that perfect competition has no title to being established as the model of dynamic efficiency. But his less cautious followers were wrong when they implied that powerful monopolies and tightly knit cartels had any stronger claim to that title. What is needed for rapid technological progress is a subtle blend of competition and monopoly, with more emphasis in general on the former than the latter, and with the role of monopolistic elements diminishing when rich technological opportunities exist.

In the cases that follow, consider the approach of the courts to the issues of: 1) market structure as a basis of innovation and 2) the exploitation of intellectual property rights by licenses that may restrict competition.

B. Royalties: The Base and Other Limitations

Since the royalty payment is the primary means by which the intellectual property rightholder can capture the economic value of the creative work, the royalty term is central to all licenses. As in the law of contracts generally, courts do not hear issues of the amount of the royalty. In *Brulotte v. Thys Co.*, 379 U.S. 29, 33 (1964), the Court in *dictum* noted: "A patent empowers the owner to exact royalties as high as he can negotiate with the leverage of that monopoly." There is, however, some authority holding that a claim of an exhorbitant royalty raises an antitrust issue as a restraint of trade. *American Photocopy Equipment Co. v. Rovico, Inc.*, 359 F.2d 745 (7th Cir. 1966). A license may lawfully require payment of a minimum fee for the license to cover the cost of negotiations, even if the patent is not used at all. *Zenith Radio Corp. v. Hazeltine Research, Inc.*, 395 U.S. 100, 139 (1969).

The royalty amount has also been subject to antitrust scrutiny as patent misuse when a different royalty is charged various licensees. There can be no Robinson-Patman issue in charging differential royalties, however, unless commodities are sold as part of the license. *See Honeywell Inc. v. Sperry Rand.*, 180 U.S.P.Q. (BNA) 673 (D. Minn. 1973). Nor is there an antitrust issue where the royalty differential can be justified by business reasons. In *Bela Seating Co. v. Poloron Products, Inc.,* 438 F.2d 733, 736 (7th Cir. 1971), the differential was the result of a determination that the first licensee's royalty was inadequate in relation to the final selling price of the product. There is some uncertain authority that royalty differentials between licensees might be actionable under § 5 of the Federal Trade Commission Act based on the "shrimp peeler" litigation, *Peelers Co. v. Wendt,* 260 F. Supp. 193 (W.D. Wash. 1966); *Laitram Corp. v. King Crab, Inc.*, 244 F. Supp. 9 (D. Ala.), *modified,* 245 F. Supp. 1019 (D. Ala. 1965). In those cases the patentee, who had a financial stake in the Gulf area shrimp sellers, licensed his peeling machine to shrimp sellers in the Northwest at twice the royalty charged the Gulf merchants. The FTC found the royalty differential to be linked to an attempt to insulate the Gulf sellers, in which the patentee had a financial interest, from competition with the Northwest sellers. Other courts have distinguished the *Shrimp Peeler* cases on this basis. *Carter-Wallace, Inc. v. United States,* 167 U.S.P.Q. (BNA) 667, 673 (Ct. Cl. 1970); *USM Corp. v. SPS Technologies, Inc.,* 694 F.2d 505, 513 (7th Cir. 1982). It is unlikely that differential royalties would be actionable in the absence of a material market impact.

Right holders have utilized a variety of methods on which to base the calculation of the payment for the right to make or to use patented subject matter. Given the manifold circumstances in which licenses are negotiated, the calculation of the royalty payment for the use right may involve both a per use charge and time term. For example, in *Brulotte,* above, it was held to be patent misuse for the patent holder to ". . . use that leverage to project those royalty payments beyond the life of the patent." 379 U.S. at 33. The patentee was entitled to royalties paid after the expiration of the patent for use during the term of the patent, but not for use after expiration. Justice Harlan pointed out the difficulty of judicial oversight of use right royalties in his dissent in *Brulotte* by giving an example of the installation of a patented coin-operated laundry machine in an apartment house subject to a $.25 charge for each use. *Id.* at 37 (Harlan, J., dissenting). Assuming a durable machine that would survive the duration of patent protection, should it be patent misuse to require a royalty for each use of the machine after the patent has expired?

An antitrust issue may be raised where the calculation of the royalty payment is not directly related to the licensee's use of the protected process or machine. In *Zenith Radio Corp. v. Hazeltine Research, Inc.,* 395 U.S. 100, 136 (1969), Zenith accepted a package license covering all of Hazeltine's domestic patents for devices used by Zenith to manufacture radios and televisions. Zenith did not want all of the patents in the package, but was told in the negotiations with Hazeltine that a license on the desired patents was conditioned on accepting a license on all patents.

The royalty was to be calculated as a percentage of all products sold by Zenith. The Supreme Court struck down the royalty provision as misuse stating:

> . . . [the patentee cannot] garner as royalties a percentage share of the licensee's receipts from sales of other products; . . . the patentee seeks to extend the monopoly of his patent to derive a benefit not attributable to use of the patent's teachings.

In *Zenith* the Court distinguished and clarified its earlier decision in *Automatic Radio Manufacturing Co., Inc. v. Hazeltine Research Inc.*, 339 U.S. 827 (1950), in which the Court permitted a royalty calculation granting Automatic Radio a non-exclusive license to use any of Hazeltine's 570 patents and its 200 applications in the manufacture of broadcasting equipment. The royalty consisted of a minimum payment of $100,000 based on a percentage of the final selling price of Automatic Radio's receivers. In rejecting a claim of patent misuse by basing a royalty on a package license under which all patents would not be used, the Court upheld the calculation of royalties based on a percentage of the sales price of the final product manufactured under a package license in which not all patents in the package were used by the licensee. The Court took the occasion in *Zenith* to clarify its holding in *Automatic Radio* by distinguishing consensual from coercive determination of the total sales term.

> It could be as the Court indicated in *Automatic Radio*, that licensee as well as the patentee would find it more convenient and efficient from several standpoints to base royalties on total sales than to face the burden of figuring royalties based on actual use. *If convenience of the parties rather than patent power dictates the total-sales royalty provision, there is no misuse of the patents. . . .*"

395 U.S. at 138 (emphasis added). This opinion emphasized the distinction between licenses in which the parties mutually agreed to total sales as a formulaic means of computing the royalty from those licenses in which, as stated in footnote 29 of the majority opinion in *Zenith*, the licensee "was forced into accepting" the total-sales royalty calculation. In 1995, the Department of Justice required Microsoft, Inc. to modify its operating system licenses to PC manufacturers by eliminating the "per processor" requirement. Under this provision, the licensee had been obligated to compute its royalty due Microsoft on all units manufactured, including units in which a competitor's operating system had been installed. *See United States v. Microsoft*, 56 F.3d 1448 (D.C. Cir. 1995). This case is discussed further at pages 840-41, *infra*.

License terms restricting the use right of the patent geographically or in application may also raise antitrust issues under the heading of "field of use," restrictions. In *General Talking Pictures Corp. v. Western Electric Co.*, 304 U.S. 175 (1938), *see* page 813, *infra*, the Supreme Court upheld a restriction limiting the licensee to the manufacturing of sound equipment for theatres, where another licensee has been granted a license to manufacture sound equipment for the private consumer market. The licensee breaching the theatre restriction and his vendee were held liable for patent infringement. Similarly, it was held that no antitrust issue arises when licensees are restricted both as to sub-licensing and to fields of use. In *Beneger Labs., Ltd. v. R.K. Laros Co.,* 209 F. Supp. 639, 648 (E.D. Pa. 1962), *aff'd per curiam*, 317 F.2d 455 (3d. Cir.), *cert. denied*, 375 U.S. 833 (1963), one licensee was granted use rights for the veterinarian market; another was granted rights for the human market. Both were denied the right to sub-license. In approving the restrictions, the trial court stated:

> . . . [I]n order to sustain a charge of violation of the antitrust laws through the instrumentality of a patent . . ., there must be evidence of an intent to create an unlawful restraint or monopoly, together with conduct effective to bring such restraint . . . into being.

In the 1995 INTELLECTUAL PROPERTY GUIDELINES (reproduced in full in Appendix C), § 2.3 Procompetitive benefits of licensing, states in part: "Field-of-use, territorial, and other limitations on intellectual property licenses may serve procompetitive ends by allowing the licensor to exploit its property as efficiently and effectively as possible." Since in many instances the license establishes a vertical relationship between the parties, it is likely that such license restrictions will be subject to rule of reason analysis under *Sylvania. See* Chapter 5.

C. Price Fixing and Licenses

United States v. General Electric Co.

272 U.S. 476 (1926)

Mr. Chief Justice TAFT delivered the opinion of the Court.

. . . The bill made two charges, one that the General Electric Company, in its business of making and selling incandescent electric lights, had devised and was carrying out a plan for their distribution throughout the United States by a number of so-called agents, exceeding 21,000, to restrain interstate trade in such lamps and to exercise a monopoly of the sale thereof; and, second, that it was achieving the same illegal purpose through a contract of license with . . . the Westinghouse Electric & Manufacturing Company. . . .

The government alleged that the system of distribution adopted was merely a device to enable the Electric Company to fix the resale prices of lamps in the hands of purchasers, that the so-called agents were in fact wholesale and retail merchants, and the lamps passed through the ordinary channels of commerce in the ordinary way, and that the restraint was the same and just as unlawful as if the so-called agents were avowed purchasers handling the lamps under resale price agreements. The Electric Company answered that its distributors were bona fide agents, that it had the legal right to market its lamps and pass them directly to the consumer by such agents, and at prices and by a system prescribed by it and agreed upon between it and its agents, there being no limitation sought as to resale prices upon those who purchased from such agents.

The second question in the case involves the validity of a license granted March 1, 1912, by the Electric Company to the Westinghouse Company to make, use, and sell lamps under the patents owned by the former. It was charged that the license in effect provided that the Westinghouse Company would follow prices and terms of sale from time to time fixed by the Electric Company and observed by it, and that the Westinghouse Company would, with regard to lamps manufactured by it under the license, adopt and maintain the same conditions of sale as observed by the Electric Company in the distribution of lamps manufactured by it.

The District Court upon a full hearing dismissed the bill . . . and this is an appeal under . . . the Expediting Act . . . .

The Electric Company is the owner of three patents . . . . These three patents cover completely the making of the modern electric lights with the tungsten filaments, and secure to the Electric Company the monopoly of their making, using, and vending.

The total business in electric lights for the year 1921 was $68,300,000, and the relative percentages of business done by the companies were: Electric, 69 per cent., Westinghouse, 16 per cent., other licensees, 8 per cent., and manufacturers not licensed, 7 per cent. The plan of distribution by the Electric Company divides the trade into three classes. The first class is that of sales to large consumers readily reached by the Electric Company, negotiated by its own salaried employees, and the deliveries made from its own factories and warehouses. The second class is of sales to large consumers under contracts with the Electric Company, negotiated by agents, the deliveries being made from stock in the custody of the agents; and the third is of the sales to general consumers by agents under similar contracts. The agents under the second class are called B agents, and the agents under the third class are called A agents. Each B agent is appointed by the Electric Company by the execution and delivery of a contract for the appointment, which lasts a year . . . unless sooner terminated. It provides that the company is to maintain on consignment in the custody of the agent a stock of lamps, the sizes, types, classes, and quantity of which and the length of time which they are to remain in stock to be determined by the company. . . . All of the lamps in such consigned stock are to be and remain the property of the company until the lamps are sold, and the proceeds of all lamps are to be held in trust for the benefit and for the account of the company until fully accounted for. The B agent is authorized to deal with the lamps on consignment with him in three ways—first to distribute the lamps to the company's A agents as authorized by the company; second, to sell lamps from the stock to any consumer to the extent of his requirements for immediate delivery at prices specified by the company; third, to deliver lamps from the stock to any purchaser under written contract with the company to whom the B agent may be authorized by the company to deliver lamps at the prices and on the terms stated in the contract. . . .

There is a basic rate of commission payable to the agent, and there are certain special supplemental and additional compensations for prompt and efficient service. . . . It appears in the evidence that since 1915 . . . the company has assumed all risk of fire, flood, obsolescence, and price decline, and carries whatever insurance is carried on the stocks of lamps in the hands of its agents and pays whatever taxes are assessed. This is relevant as a circumstance to confirm the view that the so-called relation of agent to the company is the real one. There are 400 of the B agents, the large distributors. They recommend to the company efficient and reliable distributors in the localities with which they are respectively familiar, to act as A agents, whom the company appoints. There are 21,000 or more of the A agents. They are usually retail electrical supply dealers in smaller places. The only sales which the A agent is authorized to make are to consumers for immediate delivery and to purchasers under written contract with the manufacturer, just as in the case of the B agents. The plan was, of course, devised for the purpose of enabling the company to deal directly with consumers and purchasers, and doubtless was intended to avoid selling the lamps owned by the company to jobbers or dealers and prevent sale by these middlemen to consumers at different and competing prices. The question is whether, in view of the arrangements made by the company with those who ordinarily and usually would be merchants buying from the manufacturer and selling to the public, such persons are to be treated as agents or as owners of the lamps, consigned to them under such contracts. If they are to be regarded really as purchasers, then the restriction as to the prices at which the sales are to be made is a restraint of trade and a violation of the Anti-Trust Law.

We find nothing in the form of the contracts and the practice under them which makes the so-called B and A agents anything more than genuine agents of the company, or the delivery of the stock to each agent anything more than a consignment to the agent for his custody and sale as such. . . . The agent has no power to deal with the lamps in any way inconsistent with the retained ownership of the lamps by the company. When they are delivered by him to the purchasers, the title passes directly from the company to those purchasers. . . . The circumstance that the agents were in their regular business wholesale or retail merchants, and under a prior arrangement had bought the lamps and sold them as their owners, did not prevent a change in their relation to the company. . . .

But it is said that the system of distribution is so complicated and involves such a very large number of agents, distributed throughout the entire country, that the very size and comprehensiveness of the scheme brings it within the Anti-Trust Law. . . . But under the patent law the patentee is given by statute a monopoly of making, using and selling the patented article. The extent of his monopoly in the articles sold and in the territory of the United States where sold is not limited in the grant of his patent, and the comprehensiveness of his control of the business in the sale of the patented article is not necessarily an indication of illegality of his method. As long as he makes no effort to fasten upon ownership of the articles he sells control of the prices at which his purchaser shall sell, it makes no difference how widespread his monopoly. It is only when he adopts a combination with others, by which he steps out of the scope of his patent rights and seeks to control and restrain those to whom he has sold his patented articles in their subsequent disposition of what is theirs, that he comes within the operation of the Anti-Trust Act. . . .

The government relies in its contention for a different conclusion on the case of *Dr. Miles Medical Co. v. John D. Park & Sons Co.*, 220 U. S. 373. . . .

The plan of distribution of the Miles Medical Company resembled in many details the plan of distribution in the present case, except that the subject matter there was medicine by a secret formula, and not a patented article. But there were certain vital differences. . . . This Court . . . found in the contracts themselves and their operation plain provision for purchases by the so-called agents which necessarily made the contracts as to an indefinite amount of the consignments to them, contracts of sale rather than of agency. The court therefore held that the showing made was of an attempt by the Miles Medical Company, through its plan of distribution, to hold its purchasers after the purchase at full price to an obligation to maintain prices on a resale by them. This is the whole effect of the *Miles Medical* Case. . . .

We are of opinion, therefore, that there is nothing as a matter of principle or in the authorities which requires us to hold that genuine contracts of agency like those before us, however comprehensive as a mass or whole in their effect, are violations of the Anti-Trust Act. The owner of an article patented or otherwise is not violating the common law or the

Anti-Trust Act by seeking to dispose of his articles directly to the consumer and fixing the price by which his agents transfer the title from him directly to such consumer. The first charge in the bill can not be sustained.

Second. Had the Electric Company as the owner of the patents, entirely controlling the manufacture, use and sale of the tungsten incandescent lamps, in its license to the Westinghouse Company, the right to impose the condition that its sales should be at prices fixed by the licensor and subject to change according to its discretion? The contention is also made that the license required the Westinghouse Company not only to conform in the matter of the prices at which it might vend the patented articles, but also to follow the same plan as that which we have already explained the Electric Company adopted in its distribution. It does not appear that this provision was express in the license, because no such plan was set out therein, but even if the construction urged by the government is correct, we think the result must be the same.

The owner of a patent may assign it to another and convey (1) the exclusive right to make, use, and vend the invention throughout the United States; or (2) an undivided part or share of that exclusive right; or (3) the exclusive right under the patent within and through a specific part of the United States. But any assignment or transfer short of one of these is a license giving the licensee no title in the patent and no right to sue at law in his own name for an infringement. . . . Conveying less than title to the patent or part of it, the patentee may grant a license to make, use, and vend articles under the specifications of his patent for any royalty, or upon any condition the performance of which is reasonably within the reward which the patentee by the grant of the patent is entitled to secure. . . . The patentee may make and grant a license to another to make and use the patented articles but withhold his right to sell them. The licensee in such a case acquires an interest in the articles made. He owns the material of them and may use them. But if he sells them he infringes the right of the patentee, and may be held for damages and enjoined. If the patentee goes further and licenses the selling of the articles, may he limit the selling by limiting the method of sale and the price? We think he may do so provided the conditions of sale are normally and reasonably adapted to secure pecuniary reward for the patentee's monopoly. One of the valuable elements of the exclusive right of a patentee is to acquire profit by the price at which the article is sold. The higher the price, the greater the profit, unless it is prohibitory. When the patentee licenses another to make and vend and retains the right to continue to make and vend on his own account, the price at which his licensee will sell will necessarily affect the price at which he can sell his own patented goods. It would seem entirely reasonable that he should say to the licensee, "Yes, you may make and sell articles under my patent but not so as to destroy the profit that I wish to obtain by making them and selling them myself." He does not thereby sell outright to the licensee the articles the latter may make and sell or vest absolute ownership in them. He restricts the property and interest the licensee has in the goods he makes and proposes to sell. . . .

Affirmed.

COMMENTARY

1. Consider the Vertical Aspects of the General Electric Distribution System:

General Electric distributed its light bulbs at wholesale and retail levels by consignment. No sale by GE took place until there was a purchase of the bulbs. In the interim, the wholesalers and retailers were "agents" handling the bulbs whose legal title remained in General Electric, the manufacturer. The wholesalers (or B) agents sold to large buyers and the retailers (or A) agents sold to householders and other small purchasers. As the opinion points out there were 400 B agents and 21,000 A agents.

The government argued that "the very size and comprehensiveness" of GE's distribution system should be grounds for treating the agents as purchasers for resale. This contention was successfully employed by the plaintiff in *Simpson v. Union Oil Co.*, 377 U.S. 13 (1964) (Chapter 5, *supra*). What reasons did the Court in GE give for rejecting that argument? Why did the government want the agents to be treated as purchasers for resale? What provisions of the distribution system would have become unlawful if the agents were treated as purchasers for resale? Is it realistic to make the lawfulness of GE's distribution system turn on the skill with which lawyers incorporate the formalities of agency law into distribution contracts? Did the Court distinguish *Dr. Miles*? solely on the ground that the agency contracts were defectively drafted there and were carefully drafted here? Was the Court then suggesting that the patented quality of GE's light bulbs was irrelevant? How did *Simpson* distinguish *GE*?

In 1973 the government successfully attacked General Electric's control of retail prices through its consignment distribution system. Because General Electric no longer controlled the basic patents over light bulbs, the court held that the case was governed by *Simpson v. Union Oil Co. See United States v. General Electric Co.*, 358 F. Supp. 731 (S.D.N.Y. 1973).

2. Earlier attempts at vertical price-fixing of intellectual property:

Vertical price-fixing arrangements were held to violate the Sherman Act as, for example, in *Dr. Miles,* Chapter 5, *supra*. Vertical price-fixing of protectible subject matter under the copyright and patent statutes was not authorized by those statutes.

In *Bobbs-Merrill Co. v. Straus,* 210 U.S. 339 (1908), the Bobbs-Merrill Co. owned the copyright on a novel entitled "The Castaway" and published that novel with the following notice affixed: "The price of this book at retail is one dollar net. No dealer is licensed to sell it at a less [sic] price, and a sale at a less price will be treated as an infringement of the copyright." Bobbs-Merrill sold copies of the book to wholesalers who resold to retailers. R.H. Macy & Co. purchased quantities of the book from wholesalers and resold at retail for 89¢ a copy. Bobbs-Merrill then sought to enjoin Macy from selling below the $1 price set in the notice. Justice Day, writing for the Court, rejected this claim:

> In our view the copyright statutes, while protecting the owner of the copyright in his right to multiply and sell his production, do not create the right to impose, by notice, such as is disclosed in this case, a limitation at which the book shall be sold at retail by future purchasers, with whom there is no privity of contract. . . .

Id. at 351.

In *Bauer & Cie v. O'Donnell*, 229 U.S. 1 (1913), the plaintiff manufacturer owned the United States patent on "Sanatogen," a water soluble ablumenoid, which was uniformly sold and supplied to the trade and to the public in sealed packages bearing the name "Sanatogen," the words "Patented in U.S.A., No. 601,955," and the following notice:

> Notice to the Retailer
>
> This size package of Sanatogen is licensed by us for sale and use at a price not less than one dollar ($1.00). Any sale in violation of this condition, or use when so sold, will constitute an infringement of our patent No. 601,955, under which Sanatogen is manufactured, and all persons so selling or using packages or contents will be liable to injunction and damages.
>
> A purchase is an acceptance of this condition. All rights revert to the undersigned in the event of violation.
>
> The Bauer Chemical Co.

O'Donnell was the proprietor of a retail drug store in Washington, D.C. and was selling packages of Sanatogen at retail at less than the $1 price set in the quoted notice. In upholding the defendant's right to sell the product for whatever price he set, Justice Day, speaking for the Court, said that under the patent as well as the copyright statutes:

> . . . it was the intention of Congress to secure an exclusive right to sell, and there is no grant of a privilege to keep up prices and prevent competition by notices restricting the price at which the article may be resold. The right to vend conferred by the patent law has been exercised, and the added restriction is beyond the protection and purpose of the act. This being so, the case is brought within that line of cases [holding] . . . that a patentee who has parted with a patented machine by passing title to a purchaser has placed the article beyond the limits of the monopoly secured by the patent act. . . .

Id. at 16. The Court's reference to "passing title" states a principle of patent law known as the "first sale" or "exhaustion doctrine." This caselaw principle holds that the authorized sale of a patented product exhausts the patent monopoly as to that product. A purchaser of a patented product from the patentee or its licensee may resell the patented product free of any conditions imposed by the patentee. *See* DONALD S. CHISUM, CHISUM ON PATENTS § 16.03[2][a] (1997). *See also* page 821-22, *infra*.

3. Assuming that General Electric's legal counsel considered the decision in *Bauer & Cie v. O'Donnell* to bar reliance on the GE lamp patent to control the resale prices set by its customers for the lamps, does that suggest why General Electric employed the agency-consignment method to control the retail prices of dealers handling its light bulbs?

4. The Horizontal Aspects of the *General Electric* Decision—The Licensing Arrangement:

The patent statutes confer on the holder of a patent the exclusive right to make, use and sell the patented device, 35 U.S.C. § 154(a)(1). A person who either makes or uses or sells such a device without the permission of the patentee, therefore, is liable to the patentee in an action for infringement. General Electric had licensed Westinghouse and several smaller companies to make (*i.e.,* manufacture) the patented light bulbs and to sell them. The problematic aspect of the licensing agreements was the condition in the license requiring the licensees to observe minimum selling prices set by General Electric.

Note the relationship between patent law, the law of contracts as applied to the license, and antitrust law. By conditioning a license on Westinghouse's sales prices, GE ensured that nonconforming sales by Westinghouse would fall outside of the license and therefore would be infringing sales in violation of the patent law. If Westinghouse also agreed (in a license agreement) to observe GE's directions about resale prices, a violation of the agreement would be a breach of contract. Antitrust law treats price-fixing agreements as not only void, but as a *per se* civil and criminal offense. In *GE,* however, the Court did not condemn price-fixing provisions in that patent license. Why not?

In the second part of its opinion, the Court distinguished a license from an assignment. The Court wanted to establish that GE only issued licenses in order to show that GE retained a continuing interest in the marketing of the bulbs, including the prices at which they were marketed. That continuing economic interest in the patented product, the Court believed, justified GE's assertion of control over the prices at which its licensees sold.

Observe some of the technical aspects of patent licensing present here: Westinghouse had legal title to the bulbs which it manufactured, but needed GE's permission to manufacture and sell them. Under *Bauer & Cie v. O'Donnell*, a wholesale or retailer dealer who purchased bulbs from GE could resell them without GE's permission under the first sale (exhaustion) doctrine. But since Westinghouse had not purchased the physical bulbs (but manufactured them itself) it did not fall within the first sale doctrine and, under patent law, needed GE's permission to sell them.

It is frequently asserted that licensing should be encouraged, as it is a means through which technological "know-how" is dispersed throughout society. GE would be discouraged from licensing Westinghouse and others if it could not control their prices because it would fear that one or more of the licensees would undercut GE's own prices.

Why could not GE protect itself from undercutting by charging a royalty that was large enough to ensure that the licensees could not undercut it? Were there other patented light bulbs on the market?

5. *United States v. Masonite Corp.*, 316 U.S. 265 (1942). The Masonite Corp. was a manufacturer of hardboard. Masonite brought suits against several of its principal competitors, charging them with patent infringement. The suits were settled under an arrangement in which (1) each defendant acknowledged the validity of Masonite's patents and (2) Masonite appointed each defendant as an "agent" to sell hardboard produced by Masonite at prices set by Masonite. The arrangement thus converted Masonite's former manufacturer-competitors into distributors selling Masonite-produced hardboard on consignment. The Court (through Justice Douglas) condemned the arrangement as a misuse of the agency device:

> A patentee who employs . . . [a *del credere*] agent [a *del credere* agent guarantees its principal against default of payment by the vendees of the agent—Eds.] to distribute his product certainly is not enlarging the scope of his patent privilege if it may fairly be said that that distribution is part of the patentee's own business and operates only to secure to him the reward for his invention which Congress has provided. But where he utilizes the sales organization of another business—a business with which he has no intimate relationship—quite different problems are posed since such a regimentation of a marketing system is peculiarly susceptible to the restraints of trade which the Sherman Act condemns. And when it is clear, as it is in this case, that the marketing systems utilized by means of the *del credere* agency agreements are those of competitors of the patentee and that the purpose is to fix prices at which the competitors may market the product, the device is without more an enlargement of the limited patent privilege and a violation of the Sherman Act. In such a case the patentee exhausts his limited privilege when he disposes of the product to the *del credere* agent. . . .

Id. at 279.

Masonite attempted to base its defense upon the vertical part of the *GE* case in which GE's consignment method of distribution was upheld as a lawful means through which GE could control the prices of light bulbs manufactured by it. Do you think that Masonite would have been more successful if it had issued licenses to its rivals for production under the Masonite patents?

If Masonite's patent was in fact valid and the patents of its rivals were invalid, what would be wrong with the agency arrangements? Do you think the fact that the arrangements were established in settlements affected the way that the Court reacted to them? If Masonite had pursued the patent infringement litigation to judgment, establishing the superiority of its patent, would the Court have then permitted Masonite to distribute its production through its former competitors?

A FURTHER LIMITATION OF *GENERAL ELECTRIC*

1. In *United States v. Line Material Co.,* 333 U.S. 287 (1948), complementary product patents for fuses to protect an electrical circuit from the dangers incident to a short circuit or other overload were involved. The dominant patent (George

Lemmon of Southern States Equipment Co.) and an improvement patent (Schultz of Line Material Co.) had been pending simultaneously. The Patent Office resolved the interference between these applications by awarding dominant claims to Southern States Equipment Corp. and subservient claims to Line Material Co., so that both patents were necessary for a commercially viable product. Line and Southern then cross-licensed each other under their respective patents. First Southern and then Line was given the right to issue sublicenses to others. The sublicenses contained price-fixing provisions and Southern agreed to observe the prices set by Line in the sublicenses.

When the Government challenged the price-fixing, the parties defended the arrangement as authorized by the *General Electric* decision. Four Justices agreed and wanted to extend *GE* to protect price-fixing clauses in cross-licensing agreements. Four Justices wanted to take the occasion to overrule *General Electric*. Justice Reed was the swing vote. He wrote an opinion reaffirming *General Electric*, but limiting it to a single patent license:

> While the *General Electric* case holds that a patentee may, under certain conditions, lawfully control the price the licensee of his several patents may charge for the patented device, no case of this Court has construed the patent and antimonopoly statutes to permit separate owners of separate patents by cross-licenses or other arrangements to fix the prices to be charged by them and their licensees for their respective products. Where two or more patentees with competitive, non-infringing patents combine them and fix prices on all devices produced under any of the patents, competition is impeded to a greater degree than where a single patentee fixes prices for his licenses. . . . Even when, as here, the devices are not commercially competitive because the subservient patent cannot be practiced without consent of the dominant, the statement holds good.

2. The objections to the *General Electric* decision: Justice Douglas' concurring opinion in *Line Material* identifies the problematic aspect of *General Electric*:

> . . . the *General Electric* case inverted Cl. 8 of Art. I, § 8 of the Constitution and made the inventor's reward the prime rather than an incidental object of the patent system.
>
> . . . [The patentee] and his associates get . . . an "exclusive right" to form a combination with competitors to fix the prices of the products of invention. The patentee creates by that method a powerful inducement for the abandonment of competition, for the cessation of litigation concerning the validity of patents, for the acceptance of patents no matter how dubious, for the abandonment of research in the development of competing patents. Those who can get stabilized markets, assured margins, and freedom from price cutting will find a price-fixing license an attractive alternative to the more arduous methods of maintaining their competitive positions. Competition tends to become impaired not by rea-

> son of the public's preference for the patented article but because of the preference of competitors for price fixing and for the increased profits which that method of doing business promises.

333 U.S. 287, 318-19 (1948) (Douglas, J., concurring). Justice Douglas was troubled by the fact that the *General Electric* precedent carves out an exception to the rule (of *Socony-Vacuum* and *Trenton Potteries*) condemning all price-fixing agreements among competitors as *per se* illegal. Under *General Electric* a business firm may exert contractual control over the prices of its rivals, so long as the price-fixing power is exerted through a clause in a patent license. Douglas thought that this exception to the rule of *per se* illegality might induce competing firms to accept patent licenses for the benefit of the price-fixing clauses in those licenses rather than for the benefit of the patents in themselves. Douglas thus feared that firms might accept licenses containing price-fixing clauses under economically worthless patents or under patents of doubtful validity.

3. *Standard Sanitary Mfg. Co. v. United States*, 226 U.S. 20 (1912). The Standard Sanitary Mfg. Co., a manufacturer of 50% of the enameled iron ware produced in the United States, was the owner of the Arrott patent. That patent covered an improved process for enameling iron ware with opaque white glass, an operation which was performed in the manufacture of "wash bowls, drinking fountains, sinks, closets, etc." Enameling under the Arrott process produced an invariably even distribution of the glass coating and thus eliminated the unevenness that frequently was produced by the simpler, manual techniques employed prior to the Arrott invention. Besides eliminating the production of defective pieces, the Arrott process also lessened the time required for enameling.

Although originally opposed to licensing other manufacturers to use the Arrott patent, the Standard Sanitary Mfg. Co. ultimately agreed with one Edwin L. Wayman to convey to him the Arrott patent for the purpose of licensing manufacturers of at least 83% of the enameled iron ware industry. Under the licenses each manufacturer would undertake to sell no "seconds" (*i.e.,* allegedly defective products which were said to be injuring the reputation of enameled iron ware). Each licensed manufacturer was also required by the license agreement to sell his iron ware products at set prices to licensed jobbers. Jobbers were licensed to buy enameled ware and to resell it at set prices. In condemning the licensing arrangements, the Supreme Court described the relevant circumstances in the following terms:

> . . . Before the agreements the manufacturers of enameled ware were independent and competitive. By the agreements they were combined, subjected themselves to certain rules and regulations, among others not to sell their product to the jobbers except at a price fixed not by trade and competitive conditions, but by the decision of the committee of six of their number, and zones of sales were created. And the jobbers were brought into the combination and made its subjection complete and its purpose successful. Unless they entered the combination they could

> obtain no enameled ware from any manufacturer who was in the combination, and the condition of entry was not to resell to plumbers except at the prices determined by the manufacturers. The trade was, therefore, practically controlled from producer to consumer, and the potency of the scheme was established by the co-operation of 85% of the manufacturers and their fidelity to it was secured not only by trade advantages but by what was practically a pecuniary penalty, not inaptly termed in the argument, "cash bail." The royalty for each furnace was $5.00, 80% of which was to be returned if the agreement was faithfully observed; it was to be "forfeited as a penalty" if the agreement was violated. And for faithful observance of their engagements the jobbers, too, were entitled to rebates from their purchases.

Id. at 47.

4. Compare *General Electric* with *Standard Sanitary*. A critical difference is that in *Standard Sanitary* the patent license is apparently being used as a cover for a price-fixing cartel. That is, the patent license is primarily important to the licensees not for the technology which it brings but as an excuse for price-fixing. Is there any way of testing a given patent license to determine whether the motive underlying the licensee's acceptance of the license was the value to it of the patented technology or whether the motive underlying its acceptance of the license was the prospect of entering into a price-fixing agreement? What inferences would you draw from a patent license being accepted by less than all firms in an industry? What inferences would you draw in a circumstance in which most of the firms in an industry have accepted a patent license containing price-fixing provisions and the royalty is small in comparison to the profit margins of the licensee firms? *See* George L. Priest, *Cartels and Patent License Arrangements*, 20 J.L. & ECON. 309, 327 (1977); William F. Baxter, *Legal Restrictions on Exploitation of the Patent Monopoly: An Economic Analysis*, 76 YALE L.J. 267, 336 (1966).

5. If Westinghouse had possessed its own process for producing a light bulb which did not infringe the General Electric patent, what incentives would it have for accepting a license under the General Electric patent?

6. After the *Line Material* decision, could Southern dedicate its (Lemmon) patent to the public and then accept a license from Line (under the Schultz patent) which contained a price-fixing provision? How would this result differ from the transaction disallowed in the *Line Material* decision?

7. Could Line purchase the Lemmon patent from Southern and then issue licenses containing price-fixing clauses under the combined Lemmon and Schultz patents to firms other than Southern? to Southern?

Standard Oil Co. (Indiana) v. United States
283 U.S. 163 (1931)

[Appeal from a decree of the District Court granting part of the relief sought by the government in a bill charging an illegal combination to monopolize and restrain interstate commerce by controlling that part of the supply of gasoline which is produced by the process of "cracking."]

Mr. Justice BRANDEIS delivered the opinion of the Court.

. . . It had long been known that from a given quantity of crude, additional oils of high volatility could be produced by "cracking"; that is, by applying heat and pressure to the residuum after ordinary distillation. . . . The first such process was perfected by the Indiana Company in 1913; and for more than seven years this was the only one practiced in America. . . .

Meanwhile . . . other concerns had been working independently to develop commercial processes of their own. Most prominent among these were the three other primary defendants, the Texas Company, the New Jersey Company, and the Gasoline Products Company. Each of these secured numerous patents covering its particular cracking process. Beginning in 1920, conflict developed among the four companies concerning the validity, scope, and ownership of issued patents. One infringement suit was begun; cross-notices of infringement . . . were given . . . . The primary defendants assert that it was these difficulties which led to their executing the three principal agreements which the United States attacks; and that their sole object was to avoid litigation and losses incident to conflicting patents.

. . . The three agreements differ from one another only slightly in scope and terms. Each primary defendant was released thereby from liability for any past infringement of patents of the others. Each acquired the right to use these patents thereafter in its own process. Each was empowered to extend to independent concerns, licensed under its process, releases from past, and immunity from future claims of infringement of patents controlled by the other primary defendants. And each was to share in some fixed proportion the fees received under these multiple licenses. The royalties to be charged were definitely fixed in the first contract; and minimum sums per barrel, to be divided between the Texas and Indiana companies, were specified in the second and third. . . .

. . . .

Second. The Government contends that the three agreements constitute a pooling by the primary defendants of the royalties from their several patents; that thereby competition between them in the commercial exercise of their respective rights to issue licenses is eliminated; that this tends to maintain or increase the royalty charged secondary defendants [*i.e.,* the licensees] and hence to increase the manufacturing cost of cracked gasoline; that thus the primary defendants exclude from interstate commerce gasoline which would, under lower competitive royalty rates, be produced . . . . The only restraint thus charged is that necessarily arising out of the making and effect of the provisions for cross-licensing and for division of royalties.

. . . Where there are legitimately conflicting claims or threatened interferences, a settlement by agreement, rather than litigation, is not precluded by the Act. . . . An interchange of patent rights and a division of royalties according to the value attributed by the parties to their respective patent claims is frequently necessary if technical advancement is not to be blocked by threatened litigation. If the available advantages are upon on reasonable terms to all manufacturers desiring to participate, such interchange may promote rather than restrain competition. . . .

Third. The Government . . . contends that the agreements to maintain royalties violate the Sherman Law because the fees charged are onerous. The argument is that the competitive advantage which the three primary defendants enjoy of manufacturing cracked gasoline free of royalty, while licensees must pay to them a heavy tribute in fees, enables these primary defendants to exclude from interstate commerce cracked gasoline which would, under lower competitive royalty rates, be produced by possible rivals. This argument ignores the privileges incident to ownership of patents. Unless the industry is dominated, or interstate commerce directly restrained, the Sherman Act does not require cross-licensing patentees to license at reasonable rates others engaged in interstate commerce. . . . The allegation that the royalties charged are onerous is, standing alone, without legal significance. . . .

Fourth. The main contention of the Government is [that the provisions of the three agreements providing for fixed royalties] . . . enable the primary defendants to maintain existing royalties. . . . The alleged effect of these provisions is to enable the primary defendants, because of their monopoly of patented cracking processes, to maintain royalty rates at the level established originally for the Indiana process.

The rate of royalties may, of course be a decisive factor in the cost of production. If combining patent owners effectively dominate an industry, the power to fix and maintain royalties is tantamount to the power to fix prices. . . . Where domination exists, a pooling of competing process patents, or an exchange of licenses for the purpose of curtailing the manufacture and supply of an unpatented product, is beyond the privileges conferred by the patents and constitutes a violation of the Sherman Act. The lawful individual monopolies granted by the patent statutes cannot be unitedly exercised to restrain competition. . . . But an agreement for cross-licensing and division of royalties violates the Act only when used to effect a monopoly, or to fix prices, or to impose otherwise an unreasonable restraint upon interstate commerce. . . . In the case at bar, the primary defendants own competing patented processes for manufacturing an unpatented product which is sold in interstate commerce; and agreements concerning such processes are likely to engender the evils to which the Sherman Act was directed. . . . We must, therefore, examine the evidence to ascertain the operation and effect of the challenged contracts.

Fifth. No monopoly, or restriction of competition, in the business of licensing patented cracking processes resulted from the execution of these agreements. . . . [The] development and commercial expansion of competing processes is clear evidence that the contracts did not concentrate in the hands of the four primary defendants the licensing of patented processes for the production of cracked gasoline. . . .

No monopoly, or restriction of competition, in the production of either ordinary or cracked gasoline has been proved. The output of cracked gasoline in the years in question was about 26% of the total gasoline production. Ordinary or straight run gasoline is indistinguishable from cracked gasoline and the two are either mixed or sold interchangeably. Under these circumstances the primary defendants could not effectively control the supply or fix the price of cracked gasoline by virtue of their alleged monopoly of the cracking processes, unless they could control, through some means, the remainder of the total gasoline production from all sources. . . . In the absence of proof that the primary defendants had such control of the entire industry as would make effective the alleged domination of a part, it is difficult to see how they could by agreeing upon royalty rates control either the price or the supply of gasoline, or otherwise restrain competition. . . .

Reversed.

COMMENTARY

1. The defendants controlled 55% of the cracked gasoline market and 25% of the entire gasoline market. Which market controlled? What did the Court consider credible evidence of the existence of "blocking patents"? Suppose the patents in this case had been fully competing—that is, they involved substitute processes at essentially the same cost. Should the analysis and holding of *Standard Oil* control? Suppose the parties to a patent pool had reason to believe that their improvements to a basic patent would not qualify for patent protection, should *Standard Oil* control? Lower courts have permitted horizontal agreement among competitors relating to cross-licensing of blocking patents. Under rule of reason analysis such agreements are deemed necessary in order for each patentee to practice its own patent without incurring liability for infringement. *See Carpet Seaming Tape Licensing Corp. v. Best Seam, Inc.*, 616 F.2d 1133 (9th Cir. 1980), *aff'd in part*, 694 F.2d 570 (9th Cir. 1982), *cert. denied*, 464 U.S. 818 (1983) (exchange of blocking patents a recognized legitimate purpose). However, there are at least three constraints on the legality of patent pools. First, a patent pool that creates monopoly power in a market and excludes others has been held to fall outside the scope of legitimate pooling. In *United States v. National Lead Co.,* 63 F. Supp. 513 (S.D.N.Y. 1945), *aff'd,* 332 U.S. 319 (1947), the exchange of nonexclusive licenses between the largest firms in the product market involving all patents existing and future, and excluding competitors, was held illegal. In *United States v. Krasnov*, 143 F. Supp. 184 (E.D. Pa. 1956), the cross-licensing arrangement between the two dominant firms in an industry was held to violate the antitrust laws because there was price-fixing, refusal to license, and sharing of patent litigation expenses. Second, even in the absence of monopoly power, a pooling arrangement that had the effect of excluding a competitor from a relevant (foreign) market, was held illegal in *Zenith Radio Corp. v. Hazeltine Research, Inc.,* 395 U.S. 100 (1969). Third, as noted in *United States v. Line Material*, above, a pooling arrangement containing price-fixing provisions is illegal. Similarly, exclusion of a competitor may counterbalance a cross-licensing arrangement necessitated to avoid patent blocking. *See United States v. Singer Mfg. Co.*, 374 U.S. 174 (1963), in which the trial court's finding of no antitrust violation was reversed on the basis of an ancillary finding that suppression of competition was a goal of the cross-licensing.

2. The joint Department of Justice/Federal Trade Commission ANTITRUST GUIDELINES FOR THE LICENSING OF INTELLECTUAL PROPERTY issued in April of 1995 (*see* Appendix C) state a concern by the enforcement agencies with patent cross-licensing arrangements where new technology is involved. The Guidelines expressly recognize that innovation is promoted and competition is enhanced by licensing arrangements (Guidelines 4.3) and state further that the agencies will not presume that the existence of a patent, copyright, or trade secret necessarily confers market power on the rightholder. Guidelines 2.2. The format of the Guidelines is to provide "safety zones"—general circumstances in which restraint provisions in licensing agreements will not be challenged by the enforcement agencies. The general analysis takes market share data, when available and relevant, and defines a "safety zone" as one in which the market share of all the firms subject to the license restraint account for less than a 20 percent market share. If market share data is not available or not meaningful, then a "safety zone" exists if there are at least 4 or more independently controlled firms offering the same technology at comparable cost to the licensees. Guidelines 4.3. It is assumed for purposes of these examples that the particular restraint would not be one, such as price-fixing, that would be illegal *per se*.

In Example 2 (Guidelines, 3.2.2), there is agreement between competitors having two (non-blocking) patents of different processes to make an unpatented pharmaceutical by the transfer of both patents to a joint venture. The concern expressed is for the effect of the joint venture on competition in the relevant market for the technology to manufacture the compound and ultimately on the price of the pharmaceutical. Note the two-step analysis proposed of 1) the availability of other manufacturing technologies at comparable cost and 2) the availability of near substitutes for the end product. Do the Guidelines consider such combinations of factors of production to be pro-competitive? *See* Guidelines 2.0(c); for the analysis of joint ventures, *see* 3.2.3, Example 4.

In Examples 9 and 10 (5.1), the Guidelines distinguish the analysis of cross-licensing between patents that are blocking and those that are not. Basically, non-blocking patents are viewed as horizontal agreements between competitors. If there is no evidence of efficiency-enhancing integration as a result of the cross-licensing, the restraint might be viewed as a *per se* restraint if uniform prices or territorial restrictions were involved. Where there is evidence of efficiency-enhancing benefits from the arrangement, rule of reason analysis will be applied.

NOTE: *WALKER PROCESS* AND RELATED DOCTRINES

Walker Process Equipment Inc. v. Food Machinery & Chemical Corp., 382 U.S. 172 (1965), involved a patent which the patentee had obtained on the basis of a false statement in the patent application that the invention had not been on sale for more than a year prior to the time of the filing. The patentee knew that statement to be false at the time when it made that statement. The Court held that, in addition to this conscious fraud on the patent office invalidating the patent and all infringement actions under it, such fraud could constitute the basis of actions under §§ 1 & 2 of the Sherman Act if, in addition to the fraud, the plaintiff could establish the exclusionary power of the illegal patent claim in the relevant market for the affected product. (Note that although a patent confers exclusionary rights over the subject matter of the patent, the exercise of those rights is not necessarily anti-competitive.) Similarly, in *Charles Pfizer & Co. v. FTC*, 401 F.2d 574 (6th Cir. 1968), *cert. denied,* 394 U.S. 920 (1969), the court affirmed a Commission finding that submitting false and misleading information to the Patent and Trademark

Office violated § 5 of the Federal Trade Commission Act. There, the defendants were required to grant non-exclusive licenses at specified royalties. A slightly different, but related, issue arose in *Handgards, Inc. v. Ethicon, Inc.*, 743 F.2d 1282 (9th Cir. 1984). In *Handgards*, a firm with a 90% market share sued for patent infringement on a patent, knowing the patent to be invalid. In these circumstances, the Ninth Circuit sustained a jury finding of attempting to monopolize in violation of § 2 of the Sherman Act.

In patent litigation, it is a common practice for a defendant charged with infringement to counterclaim, alleging an antitrust violation. In its most common version, the counterclaim attempts to replicate *Handgards* where the antitrust offense consisted of maintaining a monopoly through the mechanism of bringing a lawsuit to enforce a patent known to be invalid. In the version replicating *Walker Process*, the counterclaimant would allege that the plaintiff not only is consciously attempting to preserve a monopoly by enforcing an invalid patent, but that the plaintiff had obtained the patent itself by fraud on the Patent Office.

The *Walker Process* and *Handgards* cases are in tension with the *Noerr/Pennington* doctrine, which recognizes the right of individuals and corporations to seek redress from government, including a right to sue in the courts, without being subjected to antitrust liability. In *California Motor Transport Co. v. Trucking Unlimited*, 404 U.S. 508 (1972), however, the Court recognized an important exception to the right to institute proceedings before courts and agencies: a person is entitled, under the *Noerr/Pennington* line of cases, to bring lawsuits (or other proceedings) to vindicate claims, but only so long as the lawsuits are not "shams" brought for the purpose of so harassing the respondent as to deny it "free and meaningful access to agencies and courts." *Id.* at 515. This concept of "sham" recognized in *California Motor Transport* is not free from ambiguity. On the one hand, *California Motor Transport* recognizes the right of every person to use its access to agencies and courts to further its own (including competitive) interests. On the other, it excludes from the protection of the *Noerr/Pennington* doctrine, certain suits and proceedings which are "shams," without providing a workable definition of such sham litigation.

After *California Motor Transport*, then, both the *Walker Process/Handgards* and *Noerr/Pennington* lines of cases recognized that a person does not lose the right to sue, merely because the claim is doubtful. But the line between suing to enforce a patent claim of doubtful validity and suing to enforce a patent claim which is known to be invalid is sometimes difficult to identify in practice. This practical fuzziness was inherent in the application of *Handgards* from the beginning, but it was generally resolved through the use of a probable cause analogy: Was there an objectively reasonable basis for the patentee to bring its infringement action? Yet the gloss on the *Noerr/Pennington* doctrine provided by *California Motor Transport* carried some emphasis upon the plaintiff's subjective intent in bringing the lawsuit which added additional perplexity to the application of a probable cause approach.

In 1993, the Supreme Court decided *Professional Real Estate Investors, Inc. v. Columbia Pictures Industries, Inc.*, 508 U.S. 49 (1993) (*PRE*), a case involving an attempt to enforce copyrights and in which the defendants responded with an antitrust counterclaim, asserting that the copyright action was a "sham" designed to monopolize the viewing of motion pictures by hotel guests. In that case, the Supreme Court provided a comprehensive two-part test for use in identifying "sham" litigation involving all antitrust claims arising from the enforcement of intellectual property and other legal rights. Under the two part test of *PRE*, in order to constitute "a sham," the lawsuit must be objectively baseless. Only if the court determines that the lawsuit was objectively baseless, is the court permitted to reach the second part of the test. That second part of the test asks "whether the baseless lawsuit conceals an 'attempt to interfere *directly* with the business relationships of a competitor' . . . through the 'use [of] the governmental *process*—as opposed to the outcome of that process—as an anticompetitive weapon.' . . ." *Id.* at 60-61 (quoting *Columbia v. Omni Outdoor Advertising, Inc.*, 499 U.S. 365, 380 (1991)). The Court's construction of the two-part test heightens the importance of an objective standard. Indeed, the satisfaction of the objective standard is explicitly made a *sine qua non* for the "sham" analysis to go forward. *PRE*, therefore, should act as a needed corrective to uncertainty engendered by *California Motor Transport.* Some lower courts, however, have followed the gloss on the *PRE* two-part test suggested by Justice Stevens in his *PRE* concurrence: When a person brings a series of lawsuits pursuant to a policy of starting legal proceedings without regard to the merits and for the purpose of injuring a market rival, that behavior falls within the sham exception to *Noerr/Pennington. USS-POSCO Indus. v. Contra Costs County Bldg. & Constr. Trades Council*, 31 F.3d 800, 811 (9th cir. 1994) (*dicta*).

For a critical review of the impact of PRE on patent litigation, see James B. Kobak, Jr., *Professionial Real Estate Investors and the Future of Patent-Antitrust Litigation:* Walker Process *and* Handgards *Meet* Noerr-Pennington, 63 ANTITRUST L.J. 185 (1994). Kobak writes:

> What is not . . . clear is what that test will mean and how it will be applied. At the objective phase, the questions are apt often to turn on state of mind and be more factual that was the case in *PRE,* so that the Court's many different phrasings of the test may provide little guidance. At the subjective phase, the question is what, in addition to the antitrust defendants' knowing commencement of objectively baseless litigation to enforce an exclusionary right, a claimant need show—and why it need show it—simply to have a chance to to try to establish an already difficult antitrust claim.

Id. at 211. Do you think that the test of liability set forth in *Handgards* is consistent with the *PRE* test? Is it subsumed in *PRE*? *See* Chapter 18, Section D, for discussion of *Noerr* and related cases. Explain how the *PRE* opinion modifies these cases. Would *Columbia v. Omni Outdoor Advertising Inc.,* page 964, *infra*, come out the same way under the test of *PRE*?

D. Patents and Tying Arrangements; From *Mercoid* to *Dawson* and the Provisions of the Patent Act

The general antitrust law governing tying arrangements was reviewed in Chapter 6, above. Here the focus is upon special problems which arise when tying practices involve intellectual property, primarily patented products. Not all of the issues involving such tying arrangements are viewed by courts as antitrust issues. As some of the cases below illustrate, tying practices involving patented articles, may raise issues as a matter of patent law, such as the scope of patent law protection, the extent to which patent law permits conditioning a license upon the use of specified supplies, the scope of the "patent misuse" doctrine, and the validity and enforceability of contractual provisions. Consider how courts address the tension between the patent act and the antitrust laws, recalling that the antitrust laws were not enacted until 1890, at which time the courts had been dealing with patent cases for almost a century. *E.g., Evans v. Eaton*, 21 U.S. (3 Wheat.) 454 (1818); *Burr v. Duryee*, 68 U.S. (1 Wall.) 531 (1863); *Adams v. Burke*, 84 U.S. (17 Wall.) 453 (1874).

NOTE: SOME HISTORY

1. *Leeds & Catlin Co. v. Victor Talking Machine Co.*, 213 U.S. 325 (1909), involved a suit brought by the Victor Company (the owner of a patent on a phonograph) against Leeds & Catlin which made records for use on the phonograph. The Victor Company charged that the manufacture of records by Leeds & Catlin was an act of contributory infringement. The Victor Company's theory was that the record was a component part of the patented phonograph and that Leeds & Catlin sold such a component, knowing that it would be used by the purchaser to "construct" the patented invention. Since only the patentee or its licensees had a right to make the patented invention, the purchaser of a Leeds & Catlin record committed an act of direct infringement when he or she placed the record on the phonograph, and Leeds & Catlin, by facilitating the act of direct infringement, committed an act of contributory infringement. (A similar "construction" of the patented invention with the use of a Victor record would, of course, have been lawful, because Victor extended a license to all phonograph owners to "construct" or "reconstruct" the patented invention with a Victor record.)

In the *Victor* case, the Court distinguished a previous case, *Morgan Envelope Co. v. Albany Perforated Wrapping Paper Co.*, 152 U.S. 425 (1894), which had rejected a claim of contributory infringement against the supplier of paper rolls for use with a toilet-paper dispenser on the ground that the element there supplied was "an article of manufacture, perishable in its nature, which it [was] . . . the object of the mechanism to deliver, and must be renewed periodically whenever the device is put to use." By contrast, in the *Victor* case,

> [t]he disc is not a mere concomitant to the stylus; it co-acts with the stylus to produce the result. Indeed, . . . it is the distinction of the invention, constituting . . . the advance upon the prior art. [T]here is no pretense of mending broken or worn-out records, or of repairing or replacing "the operative ultimate tool of the invention" which has deteriorated by use. The sales of the petitioner . . . were not to furnish new records identical with those originally offered by the Victor Company, but . . . "more frequently in order to increase the repertory of tunes than as substituted for worn-out records." . . . The right of substitution or "resupply" of an element depends upon the same test. The license granted to a purchaser of a patented combination is to preserve its fitness for use so far as it may be affected by wear or breakage. Beyond this there is no license.

2. *Henry v. A.B. Dick Co.*, 221 U.S. 1 (1912), involved an attempt by the A.B. Dick Co. (the owner of two patents on a mimeograph machine) to control the market for paper, ink, and supplies used with that machine. In this case, the patent did not extend to the paper, ink, and supplies, so the patentee attempted to exert control over the latter by conditioning the right to use the machines it sold. The following notice was attached to a machine purchased by a Miss Christina B. Skou:

> License Restriction
>
> This machine is sold by the A.B. Dick Co. with the license restriction that it may be used only with the stencil paper, ink and other supplies made by A.B. Dick Company, Chicago, U.S.A.

The A.B. Dick Company brought suit against one Sidney Henry as a result of his selling ink to Miss Skou with knowledge of the license restriction and with the expectation that it would be used in the machine. Under the A.B. Dick Company's theory, Henry would be a contributory infringer and Miss Skou would be a direct infringer. The Court upheld the validity of the license restriction and thereby endorsed the A.B. Dick Company's theory.

3. Five years later, the Court overruled *Henry v. A.B. Dick Co.* in *Motion Picture Patents Co. v. Universal Film Manufacturing Co.*, 243 U.S. 502 (1917). In the latter case the Motion Picture Patents Co. held the patent on a mechanism for feeding motion-picture film into a projector. The Motion Picture Patents Company attached a condition to the machines sold under which the owner had a license to use the machine only with certain specified film and obligated itself to pay a royalty. The Court reviewed the theory under which the owner of a patent claimed the right to control the use of supplies to be used with its patented invention, a theory which the Court traced to *Heaton-Peninsular Button-Fastener Co. v. Eureka Specialty Co.*, 77 F. 288 (6th Cir. 1896). Influenced by the Congressional hostility to tie-ins manifested in the enactment of § 3 of the Clayton Act in 1914, the Court repudiated *Heaton-Peninsular Button-Fastener* and overruled *A.B. Dick*. The Court thus ruled that the rights conferred under patent law do not include the right to control the supplies to be used with a patented invention. Since that ruling resolved the case, the Court did not consider whether the tie (of film to the film-feeder) involved a violation of the antitrust laws.

4. *Carbice Corp. of America v. America Patents Development Corp.*, 283 U.S. 27 (1931), involved a patent on a "transportation package," a container used for shipping ice cream long distances prior to the advent of refrigerator cars. The transportation package consisted of a carton with a center compartment containing dry ice (*i.e.,* solid carbon dioxide) surrounded by an outer compartment holding ice cream. The dry ice was shielded by the ice cream and in turn kept the ice cream from melting.

The American Patents Development Corporation held the patent on the container which it licensed exclusively to the Dry Ice Corporation. The Dry Ice Corporation, which sold dry ice, was granted an exclusive royalty-free license by American Patents to use the transportation package. When the Carbice Corp. sold dry ice to customers with the knowledge that its customers were using it to construct a transportation package, the American Patents Development Corporation (the patentee) and the Dry Ice Corporation (the exclusive licensee) brought suit for contributory infringement. When the case reached the Supreme Court, the Court recognized that the Carbice Corp. was a contributory infringer, but denied relief on the ground that the patentee and its exclusive licensee were guilty of patent misuse by engaging in a tie. So long as the misuse continued, they would be barred from enforcing their patent rights:

> The invention claimed is for a particular kind of package employing solid carbon dioxide in a new combination. If the patent is valid the owner can, of course, prohibit entirely the manufacture, sale, or use of such packages. . . . Or it can grant licenses upon terms consistent with the limited scope of the patent monopoly. . . . It may charge a royalty or license fee. But it may not exact as the condition of a license that unpatented materials used in connection with the invention shall be purchased only from the licensor; and if it does so, relief against one who supplies such unpatented materials will be denied. The limited monopoly to make, use, and vend an article may not be "expanded by limitations as to materials and supplies necessary to the operation of it." *Motion Picture Patents Co. v. Universal Film Manufacturing Co.* . . .
>
> . . . The Dry Ice Corporation has no right to be free from competition in the sale of solid carbon dioxide. Control over the supply of such unpatented material is beyond the scope of the patentee's monopoly. . . . Relief is denied because the Dry Ice Corporation is attempting, without sanction of law, to employ the patent to secure a limited monopoly of unpatented material used in applying the invention. . . . [T]he plaintiffs neither sell nor license others to sell complete transportation packages. They supply merely one of the several materials entering into the com-

bination; and on that commodity they have not been granted a monopoly. Their attempt to secure one cannot be sanctioned.

283 U.S. at 30-35.

5. In 1944, the Supreme Court decided the *Mercoid* cases: *Mercoid Corp. v. Mid-Continent Investment Co.*, 320 U.S. 661 (1944), and *Mercoid Corp. v. Minneapolis-Honeywell Regulator Co.*, 320 U.S. 680 (1944). Both cases involved "combination patents," *i.e.*, patents upon the combination of several nonpatented components. The first case involved a patent on a domestic heating system composed of a motor driven stoker for feeding coal into the furnace, a thermostat, and a combustion stoker switch which overrode the thermostat to prevent the fire from being extinguished in warm weather. Honeywell was the exclusive licensee of Mid-Continent, the owner of the patent on the heating system. Honeywell did not sell the combination but rather sold the combination stoker switch and granted the right to use the patented heating system to purchasers of the stoker switch. The Mercoid Corporation produced the combination stoker switch knowing that purchasers would use it to construct the patented heating system without permission of the patentee. When Mercoid was sued for contributory infringement, the Court denied relief on the ground of patent misuse:

> Mercoid, like Mid-Continent and Minneapolis-Honeywell, does not sell or install the . . . heating system. But the Circuit Court of Appeals found that Mercoid manufactured and sold combustion stoker switches for use in the . . . combination patent. And we may assume that Mercoid did not act innocently. Indeed the Circuit Court of Appeals said that it could find no use for the accused devices other than in the . . . combination patent. . . . But though we assume the validity of the patent and accept fully the findings of the Circuit Court of Appeals, we think the judgment below should be reversed.
>
> Ever since *Henry v. A.B. Dick Co.* . . . was overruled by *Motion Picture Co. v. Universal Film Co.* . . . this Court has consistently held that the owner of a patent may not employ it to secure a limited monopoly of an unpatented material used in applying the invention. . . . [In prior] cases both direct and contributory infringement suits were disallowed on a showing that the owner of the patent was using it "as the effective means of restraining competition with its sale of an unpatented article." . . . It is true that those cases involved the use of the patent for a machine or process to secure a partial monopoly in supplies consumed in its operation or unpatented materials employed in it. But we can see no difference in principle where the unpatented material or device is itself an integral part of the structure embodying the patent.
>
> * * *

The instant case is a graphic illustration of the evils of an expansion of the patent monopoly by private engagements. The patent in question embraces furnace assemblies which neither the patentee nor the licensee makes or vends. The struggle is not over a combination patent and the right to make or vend it. The contest is solely over unpatented wares which go into the patented product. . . . [T]he competition which is sought to be controlled is not competition in the sale of the patented assembly but merely competition in the sale of the unpatented thermostatic controls. The patent is employed to protect the market for a device on which no patent has been granted. . . . Mr. Justice Brandeis, speaking for the Court, stated in the *Carbice* case that "Control over the supply of such unpatented material is beyond the scope of the patentee's monopoly; and this limitation, inherent in the patent grant, is not dependent upon the peculiar function or character of the unpatented material or on the way in which it is used." . . . We now add that it makes no difference that the unpatented device is part of the patented whole.

That result may not be obviated in the present case by calling the combustion stoker switch the "heart of the invention" or the "advance in the art." The patent is for a combination only. . . .

Leeds & Catlin v. Victor Talking Machine Co. (No. 2) . . . is authority for the conclusion that he who sells an unpatented part of a combination patent for use in the assembled machine may be guilty of contributory infringement. The protection which the Court in that case extended to the phonograph record, which was an unpatented part of the patented phonograph, is in substance inconsistent with the view which we have expressed in this case. The rule of the *Leeds & Catlin* case (No. 2) accordingly must no longer prevail against the defense[1] that a combination patent is being used to protect an unpatented part from competition. That result obtains here though we assume for the purposes of this case that Mercoid was a contributory infringer and that respondents could have enjoined the infringement had they not misused the patent for the purpose of monopolizing unpatented material. Inasmuch as their misuse of the patent would have precluded them from enjoining a direct infringement . . . they cannot stand in any better position with respect to a contributory infringer. Where there is a collision between the principle

---

[1] The Court in that case did not refer to the doctrine of misuse of a patent. That doctrine indeed was developed in this Court some years later as shown by the *Motion Picture* case. The record in the *Leeds & Catlin* case indicates that the point which we deem crucial in the instant case was adverted to only obliquely in the briefs. The Court was chiefly concerned with the proposition that a substitution or renewal of an unpatented element of a combination patent, as distinguished from its repair, is a "reconstruction" of the combination. 213 U.S. at 333, 336.

> of the *Carbice* case and the conventional rules governing either direct or contributory infringement, the former prevails.
>
> The result of this decision, together with those which have preceded it, is to limit substantially the doctrine of contributory infringement. What residuum may be left we need not stop to consider. . . .

320 U.S. at 664-69.

Mercoid Corp. v. Minneapolis-Honeywell Regulator Co., 320 U.S. 680 (1944), involved another combination patent, the Freeman patent held by Honeywell covering a system of hot air furnace control, employing three thermostats: a room thermostat which starts the stoker, a limit switch which breaks the stoker circuit when the air in the furnace reaches a predetermined temperature, irrespective of the fact that the room thermostat may still call for heat, and a third thermostat which controls a fan which forces hot air from the furnace to the rooms when the air in the furnace reaches a specified degree of heat. Honeywell licensed five of its manufacturing competitors under the Freeman patent. Each licensee was required to attach to each furnace control sold a notice that the control included a license for one installation of the Freeman heating system. The licenses also established minimum prices for the sale of the controls. Honeywell tried unsuccessfully to induce Mercoid to take a license. When Honeywell sued Mercoid, the Court not only held that the patents could not be enforced because of patent misuse but also indicated that the arrangement violated the antitrust laws:

> Neither the petitioner nor the respondent sells or installs the Freeman system in furnaces; that is to say, they do not practice the invention. They are competitors in supplying the switch to control the fan and limit circuits employed in such systems. . . . The Circuit Court of Appeals concluded that although the combustion furnace control was unpatented, it served "to distinguish the invention" and to mark the "advance in the art" achieved by the Freeman patent. . . .
>
> The fact that an unpatented part of a combination patent may distinguish the invention does not draw to it the privileges of a patent. . . . The legality of any attempt to bring unpatented goods within the protection of the patent is measured by the anti-trust laws not by the patent law. For the reasons stated in *Mercoid v. Mid-Continent Investment Co., supra*, the effort here made to control competition in this unpatented device plainly violates the anti-trust laws, even apart from the price-fixing provisions of the license agreements. It follows that petitioner is entitled to be relieved against the consequences of those acts. It likewise follows that respondent may not obtain from a court of equity any decree which directly or indirectly helps it to subvert the public policy which underlies the grant of its patent. . . .

320 U.S. at 683-84.

The *Mercoid* cases created turmoil in the law of contributory infringement by essentially abolishing it. One commentator has summarized the unsettled state of the case law after the *Mercoid* cases as follows:

> . . . [T]hree distinct positions on misuse emerged in the courts, which caused serious confusion and uncertainty for the next forty years. First, there was the Douglas thesis that because misuse defenses were based on the public policy underlying the patent laws, any cognizable misuse defense was an antitrust violation *per se* without regard to market impact. Second, there were the pronouncements in *Carbice* . . . and *Morton Salt* that a viable misuse defense could be sustained without reference to the antitrust laws or consideration of market impact. Finally, there is the court of appeals' position in *Morton Salt*, which required a showing of antitrust injury including market impact to sustain a misuse defense.

Richard Calkins, *Patent Law: The Impact of the 1988 Patent Misuse Reform Act and* Noerr-Pennington *Doctrine on Misuse Defenses and Antitrust Counterclaims,* 38 DRAKE L. REV. 175, 185 (1988-89).

6. Congress responded to this state of the misuse/contributory infringement muddle by amending the Patent Act in 1952, 66 Stat. 815, 35 U.S.C. §§ 1-376 (1952), to include the following provision:

> § 271. Infringement of patent
>
> (a) Except as otherwise provided in this title, whoever without authority makes, uses or sells any patented invention, within the United States during the term of the patent therefor, infringes the patent.
>
> (b) Whoever actively induces infringement of a patent shall be liable as an infringer.
>
> (c) Whoever sells a component of a patented machine, manufacture, combination or composition, or a material or apparatus for use in practicing a patented process, constituting a material part of the invention, knowing the same to be especially made or especially adapted for use in an infringement of such patent, and not a staple article or commodity of commerce suitable for substantial noninfringing use, shall be liable as a contributory infringer.
>
> (d) No patent owner otherwise entitled to relief for infringement or contributory infringement of a patent shall be denied relief or deemed guilty of misuse or illegal extension of the patent right by reason of his having done one or more of the following: (1) derived revenue from acts which if performed by another without his consent would constitute contributory infringement of the patent; (2) licensed or authorized another to perform acts which if performed without his consent would constitute contributory infringement of the patent; (3) sought to enforce his patent rights against infringement or contributory infringement. . . .

Congress believed that this provision had the effect of overruling the *Mercoid* cases by reinstating the doctrine of contributory infringement and restricting the scope of the misuse doctrine. Do you agree? How would the *Leeds & Catlin* case fare under the 1952 legislation?

The 1952 version of § 271 was amended in 1988, by adding clauses (4) and (5). Section 271(d) now provides that no patent owner shall be denied relief or deemed guilty of misuse or illegal extension of the patent right by reason of having "(4) refused to license or use any rights of the patent; or (5) conditioned the license of any rights to the patent or the sale of the patented product on the acquisition of a license to rights in another patent or purchase of a separate product, unless, in view of the circumstances, the patent owner has market power in the relevant market for the patent or patented product on which the license or sale is conditioned." *See* page 811, *infra*.

The 1952 version of § 271 (above) was the focus of the Court's decision in *Dawson Chemical Co. v. Rohm & Haas Co.*, considered in Part E, below.

In re Independent Service Organizations Antitrust Litigation

203 F.3d 1322 (Fed. Cir. 2000)

MAYER, Chief Judge.

CSU, L.L.C. appeals the judgment of the United States District Court for the District of Kansas, dismissing on summary judgment CSU's claims that Xerox's refusal to sell patented parts and copyrighted manuals and to license copyrighted software violate the antitrust laws. . . . Because we agree with the district court that CSU has not raised a genuine issue as to any material fact and that Xerox is entitled to judgment as a matter of law, we affirm.

Background

Xerox manufactures, sells, and services high-volume copiers. Beginning in 1984, it established a policy of not selling parts unique to its series 10 copiers to independent service organizations ("ISOs"), including CSU, unless they were also end-users of the copiers. In 1987, the policy was expanded to include all new products as well as existing series 9 copiers. Enforcement of this policy was tightened in 1989, and Xerox cut off CSU's direct purchase of restricted parts. Xerox also implemented an "on-site end-user verification" procedure to confirm that the parts ordered by certain ISOs or their customers were actually for their end-user use. Initially this procedure applied to only the six most successful ISOs, which included CSU.

To maintain its existing business of servicing Xerox equipment, CSU used parts cannibalized from used Xerox equipment, parts obtained from other ISOs, and parts purchased through a limited number of its customers. For approximately one year, CSU also obtained parts from Rank Xerox, a majority-owned European affiliate of Xerox, until Xerox forced Rank Xerox to stop selling parts to CSU and other ISOs. In 1994, Xerox settled an antitrust lawsuit with a class of ISOs by which it agreed to suspend its restrictive parts policy for six and one-half years and to license its diagnostic software for four and one-half years. CSU opted out of that settlement and filed this suit alleging that Xerox violated the

Sherman Act by setting the prices on its patented parts much higher for ISOs than for end-users to force ISOs to raise their prices. This would eliminate ISOs in general and CSU in particular as competitors in the relevant service markets for high speed copiers and printers.

Xerox counterclaimed for patent and copyright infringement and contested CSU's antitrust claims as relying on injury solely caused by Xerox's lawful refusal to sell or license patented parts and copyrighted software. Xerox also claimed that CSU could not assert a patent or copyright misuse defense to Xerox's infringement counterclaims based on Xerox's refusal to deal.

The district court granted summary judgment to Xerox dismissing CSU's antitrust claims and holding that if a patent or copyright is lawfully acquired, the patent or copyright holder's unilateral refusal to sell or license its patented invention or copyrighted expression is not unlawful exclusionary conduct under the antitrust laws, even if the refusal to deal impacts competition in more than one market. The court also held, in both the patent and copyright contexts, that the right holder's intent in refusing to deal and any other alleged exclusionary acts committed by the right holder are irrelevant to antitrust law. This appeal followed.

Discussion

. . . The district court's grant of summary judgment as to CSU's antitrust claims arising from Xerox's refusal to sell its patented parts is . . . reviewed as a matter of Federal Circuit law, while consideration of the antitrust claim based on Xerox's refusal to sell or license its copyrighted manuals and software is under Tenth Circuit law.

A.

Intellectual property rights do not confer a privilege to violate the antitrust laws. *See Intergraph Corp. v. Intel Corp.*, 195 F.3d 1346, 1362, 52 USPQ2d 1641, 1652 (Fed.Cir.1999). "But it is also correct that the antitrust laws do not negate the patentee's right to exclude others from patent property." *Id.* (citation omitted). "The commercial advantage gained by new technology and its statutory protection by patent do not convert the possessor thereof into a prohibited monopolist." *Abbott Lab. v. Brennan*, 952 F.2d 1346, 1354, 21 USPQ2d 1192, 1199 (Fed.Cir.1991). "The patent right must be 'coupled with violations of § 2,' and the elements of violation of 15 U.S.C. § 2 must be met."[1] *Id.* (citations omitted). "Determination of whether the patentee meets the Sherman Act elements of monopolization or attempt to monopolize is governed by the rules of application of the antitrust laws to market participants, with due consideration to the exclusivity that inheres in the patent grant." *Id.* at 1354-55, 952 F.2d 1346, 21 USPQ2d at 1199 (citations omitted).

A patent alone does not demonstrate market power. . . . The United States Department of Justice and Federal Trade Commission have issued guidance that, even where it exists, such "market power does not 'impose on the intellectual property owner an obligation to license the use of that property to others.'" . . . The patentee's right to exclude is further supported by section 271(d) of the Patent Act which states, in pertinent part, that "[n]o patent owner otherwise entitled to relief . . . shall be denied relief or deemed guilty of misuse or illegal extension of the patent right by reason of his having . . . (4) refused to license or use any rights to the patent . . . ." 35 U.S.C. § 271(d) (1999).

---

[1] Section 2 of the Sherman Act, 15 U.S.C. § 2, prohibits monopolization or attempts to monopolize: "Every person who shall monopolize, or attempt to monopolize, or combine or conspire with any other person or persons, to monopolize any part of the trade or commerce among the several States, or with foreign nations, shall be deemed guilty of a felony . . . ."

The patentee's right to exclude, however, is not without limit. As we recently observed in *Glass Equipment Development Inc. v. Besten, Inc.*, a patent owner who brings suit to enforce the statutory right to exclude others from making, using, or selling the claimed invention is exempt from the antitrust laws, even though such a suit may have an anti-competitive effect, unless the infringement defendant proves one of two conditions. 174 F.3d 1337, 1343, 50 USPQ2d 1300, 1304 (Fed.Cir.1999) (citing *Nobelpharma*, 141 F.3d at 1068, 46 USPQ2d at 1104). First, he may prove that the asserted patent was obtained through knowing and willful fraud within the meaning of *Walker Process Equipment, Inc. v. Food Machinery & Chemical Corp.*, 382 U.S. 172, 177, 86 S.Ct. 347, 15 L.Ed.2d 247 (1965). . . . Or he may demonstrate that the infringement suit was a mere sham to cover what is actually no more than an attempt to interfere directly with the business relationships of a competitor. *See id.* (citing *Eastern R.R. Presidents Conference v. Noerr Motor Freight, Inc.*, 365 U.S. 127, 144, 81 S.Ct. 523, 5 L.Ed.2d 464 (1961)). Here, CSU makes no claim that Xerox obtained its patents through fraud in the Patent and Trademark Office; the *Walker Process* analysis is not implicated.

"[I]rrespective of the patent applicant's conduct before the [Patent and Trademark Office], an antitrust claim can also be based on [an] allegation that a suit is baseless; in order to prove that a suit was within *Noerr*'s 'sham' exception to immunity, [see *Noerr*, 365 U.S. at 144, 81 S.Ct. 523], an antitrust plaintiff must prove that the suit was both *objectively* baseless and *subjectively* motivated by a desire to impose collateral, anti-competitive injury rather than to obtain a justifiable legal remedy." *Nobelpharma*, 141 F.3d at 1071, 46 USPQ2d at 1107 (citing *Professional Real Estate Investors, Inc. v. Columbia Pictures Indus., Inc.*, 508 U.S. 49, 60-61, 113 S.Ct. 1920, 123 L.Ed.2d 611, 26 USPQ2d 1641, 1646 (1993)). "Accordingly, if a suit is not objectively baseless, an antitrust defendant's subjective motivation is immaterial." *Id.* at 1072, 46 USPQ2d at 1107. CSU has alleged that Xerox misused its patents but has not claimed that Xerox's patent infringement counterclaims were shams.

To support its argument that Xerox illegally sought to leverage its presumably legitimate dominance in the equipment and parts market into dominance in the service market, CSU relies on a footnote in *Eastman Kodak Co. v. Image Technical Services, Inc.*, 504 U.S. 451, 480 n. 29, 112 S.Ct. 2072, 2089 n. 29, 119 L.Ed.2d 265 (1992), that "[t]he Court has held many times that power gained through some natural and legal advantage such as a patent, . . . can give rise to liability if 'a seller exploits his dominant position in one market to expand his empire into the next.'" Notably, *Kodak* was a tying case when it came before the Supreme Court, and no patents had been asserted in defense of the antitrust claims against Kodak. Conversely, there are no claims in this case of illegally tying the sale of Xerox's patented parts to unpatented products. Therefore, the issue was not resolved by the *Kodak* language cited by CSU. Properly viewed within the framework of a tying case, the footnote can be interpreted as restating the undisputed premise that the patent holder cannot use his statutory right to refuse to sell patented parts to gain a monopoly in a market *beyond the scope of the patent. See, e.g., Atari Games Corp. v. Nintendo of Am., Inc.*, 897 F.2d 1572, 1576, 14 USPQ2d 1034, 1037 (Fed.Cir.1990) ("[A] patent owner may not take the property right granted by a patent and use it to extend his power in the marketplace improperly, *i.e.* beyond the limits of what Congress intended to give in the patent laws.").

The cited language from *Kodak* does nothing to limit the right of the patentee to refuse to sell or license in markets within the scope of the statutory patent grant. In fact, we have expressly held that, absent exceptional circumstances, a patent may confer the right to exclude competition altogether in more than one antitrust market. *See B. Braun Med., Inc.*

v. Abbott Lab., 124 F.3d 1419, 1427 n. 4, 43 USPQ2d 1896, 1902 n. 4 (Fed.Cir.1997) (patentee had right to exclude competition in both the market for patented valves and the market for extension sets incorporating patented valves).

CSU further relies on the Ninth Circuit's holding on remand in *Image Technical Services* that "'while exclusionary conduct can include a monopolist's unilateral refusal to license a [patent] or to sell its patented . . . work, a monopolist's 'desire to exclude others from its [protected] work is a presumptively valid business justification for any immediate harm to consumers.'" 125 F.3d at 1218, 44 USPQ2d at 1081 (citing *Data General Corp. v. Grumman Sys. Support Corp.*, 36 F.3d 1147, 1187, 32 USPQ2d 1385, 1417 (1st Cir.1994)). By that case, the Ninth Circuit adopted a rebuttable presumption that the exercise of the statutory right to exclude provides a valid business justification for consumer harm, but then excused as harmless the district court's error in failing to give any instruction on the effect of intellectual property rights on the application of the antitrust laws. . . . It concluded that the jury must have rejected the presumptively valid business justification as pretextual. . . . This logic requires an evaluation of the patentee's subjective motivation for refusing to sell or license its patented products for pretext. We decline to follow *Image Technical Services*.

We have held that "if a [patent infringement] suit is not objectively baseless, an antitrust defendant's subjective motivation is immaterial." *Nobelpharma*, 141 F.3d at 1072, 46 USPQ2d at 1107. We see no more reason to inquire into the subjective motivation of Xerox in refusing to sell or license its patented works than we found in evaluating the subjective motivation of a patentee in bringing suit to enforce that same right. In the absence of any indication of illegal tying, fraud in the Patent and Trademark Office, or sham litigation, the patent holder may enforce the statutory right to exclude others from making, using, or selling the claimed invention free from liability under the antitrust laws. We therefore will not inquire into his subjective motivation for exerting his statutory rights, even though his refusal to sell or license his patented invention may have an anticompetitive effect, so long as that anticompetitive effect is not illegally extended beyond the statutory patent grant. *See Glass Equip. Dev.*, 174 F.3d at 1343, 50 USPQ2d at 1304. It is the infringement defendant and not the patentee that bears the burden to show that one of these exceptional situations exists and, in the absence of such proof, we will not inquire into the patentee's motivations for asserting his statutory right to exclude. Even in cases where the infringement defendant has met this burden, which CSU has not, he must then also prove the elements of the Sherman Act violation.

We answer the threshold question of whether Xerox's refusal to sell its patented parts exceeds the scope of the patent grant in the negative.[2] Therefore, our inquiry is at an end. Xerox was under no obligation to sell or license its patented parts and did not violate the antitrust laws by refusing to do so.

B.

The Copyright Act expressly grants a copyright owner the exclusive right to distribute the protected work by "transfer of ownership, or by rental, lease, or lending." 17 U.S.C. § 106(3) (1996). "[T]he owner of the copyright, if [it] pleases, may refrain from vending or licensing and content [itself] with simply exercising the right to exclude others from using [its] property." *Data General*, 36 F.3d at 1186, 32 USPQ2d at 1416 (citing *Fox Film Corp. v. Doyal*, 286 U.S. 123, 127, 52 S.Ct. 546, 547, 76 L.Ed. 1010 (1932)).

---

[2] Having concluded that Xerox's actions fell within the statutory patent grant, we need not separately consider CSU's allegations of patent misuse and they are rejected.

The Supreme Court has made clear that the property right granted by copyright law cannot be used with impunity to extend power in the marketplace beyond what Congress intended. *See United States v. Loew's, Inc.*, 371 U.S. 38, 47-48, 83 S.Ct. 97, 103-04, 9 L.Ed.2d 11 (1962) (block booking of copyrighted motion pictures is illegal tying in violation of Sherman Act). The Court has not, however, directly addressed the antitrust implications of a unilateral refusal to sell or license copyrighted expression.

The Tenth Circuit has not addressed in any published opinion the extent to which the unilateral refusal to sell or license copyrighted expression can form the basis of a violation of the Sherman Act. We are therefore left to determine how that circuit would likely resolve the issue; the precedent of other circuits is instructive in that consideration. The Fourth Circuit has rejected a claim of illegal tying, supported only by evidence of a unilateral decision to license copyrighted diagnostic software to some but not to others. *See Service & Training, Inc. v. Data General Corp.*, 963 F.2d 680, 686, 23 USPQ2d 1102, 1106 (4th Cir.1992). In reaching this conclusion, the court recognized the copyright owner's exclusive right to "sell, rent, lease, lend, or otherwise distribute copies of a copyrighted work," *id.* (citing 17 U.S.C. § 106(3)), and concluded that "Section 1 of the Sherman Act does not entitle 'a purchaser . . . to buy a product that the seller does not wish to offer for sale.'" *Id.* (citing *Jefferson Parish Hosp. Dist. v. Hyde*, 466 U.S. 2, 24 n. 40, 104 S.Ct. 1551, 80 L.Ed.2d 2 (1984)).

Perhaps the most extensive analysis of the effect of a unilateral refusal to license copyrighted expression was conducted by the First Circuit in *Data General Corp. v. Grumman Systems Support Corp.*, 36 F.3d 1147, 32 USPQ2d 1385. There, the court noted that the limited copyright monopoly is based on Congress' empirical assumption that the right to "exclude others from using their works creates a system of incentives that promotes consumer welfare in the long term by encouraging investment in the creation of desirable artistic and functional works of expression. . . . We cannot require antitrust defendants to prove and reprove the merits of this legislative assumption in every case where a refusal to license a copyrighted work comes under attack." . . . The court went on to establish as a legal standard that "while exclusionary conduct can include a monopolist's unilateral refusal to license a copyright, an author's desire to exclude others from use of its copyrighted work is a presumptively valid business justification for any immediate harm to consumers." . . . The burden to overcome this presumption was firmly placed on the antitrust plaintiff. The court gave no weight to evidence showing knowledge that developing a proprietary position would help to maintain a monopoly in the service market in the face of contrary evidence of the defendant's desire to develop state-of-the-art diagnostic software to enhance its service and consumer benefit. . . .

As discussed above, the Ninth Circuit adopted a modified version of this *Data General* standard. Both courts agreed that the presumption could be rebutted by evidence that "the monopolist acquired the protection of the intellectual property laws in an unlawful manner." *Image Technical Servs.*, 125 F.3d at 1219, 44 USPQ2d at 1082 (citing *Data General*, 36 F.3d at 1188, 32 USPQ2d at 1418). The Ninth Circuit, however, extended the possible means of rebutting the presumption to include evidence that the defense and exploitation of the copyright grant was merely a pretextual business justification to mask anticompetitive conduct. . . . The hazards of this approach are evident in both the path taken and the outcome reached. The jury in that case was instructed to examine each proffered business justification for pretext, and no weight was given to the intellectual property rights in the instructions. . . . This permitted the jury to second guess the subjective motivation of the copyright holder in asserting its statutory rights to exclude under the copyright laws without properly weighing the presumption of legitimacy in asserting its rights under the copyright laws. While concluding that the failure to weigh the intellectual property rights was an abuse of discretion, the Ninth Circuit nevertheless held the error harmless because it thought the jury must have rejected the presumptive validity of asserting the copyrights as pretextual. . . . This is in reality a significant departure from the First Circuit's central premise that rebutting the presumption would be an uphill battle and would only be appropriate in those rare cases in which imposing antitrust liability is unlikely to frustrate the objectives of the Copyright Act. *See Data General*, 36 F.3d at 1187 n. 64, 1188, 32 USPQ2d at 1417 n. 64.

We believe the First Circuit's approach is more consistent with both the antitrust and the copyright laws and is the standard that would most likely be followed by the Tenth Circuit in considering the effect of Xerox's unilateral right to refuse to license or sell copyrighted manuals and diagnostic software on liability under the antitrust laws. We therefore reject CSU's invitation to examine Xerox's subjective motivation in asserting its right to exclude under the copyright laws for pretext, in the absence of any evidence that the copyrights were obtained by unlawful means or were used to gain monopoly power beyond the statutory copyright granted by Congress. In the absence of such definitive rebuttal evidence, Xerox's refusal to sell or license its copyrighted works was squarely within the rights granted by Congress to the copyright holder and did not constitute a violation of the antitrust laws.

Conclusion

Accordingly, the judgment of the United States District Court for the District of Kansas is affirmed.

COMMENTARY

1. In *Independent Service Organizations*, the Federal Circuit criticized the Ninth Circuit's decision in *Image Technical Services, Inc. v. Eastman Kodak Co.*, 125 F.3d 1195 (9th Cir. 1997). The Federal Circuit also recently dealt with the intellectual-property/antitrust interface in *Intergraph Corp. v. Intel Corp.*, 195 F.3d 1346 (Fed. Cir. 1999).

2. In *Intergraph*, the district court had issued an injunction requiring Intel to continue to supply microprocessors, other chips, and confidential information to Intergraph during the pendency of litigation between the companies. Intergraph had first charged Intel with patent infringement and later added an antitrust charge. Intergraph had claimed that antitrust law required Intel to continue its pre-litigation supplier relationship with Intergraph. Responding to Intel's contention that much of the material affected by the district court's order was protected by patents and copyright, the Federal Circuit commented:

> In response to Intel's argument that its proprietary information and pre-release products are subject to copyright and patents, the district court observed that Intel's intellectual property "does not confer upon it a priv-

> ilege or immunity to violate the antitrust laws." That is of course correct. But it is also correct that the antitrust laws do not negate the patentee's right to exclude others from patent property. . . . In *Image Technical Services* the Ninth Circuit reported that it had found "no reported case in which a court had imposed antitrust liability for a unilateral refusal to sell or license a patent or copyright." 125 F.3d at 1216. Nor have we. . . .

3. *MAI Systems, Inc. v. Peak Computer, Inc.*, 991 F.2d 511 (9th Cir. 1993), showed another way in which intellectual property might be employed as a means of excluding independent servicing organizations from the servicing aftermarket. MAI Systems, Inc. manufactured computers and designed software (including operating system software) to run those computers and also serviced the computers in the aftermarket. Although MAI sold the computers to its customers, it retained ownership of the copyright on the software. MAI licensed its customers to use the software for their own internal information processing. Peak was an independent servicing organization which maintained computer systems for its clients. When Peak serviced computers manufactured by MAI, it turned on the computer and thereby activated the operating system. In so doing, the operating system was copied into the computer's random access memory (RAM). The Ninth Circuit upheld MAI's claim that this copying of the software into the computer's RAM constituted copyright infringement. The MAI approach was used in later cases but ultimately was overruled by legislation.

4. *Triad Systems Corp. v. Southeastern Express Co.*, 64 F.3d 1330 (9th Cir. 1995), involved a situation similar to that in *MAI*. Triad manufactured computers for use by automotive parts stores to automate their operations and designed, sold, and licensed unique software to run those computers. Triad also serviced those computers in the aftermarket. Southeastern, an independent servicing organization, competed with Triad in servicing Triad computers. In this case, the Ninth Circuit again ruled that the independent servicing organization infringed the manufacturer's software copyright when the servicing organization employee turned on the computer and loaded the software into the computer's RAM.

5. *Fonar Corp. v. Domenick*, 105 F.3d 99 (2d Cir. 1997), also lent some support to the approach of the Ninth Circuit in *MAI* and *Triad*. In this case Fonar used copyrighted diagnostic software to exclude independent servicing organizations. Fonar Corp. had manufactured magnetic resonance imaging scanners and provided maintenance services. Fonar brought suit against an independent servicing organization for copyright infringement, contending that the servicing organization infringed its copyright in diagnostic software when it operated the scanners. The Second Circuit reversed the lower court's grant of summary judgment to the defendant, ruling that the question of whether the defendant had infringed the plaintiff's copyright when diagnostic software was loaded into the equipment's RAM was an issue for trial.

6. Since most sophisticated equipment contains diagnostic software which is activated when the equipment is turned on, the *MAI*, *Triad*, and *Fonar* cases seemed to provide a means by which any manufacturer could exclude independent servicing organizations from the servicing aftermarket. Congress, however, responded to these cases in the Digital Millennium Copyright Act. There, Congress added §§ 117(c) and (d) to Title 17 of the U.S. Code (the Copyright Act):

> (c) Machine maintenance or repair.—Notwithstanding the provisions of section 106, it is not an infringement for the owner or lessee of a machine to make or authorize the making of a copy of a computer program if such copy is made solely by virtue of the activation of a machine that lawfully contains an authorized copy of the computer program, for purposes only of maintenance or repair of that machine, if—
>
> (1) such new copy is used in no other manner and is destroyed immediately after the maintenance or repair is completed; and
>
> (2) with respect to any computer program or part thereof that is not necessary for that machine to be activated, such program or part thereof is not accessed or used other than to make such new copy by virtue of the activation of the machine.
>
> (d) Definitions.—For purposes of this section—
>
> (1) the "maintenance" of a machine is the servicing of the machine in order to make it work in accordance with its original specifications and any changes to those specifications authorized for that machine; and
>
> (2) the "repair" of a machine is the restoring of the machine to the state of working in accordance with its original specifications and any changes to those specifications authorized for that machine.

7. Note, however, that the above legislation changes the law as set forth in *MAI*, *Triad*, and *Fonar* only with respect to the maintenance and repair aftermarket. Other aftermarkets are unaffected by the new §§ 117(c) and (d) and apparently are still governed by *MAI* and *Triad*, as the *Xerox* litigation shows. Consider whether and how the opinion in *Alcatel*, below, might have been written differently, if Congress had written the amendments to § 117 more broadly.

8. In *United States v. Microsoft Corp.*, 253 F.3d 34 (D.C. Cir. 2001), presented in Chapters 6 & 9, *supra*, the Court of Appeals cites *Independent Serv. Orgs. Antitrust Litig.* for the proposition that "Intellectual property rights do not confer a privilege to violate the antitrust laws." *Id.* at 55. In the Court of Appeals, Microsoft had defended its use of restrictive licensing provisions in its OEM licenses as an exercise of its rights as a holder of valid copyrights, stating: "If intellectual property rights have been lawfully acquired, their subsequent exercise cannot give rise to antitrust liability." *Id.* The Court of Appeals characterized this argument as one that "borders on the frivolous." *Id.* Microsoft then argued that it had not used its copyright unreasonably in that it was seeking only to restrict material alteration of their copyrighted software. The Court of Appeals accepted Microsoft's explanation that barring OEM's from automatically launching a substitute user interface on the completion of the boot process was justified as a means of avoiding a drastic alteration of Microsoft's copyright. The Court of Appeals, however, rejected the ancillary argument that other license restrictions were justified in order to protect the value of the copyrighted software.

In thus reviewing Microsoft's copyright claims was the Court of Appeals resolving an intellectual-property/antitrust conflict by requiring the right-holder to justify the protection of a copyright interest in the face of a claim of an anitcompetitive effect? Might this analysis be characterized as a balancing test with the burden of justification on the right-holder? Is this analysis the same as that of the Federal Circuit in *Independent Serv. Orgs. Antitrust Litig.*? Might there be a conflict between the D.C. Circuit and the Federal Circuit on the proper analysis of the intellectual-property/antitrust interface?

Alcatel USA, Inc. v. DGI Technologies, Inc.

166 F.3d 772 (5th Cir. 1999)

WIENER, Circuit Judge:

. . . .

FACTS AND PROCEEDINGS

[Alcatel USA, Inc. (formerly DSC Communications Corporation ("DSC"))] . . . designs, manufactures, and sells equipment ("switches") comprising telephone switching systems. Its customers are long-distance telephone service providers, such as MCI and Sprint. A telephone switch routes long distance telephone calls to their destinations. DSC switches are controlled by its copyrighted operating system software. DSC regularly implements new features in its switches by upgrading its software, a process that costs DSC millions of dollars.

DSC does not sell its operating system software—as it does the switches—but instead licenses its use pursuant to a licensing agreement. The licensing agreement provides that (1) the operating system software remains the property of DSC; (2) the customer has the right to use the software only to operate its switch; (3) the customer is prohibited from copying the software or disclosing it to third parties; and (4) the customers are authorized to use the software only in conjunction with DSC-manufactured equipment.

The record evidence shows that DSC's customers, like other long distance providers, frequently need to expand the call-handling capacity of their switches. One way to expand the call-handling capacity of DSC switches is to add groups of "cards" to the switch. Prior to 1989, DSC was the only manufacturer of expansion cards for its own switches. In 1989, DGI was founded to design and sell such cards for use with DSC switches.

DGI contends that it developed its cards by analyzing DSC's unpatented products and then duplicating their functionality—a process referred to as "reverse engineering." DGI initially obtained a used DSC switch containing a multitude of cards and a set of switch owners manuals ("DSPs" or "DSP manuals") from an investor. Once DGI had determined the functionality of DSC's products, it designed its own to perform these same functions using newer-generation electronics and adding additional features. DGI further insists that, from its inception, DSC repeatedly attempted to thwart DGI's entry into the market. For instance, DSC threatened to insert a software "patch" in its operating system software to render DGI's cards inoperable on DSC-manufactured switches, and in fact did insert such a patch, but was never successful in disabling the DGI products. DGI also notes that in 1991, before it had introduced its first product for sale, DSC sent a letter to its switch owners, threatening to void their switch warranties if they used DGI cards and claiming that DGI refused to provide DSC a card to test, an assertion that DGI maintains was untrue. Finally, DSC (1) refused to inform its customers of the compatibility of DGI's cards, even after testing them, and (2) hired investigators to go through DGI's trash.

DSC, on the other hand, asserts that DGI did not engage in legitimate reverse engineering, but rather misappropriated DSC's intellectual property by wrongfully obtaining schematics and manuals provided only to DSC customers on the express condition that there be no disclosure to third parties. DSC also notes that each manual contained a plainly visible copyright notice.

In any event, between 1992 and 1994, DGI developed and introduced four DSC-compatible cards—the Digital Trunk Interface ("DTI"), the Bus Terminator ("BT"), the Digital Tone Detector ("DTD"), and the Pulse Code Modulation Interface ("PCMI"). None of these initial DGI cards were microprocessor cards, however. A microprocessor card contains firmware, which is software embedded in a memory chip on the card. When installed in a switch, a microprocessor card controls the "boot up"—that is, it downloads DSC's copyrighted operating system software into its random access memory ("RAM"). A DTI, DTD, or BT card alone cannot expand the capacity of a switch; a customer must install a group of cards together with a microprocessor card to achieve expansion. For this reason, DGI obtained DSC microprocessor cards—then known as MP-2s—in the used market to sell along with three DGI cards. This enabled DGI to offer a customer a complete expansion card complement, which it did.

In 1995, as a result of a new dialing plan implemented by the Federal Communications Commission ("FCC") and customer demands for new features, DSC revised and expanded its operating system software. These changes required DSC customers to upgrade to a new microprocessor card—the MP-8. As few MP-8 cards were available on the used market, DGI was no longer able to offer a complete card complement. Its marketing problems were exacerbated by DSC's practice of offering substantial discounts to customers who purchased whole complements of cards from DSC, but charging much higher prices for individual MP-8 cards. This motivated DGI to develop its own microprocessor card—the DMP-2800.

To develop a microprocessor card, DGI had to overcome several difficulties. First, DGI needed to understand DSC's firmware. For this purpose, DGI purchased an MP-8 card and, using a "burner" to remove the DSC firmware from a memory chip, obtained the machine-readable object code. DGI engineers then used a process called "disassembly" to convert the firmware into human-readable form. In this way, DGI was able to write its own firmware—which it claims is not substantially similar to DSC's firmware—for its DMP-2800 microprocessor card. DSC asserts that DGI violated the copyright on its firmware when it copied DSC's firmware several times in this process.

Second, the DGI microprocessor card had to accept a download from the switch of the DSC operating system. To obtain the software needed for this function, several DGI engineers took an MP-8 card to NTS Communications ("NTS"), a DSC switch owner/software licensee and DGI customer. There, Ernie Carrasco, an NTS employee who also consulted for DGI, placed the MP-8 card into an NTS switch and copied the operating system to a laptop computer. DGI engineers then took the laptop back to DGI. DSC maintains that DGI never told NTS that it was copying and removing DSC's copyrighted software, only that it was "testing" MP-8 cards.

DGI engineers returned to NTS several times to test MP-8 cards containing versions of DGI's firmware. To avoid having to perform all this testing at NTS, DGI modified an MP-8 card to include a device called a "punch" card or "snooper" card, which monitored the firmware during the operating system download. Using this snooper card, DGI was able to understand which parts of the DSC firmware were accessed during the "boot" of the operating system. DSC maintains that DGI used this snooper card to copy the messages contained in DSC's copyrighted operating system software. It insists that, but for DGI's "theft" of DSC's operating system, it would have been extremely expensive and time-consuming for DGI to develop its own microprocessor card.

DGI counters that the copy was used only to discern the size of the operating system download to the MP-8 card, as it was investigating the possibility of upgrading the older MP-2 card. DGI insists that, as the content of the software was irrelevant in determining its size, it never even disassembled the operating system software from unreadable machine language.

. . . .

II
ANALYSIS

A. *DGI's Antitrust Claim*

The jury found DSC liable under § 2 of the Sherman Act for monopolization of the expansion and enhancement market for DSC-manufactured switches and awarded DGI $750,000 in lost profits and $1.5 million in future lost profits on that claim. The district court overturned this verdict, however, holding that (1) there was insufficient evidence to establish that expansion cards are the relevant market for antitrust purposes, and (2) DGI's damage model was hopelessly flawed.

. . . .

3. *Relevant Market*

"'The offense of monopoly under § 2 of the Sherman Act has two elements: (1) the possession of monopoly power in the relevant market and (2) the willful acquisition or maintenance of that power as distinguished from growth or development as a consequence of a superior product, business acumen, or historic accident.'" Thus, to prove a monopolization claim, the plaintiff must first establish the relevant product market. DGI disputes the district court's conclusion that it failed to prove that the "capacity enhancement and expansion products" market for DSC-manufactured switches is the relevant market for antitrust purposes.

As DGI stresses, in determining the relevant product market, "the reality of the marketplace must serve as the lodestar." DGI advances that market realities dictate that the relevant market in this case is the capacity expansion market. For instance, it asserts that the evidence shows that DSC's officers, employees, customers, and internal documents, as well as DGI's officers, salesmen, and economic experts, defined the relevant market as the market for expansion products. DGI insists that users of DSC switches are "locked-in" to DSC in the aftermarket. This assertion is strengthened, it maintains, by the fact that DSC's software license allows its customers to use its copyrighted software only in conjunction with the unpatented DSC hardware.

DGI adds that the district court's reference to *Kodak* is not apt, and in fact urges that *Kodak* supports DGI's claim by establishing that aftermarket monopolization is actionable under the Sherman Act. In that case, defendant Kodak sold plain paper copiers in a market with several rivals. The Court assumed that, at the time of sale, Kodak sold replacement parts, giving users the option either to repair their copiers or to hire independent service organizations ("ISOs") to do so. Later, Kodak changed its policy and refused to sell parts to ISOs. The ISOs alleged that, as Kodak's equipment was unique and its competitors' parts incompatible with Kodak machines, this altered practice allowed Kodak to capture the repair business for itself, at "supra-competitive" prices. Kodak argued that, "either presumptively or as a matter of law, vigorous competition in the copier market would prevent Kodak from raising its parts and servicing contract prices above competitive levels, because any such price increases in these 'derivative aftermarkets' would become known to copier-equipment consumers, and eventually cause Kodak to lose ground to its competitors in copier sales."

The Court rejected Kodak's argument, concluding that summary judgment was not appropriate. It reasoned that, at the time of their original copier purchases, some consumers might not have cost-efficient access to pricing information needed to evaluate the total "life-cycle" cost of the entire Kodak package, *i.e.*, the price of the copier, likely replacement parts, and product-lifetime servicing. Likewise, the Court explained that, inasmuch as Kodak's customers found it prohibitively expensive to replace their equipment with another manufacturer's product, they might tolerate some level of aftermarket price increase before changing brands. The Court thus decided that the undetermined "information costs" and "switching costs" represented material issues of fact that precluded summary judgment. DGI argues here that, in a similar manner, DSC could substantially raise its aftermarket card prices before DSC switch owners would consider replacing DSC switches, and that DSC was thus able to maintain supra-competitive prices in the expansion products aftermarket.

DGI's reliance on *Kodak* is misplaced. As we previously noted . . . "[t]he Supreme Court's decision in Kodak was a rejection of Kodak's assertion that market power could *never* exist over repair parts in any case where the defendant did not have market power over earlier-purchased machines needing those parts." We pointed out that, "[c]ritically, the plaintiffs in Kodak produced evidence that Kodak was charging above market prices for its service and was engaging in price discrimination in favor of the knowledgeable customers who could most easily obtain information or switch companies." Indeed, the Court in *Kodak* concluded that "[i]t may be that [Kodak's] parts, service, and equipment are components of one unified market, or that the equipment market does discipline the aftermarkets so that all three are priced competitively overall, or that any anti-competitive effects of Kodak's behavior are outweighed by its competitive effects." The Court simply was not prepared to permit this factual determination to be made at the summary judgment stage.

In contrast to *Kodak*, the instant case comes to us after a full-blown jury trial. Also unlike *Kodak*, here there is no evidence that DSC has a superior or unique product that allows it to charge supra-competitive prices. Indeed, although DGI presented testimony that DSC's cards are extremely expensive, it never compared DSC's prices to its competitors' prices. And unlike the plaintiffs in *Kodak*, DGI did not prove that DSC's customers face substantial information and switching costs. To the contrary, the evidence shows that many DSC switch owners engage in life-cycle pricing, that is, they factor in not only the purchase price of the equipment, but also the post-acquisition costs of operation, maintenance, and expansion at the time of purchase. By engaging in life-cycle pricing, a customer links together the primary equipment market and any aftermarket for parts and service for the equipment of particular manufacturers.

And, as noted, DGI did not prove that a change in any of DSC's pricing, warranty, or other policies served to subject DSC switch owners to substantial additional information or switching costs. From the beginning, DSC's licensing agreement for its operating system software authorized its customers to use the software only in conjunction with equipment manufactured by DSC. This was a long-standing policy, not a response to DGI's entry into the market. True, there was some evidence that DSC threatened to cancel its warranties on switches that used equipment not manufactured by DSC. The evidence also shows, however, that despite referring to DGI by name, the letter threatening to void the warranties was sent before DGI ever offered its first product for sale. As DSC was the sole manufacturer of expansion products for DSC switches before DGI entered the market, this alleged change in policy could not substantially increase the information costs for DSC customers; when they purchased the DSC switches, they could not have reasonably expected suppliers of expansion products other than DSC to enter the aftermarket. Several circuits have held that such a change in policy is a crucial factor in establishing an aftermarket monopoly claim. As the Sixth Circuit held, "an antitrust plaintiff cannot succeed on a *Kodak*-type theory when the defendant has not changed its policy after locking-in some of its customers, and the defendant has been otherwise forthcoming about its pricing structure and service policies."

We agree with the district court's determination that DGI's characterization of the expansion products market as the relevant market is at odds with market realities. The record shows that the prices for two-thirds of all of DSC's cards are set at the time a telephone company purchases a switch, either because the customer purchases the one frame that the switch must have to operate, or through a future or life-cycle pricing scheme negotiated at the time of purchase. DGI's model excludes all these cards from its relevant market, not an insignificant flaw in the model.

Furthermore, DGI's proposed market does not acknowledge that the purchase of a new frame with cards is only one of several ways a telephone company can expand its call-handling capacity. For instance, a company can purchase a new switch from DSC or from another switch manufacturer, purchase a used switch from DSC or a broker, or trade for or lease capacity in another company's network. In addition, as many of DSC's customers, such as MCI, are dual-sourced—that is, they own switches built by more than one manufacturer—they can purchase a new frame for one of their non-DSC switches. All of these capacity handling options are also omitted from DGI's relevant market.

We are convinced that DGI . . . is "trying to define the market as narrowly as possible (in order to make it look as if [defendant] had market power)." Because (1) DGI did not present legally sufficient evidence that DSC's customers faced significant information and switching costs, and (2) DGI's proffered relevant market does not comport with market realities, its aftermarket monopoly claim fails as a matter of law. As such, the district court did not err in granting DSC's motion for a JML dismissing DGI's antitrust claim.

. . . .

C. *Injunction*

. . . .

2. *Copyright Infringement*

a. Sufficiency of the Evidence

. . . .

We have no problem upholding the district court's injunction on the basis of DGI's copyright infringement. There is no question that DGI engaged in at least one act of direct copyright infringement: None dispute that DGI personnel connected a laptop computer to the DSC switch at NTS, made a copy of the DSC operating system software, and carried the laptop back to the DGI labs. This unauthorized act clearly infringed DSC's exclusive right to reproduce its software.

We also agree with DSC and the district court that DGI engaged in contributory infringement as a matter of law. The evidence shows that each time a DGI microprocessor card is booted up, it downloads (makes a copy of) the DSC operating system. By selling its DMP-2800 card, therefore, DGI knowingly induces and causes its customers—*i.e.*, DSC switch owners—to violate DSC's exclusive right to reproduce its software. Under section 117 of the Copyright Act, DGI could have avoided liability for contributory infringement by proving that its customers *owned* copies of the DSC operating system software, and were therefore *authorized* to make additional copies, provided such reproduction was "an essential step in the utilization of the computer program."[76] In a specific interrogatory, however, the jury found that DGI did not prove by a preponderance of the evidence that DSC switch owners *owned* copies of DSC software. In light of this finding—which was unappealed—the jury's conclusion that DGI did not contributorily infringe DSC's software copyright is internally inconsistent. . . . Here, the district court's injunction can be upheld solely on the basis of contributory infringement. As such, the injunctive relief is grounded not in some earlier act of infringement by DGI, but in the recognition that DGI and its customers are violating the DSC software licensing agreement each time they boot up the DSC operating system into a DGI microprocessor card.

[Although the court both dismissed DGI's antitrust claim against DSC and ruled in favor of DSC on its copyright claim, the court ruled that DSC had engaged in copyright misuse. The misuse issue is considered, *infra*, page 835.]

---

[76] 17 U.S.C. § 117 provides an exception to a copyright owner's exclusive rights in computer programs. It states:

> Notwithstanding the provisions of section 106, it is not infringement for the owner of a copy of a computer program to make or authorize the making of another copy or adaptation of that computer program provided:
>
> (1) that such a new copy or adaptation is created as an essential step in the utilization of the computer program in conjunction with a machine and that it is used in no other manner, or
>
> (2) that such new copy or adaptation is for archival purposes only and that all archival copies are destroyed in the event that continued possession of the computer program should cease to be rightful.
>
> . . .

E. Patent Misuse, Contributory Infringement, and Antitrust Standards

Dawson Chemical Co. v. Rohm and Haas Co.
448 U.S. 176 (1980)

Mr. Justice BLACKMUN delivered the opinion of the Court.

. . . The issue before us is whether the owner of a patent on a chemical process is guilty of patent misuse, and therefore is barred from seeking relief against contributory infringement of its patent rights, if it exploits the patent only in conjunction with the sale of an unpatented article that constitutes a material part of the invention and is not suited for commercial use outside the scope of the patent claims. . . .

The catalyst for this litigation is a chemical compound known to scientists as "3, 4-dichloropropionanilide" and referred to in the chemical industry as "propanil." In the late 1950's, it was discovered that this compound had properties that made it useful as a selective, "post-emergence" herbicide particularly well suited for the cultivation of rice. If applied in the proper quantities, propanil kills weeds normally found in rice crops without adversely affecting the crops themselves. . . .

Efforts to obtain patent rights to propanil or its use as a herbicide have been continuous since the herbicidal qualities of the chemical first came to light. [The Monsanto Company had filed the first of three successive applications for a patent on propanil itself in 1957 and was finally issued a patent in 1968. That patent was later declared invalid in litigation on the ground that propanil had been implicitly revealed in prior art dating back as far as 1902, even though its use as a herbicide had been discovered only recently.] . . .

Invalidation of the Monsanto patent cleared the way for Rohm & Haas, respondent here, to obtain a patent on the method of process for applying propanil. This is the patent on which the present lawsuit is founded. . . . The patent contains several claims covering a method for applying propanil to inhibit the growth of undesirable plants in areas containing established crops. . . .

Petitioners, too, are chemical manufacturers. They have manufactured and sold propanil for application to rice crops since before Rohm & Haas received its patent. . . . Petitioners did not cease manufacture and sale of propanil after that patent issued, despite knowledge that farmers purchasing their products would infringe on the patented method by applying the propanil to their crops. Accordingly, Rohm & Haas filed this suit . . . . seeking injunctive relief against petitioners on the ground that their manufacture and sale of propanil interfered with its patent rights.

The complaint alleged not only that petitioners contributed to infringement by farmers who purchased and used petitioners' propanil, but also that they actually induced such infringement by instructing farmers how to apply the herbicide. *See* 35 U.S.C. §§ 271(b) and (c). Petitioners responded to the suit by requesting licenses to practice the patented method. When Rohm & Haas refused to grant such licenses, however, petitioners raised a defense of patent misuse and counterclaimed for alleged antitrust violations by respondent. . . .

The District Court granted summary judgment for petitioners. . . . It agreed that Rohm & Haas was barred from obtaining relief against infringers of its patent because it had attempted illegally to extend its patent monopoly. The District Court recognized that 35 U.S.C. § 271(d) specifies certain conduct which is not to be deemed patent misuse. The court ruled, however, that "[t]he language of § 271(d) simply does not encompass the totality of [Rohm & Haas'] conduct in this case." . . . It held that respondent's refusal to grant licenses, other than the "implied" licenses conferred by operation of law upon purchasers of its propanil, constituted an attempt by means of a "tying" arrangement to effect a monopoly over an unpatented component of the process. . . .

The United States Court of Appeals for the Fifth Circuit reversed. . . .

We granted *certiorari* . . . to forestall a possible conflict in the lower courts and to resolve an issue of prime importance in the administration of the patent law.

. . . .

[H]ad the present case arisen prior to *Mercoid*, we believe it fair to say that it would have fallen close to the wavering line between legitimate protection against contributory infringement and illegitimate patent misuse.

III

The *Mercoid* decisions left in their wake some consternation among patent lawyers and a degree of confusion in the lower courts. . . . This state of affairs made it difficult for patent lawyers to advise their clients on questions of contributory infringement and to render secure opinions on the validity of proposed licensing arrangements. Certain segments of the patent bar eventually decided to ask Congress for corrective legislation . . . [which] eventually was enacted in 1952 as 35 U.S.C. § 271.

A

. . . .

Section 271(c) identifies the basic dividing line between contributory infringement and patent misuse. It adopts a restrictive definition of contributory infringement that distinguishes between staple and nonstaple articles of commerce. It also defines the class of nonstaple items narrowly. In essence, this provision places materials like the dry ice of the *Carbice* case outside the scope of the contributory infringement doctrine. As a result, it is no longer necessary to resort to the doctrine of patent misuse in order to deny patentees control over staple goods used in their inventions. . . .

In our view, the provisions of § 271(d) effectively confer upon the patentee, as a lawful adjunct of his patent rights, a limited power to exclude others from competition in nonstaple goods. A patentee may sell a nonstaple article himself while enjoining others from marketing that same good without his authorization. By doing so, he is able to eliminate competitors and thereby to control the market for that product. Moreover, his power to demand royalties from others for the privilege of selling the nonstaple item itself implies that the patentee may control the market for the nonstaple good; otherwise, his "right" to sell licenses for the marketing of the nonstaple good would be meaningless, since no one would be willing to pay him for a superfluous authorization. . . .

Rohm & Haas' conduct is not dissimilar in either nature or effect from the conduct that is thus clearly embraced within § 271(d). It sells propanil; it authorizes others to use propanil; and it sues contributory infringers. These are all protected activities. Rohm & Haas does *not* license others to sell propanil, but nothing on the face of the statute requires it to do so. To be sure, the sum effect of Rohm & Haas' actions is to suppress competition in the market for an unpatented commodity. But . . . in this its conduct is no different from that which the statute expressly protects.

The one aspect of Rohm & Haas' behavior that is not expressly covered by § 271(d) is its linkage of two protected activities—sale of propanil and authorization to practice the patented process—together in a single transaction. Petitioners vigorously argue that this linkage, which they characterize pejoratively as "tying," supplies the otherwise missing element of misuse. They fail, however, to identify any way in which this "tying" of two expressly protected activities results in any extension of control over unpatented materials beyond what § 271(d) already allows. Nevertheless, the language of § 271(d) does not explicitly resolve the question when linkage of this variety becomes patent misuse. In order to judge whether this method of exploiting the patent lies within or without the protection afforded by § 271(d), we must turn to the legislative history.

....

B

....

We find nothing in this legislative history to support the assertion that respondent's behavior falls outside the scope of § 271(d). To the contrary, respondent has done nothing that would extend its right of control over unpatented goods beyond the line that Congress drew. Respondent, to be sure, has licensed use of its patented process only in connection with purchases of propanil. But propanil is a *nonstaple* product, and its herbicidal property is the heart of respondent's invention. Respondent's method of doing business is thus essentially the same as the method condemned in the *Mercoid* decisions, and the legislative history reveals that § 271(d) was designed to retreat from *Mercoid* in this regard.

There is one factual difference between this case and *Mercoid*: the licensee in the *Mercoid* cases had offered a sublicense to the alleged contributory infringer, which offer had been refused. . . . Seizing upon this difference, petitioners argue that respondent's unwillingness to offer similar licenses to its would-be competitors in the manufacture of propanil legally distinguishes this case and sets it outside § 271(d). To this argument, there are at least three responses. First, as we have noted, § 271(d) permits such licensing but does not require it. Accordingly, petitioners' suggestion would import into the statute a requirement that simply is not there. Second, petitioners have failed to adduce any evidence from the legislative history that the offering of a license to the alleged contributory infringer was a critical factor in inducing Congress to retreat from the result of the *Mercoid* decisions. Indeed, the *Leeds & Catlin* decision, which did not involve such an offer to license, was placed before Congress as an example of the kind of contributory infringement action the statute would allow. Third, petitioners' argument runs contrary to the long-settled view that the essence of a patent grant is the right to exclude others from profiting by the patented invention. . . . If petitioners' argument were accepted, it would force patentees either to grant licenses or to forfeit their statutory protection against contributory infringement. Compulsory licensing is a rarity in our patent system, and we decline to manufacture such a requirement out of § 271(d).

....

It is perhaps, noteworthy that holders of "new use" patents on chemical processes were among those designated to Congress as intended beneficiaries of the protection against contributory infringement that § 271 was designed to restore. . . . We have been informed that the characteristics of practical chemical research are such that this form of patent protection is particularly important to inventors in that field. The number of chemicals either known to scientists or disclosed by existing research is vast. It grows constantly, as those engaging in "pure" research publish their discoveries. The number of these chemicals that have known uses of commercial or social value, in contrast, is small. Development of new uses for existing chemicals is thus a major component of practical chemical research. It is extraordinarily expensive. It may take years of unsuccessful testing before a chemical having a desired property is identified, and it may take several years of further testing before a proper and safe method for using that chemical is developed.

Under the construction of § 271(d) that petitioners advance, the rewards available to those willing to undergo the time, expense, and interim frustration of such practical research would provide at best a dubious incentive. Others could await the results of the testing and then jump on the profit bandwagon by demanding licenses to sell the unpatented, nonstaple chemical used in the newly developed process. Refusal to accede to such a demand, if accompanied by any attempt to profit from the invention through sale of the unpatented chemical, would risk forfeiture of any patent protection whatsoever on a finding of patent misuse. As a result, noninventors would be almost assured of an opportunity to share in the spoils, even though they had contributed nothing to the discovery. The incentive to await the discoveries of others might well prove sweeter than the incentive to take the initiative oneself.

. . . [W]e hold that Rohm & Haas has not engaged in patent misuse, either by its method of selling propanil, or by its refusal to license others to sell that commodity. The judgment of the Court of Appeals is therefore affirmed.

It is so ordered.

In 1988 Congress revised § 271 in the Patent Misuse Reform Act. As revised in 1988, § 271 appears as follows:

§ 271. Infringement of patent

(a) Except as otherwise provided in this title, whoever without authority makes, uses or sells any patented invention, within the United States during the term of the patent therefor, infringes the patent.

(b) Whoever actively induces infringement of a patent shall be liable as an infringer.

(c) Whoever sells a component of a patented machine, manufacture, combination or composition, or a material or apparatus for use in practicing a patented process, constituting a material part of the invention, knowing the same to be especially made or especially adapted for use in an infringement of such patent, and not a staple article or commodity of commerce suitable for substantial noninfringing use, shall be liable as a contributory infringer.

(d) No patent owner otherwise entitled to relief for infringement or contributory infringement of a patent shall be denied relief or deemed guilty of misuse or illegal extension of the patent right by reason of his having done one or more of the following: (1) derived revenue from acts which if performed by another without his consent would constitute contributory infringement of the patent; (2) licensed or authorized another to perform acts which if performed without his consent would constitute contributory infringement of the patent; (3) sought to enforce his patent rights against infringement or contributory infringement; (4) refused to license or use any rights to the patent; or (5) conditioned the license of any rights to the patent or the sale of the patented product on the acquisition of a license to rights in another patent or purchase of a separate product, unless, in view of the circumstances, the patent owner has market power in the relevant market for the patent or patented product on which the license or sale is conditioned.

* * *

(f)(1) Whoever without authority supplies or causes to be supplied in or from the United States all or a substantial portion of the components of a patented invention, where such components are uncombined in whole or in part, in such manner as to actively induce the combination of such components outside of the United States in a manner that would infringe the patent if such combination occurred within the United States, shall be liable as an infringer.

(2) Whoever without authority supplies or causes to be supplied in or from the United States any component of a patented invention that is especially made or especially adapted for use in the invention and not a staple article or commodity of commerce suitable for substantial non-infringing use, where such component is uncombined in whole or in part, knowing that such component is so made or adapted and intending that such component will be combined outside of the United States in a manner that would infringe the patent if such combination occurred within the United States, shall be liable as an infringer.

(g) Whoever without authority imports into the United States or sells or uses within the United States a product which is made by a process patented in the United States shall be liable as an infringer, if the importation, sale, or use of the product occurs during the term of such process patent. In an action for infringement of a process patent, no remedy may be granted for infringement on account of the noncommercial use or retail sale of a product unless there is no adequate remedy under this title for infringement on account of the importation or other use or sale of that product. A product which is made by a patented process will, for purposes of this title, not be considered to be so made after—
(1) it is materially changed by subsequent processes; or
(2) it becomes a trivial and nonessential component of another product.

(h) As used in this section, the term "whoever" includes any State, any instrumentality of a State, and any officer or employee of a State or instrumentality of a State acting in his official capacity. Any State, and any such instrumentality, officer, or employee, shall be subject to the provisions of this title in the same manner and to the same extent as any nongovernmental entity.

See Chapter 18 for a discussion of the state action exemption and related doctrines.

COMMENTARY

1. For a discussion of the legislative history of the 1988 changes, see Kenneth J. Burchfiel, *Patent Misuse and Antitrust Reform; "Blessed Be The Tie?,"* 4 HARV. J.L. & TECH. 1 (1991). Section 271(e) was modified in 1994 by § 533, Pub. L. 103-465, to conform to foreign commerce agreements of the Uruguay Round.

Notice how the 1988 Act has changed the definition of patent misuse. Unless a patentee possesses market power, is it no longer misuse to tie a patented product to a staple commodity? Did Congress in enacting the 1988 changes eliminate the standard for distinguishing between legitimate and illegitimate ties which it adopted in 1952 and which was the basis for the decision in *Dawson Chemical*? Why do you think that Congress concluded in 1988 that tying a staple under a patent license should no longer be considered misuse?

Perhaps by 1988, the Congress had absorbed some of the academic criticism of the Supreme Court's traditional hostility towards tying arrangements, namely that tying arrangements are not inherently anticompetitive arrangements. Often they serve efficiency goals or provide a practical way for a patentee to exploit a patent, as in the *Dawson Chemical* case above or in the *IBM Machine Card* case, 298 U.S. 131 (1936) (where the tie enabled the Company to engage in a kind of price discrimination which reduced the monopoly misallocation of resources which would otherwise have occurred).

Since at least 1962 the courts had determined that a patent or copyright raised a presumption of economic power for purposes of finding an antitrust tying violation. Although some courts were questioning the continuing validity of that presumption, the language added in § 271(d)(5) indicates that market power must now be proved for purposes of establishing misuse as a result of a tie. But misuse has always been understood as easier to establish than an antitrust violation. Does this new language indicate that no antitrust violation can occur unless the patentee possesses market power? The history of the presumption of market power from a patent or copyright is considered below.

2. Courts now scrutinize intellectual property licenses under traditional antitrust, patent, and patent misuse doctrines. Thus, contrary to the contentions of the licensee, the patentee's power to limit a manufacturing licensee to selling the patented product within a specified field was upheld in *General Talking Pictures Corp. v. Western Electric Co.,* 304 U.S. 175 (1938). In that case the patentee had confined the licensee to selling amplifiers containing the patented inventions for private noncommercial use, reserving the right to sell amplifiers for commercial use. The misuse doctrine, as noted above, was developed by the federal courts in patent cases prior to the enactment of the Sherman Act. *See* Jere M. Webb & Lawrence A. Locke, *Intellectual Property Misuse: Developments in the Misuse Doctrine,* 4 HARV. J.L. & TECH. 256 (1991); Donald F. Turner, *Basic Principles in Formulating Antitrust and Misuse Constraints on the Exploitation of Intellectual Property Rights,* 53 ANTITRUST L.J. 485 (1984). Procedurally, the misuse doctrine functions as an affirmative defense to an action for patent infringement or for contributory infringement. The doctrine has been described as an equitable concept designed to prevent a patent owner from using the patent in a manner contrary to public policy. *See* WILLIAM G. HOLMES, INTELLECTUAL PROPERTY AND ANTITRUST LAW § 1.07 (1994).

Developed by the federal courts in patent litigation as exercise of their equitable jurisdiction, the misuse doctrine limits the scope of patent rights. When the patent misuse doctrine is invoked against license terms that have an antitcompetitive impact, it may be applied to anticompetitive conduct of a patentee that would not be considered a full-blown antitrust violation. *Transparent-Wrap Machine Corp. v. Stokes & Smith Co.*, 329 U.S. 637, 641 (1947) (holding not illegal *per se* a required improvement grant-back provision and remanding for a determination on misuse). However, the misuse doctrine has also been invoked when the patentee's conduct involves enforcement of license conditions that fall within traditional antitrust doctrines, *e.g.*, resale price, tying arrangements, and related horizontal and vertical restraints.

Under the Sherman and Clayton Acts, courts were historically able to rely on these statutes as a basis for reviewing patent license provisions such as tying arrangements, price agreements, and territorial and other restrictions. Thus, the misuse doctrine and traditional antitrust doctrines became intertwined. To clarify the extent of the overlap of these doctrines, some courts have taken the position that misuse should now be interpreted solely by antitrust principles. In *Windsurfing International, Inc. v. AMF, Inc.*, 782 F.2d 995, 1001 (Fed. Cir.), *cert. denied*, 477 U.S. 905 (1986), the court stated:

> To sustain a misuse defense . . . a factual determination must reveal that the overall effect of the license tends to restrain competition unlawfully in an appropriately defined relevant market.

Earlier Judge Posner had written that the doctrine of misuse had been absorbed by the refinement of antitrust principles. As he put it,

> . . . [W]e must . . . consider whether the patent-misuse doctrine . . . constitutes a general code of patent licensing distinct from antitrust law.
>
> The doctrine arose before there was any significant body of federal antitrust law, and reached maturity long before that law . . . attained its present broad scope. Since the antitrust laws as currently interpreted reach every practice that could impair competition substantially, it is not easy to define a separate role for a doctrine also designed to prevent an anticompetitive practice—the abuse of a patent monopoly.

USM Corp. v. SPS Technologies, Inc., 694 F.2d 505, 511 (7th Cir. 1982). For a critical assessment of the misuse doctrine, see Note, *Economic Irrationality of the Patent Misuse Doctrine*, 78 CAL. L. REV. 1599 (1990).

The uncertain scope of the misuse doctrine is reflected in contrary interpretations by different panels of the Federal Circuit. In *Windsurfing International, supra,* Judge Markey and two colleagues interpreted patent misuse by antitrust criteria. In the same year, Judge Markey and two different colleagues applied patent misuse as an independent doctrine, stating:

> ... [A]s the Supreme Court has said, the patentee's act [of tying the use of its patented process to the purchase of unpatented equipment used in the protected process] may constitute patent misuse without rising to the level of an antitrust violation.

Senza-Gel Corp. v. Seiffhart 803 F.2d 661, 668 (Fed. Cir. 1986).

The traditional role of misuse is as a defense to an action for patent infringement. Generally, the actions constituting misuse are based on the licensing practices of the patentee and consist of conduct that would be the subject of scrutiny under antitrust principles. Some courts have allowed an affirmative claim of misuse as the basis of relief for money damages under the Declaratory Judgment Act. *See B. Braun Medical v. Abbott Laboratories,* 892 F. Supp. 115 (E.D. Pa. 1995).

The proper relationship between antitrust principles and misuse analysis remains unsettled. Recent decisions of the Seventh Circuit take the position that to constitute misuse, the challenged conduct should be found to constitute an antitrust violation. The Federal Circuit in the *Mallinkrodt* case set out at page 823, *infra*, applies antitrust rule of reason analysis to conduct that could be viewed as coming within the exhaustion doctrine under the Patent Act.

Note that the changes to § 271(d) imposed in the 1988 Patent Misuse Statute begin with clause (4). Clause (4) ratifies the result in *Rohm & Haas*. In § 271(d)(5), Congress sought to incorporate contemporary antitrust analysis of tying arrangements into a statutory expression of patent misuse. How does § 271(d)(5) relate to § 271(d)(1)? Do both provisions cover tying? Does § 271(d)(5) now permit a defendant in a patent infringement suit successfully to invoke the misuse defense only if it can establish that the patentee had market power in the tied product? Does this provision apply the same standard for establishing an illegal tying arrangement as announced by the decision in *Jefferson Parish Hospital District No. 2 v. Hyde*, 466 U.S. 2 (1984), set out in Chapter 3? Is it the state of the law that a party must establish the existence of market power to succeed in the misuse defense, but can rely on the existence of the patent to raise a presumption market power in making an antitrust claim? Do you agree with the following statement describing the state of the relationship between the legal standard for proving misuse by a tying arrangement and establishing an illegal tying arrangement under § 1 of the Sherman Act?

> ... [A]n anomalous situation exists where a plaintiff must demonstrate market power to prevail in a misuse claim, but may rely on the existence of the patent to prevail in an antitrust claim.

ABA ANTITRUST SECTION, ANTITRUST LAW DEVELOPMENTS 832 (3d ed. 1992).

Do your responses to these questions depend on how the several opinions in *Jefferson Parish* are interpreted? Note that the 1988 amendment of § 271 followed the decision in *Jefferson Parish. See also* Norman E. Rosen, *Intellectual Property and the Antitrust Pendulum: Recent Developments at the Interface Between the*

Antitrust and Intellectual Property Laws, 62 ANTITRUST L.J. 669 (1994); Note, *The Presumption of Economic Power for Patented and Copyrighted Products in Tying Arrangements,* 85 COLUM. L. REV. 1140 (1985). Writing for the Seventh Circuit, in *USM Corp. v. SPS Technologies, Inc.*, 694 F.2d 505, 511 (7th Cir. 1982), Judge Posner also pointed out that a patent is not commensurate with the possession of market power. On the relation between a patent and market power, consider the following developments.

In the 1995 Guidelines for the Licensing of Intellectual Property, the enforcement agencies take the position that:

> Although tying arrangements may result in anticompetitive effects, such arrangements can also result in significant efficiencies and pro-competitive benefits. In the exercise of their prosecutorial discretion, the agencies will consider both . . . [effects]. The Agencies will be likely to challenge a tying arrangement if: (1) the seller has market power in the tying product . . . [taking account of 35 U.S.C. § 271(d) (1988) & Supp. V 1993], (2) the arrangement has an adverse effect on competition in the relevant market for the tied product, and (3) efficiency justifications for the arrangement do not outweigh the anti-competitive effects.

Guidelines for the Licensing of Intellectual Property 5.3.

In 1996, Congress held hearings on the Intellectual Property Antitrust Protection Act of 1995, *Hearings on H.R. 2674,* 104th Cong., 2d Sess. 16 (May 14, 1996), a measure that would remove any presumption of market power from all forms of intellectual property. This measure would effectively overrule the presumption of market power from the existence of a copyright that had been made by the Supreme Court in tying cases such as *United States v. Loew's, Inc.* 371 U.S. 44, 45 (1962), and by the Ninth Circuit in *Didigidyne Corp. v. Data General Corp.*, 734 F.2d 1336 (9th Cir. 1984). Section 2 of the bill states:

> In any action in which the conduct of an owner, licensor, licensee, or other holder of an intellectual property right is alleged to be in violation of the antitrust laws in connection with the marketing or distribution of a product or service protected by such a right, such right shall not be presumed to define a market, to establish market power (including economic power and product uniqueness or distinctiveness), or to establish monopoly power.

Do the positions expressed in the 1995 DOJ/FTC Intellectual Property Guidelines and in H.R. 2674 reflect a tardy awareness that there can be competition in markets for patented, copyrighted, and trademarked products? In the case that follows, does the court anticipate the position of the Guidelines and H.R. 2674? (This bill was not enacted.)

A.I. Root Co. v. Computer/Dynamics, Inc.

806 F.2d 673 (6th Cir. 1986)

KEITH, Circuit Judge.

Plaintiff, A.I. Root Company appeals a summary judgment rendered for Computer Dynamics, Inc. (CDI) and Management Assistance, Inc. (MAI), in this anti-trust case alleging an illegal tying arrangement and group boycott. A.I. Root alleged that CDI and MAI engaged in anti-competitive activity in violation of the Sherman Antitrust Act . . . . We affirm.

I.
FACTUAL BACKGROUND

A.I. Root Company is an Ohio corporation, manufacturing beekeeper's supplies, ecclesiastical candles, and other products in Medina, Ohio. MAI is a New York corporation which manufactures Basic Four computer equipment and operating software for that equipment. CDI is an Ohio corporation and MAI's authorized dealer in Medina, Ohio. Since 1977, A.I. Root Company had purchased small business computers from MAI dealers, including CDI. In 1982, Root decided to upgrade its computer capabilities by computerizing its inventory and manufacturing processes. CDI offered Root a new MAI Model 710 computer. However, Root purchased a used Basic Four computer from Assured Systems Development, Inc. (ASD)—a dealer in used computers in Cleveland, Ohio.

Root had been using a set of computer programs known as the Basic Operating Software System (BOSS), to operate its earlier machines. These programs constitute operating software necessary to operate the computer generally and to support applications software; applications software consists of programs performing specific data-processing tasks. Root approached CDI for reconfigured BOSS software which was necessary to operate properly its newly-purchased Basic Four Model 730B. Root alleged that CDI offered to sell the reconfigured BOSS software only if Root signed licensing agreements concerning applications software.[1]

This licensing agreement would have required Root to: (1) Use only computer hardware manufactured by MAI with Root's applications software; and (2) Purchase for a "transfer fee" CDI's programming services each time Root acquired an updated or different Basic Four computer. Root contends that these terms constitute an unlawful tying arrangement by conditioning the sale of a reconfigured BOSS software (the tying product) on Root's signing the application software license (the tied product). Rather than accede to the above arrangement, Root purchased new IBM equipment and software.

II.
DISCUSSION

We uphold the summary judgment for defendants, finding no illegal tying arrangement. . . . There is no legal theory under the asserted version of facts which can support an illegal tie; summary judgment is therefore appropriate.

In *Bell v. Cherokee Aviation Corp.,* 660 F.2d 1123, 1127 (6th Cir.1981) (quoting *Fortner Enterprises v. U.S. Steel*, 394 U.S. 495, 499 (1969)), this court stated the requisites of an illegal tie-in as follows:

---

[1] Root had previously acquired applications software and programming services without any restrictions.

1. There must be a tying arrangement between two distinct products or services;
2. The defendant must have sufficient economic power in the tying market to appreciably restrain competition in the tied product market;
3. The amount of commerce affected must be "not insubstantial."

We conclude that MAI did not possess the requisite "economic power" for an illegal tie. Significantly, MAI controlled only 2-4% of the small computer market. This market share is insufficient as a matter of law to infer market dominance. *Accord Jefferson Parish Hospital District No. 2 v. Hyde,* 466 U.S. 2, 26 (1984) (30% market share insufficient to infer market power).

. . . .

Root would . . . have us confer the requisite "economic power" for a tie on BOSS, relying on *United States v. Loew's, Inc.*, 371 U.S. 38, 44 (1962), which states "[t]he requisite economic power is presumed when the tying product is patented or copyrighted." It is uncontested that the BOSS product is copyrighted. Nonetheless, we find the pronouncement in *Loew's* to be overbroad and inapposite to the instant case. Accordingly, we reject any absolute presumption of market power for copyright or patented product, based on the cogent reasoning in Note, *The Presumption of Economic Power for Patented and Copyrighted Products in Tying Arrangements*, 85 COLUM. L. REV. 1140 (1985). The article notes that the evil of tie-ins exists only when the tying product can force consumers to buy an unwanted tied product. This exists only when the tying product confers great market power, evidenced by an exceptional demand for the tying product. However, such a presumption is not warranted merely by existence of a copyright or patent.[2] "More often than not, however, a patent or copyright provides little, if any, market power." *Id.* at 1156.

The above analysis is reflected in Justice O'Connor's concurrence in *Jefferson Parish Hospital.* Although the majority cites *Loew's* for the proposition that "a patent or similar monopoly" confers market power, 466 U.S. at 16, Justice O'Connor, in a footnote, states a more realistic view of the significance of a copyright or patent in tying cases:

> A common misconception has been that a patent or copyright, a high market share, or an unique product that competitors are not able to offer suffice to demonstrate market power. While each of these factors might help to give

---

[2] The Note explains at 1150:

The mere existence of a patent or copyright does not create a demand for a product. Indeed, the majority of all patents and copyrights confer little or no monopoly power. A cursory examination of the market structure for patented or copyrighted goods bears this out. Since each seller's product is differentiated, buyers are matched with sellers on the basis of the buyer's preference. The market is thus not perfectly competitive, since a seller may raise prices without losing every buyer to another seller. The buyer may continue to purchase the goods because his preference for it outweighs the price disincentive. Even if a seller is exacting supernormal profits, it is not necessarily the patent or copyright which allows him to do so. The potential for supernormal profits exists because of barriers to entry, divergent costs, or strong consumer preferences for one of the products. Central to the issue of whether a producer can exact these profits is the existence of adequate substitutes that can be produced at roughly the same cost. If such substitutes exist, supernormal profits are impossible to sustain. However, the existence of a patent or copyright provides little, if any, evidence of supernormal profits, barriers to entry, consumer preferences, or absence of adequate substitutes.

> market power . . . a patent holder has no market power in any relevant sense if there are close substitutes for the patented product.

466 U.S. at 37 n.7. To reiterate, the equipment using BOSS software in the instant case had "close substitutes." Therefore, the fact that BOSS is copyrighted is not determinative of "market power."

. . . .

In conclusion, we find no illegal tying arrangement. MAI controlled only 2-4% of the small computer market and the BOSS system was not unique as to be a particularly sought after tying product; it could not coerce customers into buying an unwanted tied product. MAI and CDI did not engage in the type of anti-competitive conduct proscribed by the antitrust laws. In *Jefferson Parish Hospital v. Hyde,* 466 U.S. at 12, the court stated: "The essential characteristic of an invalid tying arrangement lies in the seller's exploitation of its control over the tying product to force the buyer into the purchase of a tied product that the buyer either did not want at all, or might have preferred to purchase elsewhere." Such an "essential characteristic" was palpably absent in the instant case.

. . . .

Accordingly . . . we affirm the summary judgment orders below.

COMMENTARY

1. Does the decision in the *A.I. Root Co.* case dispose of the issue of the relation between intellectual property and a presumption of market power? Did the copyright raise a presumption of power? Did the court rule that such a presumption was rebutted or that no presumption was raised?

2. How does the decision in *A.I. Root Co.* relate to the Patent Misuse Reform Act? After the Patent Misuse Reform Act, tying a staple to a patent does not constitute misuse unless the patentee possesses market power. Does the Act imply that market power must be proved for a patentee to commit a tying antitrust violation? How does the law governing tying violations differ (if at all) when the tying product is patented from when the tying product is copyrighted?

3. *An historical note:*—The appropriate antitrust enforcement posture of the Antitrust Division regarding intellectual property licensing has been much debated since 1970. In the 1970s, the Antitrust Division put out a list of nine licensing practices that it considered illegal. This list became known, if not notorious, as the "Nine-No No's." In a talk given by Bruce B. Wilson of the Intellectual Property Section of the Antitrust Division, he identified nine licensing practices which the Department of Justice considered to be "clearly unlawful." According to Wilson, "each of them has an effect on competition which extends beyond the metes and bounds of the claims of the patent." The particular practices which he identified were:

1) tying the purchase of unpatented materials as a condition of the license;
2) requiring the licensee to assign back subsequent patents;
3) restricting the right of the purchaser of the product in the resale of the product;
4) restricting the licensee's right to deal in products outside the scope of the patent;
5) a licensor's agreement not to grant subsequent licenses;
6) mandatory package licenses;
7) royalty provisions not reasonably related to the licensee's sales;
8) restrictions on a licensee's use of a product made by a patented process;
9) minimum resale price provisions for the licensed products.

In introducing this list, Mr. Wilson identified these practices by stating,

> . . . What licensing practices does the Department of Justice consider to be clearly unlawful? I believe that I can identify at least nine. Each of them has an effect on competition which extends beyond the metes and bounds of the claims of the patent.
>
> The practices which I have thus far outlined are, in the Department's view, unlawful in virtually every context.
>
> Most practices other than these, we believe, have a wider scope of justification under the rule of reason. . . ."

Bruce B. Wilson, *Patent and Know-How License Agreements: Field of Use, Territorial, Price and Quantity Restrictions*, *in* ANTITRUST PRIMER: PATENTS, FRANCHISING, TREBLE DAMAGE SUITS, 4 NEW ENG. ANTITR. CONF. 11, 15 (Proceedings 1970).

This list of practices has been given varying interpretations by subsequent commentators. One view is that the list be interpreted as a list of licensing provisions that should be subject to antitrust scrutiny. Under this view, any of the nine provisions would be illegal only if anticompetitive consequences could be proven in court. The list was not considered by its drafters as a statement of practices illegal *per se*. This is the view of Richard H. Stern, Chief of the Patent Section of the Division during this period. *See What Ever Happened to the Nine No-No's?,* an address before the American Bar Association, Section On Trademark, Patent, and Copyright Law, Aug. 10, 1993.

In the 1980s, as the post-*Sylvania* view of vertical restraints gained wide acceptance, this list of nine provisions was characterized as an outdated list of practices illegal *per se*. Roger B. Andewelt, Deputy Director of Operations, Antitrust Division, stated his perception of the earlier policy as follows:

> For a significant period of time the Division could be conservatively described as openly hostile to certain forms of intellectual property licensing. The apex of this hostility occurred during the early 1970's

> when the Division indicated that it considered each of nine specific patent license provisions to be *per se* unlawful under the antitrust laws—the so-called nine no-nos of patent licensing.
>
> The old hostility to intellectual property licensing simply was an untenable economic positions [*sic*]. . . . Advances in technology increase productivity, create new industries and improve the ability of U.S. firms to compete in foreign markets. Technological advancement therefore is viewed as a partial solution to some of the nation's most vexing economic problems; unemployment, inflation, and a negative international trade balance.

Roger B. Andewelt, *The Antitrust Division's Perspective on Intellectual Property Protection and Licensing—The Past, the Present, and the Future*, a talk given on July 16, 1985, *reprinted in* ROGER M. MILGRIM, 4 ON TRADE SECRETS, Appendix H-4, H-4-4, H-4-14 (1993).

In 1981, another Deputy Assistant in the Antitrust Division subjected the No-No's to critical review and found them wanting as fixed maxims of antitrust policy. This commentator concluded that none of the No-No's can serve as a general rule of illegality:

> Having buried the "Nine No-No's," let me perform a partial collective resurrection: I have analyzed each of these rules, and have found in almost every instance that they are overinclusive or contain at least some element of economic irrationality. Nevertheless each practice might be condemned in the type of complex multi-party, multi-patent context that seems so typical in this field. . . .
>
> In the antitrust world . . . at the patent/antitrust interface, the basic point is to prevent collusive activity unnecessary to the exploitation of a lawful monopoly.

Abbott B. Lipsky, Jr., *Current Antitrust Division Views on Patent Licensing Practices,* 50 ANTITRUST L.J. 515, 523-24 (1981).

Based on this historical experience, how should enforcement policy for the next decades be stated? How better might the Federal Trade Commission and the Antitrust Division communicate their concern over certain licensing practices to the antitrust bar? What practices should be on a current list, if any?

4. Some of the uncertainty over the misuse doctrine is generated by varying interpretations of the scope of the intellectual property limitations. Each of the principal intellectual property regimes limits the exercise of the granted exclusionary rights in the subject matter being protected. Each regime ends the rightholder's intellectual property control beyond the initial transfer of title. For example, the patentee and the initial licensee may without constraint agree on the royalty for the right to make the patented item. But the patentee may not control the price of that item when it is resold by the initial vendee. *Adams v. Burke,* 84 U.S. (17 Wall.) 453

(1874), is generally cited for the proposition that a patentee may not attach a condition to the right to manufacture by a licensee, that runs with the manufactured article and limits the price or the place at which a subsequent owner may resell the article. A current treatise states this principle as follows:

> Maintenance of the price set by the licensor is enforceable only so far as the licensee's immediate vendee. Stated in other words, the set price extends no further than the first sale. This is an example of the doctrine of domestic patent exhaustion which holds that the first sale of a patented product "exhausts" the patent control by the patentee.

3 PETER D. ROSENBERG, PATENT LAW FUNDAMENTALS 16 (1994).

Similarly, § 109(a) of the Copyright Act restricts the granted distribution right of the copyright holder as follows:

> . . . the owner of a particular copy or phonorecord lawfully made under this title . . . is entitled, without the authority of the copyright owner, to sell or otherwise dispose of the possession of that copy. . . .

17 U.S.C. § 109(a).

The leading copyright treatise characterizes the rationale for the first sale doctrine as follows:

> . . . [when § 109(a) applies] the policy favoring a copyright monopoly for authors gives way to the policy opposing restraints of trade and restraints on alienation.

2 M. NIMMER & D. NIMMER, ON COPYRIGHT 8-129 (1993).

Recall the reliance on the common law doctrine of restraints on alienation of chattels in Justice Fortas' opinion in *Schwinn* in Chapter 5. After the decision in *GTE Sylvania*, which overruled *Schwinn*, was the scope of the common law rule withdrawn from antitrust analysis in order to enhance inter-brand competition and to address the "free rider" issue? Do the intellectual property regimes retain some reliance on the common law doctrine of disfavoring restraints on alienation of property? Does the case that follows address the tension between two views of the rule against restraints on alienation? If the common law doctrine of restraints on alienation was deemed inappropriate as a basis for antitrust analysis of vertical restraints by the Supreme Court, does this suggest that it might be an equally blunt instrument as a basis for the first sale doctrine?

F. Antitrust or Intellectual Property Criteria?

Mallinckrodt, Inc. v. Medipart, Inc.

976 F.2d 700 (Fed. Cir. 1992)

NEWMAN, Circuit Judge.

This action for patent infringement and inducement to infringe relates to the use of a patented medical device in violation of a "single use only" notice that accompanied the sale of the device. Mallinckrodt sold its patented device to hospitals, which after initial use of the devices sent them to Medipart for servicing that enabled the hospitals to use the device again. Mallinckrodt claimed that Medipart thus induced infringement by the hospitals and itself infringed the patent.

The district court held that violation of the "single use only" notice cannot be remedied by suit for patent infringement, and granted summary judgment of noninfringement. [The district court also enjoined Mallinckrodt from distributing a new notice to its hospital customers. Mallinckrodt appeals the grant of summary judgment on the infringement issue and the grant of the preliminary injuction barring distribution of a new notice.]

[The district court relied on a long line of Supreme Court cases upholding the exhaustion doctrine stating:

> In sum, . . . [the precedents] stand only for the proposition that where a patent owner licenses a manufacturer to make his patented invention the patent owner can validly restrict that *manufacturing licensee's* use of the invention and enforce that restriction under the patent laws.
>
> . . . .
>
> But . . . [the precedents do] *not* stand for the broader proposition that express restrictions are per se valid, bind *purchasers*, and can be enforced by suits for infringement.
>
> . . . .
>
> . . . [T]here is a strong public interest in not stretching the patent laws to authorize restriction on the use of purchased goods. The first sale rule is, primarily, a statement about social objectives. . . . It rests on a pragmatic judgment that in, general, people both expect and should be able to use goods they purchase without restraints from merchants and manufacturers.
>
> . . . .
>
> We do not intimate any view about whether Mallinckrodt's restriction might be enforceable on a legal theory other than patent infringement—as a matter of contract law or property law or anything else. We also express no opinion about whether, upon a sufficient showing of danger to the public health, the restriction might be enforceable on equitable grounds.]

We . . . conclude that the district court misapplied precedent in holding that there can be no restriction on use imposed as a matter of law, even on the first purchaser. The restriction here at issue does not *per se* violate the doctrine of patent misuse or the antitrust law. Use in violation of a valid restriction may be remedied under the patent law, provided that no other law prevents enforcement of the patent.

. . . .

BACKGROUND

The patented device is an apparatus for delivery of radioactive or therapeutic material in aerosol mist form to the lungs of a patient, for diagnosis and treatment of pulmonary disease. Radioactive material is delivered primarily for image scanning in diagnosis of lung conditions. Therapeutic agents may be administered to patients suffering various lung diseases. The device is manufactured by Mallinckrodt, who sells it to hospitals as a unitary kit that consists of a "nebulizer" which generates a mist of the radioactive material or the prescribed drug, a "manifold" that directs the flow of oxygen or air and the active material, a filter, tubing, a mouthpiece, and a nose clip. In use, the radioactive material or drug is placed in the nebulizer, is atomized, and the patient inhales and exhales through the closed system. The device traps and retains any radioactive or other toxic material in the exhalate. The device fits into a lead-shielded container that is provided by Mallinckrodt to minimize exposure to radiation and for safe disposal after use.

The device is marked with the appropriate patent numbers, . . . and bears the trademarks "Mallinckrodt" and "UltraVent" and the inscription "Single Use Only." The package insert provided with each unit states "For Single Patient Use Only" and instructs that the entire contaminated apparatus be disposed of in accordance with procedures for the disposal of biohazardous waste. . . . The hospitals whose activities led to this action do not dispose of the UltraVent apparatus, or limit it to a single use.

Instead, the hospitals ship the used manifold/nebulizer assemblies to Medipart, Inc. Medipart in turn packages the assemblies and sends them to Radiation Sterilizers Inc., who exposes the packages to at least 2.5 megarads of gamma radiation, and returns them to Medipart. Medipart personnel then check each assembly for damage and leaks, and place the assembly in a plastic bag together with a new filter, tubing, mouthpiece, and nose clip. The "reconditioned" units, as Medipart calls them, are shipped back to the hospitals from whence they came. Neither Radiation Sterilizers nor Medipart tests the reconditioned units for any residual biological activity or for radioactivity. . . .

Mallinckrodt filed suit against Medipart, asserting patent infringement and inducement to infringe. Mallinckrodt also asserted other counts including trademark infringement, unfair competition under section 43(a) of the Lanham Trademark Act, and violation of Illinois unfair competition statutes. Both parties moved for summary judgment on all counts. . . .

Mallinckrodt appeals the grant of summary judgment on the infringement issue, and the grant of the preliminary injunction.

I

THE RESTRICTION ON REUSE

. . . .

Mallinckrodt states that the restriction to single patient use is valid and enforceable under the patent law because the use is within the scope of the patent grant, and the restriction does not enlarge the patent grant. Mallinckrodt states that a license to less than all uses of a patented article is well recognized and a valid practice under patent law, and that such license does not violate the antitrust laws and is not patent misuse. Mallinckrodt also states that the restriction here imposed is reasonable because it is based on health, safety, efficacy, and liability considerations and violates no public policy. Thus Mallinckrodt argues that the restriction is valid and enforceable under the patent law. Mallinckrodt concludes that use in violation of the restriction is patent infringement . . . and that the district court erred in holding otherwise.

Medipart states that the restriction is unenforceable, for the reason that "the *Bauer* trilogy and *Motion Picture Patents* clearly established that *no* restriction is enforceable under patent law upon a purchaser of a sold article." (Medipart's emphasis). The district court so held. The district court also held that since the hospitals purchased the device from the patentee, not from a manufacturing licensee, no restraint on the use of the device could lawfully be imposed under the patent law.

The district court described the cases sustaining field of use and other restrictions as "in tension" with the cases prohibiting restrictions such as price-fixing and tying, and with the cases holding that the patent right is exhausted with the first sale. The court stated that policy considerations require that no conditions be imposed on patented goods after their sale and that Mallinckrodt's restriction could not "convert[] what was in substance a sale into a license." . . . [T]he . . . [district] court erred in its analysis of the law, for not all restrictions on the use of patented . . . goods are unenforceable.

The enforceability of restrictions on the use of patented goods derives from the patent grant, which is in classical terms of property: the right to exclude. 35 U.S.C. § 154 [now 20 years from date of filing of the application—Eds.]. Every patent shall contain . . . a grant . . . for the term of seventeen years . . . of the right to exclude others from making, using, or selling the invention throughout the United States . . . .

. . . As in other areas of commerce, private parties may contract as they choose, provided that no law is violated thereby:

> [T]he rule is, with few exceptions, that any conditions which are not in their very nature illegal with regard to this kind of property, imposed by the patentee and agreed to by the licensee for the right to manufacture or use or sell the [patented] article, will be upheld by the courts.

E. Bement & Sons v. National Harrow Co., 186 U.S. 70, 91 (1902). The district court's ruling that Mallinckrodt's restriction on reuse was unenforceable was an application of the doctrine of patent misuse, although the court declined to use that designation. The concept of patent misuse arose to restrain practices that did not in themselves violate any law, but that drew anticompetitive strength from the patent right, and thus were deemed to be contrary to public policy. The policy purpose was to prevent a patentee from using the patent to obtain market benefit beyond that which inheres in the statutory patent right.

The district court's holding that Mallinckrodt's restriction to single patient use was unenforceable was, as we have remarked, based on "policy" considerations.

. . . .

The UltraVent device was manufactured by the patentee; but the sale to the hospitals was the first sale and was with notice of the restriction. Medipart offers neither law, public policy, nor logic, for the proposition that the enforceability of a restriction to a particular use is determined by whether the purchaser acquired the device from a manufacturing licensee or from a manufacturing patentee. We decline to make a distinction for which there appears to be no foundation. Indeed, Mallinckrodt has pointed out how easily such a criterion could be circumvented. That the viability of a restriction should depend on how the transaction is structured was denigrated as "formalistic line drawing" in *Continental T.V., Inc. v. GTE Sylvania, Inc.*, 433 U.S. 36, 57-59, 53 . . . (1977), the Court explaining, in overruling *United States v. Arnold, Schwinn & Co.*, 388 U.S. 365, . . . (1967), that the legality of attempts by a manufacturer to regulate resale does not turn on whether the reseller had purchased the merchandise or was merely acting as an agent of the manufacturer. The Court having disapproved reliance on formalistic distinctions of no economic consequence in antitrust analysis, we discern no reason to preserve formalistic distinctions of no economic consequence, simply because the goods are patented.

. . . .

. . . The . . . [antitrust] prohibitions against price-fixing and tying did not make all other restrictions *per se* invalid and unenforceable. . . .

Restrictions on use are judged in terms of their relation to the patentee's right to exclude from all or part of the patent grant, *see, e.g.,* W.F. Baxter, *The Viability of Vertical Restraints Doctrine*, 75 CALIF. L. REV. 933, 935 (1987) ("historically, legal prohibition began with [resale price control and tie-in agreements] and, with rare exceptions, now continues only with those devices"); and where an anticompetitive effect is asserted, the rule of reason is the basis of determining the legality of the provision. In *Windsurfing International, Inc. v. AMF, Inc.*, 782 F.2d 995, 228 USPQ 562 (Fed. Cir.), *cert. denied*, 477 U.S. 905 (1986), this court stated:

> To sustain a misuse defense involving a licensing arrangement not held to have been *per se* anticompetitive by the Supreme Court, a factual determination must reveal that the overall effect of the license tends to restrain competition unlawfully in an appropriately defined relevant market.

Id. at 1001-1002, 228 USPQ at 567 (footnote omitted). *See also Continental T.V. v. GTE Sylvania*, 433 U.S. at 58-59 . . . (judging vertical restrictions under the rule of reason); *Business Electronics Corp. v. Sharp Electronics Corp.*, 485 U.S. 717, 735-36 . . . (1988) (vertical non-price restraints are not *per se* illegal). The district court, stating that it "refuse[s] to limit *Bauer* and *Motion Picture Patents* to tying and price-fixing not only because their language suggests broader application, but because there is a strong public interest in not stretching the patent laws to authorize restrictions on the use of purchased goods," *Mallinckrodt*, . . . has contravened this precedent.

. . . .

. . . [T]his is not a price-fixing or tying case, and the *per se* antitrust and misuse violations . . . are not here present. The appropriate criterion is whether Mallinckrodt's restriction is reasonably within the patent grant, or whether the patentee has ventured beyond the patent grant and into behavior having an anticompetitive effect not justifiable under the rule of reason.

Should the restriction be found to be reasonably within the patent grant, *i.e.*, that it relates to subject matter within the scope of the patent claims, that ends the inquiry. However, should such inquiry lead to the conclusion that there are anticompetitive effects extending beyond the patentee's statutory right to exclude, these effects do not automatically impeach the restriction. Anticompetitive effects that are not *per se* violations of law are reviewed in accordance with the . . . rule of reason. Patent owners should not be in a worse position, by virtue of the patent right to exclude, than owners of other property used in trade. *Compare Tripoli Co. v. Wella Corp.*, 425 F.2d 932, 936-38 (3d Cir.) (*en banc*), cert. denied, 400 U.S. 831 . . . (1970) (in a non-patent action, restriction on resale of certain potentially dangerous products does not violate antitrust laws where motivation was prevention of injury to public and protection against liability risk) *with Marks, Inc. v. Polaroid Corp.*, 237 F.2d 428, 436 (1st Cir. 1956), *cert. denied*, 352 U.S. 1005 . . . (1957) (single use only restriction based on safety concerns not patent misuse, and enforceable by suit for patent infringement).

We conclude that the district court erred in holding that the restriction on reuse was, as a matter of law, unenforceable under the patent law. If the sale of the UltraVent was validly conditioned under the applicable law such as the law governing sales and licenses, and if the restriction on reuse was within the scope of the patent grant or otherwise justified, then violation of the restriction may be remedied by action for patent infringement. The grant of summary judgment is reversed, and the cause is remanded.

....

COMMENTARY

1. Did Judge Newman consider the district court's decision to be improperly rested on the misuse doctrine? Does Judge Newman reject the misuse doctrine as a statement of "policy"? In citing *Sylvania* is Judge Newman interpreting patent misuse according to antitrust principles? In applying rule of reason analysis does the opinion define the relevant market? How was it determined whether Mallinckrodt's restriction was "within" the patent grant?

2. Which outcome in this case, district court or court of appeals, is most congruent with consumer welfare? Assume that Mallinckrodt sold the UltraVent device for $50. Assume the purchasing hospital complied with the single use condition and disposed of the device as hazardous waste at a cost, say, of $1. Alternatively, the hospital ignores the single use limitation, hires the defendant which sterilizes and returns a re-usable device for $10. Assume the patient is billed at hospital cost plus 10%. This example is given by Richard H. Stern, *The Undeserved Demise of the Exhaustion Doctrine in U.S. Patent Law*, 15 EUR. INTELL. PROP. REV. 460 (1993), in an article critical of Judge Newman's decision as downgrading the exhaustion doctrine in this case. If Judge Newman had ruled in favor of the hospital, would the patentee then raise its prices on the UltraVent? Why might the patentee raise its prices on the UltraVent in response to an adverse ruling by Judge Newman while not raising them otherwise?

3. In a recent interview, the then Chief of the Antitrust Division stated: "We expect to file amicus briefs in patent cases where competition would be harmed, even if its not an antitrust issue as such." Anne K. Bingaman, 80 A.B.A. J. 36 (1994). Is *Mallinckrodt* a case where such a brief would be appropriate? Does the misuse doctrine apply also to rights granted by the Copyright Act?

Lasercomb America, Inc. v. Reynolds

911 F.2d 970 (4th Cir. 1990)

Before WIDENER and SPROUSE, Circuit Judges, and HOFFMAN, Senior United States District Judge for the Eastern District of Virginia, sitting by designation.

SPROUSE, Circuit Judge:

Appellants Larry Holliday and Job Reynolds appeal from a district court judgment holding them liable to appellee Lasercomb America, Inc., for copyright infringement and for fraud, based on appellants' unauthorized copying and marketing of appellee's software. We affirm in part, reverse in part, and remand for recomputation of damages.

I

Facts and Proceedings Below

Appellants and defendants below . . . [include] Job Reynolds, a computer programmer for . . . Holiday Steel Co. Appellee is Lasercomb America, Inc. (Lasercomb), the plaintiff below. Holiday Steel and Lasercomb were competitors in the manufacture of steel rule dies that are used to cut and score paper and cardboard for folding into boxes and cartons. Lasercomb developed a software program, Interact, which is the object of the dispute between the parties. Using this program, a designer creates a template of a cardboard cutout on a computer screen and the software directs the mechanized creation of the conforming steel rule die.

In 1983, before Lasercomb was ready to market its Interact program generally, it licensed four prerelease copies to Holiday Steel which paid $35,000 for the first copy, $17,500 each for the next two copies, and $2,000 for the fourth copy. Lasercomb informed Holiday Steel that it would charge $2,000 for each additional copy Holiday Steel cared to purchase. Apparently ambitious to create for itself an even better deal, Holiday Steel circumvented the protective devices Lasercomb had provided with the software and made three unauthorized copies of Interact which it used on its computer systems. Perhaps buoyed by its success in copying, Holiday Steel then created a software program called "PDS-1000," which was almost entirely a direct copy of Interact, and marketed it as its own CAD/CAM [computer assisted design/computer assisted software] die-making software. These infringing activities were accomplished by Job Reynolds at the direction of Larry Holliday [president and sole shareholder of Holiday Steel Co.].

There is no question that defendants engaged in unauthorized copying, and the purposefulness of their unlawful action is manifest from their deceptive practices. For example, Lasercomb had asked Holiday Steel to use devices called "chronoguards" to prevent unauthorized access to Interact. Although defendants had deduced how to circumvent the chronoguards and had removed them from their computers, they represented to Lasercomb that the chronoguards were in use. Another example of subterfuge is Reynolds' attempt to modify the PDS-1000 program output so it would present a different appearance than the output from Interact.

When Lasercomb discovered Holiday Steel's activities, it registered its copyright in Interact and filed this action against Holiday Steel, Holliday, and Reynolds on March 7, 1986. Lasercomb claimed copyright infringement, breach of contract, misappropriation of trade secret, false designation of origin, unfair competition, and fraud. Defendants filed a number of counterclaims. On March 24, 1986, the district court entered a preliminary injunction, enjoining defendants from marketing the PDS-1000 software.

The procedural history of this case is complex, with various claims and defenses experiencing both death and resurrection on various pretrial motions and at the bench trial itself. For purposes of this appeal it suffices to say that, ultimately, all of the counterclaims were dismissed; Lasercomb's claims of misappropriation of trade secret, false designation of origin, and unfair competition were dismissed as preempted by the Copyright Act; the court found the defendants liable to Lasercomb for copyright infringement, rejecting their affirmative defenses of misuse of copyright and lack of statutory copyright notice; and the court held for Lasercomb on its claims of breach of contract and fraud.

The district court awarded Lasercomb $105,000 in actual damages for copyright infringement and for fraud—plus $10,000 against Holliday and $5,000 against Reynolds as punitive damages on the fraud claim. All defendants were permanently enjoined from publishing and marketing the PDS-1000 software.

Holliday and Reynolds raise . . . [among others, the following issue on appeal]. They do not dispute that they copied Interact, but they contend that Lasercomb is barred from recovery for infringement by its concomitant culpability. They assert that, assuming Lasercomb had a perfected copyright, it impermissibly abused it. This assertion of the "misuse of copyright" defense is based on language in Lasercomb's standard licensing agreement, restricting licensees from creating any of their own CAD/CAM die-making software. . . .

II

Misuse of Copyright Defense

A successful defense of misuse of copyright bars a culpable plaintiff from prevailing on an action for infringement of the misused copyright. Here, appellants claim Lasercomb has misused its copyright by including in its standard licensing agreement clauses which prevent the licensee from participating in any manner in the creation of computer-assisted die-making software. The offending paragraphs read:

> D. Licensee agrees during the term of this Agreement that it will not permit or suffer its directors, officers and employees, directly or indirectly, to write, develop, produce or sell computer assisted die making software.
>
> E. Licensee agrees during the term of this Agreement and for one (1) year after the termination of this Agreement, that it will not write, develop, produce or sell or assist others in the writing, developing, producing or selling computer assisted die making software, directly or indirectly without Lasercomb's prior written consent. Any such activity undertaken without Lasercomb's written consent shall nullify any warranties or agreements of Lasercomb set forth herein.

The "term of this Agreement" referred to in these clauses is ninety-nine years.

. . . .

The district court rejected the copyright misuse defense for three reasons. First, it noted that defendants had not explicitly agreed to the contract clauses alleged to constitute copyright misuse. Second, it found "such a clause is reasonable in light of the delicate and sensitive area of computer software." And, third, it questioned whether such a defense exists. We consider the district court's reasoning in reverse order.

A. *Does a "Misuse of Copyright" Defense Exist?*

We agree with the district court that much uncertainty engulfs the "misuse of copyright" defense. We are persuaded, however, that a misuse of copyright defense is inherent in the law of copyright just as a misuse of patent defense is inherent in patent law.

The misuse of a patent is a potential defense to suit for its infringement, and both the existence and parameters of that body of law are well established. *E.g., United States Gypsum Co. v. National Gypsum Co.*, 352 U.S. 457, 465 (1957).... Although there is little case law on the subject, courts from time to time have intimated that the similarity of rationales underlying the law of patents and the law of copyrights argues for a defense to an infringement of copyright based on misuse of the copyright. *E.g., United States v. Loew's, Inc.*, 371 U.S. 38, 44-51 (1962); *United States v. Paramount Pictures, Inc.*, 334 U.S. 131, 157-59 (1948); *Mitchell Bros. Film Group v. Cinema Adult Theater*, 604 F.2d 852, 865 & n.27 (5th Cir. 1979), *cert. denied*, 445 U.S. 917 (1980). The origins of patent and copyright law in England, the treatment of these two aspects of intellectual property by the framers of our Constitution, and the later statutory and judicial development of patent and copyright law in this country persuade us that parallel public policies underlie the protection of both types of intellectual property rights. We think these parallel policies call for application of the misuse defense to copyright as well as patent law.

1. Overview

Because of the paucity of precedent in the copyright misuse area, some historical perspective of the elements underlying intellectual property law is helpful to our inquiry. Fortunately, respected treatise authors have captured well the essence of the relevant historical perspective.

During the sixteenth century, it became common for the English Crown to grant "letters patent" which gave individuals exclusive rights to produce, import and/or sell given items within the kingdom.... These monopolies were granted for such commonplace items as salt, vinegar, and calfskins, to name but a few. The practice of granting monopolies led to widespread abuses, such as shortages and inflated prices for items that would otherwise be easily and cheaply available. Consequently, Parliament passed the Statute of Monopolies (1623-24), prohibiting the creation of such monopolies by the Crown. An exception was made, however, to permit a patent to be granted for a period of fourteen years to the creator of a new invention....

The rationale for allowing patents for new inventions was and is to encourage their creation for the benefit of society.... The monopolies granted by the Crown had been odious because they restrained trade in articles that had previously been a part of the public domain. An invention, however, does not withdraw anything from public traffic; rather, it introduces something new. To encourage and reward inventors for increasing the inventory of useful objects, the government grants them, for a limited time, the right to exclude others from making and selling their inventions. *United States v. Dubilier Condenser Corp.*, 289 U.S. 178, 186 (1933).

The development of copyright law in England likewise grew out of a differentiation by Parliament between a monopoly that restricts publication of works and a limited copyright that encourages the efforts of authors. In sixteenth-century England, the Crown granted to the Stationers' Company the exclusive right to publish and print all published works (apparently to enable censorship of Protestant materials). In the early 1700s, the Stationer's Company petitioned Parliament to recognize that these rights inured to it in perpetuity. Instead, Parliament passed the Statute of Anne (1709-10), the first known copyright legislation. A. Latman, *The Copyright Law*: . . . That statute gave authors the sole right of publication for up to twenty-eight years. Thus, the English statutory treatment of copyright was similar to that of patent in that it granted the creator a monopoly for a limited time only.

It is significant, we think, that the framers of our Constitution continued the English development of intellectual property law and considered in tandem those property rights protectable by copyrights and those protectable by patents. In giving Congress the power to create copyright and patent laws, the framers combined the two concepts in one clause, stating a unitary purpose—to promote progress. Article I, section 8, clause 8 of the United States Constitution provides:

> [The Congress shall have power] To promote the Progress of Science and useful Arts, by securing for limited Times to Authors and Inventors the exclusive Right to their respective Writings and Discoveries.

This clause was adopted without debate, and material explaining the intention of the framers is limited. However, a comment in *The Federalist* papers indicates the public policy behind the grant of copyright and patent powers is essentially the same:

> The utility of this power will scarcely be questioned. The copyright of authors has been solemnly adjudged, in Great Britain, to be a right of common law. The right to useful inventions seems with equal reason to belong to the inventors. The public good fully coincides in both cases with the claims of individuals.

The Federalist, No. 43 at 279 (J. Madison) (Mod. Lib. ed. 1941).

Supreme Court comment has likewise equated the public policies of copyright and patent. For example, in *Mazer v. Stein*, 347 U.S. 201, 219 (1953), the Supreme Court stated:

> The economic philosophy behind the clause empowering Congress to grant *patents and copyrights* is the conviction that encouragement of individual effort by personal gain is the best way to advance public welfare through the talents of authors and inventors in "Science and useful Arts." Sacrificial days devoted to such creative activities deserve rewards commensurate with the services rendered.

(Emphasis added.) *See also Loew's*, 371 U.S. at 44-51; *Paramount Pictures*, 334 U.S. at 154-59. The philosophy behind copyright, parallel to that discussed above for patent, is that the public benefits from the efforts of authors to introduce new ideas and knowledge into the public domain. To encourage such efforts, society grants authors exclusive rights in their works for a limited time.

. . . .

3. The "Misuse of Copyright" Defense

Although the patent misuse defense has been generally recognized since *Morton Salt*, it has been much less certain whether an analogous copyright misuse defense exists. . . . This uncertainty persists because no United States Supreme Court decision has firmly established a copyright misuse defense in a manner analogous to the establishment of the patent misuse defense by *Morton Salt*. The few courts considering the issue have split on whether the defense should be recognized . . . and we have discovered only one case which has actually applied copyright misuse to bar an action for infringement. *M. Witmark & Sons v. Jensen*, 80 F. Supp. 843 (D. Minn. 1948), *appeal dismissed*, 177 F.2d 515 (8th Cir.1949).

We are of the view, however, that since copyright and patent law serve parallel public interests, a "misuse" defense should apply to infringement actions brought to vindicate either right. As discussed above, the similarity of the policies underlying patent and copyright is great and historically has been consistently recognized. Both patent law and copyright law seek to increase the store of human knowledge and arts by rewarding inventors and authors with the exclusive rights to their works for a limited time. At the same time, the granted monopoly power does not extend to property not covered by the patent or copyright. *Morton Salt*, 314 U.S. at 492; *Paramount Pictures*, 334 U.S. at 156-58; *cf. Baker v. Selden*, 101 U.S. 99, 101-04 (1880).

Thus, we are persuaded that the rationale of *Morton Salt* in establishing the misuse defense applies to copyrights. In the passage from *Morton Salt* quoted above, the phraseology adapts easily to a copyright context:

> The grant to the [author] of the special privilege of a [copyright] carries out a public policy adopted by the Constitution and laws of the United States, "to promote the Progress of Science and useful Arts, by securing for limited Times to [Authors] . . . the exclusive Right . . ." to their ["original" works]. United States Constitution, Art. I, § 8, cl. 8, [17 U.S.C.A. § 102]. But the public policy which includes [original works] within the granted monopoly excludes from it all that is not embraced in the [original expression]. It equally forbids the use of the [copyright] to secure an exclusive right or limited monopoly not granted by the [Copyright] Office and which it is contrary to public policy to grant.

Cf. Morton Salt, 314 U.S. at 492.

Having determined that "misuse of copyright" is a valid defense, analogous to the misuse of patent defense, our next task is to determine whether the defense should have been applied by the district court to bar Lasercomb's infringement action against the defendants in this case.

B. *The District Court's Finding that the Anticompetitive Clauses Are Reasonable*

In declining to recognize a misuse of copyright defense, the district court found "reasonable" Lasercomb's attempt to protect its software copyright by using anticompetitive clauses in their licensing agreement. In briefly expressing its reasoning, the court referred to the "delicate and sensitive" nature of software. It also observed that Lasercomb's president had testified that the noncompete language was negotiable.

If, as it appears, the district court analogized from the "rule of reason" concept of antitrust law, we think its reliance on that principle was misplaced. Such reliance is, however, understandable. Both the presentation by appellants and the literature tend to intermingle antitrust and misuse defenses. . . . A patent or copyright is often regarded as a limited monopoly—an exception to the general public policy against restraints of trade. Since antitrust law is the statutory embodiment of that public policy, there is an understandable association of antitrust law with the misuse defense. Certainly, an entity which uses its patent as the means of violating antitrust law is subject to a misuse of patent defense. However, *Morton Salt* held that it is not necessary to prove an antitrust violation in order to successfully assert patent misuse[.]

. . . .

So while it is true that the attempted use of a copyright to violate antitrust law probably would give rise to a misuse of copyright defense, the converse is not necessarily true—a misuse need not be a violation of antitrust law in order to comprise an equitable defense to an infringement action. The question is not whether the copyright is being used in a manner violative of antitrust law (such as whether the licensing agreement is "reasonable"), but whether the copyright is being used in a manner violative of the public policy embodied in the grant of a copyright.

Lasercomb undoubtedly has the right to protect against copying of the Interact code. Its standard licensing agreement, however, goes much further and essentially attempts to suppress any attempt by the licensee to independently implement the idea which Interact expresses. The agreement forbids the licensee to develop or assist in developing any kind of computer-assisted die-making software. If the licensee is a business, it is to prevent all its directors, officers and employees from assisting in any manner to develop computer-assisted die-making software. Although one or another licensee might succeed in negotiating out the noncompete provisions, this does not negate the fact that Lasercomb is attempting to use its copyright in a manner adverse to the public policy embodied in copyright law, and that it has succeeded in doing so with at least one licensee. . . .

The language employed in the Lasercomb agreement is extremely broad. Each time Lasercomb sells its Interact program to a company and obtains that company's agreement to the noncompete language, the company is required to forego utilization of the creative abilities of all its officers, directors and employees in the area of CAD/CAM die-making software. Of yet greater concern, these creative abilities are withdrawn from the public. The period for which this anticompetitive restraint exists is ninety-nine years, which could be longer than the life of the copyright itself.

We previously have considered the effect of anticompetitive language in a licensing agreement in the context of patent misuse. *Compton v. Metal Products, Inc.*, 453 F.2d 38 (4th Cir.1971), *cert. denied*, 406 U.S. 968 (1972). Compton had invented and patented coal auguring equipment. He granted an exclusive license in the patents to Joy Manufacturing, and the license agreement included a provision that Compton would not "engage in any business or activity relating to the manufacture or sale of equipment of the type licensed hereunder" for as long as he was due royalties under the patents. Suit for infringement of the Compton patents was brought against Metal Products, and the district court granted injunctive relief and damages. On appeal we held that relief for the infringement was barred by the misuse defense, stating:

> The need of Joy to protect its investment does not outweigh the public's right under our system to expect competition and the benefits which flow therefrom, and the total withdrawal of Compton from the mining machine business . . . everywhere in the world for a period of 20 years unreasonably lessens the competition which the public has a right to expect, and constitutes misuse of the patents.

. . . .

We think the anticompetitive language in Lasercomb's licensing agreement is . . . egregious . . . and therefore amounts to misuse of its copyright. Again, the analysis necessary to a finding of misuse is similar to but separate from the analysis necessary to a finding of antitrust violation. The misuse arises from Lasercomb's attempt to use its copyright in a particular expression, the Interact software, to control competition in an area outside the copyright, *i.e.,* the idea of computer-assisted die manufacture, regardless of whether such conduct amounts to an antitrust violation. . . .

. . . .

In its rejection of the copyright misuse defense, the district court emphasized that Holiday Steel was not explicitly party to a licensing agreement containing the offending language. However, again analogizing to patent misuse, the defense of copyright misuse is available even if the defendants themselves have not been injured by the misuse. In *Morton Salt*, the defendant was not a party to the license requirement that only Morton-produced salt tablets be used with Morton's salt-depositing machine. Nevertheless, suit against defendant for infringement of Morton's patent was barred on public policy grounds. Similarly, in *Compton*, even though the defendant Metal Products was not a party to the license agreement that restrained competition by Compton, suit against Metal Products was barred because of the public interest in free competition. . . .

Therefore, the fact that appellants here were not parties to one of Lasercomb's standard license agreements is inapposite to their copyright misuse defense. The question is whether Lasercomb is using its copyright in a manner contrary to public policy, which question we have answered in the affirmative.

In sum, we find that misuse of copyright is a valid defense, that Lasercomb's anticompetitive clauses in its standard licensing agreement constitute misuse of copyright, and that the defense is available to appellants even though they were not parties to the standard licensing agreement. Holding that Lasercomb should have been barred by the defense of copyright misuse from suing for infringement of its copyright in the Interact program, we reverse the injunction and the award of damages for copyright infringement.

. . . .

COMMENTARY

1. The acceptance by the Fourth Circuit of the copyright misuse defense represents the minority view among the circuit courts; the Supreme Court has not explicitly recognized the doctrine, which has been rejected in *Triad Systems Corp. v. Southeastern Express Co.*, 64 F.3d 1330 (9th Cir. 1995); *Data General Corp. v. Grumman Systems Support Corp.,* 36 F.3d 1146 (1st Cir. 1994*); Atari Games Corp. v. Nintendo of America.*, 975 F.2d 832 (Fed. Cir. 1992); and *BellSouth Advertising & Publishing Corp. v. Donnelley Information Publishing, Inc.*, 933 F.2d 952 (11th Cir. 1991). Although the doctrine has not been widely accepted by district courts, *Basic Books, Inc. v. Kinko's Graphics Corp.,* 758 F. Supp. (E.D. Pa. 1990), the doctrine was recently applied to dismiss an infringement claim in *Tamburo v. Calvin,* WL 121539 (N.D. Ill. 1995), in which the license of a copyrighted computer program contained clauses barring the licensee from selling copies of the licensed program and from producing a competing product for a ten year period.

The rationale of *Lasercomb* has been criticized as being ambiguous in Note, *Divorcing Public Policy from Economic Reality: The Fourth Circuit's Copyright Misuse Doctrine in* Lasercomb, 69 N.C. L. Rev. 1672 (1991); for an analysis of the copyright misuse doctrine that is critical of the application of antitrust principles to misuse analysis, see Note, *Misusing Antitrust: The Search for Functional Copyright*

Misuse Standards, 46 STAN. L. REV. 401 (1994); for an analysis of the the copyright misuse doctrine favoring the application of antitrust principles, see Note, *Clarifying the Copyright Misuse Defense: The Role of Antitrust Standards and First Amendment Values*, 104 HARV. L. REV. 1289 (1991).

2. The copyright misuse defense was used by the Fifth Circuit in *Alcatel USA, Inc. v. DGI Technologies, Inc.*, 166 F.3d 772 (5th Cir. 1999). (The facts and principal parts of the opinion are set forth on page 802.) In the following excerpt, the court considers the issue of copyright misuse:

Alcatel USA, Inc. v. DGI Technologies, Inc.

166 F.3d 772 (5th Cir. 1999)

WIENER, Circuit Judge:

. . .

b. Copyright Misuse

. . .

We recognized the copyright misuse defense in *DSC I*. We noted that "DSC *seems to be* attempting to use its copyright to obtain a patent-like monopoly over unpatented microprocessor cards." Speculating that DGI might prevail on a copyright misuse defense, we refused to expand the preliminary injunction issued by the district court.

Not surprisingly, DGI argues . . . that . . . the district court abused its discretion when it ignored the jury's finding that DSC misused its operating system copyright and entered the permanent injunction. DGI reasons that, as DSC's software is licensed to customers to be used only in conjunction with DSC-manufactured hardware, DSC indirectly seeks to obtain patent-like protection of its hardware—its microprocessor card—through the enforcement of its software copyright. DSC responds that its actions do not constitute misuse, inasmuch as its licensing agreement does not prohibit the independent development of compatible operating system software. As DSC points out, it was this "attempt[ ] to suppress any attempt by the licensee to independently implement" competing software that the court condemned in *Lasercomb*.

We agree with the *DSC I* panel's conjecture and the jury's finding that DSC's licensing agreement for its operating system constitutes misuse. . . .

A reasonable juror could conclude, based on the licensing agreement, that "DSC has used its copyrights to indirectly gain commercial control over products DSC does not have copyrighted," namely, its microprocessor cards. The facts on which we based our misuse prediction in *DSC I* have not changed substantially. As we reasoned then:

> Any competing microprocessor card developed for use on DSC phone switches must be compatible with DSC's copyrighted operating system software. In order to ensure that its card is compatible, a competitor such as DGI must test the card on a DSC phone switch. Such a test necessarily involves making a copy of DSC's copyrighted operating system, which copy is downloaded into the card's memory when the card is booted up. If DSC is allowed to prevent such

copying, then it can prevent anyone from developing a competing microprocessor card, even though it has not patented the card.

Under these facts, DSC's assertion that its licensing agreement does not prohibit the independent development of compatible software is simply irrelevant. Despite the presence of some evidence—the testimony of a DSC executive—that DGI could have developed its own software, there was also evidence that it was not technically feasible to use a non-DSC operating system because the switch has a "common control" scheme in which each microprocessor card in a network of such cards runs the same operating system. Hence, without the freedom to test its cards in conjunction with DSC's software, DGI was effectively prevented from developing its product, thereby securing for DSC a limited monopoly over its uncopyrighted microprocessor cards. Furthermore, the jury instructions never mentioned that misuse could only be present if DSC's agreement prohibited the independent development of software. Consequently, we conclude that the district court abused its discretion in awarding injunctive relief based on DGI's infringing acts.

We reach this conclusion despite the jury's finding that DGI acted with unclean hands in its acquisition and use of DSC's copyrighted software, firmware, and manuals. DSC insists that, based on this finding, DGI is barred from invoking an equitable defense, and DSC is entitled to injunctive relief notwithstanding its alleged copyright misuse. We reject this contention.

. . . In the instant case, it is DSC which seeks equitable relief in the form of an injunction, and thus it is DSC's hands alone that must pass the hygenic test. By misusing its software copyright, DSC sullied its hands, barring itself from obtaining the equitable reward of injunction on grounds of copyright infringement. This does not mean that we repudiate the jury's finding of unclean hands on the part of DGI. Indeed, the deceptive practices used by DGI to obtain a copy of DSC's software left it with very dirty mitts. Nevertheless, this finding is irrelevant given the particular posture of this case.

. . . .

III
CONCLUSION

For the foregoing reasons, we affirm the district court's grant of a JML in favor of DSC, dismissing DGI's antitrust claim. . . . Because DSC misused its copyrights, however, we reverse the portions of the injunction tailored by the district court as relief from DGI's copyright infringement. . . .

Affirmed in part; Reversed and Vacated in part; and Remanded in part.

COMMENTARY

1. DSC was at least partially successful in asserting its copyrights against an aftermarket competitor in *DSC Communications Corp. v. Pulse Communications, Inc.*, 170 F.3d 1354 (Fed. Cir. 1999). The court there recognized the copyright misuse issue, but ruled that it was not yet ripe for appellate review.

The essential facility doctrine (see pages 472 ff., *supra*) has also been invoked against a denial of access to copyrighted material—a claim recognized in some circumstances as actionable under § 2 of the Sherman Act in cases not involving intellectual property rights, *e.g., Aspen Skiing Co. v. Aspen Highlands Skiing Co.*, and *Otter Tail Power Co.* In *Data General Corp. v. Grumman Systems Support Corp.*, 761 F. Supp. 185 (D. Mass. 1991); 803 F. Supp. 487 (D. Mass. 1992), the defendant raised antitrust claims of denial of use of an essential facility in violation of § 2 of the Sherman Act. Defendant, a computer service provider used without permission the plaintiff's copyrighted diagnostic computer software program in doing its repair work. Plaintiff, a software developer and provider of maintenance and repair service for computer equipment, had brought a copyright infringement action against the defendant, a competing service provider. The antitrust defense was rejected, the Court stating,

> The Sherman Act has not been interpreted to require manufacturers . . . [of copyrighted material] to abandon their advantage. . . .
>
> * * *
>
> [Were they required to do so] the incentives of copyright and patent laws would be severely undermined.

761 F. Supp. at 192. In *Montgomery County Association of Realtors v. Realty Photo Master Corp.*, 878 F. Supp. 804 (D. Md. 1995), the court rejected the claim that a multiple listing real estate data base was an essential facility.

3. The enforcement of intellectual property rights known by the holder to be invalid can sometimes give rise to an antitrust cause of action. A related doctrine holds that the commission of intentional fraud on the patent office can, when the requisite other factors are present, also give rise to an antitrust cause of action. These matters are discussed, pages 784-86, *supra*.

G. Enforcement Policy and Intellectual Property

The dramatic expansion of computer technology during the 1980s was reflected in the following statement by the then-head of the Antitrust Division.

> When lawyers think of innovation, they tend to think of the laws protecting intellectual property, in particular patent law, but also copyright law, especially since the copyrightability of computer programs became clear. . . . It has long been common, if not necessarily accurate, to speak of the tension between patent law and the antitrust laws, and increasingly the same is heard about copyright law and the antitrust laws.
>
> * * *

> The core rights of owners of intellectual property are reasonably clear, but beyond that core, matters are a good deal less settled. Whether the holder of a patent may, for instance, tie unpatented supplies to the patented product; engage in compulsory assignment grant-backs; or place post-sale restraints on resale by purchasers are just a few of the host of issues that have been debated and litigated in the patent/antitrust field for several decades.
>
> * * *
>
> Recognizing the importance to innovation of an appropriate antitrust/intellectual property accommodation, and the inadequacy of intuitive and *ad hoc* responses, I have recently . . . [set up] a task force that will consult with leading academics, practitioners, and industry experts in the field of intellectual property to review and reformulate, where appropriate, the Division's policies on intellectual property and antitrust.

Speech by Anne K. Bingaman, Assistant Attorney General, Antitrust Division, January 1, 1994, CCH Trade Reg. Reports ¶ 50,128 at page 48,998.

On April 6, 1995, the Department of Justice and the Federal Trade Commission issued jointly Antitrust Guidelines for the Licensing of Intellectual Property, which are reproduced in full in 68 Antitrust Trade Reg. Rep. 476 (BNA) and in Appendix C. The stated objectives of the Guidelines are to provide assistance in predicting the response of the enforcement agencies to various industry practices. The Guidelines state that: "The intellectual property laws and the antitrust laws share the common purpose of promoting innovation and enhancing consumer welfare." Guidelines § 1. The introduction also notes that the enforcement agencies "do not presume that intellectual property creates market power in the antitrust context." Guidelines § 2. It is further noted that licensing arrangements that fall outside the "safety zones" are not deemed to be antitcompetitive.

In § 3.2.3 the Guidelines emphasize a concern with licensing arrangement that may impinge on the development of new or improved goods or processes. The reference is to "innovation markets," which are defined as research and development activities. Example 1 concerns licensing arrangements that might have a restrictive effect on computer software development. See the discussion of the *Microsoft* litigation, below. For further discussion of innovation markets, see Chapter 12.

The design of the Guidelines is to set out the circumstances in which one or more restraints in an intellectual property license will presumptively be immune from enforcement challenge. The conditions of qualification for such presumptive immunity from enforcement scrutiny is stated in terms of "safety zones." Where there is available data for market shares, a "safety zone" exists if, taking the license restrictions collectively among the firms in the industry, 20 percent or less of each relevant market is affected by the restraint, so long as the stated restriction is not illegal *per se*. Where there is no market share data or the existing data is deemed invalid, a "safety zone" exists if there are available at least four near substitutes at comparable cost for the technology subject to the restrictive license provision and the restrictive provision is not illegal *per se*.

The attention given by the enforcement agencies to the business practices of Microsoft Corporation starting in 1990, includes particular attention to its licensing practices, as noted below. The extended review of the licensing and related practices of Microsoft are critically reviewed by Daniel J. Gifford, in *Microsoft Corporation, the Justice Department, and Antitrust Theory,* 25 Sw. U. L. Rev. 621, 632 (1996).

The FTC had initially reviewed Microsoft's licensing practices, but concluded its review in 1993 without filing a complaint. After the FTC's review was concluded, the Antitrust Division picked up the case. In 1994, the Department's review resulted in a complaint and a consent decree that was primarily directed at several terms in Microsoft's licensing agreements with manufacturers of personal computers. *See* Complaint, § 4, *United States v. Microsoft, Corp.*, 1995 WL 505998 (D.D.C.). In the required review of consent decrees under the Tunney Act, 15 U.S.C. § 16(e) (Supp. 1994), an act designed to provide for judicial review of consent decrees according to a public interest standard, the decree was initially rejected as being too narrow in *United States v. Microsoft Corp.,* 159 F.R.D. 318 (D.D.C. 1995), but was reinstated on appeal, 56 F.3d 1448 (D.C. Cir. 1995).

The nub of the government's case was that Microsoft, a dominant (70% market share) seller of copyrighted computer operating systems, had used its license provisions to establish a large installed base of computer manufacturers so as to monopolize the market for operating systems in violation of § 2 of the Sherman Act. Microsoft's dominance stemmed from its alliance with IBM in the early 1980s to install the Microsoft MS-DOS operating system in all personal computers manufactured by IBM. The Complaint further alleged that these license provisions were contracts in restraint of trade under § 1.

The District Court opinion summarized the Complaint as follows:

> Microsoft, the Justice Department and a number of competitors who oppose the entry of the decree all agree that it is very difficult to enter the operating systems market. There are two main reasons for this, each of which reinforces the other. First, consumers do not want to buy PCs with an operating system that does not already have a large installed base because of their concern that there will not be a wide range of applications software available for that operating system. The second complementary reasons why there are large barriers to entry into the operating systems market is that ISVs . . . [independent software vendors] do not want to spend time and money developing applications for operating systems that do not have a large installed base.

> . . . As a result OEMs . . . [original equipment manufacturers (of PCs)] have little incentive to license an operating system that does not have a large installed base and include it in their PCs.
>
> In addition to these "natural" barriers to entry, the complaint identifies Microsoft's use of per processor licenses and long term commitments as "exclusionary and anti-competitive contract terms to maintain its monopoly." A per processor license means that Microsoft licenses an operating system to an OEM which pays a royalty to Microsoft for each PC sold regardless of whether a Microsoft operating system is included in that PC. . . . [U]nder a per processor license, if an OEM sells some PCs with a competitor's operating system installed (*e.g.,* IBM's OS/2), and others with MS-DOS installed, the OEM would pay Microsoft royalties on all PCs sold. In effect, the OEM pays twice every time it sells a PC with a non-Microsoft operating system—once to the company that licensed the operating system to the OEM and once to Microsoft.
>
> * * *
>
> The complaint further alleges that Microsoft's use of long-term licensing agreements with or without minimum commitments, and the rolling over of unused commitments unreasonably extended some licensing agreements with Microsoft.

United States v. Microsoft Corp., 159 F.R.D. 318, 322-3 (D.D.C. 1995).

Under Section IV of the Consent Decree, styled "Prohibited Conduct," Microsoft is enjoined and restrained as follows:

> A. Microsoft shall not enter into any License Agreement . . . that has a total Duration that exceeds one year. . .
> [The decree permitted Microsoft to include a term permitting the OEM to renew the license on the same terms for another year.]
>
> * * *
>
> C. Microsoft shall not enter into any per processor license.

United States v. Microsoft Corp., 1995 WL 505998 (D.D.C.).

COMMENTARY

1. Does the per processor license violate the royalty base computation rule of *Zenith v. Hazeltine*? Explain.

2. Professor Gifford questions the rationale of barring the use of the lump-sum license as follows:

> Why doesn't the apparent easy entry into personal computer manufacturing ensure the availability of outlets for OS/2 Warp? . . . If it is easy to enter computer manufacturing and if specialization in marketing OS/2 Warp [equipped] machines is feasible, then the exclusionary effect of Microsoft's lump-sum licenses may be minimal. Indeed, IBM (the provider of OS2/Warp) is itself a computer manufacturer. If the demand for OS2/Warp-equipped machines does not exceed IBM's personal computer production capacity, then IBM itself can be the specialized vendor of OS2/Warp-equipped personal computers. On this analysis, the restraint constituted by Microsoft's lump-sum licensing withers into insignificance.

Microsoft Corporation, the Justice Department, and Antitrust Theory, 25 Sw. U. L. Rev. 621, 636-37 (1996)

3. As to the long-term consequences of Microsoft's practices, Professor Gifford criticizes the Departments basic premise in bringing the *Microsoft* case, as follows:

> The Justice Department's objections to the exclusive-supply contracts . . . [the MS-DOS licenses] lay in their longer term effects. The Department believes that these supply contracts help to exclude Microsoft's rivals—principally IBM—from outlets for their operating systems and thus help Microsoft to acquire a monopoly in the long term. More precisely, the Department believes that Microsoft already possesses a market share legally equivalent to a monopoly, and that these contracts will further strengthen that monopoly. Then, after Microsoft has effectively eliminated IBM as a competitor, the scenario proceeds, Microsoft will exploit that monopoly in restricting output and raising prices. This long term scenario, however, is subject to criticism on at least two grounds. First, this scenario does not deal with a natural monopoly analysis. In theory, operating systems could be a natural monopoly. If they were a natural monopoly, then the exclusionary aspects of lump-sum licensing would be a matter of little concern, since a single company would eventually control the market anyway. If Microsoft is to be the prevailing "natural monopolist," then maybe its present large market position is socially beneficial. . . . Thus, there is ground to believe that society would be better off if the selection of the natural monopolist occurs sooner rather than later, since an earlier selection would minimize the amount of society's assets which are expended in providing the service. . . .
>
> Second, the scenario does not deal with the dynamic nature of technology. Operating systems are continually in process. At the stage of each new move to a higher-level technology, the market carries a potential for opening wider to new entrants and for presenting new opportunities for existing players. . . .

Id. at 638-39 (footnotes omitted).

The refusal of the District Court to accept the consent decree rested on its several perceived limitations, among them were: 1) failure to remedy the monopoly position achieved by Microsoft by illegal means, 2) failure to address practices complained of by competitors, such as advance announcement of new software products well in advance of their availability, a practice dubbed the production of vaporware, and a means of inhibiting the development of competing products, and 3) manipulating its operating system so as to make difficult the running of competing software products. The D.C. Circuit found these grounds raised issues which exceeded the scope of Tunney Act review and reversed, remanding for reinstatement of the Consent Decree, 56 F.3d 1448.

4. The concern of the enforcement agencies with computer technology was further shown by the FTC case brought against Dell Computer Corp. that resulted in a Consent Decree, FTC File No. 931-0097, 50 F.R. 57870 (Nov. 22, 1995). In 1991, Dell was issued a patent on technology for configuring its VL-bus chip into the motherboard of a computer. This chip moves instructions from the central processing unit to peripheral components, *e.g.*, the hard drive. At that time there were a variety of ways of installing it. In 1992 Dell participated in the deliberations of the non-profit trade association, Video Electronics Standards Association, that set the standard for computer bus design as that of Dell technology. At those meetings, the Dell representative certified in writing, as did the other participants, that it knew of no patent that the adopted bus design standard would violate. Subsequently, Dell threatened to sue several manufacturers adhering to the standard for infringement of Dell's patent. The majority of the Commission considered this conduct an unfair method of competition under § 5. The dissenting commissioner thought there was no evidence to support the contention that Dell intended to mislead, and alternatively, she doubted that participation in the settling of standards imposes a duty on a patentee to identify the boundaries of their intellectual property rights.

What is the harm that the majority feared? Does the dissenting commissioner have the better analysis? Explain.

5. In *United States v. Pilkington PLC,* 1994 WL 750645 (D. Ariz), the Justice Department sued Pilkington, a pioneer in the development of a process for making flat glass by floating molten glass in a bath of molten metal, under §§ 1 and 2 of the Sherman Act alleging monopolizing of the world float glass market by means of licensing provisions containing territorial restrictions and of keeping these arrangements in force after the expiration of the basic float glass patents. The Consent Decree barred the use of license provisions containing territorial or use restrictions.

6. Were you asked by the current head of the Antitrust Division to restate the Division's position on the antitrust/intellectual property accommodation, how would you respond in a manner that is neither "intuitive" nor "*ad hoc*"?

Chapter 16

Competition, Labor Policy, and Antitrust Law

A. Historical Note

The collective activity in labor negotiations over wage rates and the collective activity in the determination of selling prices of commodities has had a distinct and separate reception in Congress and in the courts. During the Nineteenth Century, state courts, applying common law principles, viewed labor unions as unlawful conspiracies. Union activities such as strikes, picketing, and boycotts were viewed as criminal conspiracies designed to raise the prices of wages and of the products that labor produced. It was not until 1842, that the decision in *Commonwealth v. Hunt*, 45 Mass. (4 Metc.) 111 (1842), held that criminal liability could not be imposed on a union without a review of the union's objectives. However, civil liability and injunctions routinely attached to union activity as an illegal combination of workers. *E.g., Vegelahn v. Gunter*, 167 Mass. 92, 44 N.E. 1077 (1896). *See* Herbert Hovenkamp, *Labor Conspiracies in American Law, 1880-1930*, 66 TEX. L. REV. 919 (1988).

During the legislative debates of the Sherman Act, Senator Sherman proposed a provision expressly stating that the statute would not apply to "... arrangements, agreements, or combinations between laborers...." 21 Cong. Rec. 2612 (1890), but this provision was dropped from the measure as enacted. Subsequently, the conspiracy language of § 1 of the Sherman Act was interpreted by the Supreme Court to be applicable to union activities in the famous *Danbury Hatters* case, *Lowe v. Lawlor*, 208 U.S. 274 (1908). In that case, the United Hatters of North America, seeking to organize a factory, struck the factory and urged wholesalers and retailers not to purchase Lowe's hats—a secondary boycott in labor law terms. The Court held this secondary boycott illegal under § 1 of the Sherman Act and assessed treble damages against the individual members of the union.

The *Danbury Hatters* case is illustrative of the difficulty of distinguishing "labor" activity from "commercial" activity by employers for Sherman Act purposes. Originally, the hat making industry employed skilled hand labor, but in 1891 the hydraulic hat presser and the steam lathe reduced the need for skilled hand labor, thus creating unemployment. The depression of 1893 put further pressure on employers to supplant skilled labor with semi-skilled and unskilled labor. These developments led the craft unions of skilled makers and finishers to merge into a single union, the United Hatters of America. In 1899, the United Hatters announced a rule restricting its members to a fifty-five hour work week as a means of reducing unemployment. The larger effect of these union activities was to convert an industry characterized by many small competitors, who engaged in cut-throat competition, into a stabilized industry. This came about because many of the small shops were unable to afford the increased costs of union wages and working conditions and left the industry. The remaining shops ended up with better paid workers and enjoyed higher profit margins. The effect of the union activity was to do change the structure of the industry—a feat which the manufacturers were unlikely to have been able to accomplish otherwise. Historians of this industry note that the union became a stabilizing force in the industry. *See* Colin Gordon, *New Deals: Business, Labor, and Politics in America, 1920-1935* 102-03 (1994); Daniel Ernst, *The* Danbury Hatters *Case, in* LABOR LAW IN AMERICA: HISTORICAL AND CRITICAL ESSAYS 185-187 (Andrew King & Christopher Tomlins eds. 1992).

Resentment of the result in the *Danbury Hatters* case coupled with a growing acceptance of labor unions, resulted in the enactment of two exemption provisions in the Clayton Act of 1914. Under § 6 of the Clayton Act, 15 U.S.C. § 17 (1994), labor is no longer deemed to be an article of commerce. Collective action by union members therefore is withdrawn from the ambit of § 1 of the Sherman Act. Section 6 of the Clayton Act legislatively reverses the *Danbury Hatters* case and ends the common law characterization of union activities as illegal conspiracies. Under § 20 of the Clayton Act, 29 U.S.C. § 352 (1994), and the Norris-LaGuardia Act of 1932, 29 U.S.C. §§ 52 and 105 (1994), a federal court may no longer follow the common practice of granting injunctive relief to employers against union activity such as striking, peaceful picketing, and advocating secondary boycotts. Taken together, these provisions grant antitrust immunity to most concerted peaceful union activity.

In addition to this statutory exemption of union activity from the antitrust laws, courts have developed a non-statutory exemption in order to accommodate the tension between the antitrust laws and subsequently enacted federal legislation over labor relations, the National Labor Relations Act, 29 U.S.C. §§ 151 *et seq.* (1996). The stated rationale for this caselaw exemption is that proper accommodation of the congressional preference for free, competitive markets with the congressional policy favoring collective bargaining requires that a limited, non-statutory exemption from antitrust scrutiny be accorded certain labor-management agreements. In *Amalgamated Meat Cutters v. Jewel Tea Co.*, 381 U.S. 676, 689 (1965), the Court stated: "The exemption for union-employer agreements is very much a matter of accommodating the coverage of the Sherman Act to the policy of the labor laws." In the materials that follow consider how the courts have accomplished this accommodation between the different policies expressed in these two federal statutes.

Allen Bradley Co. v. Local Union No. 3, International Brotherhood of Electrical Workers

325 U.S. 797 (1945)

Mr. Justice BLACK delivered the opinion of the Court.

. . . .

Petitioners are manufacturers of electrical equipment. Their places of manufacture are outside of New York City, and most of them are outside of New York State as well. They have brought this action because of their desire to sell their products in New York City, a market area that has been closed to them through the activities of respondents and others.

Respondents are a labor union, its officials and its members. The union, Local No. 3 of the International Brotherhood of Electrical Workers, has jurisdiction only over the metropolitan area of New York City. It is therefore impossible for the union to enter into a collective bargaining agreement with petitioners. . . .

The union's consistent aim for many years has been to expand its membership, to obtain shorter hours and increased wages, and to enlarge employment opportunities for its members. To achieve this latter goal—that is, to make more work for its own members—the union realized that local manufacturers, employers of the local members, must have the widest possible outlets for their product. The union therefore waged aggressive campaigns to obtain closed shop agreements with all local electrical equipment manufacturers and contractors. Using conventional labor union methods, such as strikes and boycotts, it gradually obtained more and more closed shop agreements in the New York City area. Under these agreements, contractors were obligated to purchase equipment from none but local manufacturers who also had closed shop agreements with Local No. 3; manufacturers obligated themselves to confine their New York City sales to contractors employing the Local's members. In the course of time, this type of individual employer-employee agreement expanded into industry-wide understandings, looking not merely to terms and conditions of employment but also to price and market control. Agencies were set up composed of representatives of all three groups to boycott recalcitrant local contractors and manufacturers and to bar from the area equipment manufactured outside its boundaries. The combination among the three groups, union, contractors, and manufacturers, became highly successful from the standpoint of all of them. The business of New York City manufacturers had a phenomenal growth, thereby multiplying the jobs available for the Local's members. Wages went up, hours were shortened, and the New York electrical equipment prices soared, to the decided financial profit of local contractors and manufacturers. The success is illustrated by the fact that some New York manufacturers sold their goods in the protected city market at one price and sold identical goods outside of New York at a far lower price. All of this took place, as the Circuit Court of Appeals declared (145 F.2d 218), "through the stifling of competition," and because the three groups, in combination as "co-partners," achieved "a complete monopoly which they used to boycott the equipment manufactured by the plaintiffs." . . .

Quite obviously, this combination of business men has violated both §§ 1 and 2 of the Sherman Act, unless its conduct is immunized by the participation of the union. . . . [W]e have two declared congressional policies which it is our responsibility to try to reconcile. The one seeks to preserve a competitive business economy; the other to preserve the rights of labor to organize to better its conditions through the agency of collective bargaining. We must determine here how far Congress intended activities under one of these policies to neutralize the results envisioned by the other.

Aside from the fact that the labor union here acted in combination with the contractors and manufacturers, the means it adopted to contribute to the combination's purpose fall squarely within the "specified acts" declared by § 20 [of the Clayton Act] not to be violations of federal law. For the union's contribution to the trade boycott was accomplished through threats that unless their employers bought their goods from local manufacturers the union laborers would terminate the "relation of employment" with them and cease to perform "work or labor" for them; and through their "recommending, advising, or persuading others by peaceful and lawful means" not to "patronize" sellers of the boycotted electrical equipment. Consequently, under our holdings . . . had there been no union-contractor-manufacturer combination the union's actions here, coming as they did within the exemptions of the Clayton and Norris-La Guardia Acts, would not have been violations of the Sherman Act. We pass to the question of whether unions can with impunity aid and abet business men who are violating the Act.

. . . [W]e think Congress never intended that unions could, consistently with the Sherman Act, aid non-labor groups to create business monopolies and to control the marketing of goods and services.

Section 6 of the Clayton Act declares that the Sherman Act must not be so construed as to forbid the "existence and operation of labor, agricultural, or horticultural organizations, instituted for the purposes of mutual help. . . ." But "the purposes of mutual help" can hardly be thought to cover activities for the purpose of "employer-help" in controlling markets and prices. . . . Since union members can without violating the Sherman Act strike to enforce a union boycott of goods, it is said they may settle the strike by getting their employers to agree to refuse to buy the goods. Employers and the union did here make bargaining agreements in which the employers agreed not to buy goods manufactured by companies which did not employ the members of Local No. 3. We may assume that such an agreement standing alone would not have violated the Sherman Act. But it did not stand alone. It was but one element in a far larger program in which contractors and manufacturers united with one another to monopolize all the business in New York City, to bar all other business men from that area, and to charge the public prices above a competitive level. It is true that victory of the union in its disputes, even had the union acted alone, might have added to the cost of goods, or might have resulted in individual refusals of all of their employers to buy electrical equipment not made by Local No. 3. So far as the union might have achieved this result acting alone, it would have been the natural consequence of labor union activities exempted by the Clayton Act from the coverage of the Sherman Act. . . . But when the unions participated with a combination of business men who had complete power to eliminate all competition among themselves and to prevent all competition from others, a situation was created not included within the exemptions of the Clayton and Norris-La Guardia Acts.

. . . .

Our holding means that the same labor union activities may or may not be in violation of the Sherman Act, dependent upon whether the union acts alone or in combination with business groups. . . .

The judgment of the Circuit Court of Appeals ordering the action dismissed is accordingly reversed and the cause is remanded to the district court for modification and clarification of the judgment and injunction, consistent with this opinion.

Reversed and remanded.

COMMENTARY

1. Is the Court saying, in its opinion, that the union could have entered into agreements with contractors containing clauses prohibiting the contractors from buying equipment from manufacturers which did not have an existing collective bargaining contract with that union? And that the union could have entered into agreements with manufacturers under which the manufacturers would be prohibited from selling to contractors which had no existing collective bargaining contracts with that union? How did the actual situation in the *Allen Bradley* case differ? Was it the enforcement mechanisms which distinguished the actual *Allen Bradley* situation from a situation in which the union entered into a series of separate collective bargaining contracts with contractors restricting their sources of supply and with manufacturers restricting their choice of customers? How did the Court determine that the union "participated with a combination of businessmen"? What is the test for determining whether the union acts "alone"? If the union coerced its contractor employers to boycott nonunionized suppliers by threatening strikes but without entering into agreements with the contractors, would the union be acting "alone"? If the union coerced those employers into signing agreements with the union to boycott nonunionized suppliers, would the union still be acting "alone"? Does "alone" refer to the absence of independent collective bargaining contracts involving more than one employer?

2. Would the union be deemed to be acting alone if it sought and obtained an agreement restricting contractors' sources of supply in multi-employer bargaining? if it sought and obtained an agreement restricting manufacturers' choices of customers in multi-employer bargaining?

3. In a later case, *United Mine Workers of America v. Pennington*, 381 U.S. 657 (1965), Justice Goldberg expressed a concern that the antitrust laws ought not to be interpreted to interfere with "pattern" bargaining, a process in which a union first bargains with a single employer and in which the resulting agreement forms the basic pattern for agreements between that union and other employers in the industry. Would the lawfulness of pattern bargaining be brought into question by the *Allen Bradley* decision? Does pattern bargaining embody an understanding between the union and the first employer that the union will seek to impose terms similar to the agreed-upon contract on other employers? If so, would the union be deemed to be acting in combination with a business group? Would it matter under *Allen Bradley* whether the combination with a business group sought to reduce competition only in labor or whether the combination also sought to reduce competition in items other than labor?

4. Section 6 of the Clayton Act provides that "[t]he labor of a human being is not a commodity or article of commerce. Nothing contained in the antitrust laws shall be construed to forbid the existence and operation of labor . . . organizations

. . . or to forbid or restrain individual members of such organizations from lawfully carrying out the legitimate objects thereof; nor shall such organizations, or the members thereof, be held or construed to be illegal combinations or conspiracies in restraint of trade, under the antitrust laws." Section 20 of the Clayton Act limits the use of injunctions and restraining orders by the federal courts in labor disputes, forbids those courts from enjoining or restraining work stoppages and other specified labor activities, and declares that none of those specified acts shall "be considered or held to be violations of any laws of the United States."

5. In *Duplex Printing Press Co. v. Deering*, 254 U.S. 443 (1921), the United States Supreme Court construed these provisions of the Clayton Act as permitting federal courts to enjoin secondary boycotts employed by labor unions as weapons in labor disputes.

6. In 1932 Congress enacted the Norris-LaGuardia Act which divested the federal courts, except in narrowly confined circumstances, of jurisdiction to issue injunctions and restraining orders in labor disputes. 47 Stat. 70 (1932), 29 U.S.C. §§ 101-115 (1994).

7. In *United States v. Hutcheson*, 312 U.S. 219 (1941), the Court reconsidered the Clayton Act's labor exemption in the light of the Norris-LaGuardia Act. There the Court ruled that the Sherman Act was not violated when a carpenters' union, demanding that certain construction work be performed by its members rather than by members of a machinists' union, struck a brewing company, its tenant, and the construction companies which were working for those firms. The carpenters' union also had sought to dissuade its members and others from buying beer produced by the brewery. Writing for the Court, Justice Frankfurter traced the history of the application of the antitrust laws to labor disputes and concluded that the labor exemption in § 20 of the Clayton Act could properly be construed only in the light of the Norris-LaGuardia Act:

> Congress in the Norris-LaGuardia Act has expressed the public policy of the United States and defined its conception of a "labor dispute" in terms that no longer leave room for doubt. . . . To be sure, Congress expressed this national policy and determined the bounds of a labor dispute in an act explicitly dealing with the further withdrawal of injunctions in labor controversies. But to argue . . . that the *Duplex* case still governs for purpose of a criminal prosecution is to say that that which on the equity side of the court is allowable conduct may in a criminal proceeding become the road to prison. . . . The relation of the Norris-LaGuardia Act to the Clayton Act is not that of a tightly drawn amendment to a technically phrased tax provision. The underlying aim of the Norris-LaGuardia Act was to restore the broad purpose which Congress thought it had formulated in the Clayton Act but which was

> frustrated, so Congress believed, by unduly restrictive judicial construction.

Id. at 234-36.

8. The year before its decision in *Hutcheson*, the Court in *Apex Hosiery Co. v. Leader*, 310 U.S. 469 (1940), had considered a charge that a union which had engaged in a sit-down strike, destroyed substantial amounts of the employer's property, and prevented the shipment of finished goods was thereby unlawfully restraining trade. The Court ruled that since no significant impact on the market for hosiery resulted from the union's activities, the Sherman Act was not violated. It refused to rule, however, that the Clayton Act excepted all labor union activities from the Sherman Act.

9. In considering whether a substantial market impact resulted from a labor union's activities as a guide to the applicability of the Sherman Act, *Apex Hosiery* appears to be employing a rule of reason approach to the applicability of the Sherman Act. Would such an approach aid in distinguishing the situation in which a union entered into an agreement with an employer pursuant to which the employer agreed to boycott suppliers which had no present collective bargaining agreement with that union (which the *Allen Bradley* Court assumed would not violate the Sherman Act "standing alone") from the situation which actually occurred in *Allen Bradley*? In the case of one such agreement in a competitively structured industry, the likelihood of an impact on the market as a whole for the supplies in question would tend to be small or insignificant. How would the *Apex Hosiery* approach treat a series of such agreements? How should a series of agreements be treated?

United Mine Workers of America v. Pennington
381 U.S. 657 (1965)

Mr. Justice WHITE delivered the opinion of the Court.

This action began as a suit by the trustees of the United Mine Workers of America Welfare and Retirement Fund against the respondents, individually and as owners of Phillips Brothers Coal Company, a partnership, seeking to recover some $55,000 in royalty payments alleged to be due and payable under the trust provisions of the National Bituminous Coal Wage Agreement of 1950. . . . Phillips filed an answer and a cross claim against UMW, alleging in both that the trustees, the UMW and certain large coal operators had conspired to restrain and to monopolize interstate commerce in violation of §§ 1 and 2 of the Sherman Antitrust Act. . . .

The allegations of the cross claim were essentially as follows: Prior to the 1950 Wage Agreement between the operators and the union, severe controversy had existed in the industry, particularly over wages, the welfare fund and the union's efforts to control the working time of its members. Since 1950, however, relative peace has existed in the industry, all as the result of the 1950 Wage Agreement and its amendments and the additional understandings entered into between UMW and the large operators. Allegedly the parties considered overproduction to be the critical problem of the coal industry. The agreed solution was to be the elimination of the smaller companies, the larger companies thereby controlling the market. More specifically, the union abandoned its efforts to control the working time of the miners, agreed not to oppose the rapid mechanization of the mines which would substantially reduce mine employment, agreed to help finance such mechanization and agreed to impose the terms of the 1950 agreement on all operators without regard to their ability to pay. The benefit to the union was to be increased wages as productivity increased with mechanization, these increases to be demanded of the smaller companies whether mechanized or not. Royalty payments into the welfare fund were to be increased also, and the union was to have effective control over the fund's use. The union and large companies agreed upon other steps to exclude the marketing, production, and sale of nonunion coal. Thus the companies agreed not to lease coal lands to nonunion operators, and in 1958 agreed not to sell or buy coal from such companies. . . .

A major part of Phillips' case . . . was that the union entered into a conspiracy with the large operators to impose the agreed-upon wage and royalty scales upon the smaller, nonunion operators, regardless of their ability to pay and regardless of whether or not the union represented the employees of these companies, all for the purpose of eliminating them from the industry, limiting production and pre-empting the market for the large, unionized operators. The UMW urges that since such an agreement concerned wage standards, it is exempt from the antitrust laws.

It is true that wages lie at the very heart of those subjects about which employers and unions must bargain and the law contemplates agreements on wages not only between individual employers and a union but agreements between the union and employers in a multi-employer bargaining unit. . . . The union benefit from the wage scale agreed upon is direct and concrete and the effect on the product market, though clearly present, results from the elimination of competition based on wages among the employers in the bargaining unit, which is not the kind of restraint Congress intended the Sherman Act to proscribe. . . . We think it beyond question that a union may conclude a wage agreement with the multi-employer bargaining unit without violating the antitrust laws and that it may as a matter of its own policy, and not by agreement with all or part of the employers of that unit, seek the same wages from other employers.

This is not to say that an agreement resulting from union-employer negotiations is automatically exempt from Sherman Act scrutiny simply because the negotiations involve a compulsory subject of bargaining, regardless of the subject or the form and content of the agreement. . . .

We have said that a union may make wage agreements with a multiemployer bargaining unit and may in pursuance of its own union interests seek to obtain the same terms from other employers. No case under the antitrust laws could be made out on evidence limited to such union behavior. But we think a union forfeits its exemption from the antitrust laws when it is clearly shown that it has agreed with one set of employers to impose a certain wage scale on other bargaining units. One group of employers may not conspire to eliminate competitors from the industry and the union is liable with the employers if it becomes a party to the conspiracy. This is true even though the union's part in the scheme is an undertaking to secure the same wages, hours or other conditions of employment from the remaining employers in the industry.

. . . .

[The Court then decided, contrary to the rulings in two cases below, that joint efforts of the union and coal operators to influence the Secretary of Labor to raise the minimum wage applicable to contractors selling coal to the Tennessee Valley Authority were not violations of the Sherman Act.]

The judgment is reversed and the case remanded for further proceedings consistent with this opinion.

It is so ordered.

Mr. Justice DOUGLAS, with whom Mr. Justice BLACK, and Mr. Justice CLARK agree, concurring.

. . . On the new trial the jury should be instructed that if there were an industry-wide collective bargaining agreement whereby employers and the union agreed on a wage scale that exceeded the financial ability of some operators to pay and that if it was made for the purpose of forcing some employers out of business, the union as well as the employers who participated in the arrangement with the union should be found to have violated the antitrust laws.

. . . .

Local Union No. 189, Amalgamated Meat Cutters v. Jewel Tea Co., Inc.

381 U.S. 676 (1965)

Mr. Justice WHITE announced the judgment of the Court and delivered an opinion, in which THE CHIEF JUSTICE and Mr. Justice BRENNAN join.

Like No. 48, *United Mine Workers of America v. Pennington* . . . decided today, this case presents questions regarding the application of §§ 1 and 2 of the Sherman Antitrust Act . . . to activities of labor unions. In particular, it concerns the lawfulness of the following restriction on the operating hours of food store meat departments contained in a collective bargaining agreement executed after joint multi-employer, multiunion negotiations:

> "Market operating hours shall be 9:00 a.m. to 6:00 p.m. Monday through Saturday, inclusive. No customer shall be served who comes into the market before or after the hours set forth above."

This litigation arose out of the 1957 contract negotiations between the representatives of 9,000 Chicago retailers of fresh meat and the seven union petitioners, who are local affiliates of the Amalgamated Meat Cutters and Butcher Workmen of North America, AFL-CIO, representing virtually all butchers in the Chicago area. During the 1957 bargaining sessions the employer group presented several requests for union consent to a relaxation of the existing contract restriction on marketing hours for fresh meat, which forbade the sale of meat before 9 a.m. and after 6 p.m. in both service and self-service markets. The unions rejected all such suggestions, and their own proposal retaining the marketing-hours restriction was ultimately accepted at the final bargaining session by all but two of the employers, National Tea Co. and Jewel Tea Co. (hereinafter "Jewel"). Associated Food Retailers of Greater Chicago, a trade association having about 1,000 individual and independent merchants as members and representing some 300 meat dealers in the negotiations, was among those who accepted. Jewel, however, asked the union negotiators to present to their membership, on behalf of it and National Tea, a counter offer that included provision for Friday night operations. At the same time Jewel voiced its belief, as it had midway through the negotiations, that any marketing-hours restriction was illegal. On the recommendation of the union negotiators, the Jewel offer was rejected by the union membership, and a strike was authorized. Under the duress of the strike vote, Jewel decided to sign the contract previously approved by the rest of the industry.

In July 1958 Jewel brought suit against the unions, certain of their officers, Associated, and Charles H. Bromann, Secretary-Treasurer of Associated, seeking invalidation under §§ 1 and 2 of the Sherman Act of the contract provision that prohibited night meat market operations. [The District Court dismissal of the complaint was reversed by the Court of Appeals for the Seventh Circuit.]

It is well at the outset to emphasize that this case comes to us stripped of any claim of a union-employer conspiracy against Jewel. The trial court found no evidence to sustain Jewel's conspiracy claim and this finding was not disturbed by the Court of Appeals. We therefore have a situation where the unions, having obtained a marketing-hours agreement from one group of employers, have successfully sought the same terms from a single employer, Jewel, not as a result of a bargain between the unions and some employers directed against other employers, but pursuant to what the unions deemed to be in their own labor union interests.

. . . .

We pointed out in *Pennington* that exemption for union-employer agreements is very much a matter of accommodating the coverage of the Sherman Act to the policy of the labor laws. Employers and unions are required to bargain about wages, hours and working conditions, and this fact weighs heavily in favor of antitrust exemption for agreements on these subjects. . . .

Thus the issue in this case is whether the marketing-hours restriction, like wages, and unlike prices, is so intimately related to wages, hours and working conditions that the unions' successful attempt to obtain that provision through bona fide, arm's-length bargaining in pursuit of their own labor union policies, and not at the behest of or in combination with nonlabor groups, falls within the protection of the national labor policy and is therefore exempt from the Sherman Act.[5] We think that it is.

. . . .

Contrary to the Court of Appeals, we think that the particular hours of the day and the particular days of the week during which employees shall be required to work are subjects well within the realm of "wages, hours, and other terms and conditions of employment" about which employers and unions must bargain. . . . And, although the effect on competition is apparent and real, perhaps more so than in the case of the wage agreement, the concern of union members is immediate and direct. Weighing the respective interests involved, we think the national labor policy expressed in the National Labor Relations Act places

---

[5] The crucial determinant is not the form of the agreement—*e.g.*, prices or wages—but its relative impact on the product market and the interests of union members. Thus in *Local 24 of Intern. Broth. of Teamsters Union v. Oliver*, 358 U.S. 283, we held that federal labor policy precluded application of state antitrust laws to an employer-union agreement that when leased trucks were driven by their owners, such owner-drivers should receive, in addition to the union wage, not less than a prescribed minimum rental. Though in form a scheme fixing prices for the supply of leased vehicles, the agreement was designed "to protect the negotiated wage scale against the possible undermining through diminution of the owner's wages for driving which might result from a rental which did not cover his operating costs." *Id.* at 293-294. As the agreement did not embody a "'remote and indirect approach to the subject of wages' . . . but a direct frontal attack upon a problem thought to threaten the maintenance of the basic wage structure established by the collective bargaining contract," . . . the paramount federal policy of encouraging collective bargaining proscribed application of the state law. . . .

beyond the reach of the Sherman Act union-employer agreements on when, as well as how long, employees must work. An agreement on these subjects between the union and the employers in a bargaining unit is not illegal under the Sherman Act, nor is the union's unilateral demand for the same contract of other employers in the industry.

. . . .

The unions argue that since night operations would be impossible without night employment of butchers, or an impairment of the butchers' jurisdiction, or a substantial effect on the butchers' workload, the marketing-hours restriction is either little different in effect from the valid working-hours provision that work shall stop at 6 p.m. or is necessary to protect other concerns of the union members. If the unions' factual premises are true, we think the unions could impose a restriction on night operations without violation of the Sherman Act; for then operating hours, like working hours, would constitute a subject of immediate and legitimate concern to union members.

. . . .

If it were true that self-service markets could actually operate without butchers, at least for a few hours after 6 p.m., that no encroachment on butchers' work would result and that the workload of butchers during normal working hours would not be substantially increased, Jewel's position would have considerable merit. For then the obvious restraint on the product market—the exclusion of self-service stores from the evening market for meat—would stand alone, unmitigated and unjustified by the vital interests of the union butchers which are relied upon in this case. In such event the limitation imposed by the unions might well be reduced to nothing but an effort by the unions to protect one group of employers from competition by another, which is conduct that is not exempt from the Sherman Act. Whether there would be a violation of §§ 1 and 2 would then depend on whether the elements of a conspiracy in restraint of trade or an attempt to monopolize had been proved.[6]

Thus the dispute between Jewel and the unions essentially concerns a narrow factual question: Are night operations without butchers, and without infringement of butchers' interests, feasible? The District Court resolved this factual dispute in favor of the unions. . . . [Although Jewel has challenged the unions' evidence on the practicality of night operations by employing various lines of argument,] . . . Jewel's argument—when considered against the historical background of union concern with working hours and operating hours and the virtually uniform recognition by employers of the intimate relationship between the two subjects, as manifested by bargaining proposals in 1957, 1959, and 1961—falls far short of a showing that the trial judge's ultimate findings were clearly erroneous.

Reversed.

Mr. Justice GOLDBERG, with whom Mr. Justice HARLAN and Mr. Justice STEWART join, dissenting from the opinion but concurring in the reversal in No. 48 [*Pennington*] and concurring in the judgment of the Court in No. 240 [*Jewel Tea*].

. . . While purporting to recognize the indisputable fact that the elimination of employer competition based on substandard labor conditions is a proper labor union objective endorsed by our national labor policy and that, therefore, "a union may make wage agreements with a multi-employer bargaining unit and may in pursuance of its own union interests seek to obtain the same terms from other employers," *Pennington*, *ante*, . . . the

---

[6] One issue, for example, would be whether the restraint was unreasonable. . . .

Court holds that "a union forfeits its exemption from the antitrust laws when it is clearly shown that it has agreed with one set of employers to impose a certain wage scale on other bargaining units." . . .

This rule seems to me clearly contrary to the congressional purpose manifested by the labor statutes, and it will severely restrict free collective bargaining. Since collective bargaining inevitably involves and requires discussion of the impact of the wage agreement reached with a particular employer or group of employers upon competing employers, the effect of the Court's decision will be to bar a basic element of collective bargaining from the conference room. If a union and employer are prevented from discussing and agreeing upon issues which are, in the great majority of cases, at the central core of bargaining, unilateral force will inevitably be substituted for rational discussion and agreement. Plainly and simply, the Court would subject both unions and employers to antitrust sanctions, criminal as well as civil, if in collective bargaining they concluded a wage agreement and, as part of the agreement, the union has undertaken to use its best efforts to have this wage accepted by other employers in the industry. . . .

. . . [Labor] history . . . shows that labor contracts establishing more or less standardized wages, hours, and other terms and conditions of employment in a given industry or market area are often secured either through bargaining with multi-employer associations or through bargaining with market leaders that sets a "pattern" for agreements on labor standards with other employers. These are two similar systems used to achieve the identical result of fostering labor peace through the negotiation of uniform labor standards in an industry. Yet the Court makes antitrust liability for both unions and employers turn on which of these two systems is used. It states that uniform wage agreements may be made with multi-employer units but an agreement cannot be made to affect employers outside the formal bargaining unit. I do not believe that the Court understands the effect of its ruling in terms of the practical realities of the automobile, steel, rubber, shipbuilding, and numerous other industries which follow the policy of pattern collective bargaining. . . . I also do not understand why antitrust liability should turn on the form of unit determination rather than the substance of the collective bargaining impact on the industry.

. . . .

The judicial expressions in *Jewel Tea* represent another example of the reluctance of judges to give full effect to congressional purpose . . . . In this case the Court of Appeals would have held the Union subject to the Sherman Act's criminal and civil penalties because in the court's social and economic judgment, the determination of the hours at which meat is to be sold is a "proprietary" matter within the exclusive control of management and thus the Union had no legitimate interest in bargaining over it. My Brother DOUGLAS, joined by Mr. Justice BLACK and Mr. Justice CLARK, would affirm this judgment apparently because the agreement was reached through a multi-employer bargaining unit. . . . My Brother WHITE recognizes that the issue of the hours of sale of meat concerns a mandatory subject of bargaining based on the trial court's findings that it directly affected the hours of work of the butchers in the self-service markets, and therefore, since there was a finding that the Union was not abetting an independent employer conspiracy, he joins in reversing the Court of Appeals. In doing so, however, he apparently draws lines among mandatory subjects of bargaining, presumably based on a judicial determination of their importance to the worker, and states that not all agreements resulting from collective bargaining based on mandatory subjects of bargaining are immune from the antitrust laws, even absent evidence of union abetment of an independent conspiracy of employers. Following this reasoning, my Brother WHITE indicates that he would sustain a judgment here, even absent evidence of union abetment of an independent conspiracy of employers, if the trial court had found "that self-service markets could actually operate without butchers, at least for a few hours after 6 p.m., that no encroachment on butchers' work would result and that the workload of butchers during normal working hours would not be substantially increased. . . ." . . . Such a view seems to me to be unsupportable. It represents a narrow, confining view of what labor unions have a legitimate interest in preserving and thus bargaining about. . . .

Mr. Justice DOUGLAS, with whom Mr. Justice BLACK and Mr. Justice CLARK concur, dissenting.

If we followed *Allen Bradley Co. v. Local Union No. 3*, 325 U.S. 797, we would hold with the Court of Appeals that this multiemployer agreement with the union not to sell meat between 6 p.m. and 9 a.m. was not immunized from the antitrust laws and that respondent's evidence made out a prima facie case that it was in fact a violation of the Sherman Act.

. . . .

At the conclusion of respondent's case, the District Court dismissed Associated and Bromann from the action, which was tried without a jury, on the ground that there was no evidence of a conspiracy between Associated and the unions. But in the circumstances of this case the collective bargaining agreement itself, of which the District Court said there was clear proof, was evidence of a conspiracy among the employers with the unions to impose the marketing-hours restriction on Jewel via a strike threat by the unions. . . . The unions here induced a large group of merchants to use their collective strength to hurt others who wanted the competitive advantage of selling meat after 6 p.m. Unless *Allen Bradley* is either overruled or greatly impaired, the unions can no more aid a group of businessmen to force their competitors to follow uniform store marketing hours than to force them to sell at fixed prices. . . .

COMMENTARY

1. What is the relevance that the agreement in question in *Jewel Tea* involved a mandatory subject of collective bargaining? The Court in *Pennington* suggests that even some agreements involving compulsory subjects of bargaining may fall under the Sherman Act, does it not? Does the Court furnish a test of when agreements on such subjects will fall under the Sherman Act? when the union agrees with one set of employers about the terms which it will seek to impose upon another set of employers?

In considering the application of the labor exemption, should the Court have analyzed the role of wage rates, given the structure of the coal industry at the time?

2. Do you understand the approach of Justice Douglas in *Pennington*? Is Douglas suggesting that it is lawful for a union to agree with one group of employers about the terms which it will seek to impose upon another group of employers so long as it does not promise to seek a wage scale which exceeds "the financial ability" of some employers in the second group? Would Douglas differentiate the case where an agreement was made with the objective of securing equal labor costs for all employers, even though some employers would be forced out of business, from the case where the objective of the agreement was to restructure the market in a more concentrated fashion? For an economic analysis of collective bargaining as a cost-raising strategy, see Oliver Williamson, *Wage Rates as a Barrier to Entry: The* Pennington *Case*, 82 J. ECON. 85 (1968).

3. According to Justice Goldberg, the majority opinion in *Pennington* casts doubt on the lawfulness of "pattern" collective bargaining—where the contract terms established between the union and one employer form the basis for contracts entered into later between that union and other employers. Do you agree? Do you see anything in Justice White's opinion in *Jewel Tea* which could be construed as placing limits on pattern bargaining? Would Justice Douglas' approach preserve the validity of pattern bargaining? Under some circumstances and not under others?

4. Justice White's *Jewel Tea* opinion states the "issue" in the case to be whether "the unions' successful attempt to obtain that provision [restricting marketing hours] through bona fide, arm's-length bargaining in pursuit of their own labor union policies, and not at the behest of or in combination with nonlabor groups, falls within the protection of the national labor policy and is therefore exempt from the Sherman Act." Why was the agreement which the union obtained not a combination between the union and a nonlabor group? Could the employers have lawfully agreed among themselves on marketing hours without the union? Does the participation of the union immunize employer agreements which otherwise would be illegal? Does *Jewel Tea* immunize conduct which would have been condemned under *Allen Bradley*? How does Justice White support the lawfulness of bargaining between a union and a multi-employer unit over marketing hours?

5. Does Justice Douglas' *Jewel Tea* dissent suggest that a union is necessarily conspiring with a nonlabor group when it engages in bargaining with a multi-employer unit? Is this also Justice White's view? If so, how does White uphold multi-employer bargaining? How can Douglas reconcile the *Jewel Tea* dissent with his view in *Pennington* that at least some multi-employer bargaining can be lawful? Does Douglas make the lawfulness of multi-employer bargaining depend upon the issues which are the subject of the bargaining? Would Douglas find all multi-employer bargaining unlawful whenever the bargaining issues concern prices, hours of operation or behavior which would affect market structure?

6. The Eighth Circuit has had occasion to deal extensively with the antitrust labor exemption in the context of professional sports. In *Mackey v. National Football League*, 543 F.2d 606 (8th Cir. 1976), *cert. dismissed*, 434 U.S. 801 (1977), that court considered a challenge to the National Football League's "Rozelle Rule" by a group of players. Under the League rules every player has been required to play only for the club with which he had entered a playing contract for the term of that contract plus one additional year at the option of the club. At the end of this period, a player might, if he so chose, become a free agent and seek employment by other NFL clubs. Under the NFL's so-called "Rozelle Rule," a club which hired a free agent was required to pay compensation to the club losing that player and in the absence of agreement between the affected clubs, the Commissioner of the League possessed the responsibility for determining the amount of compensation. Although the court ruled that the Rozelle Rule was an unreasonable restraint of trade, it sought to move the arena of conflict over the Rule from the courts to the collective bargaining process. The court indicated that because the Rule depressed player salaries, it constituted a mandatory subject of bargaining and hence might fall within the nonstatutory labor exemption if its terms had been the result of such bargaining rather than having been unilaterally imposed by the clubs:

> Since the Rozell Rule, as implemented, concerns a mandatory subject of collective bargaining, any agreement as to inter-team compensation for free agents moving to other teams, reached through good faith collective bargaining, might very well be immune from antitrust liability under the nonstatutory labor exemption. . . . We encourage the parties to resolve this question through collective bargaining.

Id. at 623. In *Powell v. National Football League*, 888 F.2d 559 (8th Cir. 1989), the court was again required to construe the antitrust labor exemption in the context of professional sports. In this case, the players objected to a provision in the collective bargaining contract providing that clubs could retain a veteran free agent by exercising a right of first refusal and by matching a competing club's offer. Conversely, if the club decided not to exercise its right of first refusal, it was entitled to compensation from the competing club. After the collective bargaining agreement expired, the League maintained the status quo on all mandatory subjects of bargaining, including the first refusal/compensation provision. A strike was called after negotiations proved unsuccessful in reaching a new agreement. The players then brought suit, challenging the League's continued imposition of the first refusal/compensation system as a violation of the Sherman Act. The district court ruled that the labor exemption expired after the parties had reached an impasse in bargaining. On appeal, the Eighth Circuit held that the labor exemption continued to protect the clause, even after the parties had reached an impasse in bargaining, a position later taken by the U.S. Supreme Court in *Brown v. Pro Football, Inc.*, 116 S. Ct. 2116 (1996), page 868, *infra*. The plaintiffs then dissolved their union in order to facilitate their antitrust attack, free from the labor exemption.

Connell Construction Co., Inc. v. Plumbers & Steamfitters Local Union No. 100

421 U.S. 616 (1975)

Mr. Justice POWELL delivered the opinion of the Court.

The building trades union in this case supported its efforts to organize mechanical subcontractors by picketing certain general contractors, including petitioner. The union's sole objective was to compel the general contractors to agree that in letting subcontracts for mechanical work they would deal only with firms that were parties to the union's current collective-bargaining agreement. The union disclaimed any interest in representing the general contractors' employees. In this case the picketing succeeded, and petitioner seeks to annul the resulting agreement as an illegal restraint on competition under federal and state law. The union claims immunity from federal antitrust statutes and argues that federal labor regulation pre-empts state law.

In November 1970, Local 100 asked Connell to agree that it would subcontract mechanical work only to firms that had a current contract with the union. . . . Connell . . . signed the subcontracting agreement under protest. . . . Connell sought a declaration [that the agreement violated §§ 1 and 2 of the Sherman Act] . . . and an injunction against any further efforts to force it to sign such an agreement.

[The Court of Appeals for the Fifth Circuit affirmed a District Court decision holding the union exempt from federal antitrust law and that state antitrust law was preempted by federal labor legislation.]

II

The basic sources of organized labor's exemption from federal antitrust laws are §§ 6 and 20 of the Clayton Act . . . and the Norris-LaGuardia Act. . . . These statutes declare that labor unions are not combinations or conspiracies in restraint of trade, and exempt specific union activities, including secondary picketing and boycotts, from the operation of the antitrust laws. . . . They do not exempt concerted action or agreements between unions and nonlabor parties. *Mine Workers v. Pennington*. . . . The Court has recognized, however, that a proper accommodation between the congressional policy favoring collective bargaining under the NLRA and the congressional policy favoring free competition in business markets requires that some union-employer agreements be accorded a limited nonstatutory exemption from antitrust sanctions. *Meat Cutters v. Jewel Tea Co.* . . .

The nonstatutory exemption has its source in the strong labor policy favoring the association of employees to eliminate competition over wages and working conditions. . . . Labor policy clearly does not require, however, that a union have freedom to impose direct restraints on competition among those who employ its members. Thus, while the statutory exemption allows unions to accomplish some restraints by acting unilaterally, . . . the nonstatutory exemption offers no similar protection when a union and a nonlabor party agree to restrain competition in a business market. . . . .

In this case Local 100 used direct restraints on the business market to support its organizing campaign. The agreements with Connell and other general contractors indiscriminately excluded nonunion subcontractors from a portion of the market, even if their competitive advantages were not derived from substandard wages and working conditions but rather from more efficient operating methods. Curtailment of competition based on efficiency is neither a goal of federal labor policy nor a necessary effect of the elimination of competition among workers. Moreover, competition based on efficiency is a positive value that the antitrust laws strive to protect.

. . . [This agreement] contravenes antitrust policies to a degree not justified by congressional labor policy, and therefore cannot claim a nonstatutory exemption from the antitrust laws.

[The Court then construed § 8(e) of the National Labor Relations Act. That section forbids most secondary boycotts, but permits some such boycotts in the construction industry. The Court here ruled that the type of conduct involved in this case was not authorized by § 8(e).]

. . .

We . . . hold that this agreement, which is outside the context of a collective-bargaining relationship and not restricted to a particular jobsite, but which nonetheless obligates Connell to subcontract work only to firms that have a contract with Local 100, may be the basis of a federal antitrust suit because it has a potential for restraining competition in the business market in ways that would not follow naturally from elimination of competition over wages and working conditions.

IV

Although we hold that the union's agreement with Connell is subject to the federal antitrust laws, it does not follow that state antitrust law may apply as well. . . .

Because employee organization is central to federal labor policy and regulation of organizational procedures is comprehensive, federal law does not admit the use of state antitrust law to regulate union activity that is closely related to organizational goals. . . . The governing factor is the risk of conflict with the NLRA or with federal labor policy.

V

Neither the District Court nor the Court of Appeals decided whether the agreement between Local 100 and Connell, if subject to the antitrust laws, would constitute an agreement that restrains trade within the meaning of the Sherman Act. . . . Accordingly, we remand for consideration whether the agreement violated the Sherman Act.

Reversed in part, affirmed in part, and remanded.

COMMENTARY

1. In *Connell* the court explicitly distinguished between a "statutory" exemption from the antitrust laws and a "nonstatutory" exemption and articulated the difference between them. Which of these exemptions was involved in *Jewel Tea*? Which were in issue in *Pennington*? in *Allen Bradley*? in *Mackay*? in *Powell*? Does a union's combination with a nonlabor party destroy the statutory exemption? Are all employer-union agreements outside of the protection of the statutory exemption?

2. When does a union's agreement with a nonlabor party destroy the nonstatutory exemption? How do the statutory and nonstatutory exemptions then differ?

3. Did not the *Allen Bradley* opinion indicate that, standing alone, a single union-employer agreement obligating the employer not to purchase supplies from nonunion business firms would not violate the Sherman Act? Was the lawfulness of such an agreement the result of the statutory labor exemption? the nonstatutory labor exemption? Did the Court in *Allen Bradley* make the lawfulness of certain labor activities turn upon whether the union acted alone or in combination with nonlabor groups? When the Court in *Connell* excluded all union-employer agreements from the scope of the "statutory" exemption, was it following its own earlier approach in *Allen Bradley*? Was it thereby forcing collective-bargaining agreements to be tested by a set of stricter standards incorporated in the nonstatutory exemption? If so, would this approach be compatible, in your judgment, with the Congressional objectives embodied in Clayton Act § 20 and the Norris-LaGuardia Act?

4. Does the Court's limitation of the statutory exemption to cases in which the union has not entered into a combination with a nonlabor party mean that a union is protected by the statutory exemption so long as it merely threatens an employer but does not enter into an agreement with the employer? Would such an approach thrust into the labor-antitrust arena a *Colgate*-like distinction between unilateral activity and activity constituting an agreement? Would such a distinction remain viable after the development of the meaning of "combination" in *Parke Davis*, *Albrecht*, and *Copperweld*?

5. In *Connell* the Court said that "while the statutory exemption allows unions to accomplish some restraints by acting unilaterally, . . . the nonstatutory exemption offers no similar protection when a union and a nonlabor party agree to restrain competition in a business market . . . ." Consider the agreement hypothesized in *Allen Bradley* in which an employer agreed not to buy goods manufactured by companies which did not employ the members of the union. Would such an agreement fall outside the scope of the statutory exemption? Would it fall outside the scope of the nonstatutory exemption? In *Allen Bradley*, the Court assumed "that such an agreement standing alone would not have violated the Sherman Act." Is the Court's *Allen Bradley* assumption still valid?

6. Would the agreement involved in *Connell* have been entitled to a statutory exemption if it had been the result of collective bargaining between a union representing Connell employees and Connell? Such an agreement would still "indiscriminately" exclude "nonunion subcontractors from a portion of the market, even if their competitive advantages were not derived from substandard wages and working conditions but rather from efficient operating methods," would it not?

7. How should the court on remand evaluate the reasonableness of the *Connell* agreement? What criteria should it employ? To what extent are the criteria of *Professional Engineers* applicable to the evaluation of collective bargaining contracts under the rule of reason?

8. Suppose a group of employers agreed among themselves not to enter into agreements of the *Connell* variety. Would the agreement among the employers violate the Sherman Act? *See California State Council of Carpenters v. Associated General Contractors of California, Inc.*, 648 F.2d 527 (9th Cir. 1981), *rev'd*, 459 U.S. 519 (1982). *See Associated General Contractors of California, Inc. v. California State Council of Carpenters*, 459 U.S. 519 (1982)

H.A. Artists & Associates, Inc. v. Actors' Equity Association

451 U.S. 704 (1981)

Justice STEWART delivered the opinion of the Court.

The respondent Actors' Equity Association (Equity) is a union representing the vast majority of stage actors and actresses in the United States. It enters into collective-bargaining agreements with theatrical producers that specify minimum wages and other terms and conditions of employment for those whom it represents. The petitioners are independent theatrical agents who place actors and actresses in jobs with producers. The Court of Appeals for the Second Circuit held that the respondents' system of regulation of theatrical agents is immune from antitrust liability by reason of the statutory labor exemption from the antitrust laws. . . .

. . . The terms negotiated with producers are the minimum conditions of employment (called "scale"); an actor or actress is free to negotiate wages or terms more favorable than the collectively bargained minima.

Theatrical agents are independent contractors who negotiate contracts and solicit employment for their clients. . . . If an agent succeeds in obtaining employment for a client, he receives a commission based on a percentage of the client's earnings. . . .

The essential elements of Equity's regulation of theatrical agents have remained unchanged since 1928. A member of Equity is prohibited, on pain of union discipline, from using an agent who has not, through the mechanism of obtaining an Equity license (called a "franchise"), agreed to comply with the regulations. The most important of the regulations requires that a licensed agent must renounce any right to take a commission on an employment contract under which an actor or actress receives scale wages. . . . Moreover, commissions are limited on wages within 10% of scale pay. . . . Finally, agents are required to pay franchise fees to Equity. The fee is $200 for the initial franchise, $60 a year thereafter for each agent, and $40 for any sub-agent working in the office of another. . . .

In 1977, after a dispute between Equity and Theatrical Artists Representatives Associates (TARA)—a trade association representing theatrical agents . . . —a group of agents, including the petitioners, resigned from TARA because of TARA's decision to abide by Equity's regulations. These agents also informed Equity that they would not accept Equity's regulations, or apply for franchises. The petitioners instituted this lawsuit in May 1978, contending that Equity's regulations of theatrical agents violated §§ 1 and 2 of the Sherman Act. . . .

[The District Court found that the Equity franchise system was protected by the statutory labor exemptions from the antitrust laws and the Court of Appeals affirmed.]

II

. . . .

A

. . . .

The statutory exemption does not apply when a union combines with a "non-labor group." . . .[19]

---

[19] Even where there are union agreements with nonlabor groups that may have the effect of sheltering the nonlabor groups from competition in product markets, the Court has recognized a "nonstatutory" exemption to

. . . .

B

The Court of Appeals properly recognized that the threshold issue was to determine whether or not Equity's franchising of agents involved any combination between Equity and any "non-labor groups," or persons who are not "parties to a labor dispute." . . . And the court's conclusion that the trial court had not been clearly erroneous in its finding that there was no combination between Equity and the theatrical producers[20] to create or maintain the franchise system is amply supported by the record.

The more difficult problem is whether the combination between Equity and the agents who agreed to become franchised was a combination with a "non-labor group." The answer to this question is best understood in light of *Musicians v. Carroll*, 391 U.S. 99. There, four orchestra leaders, members of the American Federation of Musicians, brought an action based on the Sherman Act challenging the union's unilateral system of regulating "club dates," or one-time musical engagements. These regulations, *inter alia*, enforced a closed shop; required orchestra leaders to engage a minimum number of "sidemen," or instrumentalists; prescribed minimum prices for local engagements; prescribed higher minimum prices for traveling orchestras; and permitted leaders to deal only with booking agents licensed by the union.

Without disturbing the finding of the Court of Appeals that the orchestra leaders were employers and independent contractors, the Court concluded that they were nonetheless a "labor group" and parties to a "labor dispute" within the meaning of the Norris-LaGuardia Act, and thus that their involvement in the union regulatory scheme was not an unlawful combination between "labor" and "nonlabor" groups. The Court agreed with the trial court that the applicable test was whether there was "job or wage competition or some other economic interrelationship affecting legitimate union interests between the union members and the independent contractors." . . .

The Court also upheld the restrictions on booking agents, who were *not* involved in job or wage competition with union members. Accordingly, these restrictions had to meet the "other economic interrelationship" branch of the disjunctive test quoted above. And the test was met because those restrictions were "'at least as intimately bound up with the subject of wages' . . . as the price floors." . . . The Court noted that the booking agent restrictions had been adopted, in part, because agents had "charged exorbitant fees, and booked engagements for musicians at wages . . . below union scale."

C

The restrictions challenged by the petitioners in this case are very similar to the agent restrictions upheld in the *Carroll* case.[24] . . .

---

shield such agreements if they are intimately related to the union's vital concerns of wages, hours, and working conditions. [Citing *Jewel Tea*, page 853, *supra*, and quoting from *Connell Construction Co.*, page 859, *supra*]. . .

20 As the employers of Equity's members, producers are plainly a "non-labor group." Employers almost always will be a "non-labor group," although an exception has been recognized, for example, when the employer himself is in job competition with his employees. *See Musicians v. Carroll*, 391 U.S. 99 (orchestra leaders who both lead an orchestra and play an instrument).

24 Several cases before *Carroll* also upheld union regulation of the practices of independent entrepreneurs affecting the wages or working conditions of union members. *See Milk Wagon Drivers v. Lake Valley Farm Products, Inc.*, 311 U.S. 91; *Teamsters v. Oliver*, 358 U.S. 283 (*Oliver I*); *Teamsters v. Oliver*, 362 U.S. 605 (*Oliver II*).

The peculiar structure of the legitimate theater industry, where work is intermittent, where it is customary if not essential for union members to secure employment through agents, and where agents' fees are calculated as a percentage of a member's wage, makes it impossible for the union to defend even the integrity of the minimum wages it has negotiated without regulation of agency fees. The regulations are "brought within the labor exemption [because they are] necessary to assure that scale wages will be paid . . . ." *Carroll* . . . They "embody . . . a direct frontal attack upon a problem thought to threaten the maintenance of the basic wage structure." *Teamsters v. Oliver*. . . . Agents must, therefore, be considered a "labor group," and their controversy with Equity is plainly a "labor dispute" as defined in the Norris-LaGuardia Act: "representation of persons in negotiating, fixing, maintaining, changing, or seeking to arrange terms or conditions of employment, regardless of whether or not the disputants stand in the proximate relation of employer and employee." . . .

Agents perform a function—the representation of union members in the sale of their labor—that in most nonentertainment industries is performed exclusively by unions. In effect, Equity's franchise system operates as a substitute for maintaining a hiring hall as the representative of its members seeking employment.

Finally, Equity's regulations are clearly designed to promote the union's legitimate self-interest. . . . In a case such as this, where there is no direct wage or job competition between the union and the group it regulates, the *Carroll* formulation to determine the presence of a nonlabor group—whether there is "'some . . . economic interrelationship affecting legitimate union interests . . .'"—necessarily resolves this issue.

D

The question remains whether the fees that Equity levies upon the agents who apply for franchises are a permissible component of the exempt regulatory system. We have concluded that Equity's justification for these fees is inadequate. . . .

III

For the reasons stated, the judgment of the Court of Appeals is affirmed in part and reversed in part, and the case is remanded for proceedings consistent with this opinion.

It is so ordered.

In *Milk Wagon Drivers*, the Court held that the union had engaged in a "labor dispute" within the meaning of the Norris-LaGuardia Act when it attempted to organize independent "vendors" who supplied milk to retail stores. There the union feared that the "vendor system" was designed to escape the payment of union wages and the assumption of union-imposed working conditions. In *Oliver I*, the *Milk Wagon Drivers* decision was invoked to protect from state antitrust challenge a union's successful efforts to prescribe through collective-bargaining agreements a wage scale for truck drivers, and minimum rental fees for drivers who owned their own trucks. The union feared that driver-owners, whose fees included not only an entrepreneurial component but also a "wage" for the labor of driving, might undercut the union scale by charging a fee that effectively included a subscale wage component. The Court stated that "[t]he regulations embod[ied] . . . a direct frontal attack upon a problem thought to threaten the maintenance of the basic wage structure established by the collective bargaining contract." . . .

COMMENTARY

Why was it the statutory exemption which was in issue in *H.A. Artists & Associates*? Why was the union not agreeing with a nonlabor party? What approach was the Court employing to determine when a party is or is not a nonlabor party?

NOTE: CASES RELIED UPON IN *H.A. ARTISTS & ASSOCIATES, INC. V. ACTORS' EQUITY ASSOCIATION*

1. *Milk Wagon Drivers' Union, Local No. 753 v. Lake Valley Farm Products, Inc.*, 311 U.S. 91 (1940). Lake Valley Farm Products and another dairy distributed milk to retail stores partially through "vendors" who purchased the milk from the dairies, delivered it in their own trucks to retail stores, and resold it to these retail stores at wholesale prices. Retail stores purchasing milk from vendors tended to offer that milk for sale to the public at lower prices than milk supplied by dairies employing Teamsters union drivers. The defendant Teamsters union believed that the vendor system facilitated this undercutting because the vendors worked longer hours and accepted lower compensation than did Teamsters union members. The Teamsters union therefore picketed the retail stores which purchased milk from the vendors. The two dairies marketing through vendors, a Wisconsin cooperative supplying milk to those dairies, and the C.I.O. union containing the vendors sought an injunction against this picketing. The plaintiffs claimed that the defendant union was engaged in a secondary boycott "of which the purpose is not to unionize the vendors but to obtain for the defendants' employers a Chicago milk monopoly at a sustained high price level, contrary to the Sherman Act." The Supreme Court, reversing a decision of the Court of Appeals, ruled that the case involved a "labor dispute" within the meaning of the Norris-LaGuardia Act and that the federal courts accordingly lacked jurisdiction to grant an injunction.

2. *Local 24, International Brotherhood of Teamsters v. Oliver*, 358 U.S. 283 (1959) (*Oliver I*). As a result of multi-employer bargaining, an agreement was entered into between the defendant union and various interstate carriers operating in twelve midwestern states. Under the agreement a minimum rental was established for the lease of a motor vehicle to a carrier by an owner who drives the vehicle in the carrier's service. An owner-driver successfully challenged the agreement in the Ohio courts as a price-fixing agreement in violation of the Ohio antitrust law. The United States Supreme Court reversed:

> The regulations [contained in the agreement] embody not the "remote and indirect approach to the subject of wages" perceived by the Court of Common Pleas but a direct frontal attack upon a problem thought to threaten the maintenance of the basic wage structure established by the

> collective bargaining contract. The inadequacy of a rental which means that the owner makes up his excess costs from his driver's wages not only clearly bears a close relation to labor's efforts to improve working conditions but is in fact of vital concern to the carrier's employed drivers; an inadequate rental might mean the progressive curtailment of jobs through withdrawal of more and more carrier-owned vehicles from service. . . . Federal law here created the duty upon the parties to bargain collectively; Congress has provided for a system of federal law applicable to the agreement the parties made in response to that duty . . . and federal law sets some outside limits . . . on what their agreement may provide. . . . We believe that there is no room in this scheme for the application of this state policy limiting the solutions that the parties' agreement can provide to the problems of wages and working conditions. . . .

3. *Local 24, International Brotherhood of Teamsters v. Oliver*, 362 U.S. 605 (1960) (*Oliver II*). The Ohio Court of Appeals set aside its previous order "as it concerns and applies to Revel Oliver, appellee, as a lessor-driver" but continued the order "as it concerns and applies to Revel Oliver, appellee, as a lessor-owner and employer of drivers of his equipment." The United States Supreme Court again reviewed the case:

> We read the judgment of the Court of Appeals as enjoining petitioners and respondents A.C.E. Transportation Co. and Interstate Truck Service, Inc., from enforcing against respondent Oliver those parts of [the agreement] . . . which provide that hired or leased equipment, if not owner-driver, shall be operated only by employees of the certified or permitted carriers and require those carriers to use their own available equipment before hiring any extra equipment. . . . While we do not think the issue was tendered to us when the case was last here, we are of the opinion that these provisions are at least as intimately bound up with the subject of wages as the minimum rental provisions we passed on then.
>
> *Reversed.*

362 U.S. at 605-06.

4. *American Federation of Musicians v. Carroll*, 391 U.S. 99 (1968). Four musicians, members of the defendant Federation and Local, who usually acted as orchestra leaders brought suit against the American Federation of Musicians and its Local 802, alleging that certain practices of the unions violated the Sherman Act as activities in combination with a "non-labor" group. When a musician arranges a one-time engagement for an orchestra (a "club-date"), the musician usually assumes the role of "leader" of the orchestra, hires other musicians as members of the orchestra ("sidemen"), and attends to the bookkeeping and other details of the engagement. The leader was viewed therefore by the lower courts as an employer, for that club-date. Among the union practices challenged was a minimum price restriction applicable to club-dates. The minimum prices for such club-dates were the total of (a) the minimum wage scales for the sidemen, (b) a "leader's fee" which was double the sideman's scale when four or more musicians compose the orchestra, and (c) an additional 8% to cover social security, unemployment insurance, and other expenses. The Court of Appeals held that all of the practices, except the minimum price restrictions, were within the labor exemption from the Sherman Act. The United States Supreme Court ruled that all of the union practices were exempt: "The critical inquiry is whether the price floors in actuality operate to protect the wages of the subleader and sidemen. . . . [T]he price floors, including the minimums for leaders, are simply a means for coping with the job and wage competition of the leaders to protect the wage scales of musicians who respondents concede are employees on club-dates, namely sidemen and subleaders."

Brown v. Pro Football, Inc.

116 S. Ct. 2116 (1996)

Justice BREYER delivered the opinion of the Court.

The question in this case arises at the intersection of the Nation's labor and antitrust laws. A group of professional football players brought this antitrust suit against football club owners. The club owners had bargained with the players' union over a wage issue until they reached impasse. The owners then had agreed among themselves (but not with the union) to implement the terms of their own last best bargaining offer. The question before us is whether federal labor laws shield such an agreement from antitrust attack. We believe that they do. This Court has previously found in the labor laws an implicit antitrust exemption that applies where needed to make the collective bargaining process work. Like the Court of Appeals, we conclude that this need makes the exemption applicable in this case.

I

We can state the relevant facts briefly. In 1987, a collective-bargaining agreement between the National Football League (NFL), a group of football clubs, and the NFL Players Association, a labor union, expired. The NFL and the Players Association began to negotiate a new contract. In March 1989, during the negotiations, the NFL adopted Resolution G-2, a plan that would permit each club to establish a "developmental squad" of up to six rookie or "first-year" players who, as free agents, had failed to secure a position on a regular player roster. . . . Squad members would play in practice games and sometimes in regular games as substitutes for injured players. Resolution G-2 provided that the club owners would pay all squad members the same weekly salary.

The next month, April, the NFL presented the developmental squad plan to the Players Association. The NFL proposed a squad player salary of $1,000 per week. The Players Association disagreed. It insisted that the club owners give developmental squad players benefits and protections similar to those provided regular players, and that they leave individual squad members free to negotiate their own salaries.

Two months later, in June, negotiations on the issue of developmental squad salaries reached an impasse. The NFL then unilaterally implemented the developmental squad program by distributing to the clubs a uniform contract that embodied the terms of Resolution G-2 and the $1,000 proposed weekly salary. The League advised club owners that paying developmental squad players more or less than $1,000 per week would result in disciplinary action, including the loss of draft choices.

In May 1990, 235 developmental squad players brought this antitrust suit against the League and its member clubs. The players claimed that their employers' agreement to pay them a $1,000 weekly salary violated the Sherman Act. . . . The Federal District Court denied the employers' claim of exemption from the antitrust laws; it permitted the case to reach the jury; and it subsequently entered judgment on a jury treble-damage award that exceeded $30 million. The NFL and its member clubs appealed.

The Court of Appeals (by a split 2-to-1 vote) reversed. The majority interpreted the labor laws as "waiv[ing] antitrust liability for restraints on competition imposed through the collective-bargaining process, so long as such restraints operate primarily in a labor market characterized by collective bargaining." . . . The Court held, consequently, that the club owners were immune from antitrust liability. We granted *certiorari* to review that determination. Although we do not interpret the exemption as broadly as did the Appeals Court, we nonetheless find the exemption applicable, and we affirm that Court's immunity conclusion.

II

The immunity before us rests upon what this Court has called the "nonstatutory" labor exemption from the antitrust laws. . . . The Court has implied this exemption from federal labor statutes, which set forth a national labor policy favoring free and private collective bargaining, . . . which require good-faith bargaining over wages, hours and working conditions, and which delegate related rulemaking and interpretive authority to the National Labor Relations Board. . . .

This implicit exemption reflects both history and logic. As a matter of history, Congress intended the labor statutes (from which the Court has implied the exemption) in part to adopt the views of dissenting Justices in *Duplex Printing Press Co. v. Deering*, 254 U.S. 443 (1921), which Justices had urged the Court to interpret broadly a different explicit "statutory" labor exemption that Congress earlier (in 1914) had written directly into the antitrust laws. . . . In the 1930's, when it subsequently enacted the labor statutes, Congress, as in 1914, hoped to prevent judicial use of antitrust law to resolve labor disputes—a kind of dispute normally inappropriate for antitrust law resolution. *See Jewel Tea*, *supra*, at 700-709 (opinion of Goldberg, J.); *Marine Cooks v. Panama S.S. Co.*, 362 U.S. 365, 370, n.7 (1960); A. Cox, Law and the National Labor Policy 3-8 (1960); *cf. Duplex*, *supra*, at 485 (Brandeis, J., dissenting) (explicit "statutory" labor exemption reflected view that "Congress, not the judges, was the body which should declare what public policy in regard to the industrial struggle demands"). The implicit ("nonstatutory") exemption interprets the labor statutes in accordance with this intent, namely, as limiting an antitrust court's authority to determine, in the area of industrial conflict, what is or is not a "reasonable" practice. It thereby substitutes legislative and administrative labor-related determinations for judicial antitrust-related determinations as to the appropriate legal limits of industrial conflict. *See Jewel Tea*, *supra*, at 709-710.

As a matter of logic, it would be difficult, if not impossible, to require groups of employers and employees to bargain together, but at the same time to forbid them to make among themselves or with each other any of the competition-restricting agreements potentially necessary to make the process work or its results mutually acceptable. Thus, the implicit exemption recognizes that, to give effect to federal labor laws and policies and to allow meaningful collective bargaining to take place, some restraints on competition imposed through the bargaining process must be shielded from antitrust sanctions. *See Connell, supra*, at 622 (federal labor law's "goals" could "never" be achieved if ordinary anticompetitive effects of collective bargaining were held to violate the antitrust laws); *Jewel Tea, supra*, at 711 (national labor law scheme would be "virtually destroyed" by the routine imposition of antitrust penalties upon parties engaged in collective bargaining); *Pennington, supra*, at 665 (implicit exemption necessary to harmonize Sherman Act with "national policy . . . of promoting 'the peaceful settlement of industrial disputes by subjecting labor-management controversies to the mediatory influence of negotiation'") (quoting *Fibreboard Paper Products Corp. v. NLRB*, 379 U.S. 203, 211 (1964)).

The petitioners and their supporters concede, as they must, the legal existence of the exemption we have described. They also concede that, where its application is necessary to make the statutorily authorized collective-bargaining process work as Congress intended, the exemption must apply both to employers and to employees. . . . Consequently, the question before us is one of determining the exemption's scope: Does it apply to an agreement among several employers bargaining together to implement after impasse the terms of their last best good-faith wage offer? We assume that such conduct, as practiced in this case, is unobjectionable as a matter of labor law and policy. On that assumption, we conclude that the exemption applies.

Labor law itself regulates directly, and considerably, the kind of behavior here at issue—the postimpasse imposition of a proposed employment term concerning a mandatory subject of bargaining. Both the Board and the courts have held that, after impasse, labor law permits employers unilaterally to implement changes in preexisting conditions, but only insofar as the new terms meet carefully circumscribed conditions. For example, the new terms must be "reasonably comprehended" within the employer's preimpasse proposals (typically the last rejected proposals), lest by imposing more or less favorable terms, the employer unfairly undermined the union's status. . . . The collective-bargaining proceeding itself must be free of any unfair labor practice, such as an employer's failure to have bargained in good faith. . . . These regulations reflect the fact that impasse and an accompanying implementation of proposals constitute an integral part of the bargaining process. . . .

Although the caselaw we have cited focuses upon bargaining by a single employer, no one here has argued that labor law does, or should, treat multiemployer bargaining differently in this respect. Indeed, Board and court decisions suggest that the joint implementation of proposed terms after impasse is a familiar practice in the context of multiemployer bargaining. . . . We proceed on that assumption.

Multiemployer bargaining itself is a well-established, important, pervasive method of collective bargaining, offering advantages to both management and labor. *See* Appendix (multiemployer bargaining accounts for more than 40% of major collective-bargaining agreements, and is used in such industries as construction, transportation, retail trade, clothing manufacture, and real estate, as well as professional sports); *NLRB v. Truck Drivers*, 353 U.S. 87, 95 (1957) (*Buffalo Linen*) (Congress saw multiemployer bargaining as "a vital factor in the effectuation of the national policy of promoting labor peace through strengthened collective bargaining"); *Charles D. Bonanno Linen Service, Inc. v. NLRB*, 454 U.S. 404, 409, n.3 (1982) (*Bonanno Linen*) (multiemployer bargaining benefits both management and labor, by saving bargaining resources, by encouraging development of industry-wide worker benefits programs that smaller employers could not otherwise afford, and by inhibiting employer competition at the workers' expense); Brief for Respondent NLRB in *Bonanno Linen*, O.T. 1981, No. 80-931, p. 10, n.7 (same); General Subcommittee on

Labor, House Committee on Education and Labor, Multiemployer Association Bargaining and its Impact on the Collective Bargaining Process, 88th Cong., 2d Sess. 10-19, 32-33 (Comm. Print 1964) (same); *see also* C. Bonnett, Employers' Associations in the United States: A Study of Typical Associations (1922) (history). The upshot is that the practice at issue here plays a significant role in a collective-bargaining process that itself comprises an important part of the Nation's industrial relations system.

In these circumstances, to subject the practice to antitrust law is to require antitrust courts to answer a host of important practical questions about how collective bargaining over wages, hours and working conditions is to proceed—the very result that the implicit labor exemption seeks to avoid. And it is to place in jeopardy some of the potentially beneficial labor-related effects that multiemployer bargaining can achieve. That is because unlike labor law, which sometimes welcomes anticompetitive agreements conducive to industrial harmony, antitrust law forbids all agreements among competitors (such as competing employers) that unreasonably lessen competition among or between them in virtually any respect whatsoever. *See, e.g., Paramount Famous Lasky Corp. v. United States*, 282 U.S. 30 (1930) (agreement to insert arbitration provisions in motion picture licensing contracts). Antitrust law also sometimes permits judges or juries to premise antitrust liability upon little more than uniform behavior among competitors, preceded by conversations implying that later uniformity might prove desirable, *see, e.g., United States v. General Motors Corp.*, 384 U.S. 127, 142-143 (1966); *United States v. Foley*, 598 F.2d 1323, 1331-1332 (4th Cir. 1979), *cert. denied*, 444 U.S. 1043 (1980), or accompanied by other conduct that in context suggests that each competitor failed to make an independent decision, *see, e.g., American Tobacco Co. v. United States*, 328 U.S. 781, 809-810 (1946); *United States v. Masonite Corp.*, 316 U.S. 265, 275 (1942); *Interstate Circuit, Inc. v. United States*, 306 U.S. 208, 226-227 (1939). *See generally* 6 P. AREEDA, ANTITRUST LAW ¶¶ 1416-1427 (1986); Turner, *The Definition of Agreement Under the Sherman Act: Conscious Parallelism and Refusals to Deal*, 75 HARV. L. REV. 655 (1962).

If the antitrust laws apply, what are employers to do once impasse is reached? If all impose terms similar to their last joint offer, they invite an antitrust action premised upon identical behavior (along with prior or accompanying conversations) as tending to show a common understanding or agreement. If any, or all, of them individually impose terms that differ significantly from that offer, they invite an unfair labor practice charge. Indeed, how can employers safely discuss their offers together even before a bargaining impasse occurs? A preimpasse discussion about, say, the practical advantages or disadvantages of a particular proposal, invites a later antitrust claim that they agreed to limit the kinds of action each would later take should an impasse occur. The same is true of postimpasse discussions aimed at renewed negotiations with the union. Nor would adherence to the terms of an expired collective-bargaining agreement eliminate a potentially plausible antitrust claim charging that they had "conspired" or tacitly "agreed" to do so, particularly if maintaining the status quo were not in the immediate economic self-interest of some. *Cf. Interstate Circuit, supra*, at 222-223; 6 AREEDA, *supra*, at ¶ 1425. All this is to say that to permit antitrust liability here threatens to introduce instability and uncertainty into the collective-bargaining process, for antitrust law often forbids or discourages the kinds of joint discussions and behavior that the collective-bargaining process invites or requires.

We do not see any obvious answer to this problem. We recognize, as the Government suggests, that, in principle, antitrust courts might themselves try to evaluate particular kinds of employer understandings, finding them "reasonable" (hence lawful) where justified by collective-bargaining necessity. But any such evaluation means a web of detailed rules spun by many different nonexpert antitrust judges and juries, not a set of labor rules enforced by a single expert administrative body, namely the Labor Board. The labor laws give the Board, not antitrust courts, primary responsibility for policing the collective-bargaining process. And one of their objectives was to take from antitrust courts the authority to determine, through application of the antitrust laws, what is socially or economically desirable collective-bargaining policy. *See supra* . . . ; *see also Jewel Tea*, 381 U.S. at 716-719 (opinion of Goldberg, J.).

III

Both petitioners and their supporters advance several suggestions for drawing the exemption boundary line short of this case. We shall explain why we find them unsatisfactory.

A

Petitioners claim that the implicit exemption applies only to labor-management *agreements*—a limitation that they deduce from caselaw language, *see, e.g., Connell*, 421 U.S., at 622 (exemption for "some union-employer *agreements*") (emphasis added), and from a proposed principle—that the exemption must rest upon labor-management consent. The language, however, reflects only the fact that the cases previously before the Court involved collective-bargaining agreements . . . ; the language does not reflect the exemption's rationale. . . .

Nor do we see how an exemption limited by petitioners' principle of labor-management consent could work. One cannot mean the principle literally—that the exemption applies only to understandings embodied in a collective-bargaining agreement—for the collective-bargaining process may take place before the making of any agreement or after an agreement has expired. Yet a multiemployer bargaining process itself necessarily involves many procedural and substantive understandings among participating employers as well as with the union. Petitioners cannot rescue their principle by claiming that the exemption applies only insofar as both labor and management consent to those understandings. Often labor will not (and should not) consent to certain common bargaining positions that employers intend to maintain. *Cf.* AREEDA & HOVENKAMP, ANTITRUST LAW, at ¶ 229d, p. 277 (Supp.1995) ("[J]oint employer preparation and bargaining in the context of a formal multi-employer bargaining unit is clearly exempt"). Similarly, labor need not consent to certain tactics that this Court has approved as part of the multiemployer bargaining process, such as unit-wide lockouts and the use of temporary replacements. . . .

Petitioners cannot save their consent principle by weakening it, as by requiring union consent only to the multiemployer bargaining process itself. This general consent is automatically present whenever multiemployer bargaining takes place. *See Hi-Way Billboards, Inc.*, 206 N.L.R.B. 22, 1973 WL 4443 (1973) (multiemployer unit "based on consent" and "established by an unequivocal agreement by the parties"), *enf. denied on other grounds*, 500 F.2d 181 (5th Cir. 1974); *Weyerhaeuser Co.*, 166 N.L.R.B. 299, 299-300 (1967). As so weakened, the principle cannot help decide which related practices are, or are not, subject to antitrust immunity.

B

The Solicitor General argues that the exemption should terminate at the point of impasse. After impasse, he says, "employers no longer have a duty under the labor laws to maintain the status quo," and "are free as a matter of labor law to negotiate individual arrangements on an interim basis with the union." . . .

Employers, however, are not completely free at impasse to act independently. The multiemployer bargaining unit ordinarily remains intact; individual employers cannot withdraw. *Bonanno Linen*, 454 U.S. at 410-413. The duty to bargain survives; employers must stand ready to resume collective bargaining. *See, e.g., Worldwide Detective Bureau*, 296 N.L.R.B. 148, 155 (1989); *Hi-Way Billboards, Inc.*, 206 N.L.R.B. at 23. And individual employers can negotiate individual interim agreements with the union only insofar as those agreements are consistent with "the duty to abide by the results of group bargaining." *Bonanno Linen, supra*, at 416. Regardless, the absence of a legal "duty" to act jointly is not determinative. This Court has implied antitrust immunities that extend beyond statutorily required joint action to joint action that a statute "expressly or impliedly allows or assumes must also be immune." 1 P. AREEDA & D. TURNER, ANTITRUST LAW ¶ 224, p. 145 (1978); *see, e.g., Gordon v. New York Stock Exchange, Inc.*, 422 U.S. 659, 682-691 (1975) (immunizing application of joint rule that securities law permitted, but did not require); *United States v. National Assn. of Securities Dealers, Inc.*, 422 U.S. 694, 720-730 (1975) (same).

More importantly, the simple "impasse" line would not solve the basic problem we have described above. . . . Labor law permits employers, after impasse, to engage in considerable joint behavior, including joint lockouts and replacement hiring. . . . Indeed, as a general matter, labor law often limits employers to four options at impasse: (1) maintain the status quo, (2) implement their last offer, (3) lock out their workers (and either shut down or hire temporary replacements), or (4) negotiate separate interim agreements with the union. *See generally* 1 HARDIN, THE DEVELOPING LABOR LAW, at 516-520, 696-699. What is to happen if the parties cannot reach an interim agreement? The other alternatives are limited. Uniform employer conduct is likely. Uniformity—at least when accompanied by discussion of the matter—invites antitrust attack. And such attack would ask antitrust courts to decide the lawfulness of activities intimately related to the bargaining process.

The problem is aggravated by the fact that "impasse" is often temporary . . . ; it may differ from bargaining only in degree . . . ; it may be manipulated by the parties for bargaining purposes . . . ; and it may occur several times during the course of a single labor dispute, since the bargaining process is not over when the first impasse is reached. . . . How are employers to discuss future bargaining positions during a temporary impasse? Consider, too, the adverse consequences that flow from failing to guess how an antitrust court would later draw the impasse line. Employers who erroneously concluded that impasse had not been reached would risk antitrust liability were they collectively to maintain the status quo, while employers who erroneously concluded that impasse had occurred would risk unfair labor practice charges for prematurely suspending multiemployer negotiations.

The Solicitor General responds with suggestions for softening an "impasse" rule by extending the exemption after impasse "for such time as would be reasonable in the circumstances" for employers to consult with counsel, confirm that impasse has occurred, and adjust their business operations, . . . by reestablishing the exemption once there is a "resumption of good-faith bargaining," . . . and by looking to antitrust law's "rule of reason" to shield—"in some circumstances"—such joint actions as the unit-wide lockout or the concerted maintenance of previously-established joint benefit or retirement plans. . . . But even as so modified, the impasse-related rule creates an exemption that can evaporate in the middle of the bargaining process, leaving later antitrust courts free to second-guess the parties' bargaining decisions and consequently forcing them to choose their collective-bargaining responses in light of what they predict or fear that antitrust courts, not labor law administrators, will eventually decide. . . .

C

Petitioners and their supporters argue in the alternative for a rule that would exempt postimpasse agreement about bargaining "tactics," but not postimpasse agreement about substantive "terms," from the reach of antitrust. . . . They recognize, however, that both the Board and the courts have said that employers can, and often do, employ the imposition of "terms" as a bargaining "tactic." . . . This concession as to joint "tactical" implementation would turn the presence of an antitrust exemption upon a determination of the employers' primary purpose or motive. . . . But to ask antitrust courts, insulated from the bargaining process, to investigate an employer group's subjective motive is to ask them to conduct an inquiry often more amorphous than those we have previously discussed. And, in our view, a labor/antitrust line drawn on such a basis would too often raise the same related (previously discussed) problems. *See* . . . *Jewel Tea*, 381 U.S. at 716 (opinion of Goldberg, J.) (expressing concern about antitrust judges "roaming at large" through the bargaining process).

D

The petitioners make several other arguments. They point, for example, to cases holding applicable, in collective-bargaining contexts, general "backdrop" statutes, such as a state statute requiring a plant-closing employer to make employee severance payments, *Fort Halifax Packing Co. v. Coyne*, 482 U.S. 1 (1987), and a state statute mandating certain minimum health benefits, *Metropolitan Life Ins. Co. v. Massachusetts*, 471 U.S. 724 (1985). Those statutes, however, "'neither encourage[d] nor discourage[d] the collective-bargaining processes that are the subject of the [federal labor laws].'" *Fort Halifax, supra*, at 21 (quoting *Metropolitan Life, supra*, at 755). Neither did those statutes come accompanied with antitrust's labor-related history. *Cf. Oliver*, 358 U.S. at 295-297 (state antitrust law interferes with collective bargaining and is not applicable to labor-management agreement).

Petitioners also say that irrespective of how the labor exemption applies elsewhere to multiemployer collective bargaining, professional sports is "special." We can understand how professional sports may be special in terms of, say, interest, excitement, or concern. But we do not understand how they are special in respect to labor law's antitrust exemption. We concede that the clubs that make up a professional sports league are not completely independent economic competitors, as they depend upon a degree of cooperation for economic survival. . . . In the present context, however, that circumstance makes the league more like a single bargaining employer, which analogy seems irrelevant to the legal issue before us.

We also concede that football players often have special individual talents, and, unlike many unionized workers, they often negotiate their pay individually with their employers. *See post* . . . (STEVENS, J., dissenting). But this characteristic seems simply a feature, like so many others, that might give employees (or employers) more (or less) bargaining power, that might lead some (or all) of them to favor a particular kind of bargaining, or that might lead to certain demands at the bargaining table. We do not see how it could make a critical legal difference in determining the underlying framework in which bargaining is to take place. . . . Indeed, it would be odd to fashion an antitrust exemption that gave additional advantages to professional football players (by virtue of their superior bargaining power) that transport workers, coal miners, or meat packers would not enjoy.

The dissent points to other "unique features" of the parties' collective bargaining relationship, which, in the dissent's view, make the case "atypical." . . . It says, for example, that the employers imposed the restraint simply to enforce compliance with league-wide rules, and that the bargaining consisted of nothing more than the sending of a "notice," and therefore amounted only to "so-called" bargaining. . . . Insofar as these features underlie an argument for looking to the employers' true purpose, we have already discussed them. . . . Insofar as they suggest that there was not a genuine impasse, they fight the basic assumption upon which the District Court, the Court of Appeals, the petitioners, and this Court, rest the case. . . . Ultimately, we cannot find a satisfactory basis for distinguishing football players from other organized workers. We therefore conclude that all must abide by the same legal rules.

. . . .

For these reasons, we hold that the implicit ("nonstatutory") antitrust exemption applies to the employer conduct at issue here. That conduct took place during and immediately after a collective-bargaining negotiation. It grew out of, and was directly related to, the lawful operation of the bargaining process. It involved a matter that the parties were required to negotiate collectively. And it concerned only the parties to the collective-bargaining relationship.

Our holding is not intended to insulate from antitrust review every joint imposition of terms by employers, for an agreement among employers could be sufficiently distant in time and in circumstances from the collective-bargaining process that a rule permitting antitrust intervention would not significantly interfere with that process. *See, e.g.,* 50 F.3d at 1057 (suggesting that exemption lasts until collapse of the collective-bargaining relationship, as evidenced by decertification of the union); *El Cerrito Mill & Lumber Co.*, 316 N.L.R.B. at 1006-1007 (suggesting that "extremely long" impasse, accompanied by "instability" or "defunctness" of multiemployer unit, might justify union withdrawal from group bargaining). We need not decide in this case whether, or where, within these extreme outer boundaries to draw that line. Nor would it be appropriate for us to do so without the detailed views of the Board, to whose "specialized judgment" Congress "intended to leave" many of the "inevitable questions concerning multiemployer bargaining bound to arise in the future." . . .

The judgment of the Court of Appeals is affirmed.

It is so ordered.

Appendix to Opinion of Breyer, J.

TABLE A
MAJOR BARGAINING UNITS AND EMPLOYMENT IN PRIVATE INDUSTRY, BY TYPE OF
BARGAINING UNIT, 1994.
(Covers bargaining units of 1,000 or more workers.)

	Number		Percent	
Type	Units	Employment	Units	Employment
I	522	2,305,478	44	43
M & S	664	3,040,159	56	57
Total	1,186	5,345,637	100	100

I = Multiemployer.
M = One company, more than one location.
S = One company, single location.
SOURCE: U.S. Dept. of Labor, Bureau of Labor Statistics, unpublished data (Feb. 14, 1996) (available in Clerk of Court's case file).

TABLE B
MAJOR MULTIEMPLOYER COLLECTIVE BARGAINING UNITS AND EMPLOYMENT IN PRIVATE INDUSTRY, BY INDUSTRY, 1994.
(Covers bargaining units of 1,000 or more workers.)

Type	Number		Percent	
	Units	Employment	Units	Employment
All industries	522	2,305,478	100	100
Manufacturing	45	210,050	9	9
Food	13	50,750	2	2
Apparel	23	141,600	4	6
Other	9	17,700	2	1
Nonmanufacturing	477	2,095,428	91	91
Mining	2	67,500	(1)	3
Construction	337	995,443	65	43
Railroads	12	189,183	2	8
Other transportation	20	156,662	4	7
Wholesale trade	6	8,500	1	(1)
Retail trade	37	314,100	7	14
Real estate	11	85,800	2	4
Hotels and motels	11	79,200	2	3
Business services	13	63,200	2	3
Health services	8	65,100	2	3
Other	20	70,740	4	3

(1)= More than 0 and less than 0.05 percent.
SOURCE: U.S. Dept. of Labor, Bureau of Labor Statistics, unpublished data (Apr. 17, 1996) (available in Clerk of Court's case file).

Justice STEVENS, dissenting.

I

. . . .

The basic premise underlying our national labor policy is that unregulated competition among employees and applicants for employment produces wage levels that are lower than they should be. . . . Whether or not the premise is true in fact, it is surely the basis for the statutes that encourage and protect the collective-bargaining process, including the express statutory exemptions from the antitrust laws that Congress enacted in order to protect union activities. Those statutes were enacted to enable collective action by union members to achieve wage levels that are higher than would be available in a free market. . . .

In my view, however, neither the policies underlying the two separate statutory schemes, nor the narrower focus on the purpose of the nonstatutory exemption, provides a justification for exempting from antitrust scrutiny collective action initiated by employers to depress wages below the level that would be produced in a free market. Nor do those policies support a rule that would allow employers to suppress wages by implementing noncompetitive agreements among themselves on matters that have not previously been the subject of either an agreement with labor or even a demand by labor for inclusion in the bargaining process. That, however, is what is at stake in this litigation.

II

In light of the accommodation that has been struck between antitrust and labor law policy, it would be most ironic to extend an exemption crafted to protect collective action by employees to protect employers acting jointly to deny employees the opportunity to negotiate their salaries individually in a competitive market. Perhaps aware of the irony, the Court chooses to analyze this case as though it represented a typical impasse in an unexceptional multiemployer bargaining process. In so doing, it glosses over three unique features of the case that are critical to the inquiry into whether the policies of the labor laws require extension of the nonstatutory labor exemption to this atypical case.

First, in this market, unlike any other area of labor law implicated in the cases cited by the Court, player salaries are individually negotiated. The practice of individually negotiating player salaries prevailed even prior to collective bargaining. The players did not challenge the prevailing practice because, unlike employees in most industries, they want their compensation to be determined by the forces of the free market rather than by the process of collective bargaining. Thus, although the majority professes an inability to understand anything special about professional sports that should affect the framework of labor negotiations, . . . in this business it is the employers, not the employees, who seek to impose a noncompetitive uniform wage on a segment of the market and to put an end to competitive wage negotiations.

Second, respondents concede that the employers imposed the wage restraint to force owners to comply with league-wide rules that limit the number of players that may serve on a team, not to facilitate a stalled bargaining process, or to revisit any issue previously subjected to bargaining. . . . The employers could have confronted the culprits directly by stepping up enforcement of roster limits. They instead chose to address the problem by unilaterally forbidding players from individually competing in the labor market.

Third, although the majority asserts that the "club owners had bargained with the players' union over a wage issue until they reached impasse," . . . that hardly constitutes a complete description of what transpired. When the employers' representative advised the union that they proposed to pay the players a uniform wage determined by the owners, the union promptly and unequivocally responded that their proposal was inconsistent with the "principle" of individual salary negotiation that had been accepted in the past and that predated collective bargaining. The so-called "bargaining" that followed amounted to nothing more than the employers' notice to the union that they had decided to implement a decision to replace individual salary negotiations with a uniform wage level for a specific group of players.

Given these features of the case, I do not see why the employers should be entitled to a judicially crafted exemption from antitrust liability. We have explained that the "[t]he nonstatutory exemption has its source in the strong labor policy favoring the association of employees to eliminate competition over wages and working conditions." *Connell Constr. Co.*, 421 U.S. at 622. I know of no similarly strong labor policy that favors the association of employers to eliminate a competitive method of negotiating wages that predates collective bargaining and that labor would prefer to preserve.

Even if some collective action by employers may justify an exemption because it is necessary to maintain the "integrity of the multiemployer bargaining unit," . . . no such justification exists here. The employers imposed a fixed wage even though there was no dispute over the pre-existing principle that player salaries should be individually negotiated. They sought only to prevent certain owners from evading roster limits and thereby gaining an unfair advantage. Because "the employer's interest is a competitive interest rather than an interest in regulating its own labor relations," . . . there would seem to be no more reason to exempt this concerted, anticompetitive employer action from the antitrust laws than the action held unlawful in *Radovich v. National Football League*, 352 U.S. 445 (1957).

. . . .

III

. . . .

We have previously considered the scope of the nonstatutory labor exemption only in cases involving challenges to anticompetitive agreements between unions and employers brought by other employers not parties to those agreements. . . . Even then, we have concluded that the exemption does not always apply. *See Mine Workers v. Pennington*, 381 U.S. at 663.

As *Pennington* explained, the mere fact that an antitrust challenge touches on an issue, such as wages, that is subject to mandatory bargaining does not suffice to trigger the judicially fashioned exemption. . . . Moreover, we concluded that the exemption should not obtain in *Pennington* itself only after we examined the motives of one of the parties to the bargaining process. . . .

The Court's only attempt to square its decision with *Pennington* occurs at the close of its opinion. It concludes that the exemption applies because the employers' action "grew out of, and was directly related to, the lawful operation of the bargaining process," "[i]t involved a matter that the parties were required to negotiate collectively," and that "concerned only the parties to the collective-bargaining relationship.". . .

As to the first two qualifiers, the same could be said of *Pennington*. Indeed, the same was said and rejected in *Pennington*. "This is not to say that an agreement resulting from union-employer negotiations is automatically exempt from Sherman Act scrutiny simply because the negotiations involve a compulsory subject of bargaining, regardless of the subject or the form and content of the agreement." . . .

The final qualifier does distinguish *Pennington*, but only partially so. To determine whether the exemption applied in *Pennington*, we undertook a detailed examination into whether the policies of labor law so strongly supported the agreement struck by the bargaining parties that it should be immune from antitrust scrutiny. We concluded that because the agreement affected employers not parties to the bargaining process, labor law policies could not be understood to require the exemption.

Here, however, the Court does not undertake a review of labor law policy to determine whether it would support an exemption for the unilateral imposition of anticompetitive wage terms by employers on a union. The Court appears to conclude instead that the exemption should apply merely because the employers' action was implemented during a lawful negotiating process concerning a mandatory subject of bargaining. Thus, the Court's analysis would seem to constitute both an unprecedented expansion of a heretofore limited exemption, and an unexplained repudiation of the reasoning in a prior, nonconstitutional decision that Congress itself has not seen fit to override.

The Court nevertheless contends that the "rationale" of our prior cases supports its approach. . . . As support for that contention, it relies heavily on the views espoused in Justice Goldberg's separate opinion in *Meat Cutters v. Jewel Tea Co.*, 381 U.S. 676 (1965). At five critical junctures in its opinion . . . the Court invokes that separate concurrence to explain why, for purposes of applying the nonstatutory labor exemption, labor law policy admits of no distinction between collective employer action taken in response to labor demands, and collective employer action of the kind we consider here.

It should be remembered that *Jewel Tea* concerned only the question whether an agreement between employers and a union may be exempt, and that even then the Court did not accept the broad antitrust exemption that Justice Goldberg advocated. Instead, Justice White, the author of *Pennington*, writing for Chief Justice Warren and Justice Brennan, explained that even in disputes over the lawfulness of agreements about terms that are subject to mandatory bargaining, courts must examine the bargaining process to determine whether antitrust scrutiny should obtain. . . . "The crucial determinant is not the form of the agreement—*e.g.,* prices or wages—but its relative impact on the product market *and the interests of union members.*" . . . (emphasis added). Moreover, the three dissenters, Justices Douglas, Clark, and Black, concluded that the union was entitled to no immunity at all. . . .

. . . .

Congress is free to act to exempt the anticompetitive employer conduct that we review today. In the absence of such action, I do not believe it is for us to stretch the limited exemption that we have fashioned to facilitate the express statutory exemption created for labor's benefit so that unions must strike in order to restore a prior practice of individually negotiating salaries. I therefore agree with the position that the District Court adopted below. . . .

COMMENTARY

1. Both the majority and dissenting opinions in *Brown v. Pro Football, Inc.* raise a number of issues about the intersection of labor and antitrust policies. Justice Breyer's opinion for the Court, holding that the nonstatutory labor exemption continues to protect the participants in a multi-employer bargaining unit, even after bargaining has reached a state of impasse, seems unexceptional on the surface. Breyer's opinion, however, highlights the latent policy conflicts hidden in the antitrust/labor law interface.

Surely, Justice Breyer is correct that the exemption must be interpreted to facilitate multi-employer bargaining, since Congress clearly intended the labor laws to accommodate multi-employer bargaining. Breyer's Appendix shows a widespread use of multi-employer bargaining. Yet when multi-employer bargaining includes all (or most) of the employers in an industry, collective bargaining effectively determines the labor costs of the industry and hence (in the absence of effective competition from abroad) the price of the industry's goods in the product market. Congress was aware that such industry-wide bargaining would be reflected in increased prices in the product market. Accordingly, the nonstatutory labor exemption (under which antitrust law bends to accommodate national labor policy) must be invoked to accommodate this product-market effect.

Justice Stevens in dissent explicitly recognizes that the National Labor Relations Act was intended not just to facilitate collective bargaining as a process. It was also expected to raise wages. Indeed, as Stevens points out, the leading supporters of that legislation thought that wages were too low and that the NLRA would encourage unionization and thereby generate upward pressure on wages. In the present context, employers are combining to impose a reduced wage upon the substitute players. Do you agree with Stevens that the employers' behavior in these circumstances is contrary to the policies of both the antitrust laws and of the labor laws? If you agree with Stevens here, how do you deal with Justice Breyer's concern that the labor exemption must be construed broadly enough to facilitate multiemployer bargaining? Does Justice Stevens take the employers' motive into account?

2. Stevens' historical reminder that the NLRA was intended to generate an upward pressure on wages, however, raises the problem of the wage/employment tradeoff which is present in most industries. An employer will hire workers so long as each worker hired produces value which exceeds the wage paid to that worker. (In economic terms, an employer will hire workers until the value of the marginal product produced by the last worker hired equals the wage rate.) Because of the extremely high revenues which professional sports generate and the relatively few players required, wages generally have not reached the level of the value of the marginal product contributed by most players. Justice Stevens was therefore able to leave the wage/employment tradeoff out of his discussion of NLRA policy as applied to professional football.

3. If labor is not an article of commerce under § 6 of the Clayton Act, how could the owners violate the Sherman Act by combining to drive down the compensation of football players?

4. Isn't it odd that a union of football players was demanding that the employers negotiate individually with each player? Commenting on *Brown* while the case was still pending before the U.S. Supreme Court, Professor Douglas Leslie argued that the economics of sports may be different from those of other industries:

> In sports labor markets, wages go up, it is thought, when teams compete against one another for players. If those suppositions are correct, a ruling in *Brown* for the employers may discourage unionization in professional team sports, but it will not do so in other labor markets. A ruling for the plaintiffs, on the other hand, will discourage and destabilize multiemployer bargaining in all markets, as employers realize that choosing to join a multiemployer unit carries a cost: the risk of antitrust liability for unilateral implementation and for a lockout. . . . Having chosen the advantages of unionization and of multiemployer bargaining, consideration of the interests of nonsports workers suggest that athletes should bear the costs as well.

Douglas L. Leslie, Brown v. Pro Football, 82 VA. L. REV. 629, 645-46 (1996). If wages go up for athletes when teams compete against each other for players, why did the players bother to form a labor union in the first place? Might competition among teams for players be most intense for stars and significantly less intense for less-talented players? One comprehensive review of the application of the antitrust laws to sports can be found in Joseph P. Bauer, *Antitrust and Sports: Must Competition on the Field Displace Competition in the Marketplace?*, 60 TENN. L. REV. 263 (1993).

5. Justice Breyer rejected the Solicitor General's suggestion that the exemption should be extended after impass "for such time as would be reasonable in the circumstances," believing that the application of such a standard would be unpredictable. The Solicitor General was calling for a dynamic approach to the interpretation of the labor exemption, under which the length of the exemption would depend upon fact-specific conditions. In your mind, would the merits of such individualized treatment outweigh Breyer's objections? Would the Solicitor General's proposal have been as predictable as other applications of antitrust's "rule of reason"? Why not?

NOTE: LABOR AND ANTITRUST POLICIES: INADEQUATE RESOLUTION OF POLICY CONFLICTS[1]

The theory of collective bargaining assumes that workers bargain over wages, hours and working conditions through a single representative (the union). The union thus controls the sole source of labor and can exert substantially more bargaining power than can any individual worker. The employer is nonetheless constrained by the wage which it can offer by competition from rivals: the employer cannot raise its costs so much that it can no longer compete. Competition from unorganized firms may thus constrain the bargaining between an employer and a union.

If and when a union successfully organizes an entire industry, that constraint is no longer present. If all rival firms pay the same union wage scale, then no firm is disadvantaged by incurring higher wage costs than its rivals. Consider, first, a competitively-structured industry in which a union has successfully organized the workers of all employers. Assume bargaining takes place between the union and all employers (in a multi-employer format). An agreed-upon wage increase will be reflected as increased labor costs. The increased labor costs will be passed on to consumers in the form of higher prices because (so long as the firms all employ the same technology) the labor-cost increase affects all firms in the same way: the marginal costs of all firms shift upwards. The supply curve of the industry (composed of the aggregate marginal costs of the individual firms) shifts upwards, intersecting at a higher point with the curve representing demand for the industry's product.

Now consider how union-employer bargaining takes place in an oligopolistically-structured industry. In such circumstances, a union controlling industry labor supply bargains with employers who themselves possess market power in the product market. This is a situation in which one monopolist is bargaining with another monpolist: it is the *Albrecht* situation in another context. As in similar contexts, the interests of all parties would be served through some form of vertical integration. In a commercial context where a monopoly input supplier is selling to a

---

[1] *See generally* Daniel J. Gifford, *Redefining the Antitrust Labor Exemption*, 72 MINN. L. REV. 1379 (1988).

monopoly output producer (as in *Albrecht*) the parties are generally aware of the problem of the double monopoly. If the input supplier is willing to sell only at its own profit-maximizing price (determined without reference to the potential vertical integration which would benefit both parties) and the output producer then determines its own profit-maximizing price, taking the input supplier's price as a given, output will be unduly constrained, price will be excessively high and profits of both parties will be lower than necessary. If the parties integrated their operations, price would be lower, output would be greater and aggregate profits would be increased. Aware of the benefits of vertical integration, the parties are likely either to integrate or to simulate the effects of integration through contractual means, thereby maximizing their joint profits.

When, however, a labor union (as the monopoly input supplier) negotiates with an employer who has power in the product market, there are a variety of factors which impede the labor union and employer from attempting to eliminate the double monopoly effects. First, the labor union does not maximize profits in the way a supplier of other inputs does. The union is, of course, interested in maximizing the welfare of its members but the welfare of its members is not easily identified. If the demand for labor declines as the wage rate rises, then there is a trade-off between higher wages and employment which cannot be resolved by pursuing a policy of attempting to maximize the aggregate return to labor in the way that a monopoly supplier of goods would attempt to maximize its profits. The union's position is complicated, *inter alia,* by the seniority system generally prevalent in American industry. Under that system, the employees with the longest service are the last to be laid off. The result is a built in bias in the membership for trading off the interests of the more recently hired workers for higher wages for the remainder. Other organizational influences may also affect the union's bargaining position. The majority with the greatest seniority is not interested in maximizing labor's aggregate return (which might involve a trade off of wages for employment) but only their own wage rate. Cooperation between the labor union and producers possessing market power in the product market to reduce the effects of the double monopoly is thereby made difficult.

The effects of the double monopoly could be mitigated by the union's accepting significant amounts of compensation in the form of profit-sharing arrangements. Such arrangements would remove the profit-determined component of compensation from marginal costs and would thus exert an expansionary effect on output. Under pressure of foreign competition, some efforts in this direction have begun in the auto and other industries.

None of these American efforts have so far been extended as far as the Japanese have taken them. Japanese workers often receive 30-40% of their compensation in the form of bonuses. *See, e.g.,* JUNICHI GOTO, LABOR IN INTERNATIONAL TRADE THEORY 65 (1990); WILLIAM B. GOULD, JAPAN'S RESHAPING OF AMERICAN LABOR LAW 7 (1984). To the extent that these companies are thus able to adjust compensation in line with their sales, they are better equipped to maintain employment in the downturns of the business cycle. (The fact that Japanese companies pay significant amounts of labor compensation in the form of bonuses also advantages them in international competition.)

When Congress enacted the National Labor Relations Act it necessarily decided that the exercise of monopoly power by labor unions over the labor supply was acceptable social policy, even though that policy results in higher product prices. It is not entirely clear, however, that Congress was aware of the double monopoly effect which occurs in concentrated industries, where employers possess monopoly power themselves. As pointed out above, the result in these industries is that the public is burdened not with a single monopoly, but with the effects of a double monopoly.

The double monopoly effects in such industries could be alleviated to the extent that increases in compensation were diverted to profit sharing rather than to hourly wage compensation. The nonstatutory labor exemption, therefore, could best reconcile the national labor and antitrust policies if the labor exemption were reconceptualized to encourage mitigation of the double monopoly effect. One way of doing this would be to condition the nonstatutory exemption in concentrated industries on collective-bargaining contracts possessing a required component of profit-sharing. Rather than taking such an economic approach to the labor exemption, however, the courts have cast the exemption in terms which are purely doctrinal and which often lack definitive content. Thus, for example, why was the union in *Allen Bradley* held to have participated in an employer conspiracy if the union itself could have bargained individually with each firm for the identical results, as Justice Black's opinion suggested? Why was the agreement over operating hours in *Jewel Tea* intimately connected with hours and working conditions if the hours of work and work rate per butcher could have been agreed upon?

COMMENTARY

Would society be better off if the monopoly power of both unions and employers were constrained? Should mergers of unions, for example, be subjected to antitrust review under § 7 of the Clayton Act? Such an approach is suggested in Robert H. Lande & Richard O. Zerbe, Jr., *Anticonsumer Effects of Union Mergers: An Antitrust Solution,* 46 DUKE L.J. 197 (1996). Suppose the NLRA were amended to permit wage increases only on a showing of productivity increases in the prior year? To achieve balance, should executive compensation be constrained by a ceiling on the deductibility of salaries for federal income tax purposes? *See* I.R.C. § 162(m)(1).

Chapter 17
Standing

A. The Statute

The standing of private parties to sue for damages under the federal antitrust laws is governed by the provisions codified in 15 U.S.C. § 15 (1994). These provisions are the successors to the original provision, enacted as § 4 of the Clayton Act of 1914, ch. 323, 35 Stat. 731. Section 4 of the Clayton Act itself succeeds the earlier standing provisions of the Sherman Act, 26 Stat. 209, 210 § 7 (1890). (In the pages which follow, these provisions will frequently be referred to as § 4 of the Clayton Act.) In its current form, 15 U.S.C. § 15 reads as follows:

> **§ 15. Suits by persons injured**
>
> (a) Amount of recovery; prejudgment interest
>
> Except as provided in subsection (b) of this section, any person who shall be injured in his business or property by reason of anything forbidden in the antitrust laws may sue therefor in any district court of the United States in the district in which the defendant resides or is found or has an agent, without respect to the amount in controversy, and shall recover threefold the damages by him sustained, and the cost of suit, including a reasonable attorney's fee. The court may award under this section, pursuant to a motion by such person promptly made, simple interest on actual damages for the period beginning on the date of service of such person's pleading setting forth a claim under the antitrust laws and ending on the date of judgment, or for any shorter period therein, if the court finds that the award of such interest for such period is just in the circumstances. In determining whether an award of interest under this section for any period is just in the circumstances, the court shall consider only—
>
> (1) whether such person or the opposing party, or either party's representative, made motions or asserted claims or defenses so lacking in merit as to show that such party or representative acted intentionally for delay, or otherwise acted in bad faith;
>
> (2) whether, in the course of the action involved, such person or the opposing party, or either party's representative,

violated any applicable rule, statute, or court order providing for sanctions for dilatory behavior or otherwise providing for expeditious proceedings; and

(3) whether such person or the opposing party, or either party's representative, engaged in conduct primarily for the purpose of delaying the litigation or increasing the cost thereof.

The standing of private parties to sue for injunctive relief under the federal antitrust laws is governed by the provisions codified in 15 U.S.C. § 26 (1994). These provisions were contained in § 16 of the original Clayton Act. In its current form, 15 U.S.C. § 26 reads as follows:

§ 26. Injunctive relief for private parties; exception; costs

Any person, firm, corporation, or association shall be entitled to sue for and have injunctive relief, in any court of the United States having jurisdiction over the parties, against threatened loss or damage by a violation of the antitrust laws, including sections 13, 14, 18, and 19 of this title, when and under the same conditions and principles as injunctive relief against threatened conduct that will cause loss or damage is granted by courts of equity, under the rules governing such proceedings, and upon the execution of proper bond against damages for an injunction improvidently granted and a showing that the danger of irreparable loss or damage is immediate, a preliminary injunction may issue. . . . In any action under this section in which the plaintiff substantially prevails, the court shall award the cost of suit, including a reasonable attorney's fee, to such plaintiff.

NOTE: THE EVOLUTION OF THE LAW GOVERNING ANTITRUST STANDING

At one time, the courts employed a test of standing which was based upon whether the plaintiff was directly (as opposed to indirectly or remotely) injured by the antitrust violation. *E.g., Loeb v. Eastman Kodak Co.*, 183 F. 704 (3d Cir. 1910). Later, some courts adopted a "target area" approach to standing. *E.g., Calderone Enterprises v. United Artists Theatre Circuit, Inc.*, 454 F.2d 1292 (2d Cir. 1971), *cert. denied*, 406 U.S. 930 (1972). Under the target-area approach, a court would inquire whether the plaintiff was a person against whom an antitrust conspiracy or other antitrust violation was aimed. In the 1970s some courts adopted a version of the approach to standing employed under the Administrative Procedure Act: they asked whether the plaintiff was injured in fact and whether the interest which the plaintiff sought to protect is arguably within the zone of interests protected by the relevant antitrust laws. *Malamud v. Sinclair Oil Corp.*, 521 F.2d 1142 (6th Cir. 1975).

In *Associated General Contractors of California, Inc. v. California State Council of Carpenters*, 459 U.S. 519 (1982) (page 913, *infra*), the Court reviewed these various approaches to antitrust standing which had been employed in the past. The Court then attempted to outline the direction that the courts should take in the future on this difficult and complex issue. *Associated General Contractors,* itself, was heavily influenced by two then-recent Supreme Court decisions: *Brunswick Corp. v. Pueblo Bowl-O-Mat, Inc.*, 429 U.S. 477 (1977) (page 891, *infra*) and *Illinois Brick Co. v. Illinois*, 431 U.S. 720 (1977) (page 909, *infra*).

B. In General

Blue Shield of Virginia v. McCready
457 U.S. 465 (1982)

Justice BRENNAN delivered the opinion of the Court.

The antitrust complaint at issue in this case alleges that a group health plan's practice of refusing to reimburse subscribers for psychotherapy performed by clinical psychologists (Ph.D.s), while providing reimbursement for comparable treatment by psychiatrists (M.D.s), was in furtherance of an unlawful conspiracy to restrain competition in the psychotherapy market. The question presented is whether a subscriber who employed the services of a psychologist has standing to maintain an action under § 4 of the Clayton Act based upon the plan's failure to provide reimbursement for the costs of that treatment.

I

From September 1975 until January 1978, respondent Carol McCready was an employee of Prince William County, Va. As part of her compensation, the county provided her with coverage under a prepaid group health plan purchased from petitioner Blue Shield of Virginia (Blue Shield). The plan specifically provided reimbursement for a portion of the cost incurred by subscribers with respect to outpatient treatment for mental and nervous disorders, including psychotherapy. Pursuant to this provision, Blue Shield reimbursed subscribers for psychotherapy provided by psychiatrists. But Blue Shield did not provide reimbursement for the services of psychologists unless the treatment was supervised by and billed through a physician. While a subscriber to the plan, McCready was treated by a clinical psychologist. She submitted claims to Blue Shield for the costs of that treatment, but those claims were routinely denied because they had not been billed through a physician.

In 1978, McCready brought this class action in the United States District Court for the Eastern District of Virginia, on behalf of all Blue Shield subscribers who had incurred costs for psychological services since 1973 but who had not been reimbursed. The complaint alleged that Blue Shield and petitioner Neuropsychiatric Society of Virginia, Inc., had engaged in an unlawful conspiracy in violation of § 1 of the Sherman Act . . . "to exclude and boycott clinical psychologists from receiving compensation under" the Blue Shield plans. McCready further alleged that Blue Shield's failure to reimburse had been in furtherance of the alleged conspiracy, and had caused injury to her business or property for which she was entitled to treble damages and attorney's fees under § 4 of the Clayton Act. . . .

II

Section 4 of the Clayton Act . . . provides a treble-damages remedy to "[a]ny person who shall be injured in his business or property by reason of anything forbidden in the antitrust laws." . . . [T]he lack of restrictive language reflects Congress' "expansive remedial purpose" in enacting § 4: Congress sought to create a private enforcement mechanism that would deter violators and deprive them of the fruits of their illegal actions, and would provide ample compensation to the victims of antitrust violations. . . .

. . . [Yet it] is reasonable to assume that Congress did not intend to allow every person tangentially affected by an antitrust violation to maintain an action to recover threefold damages for the injury to his business or property. . . . In the absence of direct guidance from Congress, and faced with the claim that a particular injury is too remote from the alleged violation to warrant § 4 standing, the courts are thus forced to resort to an analysis no less elusive than that employed traditionally by courts at common law with respect to the matter of "proximate cause." . . . In applying that elusive concept to this statutory action, we look (1) to the physical and economic nexus between the alleged violation and the harm to the plaintiff, and (2), more particularly, to the relationship of the injury alleged with those forms of injury about which Congress was likely to have been concerned in making defendant's conduct unlawful and in providing a private remedy under § 4.

. . . .

We do not think that because the goal of the conspirators was to halt encroachment by psychologists into a market that physicians and psychiatrists sought to preserve for themselves, McCready's injury is rendered "remote." The availability of the § 4 remedy to some person who claims its benefit is not a question of the specific intent of the conspirators. Here the remedy cannot reasonably be restricted to those competitors whom the conspirators hoped to eliminate from the market. McCready claims that she has been the victim of a concerted refusal to pay on the part of Blue Shield, motivated by a desire to deprive psychologists of the patronage of Blue Shield subscribers. Denying reimbursement to subscribers for the cost of treatment was the very means by which it is alleged that Blue Shield sought to achieve its illegal ends. The harm to McCready and her class was clearly foreseeable; indeed, it was a necessary step in effecting the ends of the alleged illegal conspiracy. Where the injury alleged is so integral an aspect of the conspiracy alleged, there can be no question but that the loss was precisely "'the type of loss that the claimed violations . . . would be likely to cause.'" *Brunswick Corp. v. Pueblo Bowl-O-Mat, Inc.*, 429 U.S. at 489, quoting *Zenith Radio Corp. v. Hazeltine Research, Inc.*, 395 U.S. 100, 125 (1969).

Petitioners next argue that even if the § 4 remedy might be available to persons other than the competitors of the conspirators, it is not available to McCready because she was not an economic actor in the market that had been restrained. . . . Here, petitioners contend that that market, for purposes of the alleged conspiracy, is the market in group health care plans. Thus, in petitioners' view, standing to redress the violation alleged in this case is limited to participants in that market—that is, to entities, such as McCready's employer, who were purchasers of group health plans, but not to McCready as a beneficiary of the Blue Shield plan.

Petitioners misconstrue McCready's complaint. . . . [McCready's] claim of injury is premised on a concerted refusal to reimburse under a plan that was, in fact, purchased and retained by her employer for her benefit . . . . As a consumer of psychotherapy services entitled to financial benefits under the Blue Shield plan, we think it clear that McCready was "within that area of the economy . . . endangered by [that] breakdown of competitive conditions" resulting from Blue Shield's selective refusal to reimburse. . . .

McCready charges Blue Shield with a purposefully anticompetitive scheme. She seeks to recover as damages the sums lost to her as the consequence of Blue Shield's attempt to pursue that scheme. She alleges that Blue Shield sought to induce its subscribers into selecting psychiatrists over psychologists for the psychotherapeutic services they required, and that the heart of its scheme was the offer of a Hobson's choice to its subscribers. Those subscribers were compelled to choose between visiting a psychologist and forfeiting reimbursement, or receiving reimbursement by forgoing treatment by the practitioner of their choice. In the latter case, the antitrust injury would have been borne in the first instance by the competitors of the conspirators, and inevitably—though indirectly—by the customers of the competitors in the form of suppressed competition in the psychotherapy market; in the former case, as it happened, the injury was borne directly by the customers of the competitors. McCready did not yield to Blue Shield's coercive pressure, and bore Blue Shield's sanction in the form of an increase in the net cost of her psychologist's services. Although McCready was not a competitor of the conspirators, the injury she suffered was inextricably intertwined with the injury the conspirators sought to inflict on psychologists and the psychotherapy market. In light of the conspiracy here alleged we think that McCready's injury "flows from that which makes defendants' acts unlawful" within the meaning of *Brunswick*, and falls squarely within the area of congressional concern.

. . . [W]e are unable to identify any persuasive rationale upon which McCready might be denied redress under § 4 for the injury she claims. The judgment of the Court of Appeals is

Affirmed.

COMMENTARY

Did the decision in *McCready* follow from the precedent of *Sonotone,* below, holding that consumers have antitrust standing under the "property" term in Clayton § 4? McCready, like Reiter, was a consumer. But because Reiter was an indirect purchaser, she had to show how the manufacturer was responsible for her injury. McCready dealt directly with the insurer, did she not? Was McCready's standing, therefore, easier to establish? Was McCready a purchaser? If the conspiracy had lessened competition in the psychotherapy market, the most directly injured persons would be the psychologists, would they not? Would the psychologists have standing to challenge the alleged conspiracy? Would their patients have such standing also? If successful, would not the alleged conspiracy lead to an increase in the prices charged by psychiatrists? If those increased fees resulted in increased rates for group health insurance policies, who would have paid those increased rates? McCready's employer? to whom? Blue Shield? Who would have standing to complain of the conspiracy's impact on the prices charged by psychiatrists? of resulting increased group health rates?

C. Business and Property

Reiter v. Sonotone Corp.
442 U.S. 330 (1979)

[The District Court's ruling that petitioner could establish standing as a retail customer was reversed by the Court of Appeals for the Eighth Circuit; and the Supreme Court granted *certiorari*.]

Mr. Chief Justice BURGER delivered the opinion of the Court.

. . . .

Petitioner brought a class action on behalf of herself and all persons in the United States who purchased hearing aids manufactured by five corporations, respondents here. Her complaint alleges that respondents have committed a variety of antitrust violations, including vertical and horizontal price fixing. Because of these violations, the complaint alleges, petitioner and the class of persons she seeks to represent have been forced to pay illegally fixed higher prices for the hearing aids and related services they purchased from respondents' retail dealers. . . .

. . . Section 4 of the Clayton Act . . . provides:

> "*Any person* who shall be injured in his business or *property* by reason of *anything* forbidden in the antitrust laws may sue therefor in any district court of the United States . . . without respect to the amount in controversy, and shall recover threefold the damages by him sustained, and the cost of suit, including a reasonable attorney's fee." 15 U.S.C. § 15 (emphasis added).

. . . .

When a commercial enterprise suffers a loss of money it suffers an injury in both its "business" and its "property." But neither term is rendered redundant by recognizing that a consumer not engaged in a "business" enterprise, but rather acquiring goods or services for personal use, is injured in "property" when the price of those goods or services is artificially inflated by reason of the anticompetitive conduct complained of. . . . Congress must have intended to exclude some class of injuries by the phrase "business or property." But it taxes the ordinary meaning of common terms to argue, as respondents do, that a consumer's monetary injury arising directly out of a retail purchase is not comprehended by the natural and usual meaning of the phrase "business or property." We simply give the word "property" the independent significance to which it is entitled in this context. A consumer whose money has been diminished by reason of an antitrust violation has been injured "in his . . . property" within the meaning of § 4.

. . . .

Reversed and remanded.

COMMENTARY

1. From whom did the petitioner and members of the class she was representing purchase their hearing aids? Did they purchase directly from the manufacturers or did they purchase directly from retailers and therefore only indirectly from the manufacturers? Prior to the decision in *Sonotone*, the Court had decided, in *Illinois Brick Co. v. Illinois*, 431 U.S. 720 (1977) (page 909, below), that indirect purchasers lacked standing to assert an antitrust claim against manufacturers who conspired to fix prices. Is *Sonotone* consistent with *Illinois Brick*?

2. Justice Rehnquist, concurring, expressed concern that the Court's decision would "add a substantial volume of litigation to the already strained dockets of the federal courts. . . ." Does the extent of Justice Rehnquist's concern depend upon how the effects of the standing question decided in *Sonotone* are mitigated by application of the *Illinois Brick* doctrine (limiting antitrust injury caused by price fixing to the direct purchasers)? If only initial purchasers were allowed to bring suit against manufacturers which had allegedly conspired to raise prices, how could the issue of consumer standing arise? Why did not the initial purchasers of hearing aids (*i.e.*, the distributors) bring this action?

3. Does the significance of *Sonotone* to a manufacturer depend upon the structure of the manufacturer's distribution system? whether consumer goods are sold to distributors and dealers for resale or whether they are shipped on consignment to retailers? Would consumers be allowed to sue a group of price-fixing manufacturers which distributed through a consignment method through retailers, but not allowed to sue a group of price-fixing manufacturers which sold their goods to distributors and dealers for resale to consumers? Did not the Court in *Sylvania* (Chapter 5, *supra*) express disapproval of legal rules which depend upon such formal distinctions?

4. Even under the doctrine of *Illinois Brick*, consumers would have standing to assert antitrust claims against manufacturers if the manufacturers conspired not only with each other but with retailers as well, would they not?

D. The Concept of "Antitrust Injury"

Brunswick Corp. v. Pueblo Bowl-O-Mat, Inc.

429 U.S. 477 (1977)

[Petitioner Brunswick Corp. was a manufacturer of bowling equipment. In the early 1960s the bowling industry went into a sharp decline, and the petitioner experienced great difficulty in collecting money owed to it by purchasers of its equipment. Accordingly, petitioner began acquiring and operating defaulting bowling centers when their equipment could not be resold and a positive cash flow could be expected from operating the centers. Respondents are three of the 10 bowling centers owned by the Treadway Companies, Inc.; they were independent competitors of bowling centers acquired by the petitioner. The respondents alleged that the petitioner's acquisitions of bowling centers in the markets in which respondents operated constituted violations of § 7 of the Clayton Act.]

Mr. Justice MARSHALL delivered the opinion of the Court.

. . . To establish a § 7 violation, respondents sought to prove that because of its size, petitioner had the capacity to lessen competition in the markets it had entered by driving smaller competitors out of business. To establish damages, respondents attempted to show that had petitioner allowed the defaulting centers to close, respondents' profits would have increased. . . . If the acquisitions here were unlawful, it is because they brought a "deep pocket" parent into a market of "pygmies." Yet respondents' injury—the loss of income that would have accrued had the acquired centers gone bankrupt—bears no relationship to the size of either the acquiring company or its competitors. Respondents would have suffered the identical "loss" but no compensable injury had the acquired centers instead obtained refinancing or been purchased by "shallow pocket" parents . . . . Thus, respondents' injury was not of "the type that the statute was intended to forestall." . . .

But the antitrust laws are not merely indifferent to the injury claimed here. At base, respondents complain that by acquiring the failing centers petitioner preserved competition, thereby depriving respondents of the benefits of increased concentration. The damages respondents obtained are designed to provide them with the profits they would have realized had competition been reduced. The antitrust laws, however, were enacted for "the protection of *competition* not *competitors*." . . . It is inimical to the purposes of these laws to award damages for the type of injury claimed here.

. . . [I]t is quite clear that if respondents were injured, it was not "by reason of anything forbidden in the antitrust laws": while respondents' loss occurred "by reason of" the unlawful acquisitions, it did not occur "by reason of" that which made the acquisitions unlawful.

We therefore hold that the plaintiffs to recover treble damages on account of § 7 violations, they must prove more than injury causally linked to an illegal presence in the market. Plaintiffs must prove *antitrust* injury, which is to say injury of the type the antitrust laws were intended to prevent and that flows from that which makes defendants' acts unlawful. The injury should reflect the anticompetitive effect either of the violation or of anticompetitive acts made possible by the violation. It should, in short, be "the type of loss that the claimed violations . . . would be likely to cause." . . .

The judgment of the Court of Appeals is vacated, and the case is remanded for further proceedings consistent with this opinion.

It is so ordered.

COMMENTARY

1. Was Pueblo adversely affected by Brunswick's acquisitions? If Brunswick's acquisitions violated § 7 of the Clayton Act, then Brunswick's unlawful acts caused Pueblo's injury in the sense that Pueblo's injuries would not have occurred "but for" Brunswick's unlawful acts. The Court's decision here, however, holds that "but for" causation is not enough. The injury to the plaintiff (here Pueblo) has to be "antitrust injury." The Court gave us some general guidelines as to its approach towards defining "antitrust injury" in *Brunswick*: "injury of the type the antitrust laws were intended to prevent and that flows from that which makes defendants' acts unlawful." Later judicial rulings help further to clarify this concept.

Consider the following questions: If Brunswick's acquisitions were illegal under § 7 (*see* Chapter 12, *supra*), what would be the antitrust violation(s) which would have made them illegal? Were these acquisitions vertical ones? If they were illegal, would their legality or illegality be evaluated in terms of foreclosing outlets from suppliers or foreclosing purchasers from sources of supply? How could these concerns be related to Pueblo's claimed injury? What would be the horizontal impact of Brunswick's acquisition? Would the acquisition increase or decrease concentration in bowling facilities in the area in which Pueblo operated? In fact, the acquisition prevented an increase of concentration, did it not? Did the acquisition lessen competition?

2. Could Brunswick's acquisitions be unlawful under § 2 of the Sherman Act because they were preserving excess capacity and thereby discouraging entry into the business of operating bowling alleys? Judge Hand thought that Alcoa had built excess capacity in order to deter entry in to the aluminum smelting business and thus offended the monopolization clause. *See United States v. Aluminum Co. of America, Inc.*, 148 F.2d 416 (2d Cir. 1945) (Chapter 9, *supra*). *See also E.I. du Pont de Nemours & Co.*, 96 F.T.C. 653 (1980) (dealing with an analogous issue under FTCA § 5). What facts would have to be made out, in addition to the preservation of excess capacity, to establish Brunswick's monopolization here? If such an offense could be established, would it be consistent with Pueblo's incurrence of "antitrust injury"?

3. Would you expect that labor unions might be particularly likely to experience injuries as a result of antitrust violations that were not "antitrust injuries"? Why? *See Associated General Contractors of California, Inc. v. California State Council of Carpenters*, 459 U.S. 519 (1982) (page 913, *infra*).

Cargill, Inc. v. Monfort of Colorado, Inc.

479 U.S. 104 (1986)

Justice BRENNAN delivered the opinion of the Court.

Under § 16 of the Clayton Act, 38 Stat. 737, as amended, 15 U.S.C. § 26, private parties "threatened [with] loss or damage by a violation of the antitrust laws" may seek injunctive relief. This case presents two questions: whether a plaintiff seeking relief under § 16 must prove a threat of antitrust injury, and, if so, whether loss or damage due to increased competition constitutes such injury.

I

Respondent Monfort of Colorado, Inc. (Monfort), the plaintiff below, owns and operates three integrated beef-packing plants, that is, plants for both the slaughter of cattle and the fabrication of beef.[1] Monfort operates in both the market for fed cattle (the input market) and the market for fabricated beef (the output market). These markets are highly competitive, and the profit margins of the major beef packers are low. The current markets are a product of two decades of intense competition, during which time packers with modern integrated plants have gradually displaced packers with separate slaughter and fabrication plants.

Monfort is the country's fifth-largest beef packer. Petitioner Excel Corporation (Excel), one of the two defendants below, is the second-largest packer. Excel operates five integrated plants and one fabrication plant. It is a wholly owned subsidiary of Cargill, Inc., the other defendant below, a large privately owned corporation with more than 150 subsidiaries in at least 35 countries.

On June 17, 1983, Excel signed an agreement to acquire the third-largest packer in the market, Spencer Beef, a division of the Land O'Lakes agricultural cooperative. Spencer Beef owned two integrated plants and one slaughtering plant. After the acquisition, Excel would still be the second-largest packer, but would command a market share almost equal to that of the largest packer, IBP, Inc. (IBP).[2]

Monfort brought an action under § 16 of the Clayton Act, 15 U.S.C. § 26, to enjoin the prospective merger. Its complaint alleged that the acquisition would "violat[e] Section 7 of the Clayton Act because the effect of the proposed acquisition may be substantially to lessen competition or tend to create a monopoly in several different ways . . . ." . . . Monfort described the injury that it allegedly would suffer in this way:

> "(f) Impairment of plaintiff's ability to compete. The proposed acquisition will result in a concentration of economic power in the relevant markets which threatens Monfort's supply of fed cattle and its ability to compete in the boxed beef market." . . .

. . . .

II

This case requires us to decide, at the outset, a question we have not previously addressed: whether a private plaintiff seeking an injunction under § 16 of the Clayton Act must show a threat of antitrust injury. To decide the question, we must look first to the source of the antitrust injury requirement, which lies in a related provision of the Clayton Act, § 4, 15 U.S.C. § 15.

Like § 16, § 4 provides a vehicle for private enforcement of the antitrust laws. . . . It is plain that § 16 and § 4 do differ in various ways. For example, § 4 requires a plaintiff to show actual injury, but § 16 requires a showing only of "threatened" loss or damage; similarly, § 4 requires a showing of injury to "business or property". . . while § 16 contains no

---

1 As the District Court explained, "'[f]abrication' is the process whereby the carcass is broken down into either whole cuts (referred to as 'primals,' 'subprimals' and 'portions') or ground beef." 591 F. Supp. 683, 690 (D. Colo.1983). Whole cuts that are then vacuum packed before shipment are called "boxed beef"; the District Court found that "80% of all beef received at the retail supermarket level and at the hotel, restaurant, and institutional ('HRI') level" is boxed beef. *Ibid.*

2 The District Court relied on the testimony of one of Monfort's witnesses in determining market share. . . . According to this testimony, Monfort's share of the cattle slaughter market was 5.5%, Excel's share was 13.3%, and IBP's was 24.4%. . . . Monfort's share of the production market was 5.7%, Excel's share was 14.1%, and IBP's share was 27.3%. After the merger, Excel's share of each market would increase to 20.4%. . . .

such limitation.[6] Although these differences do affect the nature of the injury cognizable under each section, the lower courts, including the courts below, have found that under both § 16 and § 4 the plaintiff must still allege an injury of the type the antitrust laws were designed to prevent. We agree.

The wording concerning the relationship of the injury to the violation of the antitrust laws in each section is comparable. Section 4 requires proof of injury "by reason of anything forbidden in the antitrust laws"; § 16 requires proof of "threatened loss or damage by a violation of the antitrust laws." It would be anomalous, we think, to read the Clayton Act to authorize a private plaintiff to secure an injunction against a threatened injury for which he would not be entitled to compensation if the injury actually occurred.

. . . Sections 4 and 16 are thus best understood as providing complementary remedies for a single set of injuries. Accordingly, we conclude that in order to seek injunctive relief under § 16, a private plaintiff must allege threatened loss or damage "of the type the antitrust laws were designed to prevent and that flows from that which makes defendants' acts unlawful." *Brunswick*, 429 U.S. at 489. We therefore turn to the question whether the proposed merger in this case threatened respondent with antitrust injury.

III

Initially, we confront the problem of determining what Monfort alleged the source of its injury to be. . . . Monfort alleged that after the merger, Excel would attempt to increase its market share at the expense of smaller rivals, such as Monfort. To that end, Monfort claimed, Excel would bid up the price it would pay for cattle, and reduce the price at which it sold boxed beef. Although such a strategy, which Monfort labeled a "price-cost squeeze," would reduce Excel's profits, Excel's parent corporation had the financial reserves to enable Excel to pursue such a strategy. Eventually, according to Monfort, smaller competitors lacking significant reserves and unable to match Excel's prices would be driven from the market; at this point Excel would raise the price of its boxed beef to supracompetitive levels, and would more than recoup the profits it lost during the initial phase. . . .

A

Monfort's first claim is that after the merger, Excel would lower its prices to some level at or slightly above its costs in order to compete with other packers for market share. Excel would be in a position to do this because of the multiplant efficiencies its acquisition of Spencer would provide. . . . To remain competitive, Monfort would have to lower its prices; as a result, Monfort would suffer a loss in profitability, but would not be driven out of business.[10] The question is whether Monfort's loss of profits in such circumstances constitutes antitrust injury.

To resolve the question, we look again to *Brunswick v. Pueblo Bowl-O-Mat, supra.* . . . *Brunswick* holds that the antitrust laws do not require the courts to protect small busi-

---

[6] Standing analysis under § 16 will not always be identical to standing analysis under § 4. For example, the difference in the remedy each section provides means that certain considerations relevant to a determination of standing under § 4 are not relevant under § 16. . . . Thus, because standing under § 16 raises no threat of multiple lawsuits or duplicative recoveries, some of the factors other than antitrust injury that are appropriate to a determination of standing under § 4 are not relevant under § 16.

[10] In this case, Monfort has conceded that its viability would not be threatened by Excel's decision to lower prices: "Because Monfort's operations were as efficient as those of Excel, only below-cost pricing could remove Monfort as an obstacle." . . .

nesses from the loss of profits due to continued competition, but only against the loss of profits from practices forbidden by the antitrust laws. The kind of competition that Monfort alleges here, competition for increased market share, is not activity forbidden by the antitrust laws. It is simply, as petitioners claim, vigorous competition. To hold that the antitrust laws protect competitors from the loss of profits due to such price competition would, in effect, render illegal any decision by a firm to cut prices in order to increase market share. The antitrust laws require no such perverse result, for "[i]t is in the interest of competition to permit dominant firms to engage in vigorous competition, including price competition." *Arthur S. Langenderfer, Inc. v. S.E. Johnson Co.*, 729 F.2d 1050, 1057 (6th Cir.), *cert. denied*, 469 U.S. 1036 (1984). The logic of *Brunswick* compels the conclusion that the threat of loss of profits due to possible price competition following a merger does not constitute a threat of antitrust injury.

B

The second theory of injury argued here is that after the merger Excel would attempt to drive Monfort out of business by engaging in sustained predatory pricing. Predatory pricing may be defined as pricing below an appropriate measure of cost for the purpose of eliminating competitors in the short run and reducing competition in the long run. . . .

Although the Court of Appeals did not explicitly define what it meant by predatory pricing, two interpretations are plausible. First, the court can be understood to mean that Monfort's allegation of losses from the above-cost "price-cost squeeze" was equivalent to an allegation of injury from predatory conduct. If this is the proper interpretation, then the court's judgment is clearly erroneous because (a) Monfort made no allegation that Excel would act with predatory intent after the merger, and (b) price competition is not predatory activity, for the reasons discussed in Part III-A, *supra*.

Second, the Court of Appeals can be understood to mean that Monfort had shown a credible threat of injury from below-cost pricing. To the extent the judgment rests on this ground, however, it must also be reversed, because Monfort did not allege injury from below-cost pricing before the District Court. . . .

IV

In its *amicus* brief, the United States argues that the "danger of allowing a competitor to challenge an acquisition on the basis of necessarily speculative claims of post-acquisition predatory pricing far outweighs the danger that any anticompetitive merger will go unchallenged." . . . On this basis, the United States invites the Court to adopt in effect a *per se* rule "denying competitors standing to challenge acquisitions on the basis of predatory pricing theories." . . .

We decline the invitation. As the foregoing discussion makes plain, . . . predatory pricing is an anticompetitive practice forbidden by the antitrust laws. While firms may engage in the practice only infrequently, there is ample evidence suggesting that the practice does occur. . . .

V

We hold that a plaintiff seeking injunctive relief under § 16 of the Clayton Act must show a threat of antitrust injury, and that a showing of loss or damage due merely to increased competition does not constitute such injury. . . . Because respondent has therefore failed to make the showing § 16 requires, we need not reach the question whether the proposed merger violates § 7. The judgment of the Court of Appeals is reversed, and the case is remanded for further proceedings consistent with this opinion.

It is so ordered.

COMMENTARY

1. How would Montfort be injured as a result of Excel's acquisition? Do you understand Montfort's theory of a "price-cost squeeze"? Did the Court deal adequately with this theory? In so far as the price-cost squeeze depends upon Excel reducing its price to some above-cost level, that behavior should be treated as procompetitive, should it not?

2. How would Excel "bid up" the price of beef? Would it buy more beef than it needed? What would it do with the excess? If Excel used the beef which it purchased, how could its purchases be deemed anticompetitive behavior?

3. This case illustrates the difficulty faced by a rival in attempting to halt a merger. The rival must establish "antitrust injury" in order to have standing. Yet the likely impact of the merger is either (a) to enhance the efficiencies of the merging firms; or (b) to facilitate the exercise of market power by the merging firms. If the merger enhances the efficiencies of the merging firms, the merger is procompetitive. Conversely, if the merger facilitates the exercise of market power by the merging firms, enabling them to raise prices above the competitive level, then the rival firm will share in the monopoly profits which are now obtainable in the industry. In the latter circumstance, the rival is not injured at all. In the former circumstance, the rival is injured because it must compete with more efficient rivals. That injury is not "antitrust injury."

4. This case goes a long way towards denying rivals standing to challenge mergers and acquisitions. As the opinion makes clear, a rival challenging a merger or acquisition must establish that the merger or acquisition is designed to facilitate post-acquisition predatory behavior. The Justice Department thought that the likelihood of such an event was too small to be recognized at all, but the Court declined to adopt the *per se* rule against competitor standing which the Department sought. What kind of evidence would a rival have to collect in order to establish standing to challenge the merger of two rivals as unlawful under the antitrust laws?

5. Note here that the antitrust injury concept is applicable to private suits for injunctions under § 16 as well as to private actions for damages under § 4.

E. Antitrust Standing in Hostile Takeovers

Consolidated Gold Fields PLC v. Minorco, S.A.

871 F.2d 252 (2d Cir.),
cert. dismissed, 492 U.S. 939 (1989)

JON O. NEWMAN, Circuit Judge:

The primary issue on this appeal is whether the target of a takeover and entities controlled by a target can demonstrate a threat of "antitrust injury" sufficient to confer standing to seek injunctive relief under section 16 of the Clayton Act against a takeover alleged to violate section 7 of the Act . . . .

We conclude that all the plaintiffs in this case—the target as well as the target-controlled entities—have demonstrated a threat of "antitrust injury" sufficient to warrant the issuance of a preliminary injunction. We therefore affirm the District Court's grant of injunctive relief under section 16 . . . .

Background

A. The Parties

Gold Fields is a British corporation with significant holdings in the United States. It is engaged primarily in the exploration, mining, and sale of natural resources, especially gold. Half of Gold Fields' $2.4 billion in assets are located in the United States. Gold Fields wholly owns GFMC, a Delaware corporation headquartered in New York with gold mining operations in California and Nevada. The crown jewel of Gold Fields' assets is its 49.3% stake in Newmont, a Delaware corporation headquartered in New York. Newmont, in turn, owns 90% of Newmont Gold, the largest gold producer in the United States. In addition to these American interests, Gold Fields has significant holdings in Australian gold mining operations, as well as a 38% ownership interest in Gold Fields of South Africa Limited, the second largest gold producer in South Africa. Gold Fields and its associated companies account for 12% of the western world's gold production, making it the second largest gold producer in the non-communist world.

Minorco is a Luxembourg corporation, whose principal assets are shareholdings in companies engaged in natural resource production and exploration, including a 29.9% interest in Gold Fields. Minorco is controlled to a large extent by co-defendants Anglo, a South African corporation, which owns 39.1% of Minorco, and De Beers, also a South African corporation, which owns 21% of Minorco. The Oppenheimer family of South Africa owns 7% of Minorco. Anglo has extensive gold mining operations in South Africa, as does the Oppenheimer family, which allegedly controls Anglo, De Beers, and Minorco. In addition to ownership interests in the three defendant companies, the Oppenheimer family has a number of its members and close associates on the boards of the companies. Considered together, the Minorco group is the largest producer of gold in the non-communist world, accounting for 20.3% of all gold production in the western world.

B. The Tender Offer

In October 1988, Minorco commenced its offer for the 70% of Gold Fields' stock it does not already own. Of the 213,450,000 Gold Fields shares outstanding, approximately 5,300,000 (2.5%) are held by United States residents. Of these shares, approximately

50,000 shares are held directly by residents, 3.1 million shares are held indirectly through nominee accounts in the United Kingdom, and about 2.15 million shares are owned through the ownership of American Depository Receipts (ADR's), documents that indicate ownership by an American of a specific number of shares in a foreign corporation held of record by a United States depository bank. . . .

1. *Likelihood of Success.* The District Court concluded that the proposed acquisition would substantially lessen competition in the non-communist gold market because it involved a combination of entities holding market shares of 20.3% (Minorco) and 12% (Gold Fields). However, the District Court determined that only two of the plaintiffs—Newmont and Newmont Gold—could demonstrate that the resulting post-acquisition entity threatened them with "antitrust injury." In order to obtain injunctive relief under section 16, plaintiffs must show a threat of "antitrust injury" . . . that is, injury "of the type the antitrust laws were designed to prevent and that flows from that which makes defendants' acts unlawful." . . . Applying the principles set forth in *Cargill*, the District Court granted standing to Newmont and Newmont Gold but denied standing to Gold Fields and GFMC.

a. *Standing.* Newmont and Newmont Gold contend that once the takeover is complete, Anglo and the Oppenheimer family, through their control of Gold Fields' 49.3% ownership in Newmont, would attempt to shut down the company. In essence, Newmont's claim is that its ability to compete in the marketplace will be reduced by anticompetitive influence, exercised from inside its own boardroom. The factual basis for this claim is that production costs in South Africa, where Anglo has its mines, are rapidly rising and considerably higher than those in the United States, where Newmont and Newmont Gold have their mines. The contention, based on these facts, is that after the acquisition Minorco, fearing the day when gold mining in South Africa will become unprofitable, would maximize its profits by concentrating in the short run on South African gold production and use its interests in Gold Fields and Newmont to limit production outside of South Africa. Anglo, it is contended, has an added incentive to have Minorco pursue this policy because its interest in South African mines and hence its share of profits on gold from those mines is much greater than its interest and hence share of profits will be in non-South African gold mined after the acquisition. Anglo thus would have an incentive, the District Court concluded, to limit production at the more efficient non-South African mines within the Gold Fields group, including the Newmont companies. Anglo, through Minorco, would cause Newmont to restrict its output, thereby reducing competition in the non-communist gold market.

We agree with the District Court that Newmont and Newmont Gold have demonstrated a threat of "antitrust injury." . . . In this case . . . Newmont contends that it would suffer reduced profits because the takeover will enable outside corporate forces to cause it to restrain its own competitiveness and thereby reduce competition in the relevant market. Newmont's threatened injury is precisely the type that the antitrust laws were designed to protect against. . . .

The question of whether the target itself, Gold Fields, and its subsidiary GFMC, have standing to seek injunctive relief under section 16 is a thornier problem. Some courts have held that target companies lack standing under the antitrust laws. . . . These cases subscribe to the theory that a target cannot claim "antitrust injury" because after a takeover it will become "part of the very entity that it claims will have a supercompetitive advantage," and it therefore suffers no antitrust harm." . . . A number of commentators support this view. *See, e.g.*, II P. AREEDA & H. HOVENKAMP, ANTITRUST LAW ¶ 340.2i, at 368-70 (Supp.1988); Easterbrook & Fischel, *Antitrust Suits by Targets of Tender Offers*, 80 MICH. L. REV. 1155 (1982).

This Circuit has previously upheld target standing to challenge takeovers alleged to violate section 7, and we reaffirm that position today. In our view, Gold Fields has demonstrated a threat of "antitrust injury." If the acquisition is permitted to go forward, Gold Fields will lose its ability to compete independently in the gold production market. Its wholly owned United States mining subsidiary, GFMC, is threatened with curtailment of its production, much like Newmont. Surely Gold Fields' loss of independence is causally linked to the injury occurring in the marketplace, where the acquisition threatens to diminish competitive forces. Though what happens to Gold Fields and what happens to competition may not be precisely the same type of injury, there is a common element in that the independent existence of a major competitor is being eliminated.[5] It is not a sufficient answer to say that even though competition is diminished, Gold Fields is not injured because of its absorption into the Minorco group. The enlarged entity that emerges from the takeover may benefit from the acquisition, but Gold Fields will have lost one of the vital components of competition—the power of independent decision-making as to price and output. It is hard to imagine an injury to competition more clearly "of the type the antitrust laws were intended to prevent," *Brunswick Corp. v. Pueblo Bowl-O-Mat, Inc.*, *supra*, 429 U.S. at 489, 97 S. Ct. at 697, than the elimination of a major competitor's power to determine its prices and output. It is precisely the loss of this power that makes a section 1 conspiracy so pernicious. . . . For this reason, a member of a section 1 conspiracy has standing to challenge the restraint upon its freedom to compete, even though, in the long run, it may enjoy the benefits of the cartel. . . .

It is possible, of course, that Gold Fields, if it remains a distinct corporation within the enlarged Minorco combination, will ultimately derive some economic benefit from the enhanced power of its corporate parent. But Gold Fields is entitled to prefer to take its chances on its capacity to prosper as an independent entity. Whether in the long run more profits will enter its corporate treasury as an independent company than as a subsidiary of Minorco is a speculative matter that need not concern us. The antitrust laws ensure the right to compete. That is what Gold Fields wishes to do, and that is what it will not be able to do if the threatened takeover succeeds.

Nor is it any of our concern whether the motivation for Gold Fields' suit is to protect competition or the job security of its senior management. We recognize that for a variety of reasons target companies may try to find refuge in the antitrust laws to fend off unwanted suitors . . . . But whether Gold Fields has standing turns on whether what it is about to lose is an injury of the type the antitrust laws were intended to prevent, not on why Gold Fields has decided to complain of this injury.

In granting standing to Gold Fields and GFMC, we rely on our pre-*Cargill* decision in *Grumman Corp. v. LTV Corp.*, 665 F.2d 10 (2d Cir.1981). In that case, Grumman sought injunctive relief to prevent an unwanted suitor from executing a tender offer for all of Grumman's shares. We affirmed the grant of a preliminary injunction, noting:

> If the effect of a proposed takeover may be substantially to lessen competition, the target company is entitled to fend off its suitor.
>
> . . . .

---

[5] The dissenting opinion of Judge Altimari points out that the injury complained of by Gold Fields would occur even if the total market share of the combining corporations were only two per cent. If suit were brought on such insubstantial facts, the target would still have standing to claim that it was injured by a section 7 violation, but it would lose on the merits, probably for failure to state a claim and surely on summary judgment. A litigant need not have a winning claim to have standing.

> If free to combine, two competitors might be expected to prefer the advantages of diminished competition. But in reality it is only the resulting entity that would enjoy such advantages. The target company is entitled under § 16 to preserve its separate existence as a competitor.

. . . A number of other courts have granted standing to targets and have either explicitly or implicitly endorsed the Grumman analysis. . . .

The District Court acknowledged the *Grumman* analysis but held that *Cargill* had weakened *Grumman*'s precedential value. In particular, the District Court noted that in *Grumman* we had acknowledged the view that "the inquiry in a suit under § 16 is not as narrowly focused as in a suit for damages under § 4." . . . *Cargill* emphasized that antitrust injury is an element of suits under both sections 16 and 4, though the Court acknowledged some differences in the standing analysis under these provisions.[6] As indicated above, however, we believe that the injury of which Gold Fields complains is antitrust injury. Moreover, the denial of standing to the plaintiff in *Cargill* does not require a similar result here. . . . [Contrary to *Cargill*] [o]ur case involves a threat of decreased competition and threatens a target with elimination as an independent competitor.

We note finally that if we fail to recognize target standing, we would substantially impair enforcement of the antitrust laws to protect against anticompetitive takeovers. The government, with its limited resources, cannot be relied upon as the sole initiator of enforcement actions. That is why Congress authorized private enforcement of the antitrust laws. . . . In the enforcement of section 7's proscription against anticompetitive acquisitions, non-target competitors claiming standing face the substantial barriers of proof erected by *Cargill*. Consumers are unlikely to face the prospect of suffering a sufficient amount of damage to justify the cost of seeking a pre-acquisition injunction. The target of a proposed takeover has the most immediate interest in preserving its independence as a competitor in the market.

For all these reasons, we hold that Gold Fields and GFMC have standing, along with Newmont and Newmont Gold, to seek relief under section 16.

. . . .

---

6 Although the Supreme Court requires a showing of "antitrust injury" in both injunction and damage cases, it has specifically said that "standing analysis under § 16 will not always be identical to standing analysis under § 4." *Cargill v. Monfort of Colorado, Inc., supra*, 479 U.S. at 111 n.6. Since section 4 allows for treble-damage recovery, courts will generally be more circumspect about granting relief: "In order to protect against multiple lawsuits and duplicative recoveries, courts should examine other factors in addition to antitrust injury, such as the potential for duplicative recovery, the complexity of apportioning damages, and the existence of other parties that have been more directly harmed, to determine whether a party is a proper plaintiff under § 4." *Id.*; *see also Associated General Contractors of California, Inc. v. Carpenters*, 459 U.S. 519, 544-45 (1983). Conversely, since relief is equitable under section 16 and "one injunction is as effective as 100," *Cargill v. Monfort of Colorado, Inc., supra*, 479 U.S. at 111 n.6 (quoting *Hawaii v. Standard Oil Co.*, 405 U.S. 251, 261 (1972)), these other factors relevant to section 4 standing analysis "are not relevant under § 16." *Id.* Thus *Cargill* supports the proposition that standing analysis under section 16 is still less rigorous than that under section 4. We therefore do not read *Cargill* to have weakened the Court's prior holding that section 16 is imbued with a special public policy dimension: Section 16 should be construed and applied with this purpose [enforcing the antitrust laws] in mind, and with the knowledge that the remedy it affords, like other equitable remedies, is flexible and capable of nice "adjustment and reconciliation between the public interest and private needs as well as between competing private claims." *Hecht Co. v. Bowles*, 321 U.S. 321, 329-30 (1944). Its availability should be "conditioned by the necessities of the public interest which Congress has sought to protect." *Id.* at 330. *Zenith Radio Corp. v. Hazeltine Research*, 395 U.S. 100, 131 (1969).

COMMENTARY

1. Did the court's decision further antitrust policy objectives? Was its decision consistent with *Cargill*?

2. Hostile takeovers are widely believed to constitute a mechanism for removing inefficient management, who are often adept at controlling the board of directors and insulating themselves from effective stockholder control. When management fails to exploit fully the profitmaking potential of corporate assets, that poor performance is reflected in the price at which the stock trades in the securities markets. Other corporations or investors who believe that they could produce higher profits with those assets then offer an appropriate price for the shares, a price which reflects their own confidence of the potential value of the corporate assets.

Does *Consolidated Gold Fields* provide a means for an entrenched board and its management to use the antitrust laws as a shield from an efficiency-enhancing takeover? Or do the facts of *Consolidated Gold Fields* significantly limit its use as a standing precedent in the takeover context? Would a target corporation have standing under *Consolidated Gold Fields* to oppose its acquisition on the ground that the acquisition would significantly increase concentration in the industry? Why should such a target corporation have standing while a competitor corporation (not a party to the acquisition) does not?

3. Other courts have considered and rejected the approach of *Consolidated Gold Fields*. Thus the Fifth Circuit in *Anago, Inc. v. Technol Medical Products, Inc.*, 976 F.2d 248 (5th Cir. 1992), expressly refused to follow the Second Circuit's holding in *Consolidated Gold Fields*. In *Anago, Inc.*, the Fifth Circuit stated:

> First, we are concerned that the Second Circuit's emphasis on a causal relationship between the loss of independence and the alleged antitrust violation does not comport with Supreme Court precedent. As the Court has stated, a plaintiff "must prove more than injury causally linked to an illegal presence in the market" [citing *Brunswick*].
>
> Second, we are not convinced, as is the Second Circuit, that the loss of independent decision making is the type of injury meant to be prevented by the antitrust laws. . . .
>
> Proof that a plaintiff will be adversely affected by the merger itself will not suffice in this Court, unless the injuries are related to the anticompetitive effects of the merger. Although Anago presented evidence that the merger will have anticompetitive effects, such as higher prices and decreased competition, it did not show that either of these effects will cause it injury. In fact, Anago will suffer a loss of independence whether or not its takeover violates antitrust principles. Moreover, once the takeover is complete, Anago and its shareholders are likely to benefit from any increased prices or decreased competition that might result.

976 F.2d at 251. *Accord Moore Corp. v. Wallace Computer Services, Inc.*, 907 F. Supp. 1545, 1567 (D. Del. 1995).

F. Standing of a Competitor to Complain of Maximum Price Fixing Agreements

Atlantic Richfield Co. v. USA Petroleum Co.
495 U.S. 328 (1990)

Justice BRENNAN delivered the opinion of the Court.

This case presents the question whether a firm incurs an "injury" within the meaning of the antitrust laws when it loses sales to a competitor charging nonpredatory prices pursuant to a vertical, maximum price-fixing scheme. We hold that such a firm does not suffer an "antitrust injury" and that it therefore cannot bring suit under § 4 of the Clayton Act. . . .

I

Respondent USA Petroleum Company (USA) sued petitioner Atlantic Richfield Company (ARCO) in the United States District Court for the Central District of California, alleging the existence of a vertical, maximum price-fixing agreement prohibited by § 1 of the Sherman Act. . . . Petitioner ARCO is an integrated oil company that, *inter alia*, markets gasoline in the western United States. It sells gasoline to consumers both directly through its own stations and indirectly through ARCO-brand dealers. Respondent USA is an independent retail marketer of gasoline which, like other independents, buys gasoline from major petroleum companies for resale under its own brand name. Respondent competes directly with ARCO dealers at the retail level. Respondent's outlets typically are low-overhead, high-volume "discount" stations that charge less than stations selling equivalent quality gasoline under major brand names.

In early 1982, petitioner ARCO adopted a new marketing strategy in order to compete more effectively with discount independents such as respondent. Petitioner encouraged its dealers to match the retail gasoline prices offered by independents in various ways; petitioner made available to its dealers and distributors such short-term discounts as "temporary competitive allowances" and "temporary volume allowances," and it reduced its dealers' costs by, for example, eliminating credit-card sales. ARCO's strategy increased its sales and market share.

In its amended complaint, respondent USA charged that ARCO engaged in "direct head-to-head competition with discounters" and "drastically lowered its prices and in other ways sought to appeal to price-conscious consumers." . . . Respondent asserted that petitioner conspired with retail service stations selling ARCO brand gasoline to fix prices at below-market levels: "ARCO and its co-conspirators have organized a resale price maintenance scheme, as a direct result of which competition that would otherwise exist among ARCO-branded dealers has been eliminated by agreement, and the retail price of ARCO-branded gasoline has been fixed, stabilized and maintained at artificially low and uncompetitive levels." . . . Respondent alleged that petitioner "has solicited its dealers and distributors to participate or acquiesce in the conspiracy and has used threats, intimidation and coercion to secure compliance with its terms." . . . According to respondent, this conspiracy drove many independent gasoline dealers in California out of business. . . . Count one of the amended complaint charged that petitioner's vertical, maximum price-fixing scheme constituted an agreement in restraint of trade and thus violated § 1 of the Sherman Act. . . .

The District Court granted summary judgment for ARCO on the § 1 claim. The court stated that "[e]ven assuming that [respondent USA] can establish a vertical conspiracy to maintain low prices, [respondent] cannot satisfy the 'antitrust injury' requirement of Clayton Act § 4, without showing such prices to be predatory." . . . The court then concluded that respondent could make no such showing of predatory pricing because, given petitioner's market share and the ease of entry into the market, petitioner was in no position to exercise market power.

A divided panel of the Court of Appeals for the Ninth Circuit reversed. . . . The court reasoned that any form of price-fixing contravenes Congress' intent that "market forces alone determine what goods and services are offered, at what price these goods and services are sold, and whether particular sellers succeed or fail." . . . The court believed that the key inquiry in determining whether respondent suffered an "antitrust injury" was whether its losses "resulted from a disruption . . . in the . . . market caused by the . . . antitrust violation." . . .

We granted *certiorari*. . . .

II

A private plaintiff may not recover damages under § 4 of the Clayton Act merely by showing "injury causally linked to an illegal presence in the market." *Brunswick Corp. v. Pueblo Bowl-O-Mat, Inc.*, 429 U.S. 477, 489 (1977). Instead, a plaintiff must prove the existence of "antitrust injury, which is to say injury of the type the antitrust laws were intended to prevent and that flows from that which makes defendants' acts unlawful." . . .

Respondent argues that, as a competitor, it can show antitrust injury from a vertical conspiracy to fix maximum prices that is unlawful under § 1 of the Sherman Act, even if the prices were set above predatory levels. In addition, respondent maintains that any loss flowing from a *per se* violation of § 1 automatically satisfies the antitrust injury requirement. We reject both contentions and hold that respondent has failed to meet the antitrust injury test in this case. We therefore reverse the judgment of the Court of Appeals.

A

In *Albrecht v. Herald Co.*, 390 U.S. 145 (1968) [overruled, *State Oil Co. v. Khan,* 66 U.S.L.W. (4001) (Nov. 4, 1997)—Eds.], we found that a vertical, maximum price-fixing scheme was unlawful *per se* under § 1 of the Sherman Act because it threatened to inhibit vigorous competition by the dealers bound by it and because it threatened to become a minimum price-fixing scheme.[5] . . . But in *Albrecht* we held such an agreement *per se* unlawful because of its potential effects on dealers and consumers, not because of its effect on *competitors*. Respondent's asserted injury as a competitor does not resemble any of the potential dangers described in *Albrecht*.[6] For example, if a vertical agreement fixes "[m]axi-

---

[5] We assume, arguendo, that *Albrecht* correctly held that vertical, maximum price-fixing is subject to the *per se* rule.

[6] *Albrecht* is the only case in which the Court has confronted an unadulterated vertical, maximum price-fixing arrangement. In *Kiefer-Stewart Co. v. Joseph E. Seagram & Sons, Inc.*, 340 U.S. 211, 213 (1951), we also suggested that such an arrangement was illegal because it restricted vigorous competition among dealers. The restraint in *Kiefer-Stewart* had an additional horizontal component, however, *see Arizona v. Maricopa County Medical Society*, 457 U.S. 332, 348, n.18 (1982), since the agreement was between two suppliers that had agreed to sell liquor only to wholesalers adhering to "maximum prices above which the wholesalers could not resell." *Kiefer-Stewart, supra*, 340 U.S. at 212.

mum prices . . . too low for the dealer to furnish services" desired by consumers, or in such a way as to channel business to large distributors, . . . then a firm dealing in a competing brand would not be harmed. Respondent was benefitted rather than harmed if petitioner's pricing policies restricted ARCO sales to a few large dealers or prevented petitioner's dealers from offering services desired by consumers such as credit card sales. Even if the maximum price agreement ultimately had acquired all of the attributes of a minimum price-fixing scheme, respondent still would not have suffered antitrust injury because higher ARCO prices would have worked to USA's advantage. . . . When a firm, or even a group of firms adhering to a vertical agreement, lowers prices but maintains them above predatory levels, the business lost by rivals cannot be viewed as an "anticompetitive" consequence of the claimed violation. A firm complaining about the harm it suffers from nonpredatory price competition "is really claiming that it [is] unable to raise prices." . . . This is not antitrust injury; indeed, "cutting prices in order to increase business often is the very essence of competition." . . .

Respondent further argues that it is inappropriate to require a showing of predatory pricing before antitrust injury can be established when the asserted antitrust violation is an agreement in restraint of trade illegal under § 1 of the Sherman Act . . . .

We reject respondent's argument. Although a vertical, maximum price-fixing agreement is unlawful under § 1 of the Sherman Act, it does not cause a competitor antitrust injury unless it results in predatory pricing. Antitrust injury does not arise for purposes of § 4 of the Clayton Act . . . until a private party is adversely affected by an *anticompetitive* aspect of the defendant's conduct, *see Brunswick*, 429 U.S. at 487; in the context of pricing practices, only predatory pricing has the requisite anticompetitive effect. . . .

B

We also reject respondent's suggestion that no antitrust injury need be shown where a *per se* violation is involved. The *per se* rule is a method of determining whether § 1 of the Sherman Act has been violated, but it does not indicate whether a private plaintiff has suffered antitrust injury and thus whether he may recover damages under § 4 of the Clayton Act. . . .

The . . . antitrust injury requirement . . . ensures that the harm claimed by the plaintiff corresponds to the rationale for finding a violation of the antitrust laws in the first place, and it prevents losses that stem from competition from supporting suits by private plaintiffs for either damages or equitable relief. Actions *per se* unlawful under the antitrust laws may nonetheless have some procompetitive effects, and private parties might suffer losses therefrom. . . . Conduct in violation of the antitrust laws may have three effects, often interwoven: in some respects the conduct may reduce competition, in other respects it may increase competition, and in still other respects effects may be neutral as to competition. The antitrust injury requirement ensures that a plaintiff can recover only if the loss stems from an competition-reducing aspect or effect of the defendant's behavior. The need for this showing is at least as great under the *per se* rule as under the rule of reason. Indeed, insofar as the *per se* rule permits the prohibition of efficient practices in the name of simplicity, the need for the antitrust injury requirement is underscored. . . .

C

. . . .

Respondent's injury, moreover, is not "inextricably intertwined" with the antitrust injury that a dealer would suffer, *McCready*, 457 U.S. at 484, and thus does not militate in favor of permitting respondent to sue on behalf of petitioner's dealers. A competitor is not injured by the *anticompetitive* effects of vertical, maximum price-fixing, . . . and does not have any incentive to vindicate the legitimate interests of a rival's dealer. *See* Easterbrook, *The Limits of Antitrust*, 63 TEXAS L. REV. 1, 33-39 (1984). A competitor will not bring suit to protect the dealer against a maximum price that is set too low, inasmuch as the competitor would *benefit* from such a situation. Instead, a competitor will be motivated to bring suit only when the vertical restraint promotes interbrand competition between the competitor and the dealer subject to the restraint. . . . . In short, a competitor will be injured and hence motivated to sue only when a vertical, maximum price-fixing arrangement has a *procompetitive* impact on the market. Therefore, providing the competitor a cause of action would not protect the rights of dealers and consumers under the antitrust laws.

III

Respondent has failed to demonstrate that it has suffered any antitrust injury. The allegation of a *per se* violation does not obviate the need to satisfy this test. The judgment of the Court of Appeals is reversed, and the case is remanded for proceedings consistent with this opinion.

It is so ordered.

COMMENTARY

1. Was USA Petroleum injured by ARCO's vertical maximum price-fixing agreements? How? USA Petroleum is claiming that the competition of ARCO dealers forced it to sell at lower levels than it otherwise would, is it not? Is this the kind of injury that the antitrust laws were designed to prevent? USA Petroleum is essentially claiming injury as a result of too much price competition, is it not? Isn't this similar to the kind of injury of which Pueblo was complaining in *Brunswick*?

2. What significance did USA Petroleum seek to attribute to the fact that the agreements between ARCO and its dealers were allegedly *per se* illegal under § 1 of the Sherman Act? Were they actually *per se* illegal? Is your answer affected at all by the Court's ruling in *Business Electronics* (Chapter 5, *supra*)? Would USA Petroleum's position regarding standing to complain of a *per se* antitrust violation be good or bad policy?

3. Would a rival retailer have standing to complain of a vertical minimum price-fixing agreement?

4. In *Caribe BMW, Inc. v. Bayerische Motoren Werke Aktiengesellschaft*, 19 F.3d 745 (1st Cir. 1994), then Judge Breyer, writing for the First Circuit, upheld the standing of an automobile dealer to challenge the lawfulness of a maximum-price agreement constraining the dealer's ability to raise its prices. Judge Breyer distinguished *USA Petroleum* on the ground that a dealer could show antitrust injury consisting of its inability to provide a combination of higher prices and greater services, a combination which its customers might be demanding. Judge Breyer believed that he was required to reach this result so long as *Albrecht* remained a viable precedent. Now that the Supreme Court has overruled *Albrecht* [in *State Oil Co. v. Khan*, page 183, *supra*], the First Circuit's decision in *Caribe BMW* has lost its significance.

G. The "Pass-On" Issue: Offensive and Defensive Pass-On

Hanover Shoe, Inc. v. United Shoe Machinery Corp.

392 U.S. 481 (1968)

[Suit by Hanover Shoe, Inc., a shoe manufacturer, against United Shoe Machinery Corp., a manufacturer of shoe machinery, alleging that the latter monopolized the shoe machinery industry by, *inter alia*, its practice of leasing and refusing to sell certain shoe machinery. Hanover sought the difference between what it paid United in shoe machinery rentals and what it would have paid had United been willing to sell those machines. The Court of appeals for the Third Circuit affirmed the District Court's finding of United's liability but disagreed on damages. The Supreme Court granted *certiorari*.]

Mr. Justice WHITE delivered the opinion of the Court.

. . . We think it sound to hold that when a buyer shows that the price paid by him for materials purchased for use in his business is illegally high and also shows the amount of the overcharge, he has made out a prima facie case of injury and damage within the meaning of [Clayton Act] § 4.

If in the face of the overcharge the buyer does nothing and absorbs the loss, he is entitled to treble damages. This much seems conceded. The reason is that he has paid more than he should and his property has been illegally diminished, for had the price paid been lower his profits would have been higher. It is also clear that if the buyer, responding to the illegal price, maintains his own price but takes steps to increase his volume or to decrease other costs, his right to damages is not destroyed. Though he may manage to maintain his profit level, he would have made more if his purchases from the defendant had cost him less. We hold that the buyer is equally entitled to damages if he raises the price for his own product. As long as the seller continues to charge the illegal price, he takes from the buyer more than the law allows. At whatever price the buyer sells, the price he pays the seller remains illegally high, and his profits would be greater were his costs lower.

. . . .

United seeks to limit the general principle that the victim of an overcharge is damaged within the meaning of § 4 to the extent of that overcharge. The rule, United argues, should be subject to the defense that economic circumstances were such that the overcharged buyer could only charge his customers a higher price because the price to him was higher. It is argued that in such circumstances the buyer suffers no loss from the overcharge. This situation might be present, it is said, where the overcharge is imposed equally on all of a buyer's competitors and where the demand for the buyer's product is so inelastic that the buyer and his competitors could all increase their prices by the amount of the cost increase without suffering a consequent decline in sales.

We are not impressed with the argument that sound laws of economics require recognizing this defense. A wide range of factors influence a company's pricing policies. . . . Equally difficult to determine, in the real economic world rather than an economist's hypothetical model, is what effect a change in a company's price will have on its total sales. . . . Even if it could be shown that the buyer raised his price in response to, and in the amount of, the overcharge and that his margin of profit and total sales had not thereafter declined, there would remain the nearly insuperable difficulty of demonstrating that the particular plaintiff could not or would not have raised his prices absent the overcharge or maintained the higher price had the overcharge been discontinued. Since establishing the applicability of the passing-on defense would require a convincing showing of each of these virtually unascertainable figures, the task would normally prove insurmountable. . . . Treble-damage actions would often require additional long and complicated proceedings involving massive evidence and complicated theories.

In addition, if buyers are subjected to the passing-on defense, those who buy from them would also have to meet the challenge that they passed on the higher price to their customers. These ultimate consumers, in today's case the buyers of single pairs of shoes, would have . . . little interest in attempting a class action. In consequence, those who violate the antitrust laws by price fixing or monopolizing would retain the fruits of their illegality because no one was available who would bring suit against them. . . .

The judgment of the Court of Appeals is affirmed in part and reversed in part, and the cases are remanded for further proceedings consistent with this opinion.

It is so ordered.

COMMENTARY

1. Does the Court's decision in *Hanover Shoe* have the effect of discouraging antitrust violations by facilitating private actions against violators? Does it simplify private action enforcement? Is the Court trying to extricate the judicial system from an onerous burden? a costly burden? Does the *Hanover Shoe* decision create windfalls for initial purchasers who have passed on the higher prices which they themselves have paid to their own customers? How are such windfalls justified? Is the Court suggesting that ultimate consumers would have little incentive to institute antitrust actions against monopolizing or price-fixing manufacturers? Why would they lack such incentives?

2. Is the *Hanover Shoe* decision an attempt to save the courts from becoming entangled in complex economic contentions about where the burden of manufacturer-level monopoly pricing would ultimately be borne? Does this mean that the Court would be unreceptive to a critique of its decision based upon economic analysis? Would you expect that the Court would be willing to carve out exceptions to the *Hanover Shoe* rule in circumstances in which it could be shown without the aid of complex analysis that the burden of manufacturer-level monopoly pricing was borne by a class of customers other than the first purchasers, say purchasers under a cost-plus contract?

Illinois Brick Co. v. Illinois
431 U.S. 720 (1977)

Mr. Justice WHITE delivered the opinion of the Court.

. . . .

Respondent State of Illinois . . . brought this antitrust treble-damages action . . . alleging that petitioners had engaged in a combination and conspiracy to fix the prices of concrete block in violation of § 1 of the Sherman Act. The complaint alleged that the amounts paid by respondents for concrete block were more than $3 million higher by reason of this price-fixing conspiracy. The only way in which the antitrust violation alleged could have injured respondents is if all or part of the overcharge was passed on by the masonry and general contractors to respondents, rather than being absorbed at the first two levels of distribution. . . .

We granted *certiorari* . . . to resolve a conflict among the Courts of Appeals on the question whether the offensive use of pass-on authorized by the decision below is consistent with *Hanover Shoe*'s restrictions on the defensive use of pass-on. We hold that it is not, and we reverse. . . .

. . . A one-sided application of *Hanover Shoe* substantially increases the possibility of inconsistent adjudications and therefore of unwarranted multiple liability for the defendant by presuming that one plaintiff (the direct purchaser) is entitled to full recovery while preventing the defendant from using that presumption against the other plaintiff; overlapping recoveries are certain to result from the two lawsuits unless the indirect purchaser is unable to establish any pass-on whatsoever. . . .

Second, the reasoning of *Hanover Shoe* cannot justify unequal treatment of plaintiffs and defendants with respect to the permissibility of pass-on arguments. The principal basis for the decision in *Hanover Shoe* was the Court's perception of the uncertainties and difficulties in analyzing price and output decisions "in the real economic world rather than an economist's hypothetical model," . . . and of the costs to the judicial system and the efficient enforcement of the antitrust laws of attempting to reconstruct those decisions in the courtroom. . . .

. . . There have been many proposals to allow pass-on theories in some . . . contexts while preserving the *Hanover Shoe* rule in others. Respondents here argue, not without support from some lower courts, that pass-on theories should be permitted for middlemen that resell goods without altering them and for contractors that add a fixed percentage markup to the cost of their materials in submitting bids. . . . Exceptions to the *Hanover Shoe* rule have also been urged for other situations in which most of the overcharge is purportedly passed on—for example, where a price-fixed good is a small but vital input into a much larger product, making the demand for the price-fixed good highly inelastic. . . .

We reject these attempts to carve out exceptions to the *Hanover Shoe* rule for particular types of markets. . . . [T]he process of classifying various market situations according to the amount of pass-on likely to be involved and its susceptibility of proof in a judicial forum would entail the very problems that the *Hanover Shoe* rule was meant to avoid. . . .

We think the longstanding policy of encouraging vigorous private enforcement of the antitrust laws . . . supports our adherence to the *Hanover Shoe* rule, under which direct purchasers are not only spared the burden of litigating the intricacies of pass-on but also are permitted to recover the full amount of the overcharge. . . . [W]e conclude that the legislative purpose in creating a group of "private attorneys general" to enforce the antitrust laws under § 4 . . . is better served by holding direct purchasers to be injured to the full extent of the overcharge paid by them than by attempting to apportion the overcharge among all that may have absorbed a part of it.

. . . .

For the reasons stated, the judgment is reversed, and the case is remanded for further proceedings consistent with this opinion.

So ordered.

COMMENTARY

1. Is the *Illinois Brick* decision compelled by *Hanover Shoe*? Could the Court have denied the pass-on defense and yet authorized indirect purchasers to sue as plaintiffs? Would this have involved the judicial system in the procedural complexities which the Court sought to avoid in *Hanover Shoe*? Would it be an acceptable course to attempt to lessen the procedural burdens on the courts by permitting antitrust violators to be exposed to liability in multiple federal antitrust suits?

2. Justice White, in his opinion, states that he recognizes "that direct purchasers sometimes may refrain from bringing a treble-damages suit for fear of disrupting relations with their suppliers." In what circumstances is this a concern? In industries in which distributors tend to purchase over the long-term from the same supplier without long-term contractual commitments from that supplier? Would that concern be greater in industries in which distributors' entire inventories consisted of brand-name goods purchased from a single supplier? Would it be less in industries in which distributors handled products of many suppliers? Would it be less in industries in which distributors had long-term contractual commitments from their suppliers?

3. To what extent is the *Illinois Brick* precedent applicable to plaintiffs asserting causes of action under the Robinson-Patman Act? In *Perkins v. Standard Oil Co.*, 395 U.S. 642 (1969) (Chapter 13, *supra*), Perkins, a wholesaler and retailer of gasoline, was allowed to sue Standard Oil Company of California for discriminating in price against it, allegedly in violation of the Robinson-Patman Act, by charging a higher price to it than Standard charged Signal Oil & Gas Co., a wholesaler which resold the gasoline to Western Hyway which, in turn, resold the gasoline to Regal Stations Co., Perkins' retail competitor. Perkins alleged that by reason of the discriminatorily favorable price to Signal, Regal was able to underprice Perkins. Would Regal have been allowed to bring a similar suit against Standard if it had been Perkins, rather than Signal, which had received the discriminatorily favorable price?

In answering this question, recall that the Robinson-Patman Act was designed to protect, *inter alia,* small retailers from the supply-cost advantages possessed by chain stores, many of which were integrated through the wholesale level. If indirect purchasers lack standing to sue a manufacturer which is discriminating against their suppliers, then one of the classes which the Act was designed to protect would be unable to obtain redress from prototypical discrimination. *But see Klein v. Lionel Corp.*, 237 F.2d 13 (3d Cir. 1956) (Chapter 13, *supra*).

In *Schwimmer v. Sony Corp. of America*, 637 F.2d 41, 48-49 (2d Cir. 1980), and *Edward J. Sweeney & Sons, Inc. v. Texaco, Inc.*, 637 F.2d 105, 122 (3d Cir. 1980), the courts applied *Illinois Brick* to the Robinson-Patman Act by barring indirect purchasers from bringing suit for price discrimination against their suppliers. Are these holdings reconcilable with the Supreme Court's rejection of the automatic damages rule of liability in the Robinson-Patman context in *J. Truett Payne Co. v. Chrysler Motors Corp.*, 451 U.S. 557 (1981) (page 923, *infra*)?

4. In *Reading Industries, Inc. v. Kennecott Copper Corp.*, 631 F.2d 10 (2d Cir. 1980), Reading claimed that it was injured as a competitor of the defendants in the sale of fabricated copper products as a result of the concerted behavior of three integrated producer-fabricators. Reading contended that the defendants conspired to maintain the producers' price at low levels, well below the London Metal Exchange (futures) price, and that this resulted in Reading's paying a higher price in the copper scrap market. Reading alleged that the defendants kept the producers' price artificially low creating a shortage of new copper and fabricators were forced to augment their copper supplies from the scrap market, thus forcing scrap prices higher and injuring Reading which obtained its supplies from the scrap market. In rejecting Reading's claim, the Second Circuit relied partially on *Illinois Brick* as an authority for keeping the courts out of cases in which the issues can be resolved only by complex economic analysis. There the court stated:

> . . . to find antitrust damages in this case would engage the court in hopeless speculation concerning the relative effect of an alleged conspiracy in the market for refined copper on the price of copper scrap, where countless other market variables could have intervened to affect those pricing decisions. The court's task of tracing would be difficult, if not impossible, raising in aggravated form the problem that *Illinois Brick* was intended to avoid. While it is true that *Illinois Brick* holds narrowly only that indirect purchasers may not recover damages for the passing-on of overcharges due to antitrust violations, it has a broader significance in indicating that there are inherent limitations in the substantive protection afforded by the antitrust laws: they exclude claims based on conjectural theories of injury and attenuated economic causality that would mire the courts in intricate efforts to recreate the possible permutations in the causes and effects of a price change. . . .

631 F.2d at 13-14. Could you also draw support for the rejection of this type of claim from the rejection in *Cargill* of an asserted injury resulting from a price squeeze? *See* page 893, *supra*.

A NOTE ON *ILLINOIS BRICK*

1. The *Illinois Brick* issue has reappeared several times in cases before the Supreme Court. In *Associated General Contractors of California, Inc. v. California State Council of Carpenters*, 459 U.S. 519 (1982) (below), a labor union brought suit against a trade association of building contractors, charging that the association was coercing owners to employ nonunion building contractors on construction contracts. In ordering the case dismissed for lack of standing, the Court relied upon a number of grounds, one of which was the complexity of the damages calculation which underlay the *Illinois Brick* decision. On this issue the Court relied explicitly upon the authority of *Illinois Brick*.

2. In *Kansas v. Utilicorp United, Inc.*, 497 U.S. 199 (1990), the Court reaffirmed the *Illinois Brick* rule in a case in which a pipeline company and five gas production companies were alleged to have conspired to inflate the price of natural gas. The two states (Kansas and Missouri), acting as *parens patriae*, asserted the claims of their residents who had purchased gas at the inflated prices. The Court acknowledged language in *Illinois Brick* that standing might be allowed to indirect purchasers buying under cost plus contracts. Nonetheless, the Court rejected the contention that utility regulation accomplished purposes similar to cost-plus contracts. It indicated that the cost-plus-contract exception, if allowed, would be the only such exception: "[W]e think it an unwarranted and counterproductive exercise to litigate a series of exceptions."

3. After the *Illinois Brick* decision, a number of states amended their own (state) antitrust laws to allow recovery by indirect purchasers in actions brought under those laws. This state of affairs raised the issue of whether inconsistent treatment of indirect purchasers by states under their own antitrust laws was compatible with federal antitrust enforcement.

This issue came to a head in *California v. Arc America Corp.*, 490 U.S. 93 (1989). In that case, a number of states had brought a federal antitrust suit based upon an alleged nationwide conspiracy to fix the price of cement. Because the states were indirect purchasers, their federal antitrust claims were dismissed under the rule of *Illinois Brick*. In their complaints, however, the states had also asserted claims under state antitrust laws. The U.S. Court of Appeals for the Ninth Circuit ruled that the inconsistent standing provisions of the state laws were preempted by federal law. The U.S. Supreme Court, however, took a different view. Under the latter Court's ruling, the allowance of standing by the states to indirect purchasers did not interfere with the enforcement of the federal antitrust laws nor did it affect at all the procedural complexity of federal actions. *Illinois Brick*, the Court indicated, was a rule governing federal procedure and was not intended to affect choices by the states of how to administer their own sets of antitrust laws.

4. *Illinois Brick* drastically reduces the importance of consumer standing, a concept recognized in *Reiter v. Sonotone*, 442 U.S. 330 (1977) (page 890, *supra*). Since consumers generally purchase through dealers (and not directly from manufacturers), consumers will rarely have standing to assert antitrust claims against manufacturers.

Associated General Contractors of California, Inc. v. California State Council of Carpenters

459 U.S. 519 (1982)

Justice STEVENS delivered the opinion of the Court.

This case arises out of a dispute between parties to a multiemployer collective bargaining agreement. The plaintiff unions allege that, in violation of the antitrust laws, the multiemployer association and its members coerced certain third parties, as well as some of the association's members, to enter into business relationships with nonunion firms. This coercion, according to the complaint, adversely affected the trade of certain unionized firms and thereby restrained the business activities of the unions. The question presented is whether the complaint sufficiently alleges that the unions have been "injured in [their] business or property by reason of anything forbidden in the antitrust laws" and may therefore recover treble damages under § 4 of the Clayton Act. . . . Unlike the majority of the Court of Appeals for the Ninth Circuit, we agree with the District Court's conclusion that the complaint is insufficient.

. . . .

IV

There is a similarity between the struggle of common-law judges to articulate a precise definition of the concept of "proximate cause," and the struggle of federal judges to articulate a precise test to determine whether a party injured by an antitrust violation may recover treble damages.[27] It is common ground that the judicial remedy cannot encompass every conceivable harm that can be traced to alleged wrongdoing. In both situations the infi-

---

[27] Some courts have focused on the directness of the injury, *e.g.*, *Loeb v. Eastman Kodak Co.*, 183 F. 704, 709 (3d Cir. 1910); *Productive Inventions, Inc. v. Trico Prods. Corp.*, 224 F.2d 678, 679 (2d Cir. 1955), *cert. denied*, 350 U.S. 936 (1956); *Volasco Products Co. v. Lloyd A. Fry Roofing Co.*, 308 F.2d 383, 394-395 (6th Cir. 1962), *cert. denied*, 372 U.S. 907 (1963). Others have applied the requirement that the plaintiff must be in the "target area" of the antitrust conspiracy, that is, the area of the economy which is endangered by a breakdown of competitive conditions in a particular industry. *E.g.*, *Pan-Islamic Trade Corp. v. Exxon Corp.*, 632 F.2d 539, 546-547 (5th Cir. 1980); *Engine Specialties, Inc. v. Bombardier Ltd.*, 605 F.2d 1, 17-18 (1st Cir. 1979); *Calderone Enterprises Corp. v. United Artists Theater Circuit, Inc.*, 454 F.2d 1292-1295 (2d Cir. 1971). Another court of appeals has asked whether the injury is "arguably within the zone of interests protected by the antitrust laws." *Malamud v. Sinclair Oil Corp.*, 521 F.2d 1142, 1151-1152 (6th Cir. 1975). . . . As a number of commentators have observed, these labels may lead to contradictory and inconsistent results. . . . Handler, *The Shift From Substantive to Procedural Innovations in Antitrust Suits*, 71 COLUM. L. REV. 1, 27-31 (1971); Sherman, *Antitrust Standing: From* Loeb *to* Malamud, 51 N.Y.U. L. REV. 374, 407 (1976) ("it is simply not possible to fashion an across-the-board and easily applied standing rule which can serve as a tool of decision for every case"). In our view, courts should analyze each situation in light of the factors set forth in the text *infra*.

nite variety of claims that may arise make it virtually impossible to announce a black-letter rule that will dictate the result in every case. Instead, previously decided cases identify factors that circumscribe and guide the exercise of judgment in deciding whether the law affords a remedy in specific circumstances.

The factors that favor judicial recognition of the Union's antitrust claim are easily stated. The complaint does allege a causal connection between an antitrust violation and harm to the Union and further alleges that the defendants intended to cause that harm. . . .

A number of other factors may be controlling. In this case it is appropriate to focus on the nature of the plaintiff's alleged injury. As the legislative history shows, the Sherman Act was enacted to assure customers the benefits of price competition, and our prior cases have emphasized the central interest in protecting the economic freedom of participants in the relevant market. Last Term in *Blue Shield of Virginia v. McCready*, . . . we identified the relevance of this central policy to a determination of the plaintiff's right to maintain an action under § 4. McCready alleged that she was a consumer of psychotherapeutic services and that she had been injured by the defendants' conspiracy to restrain competition in the market for such services. . . . After noting that her injury "was inextricably intertwined with the injury the conspirators sought to inflict on psychologists and the psychotherapy market," . . . the Court concluded that such an injury "falls squarely within the area of congressional concern." . . .

In this case . . . the Union was neither a consumer nor a competitor in the market in which trade was restrained. It is not clear whether the Union's interests would be served or disserved by enhanced competition in the market. As a general matter, a union's primary goal is to enhance the earnings and improve the working conditions of its membership; that goal is not necessarily served, and indeed may actually be harmed, by uninhibited competition among employers striving to reduce costs in order to obtain a competitive advantage over their rivals. At common law—as well as in the early days of administration of the federal antitrust laws—the collective activities of labor unions were regarded as a form of conspiracy in restraint of trade. Federal policy has since developed not only a broad labor exemption from the antitrust laws, but also a separate body of labor law specifically designed to protect and encourage the organizational and representational activities of labor unions. Set against this background, a union, in its capacity as bargaining representative, will frequently not be part of the class the Sherman Act was designed to protect, especially in disputes with employers with whom it bargains. In each case its alleged injury must be analyzed to determine whether it is of the type that the antitrust statute was intended to forestall. *See Brunswick Corp. v. Pueblo Bowl-O-Mat, Inc.* . . . In this case, particularly in light of the longstanding collective bargaining relationship between the parties, the Union's labor-market interests seem to predominate, and the *Brunswick* test is not satisfied.

An additional factor is the directness or indirectness of the asserted injury. . . . According to the complaint, defendants applied coercion against certain landowners and other contracting parties in order to cause them to divert business from certain union contractors to nonunion contractors. As a result, the Union's complaint alleges, the Union suffered unspecified injuries in its "business activities." It is obvious that any such injuries were only an indirect result of whatever harm may have been suffered by "certain" construction contractors and subcontractors.

If either these firms, or the immediate victims of coercion by defendants, have been injured by an antitrust violation, their injuries would be direct and, as we held in *McCready* . . . they would have a right to maintain their own treble damages actions against the defendants. An action on their behalf would encounter none of the conceptual difficulties that encumber the Union's claim. The existence of an identifiable class of persons whose self-interest would normally motivate them to vindicate the public interest in antitrust enforcement diminishes the justification for allowing a more remote party such as the Union to perform the office of a private attorney general. Denying the Union a remedy on the basis of its allegations in this case is not likely to leave a significant antitrust violation undetected or unremedied.

. . .

The indirectness of the alleged injury also implicates the strong interest, identified in our prior cases, in keeping the scope of complex antitrust trials within judicially manageable limits. These cases have stressed the importance of avoiding either the risk of duplicate recoveries on the one hand, or the danger of complex apportionment of damages on the other. . . . As the Court wrote in *Illinois Brick*, massive and complex damages litigation not only burdens the courts, but also undermines the effectiveness of treble-damages suits. . . . In this case, if the Union's complaint asserts a claim for damages under § 4 [of the Clayton Act], the District Court would face problems of identifying damages and apportioning them among directly victimized contractors and subcontractors and indirectly affected employees and union entities. It would be necessary to determine to what extent the coerced firms diverted business away from union subcontractors, and then to what extent those subcontractors absorbed the damage to their businesses or passed it on to employees by reducing the workforce or cutting hours or wages. In turn it would be necessary to ascertain the extent to which the affected employees absorbed their losses and continued to pay union dues.

We conclude, therefore, that the Union's allegations of consequential harm resulting from a violation of the antitrust laws, although buttressed by an allegation of intent to harm the Union, are insufficient as a matter of law. Other relevant factors—the nature of the Union's injury, the tenuous and speculative character of the relationship between the alleged antitrust violation and the Union's alleged injury, the potential for duplicative recovery or complex apportionment of damages, and the existence of more direct victims of the alleged conspiracy—weigh heavily against judicial enforcement of the Union's antitrust claim. Accordingly, we hold that, based on the allegations of this complaint, the District Court was correct in concluding that the Union is not a person injured by reason of a violation of the antitrust laws within the meaning of § 4 of the Clayton Act. The judgment of the Court of Appeals is reversed.

It is so ordered.

COMMENTARY

Is *Associated General Contractors* an appropriate application of *Illinois Brick*? of *Brunswick*? Was the union an indirect purchaser? Is *Associated General Contractors* consistent with *McCready* (page 887, *supra*)? The conspiracy alleged in *McCready* was to divert business from psychologists to psychiatrists, was it not? And the customers of the psychologists were held to have standing, were they not? What qualifications would you place on your answers to the last question? In *Associated General Contractors*, the alleged conspiracy is to divert business from union contractors to nonunion contractors. Why are the employees of the union contractors (the direct victims) not injured as much as (at least some) patients of the psychologists (the victimized class) in *McCready*? Would the Court allow standing to the employees themselves after denying it to their union?

H. Employee Standing to Complain of Antitrust Violation by Employer

Ashmore v. Northeast Petroleum Division of Cargill, Inc.

843 F. Supp. 759 (D. Me. 1994)

GENE CARTER, Chief Judge.

This action was commenced by Plaintiffs Frederick Ashmore, David Boya, William Simone, and Richard Simeone alleging that they were dismissed from employment as sales representatives for Defendants in retaliation for Plaintiffs' refusal to implement a pricing system which allegedly violated the Robinson-Patman Antidiscrimination Act of 1936. . . .

I. The Factual Allegations

Plaintiffs were employed as sales representatives by Defendant Cargill's Northeast Division. As sales representatives, Plaintiffs sold petroleum products to both small and large retailers in the northeastern United States. Plaintiff Ashmore worked out of Northeast Division's Maine office. Plaintiffs Boya and Simone were based in Northeast's Connecticut office, and Plaintiff Simeone was based in Massachusetts. All were trained at and received pricing instructions from the Chelsea, Massachusetts administrative offices of Northeast Division.

Plaintiffs allege that in 1991, Defendants adopted a discriminatory pricing system which violated the Robinson-Patman Act. Specifically they claim that:

> Northeast implemented a company-wide program of assigning customers to pricing groups based on the characteristics of customer loyalty and the ability of each customer to ascertain a fair price ("price sensitivity"). Northeast then assigned different allowances (discounts) to each pricing group. The most generous allowances were assigned to customers in the group considered to be the most able to ascertain a fair price, and the least loyal to Defendants; and the least generous allowance was granted to customers in the group considered to be the least price sensitive and the most loyal. Northeast determined the daily sale price of each product offered to a particular customer by subtracting from the rack price for the product the allowance assigned to the customer's pricing group. . . . The scheme conferred favored status on large retailers and disfavored status on small retailers. . . .

. . . Plaintiffs further allege that Northeast's sales representatives were required to take an active role in implementing this policy and "based on their familiarity with their customers, they were required to assign each customer" to one of the pricing groups. . . . Plaintiff Ashmore refused to implement the pricing system. . . . Plaintiffs Boya, Simeone, and Simone objected to the new pricing system but were allegedly "forced to implement the price grouping policy under threats of dire consequences." . . . Defendants terminated Plaintiffs' employment at Northeast on May 29, 1992. Plaintiffs allege that this discharge was in retaliation for "their refusal to engage in criminal activity, and resistance to the unlawful" discriminatory pricing system and "to make an example of them" to other employees who resisted the allegedly illegal practice. . . .

II

A

The issue of whether an employee has standing to sue under section 4 on a claim of retaliatory discharge for resisting the implementation of a policy which violates the federal antitrust laws has not been addressed by the Supreme Court and is a matter of first impression in this Circuit. As the parties point out, there is a split among federal courts on this issue.[34] The Court of Appeals for the Ninth Circuit has held that an employee subjected to retaliatory discharge for refusing to cooperate with a price-fixing conspiracy in violation of the Sherman Act has standing under section 4. *Ostrofe v. H.S. Crocker Co.*, 740 F.2d 739 (9th Cir.1984), *cert. dismissed at request of parties*, 469 U.S. 1200 (1985). The United States District Court for the Southern District of New York followed the Ninth Circuit's *Ostrofe II* holding in *Donahue v. Pendleton Woolen Mills, Inc.*, 633 F. Supp. 1423 (S.D.N.Y.1986). On the other hand, courts in the Seventh, Third, and Tenth Circuits have held that employees who allege retaliatory discharge for refusal to cooperate with policies that violate the antitrust laws do not have standing under section 4. *Bichan v. Chemetron Corp.*, 681 F.2d 514 (7th Cir.1982), *cert. denied*, 460 U.S. 1016 (1983); *Winther v. DEC International, Inc.*, 625 F. Supp. 100 (D. Colo.1985); *McNulty v. Borden, Inc.*, 542 F. Supp. 655 (E.D. Pa.1982). The Sixth Circuit has also denied standing to a sales representative who alleged his territory was reduced and later eliminated due to his refusal to cooperate in an antitrust violation. *Fallis v. Pendleton Woolen Mills, Inc.*, 866 F.2d 209, 211 (6th Cir.1989).

These different results have stemmed from varied interpretations of the Supreme Court's holdings in three recent antitrust standing cases: *Associated General Contractors v. California State Council of Carpenters*, 459 U.S. 519 (1983); *Blue Shield of Virginia v. McCready*, 457 U.S. 465 (1982); and *Brunswick Corp. v. Pueblo Bowl-O-Mat, Inc.*, 429 U.S. 477 (1977). In the most recent of this trilogy, the Supreme Court set out a comprehensive antitrust standing analysis, identifying factors which must be considered in determining whether a plaintiff may sue under section 4 of the Clayton Act. *Associated General*, 459 U.S. at 535-45. It is in this framework that this Court must evaluate Plaintiffs' claim to antitrust standing. Therefore, the Court will review the *Associated General* approach before analyzing the matter *sub judice*.

. . . .

The Court [in *Associated General*] considered each of the following factors in assessing the Union's standing to sue for treble damages under section 4:

---

[34] Northeast makes much of the fact that no court has granted standing under section 4 based on a violation of the Robinson-Patman Act. However, the analysis required by the Supreme Court to determine whether a plaintiff has standing under section 4 of the Clayton Act does not depend upon whether the underlying violation is of the Sherman Act or of the Robinson-Patman Act (see discussion of *Associated General, infra*). Therefore, the Court is not constrained to consider only those cases based on Robinson-Patman violations.

(1) the causal connection between the Union's injury and Defendant's violation of the antitrust law;
(2) the nature of the Union's alleged injury and whether it was of the type that the antitrust laws were intended to forestall;
(3) the directness of the injury particularly as it related to the tenuous and speculative nature of the harm to the Union;
(4) the danger of duplicative recoveries or complex apportionment of damages; and
(5) the existence of more immediate classes of potential plaintiffs who could be expected to vindicate the violation of the antitrust laws.

. . . .

B

. . . .

At the outset, it is clear that the allegations made by Plaintiffs, if proven, satisfy four of the five factors identified in *Associated General.* As to the first factor, Plaintiffs' allegations satisfy the causal connection required by section 4; that is, Plaintiffs allege that their employment was terminated in order for Northeast to accomplish a violation of the antitrust law. If not for the implementation of a discriminatory pricing system, Plaintiffs contend that they would not have had to resist the allegedly illegal scheme and, consequently, they would not have been discharged.

The harm to Plaintiffs in this case was direct also and, in this regard, does not implicate the concerns underlying the third factor which militated against standing in *Associated General.* . . . Here, there is nothing that is either indirect or speculative about Plaintiffs' claims. They allege that their injuries were the direct and intended result of Defendant's intentional act in furtherance of an antitrust violation. The damages claimed are in the form of lost wages and benefits. These damages are easily quantifiable and are not speculative.

The fourth factor considered by the Supreme Court in *Associated General* was the danger of duplicative treble-damage awards, or problems of complex apportionment of damages. . . . In contrast, Plaintiffs in the present case allege injuries in the form of lost compensation and benefits. These damages are wholly distinct from damages that could be claimed by other plaintiffs injured by the alleged antitrust violation. The injury is not derivative, but personal to Plaintiffs. Therefore, there is no danger of duplicative recovery.

As to the fifth factor, there is no other class more directly affected than Plaintiffs in the present case that is more likely to redress society's interest in enforcement of the antitrust laws. . . .

Here, although purchasers disadvantaged by the alleged discriminatory pricing system are also direct victims of the alleged antitrust violation, the very nature of the pricing system makes it unlikely that the victims will become aware of the price differentials unless sales representatives reveal the violation and risk discharge. The alleged pricing system discriminates against purchasers on the basis of customer loyalty and lack of accurate pricing information. It relies for concealment of this discriminatory activity upon the loyalty, expertise, and perceived self-interest of its sales employees. Those victims directly damaged by the anticompetitive effect of the pricing system are the least informed purchasers in the market and are unlikely to discover the violation in a timely manner.

. . . .

These four factors favor antitrust standing for Plaintiffs in this case. Their injuries are the direct result of actions taken in furtherance of an alleged attempt to implement a discriminatory pricing system in violation of the Robinson-Patman Act. There is no other class of plaintiffs which is more directly effected by these actions, and Plaintiffs' injuries are wholly distinct from the injuries suffered by any other class of victims; therefore, there is no danger of duplicative recoveries or complex apportionment. Finally, there is nothing speculative about the amount of damages suffered by these Plaintiffs.

C. *Antitrust Injury*

The principal standing issues raised by the Plaintiffs' claim relate to the second factor: whether the alleged injury is "antitrust injury"; that is, the type of injury that the antitrust laws were intended to forestall. In the context of the retaliatory discharge claim raised in this case, there are two relevant inquiries. First, whether the harm caused by retaliatory discharge is "antitrust injury." And second, whether failure to demonstrate "antitrust injury" in the narrowest sense is fatal to standing in every case. The Court will address these questions in turn.

. . . .

. . . [Some] courts reason that because a discharged employee's injury is not due to diminished competition in any market in which the employee is a consumer or competitor it is not "antitrust injury." . . .

Upon review of all these cases and the history of section 4 and the Robinson-Patman Act, this Court is persuaded that the more flexible approach of *Ostrofe II* is more consistent with the purposes of the antitrust laws than the extremely narrow limitations of *Bichan*. . . .

There can be no doubt that Congress was concerned with the conduct of employees and agents who assisted in carrying out antitrust violations in the discharge of their duties. The Robinson-Patman Act imposes personal criminal liability on any person engaged in commerce who knowingly assists in a discriminatory transaction of sale. 15 U.S.C.A. § 13a. Providing a remedy to those employees who suffer injury for refusing to violate this law will serve the deterrent purpose of both the criminal sanctions in the Robinson-Patman Act and the treble-damages remedy of the Clayton Act.

Finally, standing is appropriate in light of the remedial purposes of section 4. Here, unlike *Associated General* in which the Supreme Court emphasized that the Union was protected by federal labor law, it is not at all clear that employees subjected to wrongful discharge will have any remedy at law. . . .

Even if this Court reads the concept of "antitrust injury" too broadly, and if this concept is limited to injuries suffered by participants (consumers, sellers, purchasers) in the relevant market, this Court concurs with the courts that have reasoned that failure to allege participation in the relevant market, although it weighs heavily against antitrust standing, is not fatal to a claim of standing under the antitrust laws. . . . Permitting Plaintiffs' standing here will advance enforcement and deterrence, and protect competition in the affected market. All the other factors identified in *Associated General* weigh heavily in favor of standing for the Plaintiffs in this case. Therefore, this Court holds that Plaintiffs have standing on the allegations of the Complaint under the approach set out in *Associated General* and that such conclusion is consistent with the purposes of the Robinson-Patman Act.

COMMENTARY

In *Ashmore* the court followed the Ninth Circuit which had ruled in favor of an employee's standing in *Ostrofe v. H.S. Crocker Co.*, 740 F.2d 739 (9th Cir. 1984), *cert. dismissed at request of parties*, 469 U.S. 1200 (1985) (*Ostrofe II*), and in *Ostrofe v. H.S. Crocker Co.*, 670 F.2d 1378 (9th Cir. 1982), *vacated and remanded*, 460 U.S. 1007 (1983) (*Ostrofe I*). After the Ninth Circuit held that the plaintiff employee had standing in *Ostrofe I*, the Supreme Court vacated the decision and remanded the case to be reconsidered in the light of *Associated General Contractors*. The Ninth Circuit then reconsidered the case and reaffirmed its original ruling.

I. *Parens Patriae* Standing

Kansas v. UtiliCorp United, Inc.

497 U.S. 199 (1990)

Justice KENNEDY delivered the opinion of the Court.

[The respondent, UtiliCorp United, Inc., an investor-owned public utility operating in Kansas and Western Missouri, purchased natural gas from a pipeline company for its own use and for resale to its commercial and residential customers. Together with a second utility and several other gas purchasers, the respondent sued the pipeline company and five gas production companies in the United States District Court for the District of Kansas. The utilities alleged that the defendants had conspired to inflate the price of their gas in violation of the antitrust laws. They sought treble damages, pursuant to § 4 of the Clayton Act, for both the amount overcharged by the pipeline company and the decrease in sales to their customers caused by the overcharge.

The petitioners, the States of Kansas and Missouri, initiated separate § 4 actions in the District Court against the same defendants for the alleged antitrust violation. Acting as *parens patriae*, the petitioners asserted the claims of all natural persons residing within Kansas and Missouri who had purchased gas from any utility at inflated prices. They also asserted claims as representatives of state agencies, municipalities, and other political subdivisions that had purchased gas from the defendants.

In ruling upon pretrial motions, the District Court ruled that the utilities, as direct purchasers, had incurred antitrust injury, but that their customers had not. Accordingly, the District Court dismissed the petitioners' *parens patriae* claims. The Court of Appeals affirmed, and the Supreme Court granted *certiorari*.]

V

The petitioners, in their final argument, contend that § 4C of the Hart-Scott-Rodino Antitrust Improvements Act of 1976 [15 U.S.C. § 15c] . . . authorizes them to sue on behalf of consumers even though the consumers, as indirect purchasers, have no cause of action of their own. Section 4C(a)(1) provides in relevant part:

> "Any attorney general of a State may bring a civil action in the name of such state as *parens patriae* on behalf of natural persons residing in such State . . . to secure monetary relief as provided in this section for injury sustained by such natural persons to their property by reason of any violation of sections 1 to 7 of this title." 15 U.S.C. § 15c(a)(1).

Because the Act, in their view, has the clear purpose of protecting consumers, . . . the petitioners contend that it must allow the States to sue on behalf of consumers notwithstanding their status as indirect purchasers.

We have rejected this argument before. We stated in *Illinois Brick* that § 4C did not establish any new substantive liability. Instead, "[i]t simply created a new procedural device—*parens patriae* actions by States on behalf of their citizens—to enforce existing rights of recovery under § 4 [of the Clayton Act.]." . . . Section 4, as noted above, affords relief only to a person "injured in his business or property by reason of anything forbidden in the antitrust laws." 15 U.S.C. § 15(a). State attorneys general may bring actions on behalf of consumers who have such an injury. *See, e.g., Pennsylvania v. Mid-Atlantic Toyota Distributors, Inc.*, 704 F.2d 125, 128 (4th Cir. 1983) (suit on behalf of consumers injured by an alleged conspiracy to fix the price of cars). But here the respondent is the injured party under the antitrust laws, and the predicate for a *parens patriae* action has not been established. We conclude that the petitioners may not assert any claims on behalf of the customers.

Affirmed.

COMMENTARY

1. Traditionally states possess *parens patriae* standing to assert an injury to a "quasi-sovereign" interest, an interest broader than the private interests of its citizens but sufficiently concrete as to satisfy the case and controversy requirements of Article III, when the interest is asserted in a federal court. According to the Court in *Alfred L. Snapp v. Puerto Rico*, 458 U.S. 592, 607 (1982):

> . . . certain characteristics of such [quasi-sovereign] interests are so far evident. These characteristics fall into two general categories. First, a State has a quasi-sovereign interest in the health and well-being—both physical and economic—of its residents in general. Second, a State has a quasi-sovereign interest in not being discriminatorily denied its rightful status within the federal system.

2. When Congress included in the Hart-Scott-Rodino Act a provision for *parens patriae* standing by the states, it created something different from the traditional *parens patriae* standing. Under the Act, states may assert the antitrust claims of individuals. As the Court pointed out in *Utilicorp*, this does not create a new substantive right, but it does create a new procedural mechanism for the assertion of existing rights. Thus, a state's use of *parens patriae* standing may facilitate the bringing of claims which individuals might find impractical to bring separately or even in a class action.

As the cases indicate, however, the rights of consumers are limited. Generally consumers do not purchase directly from manufacturers and, accordingly, are barred by the *Illinois Brick* doctrine from making antitrust claims against the manufacturers. The state's *parens patriae* standing is also limited to natural persons, so that it cannot assert claims on behalf of businesses within its boundaries.

J. Standing to Assert a Claim Under the Robinson-Patman Act

Enterprise Industries, Inc. v. Texas Co.

240 F.2d 457 (2d Cir. 1956)

[The plaintiff was a corporation operating a retail gasoline station and brought suit against the defendant oil company for discriminating in price against the plaintiff and in favor of the plaintiff's competitors during a gasoline "price war." The defendant is appealing from a judgment for the plaintiff.]

HAND, Circuit Judge.

. . . .

The judge . . . assessed the damages by accepting as the measure of the plaintiff's loss the difference between the sale price charged the plaintiff and the lowest price charged any of the nine Texaco stations. . . . . [In a prior case] we held that the discrimination was not a proper measure of the loss . . . . There remains, however, a passage in the opinion of the Supreme Court in *Bruce's Juices, Inc. v. American Can Co.*, 330 U.S. 743, 757 . . . in which Justice Jackson said that, if the buyer showed that the prices charged were "discriminatory, . . . it would establish its right to recover three times the discriminatory difference without proving more than the illegality of the prices. If the prices are illegally discriminatory, petitioner has been damaged, in the absence of extraordinary circumstances, at least in the amount of that discrimination." The question then before the court was whether discrimination should bar a seller from recovering the contract price from the buyer and should confine him to a recovery on a *quantum meruit*; and the passage quoted was only an answer to the buyer's argument that, unless he was allowed to disaffirm the sale, he would be without any other relief. In that case the addition of 5% to the cost to the plaintiff of its cans, even if coupled with relief from "delivery charges," . . . might well not have been passed on to the consumer, and have been absorbed by the canners, who sold fruit juices in cans. If that were true, the amount of the discrimination might well be a proper measure of the buyer's damages. On the other hand, in the case at bar we have as little means of knowing whether or how far the plaintiff passed on to car owners any difference in the price charged it, as we have of knowing how far the addition affected the gallonage that it sold. In *Interstate Commerce Comm. v. United States*, 289 U.S. 385 . . . it is true that an award to the shipper of the "discrimination" would presumably have been unlawful, because by hypothesis the rate charged him had been reasonable. Nevertheless, the reasoning of Cardozo, J., in discussing the proper way to measure damages is relevant here. "If by reason of the discrimination, the preferred producers have been able to divert business that would otherwise have gone to the disfavored shipper, damage has resulted to the extent of the diverted profits. If the effect of the discrimination has been to force the shipper to sell at a lowered . . . price . . . damage has resulted to the extent of the reduction. But none of these consequences is a necessary inference from discrimination without more." . . . "Overcharge and discrimination have very different consequences, and must be kept distinct in thought" . . . .

Judgment reversed; complaint dismissed.

J. Truett Payne Company, Inc. v. Chrysler Motors Corp.
451 U.S. 557 (1981)

[Petitioner was a Chrysler-Plymouth dealer in Birmingham, Alabama and brought suit against the Chrysler Motors Corporation, claiming that as a result of the latter's "sales incentive" program, it was forced to pay more for automobiles than did its competitors. The Court of Appeals for the Fifth Circuit reversed judgment for the Petitioner; and the Supreme Court granted *certiorari*.]

Justice REHNQUIST delivered the opinion of the Court.

. . . .

Petitioner first contends that once it has proved a price discrimination in violation of § 2(a) it is entitled at a minimum to so-called "automatic damages" in the amount of the price discrimination. Petitioner concedes that in order to recover damages it must establish cognizable injury attributable to an antitrust violation and some approximation of damage. . . . It insists, however, that the jury should be permitted to infer the requisite injury and damage from a showing of a substantial price discrimination. Petitioner notes that this Court has consistently permitted such injury to be inferred in injunctive actions brought to enforce § 2(a), *e.g.*, *FTC v. Morton Salt Co.*, 334 U.S. 37 (1948), and argues that private suits for damages under § 4 should be treated no differently. We disagree.[2]

By its terms § 2(a) is a prophylactic statute which is violated merely upon a showing that "the effect of such discrimination *may be* substantially to lessen competition." (Emphasis supplied.) As our cases have recognized, the statute does not "require that the discriminations must in fact have harmed competition." . . . Section 4 of the Clayton Act, in contrast, is essentially a remedial statute. It provides treble damages to "[a]ny person who *shall be injured* in his business or property by reason of anything forbidden in the antitrust laws . . . ." (Emphasis supplied.) To recover treble damages, then, a plaintiff must make some showing of actual injury attributable to something the antitrust laws were designed to prevent. *Perkins v. Standard Oil Co.*, 395 U.S. 642 (1969) (plaintiff "must, of course, be able to show a causal connection between the price discrimination in violation of the Act and the

---

[2] The automatic-damages theory has split the lower courts. The leading case approving the theory is *Fowler Manufacturing Co. v. Gorlick*, 415 F.2d 1248 (9th Cir. 1969), *cert. denied*, 396 U.S. 1012 (1970). *See also Elizabeth Arden Sales Corp. v. Gus Blass Co.*, 150 F.2d 988 (8th Cir.) (involving §§ 2(d) and 2(e) of the Act), *cert. denied*, 326 U.S. 773 (1945); *Grace v. E. J. Kozin Co.*, 538 F.2d 170 (7th Cir. 1976) (involving § 2(c) of the Act). The leading case rejecting the theory is *Enterprise Industries, Inc. v. Texas Co.*, 240 F.2d 457 (2d Cir.), *cert. denied*, 353 U.S. 965 (1957). *Accord Edward J. Sweeney & Sons, Inc. v. Texaco, Inc.*, 637 F.2d 105 (3d Cir. 1980); *McCaskill v. Texaco, Inc.*, 351 F. Supp. 1332 (S.D. Ala. 1972), *affirmance order*, 486 F.2d 1400 (5th Cir. 1973); *Kidd v. Esso Standard Oil Co.*, 295 F.2d 497 (6th Cir. 1961).

injury suffered."). It must prove more than a violation of § 2(a), since such proof establishes only that injury *may* result.

. . . .

The legislative history buttresses this view. Both the Patman bill, H.R. 8442, § 2(d), 74th Cong., 1st Sess. (1935), as introduced in the House, and the Robinson bill, S. 3154, § 2(d), 74th Cong., 2d Sess. (1935), as introduced in the Senate, provided that a plaintiff's damages for a violation of § 2(a) shall be presumed to be the amount of the price discrimination. The provision, however, encountered such strong opposition in both Houses that the House Committee eliminated it from its bill, H.R. Rep. No.2287, 74th Cong., 2d Sess., 16 (1936), and the Senate Committee modified the provision to authorize presumptive damages in the amount of the discrimination only when plaintiff shows the "fact of damage." S. Rep. No.1502, 74th Cong., 2d Sess., 8 (1936). The Conference Committee eliminated even that compromise, and § 2(a) was passed in its present form. Congress thus has rejected the very concept which petitioner seeks to have the Court judicially legislate. . . .[3]

[The Court then remanded the case to the Court of Appeals to determine whether there was sufficient evidence in the record to establish, *inter alia,* actual injury and damage.]

COMMENTARY

1. What do you understand to be the rule for calculating Robinson-Patman damages which was employed by the Second Circuit in *Enterprise Industries*? Is that rule similar to the one which was employed in calculating damages for discrimination under the Interstate Commerce Act? Is the damages rule of *Enterprise Industries* consistent with *Illinois Brick*? Is it consistent with *Alan's of Atlanta, Inc. v. Minolta Corp.*, 903 F.2d 1414 (11th Cir. 1990) (below)?

2. Did the Court in *J. Truett Payne* adopt the damages rule of *Enterprise Industries*? How does it differ? Is the Court's approach in *J. Truett Payne* consistent with the Eleventh Circuit's decision in *Alan's of Atlanta*?

3. In order to recover under the Robinson-Patman Act, what must a plaintiff who alleges secondary-line injury show? Does such a plaintiff have to show injury to competition in addition to injury to itself? Is the *Morton Salt* presumption of competitive injury applicable in a private action brought against the discriminator by a disfavored buyer? But injury to the plaintiff for purposes of standing under § 4 of the Clayton Act is not presumed, is it? Could the Robinson-Patman Act be violated without injuring anyone? Can you reconcile *J. Truett Payne*, *Vanco*, and *Morton Salt*?

---

[3] Relying on *Bruce's Juices, Inc. v. American Can Co.*, 330 U.S. 743, 757 (1947), petitioner argues that this Court has previously accepted the automatic-damages theory. In that case the Court stated that if petitioner can show an illegal price discrimination under the Act, "it would establish its right to recover three times the discriminatory difference without proving more than the illegality of the prices." *Ibid.* But that statement is merely dictum, since the only issue before the Court was whether a violation of § 2(a) could be used as an affirmative defense to void a contract.

Alan's of Atlanta, Inc. v. Minolta Corp.

903 F.2d 1414 (11th Cir. 1990)

ESCHBACH, Senior Circuit Judge:

This case concerns the propriety of summary judgment in an antitrust action brought by a private plaintiff. The action alleges, among other things, violations of sections 2(a), 2(d), 2(e), and 2(f) of the Clayton Act, as amended by the Robinson-Patman Act, 15 U.S.C. §§ 13(a), (d), (e), and (f). The court below concluded that summary judgment was appropriate. After reviewing the record we conclude otherwise, and therefore reverse.

Alan's of Atlanta, Inc. ("AA") was an Atlanta-based "specialty" retailer of cameras and related equipment. It had stores in Atlanta and throughout Georgia and Florida. At the start of 1979 AA had a substantial share of the Atlanta market for Minolta-brand camera sales, about 33%, and an overwhelming share of specialty store sales, about 78%. By the end of 1985 AA's fortunes had taken a turn for the worse. Its Atlanta market share of Minolta camera sales had plummeted to about 4%. Its share of specialty store sales suffered a similar fate. During this same period AA witnessed the dramatic rise of a competing specialty camera retailer, Wolf Camera, Inc. Wolf Camera had captured the 29% of the Minolta camera market lost by AA and then some. Its share of that market rose from about 6% to about 41%. Even more dramatic was the rise in its share of specialty camera store sales, which rocketed from about 14% to over 65%. . . .

. . . In 1979 Robert Lathrop took over as [Minolta's] national director of sales . . . and instituted a "key dealer" program in which . . . MDF benefits were to be channeled disproportionately to "key dealers" in various cities. . . . MDF accounts were . . . [designated dealers in] a program in which these selected dealers would be given free cameras and camera equipment, free advertising, free promotions, and various other benefits not available to non-key dealers.

. . . .

Key dealers were usually the highest volume dealers within a defined market area. AA was the highest volume dealer in the Atlanta market at the time the key dealer program was instituted, but it was not chosen by Minolta as the Atlanta area key-dealer . . . [but] Wolf Camera was chosen in AA's stead.

As beneficiary of the key dealer program, Wolf Camera was slated to receive over non-key dealers a price advantage on purchases. . . . The range [allegedly] settled upon was four to seven percent per purchase dollar, generally, with specific instances of up to ten percent.[3] . . .

[The District Court dismissed Alan's of Atlanta's action, *inter alia,* on the ground that Alan's of Atlanta lacked standing because it had not suffered "antitrust injury."]

. . . .

With secondary-line RPA violations the competition/competitor distinction tends to fade. . . . As a price discrimination incipiency statute designed to "catch the weed in the seed," S. Rep. No. 1502, 74th Cong., 2d Sess. 4 (1936), the injury to secondary-line competition the RPA seeks to prevent is analogous, if not identical, to an injury to competitors

---

[3] As Wolf Camera purchased Minolta goods in the amount of $12,891,883 over a period of time comparable to that in which the price discrimination was alleged to have taken place, the purported favoritism translates into the following amounts: (1) At 4%, $537,161 (.96X = $12,891,883; X = $13,429,044; $13,429,044 - $12,891,883 = $537,161); (2) At 5%, $678,520; (3) At 6%, $822,886; (4) At 7%, $970,356.

of a favored buyer. *See* H.R. Rep. No. 2287, 74th Cong., 2d Sess. 8 (1936). . . . The effects from which the RPA injury may flow, then, are the effects one would expect to injure competitors on the wrong end of a supplier's price discrimination scheme. These effects include a lowering of price by a favored purchaser. They also include a favored purchaser's effectuation of some other means by which it uses price discrimination benefits to lure from its rivals sales or profits or present value; for example, by increasing some expenditure that ultimately leads to a lower price, enhanced product, or extra promotion. . . .

. . . [T]he RPA causation question asks whether some or all of the plaintiff's injury was derived from or materially furthered by a competitive advantage bestowed upon a favored purchaser through its receipt of discriminatory prices. . . . The evidence in this case is enough to put the question genuinely in dispute, especially in light of the substantial evidence of Appellees' wrongdoing. *See J. Truett Payne*, *supra,* 451 U.S. at 565-67. That evidence suggests that Minolta gave Wolf Camera a purchasing advantage over AA and that Wolf Camera channeled its purchasing advantage into a promotional advantage, unmatched by AA, in an industry where store sales are heavily influenced by promotional expense. It shows conclusively that during the time of this discrimination AA's share of the market dropped precipitously, that share being absorbed by Wolf Camera. And it contains, among other things, the report of an economic expert concluding that the advantage afforded Wolf Camera by the discrimination caused AA injury, and in quite a substantial amount. There is enough here for a jury to find an antitrust injury caused by Appellees "as a matter of fact and with a fair degree of certainty." *See Chrysler Credit Corp.*, *supra*, at 581 (quoting *Terrell*, *supra,* at 20). There is enough for a jury to find otherwise, too, but not so much to eliminate a triable issue.[20] At the very least the evidence gives rise to a reasonable inference that Appellees' misdeeds caused AA some harm. And where such a reasonable inference is raised by the evidence, summary judgment is uncalled for. . . .

For the foregoing reasons, the judgment of the district court is REVERSED, and its order entered October 2, 1987 is VACATED. The case is REMANDED for further proceedings consistent with this opinion.

---

[20] This conclusion stands regardless of the specific concerns advanced by the lower court. The court felt that no injury could possibly arise from the amount of price discrimination involved in the case, which it called *de minimis*. But the *de minimis* doctrine, by which a price discrimination is held to be too inconsequential to have caused competitive injury under section 2(a) or actual injury under section 4, does not depend on the large or small amount of the price discrimination *per se*. It depends on the large or small effect that the price discrimination has on business rivalry. *See Lupia*, *supra*, at 1171. To illustrate, in a competitive market the smallest increment of price advantage to one competitor would theoretically allow it to capture from its rivals as much of a market share as its output allowed. The price advantage may be *de minimis*, but the effect of it is not. We are not suggesting that the market involved here is perfectly competitive, but it is imperfectly so, and even in such markets a little price discrimination can go a long way. *See Foremost Dairies*, *supra,* at 679 (dairy industry); *Shreveport Macaroni Mfg. Co. v. FTC*, 321 F.2d 404, 409 (5th Cir. 1963), *cert. denied*, 375 U.S. 971 (1964) (pasta industry). Indeed, AA's economic expert concluded that the competitive advantage given Wolf had a substantial effect on its ability to capture market share, and as far as we know the expert's conclusions constitute evidence. Thus, the lower court's *de minimis* objection cannot keep this issue from reaching the jury. Nor can a variation on the *de minimis* theme relied on by the court: that no antitrust injury existed because Minolta products were only one line of many that AA carried. Simply because AA's injury derived from only one line of its products does not make that injury any less real. *See FTC v. Morton Salt Co.*, 334 U.S. at 49. If this particular strain of the *de minimis* argument failed in *Morton Salt*, where a grocer's potential injury came only from price differentials affecting one product amid thousands that it carried, it surely fails here. The court also seemed to think that AA's injury could only be caused from price-lowering actions by Wolf Camera. But sales in the specialty camera industry are affected by more than price; they are affected by promotion and product as well. The court found as a matter of fact that Wolf Camera channeled

COMMENTARY

1. Does *Alan's of Atlanta* suggest that Judge Hand's theory of Robinson-Patman damages articulated in *Enterprise Industries* is too narrow? Is the court's broad approach to the proof of Robinson-Patman damages in *Alan's of Atlanta* good policy? How consistent is *Alan's of Atlanta* with the Supreme Court's decision in *J. Truett Payne*?

2. How much confidence do you have that the jury can adequately sort out the amount by which Alan's of Atlanta was injured by its inability to put the savings from purchase-price discounts into promotion? If Alan's of Atlanta could have increased its profits from increased promotional spending, why didn't Alan's of Atlanta spend its own money on promotion? or borrow the money if necessary? Why isn't Alan's of Atlanta's claim essentially one based on the "automatic damages" theory rejected in *J. Truett Payne*?

---

most of its advantage into advertising and promotion, and it seems that it enhanced its product (photographic equipment and retail service combined) too. The evidence establishes that promotion and product enhancement were the primary factors affecting camera consumers' choice of sales outlet. Thus the fact that Wolf Camera did not lower its resale prices, even if true, by no means eliminates causation from jury consideration. The court felt too that no genuine issue existed about AA's antitrust injury, or lack thereof, because AA was the cause of its losses, not Appellees. There can be no liability "when the injury is the result of the plaintiff's own competitive shortcomings, rather than a merely coincidental discrimination in price." *Richard Short Oil Co. v. Texaco, Inc.*, 799 F.2d 415, 421 (8th Cir. 1986). And it is true that AA had competitive shortcomings, including its faulty computer system and its decision to blunder about unprofitably in Florida. These shortcomings could easily have been the intervening cause of all AA's sales and profit losses or some part of them, of this there is no doubt. But whether the cause of all or some of AA's problems actually was AA's discrimination-based competitive disadvantage, AA's computer, AA's managers, all of these things or none of them, is a matter of educated inference that must be left for the jury. If it finds that Appellees' price discrimination was the cause of some of AA's injury, which is certainly a reasonable inference, Appellees will be "responsible to that extent." *Falls City Indus., Inc. v. Vanco Beverage, Inc.*, 460 U.S. at 437.

Chapter 18

The State-Action Exemption: The *Noerr-Pennington* Doctrine and Related Matters

A. An Introductory Note

The state-action doctrine is a judicially created principle of substantive antitrust law, the development of which is the subject of this Chapter. Under this doctrine, many anticompetitive measures undertaken by states or their subdivisions are exempted from the prohibitions of federal antitrust law. As presented in this Chapter, the boundaries of the state-action exemption have shifted significantly over the last half century. The state-action exemption is generally understood to be grounded largely in principles of federalism. Congress is deemed to respect the rights of the states to pursue, within their own territories, economic and regulatory policies which differ from the free-market policy embodied in the Sherman Act and the other antitrust laws.

In addition to the state-action exemption, antitrust practitioners should be familiar with two doctrines of constitutional law which sometimes apply in cases in which claims to the state-action exemption are asserted. While the Commerce Clause authorizes Congress to regulate interstate commerce, that clause itself (and without congressional action)—the so-called "dormant" commerce clause—has been construed by the courts as invalidating much state and local government legislation which impedes interstate trade. State-erected barriers which act like tariffs or import or export quotas are generally labelled as "protectionist" and are treated as virtually *per se* invalid by the caselaw. *See, e.g., West Lynn Creamery, Inc. v. Healy*, 512 U.S. 186, 193, 205 (1994). A second class of restraints which impose burdens on trade flows incident to serving a legitimate state purpose are treated under a less severe balancing test. *Pike v. Bruce Church, Inc.,* 397 U.S. 137, 142 (1970). The relation of the dormant Commerce Clause to the state-action exemption of the federal antitrust laws is illustrated in litigation involving municipally-created monopolies over solid-waste treatment. In recent years many local governments have enacted ordinances requiring that locally-generated waste be treated at a municipally-franchised disposal facility, thus conferring a monopoly on the facility. Although challenges to those ordinances under the antitrust laws have generally been rebuffed under the state-action exemption, the municipally-conferred monopoly has fallen to challenges mounted under the dormant Commerce Clause when the monopoly interferes with interstate trade. *See C&A Carbone, Inc. v. Town of Clarkstown*, 511 U.S. 383 (1994); Daniel J. Gifford, *Federalism, Efficiency, the Commerce Clause, and the Sherman Act: Why We Should Follow a Consistent Free-Market Policy*, 44 EMORY L.J. 1227 (1995).

The liability of a state may be circumscribed by the Eleventh Amendment, which withdraws jurisdiction from federal courts to hear suits against a state by citizens of another state or of a foreign jurisdiction. Since the adoption of the Eleventh Amendment overruled *Chisom v. Georgia*, 2 Dall. 419 (1793), it has been generally understood that individual states are immune from suit by private parties. Although by its terms the Eleventh Amendment only prevents the federal courts from hearing suits against states by private parties resident in other states or foreign nations, the Amendment has been construed as ratifying a preexisting understanding that states are immune from suit by private parties in any federal court. Eleventh Amendment immunity has also been extended to subdivisions of state government when the state is the real party in interest. Amendments which contain provisions authorizing congressional enforcement, as does the Fourteenth Amendment (as well as most other Amendments postdating the Civil War), confer power on Congress to abrogate immunity under the Eleventh Amendment. There is, however, no such explicit grant of enforcement power to Congress under the Commerce Clause, the constitutional provision underlying the Sherman and Clayton Acts. In the recently decided *Seminole Tribe* case, the state of Florida was sued by the Seminole Tribe under the Indian Gaming Act. In ruling that the state was immune from suit, the Court formulated a two-part test, which inquires (1) whether Congress expressed an intent to abrogate state immunity, and (2) if so, whether Congress abrogated that immunity pursuant to a valid exercise of its power. In *Seminole Tribe*, the Court determined that Congress expressed an intent to abrogate state immunity, but that it lacked power to do so. In that case, Congress had legislated control over gaming under the provisions of the Commerce Clause applying to Indian Tribes. In ruling that this provision did not confer the requisite power upon Congress, the Court also apparently ruled that no legislation enacted under the Commerce Clause can subject states to suit by private parties. *Seminole Tribe of Florida v. Florida*, 116 S. Ct. 1114 (1996). Justice Stevens, in dissent, articulated his view of the ramifications of this decision for federal antitrust and other federal laws over which the federal courts possess exclusive jurisdiction:

> As federal courts have exclusive jurisdiction over cases arising under . . . federal [antitrust] laws, the majority's conclusion that the Eleventh Amendment shields States from being sued under them in federal court suggests that persons harmed by state violations of . . . antitrust laws have no remedy.

Id. at 1134 n.1 (Stevens, J., dissenting). Replying to Justice Stevens in his majority opinion, Chief Justice Rehnquist did not reject Stevens' conclusions. Rather, the Chief Justice wrote:

> Justice Stevens understands our opinion to prohibit federal jurisdiction over suits to enforce the bankruptcy, copyright, and antitrust laws against the states. . . . That conclusion is exaggerated both in its substance and in its significance. First, Justice Stevens' statement is misleadingly overbroad. We have already seen that several avenues remain open for ensuring state compliance with federal law. Most notably, an individual may obtain injunctive relief under *Ex parte Young*[, 209 U.S. 123 (1908),] in order to remedy a state officer's ongoing violation of federal law. . . . Second, contrary to the implication of Justice Stevens' conclusion, it has not been widely thought that the federal antitrust, bankruptcy, or copyright statutes abrogated the States' sovereign immunity. This Court never has awarded relief against a State under any of those statutory schemes. . . . [In *Goldfarb v. Virginia State Bar*, 421 U.S. 773, 792 n.22 (1975)] we specifically reserved the question whether the Eleventh Amendment would allow a suit to enforce the antitrust laws against a State. . . . Although . . . the antitrust laws have been in force for over a century, there is no established tradition in the lower federal courts of allowing enforcement of those federal statutes against the States.

In short, Chief Justice Rehnquist suggests (although does not hold) that the states are immune from antitrust suits by private parties. This conclusion is somewhat tempered by his recognition that, under the theory of *Ex parte Young*, the Court has allowed suits for injunctions against a state officer who is acting in violation of federal law.

The reasoning of the *Seminole Tribe* decision has been criticized for its constitutional analysis of federalism. Professor Monaghan states, ". . . *Seminole Tribe* simply perpetuates a questionable line of reasoning. . . . State sovereign immunity remains the exception, not the rule. . . ." Henry Paul Monaghan, *Commment: The Sovereign Immunity "Exception,"* 110 HARV. L. REV. 102, 133 (1996). Similarly, Professor Hovenkamp finds the majority opinion overreaching in its commitment to principles of federalism, stating, "But these commitments hardly justify striking down congressional acts on the basis of strained textual and historical interpretations of the Constitution. . . ." Herbert Hovenkamp, *Judicial Restraint and Constitutional Federalism: The Supreme Court's* Lopez *and* Seminole Tribe *Decisions*, 96 COLUM. L. REV. 2213, 2247 (1996). *See also* Susan Beth Farmer, *Altering the Balance Between State Sovereignty and Competition: A Critical Analysis of* Seminole Tribe *on the Antitrust State Action Immunity Doctrine*, 42 VILLANOVA L. REV. 100 (1997) (noting that a state is now immune from antitrust liability even if its anticompetitive conduct fails to meet the conditions of the state-action doctrine); Carlos Manuel Vásquez, *What is Eleventh Amendment Immunity?*, 106 YALE L.J. 1683, 1721 (1997).

It is difficult to assess prospectively the full ramifications of this decision. Prior to the decision in *Seminole Tribe*, the courts had evolved a doctrine of constructive or implied waiver to Eleventh Amendment immunity. Under one reading of *Seminole Tribe*, the Supreme Court has emphasized the importance of safeguarding state immunity to suit. Although states may still consent to be sued, an indirect effect of *Seminole Tribe* may be to deprive lower courts of their ability to invoke constructive or implied waiver. It is even more difficult to predict the impact, if any, of the *Seminole Tribe* decision on the antitrust state-action doctrine. While *Seminole Tribe* has no direct bearing on the state-action doctrine, lower court judges in cases involving both defenses may very well perceive the emphasis on the limited power of Congress to abrogate state sovereign immunity as also implicitly requiring a broader interpretation of the state-action doctrine. Accordingly, *Seminole Tribe* may reinforce efforts by lower court judges to expand state-action immunity in Sherman and Clayton Act cases. The *Seminole Tribe* decision may thus indirectly alter the preexisting relation between the Eleventh Amendment and the state-action doctrine that had been worked out in the caselaw. The decision provides absolute Eleventh Amendment immunity even when the antitcompetitive conduct of state actors falls outside the shelter of the state-action doctrine.

The application of the state-action exemption, the dormant Commerce Clause, and the Eleventh Amendment often arise together in litigation. Both the state-action exemption and the Eleventh Amendment are frequently raised by state defendants seeking to dismiss antitrust claims against them. Frequently, lower courts had held in cases arising prior to the *Seminole Tribe* decision, that even if a state actor fails to meet the requirements of the state-action defense, the Eleventh Amendment affords antitrust immunity. Conversely, antitrust plaintiffs often grounded their claims against anticompetitive acts of state or local governments under both the antitrust laws (where issues involving the state-action exemption are likely to arise) and the dormant Commerce Clause.

In *Crosetto v. State Bar of Wisconsin,* 12 F.3d 1396, 1401 (7th Cir. 1993), a group of Wisconsin lawyers, objecting to the Bar Association's rule of compulsory membership dues, sued the Association, its executive director, and Justices of the Wisconsin Supreme Court (who collectively administer the integrated bar), alleging violation of the First Amendment and Due Process rights. In affirming the dismissal of plaintiff's claims, the court of appeals ruled that the Eleventh Amendment shielded the Bar Association and remanded to the trial court for a finding whether the conduct met the conditions for antitrust immunity under the state-action doctrine. Some courts apply both doctrines, shielding the state under the Eleventh Amendment and individual actors under the state-action doctrine. In *Charley's Taxi Radio Dispatch Corp. v. SIDA of Hawaii, Inc.*, 810 F.2d 869 (9th Cir. 1987), the operator of a fleet of taxis sued under the Sherman Act, alleging various violations by an association of individual taxi operators, the State of Hawaii's Department of Transportation and its director as the result of the grant of an exclusive contract to the Association allowing its members to be the sole providers of taxi service at the local airport. In affirming the dismissal of the action by the lower court, the court of appeals held that the Eleventh Amendment shielded the state and its Department of Transportation and that the Department would also be immune from antitrust liability under the state-action doctrine. The director of the Department was shielded by the state-action doctrine as was the Association's action in excluding the fleet operator from membership. *See also Pennsylvania Coach Lines, Inc. v. Port Authority of Allegheny County*, 874 F. Supp. 666 (W.D. Pa. 1994), in which a limousine service operator sued the transportation authority under the Sherman Act for granting another operator the exclusive right to provide airport transportation. In declining to dismiss the latter action under the Eleventh Amendment, the court relied on a finding in unrelated litigation by the Third Circuit that the Authority was not an agency of the state of Pennsylvania. However, the court dismissed the limousine operator's case under the state-action doctrine based on a ruling of the Pennsylvania Supreme Court that the Authority was an arm of the Commonwealth of Pennsylvania. In a footnote the court stated,

> The fact that this Court has held that the defendant is not a state agency for purposes of the Eleventh Amendment does not preclude a determination that the defendant is a state agency for purposes of the state action exemption in the light of the particularized factors that courts consider when determining whether an entity is a state agency under the Eleventh Amendment.

Id. at 671 n.5. Since the decision in *Seminole Tribe* in 1996, lower courts have applied its analysis, but have not had occasion in those cases to deal with the antitrust state-action doctrine. In *College Savings Bank v. Florida Prepaid Postsecondary Education Expense Board*, 948 F. Supp. 400 (D.N.J. 1996), a patent case, the sole issue was the power of Congress to abrogate state immunity. College Savings sued the Florida Board for infringement of College Savings' patent on a method of obtaining an adequate return of prepaid college tuition, coupling the patent infringement claim with one of false advertising under the Lanham Act. Following the analytical approach of *Seminole Tribe*, the district court held that: 1) Congress had demonstrated a clear intent to abrogate Florida's immunity under patent legislation; and 2) the congressional abrogation of state immunity in these statutes was effective, because Congress was acting pursuant to a constitutional grant of power.

The constitutional grant of power to abrogate state immunity under the Patent and Plant Variety Protection Act Remedy Clarification Act is contained in § 5 of the Fourteenth Amendment. That section confers on Congress broad power to protect property against the states. Since the Patent Act grants (intellectual) property protection, Congress can subject the states to suit by private parties seeking to protect property interests created under that statute. Under this approach, however, the Congress lacks power to subject the states to suits by private parties for false advertising. Although Congress intended to subject the states to such suits in the Trademark Remedy Clarification Act of 1992, Pub. L. No. 102-542, 106 Stat. 3567, it lacked power to do so. Because the Trademark Act does not create property interests in freedom from false advertising, Congress lacked the power to abrogate state immunity to false advertising suits. As the district court put it:

> . . . [T]his case does not involve property that Congress may protect under the Fourteenth Amendment. Congress has no power under the

> Fourteenth Amendment *or any other provision of the Constitution*, to strip the states of their Eleventh Amendment immunity and subject them to suits in federal court for false advertising. Accordingly, the Trademark Remedy Clarification Act is unconstitutional as applied in this case, and plaintiff's Lanham Act Claim must be dismissed for lack of subject matter jurisdiction.

College Savings Bank, 948 F. Supp. at 427 (emphasis added).

B. The State-Action Exemption

Federal Trade Commission v. Ticor Title Insurance Co.

504 U.S. 621 (1992)

Justice KENNEDY delivered the opinion of the Court.

The Federal Trade Commission filed an administrative complaint against six of the nation's largest title insurance companies, alleging horizontal price fixing in their fees for title searches and title examinations. One company settled by consent decree, while five other firms continue to contest the matter. The Commission charged the title companies with violating § 5(a)(1) of the Federal Trade Commission Act . . . which prohibits "[u]nfair methods of competition in or affecting commerce." One of the principal defenses the companies assert is state-action immunity from antitrust prosecution, as contemplated in the line of cases beginning with *Parker v. Brown*, 317 U.S. 341 (1943). The Commission rejected this defense . . . and the firms sought review in the United States Court of Appeals for the Third Circuit. Ruling that state-action immunity was available under the state regulatory schemes in question, the Court of Appeals reversed. . . . We granted *certiorari*. . . .

I

Title insurance is the business of insuring the record title of real property for persons with some interest in the estate, including owners, occupiers, and lenders. A title insurance policy insures against certain losses or damages sustained by reason of a defect in title not shown on the policy or title report to which it refers. Before issuing a title insurance policy, the insurance company or one of its agents performs a title search and examination. The search produces a chronological list of the public documents in the chain of title to the real property. The examination is a critical analysis or interpretation of the condition of title revealed by the documents disclosed through this search.

The title search and examination are major components of the insurance company's services. . . . The Commission issued an administrative complaint in 1985. Horizontal price-fixing was alleged in these terms:

> "Respondents have agreed on the price to be charged for title search and examination services or settlement services through rating bureaus in various states. Examples of states in which one or more of the Respondents have fixed prices with other Respondents or other competitors for all or part of their search and examination services or settlement services are Arizona, Connecticut, Idaho,

Louisiana, Montana, New Jersey, New Mexico, New York, Ohio, Oregon, Pennsylvania, Wisconsin and Wyoming." 112 F.T.C. at 346.

The Commission did not challenge the insurers' practice of setting uniform rates for insurance against the risk of loss from defective titles, but only the practice of setting uniform rates for the title search, examination, and settlement, aspects of the business which, the Commission alleges, do not involve insurance.

Before the Administrative Law Judge (ALJ), the respondents . . . contended [*inter alia* that] their activities are entitled to state-action immunity, which permits anticompetitive conduct if authorized and supervised by state officials. *See California Retail Liquor Dealers Assn. v. Midcal Aluminum Inc.*, 445 U.S. 97 (1980); *Parker v. Brown*, 317 U.S. 341 (1943). As to one State, Ohio, the respondents contended that the rates for title search, examination, and settlement had not been set by a rating bureau.

Title insurance company rates and practices in thirteen States were the subject of the initial complaint. . . . Four States remain in which violations were alleged: Connecticut, Wisconsin, Arizona, and Montana.

The ALJ held that the rates for search and examination services had been fixed in these four States. . . .

The ALJ described the regulatory regimes for title insurance rates in the four States still at issue. In each one, the title insurance rating bureau was licensed by the State and authorized to establish joint rates for its members. Each of the four States used what has come to be called a "negative option" system to approve rate filings by the bureaus. Under a negative option system, the rating bureau filed rates for title searches and title examinations with the state insurance office. The rates became effective unless the State rejected them within a specified period, such as 30 days. Although the negative option system provided a theoretical mechanism for substantive review, the ALJ determined, after making detailed findings regarding the operation of each regulatory regime, that the rate filings were subject to minimal scrutiny by state regulators.

In Connecticut the State Insurance Department has the authority to audit the rating bureau and hold hearings regarding rates, but it has not done so. The Connecticut rating bureau filed only two major rate increases, in 1966 and in 1981. The circumstances behind the 1966 rate increase are somewhat obscure. The ALJ found that the Insurance Department asked the rating bureau to submit additional information justifying the increase, and later approved the rate increase although there is no evidence the additional information was provided. In 1981 the Connecticut rating bureau filed for a 20 percent rate increase. The factual background for this rate increase is better developed though the testimony was somewhat inconsistent. A state insurance official testified that he reviewed the rate increase with care and discussed various components of the increase with the rating bureau. The same official testified, however, that he lacked the authority to question certain expense data he considered quite high. . . .

In Wisconsin the State Insurance Commissioner is required to examine the rating bureau at regular intervals and authorized to reject rates through a process of hearings. Neither has been done. The Wisconsin rating bureau made major rate filings in 1971, 1981, and 1982. The 1971 rate filing was approved in 1971 although supporting justification, which had been requested by the State Insurance Commissioner, was not provided until 1978. The 1981 rate filing requested an 11 percent rate increase. The increase was approved after the office of the Insurance Commissioner checked the supporting data for accuracy. No one in the agency inquired into insurer expenses, though an official testified that substantive scrutiny would not be possible without that inquiry. The 1982 rate increase received but a cursory reading at the office of the Insurance Commissioner. The supporting materials were not checked for accuracy, though in the absence of an objection by the agency, the rate increase went into effect. . . .

In Arizona the Insurance Director was required to examine the rating bureau at least once every five years. It was not done. In 1980 the State Insurance Department announced a comprehensive investigation of the rating bureau. It was not conducted. The rating bureau spent most of its time justifying its escrow rates. Following settlement in 1981 of a federal civil suit challenging the joint fixing of escrow rates, the rating bureau went out of business without having made any major rate filings, though it had proposed minor rate adjustments. . . .

In Montana the rating bureau made its only major rate filing in 1983. In connection with it, a representative of the rating bureau met with officials of the State Insurance Department. He was told that the filed rates could go into immediate effect though further profit data would have to be provided. The ALJ found no evidence that the additional data were furnished. . . .

To complete the background, the ALJ observed that none of the rating bureaus are now active. The respondents abandoned them between 1981 and 1985 in response to numerous private treble damage suits, so by the time the Commission filed its formal complaint in 1985, the rating bureaus had been dismantled. . . . The ALJ held that the case is not moot, though, because nothing would preclude respondents from resuming the conduct challenged by the Commission. . . .

These factual determinations established, the ALJ addressed the two-part test that must be satisfied for state-action immunity under the antitrust laws, the test we set out in *California Retail Liquor Dealers Assn. v. Midcal Aluminum, Inc.*, 445 U.S. 97 (1980). A state law or regulatory scheme cannot be the basis for antitrust immunity unless, first, the State has articulated a clear and affirmative policy to allow the anticompetitive conduct, and second, the State provides active supervision of anticompetitive conduct undertaken by private actors. . . . The Commission having conceded that the first part of the test was satisfied in the four States still at issue, the immunity question, beginning with the hearings before the ALJ and in all later proceedings, has turned upon the proper interpretation and application of *Midcal*'s active supervision requirement. The ALJ found the active supervision test was met in Arizona and Montana but not in Connecticut or Wisconsin. . . .

On review of the ALJ's decision, the Commission held that none of the four states had conducted sufficient supervision, so that the title companies were not entitled to immunity in any of those jurisdictions. . . . The Court of Appeals for the Third Circuit disagreed with the Commission, adopting the approach of the First Circuit in *New England Motor Rate Bureau, Inc. v. FTC*, 908 F.2d 1064 (1990), which had held that the existence of a state regulatory program, if staffed, funded, and empowered by law, satisfied the requirement of active supervision. . . . Under this standard, the Court of Appeals for the Third Circuit ruled that the active state supervision requirement was met in all four states and held that the respondents' conduct was entitled to state action immunity in each of them. . . .

We granted *certiorari* to consider two questions: First, whether the Third Circuit was correct in its statement of the law and in its application of law to fact, and second, whether the Third Circuit exceeded its authority by departing from the factual findings entered by the ALJ and adopted by the Commission. Before this Court, the parties have confined their briefing on the first of these questions to the regulatory regimes of Wisconsin and Montana, and focused on the regulatory regimes of Connecticut and Arizona in briefing on the second question. We now reverse the Court of Appeals under the first question and remand for further proceedings under the second.

II

The preservation of the free market and of a system of free enterprise without price fixing or cartels is essential to economic freedom. . . . A national policy of such a pervasive and fundamental character is an essential part of the economic and legal system within which the separate States administer their own laws for the protection and advancement of their people. Continued enforcement of the national antitrust policy grants the States more freedom, not less, in deciding whether to subject discrete parts of the economy to additional regulations and controls. Against this background, in *Parker v. Brown*, 317 U.S. 341 (1943), we upheld a state-supervised market sharing scheme against a Sherman Act challenge. We announced the doctrine that federal antitrust laws are subject to supersession by state regulatory programs. Our decision was grounded in principles of federalism. . . .

The principle of freedom of action for the States, adopted to foster and preserve the federal system, explains the later evolution and application of the *Parker* doctrine in our decisions in *Midcal, supra*, and *Patrick v. Burget*, 486 U.S. 94 (1988). In *Midcal* we invalidated a California statute forbidding licensees in the wine trade from selling below prices set by the producer. There we announced the two-part test applicable to instances where private parties participate in a price fixing regime. "First, the challenged restraint must be one clearly articulated and affirmatively expressed as state policy; second, the policy must be actively supervised by the State itself." . . . *Midcal* confirms that while a State may not confer antitrust immunity on private persons by fiat, it may displace competition with active state supervision if the displacement is both intended by the State and implemented in its specific details. Actual state involvement, not deference to private price fixing arrangements under the general auspices of state law, is the precondition for immunity from federal law. Immunity is conferred out of respect for ongoing regulation by the State, not out of respect for the economics of price restraint. In *Midcal* we found that the intent to restrain prices was expressed with sufficient precision so that the first part of the test was met, but that the absence of state participation in the mechanics of the price posting was so apparent that the requirement of active supervision had not been met. . . .

The rationale was further elaborated in *Patrick v. Burget* [set out in Chapter 19, *infra*—Eds.]. In *Patrick* it had been alleged that private physicians participated in the State's peer review system in order to injure or destroy competition by denying hospital privileges to a physician who had begun a competing clinic. We referred to the purpose of preserving the State's own administrative policies, as distinct from allowing private parties to foreclose competition, in the following passage:

> "The active supervision requirement stems from the recognition that where a private party is engaging in the anticompetitive activity, there is a real danger that he is acting to further his own interests, rather than the governmental interests of the State. . . . The requirement is designed to ensure that the state-action doctrine will shelter only the particular anticompetitive acts of private parties that, in the judgment of the State, actually further state regulatory policies. To accomplish this purpose, the active supervision requirement mandates that the State exercise ultimate control over the challenged anticompetitive conduct. . . . The mere presence of some state involvement or monitoring does not suffice. . . . The active supervision prong of the *Midcal* test requires that state

> officials have and exercise power to review particular anticompetitive acts of private parties and disapprove those that fail to accord with state policy. Absent such a program of supervision, there is no realistic assurance that a private party's anticompetitive conduct promotes state policy, rather than merely the party's individual interests." . . .

Because the particular anticompetitive conduct at issue in *Patrick* had not been supervised by governmental actors, we decided that the actions of the peer review committee were not entitled to state-action immunity. . . .

Our decisions make clear that the purpose of the active supervision inquiry is not to determine whether the State has met some normative standard, such as efficiency, in its regulatory practices. Its purpose is to determine whether the State has exercised sufficient independent judgment and control so that the details of the rates or prices have been established as a product of deliberate state intervention, not simply by agreement among private parties. Much as in causation inquiries, the analysis asks whether the State has played a substantial role in determining the specifics of the economic policy. The question is not how well state regulation works but whether the anticompetitive scheme is the State's own.

. . . [T]he States regulate their economies in many ways not inconsistent with the antitrust laws. For example, Oregon may provide for peer review by its physicians without approving anticompetitive conduct by them. *See Patrick*. . . . Or Michigan may regulate its public utilities without authorizing monopolization in the market for electric light bulbs. *See Cantor v. Detroit Edison Co.*, 428 U.S. 579, 596 (1976). So we have held that state-action immunity is disfavored, much as are repeals by implication. . . . By adhering in most cases to fundamental and accepted assumptions about the benefits of competition within the framework of the antitrust laws, we increase the States' regulatory flexibility.

States must accept political responsibility for actions they intend to undertake. . . . Federalism serves to assign political responsibility, not to obscure it. Neither federalism nor political responsibility is well served by a rule that essential national policies are displaced by state regulations intended to achieve more limited ends. For States which do choose to displace the free market with regulation, our insistence on real compliance with both parts of the *Midcal* test will serve to make clear that the State is responsible for the price fixing it has sanctioned and undertaken to control.

Respondents contend that these concerns are better addressed by the requirement that the States articulate a clear policy to displace the antitrust laws with their own forms of economic regulation. This contention misapprehends the close relation between *Midcal*'s two elements. Both are directed at ensuring that particular anticompetitive mechanisms operate because of a deliberate and intended state policy. . . . In the usual case, *Midcal*'s requirement that the State articulate a clear policy shows little more than that the State has not acted through inadvertence; it cannot alone ensure, as required by our precedents, that particular anticompetitive conduct has been approved by the State. It seems plain, moreover, . . . that sole reliance on the requirement of clear articulation will not allow the regulatory flexibility that these States deem necessary. . . .

III

In the case before us, the Court of Appeals relied upon a formulation of the active supervision requirement articulated by the First Circuit:

> "Where . . . the state's program is in place, is staffed and funded, grants to the state officials ample power and the duty to regulate pursuant to declared stan-

> dards of state policy, is enforceable in the state's courts, and demonstrates some basic level of activity directed towards seeing that the private actors carry out the state's policy and not simply their own policy, more need not be established." . . .

Based on this standard, the Third Circuit ruled that the active supervision requirement was met in all four states, and held that the respondents' conduct was entitled to state-action immunity from antitrust liability. . . .

While in theory the standard articulated by the First Circuit might be applied in a manner consistent with our precedents, it seems to us insufficient to establish the requisite level of active supervision. The criteria set forth by the First Circuit may have some relevance as the beginning point of the active state supervision inquiry, but the analysis cannot end there. Where prices or rates are set as an initial matter by private parties, subject only to a veto if the State chooses to exercise it, the party claiming the immunity must show that state officials have undertaken the necessary steps to determine the specifics of the price-fixing or rate-setting scheme. The mere potential for state supervision is not an adequate substitute for a decision by the State. Under these standards, we must conclude that there was no active supervision in either Wisconsin or Montana.

The respondents point out that in Wisconsin and Montana the rating bureaus filed rates with state agencies and that in both States the so-called negative option rule prevailed. The rates became effective unless they were rejected within a set time. It is said that as a matter of law in those States inaction signified substantive approval. This proposition cannot be reconciled, however, with the detailed findings, entered by the ALJ and adopted by the Commission, which demonstrate that the potential for state supervision was not realized in fact. The ALJ found, and the Commission agreed, that at most the rate filings were checked for mathematical accuracy. Some were unchecked altogether. In Montana, a rate filing became effective despite the failure of the rating bureau to provide additional requested information. In Wisconsin, additional information was provided after a lapse of seven years, during which time the rate filing remained in effect. These findings are fatal to respondents' attempts to portray the state regulatory regimes as providing the necessary component of active supervision. The findings demonstrate that, whatever the potential for state regulatory review in Wisconsin and Montana, active state supervision did not occur. In the absence of active supervision in fact, there can be no state-action immunity for what were otherwise private price fixing arrangements. And as in *Patrick*, the availability of state judicial review could not fill the void. Because of the state agencies' limited role and participation, state judicial review was likewise limited. . . .

. . . .

This case involves horizontal price fixing under a vague *imprimatur* in form and agency inaction in fact. No antitrust offense is more pernicious than price fixing. . . . Our decision should be read in light of the gravity of the antitrust offense, the involvement of private actors throughout, and the clear absence of state supervision. We do not imply that some particular form of state or local regulation is required to achieve ends other than the establishment of uniform prices. *Cf. Columbia v. Omni Outdoor Advertising, Inc.*, 499 U.S. 365 (1991) (city billboard zoning ordinance entitled to state-action immunity) [set out on page 964, *infra*—Eds.]. We do not have before us a case in which governmental actors made unilateral decisions without participation by private actors. *Cf. Fisher v. Berkeley*, 475 U.S. 260 (1986) (private actors not liable without private action) [set out on page 944, *infra*—Eds.]. And we do not here call into question a regulatory regime in which sampling techniques or a specified rate of return allow state regulators to provide comprehensive supervision without complete control, or in which there was an infrequent lapse of state supervision. *Cf. 324 Liquor Corp. v. Duffy*, 479 U.S. 335, 344, n.6 (1987) (a statute specifying the margin between wholesale and retail prices may satisfy the active supervision requirement). In the circumstances of this case, however, we conclude that the acts of the respondents in the States of Montana and Wisconsin are not immune from antitrust liability.

IV

In granting *certiorari* we undertook to review the further contention by the Commission that the Court of Appeals was incorrect in disregarding the Commission's findings as to the extent of state supervision. The parties have focused their briefing on this question on the regulatory schemes of Connecticut and Arizona. We think the Court of Appeals should have the opportunity to reexamine its determinations with respect to these latter two States in light of the views we have expressed.

The judgment of the Court of Appeals is reversed and the case is remanded for further proceedings consistent with this opinion.

It is so ordered.

NOTE ON THE STATE-ACTION EXEMPTION

1. *Parker v. Brown* and its immediate aftermath.

a) *Parker v. Brown*, 317 U.S. 341 (1943). As the Court's opinion points out, the foundation case of the state-action exemption is *Parker v. Brown*. In *Parker*, a producer and packer of raisins sought to enjoin the California State Director of Agriculture and other officials from enforcing provisions of the California Agriculture Prorate Act which would have compelled the removal of a portion of that producer/packer's crop from ordinary marketing channels. The prorate program was designed to reduce the supply of a crop in order to exert upward pressure on price. It operated in the manner of a cartel, except that it was organized and administered under the auspices of the state of California. The Court ruled that because the prorate program "derived its authority and its efficacy from the legislative command of the state," it was not prohibited by the Sherman Act. That Act, the Court said, was directed against "individual and not state action." The evil at which Congress was legislating in the Sherman Act was said to be the restraint of competition and attempts to monopolize by individuals and business corporations. In reaching these conclusions, the Court injected a concern for the demands of federalism: "In a dual system of government . . . an unexpressed purpose to nullify a state's control over its officers and agents is not lightly to be attributed to Congress."

b) *Schwegmann Brothers v. Calvert Distillers Corp.*, 341 U.S. 384 (1951). The ambiguities of *Parker v. Brown* were highlighted in *Schwegmann*. That case involved so-called "fair trade" laws and the "nonsigner" provisions of those laws.

In 1937 Congress had enacted the Miller-Tydings Act which exempted from the Sherman Act certain types of vertically imposed resale price maintenance contracts entered into between suppliers of branded merchandise and their dealers in those states which had enacted exempting legislation (so-called "fair trade" acts). (One of the conditions of the exemption was that the branded merchandise had to be in competition with other brands of merchandise of the same general class. The Miller-Tydings Act is discussed in Chapter 5.) During the period in which the Miller-Tydings Act was in force (1937-75), the law governing the lawfulness of vertical price-fixing contracts varied from state to state. In those states which (pursuant to the permission of the Miller-Tydings Act) had enacted a fair trade law, vertical price-fixing contracts were lawful. In those states which had not enacted a fair trade law, vertical price-fixing contracts were *per se* illegal under the Sherman Act, as construed in *Dr. Miles*. (*See* Chapter 5.)

Louisiana had enacted a "fair trade" act authorizing such resale price maintenance contracts; the Louisiana Act, in addition, contained a "nonsigner" provision which make it illegal under Lousiana law for any noncontracting dealer to sell at a price different from the price specified in a price-fixing contract between a supplier and a dealer. The plaintiffs, out-of-state suppliers, had entered into fair trade contracts with some Louisiana retailers. The defendant, a Louisiana retailer, had refused to enter into resale price maintenance contracts with the plaintiffs and it was selling plaintiffs' brands of liquor at cut-rate prices.

The plaintiffs brought suit under the Louisiana nonsigner provision which prohibited any nonsigning retailer from selling below the price set in a fair trade contract entered into by others. The plaintiffs argued that the nonsigner provision of the Louisiana Act needed no exemption from the Sherman Act because the nonsigner provision operated where no agreements had been entered. Thus, it was the command of the state operating through the nonsigner provision rather than individual agreements upon which the plaintiffs were basing their case against the defendant retailer.

The Supreme Court (through Justice Douglas) rejected the plaintiff's contention: By compelling "retailers to follow a parallel price policy" the Louisiana Act was "demand[ing] private conduct which the Sherman Act forbids." Hence, the Louisiana nonsigner provision was declared invalid as in conflict with the Sherman Act.

2. A period of inaction followed by flux.

Parker was decided in 1943. The Court did not again deal with the interplay between state regulation and the Sherman Act until 1951 when it decided *Schwegmann*. Then the Court heard no cases in this area until 1975 when it decided *Goldfarb v. Virginia State Bar*, 421 U.S. 773 (1975). Since 1975, the Court has decided many state-action exemption cases: *Cantor v. Detroit Edison Co.*, 428 U.S. 579 (1976); *Bates v. State Bar of Arizona*, 433 U.S. 350 (1977); *City of Lafayette, Louisiana v. Louisiana Power & Light Co.*, 435 U.S. 389 (1978); *New Motor Vehicle Board of California v. Orrin W. Fox Co.*, 439 U.S. 96 (1978); *California Retail Liquor Dealers Ass'n v. Midcal Aluminum, Inc.*, 445 U.S. 97 (1980); *Community Communications Co. v. City of Bolder, Colorado*, 455 U.S. 40 (1982); *Rice v. Norman Williams Co.*, 458 U.S. 654 (1982); *Hoover v. Ronwin*, 466 U.S. 558 (1984); *Town of Hallie v. City of Eau Claire*, 471 U.S. 34 (1985); *Southern Motor Carriers Rate Conference, Inc. v. United States*, 471 U.S. 48 (1985); *Fisher v. Berkeley*, 475 U.S. 260 (1986); *324 Liquor Corp. v. Duffy*, 479 U.S. 335 (1987); *Patrick v. Burget*, 486 U.S. 94 (1988); *Columbia v. Omni Outdoor Advertising, Inc.*, 499 U.S. 365 (1991); *FTC v. Ticor Title Ins. Co.*, 504 U.S. 621 (1992).

This disproportionate number of decisions devoted to the interplay between the federal antitrust laws and nonfederal regulation reflects the Court's halting attempts to articulate standards governing the scope of the state-action exemption to the federal antitrust laws. What seems to have emerged from these cases is a formulaic standard enunciated in *Midcal*, a replay of the factual configuration of the *Schwegmann* decision, and a gloss on the *Midcal* formulation set forth in *Fisher*.

3. In the *Parker v. Brown* case, the plaintiff (Brown) brought his action against the State Director of Agriculture, Raisin Proration Zone No. 1, the members of the State Agricultural Prorate Advisory Commission and of the Program Committee for Zone No. 1, and others charged by the statute with the administration of the Prorate Act. Why do you think that Brown did not sue the state of California directly? Was he perhaps anticipating an Eleventh Amendment problem if he did? In most of the state-action cases following in the wake of *Parker v. Brown*, the plaintiffs have been careful to bring their actions against officials or individuals acting under color of state or local government authorization, rather than against the state as such. Municipalities do not share the Eleventh Amendment immunity of states. *See, e.g., Sonnenfeld v. Denver*, 100 F.3d 744, 749 (10th Cir. 1996), *petition for cert. filed*, 65 U.S.L.W. 3572 (Feb. 10, 1997) (cities and counties not entitled to Eleventh Amendment immunity). *See also Town of Hallie v. City of Eau Claire*, 471 U.S. 34, 38 (1985) (municipalities not themselves sovereign). Accordingly, antitrust actions have been brought directly against cities and other units of local government, as in the *Lafayette*, *Boulder*, *Hallie*, *Berkeley*, and *Columbia* cases listed above.

California Retail Liquor Dealers Association v. Midcal Aluminum, Inc.

445 U.S. 97 (1980)

Mr. Justice POWELL delivered the opinion of the Court.

In a state-court action, respondent Midcal Aluminum, Inc., a wine distributor, presented a successful antitrust challenge to California's resale price maintenance and price posting statutes for the wholesale wine trade. The issue . . . is whether those state laws are shielded from the Sherman Act by either the "state action" doctrine of *Parker v. Brown* . . . or § 2 of the Twenty-first Amendment. [Section 2 provides that "The transportation or importation into any State . . . for delivery or use therein of intoxicating liquors in violation of the laws thereof, is hereby prohibited."—Eds.]

. . . .

[Prior] . . . decisions establish two standards for antitrust immunity under *Parker v. Brown*. First, the challenged restraint must be "one clearly articulated and affirmatively expressed as state policy"; second, the policy must be "actively supervised" by the State itself. . . . The California system for wine pricing satisfies the first standard. The legislative policy is forthrightly stated and clear in its purpose to permit resale price maintenance. The program, however, does not meet the second requirement for *Parker* immunity. The State simply authorizes price setting and enforces the prices established by private parties. The State neither establishes prices nor reviews the reasonableness of the price schedules; nor does it regulate the terms of fair trade contracts. The State does not monitor market conditions or engage in any "pointed reexamination" of the program. The national policy in favor of competition cannot be thwarted by casting such a gauzy cloak of state involvement over what is essentially a private price-fixing arrangement. . . .

[In applying the Twenty-first Amendment, the Court sought to balance federal and state interests.] . . . Nothing in the record . . . suggests that the wine pricing system helps sustain small retail establishments. Neither the petitioner nor the State Attorney General . . . has demonstrated that the program inhibits the consumption of alcohol by Californians. We need not consider whether the legitimate state interests in temperance and the protection of small retailers ever could prevail against the undoubted federal interest in a competitive economy. . . .

Affirmed.

COMMENTARY

1. Why was *Midcal* a replay of *Schwegmann*? Was *Midcal* correctly decided? Were California's resale price maintenance and price posting statutes invalidated by the Sherman Act in *Midcal*? Under what theory were those statutes invalidated? Were those statutes preempted by the Sherman Act? Was this an application of the Supremacy Clause of the U.S. Constitution? When you read the next case (*Fisher v. Berkeley*), observe the way that Justice Marshall relates the preemption issue to the state-action doctrine.

2. In *Midcal*, the Court sought to codify the rules for determining when the state action exemption applied and when it did not. The Court probably believed that this codification was urgently required, because its prior decisions were confused and conflicting. *Midcal* set forth a two-part test. Can you state the two-part test? Do you think that you can tell when it is satisfied? What is the rationale behind each of the two parts of the *Midcal* test?

3. Do you recognize the *Midcal* test as having been applied in *Ticor*? Which part of the *Midcal* test was critical in *Ticor*? Do you think that *Ticor* properly applied the *Midcal* test?

Fisher v. Berkeley

475 U.S. 260 (1986)

Justice MARSHALL delivered the opinion of the Court.

The question presented here is whether a rent control ordinance enacted by a municipality pursuant to popular initiative is unconstitutional because pre-empted by the Sherman Act.

I

In June 1980, the electorate of the city of Berkeley, California, enacted an initiative entitled "Ordinance 5261-N.S., Rent Stabilization and Eviction for Good Cause Ordinance" (hereafter Ordinance). Section 3 of the Ordinance stated the measure's purposes.[1]

> "The purposes of this Ordinance are to regulate residential rent increases in the City of Berkeley and to protect tenants from unwarranted rent increases and arbitrary, discriminatory, or retaliatory evictions, in order to help maintain the diversity of the Berkeley community and to ensure compliance with legal obligations relating to the rental of housing. This legislation is designed to address the City of Berkeley's housing crisis, preserve the public peace, health and safety, and advance the housing policies of the City with regard to low and fixed income persons, minorities, students, handicapped, and the aged." . . .

To accomplish these goals, the Ordinance places strict rent controls on all real property that "is being rented or is available for rent for residential use in whole or in part," § 5. . . . Excepted are government-owned units, transient units, cooperatives, hospitals, certain small owner-occupied buildings, and all newly constructed buildings. For the remaining units, numbering approximately 23,000, . . . the Ordinance establishes a base rent ceiling reflecting the rents in effect at the end of May 1980. A landlord may raise his rents from these levels only pursuant to an annual general adjustment of rent ceilings by a Rent Stabilization Board of appointed commissioners or after he is successful in petitioning the Board for an individual adjustment. A landlord who fails to register with the Board units covered by the Ordinance or who fails to adhere to the maximum allowable rent set under the Ordinance may be fined by the Board, sued by his tenants, or have rent legally withheld from him. If his violations are willful, he may face criminal penalties.

Shortly after the passage of the initiative, appellants, a group of landlords owning rental property in Berkeley, brought this suit in California Superior Court [challenging the validity of the ordinance on constitutional grounds. When the case reached the California Supreme Court the question of whether the ordinance was pre-empted by the federal antitrust laws had been raised. The California Supreme Court upheld the ordinance against the antitrust challenge.] . . .

We noted probable jurisdiction limited to the antitrust pre-emption question . . . and now affirm, although on grounds different from those relied on by the California Supreme Court. . . . [W]e find traditional antitrust analysis adequate to resolve the issue presented here.

. . . .

---

[1] In 1982, while this case was pending in the California Court of Appeal, the Berkeley electorate enacted the "Tenants' Rights Amendments Act of 1982," revising certain sections of the 1980 Ordinance. Like the California Supreme Court, we review the Ordinance as amended, *see* 37 Cal.3d 644, 654, n.2, 209 Cal. Rptr. 682, 693, n.2, 693 P.2d 261, 270, n.2 (1984); all reference herein will therefore be to the 1982 version of the Ordinance.

II

A

Appellants argue that Berkeley's Ordinance is pre-empted . . . because it imposes rent ceilings across the entire rental market for residential units. Such a regime, they contend, clearly falls within the *per se* rule against price fixing, a rule that has been one of the settled points of antitrust enforcement since the earliest days of the Sherman Act . . . . That the prices set here are ceilings rather than floors and that the public interest has been invoked to justify this stabilization should not, appellants argue, save Berkeley's regulatory scheme from condemnation under the *per se* rule.

Certainly there is this much truth to appellants' argument: Had the owners of residential rental property in Berkeley voluntarily banded together to stabilize rents in the city, their activities would not be saved from antitrust attack by claims that they had set reasonable prices out of solicitude for the welfare of their tenants. . . . What distinguishes the operation of Berkeley's Ordinance from the activities of a benevolent landlords' cartel is not that the Ordinance will necessarily have a different economic effect, but that the rent ceilings imposed by the Ordinance and maintained by the Rent Stabilization Board have been unilaterally imposed by government upon landlords to the exclusion of private control.

The distinction between unilateral and concerted action is critical here. Adhering to the language of § 1, this Court has always limited the reach of that provision to "unreasonable restraints of trade effected by a 'contract, combination . . . , or conspiracy' between *separate* entities." . . . A restraint imposed unilaterally by government does not become concerted-action within the meaning of the statute simply because it has a coercive effect upon parties who must obey the law. The ordinary relationship between the government and those who must obey its regulatory commands whether they wish to or not is not enough to establish a conspiracy. Similarly, the mere fact that all competing property owners must comply with the same provisions of the Ordinance is not enough to establish a conspiracy among landlords. Under Berkeley's Ordinance, control over the maximum rent levels of every affected residential unit has been unilaterally removed from the owners of those properties and given to the Rent Stabilization Board. While the Board may choose to respond to an individual landlord's petition for a special adjustment of a particular rent ceiling, it may decide not to. There is no meeting of the minds here. . . . The owners of residential property in Berkeley have no more freedom to resist the city's rent controls than they do to violate any other local ordinance enforced by substantial sanctions.

B

Not all restraints imposed upon private actors by government units necessarily constitute unilateral action outside the purview of § 1. Certain restraints may be characterized as "hybrid," in that nonmarket mechanisms merely enforce private marketing decisions. . . . Where private actors are thus granted "a degree of private regulatory power" . . . the regulatory scheme may be attacked under § 1. Indeed, this Court has twice found such hybrid restraints to violate the Sherman Act. *See Schwegmann Bros. v. Calvert Distillers Corp.*, 341 U.S. 384 (1951); *California Retail Liquor Dealers Assn. v. Midcal Aluminum, Inc.*, 445 U.S. 97 (1980).

. . . .

The hybrid restraints condemned in *Schwegmann* and *Midcal* were thus quite different from the pure regulatory scheme imposed by Berkeley's Ordinance. While the Ordinance does give tenants—certainly a group of interested private parties—some power to trigger the enforcement of its provisions, it places complete control over maximum rent levels exclusively in the hands of the Rent Stabilization Board. Not just the controls themselves but also the rent ceilings they mandate have been unilaterally imposed on the landlords by the city.

C

There may be cases in which what appears to be a state- or municipality-administered price stabilization scheme is really a private price-fixing conspiracy, concealed under a "gauzy cloak of state involvement," *Midcal, supra*, at 106. This might occur even where prices are ostensibly under the absolute control of government officials. However, we have been given no indication that such corruption has tainted the rent controls imposed by Berkeley's Ordinance. Adopted by popular initiative, the Ordinance can hardly be viewed as a cloak for any conspiracy among landlords or between the landlords and the municipality. Berkeley's landlords have simply been deprived of the power freely to raise their rents. That is why they are here. And that is why their role in the stabilization program does not alter the restraint's unilateral nature.[2]

III

Because under settled principles of antitrust law, the rent controls established by Berkeley's Ordinance lack the element of concerted action needed before they can be characterized as a *per se* violation of § 1 of the Sherman Act, we cannot say that the Ordinance is facially inconsistent with the federal antitrust laws. *See Rice v. Norman Williams Co.* . . . We therefore need not address whether, even if the controls were to mandate § 1 violations, they would be exempt under the state-action doctrine from antitrust scrutiny. *See Hallie v. Eau Claire*, 471 U.S. 34 (1985).

The judgment of the California Supreme Court is

Affirmed.

COMMENTARY

1. Note that Justice Marshall's opinion in *Fisher* distinguishes between preemption and the state-action exemption: only if legislation fails preemption analysis must the Court resort to the state-action doctrine. In *Fisher* the Berkeley ordinance was held not to conflict with the Sherman Act and was therefore not preempted. Only if the Court had found that the ordinance was in conflict with the Sherman Act, would it be necessary to determine whether the state-action doctrine afforded an exemption.

---

[2] Though they have not pressed the point with any vigor in this Court, appellants have suggested that Berkeley's rent controls constitute attempted monopolization because the city "is clearly engaged in the provision of housing in the public sector" and using the controls to depress the prices of residential properties as a prelude to taking them over. Tr. of Oral Arg. 14-15. As to this claim, we note only that the inquiry demanded by appellants' allegations goes beyond the scope of the facial challenge presented here. *See Rice v. Norman Williams Co.*, 458 U.S. at 661.

2. As we will see below, at the time that *Fisher* was decided there was considerable uncertainty over when the state-action doctrine applied to local government regulation. Justice Marshall was able to avoid this problem by treating it initially as one of preemption where similar standards applied to state and local government legislation.

3. Try to articulate the standards governing resolution of the preemption issue. Why was the rent control ordinance not preempted? Now analyze the California legislation involved in the *Midcal* case under both preemption and state-action doctrines.

4. Justice Marshall's analysis employs the distinction between unilateral and concerted action. Are you aware of other state-action cases which employed that distinction? How did that distinction contribute to Justice Marshall's conclusion?

5. What is a so-called "hybrid" restraint? Justice Marshall identified the category of restraints in *Fisher*. How do hybrid restraints relate to the distinction between unilateral and concerted action? Of what relevance is this category of restraints? Is the fact that a restraint is a "hybrid" one relevant to the preemption issue? to the state-action exemption?

6. Are all hybrid restraints unlawful? Can you think of a hybrid restraint which is not unlawful? Are all restraints that fail the second part of the *Midcal* test hybrid restraints? Can you think of a restraint which is not a hybrid restraint which is unlawful?

7. In *Hertz Corp. v. City of New York*, 1 F.3d 121 (2d Cir. 1993), the Second Circuit considered Local Law No. 21 of New York City which prohibited car-rental companies from charging different rates to customers based upon the customer's place of residence. The court ruled that this legislation (commonly known as the "Hertz law") "on its face restrained trade within the meaning of § 1 of the Sherman act," by impeding the give and take of the market place. The court then attempted to apply Justice Marshall's reasoning in *Fisher* to an evaluation of the Hertz law:

> The Hertz law . . . lacks several features of the "unilateral" Berkeley ordinance. First, the law is not a "pure regulatory scheme," . . . because it is not a "scheme" at all; the law is simply a directive for all rental-car companies doing business in New York City to remove one factor from their competitive-pricing structures. Second, the law lacks the independent, quasi-judicial board that in Berkeley could adjust rates and provide relief in individual circumstances. Finally, the City of Berkeley was operating in an area vital to its municipal authority—housing; less vital is the rental-car industry in New York City.
>
> Nor does the Hertz law easily fit the fact pattern of the cases held to involve "hybrid" restraints—those that restrain trade through some com-

> bination of governmental and private conduct. The three Supreme Court cases in this category involved the pricing of liquor. . . . Each involved classic price-setting that was delegated by statute or regulation to private industry but was left unsupervised by the state legislature. The Hertz law, in contrast, does not purport to authorize price-setting by private industry; it simply eliminates an element of price competition among industry members.
>
> We reject the city's suggestion to apply *Fisher* expansively so as to view Local Law No. 21 as a unilateral action that lacks the degree of private-government agreement required to be a contract, combination, or conspiracy in restraint of trade. To do so would remove from the reach of the antitrust laws all local governmental actions not fitting the precise fact pattern of the liquor cases and would preclude examination of their anticompetitive effects. At the same time, we reject Hertz's contention that this case, like the "hybrid" liquor cases, presents a straight-forward example of price-fixing that is *per se* invalid.
>
> . . . [W]hile we have found no case dealing with a governmental act having attributes similar to the Hertz law, we conclude that the Hertz law is not a "unilateral" restraint. It is closer to, although not identical with, those actions categorized as "hybrid," because it removes one element of competition in car-rental pricing, but does not further regulate or review the prices set by rental companies.
>
> . . . Local Law No 21 calls for anticompetitive private conduct in setting rental rates and making rental decisions. The law thus merits hybrid treatment. . . .

Hertz, 1 F.3d at 125-29.

8. How does *Hertz* affect your understanding of Justice Marshall's distinction in *Fisher* between unilateral and concerted action? Does *Hertz* show that this distinction may be blurred at the edges? How does the *Hertz* opinion affect the usefulness of the "hybrid restraint" concept? Is the concept still useful after *Hertz*? Does *Hertz* suggest that the "hybridness" of a restraint can be a matter of degree?

C. The *Midcal* Conditions: From *Boulder* Through *Hallie* to the Present

Under *Midcal*, a restraint is entitled to the state-action exemption if it satisfies two standards:

> First, the challenged restraint must be "one clearly articulated and affirmatively expressed as state policy"; second, the policy must be "actively supervised" by the State itself.

1. The First *Midcal* Condition: Clear Articulation

Shortly after *Midcal* articulated the two standards which must be satisfied for the state-action exemption to apply, the Court decided *Community Communications Co. v. City of Boulder*, 455 U.S. 40 (1982).

Community Communications Co. v. City of Boulder, involved municipal legislation. Community Communications had provided cable service to the University Hill area of Boulder from 1966, an area which, because of the terrain, could not receive broadcast television signals. Community Communications picked up broadcast signals on an antenna located elsewhere and brought the signals to the University Hill households by cable.

By 1979, technological developments made it possible for cable television to bring a wide range of programming to subscribers. When Community Communications informed the Boulder city council that it was planning to expand its operations to other areas of the City, the council enacted an ordinance imposing a three-month moratorium on cable expansion while it sought proposals from other cable companies which were interested in doing business in Boulder.

Community Communications then brought suit in federal court, challenging the ordinance as invalid under the federal antitrust laws. The district court decided in favor of Community Communications, but its decision was reversed by a divided Court of Appeals for the Tenth Circuit. On review by the United States Supreme Court, the Court applied the *Midcal* state-action standards. The Court, however, found it necessary only to apply the first standard: the clear articulation standard. The majority ruled that the Boulder moratorium ordinance failed that standard and reversed the court of appeals decision.

The Court found the Boulder ordinance wanting because it could find no relevant state policy: the ordinance was only municipal policy. This, in the Court's view, was a critical flaw, because the state-action doctrine rests in substantial part upon an underlying concern for federalism, and federalism is concerned with the relations between the federal and state governments. The city argued that because of the Home Rule provision of the Colorado Constitution, the city speaks for the state within the confines of the city's boundaries, but the Court found that argument unconvincing.

> But plainly the requirement of "clear articulation and affirmative expression" is not satisfied when the State's position is one of mere *neutrality* respecting the municipal actions challenged as anticompetitive. A State that allows its municipalities to do as they please can hardly be said to have "contemplated" the specific anticompetitive actions for which municipal liability is sought. . . . The relationship of the State of Colorado to Boulder's moratorium ordinance is one of precise neutrality. As the majority in the Court of Appeals below acknowledged: "[W]e are here concerned with City action in the absence of any regulation whatever by the State of Colorado. Under these circumstances there is no interaction of state and local regulation. We have only the action or exercise of authority by the City." . . . [I]n Boulder's view, it can pursue its

> course of regulating cable television competition, while another home rule city can choose to prescribe monopoly service, while still another can elect free-market competition: and all of these policies are equally "contemplated," and "comprehended within the powers granted." Acceptance of such a proposition—that the general grant of power to enact ordinances necessarily implies state authorization to enact specific anticompetitive ordinances—would wholly eviscerate the concepts of "clear articulation and affirmative expression" that our precedents require.

Boulder, 455 U.S. at 55-56. The Supreme Court's *Boulder* decision gave rise to widespread fear that much municipal regulation was in conflict with the federal antitrust laws. Moreover, language in *Boulder* suggested that if this municipal regulation conflicted with the federal antitrust laws, the city and its officials might be subject to treble-damage liability. As a result, *Boulder* engendered a substantial amount of private litigation.

In response, the Congress enacted the Local Government Antitrust Act of 1984 (reproduced at pages 960-61, *infra*), restricting damages recoveries against municipalities and their officials. A common response of the lower courts to the *Boulder* decision was to find that state policy had been "clearly articulated," even in circumstances when the relevant state legislation was obscure. Finally, the Supreme Court, in *Town of Hallie v. City of Eau Claire*, 471 U.S. 34 (1985), retreating from its aggressive position in *Boulder*, adopted a broadly tolerant position towards the clear articulation requirement.

Town of Hallie v. City of Eau Claire

471 U.S. 34 (1985)

Justice POWELL delivered the opinion of the Court.

. . . .

I

Petitioners—Town of Hallie, Town of Seymour, Town of Union, and Town of Washington (the Towns)—are four Wisconsin unincorporated townships located adjacent to respondent, the City of Eau Claire (the City). Town of Hallie is located in Chippewa County, and the other three towns are located in Eau Claire County. The Towns [alleged] . . . that the City violated the Sherman Act . . . by acquiring a monopoly over the provision of sewage treatment services in Eau Claire and Chippewa Counties, and by tying the provision of such services to the provision of sewage collection and transportation services. Under the Federal Water Pollution Control Act . . . the City had obtained federal funds to help build a sewage treatment facility within the Eau Claire Service Area, that included the Towns; the facility is the only one in the market available to the Towns. The City has refused to supply sewage treatment services to the Towns. It does supply the services to individual landowners in areas of the Towns if a majority of the individuals in the area vote by referendum election to have their homes annexed by the City . . . and to use the City's sewage collection and transportation services.

Alleging that they are potential competitors of the City in the collection and transportation of sewage, the Towns contended in the District Court that the City used its monopoly over sewage treatment to gain an unlawful monopoly over the provision of sewage collection and transportation services, in violation of the Sherman Act. They also contended that the City's actions constituted an illegal tying arrangement and an unlawful refusal to deal with the Towns.

. . . .

II

. . . .

It is . . . clear from our cases that before a municipality will be entitled to the protection of the state action exemption from the antitrust laws, it must demonstrate that it is engaging in the challenged activity pursuant to a clearly expressed state policy. We have never fully considered, however, how clearly a state policy must be articulated for a municipality to be able to establish that its anticompetitive activity constitutes state action. Moreover, we have expressly left open the question whether action by a municipality—like action by a private party—must satisfy the "active state supervision" requirement. . . . We consider both of those issues below.

III

The City cites several provisions of the Wisconsin code to support its claim that its allegedly anticompetitive activity constitutes state action. We therefore examine the statutory structure in some detail.

A

Wisconsin Stat. § 62.18(1) (1981-1982) grants authority to cities to construct, add to, alter, and repair sewage systems. The authority includes the power to "describe with reasonable particularity the district to be [served]." *Ibid.* This grant of authority is supplemented by Wis. Stat. § 66.069(2)(c) (1981-1982), providing that a city operating a public utility

> "may by ordinance fix the limits of such service in unincorporated areas. Such ordinance shall delineate the area within which service will be provided and the municipal utility shall have no obligation to serve beyond the area so delineated."

With respect to joint sewage systems, Wis. Stat. § 144.07(1) (1981-1982) provides that the State's Department of Natural Resources may require a city's sewage system to be constructed so that other cities, towns, or areas may connect to the system, and the Department may order that such connections be made. Subsection(1)(m) provides, however, that an order by the Department of Natural Resources for the connection of unincorporated territory to a city system shall be void if that territory refuses to become annexed to the city.

B

The Towns contend that these statutory provisions do not evidence a state policy to displace competition in the provision of sewage services because they make no express mention of anticompetitive conduct.[5] As discussed above, the statutes clearly contemplate that a city may engage in anticompetitive conduct. Such conduct is a foreseeable result of empowering the City to refuse to serve unannexed areas. It is not necessary, as the Towns

---

[5] The Towns also rely on Wis. Stat. Ann. §§ 66.076(1) and 66.30 (1965 and Supp.1984) to argue that the State's policy on the provision of sewage services is actually procompetitive. This claim must fail because, aside from the fact that it was not raised below, the provisions relied upon do not support the contention. First, it is true

contend, for the state legislature to have stated explicitly that it expected the City to engage in conduct that would have anticompetitive effects. . . . [I]t is sufficient that the statutes authorized the City to provide sewage services and also to determine the areas to be served. We think it is clear that anticompetitive effects logically would result from this broad authority to regulate. *See New Motor Vehicle Board v. Orrin W. Fox Co.*, 439 U.S. 96, 109 (1978) (no express intent to displace the antitrust laws, but statute provided regulatory structure that inherently "displace[d] unfettered business freedom"). *Accord,* 1 P. AREEDA & D. TURNER, ANTITRUST LAW ¶ 212.3, p. 54 (Supp. 1982).

Nor do we agree with the Towns' contention that the statutes at issue here are neutral on state policy. The Towns attempt to liken the Wisconsin statutes to the Home Rule Amendment involved in *Boulder*, arguing that the Wisconsin statutes are neutral because they leave the City free to pursue either anticompetitive conduct or free-market competition in the field of sewage services. The analogy to the Home Rule Amendment involved in *Boulder* is inapposite. That Amendment to the Colorado Constitution allocated only the most general authority to municipalities to govern local affairs. We held that it was neutral and did not satisfy the "clear articulation" component of the state action test. The Amendment simply did not address the regulation of cable television. Under home rule the municipality was to be free to decide every aspect of policy relating to cable television, as well as policy relating to any other field of regulation of local concern. Here, in contrast, the State has specifically authorized Wisconsin cities to provide sewage services and has delegated to the cities the express authority to take action that foreseeably will result in anticompetitive effects. No reasonable argument can be made that these statutes are neutral in the same way that Colorado's Home Rule Amendment was.[6]

The Towns' argument amounts to a contention that to pass the "clear articulation" test, a legislature must expressly state in a statute or its legislative history that the legislature intends for the delegated action to have anticompetitive effects. This contention embodies an unrealistic view of how legislatures work and of how statutes are written. No legislature can be expected to catalog all of the anticipated effects of a statute of this kind.

Furthermore, requiring such explicit authorization by the State might have deleterious and unnecessary consequences. . . . In fact, this Court has never required the degree of specificity that the Towns insist is necessary.[7]

---

that § 66.076(1) permits certain municipalities, including towns, to operate sewage systems. The provision is simply a general enabling statute, however, not a mandatory prescription. In addition, subsection (8) of § 66.076 incorporates into the enabling statute all of the limitations of § 66.069, including the power to limit the area of service. Thus, § 66.076(1) does not express a procompetitive state attitude.

Nor does § 66.30 aid the Towns. It is a general provision concerning all utilities—not just sewage systems—that permits municipalities to enter into cooperative agreements. The statute is not mandatory, but merely permissive. Moreover, even assuming two municipalities agreed pursuant to this section to cooperate in providing sewage services, the result would not necessarily be greater competition. Rather, the two combined might well be more effective than either alone in keeping other municipalities out of the market.

[6] Nor does it help the Towns' claim that the statutes leave to the City the discretion whether to provide sewage services. States must always be free to delegate such authority to their political subdivisions.

[7] Requiring such a close examination of a state legislature's intent to determine whether the federal antitrust laws apply would be undesirable also because it would embroil the federal courts in the unnecessary interpretation of state statutes. Besides burdening the courts, it would undercut the fundamental policy of *Parker* and the state action doctrine of immunizing state action from federal antitrust scrutiny. *See* 1 P. AREEDA & D. TURNER, ANTITRUST LAW ¶ 212.3(b) (Supp.1982).

In sum, we conclude that the Wisconsin statutes evidence a "clearly articulated and affirmatively expressed" state policy to displace competition with regulation in the area of municipal provision of sewage services. These statutory provisions plainly show that "the legislature contemplated the kind of action complained of." . . . This is sufficient to satisfy the "clear articulation" requirement of the state action test.

. . . .

IV

Finally, the Towns argue that as there was no active state supervision, the City may not depend on the state action exemption. The Towns rely primarily on language in *Lafayette*. It is fair to say that our cases have not been entirely clear. The plurality opinion in *Lafayette* did suggest, without elaboration and without deciding the issue, that a city claiming the exemption must show that its anticompetitive conduct was actively supervised by the State. . . . We now conclude that the active state supervision requirement should not be imposed in cases in which the actor is a municipality.[10]

As with respect to the compulsion argument discussed above, the requirement of active state supervision serves essentially an evidentiary function: it is one way of ensuring that the actor is engaging in the challenged conduct pursuant to state policy. . . . Where a private party is engaging in the anticompetitive activity, there is a real danger that he is acting to further his own interests, rather than the governmental interests of the State. Where the actor is a municipality, there is little or no danger that it is involved in a private price-fixing arrangement. The only real danger is that it will seek to further purely parochial public interests at the expense of more overriding state goals. This danger is minimal, however, because of the requirement that the municipality act pursuant to a clearly articulated state policy. Once it is clear that state authorization exists, there is no need to require the State to supervise actively the municipality's execution of what is a properly delegated function.

V

We conclude that the actions of the City of Eau Claire in this case are exempt from the Sherman Act. They were taken pursuant to a clearly articulated state policy to replace competition in the provision of sewage services with regulation. We further hold that active state supervision is not a prerequisite to exemption from the antitrust laws where the actor is a municipality rather than a private party. We accordingly affirm the judgment of the Court of Appeals for the Seventh Circuit.

It is so ordered.

COMMENTARY

1. The Court asserted that the clear articulation requirement remained unchanged from the one employed in the *Boulder* case. Do you agree? In the *Boulder* case, the Court said that Colorado had no policy about cable television

---

[10] In cases in which the actor is a state agency, it is likely that active state supervision would also not be required, although we do not here decide that issue. Where state or municipal regulation by a private party is involved, however, active state supervision must be shown, even where a clearly articulated state policy exists. *See Southern Motor Carriers Rate Conference, Inc. v. United States, post*, at 62.

because one city might opt for free-market allocation of cable services while another city could confer a monopoly franchise upon a single provider while another city might operate a cable system as a municipal service. This demonstrated that Colorado had no state policy on the subject. Is it not true that one Wisconsin city might use a sewage treatment monopoly to force adjacent areas to agree to annexation while another Wisconsin city might freely sell sewerage treatment services (without attaching any conditions) while another city might contract out for such services? If Wisconsin cities could follow inconsistent policies in connection with sewerage treatment facilities, is it not true that Wisconsin lacks a policy for sewerage treatment in the same sense that Colorado lacked a policy for cable television?

2. What does the Court now mean by a requirement that the restraint must be "clearly articulated and affirmatively expressed as state policy"? If it can reasonably be foreseen that a power conferred by the state upon a local government can be employed in a noncompetitive way, is it now proper to say that noncompetitive behavior by the local government is taking place pursuant to a clearly articulated and affirmatively expressed state policy? Has the clear articulation requirement now been divested of most of its content?

3. Recall *Hertz Corp. v. City of New York*, 1 F.3d 121 (2d Cir. 1993) (noted on page 947, *supra*), in which a car-rental company challenged municipal legislation prohibiting car-rental companies from charging rates that varied according to the customer's place of residence. The Second Circuit ruled that the car-rental company had asserted a valid antitrust cause of action because the local legislation "restrained trade within the meaning of the Sherman Act" and remanded the case to the district court to evaluate the restraint under the rule of reason. In upholding the car-rental company's claim against a state-action defense, the court relied upon *Boulder* as authority:

> The State of New York has not granted New York City any particular authority over the car-rental field; instead the Hertz law represents an exercise of the city's home-rule powers granted by the state constitution and statutes. . . . The Supreme Court has held that a similar home-rule provision in the Colorado state constitution reflected the state's position of "mere neutrality" regarding local activities undertaken pursuant to that provision. . . . Thus, local government actions that are grounded in home-rule authority are not carried out pursuant to a clearly articulated state policy.

Hertz, 1 F3d at 128. *Hertz* may thus limit the ramifications of *Hallie*. When a state grants municipalities authority to regulate or otherwise deal with a subject matter area, *Hallie* suggests that the grant of authority will be broadly construed to authorize the municipalities to act anticompetitively. But *Hertz* suggests that when there is no grant of authority over a particular subject matter and the city is relying solely on its home-rule powers, *Boulder* may yet deny the state-action exemption.

4. In *City of Columbia v. Omni Outdoor Advertising, Inc.*, 499 U.S. 365 (1991), the Court followed the approach to the clear articulation requirement which it explained in *Hallie*. Columbia Outdoor Advertising, Inc. (COA) controlled more than 95% of the local billboard advertising market. COA was a local business owned by a family with deep roots in the community, and enjoyed close relations with the city's political leaders. When Omni Outdoor Advertising, Inc. (Omni) entered the market, the city council enacted an ordinance restricting the size, location, and spacing of billboards. The restrictions, particularly those on spacing, obviously benefitted COA, which already had its billboards in place, and severely hindered Omni's ability to compete. The Court easily upheld the city's legislative protection for COA against the inroads of the new entrant. First the Court ruled that the city possessed the requisite authority to regulate billboards:

> The South Carolina statutes under which the city acted in the present case authorize municipalities to regulate the use of land and the construction of buildings and other structures within their boundaries.[3] It is undisputed that, as a matter of state law, these statutes authorize the city to regulate the size, location, and spacing of billboards. . . . It suffices for the present to conclude that here no more is needed to establish, for *Parker* purposes, the city's authority to regulate than its unquestioned zoning power over the size, location, and spacing of billboards.

Then the Court ruled that the clear articulation requirement was satisfied:

> Besides authority to regulate, however, the *Parker* defense also requires authority to suppress competition—more specifically, "clear articulation of a state policy to authorize anticompetitive conduct" by the municipality in connection with its regulation. . . . We have rejected the contention that this requirement can be met only if the delegating statute explicitly permits the displacement of competition . . . . It is enough, we

---

3 S.C. Code § 5-23-10 (1976) ("Building and zoning regulations authorized") provides that "[f]or the purpose of promoting health, safety, morals or the general welfare of the community, the legislative body of cities and incorporated towns may by ordinance regulate and restrict the height, number of stories and size of buildings and other structures."

S.C. Code § 5-23-20 (1976) ("Division of municipality into districts") provides that "[f]or any or all of such purposes the local legislative body may divide the municipality into districts of such number, shape and area as may be deemed best suited to carry out the purposes of this article. Within such districts it may regulate and restrict the erection, construction, reconstruction, alteration, repair or use of buildings, structures or land."

S.C. Code § 6-7-710 (1976) ("Grant of power for zoning") provides that "[f]or the purposes of guiding development in accordance with existing and future needs and in order to protect, promote and improve the public health, safety, morals, convenience, order, appearance, prosperity, and general welfare, the governing authorities of municipalities and counties may, in accordance with the conditions and procedures specified in this chapter, regulate the location, height, bulk, number of stories and size of buildings and other structures. . . . The regulations shall . . . be designed to lessen congestion in the streets; to secure safety from fire, panic, and other dangers; to promote the public health and the general welfare; to provide adequate light and air; to prevent the overcrowding of land; to avoid undue concentration of population; to protect scenic areas; to facilitate the adequate provision of transportation, water, sewage, schools, parks, and other public requirements."

> have held, if suppression of competition is the "foreseeable result" of what the statute authorizes . . . . That condition is amply met here. The very purpose of zoning regulation is to displace unfettered business freedom in a manner that regularly has the effect of preventing normal acts of competition, particularly on the part of new entrants. A municipal ordinance restricting the size, location, and spacing of billboards (surely a common form of zoning) necessarily protects existing billboards against some competition from newcomers.[4]

5. What is the purpose of the clear articulation requirement? Does it have to do with ensuring that the state, the state legislators and other state officials accept responsibility for the constraints which they place on the market? Does the clear articulation requirement have a role in making state officials more accountable to their electorate? In the context of municipal antitrust liability, do *Hallie* and *Hertz* indicate that the clear articulation requirement has been reduced to a distinction between grants of authority in subject-matter terms and home rule authority?

6. Did the State of Wisconsin adopt a policy pursuant to which cities would use monopoly control over sewage treatment facilities to force adjacent areas to accept annexation? Is this the use of monopoly power in the sense contemplated in *Berkey Photo, Inc. v. Eastman Kodak Co.* (page 425, *supra*)? Is it a leveraging of monopoly power in the sense contemplated in *United States v. Griffith* (Chapter 9, *supra*)? Absent the state-action exemption, would Eau Claire have a duty, under *Aspen Skiing Co. v. Aspen Highlands Skiing Corp.* (page 436, *supra*), to trade with adjacent towns and landowners desiring sewage treatment services? When Eau Claire refuses to sell sewerage treatment services unless landowners also take

---

4 The dissent contends that, in order successfully to delegate its *Parker* immunity to a municipality, a State must expressly authorize the municipality to engage (1) in specifically "economic regulation". . . (2) of a specific industry. . . . These dual specificities are without support in our precedents, for the good reason that they defy rational implementation.

If, by authority to engage in specifically "economic" regulation, the dissent means authority specifically to regulate competition, we squarely rejected that in *Hallie v. Eau Claire* . . . . Seemingly, however, the dissent means only that the State authorization must specify that sort of regulation whereunder "decisions about prices and output are not made by individual firms, but rather by a public body.". . . But why is not the restriction of billboards in a city a restriction on the "output" of the local billboard industry? It assuredly is—and that is indeed the very gravamen of Omni's complaint. It seems to us that the dissent's concession that "it is often difficult to differentiate economic regulation from municipal regulation of health, safety, and welfare" . . . is a gross understatement. Loose talk about a "regulated industry" may suffice for what the dissent calls "antitrust parlance" . . . but it is not a definition upon which the criminal liability of public officials ought to depend.

Under the dissent's second requirement for a valid delegation of *Parker* immunity—that the authorization to regulate pertain to a specific industry—the problem with the South Carolina statute is that it used the generic term "structures," instead of conferring its regulatory authority industry-by-industry (presumably "billboards," "movie houses," "mobile homes," "TV antennas," and every other conceivable object of zoning regulation that can be the subject of a relevant "market" for purposes of antitrust analysis). To describe this is to refute it. Our precedents not only fail to suggest but positively reject such an approach. "The municipality need not 'be able to point to a specific, detailed legislative authorization' in order to assert a successful *Parker* defense to an antitrust suit." *Hallie* . . . (quoting *Lafayette v. Louisiana Power & Light Co.* . . .).

sewerage collection and transportation services, could Eau Claire's behavior be described as a tie? Would such a tie be *per se* illegal under the criteria of *Jefferson Parish Hospital District No. 2 v. Hyde* (page 249, *supra*)?

7. Is *Hallie* a case in which the antitrust laws should apply at all? The concepts of monopolization and tying are at home in commercial markets. Do they fit the issues which arise when differences arise between local governments over services which are not generally offered in commercial markets? Why did the Court not just dismiss the case on the ground that the antitrust laws were not intended to deal with the provision of services by local governments?

8. Many of the market restraints in the United States are the result of restraints imposed by local governments. Local governments frequently confer monopoly franchises on service providers or impose licensing (and hence restricted entry) where the free market would have provided the services without regulation. Many local governments license taxicabs, limiting the number of cabs which are available to serve the public. In the wake of the *Boulder* decision, the FTC had begun an investigation into municipal taxicab regulation in Minneapolis and New Orleans. After *Hallie*, it appears no longer possible to raise antitrust objections to municipal action limiting taxi service. As noted below, many municipalities have conferred monopolies upon private companies engaged in waste treatment. These municipal monopolies are, after *Hallie*, no longer vulnerable to antitrust attack. They remain, however, vulnerable to challenge under the dormant Commerce Clause.

9. Despite the prevalent liberal interpretation of state statutes to authorize anticompetitive behavior, the clear statement requirement can still be determinative. In *Surgical Care Center v. Hospital Service District No. 1*, 171 F.3d 231 (5th Cir. 1999), Judge Higginbotham, calling the clear statement doctrine vital to federalism, invoked it on behalf of the en banc Fifth Circuit to deny state-action immunity to a hospital district. In that case, a Louisiana statute had established hospital service districts as political subdivisions in which a board of five commissioners would promulgate regulations governing the conduct of the district's hospital. The commission was authorized to "contract with or engage in a joint venture with a person, corporation, partnership, or group of persons to offer, provide, promote, establish, or sell any hospital health service."

St. Luke's, a privately owned hospital, brought suit against Hospital Service District No. 1 whose North Oaks facility was managed for the district by a privately owned management firm. St. Luke's alleged that North Oaks enjoyed a monopoly in the local market for acute care services and was attempting to extend its monopoly to outpatient surgical care by entering into various exclusive contracts with five of the seven largest managed care plans in the market. North Oaks defended on the ground that its conduct was immunized by the above statute.

The Fifth Circuit, sitting en banc, rejected that defense. According to the court, the purpose of the Louisiana statute was to eliminate the competitive disadvantages to which the hospital service districts had previously been subjected: Previously, only private competitors had been able to offer integrated health services. And they had been unable to discuss business strategy in private and to enter into various business forms prevalent in the market, such as joint ventures. Thus the statute was designed to enable the hospital districts to compete on a level playing field, not to authorize anticompetitive behavior. *Surgical Care Center v. Hospital Service District No. 1*, 171 F.3d 231 (5th Cir. 1999).

---

2. The Second *Midcal* Condition: State Supervision

We saw the application of the second *Midcal* requirement of state supervision stringently applied in *Ticor* (page 934, *supra*). That requirement was also strictly applied in *Patrick v. Burget*, 486 U.S. 94 (1988). The Court in *Hallie* began a process of defining the elements of the supervision requirement.

a. *Hallie* on State Superivison

According to the Court in *Hallie*, the second *Midcal* condition (state supervision) does not apply when the actor is itself a local government. The Court suggests (but does not decide) that the same approach will be taken with state agencies. The reason that the supervision requirement does not apply, the Court said, is because local governments (and perhaps state agencies) possess the incentive to further public—rather than private—goals.

Should local governmental units be accorded such deference in the light of the new learning about public choice: that private interests are often effective in capturing the mechanisms of government to further their own narrow interests, often at the expense of the public interest? Or does the Court believe that it is effectively unable to inquire into the motivation behind official governmental action? Why would not a more stringent clear articulation requirement mitigate this problem by increasing the visibility of local government-imposed restraints? Would not this help to make local government officials more accountable to the broad electorate?

Does the Court's reference to state agencies suggest an entirely new problem? Some state "agencies" are composed of representatives of interest groups and sometimes not well-balanced ones. The state agency in the leading case of *Parker v. Brown* was composed of raisin farmers who were cooperating in running a state-authorized cartel. Surely such an agency is likely to further parochial rather than public interests. Is the supervision requirement as applied to state agencies as easily dealt with as the opinion suggests?

Compare the different judicial approaches which are now to be applied to state legislation: Legislation delegating power to municipalities and probably to some state agencies is construed as clearly articulating a state policy embracing any behavior by the local government or state agency which could reasonably be foreseen to fall within the grant. Since the supervision requirement does not apply to local governments or state agencies, broadly worded state legislation is itself sufficient to confer the state-action exemption.

b. State Supervision Updated: The Post-*Hallie* Cases

Under *FTC v. Ticor Title Ins. Co.*, supra, and its predecessor, *Patrick v. Burget*, 486 U.S. 94 (1988) (*see* Chapter 19, page 988), the supervision requirement is stringently enforced against private parties acting under a state regulatory scheme. Broadly worded state legislation is sufficient to immunize private conduct from the antitrust laws only if each activity for which immunity is sought is actively supervised. Negative approvals—in the form commonly used in rate regulation—appear to be problematic under *Ticor*.

Ticor may have been foreshadowed by *324 Liquor Corp. v. Duffy*, 479 U.S. 335 (1987). *324 Liquor*—similar to *Schwegmann* and *Midcal*—involved a state-enforced pricing system over liquor, under which wholesalers controlled retail prices. In a footnote, the Court rejected a contention that the State Liquor Authority actively supervised the liquor pricing system by virtue of its ability to respond to changing market conditions with directives allowing departures from this statutorily-established pricing system. 479 U.S. at 345 n.7.

The state supervision requirement was decisive in *Snake River Valley Electric Ass'n v. PacifiCorp*, 238 F.3d 1189 (9th Cir. 2001). An Idaho statute prohibited an electricity supplier from offering to serve an existing customer of another utility unless that utility consented. Snake River Valley Electric Association (SRVEA) sought, inter alia, the permission of PacifiCorp., a utility, to serve PacifiCorp.'s customers. PacifiCorp. refused, relying on the statute. SRVEA then sued PacifiCorp. under the Sherman Act. The Ninth Circuit ruled the statute did not confer immunity upon PacifiCorp., because the statute failed the second *Midcal* condition: it did not provide for adequate state supervision:

> Under the [Idaho statute], PacifiCorp has the power to grant written consent for another utility to serve its customers. PacifiCorp can, consistent with [that statute], avoid competition for its customers simply by declining to consent—an act undertaken without review by any state agency. By providing an option for competition, and then an "opt out" that is wholly within the utility's control and without state supervision, the state has, in effect, given the utility partial control over the no competition policy. This is the type of private regulatory power that the active supervision prong of *Midcal* is supposed to prevent.

In *Patrick v. Burget*, *infra*, a physician's hospital privileges were terminated as a result of a determination by the hospital's peer review committee that the care he provided was substandard. The peer review procedure was mandated by Oregon law. In an antitrust suit against the committee, the Court ruled that peer review procedure was inadequate to confer state-action immunity upon the physician-members of the committee because the actions of the committee were inadequately supervised by the state. The Court indicated that judicial review which ensured that the procedures were reasonable and that the decision was supported by evidence but which did not extend to the merits of the dismissal would not provide the kind of supervision required by the state-action doctrine.

Congress has provided medical peer review committees antitrust immunity in the Health Care Qualtiy Improvement Act of 1986, 42 U.S.C. § 11101-15 (1994), a fact which the Court acknowledged in a footnote. The federal legislation did not provide immunity to the defendants in the *Patrick v. Burget* case, however, because the events in question preceded the enactment of the federal legislation.

3. The Local Government Antitrust Act of 1984: Congress Responds to the *Boulder* Decision

UNITED STATES CODE
TITLE 15

§ 34. Definitions applicable to sections 34 to 36

For purposes of sections 34 to 36 of this title—

(1) the term "local government" means—

(A) a city, county, parish, town, township, village, or any other general function governmental unit established by State law, or

(B) a school district, sanitary district, or any other special function governmental unit established by State law in one or more States,

(2) the term "person" has the meaning given it in subsection (a) of the first section of the Clayton Act [15 U.S.C. § 12(a)] but does not include any local government as defined in paragraph (1) of this section, and

(3) the term "State" has the meaning given it in section 4G(2) of the Clayton Act [15 U.S.C. § 15(g)(2)].

§ 35. Recovery of damages, etc., for antitrust violations from any local government, or official or employee thereof acting in an official capacity

(a) Prohibition in general

No damages, interest on damages, costs, or attorney's fees may be recovered under section 4, 4A, or 4C of the Clayton Act [15 U.S.C. §§ 15, 15a, or 15c] of this title from any local government, or official or employee thereof acting in an official capacity.

(b) Preconditions for attachment of prohibition; prima facie evidence for nonapplication of prohibition

Subsection (a) of this section shall not apply to cases commenced before the effective date of this Act unless the defendant establishes and the court determines, in light of all the circumstances, including the stage of litigation and the availability of alternative relief under the Clayton Act, that it would be inequitable not to apply this subsection to a pending case. In consideration of this section, existence of a jury verdict, district court judgment, or any stage of litigation subsequent thereto, shall be deemed to be prima facie evidence that subsection (a) of this section shall not apply.

§ 36. Recovery of damages, etc., for antitrust violations on claim against person based on official action directed by local government, or official or employee thereof acting in an official capacity

(a) Prohibition in general

No damages, interest on damages, costs or attorney's fees may be recovered under section 4, 4A, or 4C of the Clayton Act [15 U.S.C. §§ 15, 15a, or 15c] in any claim against a person based on any official action directed by a local government, or official or employee thereof acting in an official capacity.

(b) Nonapplication of prohibition for cases commenced before effective date of provisions

Subsection (a) of this section shall not apply with respect to cases commenced before the effective date of this Act.

COMMENTARY

1. Note that the Local Government Antitrust Act provides immunity from damages liability, but does not purport to change the standards governing when the antitrust laws apply. Thus, municipalities remain subject to injunction suits under the standards embodied in the caselaw.

2. Besides conferring immunity on local governments and officials, the Act also confers immunity on private persons (individuals and corporations) because of "official action directed by a local government, or official or employee thereof acting in an official capacity."

3. When is a local government official engaged in "official action"? When is the official "acting in an official capacity"? When is official action "directed" by a local government or a local government official or employee? What standards govern the resolution of such questions? Are these questions essentially ones of agency law? Does the Act make the immunity which it confers upon private actors depend upon whether local government officials are acting within the scope of their authority? Does the Act make that immunity depend upon whether the local government is itself acting within the scope of authority delegated to it by the State? Is this authority question the same as the authority question embodied in the first *Midcal* requirement?

4. In *Columbia v. Omni Outdoor Advertising, Inc.*, 499 U.S. 365 (1991), the Court indicated that the state-action exemption would not turn upon the question of whether, as a matter of state law, the city acted within the power granted to it and in a procedurally correct manner: "We . . . believe that in order to prevent *Parker* from undermining the very interests of federalism it is designed to protect, it is necessary to adopt a concept of authority broader than what is applied to determine the legality of the municipality's action under state law."

5. Is the approach which the Court took to the authority question in *Columbia, supra*, likely to be applied to the interpretation of the Local Government Antitrust Act?

NOTE: THE FREE-MARKET POLICIES UNDERLYING THE DORMANT COMMERCE CLAUSE; HOW THE DORMANT COMMERCE CLAUSE RELATES TO THE SHERMAN ACT

The Commerce Clause of the U.S. Constitution is designed, *inter alia,* to facilitate a "common market" among the several states and, accordingly, to prevent states from erecting barriers interfering with the free flow of trade across state boundaries. In its "dormant" state, *i.e.,* in the absence of federal legislation, the Commerce Clause is effective to invalidate state legislation intended to protect or prefer local traders at the expense of out-of-state traders. One of the most recent applications of the dormant Commerce Clause took place in *C & A Carbone, Inc. v. Town of Clarkstown*, 511 U.S. 383 (1994).

In the *Carbone* case, the Town of Clarkstown, by ordinance, required that all waste generated in the town or brought into the town be deposited at a designated waste transfer station. By thus conferring a monopoly upon the waste transfer station and allowing the station to charge above-market "tipping fees," the arrangement was designed to finance the $1.4 million cost of the transfer station.

(Note that when a municipality creates a monopoly for a service provider and allows the service provider to charge above-market rates, the municipality may be attempting to finance the facility off-budget, freeing itself from budgetary and taxation limitations imposed by state government. In addition, the municipality may have rendered less visible the effective tax imposed upon its residents, through the above-market fees.)

A waste hauler prevented by the Clarkstown ordinance from disposing of waste at less expensive land fills in New Jersey challenged the validity of the Clarkstown ordinance. The Supreme Court ruled that the ordinance was a "protectionist" device, discriminating in favor of a local provider and against out-of-state providers. Accordingly, the Court invalidated the ordinance under the Commerce Clause. Similar ordinances had been invalided under the dormant Commerce Clause previously. *See, e.g., Waste Sys. Corp. v. County of Martin*, 985 F.2d 1381, 1386-89 (8th Cir. 1993).

Although municipally conferred monopoly over waste disposal is invalid under the dormant Commerce Clause when it interferes with cross-border trade, such municipally conferred monopolies have been upheld against attack under the Sherman Act. When they have been challenged under the Sherman Act, the courts (at least since the time of the Supreme Court's *Hallie* decision) have ruled that they are protected under the antitrust state-action exemption. *See, e.g., Tri-State Rubbish, Inc. v. Waste Management, Inc.*, 998 F.2d 1073, 1078-79 (1st Cir. 1993); *Kern-Tulare Water Dist. v. City of Bakersfield*, 828 F.2d 514, 519-20 (9th Cir. 1987); *L&H Sanitation, Inc. v. Lake City Sanitation*, Inc., 769 F.2d 517, 522 (8th Cir. 1985).

Thus, although both the dormant Commerce Clause and the Sherman Act incorporate federal free-market policies, they treat municipally conferred monopolies differently. For a discussion of the relation of the dormant Commerce Clause to the Sherman Act, see Daniel J. Gifford, *Federalism, Efficiency, the Commerce Clause, and the Sherman Act: Why We Should Follow a Consistent Free-Market Policy*, 44 Emory L.J. 1227 (1995).

NOTE: STATE IMMUNITY FROM SUIT UNDER THE ANTITRUST LAWS AFTER *SEMINOLE TRIBE*— A NEW BARRIER TO ANTITRUST RELIEF

As pointed out in the Introduction to this Chapter, the Supreme Court, in *Seminole Tribe of Florida v. Florida*, 517 U.S. 44 (1996), the Supreme Court ruled that the Eleventh Amendment protects unconsenting states against suit in federal courts by private parties. Since federal antitrust claims must be brought in federal court, *Seminole Tribe* apparently bars private parties from bringing antitrust actions against states as such. Chief Justice Rehnquist suggested, however, that the *Ex parte Young* procedure may remain available to private parties seeking an injunction. In *Ex parte Young*, 209 U.S. 123 (1908), the Court allowed an injunction against a state officer who was attempting to enforce an unconsitutional state statute. *Ex parte Young* dealt with the Eleventh Amendment by denying its application: Since the state could not validly authorize the officer to act, the injunction did not restrain the state. Further ramifications of *Seminole Tribe* for antitrust enforcement are raised in the Introduction.

D. The *Noerr-Pennington* Doctrine, the Now-Rejected "Conspiracy" Exception to the State-Action Doctrine, and Related Matters

Columbia v. Omni Outdoor Advertising, Inc.

499 U.S. 365 (1991)

Justice SCALIA delivered the opinion of the Court.

[In this case the City of Columbia, South Carolina had enacted an ordinance restricting the erection of new billboards. The effect of the ordinance was to entrench Columbia Outdoor Advertising, Inc. ("COA") in its dominant position in the local market, protecting it from the competition of Omni Outdoor Advertising, Inc. ("Omni"), which was attempting to enter that market. COA apparently had deep roots in the community and enjoyed close relations with the city's political leaders. Omni directed an antitrust attack against the ordinance, but the Court held that the ordinance was protected by the state-action exemption. That part of the City of Columbia decision was the focus of our attention on page 955, *supra*. In the part of the opinion reproduced below, the Court takes up Omni's claim that COA had conspired with local officials to enact the ordinance. Omni's claim is twofold: first that such a conspiracy is an exception to the state-action doctrine, and second, that such a conspiracy is in and of itself an antitrust violation.]

II

. . . The Court of Appeals upheld the jury verdict . . . by invoking a "conspiracy" exception to *Parker* that has been recognized by several Courts of Appeals. . . . That exception is thought to be supported by two of our statements in *Parker*: "[W]e have no question of the state or its municipality becoming a *participant in a private agreement* or combination by others for restraint of trade, *cf. Union Pacific R. Co. v. United States*, 313 U.S. 450." *Parker*, 317 U.S. at 351-352 (emphasis added). "The state in adopting and enforcing the prorate program made no contract or agreement *and entered into no conspiracy in restraint of trade or to establish monopoly* but, as sovereign, imposed the restraint as an act of government which the Sherman Act did not undertake to prohibit." . . . (emphasis added). *Parker* does not apply, according to the Fourth Circuit, "where politicians or political entities are involved as conspirators" with private actors in the restraint of trade. . . .

There is no such conspiracy exception. The rationale of *Parker* was that, in light of our national commitment to federalism, the general language of the Sherman Act should not be interpreted to prohibit anticompetitive actions by the States in their governmental capacities as sovereign regulators. The sentences from the opinion quoted above simply clarify that this immunity does not necessarily obtain where the State acts not in a regulatory capacity but as a commercial participant in a given market. . . . These sentences should not be read to suggest the general proposition that even governmental *regulatory* action may be deemed private—and therefore subject to antitrust liability—when it is taken pursuant to a conspiracy with private parties. The impracticality of such a principle is evident if, for purposes of the exception, "conspiracy" means nothing more than an agreement to impose the regulation in question. Since it is both inevitable and desirable that public officials often agree to do what one or another group of private citizens urges upon them, such an exception would virtually swallow up the *Parker* rule: All anticompetitive regulation would be vulnerable to a "conspiracy" charge. *See* AREEDA & HOVENKAMP, *supra,* ¶ 203.3b, at 34, and n.1; Elhauge, *The Scope of Antitrust Process,* 104 HARV. L. REV. 667, 704-705 (1991).

Omni suggests, however, that "conspiracy" might be limited to instances of governmental "corruption," defined variously as "abandonment of public responsibilities to private interests" . . . , "corrupt or bad faith decisions" . . . , and "selfish or corrupt motives." . . . Ultimately, Omni asks us not to define "corruption" at all, but simply to leave that task to the jury: "[a]t bottom, however, it was within the jury's province to determine what constituted corruption of the governmental process in their community.". . . Omni's amicus eschews this emphasis on "corruption," instead urging us to define the conspiracy exception as encompassing any governmental act "not in the public interest." . . .

A conspiracy exception narrowed along such vague lines is similarly impractical. Few governmental actions are immune from the charge that they are "not in the public interest" or in some sense "corrupt." The California marketing scheme at issue in *Parker* itself, for example, can readily be viewed as the result of a "conspiracy" to put the "private" interest of the State's raisin growers above the "public" interest of the State's consumers. The fact is that virtually all regulation benefits some segments of the society and harms others; and that it is not universally considered contrary to the public good if the net economic loss to the losers exceeds the net economic gain to the winners. *Parker* was not written in ignorance of the reality that determination of "the public interest" in the manifold areas of government regulation entails not merely economic and mathematical analysis but value judgment, and it was not meant to shift that judgment from elected officials to judges and juries. If the city of Columbia's decision to regulate what one local newspaper called "billboard jungles" . . . is made subject to *ex post facto* judicial assessment of "the public interest," with personal liability of city officials a possible consequence, we will have gone far to "compromise the States' ability to regulate their domestic commerce." . . . The situation would not be better, but arguably even worse, if the courts were to apply a subjective test: not whether the action was in the public interest, but whether the officials involved thought it to be so. This would require the sort of deconstruction of the governmental process and probing of the official "intent" that we have consistently sought to avoid. "[W]here the action complained of . . . was that of the State itself, the action is exempt from antitrust liability regardless of the State's motives in taking the action." *Hoover v. Ronwin*, 466 U.S. 558, 579-580 (1984). *See also Llewellyn v. Crothers*, 765 F.2d 769, 774 (9th Cir. 1985) (Kennedy, J.).

The foregoing approach to establishing a "conspiracy" exception at least seeks (however impractically) to draw the line of impermissible action in a manner relevant to the purposes of the Sherman Act and of *Parker*: prohibiting the restriction of competition for private gain but permitting the restriction of competition in the public interest. Another approach is possible, which has the virtue of practicality but the vice of being unrelated to those purposes. That is the approach which would consider *Parker* inapplicable only if, in connection with the governmental action in question, bribery or some other violation of state or federal law has been established. Such unlawful activity has no necessary relationship to whether the governmental action is in the public interest. A mayor is guilty of accepting a bribe even if he would and should have taken, in the public interest, the same action for which the bribe was paid. . . . When, moreover, the regulatory body is not a single individual but a state legislature or city council, there is even less reason to believe that violation of the law (by bribing a minority of the decisionmakers) establishes that the regulation has no valid public purpose. . . . To use unlawful political influence as the test of legality of state regulation undoubtedly vindicates (in a rather blunt way) principles of good government. But the statute we are construing is not directed to that end. Congress has passed other laws aimed at combatting corruption in state and local governments. *See, e.g.*, 18 U.S.C. § 1951 (Hobbs Act). "Insofar as [the Sherman Act] sets up a code of ethics at all, it is a code that condemns trade restraints, not political activity." *Eastern Railroad Presidents Conference v. Noerr Motor Freight, Inc.*, 365 U.S. 127, 140 (1961).

For these reasons, we reaffirm our rejection of any interpretation of the Sherman Act that would allow plaintiffs to look behind the actions of state sovereigns to base their claims on "perceived conspiracies to restrain trade." . . . We reiterate that, with the possible market participant exception, *any* action that qualifies as state action is "*ipso facto* . . . exempt from the operation of the antitrust laws." . . . This does not mean, of course, that the States may exempt *private* action from the scope of the Sherman Act; we in no way qualify the well established principle that "a state does not give immunity to those who violate the Sherman Act by authorizing them to violate it, or by declaring that their action is lawful." . . .

III

While *Parker* recognized the States' freedom to engage in anticompetitive regulation, it did not purport to immunize from antitrust liability the private parties who urge them to engage in anticompetitive regulation. However, it is obviously peculiar in a democracy, and perhaps in derogation of the constitutional right "to petition the Government for a redress of grievances," U.S. Const., Amdt. 1, to establish a category of lawful state action that citizens are not permitted to urge. Thus, beginning with *Eastern Railroad Presidents Conference v. Noerr Motor Freight, Inc., supra,* we have developed a corollary to *Parker*: the federal antitrust laws also do not regulate the conduct of private individuals in seeking anticompetitive action from the government. This doctrine, like *Parker*, rests ultimately upon a recognition that the antitrust laws, "tailored as they are for the business world, are not at all appropriate for application in the political arena." . . . That a private party's political motives are selfish is irrelevant: "*Noerr* shields from the Sherman Act a concerted effort to influence public officials regardless of intent or purpose." *Mine Workers v. Pennington*, 381 U.S. 657, 670 (1965).

Noerr recognized, however, what has come to be known as the "sham" exception to its rule: "There may be situations in which a publicity campaign, ostensibly directed toward influencing governmental action, is a mere sham to cover what is actually nothing more than an attempt to interfere directly with the business relationships of a competitor and the application of the Sherman Act would be justified." . . . The Court of Appeals concluded that the jury in this case could have found that COA's activities on behalf of the restrictive billboard ordinances fell within this exception. In our view that was error.

The "sham" exception to *Noerr* encompasses situations in which persons use the governmental *process*—as opposed to the *outcome* of that process—as an anticompetitive weapon. A classic example is the filing of frivolous objections to the license application of a competitor, with no expectation of achieving denial of the license but simply in order to impose expense and delay. *See California Motor Transport Co. v. Trucking Unlimited*, 404 U.S. 508 (1972). A "sham" situation involves a defendant whose activities are "not genuinely aimed at procuring favorable government action" at all, *Allied Tube & Conduit Corp. v. Indian Head, Inc.*, 486 U.S. 492, 500, n.4 (1988), not one "who 'genuinely seeks to achieve his governmental result, but does so *through improper means.*'" . . .

Neither of the Court of Appeals' theories for application of the "sham" exception to the facts of the present case is sound. The court reasoned, first, that the jury could have concluded that COA's interaction with city officials "was 'actually nothing more than an attempt to interfere directly with the business relations [*sic*] of a competitor.'" . . . This analysis relies upon language from *Noerr*, but ignores the import of the critical word "directly." Although COA indisputably set out to disrupt Omni's business relationships, it sought to do so not through the very process of lobbying, or of causing the city council to consider zoning measures, but rather through the ultimate *product* of that lobbying and consideration, *viz*., the zoning ordinances. The Court of Appeals' second theory was that the jury could have found "that COA's purposes were to delay Omni's entry into the market and even to deny it a meaningful access to the appropriate city administrative and legislative fora." . . . But the purpose of delaying a competitor's entry into the market does not render lobbying activity a "sham," unless (as no evidence suggested was true here) the delay is sought to be achieved only by the lobbying process itself, and not by the governmental action that the lobbying seeks. "If *Noerr* teaches anything it is that an intent to restrain trade as a result of government action sought . . . does not foreclose protection." Sullivan, *Developments in the* Noerr *Doctrine,* 56 ANTITRUST L.J. 361, 362 (1987). As for "deny[ing] . . . meaningful access to the appropriate city administrative and legislative fora," that may render the manner of lobbying improper or even unlawful, but does not necessarily render it a "sham." We did hold in *California Motor Transport, supra*, that a conspiracy among private parties to monopolize trade by excluding a competitor from participation in the regulatory process did not enjoy *Noerr* protection. But *California Motor Transport* involved a context in which the conspirators' participation in the governmental process was itself claimed to be a "sham," employed as a means of imposing cost and delay. ("It is alleged that petitioners 'instituted the proceedings and actions . . . with or without probable cause, and regardless of the merits of the cases.'" 404 U.S. at 512.) The holding of the case is limited to that situation. To extend it to a context in which the regulatory process is being invoked genuinely, and not in a "sham" fashion, would produce precisely that conversion of antitrust law into regulation of the political process that we have sought to avoid. Any lobbyist or applicant, in addition to getting himself heard, seeks by procedural and other means to get his opponent ignored. Policing the legitimate boundaries of such defensive strategies, when they are conducted in the context of a genuine attempt to influence governmental action, is not the role of the Sherman Act. In the present case, of course, any denial to Omni of "meaningful access to the appropriate city administrative and legislative fora" was achieved by COA in the course of an attempt to influence governmental action that, far from being a "sham," was if anything more in earnest than it should have been. If the denial was wrongful there may be other remedies, but as for the Sherman Act, the *Noerr* exemption applies.

Omni urges that if, as we have concluded, the "sham" exception is inapplicable, we should use this case to recognize another exception to *Noerr* immunity—a "conspiracy" exception, which would apply when government officials conspire with a private party to employ government action as a means of stifling competition. We have left open the possibility of such an exception . . . as have a number of Courts of Appeals. . . . At least one Court of Appeals has affirmed the existence of such an exception in dicta . . . and the Fifth Circuit has adopted it as holding . . . .

Giving full consideration to this matter for the first time, we conclude that a "conspiracy" exception to *Noerr* must be rejected. We need not describe our reasons at length, since they are largely the same as those set forth in Part II above for rejecting a "conspiracy" exception to *Parker*. As we have described, *Parker* and *Noerr* are complementary expressions of the principle that the antitrust laws regulate business, not politics; the former decision protects the States' acts of governing, and the latter the citizens' participation in government. Insofar as the identification of an immunity-destroying "conspiracy" is concerned, *Parker* and *Noerr* generally present two faces of the same coin. The *Noerr*-invalidating conspiracy alleged here is just the *Parker*-invalidating conspiracy viewed from the standpoint of the private-sector participants rather than the governmental participants. The same factors which, as we have described above, make it impracticable or beyond the purpose of the antitrust laws to identify and invalidate lawmaking that has been infected by selfishly motivated agreement with private interests likewise make it impracticable or beyond that scope to identify and invalidate lobbying that has produced selfishly motivated agreement with public officials. "It would be unlikely that any effort to influence legislative action could succeed unless one or more members of the legislative body became . . . 'co-conspirators'" in *some* sense with the private party urging such action, *Metro Cable Co. v. CATV of Rockford, Inc.*, 516 F.2d 220, 230 (7th Cir. 1975). And if the invalidating "conspiracy" is limited to one that involves some element of unlawfulness (beyond mere anticompetitive motivation), the invalidation would have nothing to do with the policies of the antitrust laws. In *Noerr* itself, where the private party "deliberately deceived the public and public officials" in its successful lobbying campaign, we said that "deception, reprehensible as it is, can be of no consequence so far as the Sherman Act is concerned." . . .

IV

Under *Parker* and *Noerr*, therefore, both the city and COA are entitled to immunity from the federal antitrust laws for their activities relating to enactment of the ordinances. . . . The judgment of the Court of Appeals is reversed, and the case is remanded for further proceedings consistent with this opinion.

It is so ordered.

NOTE: THE *NOERR-PENNINGTON* DOCTRINE

1. The *Noerr-Pennington* doctrine protects the rights of petition broadly conceived. In *Eastern Railroad Presidents Conference v. Noerr Motor Freight, Inc.*, 365 U.S. 127 (1961), an association of truckers brought suit against an association of railroads, claiming that the latter violated § 1 of the Sherman Act in cooperatively carrying on a lobbying and publicity campaign designed to disadvantage truck transport *vis-à-vis* rail transport. Through their joint lobbying and public relations efforts the railroads sought legislation imposing more restrictive weight limits on trucks and increasing truck taxes. The railroads counterclaimed that the truckers were violating the Sherman Act by cooperatively engaging in a similar lobbying and public relations campaign designed to obtain legislation improving their position *vis-à-vis* the railroads. The Supreme court ruled that the Sherman Act does not prevent business firms from cooperatively petitioning the legislature. Everyone has a right to seek legislation, even anticompetitive legislation. The Court rested this judgment upon the ground that the ordinary meaning of the Act's language does not appear to embrace petitions to the legislature and the executive; that the Sherman Act was not intended to extend to the political arena; that the operation of government requires free communication between government officials and the people; and that the constitutional problems which would be raised by a contrary holding counseled against a construction of the Act which would restrict the right of petition.

In upholding the right of the railroads to engage in joint lobbying efforts, the Court held that it made no difference to its decision that the railroads may have been dishonest in their communications with the legislature. The courts below, in holding the railroads to have violated the Sherman Act, had relied in part upon the use by the railroads of a "third party technique," a technique which the courts considered to be unethical:

> The second factor relied upon by the courts below to justify the application of the Sherman Act to the railroads' publicity campaign was the use in the campaign of the so-called third-party technique. The theory under which this factor was related to the proscriptions of the Sherman Act . . . was apparently that it involved unethical business conduct on the part of the railroads. As pointed out above, the third-party technique, which was aptly characterized by the District Court as involving "deception of the public, manufacture of bogus sources of reference, [and] distortion of public sources of information," depends upon giving propaganda actually circulated by a party in interest the appearance of being spontaneous declarations of independent groups. We can certainly agree with the courts below that this technique, though in widespread use among practitioners of the art of public relations, is one which falls far short of the ethical standards generally approved in this country. It does not follow, however, that the use of the technique in a publicity campaign designed to influence governmental action constitutes a violation of the Sherman Act. Insofar as that Act sets up a code of ethics at all, it is a code that condemns trade restraints, not political activity, and, as we have already pointed out, a publicity campaign to influence governmental action falls clearly into the category of political activity. . . . [W]e have come to the conclusion that . . . the railroads' use of the third-party technique was, so far as the Sherman Act is concerned, legally irrelevant.

365 U.S. at 140-42.

2. *United Mine Workers of America v. Pennington*, 381 U.S. 657 (1965). In this case the United Mine Workers (UMW) was charged with engaging in a conspiracy with the large coal mine operators to drive the smaller coal mine operators out of business. Part of the alleged conspiracy consisted in joint petitions by the UMW and the large operators to the Secretary of Labor asking that minimum wages be set under the Walsh-Healey Act for firms selling coal to the Tennessee Valley Authority (TVA), and another part of the conspiracy consisted in joint petitions to the TVA to curtail its spot-market purchases of coal (a substantial portion of which was exempt from Walsh-Healey regulation). The court below had ruled that the joint petitioning was unprotected if it was motivated by a purpose to drive the small operators out of business. The Supreme Court ruled that the joint petitioning of public officials by the UMW and the large coal operators was protected activity, regardless of the underlying motivations of the UMW and the operators.

3. *California Motor Transport Co. v. Trucking Unlimited*, 404 U.S. 508 (1972). In this case one group of California truckers was alleged to have conspired to oppose the grant, transfer and registration of operating rights by other truckers in agency and court proceedings. Reaffirming its ruling in *Pennington*, the Court stated that:

> . . . it would be destructive of rights of association and of petition to hold that groups with common interests may not, without violating the antitrust laws, use the channels and procedures of state and federal agencies and courts to advocate their causes and points of view respecting resolution of their businesses and economic interests *vis-à-vis* their competitors.

California Motor Transport, 404 U.S. at 510-11. Nonetheless, the Court took account of a so-called "sham" exception to the *Noerr-Pennington* doctrine, which is wider when groups acted in agency and court proceedings than when they were engaged in petitioning the legislature.

> . . . In the present case . . . the allegations are not that the conspirators sought "to influence public officials," but that they sought to bar their competitors from meaningful access to adjudicatory tribunals and so to usurp that decisionmaking process. It is alleged that petitioners "instituted the proceedings and actions . . . with or without probable cause, and regardless of the merits of the cases.". . . [S]uch a purpose or intent, if shown, would be "to discourage and ultimately to prevent the respondents from invoking" the processes of the administrative agencies and courts and thus fall within the exception to *Noerr.*

404 U.S. at 511-12. Distinguishing the unethical conduct which it held not to have violated the Sherman Act in *Noerr*, the Court went on to say:

> . . . unethical conduct in the setting of the adjudicatory process often results in sanctions. Perjury of witnesses is one example. Use of a patent obtained by fraud to exclude a competitor from the market may involve a violation of the antitrust laws, as we held in *Walker Process Equipment, Inc. v. Food Machinery & Chemical Corp.*, 382 U.S. 172, 175-177. Conspiracy with a licensing authority to eliminate a competitor may also result in an antitrust transgression. *Continental Ore Co. v. Union Carbide & Carbon Corp.*, 370 U.S. 690, 707; *Harman v. Valley National Bank*, 339 F.2d 564 (9th Cir. 1964). Similarly, bribery of a public purchasing agent may constitute a violation of § 2(c) of the Clayton Act, as amended

> by the Robinson-Patman Act. *Rangen, Inc. v. Sterling Nelson & Sons*, 351 F.2d 851 (9th Cir. 1965).
>
> There are many other forms of illegal and reprehensible practice which may corrupt the administrative or judicial processes and which may result in antitrust violations. Misrepresentations, condoned in the political arena, are not immunized when used in the adjudicatory process. Opponents before agencies or courts often think poorly of the other's tactics, motions, or defenses and may readily call them baseless. One claim, which a court or agency may think baseless, may go unnoticed; but a pattern of baseless, repetitive claims may emerge which leads the factfinder to conclude that the administrative and judicial processes have been abused. That may be a difficult line to discern and draw. But once it is drawn, the case is established that abuse of those processes produced an illegal result, *viz.*, effectively barring respondents from access to the agencies and courts. Insofar as the administrative or judicial processes are involved, actions of that kind cannot acquire immunity by seeking refuge under the umbrella of "political expression."
>
> . . . A combination of entrepreneurs to harass and deter their competitors from having "free and unlimited access" to the agencies and courts, to defeat that right by massive, concerted, and purposeful activities of the group are ways of building up one empire and destroying another. . . . If these facts are proved, a violation of the antitrust laws has been established. If the end result is unlawful, it matters not that the means used in violation may be lawful.

404 U.S. at 512-15.

4. *Professional Real Estate Investors, Inc. v. Columbia Pictures Industries, Inc.*, 508 U.S. 49 (1992). Columbia Pictures sued Professional Real Estate Investors (PRE) for alleged copyright infringement. The alleged copyright infringements consisted of PRE renting videodiscs for viewing in hotel rooms. The court determined that such rental for in-room viewing did not constitute public performance and hence that no copyright violation occurred. PRE counterclaimed, alleging that Columbia's copyright action was a sham cloaking underlying acts of monopolization and conspiracy to restrain trade.

The Supreme Court (through Justice Thomas) ruled that Columbia's suit was protected under the *Noerr* doctrine. In so ruling, the Court set forth a two-part test governing the issue of when litigation falls within the "sham" exception identified in *California Motor Transport*:

> We now outline a two-part definition of "sham" litigation. First, the lawsuit must be objectively baseless in the sense that no reasonable litigant could realistically expect success on the merits. If an objective litigant could conclude that the suit is reasonably calculated to elicit a favorable outcome, the suit is immunized under *Noerr*, and an antitrust claim

> premised on the sham exception must fail. Only if challenged litigation is objectively meritless may a court examine the litigant's subjective motivation. Under this second part of our definition of sham, the court should focus on whether the baseless lawsuit conceals "an attempt to interfere directly with the business relationships of a competitor . . . through the 'use [of] the governmental process—as opposed to the outcome of that process—as an anticompetitive weapon.'" . . . This two-tiered process requires the plaintiff to disprove the challenged lawsuit's legal viability before the court will entertain evidence of the suit's economic viability. Of course, even a plaintiff who defeats the defendant's claim to *Noerr* immunity by demonstrating both the objective and the subjective components of a sham must still prove a substantive antitrust violation. Proof of a sham merely deprives the defendant of immunity; it does not relieve the plaintiff of the obligation to establish all other elements of his claim.

Professional Real Estate Investors, 508 U.S. at 60-61.

COMMENTARY

1. In the *City of Columbia* case, Justice Scalia attempted to treat the *Parker* and *Noerr-Pennington* doctrines as consistent and complementary. Accordingly, he rejected proposed "conspiracy" exceptions to both doctrines under which the antitrust laws would apply when government officials joined a conspiracy with private parties. As construed in *City of Columbia*, business firms are entitled to cooperate in seeking anticompetitive relief from officials, tribunals and legislative bodies, to discuss and agree upon strategy with legislators, and the resulting anticompetitive legislation or orders are not invalidated by either the motives or the cooperative efforts between the private parties and the government officials.

2. Justice Scalia's opinion in *City of Columbia* states that neither the *Parker* nor the *Noerr-Pennington* doctrine embodies a conspiracy exception which would be triggered by discussions between petitioning business firms and government officials such as legislators. Is this determination consistent with *California Motor Transport*? *California Motor Transport* ruled that business firms which conspired to deny access to administrative and judicial tribunals fell within a "sham" exception to the *Noerr-Pennington* doctrine. Would denying meaningful access to a legislative body also fall within the "sham" exception? Consider the scenario described in Note 4 below.

3. To what extent does *City of Columbia* modify the "sham" exception outlined in *California Motor Transport*? Can you identify behavior which would violate the antitrust laws under the approach of *California Motor Transport*, but which would not violate the antitrust laws under Justice Scalia's approach in *City of Columbia*?

4. Suppose that in the *City of Columbia* case, COA had obtained the agreement of a majority of the members of the city council to vote for the zoning ordinance in question before the bill had even been introduced. Then the council members (who had already committed themselves to COA) refused to participate meaningfully in debate and deliberation on the bill, or went through the motions of deliberating, but in fact were already committed. Would such a scenario deny Omni resort to the legislative process?

5. Justice Scalia was aware of the possibility that such a scenario might occur, was he not? Can you identify the language in his opinion which indicates how he would deal with the scenario described in Note 4 above?

6. The *Professional Real Estate Investors* case establishes stringent standards for applying the sham exception to litigation. Do these standards also govern the application of the sham exception to the institution of administrative proceedings? to petitions directed to officials requesting them to take discretionary action disadvantaging rivals?

Chapter 19

Antitrust and the Health Care Industry

A. The Historical Background

Antitrust enforcement activity involving the health care delivery system began in 1939 with indictment of the physicians' principal trade association, the American Medical Association (AMA), two affiliated medical associations, and their officers. The indictments charged restraint of trade in the group practice of medicine by physicians in the District of Columbia in violation of § 3 of the Sherman Act, 15 U.S.C. § 3 (1994) (making illegal § 1 violations in the District of Columbia without reference to interstate commerce). Prior to this action, the practice of medicine was not generally considered as "trade" within the meaning of the Sherman Act, the position taken by the district court in dismissing these indictments in *United States v. American Medical Ass'n,* 29 F. Supp. 753 (D.D.C. 1939). The government's indictments had attacked the AMA's enforcement of its bylaws, which barred the delivery of patient care through non-profit membership associations as "unprofessional," and "unethical." In group practice, as distinguished from the traditional fee-for-service practice, the physicians were salaried employees for whose services the subscribers were charged on a pre-payment basis. Under its bylaws the AMA sanctioned members engaged in group practice and urged other physicians to sever professional connections with group practitioners.The government further charged the AMA with coordinating efforts of AMA-affiliated hospitals to deny hospital privileges to physicians engaged in group practice. The court of appeals reinstated the indictments, interpreting § 3 of the Sherman Act as applicable to the trade of group medical practice. *United States v. American Medical Ass'n,* 130 F.2d 233 (D.C. Cir. 1942). In affirming, the court of appeals decision in *American Medical Ass'n v. United States,* 317 U.S. 519 (1942), the Supreme Court held that: 1) the group practice of medicine constituted "trade" for Sherman Act purposes, 2) the conduct of the AMA was in restraint of trade under § 3 as alleged, and 3) the labor exemption from antitrust liability did not apply to the AMA, its affiliates, or its officers. This opinion marked the decline of active medical association resistance to group practice. However, group practice was not entirely free from AMA (and its local affiliated associations) scrutiny until the Federal Trade Commission's decision that the bylaws of the AMA, which characterized group practice as unethical and unprofessional, constituted an unfair method of competition. *See Federal Trade Commission v. American Medical Ass'n,* 94 F.T.C. 980 (1979), *aff'd, American Medical Ass'n v. Federal Trade Commission,* 638 F.2d 443 (2d Cir. 1980), *aff'd,* 455 U.S. 676 (1982).

Despite the government's 1942 victory against the AMA in the Supreme Court, in 1950 the Antitrust Division itself attacked a group practice arrangement in Oregon. The Division filed a civil suit under §§ 1 and 2 of the Sherman Act against the Oregon State Medical Society, several affiliated county medical societies, Oregon Physician's Services (OPS), the largest, nonprofit group practice in the state, and officers of these organizations. In its suit, the government alleged that the "contract practice" of physician-employees collectively determining fee schedules and selectively accepting patient referrals constituted price-fixing and boycotting. There was also a count of monopolizing prepaid medical services in the state and of refusing to furnish medical services in any county in Oregon which was served by a local, affiliated medical society. The government's action is not without some irony, since OPS was the survivor of a five-year bitter fight in Oregon between the local AMA membership and several small, nonprofit group practice associations, which dispute was resolved by a complete about-face on the part of the AMA and its affiliates. OPS owed its existence and dominant position to the complete acceptance of group practice by the traditional fee-for-service physicians (and their professional associations) in Oregon. The trial judge dismissed all counts without issuing a formal opinion. *United States v. Oregon State Medical Society,* 95 F. Supp. 103 (D. Ore. 1950), *aff'd, United States v. Oregon Medical Society,* 343 U.S. 326 (1952) (noting that much of the government's case rested on defendant's conduct prior to acceptance of group practice by the medical establishment in Oregon).

After 1980, all resistance to group practice ended. The acceptance of group practice began the proliferation of market actors in the delivery of health care. Adding complexity, the state and federal governments have become participants both by defining care procedures as well as by providing payment for them. In 1965 the Medicare and Medicaid programs were enacted as amendments to the Social Security Act, Pub. L. No. 89-97, § 1801, 79 Stat. 286,291, codified at 42 U.S.C. §§ 1395 and 1396 (1994). The availability of health care insurance as well as joint state/federal funding for health care, in turn, attracted the entry of a new group of service providers of institutional care in the form of nursing and convalescent homes, dialysis centers, home care providers, and free-standing emergency and surgical facilities.

Given the complex structure of the health care industry, it is difficult to determine when an arrangement or an action will produce an inefficient outcome or have an anticompetitive effect. In practice, this will require the antitrust adviser to consider the potential for antitcompetive consequences in a variety of institutional and contractual arrangements involving physicians, insurers, and hospitals. Mergers, partnerships, and joint venture arrangements may also pose antitrust issues. Various forms of "managed care" delivered through HMOs and like organizations, seem likely to continue as the principal competitive actors in health care markets.

B. The Focus of Antitrust Law

Despite the legislative failure in 1993 of the Clinton Administration's proposal for federal health legislation, some of its provisions are being adopted by private sector initiative. Looking ahead to health care over the 1994-98 period, one economist stated,

> There appears to be a revolution in the health care services industry, with dramatically aggressive competition across many market segments, ranging from reduced demand for inpatient hospital care to reduced demand for highly specialized physicians. . . . [This dynamism is attributed to the reform proposals of the Clinton Administration, which was] . . . "a strong catalyst in precipitating the private sector changes that actually gathered strength after the reform plans were dead."

Larry J. Kimball, *UCLA Business Forecasting Project, in* BNA, 4 HEALTH CARE POLICY 29 (1996).

As the structural and relational interests of the health care participants shift, the antitrust laws continue to infuse the debate. Traditional health care participants, doctors, associated professionals, and hospital managers, have historically operated from a perspective of concern with health outcomes, with a diminished emphasis on cost and price. However, as the governmental role in defining and providing health care has increased, cost has come to dominate the debates. Commentators have suggested various roles for the antitrust laws in this changing environment.

Competition, the mode of market performance that is fostered by the antitrust laws, is a method of rationalizing prices by tending to move them close to true input costs, including a reasonable rate of profit, with the ultimate result of enhancing consumer welfare. Thus, the antitrust laws become engaged in the concern for cost containment. One commentator has summed up the contribution of antitrust law to the health care debate as follows:

> The antitrust laws are important both substantively and symbolically because they eliminate non-efficiency based criteria from analytical consideration, necessarily submerging equity concerns within the public policy debate. The risk of antitrust liability will move the health care marketplace along the continuum toward market-oriented policies restraining anticompetitive actions by doctors and institutional providers. And they provide further impetus for institutional administrators to perform the traditional management functions of cost containment and economic efficiency. They encourage challenges to the traditional professional model's refusal to balance cost and quality.

James F. Blumstein, *Health Care Reform and Competing Versions of Medical Care: Antitrust and State Provider Cooperation Legislation*, 79 CORNELL L. REV. 1459, 1485-86 (1994).

Economists who have studied this industry have recommended various roles for the antitrust laws. Mancur Olson envisions antitrust review and enforcement as directly applicable to insurance arrangements. He writes,

> If I am correct in emphasizing the need for insurance plans made by insurers who are free to bargain with subsets of the fee-for-service providers . . . [prepaid group practice units] . . . and to police claims vigorously, there is also a compelling case for applying the antitrust laws more vigorously to physicians, hospitals, and the anticompetitive insurance arrangements they have created.

MANCUR OLSON, A NEW APPROACH TO THE ECONOMICS OF HEALTH CARE 25-6 (Mancur Olson ed. 1981).

Victor Fuchs, one of the pioneers among economists concerned with the health care industry, would broaden the public policy inquiry to distinguish efficiency considerations from value judgments.

> Economists are most familiar with the distinction between efficiency and distributional issues, especially greater equality of income versus greater total income. . . . [C]omprehensive changes in health policy can have . . . important distributional effects. Even for individuals at the same income level, the costs and benefits of care could change along many dimensions: rural areas versus central cities, the elderly versus the young, smokers versus nonsmokers, savers versus nonsavers. Health economists who are unanimous in approving gains in efficiency might have very different views regarding the desirability of the distributional changes and might also differ in the weights they give to the changes in efficiency versus the distributional effects.

Victor R. Fuchs, *Economics, Values, and Health Care Reforms*, 86 AM. ECON. REV. 1, 15-16 (1996).

How should considerations of cost saving be balanced against the loss of choice of one's personal physician or restrictions on alternative diagnostic procedures?

C. The Insurance Exemption

The expanding role of health care insurance poses yet another issue of antitrust concern. As health care insurance became available to individuals negotiating directly with insurance companies or through the negotiations of their employers with providers, or with their employers acting as self-insurers, more complex institutional arrangements result. Further variation and complexity is added by the advent of various managed care organizations, which combine the role of the provider with that of the insurer. These developments in health care insurance have generated pressure to modify the traditional antitrust exemption of the insurance industry.

As actors deciding which services will be covered, as well as the price of these services, health care insurers press against the boundary of the traditional antitrust insurance exemption. Under present law the "business of insurance" is expressly exempted from federal antitrust scrutiny under 15 U.S.C. §§ 1011, 1012(b), and 1013 when it is subject to state regulation. See the discussion in Chapter 4; for the latest definition of the scope of this exemption, see *FTC v. Ticor Insurance Co.*, 502 U.S. 807 (1992), in Chapter 18. During the intense debate over the Clinton Administration's health care proposals and their various alternatives during the 103rd Congress, several suggestions for modifying the insurance exemption for health insurance were offered. 67 ANTITRUST & TRADE REG. REP. For an analysis favoring retention of the McCarran-Ferguson exemption in order to permit insurers to share data, pool risks, and undertake joint product development, see, Francis Amchapong, *The McCarran Ferguson Act and the Limited Insurance Antitrust Exemption: An Indefensible Aberration?*, 15 SETON H. LEGIS. J. 141 (1991); Sarah S. Vance, *Immunity for State Sanctioned Provider Collaboration After* Ticor, 62 ANTITRUST L.J. 409 (1994).

As part of the current policy debate over health care, there have also been proposals to extend the insurance exemption to other activities in health care delivery. The American Hospital Association (AHA) issued a white paper that characterized the antitrust laws as an impediment to coordinated activities that could reduce the costs of health care and guarantee wider access to high quality health care. *See* AMERICAN HOSPITAL ASSOCIATION, HOSPITAL COLLABORATION: THE NEED FOR AN APPROPRIATE HEALTH POLICY (1992). As part of this discussion, the Legislature of the State of Washington directed the State Attorney General to undertake an investigation of the need for antitrust immunity for insurance and other aspects of current health care delivery practices. In her Report, THE ROLE OF ANTITRUST IMMUNITY IN THE WASHINGTON STATE HEALTH CARE MARKET, December 15, 1995, the Attorney General concluded that a general immunity would be inappropriate, stating:

> For most of the practices in question, the issue is not one of *per se* illegality but one characterized by a rebuttable presumption of illegality. Thus, if there were actions that a group of health care providers could document as leading to a more efficient outcome, antitrust enforcement as described by the Federal guidelines and as enforced by the courts would most certainly be permissive. No formal declaration of antitrust immunity is necessary or warranted.

Id. at 58. The Assistant Attorney General, Antitrust Division concurs in this view, stating: ". . . [T]he creation of antitrust exemptions would be fundamentally irreconcilable with the broad national agreement on the need for more competition in the health care industry." Anne K. Bingaman, *The Importance of Antitrust in Health Care*, 1995 UTAH L. REV. 373.

In the materials that follow, consider the various applications of the antitrust laws by courts and enforcement agencies.

D. The Factors of Cost and of Cost Containment

A material factor in the role of antitrust in the health care industry is the issue of the scope of antitrust scrutiny. By providing Medicare, Medicaid, and tax benefits, the state and federal governments became a significant force in that industry. Effectively, these programs provide health insurance covering a large proportion of medical costs for millions of citizens. Moreover, this state and federal support effectively subsidizes private insurance premiums paid by employers for coverage of their employees. An effective tax subsidy arises because the Internal Revenue Code permits employers to deduct premium payments for private employee health insurance as business expenses, without requiring the employee to take these amounts into gross income as wages for income and social security tax purposes. Accordingly, until the heightened concern over rising costs in the late 1980s, consumers had a diminished economic incentive to chose health care plans on the basis of lower cost.

In these circumstances, the rapid growth of costs both in the private sector and in the Medicare and Medicaid programs began to dominate the public policy debate over health care. In 1970, the total federal Medicare expenditures amounted to $7.5 billion. By 1975 this cost rose to $16.3 billion, by 1980 Medicare cost $36.7 billion, an amount that had grown to $142 billion by 1993. This same pattern was reflected in the Medicaid program. In 1970, this program cost $5.5 billion, by 1975 the cost had risen to $14.2 billion, and by 1980 this program cost $26.6 billion. *See* R.M. Gibson & D.R. Waldo, *National Health Expenditures, 1980*, 3 HEALTH CARE FINANCING REV. 1, 48 (1981). This experience led to additional federal legislation that addressed the cost issue indirectly by refining the definition of care. In 1972, Congress authorized the establishment of PSROs, Professional Standards Review Organizations that have subsequently become a system of established Peer Review Organizations, a Practicing Physicians Advisory Council, and a Provider Reimbursement Review Board, as means of monitoring the costs and quality of services to federal beneficiaries under federal health care programs. 42 U.S.C. §§ 1320c-3, 1395ee, and 1395oo (1994 Supp).

Federal regulation has also been extended beyond the performance of the participants in health care delivery to the construction and utilization of hospital facilities. This process began with the Hill-Burton programs after the Second World War. National Health Planning and Resources Development Act of 1974, 42 U.S.C. §§ 300-300e-14a (1994 & Supp. I 1995), as amended in 1979, by Pub. L. 96-79, 93 Stat. 592, 42 U.S.C. §§ 300m(d), 300m (1994). The Planning Act addressed the issue of rising hospital costs by introducing a regulatory scheme of state and federal agencies. At the local level, Health Systems Agencies (HSAs) functioned together with State Health Coordinating Councils (SHCCs) to review the decision of any hospital seeking to offer new services or to make a major capital expenditure. 42 U.S.C. § 1320a-1(b). Under this statutory scheme, a hospital seeking to expand services or facilities is required to obtain a Certificate of Need (CON).

The public policy issues generated by these developments in the health care industry have been aptly characterized by the Supreme Court in ruling on a issue in one federal regulatory statute the National Health Planning and Resources Development Act of 1974, as amended, 42 U.S.C. § 300l (1991), as follows:

> [T]here was concern that marketplace forces in this industry failed to produce efficient investment in facilities and to minimize the costs of health care. In addition, Congress sought to reduce the maldistribution of health-care facilities. . . . [In amending this statute] . . . Congress added a number of provisions requiring promotion of competition at the local, state, and federal levels.

National Gerimedical Hospital v. Blue Cross, 452 U.S. 378, 386-87 (1981).

Given the rapid structural changes in the organization of health care delivery systems, a cursory definition of the various group practice modes follows.

The Health Maintenance Organization, one popular alternative to the traditional individual doctor operating on a fee-for-service basis, has been described as follows:

> HMOs [health maintenance organizations] and preferred provider organizations [PPOs] are so-called "alternative delivery systems" which have emerged as cost-effective alternatives to traditional indemnity insurance. HMOs and PPOs are prospective reimbursement arrangements, in which a member or subscriber pays a monthly amount to medical care providers who then oversee all the health care needs of the member. In an HMO or PPO, the member typically pays less for health care coverage than under a traditional indemnity insurance plan, but is limited in . . . [the] choice of medical care providers.

Reazin v. Blue Cross and Blue Shield of Kansas, 899 F.2d 951, 956 (10th Cir. 1990).

Within the basic HMO organization, there have arisen several structural modifications as follows:

> HMO arrangements with physicians vary widely. There are, however, three basic types of HMO: a "staff" model, a "group" model, and an "individual practice association" model. In the so-called staff model, the HMO employs physicians on a salaried basis; occasionally such physician/employees have organized a labor union for purposes of collective bargaining. In the group model, the HMO entity contracts for physicians' services with an independent physician-sponsored entity. In the individual practice association model, the HMO contracts with independent practitioners individually or in small groups. HMO arrangements with hospitals range from directly owning the hospital, to contracting with independent hospitals, to using hospitals selected by contracting physicians.

Clark Havighurst, *Doctors and Hospitals: An Antitrust Perspective on Traditional Relationships*, 1984 DUKE L.J. 1071, 1073.

The PPO, preferred provider organization, is designed to meet a narrow subset of consumers and is described as follows:

> It contracts with a limited number of providers—hospitals and/or physicians—to provide care for a particular group of consumers on preferential terms. The PPO stands between a specific, defined group of consumers and a specific, defined group of providers. Consumers are offered better terms (more complete insurance and possibly price discounts and/or utilization controls) if they patronize the preferred providers—hence the name.

H.E. Frech III, *Preferred Provider Organizations and Health Care Competition*, *in* HEALTH CARE IN AMERICA 354 (H. Frech & R. Zeckhauser eds. 1988).

A variant of the HMO and the PPO is the IPA, Independent Practice Association. This an arrangement whereby a physician may act as an independent contractor to either entity, performing services for their patients on request and in conformity with their fee schedule, but may also see non-HMO and PPO patients. There are several other variants. A PCN, primary care network, is an arrangement consisting of general internists, family practice physicians, and pediatricians who agree to provide all basic services and in addition to provide, arrange, and supervise all referrals to specialists and to hospital services. The physicians are compensated by a flat fee per patient, the amount being dependent on the patient's age and gender. Another variant is the multispecialty group—an arrangement of surgeons consisting of general, orthopaedic, thoracic, and vascular surgeons that may function as an IPA or other non-prepaid basis. Yet another variation is the FMC, Foundation for Medical Care. These groups function as indemnity insurers coupled with a peer review mechanism to control costs. For further discussion of these alternative forms of health care delivery services, see ALAIN E. ENTHOVEN, HEALTH PLAN 55-69 (1980).

Coupled with these changes in the private sector, is an awareness by the Justice Department of its capability for fostering efficient outcomes by invoking antitrust analysis and without resort to litigation. The initial set of Statements describe this approach. The first is the promulgation in 1993 of the joint Department of Justice and Federal Trade Commission statements of enforcement policy in the health care area. ¶ 13,151 ANTITRUST & TRADE REG. REP. (BNA). The 1993 statements were followed by expanded statements in 1994 and in 1996. The 1996 statement is discussed in detail below. The thrust of these Statements is to foster innovative arrangements by illustrating nine major practices in which emphasis on efficient outcomes would constitute "antitrust safety zones," *i.e.*, situations in which there would not be an enforcement challenge. The statement also indicated the availability of an expedited business review letter when there are close questions relating to these practices. The second element of a competition-fostering approach is described by a Justice Department attorney in the context of mergers as follows:

> One transaction in which the Department . . . was able to promote efficiency gains was in the settlement of *United States v. Morton Plant*

Health Systems, Inc. That suit challenged the proposed merger of the two largest hospitals in Clearwater, Florida. . . .

. . . Justice Department officials met with the merging hospitals and explored ways to accomplish most of the parties' proposed efficiencies without a full-scale merger.

. . . [T]he negotiators agreed on an innovative solution that . . . promoted rather than lessened competition.

The settlement had two parts. First, the merger was prohibited, and the two hospitals agreed to remain independent providers of in-patient acute care services. Both hospitals agreed to continue to contract separately with managed care. Second, the hospitals would capture efficiencies through a production joint venture. The services that could be performed by the joint venture fell into three categories: certain tertiary services; out-patient care; and ancillary services.

Competition for the services contributed to the joint venture was protected in two important ways. First, the services in the joint venture would face competition from many other sources either because the markets . . . were broader geographically than the general in-patient services market or because organizations other than the acute-care hospitals were participants or likely entrants. . . . [A]ncillary services such as laundry, billing, . . . and purchasing were all provided in a much larger market than just the Clearwater, Florida area.

The second protection is that the venture is limited to production only. Although the venture can jointly produce services, it must sell them back to each parent hospital at cost. Each hospital will separately market those services to managed care plans and others, often in competition with one another.

. . . The hospitals have reported that the joint venture is likely to save $8 million in its first year.

Steven C. Sunshine, *How Does Antitrust Enforcement Fit In?, in* THE PROBLEM THAT WON'T GO AWAY 207, 213 (Henry J. Aaron ed. 1996).

In the light of the fluid nature of this industry, recent legislative proposals, *e.g.*, the Clinton Administration's S. 2357, 103rd Cong., 2d Sess. (1994), have adopted the suggestion of Alain Einthoven that insurers and providers join together, obtain state and federal approval as appropriate units, and then as approved regional alliances, compete for patient-subscribers. *See* ALAIN C. ENTHOVEN, THE THEORY AND PRACTICE OF MANAGED COMPETITION IN HEALTH CARE FINANCE Ch. 1 (1988); MANCUR OLSON, A NEW APPROACH TO THE ECONOMICS OF HEALTH CARE 24 (1981); *see also* HENRY J. AARON, THE PROBLEM THAT WON'T GO AWAY: REFORMING U.S. HEALTH CARE FINANCING Ch. 1 (1996). For a general reference work on antitrust issues in the health care industry, see JOHN J. MILES, HEALTH CARE AND ANTITRUST LAW: PRINCIPLES AND PRACTICE (1995).

NOTE: PRICING HEALTH CARE SERVICES

1. Review the opinion in *Arizona v. Maricopa County Medical Association*, and the questions that follow in Chapter 2. Are all forms of agreement concerning fees for medical services illegal? What is the relevant market identified by the Court in that decision? Did the complaint allege price-fixing by physicians? One commentator considers insurer services as the relevant market: "Under a rule of reason analysis, if fee schedule did in fact engender competition *among insurers*, it is doubtful that . . . anti-competitive effects cited by the . . . Court would have outweighed the procompetitive justifications. . . ." Note, *Antitrust Law—Maximum Prices and the* Per Se *Rule*, 56 TEMP. L.Q. 162, 187 (1983).

2. If a group of physicians consider an insurer's fee schedule for the physician services inadequate, may the physicians lawfully boycott that insurer? Is such a boycott illegal *per se*? Does it matter whether these physicians are associated as partners or are otherwise offering their services jointly? In examining a boycott under rule of reason analysis, is the plaintiff required to show an anticompetitive impact? For a review of these issues, see *Federal Trade Commission v. Superior Court Trial Lawyers Association v. Federal Trade Commission*, 493 U.S. 411 (1990), and *Federal Trade Commission v. Indiana Federation of Dentists*, 476 U.S. 447 (1986), in Chapter 4. Physicians' attempts to boycott insurers as a means of increasing their fees have been successfully attacked by states. *See Colorado v. Colorado Union of Physicians and Surgeons*, 1990-1 TRADE CASES (CCH) ¶ 68,968. See also *Degregorio v. Segal*, 443 F. Supp. 1257 (1979), and *American Association of Foundations for Medical Care v. FTC*, 1980-2 TRADE CASES (CCH) ¶ 63,317, where the courts held that a nursing home trade association's participation in refusing to accept Medicaid patients unless rates were increased constituted an illegal boycott.

Judge Easterbrook has criticized the opinion in *Maricopa County* because he considered it unlikely that the physicians possessed the power to organize an effective cartel. He stated:

> It seems most unlikely that a maximum price agreement is a disguised cartel if the sellers' market is not concentrated. . . . It will always be in the interest of some sellers to break with the cartel, reduce prices, and so claim a greater share of the business.

Frank H. Easterbrook, *Maximum Price-Fixing*, 48 U. CHI. L. REV. 886, 902 (1981).

Given the distinctive characteristics of the health care market, when do physicians compete by price? In what circumstances do patients shop for health care by price? Should courts determine when there is or is not price competition and make findings? In the same article, Judge Easterbook wrote ". . . third-party payments reduce the incentive for patients to search even when they can do so at low cost." *Id.* at 894. If the patient is not shopping by price, does the physician have an incentive to reduce cost?

3. How should price-fixing be defined in the context of insurer/physician cost containment negotiations? In *Barry v. Blue Cross*, 805 F.2d 866 (9th Cir. 1986), Blue Cross of California, a nonprofit corporation, issued a doctors' fee schedule under the authority of CAL. INS. CODE § 10133 (1986), which authorized Blue Cross to contract with hospitals and health care professionals to provide health care to its insureds at pre-determined prices. Under its Prudent Buyer Plan, Blue Cross contracted with hospitals and doctors to provide services at stated fees. Blue Cross negotiated a schedule of customary fees for its participating doctors and agreed to pay 90 percent of that fee, but only a lesser percentage for services provided by a nonparticipating physician. Two physicians, one who had joined the Plan and one who rejected it, filed suit alleging § 1 Sherman Act violations of price-fixing and boycott by vertical and horizontal agreements, as well as a § 2 count of monopolizing. The suit was dismissed on Blue Cross' motion for summary judgment.

On appeal, the Ninth Circuit affirmed, rejecting the plaintiffs' initial argument that Blue Cross was controlled by doctors merely because Blue Cross had solicited comments on the proposed fee schedule from several physicians prior to activating the plan. The final fee schedule was approved by the Blue Cross Physician Relations Committee, which consisted of doctors and administrators. The court of appeals rejected plaintiffs' claim of a horizontal agreement among member physicians to set fees, noting that an insurer can lawfully determine whether the proposed fee schedule is workable. The appellate court also rejected the claim of a horizontal agreement based on tacit agreement or conscious parallelism, stating,

> Conspiracy cannot be inferred from this evidence . . . because the last element of the *Interstate Circuit* test is not present. The . . . [plaintiffs] have not shown that the physicians were economically interdependent—that "cooperation was essential to successful operation of the plan." . . .
>
> The most precise test for economic interdependence involves an economic analysis of an industry's market structure. Economic interdependence exists only if an industry has relatively few competitors so that the actions of each has some impact on market price and thus on the conduct of competitors. . . . [T]he record indicates that more than 20,000 physicians practiced in Los Angeles County. . . . With such numbers, individual physicians could not possibly have had enough market power to influence the behavior of their rivals.

Barry, 805 F.2d at 869.

Similarly, the court rejected the allegation of a vertical conspiracy between Blue Cross at one level and the doctors at another, stating,

> . . . [A]lthough the vertical agreements in this case tend to foreclose nonparticipating physicians from doing business with patients insured under the Plan, the agreements do not cause impermissible market distortions. They do not prevent patients from seeing nonparticipating physicians, nor physicians from seeing nonsubscribing patients. Neither do they prevent participating physicians from referring patients to nonparticipating

> physicians, nor from contracting with other insurance companies. Therefore, the agreements do not have any prohibited anticompetitive effects.

Id. at 872.

In *United States v. A. Lanoy Alston, D.M.D., P.C.*, 974 F.2d 1206 (9th Cir. 1992), three dentists, disturbed that co-payment fees in Tucson, unlike Phoenix, had not risen in ten years, undertook to raise the amount of co-payments. They met among themselves and with other dentists to discuss higher fees. Subsequent to these meetings, Alston sent a letter to all fifty dentists in that market, stating that "a minimum acceptable fee schedule" was to be established and implemented. *Id.* at 1211.

The government obtained an indictment against the three dentists, who were convicted of price-fixing in a jury trial. The district court granted judgments of acquittal NOV to two defendants and a new trial to the third. In vacating the acquittals and affirming the new trial, Judge Kozinski wrote,

> . . . [W]hile we hold that the situation here is not sufficiently novel or unusual to escape scrutiny under the *per se* rule, the relationship between individual health care providers and medical plans is not without subtlety and complexity. In a market consisting of individual service providers and individual consumers, concerted action by the suppliers . . . is viewed with the greatest suspicion.
>
> . . . But health care providers who must deal with consumers indirectly through plans such as the one in this case face an unusual situation that may legitimate certain collective actions. Medical plans serve, effectively, as the bargaining agents for large groups of consumers; they use the clout of their consumer base to drive down health care fees. Uniform fee schedules—anathema in a normal, competitive market—are standard operating procedure when medical plans are involved. In the light of these departures from a normal competitive market, individual health care providers are entitled to take some joint action (short of price-fixing or a group boycott) to level the bargaining imbalance created by the plans and provide meaningful input into the setting of fee schedules. Thus health care providers might pool cost data in justifying a request for an increased fee schedule. . . .
>
> Providers might also band together to negotiate various other aspects of their relationship with the plans such as payment procedures, the type of documentation they must provide, the method of referring patients and the mechanism for adjusting disputes. Such concerted actions, which would not implicate the *per se* rule, must be carefully distinguished from efforts to dictate terms from explicit or implicit threats of mass withdrawals from the plans.

Id. at 1214.

How should the antitrust principles be focused to accomplish the goals stated by Judge Kozinski? Which of the partial antitrust repeal provisions in the proposed, but not enacted, health care bills (cited above) address his concerns? Could you draft a provision that would do so?

Note that much of the impetus for various managed care arrangements is designed to provide price competition between and among various health care entities. Alain Enthoven, a leading advocate of "managed competition" states the case for this approach as follows:

> What I believe is needed is not more bureaucratic controls imposed on an inherently irrational system, but rather fundamental reform of the financing and delivery system itself. *That is, we need to change from today's system dominated by cost-increasing incentives to a system in which providers are rewarded for finding ways to give better care at less cost.* . . . Government can create a system of fair economic competition in which consumers and providers of care, making decisions in an appropriately structured private market, would do the work of reorganization.

ALAIN ENTHOVEN, HEALTH PLAN xxi (1980).

Will this process be facilitated by vigorous antitrust scrutiny of the internal decisional process of insurers undertaking to review and adjust fee schedules? Where in the managed care matrix should antitrust scrutiny be directed?

4. To what extent may competing physicians exchange information among themselves in response to proposals by insurance providers relating to fees, reimbursement procedures, risk-limitation requirements, and capitation arrangements? In ¶ 5A of the Joint Department of Justice/Federal Trade Commission Statements of 1996, this problem is addressed as follows:

> In assembling information to be collectively provided to purchasers, providers need to be aware of the potential antitrust consequences of information exchanges among competitors. . . . [I]n order to qualify for the safety zone, the collection of information to be provided to purchasers must satisfy the following conditions:
>
> (1) the collection is to be managed by a third party (*e.g.*, purchaser, government agency, health care consultant, academic institution, or trade association);
>
> (2) although current fee-related information may be provided to purchasers, any information that is shared among or is available to competing providers furnishing the data must be more than three months old; and
>
> (3) for any information that is available to the providers furnishing data, there are to be at least five providers reporting data upon which each dissembled statistic is based, no individual provider's data may represent more than 25 percent on a weighted basis of that

> statistic, and any information disseminated must be sufficiently aggregated such that it would not allow recipients to identify the prices charged by any individual provider.

13 TRADE REG. REP. ¶ 13,153 (CCH), Statement 5 (1996).

E. Professional Standards as Conditions of Entry and Revocations of Privileges

Patrick v. Burget
486 U.S. 94 (1988)

[Petitioner, an Astoria, Oregon surgeon, declined an invitation by respondents to join them as a partner in the Astoria Clinic, and instead began an independent practice in competition with the Clinic. Thereafter, petitioner experienced difficulties in his professional dealings with Clinic physicians, culminating in respondents' initiation of, and participation in, peer-review proceedings to terminate petitioner's privileges at Astoria's only hospital (where a majority of whose staff members were employees or partners of the Clinic), on the ground that his care of his patients was below the hospital's standards. Petitioner filed suit in Federal District Court, alleging that respondents had violated §§ 1 and 2 of the Sherman Act by initiating and participating in the peer-review proceedings in order to reduce competition from petitioner rather than to improve patient care. Ultimately, the court entered a judgment against respondents, but the Court of Appeals reversed on the ground that respondents' conduct was immune from antitrust scrutiny under the state-action doctrine of *Parker v Brown*, 317 U.S. 341, and its progeny, because Oregon has articulated a policy in favor of peer review and actively supervises the peer-review process. (*See* Chapter 18, *supra*.)]

JUSTICE MARSHALL delivered the opinion of the Court.

The question presented in this case is whether the state-action doctrine of *Parker v. Brown*, 317 U.S. 341 (1943), protects physicians in the State of Oregon from federal antitrust liability for their activities on hospital peer-review committees.

I

. . . The only hospital in Astoria is the Columbia Memorial Hospital (CMH). Astoria also is the home of a private group-medical practice called the Astoria Clinic. At all times relevant to this case, a majority of the staff members at the CMH were employees or partners of the Astoria Clinic.

Petitioner Timothy Patrick is a general and vascular surgeon. He became an employee of the Astoria Clinic and a member of the CMH's medical staff in 1972. One year later, the partners of the Clinic, who are the respondents in this case, . . . invited petitioner to become a partner of the Clinic. Petitioner declined this offer and instead began an independent practice in competition with the surgical practice of the Clinic. Petitioner continued to serve on the medical staff of the CMH.

After petitioner established his independent practice, the physicians associated with the Astoria Clinic consistently refused to have professional dealings with him. Petitioner received virtually no referrals from physicians at the Clinic, even though the Clinic at times did not have a general surgeon on its staff. Rather than refer surgery patients to petitioner, Clinic doctors referred them to surgeons located as far as 50 miles from Astoria. In addition, Clinic physicians showed reluctance to assist petitioner with his own patients. Clinic doctors often declined to give consultations, and Clinic surgeons refused to provide backup coverage for patients under petitioner's care. At the same time, Clinic physicians repeatedly criticized petitioner for failing to obtain outside consultations and adequate backup coverage.

In 1979, respondent Gary Boelling, a partner at the Clinic, complained to the executive committee of the CMH's medical staff about an incident in which petitioner had left a patient in the care of a recently hired associate, who then left the patient unattended. The executive committee decided to refer this complaint, along with information about other cases handled by petitioner, to the State Board of Medical Examiners (BOME). Respondent Franklin Russell, another partner at the Clinic, chaired the committee of the BOME that investigated these matters. The members of the BOME committee criticized petitioner's medical practices to the full BOME, which then issued a letter of reprimand that had been drafted by Russell. The BOME retracted this letter in its entirety after petitioner sought judicial review of the BOME proceedings.

Two years later, at the request of respondent Richard Harris, a Clinic surgeon, the executive committee of the CMH's medical staff initiated a review of petitioner's hospital privileges. The committee voted to recommend the termination of petitioner's privileges on the ground that petitioner's care of his patients was below the standards of the hospital. Petitioner demanded a hearing, as provided by hospital bylaws, and a five-member *ad hoc* committee, chaired by respondent Boelling, heard the charges and defense. Petitioner requested that the members of the committee testify as to their personal bias against him, but they refused to accommodate this request. Before the committee rendered its decision, petitioner resigned from the hospital staff rather than risk termination. . . .

During the course of the hospital peer-review proceedings, petitioner filed this lawsuit in the United States District Court for the District of Oregon. Petitioner alleged that the partners of the Astoria Clinic had violated §§ 1 and 2 of the Sherman Act. . . . Specifically, petitioner contended that the Clinic partners had initiated and participated in the hospital peer-review proceedings to reduce competition from petitioner rather than to improve patient care. Respondents denied this assertion, and the District Court submitted the dispute to the jury. . . .

The jury returned a verdict against respondents Russell, Boelling, and Harris on the § 1 claim and against all of the respondents on the § 2 claim. It awarded damages of $650,000 on the two antitrust claims taken together. The District Court, as required by law, *see* 15 U.S.C. § 15(a), trebled the antitrust damages.

The Court of Appeals for the Ninth Circuit reversed. . . . It found that there was substantial evidence that respondents had acted in bad faith in the peer-review process.[1] The court held, however, that even if respondents had used the peer-review process to disadvantage a competitor rather than to improve patient care, their conduct in the peer-review

---

[1] Viewing the evidence in the light most favorable to petitioner, as appropriate in light of the verdicts rendered by the jury, the Court of Appeals characterized respondents' conduct as "shabby, unprincipled and unprofessional." 800 F.2d at 1509.

proceedings was immune from antitrust scrutiny. The court reasoned that the peer-review activities of physicians in Oregon fall within the state-action exemption from antitrust liability because Oregon has articulated a policy in favor of peer review and actively supervises the peer-review process.[2] The court therefore reversed the judgment of the District Court as to petitioner's antitrust claims.

We granted *certiorari*, . . . to decide whether the state-action doctrine protects respondents' hospital peer-review activities from antitrust challenge. . . . We now reverse.

II

In *Parker v. Brown*, 317 U.S. 341 (1943), this Court considered whether the Sherman Act prohibits anticompetitive actions of a State. Petitioner in that case was a raisin producer who brought suit against the California Director of Agriculture to enjoin the enforcement of a marketing plan adopted under the State's Agricultural Prorate Act. That statute restricted competition among food producers in the State in order to stabilize prices and prevent economic waste. Relying on principles of federalism and state sovereignty, this Court refused to find in the Sherman Act "an unexpressed purpose to nullify a state's control over its officers and agents." *Id.* at 351. The Sherman Act, the Court held, was not intended "to restrain state action or official action directed by a state." *Ibid.*

Although *Parker* involved a suit against a state official, the Court subsequently recognized that *Parker*'s federalism rationale demanded that the state-action exemption also apply in certain suits against private parties. . . . If the Federal Government or a private litigant always could enforce the Sherman Act against private parties, then a State could not effectively implement a program restraining competition among them. The Court, however, also sought to ensure that private parties could claim state-action immunity from Sherman Act liability only when their anticompetitive acts were truly the product of state regulation. We accordingly established a rigorous two-pronged test to determine whether anticompetitive conduct engaged in by private parties should be deemed state action and thus shielded from the antitrust laws. . . . First, "the challenged restraint must be 'one clearly articulated and affirmatively expressed as state policy.'" . . . Second, the anticompetitive conduct "must be 'actively supervised' by the State itself." . . . Only if an anticompetitive act of a private party meets both of these requirements is it fairly attributable to the State.

In this case, we need not consider the "clear articulation" prong of the *Midcal* test, because the "active supervision" requirement is not satisfied. The active supervision requirement stems from the recognition that "[w]here a private party is engaging in the anticompetitive activity, there is a real danger that he is acting to further his own interests, rather than the governmental interests of the State." . . . The requirement is designed to ensure that the state-action doctrine will shelter only the particular anticompetitive acts of private parties that, in the judgment of the State, actually further state regulatory policies. . . . To accomplish this purpose, the active supervision requirement mandates that the State exercise ultimate control over the challenged anticompetitive conduct. . . . The mere presence of some state involvement or monitoring does not suffice. . . . The active supervision prong

---

2 The Court of Appeals also determined that respondent Russell's activities as a member of the BOME likewise were immune from antitrust liability under the state-action doctrine. As we read the petition for writ of *certiorari* in this case, petitioner has declined to challenge this holding of the Court of Appeals. Indeed, petitioner asserts that this holding makes no difference to him because he suffered little or no damage from the BOME proceedings or respondent Russell's participation therein. Because petitioner has not brought this aspect of the Court of Appeals' decision before us, we express no view as to its correctness.

of the *Midcal* test requires that state officials have and exercise power to review particular anticompetitive acts of private parties and disapprove those that fail to accord with state policy. Absent such a program of supervision, there is no realistic assurance that a private party's anticompetitive conduct promotes state policy, rather than merely the party's individual interests.

Respondents in this case contend that the State of Oregon actively supervises the peer-review process through the State Health Division, the BOME, and the state judicial system. The Court of Appeals, in finding the active supervision requirement satisfied, also relied primarily on the powers and responsibilities of these state actors. Neither the Court of Appeals nor respondents, however, have succeeded in showing that any of these actors reviews—or even could review—private decisions regarding hospital privileges to determine whether such decisions comport with state regulatory policy and to correct abuses.

Oregon's Health Division has general supervisory powers over "matters relating to the preservation of life and health," Ore. Rev. Stat. § 431.110(1) (1987), including the licensing of hospitals, *see* § 441.025, and the enforcement of health laws, *see* §§ 431.120(1), 431.150, 431.155(1). Hospitals in Oregon are under a statutory obligation to establish peer-review procedures and to review those procedures on a regular basis. *See* §§ 441.055(3)(c), (d). The State Health Division, exercising its enforcement powers, may initiate judicial proceedings against any hospital violating this law. *See* §§ 431.150, 431.155. In addition, the Health Division may deny, suspend, or revoke a hospital's license for failure to comply with the statutory requirement. *See* § 441.030(2). Oregon law specifies no other ways in which the Health Division may supervise the peer-review process.

This statutory scheme does not establish a state program of active supervision over peer-review decisions. The Health Division's statutory authority over peer review relates only to a hospital's procedures;[3] that authority does not encompass the actual decisions made by hospital peer-review committees. The restraint challenged in this case (and in most cases of its kind) consists not in the procedures used to terminate hospital privileges, but in the termination of privileges itself. The State does not actively supervise this restraint unless a state official has and exercises ultimate authority over private privilege determinations. Oregon law does not give the Health Division this authority: under the statutory scheme, the Health Division has no power to review private peer-review decisions and overturn a decision that fails to accord with state policy. Thus, the activities of the Health Division under Oregon law cannot satisfy the active supervision requirement of the state-action doctrine.

Similarly, the BOME does not engage in active supervision over private peer-review decisions. The principal function of the BOME is to regulate the licensing of physicians in the State. As respondents note, Oregon hospitals are required by statute to notify the BOME promptly of a decision to terminate or restrict privileges. *See* Ore. Rev. Stat. § 441.820(1) (1987). Neither this statutory provision nor any other, however, indicates that the BOME has the power to disapprove private privilege decisions. The apparent purpose of the reporting requirement is to give the BOME an opportunity to determine whether addi-

---

3 Indeed, the statutory scheme indicates that the Health Division has only limited power over even a hospital's peer-review procedures. The statute authorizes the Health Division to force a hospital to comply with its obligation to establish and regularly review peer-review procedures, but the statute does not empower the Health Division to review the quality of the procedures that the hospital adopts.

tional action on its part, such as revocation of a physician's license, is warranted.[4] Certainly, respondents have not shown that the BOME in practice reviews privilege decisions or that it ever has asserted the authority to reverse them. The only remaining alleged supervisory authority in this case is the state judiciary. Respondents claim, and the Court of Appeals agreed, that Oregon's courts directly review privilege-termination decisions and that this judicial review constitutes active state supervision. This Court has not previously considered whether state courts, acting in their judicial capacity, can adequately supervise private conduct for purposes of the state-action doctrine. All of our prior cases concerning state supervision over private parties have involved administrative agencies. . . . This case, however, does not require us to decide the broad question whether judicial review of private conduct ever can constitute active supervision, because judicial review of privilege-termination decisions in Oregon, if such review exists at all, falls far short of satisfying the active supervision requirement.

As an initial matter, it is not clear that Oregon law affords any direct judicial review of private peer-review decisions. Oregon has no statute expressly providing for judicial review of privilege terminations. Moreover, we are aware of no case in which an Oregon court has held that judicial review of peer-review decisions is available. The two cases that respondents have cited certainly do not hold that a physician whose privileges have been terminated by a private hospital is entitled to judicial review. In each of these cases, the Oregon Supreme Court assumed, but expressly did not decide, that a complaining physician was entitled to the kind of review he requested. . . .

Moreover, the Oregon courts have indicated that even if they were to provide judicial review of hospital peer-review proceedings, the review would be of a very limited nature. The Oregon Supreme Court, in its most recent decision addressing this matter, stated that a court "should [not] decide the merits of plaintiff's dismissal" and that "[i]t would be unwise for a court to do more than to make sure that some sort of reasonable procedure was afforded and that there was evidence from which it could be found that plaintiff's conduct posed a threat to patient care." . . . This kind of review would fail to satisfy the state-action doctrine's requirement of active supervision. Under the standard suggested by the Oregon Supreme Court, a state court would not review the merits of a privilege termination decision to determine whether it accorded with state regulatory policy. Such constricted review does not convert the action of a private party in terminating a physician's privileges into the action of the State for purposes of the state-action doctrine.

Because we conclude that no state actor in Oregon actively supervises hospital peer-review decisions, we hold that the state-action doctrine does not protect the peer-review activities challenged in this case from application of the federal antitrust laws. In so holding, we are not unmindful of the policy argument that respondents and their *amici* have advanced for reaching the opposite conclusion. They contend that effective peer review is essential to the provision of quality medical care and that any threat of antitrust liability will

---

[4] The statutory provision requiring hospitals to inform the BOME of a decision to terminate privileges is only one of several statutory reporting requirements involving the BOME. Oregon law also provides that hospitals and licensees shall report medically incompetent conduct to the BOME. *See* Ore. Rev. Stat. § 677.415(2) (1987). Further, malpractice insurers must report all medical malpractice claims to the BOME. *See* § 743.770. All of these reporting requirements appear designed to ensure that the BOME will learn of instances of substandard medical care so that it can decide whether official action is warranted.

prevent physicians from participating openly and actively in peer-review proceedings. This argument, however, essentially challenges the wisdom of applying the antitrust laws to the sphere of medical care, and as such is properly directed to the legislative branch. To the extent that Congress has declined to exempt medical peer review from the reach of the antitrust laws,[5] review is immune from antitrust scrutiny only if the State effectively has made this conduct its own. The State of Oregon has not done so. Accordingly, we reverse the judgment of the Court of Appeals.

It is so ordered.

COMMENTARY

1. How does the result in this case make the market for health care delivery in Astoria, Oregon more competitive? Does the outcome increase the output of surgical patient treatment in this market? What goals of the antitrust laws does this case serve? Distinguish *Patrick* from *Silver v. New York Stock Exchange* on page 129, *supra.*

2. Would Justice Marshall's standard of "active supervision" (in *Parker* terms) be met by a state court's review of the peer review procedures? Would the public interest in quality medical services be better served by a complete exemption from the antitrust laws for medical care services? Would such exemption foster the enactment of state and federal legislation to control quality issues in the medical services industry?

What should antitrust Law say about physicians trained in M.D. programs at accredited medical schools, restricting entry to hospital facilities by chiropractors, osteopaths, and midwives? In *Wilk v. American Medical Association*, 719 F.2d 207 (7th Cir. 1983), the court reversed a judgment for defendant Association and remanded for a new trial on the grounds that the jury instructions failed to require that defendant's conduct be considered in terms of the effect on competition. Plaintiff-chiropractors sued under §§ 1 and 2 of the Sherman Act for access to hospital facilities, x-ray services and interpretative services of radiologists, and for referrals from members of the American Medical Association, the American Hospital Association (the AMA), the American College of Surgeons, the American College of Physicians, and the joint Committee on Accreditation of Hospitals (an

---

[5] Congress in fact insulated certain medical peer-review activities from antitrust liability in the Health Care Quality Improvement Act of 1986, 42 U.S.C. § 11101 *et seq.* (1982 ed., Supp. IV). The Act, which was enacted well after the events at issue in this case and is not retroactive, essentially immunizes peer-review action from liability if the action was taken "in the reasonable belief that [it] was in the furtherance of quality health care." § 11112(a). The Act expressly provides that it does not change other "immunities under law," § 11115(a), including the state-action immunity, thus allowing States to immunize peer-review action that does not meet the federal standard. In enacting this measure, Congress clearly noted and responded to the concern that the possibility of antitrust liability will discourage effective peer review. If physicians believe that the Act provides insufficient immunity to protect the peer-review process fully, they must take that matter up with Congress.

organization consisting of representatives of all the other named defendants). The defendants relied on Principle 3 of the AMA Principles of Medical Ethics that provides, "A physician should practice a method of healing founded on a scientific basis; and he should not voluntarily professionally associate with anyone who violates this principle."

In 1963, the AMA's "Committee on Quackery," adopted a statement in favor of containing and eliminating chiropractic as being unscientific. How should the service market for spinal manipulation be defined? By the curriculum and requirements for a Diploma in orthopaedic surgery or by the state law permitting the licensing of health delivery services, including chiropractors? Are antitrust criteria helpful in insuring the competency of health care providers?

In *Marrese v. American Academy of Orthopaedic Surgeons*, 706 F.2d 1488 (7th Cir. 1983), the court reversed a judgment favoring plaintiffs, who had alleged a boycott by Association members in denying them membership. Judge Posner described the controlling standard for reviewing an allegation of a boycott as follows:

> . . . [T]he vast majority of the nation's orthopaedic surgeons . . . are members of the Academy—10,000 members in all. The plaintiffs do not suggest that the Academy places any restrictions on its members. . . . [T]he Academy's meetings are open to nonmembers.
>
> . . . [T]he consumer interest in effective competition could not be seriously harmed by the exclusion of the plaintiffs . . . the plaintiffs do not argue that the Academy controls entry into the practice of orthopaedic surgery. Unless . . . [the members] explicitly agreed not to compete and backed up the agreement with enforcement machinery. . . . [T]he consumer would be assured the benefits of buying in a competitive market. And though there is a sense in which the exclusion of any competitor reduces competition, it is not the sense of competition that is relevant to antitrust law. . . . The plaintiffs will still have the burden at trial of showing that in these local markets the number of orthopaedic surgeons who belong to the Academy is so few that competition among them . . . cannot be relied on to give the consuming public the benefits of competition. Unless they can show this they will be unable to ask the trier of fact to draw an inference that either the exclusion of an individual orthopaedist from a local market or the possible effect of that exclusion on the competitive behavior of other aspirants to membership could result in a higher price or lower quality of orthopaedic surgery in these communities.

Id. at 497. Can you draw a workable distinction between professional qualifications and antitrust concerns? Might a family practice doctor seeking to refer a patient to an orthopedic surgeon have a preference for a Board Certified surgeon over one who was not? Is this like a potential savings bank depositor who has a preference for a federally insured institution over one that was not?

A concern for closer antitrust scrutiny over peer review has been expressed as follows:

> A large number of health care antitrust cases in the past decade have involved peer review—joint action usually by members of a speciality or by a hospital staff passing upon the qualifications and fitness of a practitioner to remain in the specialty or hospital, or to join it. Credentialing concerns a large array of private and public mechanisms for carving out and certifying institutions and personnel as qualified for providing health care. . . . Both forms of entry control can be of great significance to the level of competition among providers of a service and between providers of competing services. . . . Such conduct, as well as horizontal agreements among providers refusing to provide cost information to insurers and refusal by insurers to reimburse particular providers, have earmarks of a boycott, a joint refusal to deal for purposes of fixing prices or the adoption of regulatory power by a private group to determine who may enter the market.

John J. Flynn, *Antitrust Policy and Health Care Reform*, 39 ANTITRUST BULL. 59, 81 (1994).

How should courts distinguish conduct of private association members claiming to maintain standards of competence from conduct that results in the dampening of competition? In *Blue Shield of Virginia v. McCready*, 457 U.S. 465 (1981) (Chapter 17, *supra*), Blue Shield was accused of conspiring with physicians to exclude clinical psychologists from the market of mental health providers by reimbursing subscribers only for services of psychiatrists. The Court upheld the standing of an insured party to sue.

Is the preference for psychiatrists as opposed to clinical psychologists an example of ". . . the creation of a monopoly in medical practice through the exclusion of alternative practitioners," as suggested by one commentator, or a rational application of medical standards based on objective factors of training and experience? *See* P. STARR, THE SOCIAL TRANSFORMATION OF AMERICAN MEDICINE 227 (1982).

3. How should the exclusionary consequences stemming from the maintenance of professional standards be distinguished from restraint of trade? In *Schachar v. American Academy of Ophthalmology, Inc.*, 870 F.2d 397 (7th Cir. 1989), a group of ophthalmologists sued under § 1 of the Sherman Act alleging a conspiracy among the members of the Academy to restrain trade. The action complained against was the issuance of a press release by the Board of the Academy cautioning "patients, ophthalmologists and hospitals to approach radial keratotomy with caution until further research is completed," characterizing this surgical procedure to correct near-sightedness as "experimental." After refusal by third party payers to reimburse patients for such "experimental" procedures, the ophthalmologists sued. In affirming a jury verdict for the Academy, Judge Easterbrook wrote,

> Antitrust law is about consumers' welfare and the efficient organization of production. It condemns reduction in output that drives up prices as consumers bid for the remaining supply. . . . In a market with thousands of providers—that is, the market for ophthalmological services—what any one producer does cannot curtail output.
>
> * * *
>
> Plaintiffs say that the Academy is in the grip of professors and practitioners who favor conservative treatment, forever calling for more research. . . . [P]laintiffs portray themselves as the progressives, disdaining the Academy's fuddy-duddies in order to put the latest knowledge to work. Warfare among suppliers and their different products *is* competition. Antitrust law does not compel your competitor to praise your product or sponsor your work. . . . Unless one group of suppliers diminishes another's ability to peddle its wares, . . . there is not even the beginning an antitrust case. . . .

Id. at 399. Suppose a valid medical study of the results of this procedure showed that a statistically significant number of patients had experienced no improvement and, in addition, were susceptible to subsequent vision problems attributable to the weakening of the eyeball caused by this procedure. Suppose further that as a result of the publicity attending the release of this study, the demand for this operation fell by 88%. How would a suit by providers against the Academy come out under *Schachar*?

4. Entry into the medical specialists' market is restricted by phased professional specialty requirements, *e.g.*, a Diplomate (Board Certified in Neurosurgery), administered by a private association setting a rule of, say, 6 years of training in an approved residency program and success in an oral and written examination. In *Daniel v. American Board of Emergency Medicine*, 802 F. Supp. 912 (W.D.N.Y. 1992), the plaintiff, unable to satisfy the Board requirement of 60 months of practice in emergency medicine, was denied permission to take the examination for Board certification. The doctor sued, initially in state court, alleging denial of due process and violations of the New York State Human Rights Law. On removal to federal court, counts of antitrust violations were added and the individual members of the Board were named as parties defendant. The complaint alleged a conspiracy to restrain competition in the emergency medicine market and an attempt to monopolize the market for all emergency medicine physicians in the United States as well as the market for emergency medicine Diplomates. This complaint survived a motion for summary judgment, the court finding the requisite nexus to interstate commerce in the national scope of the Board's functions.

5. Denial of staff privileges to a licensed physician or revocation of a physician's privileges by peer review procedures of a hospital is often attacked as an antitrust conspiracy to restrain trade, but such claims rarely succeed. In 1986,

Congress responded to the rising volume of antitrust lawsuits brought on behalf of doctors who were denied hospital privileges. Many such cases were brought seeking treble damages for violations of §§ 1 & 2 of the Sherman Act based on allegations that the hospital and its staff doctors had conspired to restrain trade and monopolize the market in the specialty of the denied physician, as in *Patrick v. Burget.* The Health Care Quality Improvement Act (HCQIA) of 1986, P.L. 99-660, 100 Stat. 3748, 42 U.S.C. §§ 11101-11152 (1994), was enacted to provide limited immunity from suits for money damages as an incentive for reviewing physicians to identify and discipline incompetent physicians. H.R. REP. NO. 99-903 (1986). Section 11101(a)(4) states a Congressional finding that:

> The threat of private money damage liability under federal laws, including treble damage liability under Federal antitrust law, unreasonably discourages physicians from participating in effective professional peer review.

Section 11111 grants immunity from damages arising under any federal or state (or its political subdivision) law to a "professional review body," it members and their staff, as well as to any person who participates with or assists the review body in a "professional review action." However, immunity from damages does not extend to civil rights actions, *parens patriae* suits by a state attorney general, or to suits that do not arise from a "professional review action," which is defined by § 11151(9) as "an action based on the competence or professional conduct of a physician." Immunity from damages attaches to a reviewing body and its participants on a showing that the disciplinary action against a physician was taken "in the reasonable belief that the action was in furtherance of quality health care," 42 U.S.C. § 11112(a)(1), and the disciplined physician was accorded the due process requirements of notice, the opportunity to call and cross-examine witnesses, and to receive a record of the proceedings, § 11112(b).

Courts have granted summary judgment dismissing antitrust claims under HCQIA standards in actions brought by physicians on allegations of denial of privileges by economic competitors. In *Mathews v. Lancaster General Hospital,* 87 F.3d 624, 653 (3d Cir. 1996), the court stated: "assertions of bad faith and anticompetitive motive are irrelevant to the question of whether a decision was taken in a reasonable belief that it would further quality health care [under § 11112(b)]." Other circuits have adopted this position. *See Imperial v. Suburban Hospital Ass'n Inc.,* 37 F.3d 1026, 1330 (4th Cir. 1994); *Bryan v. James E. Holmes Regional Medical Center,* 33 F.3d 1318, 1335 (11th Cir. 1994); *Austin v. McNamara,* 979 F.2d 728, 734 (9th Cir. 1992). Can you distinguish the substantive antitrust differences between the termination of a physician's privileges to bring patients to a given hospital, from the termination of a dealer of widgets by a supplier who asserts poor merchandising and customer treatment? If asked by a trade association to draft manufacturer/wholesaler immunity legislation patterned on the HCQIA, could you use HCQIA § 11112(a) as a model? What is the best argument against extending HCQIA treatment to *Monsanto*-like relationships?

Where the HCQIA was not applicable, courts have utilized a variety of alternative grounds for effectively granting immunity from antitrust claims arising from physician access denial and disciplinary actions. Summary judgment dismissing a § 1 Sherman Act claim was granted in a revocation of surgical privileges case for failure to establish the requisite plurality of actors in *Johnson v. Nyack Hospital*, 954 F. Supp. 717 (S.D.N.Y. 1997). In *Balaklaw v. Lovell,* 14 F.3d 793 (2d Cir. 1994), the court of appeals affirmed the dismissal of an antitrust claim by an anesthesiologist denied access as a result of the hospital having signed an exclusive contract with a competing group. The holding was based on the plaintiff's failure to prove an antitrust injury. *See also Willman v. Heartland Hospital East*, 34 F.3d 605 (8th Cir. 1994); *Lee v. St. Joseph Hospital of Mt. Clemens*, 964 F.2d 567 (6th Cir. 1992). Where public hospitals are involved, some courts have based antitrust immunity on the state action doctrine, *e.g.*, *R. Ernest Cohn, DC v. Bond*, 953 F.2d 154 (4th Cir. 1991). Other courts find the state action doctrine inapplicable. *Miller v. Indiana Hospital*, 930 F.2d 334 (3rd Cir. 1991). In *Flegel v. Christian Hospital Northeast-Northwest*, 4 F.3d 682 (8th Cir. 1993), dismissal rested on the plaintiff's failure to show that the defendant hospital had power in the relevant market. There is a split among the circuits over whether a hospital and its medical staff are separate actors for § 1 purposes. Finding the medical staff an agent of the hospital and not independent of it is: *Nanavati v. Burdette Tomlin Memorial Hospital*, 857 F.2d 96 (3d Cir. 1988); finding that the medical staff have legally separate and possibly competitive interests and are thus capable of conspiring is: *Bolt v. Halifax Hospital Medical Center*, 851 F.2d 1273 (11th Cir. 1988); *Oltz v. St. Peter's Community Hospital*, 861 F.2d 1440 (9th Cir. 1988); *Oskanen v. Page Memorial Hospital*, 945 F.2d 696 (4th Cir. 1991); *Capital Imaging Associates, P.C. v. Mohawk Valley Medical Associates, Inc.*, 996 F.2d 537 (2d Cir. 1993).

Does the scope of the jurisdictional requirement of interstate commerce determine whether the Sherman Act embraces claims that could also be made as business torts? Consider the analysis of the interstate commerce requirement in the case that follows.

Summit Health, Ltd. v. Pinhas

500 U.S. 322 (1991)

[Respondent Pinhas, an ophthalmologist on the staff of petitioner Midway Hospital Medical Center, filed a suit in the District Court, asserting a violation, *inter alia,* of § 1 of the Sherman Act by Midway and other petitioners, including several doctors. The amended complaint alleged, among other things, that petitioners conspired to exclude Pinhas from the Los Angeles ophthalmological services market when he refused to follow an unnecessarily costly surgical procedure used at Midway; that petitioners initiated peer review proceedings against him which did not conform to congressional requirements and which resulted in the termination of his Midway staff privileges; that at the time he filed suit, petitioners were preparing to distribute an adverse report about him based on the peer review proceedings; that the provision of ophthalmological services affects interstate commerce because both physicians and hospitals serve nonresident patients and receive reimbursement from Medicare; and that reports from peer review proceedings are routinely distributed across state lines and affect doctors' employment opportunities throughout the Nation. The District Court dismissed the amended complaint, but the Court of Appeals reversed, rejecting petitioners' argument that the Act's jurisdictional requirements were not met because there was no allegation that interstate commerce would be affected by Pinhas' removal from Midway's staff. Rather, the court found that Midway's peer review proceedings obviously affected the hospital's interstate commerce because they affected its entire staff, and that Pinhas need not make a particularized showing of the effect on interstate commerce caused by the alleged conspiracy.]

JUSTICE STEVENS delivered the opinion of the Court.

The question presented is whether the interstate commerce requirement of antitrust jurisdiction is satisfied by allegations that petitioners conspired to exclude respondent, a duly licensed and practicing physician and surgeon, from the market for ophthalmological services in Los Angeles because he refused to follow an unnecessarily costly surgical procedure.

In 1987, respondent Dr. Simon J. Pinhas filed a complaint in District Court alleging that petitioners Summit Health, Ltd. (Summit), Midway Hospital Medical Center (Midway), its medical staff, and others had entered into a conspiracy to drive him out of business "so that other ophthalmologists and eye physicians [including four of the petitioners] will have a greater share of the eye care and ophthalmic surgery in Los Angeles." Among his allegations was a claim that the conspiracy violated § 1 of the Sherman Act. The District Court granted defendants' (now petitioners') motion to dismiss the First Amended Complaint (complaint) without leave to amend, . . . but the United States Court of Appeals for the Ninth Circuit reinstated the antitrust claim. We granted *certiorari* . . . to consider petitioners' contention that the complaint fails to satisfy the jurisdictional requirements of the Sherman Act, as interpreted in *McLain v. Real Estate Board of New Orleans, Inc.*, 444 U.S. 232 (1980) . . . , because it does not describe a factual nexus between the alleged boycott and interstate commerce.

I

Because this case comes before us from the granting of a motion to dismiss on the pleadings, we must assume the truth of the material facts as alleged in the complaint. Respondent, a diplomate of the American Board of Ophthalmology, has earned a national and international reputation as a specialist in corneal eye problems. . . . Since October 1981, he has been a member of the staff of Midway in Los Angeles, and because of his special skills, has performed more eye surgical procedures, including cornea transplants and cataract removals, than any other surgeon at the hospital.[3] Prior to 1986, most eye surgeries in Los Angeles were performed by a primary surgeon with the assistance of a second surgeon. . . . This practice significantly increased the cost of eye surgery. In February of that year, the administrators of the Medicare program announced that they would no longer reimburse physicians for the services of assistants, and most hospitals in southern California abolished the assistant surgeon requirement. Respondent, and certain other ophthalmolo-

---

[3] "One of the reasons for his success is the rapidity with which he, as distinguished from his competitors, can perform such surgeries. The speed with which such surgery can be completed benefits the patient because the exposure of cut eye tissue is drastically reduced. Some of Dr. Pinhas' competitors regularly require, on the average, six times the length of surgical time to complete the same procedures as Dr. Pinhas." App. 7

gists, asked Midway to abandon the requirement, but the medical staff refused to do so. Respondent explained that because Medicare reimbursement was no longer available, the requirement would cost him about $60,000 per year in payments to competing surgeons for assistance that he did not need. . . . Although respondent expressed a desire to maintain the preponderance of his practice at Midway, he nevertheless advised the hospital that he would leave if the assistant surgeon requirement were not eliminated. . . .

Petitioners responded to respondent's request to forgo an assistant in two ways. First, Midway and its corporate parent offered respondent a "sham" contract that provided for payments of $36,000 per year (later increased by oral offer to $60,000) for services that he would not be asked to perform. . . . Second, when respondent refused to sign or return the "sham" contract, petitioners initiated peer review proceedings against him and summarily suspended, and subsequently terminated, his medical staff privileges. . . . The proceedings were conducted in an unfair manner by biased decisionmakers, and ultimately resulted in an order upholding one of seven charges against respondent, and imposing severe restrictions on his practice. . . . When this action was commenced, petitioners were preparing to distribute an adverse report . . . about respondent that would "preclude him from continued competition in the market place, not only at defendant Midway Hospital [but also] . . . in California, if not the United States." . . . The defendants allegedly planned to disseminate the report "to all hospitals which Dr. Pinhas is a member [sic], and to all hospitals to which he may apply so as to secure similar actions by those hospitals, thus effectuating a boycott of Dr. Pinhas." . . .

The complaint alleges that petitioner Summit owns and operates 19 hospitals, including Midway, and 49 other health care facilities in California, six other States, and Saudi Arabia. Summit, Midway, and each of the four ophthalmic surgeons named as individual defendants, as well as respondent, are all allegedly engaged in interstate commerce. The provision of ophthalmological services affects interstate commerce because both physicians and hospitals serve nonresident patients and receive reimbursement through Medicare payments. Reports concerning peer review proceedings are routinely distributed across state lines and affect doctors' employment opportunities throughout the Nation. In the Court of Appeals, petitioners defended the District Court's dismissal of the complaint on the ground that there was no allegation that interstate commerce would be affected by respondent's removal from the Midway medical staff. The Court of Appeals rejected this argument because "as a matter of practical economics" the hospital's "peer review process in general" obviously affected interstate commerce. . . . The court added:

> "Pinhas need not, as appellees apparently believe, make the more particularized showing of the effect on interstate commerce caused by the alleged conspiracy to keep him from working. [*McLain v. Real Estate Bd. of New Orleans, Inc.*] He need only prove that peer-review proceedings have an effect on interstate commerce, a fact that can hardly be disputed. The proceedings affect the entire staff at Midway and thus affect the hospital's interstate commerce. Appellees' contention that Pinhas failed to allege a nexus with interstate commerce because the absence of Pinhas's services will not drastically affect the interstate commerce of Midway therefore misses the mark and must be rejected."

II

Congress enacted the Sherman Act in 1890. . . . During the past century, as the dimensions and complexity of our economy have grown, the federal power over commerce, and the concomitant coverage of the Sherman Act, have experienced similar expansion. This history has been recounted before . . . and we need not reiterate it today.[10]

We therefore begin by noting certain propositions that are undisputed in this case. Petitioner Summit, the parent of Midway as well as of several other general hospitals, is unquestionably engaged in interstate commerce. Moreover, although Midway's primary activity is the provision of health care services in a local market, it also engages in interstate commerce. A conspiracy to prevent Midway from expanding would be covered by the Sherman Act, even though any actual impact on interstate commerce would be "indirect" and "fortuitous." *Hospital Bldg. Co. v. Rex Hospital*. . . . No specific purpose to restrain interstate commerce is required. . . . As a "matter of practical economics," . . . the effect of such a conspiracy on the hospital's "purchases of out-of-state medicines and supplies as well as its revenues from out-of-state insurance companies," . . . would establish the necessary interstate nexus.

This case does not involve the full range of activities conducted at a general hospital. Rather, this case involves the provision of ophthalmological services. It seems clear, however, that these services are regularly performed for out-of-state patients and generate revenues from out-of-state sources; their importance as part of the entire operation of the hospital is evident from the allegations of the complaint. A conspiracy to eliminate the entire ophthalmological department of the hospital, like a conspiracy to destroy the hospital itself, would unquestionably affect interstate commerce. Petitioners contend, however, that a boycott of a single surgeon has no such obvious effect because the complaint does not deny the existence of an adequate supply of other surgeons to perform all of the services that respondent's current and future patients may ever require. Petitioners argue that respondent's complaint is insufficient because there is no factual nexus between the restraint on this one surgeon's practice and interstate commerce.

There are two flaws in petitioners' argument. First, because the essence of any violation of § 1 is the illegal agreement itself—rather than the overt acts performed in furtherance of it . . . proper analysis focuses, not upon actual consequences, but rather upon the potential harm that would ensue if the conspiracy were successful. As we explained in *Mclain v. Real Estate Board of New Orleans, Inc.*, . . .

> "If establishing jurisdiction required a showing that the unlawful conduct itself had an effect on interstate commerce, jurisdiction would be defeated by a demonstration that the alleged restraint failed to have its intended anticompetitive effect. This is not the rule of our cases. . . . A violation may still be found in such circumstances because in a civil action under the Sherman Act, liability may be established by proof of either an unlawful purpose or an anticompetitive effect. . . ."

Thus, respondent need not allege, or prove, an actual effect on interstate commerce to support federal jurisdiction.

---

[10] It is firmly settled that when Congress passed the Sherman Act, it "left no area of its constitutional power [over commerce] unoccupied." *United States v. Frankfort Distilleries, Inc.*, 324 U.S. 293, 298 (1945). Congress "meant to deal comprehensively and effectively with the evils resulting from contracts, combinations and conspiracies in restraint of trade, and to that end to exercise all the power it possessed." *Atlantic Cleaners & Dyers, Inc. v. United States*, 286 U.S. 427, 435 (1932).

Second, if the conspiracy alleged in the complaint is successful, "'as a matter of practical economics'" there will be a reduction in the provision of ophthalmological services in the Los Angeles market. . . . In cases involving horizontal agreements to fix prices or allocate territories within a single State, we have based jurisdiction on a general conclusion that the defendants' agreement "almost surely" had a marketwide impact and therefore an effect on interstate commerce . . . or that the agreement "necessarily affect[ed]" the volume of residential sales and therefore the demand for financing and title insurance provided by out-of-state concerns. *McLain*, 444 U.S. at 246. In the latter case, we explained:

> "To establish the jurisdictional element of a Sherman Act violation it would be sufficient for petitioners to demonstrate a substantial effect on interstate commerce generated by respondents' brokerage activity. Petitioners need not make the more particularized showing of an effect on interstate commerce caused by the alleged conspiracy to fix commission rates, or by those other aspects of respondents' activity that are alleged to be unlawful." *Id.*, at 242-243.

Although plaintiffs in *McLain* were consumers of the conspirators' real estate brokerage services, and plaintiff in this case is a competing surgeon whose complaint identifies only himself as the victim of the alleged boycott, the same analysis applies. For if a violation of the Sherman Act occurred, the case is necessarily more significant than the fate of "just one merchant whose business is so small that his destruction makes little difference to the economy." *Klor's, Inc. v. Broadway-Hale Stores, Inc.*, 359 U.S. 207, 213 (1959) (footnote omitted). The case involves an alleged restraint on the practice of ophthalmological services. The restraint was accomplished by an alleged misuse of a congressionally regulated peer review process . . . which respondent characterizes as the gateway that controls access to the market for his services. The gateway was closed to respondent, both at Midway and at other hospitals, because petitioners insisted upon adhering to an unnecessarily costly procedure. The competitive significance of respondent's exclusion from the market must be measured, not just by a particularized evaluation of his own practice, but rather, by a general evaluation of the impact of the restraint on other participants and potential participants in the market from which he has been excluded.

We have no doubt concerning the power of Congress to regulate a peer review process controlling access to the market for ophthalmological surgery in Los Angeles. Thus, respondent's claim that members of the peer review committee conspired with others to abuse that process and thereby deny respondent access to the market for ophthalmological services provided by general hospitals in Los Angeles has a sufficient nexus with interstate commerce to support federal jurisdiction.

The judgment of the Court of Appeals is affirmed.

It is so ordered.

JUSTICE SCALIA, with whom JUSTICE O'CONNOR, JUSTICE KENNEDY, and JUSTICE SOUTER join, dissenting.

The Court treats this case as involving no more than a conspiracy among eye surgeons at Midway Hospital to eliminate one of their competitors. That alone, it concludes, restrains trade or commerce among the several States within the meaning of the Sherman Act. In my judgment, the conspiracy alleged by the complaint, fairly viewed, involved somewhat more than that; but even so falls far short of what is required for Sherman Act jurisdiction. I respectfully dissent.

I

The Court has "no doubt concerning the power of Congress to regulate a peer review process controlling access to the market for ophthalmological surgery in Los Angeles," and concludes that "respondent's claim . . . has a sufficient nexus with interstate commerce to support federal jurisdiction." . . . I agree with all that. Unfortunately, however, the question before us is not whether Congress could reach the activity before us here if it wanted to, but whether it has done so via the Sherman Act. That enactment does not prohibit all conspiracies using instrumentalities of commerce that Congress could regulate. Nor does it prohibit all conspiracies that have sufficient constitutional "nexus" to interstate commerce to be regulated. It prohibits only those conspiracies that are "in restraint of trade or commerce among the several States." 15 U.S.C. § 1. This language commands a judicial inquiry into the nature and potential effect of each particular restraint. "The jurisdictional inquiry under general prohibitions like . . . § 1 of the Sherman Act, turning as it does on the circumstances presented in each case and requiring a particularized judicial determination, differs significantly from that required when Congress itself has defined the specific persons and activities that affect commerce and therefore require federal regulation." *Gulf Oil Corp. v. Copp Paving Co.*, 419 U.S. 186, 197, n.12 (1974).

Until 1980, the nature of this jurisdictional inquiry (with respect to alleged restraints not targeted at the very flow of interstate commerce) was clear: The question was whether the restraint at issue, if successful, would have a substantial effect on interstate commercial activity. . . . As I shall discuss in due course, that criterion would have called for reversal in the present case. *See United States v. Oregon State Medical Society*, 343 U.S. 326 (1952).

Unfortunately, in 1980, the Court seemed to abandon this approach. *McLain v. Real Estate Board of New Orleans, Inc.*, appeared to shift the focus of the inquiry away from the effects of the restraint itself, asking instead whether the "[defendants'] activities which allegedly have been *infected* by a price-fixing conspiracy . . . have a not insubstantial effect on the interstate commerce involved." *Id.* at 246 (emphasis added). The result in *McLain* would have been the same under the prior test, since the subject of the suit was an alleged massive conspiracy by all realtors in the Greater New Orleans area, involving price fixing, suppression of market information, and other anticompetitive practices. The Court's resort to the more expansive "infected activity" test was prompted by the belief that focusing upon the effects of the restraint itself would require plaintiffs to prove their case at the jurisdictional stage. *See id.* at 243. That belief was in error, since the prior approach had simply assumed, rather than required proof of, the success of the conspiracy.

Thus, as a dictum based upon a misconception, the "infected activities" approach was introduced into antitrust law. It was not received with enthusiasm. Most courts simply finessed the language of *McLain* and said that nothing had changed, *i.e.*, that the ultimate question was still whether the unlawful conduct *itself*, if successful, would have a substantial effect on interstate commerce. Others, however, took *McLain* at face value—and of course immediately fell into disagreement over the proper application of the new test. With respect to a restraint like the one at issue here, for example, how does one decide which "activities of the defendants" are "infected"? Are they all the activities of the hospital? . . . Only the activities of the eye surgery department? . . . The entire practice of eye surgeons who use the hospital? . . . Or, as the Ninth Circuit apparently found in this case, the peer review process itself?

Today the Court could have cleared up the confusion created by *McLain*, refocused the inquiry along the lines marked out by our previous cases (and still adhered to by most circuits), and reversed the judgment below. Instead, it compounds the confusion by rejecting the two competing interpretations of *McLain* and adding yet a third candidate to the field, one that no court or commentator has ever suggested, let alone endorsed. To determine Sherman Act jurisdiction it looks neither to the effect on commerce of the restraint, nor to the effect on commerce of the defendants' infected activity, but rather, it seems, to the effect on commerce of the activity from which the plaintiff has been excluded. As I understand the Court's opinion, the test of Sherman Act jurisdiction is whether the entire line of commerce from which Dr. Pinhas has been excluded affects interstate commerce. Since excluding him from eye surgery at Midway Hospital effectively excluded him from the entire Los Angeles market for eye surgery (because no other Los Angeles hospital would accord him practice privileges after Midway rejected him), the jurisdictional question is simply whether that market affects interstate commerce, which of course it does.[8] This analysis tells us nothing about the substantiality of the impact on interstate commerce generated by the particular conduct at issue here.

. . . .

The Court's suggestion that competition in the entire Los Angeles market was affected by this one surgeon's exclusion from that market simply ignores the "practical economics" of the matter.

II

. . . .

Charitably read, respondent's complaint alleges just such a scheme, namely, a scheme to fix prices for some of the eye surgery performed at Midway Hospital. Instead of simply agreeing to a supercompetitive price, Midway's eye surgeons have, contrary to prevailing Los Angeles practice, allegedly "padded" the cost of certain varieties of eye surgery by requiring a useless second surgeon to be present. The so-called "sham contract" was an attempt to compensate the hyperproductive Dr. Pinhas for his participation in the scheme and the concomitant reduction in his output. When that failed, the conspirators eliminated him as a competitor by terminating his medical staff privileges through the peer review process. That termination was not the totality of the conspiracy, but merely the means used to enforce it—just as, in *Monsanto v. Spray-Rite Service Corp.*, 465 U.S. 752 (1984), the elimination of the price-cutting Spray-Rite as a distributor of Monsanto's products (via termination and a boycott) was merely the means of enforcing the alleged price-fixing conspiracy between Monsanto and its other distributors. This case, like *Monsanto*, involves a "termination . . . *pursuant* to a conspiracy . . . to set . . . prices," *id.* at 757-758 (emphasis added), and for purposes of determining Sherman Act jurisdiction, what counts is the impact of that entire price-fixing conspiracy. Even when the conspiracy is viewed in this broader fashion, however, the scope of the market affected by it has nothing to do with the scope of Dr. Pinhas' exclusion from practice. If this had been a naked price-fixing conspiracy, instead of the more subtle one that it is, no one would contend that it affected prices throughout Los Angeles. Pursuant to standard antitrust analysis, the agreement itself would define the extent of the market. The market would be eye surgery at Midway (not "eye surgery in the city where Midway is located"), since the very existence of the agreement implies power over price in that defined market. . . . It is irrational to use a different analy-

---

8 Even so, I might note, it is improper for the Court to dispense with the necessary allegations to that effect. *See McLain v. Real Estate Board of New Orleans, Inc.*, 444 U.S. 232, 242 (1980).

sis, and to assume the affected market to be all of Los Angeles, simply because this more subtle price-fixing conspiracy led (incidentally) to the exclusion of Dr. Pinhas not only from Midway but from all hospitals throughout the city.

There is simply no basis for assuming that this alleged conspiracy's market power—and its consequent effect upon competition, as opposed to its effect upon *Dr. Pinhas*—extended throughout Los Angeles.

. . . .

III

In my view, the present case should be decided by applying to the price-fixing conspiracy at Midway Hospital the workable jurisdictional test that our cases had established before *McLain* confused things. On that basis, I would reverse the Court of Appeals' judgment that respondent had stated a Sherman Act claim.

. . . .

COMMENTARY

1. Are §§ 1 and 2 of the Sherman Act suited to discern the competence of a surgeon? Do some of the lower court cases that follow suggest that peer review issues ought to be immune from antitrust scrutiny? Under Justice Scalia's view of the case, what alternative remedies are available to Dr. Pinhas? Under the Health Care Quality Improvement Act of 1986, 42 U.S.C. § 11112(a)(1) (1995), a professional peer review action must be taken "in the reasonable belief that the action was in furtherance of quality health care." Could the action against Dr. Pinhas meet this standard if it were undertaken solely to punish him for his pricing practices? Might Dr. Pinhas also have a cause of action under traditional business tort doctrines, such as improper interference with the performance of obligations to patients? *See* FOWLER HARPER, FLEMING JAMES & OSCAR GRAY, 2 THE LAW OF TORTS § 6.9 (2d ed. 1986); *see also* RESTATEMENT (SECOND) OF TORTS §§ 623A, 766, 766A (1979).

2. Does the narrow "affecting commerce" aspect of *Summit Health* and the "state action" analysis of *Patrick* mask an underlying antitrust issue? Setting aside the "professional" nature of the services in both *Summit Health* and in *Patrick* was there a concerted effort by competing sellers to refuse to deal? How would this come out under *Klor's*, under *Northwest Wholesale Stationers,* or under *Indiana Federation of Dentists?* Stricter antitrust scrutiny of denials of hospital privileges is suggested by James F. Ponsoldt, in *Refusals to Deal in "Locked-in" Health Care Markets Under Section 2 of the Sherman Act After* Eastman Kodak Co. v. Image Technical Services, 1995 UTAH L. REV. 503.

3. Consider whether there is a valid refusal to deal issue in the *Marshfield Clinic* litigation that follows.

F. New Entities: Their Management and Competitive Practices

Blue Cross & Blue Shield United v. Marshfield Clinic

883 F. Supp. 1247 (W.D. Wis. 1995);
aff'd in part, rev'd and remanded,
63 F.3d 1417 (7th Cir. 1995); *cert. denied,* 116 S. Ct. 1288 (1996)

[Marshfield Clinic was established as a group practice, doctor-owned and managed, fee-for-service unit by six doctors as a non-profit treatment and research facility. In 1970, Marshfield formed an HMO as a three-way joint venture between Marshfield Clinic (the doctors), St. Joseph's Hospital (of Marshfield), and the plaintiff, Blue Cross (of Wisconsin), as insurer. The objective was to market this package of doctors, hospital, and insurer to employers and other groups seeking a health care program. The association with Blue Cross was dissolved in 1987 and Marshfield Clinic undertook to provide financing of its services by serving as its own insurer, through its subsidiary, Security Health Plan. Security Health Plan then entered into affiliation agreements with other independent practitioners in northern Wisconsin. Under these latter affiliations, the physicians remained free to take patients from other managed care groups and HMOs, as well as to treat patients on a fee-for-service basis.

In early 1990, Blue Cross began negotiations to renew its association with Marshfield Clinic offering rates not acceptable to the Clinic. After negotiations, a Blue Cross written proposal was rejected, and in February of 1994 Blue Cross and its subsidiary HMO, Compcare, sued Marshfield Clinic under §§ 1 and 2 of the Sherman Act for price-fixing, division of territories, and monopolization. The thrust of the Blue Cross suit was that Marshfield Clinic had monopolized the HMO market by obtaining the services of the large majority of physicians in the region, Blue Cross alleging that there existed an HMO market separate and distinct from other health insurance options such as indemnity insurance, or Preferred Provider Organizations.

At that time, Marshfield had grown to be owned by 400 physicians. Marshfield, Wisconsin is a town of 20,000 population in a rural, sparsely populated area of the state. The Clinic's main office is in Marshfield; it had 21 branch offices in 14 rural counties, generating annual revenue of over $200 million. The affiliated physicians consist of some 900 other physicians with whom Security has non-exclusive contracts. Blue Cross claimed that many of its insureds in north central Wisconsin are patients of the Marshfield Clinic on a fee-for-service basis and that Marshfield has fixed the price of those services to Blue Cross patients at a supracompetitive level. Plaintiff Compcare, an HMO that is a subsidiary of Blue Cross, alleged that defendants had enlisted virtually all the available doctors and hospital facilities in the 14 county, north central Wisconsin region, so that plaintiffs could not find a sufficient number of unaffiliated physicians in order to offer HMO services in competition with Marshfield.

Plaintiffs prevailed in a jury trial and were awarded damages and attorneys' fees of around $20 million. On appeal, Judge Posner set aside the monopolization and price-fixing findings and remanded for a trial on the territorial division count.

Contrast the different characterizations of the record in this case in the two opinions that follow.]

JOHN C. SHABAZ, District Judge

. . . .

There is a . . . legally sufficient evidentiary basis for a reasonable jury to find that plaintiffs established a relevant product and geographical market in HMO services. The Court acknowledges the importance of finding an HMO market. Without an HMO market, plaintiff Compcare's claim for exclusion from the market cannot stand. Plaintiff's late attempts to argue an alternative basis for liability are to no avail.

. . . .

Vicki Thoreson, sales director for Blue Cross/Blue Shield for the North Central region testified she sold products other than HMOs and that Security HMO does not compete with these products. From her testimony the jury could find that plaintiffs' PPO plan is a totally different type product than the Security HMO and that customers perceive a fee for service plan as different from an HMO which has different pricing and characteristics.

Jeffrey J. Nohl, president of Compcare which sells HMO products, specifically described those features from which the jury could reasonably find that an HMO is other than traditional indemnity insurance. Nohl stressed the managed care aspects of an HMO as a separate product. Based upon his ten years of experience in the HMO market he testified as an expert that an HMO is not a financial mechanism as is indemnity insurance. He referred also to separate federal and state laws and regulations relating to the HMO as well as those regulations which separate surplus and capital. The State of Wisconsin has a program for state employees which provides HMO health care for which HMOs may compete. . . .

The jury was advised of three distinct characteristics [of an HMO] to include, first, the gate keeper where a patient chooses a primary care doctor. The second feature provides for controls on use, monitored care a with capitation agreement and the third provides for preventive care and wellness programs where the quality of care is chosen as a part of HMO membership. . . . [T]he defendants' expert opined that an HMO market did not exist but rather a health care financing market existed of which the HMO is a part. He did not believe the Wisconsin program which requires or mandates separate HMOs to state employees and Medicaid recipients was relevant nor was the separate capital structure for companies who are able to sell HMOs. He had not considered the separate regulations and laws relating to the HMO believing them not to have made a difference in his opinion. From all of this the jury could have reasonably determined that an HMO is a distinct and unique form of health care financing for which a relevant product market exists.

. . . .

. . . HMOs may be interchangeable with indemnity insurance when they are priced at monopolistic levels, as is Security HMO, but are considerably less expensive than indemnity insurance, and correspondingly less substitutable, in competitive markets. Considering this and the consumer's convenience and preference, the jury had legally sufficient evidence upon which it could find that the consumer expects to receive a unique and distinctive service from an HMO not either envisioned or provided by indemnity insurance, all at a lower cost.

Finally, Nohl testified to a geographical market which was described as a 20 to 30 minute drive time around those primary care doctors who are "the key since each person is to select one and all care is channeled through that primary care doctor. With that selection you have a relationship with the primary care doctor. A 20 to 30 minute drive around is basically the area that an HMO can operate."

. . . .

The Court further notes that the plaintiffs' expert witness on damages, John Beyer, testified that Compcare was foreclosed from the core areas of Marshfield Clinic's service area from selling Compcare HMO Products and his opinion considering HMOs as a separate market is stated as follows: "If you mean by separate market defining it as a separate relevant product market in an antitrust setting as we heard in the prior phase of this trial, the answer is no." His testimony specifically related however to two distinct primary markets. The Greater Marshfield Health Plan which operates in the counties of Wood, Jackson, Clark, western part of Marathon, Taylor, Rusk and to a certain extent Sawyer and the Northcare Plan in the counties of Oneida, Vilas, Iron, Ashland and part of Lincoln where Security has 100% enrollment in five of the above counties. . . . Similarly, plaintiff Compcare's essential facility claim is supported by the evidence. A monopolist's refusal to deal is governed by the "essential facilities doctrine." *MCI Communications Co. v. AT&T Co.*, 708 F.2d 1081, 1132 (7th Cir. 1983).

> "Such a refusal may be unlawful because a monopolist's control of an essential facility can extend monopoly power from one stage of production to another, and from one market into another. Thus, the antitrust laws have imposed on firms controlling an essential facility the obligation to make the facility available on non-discriminatory terms.
>
> The case law sets forth four elements necessary to establish liability under the essential facilities doctrine: (1) control of the essential facility by a monopolist; (2) a competitor's inability practically or reasonably to duplicate the essential facility; (3) the denial of the use of the facility to a competitor; and (4) the feasibility of providing the facility."

. . . To be essential, a "facility need not be indispensable; it is sufficient if duplication of the facility would be economically infeasible and if denial of its use inflicts a severe handicap on potential market entrants." *Fishman v. Estate of Wirtz*, 807 F.2d 520, 539 (7th Cir. 1986). . . .

Defendants challenge Compcare's essential facility claim by stating that the Marshfield doctors are not an essential facility because Nohl testified that . . . [other] plans are in the HMO product market and plaintiffs have established . . . [another type of plan] in areas surrounding Marshfield. That plaintiff established a small . . . [alternative] plan in surrounding areas does not change the fact that the jury could reasonably find that Compcare could not establish a competing HMO in Marshfield. Moreover, there was evidence that Blue Cross could not duplicate the network of doctors. It was difficult to recruit rural doctors. . . . Obtaining new doctors or contracting with existing doctors was handicapped by Marshfield's monopolistic tactics, . . . and Marshfield's control of hospital privileges. . . . Defendants' business justifications for refusing to deal with plaintiffs are refuted by evidence of Marshfield's blanket policy of not entering contracts with other HMOs. . . . It was for the jury to decide if Marshfield offered its facility on reasonable grounds. A reasonable jury could have found it was feasible for Marshfield to offer its doctors to Compcare to form an HMO because Marshfield made physicians available to Security . . . and other clinics have contracts with multiple HMOs.

Plaintiffs also provided sufficient evidence from which a reasonable jury could have found that plaintiffs suffered antitrust injury. Defendants claim that Blue Cross did not prove it suffered antitrust injury because Blue Cross did not produce evidence that it paid a supracompetitive price, rather Blue Cross only presented evidence that it paid higher than average prices. Defendants claim that higher than average prices are not necessarily the same as supra-competitive prices because of factors like quality and investment. Defendants, however, are wrong. There was sufficient evidence from which a reasonable jury could find Blue Cross paid a supra-competitive price. Blue Cross paid charges to Marshfield that were 10% above the UCR [usual, customary, and reasonable charges]. . . . In a market basket study, the City of Marshfield's charges were the highest of 23 cities in the state. . . . This was sufficient for the jury to infer the charges were supra-competitive. Antitrust injury may be proved by inference or circumstantial evidence. *Zenith Radio Co. v. Hazeltine Research, Inc.*, 395 U.S. 100, 125 (1969). Moreover supra-competitive prices are prices that are higher than those Blue Cross would have paid in the absence of defendants' anti-competitive conduct and plaintiffs produced this type of evidence.

Similarly, Blue Cross has standing as a purchaser of physician services. This issue has been resolved in this Court's Order Denying Defendants' Motion for Summary Judgment.

Plaintiffs also produced sufficient evidence defining the other relevant markets. The relevant market must be ascertained in order to determine whether other sellers exist whose competition may limit defendants' monopoly power. *United States v. Grinnell Co.*, 384 U.S. 563, 571 (1966) A relevant geographic market is "the set of sellers to which a set of buyers can turn for supplies at existing or slightly higher prices." *A.A. Poultry Farms, Inc. v. Rose Acre Farms, Inc.*, 881 F.2d 1396, 1403 (7th Cir. 1989). In a case involving health care, the relevant market must reflect actual patient and physician practices. *SmithKline Co. v. Eli Lilly & Co.*, 427 F. Supp. 1089, 1117-18 (E.D. Pa. 1976), *aff'd*, 575 F.2d 1056 (3d Cir. 1978), *cert. denied*, 439 U.S. 838 (1978). Delineation of the relevant market is for the trier of fact. *Fishman v. Wirtz*, 807 F.2d 520, 531 (7th Cir. 1986).

Defendants first challenge the sufficiency of the geographic definition of the market for specialty care, claiming that the geographic market for specialty care includes Minnesota and plaintiffs' expert, Greenberg, erred in leaving it out. Defendants cite to *Morgenstern v. Wilson*, 29 F.3d 1291 (8th Cir. 1994), for support. Greenberg did consider Minnesota, . . . but did not include it in the market. He explained that certain communities on the edge of a market can be in two relevant markets. . . . The jury was entitled to accept this explanation. Plaintiffs distinguish *Morgenstern*, which found the jury's definition of the relevant market to be in error because it left out a city only 50 miles from the defendants' location, because Minnesota providers are close to the state border, but far from Marshfield. Duluth, the Twin Cities, and Rochester are 217, 166-200 & 160 miles away from Marshfield.

Second, defendants challenge the geographic definition of the primary and pediatric care markets because they overlap and allegedly ignore competing sellers. Plaintiffs' expert, Greenberg, considered the relevant factors: the area defendants targeted . . . , used economic and statistical tests including Elzinger [*sic*] Hogarty . . . and economic literature which indicates a 30 mile radius for primary care. Greenberg explained to the jury how markets can overlap. . . . The jury was entitled to embrace his opinion.

Third, defendants challenge the product market for specialty care asserting that there is no evidence that services in DRGs are good substitutes. Defendants claim that DRGs are merely hospital fee codes. A relevant product market is composed of products or services that are reasonably interchangeable for the purpose for which they are produced. . . . DRGs are a system developed by health economists and used by the federal and state governments and insurance carriers. [DRG means Diagnosis Related Groups, a listing of diseases and conditions classified by diagnosis and surgical procedure into major categories of treatment, on the premise that like conditions will be treated at similar costs by various hospitals—Eds.] A jury could reasonably rely on this evidence.

Plaintiffs also provided sufficient evidence from which the jury could find that defendants possessed monopoly power. In some cases, a firm's share of the relevant market indicates market power because market share may reflect a firm's ability to reduce the total output in the market and so raise prices. *Ball Memorial Hosp., Inc. v. Mutual Hosp. Ins.*, 784 F.2d 1325, 1336 (7th Cir. 1986). Part of proving market power is proving barriers to entry. Unless barriers to entry prevent rivals from entering the market at the same cost of production, even a very large market share does not establish market power. *Will v. Comprehensive Accounting Co.*, 776 F.2d 665, 672 (7th Cir. 1985). The lower the barriers to entry, and the shorter the lags of new entry, the less power existing firms have to raise prices. When the supply is highly elastic, existing market share does not signify power. . . .

Defendants have not challenged the existence of monopoly power for HMO services. Defendants do, however, challenge the jury's finding of monopoly power in other relevant markets. Defendants assert that no barriers to entry existed because a study demonstrated actual entry of new non-Marshfield doctors into the area. The jury could reasonably have disregarded this evidence because the study counted Marshfield-affiliated doctors as independent doctors, not as Marshfield doctors. . . . The study was also statistically flawed. . . . There was ample evidence from which a reasonable jury could have found barriers to entry. It is customary in rural practice to provide cross-coverage. . . . Marshfield denied cross-coverage to competitors. . . . Without cross-coverage a doctor must hire temporary doctors known as *locum tenens*. . . . This is a significant cost that Marshfield does not incur and is not incurred in other parts of the state. Marshfield also denied and restricted the hospital staff privileges of competitors. . . . Lastly, plaintiffs' expert, Greenberg, testified that there were barriers to entry.

Defendants also challenge the inclusion of Marshfield affiliated doctors within defendants' percentage of the market share. Plaintiffs presented sufficient evidence that would justify a jury adding the number of affiliated doctors to defendants' market share. The affiliation contracts are renewable or may be terminated on an annual basis. . . . Marshfield obtains the fee schedules of its affiliates and approves or disapproves them. . . . Marshfield has also allocated markets and territory with affiliated providers, Rhinelander Medical Center and Wausau Medical Center. . . . Lastly, plaintiffs' expert testified as to why affiliated providers are included in defendants' market share. . . .

Similarly there was sufficient evidence from which a reasonable jury could find that defendants engaged in anticompetitive conduct. Anti-competitive conduct is defined as the willful acquisition or maintenance of monopoly power as distinguished from growth or development as a consequence of a superior product, business acumen, or historic accident. *Aspen Skiing Co. v. Aspen Highlands Skiing Co.*, 472 U.S. 585, 596, n.19 (1984); *Olympia Equip. Leasing v. Western Union Telegraph*, 797 F.2d 370, 373 (7th Cir. 1986). In this context willful means conduct designed to maintain or enhance monopoly power improperly. *Olympia*, 797 F.2d at 373. A monopoly like any other competitor, "is permitted and indeed encouraged to compete aggressively on the merits." *Id.* at 375. Improper conduct is conduct characterized as "exclusionary," "anti-competitive" or "predatory." *Aspen Skiing Co. v. Aspen Highlands Skiing Co.*, 472 U.S. 585, 602. In determining whether conduct is exclusionary "it is relevant to consider its impact on consumers and whether it has impaired competition in an unnecessarily restrictive way." *Id.* at 605. If a firm has been "attempting to exclude rivals on some basis other than efficiency," it is fair to characterize its behavior as predatory. *Id.* It is also relevant to consider its impact on antitrust defendants and rivals. *Id.*

"Thus, 'exclusionary' comprehends at the most behavior that not only (1) tends to impair the opportunities of rivals, but also (2) either does not further competition on the merits or does so in an unnecessarily restrictive way." *Id.* at 605, n.32.

Defendants assert that there was no evidence of anticompetitive conduct because all defendants' actions have a legitimate business justification and lack anticompetitive intent. There is abundant evidence in the record from which a reasonable jury could find anticompetitive conduct. In the face of direct evidence that defendants acted with the specific intent to restrict competition, the jury was entitled to disregard defendants' alternative explanations. For example, clinics were acquired to threaten competitors. . . . Security affiliation was used to threaten doctors and to force compliance with referral policies. . . . Defendants warned potential new entrants that cross-coverage would be denied because they were competitors, . . . and hospital privileges were denied to competitors. . . . These actions excluded competitors from the market and resulted in supra-competitive prices for physician services and HMOs.

Plaintiffs' claim for attempted monopolization, however, must fail [because of inconsistency in the questions on the special verdict form].

. . . .

Defendants err in their contentions that plaintiffs did not suffer antitrust injury. Plaintiffs suffered antitrust injury for damages by paying supra-competitive prices and being excluded from the marketplace. Plaintiffs also suffered antitrust injury for injunctive relief because of the threat of continuing to pay supra-competitive prices and being excluded from the marketplace.

. . . .

There is sufficient evidence in the record of violations of section 1. For example, there was evidence that Marshfield allocated markets and territory with Rhinelander Medical Center, . . . [and] Wausau area physicians. . . . There was evidence that Marshfield allocated outpatient and urgent care services with the Ministry Corporation. . . . There was evidence of price-fixing between Marshfield and its affiliated providers. The affiliated providers had only one fee schedule for both Security and non-Security patients, . . . and Marshfield approved or disapproved it. . . . This is not a straight buyer-seller relationship, it is a relationship of competing sellers. Additional evidence suggested that although HMOs generally pay 20-40% less than list price for physician services, . . . Marshfield Clinic approved those prices at 100% of list. . . . This price fixing resulted in supra-competitive prices in the Marshfield area. . . . The overall effects of these practices were supra-competitive prices and elimination or reduction of competition. For example, the agreement between Marshfield and Rhinelander Medical Center to sign up with only one HMO, Security, and to drop . . . [others] reduced competition. . . . The contract with Wausau Medical Center which states that it cannot contract with other HMOs reduced competition. . . .

. . . .

DAMAGES

[The jury determined that $10,500,000 would fairly compensate Blue Cross for its antitrust injury].

Defendants are correct that the evidence does not support plaintiffs' claims for damages. . . .

A remittitur is appropriate in the case at bar even in light of the lower burden on a plaintiff in an antitrust action to prove the *amount* of damages. The damage award is clearly excessive, totally monstrous, contrary to the evidence presented at trial and based on a figure lacking adequate foundation. . . . The damage award to Blue Cross lacks testimony relating to the relevant markets and those markets in which defendants had market power. . . .

. . . .

[The Court ordered a new trial on the damages issue, unless the remittitur were accepted. The district court's order was rendered moot by the disposition of the court of appeals.]

COMMENTARY

1. In terms of standard antitrust analysis of relevant product and geographic market, can an HMO's services properly be defined as a market? What distinguishes an HMO from indemnity insurance or from a Preferred Provider Organization? *See* pages 980-83, *supra,* dealing with health care for a description of the various forms of group delivery of medical care. Do you agree with Judge Easterbrook, who wrote in an earlier opinion,

> The Blues, other insurance companies, hospitals offering PPOs, HMOs, and self-insuring employers all offer methods of financing health care. Employers and individual prospective patients may switch from one financing package to another. . . .

Ball Memorial Hospital v. Mutual Hospital Insurance, Inc., 784 F.2d 1325, 1331 (7th Cir. 1986).

2. If you were representing Blue Shield in this litigation, would you advise identifying HMO services as the relevant product market? Explain.

3. Do you agree or disagree with the application of the essential facility doctrine to the hospital or to the defendant's affiliated physicians? Explain.

Blue Cross and Blue Shield United of Wisconsin v. Marshfield Clinic

65 F.3d 1406 (7th Cir. 1995),
cert. denied, 116 S. Ct. 1288 (1996)

POSNER, Chief Judge.

[The Court of Appeals reversed the findings that HMOs constituted a separate market, that the defendant HMO had monopoly power, that defendant clinic was an essential facility that had engaged in price-fixing with its affiliated physicians; the award of damages and attorneys' fees was set aside *in toto;* the Court of Appeals affirmed the finding of liability for territorial divisions; and remanded for trial the issue of damages on this latter issue.]

Blue Cross & Blue Shield United of Wisconsin ("Blue Cross" for short), and its subsidiary, Compcare Health Services Insurance Corporation, a health maintenance organization (HMO), brought suit last year under sections 1 and 2 of the Sherman Act, . . . against the Marshfield Clinic and its HMO subsidiary, Security Health Plan of Wisconsin, Inc. After a two-week trial, the jury brought in a verdict for both plaintiffs that, after remittitur, trebling, and addition of attorneys' fees, produced a judgment just short of $20 million to which the judge then added a sweeping injunction that we have stayed pending the decision of the defendants' appeal, which we have heard on an expedited schedule. (The plaintiffs filed a cross-appeal, but it was dismissed by agreement of the parties.) . . .

The two plaintiffs have distinct though overlapping claims. Compcare, Blue Cross's HMO, claims that the Marshfield Clinic—a nonprofit corporation owned by the 400 physicians whom it employs—has a monopoly which it acquired and has maintained by improper practices that have excluded Compcare from the HMO "market" in the counties of north central Wisconsin in which the Marshfield Clinic and its HMO subsidiary (Security) operate. This is a section 2 monopolization charge. Blue Cross claims that Marshfield, partly through its own monopoly power and partly by collusion with other providers of medical services, charged supracompetitive prices to patients insured by Blue Cross. This is a section 2 monopolization charge combined with a section 1 price-fixing and division-of-markets charge.

Although Marshfield is a town of only 20,000 people in a largely rural region, the Marshfield Clinic is the fifth largest physician-owned clinic in North America, with annual revenues in excess of $200 million. The Clinic has its main office in Marshfield but it has 21 branch offices scattered throughout the 14 counties of north central Wisconsin. Oddly, we cannot find in the record, nor were counsel able to inform us at argument, what percentage the 400 physicians employed by the Clinic comprise of all the physicians in the 14 counties. We do know that the Clinic employs all the physicians in Marshfield itself and in several other towns—but one of these towns has only one physician—and all the physicians in one entire county—but a county that has only 12 physicians. Security, the Marshfield Clinic's HMO subsidiary, serves its subscribers through the physicians employed by the Clinic plus almost 900 other physicians with whom Security has contracts. These contracts are not exclusive—the physicians are free to work for other HMOs as well as to practice fee-for-service medicine—and in fact work for Security generates only 6 percent of these physicians' total income. (Compcare argues that the 6 percent figure is found only in a study and testimony excluded from evidence, but our reading of the objection to the testimony and the ruling on that objection is that not the figure, but only the witness's effort to characterize it as insignificant, was excluded.) In nine of the 14 counties in the north central region, Security has more than 90 percent of all subscribers to HMOs.

Compcare persuaded the jury that HMOs constitute a separate market, much as banks are a separate market from currency exchanges; and if there is a reasonable basis for this finding in the evidence, we are bound to accept it regardless of what we might think as an original matter. But we have searched the record in vain for evidence that under contemporary principles of antitrust law would justify such a finding. An HMO is not a distinctive organizational form or assemblage of skills, as is plain from the fact that the physicians retained by Security, whether they are employees of the Marshfield Clinic or completely independent, to serve its subscribers serve other patients on a fee-for-service basis. An HMO is basically a method of pricing medical services. Instead of having the patient pay separately for each medical procedure, the patient pays a fixed annual fee for all the services he needs and the HMO undertakes to provide those services with the physicians with whom it has contracts. The different method of pricing used by the HMO has, of course, consequences both for the practice of medicine and for the allocation of the risk of medical expenses. The method of pricing gives the HMO an incentive to minimize the procedures that it performs, since the marginal revenue it derives from each procedure is zero. Hence HMOs are thought to reduce "waste" and to encourage preventive care, although those hostile to the HMO concept believe that the principal effect is merely to reduce the amount of medical care that patients receive. The risk-shifting feature of the concept lies in the fact that if a subscriber incurs above-average medical expenses, the excess cost is borne by the HMO rather than by the subscriber (or by his insurer, or more likely by both because of copayment and deductible provisions in the insurance policy), while if he incurs below-average medical expense the difference enures to the benefit of the HMO rather than to him or his insurer (or, again, both). To control the upside risk that it incurs, the HMO provides medical services through physicians with whom it has contracts specifying their compensation, rather than merely reimbursing some percentage of whatever fee they might happen to charge for their services. This means that the HMO must be able to line up enough physicians with whom to contract to provide its subscribers with a more or less complete menu of medical services. Compcare complains that Security's contracts with physicians require them to refer their patients to the Clinic rather than to "independent" physicians. But that is of the essence of an HMO: the subscriber must take the service offered by the physicians whom the HMO has enlisted.

Compcare's principal argument is that Security has enlisted such a large fraction of the physicians in the 14-county north central region that Compcare cannot find enough "independent" physicians to be able to offer HMO services competitive with Security's—hence Security's huge market shares in 9 of the 14 counties. Supposing this is true—as seems unlikely since Security's almost 900 independent physicians are available to join other HMOs, along with an unknown number of physicians neither employed by the Marshfield Clinic nor retained by Security—it has monopolistic significance only if HMOs constitute a market separate from other contractual forms in which many of the same physicians sell their services. Of this we cannot find any evidence.

In defining a market, one must consider substitution both by buyers and by sellers, . . . and let us start with buyers. The record shows, what is anyway well known, that individuals, and their employers, and medical insurers (the real "buyers" of medical services, according to the plaintiffs) regard HMOs as competitive not only with each other but also with the various types of fee-for-service provider, including "preferred provider" plans (generally referred to as "PPOs," for "preferred provider organization") under which the insurer offers more generous reimbursement if the insured patronizes physicians who have contracts with the insurer to provide service at low cost to its insureds. HMOs, though they have made great strides in recent years because of the widespread concern with skyrocketing medical costs, remain relative upstarts in the market for physician services. Many people don't like them because of the restriction on the patient's choice of doctors or because they fear that HMOs skimp on service, since, as we said, the marginal revenue of a medical procedure to an HMO is zero. From a short-term financial standpoint—which we do not suggest is the only standpoint that an HMO is likely to have—the HMO's incentive is to keep you healthy if it can but if you get very sick, and are unlikely to recover to a healthy state involving few medical expenses, to let you die as quickly and cheaply as possible. HMOs compensate for these perceived drawbacks by charging a lower price than fee-for-service plans.

We do not wish to associate ourselves with the critics of HMOs. All that is important to our consideration of this appeal is that many people believe—whether rightly or wrongly is of no moment—that HMOs are not an unalloyed blessing; and this means that the price that an HMO can charge is constrained not only by competition from other HMOs but also by competition from forms of medical-services contracting that are free from the perceived perverse incentive effects of the HMO form. As far as we know or the record shows, even in areas where there is only one HMO most of the people in its service area do not subscribe to it even if its prices are lower than those of fee-for-service providers.

We do not understand Compcare to be contending that insurance companies cannot find enough physicians in the north central region willing to sign contracts with them to staff preferred-provider plans. This has a dual significance. Such plans are particularly close substitutes for HMOs, since they use the insurer's clout with physicians to drive down price. And if, as the record shows, they are feasible even in areas supposedly dominated by the Marshfield Clinic, and even without including any physicians employed by the Clinic, it is impossible to understand what barrier there could be to the formation of HMOs. All that is needed is an array of physicians who among them provide a broad range of medical services, and the same thing is needed for a preferred-provider plan. Ability to create a preferred-provider plan therefore implies ability to create an HMO, and so implies in turn that if Security raised its prices above competitive levels, and if people had a strong preference for HMOs over preferred-provider plans despite the similarities between the two systems for providing medical care, the operators of those plans would convert them to HMOs. If so, those plans are part of the same market with HMOs. . . .

As we said earlier, the definition of a market depends on substitutability on the supply side as well as on the demand side. Even if two products are completely different from the consumer's standpoint, if they are made by the same producers an increase in the price of one that is not cost-justified will induce producers to shift production from the other product to this one in order to increase their profits by selling at a supracompetitive price. . . . The services offered by HMOs and by various fee-for-service plans are both provided by the same physicians, who can easily shift from one type of service to another if a change in relative prices makes one type more lucrative than others.

We thus do not believe that a reasonable jury, confronting the record compiled in the district court, could find that HMOs constitute a separate market. (We emphasize "record compiled in the district court." Terms such as "HMO" and "PPO" are used to refer to a variety of different types of plan, which may vary in respects crucial to antitrust liability.) Nor, if we examine a more plausible market such as all physician services in north central Wisconsin and thus shift our focus from Security, the HMO, to the Marshfield Clinic itself, is there any basis in the record for treating the Clinic not as the alliance of 400 physicians that is the Marshfield Clinic but instead as the almost 1300 physicians who are either employed by the Clinic or have contracts with Security. The 900 independent contractors derive only a small fraction of their income from those contracts, as we have seen, and the contracts do not forbid them to join other HMOs or otherwise compete with Security or with the Marshfield Clinic.

It is true that because of the sparsity of the physician population in north central Wisconsin the physicians employed by the Clinic have a large share of the market for physician services, since, for primary care anyway (an important qualification—people will go a long way for a liver transplant), that market is a local one. Remember, there is one entire county in which all the physicians are employed by the Clinic. We do not understand Compcare to be arguing that this is the market that the Clinic monopolized; the damages to Compcare from being excluded (if it was excluded—we do not know) from that tiny market would be tiny. Compcare paints with a broader brush, drawing a dizzying series of concentric circles around the Clinic's offices and counting the physicians who can serve people living in the circles. It would have been much simpler and we suppose just as good—having in mind the desirability of avoiding a hunt for the snark of delusive exactness—to have treated the counties as the markets. But whatever the precise method chosen, Compcare is unable to show that in what it chooses to regard as the relevant geographic market or series of linked geographic markets for physician services the Marshfield Clinic employed 50 percent or more of the physicians serving the market. Fifty percent is below any accepted benchmark for inferring monopoly power from market share . . . and the Clinic has given us no reason for lowering the mark. Compcare is able to derive larger shares only by defining submarkets of specific, very narrowly defined medical procedures, called "Diagnostic Related Groups," such as circumcision of a male 17 years old or older, circumcision of a male under 17, hysterectomy, and reconstructive surgery for the uterine system, in a few of which (14 out of 494, according to Compcare's expert witness) the physicians employed by or under contract with the Marshfield Clinic performed most of the procedures in north central Wisconsin. As the examples we have given show, classification in a DRG is unrelated to the conditions of supply. Many, no doubt most, physicians perform or are capable of performing more than one procedure, and are therefore part of the market even if at present not active in it. If the Clinic overprices a particular procedure, other physicians capable of performing that procedure will have an added incentive to do so, knocking down the excessive price.

Compcare also asked the jury to infer monopoly power directly from the Clinic's high prices, and high rate of return, relative to the prices and rates of return of its competitors. But when dealing with a heterogeneous product or service, such as the full range of medical care, a reasonable finder of fact cannot infer monopoly power just from higher prices—the difference may reflect a higher quality more costly to provide—and it is always treacherous to try to infer monopoly power from a high rate of return. . . . As for high prices, one of the complaints against HMOs, remember, is that they skimp on service. One HMO may charge higher prices than other HMOs (and Security does charge higher prices) not because it has a monopoly but because it is offering better service than the other HMOs in its market. Compcare itself stresses the quality of the Marshfield Clinic's doctors, as part of its argument that it cannot succeed unless the Clinic is forced to join it. Generally you must pay more for higher quality.

So Security is not a monopolist of HMO services, because, subject to our earlier qualification, HMOs are not a market. The Marshfield Clinic, its parent, is not a monopolist either. It does not control its independent contractors; and once they are excluded, the Clinic (which is to say the physicians who own and are employed by it—who are the firm, functionally speaking) does not have a monopoly of physician services in the north central region or in any parts of the region other than parts too small to support more than a handful of physicians. If the Marshfield Clinic is a monopolist in any of these areas it is what is called a "natural monopolist," which is to say a firm that has no competitors simply because the market is too small to support more than a single firm. If an entire county has only 12 physicians, one can hardly expect or want them to set up in competition with each other. We live in the age of technology and specialization in medical services. Physicians practice in groups, in alliances, in networks, utilizing expensive equipment and support. Twelve physicians competing in a county would be competing to provide horse-and-buggy medicine. Only as part of a large and sophisticated medical enterprise such as the Marshfield Clinic can they practice modern medicine in rural Wisconsin.

We are mindful that a concept of essential or bottleneck facilities has been used from time to time to require a natural monopolist to cooperate with would-be competitors. . . . The principal case remains the old St. Louis terminal case. *United States v. Terminal Railroad Ass'n*, 224 U.S. 383 (1912). . . . A consortium of 14 of the 24 railroads that shipped freight across the Mississippi River at St. Louis got control of the terminal facilities at each side of the river. The Supreme Court, while assuming that the operation of these facilities as a single entity was the most efficient way to operate them (that is, they comprised a natural monopoly), held that the Sherman Act required the consortium to provide access to the terminal facilities to the 10 other railroads on nondiscriminatory terms. The decision, along with the rest of the decisions in the essential-facilities line, has been criticized as having nothing to do with the purposes of antitrust law. *E.g.*, . . . Phillip Areeda, *Essential Facilities: An Epithet in Need of Limiting Principles*, 58 ANTITRUST L.J. 841 (1990). . . . Had the terminal facilities been owned by a firm unaffiliated with any railroad, the firm could have charged whatever prices it wanted, including prices that discriminated against some of the users (monopolists frequently price discriminate), because the antitrust laws do not regulate the prices of natural monopolists. A natural monopolist that acquired and maintained its monopoly without excluding competitors by improper means is not guilty of "monopolizing" in violation of the Sherman Act, . . . and can therefore charge any price that it wants, . . . for the antitrust laws are not a price-control statute or a public-utility or common-carrier rate-regulation statute.

. . . .

. . . [Plaintiffs'] argument is not that the Marshfield Clinic "owns" some tiny natural monopolies scattered throughout its market area, to which it must admit Compcare, but that the Clinic itself is an essential facility that any HMO may demand access to on equal terms, like the excluded railroads in the terminal case. To be an essential facility, however, a facility must be essential. The terminal association controlled 100 percent of a market, assumed to be properly defined, consisting of terminal services at St. Louis. The Clinic does not control 100 percent—or even 50 percent—of any properly defined market. It did have a monopoly market share of the HMO "market," but we have held that that is not a proper market; and likewise the DRGs. Nor can the Clinic's market share be levered up to 100 percent by the argument that the Clinic's reputation is so superb that no one will sign up with an HMO or preferred-provider plan that does not have the Clinic on its roster. . . .

Since monopoly power was not proved, we need not evaluate the practices by which the Clinic acquired or maintained it. But we will not conceal our skepticism that they are exclusionary in an invidious sense. Compcare argues that the Clinic refused to allow its employees to "cross-cover" with "independent" physicians, in the sense of physicians not employed by or affiliated by contract with the Clinic (that is, agree to care for another physician's patients when that physician is on vacation or otherwise unavailable in exchange for a reciprocal agreement by the other physician), discouraged hospitals that its staff controlled from joining HMOs that compete with Security, and restricted staff privileges at those hospitals of "independent" physicians at those hospitals. All these practices are ambiguous from the standpoint of competition and efficiency. Hospitals are not public utilities, required to grant staff privileges to anyone with a medical license. The Marshfield Clinic's reputation for high quality implies selectivity in the granting of staff privileges at hospitals affiliated with the Clinic. Physicians employed by the Clinic, which has its own HMO, are hardly to be expected to steer their patients to another HMO, as they would be doing if they used their control of hospital staffs to induce the hospital to join another HMO. And given the extensive network constituted by the physicians either employed by or contracting with the Clinic, they would have little occasion to "cross-cover" with other physicians and would be reluctant to do so if, as is completely consistent with Compcare's version of the "essential facilities" doctrine, the Clinic maintains a reputation for high quality by being selective about the physicians to whom it entrusts its customers. But the important point is that, even if these practices are as we doubt tortious interferences with Compcare's business, they do not constitute monopolizing in violation of section 2 of the Sherman Act in the absence of acceptable proof, here lacking, of monopoly power.

We turn to Blue Cross's case. Blue Cross claims that it was overcharged by the Clinic. Many of the individuals whom Blue Cross insures in north central Wisconsin are customers of the Marshfield Clinic, paying for the services they receive from the Clinic on a fee-for-service basis. (The Clinic's doctors devote only a small part of their time to Security's HMO clientele.) Blue Cross pays the Clinic directly the portion of the fee that Blue Cross has agreed with its insureds to cover. The Clinic seeks to head off Blue Cross's claim at the pass, arguing that since the Clinic's fee-for-service contracts are with the patients themselves—it has no contract with Blue Cross—only the patients have "standing" (a term here not used in the jurisdictional sense . . .) to complain about the alleged overcharging.

If the patients paid the entire fees to the Clinic and then were reimbursed in whole or part by Blue Cross, the Clinic would be right: only the patients could sue. The Supreme Court has been emphatic that only the direct purchaser from an allegedly overcharging defendant has standing to maintain an antitrust suit. . . . But here the money went directly from Blue Cross to the Clinic, and although the two entities were not linked by any overarching contract, each payment and acceptance was a separate completed contract. We do not think more is required to establish Blue Cross's right to sue to collect these overcharges. . . .

. . . .

Two forms of collusion are charged. . . . The first is collusion between the Clinic and its affiliated (as distinct from employed) physicians. Here the tension between the two plaintiffs' cases again comes to the surface, since it will be recalled that Compcare in its case treats the affiliated physicians as a part of the Clinic, and a firm cannot collude with itself. Forget all that; the only evidence of collusion is that the Clinic, when buying services from the affiliated physicians either directly or through Security, would not pay them more than what these physicians charge their other patients. This is said to put a floor underneath these physicians' prices, since if they cut prices to their other patients their reimbursement from the Clinic will decline automatically. This is an ingenious but perverse argument. "Most favored nations" clauses are standard devices by which buyers try to bargain for low prices, by getting the seller to agree to treat them as favorably as any of their other customers. The Clinic did this to minimize the cost of these physicians to it, and that is the sort of conduct that the antitrust laws seek to encourage. It is not price-fixing. . . .

The other form of collusion alleged is more troublesome. The Clinic is said to have agreed with some of its competitors, in particular the North Central Health Protection Plan, an HMO that had 37,000 subscribers, to divide markets, a practice that violates section 1 of the Sherman Act. . . . The analogy between price-fixing and division of markets is compelling. It would be a strange interpretation of antitrust law that forbade competitors to agree on what price to charge, thus eliminating price competition among them, but allowed them to divide markets, thus eliminating all competition among them.

The charge of a division of markets in this case is backed up by some pretty strong documents. In one of them an executive of the Marshfield Clinic, after noting that "at the time in which management of Marshfield Clinic and North Central Health Protection Plan established the Free Flow arrangements, the parties involved purposely chose not to place in writing clear descriptions of their respective Plan service areas so as to minimize any risk in terms of violation of antitrust laws," remarks that some years ago physicians affiliated with the NCHPP "wished to establish a practice in Marshfield and we took the position that the Free Flow agreement did not support that activity"—and they backed off. The implications of this only slightly Aesopian wording are backed up by statistics showing that Security had fewer than 30 percent of the HMO subscribers in the two counties in which NCHPP was active, while in the counties surrounding those two counties on three sides it had more than 90 percent of the HMO subscribers.

We think the evidence of a division of markets, though a little scanty, was sufficient to sustain the jury's verdict on this (and only this) aspect of the case—provided this is not one of those cases in which a division of markets or other cartel-like activity is actually essential to the provision of a lawful service. . . . The "Free Flow" agreement to which the document from which we quoted refers was an agreement whereby Security's physicians and NCHPP's physicians could refer patients to each other without getting the permission of their superiors. The plan of the physician who rendered the service would bill the other plan for its cost. This was no doubt a valuable service, expanding the range of physicians to whom people enrolled in these two HMOs could turn. But the Clinic has failed to explain why, to provide this service, it was necessary for the two plans to agree not to open offices in each other's territories. . . .

We conclude that the jury verdict on liability must stand insofar as the charge of a division of markets is concerned. . . . The rest of the injunction falls with the charges that we have held to be without legal or factual basis. No part of the award of damages or of costs and attorneys' fees can stand, because these items were not segregated by offense. There must be a new trial limited to damages for dividing markets. The burden will be on Blue Cross to show how much less it would have paid the Clinic had the Clinic refrained from that illegal practice.

The judgment is affirmed in part, reversed in part, and remanded for further proceedings consistent with this opinion. . . .

COMMENTARY

Explain the difference in the criteria used by the district court and the court of appeals in characterizing HMO services as a relevant market. Which court's view of the application of the essential facilities doctrine is more persuasive? Explain. Contrast the characterization of competition among hospitals provided by the court in the *Mercy* case that follows with that of the each of the courts in the *Marshfield Clinic* litigation.

G. Hospital Mergers and Joint Ventures

For the treatment of mergers generally, see Chapter 12, *supra;* hospital mergers are subject to antitrust scrutiny under the Joint FTC/Department of Justice Health Care Policy Statement discussed below.

United States v. Rockford Memorial Corp.

898 F.2d 1278 (7th Cir.), *cert. denied*, 498 U.S. 920 (1990)

POSNER, Circuit Judge.

The United States brought suit under section 7 of the Clayton Act and section 1 of the Sherman Act to enjoin a merger of the two largest hospitals—both nonprofits—in Rockford, Illinois, a city of 140,000 people. The district judge held that the merger violated section 7, and issued the injunction; he did not reach the section 1 charge. 717 F. Supp. 1251.

The defendants appeal, arguing first that section 7 does not apply to a merger between nonprofit enterprises. Surprisingly, this is an issue of first impression at the appellate level, with the exception of an unpublished opinion by the Fourth Circuit. . . . Section 7 provides that "[1] no person . . . shall acquire . . . the whole or any part of the *stock or other share capital* and [2] no person *subject to the jurisdiction of the Federal Trade Commission* shall acquire the whole or any part of the assets of another person," where the effect may be substantially to lessen competition, or to tend to create a monopoly. (Emphasis added.) Illinois law forbids a nonprofit corporation to have, and these hospitals do not have, stock or share capital. . . . So the clause we have labeled [1] would seem not to apply. And, the defendants argue, the FTC has no jurisdiction over a nonprofit corporation—so that the merger is not covered by the clause referring to asset acquisitions, clause [2], either—because section 4 of the Federal Trade Commission Act confines the Commission's jurisdiction under the Act to a "company . . . or association, incorporated or unincorporated, which is organized to carry on business for its own profit or that of its members."

The first argument, knocking out clause [1], is strong. The second argument, however, in assuming that the reference in section 7 to "person[s] subject to the jurisdiction of the Federal Trade Commission" is to the Federal Trade Commission Act, overlooks the possibility that the reference is actually to the provision in the Clayton Act itself concerning the jurisdiction of the FTC—namely section 11. Section 11 vests authority to enforce the prohibitions of the Clayton Act in five agencies. These are the Interstate Commerce Commission, with respect to the common carriers regulated by that Commission; the Federal Communications Commission, with respect to the common carriers regulated by it; ditto for the Civil Aeronautics Board (now defunct); the Federal Reserve Board, for banks; and, for everyone else, the FTC: "Authority to enforce compliance with sections 2, 3, 7, and 8 of this Act by the persons respectively subject thereto is hereby vested in . . . the Federal Trade Commission where applicable to all other character of commerce." Section 11 goes on to prescribe the procedure to be followed by these commissions and boards that have been given jurisdiction to enforce the Act. The procedure is self-contained and does not depend on particular provisions in the agencies' organic statutes, so that when in 1950 Congress amended section 7 to broaden its reach, it amended section 11 as well. We believe that the force of the assets-acquisition provision in section 7 is, therefore, merely to exempt mergers in the regulated industries enumerated in section 11. Those industries do not include the hospital industry. The Clayton Act evinces a purpose of limiting the Federal Trade Commission's jurisdiction vis-a-vis that of other federal agencies charged with enforcing the Act in the industries that they regulate, but it evinces no purpose of exempting nonprofit firms in industries within the domain that the Act bestows on the Commission ("all other character of commerce").

. . . .

The government has a fallback position, however: the merger violates section 1 of the Sherman Act, as charged alternatively in the complaint.

. . . .

A merger with . . . [substantial anticompetitive] effects would also violate section 1. . . . [H]ere we have a far larger merger and, as we shall see, such unusual conditions as may be present in the hospital industry [so as to] reinforce rather than undermine the inference naturally to be drawn from the defendants' combined market share.

But all this is provided the district court's market definition is accepted. . . .

The district judge estimated the combined market share of the parties to the merger (hospitals of roughly equal size—the two largest in Rockford) at between 64 and 72 percent, depending on whether beds, admissions, or patient days are used as the measure of output. And he estimated the combined market share of the three largest hospitals in Rockford after the merger at 90 percent. Three firms having 90 percent of the market can raise prices with relatively little fear that the fringe of competitors will be able to defeat the attempt by expanding their own output to serve customers of the three large firms. An example will show why. To take away 10 percent of the customers of the three large firms in our hypothetical case, thus reducing those firms' aggregate market share from 90 percent to 81 percent, the fringe firms would have to increase their own output by 90 percent (from 10 to 19 percent of the market). This would take a while, surely, and would force up their costs, perhaps steeply—the fact they are so small suggests that they would incur sharply rising costs in trying almost to double their output, and that it is this prospect which keeps them small. So the three large firms could collude to raise price (within limits of course) above the competitive level without incurring the additional transaction costs and risk of exposure that would result from their trying to coordinate their actions with that of their small competitors.

This analysis, however, collapses if customers can turn to suppliers who (or products that) have been excluded from the market. The market defined by the district judge consists of the provision of inpatient services by acute-care hospitals in Rockford and its hinterland. The defendants point out correctly that a growing number of services provided by acute-care hospitals are also available from nonhospital providers. But the force of the point eludes us. If a firm has a monopoly of product X, the fact that it produces another product, Y, for which the firm faces competition is irrelevant to its monopoly unless the prices of X and Y are linked. For many services provided by acute-care hospitals, there is no competition from other sorts of provider. If you need a kidney transplant, or a mastectomy, or if you have a stroke or a heart attack or a gunshot wound, you will go (or be taken) to an acute-care hospital for inpatient treatment. The fact that for other services you have a choice between inpatient care at such a hospital and outpatient care elsewhere places no check on the prices of the services we have listed, for their prices are not linked to the prices of services that are not substitutes or complements. If you need your hip replaced, you can't decide to have chemotherapy instead because it's available on an outpatient basis at a lower price. Nor are the prices of hip replacement and chemotherapy linked. The defendants' counsel correctly noted that diet soft drinks sold to diabetics are not a relevant product market, but that is because the manufacturers cannot separate their diabetic customers from their other customers and charge the former a higher price. Hospitals can and do distinguish between the patient who wants a coronary bypass and the patient who wants a wart removed from his foot; these services are not in the same product market merely because they have a common provider. The defendants do not argue for the broader market on the basis of substitutability in supply—that is, the ability of a provider of outpatient services to switch to inpatient services should the price of the latter rise as a result of collusive pricing, making such services more profitable.

The more difficult issue is the geographical market. The defendants offered evidence, which the judge accepted, that their service area is a ten-county area of northern Illinois and southern Wisconsin centered on Rockford. Medicare records the address of all hospital patients, so it was possible to determine the zip codes from which the defendants draw their patients. The district judge noticed that 87 percent of the defendants' patients come from an area surrounding Rockford and consisting of the rest of Winnebago County (the county in which Rockford is located) and pieces of several other counties; the remaining patients are widely scattered. The defendants accept the area picked out by the district judge as a reasonable approximation of their service area (though not of the relevant market). There are four other acute-care hospitals in that area. Their output (as measured, we said, by beds, admissions, or patient days, all of which are highly correlated) plus that of the defendants is the market that the judge used to estimate the defendants' market share.

The defendants point out correctly that the hospitals in the defendants' service area may not exhaust the alternatives open to the residents of that area. Maybe a lot of people who live in Rockford, or if not in Rockford then at the edge of the Rockford hospitals' service area at the farthest possible distance from Rockford that is still within that area, use hospitals outside the area. Maybe—but the record shows that the six hospitals in the defendants' service area, plus a hospital in Beloit just north of the service area, account for 83 percent of the hospitalizations of residents of the service area, and that 90 percent of Rockford residents who are hospitalized are hospitalized in Rockford itself. For highly exotic or highly elective hospital treatment, patients will sometimes travel long distances, of course. But for the most part hospital services are local. People want to be hospitalized near their families and homes, in hospitals in which their own—local—doctors have hospital privileges. There are good hospitals in Rockford, and they succeed in attracting most of the hospital patients not only from Rockford itself but from the surrounding area delineated by the district judge. The exclusion of the Beloit hospital from the market was not adequately explained, but apparently does not affect the figures materially.

It is always possible to take pot shots at a market definition (we have just taken one), and the defendants do so with vigor and panache. Their own proposal, however, is ridiculous—a ten-county area in which it is assumed (without any evidence and contrary to common sense) that Rockford residents, or third-party payors, will be searching out small, obscure hospitals in remote rural areas if the prices charged by the hospitals in Rockford rise above competitive levels. Forced to choose between two imperfect market definitions, the defendants' and the district judge's (the latter a considerable expansion of the government's tiny proposed market), . . . we choose the less imperfect, the district judge's.

The defendants' immense shares in a reasonably defined market create a presumption of illegality. Of course many factors other than the number and size distribution of firms affect the propensity to collude. . . . Regulatory limitations on entry into the hospital industry increase the propensity to collude by preventing (or at least delaying and increasing the cost of) entry by new competitors to take advantage of an increase in prices. And neither generally nor in this instance does the existence of regulation work an implied repeal of the antitrust laws. . . . The excess capacity that is part of the motivation for the regulatory limitations is itself an incentive to collude, although excess capacity in the competitive fringe reduces the feasibility of collusion—but concerning *that* excess capacity there is no evidence in the record. The urgencies of medical care and the prevalence of third-party (insurance or governmental) payment no doubt dilute price sensitivity, but that this weakens—rather than strengthens—the importance of encouraging competition is far from obvious.

. . . .

. . . Most people do not like to compete, and will seek ways of avoiding competition by agreement tacit or explicit, depending of course on the costs of agreeing. The ideology of nonprofit enterprise is cooperative rather than competitive. If the managers of nonprofit enterprises are less likely to strain after that last penny of profit, they may be less prone to engage in profit-maximizing collusion but by the same token less prone to engage in profit-maximizing competition. . . .

The question cannot be resolved a priori, and once the government showed that the merger would create a firm having a market share approaching, perhaps exceeding, a common threshold of monopoly power—two-thirds (*United States v. Aluminum Co. of America*, 148 F.2d 416, 424 (2d Cir. 1945) (L. Hand, J.))—it behooved the defendants to present evidence that the normal inference to be drawn from such a market share would mislead.

It is regrettable that antitrust cases are decided on the basis of theoretical guesses as to what particular market-structure characteristics portend for competition, but to place on the government an insuperable burden of proof is not the answer. We would like to see more effort put into studying the actual effect of concentration on price in the hospital industry as in other industries. If the government is right in these cases, then, other things being equal, hospital prices should be higher in markets with fewer hospitals. This is a studiable hypothesis, by modern methods of multivariate statistical analysis, and some studies have been conducted correlating prices and concentration in the hospital industry. Kopit & McCann, *Toward a Definitive Antitrust Standard for Nonprofit Hospital Mergers*, 13 Journal of Health Politics, Policy & Law 635, 645-46 and n.30 (1988) (discussing studies). . . . Unfortunately, this literature is at an early and inconclusive stage, and the government is not required to await the maturation of the relevant scholarship in order to establish a prima facie case. . . . The principles of civil procedure do not require that the plaintiff make an airtight case, only that his case satisfy some minimum threshold of persuasiveness and be better than the defendant's case. The government showed large market shares in a plausibly defined market in an industry more prone than many to collusion. The defendants responded with conjectures about the motives of nonprofits, and other will o' the wisps, that the district judge was free to reject, and did. The judge's findings establish a violation of section 1 under the standards of *Columbia Steel*, and the judgment must therefore be affirmed without our needing to decide whether the district judge was correct in holding that section 7 does reach mergers between nonprofit corporations. . . .

AFFIRMED.

COMMENTARY

1. Although the district court had held that the merger violated § 7 of the Clayton Act, the court of appeals affirmed that decision under § 1 of the Sherman Act. Judge Posner held that the government had failed properly to support the application of § 7 of the Clayton Act to a merger of non-profit corporations. Accordingly, he rested the affirmance on the alternate Sherman Act count in the complaint.

2. Read the Joint FTC/Department of Justice Health Care Policy Statements in Appendix C.

Does § 1 of these Statements look first to increased concentration as measured by the HHI Index? Do the Statements assume a potential for anticompetitive conduct from a merger of hospitals, for example, that exceeds the threshold concentration levels given in the Statements? Where a proposed merger does exceed that threshold, do the Statements indicate that the merger proponents then have to address three issues: 1) Will entry into the market be made more difficult by the merger? 2) Will the merger produce efficiencies that would not otherwise be obtained? 3) Would either party be likely to fail, but for the merger?

3. Does the caselaw in Chapter 12 (Mergers) above, suggest that a major premise of enforcement activity is that a resulting dominant firm with a large market share may raise prices and restrict output? Is the reasoning of the enforcement agencies that a large market share increases the ability to raise prices because the few smaller firms in the market lack adequate capacity to accommodate customers who would like to switch from the dominant firm?

Where the merger would result in very few large firms of relatively equal size, do the Statements reflect a concern with the enhanced possibility of collusion? Is the reasoning here that although no one firm commands a sufficient market share to permit the announcement of a prevailing price that would generate supranormal profits, a small group of comparable firms may end up collusively adopting such a price? Would the conditions of entry be a relevant consideration? Does the requirement of a Certificate of Need as a condition of building a new hospital affect entry?

One commentator expressed the concern that the rapid changes in the health care organizations and in the relationships among them may overwhelm the ability of enforcement agencies properly to identify and to assess anticompetitive practices.

> Conceptual and empirical gaps hinder our ability to prevent the health care system from becoming overly concentrated. . . . [O]wnership may no longer be the critical issue in antitrust enforcement. A broad range of relationships being formed between entities such as hospitals, physician groups, laboratories, and ambulatory surgery centers do not involve cross-ownership. . . . A taxonomy of linkages must be developed that depends on the market environment and on the specific relationships being established.

Jack Zwanziger, *The Need for an Antitrust Policy for a Health Care Industry in Transition*, 20 J. HEALTH POLICY, POLITICS & LAW 171, 172 (1995).

A representative of the Department of Justice explains the methodology of the Antitrust Division in assessing hospital mergers as follows:

> The set of market participants will probably depend on the market in question. For example, if outpatient care is one product market, the providers will probably include hospitals, physician clinics, surgicenters, and perhaps even individual doctors' offices. If inpatient acute care ser-

> vices constitute a product market, the providers may be limited to acute-care hospitals.
>
> In some cases, an acute-care hospital inside the geographic market may not be a market participant. For example, because HMOs cannot send their patients to Veterans Administration hospitals, those hospitals generally should not be considered market participants. Similarly, if a hospital is owned by a staff model HMO such as Kaiser and is only used by that HMO's patients, that vertically integrated hospital should only be viewed as a market participant for the staff model HMO.

Gregory Vistnes, *Hospital Mergers and Antitrust Enforcement*, 20 J. HEALTH POLITICS, POLICY & LAW 175, 185 (1995).

4. The FTC responded to the rapid changes in the structure of the health care delivery markets. On August 28, 1996, the Department of Justice and the Federal Trade Commission issued a revision of their earlier Statements relating to the health care industry. Do these 1996 Statements, which are digested below, address the issue of rapid change in the organization and structure of the health care industry?

In the 1996 Statements of Enforcement Policy, the reason for this revision of the 1993 and 1994 Statements was given as follows:

> Since the issuance of the 1994 statements, health care markets have continued to evolve in response to consumer demand and competition in the marketplace. New arrangements and variations on existing arrangements involving joint activity by health care providers continue to emerge to meet consumers', purchasers', and payers' desire for more efficient delivery of high quality medical care services.

4 ANTITRUST & TRADE REG. REP. ¶ 20,799 (1996). Accordingly, the revised Enforcement Policy Statements addressed nine topics as follows:

Statement 1—Mergers Among Hospitals,
Statement 2—Hospital Joint Ventures Involving High-Technology or Other Expensive Medical Equipment,
Statement 3—Hospital Joint Ventures Involving Specialized Clinical or Other Expensive Health Care Services,
Statement 4—Providers' Collective Provision of Non-Fee-Related Information to Purchasers of Health Care Services,
Statement 5—Providers' Collective Provision of Fee-Related Information to Purchasers of Health Care Services,
Statement 6—Provider Participation in Exchanges of Price and Cost Information,
Statement 7—Joint Purchasing Arrangements Among Providers,
Statement 8—Physician Network Joint Ventures, and
Statement 9—Multiprovider Networks

See 4 ANTITRUST & TRADE REG. REP. (CCH) ¶ 13,153 (1996). The Statements adopt the format of setting out the agencies' antitrust concern, describing the practices and conditions of a safety zone—the circumstances under which the agencies will not challenge the practice—and finally, describing the analysis of situations that fall outside of the safety zone.

With regard to mergers, Statement one notes that the safety zone was developed ". . . in the light of the Agencies' extensive experience in analyzing hospital mergers." The stated example of a merger that is within the safety zone is the merger of two general acute-care hospitals where one hospital has an average of fewer than 100 licensed beds over the three most recent years and that hospital has had an average daily inpatient census of fewer than 40 patients over the last three years. It is a further condition that this hospital is more than five years old. Such a hospital is deemed likely to realize cost-saving efficiencies by merging with a larger hospital. There is no mention of the characteristics of the other hospital, presumably the acquiring firm.

For mergers that fall outside this safety zone, the Statement relies on the analysis of the general Merger Guidelines. Moreover, the Statement points out that since 1987, the Agencies have challenged only ". . . a handful . . . [of hospital mergers] and in several cases sought relief only as to part of the transaction." The Statement also notes that the review of most hospital mergers is completed within one month. Notice is given that hospital mergers may be presented for expedited review either through the Department's business review procedure set out in 28 C.F.R. § 50.6 (1992) or the Commission's advisory opinion procedure described in 16 C.F.R. §§ 1.1-1.4 (1993). The Statement commits the agencies to a response within 90 days from the completion of a submission.

As to hospital joint ventures to purchase and share costs of owning, operating, and marketing expensive health care equipment, Statement two announces the policy of challenging only those joint arrangements that may result in increased prices to consumers. The Statement notes, moreover, that the Agencies have never challenged a joint venture of hospitals to acquire and operate expensive equipment. The safety zone for joint ventures involving expensive hospital equipment is the case of two hospitals, neither of which was capable of recovering the cost of the equipment alone. The example of a joint venture outside the safety zone is the case involving three hospitals, one of which would have been capable of recovering the cost over the useful life of the equipment on its own. The Statement notes that joint arrangements outside the safety zone will be reviewed under traditional rule of reason analysis, with the ultimate test requiring a determination of whether the procompetitive efficiencies outweigh the anitcompetitive effects. This analysis is illuminated by several examples, apparently drawn from actual cases. The agencies make available summary review procedures, subject to the 90 day response.

The third Statement considers joint ventures to provide specialized clinical or related expensive care. Here the Statement notes that the Agencies have never challenged such arrangements. The absence of a stated safety zone for such arrangements is attributed to insufficient experience of the Agencies with these arrangements.

Instead, the Statement announces rule of reason analysis and gives the following example. In a city with a population of 75,000 situated in a rural area, there are two existing acute-care general hospitals, neither of which has an open-heart surgery unit, nor was either hospital contemplating the establishment of this unit. They propose a joint venture to share the costs of recruiting a cardiac heart surgery team and equipment; there is data to support the conclusion that such a unit is economically viable. The example notes the saving to consumers who need no longer incur the expenses of traveling to distant cities for this procedure and, the fact that the arrangement does not eliminate any existing competition. The expedited review procedures are available for these arrangements, too.

The fourth and fifth Statements are devoted to the sticky problem of providers' collective action relating to the transmission of information to purchasers of health care plans. The Statement divides such information between fee-related [consumer prices] and non-fee-related data. Thus, the fourth section is concerned with non-fee-related information and the fifth section deals with fee-related information. The fourth section deals with such information as the data about outcomes of various surgical and other treatment procedures, and practice parameters, *e.g.*, the manner in which diabetic patients are supervised and medicated. The fourth section safety zone allows providers to engage collectively in discussions with purchasers about the scientific merit of treatment data. Providers fall outside the safety zone by attempts to coerce the purchaser into accepting a mode of treatment or a stated treatment protocol. The coercion could consist of the providers threatening collectively to boycott any purchaser unwilling to accept the providers' treatment procedures. Similarly, a provider boycott of plans objecting to the providers' administrative or clinical practices would raise an antitrust issue. The example given is that of a collective refusal to provide x-rays to a purchaser who seeks them in a particular treatment regimen. Here, too, the summary review procedure is available. No further elucidation is given of the analysis of practices that fall outside the safety zone.

The fifth Statement considers collective use of data about past fees, current fees, methods of charges and reimbursements, discounts, capitation arrangements, risk-withhold fees, and all-inclusive fees. The Statement notes the benefits of providing purchasers with relevant information, as well as the potential for illegal price-fixing. The description of the safety zone under this heading is quite detailed consisting of the following conditions: 1) the collection of information provided to purchasers must be managed by an outsider (the agencies consider an outsider for these purposes to be a purchaser, a governmental agency, a health care consultant, an academic institution, or a trade association); 2) although current fee-related information may be provided to purchasers, any information that is either shared among the providers or is available to the other providers must be more than three months old; 3) any information that is shared among the providers and disseminated to purchasers must be the result of the input of at least five providers. Moreover, no individual provider's input may represent more than 25% on a weighted basis and any stated fee, and any information disseminated, must be so aggregated as to foreclose the possibility that the recipient could identify the individual provider.

Where fee-related information is disseminated under conditions determined to be outside the safety zone, the Statement again refers to an implied or threatened boycott of purchasers in order to require acceptance of collectively-determined fees. Preservation of the independence of purchasers' decisions seems to be the focus of the analysis of arrangements outside the safety zone.

The sixth Statement deals with the related topic of exchange of cost information about inputs, primarily salaries, wages, and fringe benefits of health care professionals. While recognizing the benefits for competitive conditions of survey information about salaries and related costs, the Statement expresses the need for safeguards against the use of this data to foster collusion. The safety zone for this data is the same as the description of the safety zone for fee-related information in section five of the Statement. The analysis of exchanges of input information that fall outside the safety zone emphasizes the potential for abuse involved in the exchange of information about future salaries and related costs.

The seventh Statement addresses collective information about other costs—joint purchasing agreements of supplies and non-professional services among competing providers. The costs identified under this section are those of laundry and food services, computer and data-processing services, and prescription drugs and related pharmaceutical products. The expressed concern is that buying power may be abused and become a vehicle for price-fixing. In order to minimize the risks of facilitating price-fixing, the safety zone is circumscribed by two conditions: 1) the aggregate volume of purchases subject to the joint agreement must constitute less than 35 percent of the total sales of the purchased product or services in its relevant market, and 2) the cost of the products or services purchased jointly accounts for less than 20 percent of the total revenues from all products or services sold by each competing participant in the joint purchasing arrangement. The expressed concern of this condition is the likelihood of establishing standardized costs as a predicate for fixing final prices.

For joint purchasing arrangements that fall outside of the safety zone, the Statement suggests three factors which would diminish agency concern. First, the joint purchasing agreement should not require all of a given product or service to be acquired jointly. Second, where possible, negotiations for the joint purchases should be conducted by one who is not also an employee of one of the joint purchasing participants. Finally, it is suggested that all communications between an individual seller and a member of the joint purchasing group be kept confidential, rather than being discussed with or disseminated to all of the purchasing group. The objective of this final restriction is to inhibit the emergence of a discussion group about costs that could also become a forum for discussion of and an agreement on selling prices.

The eighth Statement addresses collective arrangements among physicians to offer their services to group purchasers. This section is limited to organizations of physicians. Arrangements for health care delivery that include physicians and other professionals are designated by the Statement in the following section as multiprovider networks (*e.g.*, psychiatrists and therapists or orthopaedic surgeons and podiatrists). The phrase, "physician network joint ventures," encompasses IPAs (independent practice associations), PPOs (preferred practice providers), and the other forms of group medical practice set out on pages 980-83, *supra*. A physician network joint venture is a physician-controlled venture in which the network's physician participants collectively agree on prices or price-related terms and jointly market their services. The Statement also recognizes the rapid rate of change in these arrangements as follows:

> The Agencies emphasize that merely because a physician network joint venture does not come within a safety zone in no way indicates that it is unlawful under the antitrust laws. On the contrary, such arrangements may be procompetitive and lawful, and many such arrangments have received favorable business review letters or advisory opinions from the Agencies

4 ANTITRUST & TRADE REG. REP. (CCH) ¶ 20, 814 (1996).

The definition of the physicians network safety zone distinguishes between "exclusive" and "non-exclusive" networks. The former is a network in which the individual physician-member is restricted by the terms of the network from affiliating with, or otherwise offering medical services outside of that group; the latter permits the individual member to make such arrangements outside that network. An exclusive network will not be challenged if two conditions are met. First, the members must share substantial financial risk in the profitability of the network. Second, the members of that network comprise 20 percent or less of the total number of physicians in each specialty with active hospital staff privileges in that relevant geographic market. The 20 percent condition looks to market power in a specialty. These percentage limitations look to the existence of competition for these services in a relevant market. The goal of the Statement is to allow joint action among competitors, including joint pricing, if this activity occurs in a competitive market and there are reasonable prospects for achieving efficiencies. The substantial financial risk condition is a surrogate for efficiency. The Statement describes the significance of financial risk as follows: ". . . normally it is a clear and reliable indicator that a physician network involves sufficient integration by its physician participants to achieve significant efficiencies." *Id.* at ¶ 20,816. For non-exclusive networks, there will be no agency challenge if there is substantial financial risk and the individual physician members constitute 30 percent or less of the physicians in that specialty with active hospital privileges. For networks outside the safety zone, the Statement provides extended discussion of the rule of reason analysis it will apply to six specific examples. The approach is a wide-ranging, "all facts and circumstances" inquiry to determine whether the potential for realizing efficiences exceeds the likelihood of producing antitcompetive results. Particular attention is given to the installation by a network of cost-saving procedures, including case management protocols, economies of scale, and reduced administrative and transactions costs. *Id.* at ¶ 20,818-19.

The ninth and final Statement deals with multiprovider networks, which are defined above. Like the physician networks, multiprovider networks market their services to health plans and their subscribers and to other purchasers. Multiprovider networks are treated differently from physician networks in that the Statement provides no safety zone for multiprovider networks. The absence of a safety zone is explained as follows:

> Because multiprovider networks involve a large variety of structures and relationships among many different types of health care providers, and new arrangements are continually developing, the Agencies are unable to establish a meaningful safety zone for these entities.

Id. at ¶ 20,826. Instead of a safety zone, the Statement applies rule of reason analysis to the vertical and horizontal aspects of multiprovider arrangements in the relevant markets in which they are involved. Under these headings the potential for anticompetitive results not counterbalanced by efficiencies is examined. Efficiencies are identified for multiprovider networks by the same analysis as is applied to physician networks. Substantial financial risk-sharing as well as clinical integration are considered probative of efficiencies in operation. Cost-containment procedures and competitive conditions in that relevant market are also significant factors in permitting joint action. Given the manifold organizational arrangements of these networks, the agencies plan to apply an "all facts and circumstances" test to them, including interviewing consumers, competitors, public interest persons, and experts. The suggested analysis is applied to several examples.

Does the detailed transactional framework of these 1996 Statements (other than in the ninth Statement) warrant consideration of a like approach generally to §§ 1 & 2 of the Sherman Act in their application to other industries?

United States v. Mercy Health Services

902 F. Supp. 968 (N.D. Iowa 1995)

[This case involves the formation of a partnership between Mercy and Finley hospitals, the only acute-care hospitals in Dubuque. They are located within six blocks of each other and each of them is larger than any other acute-care hospital within a 70 mile radius of Dubuque. The new entity would be entitled Dubuque Regional Health Services, DRHS. The parties stipulated that the formation of this partnership constitutes a merger for antitrust purposes.]

Melloy, Chief Judge,

The United States has brought this action under the antitrust laws. . . . On June 10, 1994, the government filed a complaint seeking injunctive relief against the merger as a violation of § 7 of the Clayton Act and of § 1 of the Sherman Act. . . . After expedited discovery, the matter was tried to the bench. . . .

I. Findings of Fact

A. Hospital Background

Dubuque is situated within Dubuque County, Iowa, which in 1993 had a population of 86,403. Dubuque lies on the Mississippi River, at a point where Iowa adjoins the southwestern portion of Wisconsin and the northwestern portion of Illinois.

Mercy is an acute care hospital which, in 1994, had approximately 320 staffed beds, 9980 acute care patient discharges and an average daily census of 127. Mercy's acute care commercial discharges for 1994 were estimated to be 3622 and the average daily acute care commercial census was 44. Finley is also an acute care hospital and, in 1994, was estimated to have 124 staffed beds, 5247 acute care patient discharges and an average daily census of 63. Finley's acute care commercial discharges for 1994 were estimated to be 2175 and the average daily acute care commercial census was 21.

There are seven rural hospitals in the area: Galena-Stauss Hospital in Galena, Illinois, 15 minutes from Dubuque, has 25 licensed beds and an average daily census of 3. Southwest Health Center in Platteville, Wisconsin, 30 minutes from Dubuque, has 35 licensed beds and an average daily census of 11. Lancaster Memorial Hospital in Lancaster, Wisconsin, 30 minutes from Dubuque, has 35 licensed beds and an average daily census of 10. Delaware County Memorial Hospital in Manchester, Iowa, 40 minutes from Dubuque, has 58 licensed beds and an average daily census of 12. Jackson County Public Hospital in Maquoketa, Iowa, 30 minutes from Dubuque, has 99 licensed beds and an average daily census of 12.4. Guttenberg Memorial Hospital in Guttenberg, Iowa, 40 minutes from Dubuque, has 37 licensed beds and an average daily census of 7. Finally, Central Community Hospital in Elkader, Iowa, 60 minutes from Dubuque, has 29 licensed beds and an average daily census of 3-4.

These hospitals primarily serve patients who are closer to the rural hospital than to any other hospital. The rural hospitals mainly provide primary care services and do not provide the breadth of services Mercy and Finley offer. Guttenberg provides the largest array of services in that it offers 68% of the same Diagnosis Related Groups (DRGs)[1] Mercy and Finley provide. Galena-Stauss has the smallest array of services, providing care for only 11.5% of the same DRGs Mercy and Finley provide.

There are several regional hospitals within 70 to 100 miles of Dubuque which generally offer the same or greater range of services as provided by Mercy and Finley. Allen Memorial Hospital in Waterloo, Iowa has 194 staffed beds and an average daily census of 145. Covenant Medical Center in Waterloo, Iowa has approximately 322 staffed acute care beds with an average daily census of 173. St. Luke's Methodist Hospital in Cedar Rapids, Iowa has 441 staffed beds with an average daily census of 284. Mercy Medical Center in Cedar Rapids, Iowa has 353 staffed beds and an average daily census of 193. St. Mary's Medical Center in Madison, Wisconsin has 345 staffed beds and an average daily census of 265. Freeport Memorial Hospital in Freeport, Illinois has 143 staffed beds and an average daily census of 70. University of Wisconsin Hospital and Clinics in Madison, Wisconsin has 496 staffed beds and an average daily census of 386. Meriter Hospital in Madison, Wisconsin has 429 staffed beds and an average daily census of 258. The University of Iowa

---

[1] A DRG is a numerical code indicating the treatment provided to a patient or his diagnosis and severity of his illness. [DRG means Diagnostic Related Group—Eds.]

Hospitals and Clinics in Iowa City, Iowa (UIHC) has 868 staffed beds and an average daily census of 677.

Mercy and Finley's patient bases are composed of individuals covered by government insurance programs, traditional indemnity insurance and managed care payers. Managed care payers include health maintenance organizations (HMO's), and preferred provider organizations (PPO's). HMO's generally charge a set fee which covers all of an enrollee's health care needs, including hospitalizations. HMO's generally restrict the doctors and hospitals from which an enrollee can receive care to those physicians and hospitals providing a discounted rate to the HMO. HMO's often work with the hospitals when an enrollee is hospitalized to insure that the costs of the hospitalization remain as low as possible. HMO's may have their own clinics to which enrollees are obligated to go for office visits and most outpatient needs. HMO's generally stress preventative care and require preapproval prior to being hospitalized in order to keep the rate of hospitalizations low.

PPO's generally negotiate discounted rates with physicians and hospitals and then require their enrollees to receive their care from the discounted care providers or risk being denied reimbursement. PPO's generally do not have their own clinics and do not stress preventative care. In contrast to the managed care payers, the indemnity health insurers have not traditionally attempted to gain discounted rates from physicians or hospitals. Instead, these traditional insurers cover a percentage of the health care costs with the remainder being paid by the insured. HMO's and PPO's have only recently established themselves in Iowa, but already 25% of Mercy and Finley's patients are covered by managed care payers. Of the remaining 75% of Mercy and Finley's inpatients, 50% are covered by Medicare and Medicaid and the other 25% are covered by traditional indemnity insurance.

[The traditional indemnity insurers are now beginning to demand and receive discounts. In addition, traditional insurers, such as Blue Cross/Blue Shield, have formed their own PPOs or HMOs.]

A hospital will discount its stated charges to managed care payers in order to entice the managed care entity to send more enrollees to their hospital for inpatient care. Mercy currently gives discounts to . . . [many] managed care entities. . . .

Medical Associates is a physician-owned medical practice which operates the Medical Associates HMO in the Dubuque area. The HMO has approximately 30,000 enrollees. The Medical Associates HMO accounts for 11-12% of Mercy's net revenues. Physicians employed by Medical Associates refer patients to Mercy for inpatient and outpatient care constituting approximately 80% of Mercy's yearly revenue. Heritage National Health Plan operates a PPO which covers 5,000 lives in the Dubuque area. Nationally it covers 280,000 persons. It accounts for 2-3% of Mercy's net revenues. SISCO is a third-party payer which administers self-insured employee health plans and also contracts for reduced rates for some of its employer-customers. Blue Cross has a state-run managed care plan in which it offers the hospital a contract on a "take it or leave it" basis. The hospital can either agree to the stated rates or not be on the plan's preferred provider list. It accounts for 8-9% of Mercy's net revenues. Affordable accounts for less than 1% of Mercy's revenues. HMO Wisconsin accounts for less than 0.5% of Mercy's revenues. Medicare and Medicaid account for 46-47% of Mercy's net revenues. Traditional indemnity insurance accounts for 26% of Mercy's net revenues.

Medical Associates has a clinic in Dubuque in which it sees patients for regular office visits. It also operates an outpatient clinic in Dubuque which directly competes with Mercy and Finley for outpatient procedures. In addition to its Dubuque Clinic, Medical Associates has permanent facilities in Bellevue, Iowa; East Dubuque, Illinois; and Galena, Illinois. It operates outreach clinics in Bellevue, Iowa; Dyersville, Iowa; Lancaster, Wisconsin; Maquoketa, Iowa; Platteville, Wisconsin; Boscobel, Wisconsin; Elkader, Iowa; Guttenberg, Iowa; Manchester, Iowa; Oelwein, Iowa; Darlington, Wisconsin; Clinton, Iowa; and Monticello, Iowa. These outreach clinics are primarily conducted in order to obtain secondary referrals for Medical Associates' specialists.

B. Health Care Market Trends

Traditionally, hospitals competed on the basis of amenities and perceptions of quality. Only in the last ten to fifteen years have hospitals begun to compete on the basis of price. To a large degree, this competition has occurred because of the arrival of managed care. These large purchasers shop on the basis of price and are able to induce hospitals to discount stated charges in return for the managed care payer's promise to direct a larger volume of patients to the hospital. Hospitals must employ cost containment measures in order to become more cost efficient so that they can afford to give discounts to the managed care payers. Competition for Medicare, Medicaid and traditional indemnity patients still occurs on the basis of amenities and perceptions of quality.

Managed care entities are capable of inducing their enrollees to receive inpatient care at a specific hospital. The entity does this in one of the following ways: (1) by only paying the hospitalization costs if the enrollee is treated at a specified hospital, or (2) by requiring the enrollee to pay a higher percentage of the enrollee's hospitalization costs (a co-pay) if the enrollee chooses to be hospitalized at a non-preferred hospital. Managed care entities are gaining sophistication in their ability to induce patients to be hospitalized at a preferred hospital. However, the managed care entities do not always show price sensitivity when they establish requirements. For example, Medical Associates may be charged a lower rate by one hospital for a certain DRG, however, the physicians who admit the patients may not be aware of the rate differential and consequently do not encourage patients to go to the cheaper hospital.

. . . .

The advent of managed care has resulted in individuals also considering what their out-of-pocket expenses will be. Under traditional indemnity insurance a certain percentage of a hospitalization is covered without regard to the hospital used. Managed care enrollees are much more aware of their out-of-pocket expenses resulting from a hospitalization because the policies generally state that expenses incurred at certain hospitals will either not be covered or will require a higher co-pay.

. . . .

Price competition is important among the managed care groups. Generally, the managed care payer will negotiate the best rates and the greatest discounts possible with area hospitals and physician groups. Based on the rates obtained, the managed care payer determines the premium it must charge enrollees for services. The managed care group next approaches businesses to try to convince them to offer their managed care plan to their employees. Thirty-five to 40% of the managed care premium is due to inpatient hospital charges, so the rates negotiated with the hospitals significantly impact the premium charged by the managed care payer and affect the cost competitiveness of the managed care entity receiving the discount.

. . . .

Along with the rise of managed care has come the increased use of outpatient services for procedures which traditionally required overnight hospitalization. The length of hospital stays are also becoming significantly shorter because of the increased use of home care and because managed care payers closely monitor the length of time an enrollee is hospitalized. This results in less hospital utilization and a decrease in the average daily census. Because hospitals have high fixed costs, the loss of patient volume requires hospitals to broaden their service area in order to maintain patient census and resulting cash flow.

Prior to the trend in shorter and fewer hospitalizations and to the advent of cost competition, hospitals had their own "catchment area" from which they drew their patients and from which other hospitals generally did not try to encroach upon the residing population. The main competition between regional hospitals was in the "fringe area," the area half-way between two regional hospitals. However, the competitive market has changed and is continuing to change at a rapid pace.

Hospitals, needing to maintain their patient volume, have begun to establish outreach efforts in the fringe areas as well as deep in the heart of what used to be considered another hospital's catchment area. The efforts include the establishment of hospital owned clinics and the purchase of physician practices in towns up to 50-60 miles from the hospital. These clinics have succeeded in capturing patients and referring them to their associated hospital for inpatient care.

Outreach efforts also include clinics established by private physicians' groups. The physician clinics are used to broaden the referral base for the clinic's various specialties. The clinics refer patients back to the hospital where the physicians have admitting privileges for inpatient and outpatient services. Consequently, when a physicians' group extends its market area by opening an outreach clinic, it also extends the market area of the hospital with which the group is associated. Once an outreach clinic is established, the hospital and specialty referral patterns from the community where it is located change significantly within a short period of time (often within two months). Clinics can generally be established in a matter of weeks as they are often opened in existing hospitals or clinics. Both hospital and physician-owned clinics have proven they induce outreach patients to receive hospital care at the associated hospital, even if another regional hospital is closer.

There is a great deal of evidence showing that these national trends exist in the Dubuque area. Mercy's inpatient volume decreased by approximately 15% from 1990 to 1994. In order to maintain its present patient volume and revenues, Mercy must gain market share in what it considers its "secondary market," the area outside of Dubuque County. This can only be done on a significant level by establishing outreach clinics. Mercy has not established any of its own outreach clinics, but depends on the managed care payers which use Mercy to do so—primarily Medical Associates.

. . . .

Section 7 of the Clayton Act provides, in part, that "no person . . . shall acquire the whole or any part of the assets of another person . . . where . . . the effect of such acquisition may be substantially to lessen competition." (Section 7 is "designed to arrest in its incipiency . . . the substantial lessening of competition. . . .")

. . . .

II. . . .

. . . .

B. Relevant Product Market

The parties have agreed that the relevant product market is acute care inpatient services offered by both Mercy and Finley. This definition excludes inpatient psychiatric care, substance abuse treatment, rehabilitation services, and open-heart surgery. This limits the product market to those services for which Mercy and Finley currently compete for inpatients.

C. Relevant Geographic Market

The burden is on the government to prove the relevant geographic market. The relevant market is hotly disputed by the parties. The government asserts that the geographic market includes Dubuque County, Iowa and a half-circle with a 15 mile radius extending from Dubuque County's eastern edge into Illinois and Wisconsin. This geographical area would include Mercy, Finley and Galena-Strauss Hospital. Currently, 88% of the patients within the market use the three hospitals within the market. Only about 2% of the 88% use Galena-Stauss; the remainder use Mercy and Finley. Approximately 76% of the patients at the three hospitals come from within the market.

The defendants assert that the proper geographic market includes Mercy, Finley, the seven closest rural hospitals and the regional hospitals situated in Cedar Rapids, Waterloo, Iowa City, Davenport, and Madison. Mercy and Finley's market share of the patients within this geographical area is approximately 10%. The government does not contest that if this is the relevant market, the merger is not illegal.

The parties dispute whether the government has properly defined the relevant geographic market by trying to show whether DRHS could (1) profitably raise prices by 5% to managed care entities, or (2) profitably raise prices by completely eliminating present discounts to managed care entities. In the event the court finds the government has not met its burden as to the proposed geographic market, the government has proposed an alternative market encompassing only the City of Dubuque.

The government defined its market based on (1) the views of the major purchasers of health care services in the Dubuque area, (2) where physicians have privileges, (3) the views of physicians, and (4) patient flow data. Looking at the views of the major managed care providers in the Dubuque area, the government finds it significant that Medical Associates HMO and the Heritage Plan both feel their health care plans must include one of the Dubuque hospitals in order for the plan to be marketable to Dubuque employers. The government argues this is evidence that there is no market substitute for the Dubuque hospitals.

The government then looked at the overlap of physicians who were currently on staff at the area hospitals. The government showed that there is a great deal of physician staff overlap between the staffs of Mercy and Finley, but very little between the rural hospitals and Mercy or Finley. Seventy-six percent of Mercy's physicians were shown to be on staff at Finley and over 90% of Finley's physicians were on staff at Mercy. The government concludes from these statistics that (1) those patients who currently use a physician with privileges at Mercy and Finley cannot switch to a rural hospital due to their loyalty to their physician and their physician's inability to admit them at a rural facility, and (2) Mercy and Finley are seen by physicians as being comparable hospitals as physicians are willing to work out of either of them. By contrast, Dubuque physicians are not willing to work out of the rural hospitals, hence the rurals are not comparable and therefore they are not substitutes for Mercy and Finley.

The government also asserts that Dubuque physicians would not seek privileges at the rural hospitals as they do not see the rural hospitals as being able to provide the broad range of services which the majority of their patients require and because the rurals are not adequately staffed and do not have the equipment to do many inpatient surgical procedures.

The government then goes on to look at the inflow and outflow of patients from the market. The "Elzinga-Hogarty" test was employed by the government to argue that the relevant geographical market was quite limited. This test looks at the empirical data to determine (1) the area from which the hospitals draw their patients and (2) where the residents in that area go for hospital care. When both numbers are at 90%, the market definition is said to be "strong." Numbers at 75% are said to constitute a "weak" market definition. [The details of the Elzinga-Hogarty test are set out in Chapter 9—Eds.]

Looking at the government's proposed market definition—Dubuque County and a fifteen mile radius into Illinois and Wisconsin—76% of Mercy's and Finley's inpatients come from within this defined market, and 88% of those residing within the market seek care within the market. Shrinking the market to include only the City of Dubuque, 55% of Mercy and Finley's inpatients come from within the market and 91% of those residing in Dubuque seek hospital care at either Mercy or Finley. Defining the market as a twenty-five mile radius around Dubuque, 85% of Mercy's and Finley's patients come from within the market and 89% of those persons within the market seek care inside the market. Broadening the market to a 35 mile radius around Dubuque, 89% of Mercy and Finley's inpatients come from within the market and 82% of the persons within that market seek care at Mercy or Finley.

Finally, the government asserts that the regional hospitals are not in the relevant geographic market as they only compete for patients at the "fringes," the area located at the midpoint between Dubuque and a particular regional hospital. The government reasons that people will not travel greater distances than necessary for inpatient care and, therefore, only those patients at the midway point between two regional hospitals could be induced to switch hospitals due to price concerns. The government concludes that DRHS would have the ability to raise prices as the rurals do not act as a competitive alternative to DRHS and the regional centers are only a competitive force at the fringes of Mercy's and Finley's service areas and therefore could not induce enough people to switch hospitals to defeat a price rise by DRHS.

The defendants criticize the government's market definition as being dependent on incorrect assumptions, and as not accounting for current market trends. The defendants also assert that the government's geographical market is too small because a 5% price increase would be easily defeated by patients who would choose to travel to other hospitals for cheaper care. In reaching this result, the defendants challenge the government's assumptions of strong doctor-patient loyalty, that outreach clinics only have an effect on hospital use at the fringes of a hospital's service area, and that there are significant barriers to entry into this market.

1. Analysis of the Relevant Geographic Market

The court finds that the government's case rests too heavily on past health care conditions and makes invalid assumptions as to the reactions of third-party payers and patients to price changes. The government's case also fails to undergo a dynamic approach to antitrust analysis, choosing instead to look at the situation as it currently exists within a competitive market.

In determining the relevant geographic market, the court must determine "the market in which the seller operates and to which the purchaser can practicably turn for supplies." *Tampa Elec. Co. v. Nashville Coal Co.*, 365 U.S. 320, 327 (1960); *Philadelphia National Bank*, 374 U.S. at 359. The analysis must focus not merely on where patients have gone for acute inpatient services, but where they could practicably go should DRHS become anticompetitive. This requires a fluid analysis. It is not sufficient to take a snapshot of the current situation and define the relevant geographic market to be synonymous with the current service areas of the defendant hospitals. . . .

In order to determine the actual geographic market, current market behavior must be put into a dynamic analysis which looks at possible competitive responses from other hospitals, third party payers and consumers. In this light, it is important to note that the government's reliance on the Elzinga-Hogarty test is merely a starting point—it states where Mercy and Finley are currently attracting patients and the area from which most patients seek services from either Mercy or Finley. This is the snapshot of the market as it exists under current conditions and does not pretend to answer the question of what would happen if there was an attempt to exercise market power by one of the market participants. . . .

The government's case in general makes the mistake of relying too heavily on past conditions in the hospital industry and discounts the effects of outreach efforts, the strong emphasis that regional hospitals place on expanding their service areas and the willingness of managed care enrollees to make changes in their health care for financial reasons.

The government's case relies on several assumptions and conclusions that are not supported by the evidence. One of the assumptions is that there is strong doctor-patient loyalty. This assumption supports the argument that patients cannot be enticed to use a non-Dubuque hospital because the patient already has a Dubuque doctor to whom the patient is very loyal.

There are several problems with this assumption. First, the evidence shows that many hospital patients do not have an established physician relationship, or, are admitted by a specialist who is not the patient's regular physician.

Secondly, the evidence does not support a finding of strong patient-physician loyalty that prevents patient shifting for financial reasons. The medical professionals testified there is a large amount of patient shifting that occurs when an employer changes or modifies a health insurance plan so as to encourage usage of a particular physician or group of physicians. Testimony also shows that managed care entities have been very successful in enrolling patients in HMO's that require switching physicians or agreeing to be seen by any available physician.[3]

The government's assertion that the outreach clinics have little effect on hospitalization patterns is also erroneous. There are several communities where referral practices have been dramatically altered due to outreach efforts. Most notably Manchester, Independence and Clarion, Iowa. While the effect of the outreach clinics has not been quantified, the fact that they are established is significant as it is only through the generation of inpatient and outpatient referrals that these clinics become profitable. Outreach efforts have been characterized by the regional hospitals as being pivotal in their efforts to expand patient volume at a time when all other trends are causing them to lose volume. In other words, without growth in these areas most hospitals acknowledge they would incur a significant decrease in revenue. The start-up of outreach clinics cannot be justified based solely upon the direct business they obtain on site. They are economically justified due to the increased referrals they bring to the physicians and hospitals sponsoring them. Outreach clinics generally attract patients from a fifteen mile radius and these clinics have been established within twenty-five miles of Dubuque. 18.8% of Mercy and Finley's patients come from within fifteen miles of an outreach clinic associated with another regional hospital.

The government attempts to argue that outreach clinics are only effective in shifting patients from the fringe areas to other hospitals as people will not agree to be hospitalized

---

[3] Medical Associates HMO does not guarantee the availability of a particular physician for office visits and John Deere has been successful nationally even though it has a limited panel of doctors.

at a hospital a significant distance away from their home and family. The government argues that most hospitalizations require two pre-operative visits to the hospital, the actual hospitalization and two or three post-operative visits to the hospitals and patients will not want to incur the expense and inconvenience of travel for these visits. However, the evidence was clear that one reason why the outreach clinics are so effective in altering hospitalization practices is because the pre- and post-operative visits take place at the outreach clinic and the patient is only required to travel to the hospital for the actual surgical procedure.

In fact, people will use outreach clinics which are associated with hospitals that are a significant distance from their hometown. To illustrate, the Platteville and Lancaster areas are 25 miles from Dubuque and sixty to seventy miles from Madison, Wisconsin, yet Medical Associates, which refers persons back to Dubuque for inpatient care, meets strong competition in these communities from the Dean Clinic which refers its patients to St. Mary's Hospital in Madison.

The fact that the residents of southwest Wisconsin are willing to drive to Madison for their inpatient needs also shows that the government's assumption that persons within twenty-five miles of Dubuque will only go to Dubuque for their inpatient needs is an incorrect assumption. The government has also failed to account for the fact that there are several zip codes within 25 miles of Dubuque which currently send over one-third of their inpatients to other hospitals. Looking at the zip codes encompassing Cuba City, Wisconsin; Galena, Illinois; New Vienna, Iowa; Potosi, Wisconsin; and Hazel Green, Wisconsin, there were 930 discharges in a six month period from these zip codes and only 560 were discharged from Mercy or Finley (60.2%). 179 of these discharges were to hospitals other than Mercy, Finley, the seven rurals or the University of Iowa (19.2%). Obviously, these persons are already being attracted to hospitals outside the immediate area. Discharges from these five zip codes account for 7.7% of Mercy and Finley's total discharges.

The main point made by the government which the court does agree with is the inability of the rural hospitals to prevent DRHS from acting in an anticompetitive manner. The government argues that it would not be feasible for more patients to use the rural hospitals as the rural hospitals are not equipped to handle anything but the least complicated hospitalizations. The defendants counter that the rural hospitals are a practicable alternative as they have a great number of empty beds and are capable of meeting the needs of a significant number of inpatients.

Due to the high utilization rates of some of the rurals by those in the same zip code as the hospital, many of the rurals can apparently care for a wide range of diagnoses. For example, in the zip code encompassing Guttenberg, Iowa, where Guttenberg Hospital lies, 178 out of 269 hospitalizations were at the Guttenberg hospital (66.1%). Further, Guttenberg Hospital has cared for inpatients hospitalized for 68% of the DRGs for which Mercy and Finley admit patients. However, in the zip code encompassing Galena, Illinois, where Galena-Stauss lies, only 93 out of 340 hospitalizations were at Galena-Stauss Hospital (27.3%) and Galena-Stauss has admitted patients for only 27% of the DRGs for which Mercy and Finley admit patients. Therefore, the rural hospitals have a wide divergence as to each's ability to care for more patients than are currently hospitalized there.

This evidence shows that the rural hospitals are technically qualified to meet the hospitalization needs of more patients than currently choose to go there. However, other barriers exist to prevent greater utilization of the rurals, the largest barrier being individual attitudes toward the rurals. Persons living any distance from the rurals simply do not seek them out for care. For example, despite the high utilization rate by the population living within the same zip code as Guttenberg Hospital, in the rest of Clayton County, in which the Guttenberg hospital lies, only 92 out of 579 hospitalizations were at the Guttenberg Hospital (15.8%). In all of Jo Davies County, in which Galena, Illinois is a part, there were 63 out of 702 hospitalizations at Galena-Stauss (8.9%). Further, a survey done by Jackson County Public Hospital in Maquoketa found they were significantly used by persons within 20 miles of the hospital, but not by persons of any greater distance.

Another barrier to the rurals taking on a greater patient volume is the difficulty the rurals have in obtaining qualified doctors and nursing staff willing to live and work in a rural community. It is not at all apparent that the rurals could attract the staff necessary to expand patient volume.

. . . .

2. 5% Price Increase

The government also argues that there are no competitors who could defeat a 5% price increase by DRHS and that therefore, the merger would result in an anticompetitive effect. The 1984 Merger Guidelines instituted the 5% test—suggesting that if a merged entity could sustain a 5% price rise for approximately one year, the merger should be enjoined as a violation of the antitrust laws. The government concluded that a 5% price increase would be profitable, in large part, due to the following assumptions: (1) people have strong loyalties to their doctors and will not switch hospitals as this would entail switching doctors, (2) the outreach clinics only influence behavior in the "fringe areas" between two regional hospitals, and (3) persons within twenty-five miles of Dubuque will only use Dubuque hospitals.

Both parties agreed that for a 5% price increase to be unprofitable, DRHS would have to lose 8% of its present population. The government asserts that this will not happen as (1) at most, 4% of those within twenty-five miles of Dubuque would shift to a non-Dubuque hospital, and (2) at most, 3.2% of the 13% of Dubuque patients living outside this 25 mile radius might shift. The government argues that those within twenty-five miles of Dubuque would not shift as they would not travel outside of Dubuque for health care needs partly because they would find it inconvenient, and partly because a shift would necessitate changing physicians which most would be unwilling to do.

The government broke down the 13% of Mercy and Finley's patients who reside outside the 25 mile radius into categories and found that the following persons would be unlikely to switch in the event of a 5% price rise: (1) the .6% admitted who reside completely outside the area (*e.g.* California), (2) the 1.2% who are admitted through the emergency room whom the government assumes happened to be in the Dubuque area when their emergency arose, (3) the 1.1% who are admitted by Medical Associates physicians because these patients will not change hospitals due to their loyalty to their physicians and because their physicians only have privileges at Mercy and Finley, and (4) the 3.6% who were admitted by their Dubuque primary care physician, who the government assumes will not switch because they have ties to Dubuque and that particular doctor. The government asserts of the remaining 6.5% who do not fall in any of the above categories, only half, or 3.2% would switch.

The court finds the government's numerical conclusions to be incorrect, again due to the government's assumption of strong patient-physician loyalty and the government's erroneous belief that persons within twenty-five miles of Dubuque will not travel outside of Dubuque for hospital care. Adding in the percentages which the government excluded due to these assumptions puts the total of those likely to switch in the event of a 5% price rise at a number higher than the 8% necessary to make the price rise unprofitable.

3. Elimination of Managed Care Discounts

The government contends the more likely scenario is that DRHS would reduce or eliminate all current discounts to managed care entities resulting in a 15-30% increase in prices. The evidence was that such a price increase would have to be countered by a 20-35% loss of patients to make such a price increase unprofitable. The government asserts that with a total abandonment of managed care discounts, to defeat a price rise, DRHS would have to lose all of its patients residing outside of the government's proposed market area (24%) and perhaps a number of those residing within the market area. The government argues that it is inconceivable that such a large exodus from the Dubuque hospitals would occur.

The government presumably relies on its assumptions that persons within twenty-five miles of Dubuque will not shift to other facilities, that outreach clinics are largely irrelevant to the analysis, and that there is strong doctor-patient loyalty preventing shifting. For the reasons stated above, the court has already found that these assumptions are erroneous.

The government continues to fail to look at the merger within the context of current market trends. All evidence is that there is a great deal of competition for health care dollar—including stiff competition between the managed care entities. As hospitalization costs account for approximately 40% of an HMOs' fee, a 15-30% price increase in hospitalization rates would equate to a 6-12% increase in the cost of an HMO. HMOs which could avoid this increase would be much more cost competitive and presumably would be able to attract more enrollees. Therefore, if DRHS acted in a noncompetitive manner, an HMO that could successfully induce Dubuque area residents to use alternative hospitals would be at a significant cost advantage.

The government asserts that those within twenty-five miles of Dubuque cannot be induced to travel outside of Dubuque for health care; however, the court finds to the contrary for several reasons: (1) a significant portion of the population already chooses to go outside Dubuque for health care, (2) managed care entities have successfully shifted patients in the past, and (3) managed care enrollees are increasingly willing to travel for financial savings.

Turning to the first point, already, a significant number of Dubuque residents use the University of Iowa Hospitals and Clinics ("UIHC"), a ninety mile drive, due to quality concerns. The government asserts that these persons are only going to the University of Iowa for health care that cannot be obtained in Dubuque, and supports this assertion by testimony from doctors stating that they only send patients to the UIHC for care unavailable in Dubuque. However, 63% of Dubuque residents using the UIHC are self-referrals who are not going to the UIHC on the referral of a Dubuque doctors. Further, the zip code data shows a widely varied use of the UIHC across zip codes, indicative of the defendants' position that persons are not going only for care unavailable in Dubuque. Presumably, if persons were only using the UIHC for care unavailable in Dubuque, the percentages of persons going to the UIHC from each zip code would be fairly equal.

There was also testimony that a plastic surgeon from Cedar Rapids successfully induces Dubuque residents to travel to Cedar Rapids for plastic surgery by offering them lower prices on the surgery and hospitalization. Plastic surgery is not often covered by private health insurance and therefore persons wanting plastic surgery have to pay for the full cost out of their own pocket.

A final example of persons traveling outside of Dubuque for health care needs is that of a Dubuque physician who successfully directs cardiac patients needing catheterization, angioplasty and open heart surgery to Iowa City. Although this is reportedly done for political reasons and not for price considerations, it nevertheless does show that persons can be induced to travel from the Dubuque area for inpatient care available in Dubuque.

There is also evidence that managed care entities can successfully induce Dubuque residents to use other regional hospitals for their inpatient needs. Heritage shifted patients in need of open heart surgery and substance abuse treatment from Dubuque to Waterloo and Davenport in a successful attempt to obtain lower prices from Mercy in these service areas. The government vehemently argues that this evidence is irrelevant as these are services outside the product market and that there is no evidence that people who would switch for these services would switch for the services within the relevant product market. The court finds, however, that it may rely on this evidence for two reasons: (1) the evidence is that it is generally harder to induce people to travel for the longer term hospital care necessitated by these services than for the type of hospital care within the relevant product market, and (2) there is no evidence that patients distinguish these types of care when considering whether to travel for hospital care. The main basis for the government's assertion that people inside Dubuque will not travel for hospital care is that they have not done so in the past, they are not willing to go to the extra expense of having to travel and put their families through the expense and inconvenience of having to stay in a hotel to be near them during their hospitalization, and they do not want to switch physicians. Persons traveling for substance abuse treatment and open heart surgery would apparently have these same concerns, yet they are traveling.

Finally, the court turns to the third point—that financial incentives can induce people to travel. Many witnesses testified that employees are more willing to travel now that they are covering a greater portion of their health care costs. Survey results indicate that, for less than $1000.00, Dubuque residents could be induced to travel to another hospital for care. The government disputes the reliability of the surveys, but the survey outcomes are confirmed by the testimony of officers within the managed care corporations and employers purchasing health care plans.

For example, Doug Sesterhahn testified that SISCO has induced enrollees to travel an hour to an hour-and-a-half for health care by providing financial incentives. Mr. Sesterhahn also testified that he felt SISCO could provide incentives that would induce Dubuque employees to go to Platteville and Southwest Medical Center for care. James Thompson felt that for some categories of patients—nonsurgical, cancer care and heart care patients—a $200 incentive would be enough to induce some Dubuque residents to travel to another regional center for their care. While he was unsure as to the numbers of persons who would travel for a $200 inducement, Mr. Thompson also testified that, with financial inducements of between $500-1000, Heritage could shift patients from inside Dubuque to the regional hospitals for many services in the relevant product market.

The average full charge for inpatient hospitalization at Finley and Mercy is approximately $6,000. Thus, the current 20% discount to managed care payers averages $1,200. If that discount was eliminated at DRHS but available at one of the regional hospitals, the managed care payers would be able to offer a very significant financial incentive in order to get patients to travel. The managed care payers could include a Dubuque hospital in their health care package but also impose different co-pay requirements between the DRHS hospital and regional hospitals so as to induce travel by enough patients to defeat the price increase.

The court must also consider the present trend in hospitalizations toward shorter and fewer hospital stays requiring hospitals to enter into intense competitions [sic] for an increased population base. The court finds it relevant that the regional hospitals are in an intense competition to increase the population base from which they draw patients due to the trend in shorter hospital stays and less frequent stays. Mercy has recognized, beginning with its long range plan of 1990, that, to maintain its average daily patient census, it is dependent on increasing its base of patients residing beyond Dubuque County. DRHS would be under similar pressures. The current state of hospital competition would require that DRHS strongly attempt to expand the use of its hospital by those persons outside Mercy and Finley's traditional catchment areas. If DRHS raised its prices so as to become noncompetitive with other institutions, it would not be able to expand beyond its traditional service area.

The court also notes that 23.7% of Mercy and Finley's patients currently reside in a zip code in which 33% of the residents within that zip code currently use a hospital other than Mercy or Finley. In addition there are an additional 5.9% of Mercy and Finley's patients coming from other zip codes which lie within 15 miles of a regional outreach location. The government makes no attempt to state why these individuals would not be able to switch hospitals in the event of a 15-30% price rise.

4. City of Dubuque as the Relevant Market

The government has offered an alternative geographic market. It contends that the City of Dubuque is a geographic market within which DRHS would be able to exercise market power because Dubuque residents will not travel to the rurals or other regional hospitals for hospital care that is available in Dubuque. While this is a much smaller area than DRHS would service, it may be the relevant market if it is a significant market area and DRHS could successfully exert market power over this group. . . .

The validity of a horizontal merger must be determined based on the merger's "effect on competition generally in an economically significant market." *Brown Shoe Co.*, 370 U.S. at 335. How large a market must be to be economically significant has never been fully addressed. . . . However, the Supreme Court in *Brown Shoe Co.* found that, under some circumstances the relevant geographic area may be as small as a single metropolitan area. . . . For purposes of this analysis, the court will assume Dubuque is large enough to be an economically significant geographic area for purposes of the antitrust laws.

The government's argument that hospital services are local and that persons residing within Dubuque will not go elsewhere for hospital services is largely based upon the government's perception of inpatients' desires for the convenience of a local hospitalization for themselves and for their family members who will be visiting them. . . . The government contends that hospital services, like the banking services at issue in *Philadelphia National Bank* are local in nature and that people want the convenience of a local hospital. 374 U.S. at 358 ("The factor of inconvenience localizes banking competition as effectively as high transportation costs in other industries.").

The government next argues that this geographical region is relevant as DRHS could raise prices to all managed care enrollees within the immediate Dubuque area while providing more favorable pricing to those persons that might possibly switch to other hospitals. It is the government's contention that managed care entities cannot get residents of Dubuque to use hospitals outside of Dubuque, and therefore, the merger would substantially lessen competition to those persons residing within the immediate Dubuque area. The government relies heavily on its assertion that residents of Dubuque will not travel for medical care available in Dubuque. However, the court finds, as stated above, that Dubuque residents have in the past traveled for their health care needs and would travel in the future should DRHS prices become noncompetitive.

. . . .

The court does recognize that other courts have discounted the ability of third party payers to prevent price rises. *See University Health, Inc.*, 938 F.2d at 1213; *Hospital Corp. of America*, 807 F.2d at 1391. These courts found that large insurers who "purchase" hospital services on behalf of their insureds merely pass any increased cost on to the consumer. In *University Health Inc.*, the court found that the third party payer could not refuse to reimburse its insured because it deemed the price of the hospital services was too high. *University Health Inc.*, 938 F.2d at 1213. However, these cases did not focus on managed care entities, but focused instead on traditional indemnity insurers. In the case at hand, the defendants have shown that the third party payers of interest in this matter—the managed care entities—can cause their enrollees to shift to other hospitals if prices at one hospital are too high, thus avoiding having to pay the higher price and providing strong incentive for the anticompetitive hospital to lower its charges.

Further, the competition has become fierce between HMO's. If an HMO were merely to pass on increased hospitalization costs to enrollees, it will lose enrollees to plans that offer a cheaper rate. This pattern has been evidenced in Platteville, Wisconsin, an area where Medical Associates HMO has met strong competition from competing plans.

Even assuming Dubuque residents would not shift in the event of a price increase by DRHS, the government has also failed to establish that DRHS could successfully initiate a price discrimination program. Mr. Thompson testified in general terms that it would be possible for the hospitals to price discriminate on the basis of where a patient resided, but no one established the mechanics of how this would work. Generally, managed care payers contract with the hospitals at one price, but it is conceivable that they could either 1) establish different prices according to which employer the inpatient was insured through, or 2) establish different prices according to where the inpatient resided. If the hospital were to price discriminate by employer, this would presumably lead to the same rate being offered to all Dubuque employees without regard to where they reside. However, a substantial number of persons employed in Dubuque reside significant distances from Dubuque and would presumably have greater access to alternative hospital care. These employees would shift from using a managed care plan that used DRHS to a plan using other hospitals. The government did not address how many employees reside outside of Dubuque and therefore would shift to managed care entities with presumably lower premiums. Without any quantification, it is only speculation on the government's part that such a program would be feasible.

Should DRHS attempt the other option, charging different rates based on where the employee resides, this would appear to require complex accounting by both the managed care entity and the hospital. The government has not attempted to prove that employers would agree to offer the same plan to its employees at different rates depending on where the employee resides nor has it proven that the managed care payers would agree to offer such plans. Again, that such a plan is feasible is mere speculation on behalf of the government.

Further, looking specifically at those managed care entities that currently receive discounts off their hospitalizations from Mercy or Finley, there is little evidence to support the government's contention that discounts to these businesses could profitably be eliminated if the hospitals merge. Mercy gives discounts to Medical Associates, Heritage National Health Plan, SISCO, Blue Cross Alliance, HMO of Wisconsin, Wisconsin Education Association Insurance and the Affordable Health Plan.

Presumably discounts to the two Wisconsin companies would have to be maintained as there is substantial competition for the residents of southwest Wisconsin. Also, the discount to Blue Cross Alliance could not be eliminated as it offers a contract with hospitals on a "take it or leave it" basis and DRHS would either have to accept its terms or deny admittance to Blue Cross Alliance enrollees. That leaves Self Insured Systems Corporation (SISCO), Heritage National Health Plan and Medical Associates. As discussed above, Heritage has shown it has the general ability to transfer patients out of the Dubuque area to another regional hospital so it could prevent DRHS from denying it a discount. It is uncertain where SISCO's enrollees come from, but assuming they do all come from the immediate Dubuque area, it is not apparent that they could not transfer patients as does Heritage. The government has asserted no reason why SISCO would be less effective at altering hospitalization patterns than is Heritage. . . .

The government argues that Medical Associates would not shift patients to other hospitals because it is physician owned and prefers to use only the physician services of its Dubuque physicians. Shifting patients to other hospitals would require it to also pay outside physicians for services provided to their enrollees while hospitalized at a non-Dubuque hospital. However, the antitrust laws protect competition, not competitors. . . . If DRHS were to refuse to give Medical Associates a discount, but did give discounts to other managed care entities who would shift patients, Medical Associates would soon lose many of its enrollees as it would no longer be price competitive.

However, the more likely scenario would be that DRHS would continue to give discounts to Medical Associates as it would be very dependent on Medical Associates to perform outpatient services at DRHS and to attract inpatients through its outreach efforts. In 1991, Mercy recognized that because of fewer and shorter hospitalizations, its patient volume was decreasing and it needed to increase its market share of the population base outside of Dubuque County. Mercy has focused on its relationship with Medical Associates as the major method of attracting new populations. As a would-be large purchaser of DRHS's services, Medical Associates could also bargain for discounts from DRHS through threats to discontinue use of DRHS outpatient services. Currently 1/3 of Medical Associates payments to both Mercy and Finley are for outpatient services, many of which Medical Associates could potentially perform at its own facilities if DRHS prices discriminated against it.

D. Distinction from *Rockford*

The plaintiff relies heavily on *United States v. Rockford Mem. Corp.*, 898 F.2d 1278 (7th Cir. 1990), to argue that it is ridiculous to conceive of a relevant geographic market area encompassing more than a few counties. The *Rockford Mem. Corp.* court stated that:

> But for the most part, hospital services are local. People want to be hospitalized near their families and homes, in hospitals in which their own—local—doctors have hospital privileges. . . . [The defendants'] proposal is ridiculous—a ten-county area in which it is assumed (without any evidence and contrary to common sense) that Rockford residents, or third party payors, will be searching out small, obscure hospitals in remote rural areas if the prices charged by the hospitals in Rockford rise above competitive levels.

Id. at 1285. The evidence in this case shows, however, that the *Rockford Mem. Corp.* assumptions are not correct. There is strong evidence of (1) individuals' willingness to travel, given price incentives, (2) patient-doctor loyalty is not strong enough to overcome price differentials, and (3) there are options other than the rural hospitals should DRHS raise prices. A further distinction is that the *Rockford Mem. Corp.* case did not discuss how outreach clinics can impact on hospital accessibility and choice.

The court also wishes to note that other hospital merger cases have not considered the impact of outreach clinics in their discussions of barriers to entry into the relevant geographic market. Most hospital cases have stated the inability to build new hospitals as a strong barrier to entry. *See University Health, Inc.*, 938 F.2d at 1211. The parties to this dispute have stipulated that no new hospital would be built in the tri-state area within the relevant time frame. However, entry would not necessitate the building of a new hospital, but merely requires that another entity be able to enter a market it was not previously servicing. The regional hospitals are able to do this through the establishment of outreach clinics.

. . . .

F. Conclusion

The government has failed to establish the relevant geographical area and hence has failed to establish that the merger of Mercy and Finley Hospitals will likely result in anticompetitive effects.

III. Defendants' Affirmative Defenses

. . . .

A. Efficiencies Defense

. . . .

The irony of this case is, that while the government has failed to meet its burden of showing that the merger will result in anti-competitive behavior in the relevant market, the court must conclude that the defendants have fallen far short in several respects in proving the efficiencies which it claims will result from the creation of DRHS. The defendants have failed to meet this burden in several significant respects: (1) a merger is not required to achieve many of the efficiencies; (2) implementation of the steps necessary to achieve the efficiencies is highly speculative; and (3) the Gallagher Report overstates the efficiencies which can be achieved.

Each side presented an efficiencies expert who prepared various reports and testified at trial. The defendants presented Duncan Gallagher, a senior manager at Peat Marwick & Co., as their expert. The government countered with a report and testimony of Dr. Robert Taylor. On balance, the testimony and report of Dr. Taylor is far more persuasive and credible.

Mr. Gallagher estimates that the total operating efficiencies that can be achieved as a result of the merger are approximately $5.2 million per year. However, approximately $2.1 million of that figure represents savings from "best practices." Best practices is somewhat of an illusive concept. Generally it can be defined as an attempt by hospitals to become more efficient in utilization of resources and the avoidance of duplication of expenses. Best practices can be contrasted from general attempts at efficiencies by its focus on physician practices. The defendants argue that as a merged entity they can review items such as the number of x-rays a particular physician may order and compare that number to practices of other physicians in order to determine the number of tests which are most efficient while still maintaining patient care. This efficiency becomes the "best practice."

Based upon the evidence and testimony, including Dr. Taylor's analysis, it is apparent there are a number of flaws with the best practices analysis used by Mr. Gallagher. First, Mr. Gallagher concedes that this is the first time he has ever used best practices as a part of an efficiencies analysis in a hospital merger case. This points out one of the fundamental flaws with the analysis, that is, that there is little evidence a merger is necessary in order to implement the best practices savings the hospitals hope to achieve. Even one of the defendants' own witnesses, Gary Gutzko, testified that best practices does not require a merger. The hospitals argue that they need to merge in order to create a database for every department in the hospital. Dr. Taylor points out, however, there are a multitude of alternative databases available which can be used to compare the practices at Mercy and Finley in order to achieve optimum efficiencies.

There is also a serious question about the methodology used in determining the savings from best practices. Mr. Gallagher stated that the numbers he came up with for the best practices were essentially those given to him by Terry Steele.

In summary, I find the testimony of Dr. Taylor is more credible on the issue of the efficiencies which can be achieved from the merger. Dr. Taylor's report shows that the optimum efficiencies which can be achieved from the merger total approximately $2 million per year for both operating and capital expenses.

The defendants argue that even if the $2 million figure of Dr. Taylor's is used, that the efficiencies outweigh any alleged anticompetitive effects from the formation of DRHS. However, the hospitals' proof of [their] abilities to implement the efficiencies is also lacking. The government argues that the whole efficiencies issue is speculative because the DRHS Board has made no decision as to which actions will be taken in order to implement any of the changes which will result in the efficiencies. The government's argument is not well founded in this regard. The DRHS Board cannot come into existence until the merger is approved and becomes effective. Consequently, the DRHS Board can make no decisions at this time as to how it is going to operate the merged entity. The testimony shows that the proposed members of the DRHS Board are serious about obtaining optimum efficiencies from the merger and will do everything within their power to achieve all the potential efficiencies that may result from the merger.

The more serious problem, which was not adequately addressed by the hospitals, is the ability of the DRHS Board to impose on the physicians and other parties the type of changes that will be required in order to achieve the efficiencies outlined in either the Gallagher or Taylor reports. As an example, both reports envision efficiencies being achieved by merging all of the obstetrical services at Finley Hospital. It is highly questionable as to whether the DRHS Board can impose such a change on the medical community given the strong opposition of Medical Associates to the merger, and the unwillingness of Medical Associates physicians to use Finley for obstetrical services when Finely offered the Medical Associates HMO a substantial discount if more Medical Associates' patients were directed to Finley. Given the fact that Medical Associates physicians were not willing to use Finley Hospital when they had a strong personal financial incentive to do so, leads to the conclusion that there very likely will be significant opposition to eliminating the obstetrics unit at Mercy Hospital.

In summary, if the government had been successful in showing anticompetitive effects from the merger, the hospital efficiencies defense must fail. The evidence is inadequate to warrant a finding of maximum potential efficiencies in any amount in excess of the $2 million found by Dr. Taylor in his report. Moreover, there is a lack of evidence on behalf of the hospitals as to their actual ability to implement proposed efficiencies.

B. Non-Profit Status

The hospitals have also asserted as a defense their non-profit status and procompetitive intent. . . . The government points out, this is a questionable legal proposition. No other courts have explicitly adopted this theory of defense. Moreover, the facts in this case would not support the defense even if it were legally viable.

The government has presented substantial evidence to demonstrate that Mercy Hospital, in particular, has operated in a fashion similar to a for-profit corporation. Mercy Health Center of Dubuque is an operating division of Mercy Health Services of Detroit, Michigan. The evidence shows that in recent years Mercy Hospital of Dubuque has been required to return approximately 30% of its profits to the parent corporation. This figure has totaled approximately $1.5 million to $2 million per year over the past several years. Obviously, the operations of the parent corporation cannot be funded out of a percentage of the profits if there are no profits generated by the Dubuque subsidiary. This is not a criticism of the payment of money to the Detroit parent. There are legitimate business and charitable reasons for the payments to the parent corporation. However, the fact remains that the practical effect of the funds transfer is to operate the hospital as the functional equivalent of a profit making subsidiary of an out-of-state corporation.

. . . However, the fact remains, that for antitrust analysis, the court must assume that new and different Board members can take control of the corporation, and that if there is the potential for anticompetitive behavior, there is nothing inherent in the structure of the corporate board or the non-profit status of the hospitals which would operate to stop any anticompetitive behavior.

ORDER

Accordingly,

It Is Ordered:

Plaintiff's request for an injunction to block the merger of Mercy Health Center and Finley Hospital is denied. Judgment shall enter for the defendants. . . .

COMMENTARY

1. Note the reference to the Elzinga-Hogarty test on page 1035, above. For an analysis and description of this test, see Chapter 9, page 443.

2. If you had to write an opinion letter involving a hospital merger like that in *Rockford*, from which an appeal would go to the Seventh Circuit, would you favor the definition of the relevant market taken by the court in *Mercy* over that in *Rockford*? Explain.

3. How would each of these cases have fared in an agency review under the 1996 Statements which are summarized on pages 1025-30 above, and reproduced in full in Appendix C?

For further discussion of these issues, see Thomas L. Greaney, *Regulating For Efficiency in Health Care Through the Antitrust Laws*, 1995 UTAH L. REV. 465 (1995).

H. Third-Party Payer Contracts

In the preceding pages, we have seen how considerations peculiar to the healthcare industry affect the antitrust treatment of mergers and acquisitions. In the following pages, we will look at some antitrust issues arising from contractual provisions between insurers and healthcare providers.

1. Most Favored Nation Clauses

A contractual provision under which a buyer limits its obligation to its supplier to the lowest price which that supplier has charged another buyer is generally known as a "most favored nation" clause. Many healthcare insurers have employed such clauses in their contracts with physicians and other healthcare providers. These contracts have generally been upheld against antitrust attacks. In the material which follows, however, we will see some of the antitrust complexities raised by these and related kinds of contracts.

United States v. Delta Dental
943 F. Supp. 172 (D.R.I. 1996)
ORDER AND MEMORANDUM

PETTINE, Senior District Judge.

The Report and Recommendation of United States Magistrate Judge, Robert W. Lovegreen filed on July 12, 1996 in the above-captioned matter is hereby accepted pursuant to 28 U.S.C. § 636(b)(1).

Delta Dental of Rhode Island ("Delta") objects to the Magistrate Judge's ("Magistrate") Report and Recommendation, which recommended a denial of Delta's Fed.R.Civ.P. 12(b)(6) motion to dismiss for failure to state a claim upon which relief can be granted. . . . After carefully considering the Magistrate's Report and Recommendation, . . . I fully accept the Magistrate Judge's Report and Recommendation. In so doing, I incorporate in whole, and without discussion, the Magistrate's statement of facts as well as the Magistrate's discussion of Fed.R.Civ.Proc. 12(b)(6) standards, and, for reasons of clarity, I attach in full the Magistrate's Report and Recommendation.

. . . .

The gravamen of Delta's objections to the Magistrate's Report and Recommendation is that the Magistrate failed to follow the rule of law set down in the First Circuit cases, *Kartell v. Blue Shield of Massachusetts, Inc.*, 749 F.2d 922 (1st Cir.1984), *cert. denied*, 471 U.S. 1029, and *Ocean State Physicians Health Plan v. Blue Cross and Blue Shield of Rhode Island*, 883 F.2d 1101 (1st Cir.1989), *cert. denied*, 494 U.S. 1027 (1990). However, I find that the Magistrate properly concluded that:

> . . . .
>
> [d]espite *Kartell* and *Ocean State*'s broad language, these decisions, properly construed, fail to establish a *per se* validation of the MFN clauses in all cases where pricing is not predatory or below incremental costs. Such a blanket condonation of MFN clauses would ignore the context *Kartell* and *Ocean State*

were decided in, run counter to the Sherman Act's preference for fact-specific inquiries, implausibly reject the premise that MFN clauses produce substantial anticompetitive effects in particular circumstances and contradict the Sherman Act's animating concern for low consumer prices.

....

REPORT AND RECOMMENDATION

LOVEGREEN, United States Magistrate Judge.

....

As a result of Delta's significant share of insured dental patients in Rhode Island, the government contends that the MFN clause imposes a stiff financial penalty on participating dentists who want to charge fees substantially lower than Delta. . . . This financial penalty allegedly impedes the ability of existing competing plans to contract with most Rhode Island dentists at fees substantially lower than Delta's. . . . It also makes it significantly more difficult for new plans to find sufficient dentists to serve potential subscribers at reduced rates, thereby acting as a barrier to market entry. . . . Consequently, the government avers that participating dentists either disaffiliate from or refuse to join alternative dental plans offering fees less than Delta's or insist that the alternative plans match Delta's higher reimbursement levels. As a result, "Delta's MFN clause has deprived consumers of the benefits that discounted fee plans can offer: increased competition, lower premiums, and greater availability of dental care." . . .

....

Despite *Kartell* and *Ocean State*'s broad language, these decisions, properly construed, fail to establish a *per se* validation of MFN clauses in all cases where pricing is not predatory or below incremental cost. Such a blanket condonation of MFN clauses would ignore the context *Kartell* and *Ocean State* were decided in, run counter to the Sherman Act's preference for fact-specific inquiries, implausibly reject the premise that MFN clauses produce substantial anticompetitive effects in particular circumstances and contradict the Sherman Act animating concern for low consumer prices.

A generous reading of the government's Complaint reveals a plausible allegation that Delta possesses significant market power. Armed with this power, Delta applies its MFN selectively to block alternative reduced-fee plans from the dental insurance market, but has gained no discernible cost savings. Additionally, such a practice has sustained or increased consumer dental costs in the form of premiums. Thus, Delta's use of its MFN clause has had an allegedly negative market impact without any perceivable competitive benefits. Although the government may have trouble proving the severity of these alleged effects, nonetheless, at this stage of the litigation, these allegations highlight the possible detrimental, anticompetitive effects that the selective use of a MFN clause can have on a relevant market and the resulting need to approach these fact driven situations on a case by case basis, rather than with a sweeping *per se* rule.

Furthermore, a blanket rule validating MFN clauses in all contexts devoid of pricing that is predatory or below incremental cost would rest on the implausible premise that, in such cases, a MFN clause's anticompetitive effects are always *de minimis* when compared to its competitive benefits. Such a premise simply can not stand. As set forth above, the government's allegations provide a fact-specific example exposing the flaw in such reasoning. Moreover, it has been generally pointed out that in given circumstances, not limited to those where pricing is predatory or below incremental cost, MFN clauses "discourage discounting, facilitate oligopolistic pricing, and deter entry or expansion by more efficient distribution systems." Arnold Celnicker, *A Competitive Analysis of Most Favored Nation Clauses in Contracts Between Health Care Providers and Insurers*, 69 N.C. L. REV. 863, 891 (1991).

. . . .

Consequently, viewing the government's allegations in the light most favorable to the government and acknowledging the fact intensive nature of the rule of reason inquiry, the government's Complaint has sufficiently navigated the constraints of Fed.R.Civ.P. 12(b)(6), albeit precariously, to state a claim under § 1.

Conclusion

For the reasons stated, I recommend that defendant's motion to dismiss be denied.

. . . .

BACKGROUND CASES ON AGREED PAYMENT ARRANGEMENTS OR "MFN" CLAUSES

1. *Ocean State Physicians Health Plan, Inc. v. Blue Cross & Blue Shield*, 883 F.2d 1101 (1st Cir. 1989), *cert. denied*, 494 U.S. 1027 (1990). Ocean State Physicians Health Plan, Inc. (Ocean State) and a group of participating physicians brought an action against Blue Cross & Blue Shield of Rhode Island (Blue Cross), challenging, *inter alia,* Blue Cross' "Prudent Buyer Policy." Under that Policy, Blue Cross would not pay a provider physician any more for any particular service than that physician was accepting from Ocean State or any other private health care purchaser. That Policy appeared in Blue Cross' contracts with participating physicians. The First Circuit ruled that the Prudent Buyer Policy was lawful:

> We agree with the district court, however, that the Prudent Buyer policy—through which Blue Cross ensured that it would not pay a provider physician any more for any particular service than she was accepting from Ocean State or any other private health care purchaser—is, as a matter of law, not violative of section 2 of the Sherman Act.
>
> * * *
>
> We agree with the district court that such a policy of insisting on a supplier's lowest price—assuming that the price is not "predatory" or below the supplier's incremental cost—tends to further competition on the merits and, as a matter of law, is not exclusionary. It is hard to disagree with the district court's view:
>
>> As a naked proposition, it would seem silly to argue that a policy to pay the same amount for the same service is anticompetitive, even on the part of one who has market power. This, it would seem, is what competition should be all about.
>
> * * *
>
> This conclusion is also compelled by this court's holding in *Kartell v. Blue Shield of Massachusetts*, 749 F.2d 922 (1st Cir. 1984), *cert. denied*, 471 U.S. 1029 (1985) that a health insurer's unilateral decisions about the prices it will pay providers do not violate the Sherman Act—unless the prices are "predatory"

> or below incremental cost—even if the insurer is assumed to have monopoly power in the relevant market. . . .
>
> *Kartell* concerned Blue Shield of Massachusetts's ban on balance billing, a price policy according to which Blue Shield paid participating physicians only if they agreed not to make any additional charges to the subscriber. We held that, for antitrust purposes, a health insurer like Blue Shield must be viewed "as itself the purchaser of the doctors' [services]." . . . *Id.* at 924. As such, the insurer—like any buyer of goods or services—is lawfully entitled to bargain with its providers for the best price it can get. . . . "[E]ven if the buyer has monopoly power, an antitrust court . . . will not interfere with a buyer's (nonpredatory) determination of price." . . . In the present case, Ocean State does not contend that the prices paid under the Prudent Buyer policy were "predatory" or below anyone's incremental cost. As Blue Cross argues, the legality of the Prudent Buyer policy rests *a fortiori* upon the holding in *Kartell*. In that case, Blue Shield sought to limit the fees to be charged by the physician to the subscriber; here, Blue Cross is limiting the price that it pays to the physician for services it is purchasing.

Blue Cross & Blue Shield United v. Marshfield Clinic, 65 F.3d 1406 (7th Cir. 1995) [page 1006, *supra*]. In that case, the Blues charged that the Marshfield Clinic committed an antitrust violation when it refused to pay more to affiliated physicians for a service than those physicians charged their patients or other insurers. Under the Blues' theory, the Clinic's most favored nation clause placed a floor underneath physicians' prices. The Seventh Circuit, through Judge Posner, rejected the charge, labeling it an "ingenious but perverse argument":

> . . . the only evidence of collusion is that the Clinic, when buying services from the affiliated physicians either directly or through Security, would not pay them more than what these physicians charge their other patients. This is said to put a floor underneath these physicians' prices, since if they cut prices to their other patients their reimbursement from the Clinic will decline automatically. This is an ingenious but perverse argument. "Most favored nations" clauses are standard devices by which buyers try to bargain for low prices, by getting the seller to agree to treat them as favorably as any of their other customers. The Clinic did this to minimize the cost of these physicians to it, and that is the sort of conduct that the antitrust laws seek to encourage. It is not price-fixing. . . . Perhaps, as the Department of Justice believes, these clauses are misused to anticompetitive ends in some cases; but there is no evidence of that in this case.

COMMENTARY

1. Was the court correct in *Ocean State* to uphold the lawfulness of Blue Cross' Prudent Buyer Policy? How was the district court in *Delta Dental* able to distinguish *Ocean State*? Is Judge Posner's opinion in *Marshfield Clinic* consistent with *Ocean State*? with *Delta Dental*?

2. What is the "ingenious but perverse argument" made by the Blues against the Clinic's most favored nation clause in the *Marshfield Clinic* case? Was a similar contention made in *Ocean State*? in *Delta Dental*? Does Judge Posner admit that most favored nation clauses might fail to pass a rule of reason evaluation in some circumstances?

3. *Delta Dental* says that most favored nation clauses are subject to the rule of reason, but rejects the contention which would treat them as *per se* lawful. Can you identify the situation in which a most favored nation clause would produce an anticompetitive effect on the market which would outweigh any procompetitive effect which it produced? What kind of evidence would the government be required to produce in order to prove the unlawfulness of a most favored nation clause under the rule of reason?

4. The various effects of most favored nation clauses, *inter alia,* are examined in Jonathan B. Baker, *Vertical Restraints with Horizontal Consequences: Competitive Effects of "Most-Favored-Customer" Clauses*, 64 ANTITRUST L.J. 517 (1996).

5. A separate issue in *Ocean State* concerned the organization by Blue Cross of an HMO which offered equivalent coverage to the Ocean State HMO. Because Blue Cross expected that younger and healthier people would tend to opt for its HMO, thereby raising the proportion of older and sicker people in the standard Blue Cross pool, Blue Cross instituted a pricing plan which took account of that projected difference in health expenses. That pricing plan was approved by the Rhode Island Department of Business Regulation. Ocean State's challenge to this pricing plan was barred by the McCarran-Ferguson Act. (For an explanation of this Act, see Chapter 4.)

Note that the McCarran-Ferguson Act protects insurance rating and pricing, but that it does not apply to contracts between insurers and healthcare providers. The favorable terms which Blue Cross obtained in the physician provider agreements in *Kartell* and *Ocean State* were then passed on by Blue Cross to subscribers, increasing the appeal of Blue Cross insurance to subscribers. Although the contracts between Blue Cross and the physicians in *Kartell* and *Ocean State* were an important ingredient in enabling Blue Cross to compete with rival insurers, the physician/insurer contracts were subject to antitrust scrutiny, but the terms of the resulting insurance were not.

---

2. Clauses Limiting Co-Payment Insurance

In *Kartell*, Blue Cross required physicians participating in its insurance program to agree to accept as full compensation for performing a procedure, the fee set in the Blue Cross fee schedule. Accordingly, these physicians agreed not to accept additional payment from their patients. In *SmileCare*, dentists participating in the Delta Dental plan agreed not to accept payment from insurers in fulfillment of the co-payment obligations of patients. In both circumstances, the participating health-care providers were barred from accepting payments from an outside source. Consider how the economics of the Delta Plan below differ from the economics of the ban on excess billing of patients in *Kartell*.

SmileCare Dental Group v. Delta Dental Plan of California, Inc.

88 F.3d 780 (9th Cir. 1996)

T.G. NELSON, Circuit Judge:

SmileCare Dental Group ("SmileCare") and Delta Dental Plan of California, Inc. ("Delta Dental") are dental insurers offering health care plans to employers, labor unions, and individuals. Delta Dental offers a co-payment plan under which it pays participating dentists a portion of their fee and requires them in return to collect the remainder, or co-payment, from their patients at the time of service. SmileCare offers a supplemental plan which provides coverage for the co-payment. Delta Dental does not recognize co-payments made by supplemental insurers as contractually valid, and deems participating dentists who accept such payments to be in breach of contract.

SmileCare appeals the district court's dismissal for failure to state a claim, alleging that Delta Dental's policy violates Section 2 of the Sherman Act, 15 U.S.C. § 2, because it illegitimately restricts competition and is aimed at eliminating SmileCare's supplemental dental plan. . . . We . . . affirm.

FACTS AND PROCEDURAL HISTORY

Both parties are dental insurers offering a variety of health care plans to employers, labor unions and individuals. According to SmileCare, sixty percent of all California residents with dental insurance are covered by Delta Dental. Ninety-five percent of California dentists are enrolled, on a nonexclusive basis, as Delta Dental service providers. Delta Dental offers a full coverage plan, but covers most of its insureds through its co-payment plans, which are considerably cheaper. Under the co-payment plan, Delta Dental pays participating dentists a portion of their fee and requires that the dentists recover the remainder directly from the patient as a co-payment. Dentists set their own fees, subject to approval by Delta Dental, and Delta Dental determines the amount of co-payment required according to the type of treatment performed. Delta Dental's contract with its service providers prohibits them from waiving the co-payment.

SmileCare offers a variety of dental health plans, but its primary business is a coverage plan called "SmileCare Coverage Plus," which is designed to supplement co-payment plans such as Delta Dental's. By paying participating dentists the co-payment, or an agreed-upon portion of the co-payment, Coverage Plus purports to fulfill the patient's payment obligations to the dentist. Coverage Plus subscribers are thereby provided with full dental coverage. According to SmileCare, Delta Dental has acted to thwart SmileCare and injure the consumer by refusing to accept co-payments from supplemental insurers. Delta Dental providers who accept SmileCare payments in lieu of patient co-payments are deemed by Delta Dental to be in breach of contract, and are allegedly penalized with reduced fee payments, threats of termination, and, in some cases, actual termination. . . .

ANALYSIS

. . . .

I

. . . The following elements are required to establish an attempt to monopolize claim: "(1) specific intent to control prices or destroy competition; (2) predatory or anticompetitive conduct to accomplish the monopolization; (3) dangerous probability of success; and (4) causal antitrust injury." . . . Delta Dental does not dispute SmileCare's allegation that it possesses market power;[2] the remaining issue is whether SmileCare has adequately alleged intentional predatory or anticompetitive conduct and resultant injury.

. . . .

Notwithstanding its lengthy forays into the questionable market benefits of insurance co-payment plans, SmileCare repeatedly asserts that it is *not* challenging Delta Dental's co-payment scheme *per se*. Nor is it questioning Delta Dental's right to insist that providers not waive the co-payment. Rather, it is challenging Delta Dental's behavior in refusing to honor supplemental insurers' coverage of the patient's co-payment because it deems such coverage as tantamount to waiver of the co-payment. The key issue, then, is whether Delta Dental's refusal to recognize as contractually valid a participating dentist's acceptance of co-payment from a supplemental insurer rather than from the patient herself has any impermissible anticompetitive effects. *See Barry v. Blue Cross of California*, 805 F.2d 866, 871-72 (9th Cir.1986).

The district court responded to this question after visiting the merits of co-payment plans themselves. . . . The court opined that insurance creates a "moral hazard" because it desensitizes patients to cost and induces them to seek inordinate amounts of care; co-payments offset this hazard by forcing patients to reflect upon the cost of services and moderate their demands for treatment. . . . The district court denied as a matter of law SmileCare's contention that "supplemental plans are not waivers of co-payments, but rather are merely substitutes for them," based on its finding that supplemental plans create the same "moral hazard" as waivers because they render patients insensitive to cost. . . .

We need not adopt the "moral hazard" theory or reach a conclusion as to the relative market advantage of co-payment plans to decide the instant case. . . . Delta Dental concedes that if SmileCare paid the patient the co-payment, and the patient then paid the dentist, it would have no objection or cause to find its providers in breach of contract. . . . However, because SmileCare pays the dentist, the legal obligation required of the insured is eliminated, distorting the actuarial basis for Delta Dental's co-payment plan.[4]

---

[2] According to the district court, "Delta Dental concedes that SmileCare has adequately alleged market power." *SmileCare*, 858 F. Supp. at 1037. While the parties do not discuss the issue of market power on appeal, we observe that market share does not necessarily equal market or monopoly power, which further requires an assessment of such factors as ease of entry. *United States v. Syufy Enters.*, 903 F.2d 659, 664 (9th Cir.1990). *See also Ball Memorial Hosp., Inc. v. Mutual Hosp. Ins., Inc.*, 784 F.2d 1325, 1335-37 (7th Cir.1986) (where there are no barriers to entry, insurer with large market share lacked market power).

[4] The actuarial basis for Delta Dental's co-payment plan is premised on the theory that insureds will seek cheaper or less frequent treatment if they are forced to consider the pinch to their own wallets. When SmileCare pays the patient's portion of the fee, the patient has no reason to shop for a less expensive provider or to question the necessity of certain treatments. As the district court observed, "SmileCare and the patient pocket Delta Dental's loss. Of course, this windfall will be short-lived," for Delta Dental will raise its prices or abandon co-payment plans altogether as unprofitable. *SmileCare*, 858 F. Supp. at 1039.

The district court denied as a matter of law SmileCare's argument that "Delta Dental's conduct is anticompetitive because it stamps out supplemental plans," based on its finding that SmileCare's supplemental insurance plan does not compete with Delta Dental's primary plan. . . .[5] "Competitive discipline comes not from supplemental plans, but from competing primary plans." . . . The court acknowledged that employees already covered through their employers or unions by Delta Dental's mandatory co-payment plan might wish to obtain 100% coverage by purchasing supplemental coverage. "If Delta Dental overcharges for supplemental plans, competitors will induce the patient's employer to switch mandatory co-payment plan providers. . . . As long as Delta Dental does not improperly attempt to crush competition in the primary plan market, it does not act anti-competitively." . . .

SmileCare maintains that it is competing with Delta Dental because its supplemental plan threatens Delta Dental's business and provides the consumer with a better product at a lower cost. It cites *Syufy* for the proposition that competition exists where parties impose "an essential discipline [on one another] to provide the consumer with a better product at a lower cost." *United States v. Syufy Enters.*, 903 F.2d 659, 663 (9th Cir.1990). However, SmileCare's plan does not put pressure on Delta Dental to reduce the price of its co-payment plan. To the contrary, by eliminating the patient's contribution for each service, the supplemental plan eliminates the anticipated benefit of reduced demand for services. The supplemental plan thus has the potential to increase Delta Dental's costs, pressuring it to raise the cost of co-payment plans or eliminate them altogether, to the ultimate detriment of the consumer.

Instead of competing with Delta Dental directly, SmileCare would "discipline" Delta Dental by encroaching upon its method of disciplining its insureds. We therefore agree with the district court's conclusion that SmileCare and Delta Dental are not true competitors. Rather, SmileCare has found a niche in the coverage "gap" created by Delta Dental's co-payment plan, and now seeks to impose on Delta Dental its own way of doing business. SmileCare fails to cite any provision under the antitrust laws that would require Delta Dental to modify a legitimate way of doing business in order to allow SmileCare to sell its plan.

Even assuming arguendo that the parties were competitors, SmileCare's claims that Delta Dental's conduct amounted to "group boycott" or "refusal to deal" in violation of the antitrust laws are not persuasive. . . . SmileCare cites *Klor's Inc. v. Broadway-Hale Stores, Inc.*, 359 U.S. 207 (1959), and *Aspen Skiing Co. v. Aspen Highlands Skiing Corp.*, 472 U.S. 585 (1985), in support of its group boycott and refusal to deal claims. In *Klor's*, the Supreme Court held that an alleged conspiracy between Broadway-Hale and various manufacturers and distributors to refuse to sell to its competitor, or to sell to it only on unfavorable terms, stated a claim under Sections 1 and 2 of the Sherman Act. . . . The district court found *Klor's* inapposite because it "only forbade a reseller from coercing suppliers not to sell competing goods to the reseller's competitor," and SmileCare and Delta Dental are not competitors. . . . Whether or not the parties are in competition, we hold that SmileCare's failure to allege the essential element of conspiracy between Delta Dental and any other parties precludes a group boycott claim. . . .

In *Aspen*, the Supreme Court considered a decision by a ski resort to back out of a ticket-sharing arrangement it had long held with a smaller competitor. The Court held that because the larger resort's decision "to change the character of the market" was not based

---

[5] The court reasoned that moral hazard and antitrust price-fixing prohibitions require that supplemental and co-payment plans be offered by the same insurer. . . .

on efficiency or any other legitimate business reason, its conduct was in violation of Section 2 of the Sherman Act. . . . We agree with the district court that this case, too, is inapposite. Unlike the defendant skiing company in *Aspen*, Delta Dental did not discontinue a marketing arrangement with SmileCare. Delta Dental's co-payment plan pre-existed SmileCare's supplemental plan and the parties have never co-operated to supply the market with a new or better product. Nor did Delta Dental impose the prohibition against waiver of the co-payment as a response to SmileCare's plan.

. . . .

While the existence of valid business reasons is ordinarily a question of fact, in the case before us it is a foregone conclusion requiring no further analysis: The validity of Delta Dental's business reasons for requiring its dentists to collect the co-payment directly from the patient has already been established by our decision in *Davidowitz v. Delta Dental Plan of California, Inc.*, 946 F.2d 1476 (9th Cir. 1991). We therefore agree with the district court that Delta Dental's policy is supported as a matter of law by a legitimate business justification—its interest in protecting the disciplinary effect of its co-payment plan. . . .

Because Delta Dental's co-payment plan is concededly legitimate, and because SmileCare has failed to allege that Delta Dental's enforcement of its no-waiver clause has any anticompetitive effects, we affirm the district court.

AFFIRMED.

COMMENTARY

1. A concept employed in economic analysis, "moral hazard," is relevant to the situation involved in *SmileCare*. Moral hazard describes a situation in which economic actors while maximizing their own utility to the detriment of others, may not bear the full consequences of their actions due to uncertainty or to incomplete or restricted contracts. Insurance contracts provide an apt illustration of this concept. Judge Richard Posner gives the following example:

> . . . [C]omprehensive insurance against poverty is difficult to obtain, and this for two reasons: moral hazard and adverse selection. If it were possible to insure against being poor, anyone who bought such insurance would have a diminished incentive to work and to save and an increased incentive to have children and to engage in extremely risky economic behavior. That is moral hazard.

RICHARD A. POSNER, ECONOMIC ANALYSIS OF LAW 466 (4th ed. 1992). How does "moral hazard" analysis apply to the *SmileCare* case?

2. How did Delta justify its ban on the acceptance by participating dentists of payments of the co-payment amounts by insurers? Did SmileCare's insurance interfere with the actuarial basis of Delta's insurance? How did the court deal with the concept of moral hazard?

3. Was SmileCare's free riding on Delta's plan? Is SmileCare likely to be injured by Delta's ban? Why does not SmileCare respond to the Delta ban by offering primary insurance in direct competition with Delta?

4. Was Ocean State free riding on Blue Cross' supply contracts with physicians? Was SmileCare free riding in an analogous way? If the government ultimately prevails in *Delta Dental* (page 1048, *supra*), will other dental insurers be able to free ride on Delta's insurance? How is the co-insurance provision in issue in *SmileCare* critically different from the most favored nation clauses involved in *Ocean State* and *Delta Dental*?

Appendix A[1]

[1] Only the principal statutory provisions are included in this Appendix.

Sherman Act[2]

§ 1. Trusts, etc., in restraint of trade illegal; penalty

Every contract, combination in the form of trust or otherwise, or conspiracy, in restraint of trade or commerce among the several States, or with foreign nations, is hereby declared to be illegal. Every person who shall make any contract or engage in any combination or conspiracy hereby declared to be illegal shall be deemed guilty of a felony, and, on conviction thereof, shall be punished by fine not exceeding $10,000,000 if a corporation, or, if any other person, $350,000, or by imprisonment not exceeding three years, or by both said punishments, in the discretion of the court.

§ 2. Monopolizing trade a felony; penalty

Every person who shall monopolize, or attempt to monopolize, or combine or conspire with any other person or persons, to monopolize any part of the trade or commerce among the several States, or with foreign nations, shall be deemed guilty of a felony, and, on conviction thereof, shall be punished by fine not exceeding $10,000,000 if a corporation, or, if any other person, $350,000, or by imprisonment not exceeding three years, or by both said punishments, in the discretion of the court.

§ 3. Trusts in Territories or District of Columbia illegal; combination a felony

Every contract, combination in form of trust or otherwise, or conspiracy, in restraint of trade or commerce in any Territory of the United States or of the District of Columbia, or in restraint of trade or commerce between any such Territory and another, or between any such Territory or Territories and any State or States or the District of Columbia, or with foreign nations, or between the District of Columbia and any State or States or foreign nations, is declared illegal. Every person who shall make any such contract or engage in any such combination or conspiracy, shall be deemed guilty of a felony, and, on conviction thereof, shall be punished by fine not exceeding $10,000,000 if a corporation, or, if any other person, $350,000, or by imprisonment not exceeding three years, or by both said punishments, in the discretion of the court.

§ 4. Jurisdiction of courts; duty of United States attorneys; procedure

The several district courts of the United States are invested with jurisdiction to prevent and restrain violations of sections 1 to 7 of this title; and it shall be the duty of the several United States attorneys, in their respective districts, under the direction of the Attorney General, to institute proceedings in equity to prevent and restrain such violations. Such proceedings may be by way of petition setting forth

---

2 Act of July 2, 1890, ch. 687, 26 Stat. 209; citations are to 15 U.S.C. §§ 1-7.

the case and praying that such violation shall be enjoined or otherwise prohibited. When the parties complained of shall have been duly notified of such petition the court shall proceed, as soon as may be, to the hearing and determination of the case; and pending such petition and before final decree, the court may at any time make such temporary restraining order or prohibition as shall be deemed just in the premises.

§ 5. Bringing in additional parties

Whenever it shall appear to the court before which any proceeding under section 4 of this title may be pending, that the ends of justice require that other parties should be brought before the court, the court may cause them to be summoned, whether they reside in the district in which the court is held or not; and subpoenas to that end may be served in any district by the marshal thereof.

§ 6. Forfeiture of property in transit

Any property owned under any contract or by any combination, or pursuant to any conspiracy (and being the subject thereof) mentioned in section 1 of this title, and being in the course of transportation from one State to another, or to a foreign country, shall be forfeited to the United States, and may be seized and condemned by like proceedings as those provided by law for the forfeiture, seizure, and condemnation of property imported into the United States contrary to law.

§ 6a. Conduct involving trade or commerce with foreign nations

Sections 1 to 7 of this title shall not apply to conduct involving trade or commerce (other than import trade or import commerce) with foreign nations unless—

(1) such conduct has a direct, substantial, and reasonably foreseeable effect—

(A) on trade or commerce which is not trade or commerce with foreign nations, or on import trade or import commerce with foreign nations; or

(B) on export trade or export commerce with foreign nations, or a person engaged in such trade or commerce in the United States; and

(2) such effect gives rise to a claim under the provisions of sections 1 to 7 of this title, other than this section.

If sections 1 to 7 of this title apply to such conduct only because of the operation of paragraph (1)(B), then sections 1 to 7 of this title shall apply to such conduct only for injury to export business in the United States.

§ 7. "Person" or "persons" defined

The word "person", or "persons", wherever used in sections 1 to 7 of this title shall be deemed to include corporations and associations existing under or authorized by the laws of either the United States, the laws of any of the Territories, the laws of any State, or the laws of any foreign country.

Clayton Act[3]

An Act to supplement existing laws against unlawful restraints and monopolies, and for other purposes.

§ 1. Definitions; short title

(a) "Antitrust laws," as used herein, includes the Act entitled "An Act to protect trade and commerce against unlawful restraints and monopolies," approved July second, eighteen hundred and ninety; sections seventy-three to seventy-seven, inclusive, of an Act entitled "An Act to reduce taxation, to provide revenue for the Government, and for other purposes," of August twenty-seventh, eighteen hundred and ninety-four; an Act entitled "An Act to amend sections seventy-three and seventy-six of the Act of August twenty-seventh, eighteen hundred and ninety-four, entitled 'An Act to reduce taxation, to provide revenue for the Government, and for other purposes,'" approved February twelfth, nineteen hundred and thirteen; and also this Act.

"Commerce," as used herein, means trade or commerce among the several States and with foreign nations, or between the District of Columbia or any Territory of the United States and any State, Territory, or foreign nation, or between any insular possessions or other places under the jurisdiction of the United States, or between any such possession or place and any State or Territory of the United States or the District of Columbia or any foreign nation, or within the District of Columbia or any Territory or any insular possession or other place under the jurisdiction of the United States: Provided, That nothing in this Act contained shall apply to the Philippine Islands.

The word "person" or "persons" wherever used in this Act shall be deemed to include corporations and associations existing under or authorized by the laws of either the United States, the laws of any of the Territories, the laws of any State, or the laws of any foreign country.

(b) This Act may be cited as the "Clayton Act".

§ 2. Discrimination in price, services, or facilities

(a) Price; selection of customers

It shall be unlawful for any person engaged in commerce, in the course of such commerce, either directly or indirectly, to discriminate in price between different purchasers of commodities of like grade and quality, where either or any of the purchases involved in such discrimination are in commerce, where such commodities are sold for use, consumption, or resale within the United States or any Territory thereof or the District of Columbia or any insular possession or other place under the jurisdiction of the United States, and where the effect of such discrimination

---

[3] Clayton Act, October 15, 1914, ch. 323, 38 Stat. 730, sections are designated as in the Clayton Act rather than as codified in 15 U.S.C.A. §§ 12-27 (1997). This style conforms to the practice of most courts.

may be substantially to lessen competition or tend to create a monopoly in any line of commerce, or to injure, destroy, or prevent competition with any person who either grants or knowingly receives the benefit of such discrimination, or with customers of either of them: Provided, That nothing herein contained shall prevent differentials which make only due allowance for differences in the cost of manufacture, sale, or delivery resulting from the differing methods or quantities in which such commodities are to such purchasers sold or delivered: Provided, however, That the Federal Trade Commission may, after due investigation and hearing to all interested parties, fix and establish quantity limits, and revise the same as it finds necessary, as to particular commodities or classes of commodities, where it finds that available purchasers in greater quantities are so few as to render differentials on account thereof unjustly discriminatory or promotive of monopoly in any line of commerce; and the foregoing shall then not be construed to permit differentials based on differences in quantities greater than those so fixed and established: And provided further, That nothing herein contained shall prevent persons engaged in selling goods, wares, or merchandise in commerce from selecting their own customers in bona fide transactions and not in restraint of trade: And provided further, That nothing herein contained shall prevent price changes from time to time where in response to changing conditions affecting the market for or the marketability of the goods concerned, such as but not limited to actual or imminent deterioration of perishable goods, obsolescence of seasonal goods, distress sales under court process, or sales in good faith in discontinuance of business in the goods concerned.

(b) Burden of rebutting prima-facie case of discrimination

Upon proof being made, at any hearing on a complaint under this section, that there has been discrimination in price or services or facilities furnished, the burden of rebutting the prima-facie case thus made by showing justification shall be upon the person charged with a violation of this section, and unless justification shall be affirmatively shown, the Commission is authorized to issue an order terminating the discrimination: Provided, however, That nothing herein contained shall prevent a seller rebutting the prima-facie case thus made by showing that his lower price or the furnishing of services or facilities to any purchaser or purchasers was made in good faith to meet an equally low price of a competitor, or the services or facilities furnished by a competitor.

(c) Payment or acceptance of commission, brokerage, or other compensation

It shall be unlawful for any person engaged in commerce, in the course of such commerce, to pay or grant, or to receive or accept, anything of value as a commission, brokerage, or other compensation, or any allowance or discount in lieu thereof, except for services rendered in connection with the sale or purchase of goods, wares, or merchandise, either to the other party to such transaction or to an agent, representative, or other intermediary therein where such intermediary is acting in fact for or in behalf, or is subject to the direct or indirect control, of any party to such transaction other than the person by whom such compensation is so granted or paid.

(d) Payment for services or facilities for processing or sale

It shall be unlawful for any person engaged in commerce to pay or contract for the payment of anything of value to or for the benefit of a customer of such person in the course of such commerce as compensation or in consideration for any services or facilities furnished by or through such customer in connection with the processing, handling, sale, or offering for sale of any products or commodities manufactured, sold, or offered for sale by such person, unless such payment or consideration is available on proportionally equal terms to all other customers competing in the distribution of such products or commodities.

(e) Furnishing services or facilities for processing, handling, etc.

It shall be unlawful for any person to discriminate in favor of one purchaser against another purchaser or purchasers of a commodity bought for resale, with or without processing, by contracting to furnish or furnishing, or by contributing to the furnishing of, any services or facilities connected with the processing, handling, sale, or offering for sale of such commodity so purchased upon terms not accorded to all purchasers on proportionally equal terms.

(f) Knowingly inducing or receiving discriminatory price

It shall be unlawful for any person engaged in commerce, in the course of such commerce, knowingly to induce or receive a discrimination in price which is prohibited by this section.

§ 3. Sale, etc., on agreement not to use goods of competitor

It shall be unlawful for any person engaged in commerce, in the course of such commerce, to lease or make a sale or contract for sale of goods, wares, merchandise, machinery, supplies, or other commodities, whether patented or unpatented, for use, consumption, or resale within the United States or any Territory thereof or the District of Columbia or any insular possession or other place under the jurisdiction of the United States, or fix a price charged therefor, or discount from, or rebate upon, such price, on the condition, agreement, or understanding that the lessee or purchaser thereof shall not use or deal in the goods, wares, merchandise, machinery, supplies, or other commodities of a competitor or competitors of the lessor or seller, where the effect of such lease, sale, or contract for sale or such condition, agreement, or understanding may be to substantially lessen competition or tend to create a monopoly in any line of commerce.

§ 4. Suits by persons injured

(a) Amount of recovery; prejudgment interest

Except as provided in subsection (b) of this section, any person who shall be injured in his business or property by reason of anything forbidden in the antitrust laws may sue therefor in any district court of the United States in the district in which the defendant resides or is found or has an agent, without respect to the amount in controversy, and shall recover threefold the damages by him sustained, and the cost of suit, including a reasonable attorney's fee. The court may award under this section, pursuant to a motion by such person promptly made, simple interest on actual damages for the period beginning on the date of service of such person's pleading setting forth a claim under the antitrust laws and ending on the date of judgment, or for any shorter period therein, if the court finds that the award of such interest for such period is just in the circumstances. In determining whether an award of interest under this section for any period is just in the circumstances, the court shall consider only—

(1) whether such person or the opposing party, or either party's representative, made motions or asserted claims or defenses so lacking in merit as to show that such party or representative acted intentionally for delay, or otherwise acted in bad faith;

(2) whether, in the course of the action involved, such person or the opposing party, or either party's representative, violated any applicable rule, statute, or court order providing for sanctions for dilatory behavior or otherwise providing for expeditious proceedings; and

(3) whether such person or the opposing party, or either party's representative, engaged in conduct primarily for the purpose of delaying the litigation or increasing the cost thereof.

(b) Amount of damages payable to foreign states and instrumentalities of foreign states

(1) Except as provided in paragraph (2), any person who is a foreign state may not recover under subsection (a) of this section an amount in excess of the actual damages sustained by it and the cost of suit, including a reasonable attorney's fee.

(2) Paragraph (1) shall not apply to a foreign state if—

(A) such foreign state would be denied, under section 1605(a)(2) of Title 28, immunity in a case in which the action is based upon a commercial activity, or an act, that is the subject matter of its claim under this section;

(B) such foreign state waives all defenses based upon or arising out of its status as a foreign state, to any claims brought against it in the same action;

(C) such foreign state engages primarily in commercial activities; and

(D) such foreign state does not function, with respect to the commercial activity, or the act, that is the subject matter of its claim under this section as a procurement entity for itself or for another foreign state. . . .

§ 4A. Suits by United States; amount of recovery; prejudgment interest

Whenever the United States is hereafter injured in its business or property by reason of anything forbidden in the antitrust laws it may sue therefor in the United States district court for the district in which the defendant resides or is found or has an agent, without respect to the amount in controversy, and shall recover threefold the damages by it sustained and the cost of suit. The court may award under this section, pursuant to a motion by the United States promptly made, simple interest on actual damages for the period beginning on the date of service of the pleading of the United States setting forth a claim under the antitrust laws and ending on the date of judgment, or for any shorter period therein, if the court finds that the award of such interest for such period is just in the circumstances. In determining whether an award of interest under this section for any period is just in the circumstances, the court shall consider only—

(1) whether the United States or the opposing party, or either party's representative, made motions or asserted claims or defenses so lacking in merit as to show that such party or representative acted intentionally for delay or otherwise acted in bad faith;

(2) whether, in the course of the action involved, the United States or the opposing party, or either party's representative, violated any applicable rule, statute, or court order providing for sanctions for dilatory behavior or otherwise providing for expeditious proceedings;

(3) whether the United States or the opposing party, or either party's representative, engaged in conduct primarily for the purpose of delaying the litigation or increasing the cost thereof; and

(4) whether the award of such interest is necessary to compensate the United States adequately for the injury sustained by the United States.

§ 4B. Limitation of actions

Any action to enforce any cause of action under section 4, 4A, or 4C of this title shall be forever barred unless commenced within four years after the cause of action accrued. No cause of action barred under existing law on the effective date of this Act shall be revived by this Act.

§ 4C. Actions by State attorneys general

(a) Parens patriae; monetary relief; damages; prejudgment interest

(1) Any attorney general of a State may bring a civil action in the name of such State, as parens patriae on behalf of natural persons residing in such State, in any district court of the United States having jurisdiction of the defendant, to secure monetary relief as provided in this section for injury sustained by such natural persons to their property by reason of any violation of sections 1 to 7 of this title. The court shall exclude from the amount of monetary relief awarded in such action any amount of monetary relief (A) which duplicates amounts which have been awarded for the same injury, or (B) which is properly allocable to (i) natural persons who have excluded their claims pursuant to subsection (b)(2) of this section, and (ii) any business entity.

(2) The court shall award the State as monetary relief threefold the total damage sustained as described in paragraph (1) of this subsection, and the cost of suit, including a reasonable attorney's fee. The court may award under this paragraph, pursuant to a motion by such State promptly made, simple interest on the total damage for the period beginning on the date of service of such State's pleading setting forth a claim under the antitrust laws and ending on the date of judgment, or for any shorter period therein, if the court finds that the award of such interest for such period is just in the circumstances. In determining whether an award of interest under this paragraph for any period is just in the circumstances, the court shall consider only—

(A) whether such State or the opposing party, or either party's representative, made motions or asserted claims or defenses so lacking in merit as to show that such party or representative acted intentionally for delay or otherwise acted in bad faith;

(B) whether, in the course of the action involved, such State or the opposing party, or either party's representative, violated any applicable rule, statute, or court order providing for sanctions for dilatory behavior or otherwise providing for expeditious proceedings; and

(C) whether such State or the opposing party, or either party's representative, engaged in conduct primarily for the purpose of delaying the litigation or increasing the cost thereof.

(b) Notice; exclusion election; final judgment

(1) In any action brought under subsection (a)(1) of this section, the State attorney general shall, at such times, in such manner, and with such content as the court may direct, cause notice thereof to be given by publication. If the court finds that notice given solely by publication would deny due process of law to any person or persons, the court may direct further notice to such person or persons according to the circumstances of the case.

(2) Any person on whose behalf an action is brought under subsection (a)(1) of this section may elect to exclude from adjudication the portion of the State claim for monetary relief attributable to him by filing notice of such election with the court within such time as specified in the notice given pursuant to paragraph (1) of this subsection.

(3) The final judgment in an action under subsection (a)(1) of this section shall be res judicata as to any claim under section 15 of this title by any person on behalf of whom such action was brought and who fails to give such notice within the period specified in the notice given pursuant to paragraph (1) of this subsection.

(c) Dismissal or compromise of action

An action under subsection (a)(1) of this section shall not be dismissed or compromised without the approval of the court, and notice of any proposed dismissal or compromise shall be given in such manner as the court directs.

(d) Attorneys' fees

In any action under subsection (a) of this section—

(1) the amount of the plaintiffs' attorney's fee, if any, shall be determined by the court; and

(2) the court may, in its discretion, award a reasonable attorney's fee to a prevailing defendant upon a finding that the State attorney general has acted in bad faith, vexatiously, wantonly, or for oppressive reasons.

§ 4D. Measurement of damages

In any action under section 4C(a)(1) of this title, in which there has been a determination that a defendant agreed to fix prices in violation of sections 1 to 7 of this title [The Sherman Act, 15 U.S.C. §§ 1, *et seq.*], damages may be proved and assessed in the aggregate by statistical or sampling methods, by the computation of illegal overcharges, or by such other reasonable system of estimating aggregate damages as the court in its discretion may permit without the necessity of separately proving the individual claim of, or amount of damage to, persons on whose behalf the suit was brought.

§ 4E. Distribution of damages

Monetary relief recovered in an action under section 4C(a)(1) shall—

(1) be distributed in such manner as the district court in its discretion may authorize; or

(2) be deemed a civil penalty by the court and deposited with the State as general revenues;

subject in either case to the requirement that any distribution procedure adopted afford each person a reasonable opportunity to secure his appropriate portion of the net monetary relief.

§ 4F. Actions by Attorney General

(a) Whenever the Attorney General of the United States has brought an action under the antitrust laws, and he has reason to believe that any State attorney general would be entitled to bring an action under this Act based substantially on the same alleged violation of the antitrust laws, he shall promptly give written notification thereof to such State attorney general.

(b) To assist a State attorney general in evaluating the notice or in bringing any action under this Act, the Attorney General of the United States, shall, upon the request of such State attorney general, make available to him, to the extent permitted by law, any investigative files or other materials which are or may be relevant or material to the actual or potential cause of action under this Act.

§ 4G. Definitions

For the purposes of section 4C, 4D, 4E, and 4F of this Act:

(1) the term "State attorney general" means the chief legal officer of the State, or any other person authorize by State law to bring actions under section 4C of this Act, and includes the Corporation Counsel of the District of Columbia, except that such term does not include any person employed or retained on—

(A) a contingency fee based on a percentage of the monetary relief awarded under this section; or

(B) any other contingency fee basis, unless the amount of the award of a reasonable attorney's fee to a prevailing plaintiff is determined by the court under section 4C(d)(1).

(2) The term "State" means a State, the District of Columbia, the Commonwealth of Puerto Rico, and any other territory or possession of the United States.

(3) The term "natural persons" does not include proprietorships or partnerships.

§ 4H. Applicability of parens patriae actions

Sections 4C, 4D, 4E, 4F, and 4G shall apply in any State, unless such State provides by law for its nonapplicability in such State.

§ 5. Judgments

(a) Prima facie evidence; collateral estoppel

A final judgment or decree heretofore or hereafter rendered in any civil or criminal proceeding brought by or on behalf of the United States under the antitrust laws to the effect that a defendant has violated said laws shall be prima facie evidence against such defendant in any action or proceeding brought by any other party against such defendant under said laws as to all matters respecting which said judgment or decree would be an estoppel as between the parties thereto: Provided, That this section shall not apply to consent judgments or decrees entered before any testimony has been taken. Nothing contained in this section shall be construed to impose any limitation on the application of collateral estoppel, except that, in any action or proceeding brought under the antitrust laws, collateral estoppel effect shall not be given to any finding made by the Federal Trade Commission under the antitrust laws or under section 45 of this title which could give rise to a claim for relief under the antitrust laws.

(b) Consent judgments and competitive impact statements; publication in Federal Register; availability of copies to the public

Any proposal for a consent judgment submitted by the United States for entry in any civil proceeding brought by or on behalf of the United States under the antitrust laws shall be filed with the district court before which such proceeding is pending and published by the United States in the Federal Register at least 60 days prior to the effective date of such judgment. Any written comments relating to such proposal and any responses by the United States thereto, shall also be filed with such district court and published by the United States in the Federal Register within such sixty-day period. Copies of such proposal and any other materials and documents which the United States considered determinative in formulating such proposal, shall also be made available to the public at the district court and in such other districts as the court may subsequently direct. Simultaneously with the filing of such proposal, unless otherwise instructed by the court, the United States shall file with the district court, publish in the Federal Register, and thereafter furnish to any person upon request, a competitive impact statement which shall recite—

(1) the nature and purpose of the proceeding;
(2) a description of the practices or events giving rise to the alleged violation of the antitrust laws;
(3) an explanation of the proposal for a consent judgment, including an explanation of any unusual circumstances giving rise to such proposal or any provision contained therein, relief to be obtained thereby, and the anticipated effects on competition of such relief;
(4) the remedies available to potential private plaintiffs damaged by the alleged violation in the event that such proposal for the consent judgment is entered in such proceeding;
(5) a description of the procedures available for modification of such proposal; and
(6) a description and evaluation of alternatives to such proposal actually considered by the United States.

(c) Publication of summaries in newspapers

The United States shall also cause to be published, commencing at least 60 days prior to the effective date of the judgment described in subsection (b) of this section . . . in newspapers of general circulation of the district in which the case has been filed . . .

(i) a summary of the terms of the proposal for the consent judgment,
(ii) a summary of the competitive impact statement filed under subsection (b) of this section. . . .

(d) Consideration of public comments by Attorney General and publication of response

During the 60-day period as specified in subsection (b) of this section, and such additional time as the United States may request and the court may grant, the United States shall receive and consider any written comments relating to the proposal for the consent judgment submitted under subsection (b) of this section. . . . At the close of the period during which such comments may be received, the United States shall file with the district court and cause to be published in the Federal Register a response to such comments.

(e) Public interest determination

Before entering any consent judgment proposed by the United States under this section, the court shall determine that the entry of such judgment is in the public interest. . . .

(f) Procedure for public interest determination

In making its determination under subsection (e) of this section, the court may—

(1) take testimony of Government officials or experts or such other expert witnesses, upon motion of any party or participant or upon its own motion, as the court may deem appropriate; . . .

* * *

(i) Suspension of limitations

Whenever any civil or criminal proceeding is instituted by the United States to prevent, restrain, or punish violations of any of the antitrust laws, but not including an action under section 15a of this title, the running of the statute of limitations in respect of every private or State right of action arising under said laws and based in whole or in part on any matter complained of in said proceeding shall be suspended during the pendency thereof and for one year thereafter: Provided, however, That whenever the running of the statute of limitations in respect of a cause of action arising under section 15 or 15c of this title is suspended hereunder, any action to enforce such cause of action shall be forever barred unless commenced either within the period of suspension or within four years after the cause of action accrued.

§ 6. Antitrust laws not applicable to labor organizations

The labor of a human being is not a commodity or article of commerce. Nothing contained in the antitrust laws shall be construed to forbid the existence and operation of labor, agricultural, or horticultural organizations, instituted for the purposes of mutual help, and not having capital stock or conducted for profit, or to forbid or restrain individual members of such organizations from lawfully carrying out the legitimate objects thereof; nor shall such organizations, or the members thereof, be held or construed to be illegal combinations or conspiracies in restraint of trade, under the antitrust laws.

§ 7. Acquisition by one corporation of stock of another

No person engaged in commerce or in any activity affecting commerce shall acquire, directly or indirectly, the whole or any part of the stock or other share capital and no person subject to the jurisdiction of the Federal Trade Commission shall acquire the whole or any part of the assets of another person engaged also in commerce or in any activity affecting commerce, where in any line of commerce or in any activity affecting commerce in any section of the country, the effect of such acquisition may be substantially to lessen competition, or to tend to create a monopoly.

No person shall acquire, directly or indirectly, the whole or any part of the stock or other share capital and no person subject to the jurisdiction of the Federal Trade Commission shall acquire the whole or any part of the assets of one or more persons engaged in commerce or in any activity affecting commerce, where in any line of commerce or in any activity affecting commerce in any section of the country, the effect of such acquisition, of such stocks or assets, or of the use of such stock by the voting or granting of proxies or otherwise, may be substantially to lessen competition, or to tend to create a monopoly.

This section shall not apply to persons purchasing such stock solely for investment and not using the same by voting or otherwise to bring about, or in attempting to bring about, the substantial lessening of competition. Nor shall anything contained in this section prevent a corporation engaged in commerce or in any activity affecting commerce from causing the formation of subsidiary corporations for the actual carrying on of their immediate lawful business, or the natural and legitimate branches or extensions thereof, or from owning and holding all or a part of the stock of such subsidiary corporations, when the effect of such formation is not to substantially lessen competition.

Nor shall anything herein contained be construed to prohibit any common carrier subject to the laws to regulate commerce from aiding in the construction of branches or short lines so located as to become feeders to the main line of the company so aiding in such construction or from acquiring or owning all or any part of the stock of such branch lines, nor to prevent any such common carrier from acquiring and owning all or any part of the stock of a branch or short line constructed by an independent company where there is no substantial competition between the company owning the branch line so constructed and the company owning the main line acquiring the property or an interest therein, nor to prevent such common carrier from extending any of its lines through the medium of the acquisition of stock or otherwise of any other common carrier where there is no substantial competition between the company extending its lines and the company whose stock, property, or an interest therein is so acquired.

Nothing contained in this section shall be held to affect or impair any right heretofore legally acquired: Provided, That nothing in this section shall be held or construed to authorize or make lawful anything heretofore prohibited or made illegal by the antitrust laws, nor to exempt any person from the penal provisions thereof or the civil remedies therein provided. . . .

§ 7a. Premerger notification and waiting period

(a) Filing

Except as exempted pursuant to subsection (c) of this section, no person shall acquire, directly or indirectly, any voting securities or assets of any other person, unless both persons (or in the case of a tender offer, the acquiring person) file notification pursuant to rules under subsection (d)(1) of this section and the waiting period described in subsection (b)(1) of this section has expired, if—

(1) the acquiring person, or the person whose voting securities or assets are being acquired, is engaged in commerce or in any activity affecting commerce;

(2) **(A)** any voting securities or assets of a person engaged in manufacturing which has annual net sales or total assets of $10,000,000 or more are being acquired by any person which has total assets or annual net sales of $100,000,000 or more;

(B) any voting securities or assets of a person not engaged in manufacturing which has total assets of $10,000,000 or more are being acquired by any person which has total assets or annual net sales of $100,000,000 or more; or

(C) any voting securities or assets of a person with annual net sales or total assets of $100,000,000 or more are being acquired by any person with total assets or annual net sales of $10,000,000 or more; and

(3) as a result of such acquisition, the acquiring person would hold—

(A) 15 per centum or more of the voting securities or assets of the acquired person; or

(B) an aggregate total amount of the voting securities and assets of the acquired person in excess of $15,000,000.

In the case of a tender offer, the person whose voting securities are sought to be acquired by a person required to file notification under this subsection shall file notification pursuant to rules under subsection (d) of this section.

(b) Waiting period; publication; voting securities

(1) The waiting period required under subsection (a) of this section shall—

(A) begin on the date of the receipt by the Federal Trade Commission and the Assistant Attorney General in charge of the Antitrust Division of the Department of Justice (hereinafter referred to in this section as the "Assistant Attorney General") of—

(i) the completed notification required under subsection (a) of this section, or

(ii) if such notification is not completed, the notification to the extent completed and a statement of the reasons for such noncompliance, from both persons, or, in the case of a tender offer, the acquiring person; and

(B) end on the thirtieth day after the date of such receipt (or in the case of a cash tender offer, the fifteenth day), or on such later date as may be set under subsection (e)(2) or (g)(2) of this section.

(2) The Federal Trade Commission and the Assistant Attorney General may, in individual cases, terminate the waiting period specified in paragraph (1) and allow any person to proceed with any acquisition subject to this section . . . and promptly shall cause to be published in the Federal Register a notice that neither intends to take any action within such period with respect to such acquisition.

(3) As used in this section—

(A) The term "voting securities" means any securities which at present or upon conversion entitle the owner or holder thereof to vote for the election of directors of the issuer or, with respect to unincorporated issuers, persons exercising similar functions.

(B) The amount or percentage of voting securities or assets of a person which are acquired or held by another person shall be determined by aggregating the amount or percentage of such voting securities or assets held or acquired by such other person and each affiliate thereof.

(c) Exempt transactions

The following classes of transactions are exempt from the requirements of this section—

(1) acquisitions of goods or realty transferred in the ordinary course of business;

(2) acquisitions of bonds, mortgages, deeds of trust, or other obligations which are not voting securities;

(3) acquisitions of voting securities of an issuer at least 50 per centum of the voting securities of which are owned by the acquiring person prior to such acquisition;

* * *

(9) acquisitions, solely for the purpose of investment, of voting securities, if, as a result of such acquisition, the securities acquired or held do not exceed 10 per centum of the outstanding voting securities of the issuer;

(10) acquisitions of voting securities, if, as a result of such acquisition, the voting securities acquired do not increase, directly or indirectly, the acquiring person's per centum share of outstanding voting securities of the issuer;

* * *

(d) Commission rules

The Federal Trade Commission, with the concurrence of the Assistant Attorney General and by rule in accordance with section 553 of Title 5, consistent with the purposes of this section—

(1) shall require that the notification required under subsection (a) of this section be in such form and contain such documentary material and information relevant to a proposed acquisition as is necessary and appropriate to enable the Federal Trade Commission and the Assistant Attorney General to determine whether such acquisition may, if consummated, violate the antitrust laws; and . . . .

* * *

(e) Additional information; waiting period extensions

(1) The Federal Trade Commission or the Assistant Attorney General may, prior to the expiration of the 30-day waiting period (or in the case of a cash tender offer, the 15-day waiting period) specified in subsection (b)(1) of this section, require the submission of additional information or documentary material relevant to the proposed acquisition, from a person required to file notification with respect to such acquisition under subsection (a) of this section prior to the expiration of the waiting period specified in subsection (b)(1) of this section, or from any officer, director, partner, agent, or employee of such person.

(2) The Federal Trade Commission or the Assistant Attorney General, in its or his discretion, may extend the 30-day waiting period (or in the case of a cash tender offer, the 15-day waiting period) specified in subsection (b)(1) of this section for an additional period of not more than 20 days (or in the case of a cash tender offer, 10 days) after the date on which the Federal Trade Commission or the Assistant Attorney General, as the case may be, receives from any person to whom a request is made under paragraph (1), or in the case of tender offers, the acquiring person, (A) all the information and documentary material required to be submitted pursuant to such a request, or (B) if such request is not fully complied with, the information and documentary material submitted and a statement of the reasons for such noncompliance. Such additional period may be further extended only by the United States district court, upon an application by the Federal Trade Commission or the Assistant Attorney General pursuant to subsection (g)(2) of this section. . . .

(g) Civil penalty; compliance; power of court

(1) Any person, or any officer, director, or partner thereof, who fails to comply with any provision of this section shall be liable to the United States for a civil penalty of not more than $10,000 for each day during which such person is in violation of this section. Such penalty may be recovered in a civil action brought by the United States.

(2) If any person, or any officer, director, partner, agent, or employee thereof, fails substantially to comply with the notification requirement under subsection (a) of this section or any request for the submission of additional information or documentary material under subsection (e)(1) of this section within the waiting period specified in subsection (b)(1) of this section and as may be extended under subsection (e)(2) of this section, the United States district court—

(A) may order compliance;

(B) shall extend the waiting period specified in subsection (b)(1) of this section and as may have been extended under subsection (e)(2) of this section until there has been substantial compliance, except that, in the case of a tender offer, the court may not extend such waiting period on the basis of a failure, by the person whose stock is sought to be acquired, to comply substantially with such notification requirement or any such request; and

(C) may grant such other equitable relief as the court in its discretion determines necessary or appropriate, upon application of the Federal Trade Commission or the Assistant Attorney General.

* * *

Federal Trade Commission Act[4]

An Act To Create A Federal Trade Commission, to define its powers and duties, and for other purposes.

§ 1. Federal Trade Commission established; membership; vacancies; seal

A commission is created and established, to be known as the Federal Trade Commission (hereinafter referred to as the Commission), which shall be composed of five Commissioners, who shall be appointed by the President, by and with the advice and consent of the Senate. Not more than three of the Commissioners shall be members of the same political party. . . .

* * *

§ 5. Unfair methods of competition unlawful; prevention by Commission

(a) Declaration of unlawfulness; power to prohibit unfair practices; inapplicability to foreign trade

(1) Unfair methods of competition in or affecting commerce, and unfair or deceptive acts or practices in or affecting commerce, are hereby declared unlawful.

(2) The Commission is hereby empowered and directed to prevent persons, partnerships, or corporations, except banks, savings and loan institutions described in section 57a(f)(3) of this title, Federal credit unions described in section 57a(f)(4) of this title, common carriers subject to the Acts to regulate commerce, air carriers and foreign air carriers subject to part A of subtitle VII of Title 49, and persons, partnerships, or corporations insofar as they are subject to the Packers and Stockyards Act, 1921, as amended [7 U.S.C.A. § 181, *et seq.*], except as provided in section 406(b) of said Act [7 U.S.C.A. § 227(b)], from using unfair methods of competition in or affecting commerce and unfair or deceptive acts or practices in or affecting commerce.

(3) This subsection shall not apply to unfair methods of competition involving commerce with foreign nations (other than import commerce) unless—

(A) such methods of competition have a direct, substantial, and reasonably foreseeable effect—

(i) on commerce which is not commerce with foreign nations, or on import commerce with foreign nations; or

(ii) on export commerce with foreign nations, of a person engaged in such commerce in the United States; and

---

[4] Sept. 26, 1914, ch. 311, §1, 38 Stat. 717. Sections cited in conformity with customary practice rather than as in 15 U.S.C.A. §§ 41-45 (1997).

(B) such effect gives rise to a claim under the provisions of this subsection, other than this paragraph.

If this subsection applies to such methods of competition only because of the operation of subparagraph (A)(ii), this subsection shall apply to such conduct only for injury to export business in the United States.

(b) Proceeding by Commission; modifying and setting aside orders

Whenever the Commission shall have reason to believe that any such person, partnership, or corporation has been or is using any unfair method of competition or unfair or deceptive act or practice in or affecting commerce, and if it shall appear to the Commission that a proceeding by it in respect thereof would be to the interest of the public, it shall issue and serve upon such person, partnership, or corporation a complaint stating its charges in that respect and containing a notice of a hearing upon a day and at a place therein fixed at least thirty days after the service of said complaint. The person, partnership, or corporation so complained of shall have the right to appear at the place and time so fixed and show cause why an order should not be entered by the Commission requiring such person, partnership, or corporation to cease and desist from the violation of the law so charged in said complaint. . . .

* * *

(l) Penalty for violation of order; injunctions and other appropriate equitable relief

Any person, partnership, or corporation who violates an order of the Commission after it has become final, and while such order is in effect, shall forfeit and pay to the United States a civil penalty of not more than $10,000 for each violation, which shall accrue to the United States and may be recovered in a civil action brought by the Attorney General of the United States. Each separate violation of such an order shall be a separate offense, except that in the case of a violation through continuing failure to obey or neglect to obey a final order of the Commission, each day of continuance of such failure or neglect shall be deemed a separate offense. . . .

* * *

(n) Standard of proof; public policy considerations

The Commission shall have no authority under this section or section 57a [the rulemaking authority of the Commission] of this title to declare unlawful an act or practice on the grounds that such act or practice is unfair unless the act or practice causes or is likely to cause substantial injury to consumers which is not reasonably avoidable by consumers themselves and not outweighed by countervailing benefits to consumers or to competition. In determining whether an act or practice is unfair, the Commission may consider established public policies as evidence to be considered with all other evidence. Such public policy considerations may not serve as a primary basis for such determination.

Antitrust Civil Process Act[5]

* * *

§ 1312 Civil investigative demands

(a) Whenever the Attorney General, or the Assistant Attorney General in charge of the Antitrust Division of the Department of Justice, has reason to believe that any person may be in possession, custody, or control of any documentary material, or may have any information, relevant to a civil antitrust investigation, . . . he may, prior to the institution of a civil or criminal proceeding by the United States thereon, issue in writing, and cause to be served upon such person, a civil investigative demand requiring such person to produce such documentary material for inspection and copying or reproduction, to answer in writing written interrogatories, to give oral testimony concerning documentary material or information, or to furnish any combination of such material, answers, or testimony. . . .

* * *

[5] Act of Sept. 19, 1962, Pub. L. No. 87-664, § 2, 76 Stat. 548, codified at 15 U.S.C.A. §§ 1311-1314 (1982 & Supp. 1997).

Antitrust Civil Process Act*

§ 1312. Civil investigative demand

(a) Whenever the Attorney General, or the Assistant Attorney General in charge of the Antitrust Division of the Department of Justice, has reason to believe that any person may be in possession, custody, or control of any documentary material, or may have any information, relevant to a civil antitrust investigation, he may, prior to the institution of a civil or criminal proceeding by the United States thereon, issue in writing, and cause to be served upon such person, a civil investigative demand requiring such person to produce such documentary material for inspection and copying or reproduction, to answer in writing written interrogatories, to give oral testimony concerning documentary material or information, or to furnish any combination of such material, answers, or testimony.

* Act of Sept. 19, 1962, Pub. L. No. 87-664, [illegible] 76 Stat. 548, [illegible] 15 U.S.C. §§ [illegible] (1982 & Supp. [illegible]).

Local Government Antitrust Act[6]

§ 34. Definitions applicable to sections 34 to 36

For purposes of sections 34 to 36 of this title—

(1) the term "local government" means—

(A) a city, county, parish, town, township, village, or any other general function governmental unit established by State law, or

(B) a school district, sanitary district, or any other special function governmental unit established by State law in one or more States,

(2) the term "person" has the meaning given it in subsection (a) of the first section of the Clayton Act (15 U.S.C. 12(A)) [15 U.S.C.A. § 12(a)], but does not include any local government as defined in paragraph (1) of this section, and

(3) the term "State" has the meaning given it in section 4G(2) of the Clayton Act (15 U.S.C. 15g(2)).

§ 35. Recovery of damages, etc., for antitrust violations from any local government, or official or employee thereof acting in an official capacity

(a) Prohibition in general

No damages, interest on damages, costs, or attorney's fees may be recovered under section 4, 4A, or 4C of the Clayton Act (15 U.S.C. 15, 15a, or 15c) from any local government, or official or employee thereof acting in an official capacity.

(b) Preconditions for attachment of prohibition; prima facie evidence for nonapplication of prohibition

Subsection (a) of this section shall not apply to cases commenced before the effective date of this Act unless the defendant establishes and the court determines, in light of all the circumstances, including the stage of litigation and the availability of alternative relief under the Clayton Act, that it would be inequitable not to apply this subsection to a pending case. In consideration of this section, existence of a jury verdict, district court judgment, or any stage of litigation subsequent thereto, shall be deemed to be prima facie evidence that subsection (a) of this section shall not apply.

§ 36. Recovery of damages, etc., for antitrust violations on claim against person based on official action directed by local government, or official or employee thereof acting in an official capacity

(a) Prohibition in general

No damages, interest on damages, costs or attorney's fees may be recovered under section 4, 4A, or 4C of the Clayton Act (15 U.S.C. 15, 15a, or 15c) in any

---

6 Act of Oct. 24, 1984, Pub. L. No. 98-544, § 2, 98 Stat. 2750, codified at 15 U.S.C.A. §§ 34-36 (1997).

claim against a person based on any official action directed by a local government, or official or employee thereof acting in an official capacity.

(b) Nonapplication of prohibition for cases commenced before effective date of provisions

Subsection (a) of this section shall not apply with respect to cases commenced before the effective date of this Act.

* * *

The Patent Act[7]

* * *

§ 271. Infringement of patent

(a) Except as otherwise provided in this title, whoever without authority makes, uses, offers to sell, or sells any patented invention, within the United States or imports into the United States any patented invention during the term of the patent therefor, infringes the patent.

(b) Whoever actively induces infringement of a patent shall be liable as an infringer.

(c) Whoever offers to sell or sells within the United States or imports into the United States a component of a patented machine, manufacture, combination or composition, or a material or apparatus for use in practicing a patented process, constituting a material part of the invention, knowing the same to be especially made or especially adapted for use in an infringement of such patent, and not a staple article or commodity of commerce suitable for substantial noninfringing use, shall be liable as a contributory infringer.

(d) No patent owner otherwise entitled to relief for infringement or contributory infringement of a patent shall be denied relief or deemed guilty of misuse or illegal extension of the patent right by reason of his having done one or more of the following: (1) derived revenue from acts which if performed by another without his consent would constitute contributory infringement of the patent; (2) licensed or authorized another to perform acts which if performed without his consent would constitute contributory infringement of the patent; (3) sought to enforce his patent rights against infringement or contributory infringement; (4) refused to license or use any rights to the patent; or (5) conditioned the license of any rights to the patent or the sale of the patented product on the acquisition of a license to rights in another patent or purchase of a separate product, unless, in view of the circumstances, the patent owner has market power in the relevant market for the patent or patented product on which the license or sale is conditioned.

* * *

(f) **(1)** Whoever without authority supplies or causes to be supplied in or from the United States all or a substantial portion of the components of a patented invention, where such components are uncombined in whole or in part, in such manner as to actively induce the combination of such components outside of the United States in a manner that would infringe

---

[7] July 15, 1952, ch. 950, 66 Stat. 811, as amended Sept. 24, 1984, Pub. L. No. 98-417, Title II, § 202, 98 Stat. 1603, codified at 35 U.S.C.A. §§ 1-376 (1984 & Supp. 1997).

the patent if such combination occurred within the United States, shall be liable as an infringer.

(2) Whoever without authority supplies or causes to be supplied in or from the United States any component of a patented invention that is especially made or especially adapted for use in the invention and not a staple article or commodity of commerce suitable for substantial noninfringing use, where such component is uncombined in whole or in part, knowing that such component is so made or adapted and intending that such component will be combined outside of the United States in a manner that would infringe the patent if such combination occurred within the United States, shall be liable as an infringer.

* * *

(h) As used in this section, the term "whoever" includes any State, any instrumentality of a State, and any officer or employee of a State or instrumentality of a State acting in his official capacity. Any State, and any such instrumentality, officer, or employee, shall be subject to the provisions of this title in the same manner and to the same extent as any nongovernmental entity.

(i) As used in this section, an "offer for sale" or an "offer to sell" by a person other than the patentee, or any designee of the patentee, is that in which the sale will occur before the expiration of the term of the patent.

* * *

Appendix B

Department of Justice and Federal Trade Commission Revised Policy Statements of Antitrust Enforcement Policy in Health Care (1996)[1]

Introduction

In September 1993, the Department of Justice and the Federal Trade Commission (the "Agencies") issued six statements of their antitrust enforcement policies regarding mergers and various joint activities in the health care area. The six policy statements addressed: (1) hospital mergers; (2) hospital joint ventures involving high-technology or other expensive medical equipment; (3) physicians' provision of information to purchasers of health care services; (4) hospital participation in exchanges of price and cost information; (5) health care providers' joint purchasing arrangements; and (6) physician network joint ventures. The Agencies also committed to issuing expedited Department of Justice business reviews and Federal Trade Commission advisory opinions in response to requests for antitrust guidance on specific proposed conduct involving the health care industry.

The 1993 policy statements and expedited specific Agency guidance were designed to advise the health care community in a time of tremendous change, and to address, as completely as possible, the problem of uncertainty concerning the Agencies' enforcement policy that some had said might deter mergers, joint ventures, or other activities that could lower health care costs. Sound antitrust enforcement, of course, continued to protect consumers against anticompetitive activities.

When the Agencies issued the 1993 health care antitrust enforcement policy statements, they recognized that additional guidance might be desirable in the areas covered by those statements as well as in other health care areas, and committed to issuing revised and additional policy statements as warranted. In light of the comments the Agencies received on the 1993 statements and the Agencies' own experience, the Agencies revised and expanded the health care antitrust enforcement policy statements in September 1994. The 1994 statements, which superseded the 1993 statements, added new statements addressing hospital joint ventures involving specialized clinical or other expensive health care services, providers' collective provision of fee-related information to purchasers of health care services, and analytical principles relating to a broad range of health care provider networks (termed "multiprovider networks"), and expanded the antitrust "safety zones" for several other statements.

---

[1] Federal Trade Commission, World Wide Web site, http://www.ftc.gov; selected portions of this extended Statement are reproduced in this Appendix. The full Statement is summarized in Chapter 19.

Since issuance of the 1994 statements, health care markets have continued to evolve in response to consumer demand and competition in the marketplace. New arrangements and variations on existing arrangements involving joint activity by health care providers continue to emerge to meet consumers', purchasers', and payers' desire for more efficient delivery of high quality health care services. During this period, the Agencies have gained additional experience with arrangements involving joint provider activity. As a result of these developments, the Agencies have decided to amplify the enforcement policy statement on physician network joint ventures and the more general statement on multiprovider networks.

In these revised statements, the Agencies continue to analyze all types of health care provider networks under general antitrust principles. These principles are sufficiently flexible to take into account the particular characteristics of health care markets and the rapid changes that are occurring in those markets. The Agencies emphasize that it is not their intent to treat such networks either more strictly or more leniently than joint ventures in other industries, or to favor any particular procompetitive organization or structure of health care delivery over other forms that consumers may desire. Rather, their goal is to ensure a competitive marketplace in which consumers will have the benefit of high quality, cost-effective health care and a wide range of choices, including new provider-controlled networks that expand consumer choice and increase competition.

The revisions to the statements on physician network joint ventures and multiprovider networks are summarized below. In addition to these revisions, various changes have been made to the language of both statements to improve their clarity. No revisions have been made to any of the other statements.

* * *

Table of Contents

1. Statement of Department of Justice and Federal Trade Commission Enforcement Policy on Mergers Among Hospitals

Introduction

Most hospital mergers and acquisitions ("mergers") do not present competitive concerns. While careful analysis may be necessary to determine the likely competitive effect of a particular hospital merger, the competitive effect of many hospital mergers is relatively easy to assess. This statement sets forth an antitrust safety zone for certain mergers in light of the Agencies' extensive experience analyzing hospital mergers. Mergers that fall within the antitrust safety zone will not be challenged by the Agencies under the antitrust laws, absent extraordinary circumstances.[2] This policy statement also briefly describes the Agencies' antitrust analysis of hospital mergers that fall outside the antitrust safety zone.

A. Antitrust Safety Zone: Mergers of Hospitals That Will Not Be Challenged, Absent Extraordinary Circumstances, by the Agencies

The Agencies will not challenge any merger between two general acute-care hospitals where one of the hospitals (1) has an average of fewer than 100 licensed beds over the three most recent years, and (2) has an average daily inpatient census of fewer than 40 patients over the three most recent years, absent extraordinary circumstances. This antitrust safety zone will not apply if that hospital is less than 5 years old.

The Agencies recognize that in some cases a general acute care hospital with fewer than 100 licensed beds and an average daily inpatient census of fewer than 40 patients will be the only hospital in a relevant market. As such, the hospital does not compete in any significant way with other hospitals. Accordingly, mergers involving such hospitals are unlikely to reduce competition substantially.

The Agencies also recognize that many general acute care hospitals, especially rural hospitals, with fewer than 100 licensed beds and an average daily inpatient census of fewer than 40 patients are unlikely to achieve the efficiencies that larger hospitals enjoy. Some of those cost-saving efficiencies may be realized, however, through a merger with another hospital.

B. The Agencies' Analysis of Hospital Mergers That Fall Outside the Antitrust Safety Zone

Hospital mergers that fall outside the antitrust safety zone are not necessarily anticompetitive, and may be procompetitive. The Agencies' analysis of hospital

---

[2] The Agencies are confident that conduct falling within the antitrust safety zones contained in these policy statements is very unlikely to raise competitive concerns. Accordingly, the Agencies anticipate that extraordinary circumstances warranting a challenge to such conduct will be rare.

mergers follows the five steps set forth in the Department of Justice/Federal Trade Commission 1992 Horizontal Merger Guidelines.

Applying the analytical framework of the Merger Guidelines to particular facts of specific hospital mergers, the Agencies often have concluded that an investigated hospital merger will not result in a substantial lessening of competition in situations where market concentration might otherwise raise an inference of anticompetitive effects. Such situations include transactions where the Agencies found that: (1) the merger would not increase the likelihood of the exercise of market power either because of the existence post-merger of strong competitors or because the merging hospitals were sufficiently differentiated; (2) the merger would allow the hospitals to realize significant cost savings that could not otherwise be realized; or (3) the merger would eliminate a hospital that likely would fail with its assets exiting the market.

Antitrust challenges to hospital mergers are relatively rare. Of the hundreds of hospital mergers in the United States since 1987, the Agencies have challenged only a handful, and in several cases sought relief only as to part of the transaction. Most reviews of hospital mergers conducted by the Agencies are concluded within one month.

If hospitals are considering mergers that appear to fall within the antitrust safety zone and believe they need additional certainty regarding the legality of their conduct under the antitrust laws, they can take advantage of the Department's business review procedure (28 C.F.R. § 50.6 (1992)) or the Federal Trade Commission's advisory opinion procedure (16 C.F.R. §§ 1.1-1.4 (1993)). The Agencies will respond to business review or advisory opinion requests on behalf of hospitals considering mergers that appear to fall within the antitrust safety zone within 90 days after all necessary information is submitted.

---

2. Statement of Department of Justice and Federal Trade Commission Enforcement Policy on Hospital Joint Ventures Involving High-Technology or Other Expensive Health Care Equipment

Introduction

Most hospital joint ventures to purchase or otherwise share the ownership cost of, operate, and market high-technology or other expensive health care equipment and related services do not create antitrust problems. In most cases, these collaborative activities create procompetitive efficiencies that benefit consumers. These efficiencies include the provision of services at a lower cost or the provision of services that would not have been provided absent the joint venture. Sound antitrust enforcement policy distinguishes those joint ventures that on balance benefit the public from those that may increase prices without providing a countervailing benefit, and seeks to prevent only those that are harmful to consumers. The Agencies have never challenged a joint venture among hospitals to purchase or otherwise share the ownership cost of, operate and market high-technology or other expensive health care equipment and related services.

This statement of enforcement policy sets forth an antitrust safety zone that describes hospital high-technology or other expensive health care equipment joint ventures that will not be challenged, absent extraordinary circumstances, by the Agencies under the antitrust laws. It then describes the Agencies' antitrust analysis of hospital high-technology or other expensive health care equipment joint ventures that fall outside the antitrust safety zone. Finally, this statement includes examples of its application to hospital high-technology or other expensive health care equipment joint ventures.

A. Antitrust Safety Zone: Hospital High-Technology Joint Ventures That Will Not Be Challenged, Absent Extraordinary Circumstances, by the Agencies

The Agencies will not challenge under the antitrust laws any joint venture among hospitals to purchase or otherwise share the ownership cost of, operate, and market the related services of, high-technology or other expensive health care equipment if the joint venture includes only the number of hospitals whose participation is needed to support the equipment, absent extraordinary circumstances.[3] This applies to joint ventures involving purchases of new equipment as well as to joint ventures involving existing equipment.[4] A joint venture that includes additional hospitals also will not be challenged if the additional hospitals could not support the equipment on their own or through the formation of a competing joint venture, absent extraordinary circumstances.

For example, if two hospitals are each unlikely to recover the cost of individually purchasing, operating, and marketing the services of a magnetic resonance imager (MRI) over its useful life, their joint venture with respect to the MRI would not be challenged by the Agencies. On the other hand, if the same two hospitals entered into a joint venture with a third hospital that independently could have purchased, operated, and marketed an MRI in a financially viable manner, the joint venture would not be in this antitrust safety zone. If, however, none of the three hos-

---

[3] A hospital or group of hospitals will be considered able to support high-technology or other expensive health care equipment for purposes of this antitrust safety zone if it could recover the cost of owning, operating, and marketing the equipment over its useful life. If the joint venture is limited to ownership, only the ownership costs are relevant. . . .

[4] Consequently, the safety zone would apply in a situation in which one hospital had already purchased the health care equipment, but was not recovering the costs of the equipment and sought a joint venture with one or more hospitals in order to recover the costs of the equipment.

pitals could have supported an MRI by itself, the Agencies would not challenge the joint venture.[5]

Information necessary to determine whether the costs of a piece of high-technology health care equipment could be recovered over its useful life is normally available to any hospital or group of hospitals considering such a purchase. This information may include the cost of the equipment, its expected useful life, the minimum number of procedures that must be done to meet a machine's financial breakeven point, the expected number of procedures the equipment will be used for given the population served by the joint venture and the expected price to be charged for the use of the equipment. Expected prices and costs should be confirmed by objective evidence, such as experiences in similar markets for similar technologies.

B. The Agencies' Analysis of Hospital High-technology or Other Expensive Health Care Equipment Joint Ventures That Fall Outside the Antitrust Safety Zone

The Agencies recognize that joint ventures that fall outside the antitrust safety zone do not necessarily raise significant antitrust concerns. The Agencies will apply a rule of reason analysis in their antitrust review of such joint ventures.[6] The objective of this analysis is to determine whether the joint venture may reduce competition substantially, and, if it might, whether it is likely to produce procompetitive efficiencies that outweigh its anticompetitive potential. This analysis is flexible and takes into account the nature and effect of the joint venture, the characteristics of the venture and of the hospital industry generally, and the reasons for, and purposes of, the venture. It also allows for consideration of efficiencies that will result from the venture. The steps involved in a rule of reason analysis are set forth below.[7]

Step one: Define the relevant market. The rule of reason analysis first identifies what is produced through the joint venture. The relevant product and geo-

---

[5] The antitrust safety zone described in this statement applies only to the joint venture and agreements necessary to the venture. The safety zone does not apply to or protect agreements made by participants in a joint venture that are related to a service not provided by the venture. For example, the antitrust safety zone that would apply to the MRI joint venture would not apply to protect an agreement among hospitals with respect to charges for an overnight stay.

[6] This statement assumes that the joint venture arrangement is not one that uses the joint venture label but is likely merely to restrict competition and decrease output. For example, two hospitals that independently operate profitable MRI services could not avoid charges of price-fixing by labeling as joint venture their plan to obtain higher prices through joint marketing of their existing MRI services.

[7] Many joint ventures that would provide substantial efficiencies also may present little likelihood of competitive harm. Where it is clear initially that any joint venture presents little likelihood of competitive harm, the step-by-step analysis described in the text below will not be necessary. For example, when two hospitals propose to merge existing expensive health care equipment into a joint venture in a properly defined market in which many other hospitals or other health care facilities operate the same equipment, such that the market will be unconcentrated, then the combination is unlikely to be anticompetitive and further analysis ordinarily will not be required. *See* Department of Justice/Federal Trade Commission *1992 Horizontal Guidelines*.

graphic markets are then properly defined. This process seeks to identify any other provider that could offer what patients or physicians generally would consider a good substitute for that provided by the joint venture. Thus, if a joint venture were to purchase and jointly operate and market the related services of an MRI, the relevant market would include all other MRIs in the area that are reasonable alternatives for the same patients, but would not include providers with only traditional X-ray equipment.

Step two: Evaluate the competitive effects of the venture. This step begins with an analysis of the structure of the relevant market. If many providers would compete with the joint venture, competitive harm is unlikely and the analysis would continue with step four described below.

If the structural analysis of the relevant market showed that the joint venture would eliminate an existing or potentially viable competing provider and that there were few competing providers of that service, or that cooperation in the joint venture market may spill over into a market in which the parties to the joint venture are competitors, it then would be necessary to assess the extent of the potential anticompetitive effects of the joint venture. In addition to the number and size of competing providers, factors that could restrain the ability of the joint venture to raise prices either unilaterally or through collusive agreements with other providers would include: (1) characteristics of the market that make anticompetitive coordination unlikely; (2) the likelihood that other providers would enter the market; and (3) the effects of government regulation.

The extent to which the joint venture restricts competition among the hospitals participating in the venture is evaluated during this step. In some cases, a joint venture to purchase or otherwise share the cost of high-technology equipment may not substantially eliminate competition among the hospitals in providing the related service made possible by the equipment. For example, two hospitals might purchase a mobile MRI jointly, but operate and market MRI services separately. In such instances, the potential impact on competition of the joint venture would be substantially reduced.[8]

Step three: Evaluate the impact of procompetitive efficiencies. This step requires an examination of the joint venture's potential to create procompetitive efficiencies, and the balancing of these efficiencies against any potential anticompetitive effects. The greater the venture's likely anticompetitive effects, the greater must be the venture's likely efficiencies. In certain circumstances, efficiencies can be substantial because of the need to spread the cost of expensive equipment over a large number of patients and the potential for improvements in quality to occur as providers gain experience and skill from performing a larger number of procedures.

---

[8] If steps one and two reveal no competitive concerns with the joint venture, step three is unnecessary, and the analysis continues with step four described below.

Step four: Evaluate collateral agreements. This step examines whether the joint venture includes collateral agreements or conditions that unreasonably restrict competition and are unlikely to contribute significantly to the legitimate purposes of the joint venture. The Agencies will examine whether the collateral agreements are reasonably necessary to achieve the efficiencies sought by the joint venture. For example, if the participants in a joint venture formed to purchase a mobile lithotripter also agreed on the daily room rate to be charged lithotripsy patients who required overnight hospitalization, this collateral agreement as to room rates would not be necessary to achieve the benefits of the lithotripter joint venture. Although the joint venture itself would be legal, the collateral agreement on hospital room rates would not be legal and would be subject to challenge.

C. Examples of Hospital High-Technology Joint Ventures

The following are examples of hospital joint ventures that are unlikely to raise significant antitrust concerns. Each is intended to demonstrate an aspect of the analysis that would be used to evaluate the venture.

1. New Equipment That Can Be Offered Only by a Joint Venture

All the hospitals in a relevant market agree that they jointly will purchase, operate and market a helicopter to provide emergency transportation for patients. The community's need for the helicopter is not great enough to justify having more than one helicopter operating in the area and studies of similarly sized communities indicate that a second helicopter service could not be supported. This joint venture falls within the antitrust safety zone. It would make available a service that would not otherwise be available, and for which duplication would be inefficient.

2. Joint Venture to Purchase Expensive Equipment

All five hospitals in a relevant market agree to jointly purchase a mobile health care device that provides a service for which consumers have no reasonable alternatives. The hospitals will share equally in the cost of maintaining the equipment, and the equipment will travel from one hospital to another and be available one day each week at each hospital. The hospitals' agreement contains no provisions for joint marketing of, and protects against exchanges of competitively sensitive information regarding, the equipment.[9] There are also no limitations on the prices that each hospital will charge for use of the equipment, on the number of procedures that each hospital can perform, or on each hospital's ability to purchase the equipment on its own. Although any combination of two of the hospitals could afford to purchase the equipment and recover their costs within the equipment's useful life, patient volume from all five hospitals is required to maximize the efficient use of the equipment and lead to significant cost savings. In addition, patient demand would be satisfied by provision of the equipment one day each week at

---

[9] Examples of such information include prices and marketing plans.

each hospital. The joint venture would result in higher use of the equipment, thus lowering the cost per patient and potentially improving quality.

This joint venture does not fall within the antitrust safety zone because smaller groups of hospitals could afford to purchase and operate the equipment and recover their costs. Therefore, the joint venture would be analyzed under the rule of reason. The first step is to define the relevant market. In this example, the relevant market consists of the services provided by the equipment, and the five hospitals all potentially compete against each other for patients requiring this service.

The second step in the analysis is to determine the competitive effects of the joint venture. Because the joint venture is likely to reduce the number of these health care devices in the market, there is a potential restraint on competition. The restraint would not be substantial, however, for several reasons. First, the joint venture is limited to the purchase of the equipment and would not eliminate competition among the hospitals in the provision of the services. The hospitals will market the services independently, and will not exchange competitively sensitive information. In addition, the venture does not preclude a hospital from purchasing another unit should the demand for these services increase.

Because the joint venture raises some competitive concerns, however, it is necessary to examine the potential efficiencies associated with the venture. As noted above, by sharing the equipment among the five hospitals significant cost savings can be achieved. The joint venture would produce substantial efficiencies while providing access to high quality care. Thus, this joint venture would on balance benefit consumers since it would not lessen competition substantially, and it would allow the hospitals to serve the community's need in a more efficient manner. Finally, in this example the joint venture does not involve any collateral agreements that raise competitive concerns. On these facts, the joint venture would not be challenged by the Agencies.

3. Joint Venture of Existing Expensive Equipment Where One of the Hospitals in the Venture Already Owns the Equipment

Metropolis has three hospitals and a population of 300,000. Mercy and University Hospitals each own and operate their own magnetic resonance imaging device ("MRI"). General Hospital does not. Three independent physician clinics also own and operate MRIs. All of the existing MRIs have similar capabilities. The acquisition of an MRI is not subject to review under a certificate of need law in the state in which Metropolis is located.

Managed care plans have told General Hospital that, unless it can provide MRI services, it will be a less attractive contracting partner than the other two hospitals in town. The five existing MRIs are slightly underutilized—that is, the average cost per scan could be reduced if utilization of the machines increased. There is insufficient demand in Metropolis for six fully-utilized MRIs.

General has considered purchasing its own MRI so that it can compete on equal terms with Mercy and University Hospitals. However, it has decided based on its analysis of demand for MRI services and the cost of acquiring and operating the equipment that it would be better to share the equipment with another hospital. General proposes forming a joint venture in which it will purchase a 50 percent share in Mercy's MRI, and the two hospitals will work out an arrangement by which each hospital has equal access to the MRI. Each hospital in the joint venture will independently market and set prices for those MRI services, and the joint venture agreement protects against exchanges of competitively sensitive information among the hospitals. There is no restriction on the ability of each hospital to purchase its own equipment.

The proposed joint venture does not fall within the antitrust safety zone because General apparently could independently support the purchase and operation of its own MRI. Accordingly, the Agencies would analyze the joint venture under a rule of reason.

The first step of the rule of reason analysis is defining the relevant product and geographic markets. Assuming there are no good substitutes for MRI services, the relevant product market in this case is MRI services. Most patients currently receiving MRI services are unwilling to travel outside of Metropolis for those services, so the relevant geographic market is Metropolis. Mercy, University, and the three physician clinics are already offering MRI services in this market. Because General intends to offer MRI services within the next year, even if there is no joint venture, it is viewed as a market participant.

The second step is determining the competitive impact of the joint venture. Absent the joint venture, there would have been six independent MRIs in the market. This raises some competitive concerns with the joint venture. The fact that the joint venture will not entail joint price setting or marketing of MRI services to purchasers reduces the venture's potential anticompetitive effect. The competitive analysis would also consider the likelihood of additional entry in the market. If, for example, another physician clinic is likely to purchase an MRI in the event that the price of MRI services were to increase, any anticompetitive effect from the joint venture becomes less likely. Entry may be more likely in Metropolis than other areas because new entrants are not required to obtain certificates of need.

The third step of the analysis is assessing the likely efficiencies associated with the joint venture. The magnitude of any likely anticompetitive effects associated with the joint venture is important; the greater the venture's likely anticompetitive effects, the greater must be the venture's likely efficiencies. In this instance, the joint venture will avoid the costly duplication associated with General purchasing an MRI, and will allow Mercy to reduce the average cost of operating its MRI by increasing the number of procedures done. The competition between the Mercy/General venture and the other MRI providers in the market will provide some incentive for the joint venture to operate the MRI in as low-cost a manner as possible. Thus, there are efficiencies associated with the joint venture that could not be achieved in a less restrictive manner.

The final step of the analysis is determining whether the joint venture has any collateral agreements or conditions that reduce competition and are not reasonably necessary to achieve the efficiencies sought by the venture. For example, if the joint venture required managed care plans desiring MRI services to contract with both joint venture participants for those services, that condition would be viewed as anticompetitive and unnecessary to achieve the legitimate procompetitive goals of the joint venture. This example does not include any unnecessary collateral restraints.

On balance, when weighing the likelihood that the joint venture will significantly reduce competition for these services against its potential to result in efficiencies, the Agencies would view this joint venture favorably under a rule of reason analysis.

4. Joint Venture of Existing Equipment Where Both Hospitals in the Venture Already Own the Equipment

Valley Town has a population of 30,000 and is located in a valley surrounded by mountains. The closest urbanized area is over 75 miles away. There are two hospitals in Valley Town: Valley Medical Center and St. Mary's. Valley Medical Center offers a full range of primary and secondary services. St. Mary's offers primary and some secondary services. Although both hospitals have a CT scanner, Valley Medical Center's scanner is more sophisticated. Because of its greater sophistication, Valley Medical Center's scanner is more expensive to operate, and can conduct fewer scans in a day. A physician clinic in Valley Town operates a third CT scanner that is comparable to St. Mary's scanner and is not fully utilized.

Valley Medical Center has found that many of the scans that it conducts do not require the sophisticated features of its scanner. Because scans on its machine take so long, and so many patients require scans, Valley Medical Center also is experiencing significant scheduling problems. St. Mary's scanner, on the other hand, is underutilized, partially because many individuals go to Valley Medical Center because they need the more sophisticated scans that only Valley Medical Center's scanner can provide. Despite the underutilization of St. Mary's scanner, and the higher costs of Valley Medical Center's scanner, neither hospital has any intention of discontinuing its CT services. Valley Medical Center and St. Mary's are proposing a joint venture that would own and operate both hospitals' CT scanners. The two hospitals will then independently market and set the prices they charge for those services, and the joint venture agreement protects against exchanges of competitively sensitive information between the hospitals. There is no restriction on the ability of each hospital to purchase its own equipment.

The proposed joint venture does not qualify under the Agencies' safety zone because the participating hospitals can independently support their own equipment. Accordingly, the Agencies would analyze the joint venture under a rule of reason. The first step of the analysis is to determine the relevant product and geographic markets. As long as other diagnostic services such as conventional X-rays or MRI scans are not viewed as a good substitute for CT scans, the relevant product market is CT scans. If patients currently receiving CT scans in Valley Town would be unlikely to switch to providers offering CT scans outside of Valley Town in the event that the price of CT scans in Valley Town increased by a small but significant amount, the relevant geographic market is Valley Town. There are three participants in this relevant market: Valley Medical Center, St. Mary's, and the physician clinic.

The second step of the analysis is determining the competitive effect of the joint venture. Because the joint venture does not entail joint pricing or marketing of CT services, the joint venture does not effectively reduce the number of market participants. This reduces the venture's potential anticompetitive effect. In fact, by increasing the scope of the CT services that each hospital can provide, the joint venture may increase competition between Valley Medical Center and St. Mary's since now both hospitals can provide sophisticated scans. Competitive concerns with this joint venture would be further ameliorated if other health care providers were likely to acquire CT scanners in response to a price increase following the formation of the joint venture.

The third step is assessing whether the efficiencies associated with the joint venture outweigh any anticompetitive effect associated with the joint venture. This joint venture will allow both hospitals to make either the sophisticated CT scanner or the less sophisticated, but less costly, CT scanner available to patients at those hospitals.

Thus, the joint venture should increase quality of care by allowing for better utilization and scheduling of the equipment, while also reducing the cost of providing that care, thereby benefitting the community. The joint venture may also increase quality of care by making more capacity available to Valley Medical Center; while Valley Medical Center faced capacity constraints prior to the joint venture, it can now take advantage of St. Mary's underutilized CT scanner. The joint venture will also improve access by allowing patients requiring routine scans to be moved from the sophisticated scanner at Valley Medical Center to St. Mary's scanner where the scans can be performed more quickly.

The last step of the analysis is to determine whether there are any collateral agreements or conditions associated with the joint venture that reduce competition and are not reasonably necessary to achieve the efficiencies sought by the joint venture. Assuming there are no such agreements or conditions, the Agencies would view this joint venture favorably under a rule of reason analysis.

As noted in the previous example, excluding price setting and marketing from the scope of the joint venture reduces the probability and magnitude of any anticompetitive effect of the joint venture, and thus reduces the likelihood that the Agencies will find the joint venture to be anticompetitive. If joint price setting and marketing were, however, a part of that joint venture, the Agencies would have to determine whether the cost savings and quality improvements associated with the joint venture offset the loss of competition between the two hospitals. Also, if neither of the hospitals in Valley Town had a CT scanner, and they proposed a similar joint venture for the purchase of two CT scanners, one sophisticated and one less sophisticated, the Agencies would be unlikely to view that joint venture as anticompetitive, even though each hospital could independently support the purchase of its own CT scanner. This conclusion would be based upon a rule of reason analysis that was virtually identical to the one described above.

* * *

Hospitals that are considering high-technology or other expensive equipment joint ventures and are unsure of the legality of their conduct under the antitrust laws can take advantage of the Department's expedited business review procedure for joint ventures and information exchanges announced on December 1, 1992 (58 Fed. Reg. 6132 (1993)) or the Federal Trade Commission's advisory opinion procedure contained at 16 C.F.R. §§ 1.1-1.4 (1993). The Agencies will respond to a business review or advisory opinion request on behalf of hospitals that are considering a high-technology joint venture within 90 days after all necessary information is submitted. The Department's December 1, 1992 announcement contains specific guidance as to the information that should be submitted.

* * *

Appendix C

United States Department of Justice and Federal Trade Commission Horizontal Merger Guidelines (1992), as Revised (1997)*

[The Department of Justice has promulgated three complete sets of guidelines relating to mergers and acquisitions. The first such policy statement was issued in 1968 and addressed the conditions under which the Department would oppose a given merger. These guidelines have never been modified or revoked. In 1982, a new set of guidelines was issued to reflect changed economic assumptions and perspectives about mergers. The 1982 horizontal merger guidelines departed materially from the legal and economic analysis contained in the 1968 guidelines. Clarifications and refinements of the 1982 guidelines were issued in 1984. In 1992, for the first time, the Department of Justice and the Federal Trade Commission joined in promulgating horizontal merger guidelines. These guidelines were offered as a framework of analysis of the adverse competitive effects of a given merger. On April 8, 1997, a revision of Section 4 of the 1992 guidelines, which deals with efficiency considerations, was jointly issued. The 1992 guidelines, complete with the 1997 revision, are reproduced below.]

The U.S. Department of Justice ("Department") and Federal Trade Commission ("Commission") today jointly issued Horizontal Merger Guidelines revising the Department's 1984 Merger Guidelines and the Commission's 1982 Statement Concerning Horizontal Merger Guidelines. The release marks the first time that the two federal agencies that share antitrust enforcement jurisdiction have issued joint guidelines.

Central to the 1992 Department of Justice and Federal Trade Commission Horizontal Merger Guidelines is a recognition that sound merger enforcement is an essential component of our free enterprise system benefitting the competitiveness of American firms and the welfare of American consumers. Sound merger enforcement must prevent anticompetitive mergers yet avoid deterring the larger universe of procompetitive or competitively neutral mergers. The 1992 Horizontal Merger Guidelines implement this objective by describing the analytical foundations of merger enforcement and providing guidance enabling the business community to avoid antitrust problems when planning mergers. The Department first released Merger Guidelines in 1968 in order to inform the business community of the analysis applied by the Department to mergers under the federal antitrust laws. The 1968 Merger Guidelines eventually fell into disuse, both internally and exter-

* *See* Appendix B, *supra* page 1089 n.1.

nally, as they were eclipsed by developments in legal and economic thinking about mergers.

In 1982, the Department released revised Merger Guidelines which, reflecting those developments, departed dramatically from the 1968 version. Relative to the Department's actual practice, however, the 1982 Merger Guidelines represented an evolutionary not revolutionary change. On the same date, the Commission released its Statement Concerning Horizontal Mergers highlighting the principal considerations guiding the Commission's horizontal merger enforcement and noting the "considerable weight" given by the Commission to the Department's 1982 Merger Guidelines.

The Department's current Merger Guidelines, released in 1984, refined and clarified the analytical framework of the 1982 Merger Guidelines. Although the agencies' experience with the 1982 Merger Guidelines reaffirmed the soundness of its underlying principles, the Department concluded that there remained room for improvement.

The revisions embodied in the 1992 Horizontal Merger Guidelines reflect the next logical step in the development of the agencies' analysis of mergers. They reflect the Department's experience in applying the 1982 and 1984 Merger Guidelines as well as the Commission's experience in applying those guidelines and the Commission's 1982 Statement. Both the Department and the Commission believed that their respective Guidelines and Statement presented sound frameworks for antitrust analysis of mergers, but that improvements could be made to reflect advances in legal and economic thinking. The 1992 Horizontal Merger Guidelines accomplish this objective and also clarify certain aspects of the Merger Guidelines that proved to be ambiguous or were interpreted by observers in ways that were inconsistent with the actual policy of the agencies.

The 1992 Horizontal Merger Guidelines do not include a discussion of horizontal effects from non-horizontal mergers (e.g., elimination of specific potential entrants and competitive problems from vertical mergers). Neither agency has changed its policy with respect to non-horizontal mergers. Specific guidance on non-horizontal mergers is provided in Section 4 of the Department's 1984 Merger Guidelines, read in the context of today's revisions to the treatment of horizontal mergers.

A number of today's revisions are largely technical or stylistic. One major objective of the revisions is to strengthen the document as an analytical road map for the evaluation of mergers. The language, therefore, is intended to be burden-neutral, without altering the burdens of proof or burdens of coming forward as those standards have been established by the courts. In addition, the revisions principally address two areas.

The most significant revision to the Merger Guidelines is to explain more clearly how mergers may lead to adverse competitive effects and how particular market factors relate to the analysis of those effects. These revisions are found in Section 2 of the Horizontal Merger Guidelines. The second principal revision is to sharpen the distinction between the treatment of various types of supply responses and to articulate the framework for analyzing the timeliness, likelihood and sufficiency of entry. These revisions are found in Sections 1.3 and 3.

The new Horizontal Merger Guidelines observe, as did the 1984 Guidelines, that because the specific standards they set out must be applied in widely varied factual circumstances, mechanical application of those standards could produce misleading results. Thus, the Guidelines state that the agencies will apply those standards reasonably and flexibly to the particular facts and circumstances of each proposed merger.

* * *

Guidelines

0. Purpose, Underlying Policy Assumptions and Overview

These Guidelines outline the present enforcement policy of the Department of Justice and the Federal Trade Commission (the "Agency") concerning horizontal acquisitions and mergers ("mergers") subject to section 7 of the Clayton Act,[1] to section 1 of the Sherman Act,[2] or to section 5 of the FTC Act.[3] They describe the analytical framework and specific standards normally used by the Agency in analyzing mergers.[4] By stating its policy as simply and clearly as possible, the Agency hopes to reduce the uncertainty associated with enforcement of the antitrust laws in this area.

Although the Guidelines should improve the predictability of the Agency's merger enforcement policy, it is not possible to remove the exercise of judgment from the evaluation of mergers under the antitrust laws. Because the specific standards set forth in the Guidelines must be applied to a broad range of possible factual circumstances, mechanical application of those standards may provide misleading answers to the economic questions raised under the antitrust laws. Moreover, information is often incomplete and the picture of competitive conditions that develops from historical evidence may provide an incomplete answer to the forward-looking inquiry of the Guidelines. Therefore, the Agency will apply the standards of the Guidelines reasonably and flexibly to the particular facts and circumstances of each proposed merger.

---

[1] 15 U.S.C. Section 18 (1988). Mergers subject to section 7 are prohibited if their effect "may be substantially to lessen competition, or to tend to create a monopoly."

[2] 15 U.S.C. Section 1 (1988). Mergers subject to section 1 are prohibited if they constitute a "contract, combination or conspiracy in restraint of trade."

[3] 15 U.S.C. Section 45 (1988). Mergers subject to section 5 are prohibited if they constitute an "unfair method of competition."

[4] These Guidelines update the Merger Guidelines issued by the U.S. Department of Justice in 1984 and the Statement of Federal Trade Commission Concerning Horizontal Mergers issued in 1982. The Merger Guidelines may be revised from time to time as necessary to reflect any significant changes in enforcement policy or to clarify aspects of existing policy.

0.1 Purpose and Underlying Policy Assumptions of the Guidelines

The Guidelines are designed primarily to articulate the analytical framework the Agency applies in determining whether a merger is likely substantially to lessen competition, not to describe how the Agency will conduct the litigation of cases that it decides to bring. Although relevant in the latter context, the factors contemplated in the Guidelines neither dictate nor exhaust the range of evidence that the Agency must or may introduce in litigation. Consistent with their objective, the Guidelines do not attempt to assign the burden of proof, or the burden of coming forward with evidence, on any particular issue. Nor do the Guidelines attempt to adjust or reapportion burdens of proof or burdens of coming forward as those standards have been established by the courts.[5] Instead, the Guidelines set forth a methodology for analyzing issues once the necessary facts are available. The necessary facts may be derived from the documents and statements of both the merging firms and other sources.

Throughout the Guidelines, the analysis is focused on whether consumers or producers "likely would" take certain actions, that is, whether the action is in the actor's economic interest. References to the profitability of certain actions focus on economic profits rather than accounting profits. Economic profits may be defined as the excess of revenues over costs where costs include the opportunity cost of invested capital.

Mergers are motivated by the prospect of financial gains. The possible sources of the financial gains from mergers are many, and the Guidelines do not attempt to identify all possible sources of gain in every merger. Instead, the Guidelines focus on the one potential source of gain that is of concern under the antitrust laws: market power.

The unifying theme of the Guidelines is that mergers should not be permitted to create or enhance market power or to facilitate its exercise. Market power to a seller is the ability profitably to maintain prices above competitive levels for a significant period of time.[6] In some circumstances, a sole seller (a "monopolist") of a product with no good substitutes can maintain a selling price that is above the level that would prevail if the market were competitive. Similarly, in some circumstances, where only a few firms account for most of the sales of a product, those firms can exercise market power, perhaps even approximating the performance of a monopolist, by either explicitly or implicitly coordinating their actions. Circumstances also may permit a single firm, not a monopolist, to exercise market power through unilateral or non-coordinated conduct—conduct the success of which does not rely on the concurrence of other firms in the market or on coordinated responses by those firms. In any case, the result of the exercise of market power is a transfer of wealth from buyers to sellers or a misallocation of resources.

---

[5] For example, the burden with respect to efficiency and failure continues to reside with the proponents of the merger.

[6] Sellers with market power also may lessen competition on dimensions other than price, such as product quality, service, or innovation.

Market power also encompasses the ability of a single buyer (a "monopsonist"), a coordinating group of buyers, or a single buyer, not a monopsonist, to depress the price paid for a product to a level that is below the competitive price and thereby depress output. The exercise of market power by buyers ("monopsony power") has adverse effects comparable to those associated with the exercise of market power by sellers. In order to assess potential monopsony concerns, the Agency will apply an analytical framework analogous to the framework of these Guidelines.

While challenging competitively harmful mergers, the Agency seeks to avoid unnecessary interference with the larger universe of mergers that are either competitively beneficial or neutral. In implementing this objective, however, the Guidelines reflect the congressional intent that merger enforcement should interdict competitive problems in their incipiency.

0.2 Overview

The Guidelines describe the analytical process that the Agency will employ in determining whether to challenge a horizontal merger. First, the Agency assesses whether the merger would significantly increase concentration and result in a concentrated market, properly defined and measured. Second, the Agency assesses whether the merger, in light of market concentration and other factors that characterize the market, raises concern about potential adverse competitive effects. Third, the Agency assesses whether entry would be timely, likely and sufficient either to deter or to counteract the competitive effects of concern. Fourth, the Agency assesses any efficiency gains that reasonably cannot be achieved by the parties through other means. Finally the Agency assesses whether, but for the merger, either party to the transaction would be likely to fail, causing its assets to exit the market. The process of assessing market concentration, potential adverse competitive effects, entry, efficiency and failure is a tool that allows the Agency to answer the ultimate inquiry in merger analysis: whether the merger is likely to create or enhance market power or to facilitate its exercise.

1. Market Definition, Measurement and Concentration

1.0 Overview

A merger is unlikely to create or enhance market power or to facilitate its exercise unless it significantly increases concentration and results in a concentrated market, properly defined and measured. Mergers that either do not significantly increase concentration or do not result in a concentrated market ordinarily require no further analysis.

The analytic process described in this section ensures that the Agency evaluates the likely competitive impact of a merger within the context of economically meaningful markets—i.e., markets that could be subject to the exercise of market power. Accordingly, for each product or service (hereafter "product") of each merging firm, the Agency seeks to define a market in which firms could effectively exercise market power if they were able to coordinate their actions.

Market definition focuses solely on demand substitution factors—i.e., possible consumer responses. Supply substitution factors—i.e., possible production responses—are considered elsewhere in the Guidelines in the identification of firms that participate in the relevant market and the analysis of entry. See Sections 1.3 and 3. A market is defined as a product or group of products and a geographic area in which it is produced or sold such that a hypothetical profit-maximizing firm, not subject to price regulation, that was the only present and future producer or seller of those products in that area likely would impose at least a "small but significant and nontransitory" increase in price, assuming the terms of sale of all other products are held constant. A relevant market is a group of products and a geographic area that is no bigger than necessary to satisfy this test. The "small but significant and non-transitory" increase in price is employed solely as a methodological tool for the analysis of mergers: it is not a tolerance level for price increases.

Absent price discrimination, a relevant market is described by a product or group of products and a geographic area. In determining whether a hypothetical monopolist would be in a position to exercise market power, it is necessary to evaluate the likely demand responses of consumers to a price increase. A price increase could be made unprofitable by consumers either switching to other products or switching to the same product produced by firms at other locations. The nature and magnitude of these two types of demand responses respectively determine the scope of the product market and the geographic market.

In contrast, where a hypothetical monopolist likely would discriminate in prices charged to different groups of buyers, distinguished, for example, by their uses or locations, the Agency may delineate different relevant markets corresponding to each such buyer group. Competition for sales to each such group may be affected differently by a particular merger and markets are delineated by evaluating the demand response of each such buyer group. A relevant market of this kind is described by a collection of products for sale to a given group of buyers.

Once defined, a relevant market must be measured in terms of its participants and concentration. Participants include firms currently producing or selling the market's products in the market's geographic area. In addition, participants may include other firms depending on their likely supply responses to a "small but significant and nontransitory" price increase. A firm is viewed as a participant if, in response to a "small but significant and nontransitory" price increase, it likely would enter rapidly into production or sale of a market product in the market's area, without incurring significant sunk costs of entry and exit. Firms likely to make any of these supply responses are considered to be "uncommitted" entrants because their supply response would create new production or sale in the relevant market and because that production or sale could be quickly terminated without significant loss.[7] Uncommitted entrants are capable of making such quick and uncommitted

---

[7] Probable supply responses that require the entrant to incur significant sunk costs of entry and exit are not part of market measurement, but are included in the analysis of the significance of entry. See Section 3. Entrants that must commit substantial sunk costs are regarded as "committed" entrants because those sunk costs make entry irreversible in the short term without foregoing that investment; thus the likelihood of their entry must be evaluated with regard to their long-term profitability.

supply responses that they likely influenced the market premerger, would influence it post-merger, and accordingly are considered as market participants at both times. This analysis of market definition and market measurement applies equally to foreign and domestic firms.

If the process of market definition and market measurement identifies one or more relevant markets in which the merging firms are both participants, then the merger is considered to be horizontal. Sections 1.1 through 1.5 describe in greater detail how product and geographic markets will be defined, how market shares will be calculated and how market concentration will be assessed.

1.1 Product Market Definition

The Agency will first define the relevant product market with respect to each of the products of each of the merging firms.[8]

1.11 General Standards

Absent price discrimination, the Agency will delineate the product market to be a product or group of products such that a hypothetical profit-maximizing firm that was the only present and future seller of those products ("monopolist") likely would impose at least a "small but significant and nontransitory" increase in price. That is, assuming that buyers likely would respond to an increase in price for a tentatively identified product group only by shifting to other products, what would happen? If the alternatives were, in the aggregate, sufficiently attractive at their existing terms of sale, an attempt to raise prices would result in a reduction of sales large enough that the price increase would not prove profitable, and the tentatively identified product group would prove to be too narrow.

Specifically, the Agency will begin with each product (narrowly defined) produced or sold by each merging firm and ask what would happen if a hypothetical monopolist of that product imposed at least a "small but significant and nontransitory" increase in price, but the terms of sale of all other products remained constant. If, in response to the price increase, the reduction in sales of the product would be large enough that a hypothetical monopolist would not find it profitable to impose such an increase in price, then the Agency will add to the product group the product that is the next-best substitute for the merging firm's product.[9]

In considering the likely reaction of buyers to a price increase, the Agency will take into account all relevant evidence, including, but not limited to, the following:

---

[8] Although discussed separately, product market definition and geographic market definition are interrelated. In particular, the extent to which buyers of a particular product would shift to other products in the event of a "small but significant and nontransitory" increase in price must be evaluated in the context of the relevant geographic market.

[9] Throughout the Guidelines, the term "next best substitute" refers to the alternative which, if available in unlimited quantities at constant prices, would account for the greatest value of diversion of demand in response to a "small but significant and nontransitory" price increase.

(1) evidence that buyers have shifted or have considered shifting purchases between products in response to relative changes in price or other competitive variables;
(2) evidence that sellers base business decisions on the prospect of buyer substitution between products in response to relative changes in price or other competitive variables;
(3) the influence of downstream competition faced by buyers in their output markets; and
(4) the timing and costs of switching products.

The price increase question is then asked for a hypothetical monopolist controlling the expanded product group. In performing successive iterations of the price increase test, the hypothetical monopolist will be assumed to pursue maximum profits in deciding whether to raise the prices of any or all of the additional products under its control. This process will continue until a group of products is identified such that a hypothetical monopolist over that group of products would profitably impose at least a "small but significant and nontransitory" increase, including the price of a product of one of the merging firms. The Agency generally will consider the relevant product market to be the smallest group of products that satisfies this test.

In the above analysis, the Agency will use prevailing prices of the products of the merging firms and possible substitutes for such products, unless premerger circumstances are strongly suggestive of coordinated interaction, in which case the Agency will use a price more reflective of the competitive price.[10] However, the Agency may use likely future prices, absent the merger, when changes in the prevailing prices can be predicted with reasonable reliability. Changes in price may be predicted on the basis of, for example, changes in regulation which affect price either directly or indirectly by affecting costs or demand.

In general, the price for which an increase will be postulated will be whatever is considered to be the price of the product at the stage of the industry being examined.[11] In attempting to determine objectively the effect of a "small but significant and nontransitory" increase in price, the Agency, in most contexts, will use a price increase of five percent lasting for the foreseeable future. However, what constitutes a "small but significant and nontransitory" increase in price will depend on the nature of the industry, and the Agency at times may use a price increase that is larger or smaller than five percent.

1.12 Product Market Definition in the Presence of Price Discrimination

The analysis of product market definition to this point has assumed that price discrimination—charging different buyers different prices for the same product, for

---

[10] The terms of sale of all other products are held constant in order to focus market definition on the behavior of consumers. Movements in the terms of sale for other products, as may result from the behavior of producers of those products, are accounted for in the analysis of competitive effects and entry. *See* Sections 2 and 3.

[11] For example, in a merger between retailers, the relevant price would be the retail price of a product to consumers. In the case of a merger among oil pipelines, the relevant price would be the tariff—the price of the transportation service.

example—would not be profitable for a hypothetical monopolist. A different analysis applies where price discrimination would be profitable for a hypothetical monopolist.

Existing buyers sometimes will differ significantly in their likelihood of switching to other products in response to a "small but significant and nontransitory" price increase. If a hypothetical monopolist can identify and price differently to those buyers ("targeted buyers") who would not defeat the targeted price increase by substituting to other products in response to a "small but significant and nontransitory" price increase for the relevant product, and if other buyers likely would not purchase the relevant product and resell to targeted buyers, then a hypothetical monopolist would profitably impose a discriminatory price increase on sales to targeted buyers. This is true regardless of whether a general increase in price would cause such significant substitution that the price increase would not be profitable. The Agency will consider additional relevant product markets consisting of a particular use or uses by groups of buyers of the product for which a hypothetical monopolist would profitably and separately impose at least a "small but significant and nontransitory" increase in price.

1.2 Geographic Market Definition

For each product market in which both merging firms participate, the Agency will determine the geographic market or markets in which the firms produce or sell. A single firm may operate in a number of different geographic markets.

1.21 General Standards

Absent price discrimination, the Agency will delineate the geographic market to be a region such that a hypothetical monopolist that was the only present or future producer of the relevant product at locations in that region would profitably impose at least a "small but significant and nontransitory" increase in price, holding constant the terms of sale for all products produced elsewhere. That is, assuming that buyers likely would respond to a price increase on products produced within the tentatively identified region only by shifting to products produced at locations of production outside the region, what would happen? If those locations of production outside the region were, in the aggregate, sufficiently attractive at their existing terms of sale, an attempt to raise price would result in a reduction in sales large enough that the price increase would not prove profitable, and the tentatively identified geographic area would prove to be too narrow.

In defining the geographic market or markets affected by a merger, the Agency will begin with the location of each merging firm (or each plant of a multiplant firm) and ask what would happen if a hypothetical monopolist of the relevant product at that point imposed at least a "small but significant and nontransitory" increase in price, but the terms of sale at all other locations remained constant. If, in response to the price increase, the reduction in sales of the product at that location would be large enough that a hypothetical monopolist producing or selling the relevant product at the merging firm's location would not find it profitable to impose such an increase in price, then the Agency will add the location from which production is the next-best substitute for production at the merging firm's location.

In considering the likely reaction of buyers to a price increase, the Agency will take into account all relevant evidence, including, but not limited to, the following:

(1) evidence that buyers have shifted or have considered shifting purchases between different geographic locations in response to relative changes in price or other competitive variables;
(2) evidence that sellers base business decisions on the prospect of buyer substitution between geographic locations in response to relative changes in price or other competitive variables;
(3) the influence of downstream competition faced by buyers in their output markets; and
(4) the timing and costs of switching suppliers.

The price increase question is then asked for a hypothetical monopolist controlling the expanded group of locations. In performing successive iterations of the price increase test, the hypothetical monopolist will be assumed to pursue maximum profits in deciding whether to raise the price at any or all of the additional locations under its control. This process will continue until a group of locations is identified such that a hypothetical monopolist over that group of locations would profitably impose at least a "small but significant and nontransitory" increase, including the price charged at a location of one of the merging firms.

The "smallest market" principle will be applied as it is in product market definition. The price for which an increase will be postulated, what constitutes a "small but significant and nontransitory" increase in price, and the substitution decisions of consumers all will be determined in the same way in which they are determined in product market definition.

1.22 Geographic Market Definition in the Presence of Price Discrimination

The analysis of geographic market definition to this point has assumed that geographic price discrimination—charging different prices net of transportation costs for the same product to buyers in different areas, for example—would not be profitable for a hypothetical monopolist. However, if a hypothetical monopolist can identify and price differently to buyers in certain areas ("targeted buyers") who would not defeat the targeted price increase by substituting to more distant sellers in response to a "small but significant and nontransitory" price increase for the relevant product, and if other buyers likely would not purchase the relevant product and resell to targeted buyers,[12] then a hypothetical monopolist would profitably impose a discriminatory price increase. This is true even where a general price increase would cause such significant substitution that the price increase would not

---

12 This arbitrage is inherently impossible for many services and is particularly difficult where the product is sold on a delivered basis and where transportation costs are a significant percentage of the final cost.

be profitable. The Agency will consider additional geographic markets consisting of particular locations of buyers for which a hypothetical monopolist would profitably and separately impose at least a "small but significant and nontransitory" increase in price.

1.3 Identification of Firms that Participate in the Relevant Market

1.31 Current Producers or Sellers

The Agency's identification of firms that participate in the relevant market begins with all firms that currently produce or sell in the relevant market. This includes vertically integrated firms to the extent that such inclusion accurately reflects their competitive significance in the relevant market prior to the merger. To the extent that the analysis under Section 1.1 indicates that used, reconditioned or recycled goods are included in the relevant market, market participants will include firms that produce or sell such goods and that likely would offer those goods in competition with other relevant products.

1.32 Firms That Participate Through Supply Response

In addition, the Agency will identify other firms not currently producing or selling the relevant product in the relevant area as participating in the relevant market if their inclusion would more accurately reflect probable supply responses. These firms are termed "uncommitted entrants." These supply responses must be likely to occur within one year and without the expenditure of significant sunk costs of entry and exit, in response to a "small but significant and nontransitory" price increase. If a firm has the technological capability to achieve such an uncommitted supply response, but likely would not (*e.g.*, because difficulties in achieving product acceptance, distribution, or production would render such a response unprofitable), that firm will not be considered to be a market participant. The competitive significance of supply responses that require more time or that require firms to incur significant sunk costs of entry and exit will be considered in entry analysis. *See* Section 3.[13]

Sunk costs are the acquisition costs of tangible and intangible assets that cannot be recovered through the redeployment of these assets outside the relevant market, i.e., costs uniquely incurred to supply the relevant product and geographic market. Examples of sunk costs may include market-specific investments in production facilities, technologies, marketing (including product acceptance), research and development, regulatory approvals, and testing. A significant sunk cost is one which would not be recouped within one year of the commencement of the supply response, assuming a "small but significant and nontransitory" price increase in the relevant market. In this context, a "small but significant and nontransitory" price

---

13 If uncommitted entrants likely would also remain in the market and would meet the entry tests of timeliness, likelihood and sufficiency, and thus would likely deter anticompetitive mergers or deter or counteract the competitive effects of concern (see Section 3, infra), the Agency will consider the impact of those firms in the entry analysis.

increase will be determined in the same way in which it is determined in product market definition, except the price increase will be assumed to last one year. In some instances, it may be difficult to calculate sunk costs with precision. Accordingly, when necessary, the Agency will make an overall assessment of the extent of sunk costs for firms likely to participate through supply responses.

These supply responses may give rise to new production of products in the relevant product market or new sources of supply in the relevant geographic market. Alternatively, where price discrimination is likely so that the relevant market is defined in terms of a targeted group of buyers, these supply responses serve to identify new sellers to the targeted buyers. Uncommitted supply responses may occur in several different ways: by the switching or extension of existing assets to production or sale in the relevant market; or by the construction or acquisition of assets that enable production or sale in the relevant market.

1.321 Production Substitution and Extension: The Switching or Extension of Existing Assets to Production or Sale in the Relevant Market

The productive and distributive assets of a firm sometimes can be used to produce and sell either the relevant products or products that buyers do not regard as good substitutes. Production substitution refers to the shift by a firm in the use of assets from producing and selling one product to producing and selling another. Production extension refers to the use of those assets, for example, existing brand names and reputation, both for their current production and for production of the relevant product. Depending upon the speed of that shift and the extent of sunk costs incurred in the shift or extension, the potential for production substitution or extension may necessitate treating as market participants firms that do not currently produce the relevant product.[14]

If a firm has existing assets that likely would be shifted or extended into production and sale of the relevant product within one year, and without incurring significant sunk costs of entry and exit, in response to a "small but significant and nontransitory" increase in price for only the relevant product, the Agency will treat that firm as a market participant. In assessing whether a firm is such a market participant, the Agency will take into account the costs of substitution or extension relative to the profitability of sales at the elevated price, and whether the firm's capacity is elsewhere committed or elsewhere so profitably employed that such capacity likely would not be available to respond to an increase in price in the market.

---

[14] Under other analytical approaches, production substitution sometimes has been reflected in the description of the product market. For example, the product market for stamped metal products such as automobile hub caps might be described as "light metal stamping," a production process rather than a product. The Agency believes that the approach described in the text provides a more clearly focused method of incorporating this factor in merger analysis. If production substitution among a group of products is nearly universal among the firms selling one or more of those products, however, the Agency may use an aggregate description of those markets as a matter of convenience.

1.322 Obtaining New Assets for Production or Sale of the Relevant Product

A firm may also be able to enter into production or sale in the relevant market within one year and without the expenditure of significant sunk costs of entry and exit, in response to a "small but significant and nontransitory" increase in price for only the relevant product, even if the firm is newly organized or is an existing firm without products or productive assets closely related to the relevant market. If new firms, or existing firms without closely related products or productive assets, likely would enter into production or sale in the relevant market within one year without the expenditure of significant sunk costs of entry and exit, the Agency will treat those firms as market participants.

1.4 Calculating Market Shares

1.41 General Approach

The Agency normally will calculate market shares for all firms (or plants) identified as market participants in Section 1.3 based on the total sales or capacity currently devoted to the relevant market together with that which likely would be devoted to the relevant market in response to a "small but significant and nontransitory" price increase. Market shares can be expressed either in dollar terms through measurement of sales, shipments, or production, or in physical terms through measurement of sales, shipments, production, capacity, or reserves.

Market shares will be calculated using the best indicator of firms' future competitive significance. Dollar sales or shipments generally will be used if firms are distinguished primarily by differentiation of their products. Unit sales generally will be used if firms are distinguished primarily on the basis of their relative advantages in serving different buyers or groups of buyers. Physical capacity or reserves generally will be used if it is these measures that most effectively distinguish firms.[15] Typically, annual data are used, but where individual sales are large and infrequent so that annual data may be unrepresentative, the Agency may measure market shares over a longer period of time.

In measuring a firm's market share, the Agency will not include its sales or capacity to the extent that the firm's capacity is committed or so profitably employed outside the relevant market that it would not be available to respond to an increase in price in the market.

1.42 Price Discrimination Markets

When markets are defined on the basis of price discrimination (Sections 1.12 and 1.22), the Agency will include only sales likely to be made into, or capacity likely to be used to supply, the relevant market in response to a "small but significant and nontransitory" price increase.

---

15 Where all firms have, on a forward-looking basis, an equal likelihood of securing sales, the Agency will assign firms equal shares.

1.43 Special Factors Affecting Foreign Firms

Market shares will be assigned to foreign competitors in the same way in which they are assigned to domestic competitors. However, if exchange rates fluctuate significantly, so that comparable dollar calculations on an annual basis may be unrepresentative, the Agency may measure market shares over a period longer than one year.

If shipments from a particular country to the United States are subject to a quota, the market shares assigned to firms in that country will not exceed the amount of shipments by such firms allowed under the quota.[16] In the case of restraints that limit imports to some percentage of the total amount of the product sold in the United States (*i.e.*, percentage quotas), a domestic price increase that reduced domestic consumption also would reduce the volume of imports into the United States. Accordingly, actual import sales and capacity data will be reduced for purposes of calculating market shares. Finally, a single market share may be assigned to a country or group of countries if firms in that country or group of countries act in coordination.

1.5 Concentration and Market Shares

Market concentration is a function of the number of firms in a market and their respective market shares. As an aid to the interpretation of market data, the Agency will use the Herfindahl-Hirschman Index ("HHI") of market concentration. The HHI is calculated by summing the squares of the individual market shares of all the participants.[17] Unlike the four-firm concentration ratio, the HHI reflects both the distribution of the market shares of the top four firms and the composition of the market outside the top four firms. It also gives proportionately greater weight to the market shares of the larger firms, in accord with their relative importance in competitive interactions.

The Agency divides the spectrum of market concentration as measured by the HHI into three regions that can be broadly characterized as unconcentrated (HHI below 1000), moderately concentrated (HHI between 1000 and 1800), and highly concentrated (HHI above 1800). Although the resulting regions provide a useful framework for merger analysis, the numerical divisions suggest greater precision than is possible with the available economic tools and information. Other things being equal, cases falling just above and just below a threshold present comparable competitive issues.

---

16 The constraining effect of the quota on the importer's ability to expand sales is relevant to the evaluation of potential adverse competitive effects. *See* Section 2.

17 For example, a market consisting of four firms with market shares of 30 percent, 30 percent, 20 percent and 20 percent has an HHI of 2600 ($30^2 + 30^2 + 20^2 + 20^2 = 2600$). The HHI ranges from 10,000 (in the case of a pure monopoly) to a number approaching zero (in the case of an atomistic market). Although it is desirable to include all firms in the calculation, lack of information about small firms is not critical because such firms do not affect the HHI significantly.

1.51 General Standards

In evaluating horizontal mergers, the Agency will consider both the post-merger market concentration and the increase in concentration resulting from the merger.[18] Market concentration is a useful indicator of the likely potential competitive effect of a merger. The general standards for horizontal mergers are as follows:

a) Post-Merger HHI Below 1000. The Agency regards markets in this region to be unconcentrated. Mergers resulting in unconcentrated markets are unlikely to have adverse competitive effects and ordinarily require no further analysis.

b) Post-Merger HHI Between 1000 and 1800. The Agency regards markets in this region to be moderately concentrated. Mergers producing an increase in the HHI of less than 100 points in moderately concentrated markets post-merger are unlikely to have adverse competitive consequences and ordinarily require no further analysis. Mergers prodcing an increase in the HHI of more than 100 points in moderately concentrated markets post-merger potentially raise significant competitive concerns depending on the factors set forth in Sections 2-5 of the Guidelines.

c) Post-Merger HHI Above 1800. The Agency regards markets in this region to be highly concentrated. Mergers producing an increase in the HHI of less than 50 points, even in highly concentrated markets post-merger, are unlikely to have adverse competitive consequences and ordinarily require no further analysis. Mergers producing an increase in the HHI of more than 50 points in highly concentrated markets post-merger potentially raise significant competitive concerns, depending on the factors set forth in Sections 2-5 of the Guidelines. Where the post-merger HHI exceeds 1800, it will be presumed that mergers producing an increase in the HHI of more than 100 points are likely to create or enhance market power or facilitate its exercise. The presumption may be overcome by a showing that factors set forth in Sections 2-5 of the Guidelines make it unlikely that the merger will create or enhance market power or facilitate its exercise, in light of market concentration and market shares.

1.52 Factors Affecting the Significance of Market Shares and Concentration

The post-merger level of market concentration and the change in concentration resulting from a merger affect the degree to which a merger raises competitive concerns. However, in some situations, market share and market concentration data may either understate or overstate the likely future competitive significance of a firm or firms in the market or the impact of a merger. The following are examples of such situations.

---

[18] The increase in concentration as measured by the HHI can be calculated independently of the overall market concentration by doubling the product of the market shares of the merging firms. For example, the merger of firms with shares of 5 percent and 10 percent of the market would increase the HHI by 100 (5 x 10 x 2 = 100). The explanation for this technique is as follows: In calculating the HHI before the merger, the market shares of the merging firms are squared individually: $(a)^2 + (b)^2$. After the merger, the sum of those shares would be squared: $(a + b)^2$, which equals $a^2 + 2ab + b^2$. The increase in the HHI therefore is represented by 2ab.

1.521 Changing Market Conditions

Market concentration and market share data of necessity are based on historical evidence. However, recent or ongoing changes in the market may indicate that the current market share of a particular firm either understates or overstates the firm's future competitive significance. For example, if a new technology that is important to long-term competitive viability is available to other firms in the market, but is not available to a particular firm, the Agency may conclude that the historical market share of that firm overstates its future competitive significance. The Agency will consider reasonably predictable effects of recent or ongoing changes in market conditions in interpreting market concentration and market share data.

1.522 Degree of Difference Between the Products and Locations in the Market and Substitutes Outside the Market

All else equal, the magnitude of potential competitive harm from a merger is greater if a hypothetical monopolist would raise price within the relevant market by substantially more than a "small but significant and nontransitory" amount. This may occur when the demand substitutes outside the relevant market, as a group, are not close substitutes for the products and locations within the relevant market. There thus may be a wide gap in the chain of demand substitutes at the edge of the product and geographic market. Under such circumstances, more market power is at stake in the relevant market than in a market in which a hypothetical monopolist would raise price by exactly five percent.

2. The Potential Adverse Competitive Effects of Mergers

2.0 Overview

Other things being equal, market concentration affects the likelihood that one firm, or a small group of firms, could successfully exercise market power. The smaller the percentage of total supply that a firm controls, the more severely it must restrict its own output in order to produce a given price increase, and the less likely it is that an output restriction will be profitable. If collective action is necessary for the exercise of market power, as the number of firms necessary to control a given percentage of total supply decreases, the difficulties and costs of reaching and enforcing an understanding with respect to the control of that supply might be reduced. However, market share and concentration data provide only the starting point for analyzing the competitive impact of a merger. Before determining whether to challenge a merger, the Agency also will assess the other market factors that pertain to competitive effects, as well as entry, efficiencies and failure.

This section considers some of the potential adverse competitive effects of mergers and the factors in addition to market concentration relevant to each. Because an individual merger may threaten to harm competition through more than one of these effects, mergers will be analyzed in terms of as many potential adverse competitive effects as are appropriate. Entry, efficiencies, and failure are treated in Sections 3-5.

2.1 Lessening of Competition Through Coordinated Interaction

A merger may diminish competition by enabling the firms selling in the relevant market more likely, more successfully, or more completely to engage in coordinated interaction that harms consumers. Coordinated interaction is comprised of actions by a group of firms that are profitable for each of them only as a result of the accommodating reactions of the others. This behavior includes tacit or express collusion, and may or may not be lawful in and of itself.

Successful coordinated interaction entails reaching terms of coordination that are profitable to the firms involved and an ability to detect and punish deviations that would undermine the coordinated interaction. Detection and punishment of deviations ensure that coordinating firms will find it more profitable to adhere to the terms of coordination than to pursue short-term profits from deviating, given the costs of reprisal. In this phase of the analysis, the Agency will examine the extent to which post-merger market conditions are conducive to reaching terms of coordination, detecting deviations from those terms, and punishing such deviations. Depending upon the circumstances, the following market factors, among others, may be relevant: the availability of key information concerning market conditions, transactions and individual competitors; the extent of firm and product heterogeneity; pricing or marketing practices typically employed by firms in the market; the characteristics of buyers and sellers; and the characteristics of typical transactions. Certain market conditions that are conducive to reaching terms of coordination also may be conducive to detecting or punishing deviations from those terms. For example, the extent of information available to firms in the market, or the extent of homogeneity, may be relevant to both the ability to reach terms of coordination and to detect or punish deviations from those terms. The extent to which any specific market condition will be relevant to one or more of the conditions necessary to coordinated interaction will depend on the circumstances of the particular case.

It is likely that market conditions are conducive to coordinated interaction when the firms in the market previously have engaged in express collusion and when the salient characteristics of the market have not changed appreciably since the most recent such incident. Previous express collusion in another geographic market will have the same weight when the salient characteristics of that other market at the time of the collusion are comparable to those in the relevant market. In analyzing the effect of a particular merger on coordinated interaction, the Agency is mindful of the difficulties of predicting likely future behavior based on the types of incomplete and sometimes contradictory information typically generated in merger investigations. Whether a merger is likely to diminish competition by enabling firms more likely, more successfully or more completely to engage in coordinated interaction depends on whether market conditions, on the whole, are conducive to reaching terms of coordination and detecting and punishing deviations from those terms.

2.11 Conditions Conducive to Reaching Terms of Coordination

Firms coordinating their interactions need not reach complex terms concerning the allocation of the market output across firms or the level of the market prices but may, instead, follow simple terms such as a common price, fixed price differentials, stable market shares, or customer or territorial restrictions. Terms of coordination need not perfectly achieve the monopoly outcome in order to be harmful to consumers. Instead, the terms of coordination may be imperfect and incomplete—inasmuch as they omit some market participants, omit some dimension of competition, omit some customers, yield elevated prices short of monopoly levels, or lapse into episodic price wars—and still result in significant competitive harm. At some point, however, imperfections cause the profitability of abiding by the terms of coordination to decrease and, depending on their extent, may make coordinated interaction unlikely in the first instance.

Market conditions may be conducive to or hinder reaching terms of coordination. For example, reaching terms of coordination may be facilitated by product or firm homogeneity and by existing practices among firms, practices not necessarily themselves antitrust violations, such as standardization of pricing or product variables on which firms could compete. Key information about rival firms and the market may also facilitate reaching terms of coordination. Conversely, reaching terms of coordination may be limited or impeded by product heterogeneity or by firms having substantially incomplete information about the conditions and prospects of their rivals' businesses, perhaps because of important differences among their current business operations. In addition, reaching terms of coordination may be limited or impeded by firm heterogeneity, for example, differences in vertical integration or the production of another product that tends to be used together with the relevant product.

2.12 Conditions Conducive to Detecting and Punishing Deviations

Where market conditions are conducive to timely detection and punishment of significant deviations, a firm will find it more profitable to abide by the terms of coordination than to deviate from them. Deviation from the terms of coordination will be deterred where the threat of punishment is credible. Credible punishment, however, may not need to be any more complex than temporary abandonment of the terms of coordination by other firms in the market.

Where detection and punishment likely would be rapid, incentives to deviate are diminished and coordination is likely to be successful. The detection and punishment of deviations may be facilitated by existing practices among firms, themselves not necessarily antitrust violations, and by the characteristics of typical transactions. For example, if key information about specific transactions or individual price or output levels is available routinely to competitors, it may be difficult for a firm to deviate secretly. If orders for the relevant product are frequent, regular and small relative to the total output of a firm in a market, it may be difficult for the firm to deviate in a substantial way without the knowledge of rivals and without the opportunity for rivals to react. If demand or cost fluctuations are relatively infrequent and small, deviations may be relatively easy to deter.

By contrast, where detection or punishment is likely to be slow, incentives to deviate are enhanced and coordinated interaction is unlikely to be successful. If demand or cost fluctuations are relatively frequent and large, deviations may be relatively difficult to distinguish from these other sources of market price fluctuations, and, in consequence, deviations may be relatively difficult to deter.

In certain circumstances, buyer characteristics and the nature of the procurement process may affect the incentives to deviate from terms of coordination. Buyer size alone is not the determining characteristic. Where large buyers likely would engage in long-term contracting, so that the sales covered by such contracts can be large relative to the total output of a firm in the market, firms may have the incentive to deviate. However, this only can be accomplished where the duration, volume and profitability of the business covered by such contracts are sufficiently large as to make deviation more profitable in the long term than honoring the terms of coordination, and buyers likely would switch suppliers.

In some circumstances, coordinated interaction can be effectively prevented or limited by maverick firms—firms that have a greater economic incentive to deviate from the terms of coordination than do most of their rivals (*e.g.*, firms that are unusually disruptive and competitive influences in the market). Consequently, acquisition of a maverick firm is one way in which a merger may make coordinated interaction more likely, more successful, or more complete. For example, in a market where capacity constraints are significant for many competitors, a firm is more likely to be a maverick the greater is its excess or divertable capacity in relation to its sales or its total capacity, and the lower are its direct and opportunity costs of expanding sales in the relevant market.[19] This is so because a firm's incentive to deviate from price-elevating and output-limiting terms of coordination is greater the more the firm is able profitably to expand its output as a proportion of the sales it would obtain if it adhered to the terms of coordination and the smaller is the base of sales on which it enjoys elevated profits prior to the price cutting deviation.[20] A firm also may be a maverick if it has an unusual ability secretly to expand its sales in relation to the sales it would obtain if it adhered to the terms of coordination. This ability might arise from opportunities to expand captive production for a downstream affiliate.

[19] But excess capacity in the hands of non-maverick firms may be a potent weapon with which to punish deviations from the terms of coordination.

[20] Similarly, in a market where product design or quality is significant, a firm is more likely to be an effective maverick the greater is the sales potential of its products among customers of its rivals, in relation to the sales it would obtain if it adhered to the terms of coordination. The likelihood of expansion responses by a maverick will be analyzed in the same fashion as uncommitted entry or committed entry (*see* Sections 1.3 and 3) depending on the significance of the sunk costs entailed in expansion.

2.2 Lessening of Competition Through Unilateral Effects

A merger may diminish competition even if it does not lead to increased likelihood of successful coordinated interaction, because merging firms may find it profitable to alter their behavior unilaterally following the acquisition by elevating price and suppressing output. Unilateral competitive effects can arise in a variety of different settings. In each setting, particular other factors describing the relevant market affect the likelihood of unilateral competitive effects. The settings differ by the primary characteristics that distinguish firms and shape the nature of their competition.

2.21 Firms Distinguished Primarily by Differentiated Products

In some markets the products are differentiated, so that products sold by different sellers in the market are not perfect substitutes for one another. Moreover, different products in the market may vary in the degree of their substitutability for one another. In this setting, competition may be non-uniform (*i.e.,* localized), so that individual sellers compete more directly with those rivals selling closer substitutes.[21]

A merger between firms in a market for differentiated products may diminish competition by enabling the merged firm to profit by unilaterally raising the price of one or both products above the premerger level. Some of the sales loss due to the price rise merely will be diverted to the product of the merger partner and, depending on relative margins, capturing such sales loss through merger may make the price increase profitable even though it would not have been profitable premerger. Substantial unilateral price elevation in a market for differentiated products requires that there be a significant share of sales in the market accounted for by consumers who regard the products of the merging firms as their first and second choices, and that repositioning of the non-parties' product lines to replace the localized competition lost through the merger be unlikely. The price rise will be greater the closer substitutes are the products of the merging firms, *i.e.,* the more the buyers of one product consider the other product to be their next choice.

2.211 Closeness of the Products of the Merging Firms

The market concentration measures articulated in Section 1 may help assess the extent of the likely competitive effect from a unilateral price elevation by the merged firm notwithstanding the fact that the affected products are differentiated. The market concentration measures provide a measure of this effect if each prod-

---

[21] Similarly, in some markets sellers are primarily distinguished by their relative advantages in serving different buyers or groups of buyers, and buyers negotiate individually with sellers. Here, for example, sellers may formally bid against one another for the business of a buyer, or each buyer may elicit individual price quotes from multiple sellers. A seller may find it relatively inexpensive to meet the demands of particular buyers or types of buyers, and relatively expensive to meet others' demands. Competition, again, may be localized: sellers compete more directly with those rivals having similar relative advantages in serving particular buyers or groups of buyers. For example, in open outcry auctions, price is determined by the cost of the second lowest-cost seller. A merger involving the first and second lowest-cost sellers could cause prices to rise to the constraining level of the next lowest-cost seller.

uct's market share is reflective of not only its relative appeal as a first choice to consumers of the merging firms' products but also its relative appeal as a second choice, and hence as a competitive constraint to the first choice.[22] Where this circumstance holds, market concentration data fall outside the safeharbor regions of Section 1.5, and the merging firms have a combined market share of at least thirty-five percent, the Agency will presume that a significant share of sales in the market are accounted for by consumers who regard the products of the merging firms as their first and second choices.

Purchasers of one of the merging firms' products may be more or less likely to make the other their second choice than market shares alone would indicate. The market shares of the merging firms' products may understate the competitive effect of concern, when, for example, the products of the merging firms are relatively more similar in their various attributes to one another than to other products in the relevant market. On the other hand, the market shares alone may overstate the competitive effects of concern when, for example, the relevant products are less similar in their attributes to one another than to other products in the relevant market.

Where market concentration data fall outside the safeharbor regions of Section 1.5, the merging firms have a combined market share of at least thirty-five percent, and where data on product attributes and relative product appeal show that a significant share of purchasers of one merging firm's product regard the other as their second choice, then market share data may be relied upon to demonstrate that there is a significant share of sales in the market accounted for by consumers who would be adversely affected by the merger.

2.212 Ability of Rival Sellers to Replace Lost Competition

A merger is not likely to lead to unilateral elevation of prices of differentiated products if, in response to such an effect, rival sellers likely would replace any localized competition lost through the merger by repositioning their product lines.[23]

In markets where it is costly for buyers to evaluate product quality, buyers who consider purchasing from both merging parties may limit the total number of sellers they consider. If either of the merging firms would be replaced in such buyers' consideration by an equally competitive seller not formerly considered, then the merger is not likely to lead to a unilateral elevation of prices.

2.22 Firms Distinguished Primarily by Their Capacities

Where products are relatively undifferentiated and capacity primarily distinguishes firms and shapes the nature of their competition, the merged firm may find it profitable unilaterally to raise price and suppress output. The merger provides the

---

[22] Information about consumers' actual first and second product choices may be provided by marketing surveys, information from bidding structures, or normal course of business documents from industry participants.

[23] The timeliness and likelihood of repositioning responses will be analyzed using the same methodology as used in analyzing uncommitted entry or committed entry (*see* Sections 1.3 and 3), depending on the significance of the sunk costs entailed in repositioning.

merged firm a larger base of sales on which to enjoy the resulting price rise and also eliminates a competitor to which customers otherwise would have diverted their sales. Where the merging firms have a combined market share of at least thirty-five percent, merged firms may find it profitable to raise price and reduce joint output below the sum of their premerger outputs because the lost markups on the foregone sales may be outweighed by the resulting price increase on the merged base of sales.

This unilateral effect is unlikely unless a sufficiently large number of the merged firm's customers would not be able to find economical alternative sources of supply, *i.e.,* competitors of the merged firm likely would not respond to the price increase and output reduction by the merged firm with increases in their own outputs sufficient in the aggregate to make the unilateral action of the merged firm unprofitable. Such non-party expansion is unlikely if those firms face binding capacity constraints that could not be economically relaxed within two years or if existing excess capacity is significantly more costly to operate than capacity currently in use.[24]

3. Entry Analysis

3.0 Overview

A merger is not likely to create or enhance market power or to facilitate its exercise, if entry into the market is so easy that market participants, after the merger, either collectively or unilaterally could not profitably maintain a price increase above premerger levels. Such entry likely will deter an anticompetitive merger in its incipiency, or deter or counteract the competitive effects of concern.

Entry is that easy if entry would be timely, likely, and sufficient in its magnitude, character and scope to deter or counteract the competitive effects of concern. In markets where entry is that easy (*i.e.,* where entry passes these tests of timeliness, likelihood, and sufficiency), the merger raises no antitrust concern and ordinarily requires no further analysis.

The committed entry treated in this Section is defined as new competition that requires expenditure of significant sunk costs of entry and exit.[25] The Agency employs a three step methodology to assess whether committed entry would deter or counteract a competitive effect of concern.

The first step assesses whether entry can achieve significant market impact within a timely period. If significant market impact would require a longer period, entry will not deter or counteract the competitive effect of concern.

The second step assesses whether committed entry would be a profitable and, hence, a likely response to a merger having competitive effects of concern.

---

[24] The timeliness and likelihood of non-party expansion will be analyzed using the same methodology as used in analyzing uncommitted or committed entry (*see* Sections 1.3 and 3) depending on the significance of the sunk costs entailed in expansion.

[25] Supply responses that require less than one year and insignificant sunk costs to effectuate are analyzed as uncommitted entry in Section 1.3.

Firms considering entry that requires significant sunk costs must evaluate the profitability of the entry on the basis of long term participation in the market, because the underlying assets will be committed to the market until they are economically depreciated. Entry that is sufficient to counteract the competitive effects of concern will cause prices to fall to their premerger levels or lower. Thus, the profitability of such committed entry must be determined on the basis of premerger market prices over the long-term.

A merger having anticompetitive effects can attract committed entry, profitable at premerger prices, that would not have occurred premerger at these same prices. But following the merger, the reduction in industry output and increase in prices associated with the competitive effect of concern may allow the same entry to occur without driving market prices below premerger levels. After a merger that results in decreased output and increased prices, the likely sales opportunities available to entrants at premerger prices will be larger than they were premerger, larger by the output reduction caused by the merger. If entry could be profitable at premerger prices without exceeding the likely sales opportunities—opportunities that include pre-existing pertinent factors as well as the merger-induced output reduction—then such entry is likely in response to the merger.

The third step assesses whether timely and likely entry would be sufficient to return market prices to their premerger levels. This end may be accomplished either through multiple entry or individual entry at a sufficient scale. Entry may not be sufficient, even though timely and likely, where the constraints on availability of essential assets, due to incumbent control, make it impossible for entry profitably to achieve the necessary level of sales. Also, the character and scope of entrants' products might not be fully responsive to the localized sales opportunities created by the removal of direct competition among sellers of differentiated products. In assessing whether entry will be timely, likely, and sufficient, the Agency recognizes that precise and detailed information may be difficult or impossible to obtain. In such instances, the Agency will rely on all available evidence bearing on whether entry will satisfy the conditions of timeliness, likelihood, and sufficiency.

3.1 Entry Alternatives

The Agency will examine the timeliness, likelihood, and sufficiency of the means of entry (entry alternatives) a potential entrant might practically employ, without attempting to identify who might be potential entrants. An entry alternative is defined by the actions the firm must take in order to produce and sell in the market. All phases of the entry effort will be considered, including, where relevant, planning, design, and management; permitting, licensing, and other approvals; construction, debugging, and operation of production facilities; and promotion (including necessary introductory discounts), marketing, distribution, and satisfaction of customer testing and qualification requirements.[26] Recent examples of

---

[26] Many of these phases may be undertaken simultaneously.

entry, whether successful or unsuccessful, may provide a useful starting point for identifying the necessary actions, time requirements, and characteristics of possible entry alternatives.

3.2 Timeliness of Entry

In order to deter or counteract the competitive effects of concern, entrants quickly must achieve a significant impact on price in the relevant market. The Agency generally will consider timely only those committed entry alternatives that can be achieved within two years from initial planning to significant market impact.[27] Where the relevant product is a durable good, consumers, in response to a significant commitment to entry, may defer purchases by making additional investments to extend the useful life of previously purchased goods and in this way deter or counteract for a time the competitive effects of concern. In these circumstances, if entry only can occur outside of the two year period, the Agency will consider entry to be timely so long as it would deter or counteract the competitive effects of concern within the two year period and subsequently.

3.3 Likelihood of Entry

An entry alternative is likely if it would be profitable at premerger prices, and if such prices could be secured by the entrant.[28] The committed entrant will be unable to secure prices at premerger levels if its output is too large for the market to absorb without depressing prices further. Thus, entry is unlikely if the minimum viable scale is larger than the likely sales opportunity available to entrants.

Minimum viable scale is the smallest average annual level of sales that the committed entrant must persistently achieve for profitability at premerger prices.[29] Minimum viable scale is a function of expected revenues, based upon premerger prices,[30] and all categories of costs associated with the entry alternative, including an appropriate rate of return on invested capital given that entry could fail and sunk costs, if any, will be lost.[31]

---

27 Firms which have committed to entering the market prior to the merger generally will be included in the measurement of the market. Only committed entry or adjustments to pre-existing entry plans that are induced by the merger will be considered as possibly deterring or counteracting the competitive effects of concern.

28 Where conditions indicate that entry may be profitable at prices below premerger levels, the Agency will assess the likelihood of entry at the lowest price at which such entry would be profitable.

29 The concept of minimum viable scale ("MVS") differs from the concept of minimum efficient scale ("MES"). While MES is the smallest scale at which average costs are minimized, MVS is the smallest scale at which average costs equal the premerger price.

30 The expected path of future prices, absent the merger, may be used if future price changes can be predicted with reasonable reliability.

31 The minimum viable scale of an entry alternative will be relatively large when the fixed costs of entry are large, when the fixed costs of entry are largely sunk, when the marginal costs of production are high at low levels of output, and when a plant is underutilized for a long time because of delays in achieving market acceptance.

Sources of sales opportunities available to entrants include: (a) the output reduction associated with the competitive effect of concern,[32] (b) entrants' ability to capture a share of reasonably expected growth in market demand,[33] (c) entrants' ability securely to divert sales from incumbents, for example, through vertical integration or through forward contracting, and (d) any additional anticipated contraction in incumbents' output in response to entry.[34] Factors that reduce the sales opportunities available to entrants include: (a) the prospect that an entrant will share in a reasonably expected decline in market demand, (b) the exclusion of an entrant from a portion of the market over the long term because of vertical integration or forward contracting by incumbents, and (c) any anticipated sales expansion by incumbents in reaction to entry, either generalized or targeted at customers approached by the entrant, that utilizes prior irreversible investments in excess production capacity. Demand growth or decline will be viewed as relevant only if total market demand is projected to experience long-lasting change during at least the two year period following the competitive effect of concern.

3.4 Sufficiency of Entry

Inasmuch as multiple entry generally is possible and individual entrants may flexibly choose their scale, committed entry generally will be sufficient to deter or counteract the competitive effects of concern whenever entry is likely under the analysis of Section 3.3. However, entry, although likely, will not be sufficient if, as a result of incumbent control, the tangible and intangible assets required for entry are not adequately available for entrants to respond fully to their sales opportunities. In addition, where the competitive effect of concern is not uniform across the relevant market, in order for entry to be sufficient, the character and scope of entrants' products must be responsive to the localized sales opportunities that include the output reduction associated with the competitive effect of concern. For example, where the concern is unilateral price elevation as a result of a merger between producers of differentiated products, entry, in order to be sufficient, must involve a product so close to the products of the merging firms that the merged firm will be unable to internalize enough of the sales loss due to the price rise, rendering the price increase unprofitable.

4. Efficiencies (as revised April 8, 1997)

Competition usually spurs firms to achieve efficiencies internally. Nevertheless, mergers have the potential to generate significant efficiencies by permitting a

---

[32] Five percent of total market sales typically is used because where a monopolist profitably would raise price by five percent or more across the entire relevant market, it is likely that the accompanying reduction in sales would be no less than five percent.

[33] Entrants' anticipated share of growth in demand depends on incumbents' capacity constraints and irreversible investments in capacity expansion, as well as on the relative appeal, acceptability and reputation of incumbents' and entrants' products to the new demand.

[34] For example, in a bidding market where all bidders are on equal footing, the market share of incumbents will contract as a result of entry.

better utilization of existing assets, enabling the combined firm to achieve lower costs in producing a given quantity and quality than either firm could have achieved without the proposed transaction. Indeed, the primary benefit of mergers to the economy is their potential to generate such efficiencies.

Efficiencies generated through merger can enhance the merged firm's ability and incentive to compete, which may result in lower prices, improved quality, enhanced service, or new products. For example, merger-generated efficiencies may enhance competition by permitting two ineffective (*e.g.*, high cost) competitors to become one effective (*e.g.*, lower cost) competitor. In a coordinated interaction context (*see* Section 2.1), marginal cost reductions may make coordination less likely or effective by enhancing the incentive of a maverick to lower price or by creating a new maverick firm. In a unilateral effects context (*see* Section 2.2), marginal cost reductions may reduce the merged firm's incentive to elevate price. Efficiencies also may result in benefits in the form of new or improved products, and efficiencies may result in benefits even when price is not immediately and directly affected. Even when efficiencies generated through merger enhance a firm's ability to compete, however, a merger may have other effects that may lessen competition and ultimately may make the merger anticompetitive.

The Agency will consider only those efficiencies likely to be accomplished with the proposed merger and unlikely to be accomplished in the absence of either the proposed merger or another means having comparable anticompetitive effects. These are termed merger-specific efficiencies.[35] Only alternatives that are practical in the business situation faced by the merging firms will be considered in making this determination; the Agency will not insist upon a less restrictive alternative that is merely theoretical.

Efficiencies are difficult to verify and quantify, in part because much of the information relating to efficiencies is uniquely in the possession of the merging firms. Moreover, efficiencies projected reasonably and in good faith by the merging firms may not be realized. Therefore, the merging firms must substantiate efficiency claims so that the Agency can verify by reasonable means the likelihood and magnitude of each asserted efficiency, how and when each would be achieved (and any costs of doing so), how each would enhance the merged firm's ability and incentive to compete, and why each would be merger-specific. Efficiency claims will not be considered if they are vague or speculative or otherwise cannot be verified by reasonable means.

Cognizable efficiencies are merger-specific efficiencies that have been verified and do not arise from anticompetitive reductions in output or service. Cognizable efficiencies are assessed net of costs produced by the merger or incurred in achieving those efficiencies.

---

[35] The Agency will not deem efficiencies to be merger-specific if they could be preserved by practical alternatives that mitigate competitive concerns, such as divestiture or licensing. If a merger affects not whether but only when an efficiency would be achieved, only the timing advantage is a merger-specific efficiency.

The Agency will not challenge a merger if cognizable efficiencies are of a character and magnitude such that the merger is not likely to be anticompetitive in any relevant market.[36] To make the requisite determination, the Agency considers whether cognizable efficiencies likely would be sufficient to reverse the merger's potential to harm consumers in the relevant market, *e.g.*, by preventing price increases in that market. In conducting this analysis,[37] the Agency will not simply compare the magnitude of the cognizable efficiencies with the magnitude of the likely harm to competition absent the efficiencies. The greater the potential adverse competitive effect of a merger—as indicated by the increase in the HHI and post-merger HHI from Section 1, the analysis of potential adverse competitive effects from Section 2, and the timeliness, likelihood, and sufficiency of entry from Section 3—the greater must be cognizable efficiencies in order for the Agency to conclude that the merger will not have an anticompetitive effect in the relevant market. When the potential adverse competitive effect of a merger is likely to be particularly large, extraordinarily great cognizable efficiencies would be necessary to prevent the merger from being anticompetitive.

In the Agency's experience, efficiencies are most likely to make a difference in merger analysis when the likely adverse competitive effects, absent the efficiencies, are not great. Efficiencies almost never justify a merger to monopoly or near-monopoly.

The Agency has found that certain types of efficiencies are more likely to be cognizable and substantial than others. For example, efficiencies resulting from shifting production among facilities formerly owned separately, which enable the merging firms to reduce the marginal cost of production, are more likely to be susceptible to verification, merger-specific, and substantial, and are less likely to result from anticompetitive reductions in output. Other efficiencies, such as those relating to research and development, are potentially substantial but are generally less susceptible to verification and may be the result of anticompetitive output reductions. Yet others, such as those relating to procurement, management, or capital cost are less likely to be merger-specific or substantial, or may not be cognizable for other reasons.

---

[36] Section 7 of the Clayton Act prohibits mergers that may substantially lessen competition "in any line of commerce . . . in any section of the country." Accordingly, the Agency normally assesses competition in each relevant market affected by a merger independently and normally will challenge the merger if it is likely to be anticompetitive in any relevant market. In some cases, however, the Agency in its prosecutorial discretion will consider efficiencies not strictly in the relevant market, but so inextricably linked with it that a partial divestiture or other remedy could not feasibly eliminate the anticompetitive effect in the relevant market without sacrificing the efficiencies in the other market(s). Inextricably linked efficiencies rarely are a significant factor in the Agency's determination not to challenge a merger. They are most likely to make a difference when they are great and the likely anticompetitive effect in the relevant market(s) is small.

[37] The result of this analysis over the short term will determine the Agency's enforcement decision in most cases. The Agency also will consider the effects of cognizable efficiencies with no short-term, direct effect on prices in the relevant market. Delayed benefits from efficiencies (due to delay in the achievement of, or the realization of consumer benefits from, the efficiencies) will be given less weight because they are less proximate and more difficult to predict.

5. Failure and Exiting Assets

5.0 Overview

Notwithstanding the analysis of Sections 1-4 of the Guidelines, a merger is not likely to create or enhance market power or to facilitate its exercise, if imminent failure, as defined below, of one of the merging firms would cause the assets of that firm to exit the relevant market. In such circumstances, post-merger performance in the relevant market may be no worse than market performance had the merger been blocked and the assets left the market.

5.1 Failing Firm

A merger is not likely to create or enhance market power or facilitate its exercise if the following circumstances are met: 1) the allegedly failing firm would be unable to meet its financial obligations in the near future; 2) it would not be able to reorganize successfully under Chapter 11 of the Bankruptcy Act;[38] 3) it has made unsuccessful good-faith efforts to elicit reasonable alternative offers of acquisition of the assets of the failing firm[39] that would both keep its tangible and intangible assets in the relevant market and pose a less severe danger to competition than does the proposed merger; and 4) absent the acquisition, the assets of the failing firm would exit the relevant market.

5.2 Failing Division

A similar argument can be made for "failing" divisions as for failing firms. First, upon applying appropriate cost allocation rules, the division must have a negative cash flow on an operating basis. Second, absent the acquisition, it must be that the assets of the division would exit the relevant market in the near future if not sold. Due to the ability of the parent firm to allocate costs, revenues, and intra-company transactions among itself and its subsidiaries and divisions, the Agency will require evidence, not based solely on management plans that could be prepared solely for the purpose of demonstrating negative cash flow or the prospect of exit from the relevant market. Third, the owner of the failing division also must have complied with the competitively-preferable purchaser requirement of Section 5.1.

---

[38] 11 U.S.C. Sections 1101-1174 (1988).

[39] Any offer to purchase the assets of the failing firm for a price above the liquidation value of those assets—the highest valued use outside the relevant market or equivalent offer to purchase the stock of the failing firm—will be regarded as a reasonable alternative offer.

Appendix D

United States Department of Justice Intellectual Property Guidelines

ISSUED BY THE U.S. DEPARTMENT OF JUSTICE[1] AND THE FEDERAL TRADE COMMISSION (April 6, 1995)

INTELLECTUAL PROPERTY PROTECTION AND THE ANTITRUST LAWS

1.0 These Guidelines state the antitrust enforcement policy of the U.S. Department of Justice and the Federal Trade Commission (individually, "the Agency," and collectively, "the Agencies") with respect to the licensing of intellectual property protected by patent, copyright, and trade secret law, and of know-how.[2] By stating their general policy, the Agencies hope to assist those who need to predict whether the Agencies will challenge a practice as anticompetitive. However, these Guidelines cannot remove judgment and discretion in antitrust law enforcement. Moreover, the standards set forth in these Guidelines must be applied in unforeseeable circumstances. Each case will be evaluated in light of its own facts, and these Guidelines will be applied reasonably and flexibly.[3]

In the United States, patents confer rights to exclude others from making, using, or selling in the United States the invention claimed by the patent for a period of seventeen years from the date of issue.[4] To gain patent protection, an invention (which may be a product, process, machine, or composition of matter) must be novel, nonobvious, and useful. Copyright protection applies to original works of authorship embodied in a tangible medium of expression.[5] A copyright protects only the expression, not the underlying ideas.[6] Unlike a patent, which protects an inven-

---

1 These Guidelines supersede section 3.6 in Part I, "Intellectual Property Licensing Arrangements," and cases 6, 10, 11, and 12 in Part II of the U.S. Department of Justice 1988 Antitrust Enforcement Guidelines for International Operations. [The full text can be found at <www.usdoj.gov/atr/public/guidelines/ipguide.htm>—Eds.]

2 These Guidelines do not cover the antitrust treatment of trademarks. Although the same general antitrust principles that apply to other forms of intellectual property apply to trademarks as well, these Guidelines deal with technology transfer and innovation-related issues that typically arise with respect to patents, copyrights, trade secrets, and know-how agreements, rather than with product-differentiation issues that typically arise with respect to trademarks.

3 As is the case with all guidelines, users should rely on qualified counsel to assist them in evaluating the antitrust risk associated with any contemplated transaction or activity. No set of guidelines can possibly indicate how the Agencies will assess the particular facts of every case. Parties who wish to know the Agencies' specific enforcement intentions with respect to any particular transaction should consider seeking a Department of Justice business review letter pursuant to 28 C.F.R. § 50.6 or a Federal Trade Commission Advisory Opinion pursuant to 16 C.F.R. §§ 1.1-1.4.

4 *See* 35 U.S.C. § 154 (1988). Section 532(a) of the Uruguay Round Agreements Act, Pub. L. No. 103-465, 108 Stat. 4809, 4983 (1994) would change the length of patent protection to a term beginning on the date at which the patent issues and ending twenty years from the date on which the application for the patent was filed.

5 *See* 17 U.S.C. § 102 (1988 & Supp. V 1993). Copyright protection lasts for the author's life plus 50 years, or 75 years from first publication (or 100 years from creation, whichever expires first) for works made for hire. *See* 17 U.S.C. § 302 (1988). The principles stated in these Guidelines also apply to protection of mask works fixed in a semiconductor chip product (*see* 17 U.S.C. § 901 *et seq.* (1988)), which is analogous to copyright protection for works of authorship.

6 *See* 17 U.S.C. § 102(b) (1988).

tion not only from copying but also from independent creation, a copyright does not preclude others from independently creating similar expression. Trade secret protection applies to information whose economic value depends on its not being generally known.[7] Trade secret protection is conditioned upon efforts to maintain secrecy and has no fixed term. As with copyright protection, trade secret protection does not preclude independent creation by others.

The intellectual property laws and the antitrust laws share the common purpose of promoting innovation and enhancing consumer welfare.[8] The intellectual property laws provide incentives for innovation and its dissemination and commercialization by establishing enforceable property rights for the creators of new and useful products, more efficient processes, and original works of expression. In the absence of intellectual property rights, imitators could more rapidly exploit the efforts of innovators and investors without compensation. Rapid imitation would reduce the commercial value of innovation and erode incentives to invest, ultimately to the detriment of consumers. The antitrust laws promote innovation and consumer welfare by prohibiting certain actions that may harm competition with respect to either existing or new ways of serving consumers.

GENERAL PRINCIPLES

2.0 These Guidelines embody three general principles: (a) for the purpose of antitrust analysis, the Agencies regard intellectual property as being essentially comparable to any other form of property; (b) the Agencies do not presume that intellectual property creates market power in the antitrust context; and (c) the Agencies recognize that intellectual property licensing allows firms to combine complementary factors of production and is generally procompetitive.

STANDARD ANTITRUST ANALYSIS APPLIES TO INTELLECTUAL PROPERTY

The Agencies apply the same general antitrust principles to conduct involving intellectual property that they apply to conduct involving any other form of tangible or intangible property. That is not to say that intellectual property is in all respects the same as any other form of property. Intellectual property has important characteristics, such as ease of misappropriation, that distinguish it from many other forms of property. These characteristics can be taken into account by standard antitrust analysis, however, and do not require the application of fundamentally different principles.[9]

---

[7] Trade secret protection derives from state law. *See generally Kewanee Oil Co. v. Bicron Corp.*, 416 U.S. 470 (1974).

[8] "[T]he aims and objectives of patent and antitrust laws may seem, at first glance, wholly at odds. However, the two bodies of law are actually complementary, as both are aimed at encouraging innovation, industry and competition." *Atari Games Corp. v. Nintendo of America, Inc.*, 897 F.2d 1572, 1576 (Fed. Cir. 1990).

[9] As with other forms of property, the power to exclude others from the use of intellectual property may vary substantially, depending on the nature of the property and its status under federal or state law. The greater or lesser legal power of an owner to exclude others is also taken into account by standard antitrust analysis.

Although there are clear and important differences in the purpose, extent, and duration of protection provided under the intellectual property regimes of patent, copyright, and trade secret, the governing antitrust principles are the same. Antitrust analysis takes differences among these forms of intellectual property into account in evaluating the specific market circumstances in which transactions occur, just as it does with other particular market circumstances.

Intellectual property law bestows on the owners of intellectual property certain rights to exclude others. These rights help the owners to profit from the use of their property. An intellectual property owner's rights to exclude are similar to the rights enjoyed by owners of other forms of private property. As with other forms of private property, certain types of conduct with respect to intellectual property may have anticompetitive effects against which the antitrust laws can and do protect. Intellectual property is thus neither particularly free from scrutiny under the antitrust laws, nor particularly suspect under them.

The Agencies recognize that the licensing of intellectual property is often international. The principles of antitrust analysis described in these Guidelines apply equally to domestic and international licensing arrangements. However, as described in the 1995 Department of Justice and Federal Trade Commission Antitrust Enforcement Guidelines for International Operations, considerations particular to international operations, such as jurisdiction and comity, may affect enforcement decisions when the arrangement is in an international context.

INTELLECTUAL PROPERTY AND MARKET POWER

Market power is the ability profitably to maintain prices above, or output below, competitive levels for a significant period of time.[10] The Agencies will not presume that a patent, copyright, or trade secret necessarily confers market power upon its owner. Although the intellectual property right confers the power to exclude with respect to the *specific* product, process, or work in question, there will often be sufficient actual or potential close substitutes for such product, process, or work to prevent the exercise of market power.[11] If a patent or other form of intellectual property does confer market power, that market power does not by itself

---

[10] Market power can be exercised in other economic dimensions, such as quality, service, and the development of new or improved goods and processes. It is assumed in this definition that all competitive dimensions are held constant except the ones in which market power is being exercised; that a seller is able to charge higher prices for a higher-quality product does not alone indicate market power. The definition in the text is stated in terms of a seller with market power. A buyer could also exercise market power (*e.g.*, by maintaining the price below the competitive level, thereby depressing output).

[11] The Agencies note that the law is unclear on this issue. *Compare Jefferson Parish Hospital District No. 2 v. Hyde*, 466 U.S. 2, 16 (1984) (expressing the view in dictum that if a product is protected by a patent, "it is fair to presume that the inability to buy the product elsewhere gives the seller market power") *with id.* at 37 n.7 (O'Connor, J., concurring) ("[A] patent holder has no market power in any relevant sense if there are close substitutes for the patented product."). *Compare also Abbott Laboratories v. Brennan*, 952 F.2d 1346, 1354-55 (Fed. Cir. 1991) (no presumption of market power from intellectual property right), *cert. denied*, 112 S. Ct. 2993 (1992) *with Digidyne Corp. v. Data General Corp.*, 734 F.2d 1336, 1341-42 (9th Cir. 1984) (requisite economic power is presumed from copyright), *cert. denied,* 473 U.S. 908 (1985).

offend the antitrust laws. As with any other tangible or intangible asset that enables its owner to obtain significant supracompetitive profits, market power (or even a monopoly) that is solely "a consequence of a superior product, business acumen, or historic accident" does not violate the antitrust laws.[12] Nor does such market power impose on the intellectual property owner an obligation to license the use of that property to others. As in other antitrust contexts, however, market power could be illegally acquired or maintained, or, even if lawfully acquired and maintained, would be relevant to the ability of an intellectual property owner to harm competition through unreasonable conduct in connection with such property.

PROCOMPETITIVE BENEFITS OF LICENSING

Intellectual property typically is one component among many in a production process and derives value from its combination with complementary factors. Complementary factors of production include manufacturing and distribution facilities, workforces, and other items of intellectual property. The owner of intellectual property has to arrange for its combination with other necessary factors to realize its commercial value. Often, the owner finds it most efficient to contract with others for these factors, to sell rights to the intellectual property, or to enter into a joint venture arrangement for its development, rather than supplying these complementary factors itself.

Licensing, cross-licensing, or otherwise transferring intellectual property (hereinafter "licensing") can facilitate integration of the licensed property with complementary factors of production. This integration can lead to more efficient exploitation of the intellectual property, benefiting consumers through the reduction of costs and the introduction of new products. Such arrangements increase the value of intellectual property to consumers and to the developers of the technology. By potentially increasing the expected returns from intellectual property, licensing also can increase the incentive for its creation and thus promote greater investment in research and development.

Sometimes the use of one item of intellectual property requires access to another. An item of intellectual property "blocks" another when the second cannot be practiced without using the first. For example, an improvement on a patented machine can be blocked by the patent on the machine. Licensing may promote the coordinated development of technologies that are in a blocking relationship.

Field-of-use, territorial, and other limitations on intellectual property licenses may serve procompetitive ends by allowing the licensor to exploit its property as efficiently and effectively as possible. These various forms of exclusivity can be used to give a licensee an incentive to invest in the commercialization and distribution of products embodying the licensed intellectual property and to develop

---

[12] *United States v. Grinnell Corp.*, 384 U.S. 563, 571 (1966); *see also United States v. Aluminum Co. of America*, 148 F.2d 416, 430 (2d Cir. 1945) (Sherman Act is not violated by the attainment of market power solely through "superior skill, foresight and industry").

additional applications for the licensed property. The restrictions may do so, for example, by protecting the licensee against free-riding on the licensee's investments by other licensees or by the licensor. They may also increase the licensor's incentive to license, for example, by protecting the licensor from competition in the licensor's own technology in a market niche that it prefers to keep to itself. These benefits of licensing restrictions apply to patent, copyright, and trade secret licenses, and to know-how agreements.

EXAMPLE 1[13]

Situation: ComputerCo develops a new, copyrighted software program for inventory management. The program has wide application in the health field. ComputerCo licenses the program in an arrangement that imposes both field of use and territorial limitations. Some of ComputerCo's licenses permit use only in hospitals; others permit use only in group medical practices. ComputerCo charges different royalties for the different uses. All of ComputerCo's licenses permit use only in specified portions of the United States and in specified foreign countries.[14] The licenses contain no provisions that would prevent or discourage licensees from developing, using, or selling any other program, or from competing in any other good or service other than in the use of the licensed program. None of the licensees are actual or likely potential competitors of ComputerCo in the sale of inventory management programs.

Discussion: The key competitive issue raised by the licensing arrangement is whether it harms competition among entities that would have been actual or likely potential competitors in the absence of the arrangement. Such harm could occur if, for example, the licenses anticompetitively foreclose access to competing technologies (in this case, most likely competing computer programs), prevent licensees from developing their own competing technologies (again, in this case, most likely computer programs), or facilitate market allocation or price-fixing for any product or service supplied by the licensees. (*See* section 3.1.) If the license agreements contained such provisions, the Agency evaluating the arrangement would analyze its likely competitive effects as described in parts 3-5 of these Guidelines. In this hypothetical, there are no such provisions and thus the arrangement is merely a subdivision of the licensor's intellectual property among different fields of use and territories. The licensing arrangement does not appear likely to harm competition among entities that would have been actual or likely potential competitors if ComputerCo had chosen not to license the software program. The Agency therefore would be unlikely to object to this arrangement. Based on these facts, the result of the antitrust analysis would be the same whether the technology was protected by patent, copyright, or trade secret. The Agency's conclusion as to likely competitive

---

13 The examples in these Guidelines are hypothetical and do not represent judgments about, or analysis of, any actual market circumstances of the named industries.

14 These Guidelines do not address the possible application of the antitrust laws of other countries to restraints such as territorial restrictions in international licensing arrangements.

effects could differ if, for example, the license barred licensees from using any other inventory management program.

ANTITRUST CONCERNS AND MODES OF ANALYSIS

NATURE OF THE CONCERNS

While intellectual property licensing arrangements are typically welfare-enhancing and procompetitive, antitrust concerns may nonetheless arise. For example, a licensing arrangement could include restraints that adversely affect competition in goods markets by dividing the markets among firms that would have competed using different technologies. *See, e.g.*, Example 7. An arrangement that effectively merges the research and development activities of two of only a few entities that could plausibly engage in research and development in the relevant field might harm competition for development of new goods and services. *See* section 3.2.3. An acquisition of intellectual property may lessen competition in a relevant antitrust market. *See* section 5.7. The Agencies will focus on the actual effects of an arrangement, not on its formal terms.

The Agencies will not require the owner of intellectual property to create competition in its own technology. However, antitrust concerns may arise when a licensing arrangement harms competition among entities that would have been actual or likely potential competitors[15] in a relevant market in the absence of the license (entities in a "horizontal relationship"). A restraint in a licensing arrangement may harm such competition, for example, if it facilitates market division or price-fixing. In addition, license restrictions with respect to one market may harm such competition in another market by anticompetitively foreclosing access to, or significantly raising the price of, an important input,[16] or by facilitating coordination to increase price or reduce output. When it appears that such competition may be adversely affected, the Agencies will follow the analysis set forth below. *See generally* sections 3.4 and 4.2.

MARKETS AFFECTED BY LICENSING ARRANGEMENTS

Licensing arrangements raise concerns under the antitrust laws if they are likely to affect adversely the prices, quantities, qualities, or varieties of goods and services[17] either currently or potentially available. The competitive effects of licensing arrangements often can be adequately assessed within the relevant markets for the goods affected by the arrangements. In such instances, the Agencies will delineate and analyze only goods markets. In other cases, however, the analysis may

---

15 A firm will be treated as a likely potential competitor if there is evidence that entry by that firm is reasonably probable in the absence of the licensing arrangement.

16 As used herein, "input" includes outlets for distribution and sales, as well as factors of production. *See, e.g.*, sections 4.1.1 and 5.3-5.5 for further discussion of conditions under which foreclosing access to, or raising the price of, an input may harm competition in a relevant market.

17 Hereinafter, the term "goods" also includes services.

require the delineation of markets for technology or markets for research and development (innovation markets).

GOODS MARKETS

A number of different goods markets may be relevant to evaluating the effects of a licensing arrangement. A restraint in a licensing arrangement may have competitive effects in markets for final or intermediate goods made using the intellectual property, or it may have effects upstream, in markets for goods that are used as inputs, along with the intellectual property, to the production of other goods. In general, for goods markets affected by a licensing arrangement, the Agencies will approach the delineation of relevant market and the measurement of market share in the intellectual property area as in section 1 of the U.S. Department of Justice and Federal Trade Commission Horizontal Merger Guidelines.[18]

TECHNOLOGY MARKETS

Technology markets consist of the intellectual property that is licensed (the "licensed technology") and its close substitutes—that is, the technologies or goods that are close enough substitutes significantly to constrain the exercise of market power with respect to the intellectual property that is licensed.[19] When rights to intellectual property are marketed separately from the products in which they are used,[20] the Agencies may rely on technology markets to analyze the competitive effects of a licensing arrangement.

. . . .

---

[18] U.S. Department of Justice and Federal Trade Commission, Horizontal Merger Guidelines (April 2, 1992) (hereinafter "1992 Horizontal Merger Guidelines"). As stated in section 1.41 of the 1992 Horizontal Merger Guidelines, market shares for goods markets "can be expressed either in dollar terms through measurement of sales, shipments, or production, or in physical terms through measurement of sales, shipments, production, capacity or reserves."

[19] For example, the owner of a process for producing a particular good may be constrained in its conduct with respect to that process not only by other processes for making that good, but also by other goods that compete with the downstream good and by the processes used to produce those other goods.

[20] Intellectual property is often licensed, sold, or transferred as an integral part of a marketed good. An example is a patented product marketed with an implied license permitting its use. In such circumstances, there is no need for a separate analysis of technology markets to capture relevant competitive effects.